A GUIDE BOOK OF

UNITED STATES COINS

MEGA RED™

In 1792, one of the new country's most renowned scientists and public servants, David Rittenhouse, was appointed the first director of the United States Mint. He personally oversaw the construction of the new Mint facility and the production of the nation's first coinage. (See the special feature on Rittenhouse by Eric Brothers.) *Inset:* In 1871 the Mint produced this 46-mm medal, engraved by William Barber, in honor of its founder.

The Official Red Book®

A GUIDE BOOK OF

UNITED STATES COINS

MEGA RED™

EXPANDED DELUXE EDITION OF THE BEST-SELLING RED BOOK®

10TH EDITION

R.S. YEOMAN

$5 GOLD FEATURE

JEFF GARRETT
SENIOR EDITOR

JOHN FEIGENBAUM
PUBLISHER

A Guide Book of United States Coins™, Deluxe Edition

THE OFFICIAL RED BOOK and
THE OFFICIAL RED BOOK OF UNITED STATES COINS
are registered trademarks of Whitman-CDN Publishing, LLC.

©2026 Whitman®
4001 Helton Dr., Florence, AL 35630
whitman.com

Hardcover ISBN: 978-07948-55734 / Softcover ISBN: 978-07948-50647 / ZT2031 01/26
Printed in China.

Correspondence concerning this book may be directed
to the publisher, Attn: *Mega Red*, at the address above.

The values shown here are not offers to sell or buy but are included only as general information. Descriptions of coins are based on the most accurate data available, but could contain beliefs that may change with further research or discoveries.

Advertisements within this book: Whitman does not endorse, warrant, or guarantee any of the products or services of its advertisers. All warranties, statements, and guarantees are the responsibility of the advertiser.

The precious-metal spot prices in use for this edition are as follows:

Silver—$45 **Gold—**$3,746 **Platinum—**$1,527.50 **Palladium—**$1,545

For a complete catalog of numismatic reference books, supplies, and storage products, visit Whitman online at Whitman.com.

If you enjoy United States coins, visit Greysheet.com for up-to-date news, pricing, and research.

U.S. COINS
AND JEWELRY
HOUSTON'S TRUSTED DEALER SINCE 1985
Since 1985, Houston's U.S. Coins & Jewelry has been the go-to for rare coins, bullion, certified diamonds, fine jewelry, and luxury Swiss watches. Family-owned, licensed, and BBB-A+ rated, they offer free expert appraisals and an exceptional, ever-rotating inventory for collectors and sellers alike.
1880
$1
PCGS PR66CAM
CAC
87315.66/51146474
FRESH COINS UPDATED WEEKLY
USCOINSANDJEWELRY.COM
713.597.6367
8435 Katy Freeway Houston, TX 77024

CONTENTS

ADVISORY PANEL . . . . . **xiv**

LETTER FROM THE PUBLISHER . . . . . **xv**

THE HISTORY OF COINS IN AMERICA, 1607 TO DATE **1**

COLLECTING U.S. COINS **74**

A Seminar on the Grading of Coins 74

Aspects of Authenticity 82

Chinese Counterfeits *by Beth Deisher* 84

2026 Coin Market Report 84

HOW TO USE THIS BOOK **89**

SPECIAL FEATURE: David W. Rittenhouse, First Director of the United States Mint **96**

SPECIAL FEATURE: United States Semiquincentennial Coinage **100**

PRE-FEDERAL ISSUES **106**

Colonial Issues 106

Post-Colonial Issues 131

FEDERAL ISSUES **164**

Contract Issues and Patterns 164

Half Cents 170

Liberty Cap, Head Facing Left (1793) 172

Liberty Cap, Head Facing Right (1794–1797) 176

Draped Bust (1800–1808) 182

Classic Head (1809–1836) 188

Braided Hair (1840–1857) 194

Large Cents 198

Flowing Hair, Chain Reverse (1793) 200

Flowing Hair, Wreath Reverse (1793) 204

Liberty Cap (1793–1796) 208

Draped Bust (1796–1807) 215

Classic Head (1808–1814) 227

Coronet Head (1816–1839) 231

Braided Hair (1839–1857) 245

Small Cents 260

Flying Eagle (1856–1858) 262

Indian Head (1859–1909) 267

Lincoln, Wheat Ears Reverse (1909–1958) 282

Lincoln, Memorial Reverse (1959–2008) 305

Lincoln, Birth Bicentennial Reverses (2009) 313

Lincoln, Shield Reverse (2010–2025) 316

Two-Cent Pieces . . . 318
Shield (1864–1873) . . . 319
Three-Cent Pieces . . . 325
Silver Three-Cent Pieces (Trimes) (1851–1873) . . . 327
Nickel Three-Cent Pieces (1865–1889) . . . 333
Nickel Five-Cent Pieces . . . 338
Shield (1866–1883) . . . 339
Liberty Head (1883–1913) . . . 345
Indian Head or Buffalo (1913–1938) . . . 351
Jefferson (1938–2003) . . . 359
Westward Journey (2004–2005) . . . 372
Jefferson, Modified Portrait (2006 to Date) . . . 374
Half Dismes . . . 378
Half Disme (1792) . . . 379
Half Dimes . . . 382
Flowing Hair (1794–1795) . . . 384
Draped Bust, Small Eagle Reverse (1796–1797) . . . 388
Draped Bust, Heraldic Eagle Reverse (1800–1805) . . . 392
Capped Bust (1829–1837) . . . 396
Liberty Seated (1837–1873) . . . 403
Dimes . . . 413
Draped Bust, Small Eagle Reverse (1796–1797) . . . 415
Draped Bust, Heraldic Eagle Reverse (1798–1807) . . . 419
Capped Bust (1809–1837) . . . 424
Liberty Seated (1837–1891) . . . 433
Barber (1892–1916) . . . 444
Mercury (Winged Liberty Head) (1916–1945) . . . 450
Roosevelt (1946 to Date) . . . 460
Twenty-Cent Pieces . . . 473
Liberty Seated (1875–1878) . . . 474
Quarter Dollars . . . 478
Draped Bust, Small Eagle Reverse (1796) . . . 481
Draped Bust, Heraldic Eagle Reverse (1804–1807) . . . 485
Capped Bust (1815–1838) . . . 489
Liberty Seated (1838–1891) . . . 498
Barber (1892–1916) . . . 509
Standing Liberty (1916–1930) . . . 515
Washington, Eagle Reverse (1932–1998) . . . 522
Washington, State (1999–2008) . . . 535
Washington, D.C. and U. S. Territories (2009) . . . 542

Washington, America the Beautiful (2010–2021) 545
Washington, Crossing the Delaware (2021) 557
Washington, American Women (2022–2025) 559
Half Dollars 564
Flowing Hair (1794–1795) 568
Draped Bust, Small Eagle Reverse (1796–1797) 574
Draped Bust, Heraldic Eagle Reverse (1801–1807) 578
Capped Bust, Lettered Edge (1807–1836) 585
Capped Bust, Reeded Edge (1836–1839) 609
Liberty Seated (1839–1891) 614
Barber (1892–1915) 626
Liberty Walking (1916–1947) 632
Franklin (1948–1963) 638
Kennedy (1964 to Date) 645
Silver Dollars 655
Flowing Hair (1794–1795) 659
Draped Bust, Small Eagle Reverse (1795–1798) 664
Draped Bust, Heraldic Eagle Reverse (1798–1804) 670
Gobrecht (1836–1839) 681
Liberty Seated (1840–1873) 685
Trade Dollars (1873–1885) 692
Morgan (1878–1921) 698
Peace (1921–1935) 718
Modern Dollars 724
Eisenhower (1971–1978) 726
Susan B. Anthony (1979–1999) 730
Sacagawea (2000–2008, 2025) 733
Presidential (2007–2020) 736
Native American (2009 to Date) 742
American Innovation (2018–2032) 746
1921 Silver Anniversary Coins (2021, 2023 to Date) 751
Gold Dollars 754
Liberty Head (1849–1854) 755
Indian Princess Head, Small Head (1854–1856) 759
Indian Princess Head, Large Head (1856–1889) 762
Gold Quarter Eagles ($2.50) 766
Draped Bust to Right (1796–1807) 767
Capped Bust to Left (1808) 770
Capped Head to Left (1821–1834) 772
Classic Head (1834–1839) 775

Liberty Head (1840–1907) . . . 778
Indian Head (1908–1929) . . . 785
Three-Dollar Gold Pieces . . . 788
Indian Princess Head (1854–1889) . . . 789
Four-Dollar Gold Pieces . . . 793
Stella, Flowing Hair and Coiled Hair (1879–1880) . . . 794
Gold Half Eagles ($5) . . . 796
Draped Bust to Right, Small Eagle Reverse (1795–1798) . . . 804
Draped Bust to Right, Heraldic Eagle Reverse (1795–1807) . . . 807
Capped Bust to Left (1807–1812) . . . 811
Capped Head to Left (1813–1834) . . . 814
Classic Head (1834–1838) . . . 819
Liberty Head (1839–1908) . . . 822
Indian Head (1908–1929) . . . 833
Gold Eagles ($10) . . . 837
Draped Bust to Right, Small Eagle Reverse (1795–1797) . . . 839
Draped Bust to Right, Heraldic Eagle Reverse (1797–1804) . . . 842
Liberty Head (1838–1907) . . . 845
Indian Head (1907–1933) . . . 854
Gold Double Eagles ($20) . . . 859
Liberty Head (1849–1907) . . . 861
Saint-Gaudens, High Relief and Ultra High Relief, MCMVII (1907) . . . 870
Saint-Gaudens, Flat Relief, Arabic Numerals (1907–1933) . . . 873
U.S. Commemoratives (1892–1954; 1982 to Date) . . . 879
Classic Commemoratives (1892–1954) . . . 879
Modern Commemoratives (1982 to Date) . . . 893
Centennial Gold (2016) . . . 927
Best of the Mint Gold (2026) . . . 928
Proof and Mint Sets . . . 929
Modern Proof Sets (1936 to Date) . . . 933
Uncirculated Mint Sets (1947 to Date) . . . 936
Special Mint Sets (1965–1967) . . . 937
U.S. Mint Bullion Coins . . . 938
American Eagle Program . . . 939
American Buffalo Gold Bullion Program . . . 960
First Spouse Gold Bullion Program . . . 963
America the Beautiful Silver Bullion Program . . . 969
American Liberty High Relief Gold Coins . . . 973
MMIX Ultra High Relief Gold Coins . . . 975
Liberty and Britannia Gold Coins . . . 976

230th Anniversary Flowing Hair High Relief Gold Coins 977
Comic Art Gold Coins 978

PRIVATE AND TERRITORIAL GOLD 979

PRIVATE TOKENS 1009
Hard Times Tokens (1832–1844) 1009
Feuchtwanger Tokens (1837–1864) 1012
Civil War Tokens (1860s) 1012
Lesher Referendum Dollars (1900–1901) 1016

CONFEDERATE ISSUES 1017

HAWAIIAN AND PUERTO RICAN ISSUES 1019

PHILIPPINE ISSUES 1023
Philippines Under U.S. Sovereignty (1903–1936) 1025
Commonwealth Issues for Circulation (1937–1945) 1039
Commonwealth Commemorative Issues 1046

APPENDICES 1048
Appendix A: Misstrikes and Errors 1048
Appendix B: Collectible Red and Blue Books 1054
Appendix C: Top 100 U.S. Coin Prices Realized at Auction 1060
Appendix D: Numismatic Glossary 1063

BIBLIOGRAPHY 1065

IMAGE CREDITS 1065

INDEX 1066

MEGA RED 10TH ADVISORY PANEL

SENIOR EDITOR	PUBLISHER
Jeff Garrett	John Feigenbaum

EDITORS EMERITI
Ken Bressett and Q. David Bowers

CREATIVE DIRECTOR AND COVER DESIGNER
Matt Jeffirs

COORDINATING EDITOR
Diana Plattner

EDITING, GRAPHIC DESIGN, AND LAYOUT
Matthew Heller

PRICING EDITORS
John Feigenbaum and Patrick Ian Perez

ADVERTISING COORDINATOR
Billie Blattel

2026 ADVISORY PANEL

John Agre
John Albanese
Ted Ancher
Justin Atkins
Len Augsberger
Bjorn Bergstrom
Mark Borckardt
Q. David Bowers
Ken Bressett
William Bugert
Roger Burdette
John Butler
H. Robert Campbell
Seth Chandler
Elizabeth Coggan
Marc Crane
John Dannreuther
Charles Davis
Dan Decker
Beth Deisher
Ron Drzewucki
Blake Duncan
Kenny Duncan Jr.
Steven Ellsworth
David Fanning
Bill Fivaz
Gerry Fortin
Pierre Fricke
Paul Gilkes
Ronald J. Gillio
Rusty Goe
Ron Guth
James Halperin
Stephen Hayden
Brian Hodge
Todd Imhoff
Steve Ivy
Donald H. Kagin
Bradley S. Karoleff
Sean Kelly
John Kraljevich
Kevin Lipton
Andy Lustig
Dwight N. Manley
Olivia Marino
David McCarthy
Joshua McMorrow-Hernandez
Harry Miller
Lee S. Minshull
Robert Rhue
Greg Roberts
Greg Rohan
Allen Rowe
P. Scott Rubin
Ian Russell
David Ryder
Stephanie Sabin
Mark Salzberg
Scott Schechter
Jeff Shevlin
Craig Sholley
Roger Siboni
Richard Snow
Laura Sperber
Jon Sullivan
Saul Teichman
Anthony Terranova
Scott Thomas
Troy Thoreson
Brian Timmons
Rick Tomaska
Tom Uram
Tom Warren
Noal White

ORGANIZATIONS

American Numismatic Assocation
American Numismatic Society
Central States Numismatic Society
Colonial Coin Collectors Club (C4)
Florida United Numismatists
Pennsylvania Association of Numismatists
Professional Numismatists Guild
Rittenhouse Society

SPECIAL PHOTO CREDITS

CAC Grading
GreatCollections
Robert Harwell
Heritage Auctions
NGC
PCGS
Smithsonian Institution
Stack's Bowers Galleries
United States Mint
United Stated Department of the Treasury

LETTER FROM THE PUBLISHER

Dear Reader,

Welcome to the 10th edition of *A Guide Book of United States Coins: MEGA RED*™. In publishing this book, we stand on the shoulders of the numismatic editorial giants that precede us: namely, R.S. Yeoman, Q. David Bowers, and Kenneth Bressett. This edition was simply not possible without their scholarship.

This 10th edition of *Mega Red* represents something of a departure from previous editions. It is the first Mega Red to benefit from the massive catalog and pricing database at our sister company, Greysheet®. This edition carries distinct entries for approximately 18,000 coins and more than 100,000 individual values.

For the first time ever in a single publication, the reader has access to established variety listings for the specialty catalogs from Cohen (half cents), Sheldon and Newcomb (large cents), Logan & McCloskey (half dimes), Overton (Bust half dollars), Van Allen & Mallis (Morgan & Peace dollars), and so on. Of course, we have also included the listings from our popular *Cherrypickers' Guide* series (FS numbers).

The result is that this is now one of the most important and vital catalogs ever published on United States coins. I want to thank our team for their amazing work to assemble this monster—Greg Bradley, Diana Plattner, Patrick Ian Perez, Billie Blattel, and Matt Jeffirs—who put in countless hours to bring this volume to life. Jeff Garrett, our fearless senior editor, oversaw the editorial contents of the book, but nobody deserves more credit for this full makeover than Matt Heller, who is responsible for the layout. Try to imagine redesigning a 1,100-page book in three weeks!

Now for the caveats. Given the time constraints and the radical restructuring of this 10th edition, I fully expect there will be errors. While Patrick and I have been assembling pricing for these 18,000 listings for the past decade, they have never before appeared in print to this extent. I have no doubt Overton collectors will advise me that certain varieties don't exist in the grades provided. That's okay. In this case, perfection is the enemy of very good, but we want to hear from you. Please email editor@redbook.com with your feedback (positive or critical) so we can make corrections for the 11th edition.

Thank you, our readers, for supporting this project and the many other ambitions of the Whitman-Greysheet team!

Sincerely,

John Feigenbaum
Publisher and Pricing Editor

THE HISTORY OF COINS IN AMERICA, 1607 TO DATE

An NE (New England) shilling from the first coinage series struck in what is now the United States, by the Massachusetts Bay Colony in 1652.

Settlers in America from the Jamestown Colony in 1607 and the landing of the Pilgrims in Plymouth in 1620, continuing with immigrants from many lands, were mostly of European stock. The New World promised land for settlement and the pursuit of hunting and agriculture for most. For others such as settlers in what became Pennsylvania and Rhode Island, religious freedom prompted their settling on the far side of the Atlantic Ocean.

During most of the seventeenth century, the first century of permanent North American colonization by Europeans, coins were scarce. To fill the demand for media of exchange many commodities and commercial products were used. In Maryland and Virginia tobacco, powder, and shot traded at set rates. As an example, on March 4, 1635, the Massachusetts General Court adopted legislation that provided: "It is likewise ordered that musket bullets of a full bore shall pass currently for a farthing apiece, provided that no man be compelled to take above XII [one shilling] at a time in them."

In the early days in some colonies grain (a general term for corn, peas, and wheat), oat meal, cattle, furs, and fish were also used in payment of debt. Each of these had a utility value. Tobacco could be smoked, or if the recipient did not indulge, a neighbor might. Fish could be eaten, fur could be made into caps and clothing. Such commodities were often referred to as "country pay," or barter items.

In New Hampshire dried and salted fish, lumber, and agricultural products saw service as currency as did gunpowder and cattle. Citizens of the Carolinas often used tobacco, corn, peas, rice, and even pine tar for the same purpose. In New York beaver skins were sometimes specified as payment in contracts. Each of these things required effort to find or produce. Accordingly, the market could not be disturbed by an unexpected flood of animal skins or musket balls. Counterfeiting was not a problem. Unfortunately, tobacco depreciated so badly from overproduction in Virginia that, in 1640 (21 years after tobacco was made the official currency), all the "bad" and half the "good" was ordered burned. This was not successful in decreasing the flood of tobacco on the market, so in 1666 both Virginia and Maryland banned the planting of tobacco entirely for a year. Prices in 1683 were so low from overproduction that there were riots when Virginia refused to order another one-year ban. Beaver skins fluctuated also.

Cattle served as currency in certain areas of colonial America as did other perishable goods such as agricultural products.

In the meantime, and since the earliest days, gold and silver coins of all nations were accepted in normal dealings by the colonists who in turn used them to purchase imported goods. English silver coins were familiar and desirable, but of equal value were the

German thalers, Dutch silver Lyon (lion) dollars and gold ducats, French louis, and of course, the ever-present gold doubloons and silver pieces-of-eight and their fractions from Spain as well as mints from Mexico to South America. English copper coins served the need for small change, but even these were scarce and rarely adequate for commercial needs.

A Dutch silver Lyon dollar of 1589 representative of many European crown- or dollar-size coins in circulation in America in the early years of colonization.

On November 15, 1637, the Massachusetts General Court ordered that particular shell beads called wampum (shortened from the Algonquin *wampumpeage*, or "white beads") should pass at six per penny for any sum under 12 pence. From that year to 1661, Indian wampum became a standard medium of exchange for trade with the Native Americans. Strings of wampum were highly coveted and could be exchanged for furs. Six white beads or three blue beads equaled one English penny. All financial records were kept in the traditional English pounds, shillings, and pence, but debts and taxes were often paid in corn, beaver, peas, or whatever foreign coins were available.

On October 7, 1640, the General Court directed that white wampum should pass at four per penny and blue at two per penny, with no more than 12 pence worth to be used at one time unless the receiver desired more. Wampum had its problems, for it developed that similar glass beads could be made cheaply in factories, and wampum of quahog clam shells counterfeited from seashells. What had become an accepted medium of exchange among Indians became devalued when interfered with by white settlers.

Although country pay faded in the early nineteenth century and was largely replaced in cities and larger settlements by coins, the barter system endured. There are many nineteenth-century accounts of businesses in rural areas of America taking goods and services in trade for merchandise.

A string of wampum beads.

COINS USED IN THE COLONIES

Prior to establishment of the United States Mint in Philadelphia in 1792 and its subsequent production of coinage for circulation in 1793, metallic money in the American colonies came in many forms. Foreign coins comprised a wide variety of copper, silver, and gold issues from Spanish America, England, Portugal, Holland, France, Germany, and elsewhere. Many of these were made legal tender by federal law.

As a general rule, in the eighteenth century copper coins used for small change were apt to be British. Silver and gold issues, used in larger transactions, were typically struck by Spanish-American mints in Mexico (in particular), Chile, Peru, and elsewhere. These were denominated in reales (sometimes given as *reals*), with eight reales equaling a Spanish dollar. Gold coins were reckoned in escudos, with 8 escudos equaling a gold doubloon, worth about 16 Spanish dollars. Deeds, contracts, and other documents involving money were usually drawn in English or Spanish money. Brazilian gold coins were important as well as were scattered other European issues.

The popular Spanish milled dollar, or eight-reales piece, was divided into eighths or bits, the one-real worth 12-1/2¢. From this, the term "two bits" for a 25¢ coin passed into the modern idiom.

Indeed, long after the Philadelphia Mint and its several branches were in operation, most silver coins in circulation in the United States were still the Spanish-American types. In New York City, Boston, or Philadelphia in the 1850s, silver two-reales coins were much more common than federal Liberty Seated coins.

From 1821 until August 1834 there were no United States gold coins in circulation as the value of that metal had risen to the point that it cost more than face value to mint a $5 gold coin. These continued to be struck to the order of those who deposited sufficient gold to make them. After they were delivered, the coins were used in international trade where the face value made no difference. A $5 gold coin containing, for example, $5.05 worth of precious metal would be valued at $5.05 at a destination such as London, Paris, or Vienna. In the meantime, Spanish-American doubloons and other gold coins were widely used.

1745 Peru eight escudos or doubloon, one of many issues of Spanish-American gold coins that facilitated trade in early America.

Selected foreign silver and gold coins remained legal tender until after the Act of February 21, 1857, mandated their retirement. An extension was granted for two years, then another for six months, making them useful in commerce well into the year 1859. In 1857 the Treasury began large-scale redemption of foreign silver and gold issues, exchanging them for federal coins.

It was difficult, if not impossible, for the average merchant or banker to know the exchange value of an eight-escudo gold doubloon from Mexico, as compared to one from Peru or Chile, or to figure the trade worth of a French silver five-franc coin. Exchange-rate tables published in newspapers and almanacs were a help as were charts and publications known as cambists. Most city newspapers had a "prices current" column giving values of popular gold and silver coins as well as market values for commodities. A wide class of publications known as counterfeit detectors and bank-note reporters developed. These told the value of paper money in particular (in addition to endeavoring to identify counterfeits), but often gave exchange values for foreign coins.

Spanish-American two-reales coins were the most plentiful silver coins in day-to-day commerce into the 1850s, by which time most were worn nearly smooth, as was this 1781 Mexico City Mint coin counterstamped in the 1850s in New York City to advertise a hair product.

Beyond that, values of coins varied from colony to colony. A Mexican doubloon had one value in New York City and a slightly different value in Charleston.

When the first issues of the Continental Congress appeared in 1775 they specified payment in Spanish coins. For example, a typical note reads: "This Bill entitles the Bearer to receive EIGHT Spanish milled DOLLARS, or the Value thereof in Gold or Silver, according to the Resolutions of the CONGRESS, held at Philadelphia the 10th of May, 1775."

Paper money of various kinds, issued in large amounts during the eighteenth century, was often viewed with distrust. Counterfeiting was rife, notes or bills good in one area were often valueless or deeply depreciated in another, and many other problems surfaced. Bills were often altered by removing one denomination and inking in a higher value. Counterfeits were made by various processes, including carefully drawing notes by hand as well as the more expedient making of a false printing plate. Because of counterfeits, official designs were often changed at short intervals, at which time earlier currency was called in, inspected for genuineness, and exchanged for the new. Very few people could tell counterfeits from the genuine, some of which were so clever that numismatists today need to look for secret privy marks and other signs. Despite the warning "To Counterfeit Is Death" printed on many notes, the game continued. In practice, very few makers of false notes were ever executed, as juries were reluctant to apply the ultimate penalty.

Moreover, much paper money became devalued. It took ever-increasing amounts of paper to buy a given item. Such currency generally stayed within the colony of issue, or, if taken across borders, was apt to sell at a deep discount. Older paper money of higher value was often referred to as "old tenor," as were earlier coins of higher weight. The quality and acceptance of paper varied from colony to colony—with some keeping tighter rein than others.

Making matters even more difficult, the value of a given note varied from colony to colony, much more so than changing values of silver and gold coins for paper had no intrinsic or melt-down worth.

The saying, "never keep a paper dollar in your pocket till tomorrow," popularized by Aaron White in a token he issued in 1857, was just as applicable in colonial days. A citizen holding Spanish coins worth five pounds and an equivalent amount of paper money with the same value would nearly always spend the paper money first.

Continental currency was authorized by the Continental Congress and was issued in five series with 11 different authorization dates, in denominations from fractions of a dollar up to, eventually, $80. Although these notes were payable in Spanish milled dollars, as related above, the federal treasury was empty. Accordingly, the bills depreciated rapidly from their first issue in 1775 to the last in 1779. In January 1777 it took $105 in Continental paper money to buy $100 in Spanish silver dollars at an exchange office. By February 1781 it took $7,500! After this time, the bills became virtually worthless. Some smart speculators made a market in them and were rewarded when on August 4, 1790, Congress passed an act providing that Continental currency would be received at the Treasury until September 1, 1791, at the rate of $100 in bills to $1 in silver or gold coins. Among those profiting on a large scale seems to have been "Lord" Timothy Dexter, a wealthy entrepreneur in Newburyport, Massachusetts, who decorated his front lawn with statues of prominent historical figures.

A February 17, 1776, $8 Continental currency note. Each bill was signed by hand.

The Act of May 8, 1792, extended the redemption period of March 7, 1792, after which time the bills were repudiated, the status they retain today, although in all instances a well-preserved note has a numismatic value higher than its face value. Later paper-money issues of the various states, similar in design to certain Continental notes, were guaranteed by the state governments. It is an arguable point as to the legal-tender status today of signed, unredeemed bills. Again, that problem is solved by their numismatic worth.

In April 1782 the Commonwealth of Pennsylvania affirmed the charter of the Bank of North America, the first such institution authorized by a state, although banks and money-exchange offices were hardly new. Soon the bank issued paper money with its imprint, redeemable in specie (gold and silver coins) at its office. This set the pace for more than 3,000 banks to gain state charters and issue paper money from that time until the mid-1860s. In addition many private notes were issued by merchants and towns, particularly in times of economic stress, such as after the War of 1812 and following the Panic of 1837.

As federal paper money developed, bills of banks ranged from worthless to fully redeemable in gold or silver, depending on the reputation and capital of the institution involved. It was not until 1861 that the federal government again issued currency in quantity for public use. During the entire colonial era, and extending well into the mid-nineteenth century, gold and silver coins were always preferable to paper money.

Front of the mansion of "Lord" Timothy Dexter on High Street in Newburyport, Massachusetts. He speculated in Continental currency. The building (without statues) still stands today.

EUROPEAN COINAGE FOR AMERICA

In the eighteenth century, as part of the flood of European coins brought to America, such low-denomination coins as Mark Newby farthings and halfpence featuring St. Patrick and British coppers were used here, although they were not made specifically for this side of the Atlantic, nor did they bear any inscriptions relating to the colonies. Mark Newby's coppers were legal tender for a time in West Jersey (largely today's New Jersey), but no such mantle was ever placed on other English or Irish coppers. The legislature of the colony made them legal tender.

Various coins were produced in England for specific distribution in America.

In 1688 Richard Holt, a British entrepreneur, caused a quantity of 1/24th-real tin coins to be made for the American plantations, but these never reached circulation this side of the Atlantic.

For Maryland, Cecil Calvert, the second Lord Baltimore, caused a series of silver coins ranging from the groat (fourpence) to the shilling to be struck. He also had struck a copper denarium or penny.

William Wood, under a royal patent, produced the distinctive Rosa Americana issues, these in addition to his Hibernia coppers made for circulation in Ireland, but some found their way to America. To the coins in circulation were added coins and tokens of private issuers.

St. Patrick halfpennies (illustrated here) and farthings made for circulation in Ireland were imported to West Jersey in America and declared legal tender.

Silver sixpence struck in England for circulation in the colony of Maryland.

Rosa Americana coins intended for circulation in America were made under contract by William Wood beginning in 1722. Shown is a 1722 penny.

Halfpence for circulation in America were made in London and circulated widely.

Copper halfpence for Virginia were struck at the Tower Mint in London in 1773 and shipped to that colony.

Mention is made of the brass pieces produced in England circa 1616 for the Sommer Islands (Bermuda). At the time these were under the authority of the Virginia Company, but that division was separate from the colony on the American mainland. The authorization provided that these little coins, each depicting a wild hog, only be used on those islands. These are detailed in the present text by "numismatic tradition" although they are not part of coinage made for land that later became the United States. The main "currency" of the Sommer Islands during that time was tobacco.

Curiously, the many other issues that were legal tender on this side of the Atlantic—various foreign gold and silver issues—are *not* collected as part of the American colonial series. Many are of significant related interest, however. Extensive collections could be made of Spanish-American dollars and their fractional parts, as these were the main coins in American circulation in the eighteenth and early nineteenth centuries, and were given legal-tender status.

EARLY COINAGE IN AMERICA

It was not until 1652, during the reign of Oliver Cromwell, three years after King Charles was removed from the British throne, that the Massachusetts Bay Colony faced and attempted to correct the shortage of circulating coins. A mint was established in Boston to provide a coinage that could be used to satisfy local needs and to counteract debased-alloy Spanish-American silver coins. The coins that were made at that historic facility were produced over the next 30 years in defiance of British law. The date 1652 was continued in use on them by convention, representing the date of authorization by the colony. Designs included the NE (New England), Willow Tree, Oak Tree, and Pine Tree motifs.

In Simsbury, Connecticut, in 1737, Dr. Samuel Higley struck copper threepence pieces made from metal taken from local mines, a coinage that was continued after his death the same year. The first issues were denominated as three pence. Objection arose among locals who disputed the value of the tokens, and later varieties said VALUE ME AS YOU PLEASE. Today all such coins are very rare.

In 1783 John Chalmers, an Annapolis, Maryland, silversmith, issued his own high-quality coins that were readily accepted in regional commerce. The dies were made by Thomas Sparrow, who also engraved plates for bank notes.

The 1652 Pine Tree shilling is perhaps the most famous American colonial coin. Nathaniel Hawthorne once wrote a story about it.

Higley coppers were struck in Simsbury, Connecticut, in 1737 and 1739. This early issue is lettered THE VALUE OF THREE PENCE.

After the Declaration of Independence made the case for American freedom from British rule, the first of the emerging states to consider the subject of coinage was New Hampshire. The State House of Representatives authorized a limited quantity of pure-copper coins. Silversmith William Moulton was empowered to make them; he prepared cast patterns featuring a pine tree and a harp, and the date 1776. Historians believe these patterns were not accepted by the public, and few of them entered circulation. Still, they marked the beginning of a new period in American money.

1783 silver shilling made in Annapolis, Maryland, by silversmith John Chalmers. Two birds compete for a worm, while behind a fence a dangerous snake (an allegory for Britain) lurks unnoticed amidst their squabble.

During the pre-federal period each die was made of distinctive character, so the finished coins would indicate the authority of the issuer and be familiar as to value. By the time that state coinage commenced in 1785 (by Connecticut and Vermont) the most familiar foreign copper coins in circulation were British halfpence. These depicted the king on the obverse and the seated figure of Britannia, the personification of Great Britain, on the reverse. It was logical that Connecticut and Vermont (beginning in 1786, after its "landscape" coinage) placed a portrait on the one side of their coins and a seated figure on the other. Such motifs gave instant familiarity and credibility to new issues and implied that they were worth as much as a British halfpenny.

British halfpence and counterfeits thereof were the most often seen copper coins in circulation in the United States in the late eighteenth century. Shown is a genuine 1771 halfpenny.

A 1786 "landscape" motif copper issued by the Republic of Vermont. QUARTA DECIMA STELLA or "14th star" reflected the desire of many Vermont citizens to join the 13 colonies in the Union, which happened later in 1791.

To facilitate their use in commerce the design of Vermont coppers was changed to the portrait of King George III and the figure of Britannia, now with Vermont-related legends translating to "By the Authority of Vermont" and "Independence and Liberty."

Copper coins for Connecticut were struck under contract from 1785 to 1788 and circulated widely. Most bore portraits of King George II or, as seen here, III.

Other coppers of the 1780s had IMMUNIS COLUMBIA, NON VI VIRTUTE VICI, E PLURIBUS UNUM, LIBER NATUS LIBERTATEM DEFENDO, and other Latinized inscriptions, the meanings of which were probably unknown to the majority of the overall population. INDE ET LIB on the reverse of Connecticut and Vermont coppers meant "Independence and liberty," from Latin, later also related to 'Indépendence Et Liberté" used on certain French coins of the nineteenth century.

TOWARD A FEDERAL COINAGE

Fugio cents, struck under the authority of Congress under contract with the Connecticut mint, made their appearance in 1788 but were back-dated 1787, and used a sundial motif earlier found on certain Continental paper-money issues. Taken together, these diverse coinages and others are often referred to as "colonials" by numismatists today. As to when the colonial era ended can be debated. The Declaration of Independence, dated July 4, 1776, proclaimed that the colonies were henceforth independent. Therefore, they were no longer colonies. The Battle of Yorktown, 1781, marked the end of the war. The Treaty of Paris, signed in 1783, resulted in all countries, including Britain, recognizing the independence of the United States of America.

The 1787 Fugio copper cent.

In 1782 Robert Morris, the Confederation's superintendent of finance, proposed to Congress a curious money system of 1,440 "units" making up a dollar. This was calculated to figure (to the smallest fraction) into the many different valuations of the Spanish dollar, which varied throughout the states. Thomas Jefferson favored a simpler dollar unit and a decimal system. "The most easy ratio of multiplication and division is that of ten," he noted in 1784. George Washington referred to the decimal system as "a measure, which in my opinion has become indispensably necessary."

In 1783 Morris submitted to Congress a series of patterns, designed by Benjamin Dudley, as a proposal along the decimal line. The largest piece, with a denomination of 1,000 "units" (each unit being a quarter grain of silver), he called a *mark*. The 500-unit piece was a *quint* and the

Silver 1783 pattern for 1,000 units or one mark.

100-unit a *bit*. These silver patterns were proposed along with a copper 5-unit piece. The system never went beyond the experimental stage.

Actual statehood commenced when the various former colonies ratified the United States Constitution. Delaware was the first in 1787. Complicating the discussion is the issuance of paper money by the Continental Congress in the late 1770s, specifically marked "United States."

Coins and tokens of George Washington, mostly struck in England from 1783 through the mid-1790s, are often collected with colonial issues and are included herein.

FEDERAL COINAGE IN THE EARLY YEARS

By the late 1780s the individual states had ceased to issue their own coins and paper money. The sinews of commerce were secured by foreign silver and gold coins authorized as legal tender by Congress (the authorization of most did not expire until 1860, as noted earlier). Dominating the activity were coins of Spanish America, with those from the Mexico City Mint being the most prevalent. Coins of Great Britain, France, the Netherlands, and certain other European countries were legal tender as well. Joining the legitimate silver and copper issues was a flood of copper coins, mostly genuine and counterfeit British halfpence that had no legal-tender status but were widely accepted in commerce. The value of such coppers in quantity fluctuated, and in the late 1790s there had been a deep depression. However, the coins singly and in small groups continued to pass readily.

Alexander Hamilton.

In planning for a federal coinage Alexander Hamilton, who would become the nation's first secretary of the Treasury, agreed fundamentally with the decimal concept and urged that gold and silver be used in the nation's standard money. On March 3, 1791—during George Washington's first presidential term—Congress authorized the president to hire artists and acquire machinery for coinage in order to establish a federal mint. Some initial steps were taken, and that October, in his annual address, Washington stated, "The disorders in the existing currency, and especially the scarcity of small change, a scarcity so peculiarly distressing to the poorer classes, strongly recommend the carrying into immediate effect the resolution already entered into concerning the establishment of a mint."

Philadelphia in the 1790s, when it was the seat of the United States government.

Five months later, the Mint Act of April 2, 1792, provided that "the money of account of the United States should be expressed in dollars or units, dismes or tenths, cents or hundredths, and milles or thousandths; a disme being the tenth part of a dollar, a cent the hundredth part of a dollar, a mille the thousandth part of a dollar. . . ." The Mint Act also established the metal content of the coins, and their imagery; identified the "seat of government," Philadelphia, as the site of the new mint; and guaranteed that silver and gold would be made into coins free of charge to those who brought the metal in.

> The latter provision would save the Mint from having to source its own raw gold and silver. It also offered banks, merchants, and others a way to transform bullion and miscellaneous foreign specie into official, spendable U.S. coins, and thereby inject larger-denomination coins into commerce. (The conversion, while convenient, was not automatic; refining and coining took time. Alternately, one could deliver bullion to the Mint and exchange it immediately for equivalent U.S. coins, with one-half of 1 percent deducted for expenses.) The act also provided for a coinage of copper small-change coins.[3]

Copper coinage was extremely important for the early Mint. There was no profit to be made on coining silver and gold, but copper half cents and cents yielded any profit that could be made between the cost of copper stock and the face value of the coins. It was more expedient to coin a single cent than two half cents, with the result that cents were made in large quantities as compared to sporadic lower quantities for half cents.

The coins specified in the Mint Act of 1792 included these:

Denomination	Value	Fineness	Denomination	Value	Fineness
eagle	$10.00	91.7% pure gold (22k)	quarter dollar	$0.25	89.2% pure silver
half eagle	$5.00	91.7% pure gold (22k)	disme	$0.10	89.2% pure silver
quarter eagle	$2.50	91.7% pure gold (22k)	half disme	$0.05	89.2% pure silver
dollar	$1.00	89.2% pure silver	cent	$0.01	100% pure copper
half dollar	$0.50	89.2% pure silver	half cent	$0.005	100% pure copper

COINAGE OF THE 1790s

On July 31, 1792, the cornerstone was laid for the Philadelphia Mint, the second building created by the United States government (the first was a lighthouse). In attendance were President George Washington, Mint Director David Rittenhouse, and others. At the time Rittenhouse, a maker of clocks and scientific apparatus, was one of the Americans most skilled in mechanics and was an ideal choice. Philadelphia was the seat of the federal government, and the president resided just a short walk away.

By that time there was a coining press and some other equipment on hand, stored in an old carriage house on Sixth Street, above Chestnut, owned by John Harper, a saw maker and mechanic. Thomas Jefferson, in his Memorandum Book July 11, 1792, entry, noted that he took $75 in silver to the Mint to be coined. His July 13, 1792, entry records receiving 1,500 half dismes from the Mint. In the autumn the Mint was in operation, and additional silver half dismes were produced.

Thomas Jefferson's memorandum book states that he personally purchased and distributed 1,500 1792 half dismes.

In December some pattern one-cent pieces and other proposals were made. Dies for some early patterns were made by Robert Birch, and Joseph Wright created a quarter-dollar pattern.

Copper one-cent pieces were first made for circulation in February 1793. The earliest versions had a head of Liberty on the obverse and a chain of 15 links on the reverse, one for each state (by this time Vermont had joined the Union, in 1791, and Kentucky in 1792). To some the design was less than pleasing. One newspaper account described Liberty as being "in a fright," and the chain on the reverse as an ill omen for a land of freedom. The motif was changed to a different face of Liberty, and, on the reverse, a wreath. That summer, copper half cents were made for the first time. Some early dies were made by Joseph Wright (who died of yellow fever that September), and possibly by Henry Voigt, an engraver on the Mint staff. In the autumn Robert Scot, a British immigrant who was important as a local maker of copper plates for bank-notes, maps, and illustrations, was hired as engraver. In the first year the fledgling Mint struck 35,334 half cents and 111,512 cents, a creditable output. Sources of copper were erratic and problematical and ranged from new sheets to old roofing, some acquired through local advertisements.

1792 half dismes were first struck in July of that year, the first circulating coinage minted by the federal government.

On October 15, 1794, the first silver dollars were struck for circulation, comprising 1,578 coins that were found satisfactory and some others with defects that were held back for recoinage of the metal. Half dollars were also struck in the autumn. Dies dated 1794 for the half dime were made, but were not used until 1795. It was not until 1795 that a press of sufficient size to strike dollars properly was installed. These were of the Flowing Hair design from dies by Robert Scot.

A view of the first Mint as envisioned by painter Edwin Lamasure in 1914. The front structure was two joined buildings that had earlier served as a brewery and for other purposes. The rear buildings are depicted with some artistic license on Lamasure's part. This facility was used through the year 1832.

The first cents struck for circulation at the Mint were made in March 1793 and depicted Liberty on the obverse and a chain of 15 links on the reverse. On the first die the abbreviation AMERI. was used on the reverse.

David Rittenhouse, in poor health, resigned as Mint director in June 1795 and was replaced by Henry William de Saussure, who served only to the following November. Replacing him in the same month was Elias Boudinot, who remained in the post until July 1805.

The Draped Bust design was introduced on the dollar in autumn 1795 and was later used on half cents (starting in 1800) and on cents and other silver coins (1796). This was from a portrait of socialite Mrs. William Bingham drawn by Gilbert Stuart.

In July of 1795 the first federal gold coins, half eagles ($5 gold pieces), were delivered, soon followed by eagles ($10), the largest denomination. Designs changed and evolved over the years. It was general practice to have copper coins bear one common design, silver coins another standard motif, and gold coins to share still another, although sometimes there was overlapping. The Draped Bust obverse was first used on silver coins of 1795 as noted, while gold coins of that and succeeding years into the next century depicted Liberty wearing a conical cloth cap.

In 1796 the first silver dimes and quarter dollars were struck and also the first quarter eagles ($2.50 gold coins), completing all of the denominations authorized by the 1792 Mint Act. While half cents and cents were struck for the account and profit of the Mint, silver and gold coins were made only on the request of depositors of such precious metals. This was usually deposited in the form of foreign coins, but sometimes in other forms, including worn-out utensils and old ornaments.

In the early days dies for all denominations were cut by hand, with separate punches used to add numerals, letters, stars, and devices such as eagles and Liberty heads. No two dies were ever precisely alike, creating a wide panorama of varieties usually differing from each other slightly. However, more than just a few had interesting errors or blunders, such as having a word spelled as IINITED instead of UNITED, or having a fraction read 1/000, which is mathematically meaningless, instead of 1/100. While 13 stars, or one for each of the original colonies, has been the standard count on federal silver and gold coins up to the modern day, some of 1796 were given 15 stars, representing the current number of states

The first silver dollars were of the Flowing Hair type and were struck in one day on October 15, 1794.

The Draped Bust design was first used on silver dollars in 1795 and was later the motif on other copper and silver coins.

Half eagles first made in July 1795 were the first federal gold coins.

A famous reverse die for an 1801 cent had three errors: the left stem at the bottom of the wreath was missing, UNITED was spelled as IINITED, and the fraction was a meaningless 1/000 instead of 1/100.

in the Union. Tennessee joined in this year, raising the count to 16, and some coins were made with this number of stars. Soon, the idea was abandoned, and 13 became the standard.

During the 1790s continuing into the new century epidemics of yellow fever swept Philadelphia on several occasions, resulting in many deaths (including of engraver Joseph Wright in 1793). The Mint was closed during these periods and the dies stored in the vaults of a local bank. The Bank of America and the Bank of Pennsylvania were especially important in the early years of the Mint and made deposits of foreign gold and silver coins and received quantities of newly made federal issues.

An engraver at the Philadelphia Mint. (Concept by Marcia Davis, 1984)

Most dies of the era continued to be made by Robert Scot, with the assistance in earlier years of Henry Voigt and John Smith Gardner. Copper cents in circulation were augmented by many private tokens imported from England, mostly notably those bearing the advertisement of Talbot, Allum & Lee, New York City merchants in the India trade. In the spring of 1795 about 52,000 of them were bought by the Mint, and planchets for half cents were cut from them. Later, an arrangement was made for Boulton & Watt in Birmingham, England, to supply ready-made copper planchets, a practice that was maintained until the War of 1812. There were some schedule problems in 1799 that resulted in a smaller coinage of cents that year; no half cents were made in 1798 or 1799. In 1800 Johann (John) Matthias Reich was hired on contract to make medals, thus assisting engraver Robert Scot.

Despite the output of the Philadelphia Mint the Spanish-American 8-reales or piece-of-eight coin dominated domestic as well as world commerce well into the early nineteenth century. Shown is a 1761 Mexico City Mint 8-reales.

"Despite the Mint's best efforts in its early years, its coinage remained scarce in circulation. Gold and silver in particular were rarely seen in commerce, but the problem extended to small change, as well. By 1799 only about $50,000 worth of copper cents and half cents had been pumped into the economy—roughly one coin for every citizen, not nearly enough for the nation's day-to-day business." Filling the void, earlier tokens and coins of the colonies and states continued to circulate. Silver and gold coins were seldom seen in commerce, except in large cities. Many if not most silver dollars and gold $10 eagles were used in the export trade and never returned.

Legal-tender silver and gold coins of European and Central and South American countries continued to fill nearly all of the need for large denominations in circulation. The Spanish-American silver 8-reales, dollar sized, was the world's most popular trade coin. Vast quantities were purchased by American merchants and exported in exchange for goods. Whaling and merchant ships headed to the Pacific and Far East carried thousands of these coins as they were accepted at all foreign ports. A common arrangement for security was to store thousands of coins in a compartment near the captain's stateroom.

THE EARLY NINETEENTH CENTURY

At the beginning of the nineteenth century, officially 1801, these coins were being struck: cent, half dime, dime, and silver dollar, each with the Draped Bust obverse, and $5 and $10 gold of the Capped Bust motif. Yellow fever continued to be a problem, resulting in Mint closings. Another problem was the opposition of certain members of Congress to the Mint itself, and several proposals were made to close it and have coinage done under private contract. Those situations were resolved and the Mint continued operations.

Elias Boudinot, Mint director from 1795 to 1805.

Robert Maskell Patterson was appointed Mint director by President Thomas Jefferson on January 1, 1806. He served until July 1834, the longest tenure of anyone ever holding the office.

In 1806 John Reich was given a position on the Mint staff as assistant engraver. He created a version of Liberty in a floppy mob cap, called the Capped Bust motif. This was first used on half dollars and half eagles of 1807 and later on the cent (1808), half cent (1809), half dime (1829), dime (1809), and quarter (1815). Today Capped Bust half dollars, made in large quantities, are especially popular with numismatists. Reich also redesigned the reverses of silver and gold coins to incorporate a perched eagle holding arrows and an olive branch.

America was prosperous from the early 1790s until 1808, when the effects of Thomas Jefferson's 1807 Embargo Act were felt. By that time the French, then the British, had seized many American ships on the high seas, the British often kidnapping our sailors and forcing them to serve on their ships. The Embargo Act prohibited nearly all trade with foreign ports, in effect freezing the economy of most coastal cities. Many businesses failed, and other hardships were experienced. The War of 1812 created more chaos. The United States Navy was not strong, and to help fight the enemy, the government gave letters of

The Capped Bust design by John Reich was introduced on the 1807 half dollar (as shown) and half eagle and was used on certain coins as late as 1838.

Robert M. Patterson served as Mint director from 1806 to 1834.

marque, as they were called, to the captains of and owners of ships. They then engaged in privateering under the American flag, capturing whatever enemy prizes they could find and taking the ships to ports where they and their contents were sold at auction—with the money divided among the ship crews and owners. This was a rich undertaking for many, and more than a few family fortunes in Portsmouth, Baltimore, and other cities were augmented in this manner.

In a famous battle at sea in the War of 1812 the USS *Constitution* vanquished the HMS *Guerriere.* (Anton Otto Fischer)

The monetary situation in the United States was tumultuous. The supply of copper planchets from England was exhausted in 1814, and no copper coins were made in 1815. Deposits of silver and gold coins were small, and relatively few coins of these metals were struck in mid-decade. In 1816 only copper cents were made.

Gold and silver coins were in circulation in some periods in the 1810s, then one or another of these metals would rise in value, and many coins would disappear. Meanwhile, a flood of paper bills was issued by banks, merchants, and others.

John Reich left the Mint in 1817 to pursue other opportunities. Engraving was primarily continued by Robert Scot, in service since 1793, but his eyesight was failing. There were no new designs to be created for the next several years, and the design hubs and punches on hand remained in use for new dies. Economic times were difficult in 1818 and 1819, what would be called a recessionary period by later economists.

By this time only a few dozen collectors and museums pursued the art and history of numismatics. In coming years their numbers would increase.

The 1816 cent of the new Matron Head design was the only federal coinage of this year.

A $1 note issued by the Owl Creek Bank of Mount Vernon, Ohio, in 1816, a time of monetary crisis.

THE 1820s AND 1830s

The financial matters improved in the 1820s, in part spawning the creation of historical societies, athenaeums, and libraries that often included coins in their holdings and exhibits.

The first professional numismatist in the United States seems to have been John Allan, born in Scotland. In 1820 he was just one of three American subscribers to Mudie's set of National Medals, published in England. Philip Hone, a wealthy New Yorker who served as mayor of the city in 1826, is known to have been an active coin collector in New York City circa 1822–1827. The private collection of Benjamin H. Watkins, auctioned in Salem, Massachusetts, on June 12 and 13, 1828, is thought to be the first significant cataloged sale of coins in the United States, although the descriptions were poor by later standards.

In the meantime the international price of gold rose in relation to silver, and gold coins became worth more in melt value than face value. Large quantities were coined to the order of depositors who shipped them overseas, where they were received on the basis of weight, with the stamped value being of no importance. In the United States anyone desiring gold coins had to pay a premium for them to a money broker or exchange office. There were no federal gold coins in domestic circulation after 1820. Mintages of half eagles were nearly all to the order of merchants and others who exported them to Europe, where they were melted.

From 1821 to June 1834 all newly minted federal gold coins such as this half eagle cost more than face value to make. Depositors were charged a premium for them. Nearly all were shipped overseas and melted for bullion value, as the face value made no difference.

Robert Scot continued as engraver at the Mint until his death on November 3, 1823. William Kneass, a local engraver of copper plates for bank notes and other items, was appointed engraver in 1824. Christian Gobrecht, who did some contract work in the 1820s, hoped to be appointed but was not considered. Beginning about this year Adam Eckfeldt and perhaps one or two others working at the Philadelphia Mint began saving current coinage. It is said that copper cents and other items were kept on hand for sale or exchange with interested collectors. Interesting rare coins were picked out of incoming deposits and saved. Many old dies were still at the Mint, and on occasion restrikes would be made to supply pieces needed by collectors. No records were kept of such activities, and today we can only speculate as to what occurred.

On July 4, 1829, the cornerstone was laid for a new Philadelphia Mint building. For the occasion, half dimes of the Capped Bust type were struck for the first time, there having been no coinage of this denomination since 1805.

Andrew Jackson, elected president in 1828, took office on March 4, 1829. The first Bank of the United States had operated from 1791 to 1811, after which its 20-year charter was not renewed. The second Bank of the United States was chartered in 1816, to operate until 1836. This bank was mainly owned by private stockholders, although the government had a significant interest. It had many branches in the East and Midwest and issued paper money. Great resistance to it was made by the politicians of many states whose state-chartered banks felt it was unfair competition.

Jackson disliked the bank and resolved to veto any charter extension. His opponents in Congress passed a bill well in advance, in 1830, to assure that renewal would take place in 1836. Jackson kept his word, and in the 1830s the bank wound down its operations to the point that most activity ended in 1835. This was the great political issue of the era. From that time onward, politicians, newspapers, and others were largely divided into two groups: pro-Jackson and anti-Jackson. As if that was not enough, John C. Calhoun, senator from South Carolina, frequently suggested that South Carolina withdraw from the Union, and other Southern states do so as well, as the commercial interests of the South (cotton, tobacco, and other agricultural products) were so different from those of the North (manufacturing, banking, etc.). In particular, high tariffs had diminished exports of cotton, to the detriment of the South, while restricting imports from Europe and thus bringing great prosperity to factories in the North.

The charter to renew the second Bank of the United States was vetoed by President Andrew Jackson in 1830, after which the institution wound down its business, closing in 1836.

Extensive gold strikes were made in Georgia and North Carolina in the 1820s, the first time that significant quantities of that metal were discovered in the United States. In 1830 Templeton Reid issued his own $2.50, $5, and $10 gold coins, and in Rutherfordton, North Carolina, Christopher Bechtler and his family operated a private mint that would remain in business until the early 1850s and would make $1, $2.50, and $5 coins. In 1833 the new Philadelphia Mint went into operation and would remain the center of coinage activity until 1901.

A $2.50 gold coin minted by Templeton Reid in Georgia following the most important gold strike to that date on United States soil.

Prosperity continued apace, aided by the enthusiasm for building canals and railroads, the opening up of new lands in the West and making them easy to buy, and a general atmosphere of well-being. The age of steam was beginning in a large way and would soon revolutionize industrial America.

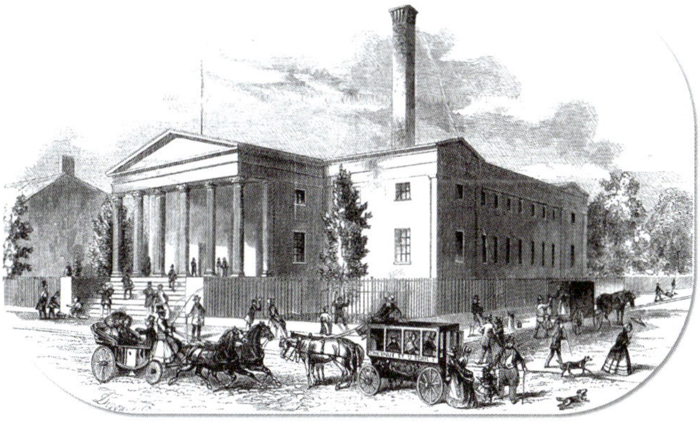

The second Philadelphia Mint operated from 1833 to 1901.

The Act of June 28, 1834, reduced the amount of gold in coins, and the lightweight issues made beginning in August of that year circulated readily. Gold had not been seen in domestic commerce since 1820.

The expansion of America and continuing prosperity brought an increased need for coinage. In 1835 Congress authorized the opening of three branch mints. Each was opened for business several years later in 1838.

The New Orleans Mint was located near the mouth of the Mississippi River, the gateway to inland commerce. Mints at Charlotte, North Carolina, and Dahlonega, Georgia, were in gold-mining regions and provided convenient facilities for converting bullion to coins. The alternative would have been to ship it to distant Philadelphia. The mintmarks O, C, and D were added to each coin to signify their origin.

In August 1835, Chief Engraver Kneass was paralyzed by a stroke. In the next month Christian Gobrecht, a Philadelphia engraver of bank-notes, book plates, and other items, and an inventor, was hired as second engraver. A man of formidable artistic ability, Gobrecht did not want to be called "assistant," and thus the "second" in his title. As it turned out, he did most of the engraving work from that point onward, although Kneass retained the primary engravership until his death in 1840.

The New Orleans Mint operated from 1838 to 1861 and again from 1879 to 1909 and produced silver and gold coins. The facility houses a museum today.

The Charlotte Mint coined gold from 1838 to 1861. Today the building, disassembled and moved to a park, is the Charlotte Art Museum.

Georgia's Dahlonega Mint produced gold coins from 1838 to 1861. The building burned in 1878. Today the Dahlonega Gold Museum Historic Site, housed in the historic Old Lumpkin County Courthouse, celebrates the region's importance in mining and private gold coinage.

An 1838-C quarter eagle, with Charlotte's C mintmark above the date.

Coinage presses were operated by hand. In 1836 steam power was introduced and in 1837 would be used on all presses for circulating coinage. Proofs made for collectors continued to be made on hand-operated equipment. Called "master coins" in the early days, Proofs would become increasingly important at the Mint, to the point in later years some coins were struck only in that format for collectors, and none for circulation (the earliest example may be the 1827 quarter dollar, for which information is incomplete, or may be the 1804 silver dollar, made in 1834 and backdated 20 years).

An early steam-powered knuckle-action coining press made for the Philadelphia Mint by a local manufacturer.

Prosperity continued in America through 1836, the year that the Bank of the United States charter expired. Speculation in real estate in the prairie beyond Pennsylvania was wildly out of control. Vast tracts were purchased through credits and drafts, paper money of depreciated or uncertain value, and promissory notes. This set the scene for Andrew Jackson's Specie Circular, July 11, 1836, one of the most pivotal documents in American financial history. This decree mandated that lands be paid for in gold and silver coins, instead of paper money and credits, that buyers be bona-fide residents or settlers, and that the amount of acreage be restricted for each purchaser. Very few buyers of land had silver half dollars or gold half eagles, and speculation came to an abrupt halt. Loans were called, but debtors could not pay. By early 1837 there was a chill in the American economy, and European bankers, who held many investments, were becoming concerned.

In the same year, 1836, the Liberty Seated design made its debut on the silver dollar, the first of this denomination coined for circulation since 1804. By 1839 it was used on all silver denominations.

After the charter of the second Bank of the United States expired, many banks were formed with reckless abandon. The bank-note companies in New York and Philadelphia were eager to print as many bills as they could sell, with little notice taken as to whether the banks were chartered or legitimately established. The system of banks issuing large amounts of paper money worked perfectly fine in the heady days of 1835 and 1836. However, in early 1837 many people became wary of banks, and sought to redeem bills for gold and silver. It was quickly learned that while some banks could redeem a small percentage of their currency, no bank was able to exchange for all. On May 10, 1837, specie payments were suspended by most Eastern banks, and within weeks most banks in the South and West also stopped paying out coins.

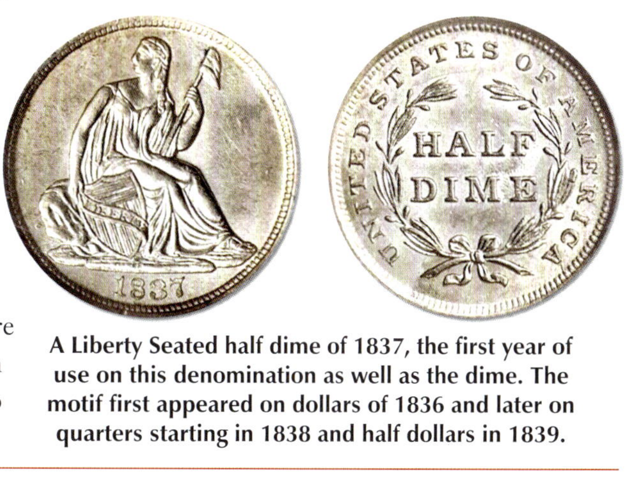

A Liberty Seated half dime of 1837, the first year of use on this denomination as well as the dime. The motif first appeared on dollars of 1836 and later on quarters starting in 1838 and half dollars in 1839.

Soon, silver and gold coins disappeared completely from circulation, although copper cents remained. To facilitate commerce, countless cent-size Hard Times tokens (as we call them today) were issued, in a wide variety of designs, including advertisements for merchants, caricatures and comments about Jackson and his veto of the Bank of the United States, and more.

In 1837 coins became scarce and many Hard Times tokens were privately issued, such as this one mentioning the suspension of specie payments.

In June 1838 the Mint Cabinet was authorized by Congress—a display of American coins old and new, together with foreign and ancient coins and medals, and mineral specimens and ores. While a few coins were purchased, the main source of supply continued to be the extraction of interesting pieces from deposits made at the Mint. Veteran Mint employee Adam Eckfeldt supplied details of Mint history to interested visitors. Numismatics was becoming increasingly important, and there were at least several hundred serious collectors in America.

THE 1840s TO THE CIVIL WAR

By the early 1840s, Jacob Reese Eckfeldt and William DuBois were curators of the pieces on display in the Mint Cabinet. In 1842 a book by these two men, *A Manual of Gold and Silver Coins of All Nations*, was published by the Mint. The text did not contain numismatic text or comments of use to collectors, but dealt with the weights and designations of coins in these metals. The main audiences were banks and counting houses.

The gold districts of North Carolina and Georgia continued to supply the Charlotte and Dahlonega mints. The Bechtler family in North Carolina, which had begun producing $1, $2.50, and $5 gold coins from regional metal since the early 1830s, continued in business without interference from the Treasury Department, seemingly as their coins were of full weight and value and helped with commerce in the Southeast.

By 1844 the Hard Times era had ended, and American commerce was flourishing. Railroad stocks led the securities market. Year by year, towns and cities throughout the East and Midwest were connected. Many new lines were formed, many of which had banking support. Some even issued paper money. Meanwhile, canals, so important earlier, were fading from the scene with many old waterways and new projects abandoned. The Erie Canal connecting the Hudson River with Lake Erie remained important. On inland waterways and on the high seas sidewheel steamships carried most of the maritime passenger traffic and much cargo. Sailing vessels were still important on routes in which speed was important. In the 1850s fast-sailing clipper ships became important in long-distance freight.

Commerce on the Erie Canal.

In 1844 Christian Gobrecht, engraver at the Mint since autumn 1835 and responsible for the Liberty Seated design and other motifs, passed away. James B. Longacre, a highly accomplished engraver in the field of portraits and bank notes, was

Railroads were the growth industry of the 1840s and 1850s.

appointed in his place. He would serve until his death on January 1, 1869. During his tenure he would create many designs for pattern and regular coinage. Interest in numismatics moved another step forward in 1846 with William DuBois's 138-page *Pledges of History*, a carefully prepared volume describing coins and other items in the Mint Cabinet. The War with Mexico in 1846 and 1847 resulted in victory for the United States. As had been the case with earlier wars, medals were struck to commemorate leaders and battles. The West was expanding in population, most notably by emigrants on the Oregon Trail.

America changed dramatically following the discovery of a gleaming flake of gold in California in the tail race at Sutter's Mill, on the American River, January 24, 1848. This ignited the California Gold Rush, the travel westward of Forty Niners the following year, and the establishment of California as a state in 1850. This transformed the boundaries and encouraged settlement more than any other single event in American history. Now the country extended from sea to shining sea.

The vast discoveries of precious metal engendered the establishment of several private mints in San Francisco, Sacramento, and elsewhere in 1849 and 1850. Large quantities of gold were sent to the East for coinage, usually by sidewheel steamship from San Francisco to Panama, then across land for about 48 miles, then connecting to another ship on the Atlantic side at the port of Aspinwall (today's Colón).

The dramatic influx of gold resulted in the Act of March 3, 1849, which introduced two new denominations—the gold dollar and $20 double eagle. The unprecedented quantity of new gold upset the traditional ratio

In 1849 the U.S. Mint introduced the gold dollar to facilitate the coining of gold arriving from California.

Sutter's Mill on the American River, the site of the first large-scale discovery of gold in California.

of 1 ounce of gold being equal to about 15.5 ounces of silver. Silver became relatively rarer than before, causing federal silver coins in circulation to increase in value to the point at which, by December 1849, they could be melted down to yield more in bullion value than face value. Nearly all disappeared from circulation. The situation would become even more acute.

The first California private gold coins were issued by Norris, Gregg, and Norris in Benecia City with the imprint of San Francisco.

In California beginning in spring 1849 and continuing through 1855 more than a dozen private companies and banks issued their own gold coins of varied design. Although these were not official legal tender they passed readily in commerce. From 1851 to 1853 Augustus Humbert, appointed by the Treasury Department as the official United States assayer of gold in California, supervised the striking of gold coins of denominations from $10 to $50, including at the United States Assay Office of Gold, the activity being conducted by arrangement and under the aegis of Moffat & Company, a firm which separately issued its own coins.

Octagonal $50 gold coins called slugs were issued under the supervision of Augustus Humbert in 1851 (as shown here) and 1852.

In 1850 the California state constitution was adopted. It forbade the use of paper money at face value in the channels of commerce. Only coins had legal-tender value. This would have important implications in the following decade of the 1860s.

In the early 1850s there was the strange situation that in the channels of commerce in the East and Midwest, Liberty Seated coins were nowhere to be seen as they had been gathered by hoarders and speculators in silver metal, and their place was nearly completely taken by Spanish-American silver coins, with the 2-reales coin being the denomination most often seen.

In 1850 double eagles were introduced and were struck at the Philadelphia and New Orleans mints. These coins became exceedingly popular, and during the next 75 years, more value was minted in this denomination than of all other United States gold coins combined.

***Placer Operations at Foster's Bar*, an 1851 oil by Ernest Narjot, depicted gold mining on the American River east of Sacramento. (Bancroft Library)**

In 1850 Jacob Reese Eckfeldt and William DuBois, continuing assayers at the Mint and keepers of the Mint Cabinet, published a small book of 61 pages, *New Varieties of Gold and Silver Coins, Counterfeit Coins, Bullion with Mint Values.* Included was information on gold coins privately minted in California. This work was also issued in modified form in 1851 and 1852. The two later versions also included the text of DuBois's 1846 *Pledges of History* work, the latter being out of print at the time.

The first truly important American auction sale featuring rare coins was that of the late Dr. Lewis Roper, a Philadelphia physician who had gone west to seek his fortune in the gold fields, but died of cholera at sea off of Panama on his return voyage in 1850. The coins were offered on February 20, 1851, in the sale room of Moses Thomas & Son, Philadelphia, a popular location for the sale of antiques, books, and other items.

In 1851 with Liberty Seated coins still absent from circulation the silver three-cent piece, or *trime*, was issued. Of 75 percent silver and 25 percent copper (instead of the standard 90:10 ratio), these coins were not profitable to melt, and thus they circulated in commerce at a time when other federal silver coins were being hoarded or melted.

In 1852 *Uncle Tom's Cabin*, a novel by Harriet Beecher Stowe describing the life of slaves on Southern plantations, was published. By decade's end it was the best-selling novel in American history. Perhaps more than any other single factor the book influenced millions of Americans, mostly in the North, to condemn slavery and campaign for abolition. Relations of Northern politicians with those in the South worsened, with the result that the presidential administrations of Franklin Pierce (1853–1857) and James Buchanan (1857–1861) would be viewed as by historians as two of the most ineffective in American history. Each attempted to please both the North and South, to the dissatisfaction of all.

The silver coinage problem ended with the implementation of the Act of February 21, 1853, in which the authorized weights of the silver half dime, dime, quarter, and half dollar were reduced. Coins made under the new standard had arrowheads added to each side of the date to distinguish them. These lightweight coins circulated, thus ending the money problems that had plagued the market since 1850. The Liberty Seated dollar weight was unchanged and those coins remained available for bullion value, or more than face value, for those who acquired them for export, in which transactions the imprinted face value made no difference.

The three-cent piece or trime was introduced in 1851. With a silver content of only 75 percent (unlike the 90 percent of other denominations) it had less than face value in metal and was not attractive to speculators.

Slaves at work in a cotton field under the gaze of the plantation owner and his family. (Vignette from a bank note of the Farmers Banking Association, Demopolis, Alabama)

In 1853 the Treasury Department acquired the building and facilities of private coiner Moffat & Company and its associates and remodeled it to become the San Francisco Mint. It opened in March 1854 and commenced striking coins with S mintmarks. Commercial connections between the Atlantic and Pacific coasts were mainly by ship, interrupted by a land crossing at Panama or, less often, Nicaragua, or entirely by sea, around the tip of South America. In the same year the new $3 gold denomination was introduced at the Philadelphia, Dahlonega, and Charlotte mints, but this met with only a lukewarm reception, as the value was too close to the long-established $2.50 quarter eagle. Over the years the mintage figures declined, and in 1889 it was discontinued.

An 1853 quarter dollar with arrows at the date to indicate reduced silver content.

The American economy was enjoying a new era of prosperity brought on by the gold excitement, the continued expansion of railroads (their shares dominated the stock exchanges), and excellent business conditions everywhere. Land investment and speculation was back in vogue, and real-estate agents were literally doing a land-office business in what was by then known as the Midwest, the term *West* being descriptive of the Rocky Mountains to the Pacific shore.

The Mint had been experimenting since 1850 with ways to reduce the size and weight of the large-diameter one-cent piece, to increase profits. The price of copper had been rising. In 1856, Engraver Longacre created a cent which was proposed for adoption. The obverse featured a flying eagle (adapted from the reverse of Gobrecht's silver dollar of 1836), and the reverse used an "agricultural wreath" from the $3 gold coin of 1854. An estimated 800 to 1,000 coins were struck in late 1856 and early 1857, all dated 1856, and sent to congressmen, newspaper editors, and others to acquaint them with the new design.

The Philadelphia Mint remained the primary facility for federal coinage. The director of the Mint had his office there

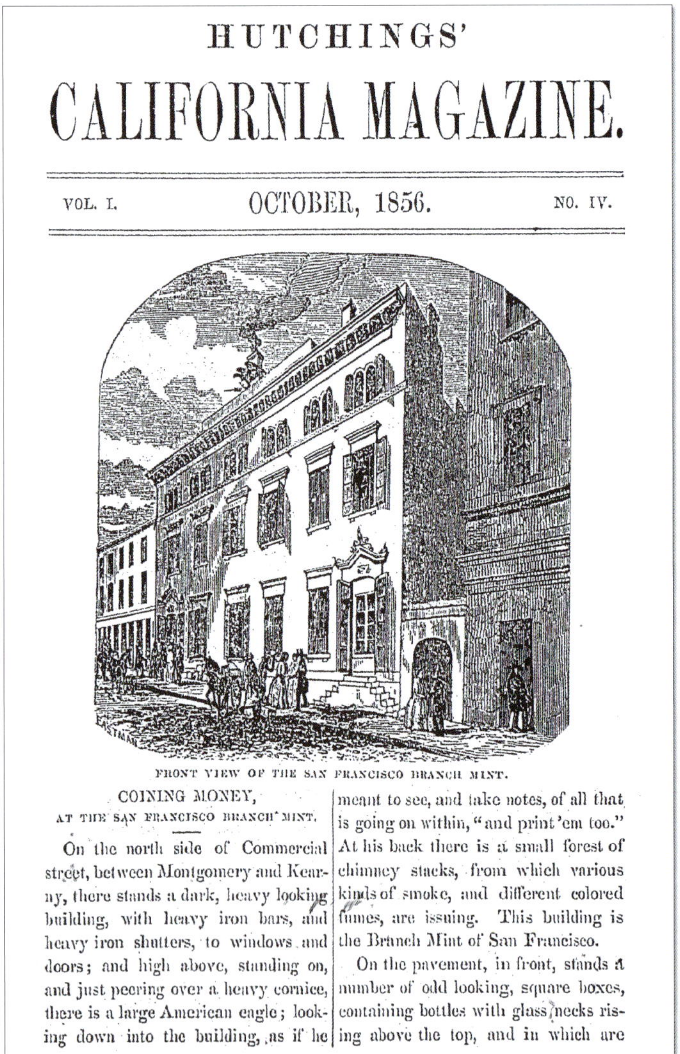

HUTCHINGS'

CALIFORNIA MAGAZINE.

VOL. I. OCTOBER, 1856. NO. IV.

FRONT VIEW OF THE SAN FRANCISCO BRANCH MINT.

COINING MONEY,

AT THE SAN FRANCISCO BRANCH MINT.

On the north side of Commercial street, between Montgomery and Kearny, there stands a dark, heavy looking building, with heavy iron bars, and heavy iron shutters, to windows and doors; and high above, standing on, and just peering over a heavy cornice, there is a large American eagle; looking down into the building, as if he meant to see, and take notes, of all that is going on within, "and print 'em too." At his back there is a small forest of chimney stacks, from which various kinds of smoke, and different colored fumes, are issuing. This building is the Branch Mint of San Francisco.

On the pavement, in front, stands a number of odd looking, square boxes, containing bottles with glass necks rising above the top, and in which are

The San Francisco Mint as depicted in *Hutchings' California Magazine*. This facility operated until 1874 when it was replaced by a new structure.

and supervised the operations of the branches at Charlotte, Dahlonega, New Orleans, and San Francisco. Coins in circulation or currently being minted included the copper half cent and cent, the silver three-cents, half dime, dime, quarter dollar, half dollar, and dollar, and the gold $1, $2.50, $3, $5, $10, and $20. Gold from California was still arriving in quantity, although the peak year was 1853.

A gold ingot issued by the assaying firm of Harris & Marchand in Sacramento. Such ingots facilitated the shipment of gold in quantity.

The Act of February 21, 1857, abolished the copper half cent and cent and mandated other changes, including the planned expiration of the legal-tender privilege for certain foreign silver and gold coins. New cents of the Flying Eagle design, of smaller diameter and made of copper-nickel, soon began rolling off the presses. On May 25, the first small cents were available to the public in exchange for old coppers and Spanish silver.

The passion for coin collecting spread rapidly, with numismatologists, as they were called, seeking rare early cents such as 1793 and 1799, while noticing other interesting old coins as well. Within several years important reference books would be published on coins, dealers would set up shop in major cities, and coin auctions would be held frequently. Thus was born an active market for rare coins, tokens, and medals. The *Historical Magazine* was launched in January 1857 and went on to include many articles about coins, including, in August, the first installment of "The First Coinage of America," by Jeremiah Colburn, who in the same year wrote articles about old copper cents for the Boston *Evening Transcript*. In New York City, Augustus B. Sage and Charles I. Bushnell engaged in a lively debate about rare coins in the pages of the *New-York Dispatch*. In the autumn the first issue of *Norton's Literary Letter*, mostly about books, but with much information on coins, was welcomed by collectors. Thus was born a new market with many thousands of numismatists participating.

The economy had enjoyed good times since 1844 and the passing of the Hard Times era. That changed on August 24, 1857, when the Ohio Life Insurance & Trust Company failed. With offices in Cincinnati and New York, it had been a big player in loans, credit, and the processing of paper relating to real estate. By then there had been some shivers in the money market, and some people were apprehensive concerning seemingly unwise investments, but little was said. On the same day the Mechanics Banking Association suspended specie payments. Fear spread, and those holding stocks and investment paper rushed to cash it in at current rates, but found few buyers. Within days, several stock brokers and money dealers failed. This was disturbing but exciting news, and papers in major cities lost no time printing "scare" headlines, which sold more papers, but also helped spread fear. In a domino effect, one failure created another, and soon the Panic of 1857 was underway. In October all of the banks in New York City suspended specie payments, except for the Chemical Bank. Unlike previous economic disturbances, the Panic of 1857 had little effect on the production of federal coinage.

On January 1, 1858, the Philadelphia Numismatic Society was formed, becoming the first such group in the United States. In March, teenaged Augustus B. Sage and friends founded the American Numismatic Society in New York City. By late summer 1858 there were nearly a dozen coin dealers active in the United States, including, in New York City alone, the venerable John Allan, and at least three young men: Augustus Sage, Henry Bogert, and John Curtis. In the same year the first important American numismatic book was published, *An Historical Account of American Coinage*, by John H. Hickcox. The slim volume included 151 numbered pages plus five pages of illustrations by John Gavit, a well-known engraver of bank note plates. Hickcox had spent some time in research and had contacted historical societies and several numismatists as well as Mint Director James Ross Snowden. Only 200 regular copies were printed, and these were mostly sent to libraries and historical societies. For collectors there was no single readily available source for information, and many still sought the elusive copper cent of 1815, not realizing that none were minted that year.

The issuance of medalets depicting historical events achieved wide popularity in 1858 and 1859 with the creation of hundreds of different privately minted varieties, most in copper and about 32 mm diameter.

A copper medalet depicting Charles I. Bushnell, one of America's most prominent numismatists in 1859. (Augustus Sage's Numismatic Gallery No. 1)

Proof coins became popular in 1858, and an estimated 210 sets of silver denominations were sold, plus a larger number of copper-nickel Flying Eagle cents. Proof gold coins were available singly, and the dollar was the most popular denomination in this metal, probably with a sale of a few dozen or so.

In the meantime James Ross Snowden, Mint director since 1853, was receiving continuous requests for restrikes of earlier coins (heretofore usually granted) and new patterns. Snowden was a numismatist and decided to vastly expand the Mint Cabinet's holding of George Washington–related tokens and medals. He offered to exchange restrikes and rarities for needed pieces. In the spring of 1859 the coining of special coins went "underground," no information was released, and *The Nation*, a popular journal, later estimated that by 1860 Mint officials had pocketed at least $60,000 secretly and without benefit to the government. This largesse would continue unabated until the summer of 1885.

In a way numismatists can be grateful for this illegal activity, for probably at least 90 percent of the nineteenth-century pattern pieces in existence today were produced secretly! The logic of this can be contemplated.

Meanwhile, coin auctions became more frequent, and in 1859 dealer Sage cataloged four sales in New York City, more than any other professional. In Philadelphia, Edward Cogan and William K. Idler became important in the coin trade. Henry Cook bought and sold coins in Boston, another shop was open in Baltimore, and a few more were scattered here and there. The first really large and impressive book for coin collectors was published that year, the *American Numismatical Manual*, by Dr. Montroville W. Dickeson.

A wooden cabinet with sliding drawers was the standard way to store and display a rare-coin collection, as seen in this 1859 illustration in the *American Numismatical Manual.*

THE 1860s AND THE CIVIL WAR

In 1860 and 1861 in Denver the banking firm of Clark, Gruber & Co., headquartered in Leavenworth, Kansas, set up a private mint and bank, and coined $2.50, $5, $10, and $20 gold pieces from local bullion. The district was in the middle of the "Pikes Peak or Bust" gold boom. Such coins were also made in 1861.

The swelling number of incoming enthusiasts electrified the coin market. Most in demand were the old copper cents, but the hottest area in terms of rapid price appreciation was the specialty of Washington pieces. Collectors scrambled to buy them in competition with Director Snowden. Prices multiplied, and specimens were hard to find.

The Clark, Gruber & Co. bank and mint in Denver in 1861. In 1862 the facility was acquired by the Treasury Department. It was renamed the Denver Mint but functioned only as an assay office and did not produce coins.

The 1860 presidential election fielded four candidates: Abraham Lincoln, Republican Party from Illinois; John C. Breckinridge, Southern Democratic Party from Kentucky; John C. Bell, Constitution Union Party from Tennessee; and Stephen A. Douglas, Northern Democratic Party from Illinois. In the November contest Lincoln, who campaigned as a staunch abolitionist, won by a landslide. This prompted South Carolina to secede from the Union on December 20, followed by six other Southern states in short order. These formed the Confederate States of America (CSA) in January 1861, with its capital in Montgomery, Alabama (moved later in the year to Richmond, Virginia).

An 1860 Lincoln token for the presidential campaign.

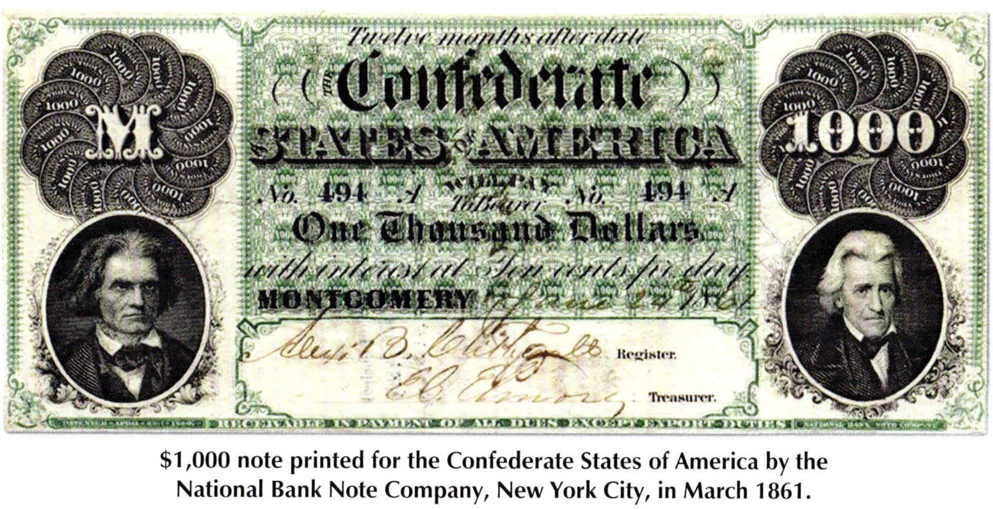

$1,000 note printed for the Confederate States of America by the National Bank Note Company, New York City, in March 1861.

At first, many in the Confederacy hoped to have favorable relations with the Union as a separate nation and trading partner. The first CSA issues of paper money and the first bonds were printed to its order by the National Bank Note and American Bank Note companies in New York City. Lincoln was inaugurated on March 4, 1861. Relations deteriorated. In the second week of April CSA forces at Fort Moultrie on the shore of Charleston Harbor bombarded and destroyed federal Fort Sumter, but allowed the men there to escape under a white flag to board a steamship for the North.

The War of the Rebellion, later generally called the Civil War (or, in the South, the War of Northern Aggression), began. The Northerners or Yankees perceived this as a quick win—the mighty industrial North against the primarily agricultural South. President Lincoln called for 90-day enlistments, by which time it was thought the war would certainly be over. Reality proved otherwise, and it was not until late July that the first important battle took place, at Bull Run in Manassas, Virginia, not far from the Union capital of Washington, D.C. To the surprise of the North, the Confederate troops won.

Under the Act of July 17, 1861, the Treasury Department issued $50,000,000 in Demand Notes, the first widely circulated paper money since Revolutionary times. To facilitate their acceptance, they could be exchanged at par for gold coins. Additional Demand Notes were authorized in February 1862. The story of federal paper money from this point onward is extensive and complex, beyond the purview of *Mega Red*, although scattered mentions are included here.

Meanwhile, in the Confederate States of America, coins all but disappeared. The Confederacy contemplated issuing a new series of half dollars with a unique design, but the coinage amounted to only four patterns. The *Richmond Enquirer*, December 31, 1861, reported that entrepreneurs were paying 30 to 50 percent premium in paper money to buy silver and gold coins: "The present price of specie will be hereafter quoted through all time as a damning stigma upon the character of Southern merchants." By that time Confederate paper money circulated widely through the region. Such bills continued to be issued into 1864 and steadily depreciated in value.

The bombardment of federal Fort Sumter in the harbor of Charleston, South Carolina on April 12, 1861, by cannon at Fort Moultrie on the shore.

By December 1861 the war was not going well for either side. In the North, citizens became apprehensive and began to hoard gold and silver. By early 1862, such coins were worth a small premium in terms of paper money, the latter being in the form of bills issued by banks. Things went from bad to worse after the Act of February 25, 1862, authorized the issue of a new series of paper money, Legal Tender notes, not redeemable in coins, but only exchangeable for other paper money.

Jefferson Davis, president of the Confederate States of America. (portrait by Mathew Brady)

General Robert E. Lee, commander of the Confederate forces.

Union soldiers taking a break.

The Confederate ironclad CSS *Merrimac* (center) and the Union USS *Monitor*, in the first battle of ironclad ships, off of Norfolk, Virginia, ended in a draw but revolutionized naval warfare.

Legal Tender Notes authorized in early 1862 were exchangeable at par only for other bank notes and not for gold or silver coins. The monetary system became disruptive.

Coin hoarding increased, and by summer 1862 no silver or gold coins were to be seen anywhere in circulation in the East or Midwest. Money brokers conducted a lively exchange business with investors and speculators, and daily prices were quoted for silver and gold coins. Proof coins continued to be minted for collectors, but the Philadelphia Mint would not accept Legal Tender notes at par for them. Instead, numismatists had to go to money brokers and buy regular coins for a premium, then send these coins to the Mint, with extra coins for the proofing charge, to obtain such sets. As a result mintages were low.

Postage Currency notes with stamp designs, 5 cents to 50 cents, were issued by the Treasury in the summer of 1862 at a time when no coins were in circulation.

On the West Coast it was a different monetary story from the scenario in the East. The California State Legislature had made the use of paper money *illegal* in commerce, beginning in 1850. When the federal government started sending Legal Tender and other notes to the West, such as to pay soldiers and government employees, these bills were accepted only at a deep discount. "Hard money" in the form of silver and gold coins continued to trade there at face value during the conflict, continuing into the 1870s.

More than 30 merchants issued encased postage stamps beginning in the summer of 1862, using stamps from 1¢ to 90¢ values.

By the second week of July, 1862, even one-cent pieces were hoarded in the East and Midwest. To facilitate commerce, a flood of paper scrip notes (3¢, 5¢, 10¢, and 25¢ were the most popular denominations) and even postage stamps was used as money. John Gault patented his encased postage stamps, with a regular stamp, from 1¢ to 90¢, mounted behind clear mica in a brass case—intended to be durable in circulation. Soon a flood of federal Postage Currency notes appeared, followed by Fractional Currency, eventually swelling to many millions of dollars in 3¢, 5¢, 10¢, 15¢, 25¢, and 50¢ denominations. Legal Tender notes rolled off the printing presses, and a new series of National Bank notes appeared.

Civil War tokens of bronze and brass were issued by the millions. Dates range from 1861 to 1864 but most bear the year 1863. These featured many different motifs, ranging from historical portraits to war heroes and scenes, to advertisements for more than 900 stores and services. Sutlers—licensed merchants who mostly traveled with the troops—issued tokens as well. At the very outset these became popular with numismatists and have remained a popular specialty ever since.

In 1862 the United States government purchased the private mint of Clark, Gruber & Co. and designated it as the Denver Mint in its reports for the next several decades, but no coins were struck there. Years later in 1906 another Denver Mint was opened and was the first facility there to make coins.

The Act of April 22, 1864, provided that bronze alloy be used for cents and the new two-cent denomination, and it made the cent legal tender up to the amount of 10¢ and the two-cent piece legal tender up to 20¢. Thus, for the first time, coins other than silver or gold became legal tender in the United States. It is a curious fact that the old copper half cents and cents (of 1793–1857) were not legal tender, and anyone had the right to refuse them in payment for debts. The motto IN GOD WE TRUST was employed on the two-cent piece, the first use of this for circulating coins. Later, it would be added to most other coins. After the spring of 1864 federal cents returned to circulation, including millions of hoarded pieces.

A Civil War token issued by Sherwood & Hopson, Utica, New York.

In July 1864 in the East it took $285 in Legal Tender bills to buy $100 in gold coins from a money broker or exchange office, the all-time high for the Civil War period. On the West Coast the situation was the opposite: coins were plentiful in stores, banks, and elsewhere; paper bills brought from the East remained illegal in commerce, but could be bought or sold to money brokers at a discount deep enough to equal the premium on gold and silver coins in the East. If at a particular time it took $285 in Legal Tender notes to buy $100 in gold coins in New York, then in San Francisco anyone with $100 in gold coins could go to an exchange dealer and buy $285 in Legal Tender notes.

A token issued by Harvey Lewis, sutler to the 23rd Massachusetts regiment.

Silver and gold coins were anticipated to soon return to circulation when the Civil War ended in April 1865. However, the public remained wary of all of the paper bills in commerce, and silver and gold remained at a premium. It was not until years later, in April 1876, that silver coins were again exchangeable at par with paper, and not until December 1879 that gold and paper were equal. By those times in the 1870s a generation of children had grown into adulthood without seeing a single silver or gold coin in circulation!

In 1864 the two-cent piece was introduced, the first circulating coin to have the motto IN GOD WE TRUST. These did not prove to be popular and were discontinued in 1873.

In the meantime in the 1860s numismatics prospered. On February 22, 1860, the Washington Cabinet was opened at the Mint and featured the vastly

MASON'S PHOTOGRAPHIC GALLERY

OF THE

COIN COLLECTORS OF THE UNITED STATES.

No. 1.

B. F. REIMER, ARTIST, PHILA.

1 J. J. Mickley, Philadelphia, Pa.
2 M. W. Dickeson, " "
3 W. H. Nevil, " "
4 Robert C. Davis, " "
5 E. J. B. Thomas, " "
6 F. D. Watson, " "
7 Wm. J. Jenks, " "
8 Joel Modot, G. Island, N. Y.
9 A. H. Johnson, Springfield, Mass.
10 J. Parker, " "
11 J. Hocker, Philadelphia, Pa.
12 G. F. Jones " "
13 G. H. Wells, " "
14 N. C. Folwell, " "
15 H. W. Lloyd, " "
16 C. P. Nichols, Springfield, Mass.
17 A. S. Bryant, Springfield, Mass.
18 Wm. Clogston, " "
19 Wm. Jester, Philadelphia, Pa.
20 J. W. Haseltine, " "
21 Chas. English, Jr., Camden, N. J.
22 F. P. Randall, Fort Wayne, Ind.
23 J. A. Bolen, Springfield, Mass.
24 M. Littlefield, Woburn, Mass.
25 L. H. Caldwell, New York.
26 Thomas Martin, Philadelphia, Pa
27 G. M. Payfer, Troy, N. Y.
28 C. A. Bulkley, Granville, N. Y.
29 J. E. Westcoat, Westfield, Mass.
30 E. S. Nott, W. Corners, N. Y.
31 R. S. Emerson, Westfield, N. Y.
32 F. M. Yeager, Reading, Pa.
33 D. O. W. Ufford, W. Troy, N. Y.
34 C. H. Davis, Troy. N. Y.
35 J. A. Shafer, Allentown, Pa.
36 C. B. Romans, Mortonville, Pa.
37 F. W. Ferry, Bethel, Conn.
38 C. W. Carhartt, Jackson, Mich.
39 C. R. Scott, Mortonville, Pa.
40 G. D. Rollins, Springfield, Mass.
41 F. R. Smith, Grand Rapids, Mich.
42 N. Landry, San F. California.
43 T. T. Bates, G. Traverse, Mich.
44 E. Mason, Jr., Philadelphia, Pa.
45 L. W. Durbin, St. Louis, Mo.
46 C. A. V. Snyder, Reading, Pa.
47 E. B. Trernan, Elmira, N. Y.
48 A. C. Kline, Philadelphia, Pa.

In 1869 Ebenezer Locke Mason Jr., a prominent coin dealer in Philadelphia, published *Mason's Photographic Gallery of the Coin Collectors of the United States.*

expanded display gathered by Director James Ross Snowden. Auctions became a regular feature in the 1860s, and dozens of important sales were conducted by W. Elliot Woodward, Edward D. Cogan, and others. Usually, the sales were held in commercial auction rooms and conducted by a professional auctioneer, not the writer of the catalog. Such auction firms usually sold other things as well, including books, art, and furniture.

In 1865 the nickel three-cent piece was introduced to facilitate commerce, as silver coins were still being hoarded.

In 1866 the first regularly issued coin magazine, the *American Journal of Numismatics*, was published by the American Numismatic and Archaeological Society, successor in 1864 to the short-lived 1858–1859 American Numismatic Society. In the same decade Ebenezer Locke Mason Jr., a Philadelphia coin dealer, issued his own combined news magazine and price list. There were no grading standards and no single source to learn coin mintages and market prices. Accordingly, it devolved upon every successful collector and dealer to spend time to learn the intricacies of the hobby. This resulted in deep bonding with numismatics, and most serious numismatists remained in the field for many years.

The nickel five-cent piece made its debut in the summer of 1865 and largely replaced the three-cent piece. The larger denomination proved to be popular and has been made nearly continuously ever since.

THE 1870S AND 1880S

The Carson City Mint was opened in Nevada 1870 to coin silver and gold from Virginia City and the Comstock Lode. Each coin bore a CC mintmark. The facility produced silver and gold coins through 1885 and again from 1889 to 1893. The career of the mint was somewhat checkered—interlaced with politics. Much silver and gold was shipped from Virginia City to the distant San Francisco Mint instead of 15 miles away to the Carson City Mint. Today the Nevada State Museum is housed there. CC-mintmark coins are especially highly prized by numismatists.

In the 1870s the prices of most coins, tokens, and medals rose steadily, although Washington pieces, once the darlings of the market, fell from favor. Changes were in the wind, and among many other provisions, the Coinage Act of 1873 abolished the two-cent piece, silver three-cent piece, and half dime, provided for the new trade dollar denomination, and slightly increased the authorized weights of dimes, quarter dollars, and half dollars

The Carson City Mint.

(which subsequently were made with arrowheads at the date to indicate the different standard). The standard silver dollar was not treated in the act, and this denomination therefore lapsed.

The Gould & Curry mine and mill in Virginia City, the largest producer of silver and gold in the Comstock Lode.

Soon, there was a popular outcry that the act was unfavorable to silver-mining interests and citizens of Western states, and the legislation became known as the "Crime of '73." Some politicians said that the act was rushed through passage, they did not have time to study it, did not realize the standard dollar would be discontinued, did not like the idea of the gold dollar becoming important by this default, would not have voted for it if they had been aware of its implications, etc. However, the *Congressional Record* shows very clearly that Western legislators studied and debated the bill at length before its passage. Later historians have been largely unaware of this.

In 1874 the San Francisco Mint was relocated to a new facility that would remain in operation until 1937. Modern equipment and the latest amenities were put in place. The cornerstone was laid in 1870 and included examples of the coinage of that year. Of the 1870-S half dime and $3 gold coin only one example of each is known today and of the 1870-S silver dollar only about a dozen.

In 1875 a new denomination, the 20-cent piece, was introduced with the expectation that it would be useful in the West, but the public confused the coins with quarter dollars, and in 1876 the mintage was sharply decreased. Only Proofs were made for collectors in 1877 and 1878, after which production was discontinued.

During the decade the price of silver declined on world markets. In the United States, increasing production in Nevada plus new discoveries, includ-

The second San Francisco Mint opened in 1874.

An 1875-S 20-cent piece.

ing in the Leadville, Colorado, district, resulted in a glut of the metal. Free Silverites, as pro-silver advocates were called, pressured politicians to abandon gold and institute silver as the dominant coinage metal. From the late 1870s onward this was the overwhelming political question in America, and it remained so until the presidential election of 1896.

After about April 20, 1876, the price of silver coins reached parity with Silver Certificates and other paper money. Citizens, exchange brokers, and banks who had been hoarding quantities of coins since 1862 turned them loose, resulting in a large glut of coins from half dimes to half dollars flooding circulation. Because of this, most mintages of quarters and half dollars dropped to low levels through the end of the Liberty Seated design in 1891.

A notable political boondoggle to support the sagging market for silver bullion, the Bland-Allison Act of February 28, 1878, directed the government to purchase millions of ounces of silver each year and coin the metal into dollars. The talents of assistant engraver George T. Morgan were tapped for the design, based on an 1877 pattern half dollar. Hundreds of millions of these dollars were made through 1921 and mainly stored in bank vaults. Today Morgan silver dollars are the most popular nineteenth-century coins from a numismatic viewpoint, from the later release of millions of coins.

The new 1878 Morgan silver dollar.

In December 1879 the value of gold coins achieved parity with Legal Tender Notes on the markets, and long-stored gold coins came out of hiding and were once again seen in commerce. By this time the public had good faith in paper money with the result that the widespread use of gold in everyday transactions was mainly confined to the Western states.

A great speculation arose in gold dollars. All available supplies were bought, and the market price rose to a modest premium. New pieces produced at the Philadelphia Mint yielded instant profits for those who were lucky enough to obtain and resell them. Investment interest in gold dollars continued for the rest of the decade. As a result in today's market Mint State gold dollars of 1879 to 1889 are plentiful in relation to their low mintages, while most earlier dates are rare in this state of preservation. At the same time a "bubble" rose in the market for Proof silver trade dollars, a denomination that had not been made in circulation-strike form after early 1878. Speculators scrambled to order 1879 Proofs from the Mint, and the production jumped up to 1,541 pieces (as compared to only 900 Proofs in 1878). The excitement continued, and in 1880 the Mint set a record of 1,987 Proofs. The passion faded, and in 1881 just 960 Proofs were struck.

The New Orleans Mint, closed since early 1861, was refurbished in 1878 and reopened for business in 1879. Silver and gold coins would be made there until 1909, after which time the building was used for other purposes. Today it houses a museum.

In January 1883 the new Liberty Head nickel without CENTS on the reverse created a nationwide sensation. Sharpers gold-plated them and passed them off as $5 gold coins. It was stated in many newspaper articles that the Mint had made a terrible mistake and would be recalling all examples, after which they would have great value. Excitement prevailed, and thousands of newcomers entered the hobby. In the meantime, the coins never did become

The first 1883 Liberty Head nickels had the denomination expressed only by the letter V, prompting some sharpers to gold-plate them and pass them as $5 gold coins.

rare, as many were minted and large quantities were saved. Still, the craze was good for the hobby, as countless thousands of citizens went from the new nickels to collect other coins.

The market went into overdrive. Many dealers opened up shops, several issued their own magazines (Ed Frossard's *Numisma* and Scott Stamp & Coin Company's *Coin Collector's Journal* notable among them), and the field of auction catalogers grew as well. John W. Haseltine and the Chapman brothers (S. Hudson and Henry) created many memorable sales, with the 1882 Bushnell Collection by the Chapmans being the most exciting auction event of the decade.

T. Harrison Garrett, of Baltimore, and Lorin G. Parmelee, of Boston, became known as super-collectors, snatching up rarities. Rare coins furnished fodder for newspapers, and metropolitan dailies carried many accounts of rare 1804 silver dollars being sold at auction, or old Massachusetts Pine Tree shillings being found buried in the ground, and more. All during this scenario, the prices of scarce and rare early United States coins continued to rise. During the 1880s a dozen or more newspapers devoted to collecting coins, stamps, Indian relics, and other things were published, often with news on multiple fields of interest.

In 1888 *The Numismatist* began publication under the auspices of Dr. George F. Heath, a Monroe, Michigan, physician who was a deeply knowledgeable collector and a skilled writer. It has endured and today is the official publication of the American Numismatic Association, as it has been for many years.

The Coinage Act of 1889 discontinued the nickel three-cent piece and the gold $1 and $3.

The decade of the 1880s had been a golden era for many activities. More county and other history books were published than in any such period before, railroad and ocean-travel facilities were more elegant than ever, and the outlook was rosier than it had been in a long time. In the Midwest many towns rose from the land as boulevards, buildings, rail lines, and other construction took place.

Things changed. Late in the decade storm clouds rose on the economic horizon, mainly due to over-speculation in land and buildings in the prairie states. Bonds to furnish large-scale expansion had been issued at interest rates of 8 to 10 percent, several points more than comparable securities issued in the East paid. Large amounts of money flowed into Iowa, Nebraska, and other states. Then came reality. Municipalities and others were not able to maintain interest payments and there were many bankruptcies.

THE 1890s INTO THE 1900s

By 1890 there were coin dealers in most cities in the eastern part of the United States, with Boston, New York City, and Philadelphia the central points of activity. J.W. Scott. W. Elliot Woodward, the auction firm of Bangs, Merwin & Co., the Chapman brothers, John Haseltine, Lyman H. Low, Ed. Frossard, and Charles Steigerwalt were among the leading professionals of the day. In 1890 New York Coin & Stamp Co. conducted the sale of the Lorin G. Parmelee Collection, the second finest cabinet (after T. Harrison Garrett's) in private hands in America. Results were mixed, and Parmelee, hardly a motivated seller, bought many of the rarities back. The coin market was entering a chilly period as was the national economy. Difficult times lay ahead.

In November 1891 in Chicago the American Numismatic Association (ANA) was formed, thus providing a common meeting place for the exchange of ideas and values among collectors from all parts of the United States and elsewhere. Beginners and amateurs were encouraged to join, while some other societies preferred numismatists with experience. Charles E. Barber's Liberty Head silver dime, quarter, and half dollar, called "Barber coins" today, were first issued in 1892. Public and numismatic interest was lukewarm.

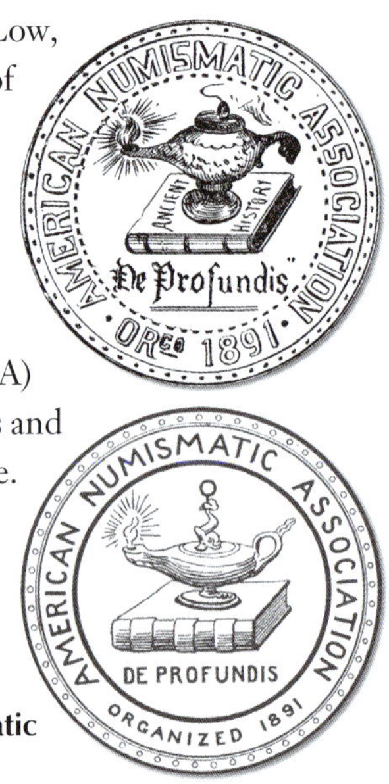

An 1894 proposal for the American Numismatic Association seal, and one later adopted.

An 1892-O Barber dime. Dimes, quarters, and half dollars designed by Chief Engraver Charles E. Barber were introduced in this year and remained in use until 1916 for the dime and quarter and 1915 for the half dollar.

The 1892 Columbian souvenir half dollar, as it was called, was produced in the year before the World's Columbian Exposition opened to the public. This was the first United States commemorative coin.

The World's Columbian Exposition was planned to open in Chicago in 1892 to celebrate the 400th anniversary of Christopher Columbus's landing in the New World. Progress was slower than anticipated, and it did not open to the public until 1893. Attractions included dozens of impressive buildings, the gigantic Ferris Wheel, and extensive exhibits of art, culture, and industry. America's first commemorative coins were issued for this event, initiating a numismatic specialty that eventually included hundreds of varieties and remains dynamic to the present day.

To this point numismatists had little interest in collecting coins by mintmark varieties. Whether a coin had an S, D, or other letter was of no importance. It was just the date of the coin that mattered. This began to change in 1893 when Augustus G. Heaton, a professional artist by trade and a numismatist by avocation, published a treatise on coins from the United States branch mints. In time such branch-mint rarities as the 1894-S dime and 1876-CC twenty-cent piece attracted notice. Interest in mintmarked gold coins developed much more slowly and did not become widely popular until decades later in the 1930s.

Speculation in prairie lands, unwise loans, and unbridled growth of the 1880s came together in the Panic of 1893. Times were difficult, many banks failed, and there was political unrest. Participants in the Free Silver movement, a political philosophy which had been gaining adherents since the 1870s, became especially vocal. It was felt by this faction that reliance on gold was hindering national growth and prosperity, and that American coinage and international trade should be based on silver, a metal in oversupply.

Silver, in oversupply in relation to the market, continued to be produced in large quantities. Shown are silver ingots at the American Smelter in Leadville, Colorado, in 1893.

The government policy of coining large amounts of silver into dollar coins was part of the "Silver Question," the pivotal political debate of the era. As the poor economic climate continued, the supply of gold coins in the United States Treasury fell to $41 million due to large exports of double eagles. Foreign interests were fearful that the Silverites would convince the government to allow overseas debts to be paid in silver dollars (the intrinsic worth of which kept declining and were worth about 48 cents each) and demanded gold. Banker J.P. Morgan and his associates stepped in to augment the gold reserves, one of the most embarrassing points in American financial history.

Several conventions were staged by advocates of free and unlimited coinage of silver to support the diminishing market. In an 1895 cartoon, "turtles" of silver dollars, marked "Real Value 50 Cents," are about to plunge into financial oblivion over a waterfall—suggesting what might happen to the American economy if such practice was continued. The presidential election of 1896 focused on silver and pitted Democrat William Jennings Bryan against Republican William McKinley. Bryan's "Cross of Gold" speech electrified the nation and gave momentum to the Free Silver movement and "easy money," promising Midwesterners and others in distress the ability to pay their debts more readily. McKinley won, and the silver movement faded sharply, although remnants lingered into the new century. Bryan ran for president on the Democratic ticket in 1900 and 1908 and lost both times.

In the 1890s gold strikes in the Cripple Creek District of Colorado starting early in the decade, followed by the Klondike Gold Rush of the late 1890s, yielded vast quantities of precious metals, much of which were coined into double eagles at the San Francisco Mint. Both events electrified the country with tales of adventures and fortunes and newspaper coverage knew no limits.

The discovery in the early 1890s of gold-bearing calaverite and telluride ore in the Cripple Creek District on the west side of Pikes Peak created a great rush that resulted in a population of more than 100,000 people by the turn of the century. An estimated $400 million in gold was extracted in an era in which the metal was worth $20.67 per ounce. The Cripple Creek District included Victor, Altman, and other communities. Shown is the panorama in 1895.

The Portland Mine on Battle Mountain, Victor, in 1896, the largest mine in the Cripple Creek District.

Main Street in Dawson City in 1898, the largest settlement in the Klondike district.

The Klondike on the Yukon River in British Columbia and Alaska yielded large amounts of gold late in the 1890s, much of which went to the San Francisco Mint to be coined into double eagles. Shown are adventurers in Chilkoot Pass, above Skagway, Alaska, on the way to the gold district.

In 1901 the third Philadelphia Mint was opened and would remain in use until 1966. All equipment and facilities were state of the art. The engraving and die-making departments continued to be centered there and served the branch mints.

In September of the same year President William McKinley was assassinated while attending the Pan-American Exposition in Buffalo, New York. Vice President Theodore Roosevelt succeeded him in the post.

In 1903 the United States began minting coins specifically for the Philippines, which had been a U.S. possession since the conclusion of the Spanish-American War in 1898. The coins featured the name UNITED STATES OF AMERICA and also the Spanish name FILIPINAS, along with designs by Filipino artist Melecio Figueroa.

The new Philadelphia Mint opened in 1901.

A silver peso minted for the Philippines under U.S. administration.

The Main Coining Room in the new Mint, with rows of electrically driven presses.

In 1904 the Louisiana Purchase Exposition opened in St. Louis. In connection with it two varieties of 1903 gold dollars were minted, the first U.S. commemoratives in that metal.

In 1906 the new Denver Mint opened for business and struck silver and gold coins. It was not until 1911 that copper coins were made there. Its coins bore a D mintmark, a letter that had been used earlier by the Dahlonega Mint from 1838 to 1861.

In April 1906 San Francisco was ravaged by a strong earthquake followed by a fire that leveled most of the commercial district of the city. The Mint was the only building remaining intact in its area and served as a headquarters for relief efforts as well as financial activity.

In 1904 President Roosevelt visited the Smithsonian Institution, a short distance from the White House, and was impressed with the beautiful artistry of ancient Greek coins on display. Not long afterward he determined to make American coins more attractive than ever before, replacing the current designs. He tapped Augustus Saint-Gaudens, America's most famous sculptor, to redesign the entire coinage spectrum from the cent to the double eagle. The artist's first effort was the $20 coin, the new design being in medallic high relief and the 1907 date in Roman numerals as MCMVII. On the obverse was *Victory* holding a palm branch, and on the reverse was a flying eagle. The sculptor redesigned he $10 eagle with an

The Denver Mint with the Colorado State Capitol in the distance. The facility was greatly expanded in 1937 and remains in use today.

Looking toward Market Street in San Francisco after the earthquake of April 18, 1906, with the fire beginning to consume most of the city.

After the fire the San Francisco Mint was the only building that remained standing. It served as a relief center and also assisted with banking.

Indian Head. Saint-Gaudens passed away in August 1907. The redesign of coinage by artists in the private sector was continued in later years with all other denominations.

The high relief of the MCMVII $20 caused production problems, and Chief Engraver Charles E. Barber changed the design to low relief and the date to regular numerals. Only 12,367 of the MCMVII coins were made, but they were so popular with the public and with numismatists that enough were saved that about half the mintage survives today.

In the same year the $2.50 and $5 gold coins were redesigned by Bela Lyon Pratt, with a recessed relief design. This met with uniformly negative reaction by collectors and dealers as expressed in pages of *The Numismatist.* Starting with each of the four gold denominations in 1908 the Sand Blast Proof finish took the place of the mirror style used in earlier years. These new Proofs were unpopular with collectors, and in the next year Satin Finish Proofs succeeded them. These also generated complaints, and in 1911 the Sand Blast Proofs were resumed, to continue in the gold series to 1915.

The MCMVII (1907) High Relief double eagle by Augustus Saint-Gaudens.

In 1908 Indian Head cents were struck at the San Francisco Mint, the first branch mint coinage of a minor (non–precious metal) denomination. In the same year the American Numismatic Society ("and Archaeological" having been dropped from its name) moved into a handsome new stone building, largely financed by Archer M. Huntington (stepson of railroad magnate Collis P. Huntington), on Audubon Terrace, Morningside Heights, New York City. An additional gift from Huntington added an adjacent matching building in the early 1930s.

The 1908 $2.50 designed by Bela Lyon Pratt. $5 coins were made with the same motif.

The 1907 Indian Head $10 by Saint-Gaudens.

In August 1909 the new Lincoln design for the cent was issued, created by Victor D. Brenner, a sculptor and medalist of renown. It the latest in the series of motifs designed by artists in the private sector. The first issues had the initials V.D.B. on the reverse, but a controversy arose, and they were soon removed, by which time 27,995,000 had been made at the Philadelphia Mint. Only 484,000 were made of the San Francisco issue (1909-S V.D.B.), creating a numismatic rarity. Proofs for collectors were in the Matte style, not much different from circulation strikes upon quick glance, and were not popular.

The 1909-S V.D.B. Lincoln cent became the key to the series and remains a numismatic favorite today.

The rare-coin market had been very strong during the decade, with steady rises in the number of collectors and in values. Collecting coins by mintmarks had not become widely popular yet, but the 1909-S V.D.B. cent, which quickly went up in value to 5¢, then 10¢, then higher, prompted many more numismatists to pay attention to branch-mint issues.

The decade saw many innovations and expansions including the vastly increased popularity of the automobile and the dawn of the age of aviation. Prosperity was the order of the era, and the difficulties of the 1890s were largely forgotten.

Orville Wright and the first powered heavier-than-air craft at Kill Devil Hill on December 17, 1903, inaugurating the aviation age.

By 1910, automobiles were a familiar sight all across America. Shown is a Hupmobile of that year.

THE 1910s AND 1920s

In 1912 the first branch-mint nickel coins were struck at the Denver and San Francisco mints. This was the last year of the Liberty Head design (although a few 1913 coins were privately made the next year). In 1913 the Buffalo or Indian Head five-cent piece, by sculptor James Earle Fraser, was released and achieved wide popularity.

To observe the opening of the Panama Canal (in 1914) and the rebirth of the city after the fire and earthquake of 1906, the Panama-Pacific Exposition in San Francisco offered a grand "city" of elegant buildings with many displays and attractions. Coin dealer Farran Zerbe had charge of selling commemorative coins of the half dollar, gold dollar, $2.50, and two varieties of the $50 denominations. The American Numismatic Association held its annual convention in the same city this year, but attendance was very low, due in part to the unpopularity of Zerbe and certain questionable actions he had with the ANA earlier when he served as president (such as rigging an election).

Production of Sand Blast Proof gold coins ended in 1915, and 1916 was the last year for Matte Proof cents and nickels. These finishes were very unpopular with collectors, who preferred the older style "brilliant" or "mirror" field type. Protests to no avail had been made to the Mint by the New York Numismatic Club and others. It was not until 1936 that Proof coins, then of the popular mirror finish, were again available to collectors.

In 1916 the denominations of silver coins then being struck were given new designs, much to the enthusiasm and acclamation not only of the numismatic community but of the public as well. The new "Mercury" or Winged Liberty Head dime was created by Adolph A. Weinman, the Standing Liberty quarter dollar by Hermon A. MacNeil, and the Liberty Walking half dollar by Weinman. The 1916-D dime and the 1916 Standing Liberty quarter became rarities due to their low mintages.

The World War had been raging in Europe since August 1914. In 1916 many Americans joined the English and French and other forces opposing the German troops of Kaiser Wilhelm II and his allies.

In 1913 the Buffalo nickel, as it came to be called, was introduced with a design by sculptor James Earle Fraser. The obverse depicted a Native American and the reverse a bison. The motif was continued through 1938.

The 1916 Winged Liberty Head or "Mercury" dime by Adolph A. Weinman.

The 1916 Standing Liberty quarter by Hermon A. MacNeil.

The 1916 Walking Liberty half dollar by Adolph A. Weinman.

This was on a voluntary basis, such as service with the Red Cross and the airborne Lafayette Escadrille. In 1917 the United States declared war and many soldiers, sailors, and aviators volunteered for service. Liberty Bond campaigns were conducted across the land. Truce finally took place on November 11, 1918. The terms the victorious allies demanded of the Germans were very harsh, creating much turmoil during the next 15 years, including runaway inflation, which led to the rise of Adolph Hitler and the Nazi party in the early 1930s.

A Liberty Loan poster for the World War, 1917, designed by Howard Chandler Christy.

The war brought great prosperity to American industries supplying munitions, equipment, and other necessities of combat. Coin mintages reached record highs. The good times did not last, and from 1921 into 1923 the American economy took a nap. Coin mintages dropped precipitately. In 1922 no nickels, dimes, quarters, or regular-issue half dollars were made (although within the latter denomination there were some commemoratives).

In 1918 the Pittman Act resulted in the melting of 270,232,722 silver dollars in Treasury storage, to supply bullion to England to ship to India. None had been minted since 1904, and the denomination was believed to have been discontinued. At the Mint the models and master dies had been destroyed in 1910.

In February 1918 the Philippine Legislature passed an appropriations bill for construction of machinery for a new mint. The Philippines in that era was still under the administration of the United States, but moving steadily toward independence. The Manila Mint opened on July 15, 1920. Earlier U.S./Philippine coins had been struck in Philadelphia, San Francisco, and Denver. Now the islands had a domestic source for coinage, which would continue to operate until the Japanese military invaded in 1941.

In 1921 the Treasury gave a hurry-up call to mint more silver dollars to provide backing for Silver Certificates. The old Morgan design was remodeled slightly, and more than 85 million new dollars were struck at the Philadelphia, Denver, and San Francisco mints. The Treasury hoped for a new design, but that was not ready until December 1921, when 1,006,473 coins of the Peace design by sculptor Anthony de Francisci were struck. The Peace dollar design was continued to 1928 and again in 1934 and 1935.

Florida experienced a wild boom in real estate in 1924 and 1925, but the end came soon, in 1926. Acres of vacant home lots were left in planned communities. Not to worry, as overall the American economy experienced boom times—the "Roaring Twenties." Many skyscrapers were built in cities, luxury automobiles were all the rage, mansions were constructed—an era epitomized by novelist F. Scott Fitzgerald in *The Great Gatsby* and in a later retrospective history, *Only Yesterday*, by Frederick Lewis Allen. Riding along with the crest, in the next several years, rare books, art, and common stocks became investment sensations.

An official commemorative medal popularly known as the "Wilson Dollar" was struck to celebrate the 1920 opening of the Manila Mint.

The rare-coin market did not participate in the boom economy and remained very quiet. New York City dealer Thomas L. Elder lamented that the great collectors of yesteryear had not been replaced by a new generation of moneyed buyers. This had a bright side, in a way. When other markets collapsed in 1929, coins held their values fairly well. Several wealthy people who were hurt by the economic conditions of the early 1930s found comfort in the value of their coin collections—Waldo C. Newcomer of Baltimore being one. Great numismatic rarities sold slowly, but not at significant discounts.

In 1929 small-size bills replaced the large-size federal paper money in use since 1861.

Architect's illustration of the Empire State Building in New York City. Envisioned and designed during the late 1920s, it was built on the site of the first Waldorf-Astoria Hotel and opened in 1931. The top featured a mooring mast for passenger zeppelins but was never used for that purpose.

The Peace design silver dollar designed by Anthony de Francisci was first issued in 1921. With the design modified to lower relief in 1922, the motif continued in use through 1935.

THE 1930s AND THE DEPRESSION ERA

In the early 1930s the rare-coin market continued on a consistent basis. The only notable bankruptcy was the firm of Guttag Brothers, leading coin dealers in the 1920s whose main business was investment securities. In 1929 they moved into their new multi-story building in New York City. The business ran into trouble early that year and collapsed in early 1930, sustaining a loss reported as $9 million. In contrast other leading dealers such as B. Max Mehl in Texas, who had been prominent since the early 1900s, Thomas L. Elder, Wayte Raymond, John Macallister, and others continued to be profitable. Coin prices softened, as noted, but demand remained fairly strong.

Franklin D. Roosevelt entered the presidential race in 1932, running against incumbent Herbert Hoover. The latter promised that "recovery is just around the corner," but economic conditions worsened. Roosevelt promised the "New Deal," a change in policies. In November he won in a landslide. Inaugurated on March 4, 1933, he set about creating many new programs. He prohibited the further issuance of gold coins by the Treasury, although mintage of $10 and $20 gold coins continued for a while. Next came the demand that all citizens turn in gold coins, those of numismatic value and a small allowance per person excepted. In January 1934 America

The $10 and $20 denominations were the only gold coins struck in 1933.

abandoned the gold standard, resulting in runaway inflation of the prices of goods and services, particularly starting in the late 1930s when the Depression wound down.

The change in gold regulations had a dramatic effect on the numismatic market. All of a sudden collectors who had not paid much attention to gold coins set about forming sets and collections. Floyd Starr of Philadelphia and Louis E. Eliasberg of Baltimore were among the best known. Thomas L. Elder issued a premium guide he sent to bank tellers and others advising that many varieties of gold coins turned in to banks by the public had significant numismatic value. Countless thousands of scarce and rare coins were thus saved from destruction.

In New York City in 1933 Morton and Joseph Stack relocated from Wheeling, West Virginia, to set up a rare-coin dealership that soon expanded by leaps and bounds. In 1935 the firm held its first auction. In the meantime Thomas L. Elder and Wayte Raymond held many public auctions, and in Fort Worth, Texas, B. Max Mehl turned out a stream of mail auctions. He also published the *Star Rare Coin Encyclopedia* with buying prices, suggesting that treasures such as a 1913 Liberty Head nickel might be found in pocket change.

As curious as the scenario may seem to an economist or historian without numismatic knowledge, the 1930s saw the greatest market boom in coin-collecting history!

In the early 1930s the Scott Stamp & Coin Company under the direction of Wayte Raymond published the National line of cardboard coin-album pages. These had openings faced on the front and back with cellulose acetate slides, permitting coins to be easily stored and the obverse and reverse to be viewed. Dates and mintages were printed below each opening. This revolutionized numismatics. Now, instead of storing coins in wooden cabinets with trays, collectors could house them in convenient pages that fit into a notebook binder, and could examine the coins from both sides.

The race was on! In the depth of the Depression the hope was held to find in pocket change many coins that had numismatic value, such as the 1877 and 1909-S Indian Head cents, 1909-S V.D.B. and 1914-D Lincoln cents, and many others. The recently issued 1931-S cent with a low mintage of 866,000 coins created excitement, and nearly all were bought by dealers and collectors. Barber dimes, quarters, and half dollars could be found dating back to 1892, usually in About Good or Good grades, well-worn but exciting to collect and enjoy as hole after hole was filled in albums.

Helping matters was that hobbies were all the rage during this era. Crossword puzzles, games, hunting and fishing, and other pursuits drew many new participants. Many towns had shops that sold or rented jigsaw puzzles. Collecting scenic postcards achieved unprecedented popularity.

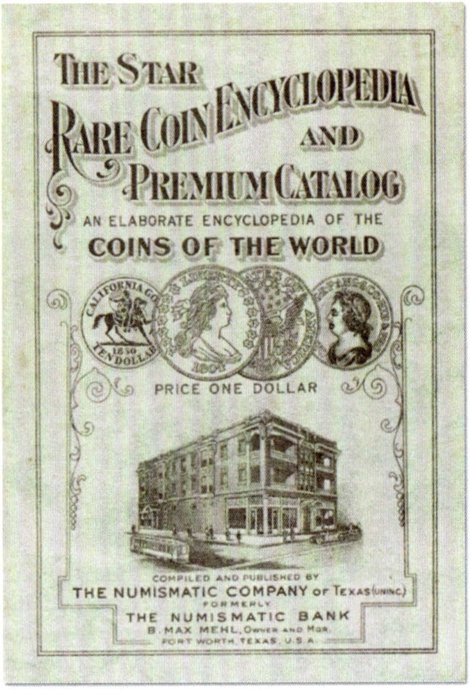

The *Star Rare Coin Encyclopedia* published by B. Max Mehl offered premiums for rare coins, including certain issues in circulation. In the 1930s the book was promoted by print advertising as well as a weekly radio program.

The National Coin Album line published by Scott Stamp & Coin Company, later by Wayte Raymond, Inc., did much to popularize the collecting of coins by dates and mintmarks.

Meanwhile in 1932 the new Washington quarter design by John Flanagan replaced the Standing Liberty motif in use since 1916 (excepting 1922 and 1931). It was intended as a circulating commemorative coin to honor the 200th anniversary of Washington's February 22, 1732, birth, but the Treasury Department decided to continue it as a regular design. Due to economic conditions, relatively few 1932 coins were saved by the general public and not many by numismatists either.

J.K. Post of Neenah, Wisconsin, in 1934 launched the Penny Collector board, a cardboard sheet with openings for each date and mintmark of Lincoln cent from 1909 to date. Western Publishing of Racine, Wisconsin, acquired the product and expanded it to include the Whitman line of boards and, in time, folders and albums.

While the preceding innovations were still in progress the commemorative-coin boom came next. This was launched by one man, Frank Dunn of Lexington, Kentucky, who was in charge of ordering and selling half dollars for the Boone Bicentennial in 1934. From his second-floor office in the Phoenix Hotel he sold 10,000 pieces for $1.60 each. At the time such coins could be ordered by various commissions (some of which were very questionable) who persuaded Congress to pass authorization. Coins were sent to the commissions for face value plus a small charge. The commissions were in charge of setting prices and policies—like coining your own money!

The year 1935 began in a normal way when 10,010 Boone halves were struck in Philadelphia in March and 5,005 each at the Denver and San Francisco mints in May. These were dated 1935 on the reverse of the coin, representing the issue date. Philadelphia coins were offered for $1.10 each, and $1.50 was charged for each Denver and San Francisco coin. A 1935 Boone set of three coins cost a total of $4.10. So far the only problem was that it was no longer the bicentennial of Boone's birthday, and there was no reason to continue celebrating a 1934 anniversary in 1935.

Unexpectedly, in October 1935 at the Philadelphia Mint 10,008 more 1935-dated Boone half dollars were made but with the addition of 1934 / PIONEER YEAR in small numerals on the right side of the reverse. No excitement here, but why create the variety? Then came excitement that knew no bounds. In November the Denver and San Francisco mints produced the very small quantity of just 2,003 and 2,004, respectively, of the modified design. News releases calling attention to the rare issues were sent

A 1932-S Washington quarter.

Whitman Publishing entered the coin-supply business in 1934 and soon offered a line of boards, later followed by folders, as seen here. More people entered numismatics through the use of Lincoln cent folders than by any other method.

out by Dunn. New York City newspapers, among others, carried the information that a pair of low-mintage Boone half dollars had been created at the Denver and San Francisco mints and could be ordered for $3.70 by sending remittances to Dunn. This equaled $1.85 per coin—a truly affordable rarity. These were also advertised in *The Numismatist.* As might be expected for such an incredibly low mintage, orders rushed in. Not so fast! There was a problem. So far as is known (per research conducted years ago by Lee F. Hewitt) *everyone* who ordered received a "Sorry, sold out" letter. No exceptions! Dunn said that they had all been sold to those who had read newspaper accounts.

Detail of the reverse of the 1935-S Boone Bicentennial half dollar with small 1934, of which 2,000 were offered.

No collection was complete without these two coins. In an undisclosed way, some came on to the market, and the price rose to $50 per pair! Not long afterward it was discovered that most of the coins had been retained by Dunn! He was accused of fraud, and transferred many assets to his wife. However, he was never prosecuted, and he continued selling three-coin Boone sets yearly through 1938!

Thus was set the scene for much excitement, with the details of various issues being given later in this book. Many abuses took place. In late 1936, after *dozens* of new varieties had been introduced in that year, the market cooled. In 1939 Congress ended the largess by prohibiting further issues.

After the commemorative slump of late 1936 the overall coin market remained robust. A new monthly publication, *The Numismatic Scrapbook*, was launched by Lee F. Hewitt. Unlike *The Numismatist*, the *Scrapbook* emphasized the human interest side of numismatics rather than technical points and history. Reports of rare coins found in circulation, collector and dealer activities, and such make up most of the content. Quickly, it gained the largest subscription base of any numismatic publications. In the meantime *Hobbies* magazine had a monthly coin section.

In 1937 the third San Francisco Mint opened, replacing the facility in use since 1874. The building, with modernization in the intervening years, is still in use today.

In the same year the Federal Bullion Depository opened on the grounds of the Fort Knox military base in Kentucky. Double eagles and other federal gold coins dating back many years that had been stored in the Philadelphia Mint were melted and the metal was cast into gold ingots and shipped to Fort Knox. During this procedure some Mint employees substituted common-date $20 and other coins for those scheduled for melting, thus rescuing them for numismatic posterity. New York City dealers of the era eagerly purchased most of these coins, including 1933 $10 and $20 issues.

The third San Francisco Mint opened in 1937 on a prominent site overlooking the city.

The Federal Bullion Depository at Fort Knox, Kentucky.

In 1938 Felix O. Schlag entered a nationwide competition of about 300 artists vying to create a new design to replace the Buffalo nickel. His design won, and the obverse was selected. His reverse was considerably modified at the Mint.

In 1939 Nazi Germany went to war and overran Czechoslovakia. Other countries fell to the Nazis. Once again, American industries rose to supply forces opposing the Germans. The Depression ended, and the economy recovered, to go on to new highs.

The Jefferson nickel was introduced in 1938. Revised versions are still coined today.

The B-17 Flying Fortress bomber was developed in the 1930s and saw extensive use in Europe during World War II, especially with the 8th Air Force.

THE 1940s AND 1950s

In Europe World War II, as it was called, expanded as Adolf Hitler's Nazi troops overran France, Holland, Belgium, and other countries, meanwhile persecuting Jews, religious figures, and others, sending many to confinement and eventual death in concentration camps. Those who were fortunate fled, many finding asylum in America, including scientist Albert Einstein and professional numismatist Hans M.F. Schulman (whose other family members in Amsterdam perished). The Battle of Britain took place in 1940 with German bombers laying waste to large portions of London and with destruction in other areas (such as the famous cathedral in Coventry). America rushed to help with the Lend-Lease Act providing ships, exports of munitions, and more, including American men and women volunteers.

The United States officially entered the war after the "day of infamy," so called for Japan's unprovoked surprise attack on Pearl Harbor on December 7, 1941. War was also declared against other members of the Axis Powers—Germany and Italy (under dictator Benito Mussolini). In the Pacific Theater, more than a quarter million Filipino volunteers joined the American armed forces to fight off the Japanese. Then followed four more years of domestic and worldwide sacrifices, the details of which are well-known and beyond the scope of the present text.

After Proof sets were sold in 1942, production was stopped so as not to detract from the Mint's activity in providing record quantities of coins for circulation. To save copper, Lincoln cents were made of zinc-coated steel in 1943. The coins quickly tarnished and spotted, and bronze was resumed

In 1943 Lincoln cents were made of zinc-coated steel while copper was directed toward the war effort.

in 1944. The alloy of five-cent pieces was changed to eliminate nickel and to make silver the main metal, a policy continued through 1945.

By 1943 cash was plentiful, but consumer goods were scarce. Inflation was everywhere, despite federal efforts to control it. On September 10 and 11, 1943, New York City dealer Abe Kosoff conducted an auction of the Michael F. Higgy Collection. A bidding frenzy took place, and many coins sold for 5 to 10 times their pre-sale estimates! From that point, prices went onward and upward all across the market. Common-date double eagles were in particular demand, a place to put extra money, and sold for about $65 each.

A World War II centavo of the Philippines, minted in the United States.

In 1944 and 1945, the San Francisco, Denver, and Philadelphia mints were used to produce coins for the Philippines. These were then brought over by American military transport to aid commerce during the liberation of the islands from Japanese control.

In November 1946 *A Guide Book of United States Coins*, written by Richard S. Yeo (under the pen name of "R.S. Yeoman") with the technical assistance of Stuart Mosher, was published with a 1947 cover date. It went on to be published annually, selling tens of millions of copies over the ensuing decades. Although World War II was over, consumer goods were still scarce. There was much uncertainty as to the future of the economy—would it be booming, or would it bust? The rare-coin market continued to be a refuge for spare cash.

In 1946 Whitman Publishing launched *A Guide Book of United States Coins* with the cover date of 1947. It went on to become the best-selling book in numismatic history.

President Franklin D. Roosevelt, in office since 1933, died of natural causes while at Warm Springs, Georgia, in early 1945. The Treasury decided to honor him by changing the Mercury dime to his portrait as modeled by Chief Engraver John R. Sinnock. The 10-cent denomination was chosen because Roosevelt, stricken with a paralytic illness as young man, was the founder of the March of Dimes, a non-profit organization that raised money to combat polio (this was finally accomplished in 1955 with the vaccine of Dr. Jonas Salk).

Before long the coin market went into a slump. By 1947 consumer goods were becoming widely available. Money went to buy appliances,

The Roosevelt dime made its debut in 1946.

Levittown, New York, in 1947, one of many communities and developments that sprung up to provide affordable housing for returning veterans and other buyers.

new homes springing up in vast developments, and other goods, and automobiles were beginning to be available. In this year and in 1948, prices of coins dropped across the board. Common-date double eagles that sold for $65 during the war now wholesaled below $40. Convention attendance dwindled. In retrospect, if there was ever a good time to *buy* coins in the postwar era it was now!

The very bottom was probably in early 1949.

Not related to market prices at all, but in terms of numismatic history, 1949 is one of the most memorable years for it saw the publication of *Early American Cents*, by Dr. William H. Sheldon. The author, a psychologist and medical professor, billed himself as a scientist with the ability to analyze and make changes. With an office at Columbia University he had developed a new version of somatotypology by classifying people as *endomorphic*, *mesomorphic*, and *ectomorphic*, based on many photographs and measurements of nude figures taken at Ivy League schools. (Today this is dismissed as pseudo-science.) In numismatics he was a grand figure and respected for his knowledge.

For years the grading of coins was a problem, with no firmly established and globally recognized standards, and establishing market values involved a lot of guesswork. In the August 1949 issue of *The Numismatist* Abe Kosoff, one of America's leading coin dealers, told about Sheldon's forthcoming book, *Early American Cents:*

> Now comes one book that is complete within itself and is not only a list—it is a new treatment of the series. Order and system were applied to the identification, grading, and valuing of every known variety of early cent. Reference to the plates and tables makes it simple for even a novice to accurately identify and appraise the value of any of the early copper cents.

Guesswork was now replaced by science! His grading system was expanded beyond early cents to include coins in all series.

B. Max Mehl's sale of April 26, 1949, the Dr. Charles W. Green Collection, billed as the greatest gold coin sale ever held, broke price records left and right. Among the greatest rarities was a 1926-S double eagle, of which only three were said to be known. It realized $1,525, or more than double expectations.

All bets were off, and the room was up for grabs. All of a sudden, many collectors who had been inactive during the slump jumped back into the market with vigor. The market became dynamic—more so than ever before when considered on a widespread basis from colonial coinage onward.

In 1949 it was thought that only three examples existed of the 1926-S double eagle. This led to a treasure hunt in Europe and elsewhere to find coins shipped to foreign banks and governments earlier in the century. Today several hundred 1926-S $20 coins are known.

Secretly, James F. Kelly, a prominent Dayton, Ohio, dealer, had enlisted Paul Wittlin, a professional numismatist from California, to go to Europe and investigate reports of hoards of American gold coins shipped there before 1933, with some said to be intact. Wittlin struck gold—literally and figuratively—in bank vaults, primarily in Switzerland. Success attended his efforts. Surprisingly, banks in France also yielded many coins, especially double eagles that had been kept "underground" during the war. The rare became common. This set the scene for a broad and enthusiastic market in double eagles which exists to the present day.

In the 1950s thousands of newcomers entered the market and, following the tradition of years earlier, bought blue Whitman folders, and started looking for treasures in pocket change—the 1909-S V.D.B. cent, 1916-D dime, and 1916 Standing Liberty quarter being targets. Some Indian Head cents and Liberty Head nickels were in circulation, and there were many Barber silver coins, particularly half dollars.

The Franklin half dollars introduced in 1948 remained the standard design through 1963.

Bank-wrapped rolls, gold coins, copper coins, and just about all other federal series were in unprecedented demand. The Philadelphia Mint, which had stopped making Proofs in 1942, resumed the tradition in 1950 and produced 51,386 Proof sets. In 1950 the Denver Mint produced only 2,630,030 nickels—the smallest nickel five-cent piece coinage since 1931. When the mintage figures were released, excitement prevailed! These and the new Proofs gave a further boost to the market.

In 1951, 57,500 Proof sets were made. As production climbed year by year, there began to be considerable interest in Proof sets from an investment viewpoint. In this decade buy and sell prices were posted of these and for bank-wrapped rolls of modern circulation coins.

In Iola, Wisconsin, in 1952, Chet Krause started *Numismatic News* as a monthly publication devoted to classified advertisements. In time the emphasis changed, and news articles and announcements were carried. Later, in the early 1960s, it went to a weekly. Krause Publications, as it came to be called, included Cliff Mishler as a key executive. The parent company became one of America's most important publishers of magazines and reference books in many hobby and sports areas, one of the largest in the world.

Beginning with the 1952 ANA Convention sale (the work of a combination of four dealers with different specialties), the New Netherlands Coin Co. of New York City, owned by Charles M. Wormser (business manager) and John J. Ford Jr. (numismatic expert), with Walter Breen as a key employee, produced catalogs with extremely detailed descriptions. Coins came to life, the New Netherlands sales had an almost cult following, and the combination of salesmanship, history, market and coin-collecting gossip and remarks, and detailed descriptions of the offered pieces initiated a new trend. This methodology was later adopted by several other auction firms. In the meantime most retail sales were through shops, price lists, and advertisements.

In 1954 a Proof set of 1936 had a market value of $100, increasing to $300 in 1955, onward and upward to $500, then to $600. At several large coin shows, Cincinnati dealer Sol Kaplan posted "bid" and "ask" prices for sets from 1936 to 1942, and 1950 to date, and prices sometimes changed hourly. A 1956 Proof set, available from the Mint that year for $2.10, was worth $2.50 to those who did not want to wait for sets to arrive in the mail. In that year a record 669,384 sets were struck, nearly doubling the preceding year's total and exceeding by more than a dozen times the number struck six years earlier in 1950. In 1957 the market for Proof sets crashed. The 1936 set dropped all the way back to $300, with scarcely a buyer in sight. Latecomers to the market racked up large losses, and many left in a hurry—perhaps muttering that coin investment was for gullible people only. While the market for Proof sets busted in 1957, time healed the wounds, recovery took place in succeeding years, and today a gem 1936 Proof set is worth well into five figures!

An 1894-S dime, one of only 24 minted and of only 10 or so known today.

In the meantime, anyone who diversified their holdings did well—as large copper cents, silver dollars, paper money, territorial gold, and Liberty Head nickels, along with just about everything else, continued to rise in price. Many records were set. In the autumn of 1957 in Stack's Empire Sale a rare 1894-S dime sold for an amazing $4,750, an event publicized in newspapers nationwide. The coin was later acquired by Emery May Holden Norweb, a leading collector of the era.

The Professional Numismatists Guild, formally organized in 1955, would go on to become America's leading organization of dealers in numismatic items. The Guild (online today at PNGdealers.org) has helped with many educational, authentication, and other matters of interest to the collecting community.

In 1955 the San Francisco Mint struck only cents and dimes, after which the Treasury Department stated that coinage there would end and it would become known as the San Francisco Assay Office. That changed in the 1960s when it again was designated as a mint, and was kept busy striking coins.

In 1955 at the Philadelphia Mint an obverse die was impressed twice, slightly off-register, by a hub die. The result was that the date was blurred and appeared as 11995555. Several presses were coining cents, dumping the coins into a box where they were then collected and mixed with the cents from other coining presses. Late in the afternoon, a Mint inspector noticed the bizarre doubled cents and removed the offending die. By that time, somewhat more than 40,000 cents had been produced, about 24,000 of which had been mixed with normal cents from other presses. The decision was made to destroy the cents still in the box, and to release into circulation the 24,000 or so pieces that were mixed with other cents. The Mint had no reason to believe that these would attract attention or have value with collectors. They were simply viewed as defective coins. It is likely that about 3,000 to 4,000 1955 Doubled Die cents exist. This variety launched in a large way the numismatic passion, today dynamic, for unusual die errors and varieties. The *Cherrypickers' Guide to Rare Die Varieties of United States Coins*, published in staggered multiple volumes covering half cents through gold, commemoratives, and bullion, is the main guide.

The obverse of the 1955 Doubled Die Lincoln cent.

Coin collecting in the 1950s was becoming an increasingly popular pastime, conventions enjoyed record attendance (the 1955 ANA show in Omaha totaled an unprecedented 49 dealers and 510 total registrants), and dealers enjoyed excellent business as well. Proof sets, bank-wrapped rolls of

Mint State coins, and commemoratives were especially popular with investors, as they were easy to understand—quite unlike esoteric colonial or pattern pieces.

Without earlier notice to the numismatic periodicals—the *Numismatic Scrapbook Magazine*, *The Numismatist*, and *Numismatic News*—the Treasury Department announced in December 1958 that the traditional wheat-ears reverse of the Lincoln cent in use since 1909 would be replaced by the Lincoln Memorial design in 1959. The new motif by Frank Gasparro drew mixed reviews, with numismatic writer Don Taxay saying that it looked like a trolley car. The design was continued through 2008.

The 1959 cent introduced the Lincoln Memorial reverse by Frank Gasparro, an engraver at the Mint.

1958 and 1959 were good years for the collector, investor-speculator, and dealer alike. Interest in early coins expanded, and colonial coins, copper cents and half cents, Capped Bust half dollars, and other series attracted many specialists, in time generating new reference books. Thousands of citizens took up the pursuit of numismatics, usually starting by filling in holes in blue Whitman folders. Coin clubs with monthly meetings expanded. Many regional associations were formed while others expanded. A short list includes the Central States Numismatic Association, Empire State Numismatic Association, Florida United Numismatists, Mid-Atlantic Numismatic Association, New England Numismatic Association, Penn-Ohio Coin Clubs, and Southern California Numismatic Association.

The Rittenhouse Society was organized in the late 1950s as an organization of young numismatic researchers (including Q. David Bowers, Kenneth Bressett, Walter Breen, George Fuld, Ken Rendell, and others). It would continue as an honorary society to the present day, with its original age limitation for membership removed.

By 1959 the market was very strong in all areas from colonial coins to private and territorial gold and all series in between.

THE 1960S AND 1970S

1960 was a watershed year in the coin market, leaving behind the older scenario of collectors and dealers, plus a limited number of investors, participating in a relatively small market. *Coin World* was launched by the Sidney Printing and Publishing Co. (now Amos Media), an entrepreneurial company that sought to establish a weekly paper in a hobby field. The choice was narrowed to antiques, bowling, and coins, with the latter winning out.

Coin World became an instant success, fueled greatly by the nationwide publicity given to the 1960 Small Date Lincoln cents. Television and newspaper coverage reported on lucky people getting $50 bags of these new cents and selling them for $10,000 to $12,000 each. To put matters in perspective, in 1960 $12,000 was about twice the price of a new Cadillac Seville convertible, one of America's most popular top-of-the-line automobiles. The cost of the average American home was $11,900. Within this year the coin market probably doubled or tripled the number of participants.

Fueled by the launch of *Coin World* in 1960 and the excitement of the Small Date Lincoln cents of that year, the coin market took off like a rocket. Hundreds of thousands of new participants entered, and the circulation of *Coin World* alone crossed the 150,000 mark at one time, with D. Wayne ("Dick") Johnson as founding editor, soon followed in the post by Margo Russell (who went on to nearly 25 years of service). The *Coin World* "Trends" column, conducted by James F. Kelly, gave coin-market prices on a *weekly* basis—the first time ever. Teletype systems linked several hundred dealers by 1962–1963, and at one time the Professional Numismatists Guild even had its own network. Dealers posted bid and ask prices as well as market news and lots of gossip, printed out by noisy, clacking keys on rolls of yellow paper. To many, this was like the stock exchange—instant price information from Chicago could be printed out in New York or Los Angeles.

The Coin Dealer Newsletter was started in 1963, listing bid and ask prices for rolls, Proof sets, and other items, using Teletype data as a basis. The great silver dollar bonanza of 1962 to 1964 added more excitement. Leading the market activity were bank-wrapped rolls of coins (with the 1950-D nickel being the hottest item of all, a 40-coin roll rising during the period from below $200 to over $1,200), Proof sets 1936 to date, common-date gold coins (owning a common-date Mint State double eagle for less than $50 was very exciting), 1,000-coin bags of silver dollars, and more. The Coin and Currency Institute featured its new "Library of Coins" albums, more compact and attractive than any on the market at the time. Many interesting and attractive holders and albums were produced by others.

Confederation Convention Dates Chosen

Coin World

THE WEEKLY NEWSPAPER OF THE ENTIRE NUMISMATIC FIELD

National Coin Week Opens Sunday, April 24

Jack Rand Of Tacoma Wash., General Chairman

R. I. Group Forms Coin, Stamp Assn.

Weekly Price Sheet Offered

Mississippian Finds Possible 1956 Dot Coin

Confederate Money Man, Criswell, Is Named Mayor Of St. Petersburg Beach, Fla.

Rolls Popular At Penn-Ohio Kelly Auction

The first issue of *Coin World,* April 21, 1960.

Many traditional market areas such as tokens, medals, colonials, copper half cents and cents, paper money, and just about any other area requiring study and knowledge, were ignored by investors and speculators not interested in numismatic art, science, and history. At the same time the interest in such specialties was growing, surely but slowly, aided by an unprecedented interest in numismatic history, tradition, and die varieties, and with special-interest groups adding to the growing excitement. The Token and Medal Society, Civil War Token Society, Early American Coppers, Liberty Seated Collectors Club, and other groups formed during the decade went on to become very important to the hobby.

The *Colonial Newsletter* was established in 1960 by Alfred D. Hoch, of Lexington, Massachusetts, to "provide in permanent form an exchange of information, opinions and discoveries concerning early American numismatics." Later in the decade the editorship passed to Jim Spilman, a true rocket scientist (he worked at the NASA facility in Huntsville, Alabama). From that time to the present, under several editors, the publication became the standard source for research on colonial and early American coins. Early American Coppers launched *Penny-Wise* under the editorship of Warren Lapp, in time succeeded by Harry Salyards, both medical doctors. Other specialized societies attracted editors and members of a generally high degree of education and intellectual curiosity.

Large (top) and small dates on 1960 Philadelphia Mint Lincoln cents. The Small Date cents were perceived as rarities and created nationwide attention.

In November 1962 a long-sealed (since 1929) vault at the Philadelphia Mint was opened in order to tap reserves of silver dollars, popular for banks to pay out during the holiday season. A few hundred 1,000-coin bags of sparkling new 1903-O Morgan dollars were casually given out, this being the rarest and most famous of all coins in the series—so rare that it was estimated that no more than a dozen or two Mint State coins existed! The 1903-O listed for $1,500 in the *Red Book*, the top price level. This was like finding money in the streets, a nationwide silver rush occurred, and several hundred million silver dollars were paid out from Treasury and bank vaults.

Prior to November 1962 the 1903-O was considered to be the rarest Morgan silver dollar in Mint State. Most dealers had never seen or handled one.

In Washington at the Treasury Building people formed long lines with wheelbarrows and sacks for silver dollars to wait their turn to get coins from the Cash Room. Coins had been stored there for generations, including large quantities of dollars brought from the closed Carson City Mint in 1911.

Finally, in March 1964, the supply ran out, at which time the Treasury took stock of its remaining pieces and found about 3,000,000 CC dollars on hand—Mint State, low-mintage issues that were later auctioned over a period of time. This dollar bonanza inspired tens of thousands of people to discover numismatics and become serious collectors, while hundreds of thousands more developed a casual interest—perhaps setting aside a few dozen or even a bag or two of dollars.

About the same time the Kennedy half dollar made its debut. After the assassination of President John F. Kennedy in November 1963, the Treasury abandoned the Benjamin Franklin motif and replaced it with a Kennedy portrait made by Chief Engraver Gilroy Roberts and a Heraldic Eagle reverse

The United States Treasury in Washington, D.C.

One of the Treasury Building silver dollar vaults as photographed in 1904.

by Frank Gasparro, an assistant engraver on the Mint staff. Not long afterward Roberts resigned to take a position with the Franklin Mint, a private coiner of medals, and Gasparro became chief engraver, a position he held until his resignation in 1982.

The Kennedy half dollar was released in March 1964.

In 1965 the coin-investment market, mostly driven by speculators with little interest in the hobby of coin collecting, ran out of new players. Rolls of 1950-D nickels seem to have stopped in their tracks at the $1,200 level or so, and holders of quantity could find few buyers at this figure. Rolls, Proof sets, 1960 Small Date Lincoln cents, and the number of subscribers to coin newspapers and magazines slumped. In the meantime, other areas that did not participate in the investment boom were doing just fine—colonials, paper money, early copper, and more. Silver dollars continued their popularity as the majority of the nearly 125 different dates and mintmarks of Morgan and Peace dollars could be obtained in Mint State for just a few dollars up to $50. It was realized that the vaults were empty, and there would be no more "surprise" bags of rarities coming on the market. Many dealers set up as to specialize in these coins.

One of the most dramatic changes in both coin production and in numismatics took place in 1965. The price of silver rose on international markets, and in that year the Treasury Department abandoned this traditional metal for use in the dime and quarter, and created a reduced-silver version of the half dollar (until 1970). New copper-nickel–clad metal compositions were used instead. The price of silver continued to rise, and all silver coins in circulation became worth more than face value—and profitable to melt down, a repeat of the 1850 to 1853 situation in American history. Copper-nickel coins have remained standard for circulation since.

Within a short time most silver coins disappeared from circulation. No longer was it possible to fill a folder or album with Mercury and Roosevelt dimes, Standing Liberty and Washington quarters, or Walking Liberty and Franklin half dollars, as no more were to be found in change. The idea of finding a 1916-D or 1942, 2 Over 1, dime or a 1932-D or -S quarter "treasure" in pocket change was gone forever. Henceforth, coins had to be purchased from dealers or found here and there by chance.

For some illogical reason, as silver coins were quickly withdrawn from circulation the general public decided to hoard cents and nickels. These became scarce in circulation, and some stores offered to pay a premium for quantities of "pennies"! Mint Director Eva Adams blamed this on coin collectors, and "punished" them by removing mintmarks from branch-mint (Denver) coins and also discontinuing the making of Proof sets. Later, Miss Adams "got religion," realized it was really the fault of the general public, became interested in numismatics, and actually sought and was elected to the office of governor of the American Numismatic Association.

A 1968-S Proof cent, the first Proof of this denomination ever to bear an S mintmark.

In 1968 Proof sets were again made available for collectors. For the first time they were struck at the San Francisco Mint and bore S mintmarks. Interest in collecting and investing in coins entered a new period of growth. Investors had been absent from the market for several years. In 1969 and 1970 and again in 1973 and 1974 the stock market was weak—at a period when the coin market exhibited great strength, making coins all the more attractive as an alternate investment. In particular, gold was a hot item.

Silver dollars had not been issued for circulation since 1935. The Treasury decided that a new issue of dollars would be desirable, now of copper-nickel metal. These would find use on gaming tables but, much more importantly, as a substitute for the paper dollar. Paper bills lasted only about 18 months in circulation while a metal dollar was expected to be used for 20 years or more. The Eisenhower dollar designed by Chief Engraver Frank Gasparro was introduced in 1971. While collectors were enthusiastic, the coins found little use in commerce and were discontinued in 1978. In 1979 a new mini-dollar was introduced, again by Gasparro, this time with the portrait of Susan B. Anthony. It was hoped that at last the public would use them due to their convenient small size. The relatively few used in circulation were often confused with quarters of just slightly smaller size. These coins were discontinued in 1981, followed by a curious additional coinage of the same design in 1999.

A 1971-S Eisenhower dollar, designed by Frank Gasparro, a Proof from the set of this year.

The government provisions of 1933 and 1934 prohibiting citizens from holding non-numismatic gold coins (and a small personal allowance) did not include Proofs of various countries, and an exception was made for modern Krugerrands from South Africa, first minted in 1967. Pegged at $35 per ounce, gold had remained at this level for decades, until the 1960s, when it began going upward. In the early 1970s, the price of gold bullion continued to rise steadily. In America where investors could not buy bulk, they could and did buy quantities of Krugerrands. In 1974 there was great excitement as the restriction was to end on December 31. The prices of common gold coins escalated. The price of bulk gold varied.

In 1975 there was not much joy in the coin market. Many dealers had been caught up, and profitably so, in the boom market for Krugerrands, double eagles, and other gold-coin investments, and, to the public "coin investment" was still a bad term, with memories of the boom-and-bust of the early 1960s. Even serious collectors pulled in their horns, with the result that many fine-quality coins, including such things as Proof gold, slumped during this time.

The 1776–1976 Bicentennial coins, which would have been as hot as a pistol in normal "up" periods of the investment cycle, laid an egg, and the Mint had a hard time pushing Proofs and special strikes out the door—and had a supply on hand for several years afterward. Serious collectors and alert investors with a contrarian turn of mind bought quietly during this period, and were to reap great profits later. Harry W. Bass Jr., who later formed one of the greatest coin collections ever, began his numismatic interest this year.

In 1978 and 1979 there was a mad rush to speculate in silver and gold bullion, sparked by the Hunt brothers, wealthy Texans seeking to buy all the silver and silver futures they could. Coin dealers who had shops and stores bought large quantities of worn silver coins, tableware, and other items, as well as scrap silver and gold jewelry, to make profits by selling to refiners. Many profited handsomely and used their gains to buy trophy coins and rarities in the coin market, which was as hot as a firecracker. Runaway inflation in the American economy and high interest rates made homes and other items less affordable than before, prompting many people to invest in tangible assets, hoping to yield more than bank interest. The first of four sessions of the Garrett Collection was auctioned by Bowers and Ruddy Galleries in November 1979 and set many records.

Numismatists found artistic fault with the Bicentennial half dollar and dollar, but the quarter dollar, shown here, was widely acclaimed. The market was in the doldrums and many fewer coins were distributed than had been hoped.

The 1960s and 1970s also saw vast changes in American society, including the gaining of improved civil rights by African-Americans and others, the popularization of passenger-jet aircraft that facilitated travel to foreign countries, and the space race between the United States and the Soviet Union. With the assassination of President John F. Kennedy in 1963, the resignation of President Richard M. Nixon in 1974, the election of former movie actor Ronald Reagan as president in 1980, and other events it was a time to remember. That was done and in spades by books and articles written by many people who had served in the White House and elsewhere in government. Detroit was still the epicenter of the automobile industry with Cadillac and Lincoln being the favorite marques for those who wanted an expensive vehicle.

A uniform patch for the Apollo 11 mission that on July 20, 1969, achieved the first landing of humans on the Moon. Adaptations of this insignia were used on several coin types.

The American Numismatic Association underwent transition as well. In the early 1960s members of the Professional Numismatist Guild and others in the field raised donations to build a permanent headquarters for the ANA. In 1965 the Home and Headquarters Committee interviewed representatives from cities desiring to be the location. In early 1965 Chairman Charles Johnson reported that one or more of the three committeemen had visited most of the 16 locations from which bids were received prior to February 1.

The Boeing 707 revolutionized air travel in the 1960s and was joined by the much larger 747 jumbo jet in the early 1970s.

Omaha was selected as the preferred site, with Colorado Springs, Oklahoma City, and Kansas City following in that order. This was reconsidered, and not long afterward the committee started negotiations for an ANA site at Colorado Springs. Satisfactory progress was being made for a site offered to the Association on the campus of Colorado College. The site included in excess of 30,000 square feet of choice space and was offered on a 99-year lease at $1 annual rental. The proposed agreement included an option for renewal of the lease prior to its expiration. This was finalized, and the Home and Headquarters had its dedication on June 10, 1967.

THE 1980s AND 1990s

Going into 1980 the coin market was still riding a crest. The price of bullion gold peaked at $873 an ounce in January 1980. The price of silver topped out at $50.35 per ounce on January 18. In early 1980 a longtime client, Dr. Collier, told me that he had been offered $15,000 *per coin* for the set of Barber Proof half dollars, 1892–1915, purchased from me a few years earlier for less than $2,000 per coin. In March 1980, some say even during the Central States convention itself, the speculation-driven market for rare coins collapsed, and the prices of many "investment grade" coins (generally, MS-65 and Proof-65 or finer silver and gold coins) fell sharply.

Most series that were the darlings of speculators dropped sharply in price. The *investment market* for coins was in a funk for the next several years. In the meantime, scarce and rare Capped Bust and Liberty Seated silver coins, large copper cents, colonials, Charlotte and Dahlonega mint gold, and other collector-oriented series continued to play to a solid market. Established dealers in rare coins persevered and expanded as the decade progressed, and most auctions were very successful. Much dealer-to-dealer business was conducted on Teletype machines.

A perspective on what happened was given by David Hall in the Monthly Summary of the *Coin Dealer Newsletter*, January 1981 (excerpted):

> "Black Friday": The April 1980 Central States Numismatic Society convention was like no other coin show in history. At that show the four-year bull market literally "stopped on a dime." In retrospect, undoubtedly there were several reasons for the sudden slowdown. Dealers had become very sloppy with their purchase policies and many dealers were financially overextended. Bullion prices were crashing. Interest rates had soared to 20%. . . . In looking back, it's also evident that there were rumblings of a market slowdown, subtle hints if you will, in the weeks preceding the Central States Show. However, no one expected it to happen when it did and every dealer I know was stunned at how incredibly sudden and incredibly hard the brakes came on.

The market recovered, and today just about all coins are worth more than they were in April 1980.

Due to rising copper prices the Mint in 1982 changed the composition of Lincoln cents from bronze to copper-coated zinc, the standard still used today. In the same year the Treasury Department resumed the issuance of commemorative coins, the first since 1954. The Washington commemorative half dollar, designed by Chief Engraver Elizabeth Jones, recent successor to Frank Gasparro, accompanied by publicity and enthusiasm generated by Mint director Donna Pope, was issued to observe the 250th anniversary of the birth of our first president. The pieces, made with Proof finish by the San Francisco Mint and with Mint State finish by the Denver Mint, were very well received, and within a year or so most were sold. This set the scene for hundreds of later commemoratives, production of which continues to be important today. During the decade the Marketing Department of the Mint was expanded, put new policies in place, and became more interactive with the numismatic community than ever before.

ANA President Matthew Rothert conducted the dedication ceremony on June 10, 1967. The officers and others are listed to the left. One success led to another, the ANA grew and prospered, and in 1982 a second story was added to the building, dedicated on June 10 (15th anniversary of the first event).

The expanded ANA headquarters in 1982.

The plaque for the 1982 dedication.

The American Numismatic Association headquarters building in 1967.

The United States Silver Bullion Depository, often referred to as the West Point Bullion Depository and today as the West Point Mint, officially opened on June 13, 1938. Its purpose was to store silver bullion, while at Fort Knox, Kentucky, the recently opened building stored most of the nation's gold reserve. In 1980 Lincoln cents were made at the Depository. Lacking mintmarks, they appeared similar to Philadelphia coins.

The first commemorative coin issued since 1954 was the 1982 half dollar observing the 250th anniversary of George Washington's birth.

In the same year the facility began striking gold pieces for the American Arts Commemorative Series gold medallion program. Produced were half-ounce and one-ounce gold medals depicting famous American painters, writers, performers, and other artists. Marketing was encumbered by frequent changes of price in step with bullion values and a complex procedure to order. The program went through its legislated run, ending in 1984, and wasn't renewed.

Beginning in 1984, the W mintmark was first used on coins—$10 gold commemoratives for the Olympic Games. Since that time many W-mint-marked coins have been struck there.

Investing in gold and silver bullion became very important. The market fall in 1980 was history, and in 1986 there were many new players buying Krugerrands, Canadian Maple Leafs, common-date double eagles, and other coins. The U.S. Mint entered the field with its own bullion coins—the American Eagle made in one-ounce silver and tenth-ounce to one-ounce gold formats. The date for the American Silver Eagle was 1986 but for the American Gold Eagle it was in Roman numerals the first year, MCMLXXXVI, later changed to Arabic for each year. Bullion strikes were produced for mass sale and Proofs for collectors. The 1995-W Proof American Silver Eagle was a special issue sold at a premium and set the stage for many "special" Proof coins and West Point coins that would be made in various series in the twenty-first century, new varieties that met with mixed reviews from buyers. The basic program was an immediate success and continues as such to the present day.

A 1980 one-ounce gold American Arts Gold Medallion depicting artist Grant Wood.

1986 American Silver Eagle.

The 1984-W commemorative $10 gold piece made the first use of the W mintmark on a legal-tender coin.

MCMLXXXVI (1986) American Gold Eagle.

In 1986 David Hall and a group of dealer associates formed the Professional Coin Grading Service (PCGS), which offered for a fee to receive coins, give an opinion of grade via several experts, and sonically seal the coin in a hard plastic holder, which became known as a "slab." In 1987 John Albanese, earlier with PCGS, established the Numismatic Guaranty Corporation of America (now the Numismatic Guaranty Company, or NGC), which also became spectacularly successful. Other services were founded, and some enjoyed niches in the marketplace. ANACS with its paper certificates and photographs faded in importance and was later sold by the ANA, eventually reestablishing itself.

A 1926 Sesquicentennial of American Independence commemorative half dollar in MS-65 had a market value of $14,500 in the spring of 1990. Years later in the 2019 edition of *A Guide Book of United States Coins* it was listed as $600.

Certified grading did wonders for the investment market as sellers found that newcomers to numismatics would readily buy coins in holders and not worry about the grade.

Several mutual funds were formed to simplify the buying of coins, including one by Merrill Lynch (it was later dissolved and participants reimbursed).

The market for investment coins reached a high in 1989 and early 1990, at which time commemoratives (most of which in the market are in Mint State) and related coins were trading to speculators (or the more popular term, investors) at prices far beyond what any seasoned collector would pay. Finally, the runaway train ran out of steam, and in early 1990 few investors wanted to get on board. The market crashed, and prices fell back to basic or foundational levels reflecting collector demand.

Although many 1989 investments were great disasters, most high-grade federal coins have increased in value since that time, and many high-level Mint State coins of the mid-nineteenth century and earlier have multiplied in price.

In 1990 the World Wide Web was initiated, but few people paid attention to the news.

The Eliasberg 1913 Liberty Head nickel, the finest of five known specimens.

The market regained strength by 1996 when the second part of the Louis E. Eliasberg Collection crossed the auction block. A Gem Proof 1913 Liberty Head nickel sold for $1,485,000, the first time in world numismatic history that any coin sold for more than a million dollars.

In 1997 the price of gold tumbled. On November 27 an ounce fell to $295.95, its lowest price since March 1985.

The 1999-P Delaware quarter, the first in the State quarter program.

In 1999 the State quarter program was launched. It was one of the most dramatic programs ever instituted by the Treasury Department. Five different states would be honored each year, in the order in which they ratified the Constitution, the first being Delaware. The program was planned to continue for ten years, until all states had been covered. The plan called for designs to be created within the individual states, by artists, members of the public, and others who were to submit ideas, to be reviewed and then finalized by the governors of the states. The eventual result was fifty different designs, no two alike, which delighted numismatists who gave many reviews and opinions concerning the beauty or lack thereof. Each of the quarters had a special launch ceremony covered with fanfare. Great excitement prevailed from beginning to end, and much was done for the entire numismatic hobby, with books published about the coins, and folders, albums, maps, and other holders and display cases made for eager collectors.

The American Numismatic Association headquarters in Colorado Springs on the campus of Colorado College.

In the same year the euro became the standard currency of many European nations.

By the last year of the twentieth century, 2000, the hobby was quite strong in most areas. Personal computers were gaining in popularity, and by this time there were many numismatic applications. Chat rooms and message boards were set up and provided many exchanges as well as instant information.

The American Numismatic Association remained the leading worldwide organization of numismatists and had slightly more than 30,000 paid members. In the United States the American Numismatic Society in New York City was a smaller group mostly devoted to advanced collectors and research. Its Coinage of the America Conference programs were held yearly with leading presenters discussing and displaying coins, tokens, and medals of the Western Hemisphere, followed by a reference book. This illustrious series ran into the early twenty-first century, after which time most conferences related to ancient coins. Across the nation several hundred local and regional coin clubs met monthly.

2000 TO DATE

The years from 2000 to date, including the official start of the twenty-first century in 2001, have seen countless changes and events on the national and international scenes. A short list includes the Y2K monetary excitement of 2000, the NASDAQ stock-market crash, the World Trade Center disaster and its vast effects on security and travel, CDs and DVDs, presidential administrations from the end of Bill Clinton to that of Donald Trump. Important events include the fall of Enron, artificial intelligence, home theaters, space shuttles, federal budget, interest rates, LGBTQ, the rebirth of Apple, iPhones and other electronic devices, electronic credit and bill paying, domestic shootings, robots, Uber and Lyft, racial equality, the securities market and the rise and fall of various companies and industries, nanotechnology, video streaming, global warming, self-driving cars, weather and natural disasters, the global COVID-19 pandemic and its aftershocks, and more.

The year 2000 began with a healthy, indeed dynamic rare-coin market mainly driven by speculator interest in coins common and rare certified in ultra-high grades. More broadly spread, and on a much more permanent basis, was well-studied *collector* interest in copper, silver, and gold coins.

The Sacagawea "golden dollar" was launched in 2000 and proved to be a numismatic favorite. Circulation strikes were made at the Philadelphia and Denver mints. Proofs (as shown) were struck in San Francisco.

The year started with the launch of the first "golden dollar," a mini-dollar in manganese-brass alloy. The obverse design featured Sacagawea, a translator who traveled with the Lewis and Clark expedition in the upper reaches of the Missouri River, carrying her baby, Pomp. The design was by artist Glenna Goodacre. The reverse depicted a flying eagle by Mint engraver Thomas D. Rogers Sr.

The Mint was eager to promote public interest and acceptance of the new dollar. It arranged with General Mills, Inc., the Minneapolis manufacturer of cereals and other foods, to supply 5,500 coins struck in late summer or early autumn 1999 with a 2000-P obverse and the prototype reverse. The difference in the reverse details was not disclosed to the numismatic community at the time. General Mills advertised a "treasure hunt"—one in every 2,000 boxes of Cheerios would contain a new Sacagawea dollar, not yet in general release, and a 2000-dated Lincoln cent. "The only place to get either coin is in a box of Cheerios." Further, one box in every 4,400 had a certificate redeemable for 100 Sacagawea dollars (finders who redeemed them received the dollars with the later-type reverse). It was not until February 2005 that the differences distinguishing this variety was noticed by a numismatist and publicized. The first one auctioned sold for nearly $35,000.

Detail of the tail feathers with cross-vanes used only on the rare 2000-P "Cheerios" dollar, the "poster rarity" of the turn of the century.

The regular reverse with plain tail feathers (no vanes), as used on all regular Sacagawea dollars 2000 to 2008.

In August 2000 the ANA World's Fair of Money convention was held in Philadelphia and drew more than 20,000 attendees, an all-time record. Across the front of the bourse area the California Gold Marketing Group set up the 50-foot-wide Ship of Gold display. This was a reproduction of the *SS Central America*, the treasure-laden ship that sank on September 12, 1857, and from which the Columbus-America Discovery Group recovered gold coins and ingots in the late 1980s. Shown were many items recovered, and a mini-theater projected films of the find. A program by treasure-finding scientist Bob Evans had an attendance of more than 400 visitors. Marketing of the treasure had begun in 1999 and continued for several years, by which time about $100 million was realized. The treasure and its publicity electrified the market and were called by *Coin World* "the story of the year."

More than 7,400 mint-fresh 1857-S double eagles have been recovered from the wreck of the SS *Central America.*

How many people collect coins? How many are serious numismatists? Beth Deisher, editor of *Coin World*, provided comments on this in the issue of March 12, 2001. She suggested that most numismatists and related organizations define a collector as "one who spends time and money to systematically gather coins for the purpose of forming a collection. Using that definition, we can begin to build a total that has some facts behind it." She suggested that about 450,000 people were serious about numismatics but noted that the United States Mint had 1,800,000 names on its mailing list. Further, "The U.S. Mint reports that its marketing surveys show that up to 110 million adults are actively collecting the State quarters."

The formation of registry sets, a collecting concept pioneered by PCGS and picked up by NGC, went into high gear. The challenge was to have the highest-graded coin or set of coins certified. In *COINage*, April 2003, editor Ed Reiter reported:

> Recently, one of these "modern rarities" brought $39,100 at an auction at the Florida United Numismatists convention in Orlando. The coin was a 1963 Lincoln cent graded Proof-70 Deep Cameo by the Professional Coin Grading Service (PCGS). It is said to be the only Proof Lincoln cent of that date ever to receive a perfect grade from one of the leading coin-certification services.

Registry set participation would eventually involve more than 10,000 people at the various services and would be responsible in coming years for many coins that are common in, say, MS-65 grade and priced at below $10 to sell for thousands of dollars in ultra-grades. Sets have contributed much to the strength of the market in recent years.

A renaissance in numismatic research and publishing was kindled in the early 2000s under the management and inspiration of Anderson Press. By 2003 Whitman Coin Products, after many years as a division of Western Publishing Company in its hometown of Racine, Wisconsin, and after later sales to various other firms, was operated by St. Martin's Press in New York City. Whitman had continued to publish the *Red Book* (its guide to retail coin prices) and the *Blue Book* (its guide to wholesale coin prices) under the editorial direction of Kenneth Bressett, but in recent years had done little in the way of new titles. This changed dramatically when H.E. Harris & Co., an Anderson Press company, bought Whitman from St. Martin's. Under new management and ownership, the combined firm took the name Whitman Publishing, LLC, under which it published hundreds of new books for collectors, investors, and researchers. These included nearly 30 volumes in the Bowers Series; the *Cherrypickers' Guide to Rare Die Varieties of United States Coins*; the 100 Greatest™ library of books; and many other titles, ranging from 96-page monographs to multiple-volume encyclopedias and *Mega Red*. These books covered American and world coins, ancient coins, paper currency, medals, tokens, bullion, and other numismatic and historical topics. Whitman also dramatically increased its line of folders, albums, display cases, magnifiers, and other storage, display, and research products for collectors.

Whitman purchased the Baltimore Coin and Currency Convention and rebranded it as the Whitman Coin & Collectibles Expo, expanding the show and adding new features, with three events held annually in Baltimore.

In 2003 the United States Mint implemented the novel Artistic Infusion Program, an effort to bring the talents of private-sector artists under the wing of the government. Eighteen "master" designers and six "associate" designers were selected from applications received, to create motifs for American coins and medals. By this time State quarters at the rate of five per year plus new medals put pressure on the Engraving Department. The program worked out well, and over the years various early artists departed and new ones were selected. The AIP has injected new artistry and creativity into American coinage and medal design.

The Whitman Coin & Collectibles Expo is held in Baltimore three times a year.

The two reverse designs for the 2004 Westward Journey nickels and the shared obverse.

The two reverse designs for the 2005 Westward Journey nickels and the shared obverse with a revised portrait of Jefferson.

Also in 2003, the Citizens Coinage Advisory Committee (CCAC.gov) was established by Act of Congress to advise the secretary of the Treasury on themes and design proposals for circulating coinage, bullion coins, Congressional Gold Medals, and national and other medals.

In 2004 and 2005 Westward Journey nickel five-cent pieces were made at the mints to honor the Lewis and Clark expedition. Beyond the coins themselves, special sets including medals were marketed, not to the pleasure of some collectors who believed that coin issues should be simple and straightforward. The portrait of President Thomas Jefferson was changed in 2005 from that created in 1938.

The Mint reported in early 2005 that sales of platinum coins were sagging. The program had never caught on with enthusiasm, and a redesign of the series was being considered. High prices were a deterrent to buying, but for the Mint the coins produced a nice profit.

Around this time increased numbers of sophisticated Chinese counterfeits of United States coins began appearing in quantity on the market. Buying coins that were professionally certified as authentic became a necessity for many advanced collectors.

In 2005 the Mint announced that "Satin Finish" would be available on circulating coins included in Mint sets sold to collectors.

In late 2006 extending to August 19, 2007, the American Museum of Natural History in New York City mounted a large exhibit, "Gold." The display included coins from ancient times to present, mostly on loan from the American Numismatic Society, and ingots and coins from the SS *Central America*, among many other sections.

The American Museum of Natural History mounted the spectacular "Gold" exhibit in 2006 and 2007.

Overall attendance at auctions and conventions declined in the early 2000s as buying and selling via the Internet was much more comfortable and convenient.

In 2007 the Mint issued a Proof $20 gold coin of the Saint-Gaudens design with the date as MMVII on the 100th anniversary of the original MCMVII (1907) issue, much to the acclaim of the numismatic community. It was of smaller diameter than the 1907 original but was thicker, thus maintaining the same weight. During this era Mint Director Edmund C. Moy was very involved in numismatic activities and was a regular attendee of major coin conventions.

The Presidential series of "golden dollars" was introduced in 2007 with the dates and mintmarks on the edge, a curious change.

In 2007 the Presidential series of "golden dollars" was introduced, overlapping slightly with the Sacagawea dollar series that ended in 2008. Presidents were featured from George Washington onward, living presidents excluded. The obverse designs featured a portrait (by various artists) and the reverse the Statue of Liberty (by Mint sculptor- engraver Don Everhart).

In 2009 the Sacagawea obverse was continued in a new series with Native American reverse motifs. Both of these new series had a major numismatic liability, according to nearly everyone: the dates and mintmarks were placed on the *edges* of the coins, where they could not be seen in holders or albums! Other new series included 24-karat American Buffalo gold bullion coins and First Spouse coins. It cost more than $20,000 in Mint-issue prices to keep current with every legal-tender coin variety produced in a given year. Sales of platinum coins continued to fall below Mint expectations and there was discussion as to what to do, such as changing the designs.

In 2009 the golden dollar was continued, now with a *dateless* obverse, combined with a yearly change of reverse in the Native American series. Dates and mintmarks were placed on the edge.

The State quarter program wound down in 2008, after which in one year six quarters for the District of Columbia and U.S. territories were made, followed in 2010 by the new America the Beautiful quarters. The latter program features national parks, national historic sites, wildernesses, forests, and other "national" locations. In connection with these a parallel series of five-ounce silver bullion coins is being produced.

In 2008 the American economy was entering a recession, with the second week in October being the worst week in the 112-year history of the Dow-Jones Industrial Average, but this and the collapse of several major Wall Street firms had no measurable effect on the numismatic market.

Despite repeated predictions that "pennies" were no longer needed in commerce, the Mint continued to turn out billions, including four commemorative reverse designs in 2009 observing the bicentennial of Abraham Lincoln's 1809 birth. At this time the recession resulted in erratic distribution through the Federal Reserve Banks and less public interest than might have been the case in good times.

The four reverse designs used on Lincoln cents in 2009.

A 2010-D cent with the new reverse adopted as standard that year.

In 2010 the Union Shield design (by AIP artist Lyndall Bass, modeled by Mint medallic sculptor Joseph Menna) became the cent's new reverse motif.

In 2009 the price of gold bullion ranged from a low of $810.00 per ounce on January 15 to a high of $1,212.50 on December 2. American Eagle silver and gold issues remained very popular. In 2010 the year started on a high note with nearly 10,000 hobbyists attending the Florida United Numismatists convention in Orlando. The Whitman Coin & Collectibles Expo conventions in Baltimore remained a strong drawing card three times a year—March, June, and November. On the West Coast the Long Beach shows were popular. Regional conventions were held by some clubs. Early American Coppers had its own stand-alone gathering each year, complete with "happenings" in which members shared particular coin types or years and compared them with others.

Throughout this era the Citizens Coinage Advisory Committee met several times a year at the U.S. Mint's executive offices in Washington, D.C., and at other venues. Proposed coinage and medallic designs were reviewed and discussed in depth. For example, on March 23, 2010, the CCAC overwhelmingly and enthusiastically endorsed a motif featuring a modern woman as Justice on the reverse of the Proof platinum series that year. The committee in its two-hour session had a prolonged discussion on the lack of interest by *collectors* in these and other non-circulating coins.

Elsewhere in Mint news it was noted that its customer mailing list had slipped below one million names. Apart from the CCAC quite a few people wondered why the Mint kept using early twentieth-century motifs instead of creating new classics. However, the recycled early-twentieth-century designs of James Earle Fraser (1913 Buffalo nickel) and Adolph A. Weinman (1916 Walking Liberty half dollar) were considered by many numismatists to be the most beautiful designs used by the Mint in the early twenty-first century.

There was not much of an aftermarket for modern Mint commemoratives, and dealers were often paying just melt value or slightly less in the secondary market. Hobbyists who were building collections and desired to buy coins for little more than melt value had a great opportunity, commented editor Steve Roach in *Coin World*, March 7, 2011. He observed that 38 varieties of commemorative silver dollars were thus available.

That situation did not change in later years. Of course, this strategy was and is not risk-free from a resale viewpoint. On April 25, 2001, the closing price of silver was $48.70, its highest in 31 years. Anyone who bought silver dollars at bullion value then would have lost money. In late February 2019, an ounce of silver was $16.

It was reported that Presidential dollars had proved to be a dud with regard to public acceptance, and with many numismatists they achieved low marks as well. In the three and a half years since the program started, 1,252,000,000 unwanted coins were placed in Treasury storage, and $650,000 was to be spent at the Federal Reserve Bank of Dallas to store them, with the expectation that there would be two billion coins by the time the program ended. The main reason for this seemingly illogical situation

The price of a common 1884 Morgan dollar in Very Fine grade varies with the value of silver metal as a commodity.

is that the Treasury booked a handsome profit on each coin—the difference between the low cost of metal and coinage and the face value.

As to numismatics, in 2011 it cost $23,500 for a completist to buy every 2011 coin variety offered by the Mint, a figure that did not include every packaging option.

Mint Director Edmund C. Moy at a launch ceremony for the John Adams Presidential dollar.

In 2010 Edmund Moy announced his resignation as director of the Mint, effective January 2011. No successor was immediately appointed. Several deputy directors filled the leadership position as acting director or principal deputy director over the next few years. Deputy Director Richard Peterson acted as director for a time. Rhett Jeppson served as principal deputy director, and David Motl and Dave Croft were acting deputy directors in turn, by dint of their positions as senior career officials within the Mint management structure. Finally in 2017 David J. Ryder, who had served as Mint director in 1992 and 1993, was nominated to again take the post of director. He was confirmed by the Senate in March 2018.

In 2010 the Mint decided to discontinue most launch ceremonies for the America the Beautiful quarters. Public interest had reached a low, and the cost of sending Mint officials to distant locations was not effective. Launches were resumed later. Tom Jurkowsky, the Mint's director of corporate communications, working with Deputy Director Richard Peterson, interfaced with the numismatic community and helped with much research, including for multiple Whitman Publishing projects.

Mint products for numismatists such as Reverse Proofs and special issues with W mintmarks drew mixed reviews, and the continued placement of dates and mintmarks on the edge of dollars remained unfortunate. The Presidential dollars program received few glowing comments. The Sacagawea and Native American dollars earned complimentary notices and were and are well liked for their designs.

Mint Deputy Director Richard Peterson emcees the 2013 White Mountain New Hampshire quarter dollar launch.

Chinese counterfeits continued to plague the hobby (as they do to an even greater degree today—see Beth Deisher's essay on the subject on page 74). These extended to coins such as common Morgan dollars in grades of Extremely Fine and About Uncirculated as well as to common large copper cents and other coins. Gold ingots and American Gold Eagles were faked and fooled many people. One American importer offered Eagles at a third of bullion value. It became a dangerous procedure to buy gold coins and ingots and store them without having them examined or assayed. Beth Deisher, who retired from *Coin World* in 2012, held seminars on the subject. Leading third-party grading services guaranteed authenticity, making the premium for encapsulation a worthwhile precaution for many buyers.

The 1964–2014 gold Proof Kennedy half dollar.

In the market for rare and expensive federal coins, certification was the rule, not the exception. In the marketplace certified coins attracted many buyers and bidders who lacked experience and would not otherwise participate. CAC stickers became more popular than ever for selected rarities.

In 2014, on the 50th anniversary of the Kennedy half dollar, the Mint struck Proof dual-dated 1964–2014 coins in gold. Distribution began on August 4, including at the World's Fair of Money in Chicago, for the issue price of $1,240.

One of 45 gold ingots recovered from the SS *Central America* in 2014, adding to the over 400 recovered in the 1980s.

In 2014 Bob Evans, the scientist who led the earlier discovery of the long-lost *SS Central America*, returned to the site off of the coast of North Carolina in a new expedition. The recovery of gold coins, ingots, and other items was substantial, in the tens of millions of dollars in numismatic value, but much less than the first find.

Several important collections were marketed in this era, including selections from the cabinets of Eugene Gardner, Donald Partrick, Eric P. Newman, D. Brent Pogue, and Bernard Edison, each one playing to a wide audience with strong bidding and many record prices. However, the overall prices for many series were lower as supply in the marketplace exceeded numismatic demand.

In 2016 the Mint issued tribute coins of the 1916 dime, quarter, and half dollar, in gold with a 2016 date. This time, sales were orderly. These coins, like the 2014 Kennedy gold half dollar, were well received.

In 2008 Representative Michael Castle, longtime congressional friend of numismatists and the legislator who facilitated the 1999 and later special quarter issues, introduced a bill for palladium coins. That gained no traction, but years later in 2017 Eagles were made in that metal. Comments concerning palladium coins as well as platinum coins were mixed among numismatists. Neither metal had anything to do with regular American circulating coins (although in 1815 an experimental platinum half dollar had been struck from regular dies). As to whether coins in either metal appealed more to numismatists or to speculators in bullion metal was debatable.

In the twenty-first century the Internet and computer have wrought major structural changes in the market. Today as you read these words, a large percentage of the membership of the American Numismatic Association, about 25,000 people, receive *The Numismatist* in virtual form on the Internet. *Coin World* and other magazines are far thinner than they were a generation ago as most dealers no longer list coins for sale in print. The Internet is faster, and cheaper, and allows instant transactions.

The three different gold denominations struck in 2016 on the 100th anniversary of the release of the silver coins of the same motifs in 1916.

The American Liberty series of $100 denomination one-ounce gold coins was launched in 2015. Shown are the 2017 obverse, designed by Justin Kunz and sculpted by Phebe Hemphill; and reverse, designed by Chris Costello and sculpted by Michael Gaudioso.

A 2017 American Palladium Eagle with imprinted value of $25, much lower than its bullion value. Apparently Congress felt the best choice for a design was not to tap the current Mint Engraving Department staff but to resurrect the Mercury dime motif created by Adolph A. Weinman in 1916, and a high-relief version of his 1907 American Institute of Architects gold medal reverse.

In recent years many sales of scarce and rare coins that might have been made privately by dealers to clients have been consigned to public auction instead. This has resulted in a rearrangement of retail practices that were in effect a generation ago.

Books in print remain important (*Mega Red* has had record sales), but information on the Internet offers competition to traditional numismatic publishing.

Instant communications bring the world of numismatics to everyone, even on cell phones when traveling. More data are available than ever before. On the negative side, anyone collecting a popular coin series such as Morgan dollars and who has a modest budget can complete most of their collection on the Internet in a day—and with the coin budget exhausted, the fun of months or years of measured collecting might not lie ahead. On the other hand, for tokens, medals, die varieties, and other specialties, many items are inexpensive. A budget of $10,000 can build a memorable display in certain token, medal, and die variety series. Many modern series are very affordable in, say, MS-65 or Gem Mint State—such as modern dollars, Eisenhower to date, State quarters, and America the Beautiful quarters. Current Mint products such as commemoratives, Proofs, and modern medals are interesting to own and contemplate, with many beautiful and historic designs.

A working library of interesting and useful numismatic books can be a treasure and resource. As an example, it is enjoyable to read about numismatic treasures, from hoards to shipwrecks, without owning any of the coins. The Newman Numismatic Portal on the Internet, coordinated by Leonard Augsburger, provides free and unlimited access to thousands of magazines, newspapers, price lists, auction catalogs, and other material, an unprecedented incredible asset for research, effectively taking the place of a library that would require a lifetime and hundreds of thousands of dollars to form—and even then it would not match the NNP. The Internet is a gateway to explore many numismatic side roads and to gain knowledge on any coin or series.

The March 2020 American Numismatic Association's National Money Show in Atlanta was one of the last big conventions before the COVID-19 pandemic shut down all such venues for a time. The pandemic's effects on the numismatic scene are still being felt and analyzed. Beyond the human toll of numismatists lost to the virus, businesses have been disrupted and normal hobby events and activities have been curtailed. At the same time, the hobby community has found ways to survive and in some ways even flourish. Videoconferencing has been a boon for club meetings and educational programs in a time when large in-person gatherings are prohibited. (Online meetings will undoubtedly continue to be a large factor in the numismatic landscape even after society "opens up" again.) Book sales have been strong, with Whitman Publishing reporting early sellouts of print runs, and increased demand for popular titles. (The *Red Book* celebrated its 75th anniversary in 2021, and the sale of more than 25 million copies since its first edition.) In the coin market, dealers and collectors have found creative ways to respond to restrictions caused by the coronavirus pandemic. Online trading, already strong, has become a flourishing market for many buyers and sellers unable to physically attend coin shows. The bullion markets have brought new attention to coins as collectibles and investments. Modern coinage has become an even more exciting and innovative arena, with the introduction of 2021 "centennial" coins honoring the Morgan and Peace dollars and the promise of remarkable, unprecedented new coinage programs on the horizon. All of these dynamic forces and factors combine at a time when numismatics is poised for change and growth.

Whitman Publishing changed hands in 2023 when CDN Publishing purchased the company. The merger allowed the considerable data expertise of CDN to greatly enhance Whitman's library of titles and ensured the continued success of a publishing brand that is vital to collectors.

Also in 2023, Certified Acceptance Corporation Grading (CACG) began operations. The company is building on the tremendous success of CAC and has become an important player in third-party grading.

Gold and silver prices began to rise in 2024, and as of press time reached record levels. Gold broke the $4,000 level for the first time in October 2025. The rare-coin market is just now adjusting to these new levels, and the impact for numismatics remains to be seen. The incredibly high bullion prices will make many rare coins unaffordable for the average collector.

The timing has been unfortunate for a collectors who were highly anticipating the Mint's new precious-metal series. In 2025, through a licensing agreement with DC Comics, the U.S. Mint launched the three-year Comic Art Coin and Medal Program. Each year, three different iconic DC characters will be featured on $50 half-ounce gold Proof coins, for a total of nine coins. Silver medals in two sizes accompany each .9999-gold issue.

Next year will be the 250th anniversary of the United States. The U.S. Mint has planned several exciting releases for the Semiquincentennial (for details, see the special feature by Paul Gilkes on page 100). The Mint has also announced that it will no longer produce one-cent coins starting in 2026. Further, 2026 will be the 40th anniversary of the American Gold and Silver Eagle programs. The year 2026 could be one of the most exciting ones for numismatics in quite some time.

As has always been true, a collecting instinct is needed to be a longtime numismatist and an intellectual curiosity is essential to keep exploring the endless byways of numismatics to discover new things. In recent years the number of leading buyers building large collections has been greater than ever before in numismatic history. The hobby is alive and well. At Whitman Publishing all of us are enthusiastic about the future.

COLLECTING U.S. COINS

Coin collecting is a wonderful pastime. In the United States, as it developed into a widespread pursuit during the latter half of the 20th century, it was frequently referred to as the *Hobby of Kings*. Superficially, this was true. Kings did collect coins. The collection of King Farouk of Egypt was sold in 1954 by Sotheby's. The Farouk pedigree and the great rarities from his collection are much coveted to this day. The last king of Italy, Umberto II, sold selections from his collection in 1967 at a Hans M.F. Schulman auction in New York. Yet even with royalty among their ranks, coin collectors have always come from all walks of life and from all places. The hobby took this name not only because of those who pursued it, but because coin collecting at its best is a sophisticated endeavor. It involves a knowledge of history. It requires an understanding of money and value, and of how they differ. Above all, it requires an appreciation of things that not everyone can see.

Cultivating a passion for numismatics is available to all. We are very fortunate here in America to have coin shops and collecting clubs in most towns, and online buying has made collecting easier and more accessible than ever. We have the American Numismatic Association, chartered by Congress in 1891, to promote the study of numismatics with education and collector outreach as its core mission. We have reference works like the *Red Book* and *Mega Red*, in themselves institutions that provide information to U.S. coin collectors in exacting detail. For many, their fascination with numismatics blossomed as they studied the pages of an edition of this very book.

The most fundamental component of what is needed to become a good collector is learning. The best advice is to go slowly, hone your interests, specialize, and develop a deeper familiarity with a coinage series. One oft-repeated aphorism in numismatics is, "Buy the book before the coin." Study the pages of a coinage series here in *Mega Red* to understand its intricacies. Then look at as many coins as possible, online and preferably in person, by visiting coin shops and attending coin shows and auction viewings.

Cultivating expertise involves developing knowledge of other topics that relate not to the coins themselves but to the hobby. The following sections include an inside view of grading, authentication, cleaning, conservation, and more—elements that are known to most experienced professionals and long-time collectors. Developing understanding in these areas will further guide your purchasing decisions, help you to avoid mistakes, and allow you to better allocate your collecting budget. In other words, you will build the best collection you can.

One rule always will hold true: Above all, buy what you love.

A SEMINAR ON THE GRADING OF COINS

There is no area of coin collecting in the current market that has the potential to add more enjoyment and value to your collection than grading. As collectors become more advanced, they grow to appreciate coins that are especially nice for the issue. As with any collectible made in multiples, examples in better condition are worth more. For coins, which are often produced in very large quantities, the finest-known examples are worth exponentially more than pieces of average quality. These are attributes that often cannot be seen or appreciated by those just starting out.

Fortunately, all collectors can learn to grade. It's a topic that has been unnecessarily and overly complicated. Today, high-value U.S. coins are always independently graded by third-party grading companies and encapsulated in their holders. This has been true for about 30 years, and many collectors have never handled uncertified (or "raw") coins. Even in this environment, understanding how to grade coins is an important part of collecting. The goal of these pages is to describe how professionals grade coins, both in the grading rooms of leading certification companies and as dealers on the bourse floor, and to remove the mystery of this basic endeavor.

Coin grading has a language. A *grade* describes the condition of coin very succinctly while still being very precise. The vocabulary and syntax of this language are found in the coin grading scale, and today we use a numerical one. With the grade alone—a single number—a knowledgeable collector can envision a good approximation of what a coin looks like and its market value. It is at once very powerful and very simple.

Let's clarify this with an example. Assume there is an advertisement for a Morgan dollar graded MS-63. (This grade can also be referred to as Choice Uncirculated.) From that grade, what do we know about the condition of this coin? We know that it has never been used in commerce and shows no wear or evidence of circulation handling. We know that this coin retains its Mint luster but isn't necessarily flashy. It has contact marks and abrasions, but no heavy or distracting marks. Its strike is at least typical of this issue. A lot of information is conveyed from "MS-63." But how do we know all this? Because on the coin grading scale, MS-63 describes a coin with these attributes.

Coin grading involves three steps. The first step of coin grading is learning and understanding the grading scale, a brief overview of which follows in the next section. The introductory text for each coin series included in *Mega Red* has an interpretation of the grading scale for that coinage series along with photo illustrations. More than enough is here to gain a foundational understanding. Looking at coins in holders graded by reputable third-party companies will reinforce your learning and make you more comfortable with the grading scale.

The second part of grading is to perform a visual examination. The physical act of grading involves looking at the coin. This is straightforward, but there is actually a right and a wrong way to do this. There are best practices. A discussion of ideal lighting, proper technique and correct magnification follows below.

During and after examination, the third step is to assign a grade to the coin that accords with the grading scale. Every coin is different. Consider a small group of uncirculated 1921 Peace dollars. One coin may have many small, scattered marks throughout, none of them deep or disturbing. Another coin may be mostly free from marks but have a few larger, centrally located hits caused by making contact with the reeded edge of another coin. A third may be especially well struck with good hair detail in the central obverse (an uncommon feature), but have dull luster and a dark, splotchy patina. A final coin may have very clean, pleasing, satiny surfaces but be flatly struck, "like a pancake." For each of these coins, we must interpret these characteristics to arrive at a grade. The grading standard doesn't address every scenario one may encounter. Instead, the significance of various flaws must be assessed based on the individual grader's understanding of the standards.

Former *Mega Red* senior editor Q. David Bowers says, "Grading is an art, not a science." And then he repeats it. He is describing this act of subjectively interpreting an objective standard. The most skilled graders can do this accurately and consistently.

Coin-Grading Scale

The scale we use today is a 70-point numerical scale first published in 1949 by Dr. William H. Sheldon. For circulated coins, he used essentially the same terms that we use today. There were fewer gradations, and intermediate grades were not explicitly described. For uncirculated coins, he described three numerical grades, 60, 65, and 70, calling them all Uncirculated. New terminology was introduced in 1958, when dealers Martin R. Brown and John W. Dunn published the first coin-grading guide, popularizing terms like Choice and Gem for levels of Uncirculated condition. James F. Ruddy's *Photograde*, which followed in 1970, included pictures and descriptions of coins in every grade for each U.S. coinage series. The book was immensely popular, but early editions still didn't use a numerical scale.

Then, in the early 1970s, the *Coin Dealer Newsletter* added Sheldon 70-point grade numbers to the Uncirculated grades in its price guide, firmly connecting numbers with grades. Finally, in 1977, the American Numismatic Association published its official grading standards, authored by Abe Kosoff, Kenneth Bressett, and Q. David Bowers, codifying the numerical grading scale that we use today. In recognition of its origin, it's referred to as the Sheldon scale.

The highest grade assigned to an Uncirculated coin is 70. This is for a coin that doesn't have any post-production imperfections visible under light magnification. For circulating coinage and coins struck without special surface finishes, this grade is often expressed as MS-70, shorthand for Mint State–70. For Proof coins, which are made for presentation purposes, this is expressed as PF-70 (for Proof-70). It's important to remember that *Proof* is not a grade. It describes a method of manufacturing. Logically, the grades MS-70 and PF-70 are assigned almost exclusively to coins of relatively recent issue.

Most coins do have imperfections. For these, the grading scale is decremental: From 70, the numerical grade is lowered to account for various surface attributes or flaws, and more significantly to account for wear from handling in circulation. While it may seem daunting to conceive of a 70-point scale, understanding the major divisions between grade categories makes it much easier to understand the various numbers and how they are used. In *Mega Red*, versions of this scale are provided for each coin type along with photographs. The following is a generalized overview of the grading scale regular-issue coins and describes the main features of each grade.

The grades MS-60 through MS-70 are used for Uncirculated coins. These coins weren't handled in commerce, and one grades them by evaluating, in tandem, four different attributes.

Surface. How many marks or how much abrasion does the coin have? Coins stuck for use as currency are ejected from the dies into bins, transported in bags, and wrapped into rolls by large sorting machines. They can have marks. Are these marks deep or shallow, large or small? And are they located in central focal areas? On higher-grade coins, there are fewer and less-prominent marks.

Luster. How do the coin's surfaces react to light? Are they flashy or dull? Distortions of luster can often reveal how a coin has been treated or if it has been mistreated. Full luster or an original mint "bloom" is desirable and unimpaired on higher-grade Uncirculated coins.

Strike. How sharply and fully was the coin impressed during minting? Are the high points well detailed? Are there area of weakness on the peripheries on either side? To achieve a high Mint State grade, a coin must be well struck.

Eye Appeal. Are there spots, splotches, or dark areas that detract from the coin's overall appeal? Negative eye appeal can preclude a coin from achieving a high grade even if it otherwise has strong technical merit—high-grade coins must be attractive to merit their lofty grades.

The grading scale for Uncirculated coins is as follows (selected grades are illustrated for reference):

Superb Gem Uncirculated

MS-70 No post-production imperfections are visible at 5x magnification.

MS-69 Minute imperfections are visible under magnification or with careful examination.

MS-67, 68 Only very small flaws are evident. The coin should have full strike, full luster, and superior eye appeal.

MS-65+

Gem Uncirculated

MS-65, 66 Slight contact marks, including hidden marks, are present. The coin is fully lustrous, well struck, and visually appealing.

Near Gem Uncirculated

MS-64 Small marks and abrasions may be evident, including in the focal areas, but do not detract from the overall appeal. Luster and strike should be at least typical for the issue.

Choice Uncirculated

MS-63 The coin has marks and abrasions but should be a good representative of the issue. The strike can have some softness or the luster may be impaired. Eye appeal should be at least average.

Uncirculated

MS-60, 61, 62 The coin can have heavy marks, spotting or staining, or a weak strike. Above all, there should be no evidence of handling from circulation.

When coins circulate, metal is moved and removed from its surface, causing the coin to lose detail. We call this wear. Circulated coins are graded largely by the amount of wear, or more specifically by how much detail remains in spite of wear. The grades from 58 down to 1 are used for circulated coins, as follows.

AU-58

About Uncirculated

AU-50, 53, 55, 58 This is the first grade level where coins exhibit evidence of circulation. The four gradations, working down from AU-58 to AU-50, describe the loss of luster from the highest points to more of the design.

EF-40

Extremely Fine
EF-40, 45

While About Uncirculated is concerned with luster loss, coins graded Extremely Fine exhibit true wear. Areas of the highest points will show loss of detail. Luster will be confined to the protected areas of the design.

VF-20

Very Fine
VF-20, 25, 30, 35

At this level the wear has increased to the point that portions of the coin show true flatness. Very Fine grades vary by the amount of the design that is affected by this flatness. Importantly, all the elements of the design should be present, if only in outline. For example, leaves on a laurel headdress should all be present and fully outlined, although their veins may have worn away.

F-15

Fine
F-12, 15

This is the first grade where major elements of the design are starting to wear away. Leaves on a headdress merge into the hair seamlessly. Small design features are only partially present.

VG-8

Very Good
VG-8, 10 — Design elements are now totally lost, but the central device is still more than just an outline. For example, for a coin that depicts a bust, the eye is fully present and portions of the hairline are present.

G-4

Good
G-4, 6 — The major design elements are all readable but may be present in outline only. The rim is full (G-6) or mostly full (G-4).

About Good
AG-3 — The rims merge into the peripheral legends. Central design elements are starting to merge into the fields.

Fair
FR-2 — Major portions of the design are missing.

Poor
PO-1 — The coin is identifiable, but no additional detail is present.

The process of grading Proof coins is a little different. Proof coinage is often struck multiple times by specially prepared dies on high-quality planchets, and, with rare exceptions, Proofs have not been used in circulation. A Proof coin is always a Proof, and thus its numerical grade is always preceded by the letters PF (or sometimes PR) regardless of whether the coin displays evidence of circulation. Instead of circulating, Proof coins were kept by collectors and (especially with older coins) subjected to the occasional wiping with a cloth, which could cause fine hairlines. Stains and spotting from improper storage may also be present. The number of hairlines and their severity account for the main differences between a coin graded PF-63 and one graded PF-67—grades that have vastly different values in the marketplace. Learning to grade Proof coins can be very straightforward because they exhibit a smaller range of flaws that must be considered. It is vitally important, however, to examine Proof coins correctly under a light to grade them accurately. Indeed, visual examinations must be conducted properly to grade all coins well.

Proper Visual Examination for Coin Grading

Assessment of a coin's condition is performed by visual examination. This requires very few tools, but there are practices and techniques that distinguish a good grader from a poor one.

The first and most important thing to consider are lighting conditions. Coin grading is performed in a dark room illuminated only by a single point light source, usually a desk lamp. Reducing ambient light is essential because marks or hairlines on a coin's surface can be directional and faceted. This means that they are visible only when light is reflected to the viewer at a constrained and direct angle. In a bright room, light bounces every which way, obscuring flaws on a coin's surface.

Professional coin graders and many dealers are fanatical about light. They can tell you which wattage and color spectrum bulb they prefer, and they will work only under that light. Graders even purchase and maintain their own supply of bulbs if they become partial to a particular brand. For years, graders worked under 75W or 100W incandescent light, but most have transitioned to LED equivalents. When buying coins from a shop or at a coin show, it is acceptable to ask for a lamp so that you can examine the coin optimally if none is set up for you.

On the bourse floor of a major coin show, you may see some dealers use a halogen or tensor lamp to overcome the bright ambient room light, but this is seldom necessary and carries a word of caution: using too bright a light makes small marks and flaws appear overly significant. You must always look at the whole coin and avoid any tendency to micrograde. *Micrograding* is assigning a grade based on a small impairment or just one fractional area of the coin. The grade assigned must consider the entire obverse, reverse, and edge as a whole.

Once lighting conditions are optimized, look at the coin and assign a "flash" grade. This is a first impression. When you first look at the coin, quickly form an opinion of where on the scale it ranks. If you are a novice your assessment might be vague: "It's a nice Uncirculated coin," or "It's a little bit circulated," or "It's heavily worn." The flash grade of an expert will be much closer, within a point or two of the final grade assigned. After flash grading, the examination progresses to refine the grade.

During the next part of grading, the examine the coin while rotating it under the light. When holding a raw coin, by its edge, move your hand back and forth. Look for flaws that react to the light. Rotate the coin a little bit, a quarter turn, and repeat moving it back and forth while assessing the surface. Continue in this way until you've covered the whole coin, obverse and reverse. These movements require a little practice, but the more coins you examine the faster and more comfortable it becomes. When a coin is encapsulated, you can play around with different angles and speeds of movement. You can hold the coin at very sharp angles to the light and see if it looks different. Learning how to roll and rotate coins under the light will allow you to see it better. This is an essential component of coin grading. Professional coin graders refer to this as "hitting all the angles." It is considered a big mistake in professional coin grading to miss a wipe or some hairlines because you did not thoroughly and properly examine the coin.

During this phase of examination, if any area of the coin looks lighter or darker or otherwise different when rotated under the light, the next step is to examine the coin under magnification. For all coin grading, there is little need to use more than 5x magnification. Higher levels are used only for authentication and variety attribution. Coins cannot be graded properly under high levels of magnification. This is a common misconception of beginners.

A 5x magnifier is essential for grading—but anything higher than 5x is counterproductive and can lead to "micrograding."

Continue to refine the grade during each phase of purposeful examination, moving up or down from the original flash impression.

Move on to examine the rim and edge for filing or other irregularities. And finally, for older vintage coins especially, examine the entire surface under 5x magnification to look for alterations. At this stage, a final grade can be assigned. Any major surface impairments that preclude a coin from being numerically graded will also have been identified. The entire process may take less than a minute for an experienced grader.

During this process, the grader may discover reasons that a coin cannot be graded using the grading scale. These are coins with detrimental surface conditions. For example, if a Bust half dollar has graffiti because a prior owner engraved his initials in the obverse of the coin, there is no standardized way to account for this using the above grading scale. Grading is a language, after all, and the shorthand "AU-50" doesn't describe a lightly circulated coin with initials carved into it! For that reason, we use details grades. The Bust half dollar in this example would thus be called, "AU Details, Obverse Graffiti." Recognizing various detrimental surface conditions is another part of grading. Taking time to examine coins graded by professional grading services with terms such as Cleaned, Environmentally Damaged, Tooled, and so on is perhaps the best way to learn this important skill.

Today's Grading Landscape

Collectors entering the rare-coin market in the United States today will discover that most valuable coins have been graded by a third-party company. These companies are "third-party" because they are neither the seller nor the prospective buyer. Instead, they are an independent party that only renders an independent opinion on the grade of the coin. This is an immensely valuable proposition. In the days before third-party grading, a collector might pay a premium for a coin described as Gem Uncirculated, only to find that when he or she tried to sell the coin years later, another dealer would say, "It's an Uncirculated coin, but not nice enough for Gem," and accordingly offer a lower price. Today, collectors know that the coins they buy will always carry the same representations of grade and authenticity when they sell them as they did when they bought them.

Third-party grading companies encapsulate coins in holders, colloquially referred to as slabs. These are tamper-evident and designed for long-term storage. Slabbing is also an essential part of independent certification because, in which companies provide a guarantee of grade and authenticity. To do this they must have certainty that a coin inside a holder is the coin they graded and that it has not been altered in any way.

Professionally graded and slabbed coins.

Among graded coins, there are several different prominent grading companies. The largest and most well-established are Professional Coin Grading Service (PCGS) and Numismatic Guaranty Company (NGC), founded in 1986 and 1987, respectively. Better known by their acronyms, they offer a wide range of services and grade both U.S. and foreign coins on a 70-point numerical scale. ANACS has an even longer history, starting as a division of the American Numismatic Association that offered only photo certificates. It's now an independent company with standard-format holders. A more recent entrant is Certified Acceptance Corporation Grading (CACG), which is owned partly by a syndicate of U.S. coin dealers. Each of these companies has different tendencies, and dealers and collectors may prefer the grading standards, holders, guarantees, or submission processes of one company over another. Since it's a matter of preference, it's perfectly acceptable for a collector to include coins graded by only one, or two, or three or more of these companies. Coins certified by these companies also have different values in the marketplace, sometimes vastly different. For that reason, it is still vitally important that collectors learn about grading even if professional third-party grading is widely available in the marketplace.

Independent certification has been around for nearly 40 years. In the very early days of coin grading, graders had less comfort with the upper register of the grading range and seldom assigned grades above MS-65. Rapidly, knowledge grew, and within a few years grading standards normalized. This has led to a characterization by some that grading used to be tighter and that these standards have loosened, a phenomenon called *gradeflation*. The truth is much more nuanced.

An apt analogy is to think of older certifications from the 1980s in the same way we think of movies from that era. There are some iconic films, great pieces of storytelling. There are also scores of average films, and there are some real clunkers, too. They are all accessible to today's audiences, and most of them offer a perfectly fine moviegoing experience when watched today. Visually and stylistically, they are a little different. There has been an evolution. The tastes of the audience have changed. And new movies are informed by those from years ago.

Collectors will encounter coins that have been graded by different individuals over several different eras. Not all grading services are equivalent, and not all graded coins of the same grade are equivalent. Most professional coin graders work for 10, 20, 30 years or even longer in the field, and this has given a grading in numismatics a level of consistency and accuracy not seen with other collectibles. There is still a great opportunity for a specialized collector who is knowledgeable at grading to find and purchase third-party graded coins that represent exceptional quality, and therefore value, for their respective grade. Cherrypicking for quality in this way is very rewarding pursuit for advanced collectors.

ASPECTS OF AUTHENTICITY

In the marketplace there are many counterfeit coins, or coins that have been altered so that they appear to be something other than what they really are. Many of these are sold by vendors who are not aware of their false nature. Others are deliberately, fraudulently sold. If a coin is found to be counterfeit, getting your money back may be difficult or impossible. Exceptions are coins certified by third-party grading services that have guaranteed authenticity.

Authenticity refers only to a coin's being genuine and struck at the place and in the era as expected. As an example, a rare 1893-S Morgan dollar is expected to be a coin made by the San Francisco Mint in the year 1893. A 1916-D Mercury dime is expected to be a coin made at the Denver Mint in the year 1916. A one-ounce 2011-W American Gold Eagle is expected to be a one-ounce, .9167-fine gold coin struck at the West Point Mint in the year 2011.

Authenticity does not refer to the grade of a coin, such as whether it is MS-63, or to the character of its surface (i.e., whether it is Mint State, prooflike, or a Proof). Authenticity refers only to originality.

Your risk of purchasing a spurious coin can be minimized if you are aware of certain factors. If a coin is priced significantly below market value, beware. If a deal on a coin seems too good to be true, it is! Coins have exceptional liquidity. Knowledgeable buyers who will pay a fair market price are accessible. Being offered a coin at a fraction of its real value should be a red flag.

Some professional organizations such as the Professional Numismatists Guild (PNGdealers.org) or the International Association of Professional Numismatists (iapn-coins.org) have binding rules of conduct surrounding counterfeit items. While many fine dealers do not belong to these groups, if the seller is not a recognized professional numismatist with a written guarantee of authenticity, be careful.

False Coins

False coins can include the following.

Struck copies from false dies. These are often crude, but in modern generations there have been a lot of fakes that almost defy detection. Many have come from China and include coins from commonplace to rare, as well as American Silver and Gold Eagles. Beth Deisher, former editor of *Coin World*, worked with the Anti-Counterfeiting Educational Foundation's Anti-Counterfeiting Task Force to combat these. EAC (Early American Coppers) is doing research as well, led by Jack Young.

Electrotypes. The person who produces these items uses a genuine coin to create molds of the obverse and reverse, and electro-deposits metal into each mold. They then join the two pieces together are smooth the resulting seams. Most coins made in this fashion can be identified by a microscopic seam on the edge. Many rare copper half cents, cents, early medals, and other issues have been electrotyped. Both the British Museum and the American Numismatic Society furnished electrotypes years ago to collectors for display purposes, these being offered openly as such.

Altered genuine coins. These coins are made by the addition of a mintmark to a Philadelphia Mint coin, the reengraving of a date to change it to another year, or some other changing to a feature. One researcher reported that in the late 1950s more than half of the purported 1916-D Mercury dimes seen at a leading convention had added D mintmarks. At a convention in 2018, this author was shown a "1934-S" dollar with an added S. Many alterations can often be detected by examination under a high-power stereomicroscope.

Coins of the wrong weight. Silver and gold coins, if in Mint State, should conform to their authorized weights. Worn coins can show a slight reduction. Any off-weight coins should be viewed with suspicion.

Replicas of colonial and other coins. Replicas may be made in quantity and sold as souvenirs, including at historical sites maintained by the Department of the Interior. Many have wound up with new owners who were not aware of their status. Some are marked COPY, but not all are, and some have had that word removed.

Coins with Altered Surfaces

For genuine coins, there are other elements that can decrease value.

Whizzing, or the polishing of the surface of a coin with a high-speed wire brush, can give false luster. This problem was endemic before third-party certification. Today newly whizzed coins are rare, but some older ones linger in the marketplace.

One can also alter a coin's surface by plugging a hole, removing stamped initials or cuts, strengthening the hair details on Liberty's portrait, etching to remove wear, or other doctoring. Such actions might improve a damaged or worn coin's visual appeal, but they are detectable, and they will nearly always decrease rather than increase its value.

Recommendations and Caveats

Buying coins from a trusted source is the best way to ensure authenticity, as many of the most obvious fakes (as described above) are recognized and not sold by reputable professionals and firms. However, even the most experienced expert can be fooled.

The Uniform Commercial Code (UCC) and various state regulations provide statues of limitation that limit the time during which the buyer of a false coin has recourse against the seller.

Major U.S. third-party grading companies such as NGC and PCGS offer comprehensive guarantees of authenticity on the coins they grade. Most leading collectors and dealers today agree that buying a coin certified for its authenticity is the best protection against counterfeits and altered coins. Collectors of certified coins should review the guarantees published on grading-service websites to learn more about the level of protection and possible limitations.

To the above, Beth Deisher has contributed the following.

Chinese Counterfeits

by Beth Deisher

For nearly 230 years large-scale counterfeiting of U.S. coins was virtually unheard of because those who attempted to manufacture fakes rarely had access to the die-making equipment or production presses necessary to succeed. Nor did they have instant access to coin buyers worldwide, particularly the largest coin market, which is in the United States.

The situation changed dramatically in the early years of the 21st century. By 2005 most sovereign mints around the world had begun embracing computer technology and robotics in their die-making and coin-production processes. It was not a matter of simply installing and adapting modern manufacturing methods. Rather, competition—especially in the commemorative-coin sector—demanded cost-effective manufacturing and innovative features in design and metallurgy.

The search for both efficiency and innovation led to the U.S. Mint's transition in 2008 to digital technology in its die-making operation, producing never-before-experienced efficiencies and precision. During the same period, the Mint increased use of computer-controlled processes and robotics throughout its manufacturing and packaging operations.

Ironically, rather than making counterfeiting more difficult, the transition to computers and digital technology opened new opportunities for counterfeiters because rapid leaps in technology and knowledge of how to use it spread throughout the world at levels unprecedented in human history. The same is true for the availability of computers and access to unregulated e-commerce platforms. Thus, costs and availability were no longer barriers for counterfeiters.

During 2007 and 2008 it became apparent to the U.S. numismatic community that the numbers of counterfeit coins in the United States marketplace were increasing at a rapid pace. Specialists in early American copper coins, trade dollars, and Morgan dollars were among the first to sound the alarm. The weekly *Coin World* joined the *New York Times* in a year-long investigation, resulting in *Coin World*'s publication of a December 2008 series revealing more than 100 thriving coin-counterfeiting operations in China. Most were small, cottage-type operations. The largest, owned by a 26-year-old entrepreneur, relied on vintage 1870s U.S. coin presses salvaged from "scrap metal" sold by the Chinese government. (The U.S. government in the 1920s sold old coining presses to China, which after using the presses stored them in the 1950s and had recently sold them as scrap.)

The proprietor of the largest operation said in 2008 he was licensed by the Chinese government to make "replicas" of any coins in the world except current circulating Chinese coins. He claimed he had the capacity to produce 100,000 coins a month, most of which were older Chinese coin types and sold in China. However, he was expanding a new line of counterfeit U.S. coins and selling about 1,000 per month in the United States via eBay. He had established a network of "wholesale" buyers in the United States who would buy in bulk and identify the most popular sellers. Most of his "replica" coins could be identified because he used iron-based planchets plated with silver or the proper alloy to match the authentic coin. He also accepted orders for counterfeits made of 90% silver and gold, but they were priced to reflect the higher-quality planchets and constituted a very small portion of his business.

By 2021 about a dozen large-scale Chinese manufacturers had forced the small businesses out of the market with production capacities of more than 500,000 per month of highly sophisticated and deceptive gold and silver counterfeits of virtually every denomination and design type of U.S. coins. By the end of 2025 they had more than doubled their capacities.

A major factor in the accelerating growth of Chinese coin counterfeiters was their ability to market their wares worldwide via Alibaba, the e-commerce company that in 1999 entered the marketplace to connect Chinese manufacturers with overseas buyers. In April 2016 Alibaba became the world's largest retailer and one of the largest Internet companies, reaching into more than 200 countries. Other Chinese internet companies such as AliExpress, DHgate, and Wish soon followed. Counterfeit coins saturated the Chinese platforms, and U.S. coin buyers were alerted to that reality.

Eager to gain market share in all products, the American e-commerce platform Amazon opened its doors to Chinese merchants, including coin counterfeiters, giving them direct access to the vast U.S. marketplace. Amazon began wooing Chinese merchants to sell on its global sites in 2007 and began actively recruiting and facilitating sales through its Global Selling Program beginning around 2013. Amazon intensified its efforts in 2015 to attract Chinese sellers for its U.S. and European marketplaces. Estimates in 2025 place the number of Chinese merchants on Amazon selling directly to U.S. consumers at approximately 54% of all merchants on the platform.

Other U.S. e-commerce platforms such as eBay, Facebook, and Etsy followed Amazon's lead, resulting in virtually all e-commerce platforms' saturation with counterfeit collectible and investment coins.

Usually, Chinese counterfeiters focus on products with high brand-name recognition. However, no U.S. coin is too cheap or too common for the Chinese to counterfeit. Conventional wisdom, long held in the numismatic community, was that "the coin has to be real since it is not worth faking"; this simply no longer applies. The Chinese counterfeiters make their profits on volume and on the wide range of counterfeit coins they manufacture and sell. For U.S. coins, the categories include:

- Historic collectible coins—every design type and denomination made by the U.S. Mint since 1793.
- Commemorative coins—specially made collector coins, usually of silver and gold, issued in limited quantities to honor a person, place, or event; early commemoratives, 1892 through 1954, and modern commemoratives, 1982 through the current year.
- Bullion coins—investment coins made of silver, gold, platinum, and palladium, traded on exchanges and sold based on the world market price for the coins' precious metal.
- Circulating (transactional) coins—the coins in your pocket used in daily commerce.

Fake Coins, Fake Holders

Chinese counterfeiters are also producing fakes of the most trusted brands of grading-service holders. Since the mid-1980s, independent third-party grading services have authenticated, graded, and encapsulated high-value collectible and bullion coins. Though these services' plastic holders have incorporated anti-counterfeiting devices essentially from the beginning, counterfeiters have become increasingly adept in recent years at mimicking these devices within months of their introduction. Counterfeiters particularly target Professional Coin Grading Service (PCGS) and Numismatic Guaranty Company (NGC) holders because they are the market leaders in grading, not only in the United States but worldwide. Virtually all of the counterfeit holders also contain counterfeit coins.

Since approximately 2015, gold and silver American Eagles have been among the most widely counterfeited bullion coins in the world. In 2021 the U.S. Mint introduced new silver and gold American Eagle bullion coin reverse designs that incorporate new anti-counterfeiting features—the first step in the U.S. Mint's efforts to thwart counterfeiters. However, there are no measurable indications that the counterfeiters have slowed their production of counterfeit American Eagle bullion coins, especially of coins dated prior to 2021.

The combination of the Trump administration's high tariffs imposed on China and ending the U.S. *de minimis* policy in May 2025 prompted a noticeable shift in Chinese coin counterfeiters' marketing strategy.

The *de minimis* provision had for years exempted packages valued at $800 or less from import duties for goods made in China and Hong Kong. The change left most shipments, including those carried by FedEx or United Parcel Service, subject to a new, 145% base tariff on all Chinese products, as well as additional levies based on the nature of the products. Steep fees on packages containing merchandise from China shipped via the international postal network are also applicable.

In recent years, use of the *de minimis* provision had skyrocketed with a surge of goods from Chinese e-commerce platforms Shein and Temu. About 1.36 billion shipments using the *de minimis* provision entered the U.S. in fiscal year 2024, up from 637 million four years earlier, according to U.S. Customs and Border Protection.

When the holder makes it difficult to inspect the coin directly, go to the source for confirmation—and buy only from reputable companies that guarantee the authenticity of their products. *(left)* Fake 2025-S Reverse Proof Morgan dollar in a fake PCGS slab. Click the Verify link at PCGS.com (or for NGC-certified coins, ngccoin.com/certlookup/)to check for authenticity. The certification number should match the coin and the number on the holder. (In this case, the number on the fake slab corresponds to a 2023-S Proof Morgan dollar, not a 2025-S Reverse Proof.) If the coin in the holder isn't shown, use the CoinFacts link for images of the real thing. *(right)* Genuine 2024-S Reverse Proof Morgan dollar in a genuine holder.

Chinese coin counterfeiters reacted to the tariffs and the end of the *de minimis* policy by establishing networks in countries in Eastern Europe and Africa that are subject to much lower tariffs. By shipping counterfeit coins to network "affiliates" who in turn ship to the United States, they have been able to continue saturating the U.S. market with counterfeit coins. Their "affiliates," skilled in creating fake websites designed to make buyers think they're purchasing from a seller in the United States, appear to have added a new marketing tactic.

The nonprofit Anti-Counterfeiting Educational Foundation (ACEF), founded in 2108, initially focused its efforts on educating law-enforcement authorities and policymakers about the threat of counterfeit coins. However, due to the increasing volume of counterfeit coins flooding the U.S. marketplace, ACEF has redirected its efforts and resources with the goal of creating more awareness, particularly among the buying public seeking a "bargain" who fall victim to counterfeiters operating on e-commerce platforms. As part of its education mission, ACEF presents anti-counterfeiting educational seminars and forums at major coin shows. ACEF also maintains a robust website (acefonline.org) featuring basic information on how to identify counterfeit coins, and offers news and alerts for all active in the coin market. ACEF is funded entirely by donations.

Online Buyer Beware

There are many things you can do to protect yourself when purchasing coins and other numismatic collectibles online. At a minimum you should follow these simple steps to avoid being scammed into buying counterfeit coins.

1. If the price is "too good to be true," do the math. Know about the coins you want to purchase, including how much precious metal they contain, and look up the current spot price of that metal. Say, for example, that the current spot price of silver is $49.97 an ounce, and the online seller has priced a 40-piece set of American Silver Eagle coins (1986–2024) at $239.99. American Silver Eagles are .999 fine and contain one ounce of pure silver. At the very least, each coin would have a silver value of $49.97. Dividing $239.99 by 40 equals about $6. At this price, the seller would lose $43.97 per coin.

Here's another example: A set of 28 Morgan dollars, which are 90 percent silver, is offered at $99.99. With the spot price of silver at $49.97, each Morgan dollar would have a silver value of $44.97, plus any premium for a rare date, variety, or high grade. Would the owner of genuine Morgan dollars sell 28 pieces for $3.57 each? Such offers are "bargain bait," and it's a sure bet the coins are counterfeit!

2. Verify telephone numbers and addresses in the Contact Us section. Often counterfeiters and scammers steal images and logos from genuine coin-dealer websites to dupe buyers into believing they are purchasing genuine coins from real sellers in the United States. Always verify the telephone number listed and talk with a real person. Always verify the physical address as well; tools like Google's Maps, Earth, and Street View are useful for this. At first glance, the address may seem real, but check carefully. Most scammers and counterfeiters use addresses of graveyards, vacant lots, or the like, or simply invent addresses that do not exist. Another favorite trick is to use the street address of a shopping mall. In that case, search for the mall's own website, and confirm that the storefront—with matching contact information—is really inside it.

The Contact Us page on the illustrated "Mint" website is a perfect example of these practices, although it's cleverer than most: Its physical address does correspond to the "Mail Correspondence for Product Inquiries" address on the real U.S. Mint's website. However, the real website lists 15 different phone numbers, including a 1-800 number for the help center and numbers for the bulk-purchase program, mutilated-coin redemption, and other issues. All of these numbers lead to legitimate government call centers. The fake website does not have a single phone number.

And finally, if the purported coin store's website does not provide any contact information, do not purchase anything from it. An email address or URL redirected from China, Africa, or an Eastern European country is also highly suspect.

3. Check the URL of the website. Counterfeiters and scammers often copy the URLs of legitimate websites and add a character, or else swap a character with a lookalike (e.g., replacing an "o" with a zero).

The image shown here is of a very high-quality fake website pretending to be that of the U.S. Mint. The Mint's real web address is https://www.usmint.gov (or simply usmint.gov); the address here, ustmint.com, is meant to capture buyers attempting to find the U.S. Mint's official website. Having entered the bogus site, the user continues to think he's purchasing from the U.S. Mint because the scammer has used stolen images and official seals of the U.S. Mint as and its products. The smart user will always double-check the URL for obvious errors (like the "t" in "ustmint"), including the extension. A ".com" extension might be expected for a private business, but the U.S. Mint is a government agency, so its extension is ".gov."

The scammers behind this website took great pains to make it look real, mimicking the Mint site's style, copying its artwork, even making sure the protocol (the part before the colon) is "https," indicating the site is secure. This is a must for any website that handles sensitive information like credit-card numbers. However, "secure" does not mean "legitimate"; it simply means information entered on the site is encrypted and can't be read by an outside party trying to steal data. Always inspect the web address closely. This one has an extra character in the domain name, and the domain extension is ".com." With rare exceptions, all official websites of the U.S. government end with ".gov."

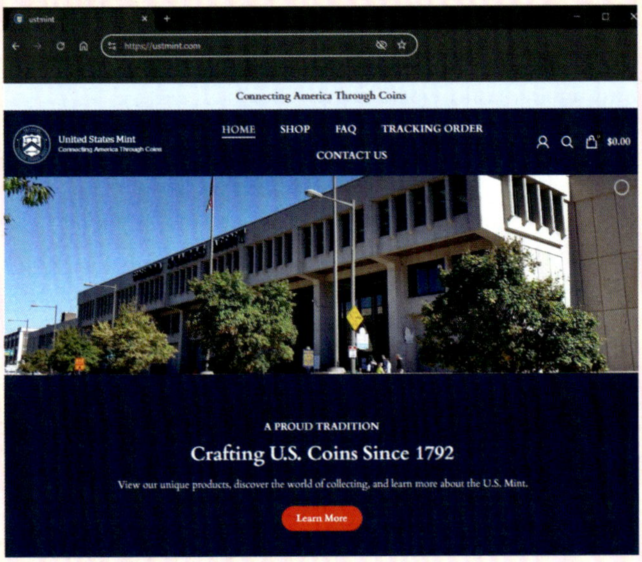

U.S. Counterfeiting Laws And Compliance

It is a federal crime to knowingly possess, buy, sell, or import into the United States counterfeit coins or precious-metal bars (U.S. Code, Title 18, Part I, Chapter 25, Sections 485 through 492). There are no exceptions for possessing counterfeit coins for "educational" purposes.

Many collectors and coin dealers mistakenly believe they have a special dispensation to keep a "reference collection" of counterfeits. While such has been longstanding practice in the hobby, be aware that such "reference collections" could be confiscated and you could be charged with federal crimes punishable by fines and sentences ranging from 5 to 15 years in federal prison. Also, don't get caught up in purchasing so-called "replica" coins online from a seller in a foreign country because you are curious as to how deceptive the coins may be. Knowingly importing counterfeit coins into the United States is a federal crime punishable by up to 15 years in federal prison.

2026 MARKET REPORT

by Jeff Garrett

Since the last edition of this book, the prices of precious metals have dominated the numismatic news. The dramatic rise in the prices for gold and silver has greatly impacted the collecting habits of collectors. Gold prices alone have jumped nearly 40% since January 1, 2025. With gold fast approaching $4,000 per ounce, many once-popular U.S. gold coins have become unaffordable for a lot of collectors.

This lack of demand for common issues of U.S. gold coins can be seen in the sharp drop in premiums. Many double eagles and half eagles now trade wholesale for about the coins' melt value. Even MS-60 to MS-63 double eagles are now considered bullion items. This would have been unthinkable five to ten years ago.

There has also been a tremendous amount of U.S. gold being repatriated from overseas, the famous Fairmont Collection being just one example. The increased supply and the rising bullion prices have driven premiums to all-time lows.

If bullion prices stabilize to a "new normal" level, and the flow of new coins subsides, premiums may once again return for U.S. gold coins. This will probably take a few years to materialize. If you have bullion such as U.S. gold eagles or in other forms, it would be a great idea to trade into vintage gold coins. The premiums can only go up from here.

Silver bullion prices had been lagging gold in this most recent rise, but have now started to ascend as well. Silver bullion prices have exceeded $40 per ounce and seem on the way to their previous highs above $50. The premiums for coins such as Morgan and Peace silver dollars have fallen, as would be predicted.

The rising bullion prices have also impacted the sales of many modern-issue coins, including output from the U.S. Mint. Many of the mass-market companies have all but abandoned trying to sell modern one-ounce gold coins. With marketing costs and the profits required to support many of these large companies, they have to price one-ounce gold coins above $6,000 each. This has predictably been a serious headwind for sales. The U.S. Mint has recently begun issuing coins under its licensed agreement with DC Comics. The first release, featuring Superman, did not sell out in the half-ounce gold version (issue price $2,950) as had been anticipated. There has been an understandable shift to lower-weight gold coins and silver issues. Look for this trend to continue.

Another major trend in the last year or two has been the explosion of sales through social media and online streaming auctions. There is now more business in rare coins being conducted everyday on cellphones than in coin shops around the country. Two major players in this space have been Whatnot and eBay Live. Sales volume has exploded as buyers and sellers have discovered these platforms. The barrier to entry for anyone wanting to participate is simply owning a cellphone. The action is also non-stop with some companies holding 24-hour marathon auctions.

The social-media aspect of these streaming auctions plays into the addictive nature of these platforms. Many of the auctions are rapid-fire, some lasting only a few seconds. Some coins are sold way too cheaply, and others bring way too much. It will be interesting to see how these streaming auctions perform in a year or two as their novelty wears off and more competition arises.

Several of the sellers on these streaming platforms have also introduced gamification into the equation, with pop-up "roulette wheels" and mystery boxes for those looking to get lucky. Many of the most successful sellers have added layers of entertainment into the mix to keep buyers engaged. The success of coin "breakouts" has also had a tremendous impact on the demand for rare coins. Most of the sellers for the above-mentioned sales channels need huge numbers of coins to support their business. This has generated strong price increases for coins in the $10–$1,000 price range. Any coins with good stories behind them fly out of the cases at coin shows.

Social media has also brought a wave of young participants into the coin business—there are now more young dealers prowling the bourse floor than I have ever seen in my 50 years of doing business. This infusion of youth into the hobby has been amazing, and most attribute the phenomenon to social media and the Internet. Some organizations such as the Professional Numismatists Guild (PNG) and the American Numismatic Association (ANA) have also invested significantly in fostering the next generation of young dealers. The intersection of new technology and more young participants has certainly stimulated the hobby.

The demand for rare coins at the top end of the market continues to be strong as "the rich get richer." There is staggering wealth in this country, and many of the super-rich have discovered rare coins. At least five to ten collectors in the United States have invested over $100 million into their collections in the last several years. This competition among the wealthy creates super-strong prices whenever great coins cross the auction block. Million-dollar auction prices realized now hardly make the news. The recently completed sales around the ANA convention saw many coins cross this threshold.

The demand for top population coins, otherwise referred to as "finest-known examples," continues to be strong as well. Collectors across the spectrum of U.S. coins continue to battle for points in set-registry competitions. Finest-known examples of common coins such as Jefferson nickels and Roosevelt dimes continue to amaze when they are offered at auction.

Years ago, the rare-coin market was dominated by rare-coin dealers, who would buy rare coins at shows and conventions and then offer those coins to collectors via catalogs or other venues. In the 1980s and 1990s, about 80% to 90% of coin sales in major auctions were to dealers. As third-party grading and the Internet transformed the business, the equation has flipped. Now, about 80% or more of the coins sold at auction are purchased by collectors. The rare-coin market is now dominated by collectors, and they want quality.

This can be seen very clearly when two coins that have graded exactly the same bring very divergent prices when they are sold. Collectors appreciate quality and are willing to pay for it. This is one of the factors that help Certified Acceptance Corporation (CAC) and now CAC Grading (CACG) coins to continue performing well when offered. An understanding of quality and the nuances of rare-coin grading is now one of the most important tools for any successful collector, which is one of the reasons my class on advanced coin grading sells out each year at the ANA Summer Seminar.

Several years ago, the ANA made the brave decision to hold its World's Fair of Money in Oklahoma City, Oklahoma. Following Covid-19 restrictions, the number of cities willing to host the show had dwindled, and there was considerable "Rosemont, Illinois" fatigue. For the last few years, the board members who had made the decision were heavily second-guessed, to say the least. As the show approached, the bourse sold out and there was a glimmer of hope. What was to follow surprised almost everyone—the Oklahoma City World's Fair of Money was a resounding success. Many dealers stated it was their best show ever! The host city was beautiful and welcoming and was thoroughly enjoyed by everyone who made the trip. One of the largest dealers in the world, APMEX, has its headquarters there, and the company made huge efforts to promote the convention. The above-mentioned demand for coins that are being sold in streaming auctions also juiced selling activity substantially. By the end of the show, many were asking when the ANA would come back to Oklahoma!

Despite the demand online for coins, there are still considerable numbers of collectors and dealers who appreciate rare-coin conventions. Over the last few years, nearly every major coin show in the country has been experiencing robust participation. Shows such as the winter F.U.N. show in Orlando, Florida, and the Central States Numismatic Society Convention in Schaumburg, Illinois, are seeing throngs of veteran and new collectors filling the bourse. Long-standing commercial shows such as the Whitman Expo in Baltimore also have been well attended. Whenever I feel concerned about the health of the hobby, all I need to do is attend a major coin show. The bourse filled with collectors buying coins is a great indicator of hobby's strength.

In the last several months, publisher John Feigenbaum and I have been conducting interviews for the *Red Book* podcast. We have been able to secure many wonderful interviews with hobby leaders, including the top management for Professional Coin Grading Service (PCGS), Numismatic Guaranty Company (NGC), and CAC. We have also interviewed David Ryder, the former U.S. Mint director, and Kristie McNally, the acting director of the U.S. Mint. These interviews have been extremely insightful and are highly recommended. They can be found on YouTube with a search for "Red Book Podcast."

One topic that comes up during most of the interviews is the impact that artificial intelligence (AI) will have on interviewees' businesses and the hobby in general. The grading and authentication companies have weighed in on AI grading coins. None of the big three think this will be a reality anytime soon, but none rule it out in the future completely. There is now doubt that our hobby will be impacted greatly by advances in AI. Sophisticated tools for writing rare-coin descriptions already exist and can be used by everyone from mom-and-pop operations to mega-companies with hundreds of employees. If you have bought rare coins recently, the descriptions you've read may have been created by AI. (One of my close friends who wrote copy for a large marketing company recently lost his job to AI.)

The entire world is waiting to see how artificial intelligence will impact their lives. There will be many great gains in productivity, but possibly at the cost of people's jobs. Hopefully, it will be transformative in a positive way for numismatics, with an impact similar to that of the Internet. The above-mentioned young dealers are already trying to figure out how to use the promise of AI to give them a competitive advantage. Look for a lot of change in the hobby over the next few years.

One of the most exciting aspects of numismatics is the discovery of something new. Often times it is a shipwreck or other buried treasure that has been uncovered. A few months ago, one of the most exciting numismatic discoveries of the last several decades was found in a safety deposit box. Most of the famous James A. Stack collection had been sold at auction in the early 1990's. The collection was known for its incredible quality—he clearly sought only the finest. Ever since I have been involved in numismatics, there have been exactly fifteen 1804 silver dollars known, in three types. The long-held number of 15 examples was upended when an unreported 1804 recently surfaced in a group of about 200 coins held by descendants of James A. Stack. The previously unknown example of the Class-3 1804 dollar graded PF-65 by PCGS, and it will be sold at auction for the first time ever in the near future.

The overall health of the rare-coin market is solid, with increasing demand and increasing numbers of participants. For the last decade or two the market for rare coins has been steady, with no major spikes up or down. With record bullion prices and swelling numbers of new participants, there is even the possibility of a boom in rare coins. Many coins have been somewhat flat in prices for several years. The last real boom in the market was in the 1990s. History does have a tendency to repeat itself. Next years will be the 250th anniversary of the United States. The Semiquincentennial (get used to saying it) could be transformative for the hobby. The U.S. Mint will be issuing an array of coins celebrating its past, and the pending elimination of the cent is also big news.

Next year could become one of the most important years ever for the hobby!

HOW TO USE THIS BOOK

Numismatics, in its purest sense, is the study of items used as money. Today in the United States, as around the world, the term embraces the activities of a diverse community of hobbyists, historians, researchers, museum curators, and others who collect and study coins, tokens, paper money, and similar objects.

Since 1946 the *Guide Book of United States Coins* has served this community as the preeminent annual reference for coin specifications, mintages, values, photographs, and other information important to collectors and students. With more than 23 million copies in print since the first edition, the *Guide Book* (commonly known as the *Red Book*) is well established as the most popular reference in numismatics—not to mention one of the best-selling nonfiction books in the history of American publishing. (In 1964 the eighteenth edition of the *Red Book* ranked number 5 on the national sales lists, at 1.2 million copies—higher than Dale Carnegie's *How to Win Friends and Influence People* at number 6, and John F. Kennedy's *Profiles in Courage* at number 9.)

Building on this strong foundation, *Mega Red* (the Deluxe Edition of the *Guide Book of United States Coins*) is an expanded and enlarged volume intended to serve not only beginning collectors, but also intermediate to advanced coin collectors, professional coin dealers and auctioneers, researchers, and investors. It features more photographs, detailed higher-grade valuations, additional listings of die varieties and rare early Proof coins, certified-coin population data, auction records, and other resources that provide a wealth of information on every coin type ever made by the U.S. Mint. *Mega Red* also expands on the regular edition's coverage of collectible die varieties, with close-up photographs, valuations, and chart notes. It is a handy single-source guide that educates its users in auction and certification trends, retail valuations, and similar aspects of the marketplace.

Like the regular-edition *Red Book*, *Mega Red* includes information on colonial and early American coins and tokens as well as all federal series (copper half cents through gold double eagles). It also covers private and territorial gold pieces; Hard Times tokens; Civil War tokens; Confederate coins; Hawaiian, Puerto Rican, and Philippine coins; Alaskan tokens; misstrikes and errors; numismatic books; Proof and Mint sets; commemorative coins from 1892 to date; silver, gold, and platinum bullion coins; and other topics.

Readers of *Mega Red* benefit from the following useful information.

The *Red Book* has become a popular collectible itself, with fans striving to acquire one of each edition dating back to number 1, published in November 1946 with a 1947 cover date. Rare early volumes can be worth $1,000 or more.

R.S. Yeoman (right), author of the original *Guide Book of United States Coins*; Ken Bressett, who would succeed him as Red Book editor; and Leroy Foerster.

Denomination Introductions

Each coinage denomination is discussed first in an overview of its history, major design types and subtypes, and general collectability by type. (The dollar denomination is divided into silver dollars, modern dollars, and gold dollars.) A second essay gives collectors a more in-depth analysis of specializing in that denomination. *These sections encapsulate decades of numismatic research and market observation, and they should be read in conjunction with the charts, photographs, and other information that follow.*

Type-by-Type Studies

Within each denomination, each major coin type is laid out in chronological order. As with the *Red Book*'s regular edition, the type's designer and its specifications (weight, composition, diameter, edge treatment, and production facilities) are given. Type-coin values are provided at the beginning of the first pricing chart for that type. Coinage designs are pictured at actual size except commemorative designs, which are standardized (one Mint State example and one Proof example, when available). Each type section includes summary text on the type's history; aspects of its striking, sharpness, and related characteristics; and its market availability. In-depth grading instructions, with enlarged illustrations, show how to grade each coin type, covering circulation strikes as well as Proofs.

Charts

The data charts include these elements:

	Mintage	GSID	AG-3	G-4	VG-8	F-12	VF-20	EF-40	AU-50	MS-60	MS-63
Draped Bust, Small Eagle Reverse (1796–1797)	**n/a**	**72453**	**$3,500**	**$4,400**	**$5,000**	**$6,250**	**$8,000**	**$11,000**	**$15,000**	**$25,000**	**$43,000**
1796	22,135	3957	3,500	4,400	5,000	6,250	8,000	11,000	15,000	25,000	43,000
	Auctions: $881,250, PCGS MS-67 HA 06/14										
↳1796, JR-1	*	213014	3,500	4,400	5,000	6,250	8,000	11,000	15,000	25,000	43,000
	Auctions: $144,000, PCGS MS-66 HA 04/25; $750,000, PCGS MS-67 HA 04/25										
↳1796, JR-6	*	241023	3,500	4,400	5,000	6,250	8,000	11,000	15,000	25,000	43,000
	Auctions: $793,125, PCGS MS-68 HA 08/14										
↳1796, JR-7	*	213019	—	—	—	—	—	—	—	—	—
1797, 16 Stars	25,261	3958	3,500	4,400	5,000	6,250	8,000	12,000	17,500	38,500	57,500
↳1797, 16 Stars, JR-1	*	374671	3,500	4,400	5,000	6,250	8,000	12,000	17,500	38,500	57,500
	Auctions: $199,750, PCGS MS-66 SBG 05/15										
1797, 13 Stars	*	3959	3,850	4,800	5,500	7,000	8,500	15,500	22,000	57,500	90,000
	Auctions: $402,500, NGC MS-65 HA 08/08										

* Included in number above.

Mintages. Mintage data is compiled from official Mint records whenever possible, and in other cases from more than 70 years of active numismatic research. In instances where the Mint's early records are in question or have been proven faulty, the official numbers are provided and further information is given in chart notes. For some early Proof coins for which no official mintage records exist, an estimated mintage, or the number of coins known in collections, is given. For modern issues (usually those minted within the past five years), the Mint has released production and/or sales numbers that are not yet officially finalized; these are given in italics.

Note that Mint reports are not always reliable for estimating the rarities of coins. In the early years of the Mint, coinage dies of previous years often were used until they became worn or broken. Certain reported quantities, particularly for gold and silver coins, cover the number of pieces struck and make no indication of the quantity that actually reached circulation. Many issues were deposited in the Treasury as backing for paper currency and later were melted without ever being released to the public.

Gold coins struck before August 1, 1834, are rare today because from 1821 onward (and at times before 1821) the gold in the coins was worth more than their face values, so they were struck as bullion and traded at a premium. Many were exported and melted for their precious-metal value.

Mintage figures shown for 1964 through 1966 are for coins bearing those dates. Some of these coins were struck in more than one year and at various mints, both with and without mintmarks. In recent years, mintage figures reported by the Mint have been revised several times and precise amounts remain uncertain.

Whatever their sources, all mintages are speculative to one degree or another. The mintage figures herein are based on the best available information and updated as needed based on expert scholarship.

Valuations. Beginning with this edition, the values in this book are derived directly from the industry-standard pricing curated by Greysheet®. The *Monthly Greysheet* has been the standard pricing reference for coin dealers since 1963. In coin shops and on bourses all over the country, professionals can be seen referring to this guide for pricing when buying and selling. *Mega Red* now relies on a carefully calculated retail value called the Collector's Price Guide (CPG) Value, which is an estimation of what a collector might expect to pay for a specific coin in a specific grade. Because the CPG directly corresponds to the *Greysheet*, readers of *Mega Red* can feel more confident in these published prices than ever before.

In general, it is critical to know that in the world of collectibles, items are worth what both a seller and buyer agree on. The values listed in the *Greysheet*, CPG, and *A Guide Book of United States Coins: MEGA RED*™ form a starting point for this price discovery, so the reader can be as informed as possible when spending money on collectible coins.

Keep in mind that the values published in this edition are a snapshot of the market from a specific point in time (September 2025, to be exact). For a serious effort to research values, the reader is highly encouraged to visit Greysheet.com and select one of the monthly subscription plans. More than 1 million prices are updated every 60 minutes, and serious collectors simply cannot afford to use old pricing information.

Auction Records. Multiple recent auction records are provided for selected coins. Each record indicates:

the price paid for the coin (including any fees)
the grade of the coin
the date (month and year) of the auction

This combination of auction data gives valuable market information for each coin. It also serves as a springboard for further research. Many auction firms have online archives of coins sold, or else their auction catalogs can be studied using the information provided. Note this information is not comprehensive and is provided as a glimpse into sample high-value results for a specific coin. Online information atgreysheet.com is much more accurate.

Chart notes. Additional information is provided for certain coins in chart notes. Historical background, die-variety diagnostics, notable market conditions, and other specific details are intended to further guide the collector and investor.

Abbreviations. These are some of the abbreviations you'll find in the charts.
/ (slash)—In names of individual coins, a slash indicates an overstrike
ANR—American Numismatic Rarities
BN—Brown; descriptive of the coloration or toning on certain copper coins
BON—Bonhams [comp: no apostrophe]
Bz—Bronze
CAM—Cameo
DCAM—Deep Cameo
DDO, DDR—Doubled-Die Obverse, Doubled-Die Reverse
DLRC—David Lawrence Rare Coins
Dt—Date
Enh Unc—Enhanced Uncirculated
FH—Full Head
GLDB—Goldberg Coins and Collectibles
HA—Heritage Auctions
Lg—Large
LGND—Legend Rare Coin Auctions
MPD—Misplaced Date
MS—Mint State
RB—Red and brown; describes the mixture of mint red and brown coloration or toning on a copper coin
RD—Red; descriptive of the mint red color on an untoned copper coin
RevPf—Reverse Proof
RPD—Repunched Date
RPM—Repunched Mintmark
SBG—Stack's Bowers Galleries
SC—Scotsman Coin and Jewelry
Sm—Small
SOTH—Sotheby's
SU—Superior Galleries
TDO, TDR—Tripled-Die Obverse, Tripled-Die Reverse
Uncert—Uncertified

DAVID RITTENHOUSE, FIRST DIRECTOR OF THE UNITED STATES MINT

by Eric Brothers

Great men tell great stories. However, such stories are not written down on paper. They are lived, over the course of many years—in flesh and blood. Therefore, great men live great stories. An example of a man who lived a great story is David W. Rittenhouse (1732–1796), the first director of the United States Mint. He did not tackle the challenge of forging a new mint in his youth, but in the autumn of his life, taking on this great responsibility at the age of 60.

MECHANICAL AND SCIENTIFIC PIONEER

Before becoming our first Mint director, Rittenhouse accomplished in life what would have taken someone else several lifetimes to accomplish. He was an astronomer, instrument maker, mathematician, and public servant. Born near Germantown, Pennsylvania, he displayed an advanced scientific and mechanical aptitude but had no opportunity to pursue a formal education. Nonetheless, self-taught and with assistance from his brother-in-law, at the age of 19 he opened a clock-making business before branching out to inventing and manufacturing scientific instruments. He conducted many boundary surveys, including an extension of the Mason-Dixon Line.

The famous portrait of Rittenhouse by Charles Willson Peale was painted around 1780, when the scientist was about 50 years old. The engraving was taken from the painting by James B. Longacre.

As a member of the American Philosophical Society (APS) of Philadelphia, Rittenhouse played an important role in observing the most significant astronomical event of his day: the transit of Venus of 1769. The APS used Rittenhouse's calculations to construct three observatories. He designed and built many of the instruments within them, including the very first telescope made in America. The year 1770 saw him move to Philadelphia, where he recorded eclipses, comets, and the new planet Uranus. He also solved complex mathematical equations, experimented with magnetism and electricity, and improved upon the Franklin stove. It was in 1771 that Rittenhouse built his most famous instrument: an orrery—or mechanical model of the solar system in motion.

LEADING REVOLUTIONARY WAR PATRIOT

During the American War of Independence, he played several important roles. As the president of the Council of Safety, he supervised the production of cannons and gunpowder, as well as surveying for defensive positions along the Delaware River. Rittenhouse was a member of the Pennsylvania Assembly and was chairman of the convention that developed Pennsylvania's new state constitution. He also served on the Board of War, the Loan Fund, and as state treasurer (1779–1789). He was a professor of astronomy at the University of Pennsylvania (1780–1781) and served on its board of trustees (1779–1796). He even helped organize the First Bank of the United States. However, his most important role to numismatists was that of the first United States Mint director.

RITTENHOUSE BECOMES MINT DIRECTOR

It was in 1792 that David Rittenhouse was solicited to become the first Mint director. This was due to his stellar reputation as a scientist, mathematician, and inventor. The president saw Rittenhouse as the perfect candidate to establish the national mint. Washington's secretary of state, Thomas Jefferson, worked closely with him and was directly involved in the process of selecting the Mint director, for the Mint was under the jurisdiction of the Department of State. On behalf of Washington, both Jefferson and Alexander Hamilton approached Rittenhouse to recruit him to run the United States Mint.

On April 13, 1792, a message was sent to the U.S. Senate: "Gentlemen of the Senate, I nominate David Rittenhouse, of Pennsylvania, to be Director of the Mint." It was signed, "Go: Washington."

Even though he was not in the best of health, Rittenhouse, at the age of 60, accepted the position in order to serve his president and nation. In that role, the duties that fell upon his shoulders were arduous and complicated. He located a series of buildings located on Seventh Street between Arch and Filbert Streets in Philadelphia to serve as the new mint facility and arranged for their purchase by the government. Rittenhouse directed the construction of the machinery and made arrangements for purchasing the necessary equipment. In daily visits to the facility, when he felt strong enough, he would personally supervise, with absolute, painstaking precision, not only the financial well-being of the institution but also the technical operations of the various departments. Such duties, with his love of system and order, his wide knowledge, and his hands-on skill in mechanics, made him the ideal man for the job, which he executed flawlessly. When poor health prevented Rittenhouse from being present, reports were presented to him—either spoken or in writing—on Mint operations and the progress of its business. In response, he gave Mint officers detailed instructions for their departments.

When conducting the affairs of the Mint, Rittenhouse was assisted by capable and trustworthy officers. They included Chief Coiner Henry Voight and Dr. Nicholas Way, the treasurer of the Mint, who provided testimony of the Mint director's honorable attention to the public interest. "I have been informed by his colleague in office, Dr. Way," writes Dr. Benjamin Rush, who succeeded Way as Mint Treasurer, "that in several instances, [Rittenhouse] paid for work done at the Mint out of his salary, where he thought the charges for it would be deemed extravagant by the United States."

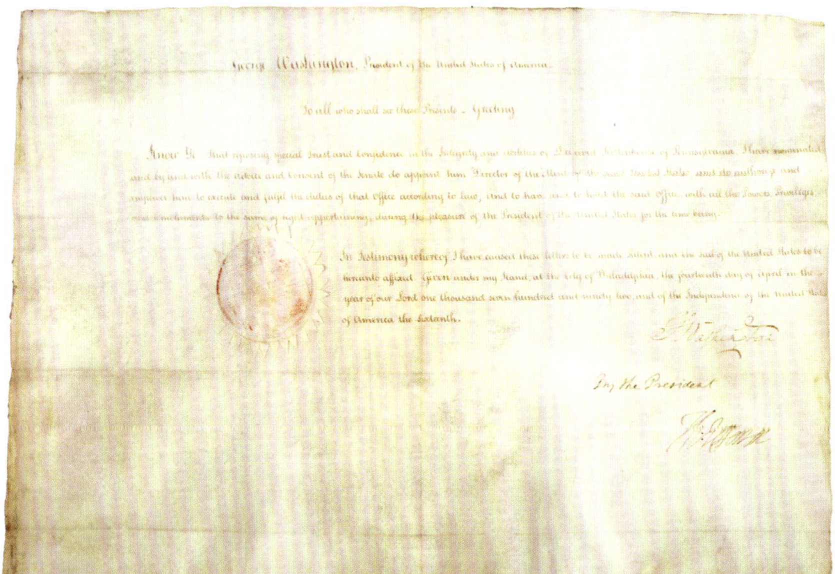

The document appointing David Rittenhouse director of the United States Mint, signed by President George Washington and Secretary of State Thomas Jefferson on April 14, 1792.

RITTENHOUSE AND THE 1794 DOLLAR

As per the Coinage Act of 1792, the silver dollar was the most important coin, for it was the standard upon which America's monetary system would be based. For that reason, the silver dollar has long held a place of honor in the annals of numismatic history. The most important silver dollar ever produced—and among the rarest—is the 1794 Flowing Hair dollar. And it was David Rittenhouse's efforts that brought it to the light of day.

Considering the importance of the dollar, Rittenhouse wanted to begin production as soon as possible. However, the necessary bullion was nonexistent, for the early U.S. Mint depended on private deposits of silver and gold; coins were not struck on government account at that time. Consequently, in order to ensure that dollar production could begin, on August 29, 1794, Rittenhouse deposited his own money: $2,001.34 worth of silver bullion. But there was a problem.

Congress was resolved to produce silver coins at the fineness of 1485/1664 (.89243), per Hamilton's Mint Report of 1791. However, assayer Albion Cox complained that the calculations were difficult to work with, and that such an alloy would prevent correct rolling of the strips. Cox also claimed to Rittenhouse that the alloy made coins too black. Perhaps that was a bit of hyperbole on the part of the assayer.

Responding to Cox, the Mint director suggested that Congress increase the fine silver in coins from 371.25 to 374.75. That would lessen the alloy to one-tenth and raise the fineness by 3.5 grains. Both Hamilton and Jefferson gave Rittenhouse approval for this change. Expecting Congress to legalize the new silver fineness, the Mint director started producing silver dollars at the new standard in October of 1794. However, Congress did not, and this new fineness was unauthorized.

At that point, the Mint used Rittenhouse's bullion and a single set of dies to mint 2,000 silver dollars. However, 242 of them were found to be unacceptable. That left a net mintage of 1,758 examples of the 1794 Flowing Hair dollar, all of which were delivered to the Mint director on October 15, 1794. Therefore, all surviving 1794 silver dollars have a David Rittenhouse pedigree. What did he do with those coins? Writes R.W. Julian, "The director made every effort to spend the coins or exchange them for Spanish dollars so that as many persons as possible would learn of the new American silver dollar."

LEGACY OF DAVID RITTENHOUSE

After Rittenhouse retired on June 30, 1795, he was succeeded by Henry William de Saussure. The latter resigned after only a few months, for members of Congress had made false accusations about the Mint and how it carried out its business. For some reason, members of the government held great hostility toward the institution. Congressmen had also launched attacks against his predecessor, David Rittenhouse.

After receiving written praise from President Washington for his tenure at the Mint, de Saussure wrote a detailed letter that was published in the Charleston City Gazette. It discussed the harsh criticism leveled at the Mint and its officers. De Saussure vindicated himself, and Rittenhouse, in his published letter. He wrote:

> The solid talents of Mr. Rittenhouse will be remembered with pride, and his mild virtue recollected with tenderness, by his countrymen, when many of his censors will be forgotten in the silent dust. His lofty and correct mind, capable alike of ascending to the sublimest heights of science, and of condescending to regulate the minute movements of mechanical machinery, organized the Mint, and created the workmen and the apparatus; amidst the complicated difficulties from which the most persevering minds might have shrunk without dishonour. A very long and debilitating state of ill health prevented him from giving the establishment all the activity of which it was susceptible; and he long wished to retire before he was permitted.

David Rittenhouse played a crucial role in shaping America's early coinage system. A distinguished astronomer, mathematician, and surveyor, his scientific precision ensured the Mint's operational accuracy. His contributions laid the foundation for the Mint's credibility, significantly influencing numismatic history and the development of a stable national coinage.

Rittenhouse deposited his own money to ensure production of the first U.S. silver dollar would take place.

Sources

Barton, William. *Memoirs of the Life of David Rittenhouse, L.L.D.F.R.S.* Philadelphia: Edward Parker, 1813.

Finkelstein, David, Joel J. Orosz, and Leonard Augsburger. "The Director's Deposits." *The Numismatist*, September 2017.

"David Rittenhouse." APS [American Philosophical Society] Members Biography. membib.amphilsoc.org/member/pub/61

Don Taxay. *The U.S. Mint and Coinage. An Illustrated History from 1776 to the Present.* New York: Arco, 1983.

SEMIQUINCENTENNIAL COINAGE OF THE UNITED STATES MINT

by Paul Gilkes

As part of its 2026 celebration of the Semiquincentennial (250th) Anniversary of the United States of America, the U.S. Mint will strike examples of its top five American coins in .9999 fine gold. The Mint is also redesigning, for one year only, all of the circulating coin denominations. To identify circulating and numismatic coins and collector medals as belonging to the Semiquincentennial series, the Mint will use a special privy mark: a silhouette of the Liberty Bell suspended from its wooden crossmember, with the numerals 250 incused vertically on its surface.

Planning for the nation's 250th anniversary began in 2016 with the congressionally authorized U.S. Semiquincentennial Commission's establishment under P.L. 114-196, enacted July 22, 2016, after being signed into law by President Barack Obama. The commission is coordinating the celebratory activities.

The Circulating Collectible Coin Redesign Act of 2020 (P.L. 116-330) was signed into law on January 13, 2021, by President Donald Trump. It authorized the American Women quarters (the program that began in 2022 and concluded in 2025), and it further authorizes special Semiquincentennial coinage in 2026 and additional programs involving the quarter dollar, half dollar, and dollar denominations beginning in 2027.

The Mint's official "Countdown to America's 250th Anniversary" commenced on July 4, 2025. To celebrate the anniversary, the Mint will be making changes to "select circulating coin designs for 2026," as authorized by the act. The designs will commemorate 250 years of American liberty, reflecting the country's founding principles and honoring American history. Per the act, up to five quarter dollars may be issued under this program; at least one of their designs "must be emblematic of a woman's or women's contribution to the birth of the Nation or the Declaration of Independence or any other monumental moments in American History." Semiquincentennial dollar coins are authorized but must be produced concurrently with (not in place of) the ongoing Native American and American Innovation dollar coin programs.

In 2027, all coins redesigned in 2026 will revert to their pre-2026 states, with the exception of the quarter dollars and half dollars. From 2027 to 2030, the reverses of the quarter dollars will feature designs "emblematic of sports played by American youth," with up to five different sports designs (one sport per coin) issued each year. Half dollar reverses will be "emblematic of a sport tailored to athletes with a range of disabilities, including physical impairment, vision impairment, and intellectual impairment" (one Paralympic sport per year, in consultation with the U.S. Paralympics).

In addition, the quarter dollar obverse is to bear a likeness of George Washington, but one that differs from that employed on the American Women quarter dollars from 2021 through 2025. The half dollar obverse is to bear a likeness of John F. Kennedy, but one that will distinguish it from the design used on half dollars from 1964 through 2025.

THE "BEST OF THE MINT" GOLD SERIES

The U.S. Mint will issue five different Best of the Mint two-piece sets, each comprising a .9999 gold version of a silver coin from the bureau's numismatic legacy (based on the results of a 2023 public survey) and a companion .999 silver medal featuring designs that reflect a modern take on the gold coins' themes. Each coin will bear its original date of issue and the Semiquincentennial privy mark.

The first four of the five coins in the series were originally produced by the Mint in .900 silver:

- the 1916 Mercury (Winged Liberty Head) dime
- the 1916 Standing Liberty quarter dollar
- the 1916 Walking Liberty half dollar
- the 1804 Draped Bust, Class I dollar

The fifth coin will reproduce the 1907 Saint-Gaudens, Roman Numerals (MCMVII), High Relief $20 double eagle, which was originally produced in .900 gold. The 1916-dated coins are effectively reissues of the Mint's 2016 Centennial Anniversary coins, but with their original date of issue and the addition of the privy mark.

The gold coins will be struck at the West Point Mint in New York, and the silver medals at the Philadelphia Mint and/or the San Francisco Mint. As of press time, the Mint had released digital composite images of the first four coins and silver medals (see the image gallery).

1916 Mercury Dime Set. The first Best of the Mint Coin and Medal Set for 2026 will feature an Uncirculated, 1916-dated Mercury dime, struck on a tenth-ounce, .9999-fine gold planchet. Its 2016-W Centennial Anniversary counterpart sold through its maximum release of 125,000.

The gold 2026 issue will bear the W mintmark of the West Point Mint on the reverse, below left of the fasces. The privy mark will appear in the field on the obverse, to the right of Liberty's head. What appears to be a W in the lower right obverse field are the initials AW for sculptor Adolph A. Weinman, who designed the Mercury dime.

The dime's Uncirculated companion medal will bear all-new modern designs inspired by elements on the original 1916 coin. The medal was designed by U.S. Mint Artistic Infusion Program designer Kathryn Hudson, whose initials, KH, appear on both obverse and reverse. Hudson's designs were sculpted by U.S. Mint medallic artist Craig A. Campbell, whose initials, CAC, also appear on both obverse and reverse.

Per the Mint, the medal's designs "recall the period of 1916 through 1945, when the Mercury [Winged Liberty Head] dime was in circulation, representing years of great change and upheaval, both foreign and domestic, for the United States. Observing that during this period the United States would enter two world wars, the artist depicts Liberty in both defensive and offensive positions. The obverse design extends to the reverse with rays emitting from the tip of the sword, symbolic of hope at the end of conflict. The Great Depression is represented by the 'Hooverville' shacks and the Dust Bowl by the swirling waves in the background."

1916 Standing Liberty Quarter. The second Best of the Mint set will feature an Uncirculated, 1916-dated Standing Liberty quarter dollar, struck on a quarter-ounce gold planchet. The original design was produced by American sculptor Hermon A. MacNeil, whose 1916 effigy of Liberty had an exposed breast. (In mid-1917, in the run-up to the United States' entry into World War II, the obverse design was modified, with chain mail covering Liberty's torso.) MacNeil's Liberty holds a shield in an attitude of protection and an olive branch of peace.

On the 2026 gold issue, the privy mark will be placed in the right quarter panel below WE TRVST. The coin will be struck at the West Point Mint but without with the facility's W mintmark. The net sales figure for the coin's 2016-W Centennial Anniversary counterpart was 91,752, which fell short of the 100,000 maximum authorized mintage.

The accompanying silver medal's designs were inspired by elements of MacNeil's quarter dollar but bring "a modern interpretation and new life to a timeless symbol," according to the Mint's design narratives. "Together, the designs embody strength, diplomacy, and America's enduring ideals. Liberty, then, now, and forever."

The medal's designer for both the obverse and the reverse was U.S. Mint Artistic Infusion Program designer Esao Andrews. His initials, EA, appear just above the foliage on the left side of the obverse and just above the clouds on the left side of the reverse. The sculptor of the obverse design was U.S. Mint Chief Engraver Joseph F. Menna, whose initials, JFM, appear at the 4 o'clock position. The reverse was sculpted by U.S. Mint medallic artist Darla Jackson, whose initials, DJ, appear just above the first star at the right.

1916 Liberty Walking Half Dollar. The third set will feature the final of the three designs in the 2016-W Centennial Anniversary series: that of the 1916 Liberty Walking half dollar, rendered in an Uncirculated, half-ounce-gold format. The powerful design, by German-born American sculptor Adolph A. Weinman, shows Liberty striding toward the rising sun, draped in a billowing American flag, just as on the 1916 silver half dollar. On the reverse, a fierce-looking eagle stands on a rocky mountain crag. The W mintmark of the West Point Mint appears on the obverse, in the field below IN GOD WE TRUST. Like the Mercury dimes, these silver half dollars were workhorses of American business through the Roaring Twenties, the Great Depression, two global wars, and beyond.

On the obverse, the privy mark has been placed above the motto, while in the right field is a monogram of the intertwined initials AW (for sculptor Adolph Weinman); while this could be mistaken for a W mintmark, it is not.

The designs on the companion silver medal reimagine elements from the Liberty Walking coin as a single scene across the obverse and reverse, and in the art deco style that succeeded Weinman's neoclassical style. The obverse and reverse were designed by U.S. Mint Artistic Infusion Program designer Andrew Sides, and his initials, AS, are placed at far left on each design. The obverse was sculpted by U.S. Mint medallic artist Renata Gordon (initials RG at far right); the reverse, by U.S. Mint medallic artist Eric Custer (initials EC at about 4 o'clock, where the sun meets the landscape). The medal will be struck at the Philadelphia Mint, but without the facility's P mintmark.

Mint officials have not yet announced the mintages for either the gold coin or the silver medal. The 2016-W Centennial issue sold 65,512 of its maximum 70,000 mintage.

1804 Draped Bust, Class I Silver Dollar. The fourth Best of the Mint set centers on a high-relief reproduction of the Class I 1804 Draped Bust, Heraldic Eagle dollar. The original, produced in .900 silver in 1834 for inclusion in diplomatic presentation sets, is an extreme rarity today, and is often called "the King of American Coins." The 1804-dated Semiquincentennial edition, to be struck as a one-ounce gold Proof coin, will capture the original designs as created and engraved by Robert Scot, the first chief engraver of the U.S. Mint.

The obverse for the gold dollar depicts the Draped Bust of Liberty facing to the right, with LIBERTY inscribed along the top border and the 1804 date below the portrait. Seven 6-pointed stars appear to the left of the portrait and six to the right. The privy mark appears in the right field.

The reverse illustrates a heraldic eagle at center with UNITED STATES OF AMERICA inscribed in a circle inside the border of dentils. In its beak, the eagle holds a ribbon with the motto E PLURIBUS UNUM. The eagle's right talons clutch 13 arrows, while the left talons grasp an olive branch. On its breast is a striped shield. In the field above the eagle's head, eight clouds form an arc above 13 six-pointed stars.

The obverse of the companion silver medal depicts Liberty as a young woman with flowing hair. Above the portrait, the word LIBERTY is flanked by a border of 5-pointed stars, seven on the left and six on the right; the date 2026 is below the portrait.

On the reverse, UNITED STATES OF AMERICA arcs around the top border. A sun with rays illuminating the dawn of a new age appears as a background device, in front of which an eagle flies above a rendition of Earth encircled by cloud formations.

Best of the Mint

Five iconic American coin designs, rendered in .9999 fine (24-karat) gold in an Uncirculated format, will be included in the Mint's Semiquincentennial offerings. Each coin will be issued as part of a set that includes a one-ounce silver medal in a companion design (see the main text). Although these items are not included among the issues authorized by the Circulating Collectible Coin Redesign Act of 2020, all share the same goal of celebrating the 250th anniversary of the America, and the gold coins will bear the official 250 / Liberty Bell privy mark. The color images of the dime, quarter, half dollar, dollar, and silver medals are U.S. Mint digital renderings, not photographs. As of press time, official Mint images of the 1907 (MCMVII) High Relief Saint-Gaudens double eagle designs were not available. The black-and-white illustration is from the CCAC.

The iconic coinage dime, quarter, and half dollar coinage of 1916, celebrated in gold for their centennial in 2016, return for the Best of the Mint Semiquincentennial coinage. The first issue will be a reproduction of the 1916 Mercury (Winged Liberty Head) dime, struck on a tenth-ounce gold planchet. The swords on the obverse and reverse of the companion silver medal's design will be aligned, as the Mint's overlapping images show. The overall design evokes the Mercury dime's spirit of national resilience in a time of hardship.

Originally produced in 1916 as a silver quarter dollar, the Standing Liberty Best of the Mint reproduction will be reflected in a quarter-ounce gold format. The companion silver medal's design expands on the sense of vigilance, diplomacy, and enduring American ideals suggested by the design of the Standing Liberty quarter.

The Walking Liberty half dollar, issued as a silver coin in 1916, will be reproduced as a half-ounce gold coin. The silver medal's design captures the sense of legacy and of progress toward a new day seen in Adolph Weinman's famous design.

Best of the Mint

The fourth Best of the Mint issue will be the 1804, Class I Draped Bust silver dollar, realized on a one-ounce gold planchet. The companion medal's design suggests the global reach of the silver dollar and its lasting diplomatic legacy.

As of this writing, no official design images have been released for the Best of the Mint coin to honor the 1907 (MCMVII) Saint-Gaudens High Relief double eagle (actual coin shown here). Like the 1804, Draped Bust, Class I Draped Bust silver dollar replica, it will contain one ounce of gold. The CCAC's favored designs for the companion silver medal include a flying eagle with its wings stylized with elements of the American flag—the artist's vision of the Mint's narrative of "a new vision of strength and pride."

Both sides of the medal were designed and sculpted by U.S. Mint medallic artist Joseph V. Noorigian. His initials, JVN, appear in the field below Liberty's flowing hair (obverse) and in the right field at about the 4 o'clock position (reverse).

1907 (MCMVII) High Relief Double Eagle. As of press time, the Mint has not yet released images of the coin and medal comprising the fifth and final set in the Best of the Mint lineup. The coin represented in that set, Augustus Saint-Gaudens's 1907, High Relief $20 gold coin with roman-numeral date, is the only Best of the Mint coin that was not originally a silver issue. Originally .900 fine, it will be reproduced with a fineness of .9999, and struck on a one-ounce gold planchet. The silver companion medal's design has not been finalized, but the designs favored by the CCAC feature a waist-up view of Liberty with her torch held forward on the obverse, and a flying eagle whose visible wing is represented by a rippling American flag.

CIRCULATING COINS

Due to high production costs for the Lincoln cent, the year 2026 is expected to be the last year it is struck for general circulation. Production likely will end around the first quarter of 2026. Coin experts anticipate the 2026 cent will be a rare collector's item due to the limited number of coins produced and to the possibility of a special design commemorating the United States' 250th anniversary.

Early in 2025, at the insistence of President Trump, Treasury Secretary Scott Bessent directed U.S. Mint officials to suspend orders for ready-to-strike planchets for circulating Lincoln cents from vendor Artazn in Greeneville, Tennessee. As of press time, Artazn is still expected to supply planchets for cents to be included in annual Uncirculated Mint Sets and Proof Sets.

As shown in the illustrations, the 2026 Lincoln cent and Jefferson nickel may be dual-dated 1776–2026, with the inclusion of a the Semiquincentennial privy mark. No final design changes for the Roosevelt dime have been announced.

Circulating Coin Illustrations

Options for the Semiquincentennial Lincoln cent in its final year of issue: With dual date range 1776–2026 but no privy mark; with the single date 2026 and 250 privy mark; and two different versions with both the dual dates and the privy mark.

Options for the Semiquincentennial nickel: With dual date range 1776–2026 but no privy mark; with the single date 2026 and 250 privy mark; and with both the dual dates and the privy mark.

Colonial Issues

FOREIGN ISSUES IN THE NEW WORLD

Money had a rich history in America prior to the advent of the United States' national coinage. When coins tumbled off the presses from the first Philadelphia Mint in 1793, the country was much more accustomed to coins from other lands. Prior to 1652 there was no local coinage and the only money in circulation was whatever came here from Europe through trade or travel. People were content to use currency, both old and new, whose value was based more on the metal content than on the issuer's reliability. Foreign money in America during the colonial period had become so embedded that it continued to be accepted as legal tender until discontinued by the Coinage Act of February 21, 1857. Coins of this era are so fundamental to American numismatics that every collection should include at least a sampling.

Scan for additional information.

From the very beginning of commerce in America "hard money" was needed for trade with overseas nations. The largest quantity of coinage consisted of English crowns, shillings, and pence, and Spanish and Spanish-American silver pieces of eight, all of which circulated throughout colonial settlements until being sent back to England for critically needed supplies. Additional quantities of coins came from trading furs, lumber, and other exports that provided a limited but much needed supply of hard currency. Of equal importance to commerce were similar coins of other European countries. The large silver Dutch *leeuwendaalder* (Lyon or Lion dollar) and French *écu* saw extensive circulation, as did the Brazilian gold *peças*. Some New York bills of 1709 were even denominated in Lyon dollars. Distinguishing between the relative values of the multitude of different foreign currencies was not a simple task. To facilitate conversions, books and tables showed comparison prices for each currency.

The popular Spanish-American silver eight reales, Pillar dollar, or piece of eight, which was a radical departure from denominations in terms of English pounds, shillings, and pence, became a model for the American silver dollar, and its fractional parts morphed into the half-dollar and quarter-dollar coins that

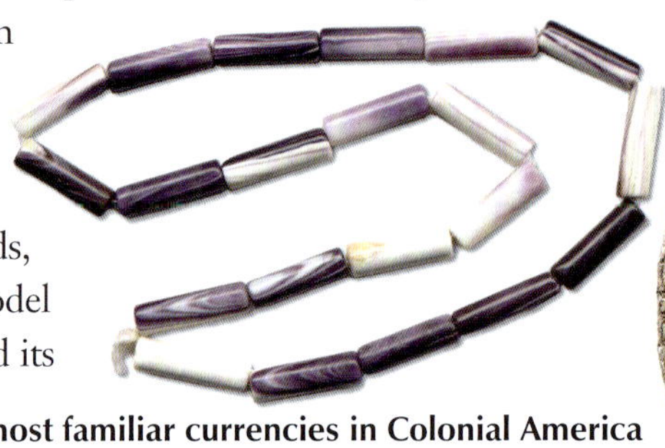

The most familiar currencies in Colonial America were the Spanish-American piece of eight, the Dutch Lion dollar, and Native American wampum.

are now considered decimal fractions of the dollar. The American quarter dollar, which was similar in size and value to the Spanish two-real coin, took on the nickname "two bits"—a moniker that remains today. Similarly, the American one-cent coin has never totally lost its association with the English penny, and is still called that by anyone indifferent to numismatic accuracy.

Coins, tokens, paper money, and promissory notes were not the only media of exchange used during the early formation of the country. Many day-to-day transactions were carried on by barter and credit. Mixed into this financial morass were local trade items such as native wampum, hides, household goods, and tools. Records were kept in the traditional English pounds, shillings, and pence, but debts and taxes were paid in corn, beaver pelts, or money—money being whatever foreign coins were available. The terms "country pay" or "corn" referred to a number of different kinds of grain or even peas. Standard exchange rates were established and country pay was lawfully received at the colonial treasury for taxes.

Beyond these pre-federal considerations are the many kinds of private and state issues of coins and tokens that permeate the colonial period from 1616 to 1776. These are items that catch the attention and imagination of everyone interested in the history and development of early America. Yet, despite their enormous historical importance, forming a basic collection of such items is not nearly as daunting as one might expect.

The coins and tokens described in the next three sections of this book are fundamentally a major-type listing of the metallic money used throughout the pre-federal period. Many collectors use this as a guide to forming a basic set of these pieces. It is not encyclopedic in its scope. Beyond the basic types are numerous sub-varieties of some of the issues, and a wider range of European coins. Some collectors aim for the finest possible condition, while others find great enjoyment in pieces that saw actual circulation and use during the formative days of the country. There are no rules about how or what to collect other than to enjoy owning a genuine piece of early American history.

Other items frequently used as money in early America included cut fractions of various silver coins. These were cut by private individuals. The quarter 8-reales coin was "two bits." Worn and cut portions of coins usually passed for change according to their weight.

Spanish-American Coinage in the New World

Values shown for these silver coins are for the most common dates and mintmarked pieces of each issue. Similar pieces were struck at Spanish-American mints in Bolivia, Chile, Colombia, Guatemala, Mexico, Panama, Peru, and Santo Domingo.

Cob Coinage – King Philip II (1556–1598) to King Philip V (1700–1724 and 1724–1746), and King Louis I (1724)

1 real cob of Mexico from the reign of Philip III.

1668 2 reales cob struck in Potosi, from the reign of Charles II.

8 escudos of Mexico from the reign of Charles II.

	GSID	VG-8	F-12	VF-20	EF-40
Cob Type, 1/2 Real (1556–1733)	393522	$80	$130	$160	$455
Cob Type, 1 Real (1556–1732)	393523	95	155	210	525
Cob Type, 2 Reales (1556–1734)	393524	160	260	360	675
Cob Type, 4 Reales (1556–1734)	393525	195	325	550	1,100

Values are for coins with partial or missing dates. Fully dated coins are valued much higher. Some cobs were also issued beyond these dates and until as late as 1773 in Bolivia.

	GSID	VG-8	F-12	VF-20	EF-40
Cob Type, 8 Reales (1556–1734)	393526	$230	$390	$550	$1,100
Cob Type, 2 Escudos, Gold (1691–1732)	393527	2,500	2,750	3,100	5,000
Cob Type, 4 Escudos, Gold (1691–1732)	393528	7,000	7,500	8,750	11,000
Cob Type, 8 Escudos, Gold (1691–1732)	393529	9,500	10,000	11,000	14,500

Values are for coins with partial or missing dates. Fully dated coins are valued much higher. Some cobs were also issued beyond these dates and until as late as 1773 in Bolivia.

Pillar Type – King Philip V (Second Reign: 1732–1747), King Ferdinand VI (1747–1760), and King Charles III (1760–1772)

1735 8 escudos, Pillar type, from the second reign of Philip V.

1734 8 reales Pillar dollar from the second reign of Philip V.

1761 2 reales "pistareen" from the reign of Charles III.

	GSID	VG-8	F-12	VF-20	EF-40
Pillar Type, 1/2 Real (1732–1771)	393516	$34	$55	$115	$195
Pillar Type, 1 Real (1732–1771)	393517	40	100	130	230
Pillar Type, 2 Reales (1732–1771)	393518	55	115	160	325
Pillar Type, 4 Reales (1732–1771)	393519	160	325	525	1,000
Pillar "dollar" Type, 8 Reales (1732–1772)	81057	260	390	650	850
"Pistareen" 2 Reales (1716–1771)	393520	55	80	130	260
Pillar Type, 2 Escudos, Gold (1716–1771)	393521	—	—	—	—

Bust Type – King Charles III (1772–1789), King Charles IV (1789–1808), and King Ferdinand VII (1808–1825)

1807 8 reales Bust dollar from the reign of Charles IV.

1809 8 escudos from the reign of Ferdinand VII.

	GSID	VG-8	F-12	VF-20	EF-40
Bust Type, 1/2 Real (1772–1821)	393530	$27	$34	$55	$120
Bust Type, 1 Real (1772–1821)	393531	34	55	80	130
Bust Type, 2 Reales (1772–1821)	393532	47	70	115	230
Bust Type, 4 Reales (1772–1821)	393533	130	290	575	900
Bust Type, 8 Reales (1772–1821)	393534	80	100	130	260
Bust, 2 Escudos, Gold (1732–1821)	393535	850	900	950	1,250
Bust, 4 Escudos, Gold (1732–1821)	393536	1,600	1,900	2,200	2,500
Bust, 8 Escudos, Gold (1732–1821)	393537	2,600	2,800	3,100	3,750

The New World began its first coinage in 1536 in Mexico City. By 1732 the first round coins were made and the *columnario*. or Pillar coinage, became the coin of trade internationally. In 1772 the Bust dollars with the effigy of the king of Spain were placed in circulation. These coins and the Republican style of later Latin American countries circulated legally in the United States until 1857.

Parallel issues of Spanish-American gold coins were made during this period. They saw extensive use for international trade and somewhat lesser use in domestic transactions in America. The Spanish silver pistareen was also a popular and convenient coin in circulation.

TYPICAL WORLD COINAGE USED IN COLONIAL AMERICA

NETHERLANDS SILVER COINAGE, 1601–1693

1616 leeuwendaalder.

	GSID	VG-8	F-12	VF-20	EF-40
Netherlands, 1/2 Leeuwendaalder "Lion Half Dollar" (1577–1653)	393538	$160	$260	$550	$1,100
Netherlands, Leeuwendaalder "Lion Dollar" (1576–1693)	393539	130	195	360	850

FRENCH COINAGE OF KING LOUIS XV (1715–1774) AND KING LOUIS XVI (1774–1792)

1791 écu from the reign of Louis XVI.

1749 louis d'or from the reign of Louis XV.

	GSID	VG-8	F-12	VF-20	EF-40
France, 1/2 Écu (1715–1792)	393540	$70	$95	$160	$390
France, Écu (1715–1792)	393541	110	130	325	420
France, Louis d'Or, Gold (1761–1774)	393542	775	950	1,000	1,200
France, Double Louis d'Or, Gold (1761–1774)	393543	1,100	1,400	1,600	2,200

See additional listings of silver, billon, and copper French coins authorized for use in North America under "French New World Issues."

British Coinage of King Charles I (1625–1649) to King George III (1760–1820)

1639 sixpence from the reign of Charles I.

1787 shilling from the reign of George III.

1798 Spade Guinea from the reign of George III.

	GSID	VG-8	F-12	VF-20	EF-40
England, Threepence (1625–1786)	393544	$27	$40	$70	$115
England, Sixpence (1625–1787)	393545	34	47	95	130
England, Shilling (1625–1787)	393546	40	70	130	240
England, Half Crown (1625–1750)	393547	100	160	360	650
England, Crown (1625–1730)	393548	245	490	875	1,200
England, Spade Guinea (1787–1799)	393549	850	900	1,100	1,900

English copper coins and their imitations circulated extensively in early America and are described under "British Copper Coins and Their Imitations."

BRITISH NEW WORLD ISSUES

Sommer Islands (Bermuda)

This coinage, the first struck for the English colonies in the New World, was issued circa 1616. The coins were known as *Hogge Money* or *Hoggies*, from the wild hogs depicted on their obverses.

The Sommer Islands, as Bermuda was known at the time, were under the jurisdiction of the Virginia Company, a joint-stock mercantile venture formed under a British royal patent and headquartered in London. (This venture was actually undertaken by two companies: the Virginia Company of Plymouth, for what is now New England; and the Virginia Company of London, for the American South.)

English government of the islands had started a few years before the coins were issued—by accident! In 1609 Admiral Sir George Somers led a fleet bound from England to the New World, laden with relief supplies for the Virginia settlement of Jamestown. Somers and his ship were separated from the rest of the fleet in a strong storm, and they ran onto the reefs of the Bermuda Islands, some 700 miles from Virginia. (The islands were named for Juan de Bermúdez, who is believed to have stopped there some hundred years earlier.) For ten months Somers and his party were able to live on wild hogs and birds, local plants, and fish, building houses and a church. During this time they also constructed two small ships, in which, in May 1610, most of the shipwrecked colonists continued their interrupted journey to Virginia.

Bermuda became a separate entity of the Virginia Company of London, from November 1612 until June 29, 1615, when "the Governour and Company of the City of London for the Plantacon of the Somer Islands" (often called the Bermuda Company by historians) was officially incorporated under royal charter. This incorporation granted the right of coinage. The coins did not arrive in the islands until May 16, 1616, at the earliest, a year after Bermuda was under its new charter.

The pieces were struck on thin planchets of brass or copper, lightly silvered, in four denominations: shilling, sixpence, threepence, and twopence, each indicated by Roman numerals. A wild hog is the main device and appears on the obverse side of each coin. SOMMER ISLANDS is inscribed (misspelling both the English admiral's name and the corporation's) within beaded circles on the larger denominations. The reverse shows a full-rigged galleon, or carrack, with the flag of St. George on each of four masts. Many examples of these coins show signs of oxidation or pitting.

Scan for additional information.

"In an era when British silver shillings and fractions traded in commerce based on their intrinsic value," writes Q. David Bowers, "the Bermuda pieces were tokens of little value, a fiat currency that circulated in the manner that paper money would later be used worldwide—good as long as both parties had confidence in the value. As might be expected, these coins had little or no trade value other than within the islands, where they were mostly used at the company storehouse, exchanged for supplies" (*Whitman Encyclopedia of Colonial and Early American Coins*).

These coins of Bermuda did not circulate in North America, but they have traditionally been considered part of early "American" coinage. Sylvester S. Crosby, writing in his 1875 masterwork *Early Coins of America*, insisted that the Bermuda coins laid claim to being "the first ever struck for the English colonies in America," this despite the fact that the islands were not a part of the Virginia colony proper. The regular edition of the *Guide Book of United States Coins* has included them in its pre-federal coverage since the first edition, published in 1946.

Twopence

Sixpence Obverse

Large Portholes Reverse

Small Portholes Reverse

Threepence

Shilling Obverse

Small Sail Reverse

Large Sail Reverse

	GSID	VG-8	F-12	VF-20	EF-40	AU-50
Twopence, Large Star Between Legs	402	$12,500	$18,000	$31,000	$53,000	—
Twopence, Small Star Between Legs	374723	24,000	48,000	79,000	—	—
Threepence	403	—	—	162,000	192,000	—
	Auctions: $205,625, NGC VF-20 HA 05/14					
Sixpence, Small Portholes Reverse	404	—	18,000	36,000	60,000	$96,000
Sixpence, Large Portholes Reverse	405	—	18,000	36,000	60,000	96,000
	Auctions: $129,250, NGC AU-50 HA 05/14					
Shilling, Small Sail Reverse	406	14,500	31,000	41,000	72,000	228,000
	Auctions: $105,750, PCGS EF-45 HA 01/17					
Shilling, Large Sail Reverse	407	—	43,000	50,500	—	—
	Auctions: $258,500, NGC AU-55 HA 05/14					

MASSACHUSETTS

"NEW ENGLAND" COINAGE (1652)

The earliest authorized medium of exchange in the New England settlements was wampum. The General Court of Massachusetts in 1637 ordered "that wampamege should passe at 6 a penny for any sume under 12 d." Wampum consisted of shells of various colors, ground to the size of kernels of corn. A hole was drilled through each piece so it could be strung on a leather thong for convenience and adornment.

Corn, pelts, and bullets were frequently used in lieu of coins, which were rarely available. Silver and gold coins brought over from England, Holland, and other countries tended to flow back across the Atlantic to purchase needed supplies. The colonists, thus left to their own resources, traded with the friendly Native Americans in kind. In 1661 the law making wampum legal tender was repealed.

Agitation for a standard coinage reached its height in 1651. England, recovering from a civil war between the Puritans and Royalists, ignored the colonists, who took matters into their own hands in 1652.

The Massachusetts General Court in 1652 ordered the first metallic currency—the New England silver threepence, sixpence, and shilling—to be struck in the English Americas (the Spaniards had established a mint in Mexico City in 1535). Silver bullion was procured principally in the form of mixed coinage from the West Indies. The mint was located in Boston, and John Hull was appointed mintmaster; his assistant was Robert Sanderson (or Saunderson). At first, Hull received as compensation one shilling threepence for every 20 shillings coined. This fee was adjusted several times during his term as mintmaster.

The planchets of the New England coins were struck with prepared punches twice (once for the obverse, and once for the reverse). First the letters NE were stamped, and then on the other side the numerical denomination of III, VI, or XII was added.

These are called "NE coins" today.

NE Threepence

NE Sixpence

NE Shilling

Massachusetts silver coins are often found weakly or unevenly struck on inferior or irregular planchets. Well-made, evenly struck specimens with full details on nice planchets command premium prices.

		GSID	VG-8	F-12	VF-20	EF-40	AU-50	MS-60	MS-63
NE Threepence	2 known	385	—	—	—	—	—	—	—
	Auctions: $2,520,000, PCGS EF-45 SBG 11/24								
NE Sixpence	8 known	386	—	—	—	$480,000	—	—	—
	Auctions: $646,250, NGC AU-58 HA 05/14								
NE Shilling		387	—	$54,000	$65,000	120,000	$156,000	$330,000	—
	Auctions: $192,000, NGC AU-58 SBG 11/24; $517,734, PCGS AU-55 SBG 11/24								

Willow Tree Coinage (1653–1660)

The simplicity of the designs on the NE coins invited counterfeiting, and clipping or shaving of the edges by charlatans who sought to snip a little bit of metal from a lot of coins and thereby accumulate a pile of silver. Therefore, they were soon replaced by the Willow Tree series.

All of the Willow Tree coins bore the date 1652, when Oliver Cromwell was in power in Britain, after the English civil war and during the Interregnum government. In fact they were minted from 1653 to 1660. The date 1652 may have been used simply because this was the year the coinage was authorized. Output increased over the years, and the coins were plentiful in circulation.

These pieces, like all early American coins, were produced from handmade dies that are often individually distinctive. The tree in the design is known as a "willow" not from any official legislative records, and certainly not from lifelike resemblance to an actual willow tree, but from terminology dating from 1867 in an auction catalog of the Joseph Mickley Collection. To make the coins, a worker likely placed a silver planchet into a rocker press, which forced a curved upper die against a curved or flat bottom die. This would explain the slight elongation and gentle bend of many Willow Tree coins.

NEW ENGLAND is spelled out, instead of being abbreviated, as on the earlier NE coinage.

Among the four classes of Massachusetts silver coins—NE, Willow Tree, Oak Tree, and Pine Tree—the Willow Tree pieces are far and away the rarest today. The die varieties that can be found and identified are of interest to collectors who value each according to individual rarity. Values shown for type coins are for the most frequently seen die variety.

Threepence

Sixpence

Shilling

		GSID	VG-8	F-12	VF-20	EF-40	AU-50	MS-60	MS-63
1652 Willow Tree Threepence	3 known	1	—	—	—	—	$660,000	—	—
	Auctions: $587,500, PCGS AU-50 SBG 03/15								
1652 Willow Tree Sixpence	14 known	4	—	$37,000	$78,000	$144,000	264,000	—	—
	Auctions: $317,544, PCGS AU-53 SBG 11/13								
1652 Willow Tree Shilling		7	$19,000	36,000	66,000	114,000	150,000	$192,000	—
	Auctions: $381,875, PCGS AU-55 SBG 03/15								

Oak Tree Coinage (1660–1667)

The Oak Tree coins of Massachusetts were struck from 1660 to 1667, following the Willow Tree coinage. The 1662-dated twopence of this type was the only coin of the Willow Tree, Oak Tree, and Pine Tree series that did not bear the date 1652. Numismatists are divided on whether the twopence date of 1662 is an error, or a deliberate use of the year that the new denomination was authorized.

The obverse of these coins features a tree traditionally described by numismatists as an oak tree. Although it is deciduous, it does not closely resemble a specific species. On the reverse, NEW ENGLAND is spelled out, surrounding the date and denomination.

In 1660 the Commonwealth of England was dissolved and the British monarchy was restored under King Charles II. At the time, following longstanding tradition and law, the right to produce coins was considered to be a royal sovereign prerogative. Sylvester Crosby in *Early Coins of America* suggested that during the Massachusetts silver coinage period, numerous tributes—including ship masts, 3,000 codfish, and other material items—were sent to the king to placate him and postpone any action on the Massachusetts coinage question. As with many situations involving early American coinage, facts are scarce.

As with other types of Massachusetts silver, a number of die varieties of Oak Tree coinage can be collected and studied. In the marketplace they are seen far more often than are the two earlier types. They are valued according to their individual rarity. Values shown here are for the most frequently seen die varieties.

Twopence

Threepence

Sixpence

Shilling

	GSID	VG-8	F-12	VF-20	EF-40	AU-50	MS-60	MS-63
1662 Oak Tree Twopence, Small 2	11	$1,400	$1,700	$2,000	$3,500	$4,100	$8,750	$14,500
	Auctions: $119,025, PCGS MS-65 SBG 11/10							
1662 Oak Tree Twopence, Large 2	375052	—	—	—	—	—	—	—
1652 Oak Tree Threepence, No IN on Obverse	2	1,750	2,500	3,550	6,500	11,000	31,000	51,000
1652 Oak Tree Threepence, IN on Obverse	375053	—	—	—	—	—	—	—
1652 Oak Tree Sixpence, IN on Reverse	5	1,550	2,050	3,100	5,750	7,250	19,000	41,000
1652 Oak Tree Sixpence, IN on Obverse	375054	1,550	2,050	3,100	5,750	7,250	19,000	41,000
	Auctions: $132,000, NGC MS-66 HA 08/25							
1652 Oak Tree Shilling	8	1,550	2,050	3,100	5,750	7,250	19,000	41,000
	Auctions: $161,000, PCGS MS-66 HA 08/10							
↳1652 Oak Tree Shilling, IN at Left	375055	—	3,250	4,000	5,750	8,250	17,000	48,000
	Auctions: $117,500, NGC MS-65 HA 08/16							
↳1652 Oak Tree Shilling, IN at Bottom	375056	2,050	2,450	2,800	4,750	7,000	12,000	24,000
↳1652 Oak Tree Shilling, ANDO	285894	2,500	3,750	5,000	7,500	9,750	15,000	30,000
↳1652 Oak Tree Shilling, Spiny Tree	285895	—	4,050	5,750	8,750	13,000	—	—

Pine Tree Coinage (1667–1682)

The first Pine Tree coins were minted on the same-size planchets as the Oak Tree pieces, in denominations of threepence, sixpence, and shilling. Subsequent issues of the shilling were narrower in diameter and thicker. Large Planchet shillings ranged from 27 to 31 mm in diameter; Small Planchet shillings ranged from 22 to 26 mm in diameter.

The design of the Pine Tree coins borrowed from the flag of the Massachusetts Bay Colony, which featured a pine tree. On the reverse, NEW ENGLAND is spelled out, surrounding the date and a Roman numeral indicating the denomination (III, VI, or XII).

Large quantities of Pine Tree coins were minted. The coinage was abandoned in 1682. A proposal to renew coinage in 1686 was rejected by the General Court of Massachusetts.

As with other types of Massachusetts silver, a number of die varieties of Pine Tree coins are available for collecting and study. In the marketplace, they are valued according to their individual rarity. Values shown here are for the most often seen die varieties.

Threepence

Sixpence

Shilling, Large Planchet (1667–1674)

Shilling, Small Planchet (1675–1682)

	GSID	VG-8	F-12	VF-20	EF-40	AU-50	MS-60	MS-63
1652 Pine Tree Threepence	3	$1,300	$1,600	$2,300	$3,450	$3,900	$12,000	$33,500
↳1652 Pine Tree Threepence, Pellets at Trunk	375057	1,400	1,950	2,500	5,250	7,750	12,000	33,500
↳1652 Pine Tree Threepence, Without Pellets	375058	1,300	1,900	2,400	5,000	7,500	12,000	33,500
1652 Pine Tree Sixpence	6	2,000	2,450	2,800	4,100	4,500	12,000	33,500
↳1652 Pine Tree Sixpence, Pellets at Trunk	375059	—	2,450	2,800	4,100	4,500	12,000	33,500
↳1652 Pine Tree Sixpence, Without Pellets	375060	—	—	—	5,000	6,250	—	—
1652 Pine Tree Shilling, Large Planchet (a)	9	2,100	2,400	3,000	5,500	8,250	15,500	33,500
	Auctions: $141,000, PCGS MS-65 HA 06/17							
↳1652 Pine Tree Shilling, Large Planchet, Pellets at Trunk	375061	—	—	—	8,750	16,000	26,500	38,500
↳1652 Pine Tree Shilling, Large Planchet, Without Pellets	375062	2,100	2,400	3,500	5,500	8,250	15,500	33,500
	Auctions: $111,625, NGC MS-65 HA 02/17							
↳1652 Pine Tree Shilling, Large Planchet, No H in MASATVSETS	375063	—	—	3,500	6,250	9,500	—	—
1652 Pine Tree Shilling, Large Planchet, Ligatured NE in Legend (a)	70725	—	—	—	6,000	7,500	22,000	29,000
1652 Pine Tree Shilling, Small Planchet (a)	10	1,750	2,750	3,500	4,750	9,750	15,000	33,500

a. Large Planchet, 27–31 mm. Small Planchet, 22–26 mm.

MARYLAND

LORD BALTIMORE COINAGE

Cecil Calvert, the second Lord Baltimore, inherited from his father nearly absolute control over Maryland. Calvert believed he had the right to coin money for the colony, and in 1659 he ordered shillings, sixpences, and groats (four-penny pieces) from the Royal Mint in London and shipped samples to Maryland, to his brother Philip, who was then his secretary for the colony. Calvert's right to strike coins was upheld by Oliver Cromwell's government. The whole issue was small, and while his coins did circulate in Maryland at first, by 1700 they had largely disappeared from commerce.

Calvert's coins bear his portrait on the obverse, with a Latin legend calling him "Lord of Mary's Land." The reverses of the larger denominations bear his family coat of arms and the denomination in Roman numerals. There are several die varieties of each. Some of these coins are found holed and repaired. The copper penny, or denarium, is the rarest denomination, with only nine reported specimens, including some found in recent times by detectorists using electronic devices.

The silver groats (fourpence), sixpence, and shillings were used extensively in commerce, and today most examples show considerable wear. Typical grades include VG, Fine, and VF, often with surface marks or damage. Those graded AU or higher are major rarities. The silver pieces have an engrailed edge.

Penny (Denarium)

Fourpence (Groat)

Sixpence

Shilling

		GSID	F-12	VF-20	EF-40	AU-50	MS-60
Denarium, Copper	7–9 known	382	—	—	$120,000	—	—
	Auctions: $241,500, Uncert AU-50 SBG 05/04						
Fourpence		378	$10,000	$11,000	21,000	$36,000	$78,000
	Auctions: $132,000, NGC AU-53 HA 08/19						
Fourpence, Small Bust	unique	374724	—	—	—	—	—
Sixpence		379	—	8,000	10,000	14,000	42,000
Shilling		383	10,500	12,000	15,000	20,500	57,500
	Auctions: $126,500, PCGS AU-58 HA 01/08						

NEW JERSEY

ST. PATRICK OR MARK NEWBY COINAGE

Mark Newby was a shopkeeper in Dublin, Ireland, in the 1670s and came to America in November 1681, settling in West Jersey (today's New Jersey). He brought with him a quantity of copper pieces, of two sizes, believed by numismatists to have been struck in Dublin circa 1663 to 1672. These are known as *St. Patrick coppers*. (Alternatively, they may have been struck for circulation in Ireland by Pierre Blondeau to fill an order made by the duke of Ormonde, but this has not been confirmed.) The larger-sized piece, called by collectors a *halfpenny*, bears the arms of the City of Dublin on the shield on the reverse. The smaller-sized piece, called a *farthing*, does not. Although neither bears a denomination, these are designations traditionally assigned by numismatists. Both sizes have reeded edges.

Newby became a member of the legislature of West Jersey, and under his influence the St. Patrick coinage was made legal tender by the General Assembly of New Jersey in May 1682. The legislature did not specify which size piece could circulate, only that the coin was to be worth a halfpenny in trade and that no one would be obliged to accept more than five shillings' worth (120 coins) in one payment. Some numismatists believe the larger-size coin was intended. However, many more farthing-size pieces are known than halfpennies, and numerous coins of the farthing size have been excavated by detectorists in New Jersey, while none of the larger coins have been found this way. Most numismatists believe that the smaller-sized piece was the one authorized as legal tender. Copper coins often circulated in the colonies at twice what they would have been worth in England.

The obverses show King David crowned, kneeling and playing a harp. The legend FLOREAT REX ("May the King Prosper") is separated by a crown. The reverse side of the halfpence shows St. Patrick with a crozier in his left hand and a trefoil in his right, and surrounded by people. At his left side is a shield. The legend is ECCE GREX ("Behold the Flock"). The farthing reverse shows St. Patrick driving away serpents and a dragon as he holds a metropolitan cross in his left hand. The legend reads QUIESCAT PLEBS ("May the People Be at Ease").

The decorative brass insert found on the coinage, usually over the crown on the obverse, was put there to make counterfeiting more difficult. On some pieces this decoration has been removed or does not show. Numerous die variations exist (more than 140 of the smaller coins, and 9 of the larger). The silver strikings, and a unique gold piece, were not authorized as legal tender, although many of the silver coins are heavily worn, suggesting that they were passed many times from hand to hand in commerce, perhaps at the value of a shilling.

St. Patrick "Farthing"

St. Patrick "Halfpenny"

		GSID	F-12	VF-20	EF-40	AU-50	MS-60
St. Patrick "Farthing"		409	$470	$550	$850	$1,250	—
↳St. Patrick "Farthing," Halo Around Saint's Head		373802	—	5,750	—	—	—
↳St. Patrick "Farthing," No C in QUIESCAT		373803	3,900	5,750	—	—	—
St. Patrick "Farthing," Silver		410	5,250	7,500	11,000	12,500	$36,000
St. Patrick "Farthing," Gold	unique	374725	—	—	—	—	—
St. Patrick "Halfpenny"		408	725	1,250	3,500	9,500	—

COINAGE AUTHORIZED BY BRITISH ROYAL PATENT

American Plantations Coins (1688)

These tokens, struck in nearly pure tin, were the first royally authorized coinage for the British colonies in America. They were made under a franchise granted in August 1688 to Richard Holt, an agent for the owners of several tin mines. Holt proposed that the new issues be made with a Spanish monetary designation to increase their acceptance in the channels of American commerce, where Spanish-American coins were often seen. Thus the tokens are denominated as 1/24 part of a Spanish real.

The obverse shows an equestrian portrait of King James II in armor and flowing garments. The reverse features four heraldic shields (English, Scottish, French, and Irish) connected by chains. The edge is decorated with dots.

Numismatist Eric P. Newman has identified seven different obverse dies and an equal number of reverse dies. Most American Plantation tokens show black oxidation of the tin. Bright, unblemished original specimens are more valuable. (Around 1828 a London coin dealer acquired the original dies and arranged for restrikes to be made for sale. In high grades these pieces are seen more frequently in the marketplace than are originals. They are valuable but worth less than original strikes.)

	GSID	VF-20	EF-40	AU-50	MS-60	MS-63
(1688) James II Plantation 1/24 Part Real (illustrated)	347	$650	$1,450	$1,900	$2,500	$6,250
↳(1688) James II Plantation 1/24 Part Real, ET. HB. REX	373804	—	7,000	9,500	14,000	—
(1688) James II Plantation 1/24 Part Real, Sideways 4 in 24	348	3,750	5,000	6,250	12,000	—
(1688) James II Plantation 1/24 Part Real, Arms Transposed	349	7,500	10,000	11,000	—	—
(1688) James II Plantation 1/24 Part Real, Restrike	350	360	550	725	1,000	2,000

Coinage of William Wood (1722–1733)

William Wood, an English metallurgist, experimented with the production of several pattern coins (of halfpenny, penny, and twopence size) in 1717. In 1722 he was granted royal patents to mint coins for America and Ireland. At the time his productions were largely unpopular as money, but later generations of coin collectors have sought his Rosa Americana coins for their connections to colonial America. The Hibernia coins are similar in some respects; they have no connection with America but are sought as companion pieces.

Rosa Americana Coins (1722–1723, 1733)

On July 12, 1722, William Wood obtained a patent from King George I to make coins for the American colonies. At the time the colonies were facing a serious shortage of circulating coins.

The first pieces Wood struck were undated. Later issues bear the dates 1722, 1723, 1724, and 1733. The Rosa Americana pieces were issued in three denominations—half penny, penny, and twopence—and were intended for America. This type had a fully bloomed rose on the reverse with the words ROSA AMERICANA UTILE DULCI ("American Rose—Useful and Sweet").

The obverse, common to both Rosa Americana and Hibernia pieces, shows the head of George I and the legend GEORGIUS D:G MAG: BRI: FRA: ET. HIB: REX ("George, by the Grace of God, King of Great Britain, France, and Ireland") or abbreviations thereof.

Despite Wood's best efforts, these Rosa Americana coins circulated in the colonies only to a limited extent. They eventually did see use as money, but it was back in England, and likely at values lower than their assigned denominations. (Each was about half the weight of its English counterpart coin.)

The 1733 twopence is a pattern that bears the bust of King George II facing to the left. It was issued by the successors to the original coinage patent, as William Wood had died in 1730.

The coins are made of a brass composition of copper and zinc (sometimes mistakenly referred to as *Bath metal*, an alloy proposed by Wood that would have also included a minute portion of silver). Planchet quality is often rough and porous because the blanks were heated prior to striking. Edges often show file marks.

Undated Twopence, Motto in Ribbon

1722 Halfpenny

1722 Penny

1722 Twopence

1723 Halfpenny, Uncrowned Rose

1723 Halfpenny, Crowned Rose

1723 Penny

1724, 4 Over 3, Penny (pattern)

(1724) Penny, ROSA: SINE: SPINA

1724 Twopence (pattern)

1733 Twopence, Proof (pattern)

		GSID	VG-8	F-12	VF-20	EF-40	AU-50	MS-60	MS-63
1720 12 Deniers, Crowned Arms on Reverse, Copper		400	—	$470	$575	$850	$1,000	$1,550	$3,000
(No Date) Twopence, Motto Without Ribbon	2 known	401	$5,250	—	8,000	10,000	12,000	—	—
1722 Halfpenny, VTILE DVLCI		17	650	1,300	2,500	3,750	5,250	—	—
1722 Halfpenny, D.G.REX ROSA AMERI. UTILE DULCI		18	285	390	525	925	1,350	2,500	4,750
1722 Halfpenny, DEI GRATIA REX UTILE DULCI		19	195	285	390	600	775	2,250	3,450

		GSID	VG-8	F-12	VF-20	EF-40	AU-50	MS-60	MS-63
1722 Penny, GEORGIVS		25	—	—	—	—	—	—	—
1722 Penny, VTILE DVLCI		26	$235	$325	$525	$850	$1,550	$3,750	$5,500
1722 Penny, UTILE DULCI		27	155	260	360	470	725	1,500	4,700
1722 Twopence, Period After REX		375049	230	340	455	625	775	1,750	—
1722 Twopence, No Period After REX		23	365	490	775	950	1,200	1,550	—
1723 Halfpenny, Uncrowned Rose		30	675	850	950	1,500	2,250	4,000	—
1723 Halfpenny, Crowned Rose		29	235	310	440	675	825	1,900	5,500
1723 Penny		40	130	190	310	525	650	1,100	3,750
1723 Twopence		35	180	235	360	725	1,050	1,400	2,900
1724, 4 Over 3 Penny, DEI GRATIA, Pattern		320	—	18,000	—	—	—	—	—
1724, 4 Over 3 Penny, D GRATIA, Pattern		321	—	—	—	—	—	—	—
(1724) Penny, ROSA: SINE: SPINA.	5 known	47	—	—	17,000	—	—	—	—
1724 Twopence, Pattern		45	—	—	—	—	12,000	19,000	—
1733 Twopence, Pattern, Proof		51	—	—	—	—	—	—	—

Wood's Hibernia Coinage (1722–1724)

Around the same time that his royal patent was granted to strike the Rosa Americana coins for the American colonies, William Wood received a franchise to produce copper coins for circulation in Ireland. This was ratified on July 22, 1722. The resulting coins, likely struck in Bristol, England, featured a portrait of King George and, on the reverse, a seated figure with a harp and the word HIBERNIA. Their edges are plain. Denominations struck were farthing and halfpenny, with dates of 1722, 1723, and 1724. These Hibernia coins were unpopular in Ireland and faced vocal public criticism, including from satirist Jonathan Swift. "It was asserted that the issues for Ireland were produced without Irish advice or consent, that the arrangements were made in secret and for the private profit of Wood, and that the pieces were seriously underweight" (*Whitman Encyclopedia of Colonial and Early American Coins*). As a result, King George reduced the number of coins allowed by Wood's patent, and the franchise was retired completely in 1725 in exchange for Wood receiving a £24,000 pension over eight years. Some of the unpopular Hibernia coins, meanwhile, may have been sent to the American colonies to circulate as small change. Their popularity with American numismatists stems from the similarity of their obverses to those in the Rosa Americana series.

Numerous varieties exist.

1722, Hibernia Farthing

1722, Hibernia Halfpenny, First Type

1722, Hibernia Halfpenny, Second Type

1723, 3 Over 2, Halfpenny

1724, Hibernia Farthing

1724, Hibernia Halfpenny

	GSID	VG-8	F-12	VF-20	EF-40	AU-50	MS-60	MS-63	MS-65
1722 Farthing, D: G: REX	24	—	—	$2,750	$6,000	—	—	$18,000	$24,000
1722 Halfpenny, D: G: REX, Rocks at Right, Pattern	20	$3,250	$4,000	5,500	8,750	$11,500	—	—	—
1722 Halfpenny, First Type, Harp at Left	21	130	150	170	310	455	$650	900	4,400
1722 Halfpenny, Second Type, Harp at Right	22	100	130	190	275	325	650	1,400	—
1722 Halfpenny, Second Type, Harp at Right, DEII (blunder)	194486	210	365	525	950	1,250	—	—	—
1723 Farthing, D.G.REX	36	100	130	155	260	340	490	950	—
1723 Farthing, DEI. GRATIA. REX	37	100	125	150	215	260	470	625	1,500
1723 Farthing, Silver Pattern	39	1,600	2,000	2,250	2,950	3,400	5,000	7,500	10,500
1723 Halfpenny	31	80	95	155	215	245	320	525	1,500
1723 Halfpenny, 3 Over 2 (varieties exist)	319	110	150	180	490	750	1,250	2,750	4,250
1723 Halfpenny, Silver Pattern	34	—	—	—	—	—	—	—	—
1724 Farthing	46	—	235	310	440	1,150	3,250	6,250	10,000
1724 Halfpenny	42	100	120	155	260	375	750	1,500	4,400
1724 Halfpenny, DEI Above Head	375050	—	—	—	—	—	—	—	—

VIRGINIA HALFPENNIES (1773–1774)

In 1773 the British Crown authorized coinage of copper halfpennies for the colony of Virginia, not to exceed 25 tons' weight. "This was the first and only colonial coinage authorized and produced in Britain for use in an American colony, thereby giving the Virginia pieces the unique claim of being the only true American colonial coinage" (*Whitman Encyclopedia of Colonial and Early American Coins*). The designs included a laureled portrait of King George III and the royal coat of arms of the House of Hanover. The coins were struck at the Tower Mint in London. Their edges are plain.

Most Mint State pieces available to collectors today are from a hoard of some 5,000 or more of the halfpennies held by Colonel Mendes I. Cohen of Baltimore, Maryland, in the 1800s. Cohen came from a prominent banking family. His cache was dispersed slowly and carefully from 1875 until 1929, as the coins passed from his estate to his nieces and nephews. Eventually the remaining coins, numbering approximately 2,200, the property of Bertha Cohen, were dispersed in one lot in Baltimore. These pieces gradually filtered out, in groups and individually, into the wider numismatic marketplace.

The Proof patterns that were struck on a large planchet with a wide milled border are often referred to as pennies. The silver pieces dated 1774 are referred to as shillings, but they may have been patterns or trials for a halfpenny or a guinea.

1773 Halfpenny

1773 "Penny"

1774 "Shilling"

		GSID	VF-20	EF-40	AU-50	MS-60	MS-63	MS-65
1773 Halfpenny, Period After GEORGIVS		67	$210	$375	$455	$800	$1,150	$2,000
1773 Halfpenny, No Period After GEORGIVS		70	260	455	575	950	1,250	2,500
1773 "Penny," Proof		73	—	—	—	—	20,000	29,000
1774 "Shilling," Proof	6 known	326	—	—	—	—	—	—

EARLY AMERICAN AND RELATED TOKENS

Elephant Tokens (ca. 1672–1694)

London Elephant Tokens

The London Elephant tokens were struck in London circa 1672 to 1694. Although they were undated, two examples are known to have been struck over 1672 British halfpennies. Most were struck in copper, but one was made of brass. Their legend, GOD PRESERVE LONDON, may have been a general plea for divine aid and not a specific reference to the outbreak of plague in 1665 or the great fire of 1666.

These pieces were not struck for the colonies, and they probably did not circulate widely in America, although a few may have been carried there by colonists. They are associated, through a shared obverse die, with the 1694 Carolina and New England Elephant tokens. They have a plain edge but often show the cutting marks from planchet preparation.

		GSID	VG-8	F-12	VF-20	EF-40	AU-50	MS-60	MS-63
(1694) Halfpenny, GOD PRESERVE LONDON, Thick Planchet		353	$490	$575	$900	$1,250	$1,750	$3,450	$5,500
Similar, Brass	unique	376444	—	—	—	—	—	24,000	—
(1694) Halfpenny, GOD PRESERVE LONDON, Thin Planchet		355	—	—	—	3,100	3,750	5,500	9,750
(1694) Halfpenny, GOD PRESERVE LONDON, Diagonals in Center of Shield		356	—	4,250	5,000	7,500	18,000	33,000	48,000
(1694) Halfpenny, GOD PRESERVE LONDON, Sword in Second Quarter of Shield		357	—	—	15,500	—	—	—	—
(1694) Halfpenny, LON DON		358	—	2,050	2,500	9,500	—	—	—

Carolina Elephant Tokens

Although no law is known authorizing coinage for Carolina, two very interesting pieces known as Elephant tokens were made with the date 1694. These copper tokens are of halfpenny denomination. The reverse reads GOD PRESERVE CAROLINA AND THE LORDS PROPRIETERS 1694.

The second and more readily available variety has the last word spelled PROPRIETORS. The correction was made on the original die, for the E shows plainly beneath the O. On the second variety the elephant's tusks nearly touch the milling.

The Carolina pieces were probably struck in England and perhaps intended as advertising to heighten interest in the Carolina Plantation. Another theory suggests they may have been related to or made for the Carolina coffee house in London.

	GSID	VG-8	F-12	VF-20	EF-40	AU-50	MS-60	MS-63
1694, PROPRIETERS	12	—	$21,500	$26,500	$31,000	$36,000	$48,000	—
1694, PROPRIETORS, O Over E	13	$7,250	8,750	11,000	17,000	21,000	43,000	—

New England Elephant Tokens

Like the Carolina tokens, the New England Elephant tokens are believed to have been struck in England, possibly as promotional pieces to increase interest in the American colonies, or perhaps related to the New England coffee house in London

		GSID	VG-8	F-12	VF-20	EF-40	AU-50	MS-60	MS-63
1694, NEW ENGLAND	3 known	14	$101,000	$132,000	—	—	—	—	—
	Auctions: $141,000, PCGS VG-8 SBG 03/15								

New Yorke in America Tokens (1660s or 1670s)

The New Yorke in America tokens are farthing or halfpenny tokens intended for New York, issued by Francis Lovelace, who was governor from 1668 until 1673. The tokens use the older spelling with a final "e" (YORKE), which predominated before 1710. The obverse shows Cupid pursuing the loveless butterfly-winged Psyche—a rebus on the name Lovelace. The reverse shows a heraldic eagle, identical to the one displayed in fesse, raguly (i.e., on a crenellated bar) on the Lovelace coat of arms. In weight, fabric, and die axis the tokens are similar to certain 1670 farthing tokens of Bristol, England, where they may have been struck. There is no evidence that any of these pieces ever circulated in America. Fewer than two dozen are believed to now exist.

	GSID	F-12	VF-20	EF-40	AU-50
(Undated), Brass or Copper	388	$10,000	$18,000	$43,000	$54,000
	Auctions: $110,450, PCGS EF-40 SBG 03/13				
(Undated), Pewter	389	—	—	—	—

Gloucester Tokens (1714)

Sylvester S. Crosby, in his book *The Early Coins of America*, stated that these tokens appear to have been intended as a pattern for a shilling—a private coinage by Richard Dawson of Gloucester (county), Virginia. The only specimens known are struck in brass, although the denomination XII indicates that a silver coinage (one shilling) may have been planned. The building depicted on the obverse may represent some public building, possibly the courthouse.

Although neither of the two known examples shows the full legends, combining the pieces shows GLOVCESTER COVRTHOVSE VIRGINIA / RIGHAVLT DAWSON. ANNO.DOM. 1714. This recent discovery has provided a new interpretation of the legends, as a Righault family once owned land near the Gloucester courthouse. A similar, but somewhat smaller, piece possibly dated 1715 exists. The condition of this unique piece is too poor for positive attribution.

		GSID	F-12
1714 Shilling, Brass	2 known	16	$108,000
	Auctions: $180,000, NGC VF-25 HA 01/21		

Higley or Granby Coppers (1737–1739)

Dr. Samuel Higley owned a private copper mine near Granby, Connecticut, in an area known for many such operations. Higley was a medical doctor, with a degree from Yale College, who also practiced blacksmithing and experimented in metallurgy. He worked his mine as a private individual, extracting particularly rich copper, smelting it, and shipping much of it to England. He also made his own dies for plain-edged pure-copper "coins" that he issued.

Legend has it that a drink in the local tavern cost three pence, and that Higley paid his bar tabs with his own privately minted coins, denominated as they were with the legend THE VALUE OF THREEPENCE. When his supply of such coppers exceeded the local demand, neighbors complained that they were not worth the denomination stated, and Higley changed the legends to read VALUE ME AS YOU PLEASE and I AM GOOD COPPER (but kept the Roman numeral III on the obverse).

After Samuel Higley's death in May 1737 his older brother John continued his coinage.

The Higley coppers were never officially authorized. There were seven obverse and four reverse dies. All are rare. Electrotypes and cast copies exist.

1737, "THE VALVE OF" Obverse, CONNECTICVT / Hammers Reverse

1737, "VALUE ME AS YOU PLEASE" Obverse, I AM GOOD COPPER / Hammers Reverse

(1737), "J CUT MY WAY THROUGH" Reverse

(1737), "THE WHEELE GOES ROUND" Obverse

		GSID	F-12	VF-20	VF-30	EF-40
1737, THE • VALVE • OF • THREE • PENCE, CONNECTICVT, 3 Hammers		52	$79,000	$101,000	$132,000	—
	Auctions: $470,000, NGC AU-50 HA 05/14					
1737, THE • VALVE • OF • THREE • PENCE, I • AM • GOOD • COPPER, CONNECTICVT, 3 Hammers	3 known	53	—	—	—	—
	Auctions: $218,500, Uncert EF-45 SBG 05/04					
1737, VALUE • ME • AS • YOU • PLEASE, I • AM • GOOD • COPPER, 3 Hammers		54	60,000	90,000	126,000	$204,000
	Auctions: $192,000, PCGS VF-30 SBG 08/22					
1737, VALVE • ME • AS • YOU • PLEASE, I • AM • GOOD • COPPER, 3 Hammers	3 known	55	60,000	90,000	126,000	204,000
(1737), VALUE • ME • AS • YOU • PLEASE, J • CUT • MY • WAY • THROUGH, Broad Axe		359	60,000	90,000	126,000	204,000
	Auctions: $199,750, NGC VF-30 HA 05/14					
(1737), THE • WHEELE • GOES • ROUND, Reverse as Above	unique	360	—	—	360,000	—
	Auctions: $376,000, NGC VF-30 HA 01/15					
1739, VALUE • ME • AS • YOU • PLEASE, J • CUT • MY • WAY • THROUGH, Broad Axe		56	—	79,000	—	—

Hibernia–Voce Populi Coins

These coins, struck in the year 1760, were prepared by Roche, of King Street, Dublin, who was at that time engaged in the manufacture of buttons for the army. Like other Irish tokens, some could have found their way to colonial America and possibly circulated in the colonies with numerous other counterfeit halfpence and "bungtown tokens." There is no evidence to prove that Voce Populi pieces, which bear the legend HIBERNIA (Ireland) on the reverse, ever circulated in North America. Sylvester S. Crosby did not include them in *The Early Coins of America*, 1875. Nor were they covered in Wayte Raymond's *Standard Catalogue of United States Coins* (until Walter Breen revised the section on colonial coins in 1954, after which they were "adopted" by mainstream collectors). Various theories exist regarding the identity of the bust portrait on the obverse, ranging from kings and pretenders to the British throne, to the provost of Dublin College.

There are two distinct issues. Coins from the first, with a "short bust" on the obverse, ranged in weight from 87 to 120 grains. Those from the second, with a "long bust" on the obverse, ranged in weight from 129 to 154 grains. Most of the "long bust" varieties have the letter P on the obverse. None of the "short bust" varieties bear the letter P, and, judging from their weight, they may have been contemporary counterfeits.

1760 Farthing, Large Letters

1760 Halfpenny

1760 Halfpenny, "P" Before Face

1760 Halfpenny, VOOE POPULI Obverse

	GSID	F-12	VF-20	EF-40	AU-50	MS-60	MS-63
1760 Farthing, Large Letters	61	$950	$1,250	$1,550	$2,000	$3,750	$6,250
1760 Farthing, Small Letters	62	—	—	—	21,500	—	—
1760 Halfpenny	57	130	245	470	575	1,000	3,000
1760 Halfpenny, VOOE POPULI	58	230	260	490	850	1,400	2,250
1760 Halfpenny, P Below Bust	59	290	390	1,000	1,450	3,750	8,000
1738–1748 Half Sou Marque, various mints	60	290	365	900	1,300	3,250	—

Pitt Tokens (ca. 1769)

William Pitt the Elder, the British statesman who endeared himself to America, is the subject of these brass or copper pieces, probably intended as commemorative medalets. The so-called halfpenny (the larger of the type's two sizes) served as currency during a shortage of regular coinage. The farthing-size tokens are rare.

The reverse legend (THANKS TO THE FRIENDS OF LIBERTY AND TRADE) refers to Pitt's criticism of the Crown's taxation of the American colonies, and his efforts to have the Stamp Act of March 22, 1765, repealed in 1766. The obverse bears a portrait and the legends THE RESTORER OF COMMERCE and NO STAMPS.

"Little is known concerning the circumstances of issue. Robert Vlack suggests that the pieces may have been designed by Paul Revere. Striking may have been accomplished around 1769 by James Smither (or Smithers) of Philadelphia" (*Whitman Encyclopedia of Colonial and Early American Coins*).

Farthing

Halfpenny

	GSID	F-12	VF-20	EF-40	AU-50	MS-60
1766 Farthing	65	$6,250	$10,500	$21,500	$31,000	—
1766 Halfpenny	63	650	1,000	1,300	2,050	$5,250

Rhode Island Ship Medals (ca. 1779)

The circumstances of the issue of these medals (or tokens) are mysterious. They were largely unknown to American coin collectors until 1864, when a specimen was offered in W. Elliot Woodward's sale of the Seavey Collection. It sold for $40—a remarkable price at the time.

The obverse shows the flagship of British admiral Lord Richard Howe at anchor, while the reverse depicts the American retreat from Rhode Island in 1778. The inscriptions show that the coin was meant for a Dutch-speaking audience. The word *vlugtende* ("fleeing") appears on the earlier issues below Howe's flagship—an engraving error. After a limited number of pieces were struck with this word, it was removed on all but two surviving examples by adding a wreath over the word on the dies or physically obliterating the word by grinding it off. It is believed the medal was struck in Holland as a jetton, but some think it was struck in England as a propaganda piece. Specimens are known in brass, pewter, and with a silvered (actually tin) wash.

Rhode Island Ship Medal (1778–1779)

Legend "vlugtende" Below Ship

Wreath Below Ship

	GSID	VF-20	EF-40	AU-50	MS-60
Wreath Below Ship, Pewter	394	$3,450	$5,000	$6,000	$10,000
Wreath Below Ship, Brass	396	1,300	1,950	2,500	4,750
Wreath Below Ship, Copper	391	1,400	2,000	2,600	5,000
Wreath Below Ship, Silvered	390	2,200	2,800	3,750	—
With "vlugtende" (fleeing) Below Ship, Brass	393	—	—	144,000	—
	Auctions: $132,000, PCGS AU-55 SBG 08/22				
Without Wreath Below Ship, Copper	392	1,400	2,200	3,000	5,000
Without Wreath Below Ship, Pewter	395	7,500	10,000	12,000	27,000
Without Wreath Below Ship, Brass	397	1,550	2,250	2,750	5,750

JOHN CHALMERS ISSUES (1783)

John Chalmers, a Maryland goldsmith and silversmith, struck a series of silver tokens of his own design in Annapolis in 1783. The dies were by Thomas Sparrow, another silversmith in the town. The shortage of change in circulation and the refusal of the American people to use underweight cut Spanish coins prompted the issuance of these pieces. (Fraudsters would attempt to cut five "quarters" or nine or ten "eighths" out of one Spanish silver dollar, thereby realizing a proportional profit when they were all spent.)

On the Chalmers threepence and shilling obverses, two clasped hands are shown, perhaps symbolizing unity of the several states; the reverse of the threepence has a branch encircled by a wreath. A star within a wreath is on the obverse of the sixpence, with hands clasped upon a cross utilized as the reverse type. On this denomination, the designer's initials TS (for Thomas Sparrow) can be found in the crescents that terminate the horizontal arms of the cross. The reverse of the more common shilling varieties displays two doves competing for a worm underneath a hedge and a snake. The symbolic message is thought to have been against the danger of squabbling with brethren over low-value stakes while a dangerous mutual enemy lurked nearby. The edges of these tokens are crudely reeded. There are only a few known examples of the shilling type with 13 interlinked rings, from which a liberty cap on a pole arises.

Threepence

Sixpence, Small Date

Sixpence, Large Date

Shilling, Birds, Short Worm

Shilling, Rings

	GSID	VG-8	F-12	VF-20	EF-40	AU-50
1783 Threepence	86	—	$5,500	$8,000	$13,500	$15,500
	Auctions: $111,625, PCGS MS-63 HA 01/14					
1783 Sixpence, Small Date	87	$3,750	5,000	8,250	30,000	—
1783 Sixpence, Large Date	88	—	12,000	15,000	18,000	42,000
1783 Shilling, Birds, Long Worm	101	1,150	2,750	3,750	9,500	12,000
1783 Shilling, Birds, Short Worm (illustrated)	102	2,200	2,800	4,050	10,000	15,500
1783 Shilling, Rings	103	—	120,000	150,000	—	—
	Auctions: $172,500, Uncert EF-40 SBG 05/04					

FRENCH NEW WORLD ISSUES

None of the coins of the French regime relate specifically to territories that later became part of the United States. They were all general issues for the French colonies of the New World. The coinage of 1670 was authorized by an edict of King Louis XIV dated February 19, 1670, for use in New France, Acadia, the French settlements in Newfoundland, and the French West Indies. The copper coinage of 1717 to 1722 was authorized by edicts of 1716 and 1721 for use in New France, Louisiana, and the French West Indies.

Coinage of 1670

The coinage of 1670 consisted of silver 5 and 15 sols and copper 2 deniers (or "doubles"). A total of 200,000 of the 5 sols and 40,000 of the 15 sols was struck at Paris. Nantes was to have coined the copper, but did not; the reasons for this may never be known, since the archives of the Nantes Mint before 1700 were destroyed. The only known specimen is a pattern struck at Paris. The silver coins were raised in value by a third in 1672 to keep them circulating, but in vain. They rapidly disappeared, and by 1680 none were to be seen. Later they were restored to their original values. This rare issue should not be confused with the common 1670-A 1/12 écu with reverse legend SIT. NOMEN. DOMINI. BENEDICTUM.

The 1670-A double de l'Amerique Françoise was struck at the Paris Mint along with the 5- and 15-sols denominations of the same date. All three were intended to circulate in France's North American colonies. Probably due to an engraving error, very few 1670-A doubles were actually struck. Today only one is known to survive.

Copper Double

Silver 5 Sols

		VG	F	VF	EF	AU	Unc.
1670-A Copper Double	unique			$500,000			
1670-A 5 Sols		$750	$1,000	2,000	$7,000	$10,000	$20,000
1670-A 15 Sols		13,000	35,000	65,000	85,000	105,000	150,000

Coinage of 1717–1720

The copper 6 and 12 deniers of 1717 were authorized by an edict of King Louis XV (by order of the six-year-old king's regent, the duke of Orléans) dated December 1716, to be struck at Perpignan (mintmark Q). The order could not be carried out, for the supply of copper was too brassy, and only a few pieces were coined. The issues of 1720, which were struck at multiple mints, are popularly collected for their association with the John Law "Mississippi Bubble" venture.

1720 6 Deniers

1717-Q 12 Deniers

1720 20 Sols

	F	VF	EF
1717-Q 6 Deniers, No Crowned Arms on Reverse (a)			—
1717-Q 12 Deniers, No Crowned Arms on Reverse	$50,000		—
1720 Liard, Crowned Arms on Reverse, Copper	350	$500	$900
1720 6 Deniers, Crowned Arms on Reverse, Copper	550	900	1,750
1720 12 Deniers, Crowned Arms on Reverse, Copper	400	900	1,600
1720 20 Sols, Silver	375	700	1,500

a. Extremely rare.

Billon Coinage of 1709–1760

The French colonial coins of 30 deniers were called *mousquetaires* because of the outlined cross on their reverse, evocative of the design on the short coats worn by French musketeers. These coins were produced at Metz and Lyon. The 15 deniers was coined only at Metz. The sou marque and the half sou were coined at almost every French mint, those of Paris being most common. The half sou of 1740 is the only commonly available date. Specimens of the sou marque dated after 1760 were not used in North America. A unique specimen of the 1712-AA 30 deniers is known in the size and weight of the 15-denier coins.

30 Deniers "Mousquetaire"

Sou Marque (24 Deniers)

	VG	F	VF	EF	AU	Unc.
1711–1713-AA 15 Deniers	$150	$300	$500	$1,000	$1,750	$4,000
1709–1713-AA 30 Deniers	75	100	250	400	675	1,500
1709–1713-D 30 Deniers	75	100	250	400	675	1,500
1738–1748 Half Sou Marque, various mints	60	100	200	350	575	1,200
1738–1760 Sou Marque, various mints	50	80	125	175	300	500

Coinage of 1721–1722

The copper coinage of 1721 and 1722 was authorized by an edict of King Louis XV dated June 1721. The coins were struck on copper blanks imported from Sweden. Rouen and La Rochelle struck pieces of nine deniers (one sou) in 1721 and 1722. New France received 534,000 pieces, mostly from the mint of La Rochelle, but only 8,180 were put into circulation, as the colonists disliked copper. In 1726 the rest of the issue was sent back to France.

In American coin catalogs of the 1800s, these coins were often called "Louisiana coppers."

	VG	F	VF	G	AU
1721-B (Rouen)	$500	$1,000	$3,500	$6,000	$12,000
1721-H (La Rochelle)	100	200	1,000	2,500	5,000
1722-H	100	200	1,000	2,500	5,000
1722-H, 2 Over 1	175	275	1,200	4,000	7,000

French Colonies in General (1767)

These copper coins were produced for use in the French colonies and only unofficially circulated in Louisiana along with other foreign coins and tokens. Most were counterstamped RF (République Française) for use in the West Indies. The mintmark A signifies the Paris Mint. The edge is decorated with a double row of dots.

	VG	VF	EF	AU
1767 French Colonies, Sou	$120	$400	$750	$1,500
1767 French Colonies, Sou, counterstamped RF	100	180	250	600

Post-Colonial Issues

The coins explored in this section are classified as "post-colonial" because they came after the colonial period (some during the early months of rebellion; most after the official declaration of independence) but before the first federal Mint was established in Philadelphia in 1792.

Early American coins were produced from hand-engraved dies, which are often individually distinctive. For many types, the great number of die varieties that can be found and identified are of interest to collectors who value each according to its individual rarity. Values shown for type coins in this section are for the most common die variety of each.

Scan for additional information.

CONTINENTAL CURRENCY PIECES (1776)

The Continental Currency dollars (as they are known to numismatists) were made to serve in lieu of a paper dollar, but the exact nature of their monetary role is still unclear. They were the first dollar-sized coins ever attributed to the United States. One obverse die was engraved by someone whose initials were E.G. (thought to be Elisha Gallaudet) and is marked EG FECIT ("EG Made It"). Studies of the coinage show that there may have been two separate emissions made at different mints, one in New York City. The link design on the reverse was suggested by Benjamin Franklin and represents the former colonies.

Varieties result from differences in the spelling of the word CURRENCY and the addition of EG FECIT on the obverse. These coins were struck in pewter, brass, and silver. Pewter pieces served as a dollar, taking the place of a Continental Currency paper note. Brass and silver pieces may have been experimental or patterns. The typical grade encountered for a pewter coin is VF to AU. Examples in original bright Uncirculated condition are worth a strong premium.

Numerous copies and replicas of these coins have been made over the years. Authentication is recommended for all pieces.

CURRENCY

CURENCY

Reverse

		GSID	F-12	VF-20	EF-40	AU-50	MS-60	MS-63
1776, CURENCY, Pewter (2 varieties)		76	$22,000	$27,000	$33,500	$39,000	$56,500	$113,000
	Auctions: $246,750, NGC MS-65 HA 01/15							
1776, CURENCY, Brass (2 varieties)	15 known	77	—	—	144,000	180,000	—	462,000
	Auctions: $440,625, NGC MS-62 HA 11/14							
1776, CURENCY, Silver	4 known	78	—	—	1,740,000	—	—	—
	Auctions: $1,527,500, NGC EF-40 HA 01/15							
1776, CURRENCY, Pewter		79	21,500	25,000	31,000	36,000	55,000	108,000
	Auctions: $264,500, NGC MS-65 SBG 06/08							
1776, CURRENCY, EG FECIT, Pewter		80	22,000	27,000	33,500	39,000	56,500	113,000
	Auctions: $546,250, NGC MS-67 HA 01/12							
1776, CURRENCY, EG FECIT, Silver	4 known	81	—	—	—	—	—	1,500,000
	Auctions: $1,527,500, NGC MS-62 HA 01/15							
1776, CURRENCEY, Pewter		82	—	—	—	—	—	420,000
	Auctions: $381,875, NGC MS-63 HA 11/14							
1776, CURRENCY, Pewter, Ornamented Date	3 known	83	—	—	—	—	—	—
	Auctions: $329,000, NGC AU-58 HA 01/15							

SPECULATIVE ISSUES, TOKENS, AND PATTERNS

NOVA CONSTELLATIO COPPERS (1783–1786)

The Nova Constellatio coppers, dated 1783 and 1785 and without denomination, were struck in fairly large quantities in Birmingham, England, and were shipped to New York where they entered circulation. Apparently they resulted from a private coinage venture undertaken by Constable, Rucker & Co., a trading business formed by William Constable, John Rucker, Robert Morris, and Gouverneur Morris as equal partners. The designs and legends were copied from the denominated patterns dated 1783 made in Philadelphia (see "Nova Constellatio Patterns"). A few additional coppers dated 1786 were made by an inferior diesinker.

"The Nova Constellatio coppers were well received and saw extensive use in commerce, as evidenced by the wear seen on typically specimens today," writes Q. David Bowers in the *Whitman Encyclopedia of Colonial and Early American Coins*. "Later, they were devalued, and many were used as undertypes (planchets) for Connecticut and, to a lesser extent, New Jersey and Vermont coppers."

1783, CONSTELLATIO, Pointed Rays, Small U.S.

1783, CONSTELLATIO Pointed Rays, Large U.S.

1783, CONSTELATIO, Blunt Rays

1785, CONSTELATIO, Blunt Rays

1785, CONSTELLATIO, Pointed Rays

	GSID	F-12	VF-20	EF-40	AU-50	MS-60	MS-63
1783, CONSTELLATIO, Pointed Rays, Small U.S.	89	$260	$390	$875	$1,100	—	$5,250
1783, CONSTELLATIO, Pointed Rays, Large U.S.	90	260	455	1,000	1,600	$3,900	—
1783, CONSTELATIO, Blunt Rays	91	325	575	1,100	2,100	5,000	11,000
1785, CONSTELATIO, Blunt Rays	110	345	575	950	1,600	—	9,500
1785, CONSTELLATIO, Pointed Rays	112	325	550	1,000	1,400	2,100	3,900
1786, CONSTELLATIO, Small Date	128	—	26,500	54,000	—	—	—
1786, CONSTELLATIO, Small Date	128	—	26,500	54,000	—	—	—

Immune Columbia Pieces (1785)

These pieces are considered private or unofficial coins. No laws describing them are known. There are several types bearing the seated figure of Justice. These pieces are stylistically related to the Nova Constellatio coppers, with the Immune Columbia motif with liberty cap and scale replacing the LIBERTAS and JUSTITIA design.

1785, Silver, 13-Star Reverse

1785, Pointed Rays, CONSTELLATIO

1785, George III Obverse

1787, IMMUNIS COLUMBIA, Eagle Reverse

		GSID	F-12	VF-20	EF-40	AU-50	MS-60
1785, Copper, 13-Star Reverse		118	—	—	$30,000	$41,000	$90,000
1785, Silver, 13-Star Reverse		119	—	$45,500	72,000	90,000	—
	Auctions: $135,125, NGC AU-53 HA 11/14						
1785, Pointed Rays, CONSTELLATIO, Extra Star in Reverse Legend, Copper		120	—	—	36,000	54,000	—
1785, Pointed Rays, CONSTELLATIO, Gold (in Smithsonian Collection) (a)	unique	122	—	—	—	—	—
1785, Blunt Rays, CONSTELATIO, Copper	2 known	121	—	60,000	96,000	—	—
	Auctions: $114,000, PCGS EF-40 SBG 03/23						
1785, Copper, GEORGE III Obverse		123	$17,000	20,000	43,000	54,000	—

a. The gold specimen in the National Numismatic Collection (now maintained by the Smithsonian) was acquired in 1843 from collector Matthew A. Stickney in exchange for an 1804 dollar.

	GSID	F-12	VF-20	EF-40	AU-50	MS-60
1786, IMMUNIS COLUMBIA, Eagle Reverse	135	—	—	$96,000	—	—
	Auctions: $152,750, NGC MS-64 HA 11/14					
1786, IMMUNIS COLUMBIA, Shield Reverse	136	—	—	60,000	$72,000	$120,000
	Auctions: $141,000, NGC MS-62 HA 11/14					
1787, IMMUNIS COLUMBIA, Eagle Reverse (b)	206	$1,550	$2,750	3,600	6,250	18,000
	Auctions: $129,250, NGC MS-64 HA 01/15					

b. Believed to be a prototype for federal coinage; some were coined after 1787.

Confederatio and Related Tokens

The Confederatio and associated coppers have patriotic motifs and were made in small quantities for circulation. The 1785, Inimica Tyrannis America, variety may owe its design to a sketch by Thomas Jefferson. In all, 12 dies were presumed struck in 13 combinations. No one knows for certain who made these pieces. The combination with a standard reverse die for a 1786 New Jersey copper is especially puzzling.

Inimica Tyrannis America

Inimica Tyrannis Americana

Gen. Washington

Immunis Columbia

Eagle

Libertas et Justitia

Large Circle

Small Circle

Narrow Shield

1786, Immunis Columbia, Scrawny Eagle Reverse

		GSID	VF-20	VF-30	EF-40	EF-45	AU-50
1785, Inimica Tyrannis America, Large Circle	6 known	117	$48,000	$72,000	$108,000	$115,000	$132,000
	Auctions: $116,331, PCGS AU-50 HA 05/16						
1785, Inimica Tyrannis America, Large Circle, Silver	unique	375343	—	—	—	—	—
1785, Inimica Tyrannis Americana, Small Circle	8 known	116	31,000	33,500	48,000	57,500	72,000
	Auctions: $149,500, PCGS MS-64 HA 08/07						
1785, Gen. Washington, Large Circle	6 known	137	108,000	120,000	132,000	—	150,000
	Auctions: $129,250, NGC AU-50 HA 01/15						
1786, Gen. Washington, Eagle	2 known	134	90,000	101,000	120,000	—	—

		GSID	VF-20	VF-30	EF-40	EF-45	AU-50
(No Date), Gen. Washington, Narrow Shield (a)	3 known	375344	—	—	—	—	—
1786, Immunis, Narrow Shield (a)	17 known	375345	—	—	—	—	—
1786, Immunis, 1785 Large Circle	2 known	178	—	—	—	—	—
1786, Eagle, Narrow Shield (a,b)		375346	—	—	—	—	—
1786, Eagle, 1785 Large Circle	2 known	375347	—	—	—	—	—
1785, Libertas et Justitia, 1785 Large Circle (b)		375348	—	—	—	—	—
1785, Small Circle, 1787 Excelsior Eagle (c)	2 known	375349	—	—	—	—	—
1786, Immunis Columbia, Scrawny Eagle	3 known	375350	—	—	—	—	—

a. The Narrow Shield was formerly known as the Pattern Shield. **b.** Damaged. **c.** The 1787 Excelsior Eagle is pictured under "New York Copper Coinage."

COINAGE OF THE STATES AND VERMONT

Republic of Vermont (1785–1788)

The Republic of Vermont was not formally part of the Union in the 1780s. However, it considered itself American and allied with the original 13 colonies, having declared independence from Britain in January 1777 and having fought in the Revolutionary War. After the war Vermont sought political connection with the United States. Territorial disagreements with New York delayed its entry into the Union, but this was finally accomplished in 1791, when it was admitted as the 14th state. In the meantime, Vermont had already embarked on its own experiments in local coinage.

Reuben Harmon Jr., a storekeeper and entrepreneur of Rupert, Vermont, was granted permission by the Vermont House of Representatives to coin copper pieces for a period of two years beginning July 1, 1785. The well-known Vermont "Landscape" coppers were first produced in that year. The franchise was extended for eight years in 1786.

Harmon's mint was located in the northeast corner of Rupert near a stream known as Millbrook. Colonel William Coley, a New York goldsmith, made the first dies. Some of the late issues were made near Newburgh, New York, by the Machin's Mills coiners.

Most coppers made in Vermont were struck on poor and defective planchets. These included the landscape and Draped Bust Left varieties. Well-struck coins on smooth, full planchets command higher prices. Later pieces made at Machin's Mills are on high-quality planchets but usually have areas of weak striking.

1785, IMMUNE COLUMBIA

1785, VERMONTS

1785, VERMONTIS

1786, VERMONTENSIUM

1786, Baby Head

1786, Bust Left

1787, Bust Left

1787, BRITANNIA

1787, 1788, Bust Right (several varieties)

1788, GEORGIVS III REX / INDE* ET•LIB*

	GSID	VG-8	F-12	VF-20	EF-40	AU-50
1785, IMMUNE COLUMBIA	125	$8,000	$18,000	$30,000	$60,000	—
1785, VERMONTS	126	575	1,000	1,950	3,100	$5,000
1785, VERMONTIS	127	1,250	1,500	2,000	4,700	5,500
1786, VERMONTENSIUM	148	325	650	1,500	2,750	4,400
1786, Baby Head	149	—	1,250	2,500	7,500	14,500
1786, Bust Left	150	650	1,150	1,750	3,100	—
1787, BRITANNIA (a)	221	—	210	325	950	1,550
1787, Bust Left	222	17,000	21,500	29,000	—	—
1787, Bust Right (several varieties)	223	260	325	625	1,800	2,750
1788, Bust Right (several varieties)	240	245	290	575	1,450	2,200
1788, Bust Right, Backward C in AUCTORI	241	12,500	15,500	32,000	42,000	54,000
1788, Bust Right, *ET LIB* *INDE	242	1,100	1,550	2,250	13,000	—
1788, GEORGIVS III REX (b)	243	525	950	1,700	3,500	—

a. The reverse of this coin is always weak. **b.** This piece should not be confused with the common English halfpence with similar design and reverse legend BRITANNIA.

NEW HAMPSHIRE (1776)

New Hampshire was the first of the states to consider the subject of coinage following the Declaration of Independence. On March 13, 1776, by which time the colonies were in rebellion but had not yet formally declared their independence, the New Hampshire House of Representatives established a committee to consider the minting of copper coins. The committee recommended such coinage as a way to facilitate small commercial transactions.

William Moulton was empowered to make a limited quantity of coins of pure copper authorized by the State House of Representatives in 1776. Although cast patterns were prepared, it is believed that they were not approved. Little of the proposed coinage was ever actually circulated.

Other purported patterns are of doubtful origin. These include a unique engraved piece and a rare struck piece with large initials WM on the reverse.

	GSID	G-6	VG-8	VG-10
1776 New Hampshire Copper	84	$72,000	$78,000	$86,500
	Auctions: $198,375, PCGS VG-10 SBG 03/12			

MASSACHUSETTS

MASSACHUSETTS UNOFFICIAL COPPERS (1776)

Presumably, in 1776, the year the colonies proclaimed their independence from Britain, three types of Massachusetts coppers were created. Very little is known about their origins or the circumstances of their production. Numismatic historians deduced them to be patterns until recent scholarship cast doubt on their authenticity as coppers of the Revolutionary War era.

The obverse of one of these coppers has a crude pine tree with "1d LM" at its base and the legend MASSACHUSETTS STATE. The reverse has a figure probably intended to represent the Goddess of Liberty, seated on a globe and holding a liberty cap and staff. A dog sits at her feet. The legend LIBERTY AND VIRTUE surrounds the figure, and the date 1776 is situated beneath.

Sylvester S. Crosby, writing in 1875 in *The Early Coins of America*, traced the provenance of this unique copper back to a grocer who sold it to a schoolboy around 1852. The grocer was from "the northerly part" of Boston, and he had "found it many years before while excavating on his premises, in the vicinity of Hull or Charter Street."

A similar piece, probably from the same source as the Pine Tree copper, features a Native American standing with a bow on the obverse, with a worn legend that may read PROVINCE OF MASSA or similar. On the reverse is a seated figure and globe, visible partially visible legend (LIBERTATIS), and the date 1776 at bottom. The only known example was overstruck on a 1747 English halfpenny, and is holed.

A third Massachusetts piece is sometimes called the *Janus copper*. On the obverse are three heads, facing left, front, and right, with the legend STATE OF MASSA. 1/2 D. The reverse shows the Goddess of Liberty facing right, resting against a globe. The legend is GODDESS LIBERTY 1776.

1776 Pine Tree Copper

1776 Indian Copper

1776 Halfpenny, "Janus Copper"

		GSID	VG-8	F-12	VF-20	EF-40	AU-50	MS-60
1776 Pine Tree Copper (in Massachusetts Historical Society Collection)	unique	376445	—	—	—	—	—	—
1776 Indian Copper	unique	376446	—	—	—	—	—	—
1776 Halfpenny, Janus Copper, 3 Heads on Obverse	unique	376447	—	—	—	—	—	—

MASSACHUSETTS AUTHORIZED ISSUES (1787–1788)

An "Act for establishing a mint for the coinage of gold, silver and copper" was passed by the Massachusetts General Court on October 17, 1786. The next year, the council directed that the design of the copper coins should incorporate ". . . the figure of an indian with a bow & arrow & a star on one side, with the word 'Commonwealth,' the reverse a spread eagle with the words—'of Massachusetts A. D. 1787'—" (this wording would be slightly different in the final product).

The coinage of Massachusetts copper cents and half cents in 1787 and 1788 was under the direction of Captain Joshua Witherle of Boston. These were the first coins bearing the denomination *cent* as would be later established by Congress. They were produced in large quantities and are fairly plentiful today. The wear seen on many of the Massachusetts cents and half cents indicates that they enjoyed long circulation in commerce. Many varieties exist, the most valuable being that with arrows in the eagle's right talon.

Most of the dies for these coppers were made by Joseph Callender. Jacob Perkins of Newburyport also engraved some of the 1788 dies.

The mint was abandoned early in 1789, in compliance with the newly ratified U.S. Constitution, and because its production was unprofitable.

1787 Half Cent

1787 Cent, Obverse

1787 Cent, Arrows in Right Talon

1787 Cent, Arrows in Left Talon

1788 Half Cent

1788 Cent, Period After MASSACHUSETTS

	GSID	VG-8	F-12	VF-20	EF-40	AU-50	MS-60	MS-63	MS-65
1787 Half Cent	151	$360	$470	$575	$1,050	$1,450	$2,200	$3,750	$10,500
1787 Cent, Arrows in Right Talon	153	15,500	24,000	39,000	51,500	102,000	—	—	240,000
	Auctions: $258,500, NGC MS-65 HA 01/15								
1787 Cent, Arrows in Left Talon	154	345	415	550	1,000	1,500	3,500	8,000	26,500
1787 Cent, "Horned Eagle" (die break)	156	235	310	525	1,500	2,250	4,750	7,500	17,000
1788 Half Cent	225	300	420	525	950	1,300	2,000	3,400	9,500
1788 Cent, Period After MASSACHUSETTS	227	285	340	575	1,000	1,500	3,750	6,500	12,000
1788 Cent, No Period After MASSACHUSETTS	74462	230	360	525	1,000	1,900	3,750	6,250	—

Connecticut (1785–1788)

Authority for establishing a mint near New Haven was granted by the state of Connecticut to Samuel Bishop, Joseph Hopkins, James Hillhouse, and John Goodrich in October 1785. They had petitioned the state's General Assembly for this right, noting the public need—small coins were scarce in circulation and many of those seen were counterfeits. Under the Assembly's grant, the four minters would pay the state's treasury an amount equal to 5 percent of the copper coins they produced. To make a profit, the minters would deduct this royalty, plus their other expenses (including materials, labor, and distribution), from the face value of the coins they struck.

Available records indicate that most of the Connecticut coppers were coined under a subcontract, by Samuel Broome and Jeremiah Platt, former New York merchants. Abel Buell was probably the principal diesinker. Many others were struck by Machin's Mills in Newburgh, New York, and were not authorized by Connecticut. These are as highly prized by collectors as are regular issues.

The Connecticut coppers were often struck crudely and on imperfect planchets. Numerous die varieties exist; over the years, collectors have given many of them distinctive nicknames.

1785 Copper, Bust Facing Left

1785 Copper, Bust Facing Right

1785 Copper, African Head

1786 Copper, ETLIB INDE

1786 Copper, Large Head Facing Right

1786 Copper, Mailed Bust Facing Left

1786 Copper, Draped Bust

1786 Copper, Mailed Bust Facing Left, Hercules Head

1787 Copper, Small Head Facing Right, ETLIB INDE

1787 Copper, Muttonhead Variety, Topless Liberty

1787 Copper, Mailed Bust Facing Left

1787 Copper, Laughing Head

1787 Copper, Reverse

1787 Copper, Horned Bust

1787 Copper, Draped Bust Facing Left

1788 Copper, Mailed Bust Facing Right

1788 Copper, Mailed Bust Facing Left

1788 Copper, Draped Bust Facing Left

		GSID	VG-8	F-12	VF-20	EF-40	AU-50	MS-60	MS-63
1785, Bust Facing Left		115	$470	$750	$1,150	$5,000	$8,500	—	—
1785, Bust Facing Right		113	160	230	340	750	1,250	$3,100	$11,000
1785, Bust Facing Right, African Head		114	415	550	650	2,000	3,550	—	—
	Auctions: $115,000, NGC VF-30 HA 10/10								
1786, Small Head Facing Right, ETLIB INDE		129	390	470	650	2,500	3,750	—	—
1786, Large Head Facing Right		130	1,750	2,400	3,750	9,500	15,000	—	—
1786, Mailed Bust Facing Left		131	130	260	365	950	1,200	3,750	7,500
1786, Mailed Bust Facing Left, Sword Hilt and Guard Reverse	unique	377258	24,000	—	—	—	—	—	—
1786, Draped Bust Facing Left		133	360	650	2,000	6,250	12,000	—	—
1786, Mailed Bust Facing Left, Hercules Head		132	360	575	950	2,500	12,000	—	—
1787, Small Head Facing Right, ETLIB INDE		159	340	575	825	1,600	2,050	4,250	—
	Auctions: $164,500, NGC F-12 HA 05/14								
1787, Liberty Seated Facing Right	2 known	375239	—	—	144,000	—	—	—	—
	Auctions: $120,000, NGC VF-20 HA 01/21								
1787, Mailed Bust Facing Right, INDE ET LIB		157	2,000	2,400	5,000	9,500	—	—	—
1787, Mailed Bust Facing Right, Muttonhead		158	390	525	775	1,600	3,750	10,000	—
1787, Mailed Bust Facing Left		160	160	235	305	455	900	2,800	—
1787, Mailed Bust Facing Left, Laughing Head		161	260	360	455	650	2,050	7,500	12,000

	GSID	VG-8	F-12	VF-20	EF-40	AU-50	MS-60	MS-63
1787, Mailed Bust Facing Left, Horned Bust	163	$160	$275	$365	$650	$1,150	$3,750	$5,500
1787, Mailed Bust Facing Left, Hercules Head	162	2,050	2,750	3,550	6,250	—	—	—
1787, Mailed Bust Facing Left, Dated 1787 Over 1877	341	290	390	775	1,900	5,000	—	—
1787, Mailed Bust Facing Left, Dated 1787 Over 88	340	525	1,000	1,250	2,750	4,500	—	—
1787, Mailed Bust Facing Left, CONNECT, INDE	164	390	490	650	1,150	1,700	3,750	—
1787, Mailed Bust Facing Left, CONNECT, INDL	375240	725	1,550	3,100	6,250	—	—	—
1787, Draped Bust Facing Left	165	100	150	260	650	850	2,000	6,250
1787, Draped Bust Facing Left, AUCIORI	166	180	240	325	725	1,500	4,250	—
1787, Draped Bust Facing Left, AUCTOPI	167	260	365	525	1,250	3,000	—	—
1787, Draped Bust Facing Left, AUCTOBI	168	300	375	550	950	1,400	—	—
1787, Draped Bust Facing Left, CONNFC	169	130	195	280	900	1,550	2,750	10,500
1787, Draped Bust Facing Left, CONNLC	170	390	525	650	1,150	1,750	—	—
1787, Draped Bust Facing Left, FNDE	171	260	340	390	850	1,250	—	—
1787, Draped Bust Facing Left, ETLIR	172	145	195	310	550	1,500	3,250	—
1787, Draped Bust Facing Left, ETIIB	173	145	290	550	2,600	3,750	—	—
1787, GEORGIVS III Obverse, INDE*ET Reverse	375241	3,250	4,500	6,250	—	—	—	—
1788, Mailed Bust Facing Right	229	325	360	390	725	1,250	7,500	31,000
1788, GEORGIVS III Obverse, INDE*ET Reverse	375242	230	490	1,100	2,500	—	—	—
1788, Mailed Bust Facing Right, Small Head	230	3,000	6,000	8,000	14,500	—	—	—
1788, Mailed Bust Facing Left	231	130	195	390	650	1,600	3,750	7,500
1788, Mailed Bust Facing Left, CONNLC	232	260	470	850	4,400	—	—	—
1788, Draped Bust Facing Left	233	155	260	360	470	1,250	3,600	11,000
1788, Draped Bust Facing Left, CONNLC	235	260	490	725	2,300	3,900	12,000	31,000
1788, Draped Bust Facing Left, INDL ET LIB	236	455	650	1,100	1,900	2,500	5,500	—

New York and Related Issues (1780s)

No official state coinage for New York is known to have been authorized. However, a number of issues in copper and gold were made relating to the state, by a variety of different issuers.

Brasher Doubloons (1786–1787)

Among the most famous early American pieces coined before establishment of the U.S. Mint at Philadelphia were those produced by the well-known New York City silversmith, goldsmith, and jeweler Ephraim Brasher, who was a neighbor and friend of George Washington's when that city was the seat of the federal government. The gold pieces Brasher made weighed about 408 grains and were valued at $15 in New York currency. They were approximately equal to the Spanish doubloon, which was equal to 16 Spanish dollars.

Pieces known as *Lima Style doubloons* were dated 1742, but it is almost certain that they were produced in 1786, and were the first efforts of Brasher to make a circulating coin for regional use. Neither of the two known specimens shows the full legends; but weight, gold content, and hallmark are all identical to those for the 1787-dated Brasher coins. An analogous cast imitation Lima style doubloon dated 1735 bears a hallmark attributed to Standish Barry of Baltimore, Maryland, circa 1787.

The design used on the 1787 Brasher doubloon features an eagle on one side and the arms of New York on the other. In addition to his impressed hallmark, Brasher's name appears in small letters on each of his coins. The unique 1787 gold half doubloon is struck from doubloon dies on an undersized planchet that weighs half as much as the larger coins. It is in the National Numismatic Collection in the Smithsonian Institution. It is uncertain why Brasher produced these pieces. He may have produced them for his own account, charging a nominal fee to convert metal into coin. He was later commissioned by the government to test and verify other gold coins then in circulation. His hallmark EB was punched on each coin as evidence of his testing and its value. In some cases the foreign coins were weight-adjusted by clipping.

		GSID	AU-50	AU-55	MS-61	MS-63	MS-65
"1742" (1786) Lima Style doubloon, Gold	2 known	377	—	—	$2,520,000	—	—
	Auctions: $2,100,000, NGC MS-61 HA 01/21						
1787 New York doubloon, Gold, E•B on Breast	unique	180	$7,320,000	—	—	—	—
	Auctions: $2,990,000, NGC EF-45 HA 01/05						
1787 New York doubloon, Gold, E•B on Wing	7 known	179	—	$3,000,000	—	$4,800,000	$11,220,000
	Auctions: $9,360,000, NGC MS-65 HA 01/21						
1787 New York half doubloon, Gold (in Smithsonian Collection)	unique	152	—	—	—	—	—
Various foreign gold coins with Brasher's E•B hallmark		375243	—	—	—	—	—

New York Copper Coinage

Several individuals petitioned the New York Legislature in early 1787 for the right to coin copper for the state, but a coinage was never authorized. Instead, a law was passed to regulate the copper coins already in use. Nevertheless, various unauthorized copper pieces were made privately and issued within the state.

One private mint known as Machin's Mills was organized by Captain Thomas Machin, a distinguished veteran of the Revolutionary War, and situated at the outlet of Orange Pond near Newburgh, New York. Shortly after this mint was formed, on April 18, 1787, it was merged with the Rupert, Vermont, mint operated by Reuben Harmon Jr., who held a coinage grant from the Republic of Vermont. The combined partnership agreed to conduct their business in New York, Vermont, Connecticut, or elsewhere if they could benefit by it (though their only known operation was the one at Newburgh).

The operations at Machin's Mills were conducted in secret and were looked upon with suspicion by the local residents. They minted several varieties of imitation George III halfpence, as well as counterfeit coppers of Connecticut and New Jersey. Only their Vermont coppers had official status.

Mints located in or near New York City were operated by John Bailey and Ephraim Brasher. They had petitioned the legislature on February 12, 1787, for a franchise to coin copper. The extent of their partnership, if any, and details of their operation are unknown. Studies of the state coinage show that they produced primarily the EXCELSIOR and NOVA EBORAC pieces of New York, and possibly the "running fox" New Jersey coppers.

1786, NON VI VIRTUTE VICI
Believed to be the bust of George Washington.

1787, EXCELSIOR, Eagle on Globe Facing Left

1787, EXCELSIOR, Large Eagle on Obverse

1787, George Clinton

1787, Indian and New York Arms

1787, Indian and Eagle on Globe

1787, Indian and George III Reverse

		GSID	VG-8	F-12	VF-20	EF-40	AU-50	AU-55
1786, NON VI VIRTUTE VICI, Large Head		146	—	—	—	—	$264,000	$312,000
	Auctions: $264,000, NGC AU-55 HA 01/21							
1786, NON VI VIRTUTE VICI, Small Head		147	$12,000	$14,500	$17,000	$24,000	31,000	48,000
	Auctions: $180,000, NGC MS-64 HA 01/21							
1787 EXCELSIOR, Eagle on Globe Facing Right		213	—	11,000	14,500	31,000	54,000	—
	Auctions: $105,000, NGC AU-58 HA 05/22							
1787 EXCELSIOR, Eagle on Globe Facing Left		214	—	10,500	14,500	24,000	31,000	48,000
1787 EXCELSIOR, Large Eagle on Obverse, Arrows and Branch Transposed		215	—	17,000	24,000	54,000	120,000	—
	Auctions: $144,000, PCGS AU-53 SBG 03/23							
1787, George Clinton		216	30,000	72,000	101,000	210,000	—	—
	Auctions: $499,375, NGC MS-63 HA 05/14							
1787, Indian and New York Arms		217	27,500	36,000	41,000	50,500	57,500	—
	Auctions: $204,000, NGC MS-64 HA 01/21							
1787, Indian and Eagle on Globe		218	—	14,500	19,000	67,000	90,000	132,000
	Auctions: $228,000, NGC MS-65 HA 01/21							
1787, Indian and George III Reverse	4 known	219	—	—	—	—	—	—

British Copper Coins and Their Imitations
(Including Machin's Mills and Other Underweight Coinage of 1786–1789)

The most common copper coin used for small transactions in early America was the British halfpenny. Wide acceptance and the non–legal-tender status of these copper coins made them a prime choice for unauthorized reproduction by private individuals.

Many such counterfeits were created in America by striking from locally made dies, or by casting or other crude methods. Some were made in England and imported into this country. Pieces dated 1781 and 1785 seem to have been made specifically for this purpose, while others were circulated in both countries.

Genuine regal British halfpence and farthings minted in London and dated 1749 are of special interest to collectors because they were specifically sent to the North American colonies as reimbursement for participation in the expedition against Cape Breton, and circulated extensively throughout New England.

Genuine British halfpenny coppers of both George II (dated 1729–1754) and George III (dated 1770–1775) show finely detailed features within a border of close denticles; the 1 in the date looks like a J. They are boldly struck on good-quality planchets. Their weight is approximately 9.5 grams; their diameter, 29 mm.

British-made lightweight imitation halfpence are generally smaller in diameter and thickness, and weigh less than genuine pieces. Details are crudely engraved or sometimes incomplete. Inscriptions may be misspelled. Planchet quality may be poor.

	G	VG	F	VF	EF
1749, George II British farthing	$20	$40	$75	$175	$250
1749, George II British halfpenny	25	50	100	200	300
1770–1775, George III British halfpenny (a)	15	20	50	100	250
1770–1775, British imitation halfpenny (a)	15	20	25	100	250

a. Values shown are for the most common variety. Rare pieces are sometimes worth significantly more.

During the era of American state coinage, New York diemaker James F. Atlee and/or other coiners minted unauthorized, lightweight, imitation British halfpence. These American-made false coins have the same or similar devices, legends, and, in some cases, dates as genuine regal halfpence, but they contain less copper. Their details are often poorly rendered or missing. Identification of American-made imitations has been confirmed by identifying certain punch marks (such as letters and numerals) and matching them to the distinct punch marks of known engravers.

There are four distinct groups of these halfpence, all linked to the regular state coinage. The first group was probably struck in New York City prior to 1786. The second group was minted in New York City in association with John Bailey and Ephraim Brasher during the first half of 1787. The third group was struck at Machin's Mills during the second half of 1787 and into 1788 or later. A fourth group, made by the Machin's Mills coiners, consists of pieces made from dies that were muled with false dies of the state coinages of Connecticut, Vermont, and New York. Pieces with very crude designs and other dates are believed to have been struck elsewhere in New England.

Georgivs/Britannia

"Machin's Mills" Copper Halfpennies Made in America

Dates used on these pieces were often "evasive," as numismatists describe them today. They include dates not used on genuine pieces and, sometimes, variations in spelling. They are as follows: 1771, 1772, 1774, 1775, and 1776 for the first group; 1747 and 1787 for the second group; and 1776, 1778, 1787, and 1788 for the third group. Pieces generally attributed to James Atlee can be identified by a single outline in the crosses (British Union) of Britannia's shield and large triangular denticles along the coin circumference. The more-valuable American-made pieces are not to be confused with the similar English-made George III counterfeits (some of which have identical dates), or with genuine British halfpence dated 1770 to 1775.

The muled coins of Group IV are listed separately with the Immune Columbia pieces and with the coins of Connecticut, Vermont, and New York. Other imitation coppers made by unidentified American makers are generally very crude and exceedingly rare. Cast copies of British coins probably circulated along with the imitations without being questioned. Counterfeits of silver Spanish-American coins and Massachusetts tree coins may have also been coined by American minters.

Group I coins dated 1771, 1772, 1774, 1775, and 1776 have distinctive bold designs but lack the fine details of the original coins. Planchets are generally of high quality.

Group II coins dated 1747 and 1787 are generally poorly made. The 1 in the date is not J-shaped, and the denticles are of various sizes. There are no outlines to the stripes in the shield.

Group III coins dated 1776, 1778, 1787, and 1788, struck at Machin's Mills in Newburgh, New York, are similar to coins of Group II, with their triangular-shaped denticles. Most have large dates and berries in the obverse wreath.

	GSID	VG-8	F-12	VF-20	EF-40	AU-50	MS-60
1747, GEORGIVS II, Group II	322	$490	$625	$1,150	$4,700	$7,500	—
1771, GEORGIVS III, Group I	323	310	525	775	2,000	—	—
1772, GEORGIVS III, Group I	69671	825	1,150	2,400	5,500	—	—
1772, GEORGIUS III, Group I	70496	—	3,750	—	—	—	—
1774, GEORGIVS III, Group I	70493	340	495	650	3,450	—	—
1774, GEORGIUS III, Group I	69674	440	—	775	—	—	—
1775, GEORGIVS III, Group I	327	310	390	575	1,600	—	—
1776, GEORGIVS III, Group III, Large Date	328	340	525	875	2,500	5,500	—
1776, GEORCIVS III, Group III, Small Date	329	7,250	8,750	12,000	19,000	—	—
1778, GEORGIVS III, Group III	331	210	285	340	950	1,900	$7,000
1784, GEORGIVS III	213349	825	1,150	2,500	4,500	—	—
1787, GEORGIVS III, Group II and III	338	155	180	245	575	900	3,000
1788, GEORGIVS III, Group III	342	195	370	525	1,200	1,550	5,000

Note: Values shown are for the most common varieties in each category. Rare pieces can be worth significantly more. Also see related George III combinations under Connecticut, Vermont, and New York.

NOVA EBORAC COINAGE FOR NEW YORK

An extensive issue of 1787-dated copper coins appeared, each with a bust on the obverse surrounded by NOVA EBORAC ("New York"). The reverse showed a seated goddess with a sprig in one hand and a liberty cap on a pole in the other hand, with the legend VIRT. ET. LIB. ("Virtue and Liberty") surrounding, and the date 1787 below. The letter punches used on this issue are identical to those used on the Brasher doubloon die. It is likely that John Bailey and Ephraim Brasher operated a minting shop in New York City and produced these and possibly other issues.

1787, NOVA EBORAC, Reverse: Seated Figure Facing Right

1787, NOVA EBORAC, Reverse: Seated Figure Facing Left

1787, NOVA EBORAC, Small Head

1787, NOVA EBORAC, Large Head

	GSID	G-4	VG-8	F-12	VF-20	EF-40	AU-50	MS-60
1787, NOVA EBORAC, Seated Figure Facing Right	174	$155	$210	$340	$525	$1,000	$1,750	$5,000
1787, NOVA EBORAC, Seated Figure Facing Left	175	230	290	340	495	900	1,100	4,000
1787, NOVA EBORAC, Small Head	176	2,800	3,750	6,250	10,500	29,000	—	—
1787, NOVA EBORAC, Large Head	177	950	1,250	1,750	3,000	8,000	10,500	16,000

NEW JERSEY (1786–1788)

On June 1, 1786, the New Jersey General Assembly granted to businessman and investor Thomas Goadsby, silversmith and assayer Albion Cox, and minter Walter Mould authority to coin three million coppers weighing six pennyweight and six grains (150 grains total, or 9.72 grams) apiece, to be completed by June 1788, on condition that they deliver to the state treasurer "one Tenth Part of the full Sum they shall strike." These coppers were to pass current at 15 to the shilling. Revolutionary War hero and New Jersey state legislator Matthias Ogden also played a significant financial and political role in the operation.

In an undertaking of this kind, the contractors purchased the metal and assumed all expenses of coining. The difference between these expenses and the total face value of the coins issued represented their profit.

Later, Goadsby and Cox asked authority to coin two-thirds of the total independently of Mould. Their petition was granted November 22, 1786. Mould was known to have produced his coins at Morristown, while Cox and Goadsby operated in Rahway. Coins with a diameter of 30 mm or more are generally considered Morristown products. Coins were also minted in Elizabethtown by Ogden and, without authority, by Machin's Mills.

The obverse shows design elements of the state seal, a horse's head with plow, and the legend NOVA CÆSAREA (New Jersey). The reverse has a United States shield and, for the first time on a coin, the legend E PLURIBUS UNUM (One Composed of Many). More than 140 varieties exist. The majority have the horse's head facing to the right; however, three of the 1788 date show the head facing left. Other variations have a sprig beneath the head, branches below the shield, stars, cinquefoils, a running fox, and other ornaments.

1786, Date Under Plow Beam

1786 and 1787, Narrow Shield

1786, Date Under Plow, No Coulter

1786, Straight Plow Beam, Protruding Tongue

1786, Wide Shield

1786, Curved Plow Beam, Bridle Variety

1787, Sprig Above Plow

1787, WM Above Plow

1787, PLURIBS Error

1787, U Over S in PLURIBUS

1787, PLURIRUS Error

1787, Hidden WM

1787 Over 1887

1787, Camel Head

1787, Serpent Head

1788, Fox Before Legend

1788, Indistinct Coulter

1788, Fox After Legend

1788, Braided Mane

1788, Head Facing Left

		GSID	G-4	VG-8	F-12	VF-20	EF-40	AU-50	MS-60	MS-63
1786, Date Under Plow Beam		140	—	—	$120,000	$228,000	$360,000	$552,000	—	—
	Auctions: $552,000, NGC AU-55 HA 01/21									
1786, Date Under Plow, No Coulter		141	$650	$950	2,250	3,000	12,000	21,500	—	—
	Auctions: $114,000, NGC MS-61 HA 01/21									
1786, Narrow Shield (a)		142	160	230	340	650	1,100	1,600	$5,750	—
1786, Straight Plow Beam (b)		374102	130	155	340	600	825	1,250	5,000	$11,000
1786, Curved Plow Beam (b)		374103	130	155	340	600	825	2,500	7,500	17,000
1786, Protruding Tongue		376452	145	175	365	650	1,000	3,450	24,000	43,000
1786, Wide Shield		143	145	175	365	650	1,400	2,000	4,000	11,000
1786, Bridle variety		145	145	175	360	650	1,900	3,450	—	—
1786, PLUKIBUS		376453	260	490	775	1,000	3,250	7,500	—	—
1787, PLURIBS		210	260	490	775	1,000	3,250	8,000	—	—
1787, Second U Over S in PLURIBUS		376454	240	420	650	875	4,500	—	—	—
1787, First U Over S in PLURIBUS		376455	—	—	—	—	—	—	—	—
1787, Sprig Above Plow (b)		376456	145	175	365	650	1,000	3,450	19,000	43,000
1787, No Sprig Above Plow (b)		376457	145	175	365	650	1,000	3,450	19,000	43,000
1787, WM Above Plow	unique	339	—	—	300,000	—	—	—	—	—
	Auctions: $264,000, NGC F-15 HA 03/21									
1787, Hidden WM in Sprig		376458	155	195	405	725	1,150	3,750	10,500	—
1787, Date Over 1887		376459	—	3,750	5,000	8,750	—	—	—	—
1787, Camel Head, Snout in High Relief		211	215	390	525	650	1,000	2,100	4,050	6,500
1787, Serpent Head		212	260	360	405	575	1,500	3,750	—	—
1787, Goiter Variety		376460	575	950	1,250	1,700	3,750	8,000	—	—
1788, Horse's Head Facing Right (several varieties)		237	155	195	260	455	1,000	2,300	—	—
1788, Horse's Head Facing Right, Running Fox Before Legend		238	290	390	525	650	2,500	5,500	—	—
	Auctions: $105,750, NGC MS-65 HA 05/14									
1788, Similar, Indistinct Coulter		376461	2,000	3,750	6,250	14,500	—	—	—	—
1788, Horse's Head Facing Right, Running Fox After Legend		376462	—	—	—	53,000	72,000	—	—	—
1788, Braided Mane		376463	1,250	2,000	3,100	5,000	10,500	18,000	—	—
1788, Horse's Head Facing Left		239	525	725	1,250	3,250	12,000	29,000	—	216,000

a. The Narrow (formerly known as "Pattern") Shield reverse was also used on several speculative patterns; see "Confederatio and Related Tokens." **b.** Common varieties.

PRIVATE TOKENS AFTER CONFEDERATION

The formal ratification of the Articles of Confederation—the document signed amongst the original 13 colonies, which established the United States of America as a confederation of sovereign states and served as its first constitution—was accomplished in early 1781. A number of private coinages sprang up after confederation, intended to facilitate local commerce. These were not the products of the federal government, but were tokens issued by businesses and other private concerns.

North American Tokens (Dated 1781)

These tokens were struck in Dublin, Ireland. The obverse shows the seated figure of Hibernia, the personification of Ireland, facing left. The date of issue is believed to have been much later than that shown on the token (1781). Like many Irish tokens, this issue found its way to America in limited quantities and was accepted in commerce near the Canadian border.

	GSID	VG-8	F-12	VF-20	EF-40	AU-50
1781, Copper or Brass	85	$115	$160	$180	$290	$725

Bar Coppers (ca. 1785)

The Bar coppers are undated and of uncertain origin. They have 13 parallel and unconnected bars on one side. On the other side is the large roman-letter USA monogram. The design is virtually identical to that used on a Continental Army uniform button.

The significance of the design is clearly defined by its extreme simplicity. The separate 13 states (bars) unite into a single entity as symbolized by the interlocking letters (USA).

These pieces are believed to have first circulated in New York during November 1785, as mentioned in a report in the *New Jersey Gazette* of November 12, 1785. They may have been made in England. Although they are scarce, examples enter the marketplace with regularity, and nearly all are in higher grades.

John Adams Bolen (1826–1907), a numismatist and a master diesinker in Springfield, Massachusetts, struck copies of the Bar copper around 1862. On these copies, the letter A passes under, instead of over, the S. Bolen's intent was not to deceive, and he advertised his copies plainly as reproductions. But his skills were such that W. Elliot Woodward, a leading auctioneer of tokens and medals in the 1860s, vacillated between selling Bolen's copies and describing them as "dangerous counterfeits." Bolen copies of the Bar copper are highly collectible in their own right, but they are less valuable than the originals.

	GSID	F-15	VF-20	EF-40	AU-50	MS-60	MS-63
(Circa 1785) Bar Copper	351	$6,000	$6,750	$9,250	$11,000	$21,500	$38,500

Auctori Plebis Tokens (1787)

These tokens are sometimes included with the coins of Connecticut, as they greatly resemble issues of that state. (The obverse features a draped male bust, possibly King George II, wearing laurels and facing left.) They were struck in England by an unknown maker, possibly for use in America.

	GSID	VG-8	F-12	VF-20	EF-40	AU-50	MS-60
1787, AUCTORI PLEBIS	220	$150	$210	$310	$440	$575	$3,250

Mott Store Cards (Dated 1789)

These nineteenth-century store cards have long been included in Early American coin collections because of the date they bear (1789). Most scholars believe these were produced no earlier than 1807 (and possibly in the Hard Times era of the late 1830s) as commemoratives of the founding of the Mott Company, and served as business cards. The firm, operated by Jordan Mott, was located at 240 Water Street, a fashionable section of New York at that time.

The obverse of the token features an eagle with wings spread and an American shield as a breastplate. The eagle holds an olive branch and arrows in his talons. Above is the date 1789, and around the rim is the legend CLOCKS, WATCHES, JEWELRY, SILVERWARE, CHRONOMETERS. The reverse of the token features a regulator clock with the legend MOTT'S N.Y. IMPORTERS, DEALERS, MANUFACTURERS OF GOLD & SILVER WARES.

		GSID	F-12	VF-20	EF-40	AU-50	MS-60	MS-63
"1789," Mott Token, Thick Planchet, Plain Edge		244	$195	$235	$325	$430	$725	$1,000
"1789," Mott Token, Thin Planchet, Plain Edge		245	215	310	420	525	1,100	1,500
"1789," Mott Token, Cent Weight		246	390	650	1,750	2,750	—	3,750
"1789," Mott Token, Thick Planchet, Engrailed Edge		247	260	360	725	1,000	1,750	2,600
"1789," Mott Token, Thin Planchet, Engrailed Edge		248	—	—	—	650	1,150	2,000
"1789," Mott Token, White Metal	unique	249	—	—	—	—	14,500	—

Standish Barry Threepence (1790)

Standish Barry, of Baltimore, was a watch- and clockmaker, an engraver, and, later, a silversmith. In 1790 he circulated a silver threepence of his own fabrication. The tokens are believed to have been an advertising venture at a time when small change was scarce. The precise date on this piece may indicate that Barry intended to commemorate Independence Day, but there are no records to prove this. The head on the obverse is probably that of James Calhoun, who was active in Baltimore politics in the 1790s. The legend BALTIMORE TOWN JULY 4, 90, appears in the border. An enigmatic gold doubloon is also attributed to Barry (see "Brasher Doubloons").

Nearly all examples of the silver threepence show significant wear, suggesting that they circulated for a long time.

	GSID	F-12	VF-20	EF-40	EF-45	AU-50
1790 Threepence	250	$12,500	$14,500	$29,000	$33,000	$38,500
	Auctions: $143,750, NGC AU-55 GLDB 09/08					

Albany Church Pennies (1790)

The First Presbyterian Church of Albany, New York, authorized an issue of 1,000 copper uniface tokens in 1790. These passed at 12 to a shilling. They were used to encourage parishioner donations (at that time, there was a scarcity of small change in circulation). They were also intended to stop contributions of worn and counterfeit coppers (in the words of the church elders' resolution, "in order to add respect to the weekly collections"). Two varieties were made, one with the addition of a large D (the abbreviation for *denarium*, or penny, in the British monetary system) above the word CHURCH. All are rare, with fewer than a dozen of each variety known.

	GSID	VG-10	F-12	VF-20	EF-40	EF-40	AU-50
(1790) Without D	346	$12,500	$15,000	$18,000	$23,000	$25,000	$30,000
(1790) With D Added	345	17,000	—	24,000	54,000	60,000	62,500
	Auctions: $115,000, PCGS EF-45 HA 01/12						

Kentucky Tokens (ca. 1792–1794)

These tokens were struck in England circa 1792 to 1794. Their obverse legend reads UNANIMITY IS THE STRENGTH OF SOCIETY; the central motif is a hand holding a scroll with the inscription OUR CAUSE IS JUST. The reverse shows a pyramid of 15 starbursts surrounded by rays. Each star in the triangle represents a state, identified by its initial letter. These pieces are usually called *Kentucky cents* or *Kentucky tokens* because the letter K (for Kentucky) happens to be at the top. Some of the edges are plain; others are milled with a diagonal reeding; and some have edge lettering that reads PAYABLE IN LANCASTER LONDON OR BRISTOL, PAYABLE AT BEDWORTH NUNEATON OR HINKLEY, or PAYABLE AT I. FIELDING, etc.

These are not known to have circulated in America. Rather, they were made as produced as collectibles, popular among English numismatists and others at the time. Likely more than 1,000 Kentucky tokens are in the hands of numismatists today.

	GSID	VF-20	EF-40	AU-50	MS-60	MS-63
(1792–1794), Plain Edge	361	$195	$300	$435	$575	$850
(1792–1794), Lettered Edge, PAYABLE AT BEDWORTH, etc.	367	—	—	3,100	—	—
(1792–1794), Lettered Edge, PAYABLE AT LANCASTER, etc.	370	195	325	390	650	850
(1792–1794), Engrailed Edge	364	525	675	900	1,250	2,000
(1792–1794), Lettered Edge, PAYABLE AT I FIELDING, etc.	373	—	—	—	2,300	3,000
(1792–1794), Birmingham Edge	373806	—	—	3,000	—	—
(1792–1794), PAYABLE AT W. PARKER, etc.	376	—	—	—	—	—

FRANKLIN PRESS TOKENS (1794)

These were English tradesman's tokens of the kind collected by English numismatists in the late 1700s and early 1800s. (As a group, they were popularly called Conder tokens, after James Conder, the man who first cataloged them for collectors.) The Franklin Press tokens did not circulate as money in America, but, being associated with a London shop where Benjamin Franklin once worked, they have long been included in American coin collections.

The obverse features a wood-frame printing press of the style that Benjamin Franklin would have operated by hand as a printer in England in 1725. He had left Philadelphia at the age of 18 to buy printing supplies in London and look for work. Around the central design is the legend SIC ORITOR DOCTRINA SURGETQUE LIBERTAS ("Thus Learning Advances and Liberty Grows"), and below is the date, 1794. The reverse legend reads PAYABLE AT THE FRANKLIN PRESS LONDON.

Most are plain-edged, but rare lettered-edge varieties exist, as well as a unique piece with a diagonally reeded edge.

	GSID	VF-20	EF-40	AU-50	MS-60	MS-63
1794, Franklin Press Token	282	$340	$415	$525	$800	$1,250

TALBOT, ALLUM & LEE CENTS (1794–1795)

Talbot, Allum & Lee was a firm of importers engaged in the India trade and located at 241 Pearl Street, New York. It placed a large quantity of English-made coppers in circulation during 1794 and 1795.

ONE CENT appears on the 1794 issue, and the legend PAYABLE AT THE STORE OF on the edge. The denomination is not found on the 1795 reverse but the edge legend was changed to read WE PROMISE TO PAY THE BEARER ONE CENT. Rare plain-edged specimens of both dates exist. Exceptional pieces have edges ornamented or with lettering CAMBRIDGE BEDFORD AND HUNTINGDON.X.X.

It is estimated that more than 200,000 of these tokens were minted, though no original records have been located. Varieties and mulings are known; the values shown here are for the most common types.

Many undistributed tokens were sold to the Philadelphia Mint in a time of copper shortage. These were cut down and used by the Mint as planchets for coining 1795 and 1797 half cents.

1794 Cent, With NEW YORK

1795 Cent

	GSID	VG-8	F-12	VF-20	EF-40	AU-50	MS-60	MS-63	MS-65
1794 Cent, With NEW YORK	275	$130	$260	$300	$415	$495	$875	$1,250	$3,250
1794 Cent, Without NEW YORK	278	—	1,550	2,000	3,000	6,000	—	—	—
1795 Cent	299	—	—	—	310	365	650	875	2,100

Myddelton Tokens (1796)

Philip Parry Price Myddelton was an Englishman who bought land in America after the Revolutionary War. He hoped to begin a vibrant farming community along the Ohio River and entice English craftsmen and workers to move there. To this end he contracted the design of a promotional token and had examples made in copper and silver. These tokens were struck at the Soho Mint of Boulton and Watt near Birmingham, England. Although their obverse legend reads BRITISH SETTLEMENT KENTUCKY, and Myddelton planned to order large quantities of the copper version for shipment to the United States, they were never actually issued for circulation in Kentucky. The entrepreneur was arrested in August 1796 and convicted in London for the crime of convincing hundreds of workers to leave England for America. He was jailed in Newgate prison for three and a half years, which ended his Kentucky plans.

The obverse of Myddelton's token shows Hope presenting two "little genii" (his description) to the goddess Liberty. She welcomes them with an open hand. At her feet is a flourishing sapling and a cornucopia representing America's bounty, and she holds a pole with a liberty cap. On the reverse, seated Britannia leans wearily on a downward-pointing spear, looking at the broken scale and fasces—symbols of unity, justice, and liberty—scattered at her feet.

Sylvester S. Crosby, in *The Early Coins of America*, remarked that "In beauty of design and execution, the tokens are unsurpassed by any piece issued for American circulation."

	GSID	PF-60	PF-63	PF-65
1796, Copper	310	$12,000	$16,500	$22,000
1796, Silver	313	12,000	16,000	33,000
	Auctions: $149,662, Uncert AG-0 SC 07/11			

Copper Company of Upper Canada Tokens (Early 1800s)

These pieces were struck some time in the early 1800s. The obverse is the same as that of the Myddelton token. The new reverse refers to a Canadian firm, the Copper Company of Upper Canada, with the denomination ONE HALF PENNY. These tokens may have been made for numismatic purposes (for sale to collectors), or as part of the coiner's samples. Their maker is unknown. Restrikes were made in England in the 1890s.

	GSID	PF-60	PF-63	PF-65
1796, Copper Company of Upper Canada	314	$4,750	$5,500	$7,000

CASTORLAND MEDALS (1796)

These medals, or "jetons," are dated 1796 and allude to a proposed French settlement known as Castorland. This was to be located on the Black River, in northern New York, not far from the Canadian border. Peter Chassanis of Paris had acquired land that he and others intended to parcel into large farms, with Chassanis heading the settlement's government, two commissaries residing at its seat, Castorville, and four commissaries headquartered in Paris. The medals were to be given as payment ("in recognition of the care which they may bestow upon the common concerns") to the Parisian directors of the colonizing company for their attendance at board meetings.

Some 20 French families, many of them aristocratic refugees from the French Revolution, moved to the settlement between 1796 and 1800. Challenges including sickness, harsh northern New York winters, loss of livestock, and theft of finances proved too much for the company, and Castorland was dissolved in 1814. Many of the surviving settlers moved to more prosperous American communities or returned to Europe.

The obverse of the Castorland medal features a profile portrait of the ancient goddess Sybele, associated with mountains, town and city walls, fertile nature, and wild animals. She wears a *corona muralis* ("walled crown"), laurels, and a draped head covering. The legend reads FRANCO-AMERICANA COLONIA, with CASTORLAND 1796 below. On the reverse the goddess Ceres, patroness of agriculture, stands at a maple with a sap drill while the tree's bounty flows into a waiting bucket. Ceres holds a cornucopia; at her feet are a sickle and a sheaf of wheat. A beaver at the bottom of the reverse further symbolizes Castorland and its resources (*castor* is French for "beaver," an animal crucial to the very profitable North American fur trade in the early 1800s). The legend, in Latin, is SALVE MAGNA PARENS FRUGUM—"Hail, Great Mother of Crops" (from Virgil).

Copy dies of the Castorland medal are still available and have been used at the Paris Mint for restriking throughout the years. Restrikes have a more modern look than originals; their metallic content (in French) is impressed on the edge: ARGENT (silver), CUIVRE (copper), or OR (gold).

	GSID	F-12	VF-20	EF-40	AU-50	MS-60	MS-63
1796, Original, Silver (reeded edge, unbroken dies)	306	$1,750	$2,100	$4,500	$6,500	$9,000	$11,000
1796, Original, Silver (reverse rusted and broken)	375351	—	—	—	—	2,250	2,800
1796, Original, Bronze (reverse rusted and broken)	307	—	2,200	2,500	2,800	3,550	4,400
(1796), Restrike, Silver (Paris Mint edge marks)	375352	—	—	—	—	130	455
(1796), Restrike, Bronze (Paris Mint edge marks)	375353	—	—	—	—	175	235

THEATRE AT NEW YORK TOKENS (CA. 1798)

These penny tokens were issued by Skidmore of London and illustrate the New Theatre (later known as the Park Theatre) in Manhattan, as it appeared circa 1797. The theater was New York City's attempt at a prestigious new level of entertainment, as the famous John Street Theatre (the "Birthplace of American Theater") was suffering from poor management and physical decay in the 1790s. The building's cornerstone was laid on May 5, 1795, and the theater opened on January 29, 1798, with a presentation of entertainments including Shakespeare's *As You Like It*.

The obverse of this copper token features a view of the playhouse building with the legend THE THEATRE AT NEW YORK AMERICA. The reverse shows an allegorical scene of a cornucopia on a dock, with bales, an anchor, and sailing ships. The legend reads MAY COMMERCE FLOURISH. The edge is marked I PROMISE TO PAY ON DEMAND THE BEARER ONE PENNY.

All known examples are struck in copper and have a Proof finish. They were made for collectors, not for use as advertising. Today examples are scarce, with about 20 known.

		GSID	AU-50	PF-60	PF-63	PF-65
Penny, THE THEATRE AT NEW YORK AMERICA	20 est. known	315	$10,500	$13,000	$17,000	$30,000

New Spain (Texas) Jola Tokens (1817–1818)

In 1817 the Spanish governor of Texas, Colonel Manuel Pardo, authorized Manuel Barrera to produce 8,000 copper coins known as jolas. These crudely made pieces show the denomination 1/2 [real], the maker's initials and the date on the obverse, and a five-pointed star on the reverse.

The 1817 coins were withdrawn from circulation the following year and replaced by a similar issue of 8,000 pieces. These bear the date 1818 and the initials, JAG, of the maker, José Antonio de la Garza. Several varieties of each issue are known. All are rare.

	GSID	F-12	VF-20	EF-40	AU-50
1817 1/2 Real	375264	$14,500	$24,000	$42,000	—
1818 1/2 Real, Large Size	316	15,000	27,000	36,000	$48,000
1818 1/2 Real, Small Size	317	15,000	24,000	34,000	54,000

North West Company Tokens (1820)

These tokens were probably valued at one beaver skin and struck in Birmingham, England, in 1820 by John Walker & Co. All but two known specimens are holed. Most have been found in Oregon in the region of the Columbia and Umpqua river valleys. They feature a portrait of King George IV on the obverse, with the legend TOKEN and the date 1820. The reverse shows a beaver in the wild, with the legend NORTH WEST COMPANY.

Holed Brass Token

James A. Haxby, in the *Guide Book of Canadian Coins and Tokens*, writes, "The pieces actually issued for circulation were pierced at the top for suspension or stringing. Unholed copper strikes are known with plain or engrailed edge and are very rare. A number of pieces have been found buried in western Canada and as far south as central Oregon."

Unholed Copper Token

	GSID	G-4	VG-8	F-12	VF-20	EF-40	AU-50
1820, Brass, Holed	213350	$1,900	$2,500	$4,050	$6,250	$10,000	$18,000
1820, Copper, Holed	318	3,750	5,500	8,250	11,000	18,000	—
1820, Copper, Unholed, Plain or Engrailed Edge	375265	—	—	—	—	—	24,000

WASHINGTON PIECES

Medals, tokens, and coinage proposals in this interesting series dated from 1783 to 1795 bear the portrait of George Washington. The likenesses in most instances were faithfully reproduced and were designed to honor the first president. Many of these pieces were of English origin and, although dated 1783, probably were made in the 1820s or later.

The legends generally signify a strong unity among the states and the marked display of patriotism that pervaded the new nation during that period. We find among some of these tokens an employment of what were soon to become the nation's official coin devices, namely, the American eagle, the United States shield, and stars. The denomination ONE CENT is used in several instances, while on some of the English pieces HALFPENNY will be found. Several of these pieces were private patterns for proposed coinage contracts.

Georgivs Triumpho Tokens

Although the head shown on these tokens bears a strong resemblance to that on some coins of King George III, many collectors consider the Georgivs Triumpho ("Triumphant George") tokens a commemorative of America's victory in the Revolutionary War.

The reverse side shows the Goddess of Liberty behind a framework of 13 bars and fleurs-de-lis. Holding an olive branch in her right hand and staff of liberty in her left, she is partially encircled by the words VOCE POPOLI ("By the Voice of the People") 1783. An example is known used as an undertype for a 1787 New Jersey copper.

	GSID	VG-8	F-12	VF-20	EF-40	AU-50	MS-60	MS-63	MS-65
1783, GEORGIVS TRIUMPHO	92	$195	$290	$325	$575	$850	$2,800	$7,500	—

Washington Portrait Pieces (1780s to Early 1800s)

Military Bust. "The 1783-dated Washington Military Bust coppers bear a portrait, adapted (with a different perspective on the coin and a wreath added to the head) from a painting by Edward Savage," writes Q. David Bowers in the *Whitman Encyclopedia of Colonial and Early American Coins*. "These seem to have circulated in England as well as America. . . . Many varieties exist, but they are not well known outside of a circle of specialists. Accordingly, the opportunity exists to acquire rare die combinations for little premium over a regular issue."

The reverse features a seated female figure holding an olive branch and a pole topped by a liberty cap. Values shown are for the most common varieties.

1783, Large Military Bust, Point of Bust Close to W

1783, Small Military Bust

	GSID	VG-8	F-12	VF-20	EF-40	AU-50	MS-60	MS-63	MS-65
1783, Large Military Bust	93	$155	$195	$260	$390	$470	$1,150	$2,500	—
1783, Small Military Bust, Plain Edge	96	130	170	230	440	525	1,200	—	—
1783, Small Military Bust, Engrailed Edge	97	150	190	285	550	900	2,500	—	—

Draped Bust. Draped Bust coppers dated 1783 depict Washington with the top of a toga draped over his shoulder. One variety includes a button at the folds in front of the toga. Another variety has no button, and has the initial "I" (for Ingram) in the toga, above the right side of the numeral 3 in the date. Both varieties feature a similar reverse design with a female figure seated on a rock, holding an olive branch and a pole surmounted by a liberty cap.

1783, Draped Bust, No Button

With Button

	GSID	VG-8	F-12	VF-20	EF-40	AU-50	MS-60	MS-63	MS-65
1783, Draped Bust, No Button	98	$155	$180	$215	$470	$525	$900	$1,350	$5,000
1783, Draped Bust, With Button (on Drapery at Neck)	99	150	215	325	525	1,400	—	—	—
1783, Draped Bust, Copper Restrike, Plain Edge, Proof	332	—	—	—	—	—	525	725	1,000
1783, Draped Bust, Copper Restrike, Engrailed Edge, Proof	334	—	—	—	—	—	575	725	1,000
1783, Draped Bust, Silver Restrike, Engrailed Edge, Proof	337	—	—	—	—	1,400	3,250	4,750	8,750

Unity States. The 1783-dated coppers with the legend UNITY STATES OF AMERICA were likely coined in the early 1800s at the Soho Mint in Birmingham, England. The obverse features a portrait of Washington in a toga and wearing laurels. The reverse is a copy of the wreath design on the copper cent produced by the Philadelphia Mint from 1796 to 1807, with UNITED spelled UNITY, perhaps as a way to evade charges of counterfeiting.

Despite the American denomination of this piece, they likely circulated in England (at the value of a halfpenny), as reflected by examples being found there in quantity in later years. They were imported into the United States as well, for use as a cent, and are mentioned in several counterfeit-detector publications in the 1850s.

1783, Unity States

	GSID	VG-8	F-12	VF-20	EF-40	AU-50	MS-60	MS-63	MS-65
1783, UNITY STATES	100	$135	$180	$220	$340	$430	$1,000	$2,400	—

Double Head. Although the Washington Double Head cents are undated, some numismatists assign them a date of 1783, given their resemblance to the Military Bust coppers that bear that date (even though those were probably struck years later). They were likely struck in Birmingham, England, by Edward Thomason sometime in the 1820s or later. They were made in England, as evidenced by many having been found there, but long after the Conder token era. They are denominated ONE CENT and, when exported to the United States, circulated along with Hard Times tokens of the 1830s.

Undated Double-Head Cent

	GSID	VG-8	F-12	VF-20	EF-40	AU-50	MS-60	MS-63	MS-65
(Undated) Double-Head Cent	352	$155	$180	$260	$390	$525	$1,400	$2,900	—

Ugly Head. The so-called Ugly Head token is a medalet struck in copper and white-metal varieties, possibly satirical, and presumably of American origin. The token's legend reads WASHINGTON THE GREAT D.G. The abbreviation "D.G." on English coins stands for Dei Gratia ("By the Grace of God"), and the portrait appears to be wigless and possibly toothless, leading some numismatists to opine that the token is a satire on George Washington. Bowers notes that the token's date, 1784, has no particular significance in Washington's life. By that year the American Revolution was over and the general had retired his commission as commander-in-chief of the Continental Army. He would not assume the presidency until 1789. The reverse of the token features a design of linked rings with abbreviations for the British colonies, reminiscent of the 1776 Continental dollar.

1784, Ugly Head

		GSID	VG-8	F-12	VF-20	EF-40	AU-50	MS-60	MS-63	MS-65
1784, Ugly Head, Pewter	unique	373809	—	—	$48,000	—	—	—	—	—
1784, Ugly Head, Copper		109	—	—	37,000	—	—	—	—	—

Small and Large Eagle. Small Eagle and Large Eagle one-cent tokens dated 1791 were made in Birmingham, England, sponsored by merchants W. and Alex Walker of that city as proposals for official American coinage. Bowers writes in the *Whitman Encyclopedia of Colonial and Early American Coins* that the Walker firm "shipped a cask filled with these cents, estimated to be about 2,500 Large Eagle and 1,500 Small Eagle coins, to Thomas Ketland & Sons, a Philadelphia contact, to be distributed to legislators. The depiction of Washington was contrary to the president's own desires, who felt that having his image on coins would appear to have the 'stamp of royalty.'"

1791 Cent, Small Eagle Reverse,
Edge Lettered UNITED STATES OF AMERICA

1791 Cent, Large Eagle Reverse

	GSID	VG-8	F-12	VF-20	EF-40	AU-50	MS-60	MS-63	MS-65
1791 Cent, Small Eagle (Date on Reverse)	255	$340	$420	$525	$900	$1,250	$2,000	$3,500	$5,500
1791 Cent, Small Eagle, Brass	343	—	—	—	—	—	—	—	—
1791 Cent, Large Eagle (Date on Obverse)	253	415	525	775	1,000	1,450	1,900	3,250	5,500

Liverpool. The Liverpool Halfpenny tokens were most likely made around 1793. They were intended for circulation as small change in England, although numismatists of the time also sought them for their collections. The obverse shows a uniformed bust of George Washington, as used on the Large Eagle one-cent tokens of 1791. The reverse features a sailing ship and the legend LIVERPOOL HALFPENNY, a design used on various English Conder tokens.

1791 Liverpool Halfpenny

	GSID	VG-8	F-12	VF-20	EF-40	AU-50	MS-60	MS-63	MS-65
1791 Liverpool Halfpenny, Lettered Edge	251	$850	$1,200	$1,300	$2,050	$2,750	—	—	—
1791 Liverpool Halfpenny, Pewter	252	—	—	—	30,000	50,500	—	—	—

1792. An extensive series of 1792-dated Washington pieces was produced in many varieties, bearing no denomination. These apparently were made in England, and were collected by numismatists in addition to circulating as coinage substitutes in America.

1792 Cent, Eagle with 13 Stars Reverse

1792, WASHINGTON PRESIDENT

Legend Reverse

(1792) Undated, WASHINGTON BORN VIRGINIA

1792, Small Eagle Reverse

Large Eagle Reverse

		GSID	VG-8	F-12	VF-20	EF-40	AU-50	MS-60	MS-63	MS-65
1792, WASHINGTON PRESIDENT, Eagle With 13 Stars Reverse, PRESIDENT at Side of Bust, Lettered Edge, Copper		265	—	$90,000	—	$144,000	$192,000	—	—	—
	Auctions: $253,000, PCGS AU-53 SBG 11/06									
1792, WASHINGTON PRESIDENT, Eagle With 13 Stars Reverse, PRESIDENT at Side of Bust, Plain Edge, Copper		266	—	—	$11,000	18,000	26,500	—	—	—
1792, WASHINGTON PRESIDENT, Eagle With 13 Stars Reverse, PRESIDENT at Side of Bust, Lettered Edge, Silver		263	—	—	—	210,000	—	—	—	—
	Auctions: $288,000, NGC EF-45 HA 01/21									
1792, WASHINGTON PRESIDENT, Eagle With 13 Stars Reverse, PRESIDENT at Side of Bust, Plain Edge, Silver		264	—	—	—	—	—	—	—	—
1792, WASHINGTON PRESIDENT, Eagle With 13 Stars Reverse, PRESIDENT at Side of Bust, Plain Edge, Gold	unique	258	—	—	—	2,100,000	—	—	—	—
	Auctions: $1,740,000, NGC EF-45 HA 08/18									
1792, WASHINGTON PRESIDENT, Eagle With 13 Stars Reverse, PRESIDENT Extends Below Bust, Copper	unique	375340	—	—	—	—	—	—	—	—
1792, WASHINGTON PRESIDENT, Legend Reverse, Plain Edge, Copper		267	—	12,000	29,000	48,000	—	—	—	—
1792, WASHINGTON PRESIDENT, Legend Reverse, Lettered Edge, Copper		268	$7,000	12,000	30,000	54,000	84,000	—	—	—
(1792) Undated, WASHINGTON BORN VIRGINIA, Eagle With 13 Stars Reverse, Copper	3 known	414	—	—	—	—	240,000	—	—	—
	Auctions: $212,750, PCGS AU-53 SBG 11/06									
(1792) Undated, WASHINGTON BORN VIRGINIA, Legend Reverse, Plain Edge, Copper		413	1,600	2,100	3,250	6,500	8,000	$17,500	$42,000	$84,000
	Auctions: $172,500, NGC MS-67 SBG 02/08									
(1792) Undated, WASHINGTON BORN VIRGINIA, Legend Reverse, Lettered Edge, Copper	1 known	375341	—	—	—	—	—	—	—	—
(1792) Undated, WASHINGTON BORN VIRGINIA, Legend Reverse, Plain Edge, Silver		411	—	—	—	78,000	—	—	120,000	—
	Auctions: $102,000, NGC MS-64 HA 01/21									
(1792) Undated, WASHINGTON BORN VIRGINIA, Legend Reverse, Lettered Edge, Silver		412	—	—	—	—	—	—	—	—

Peter Getz. Dies engraved by silversmith, mechanic, and inventor Peter Getz of Lancaster, Pennsylvania, are believed to have been made to produce a half dollar and a cent as a proposal to Congress for a private contract coinage before the Philadelphia Mint became a reality. These feature George Washington, in a military bust portrait, and a heraldic eagle.

The 1792-dated Roman Head cents show Washington in the style of an ancient Roman dignitary. These copper pieces were struck in England for collectors, as opposed to being intended for circulation. Their edge is lettered UNITED STATES OF AMERICA.

The 1793 Ship Halfpenny tokens were struck from an overdated (3 Over 2) reverse die. These copper pieces were intended for collectors, but nearly all of them ended up in circulation in England. The more common lettered-edge variety reads PAYABLE IN ANGLESEY LONDON OR LIVERPOOL.

Copper tokens dated 1795 were made in large quantities as promotional pieces for the London firm of Clark & Harris, dealers in stoves and fireplace grates. The die work is attributed to Thomas Wyon, and numismatists believe the pieces were struck in Birmingham, England, for circulation in the British Isles (although collectors saved them as well).

The obverse features a right-facing portrait of George Washington in military uniform. Two varieties exist, Small Buttons and Large Buttons (describing the coats on his frock). The legend reads G. WASHINGTON: THE FIRM FRIEND TO PEACE & HUMANITY.

The reverse shows a fireplace with a coal grate, with legends PAYABLE BY CLARK & HARRIS 13. WORMWOOD St. BISHOPSGATE and LONDON 1795.

Most have a diagonally reeded edge, although some are edge-lettered as PAYABLE AT LONDON LIVERPOOL OR BRISTOL.

1792 Getz Pattern, Small Eagle Reverse

1792, Large Eagle Reverse

1792 Getz Pattern Cent, Roman Head, Edge Lettered UNITED STATES OF AMERICA

1793 Getz Pattern Ship Halfpenny

1795 Getz Pattern Halfpenny, Grate Token, Large Buttons

1795 Getz Pattern Halfpenny, Grate Token, Small Buttons

	GSID	VG-8	F-12	VF-20	EF-40	AU-50	MS-60	MS-63	MS-65
1792, Small Eagle, Plain Edge, Copper	269	$11,000	$12,500	$14,500	$26,500	$36,000	$102,000	$144,000	—
	Auctions: $299,000, PCGS MS-64 SBG 11/06								
1792, Small Eagle, Ornamented Edge (Circles and Squares), Copper	375342	—	—	—	—	—	—	—	—
1792, Large Eagle, Silver	259	—	—	—	—	—	—	—	—
1792, Small Eagle, Silver	260	—	60,000	93,500	144,000	162,000	396,000	—	—
	Auctions: $312,000, NGC AU-58 HA 01/21								
1792, Small Eagle, Ornamented Edge (Circles and Squares), Silver	261	—	—	—	—	—	—	432,000	—
1792, Small Eagle, Ornamented Edge (Leaves), Silver	262	—	—	96,000	—	—	—	—	—
	Auctions: $391,000, Uncert MS-64 SBG 05/04								
1792 Cent, Roman Head, Edge Lettered UNITED STATES OF AMERICA	270	21,500	24,000	29,000	31,000	36,000	48,000	77,000	$108,000
	Auctions: $185,150, PCGS PF-65 SBG 08/11								
1793 Ship Halfpenny, Lettered Edge	272	260	340	390	725	900	2,250	12,000	—
1793 Ship Halfpenny, Plain Edge	273	—	6,000	7,500	9,500	—	—	—	—
1795, Large Buttons, Lettered Edge	287	—	360	430	575	750	950	1,500	5,000
1795, Large Buttons, Reeded Edge	289	135	170	245	390	420	525	650	1,600
1795, Small Buttons, Reeded Edge	291	170	210	260	305	390	775	2,000	—

Liberty and Security. The Liberty and Security halfpenny and penny tokens were made in England in 1795 as collectibles, although the halfpence also circulated widely there as small change. Their designs consist of a portrait of George Washington, identified by name, and a heraldic eagle surmounting a stylized American shield, holding a sprig of olive and several arrows. Some of their edges are plain, and some are lettered with various phrases such as AN ASYLUM FOR THE OPPRESS'D OF ALL NATIONS and BIRMINGHAM REDRUTH & SWANSEA.

Varieties exist in copper and white metal, and with mulings of different reverses.

The common name of this series derives from the reverse legend, LIBERTY AND SECURITY.

1795, Liberty and Security Halfpenny

(1795) Undated, Liberty and Security Penny, ASYLUM Edge

	GSID	VG-8	F-12	VF-20	EF-40	AU-50	MS-60	MS-63	MS-65
1795 Halfpenny, Plain Edge	292	—	$260	$340	$490	$650	—	—	—
1795 Halfpenny, LONDON Edge	293	$215	275	310	405	650	$1,700	$3,250	—
1795 Halfpenny, BIRMINGHAM Edge	294	235	285	360	625	750	1,450	2,750	—
1795 Halfpenny, ASYLUM Edge	295	—	575	775	1,000	1,200	1,900	2,500	—
1795 Penny, ASYLUM Edge	302	—	490	650	850	1,150	—	—	—
(1795), Liberty and Security Penny	415	160	310	420	575	775	1,250	2,000	$5,000
(1795), Liberty and Security Penny, Corded Outer Rims	418	—	—	1,550	2,050	2,250	3,000	3,900	9,500

North Wales. "The undated North Wales halfpenny issues, believed to have been struck in England in the early 1790s (usually listed as 1795, although this may be two or three years after they were coined), are part of the 'evasion halfpence' series. Accordingly, unlike Conder tokens, they were not created for collectors. None are known to have survived with sharp features and in high grades, as is characteristic of cabinet pieces" (*Whitman Encyclopedia of Colonial and Early American Coins*).

(1795) Undated, NORTH WALES Halfpenny

	GSID	VG-8	F-12	VF-20	EF-40	AU-50	MS-60	MS-63	MS-65
(1795), NORTH WALES Halfpenny, Plain Edge	296	$235	$245	$285	$495	$1,150	—	—	—
(1795), Lettered Edge	297	—	1,550	2,500	3,750	6,250	—	—	—
(1795), Two Stars at Each Side of Harp	298	2,100	2,600	4,600	6,000	—	—	—	—

Success Tokens. Small and large types exist of these mysterious pieces of unknown date and purpose. Today known as Success tokens, they may have been souvenirs, perhaps struck to commemorate George Washington's second inauguration (March 1793), or nineteenth-century gaming tokens. They were struck in copper or brass and most likely were made in the mid-1800s. Specimens with original silvering are rare and are valued 20 percent to 50 percent higher than others. Varieties exist.

(Undated) SUCCESS Token, Large

(Undated) SUCCESS Token, Small

	GSID	VG-8	F-12	VF-20	EF-40	AU-50	MS-60	MS-63	MS-65
(Undated) SUCCESS Medal, Large, Plain Edge	421	$275	$325	$490	$1,250	$1,500	$2,100	$5,000	—
(Undated) SUCCESS Medal, Large, Reeded Edge	422	—	575	775	1,000	1,250	2,750	3,900	—
(Undated) SUCCESS Medal, Small, Plain Edge	423	305	365	470	1,150	1,400	1,900	3,750	—
(Undated) SUCCESS Medal, Small, Reeded Edge	424	325	420	470	1,100	1,900	2,200	3,750	—

Contract Issues and Patterns

NOVA CONSTELLATIO PATTERNS (1783)

These Nova Constellatio pieces represent the first official patterns for a coinage of the United States. They were designed by Benjamin Dudley for Gouverneur Morris to carry out his ideas for a decimal coinage system. The 1,000-unit coin is a mark, the 500 a quint. These denominations, together with the small 100-unit piece, were designed to fit in with the many different values for foreign coins that constituted money in America at the time. These pattern pieces represent the first attempt at a decimal ratio, and were the forerunners of our present system of money values. Neither the proposed denominations nor the coins advanced beyond the pattern stage. These unique pieces are all dated 1783. There are two types of the quint. The copper "five" was first brought to the attention of collectors in 1980. Electrotype and cast copies exist.

Scan for additional information.

5 Units

Quint, Plain Obverse

Quint, Legend on Obverse

Quint Reverse

Bit (100 Units)

Mark

		GSID	AU-55	PF-60
1783 (Five) "5," Copper	unique	106	$1,080,000	—
1783 (Bit) "100," Silver, Decorated Edge	2 known	104	900,000	—
1783 (Bit) "100," Silver, Plain Edge	unique	375220	1,020,000	—
1783 (Quint) "500," Silver, Plain Obverse	unique	108	—	—
	Auctions: $1,175,000, PCGS AU-53 HA 04/13			
1783 (Quint) "500," Silver, Legend on Obverse	unique	107	—	$1,500,000
1783 (Mark) "1000," Silver	unique	105	—	1,920,000

FUGIO CENTS (1787)

The first coins issued under U.S. authority for which contract information is known today were the Fugio pieces, which were valued at one cent each. They were made under contract with James Jarvis, owner of a controlling interest in the Connecticut mint, which was then striking Connecticut coppers in New Haven. Jarvis obtained the federal contract with a $10,000 bribe to Col. William Duer, then head of the Board of Treasury. The contract called for Jarvis to deliver 345 tons of copper coins to the federal government. Congress, which was ignorant of the bribe, directed on July 7, 1787, "that the Board of Treasury direct the contractor for the copper coinage to stamp on one side of each piece the following device, viz: thirteen circles linked together, a small circle in the middle, with the words 'United States,' around it; and in the centre, the words 'We are one'; on the other side of the same piece the following device, viz: a dial with the hours expressed on the face of it; a meridian sun above on one side of which is the word 'Fugio,' ["time flies"] and on the other the year in figures '1787,' below the dial, the words 'Mind Your Business.'"

Jarvis was only able to mint 11,910 pounds of Fugios (equal to around 554,741 coins). Not all of these were shipped to the government, which canceled the contract for failure to meet the delivery schedule.

All Fugios were minted in 1788 and back-dated 1787. The dies were engraved by Abel Buell.

1787, With Pointed Rays

The 1787, With Pointed Rays, was later replaced by the With Club Rays variety.

American Congress Pattern

Cross After Date

Label With Raised Rims

Cinquefoil After Date

These types, with pointed rays, have regular obverses punctuated with four cinquefoils (five-leafed ornaments).

		GSID	F-12	VF-20	EF-40	AU-50	MS-60	MS-63
Obverse Cross After Date, No Cinquefoils, Reverse Rays and AMERICAN CONGRESS	3 or 4 known	181	—	—	$240,000	—	—	—
Obverse Cross After Date, No Cinquefoils, Reverse Label With Raised Rims	7 est. known	183	$13,500	$18,000	30,000	—	—	—
Obverse Cross After Date, No Cinquefoils, Reverse STATES UNITED		182	1,500	2,500	4,750	$8,000	—	—
Obverse Cross After Date, No Cinquefoils, Reverse UNITED STATES		184	1,150	1,900	3,750	7,000	—	—
STATES UNITED at Sides of Circle, Cinquefoils on Label		186	800	1,200	1,900	2,500	$3,100	$4,100
STATES UNITED, 1 Over Horizontal 1		188	1,250	2,450	4,250	12,000	—	—
UNITED STATES at Sides of Circle		189	900	1,450	2,100	2,750	3,300	4,100
	Auctions: $109,250, Uncert F-15 SBG 01/08							
UNITED STATES, 1 Over Horizontal 1		191	1,750	3,750	5,000	—	—	—
STATES UNITED, Label With Raised Rims, Large Letters in WE ARE ONE		192	950	1,600	3,100	4,700	6,250	11,500
STATES UNITED, 8-Pointed Star on Label		193	950	1,550	3,100	4,700	8,500	15,000
UNITED Above, STATES Below		194	—	—	15,000	18,000	22,000	28,000

1787, With Club Rays

The 1787, With Club Rays, is differentiated between concave and convex ends.

The so-called New Haven "restrikes" were made for Horatio N. Rust from dies recreated in 1859. These are distinguished by narrow rings on the reverse. At the time the fanciful story was given that teenaged C. Wyllys Betts discovered original dies in 1858 on the site of the Broome & Platt store in New Haven, where the original coins had been made.

1787, Club Rays, Rounded Ends

Concave Ends

New Haven Restrike
Note narrow rings.

		GSID	F-12	VF-20	EF-40	AU-50	MS-60	MS-63
Club Rays, Rounded Ends		196	$950	$1,550	$2,500	$5,250	$9,500	—
Club Rays, Concave Ends to Rays, FUCIO (C instead of G)		197	—	12,500	20,000	—	—	—
Club Rays, Concave Ends to Rays, FUGIO, UNITED STATES		198	14,000	20,000	36,000	—	—	—
Club Rays, Concave Ends to Rays, FUGIO, STATES UNITED		199	—	26,500	—	—	—	—
New Haven Restrike, Gold	2 known	200	—	43,000	—	—	—	—
New Haven Restrike, Silver		201	—	—	7,000	7,750	8,500	$11,000
New Haven Restrike, Copper		202	—	—	675	850	1,500	1,800
New Haven Restrike, Brass		205	—	—	1,000	1,200	1,950	2,400

1792 PROPOSED COINAGE

Many members of the House of Representatives favored a depiction of the president's head on the obverse of each federal coin; others considered the idea an inappropriately monarchical practice. George Washington himself is believed to have expressed disapproval of the use of his portrait on American coins. The majority considered a figure emblematic of Liberty more appropriate, and the Senate finally concurred in this opinion. Robert Birch was an engraver employed to design proposed devices for American coins. He, perhaps together with others, engraved the dies for the disme and half disme. He also cut the dies for the large copper patterns known today as *Birch cents*. Most 1792 half dismes circulated; they are summarized here and discussed in more detail under "Half Dismes."

1792 Silver Center Cent

The dies for the 1792 cent with a silver center may have been cut by Henry Voigt. The coins are copper with a silver plug in the center. The idea was to create a coin with an intrinsic or melt-down value of a cent, but of smaller diameter than if it were made entirely of copper. On the obverse is a right-facing portrait of Liberty, the legend LIBERTY PARENT OF SCIENCE & INDUSTRY, and the date 1792.

		GSID	VG-10	F-15	VF-30	EF-40	EF-45	AU-50	AU-53	AU-58	MS-61	MS-63	MS-64
1792, Silver Center	14 known	11902	—	—	$396,000	$480,000	$540,000	$600,000	$630,000	$750,000	$840,000	$1,200,000	$1,620,000
	Auctions: $576,000, PCGS EF-45 HA 01/25; $2,520,000, PCGS MS-67 HA 01/25												
1792, No Silver Center	9 known	11905	$150,000	$270,000	390,000	468,000	—	—	630,000	—	—	—	—
	Auctions: $603,750, PCGS VF-30 HA 01/08												

† Ranked in the *100 Greatest U.S. Coins* (fifth edition).

1792 Birch Cent

On the large-diameter copper Birch cent, the portrait of Liberty is "bright-eyed and almost smiling," as described in *United States Pattern Coins* (10th edition). The legend LIBERTY PARENT OF SCIENCE & INDUSTRY surrounds the portrait. BIRCH is lettered on the truncation of her neck, for the engraver. On the reverse is a ribbon-tied wreath with the legend UNITED STATES OF AMERICA and the denomination in fractional terms of a dollar: 1/100. The edge of some examples is lettered TO BE ESTEEMED BE USEFUL (with punctuating stars).

G★W.Pt.

		GSID	VG-10	F-15	VF-30	EF-40	EF-45	AU-50	AU-53	AU-58	MS-61	MS-63	MS-64
1792, Copper, Plain Edge	2 known	11908	—	—	—	—	—	—	—	—	—	—	—
1792, Copper, Lettered Edge, TO BE ESTEEMED ★ BE USEFUL ★	6–7 known	11911	$360,000	—	—	—	—	—	—	$1,380,000	—	—	—
	Auctions: $1,175,000, PCGS AU-58 SBG 03/15												
1792, Copper, Lettered Edge, TO BE ESTEEMED BE USEFUL ★	2 known	11914	—	—	—	—	—	—	—	—	$660,000	—	—
	Auctions: $564,000, NGC MS-61 HA 01/15												
1792, White Metal, G★W Pt. (George Washington President) Below Wreath	unique	11917	—	—	—	—	—	—	—	—	—	—	—

1792 Half Disme

About 1,500 silver half dismes were struck in mid-August 1792 in the shop of John Harper, using equipment ordered for the Philadelphia Mint (the foundation stones of which would be laid on July 31). Nearly all were placed into circulation. In his annual address that autumn, President George Washington noted that these had been so distributed. Their obverse design is a portrait of Liberty similar to the Birch cent's, but facing left. Its legend is abbreviated as LIB. PAR. OF SCIENCE & INDUSTRY. The reverse shows an eagle in flight, with UNI. STATES OF AMERICA around the top, and HALF DISME below.

	GSID	VG-10	F-15	VF-30	EF-40	EF-45	AU-50	AU-53	AU-58	MS-61	MS-63	MS-64
1792, Half Disme	11892	$72,000	$93,500	$132,000	$156,000	$168,000	$180,000	$192,000	$222,000	$252,000	$360,000	$510,000

1792 Disme

The 1792 pattern disme occurs in one silver variety and two copper varieties (plain-edged and the more readily available reeded-edge). The obverse legend is abbreviated as LIBERTY PARENT OF SCIENCE & INDUST., with the date 1792 below Liberty's neck. The reverse features an eagle in flight, different in design from that of the half disme, with UNITED STATES OF AMERICA around the top of the coin and the denomination, DISME, below.

		GSID	F-15	AU-50	MS-64
1792, Silver	3 known	11901	$420,000	$1,200,000	—
	Auctions: $998,750, NGC AU-50 HA 01/15				
1792, Copper (illustrated)	15 est. known	11898	180,000	—	$1,080,000

1792 Quarter Dollar

Today these mysterious undenominated pieces are commonly called "quarter dollars"; in the 1800s they were often called "cents." Little is known of their origins or who designed and engraved their portrait of Liberty and "eagle on globe" motif. One was added to the Mint Cabinet by Chief Coiner Adam Eckfeldt.

		GSID	VG-10	F-15	VF-30	EF-40	EF-45	AU-50	AU-53	AU-58	MS-61	MS-63	MS-64
1792, Copper (illustrated)	2 known	11918	—	—	—	—	—	—	—	—	—	$2,400,000	—
	Auctions: $2,232,500, NGC MS-63 HA 01/15												
1792, White Metal	4 known	11921	—	—	—	—	$510,000	—	—	$1,500,000	—	—	—
	Auctions: $1,260,000, NGC AU-58 HA 04/21												

THE LIBERTAS AMERICANA MEDAL (1782)

The Liberty Cap coinage of the fledgling United States was inspired by the famous Libertas Americana medal, whose dies were engraved by Augustin Dupré in Paris in 1782 from a concept and mottoes proposed by Benjamin Franklin. To Franklin (then U.S. minister to France), the infant Hercules symbolized America, strangling two serpents representing the British armies at Saratoga and Yorktown. Minerva, with shield and spear, symbolized France as America's ally, keeping the British Lion at bay. Franklin presented gold examples of the medal to the French king and queen and silver strikings to their ministers, "as a monumental acknowledgment, which may go down to future ages, of the obligations we are under to this nation."

Between 100 and 125 original copper medals exist, and two dozen or more silver; the location of the two gold medals is unknown. Over the years the Paris Mint has issued additional medals that are appreciated and collected at a fraction of the cost for originals.

		GSID	AU-50	MS-61	MS-63	MS-64	MS-65
Libertas Americana Medal, Copper	100–125 est. known	200006	$15,500	$27,500	$33,500	$50,500	$72,000
Libertas Americana Medal, Silver	25–30 est. known	200005	81,500	168,000	258,000	336,000	—
	Auctions: $336,000, PCGS MS-64 SBG 08/24; $180,000, PCGS MS-62 SBG 08/24						

Half Cents
1793–1857

AN OVERVIEW OF HALF CENTS

Building a type set of the six different major designs in the half cent series can be a challenging and rewarding pursuit. The first design, with Liberty Head facing left with pole and cap, minted only in 1793, is scarce in all grades and will be the most difficult to locate. However, hundreds exist of this American classic, and many are fairly attractive.

Scan for additional information.

The second type, with a *large* Liberty Head facing right with pole and cap, made only in 1794, is scarce with good eye appeal. Most are dark and rough. The next type, the *small* Liberty Head facing right, with pole and cap, is scarce, but enough are on the market that a collector can find a specimen without difficulty.

The Draped Bust half cents, struck from 1800 to 1808, are easily available as a type, including in higher grades. The Classic Head (1809–1836) and Braided Hair (1840–1857) are plentiful as types.

For the earlier half cent types there is ample opportunity for connoisseurship, for quality often varies widely, and every coin is apt to have a different appearance and "personality," even within the same grade.

For the Collector and Investor: Half Cents as a Specialty

Collecting half cents by dates and major varieties has been a popular niche specialty for a long time. Some key issues in the series are the 1793; 1796, With Pole to Cap; 1796, Without Pole to Cap, (the most famous of all the rarities); 1802, 2 Over 0, With Reverse of 1800, (a single leaf at each side of the wreath apex, rare but somewhat obscure); 1831; and the Proof-only issues of 1836, 1840 through 1848, Small Date, and 1852.

As there are so many Proof varieties, and each of these is rare as well as expensive, many collectors opt to acquire only the circulation strikes. However, the Proofs are not nearly as expensive as one might think, probably because with so many different dates and varieties needed to complete a Proof collection, the prospect is daunting to many buyers. Proofs of most dates are available in both original and restrike forms. Although this rule is not without exceptions, the original strikings of the 1840–1848 and 1849, Small Date, half cents are usually described as having the Large Berries reverse, while restrikes are of the Small Berries reverse (within the Small Berries issues there are two dies—one with diagonal die striae below RICA, and the other with doubling at the ribbon wreath). Assembling Proofs by reverse varieties is a somewhat esoteric pursuit.

For an exhaustive study of die varieties of circulation strikes and Proofs, *Walter Breen's Encyclopedia of United States Half Cents, 1793–1857*, is definitive. Roger S. Cohen Jr.'s study, *American Half Cents, The "Little Half Sisters,"* gives detailed information on circulation strikes, but omits Proofs.

Die varieties are especially abundant among half cents of the first several types, 1793 to 1808. The year 1804 offers a panorama of dies, some of which have been studied as to die states, referring to the progression of use of a die as it develops wear, cracks, etc. Varieties of 1795 exist with and without the pole to the liberty cap, the Without Pole half cents being the result of a die being relapped (reground to dress the surface), during which process the pole was removed. On the other hand, the 1796, Without Pole, half cent was the result of a die-engraving error—the diecutter forgot to add it. Some half cents of 1795 and 1797 were struck on planchets cut from copper tokens issued by the New York City firm of Talbot, Allum & Lee. Upon close inspection, some of the design details of the tokens can still be seen.

One curious and readily available variety of the 1828 half cent has 12 stars instead of the standard 13. However, in choice Mint State the 12-stars issue becomes a rarity, for, unlike the 13-stars issue, none were ever found in hoards.

The Early American Coppers Club is a special-interest group emphasizing copper half cents and large cents. Its journal, *Penny-Wise*, provides much research, social, and collecting news and information.

EXPLORING VARIETIES

Roger S. Cohen's book organizes the die varieties of U.S. half cents from 1793 to 1857. Collectors use Cohen numbers to identify each variety, much as they use Browning numbers for early U.S. quarters. These numbers are important because they provide a standard way to attribute and compare coins in this small but historic denomination.

Cohen, Roger S., Jr. *American Half Cents–The "Little Half Sisters."* Second edition. 1982.

LIBERTY CAP, HEAD FACING LEFT (1793)

Designer: *Henry Voigt.* **Weight:** *6.74 grams.*
Composition: *Copper.* **Diameter:** *21.2 to 24.6 mm.*
Edge: *Lettered TWO HUNDRED FOR A DOLLAR.* **Mint:** *Philadelphia.*

History. Among U.S. coinage, the Liberty Cap, Head Facing Left, design belongs to the small class of one-year-only types. Its design was inspired by Augustin Dupré's Libertas Americana medal. The Liberty Cap dies are often credited to Joseph Wright, who also cut the dies for the related cent, but they were more likely done by Henry Voigt.

Striking and Sharpness. Good-quality copper was used in these half cents, so they are often found light brown and on fairly smooth planchets. Unlike in later types, the borders on both sides are raised beads; certain of these beads can be weak, though this is not the norm. Some varieties are lightly defined at HALF CENT on the reverse, due to a combination of striking and shallow depth of letters in the die. This feature cannot be used in assigning a grade, as in lower grades (up to and including VG-8) these words may be completely missing.

Availability. Most half cents of 1793 are AG-3 to F-12. EF and AU examples are rare, and MS very rare (most being MS-60 to 63). Market grading is often liberal. Early American Coppers Club (EAC) "raw" grades often are lower than those of the certification services.

Grading Standards

MS-60 to 65 (Mint State). ***Obverse:*** In the lower ranges, MS-60 and 61, some light abrasions can be seen on the higher areas of the portrait. Luster in the field is incomplete, particularly in the center of the open areas. At the MS-63 level, luster should be complete, with no abrasions evident. In higher levels, the luster is deeper, and some original mint color may be seen. ***Reverse:*** In the lower ranges some abrasions are seen on the higher areas of the leaves. Generally, luster is complete in all ranges, as the open areas are protected by the lettering and wreath. Otherwise, the same comments apply as for the obverse.

MS-60BN

Illustrated coin: Well struck and nicely centered on the planchet, this example shows no sign of wear. Its color is a rich orange-brown overall, with a bit of darker gray-brown on the lower-right edge and field of the obverse. The faint roughness on the obverse is a flaw of the original planchet, and is not related to wear.

AU-50, 53, 55, 58 (About Uncirculated). ***Obverse:*** Friction is seen on the higher parts, particularly on the rounded cheek and on the higher strands of the hair. Friction and scattered marks are in the field, ranging from extensive at AU-50 to minimal at AU-58. Luster may be seen in protected areas, minimal at AU-50, but sometimes extensive on an AU-58 coin. Border beads, if well struck, are separate and boldly defined. ***Reverse:*** Friction is seen on the higher wreath leaves and (not as easy to discern) on the letters. The fields, protected by the designs, show friction, but not as noticeably as on the obverse. At AU-55 and 58 little if any friction is seen. The reverse may have original luster, toned brown, minimal on lower About Uncirculated grades, sometimes extensive at AU-58. Border beads, if well struck, are separate and boldly defined. Grading at the About Uncirculated level is mainly done by viewing the obverse.

AU-58

Illustrated coin: Two tiny rim bruises can be seen, and some nicks can be seen as well under low magnification, none of which immediately draw the eye. This coin is about as good as can be found in this grade, as many examples of the date are porous.

EF-40, 45 (Extremely Fine). ***Obverse:*** Wear is seen on the portrait overall, with reduction or elimination of some separation of hair strands on the highest part. The cheek is ever so slightly flat on the highest part. Some leaves will retain some detail, especially where they join the stems. Luster is minimal or non-existent at EF-40 and may survive in traces in protected areas at EF-45. ***Reverse:*** Wear is seen on the highest wreath and ribbon areas and the letters. Luster is minimal, but likely more noticeable than on the obverse, as the fields are protected by the designs and lettering.

EF-45

Illustrated coin: The devices are crisp for the grade. Note the glossy golden-tan surfaces and the lack of meaningful contact marks.

VF-20, 30 (Very Fine). ***Obverse:*** Wear on the portrait has reduced the hair detail to indistinct or flat at the center on a VF-20 coin, with slightly more detail at VF-30. The thin, horizontal (more or less) ribbon near the top of the hair is distinct. The border beads are blended together, with many blurred or missing. No luster is seen. ***Reverse:*** The leaf details are nearly completely worn away at VF-20, and with slight detail at VF-30. The border beads are blended together, with many indistinct. Some berries in the sprays may be worn away, depending on the strike (on strong strikes they can be seen down into Very Good and Good grades). No luster is seen. HALF CENT may be weak, but is fully readable, on certain coins (such as BW-1, C-1, B-1) in which this feature was shallowly cut into the dies.

VF-30

Illustrated coin: A small planchet crack at 8 o'clock on the obverse rim appears as struck. This planchet crack explains the softness of detail at the borders both in that area at 10 o'clock on the reverse.

F-12, 15 (Fine). ***Obverse:*** The hair details are mostly worn away, with about one-third visible, mainly at the edges. Border beads are weak or worn away in areas. F-15 shows slightly more detail. ***Reverse:*** The wreath leaves are worn flat, but their edges are distinct. HALF CENT may be missing on 1793 (Bowers-Whitman–1)—also true of lower grades given below. Border beads are weak or worn away in areas. F-15 shows slightly more detail.

F-15

Illustrated coin: Under magnification the surfaces are seen to be lightly porous.

VG-8, 10 (Very Good). ***Obverse:*** The portrait is well worn, although the eye can be seen, and the hair tips at the right show separation. Border beads are worn away, and the border blends into the field in most if not all of the periphery. LIBERTY and 1793 are bold. VG-10, not an official ANA grading designation, is sometimes applied to especially nice Very Good coins. ***Reverse:*** The wreath, bow, and lettering are seen in outline form, and some leaves and letters may be indistinct in parts. Border beads are worn away, and the border blends into the field in most if not all of the periphery.

VG-8

Illustrated coin: The scratch from the E of LIBERTY to the base of the cap behind Liberty's head is less evident at the coin's unmagnified size.

G-4, 6 (Good). ***Obverse:*** The portrait is worn smooth and is seen only in outline form, although the eye position can be discerned. LIBERTY and 1793 are complete, although the date may be weak. ***Reverse:*** Extensive wear is seen overall. From half to two-thirds of the letters in UNITED STATES OF AMERICA and the fraction numerals are worn away. The reverse shows more evidence of wear than does the obverse, and is key in assigning this grade. G-6 is often assigned to finer examples in this category.

G-6

AG-3 (About Good). ***Obverse:*** Wear is more extensive than on the preceding. The portrait is visible only in outline. LIBERTY is weak but usually fully discernible. 1793 is weak, and the bottoms of the digits may be worn away. ***Reverse:*** Parts of the wreath are visible in outline form, and all but a few letters are gone. Grading of AG-3 is usually done by the reverse.

AG-3

Fair-2 (Fair). ***Obverse:*** Worn nearly smooth. Date is partly visible, not necessarily clearly. Head of Liberty is in outline form. Some letters of LIBERTY are discernible. ***Reverse:*** Worn nearly smooth. Peripheral letters are nearly all gone, with only vestiges remaining. Wreath is in outline form. HALF CENT ranges from readable to missing (the latter on certain die varieties as struck).

Fair-2

Circulation Strikes

	Mintage	GSID	AG-3	G-4	VG-8	F-12	VF-20	EF-40	AU-50	MS-60	MS-63
Liberty Cap, Head Facing Left (1793)	**n/a**	**73819**	**$3,400**	**$5,000**	**$6,000**	**$9,250**	**$14,000**	**$21,000**	**$27,500**	**$53,000**	**$96,000**
1793	35,334	429	3,400	5,000	6,000	9,250	14,000	21,000	27,500	53,000	96,000
	Auctions: $126,500, PCGS MS-61 HA 01/09										
↳1793, C-1	*	80835	3,400	5,000	6,000	9,250	14,000	21,000	27,500	58,000	105,500
	Auctions: $111,000, PCGS MS-64 HA 08/22										
↳1793, C-2	*	80836	3,400	5,000	6,000	9,250	14,000	21,000	27,500	58,000	105,500
	Auctions: $336,000, PCGS MS-65 HA 08/22										
↳1793, C-3	*	80837	3,400	5,000	6,000	9,250	14,000	21,000	27,500	53,000	96,000
	Auctions: $1,005,000, PCGS MS-66 HA 08/22										
↳1793, C-4	*	80838	3,400	5,000	6,000	9,250	14,000	21,000	27,500	58,000	105,500
	Auctions: $240,000, PCGS MS-65 SBG 02/25										

* Included in number above.

LIBERTY CAP, HEAD FACING RIGHT (1794–1797)

Designer: *1794—Robert Scot; 1795–1797—Possibly Scot, John Smith Gardner, or other.* **Weight:** *1794, thick planchet—6.74 grams; 1795–1797—5.44 grams.* **Composition:** *Copper.* **Diameter:** *23.5 mm.* **Edge:** *1794, some of 1795, some of 1797—Lettered TWO HUNDRED FOR A DOLLAR; 1795, 1796, most of 1797—Plain; some of 1797—Gripped.* **Mint:** *Philadelphia.*

History. The design of the half cent changed in 1794 to a depiction, by Robert Scot, of Liberty facing right. A smaller-headed portrait was used from 1795 on.

Striking and Sharpness. Half cents of 1794 usually are dark, with rough surfaces, and of low aesthetic quality. Most 1795's are on high-quality planchets, smooth and attractive, this being truer of the later plain-edge type than the early thick-planchet issue. Striking can be weak in areas. Often the denticles are incomplete on one or both sides. Many Small Head coins, particularly of 1795 to 1797, have very little detail on the hair, even in higher grades. Half cents of 1796 vary in quality; higher-grade pieces are usually attractive. Half cents of 1797 are usually seen in low grades and on poor planchets; striking varies widely, but is usually weak in areas. Denticles can be weak or can be prominent in various circulated grades, down to the lowest; on certain varieties of 1795 they are prominent even on well-worn coins. Grades must be assigned carefully, and expertise is recommended—combining knowledge of a given die variety and its relief or sharpness in the die, with observations of actual circulation wear. Grades of certified coins can vary widely in their interpretations.

Availability. As a general type, this issue is scarce, but available. Most are in lower grades, but VF and EF coins appear in the market with regularity.

Grading Standards

MS-60 to 70 (Mint State). ***Obverse:*** On MS-60 and 61 coins there are some traces of abrasion on the higher areas of the portrait. Luster in the field is incomplete, particularly in the center of the open areas. At MS-63, luster should be complete, and no abrasion is evident. At higher levels, the luster is deeper, and some original mint color may be seen. At MS-65 there are some scattered contact marks and possibly some traces of fingerprints or discoloration, but these should be minimal and not at all distracting. Above MS-65, a coin should approach perfection. ***Reverse:*** In the lower ranges some abrasions are seen on the higher areas of the leaves. Generally, luster is complete in all ranges, as the open areas are protected by the lettering and wreath. Otherwise, the same comments apply as for the obverse.

MS-65

Illustrated coin: A spectacular coin of a year seldom seen in Mint State. Both sides have rich, brown surfaces. On the obverse the luster is light, while on the reverse it is not as noticeable. Note that the obverse die is in very high relief and of the Large Head style, while the reverse is in shallower relief.

AU-50

AU-50, 53, 55, 58 (About Uncirculated). ***Obverse:*** Friction is seen on the higher parts, particularly the center of the portrait. Friction and scattered marks are in the field, ranging from extensive at AU-50 to minimal at AU-58. To reiterate: knowledge of the die variety is important. For certain shallow-relief dies (such as those of 1797) an About Uncirculated coin may appear to be in a lower grade. Luster may be seen in protected areas, minimal at AU-50, but sometimes extensive on an AU-58 coin. ***Reverse:*** Friction is seen on the higher wreath leaves and (not as easy to discern) on the letters. The fields, protected by the designs, show friction, but not as noticeably as on the obverse. At AU-55 and 58 little if any friction is seen. The reverse may have original luster, toned brown, minimal on lower About Uncirculated grades, sometimes extensive on higher. Grading at the About Uncirculated level is mainly done by viewing the obverse.

Illustrated coin: Note faint ruddy highlights in the protected areas. The devices are boldly impressed. On this variety the 179 in the date was punched low into the die, partly effaced, then repunched in a higher position. On the reverse, a natural planchet fissure, small and as struck, runs from the rim through the M of AMERICA, and a smaller fissure runs from the rim to the E of AMERICA.

EF-45

EF-40, 45 (Extremely Fine). ***Obverse:*** Wear is seen on the portrait overall, with some reduction or elimination of the separation of hair strands on the highest part. This varies by die variety, as some are better delineated than others. The cheek shows light wear. Luster is minimal or nonexistent at EF-40, and may survive in traces in protected areas (such as between the letters) at EF-45. ***Reverse:*** Wear is seen on the highest wreath and ribbon areas and the letters. Luster is minimal, but likely more noticeable than on the obverse, as the fields are protected by the designs and lettering. Sharpness will vary depending on the die variety. Expect certain issues of 1794 and 1797 to be lighter.

Illustrated coin: This coin has bold details and excellent centering.

VF-30

VF-20, 30 (Very Fine). ***Obverse:*** Wear on the portrait has reduced the hair detail to indistinct or flat at the center. The border denticles are blended together, with many indistinct. No luster is seen. Again, knowing details of the die variety is important. A VF-20 or 30 1797 is very different in appearance from a 1794, Large Head, in the same grade. ***Reverse:*** The leaf details are nearly completely worn away at VF-20, with slight detail at VF-30. The border denticles are blended together, with many indistinct. No luster is seen. The sharpness of details depends on the die variety. Half cents of 1797 require special care in their study.

Illustrated coin: Minor roughness is apparent at the center of both sides, undoubtedly a trace of microporosity from the blank planchet, although the devices are overall bold from a well executed strike.

F-12, 15 (Fine). ***Obverse:*** The hair details are mostly worn away, with about one-third visible, mainly at the edges. Border denticles are weak or worn away in areas. F-15 shows slightly more detail. ***Reverse:*** The wreath leaves are worn flat, but their edges are distinct. Border denticles are weak or worn away in areas. F-15 shows slightly more detail.

F-15

Illustrated coin: This late-die-state variety has a noticeable die crack in the E of UNITED.

VG-8, 10 (Very Good). ***Obverse:*** The portrait is well worn, although the eye can be seen, and the hair tips at the left show separation. Border denticles are worn away on some issues (not as much for 1795 coins), and the border blends into the field in most if not all of the periphery. LIBERTY and the date are bold. VG-10, not an official ANA grading designation, is sometimes applied to especially nice Very Good coins. ***Reverse:*** The wreath, bow, and lettering are seen in outline form, and some leaves and letters may be indistinct in parts. Border denticles are worn away, and the border blends into the field in most if not all of the periphery. In certain die varieties and die states, especially of 1797, some letters may be very weak or missing.

VG-8

Illustrated coin: This coin exhibits roughness in the fields, but the same does not apply to the devices.

G-4, 6 (Good). ***Obverse:*** The portrait is worn smooth and is seen only in outline form, although the eye position can be discerned. LIBERTY and the date are complete, although the date may be weak. Denticles are gone on some, but not all, die varieties. ***Reverse:*** Extensive wear is seen overall. From half to two-thirds of the letters in UNITED STATES OF AMERICA, and the fraction numerals, are worn away. Certain shallow-relief dies may have letters missing. G-6 is often assigned to finer examples in this category.

G-4

Illustrated coin: On this coin the surfaces are heavily worn, yet with considerable boldness of detail remaining on the obverse.

AG-3 (About Good). ***Obverse:*** Wear is more extensive than on the preceding. The portrait is visible only in outline. LIBERTY is weak but usually fully discernible. The date is weak, and the bottoms of the digits may be worn away. ***Reverse:*** Parts of the wreath are visible in outline form, and all but a few letters are gone. Grading of AG-3 is usually done by the reverse, as the obverse typically appears to be in a slightly higher grade. If split grading were used, more than just a few half cents of this type could be designated as G-4 / AG-3 or even G-6 / AG-3.

AG-3

1794, Normal Head

1794, High-Relief Head

Circulation Strikes

	Mintage	GSID	AG-3	G-4	VG-8	F-12	VF-20	EF-40	AU-50	MS-60	MS-63
Liberty Cap, Head Facing Right (1794–1797)	**n/a**	**72297**	**$390**	**$575**	**$1,000**	**$1,550**	**$2,400**	**$5,250**	**$6,500**	**$17,000**	**$27,500**
1794, Normal Head	81,600	432	415	625	1,200	1,750	2,650	6,000	10,500	18,000	50,500
	Auctions: $408,000, PCGS MS-66 HA 08/22										
1794, Low-Relief Head	*	213364	415	625	1,200	1,750	2,650	6,000	10,500	18,000	50,500
↳1794, Low-Relief Head, Large Edge Letters, C-1a	*	80839	415	625	1,200	1,750	2,650	6,000	10,500	18,000	50,500
↳1794, Low-Relief Head, Small Edge Letters, C-1b	*	80840	—	1,900	2,500	6,250	12,000	30,000	—	—	—
↳1794, Low-Relief Head, Small Edge Letters, C-2a	*	80841	415	625	1,200	1,750	2,650	6,000	10,500	18,000	50,500
↳1794, Low-Relief Head, Large Edge Letters, C-2b	*	80842	—	5,000	9,500	15,000	24,000	36,000	48,000	—	—
↳1794, Low-Relief Head, Small Edge Letters, C-3a	*	80843	—	1,250	1,750	3,000	5,000	9,500	14,500	—	—
↳1794, Low-Relief Head, Large Edge Letters, C-3b	*	80844	—	24,000	—	60,000	—	—	—	—	—
↳1794, Low-Relief Head, Small Edge Letters, C-4a	*	80845	575	850	1,400	2,100	3,750	7,750	12,000	21,500	50,500
	Auctions: $240,000, PCGS MS-66 HA 08/22										
↳1794, Low-Relief Head, Large Edge Letters, C-4b	*	80846	6,500	10,500	18,000	24,000	36,000	48,000	66,000	—	—
↳1794, Low-Relief Head, Small Edge Letters, C-5a	*	80847	—	1,250	1,900	2,750	3,750	8,250	12,000	36,000	50,500
↳1794, Low-Relief Head, Large Edge Letters, C-5b	*	80848	—	—	60,000	—	180,000	—	—	—	—
↳1794, Low-Relief Head, Small Edge Letters, C-6a	*	80849	—	1,900	5,000	12,000	24,000	60,000	—	—	—
↳1794, Low-Relief Head, Large Edge Letters, C-6b	*	80850	—	60,000	—	120,000	—	—	—	—	—
1794, High-Relief Head	*	213365	440	675	1,250	1,850	2,800	6,500	11,500	19,000	53,500
	Auctions: $119,025, NGC MS-65 SBG 08/10										
↳1794, High Relief Head, C-7	*	80851	—	1,900	3,100	7,500	18,000	36,000	42,000	—	—
↳1794, High Relief Head, C-8	*	80852	—	1,900	3,100	7,500	18,000	29,000	38,500	—	—
↳1794, High Relief Head, C-9a	*	80853	440	675	1,250	1,850	2,800	6,500	11,500	19,000	53,500
	Auctions: $204,000, PCGS MS-65 HA 08/18										
↳1794, High Relief Head, Thin Planchet, C-9b	5–10 known	81465	—	1,900	3,750	—	—	—	—	—	—

* Included in number above.

1795, With Pole

1795, No Pole

1795, Punctuated Date

Circulation Strikes *(continued)*

	Mintage	GSID	AG-3	G-4	VG-8	F-12	VF-20	EF-40	AU-50	MS-60	MS-63
1795, With Pole, Lettered Edge	139,690	435	$430	$625	$1,200	$1,750	$2,750	$7,250	$14,000	$21,500	$66,000
	Auctions: $115,000, PCGS MS-64 GLDB 01/14										
↳1795, With Pole, Lettered Edge, C-1a	5–10 known	80854	430	625	1,200	1,750	2,750	7,250	14,000	21,500	66,000
	Auctions: $408,000, PCGS MS-67 HA 08/22										
↳1795, With Pole, Lettered Edge, Thin Planchet, C-1b	*	81466	—	2,500	—	6,250	—	—	—	—	—
1795, With Pole, Lettered Edge, Punctuated Date	*	438	470	700	1,450	1,950	3,100	8,000	15,000	26,000	84,000
↳1795, With Pole, Lettered Edge, Punctuated Date, C-2a	*	80855	470	700	1,450	1,950	3,100	8,000	15,000	26,000	84,000
	Auctions: $174,000, PCGS MS-65 HA 08/22										
1795, With Pole, Plain Edge, Punctuated Date	*	444	420	600	1,050	1,800	2,700	6,000	10,000	23,000	96,000
	Auctions: $120,750, PCGS MS-63 GLDB 01/14										
↳1795, With Pole, Plain Edge, Punctuated Date, C-2b	*	80856	—	5,000	7,500	12,000	24,000	36,000	48,000	—	—
↳1795, With Pole, Plain Edge, Punctuated Date, C-3	*	80857	—	1,500	2,250	4,250	7,500	15,000	24,000	—	—
↳1795, With Pole, Plain Edge, Punctuated Date, C-4a	*	80858	420	600	1,050	1,800	2,700	6,000	10,000	23,000	96,000
↳1795, With Pole, Plain Edge, Punctuated Date, Thick Planchet, C-4b	1–2 known	81467	—	—	—	120,000	—	—	—	—	—
1795, No Pole, Plain Edge (a)	*	441	390	575	1,000	1,550	2,400	5,250	7,750	17,000	27,500
	Auctions: $132,250, PCGS MS-65 GLDB 01/14										
↳1795, No Pole, Plain Edge, C-5a	*	80859	390	575	1,000	1,550	2,400	5,250	7,750	17,000	27,500
↳1795, No Pole, Plain Edge, C-5b	*	80860	390	575	1,000	1,550	2,400	5,250	11,500	—	—
↳1795, No Pole, Plain Edge, C-6a	*	80861	390	575	1,000	1,550	2,400	5,250	7,750	17,000	27,500
	Auctions: $235,000, PCGS MS-66 SBG 02/16										
↳1795, No Pole, Plain Edge, C-6b	1–2 known	80862	—	1,900	3,750	9,500	—	18,000	24,000	—	—
↳1795, No Pole, Plain Edge, Thin Planchet, C-6c	*	81468	—	—	—	—	—	—	—	—	—
1796, With Pole	5,090	447	14,000	20,000	30,000	37,000	48,000	72,000	114,000	192,000	228,000
	Auctions: $472,938, PCGS MS-64 SBG 08/12										
↳1796, With Pole, C-2	*	80864	14,000	20,000	30,000	37,000	48,000	72,000	114,000	192,000	228,000
	Auctions: $192,000, NGC MS-62 HA 04/21										
↳1796, With Pole, Lettered Edge, Thick Planchet, C-2b	*	81469	—	—	—	42,000	—	—	—	—	—
1796, No Pole	*	450	36,000	54,000	70,000	114,000	180,000	252,000	312,000	408,000	528,000
	Auctions: $891,250, PCGS MS-65 GLDB 01/14										
↳1796, No Pole, C-1	*	80863	36,000	54,000	70,000	114,000	180,000	252,000	312,000	408,000	528,000
	Auctions: $552,000, PCGS MS-63 HA 08/22										

* Included in number above. **a.** Many of this date/variety were struck on cut-down cents (coins that had been rejected for circulation by Mint workers), or on planchets cut from English-made Talbot, Allum & Lee tokens.

1796, "Dr. Edwards" Copy

1797, 1 Above 1

1797, Low Head

Circulation Strikes *(continued)*

	Mintage	GSID	AG-3	G-4	VG-8	F-12	VF-20	EF-40	AU-50	MS-60	MS-63
1796, Edwards Copy (b)	12 known	81470	—	—	—	—	$6,250	$8,750	$11,000	$18,000	$24,000
1797, 1 Over 1, Plain Edge	127,840	462	$390	$575	$1,000	$1,550	2,400	5,250	6,500	17,000	27,500
	Auctions: $299,000, PCGS MS-66 GLDB 01/14										
↳1797, 1 Above 1, C-1	*	80865	390	575	1,000	1,550	2,400	5,250	6,500	17,000	27,500
	Auctions: $156,000, NGC MS-65 HA 04/21										
1797, Plain Edge, Centered Head	*	456	575	750	1,500	2,000	2,750	6,000	9,750	33,000	48,000
	Auctions: $402,500, PCGS MS-66 GLDB 01/14										
↳1797, Plain Edge, Centered Head, C-2	*	80866	575	750	1,500	2,000	2,750	6,000	9,750	33,000	48,000
	Auctions: $293,750, PCGS MS-66 SBG 02/16										
1797, Plain Edge, Low Head	*	213368	525	700	1,200	1,750	5,000	11,000	24,000	—	—
↳1797, Plain Edge, Low Head, C-3a	*	80867	525	700	1,200	1,750	5,000	11,000	24,000	—	—
1797, Lettered Edge, Low Head	*	453	1,500	2,500	4,400	8,500	12,000	29,000	60,000	—	—
↳1797, Lettered Edge, Low Head, C-3b	*	80868	1,500	2,500	4,400	8,500	12,000	29,000	60,000	—	—
1797, Gripped Edge	13 est. known	459	78,000	108,000	156,000	—	—	—	—	—	—
	Auctions: $195,500, PCGS G6 GLDB 09/11										
↳1797, Gripped Edge, C-3c	*	80869	78,000	108,000	156,000	—	—	—	—	—	—
	Auctions: $102,000, NGC VG-8 HA 04/21										

* Included in number above. **b.** The deceptive "Dr. Edwards" struck copy of this coin has a different head and larger letters, as pictured.

DRAPED BUST (1800–1808)

Designer: *Robert Scot.* **Weight:** *5.44 grams.* **Composition:** *Copper.* **Diameter:** *23.5 mm.* **Edge:** *Plain.* **Mint:** *Philadelphia.*

History. By the turn of the century the Draped Bust design was already familiar to Americans from its use on cents and silver coins. The motif was introduced to the half cent in 1800, and was used through 1808.

Striking and Sharpness. Striking varies. Weakness is often seen at the center of the obverse and on the wreath leaves on the reverse. Planchet quality is often porous and dark for 1802, 1803, 1807, and 1808 due to the copper stock used.

Availability. As a type, Draped Bust half cents are available in any grade desired, up to and including Mint State, the latter usually dated 1806 (occasionally 1800 and, less often, 1804). The year 1804 includes many different die varieties and die states. Apart from aspects of strike, cherrypicking for planchet quality is essential for 1802, 1803, 1807, and 1808.

Grading Standards

MS-62

MS-60 to 70 (Mint State). ***Obverse:*** In the lower grades, MS-60 and 61, some slight abrasions can be seen on the higher areas of the portrait. Luster in the field is incomplete, particularly in the center of the open areas, which on this type are very extensive. At the MS-63 level, luster should be nearly complete, and no abrasions evident. In higher levels, the luster is complete and deeper and some original mint color may be seen. MS-64 coins may have some slight discoloration or scattered contact marks. A well-graded MS-65 or higher coin has full, rich luster; no marks visible except under magnification; and a blend of brown toning or nicely mixed (not stained or blotchy) mint color and natural brown toning. ***Reverse:*** In the lower Mint State ranges some abrasions are seen on the higher areas of the leaves. Generally, luster is complete in all ranges, as the open areas are protected by the lettering and wreath. Sharpness of the leaves can vary by die variety, so check this aspect. Otherwise, the same comments apply as for the obverse.

AU-58

AU-50, 53, 55, 58 (About Uncirculated). ***Obverse:*** Friction is seen on the higher parts, particularly the hair of Liberty. Friction and scattered marks are in the field, ranging from extensive at AU-50 to minimal at AU-58. Luster may be seen in protected areas, minimal at AU-50, with more at AU-58. At AU-58 the field may retain some luster, as well. In all instances, the luster is lesser in area and in "depth" than on the reverse of this type. ***Reverse:*** Friction is evident on the higher wreath leaves and (not as easy to discern) on the letters. Again, the die variety should be checked. The fields, protected by the designs, show friction, but not as noticeably as on the obverse. At AU-55 and 58, little if any friction is seen. The reverse may have original luster, toned brown, minimal on lower About Uncirculated grades, often extensive at AU-58.

Illustrated coin: The motifs are very boldly rendered, except for partial weakness on the lower obverse and OF on the upper reverse, which is virtually missing due to the late die state.

EF-40

EF-40, 45 (Extremely Fine). ***Obverse:*** Wear is seen on the portrait overall, with reduction or elimination of some separation of hair strands on the highest part. The cheek shows light wear. Luster is minimal or nonexistent at EF-40, and may survive among the letters of LIBERTY at EF-45. ***Reverse:*** Wear is seen on the highest wreath and ribbon areas, and the letters. Luster is minimal, but likely more noticeable than on the obverse, as the fields are protected by the designs and lettering.

VF-20

VF-20, 30 (Very Fine). ***Obverse:*** Wear on the portrait has reduced the hair detail to indistinct or flat at the center. The border denticles are blended together, with many indistinct. No luster is seen. ***Reverse:*** The leaf details are nearly completely worn away at VF 20, and with slight detail at VF-30. The border denticles are blended together, with many indistinct. No luster is seen.

Illustrated coin: Struck from a later die state, the reverse shows a bisecting die crack.

F-12, 15 (Fine). ***Obverse:*** The hair details are mostly worn away, with about one-third visible, mainly at the edges. Border denticles are weak or worn away in areas. F-15 shows slightly more detail. ***Reverse:*** The wreath leaves are worn flat, but their edges are distinct. HALF CENT may be missing on weakly struck varieties (also true of lower grades given below). Border denticles are weak or worn away in areas. F-15 shows slightly more detail.

F-15

Illustrated coin: This is the "Spiked Chin" variety, so called because of a thorn-like projection from the chin. The variety does not affect the grade.

VG-8, 10 (Very Good). ***Obverse:*** The portrait is well worn, although the eye can be seen, as can hints of hair detail (some at the left shows separation). Curls now appear as mostly solid blobs. Border denticles are worn away on most varieties, and the rim, although usually present, begins to blend into the field. LIBERTY and the date are bold. VG-10, not an official ANA grading designation, is sometimes applied to especially nice Very Good coins. ***Reverse:*** The wreath, bow, and lettering are seen in outline form, and some leaves and letters may be indistinct in parts. The border may blend into the field on some of the periphery.

VG-10

Illustrated coin: This coin is has many scratches, which detract from overall eye appeal.

G-4, 6 (Good). ***Obverse:*** The portrait is worn smooth and is seen only in outline form, although the eye position can be discerned. LIBERTY and the date are complete, although the date may be weak. The border blends into the field more extensively than on the preceding, but significant areas are still seen. ***Reverse:*** Extensive wear is seen overall. From one-half to two-thirds of the letters in UNITED STATES OF AMERICA and the fraction numerals are worn away. G-6 is often assigned to finer examples in this category.

G-4

Illustrated coin: A slightly off-center strike has allowed areas of heavier wear to creep in near the borders. There are many noticeable scratches on the obverse.

AG-3 (About Good). ***Obverse:*** Wear is more extensive than on the preceding. The portrait is visible only in outline. LIBERTY is weak but usually discernible. The date is weak, and the bottoms of the digits may be worn away, but must be identifiable. ***Reverse:*** Parts of the wreath are visible in outline form, and all but a few letters are gone.

AG-3

1st Reverse (Style of 1800)

2nd Reverse (Style of 1802)

1803, Normally Spaced 3

1803, Widely Spaced 3

1804, Plain 4

1804, Crosslet 4

Stems to Wreath

Stemless Wreath

Circulation Strikes

	Mintage	GSID	AG-3	G-4	VG-8	F-12	VF-20	EF-40	AU-50	MS-60	MS-63
Draped Bust (1800–1808), Brown	**n/a**	**72299**	**$65**	**$105**	**$120**	**$150**	**$200**	**$395**	**$625**	**$1,150**	**$2,750**
Same, Red Brown	**n/a**	**72300**	**—**	**—**	**—**	**—**	**—**	**—**	**—**	**—**	**4,500**
Same, Red	**n/a**	**72301**	**—**	**—**	**—**	**—**	**—**	**—**	**—**	**—**	**11,000**
1800	202,908	465	90	120	145	210	340	875	1,450	3,100	5,500
↳1800, C-1	*	80870	90	120	145	210	340	875	1,450	3,100	5,500
1802, 2 Over 0, Reverse of 1800	20,266	696	16,000	21,000	32,000	50,500	78,000	144,000	—	—	—
↳1802, 2 Over 0, Reverse of 1800, C-1	*	80871	16,000	21,000	32,000	50,500	78,000	144,000	—	—	—
	Auctions: $114,000, NGC VF-30 HA 04/21										
1802, 2 Over 0, Reverse of 1802	*	699	900	1,300	2,000	4,400	8,750	20,000	35,000	—	—
	Auctions: $138,000, PCGS EF-45 GLDB 01/14										
↳1802, 2 Over 0, Reverse of 1802, C-2	*	80872	900	1,300	2,000	4,400	8,750	20,000	35,000	—	—
1803	92,000	468	85	125	165	240	390	1,000	1,900	4,000	5,750
↳1803, C-1	*	80873	85	125	165	240	390	1,000	1,900	4,000	5,750
↳1803, C-2	*	80874	—	325	725	1,150	6,250	14,500	31,000	—	—
↳1803, C-3	*	80875	85	125	165	240	390	1,000	1,900	4,000	5,750
↳1803, C-4	*	80876	85	125	165	240	390	1,000	1,900	—	—
1804, Plain 4, Stems to Wreath	1,055,312	474	120	195	325	525	725	1,600	3,100	6,250	11,000
↳1804, Plain 4, Stems to Wreath, C-11	*	80887	120	195	325	525	725	1,600	3,100	6,250	11,000

* Included in number above.

1804, "Spiked Chin"

1805, Medium 5

1805, Small 5

1805, Large 5

1806, Small 6

1806, Large 6

Circulation Strikes *(continued)*

	Mintage	GSID	AG-3	G-4	VG-8	F-12	VF-20	EF-40	AU-50	MS-60	MS-63
1804, Plain 4, Stemless Wreath	*	471	$65	$105	$120	$150	$200	$395	$650	$1,250	$2,750
↳1804, Plain 4, Stemless Wreath, C-13	*	80889	65	105	120	150	200	395	650	1,250	2,750
1804, Crosslet 4, Stems to Wreath	*	477	65	120	135	180	260	550	1,000	1,550	3,000
	Auctions: $120,750, PCGS VF-30 GLDB 01/14										
↳1804, Crosslet 4, Stems to Wreath, C-1	*	80877	65	120	210	340	525	775	2,250	6,250	12,000
↳1804, Crosslet 4, Stems to Wreath, C-2	*	80878	—	14,500	19,000	24,000	50,500	96,000	—	—	—
↳1804, Crosslet 4, Stems to Wreath, C-4, FS-302	*	80880	—	1,250	2,500	5,000	10,000	21,500	36,000	—	—
↳1804, Crosslet 4, Stems to Wreath, C-9	*	80885	65	120	135	180	260	550	1,000	1,550	3,000
↳1804, Crosslet 4, Stems to Wreath, C-10	*	80886	65	120	135	180	260	550	1,000	1,550	3,000
1804, Crosslet 4, Stemless Wreath	*	480	80	115	135	180	245	415	725	1,350	3,750
↳1804, Crosslet 4, Stemless Wreath, C-12	*	80888	80	115	135	180	245	415	725	1,350	3,750
1804, "Spiked Chin"	*	483	70	130	155	210	310	600	950	1,900	3,900
↳1804, "Spiked Chin", C-5	*	80881	75	135	170	230	345	650	1,050	2,450	7,750
↳1804, "Spiked Chin", C-6	*	80882	75	135	170	230	345	650	1,050	2,500	4,400
↳1804, "Spiked Chin", C-7	*	80883	—	390	775	1,250	1,600	3,500	6,250	14,500	—
↳1804, "Spiked Chin", C-8	*	80884	70	130	155	210	310	600	950	1,900	3,900
1805, Small 5, Stemless Wreath	814,464	486	100	130	175	245	325	625	1,250	2,400	4,000
↳1805, Small 5, Stemless Wreath, C-1	*	80890	100	130	175	245	325	625	1,250	2,400	4,000
1805, Small 5, Stems to Wreath	*	489	650	1,000	1,650	2,900	7,000	16,000	33,500	—	—
↳1805, Small 5, Stems to Wreath, C-2	*	80891	3,000	4,000	5,500	8,750	12,000	29,000	50,500	—	—
↳1805, Small 5, Stems to Wreath, C-3	*	80892	650	1,000	1,650	2,900	7,000	16,000	33,500	—	—
1805, Large 5, Stems to Wreath	*	492	70	120	140	210	365	575	1,000	2,500	7,000
↳1805, Large 5, Stems to Wreath, C-4	*	80893	70	120	140	210	365	575	1,000	2,500	7,000
1806, Small 6, Stemless Wreath	356,000	495	65	105	120	150	200	395	625	1,150	2,750
↳1806, Small 6, Stemless Wreath, C-1	*	80894	65	105	120	150	200	395	625	1,150	2,750

* Included in number above.

1808, Normal Date

1808, 8 Over 7

Circulation Strikes *(continued)*

	Mintage	GSID	AG-3	G-4	VG-8	F-12	VF-20	EF-40	AU-50	MS-60	MS-63
1806, Small 6, Stems to Wreath	*	498	$120	$230	$455	$850	$1,300	$2,700	$4,400	$13,000	$36,000
↳1806, Small 6, Stems to Wreath, C-2	*	80895	120	230	455	850	1,300	2,700	4,400	13,000	36,000
↳1806, Small 6, Stems to Wreath, C-3, FS-301	*	80896	—	13,000	15,500	—	—	—	—	—	—
1806, Large 6, Stems to Wreath	*	501	65	105	120	150	200	395	625	1,300	3,100
↳1806, Large 6, Stems to Wreath, C-4	*	80897	65	105	120	150	200	395	625	1,300	3,100
1807	476,000	504	70	120	135	175	260	575	1,250	3,100	8,500
↳1807, C-1	*	80898	70	120	135	175	260	575	1,250	3,100	8,500
1808, Normal Date	400,000	507	90	130	170	235	390	775	2,000	6,250	12,000
↳1808, Normal Date, C-3	*	80901	90	130	170	235	390	775	2,000	6,250	12,000
1808, 8 Over 7	*	702	170	260	365	725	2,000	6,250	12,500	48,000	—
	Auctions: $483,000, PCGS MS-64 GLDB 01/14										
↳1808, 8 Over 7, C-1	*	80899	34,000	45,500	54,000	96,000	168,000	216,000	—	—	—
	Auctions: $180,000, PCGS EF-40 HA 08/22										
↳1808, 8 Over 7, C-2	*	80900	170	260	365	725	2,000	6,250	12,500	48,000	—

* Included in number above.

CLASSIC HEAD (1809–1836)

Designer: *John Reich.* **Weight:** *5.44 grams.* **Composition:** *Copper.* **Diameter:** *23.5 mm.* **Edge:** *Plain.* **Mint:** *Philadelphia.*

Circulation Strike

Proof Strike

History. The Classic Head design (by Mint engraver John Reich) made its first appearance on the half cent in 1809, a year after it was adopted for the one-cent coin. A very similar motif of Liberty was used on the quarter eagles and half eagles of the 1830s.

Striking and Sharpness. Coins of 1809 to 1811 usually have areas of light or incomplete striking. Grading coins of the early years requires special care and expertise. Sometimes coins as high as MS appear "blurry" in areas, due to the dies and striking. Those of later years are often found well struck and are easier to grade. Areas to check include the denticles and rims on both sides, the star centers and hair detail on the obverse, and the leaf detail on the reverse.

Availability. As a type this issue is found easily enough, although 1811 is scarce and 1831 and 1836 are notable rarities. MS coins from old hoards exist for certain of the later dates, particularly 1828, 1833, and 1835, but often have spotting, and many seen in the marketplace are cleaned or recolored. Care is advised. Although 1809–1811 half cents are often seen with extensive wear, those of the 1820s and 1830s are not often seen less than VF, as they did not circulate extensively.

Grading Standards

MS-64BN

MS-60 to 70 (Mint State). ***Obverse:*** In the lower grades, MS-60 and 61, some slight abrasions can be seen on the portrait, most evident on the cheek, as the hair details are complex on this type. Luster in the field is complete or nearly complete. At MS-63, luster should be complete, and no abrasions are evident. In higher levels, the luster is complete and deeper, and some original mint color may be seen. MS-64 coins may have some slight discoloration or scattered contact marks. A well-graded MS-65 or higher coin has full, rich luster, with no marks visible except under magnification, and has a nice blend of brown toning or nicely mixed (not stained or blotchy) mint color and natural brown toning. Coins dated 1809 to 1811 may exhibit significant weakness of details due to striking (and/or, in the case of most 1811s, porous planchet stock). ***Reverse:*** In the lower Mint State grades, some abrasions are seen on the higher areas of the leaves. Mint luster is complete in all Mint State grades, as the open areas are protected by the lettering and wreath. Sharpness of the leaves can vary by die variety, so check this aspect. Otherwise, the same comments apply as for the obverse. Coins dated 1809 to 1811 may exhibit significant weakness of details due to striking (and/or, in the case of most 1811s, porous planchet stock).

Illustrated coin: Some surface marks on the coin holder obscure the reverse, but no such marks mar the surface of this sharply struck coin.

AU-50, 53, 55, 58 (About Uncirculated). ***Obverse:*** Friction is seen on the higher parts, particularly the cheek and hair (under magnification) of Liberty. Friction and scattered marks are in the field, ranging from extensive at AU-50 to minimal at AU-58. Luster may be seen in protected areas, minimal at the AU-50 level, with more showing at AU-58. At AU-58 the field may retain some luster as well. ***Reverse:*** Friction is seen on the higher wreath leaves and (not as easy to discern) on the letters. Again, half cents of 1809 to 1811 require special attention. The fields, protected by the designs, show friction, but not as noticeably as on the obverse. At AU-55 and 58, little if any friction is seen. The reverse may have original luster, toned brown, minimal on lower About Uncirculated grades, often extensive at AU-58.

AU-58

EF-40, 45 (Extremely Fine). ***Obverse:*** Wear is seen on the portrait overall, with reduction or elimination of some separation of hair strands. The cheek shows light wear. Luster is minimal or nonexistent at EF-40 but may survive among the letters of LIBERTY at EF-45. ***Reverse:*** Wear is seen on the highest wreath and ribbon areas and the letters. Luster is minimal, but likely more noticeable than on the obverse, as the fields are protected by the designs and lettering.

EF-45

VF-20, 30 (Very Fine). ***Obverse:*** Wear on the portrait has reduced the hair detail, but much can still be seen (in this respect the present type differs dramatically from earlier types). ***Reverse:*** The wreath details, except for the edges of the leaves, are worn away at VF-20, and have slightly more detail at VF-30.

Illustrated coin: This coin is lightly struck at the left-reverse border, despite overall bold striking elsewhere.

VF-30

F-12, 15 (Fine). ***Obverse:*** The hair details are fewer than at the preceding level, but many are still present. Stars have flat centers. F-15 shows slightly more detail. ***Reverse:*** The wreath leaves are worn flat, but their edges are distinct. F-15 shows slightly more detail.

F-15

VG-10

VG-8, 10 (Very Good). ***Obverse:*** The portrait is well worn, although the eye and ear can be seen, as can some hair detail. The border is well defined in most areas. ***Reverse:*** The wreath, bow, and lettering are seen in outline form, and some leaves and letters may be indistinct in parts. The border is well defined in most areas.

G-6

G-4, 6 (Good). ***Obverse:*** The portrait is worn smooth and is seen only in outline form. Much of LIBERTY on the headband is readable, but the letters are weak. The stars are bold in outline. Much of the rim can be discerned. ***Reverse:*** Extensive wear is seen overall. Lettering in UNITED STATES OF AMERICA ranges from weak but complete (although the ANA grading guidelines allow for only half to be readable; the ANA text illustrates the words in full) to having perhaps a third of the letters missing. HALF CENT is usually bold.

Illustrated coin: While ultimately well-preserved for the grade, this coin is a bit rough in texture, with light pitting and traces of old, inactive surface build up.

AG-3

AG-3 (About Good). ***Obverse:*** Wear is more extensive than on the preceding. The portrait is visible only in outline. A few letters of LIBERTY are discernible in the headband. The stars are weak or worn away on their outer edges. The date is light. ***Reverse:*** The wreath is visible in outline form. Most or even all of UNITED STATES OF AMERICA is worn away. HALF CENT is usually readable.

PF-66

PF-60 to 70 (Proof). Proofs were struck of various years in the 1820s and 1830s, with 1831 and 1836 being great rarities (these dates were also restruck at the Mint circa 1859 and later). Some prooflike circulation strikes (especially of the 1833 date) have been certified as Proofs. Except for the years 1831 and 1836, for which Proofs are unequivocal, careful study is advised when contemplating the purchase of a coin described as Proof. Blotchy and recolored Proofs are often seen, but hardly ever described as such. Probably fewer than 25 of the Proofs of this type are truly pristine—without one problem or another. ***Obverse and Reverse:*** Proofs that are extensively hairlined or have dull surfaces, this being characteristic of many issues (1831 and 1836 usually excepted), are graded PF-60 to 62 or 63. This includes artificially toned and recolored coins, a secret that isn't really secret among knowledgeable collectors and dealers, but is rarely described in print. To qualify as PF-65 or higher, hairlines should be microscopic, and there should be no trace of friction. Surfaces should be prooflike or, better, fully mirrored, without dullness.

Illustrated coin: Note the traces of mint red throughout and the blue iridescence of the reverse. The reverse die is severely cracked from the F in OF to the T of UNITED.

1809, Normal Date

1809, Small 0 Inside 0

1809, 9 Over Inverted 9

1811, Wide Date

1811, Close Date

Circulation Strikes

	Mintage	GSID	AG-3	G-4	VG-8	F-12	VF-20	EF-40	AU-50	MS-60	MS-63
Classic Head (1809–1836), Brown	**n/a**	**72294**	**$80**	**$90**	**$95**	**$120**	**$130**	**$145**	**$180**	**$285**	**$575**
Same, Red Brown	**n/a**	**72295**	—	—	—	—	—	—	—	—	**775**
Same, Red	**n/a**	**72296**	—	—	—	—	—	—	—	—	**2,000**
1809, Normal Date	1,154,572	510	80	90	95	120	145	210	415	925	1,900
↳1809, Normal Date, C-1, FS-301	*	80902	550	850	1,500	3,750	6,500	14,500	29,000	54,000	—
↳1809, Normal Date, C-2	*	80903	85	130	210	340	575	1,150	3,000	—	—
↳1809, Normal Date, C-3	*	80904	80	90	95	120	145	210	415	925	1,900
↳1809, Normal Date, C-6	*	80907	80	90	95	120	145	210	415	925	1,900
1809, Small o Inside 0	*	513	110	120	160	290	435	950	1,400	5,500	—
↳1809, Small o Inside 0, C-4	*	80905	110	120	160	290	435	950	1,400	5,500	—
1809, 9 Over Inverted 9	*	705	85	100	105	130	150	290	525	1,000	2,500
↳1809, 9 Over Inverted 9, C-5	*	80906	85	100	105	130	150	290	525	1,000	2,500
1810	215,000	516	95	125	130	245	430	1,000	1,400	2,250	3,500
	Auctions: $109,250, PCGS MS-66 GLDB 01/14										
↳1810, C-1	*	80908	95	125	130	245	430	1,000	1,400	2,250	3,500
1811	63,140	519	235	390	850	1,250	1,800	4,400	8,500	36,000	81,500
	Auctions: $299,000, PCGS MS-65 GLDB 01/14										
↳1811, Wide Date, C-1	*	80909	235	390	850	1,250	1,800	4,400	8,500	36,000	81,500
↳1811, Close Date, C-2	*	80910	265	455	950	1,400	2,000	4,550	8,500	36,000	81,500
1811, Reverse of 1802, Mickley Restrike	12 est. known	522	—	—	—	—	—	—	4,400	6,250	9,500
1825	63,000	525	85	95	110	130	145	230	415	900	2,000
↳1825, C-1	*	80911	105	115	130	150	170	275	500	2,050	5,500
↳1825, C-2	*	80912	85	95	110	130	145	230	415	900	2,000
1826	234,000	528	80	90	95	120	130	160	230	550	1,150
↳1826, C-1	*	80913	80	90	95	120	130	160	230	550	1,150
↳1826, C-2	*	80914	80	90	95	120	130	160	230	550	1,150

* Included in number above.

1828, 13 Stars

1828, 12 Stars

Circulation Strikes *(continued)*

	Mintage	GSID	AG-3	G-4	VG-8	F-12	VF-20	EF-40	AU-50	MS-60	MS-63
1828, 13 Stars	606,000	531	$80	$90	$95	$120	$130	$145	$180	$285	$575
↳**1828, 13 Stars, C-1**	*	80915	80	90	95	120	130	145	180	285	575
↳**1828, 13 Stars, C-3**	*	80917	80	90	95	120	130	145	180	285	575
1828, 12 Stars	*	534	80	90	95	120	145	215	390	1,100	2,100
↳**1828, 12 Stars, C-2**	*	80916	80	90	95	120	145	215	390	1,100	2,100
1829	487,000	537	80	90	95	120	130	170	215	435	650
↳**1829, C-1**	*	80918	80	90	95	120	130	170	215	435	650
1831, Original (a)	2,200	540	5,500	9,500	12,000	15,000	24,000	38,500	57,000	84,000	—
↳**1831, Original, C-1** (a)	*	80919	5,500	9,500	12,000	15,000	24,000	38,500	57,000	84,000	—
1832 (b)	51,000	552	80	90	95	120	130	145	180	285	575
↳**1832, C-1**	*	80920	90	100	105	130	145	160	200	315	625
↳**1832, C-2**	*	80921	80	90	95	120	130	145	180	285	575
↳**1832, C-3**	*	80922	80	90	95	120	130	145	180	285	575
1833 (b)	103,000	558	80	90	95	120	130	145	180	285	575
↳**1833, C-1**	*	80923	80	90	95	120	130	145	180	285	575
1834 (b)	141,000	564	80	90	95	120	130	145	180	285	575
↳**1834, C-1**	*	80924	80	90	95	120	130	145	180	285	575
1835 (b)	398,000	570	80	90	95	120	130	145	180	285	575
↳**1835, C-1**	*	80925	80	90	95	120	130	145	180	285	575
↳**1835, C-2**	*	80926	80	90	95	120	130	145	180	285	575

* Included in number above. **a.** Opinions differ as to whether some of the 1831, Original half cents were circulation strikes or were Proofs that entered circulation. Beware of altered date. **b.** The figures given here are thought to be correct, although Mint records report these quantities for 1833 through 1836 rather than 1832 through 1835.

1831, Proof, Restrike

Reverse of 1831–1836

Reverse of 1840–1857

Proof Strikes

	Mintage	GSID	PF-60	PF-63	PF-65
Classic Head (1809–1836), Proof, Brown	**n/a**	**74201**	**$3,600**	**$6,000**	**$12,000**
Same, Red Brown	**n/a**	**74202**	**—**	**8,750**	**19,000**
Same, Red	**n/a**	**74203**	**—**	**10,500**	**31,000**
1831, Original (beware of altered date)	2,200	543	57,500	72,000	120,000
	Auctions: $155,250, PCGS PF-66 GLDB 01/14				
1831, Restrike, Large Berries (Reverse of 1836)	25–35	546	—	12,000	19,000
1831, Restrike, Small Berries (Reverse of 1840–1857)	10–15 known	549	9,500	18,000	36,000
1832	10–15 known	555	—	14,500	43,000
↳1832, C-1	*	213453	—	14,500	43,000
↳1832, C-2	*	213456	—	14,500	43,000
1833	25–35	561	3,600	8,000	14,500
↳1833, C-1	*	213459	3,600	8,000	14,500
1834	25–35	567	3,900	6,750	14,500
↳1834, C-1	*	213462	3,900	6,750	14,500
1835	15–20	573	3,900	6,000	12,000
↳1835, C-2	*	213465	3,900	6,000	12,000
1836, Original	140–240	576	5,500	9,000	14,500
1836, Restrike (Reverse of 1836)	20 est. known	213370	—	18,000	24,000
1836, Restrike (Reverse of 1840–1857)	*	579	—	10,000	17,500

* Included in number above.

BRAIDED HAIR (1840–1857)

Designer: *Christian Gobrecht.* **Weight:** *5.44 grams.* **Composition:** *Copper.* **Diameter:** *23 mm.* **Edge:** *Plain.* **Mint:** *Philadelphia.*

Circulation Strike

Proof Strike

History. The Braided Hair half cent debuted in 1840, a year after the same design was introduced on copper cents. There was scant commercial demand for this denomination, so only Proofs were struck from 1840 to 1848 and in 1852. (In 1849–1851 and 1853–1857 both Proofs and circulation strikes were made.) Ultimately the half cent was discontinued by the Act of February 21, 1857. After that point the coins were rapidly withdrawn from circulation, and by 1860 virtually all had disappeared from commerce.

Striking and Sharpness. Many if not most Braided Hair half cents are well struck, and nearly all are on good planchet stock. Check these points for sharpness: the denticles on both sides; the star centers and hair detail on the obverse; and the leaf detail on the reverse.

Availability. Because Braided Hair half cents were not struck for circulation until 1849 and they did not circulate after the 1850s, they never acquired extensive wear. Most coins grade EF-40 and finer. Lower grades are sometimes seen, but are not in demand.

Grading Standards

MS-63BN

MS-60 to 70 (Mint State). ***Obverse:*** In the lower Mint State grades, MS-60 and 61, some slight abrasion can be seen on the portrait, most evidently on the cheek. Check the tip of the coronet as well. Luster in the field is complete, or nearly so. At MS-63, luster should be complete, and no abrasions evident. At higher levels, the luster is complete and deeper, and some original mint color may be seen. Mint frost on this type is usually deep, sometimes satiny, but hardly ever prooflike. MS-64 coins may have some slight discoloration or scattered contact marks. A well-graded MS-65 or higher coin has full, rich luster; no contact marks visible except under magnification; and a nice blend of brown toning or nicely mixed (not stained or blotchy) mint color and natural brown toning. The late Walter Breen stated that he had never seen an 1853 (common date) half cent with extensive original mint color, but these are plentiful with brown-toned surfaces. ***Reverse:*** In the lower Mint State grades some abrasions are seen on the higher areas of the leaves. Mint luster is complete in all Mint State grades, as the open areas are protected by the lettering and wreath.

AU-50

AU-50, 53, 55, 58 (About Uncirculated). ***Obverse:*** Wear is evident on the cheek, the hair above the forehead, and the tip of the coronet. Friction is evident in the field. At AU-58, luster may be present except in the center of the fields. As the grades go down to AU-50, wear is more evident on the portrait. Wear is seen on the stars, but is not as easy to discern as it is elsewhere. At AU-50 there is either no luster or only traces of luster close to the letters and devices. ***Reverse:*** Wear is most evident on the highest areas of the leaves and the ribbon bow. Luster is present in the fields. As the grades go downward from AU-58 to 50, wear increases and luster decreases. At the AU-50 level there is either no luster or traces of luster close to the letters and devices.

Illustrated coin: This coin shows Full Details on both sides, and has eye-pleasing, light-brown surfaces.

EF-40

EF-40, 45 (Extremely Fine). ***Obverse:*** Wear is more extensive on the portrait, including the cheek, hair, and coronet. The star centers are worn down slightly. Traces of luster are minimal, if at all existent. ***Reverse:*** The centers of the leaves are well worn, with detail visible only near the edges of the leaves and nearby, with the higher parts worn flat. Letters show significant wear. Luster, if present, is minimal.

VF-30

VF-20, 30 (Very Fine). ***Obverse:*** Wear is more extensive than at the preceding levels. Some of the strands of hair are fused together. The center radials of the stars are worn nearly completely away. ***Reverse:*** The leaves show more extensive wear, with details visible at the edges, and only minimally and not on all leaves. The lettering shows smooth, even wear.

Braided Hair half cents are seldom collected in grades lower than VF-20.

PF-64RB

PF-60 to 70 (Proof). For the issues of 1840 to 1848, the 1849, Small Date, and the issues of 1852, only Proofs were made, without related examples for circulation. All were restruck at the Mint. Generally, the quality of these Proofs is very good, with excellent striking of details and nice planchet quality. ***Obverse and Reverse:*** Superb gems at PF-65 and 66 show hairlines only under high magnification, and at PF-67 none are seen. The fields are deeply mirrorlike. There is no evidence of friction. At lower levels, hairlines increase, with a profusion at PF-60 to 62 (and also a general dullness of the fields). Typical color for an undipped coin ranges from light or iridescent brown to brown with some traces of mint color. Except for issues in the 1850s, Proofs are nearly always BN or, less often, RB. The rare Proofs of the 1840s are sometimes seen with light wear and can be classified according to the About Uncirculated and Extremely Fine comments above, except in place of "luster" read "Proof surface."

Illustrated coin: Overall this coin's surfaces are smooth, and the dominant sandy-olive patina belies semi-reflective tendencies in the fields and gold, apricot and lilac undertones when viewed under direct light.

Large Berries (Original Strike)

Small Berries (Restrike)

1849, Small Date (Proof Only)

1849, Large Date

Circulation Strikes

	Mintage	GSID	AG-3	G-4	VG-8	F-12	VF-20	EF-40	AU-50	MS-60	MS-63
Braided Hair (1840–1857), Brown	**n/a**	**72302**	**$70**	**$95**	**$110**	**$120**	**$130**	**$135**	**$160**	**$230**	**$430**
Same, Red Brown	**n/a**	**72303**	**—**	**—**	**—**	**—**	**—**	**—**	**—**	**285**	**575**
Same, Red	**n/a**	**72304**	**—**	**—**	**—**	**—**	**—**	**—**	**—**	**—**	**1,300**
1849, Large Date	39,864	639	70	95	110	120	135	180	285	550	975
↳1849, Large Date, C-1	*	80927	70	95	110	120	135	180	285	550	975
1850	39,812	651	75	120	180	260	390	650	775	1,300	3,000
↳1850, C-1	*	80928	75	120	180	260	390	650	775	1,300	3,000
1851	147,672	657	70	95	110	120	130	135	160	230	430
↳1851, C-1	*	80929	70	95	110	120	130	135	160	230	430
1853	129,694	666	70	95	110	120	130	135	160	230	430
↳1853, C-1	*	80930	70	95	110	120	130	135	160	230	430
1854	55,358	672	70	95	110	120	130	135	160	230	430
↳1854, C-1	*	80931	70	95	110	120	130	135	160	230	430
1855	56,500	678	70	95	110	120	130	135	160	230	430
↳1855, C-1	*	80932	70	95	110	120	130	135	160	230	430
1856	40,430	684	70	95	110	120	130	135	160	230	430
↳1856, C-1	*	80933	70	95	110	120	130	135	160	230	430
1857	35,180	690	70	95	110	120	135	175	260	390	650
↳1857, C-1	*	80934	70	95	110	120	135	175	260	390	650

* Included in number above.

Proof Strikes

		GSID	PF-60	PF-63	PF-65
Braided Hair (1840–1857), Proof, Brown	**n/a**	**74204**	**$2,750**	**$4,100**	**$7,250**
Same, Proof, Red Brown	**n/a**	**74205**	**3,750**	**4,500**	**10,500**
Same, Red	**n/a**	**74206**	**—**	**12,000**	**26,500**
1840, Original	20–25 est. known	582	4,500	8,250	14,000
↳1840, Restrike (Reverse of 1840)	7–9 est. known	201961	3,750	7,500	11,000
↳1840, Restrike (Reverse of 1856)	14–17 est. known	585	5,000	7,500	10,000
1841, Original	35–50 est. known	588	5,000	8,750	17,500
↳1841, Restrike (Reverse of 1840)	5–7 est. known	201963	5,750	8,750	12,000
↳1841, Restrike (Reverse of 1856)	10–12 est. known	591	5,500	8,000	12,000
1842, Original	15–20 est. known	594	6,000	10,000	29,000
↳1842, Restrike (Reverse of 1840)	15–20 est. known	213377	2,750	4,100	7,250
↳1842, Restrike (Reverse of 1856)	20–25 est. known	213374	2,750	4,100	7,250
1843, Original	25–35 est. known	600	5,000	9,000	21,500
↳1843, Restrike (Reverse of 1840)	30–35 est. known	213384	5,000	8,000	10,500
↳1843, Restrike (Reverse of 1856)	7–9 est. known	213381	5,000	8,000	10,500
1844, Original	19–24 est. known	606	7,000	12,500	19,000
↳1844, Restrike (Reverse of 1840)	7–9 est. known	213391	4,750	7,250	12,500
↳1844, Restrike (Reverse of 1856)	14–17 est. known	213388	4,750	7,250	12,500
1845, Original	16–20 est. known	612	12,000	17,000	33,500
↳1845, Restrike (Reverse of 1840)	8–10 est. known	213398	4,500	6,000	10,000
↳1845, Restrike (Reverse of 1856)	12–14 est. known	213395	4,500	6,000	10,000
1846, Original	20–25 est. known	618	5,750	10,000	27,000
↳1846, Restrike (Reverse of 1840)	5–7 est. known	213405	4,000	7,500	11,000
↳1846, Restrike (Reverse of 1856)	14–17 est. known	213402	4,000	7,500	11,000
1847, Original	20–25 est. known	624	4,400	7,750	19,000
↳1847, Restrike (Reverse of 1840)	3–4 est. known	213411	4,000	6,000	11,500
↳1847, Restrike (Reverse of 1856)	30–40 est. known	213408	4,000	6,000	11,500
1848, Original	15–20 est. known	630	6,250	12,000	29,000
↳1848, Restrike, Large Berries (Reverse of 1840)	30–35 est. known	213417	2,750	4,100	8,750
↳1848, Restrike, Large Berries (Reverse of 1856)	10–12 est. known	213414	2,750	4,100	8,750
1849, Original, Small Date	12–14 est. known	642	6,250	12,000	38,500
1849, Original, Large Date	2–4 est. known	648	—	33,500	48,000
1849, Restrike, Small Date (Reverse of 1856)	18–22 est. known	645	3,000	6,000	11,000
1850	10–12 est. known	654	4,750	8,000	48,000
1851	3–5 est. known	660	—	—	60,000
1852, Original, Large Berries	5 known	663	—	—	576,000
↳1852, Restrike, Small Berries	100–125 est. known	81162	3,000	6,000	8,750
↳1852, Restrike, Large Berries		81165	—	—	210,000
	Auctions: $192,000, PCGS PF-64 HA 08/22				
↳1852, Restrike (Reverse of 1840)	100–125 est. known	81168	3,000	6,000	8,750
↳1852, Restrike (Reverse of 1856)	10–15 est. known	81171	3,000	6,000	8,750
1854	25–30 est. known	675	5,750	8,000	15,500
1855	40–60 est. known	681	2,750	4,100	7,250
1856, Reverse of 1854	70–90 est. known	226297	3,250	4,750	8,250
1856, Reverse of 1856	50–60 est. known	687	2,750	4,100	7,250
1857	120–150 est. known	693	2,750	4,100	7,250

Large Cents
1793–1857

AN OVERVIEW OF LARGE CENTS

Collecting one each of the major types of 1793–1857 copper cents can be a fascinating challenge. Early varieties were struck from hand-engraved dies, often on copper planchets of uncertain quality. It was not until 1836 that steam power was used to run coining presses at the Mint. All earlier issues were made by hand, by two men tugging on the weighted lever arm of a small screw-type press. As might be expected, this resulted in many variations in striking quality.

Scan for additional information.

The first cents of 1793, the Chain varieties, are found with two major differences: AMERI. on the reverse, and the later version with AMERICA spelled out in full. These early issues have been highly desired from the beginning days of the numismatic hobby in America, and remain in the limelight today.

Wreath cents of 1793 occur with the edge displaying a vine and bars motif and also with lettering ONE HUNDRED FOR A DOLLAR. Liberty Cap cents of the 1793–1796 years have lettered edges (ONE HUNDRED FOR A DOLLAR) used in 1793, 1794, and part of 1795, and plain edges for most 1795 coins and all of 1796.

The Draped Bust type commenced partway through 1796 and was continued through 1807. This span includes the notably rare 1799, 9 Over 8, overdate and the 1799 as well as the somewhat rare 1804. Many interesting die varieties occur in this type, particularly with regard to errors on the reverse. The Classic Head cent, designed by John Reich, was introduced in 1808, and was continued through 1814. In 1815 no cents of this date were produced. Then in 1816 the Coronet Head commenced, a new motif with a new reverse as well. With modifications this was continued through 1839, in which year the Braided Hair design by Christian Gobrecht made its appearance. Large cents were made continually through January 1857 and then discontinued.

For the Collector and Investor: Large Cents as a Specialty

For the enjoyment of copper cents 1793–1857 it is possible to go far beyond a type set. Today, varieties of the 1793–1814 cents are generally collected by Sheldon numbers (S-1, S-2, etc.), given first in *Early American Cents* and, later, in its revision, *Penny Whimsy*. Building upon this foundation, *Walter Breen's Encyclopedia of Early United States Large Cents, 1793–1814*, gives more information on this date range than available in any other single source.

Among dates and major varieties in the early range of the series, the 1793 issues Chain AMERI., Chain AMERICA, Wreath, and Liberty Cap, the 1799 (far and away the rarest date in the series), and the 1804 are key issues, each a part of an extensive series of more than 300 die varieties through and including 1814.

The most popular way to collect large cents is by basic varieties, mainly dates, overdates, and major varieties. Sometimes, a particular date is selected as a specialty for collecting die varieties by Sheldon numbers.

Generally, grades from Good to VF are popular objectives for the early series from 1793 to 1814, and for some varieties no better coins exist. EF, AU, and Mint State coins are available and are more likely to be sought by collectors of basic dates and major varieties, rather than by specialists seeing long runs of Sheldon numbers. Type-set collectors are also important in the market for high-grade pieces, where sights can be set high as there are fewer varieties to obtain. Accordingly, as a type-set collector one may aspire to own an AU or Mint State cent of the 1796–1807 Draped Bust type. However, for a specialist in die varieties, who wants to acquire more than 100 different specimens from this date range, such high grades might not be feasible to acquire.

Collecting cents of the later dates by basic varieties is an interesting pursuit, and one that is quite attainable in such grades as EF, AU, or even MS-60, most dates after the 1820s being readily available for relatively inexpensive prices. Key issues among 1816–1857 cents include 1823, 3 Over 2; 1823; 1824, 4 Over 2; 1839, 9 Over 6; and a few others. Collecting Braided Hair cents toward the end of the series, 1839 to 1857, is least expensive of all, and most major varieties can be obtained in such grades as MS-60 to 63, with lustrous brown surfaces, for reasonable figures.

EXPLORING VARIETIES

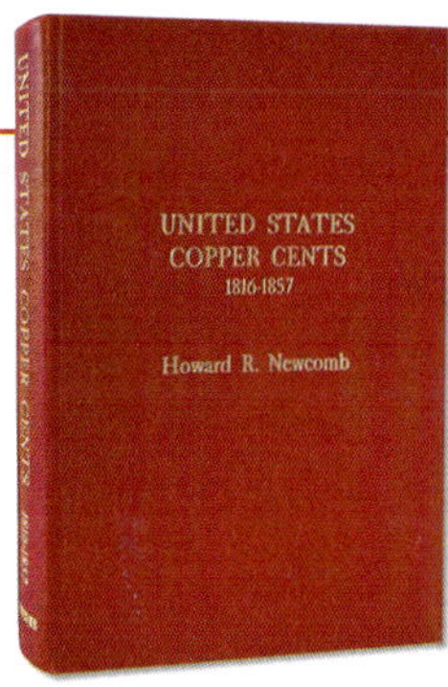

H.R. Newcomb's book catalogs later (1816–1857) die varieties of large cents. His Newcomb numbers identify the varieties of this period and remain the standard references today. Collectors use them in much the same way as they do Sheldon numbers to classify and compare coins consistently.

Newcomb, H.R. *United States Copper Cents 1816–1857.* New York, NY: 1944 (reprinted 1983).

EXPLORING VARIETIES

William H. Sheldon's *Penny Whimsy* catalogs the early large cents of 1793–1814, and it introduced the Sheldon numbers that are still the universal attributions for varieties in this series. Each Sheldon number points to a specific die marriage, and collectors rely on these numbers for study and trading. This book also popularized the 70-point grading scale and set the foundation for rarity ratings in U.S. copper coinage.

Sheldon, William H. *Penny Whimsy (1793–1814).* New York, NY: 1958 (reprinted 1965, 1976). (Formerly Early American Cents. New York, NY: 1949.)

FLOWING HAIR, CHAIN REVERSE (1793)

Designer: *Henry Voigt.* **Weight:** *13.48 grams.* **Composition:** *Copper.*
Diameter: *Average 26 to 27 mm.* **Edge:** *Vine and bars design.* **Mint:** *Philadelphia.*

Chain AMERI. Reverse

Chain AMERICA Reverse

Vine-and-Bars Edge

History. The first U.S. cents intended for circulation were struck at the Mint in Philadelphia from February 27 through March 12, 1793. These were of the Flowing Hair design, with a Chain reverse. Several varieties were struck, today these can be attributed by Bowers-Whitman numbers or Sheldon numbers. The first, or Bowers-Whitman–1, Sheldon-1, had AMERICA abbreviated as AMERI. A contemporary account noted that Liberty appeared to be "in a fright," and that the chain motif on the reverse, 15 links intended to symbolize unity of the states in the Union, was an "ill omen" for a land of liberty; accordingly, the design was used for only a short time. The rims on both sides are raised, without denticles or beads.

Striking and Sharpness. The details of Liberty's hair are often indistinct or missing, including on many higher-grade specimens. For all grades and varieties, the reverse is significantly sharper than the obverse. The portrait of Liberty is shallow and is often weak, especially on the BW-1, S-1, variety (which is often missing the date). Note that early copper coins of all kinds may exhibit "tooling" (engraving done outside the Mint in order to simulate details that were worn away or weakly struck to begin with). Also, these old coppers have sometimes been burnished to smooth out areas of porosity. These alterations are considered to be damage, and they significantly decrease a coin's value.

Availability. Demand is higher than supply for all varieties, with fewer than 1,000 or so examples surviving today. Most are in lower grades, from Fair-2 to VG-8. Even heavily worn coins (still identifiable by the chain device) are highly collectible. VF and EF coins are few and far between, and AU and MS are very rare.

Grading Standards

MS-66BN

MS-60 to 70 (Mint State). ***Obverse:*** In the lower Mint State grades, MS-60 and 61, some slight abrasions can be seen on the higher areas of the portrait. The large open field shows light contact marks and perhaps a few nicks. At MS-63 the luster should be complete, although some very light abrasions or contact marks may be seen on the portrait. At MS-64 or higher—a nearly impossible level for a Chain cent—there is no sign of abrasion anywhere. Mint color is not extensive on any known Mint State coin, but traces of red-orange are sometimes seen around the rim and devices on both sides. ***Reverse:*** In the lower Mint State grades some abrasions are seen on the chain links. There is some abrasion in the field. At MS-63, luster should be unbroken. Some abrasion and minor contact marks may be evident. In still higher grades, luster is deep and there is no sign of abrasion.

Illustrated coin: This coin is sharply struck with full hair detail. It is the Cleneay-Jackman-Ryder specimen mentioned in Sheldon's *Penny Whimsy* as the unrivalled, finest-known example of this variety.

AU-50, 53, 55, 58 (About Uncirculated). ***Obverse:*** Light wear is seen on the highest areas of the portrait. Some luster is seen in the large open fields at the AU-58 level, less at AU-55, and little if any for AU-53 and 50. Scattered marks are normal and are most evident in the field. At higher levels, some vestiges of luster may be seen among the letters, numerals, and between the hair tips. ***Reverse:*** Light wear is most evident on the chain, as this is the most prominent feature. The letters show wear, but not as extensive. Luster may be seen at the 58 and 55 levels, usually slightly more on the reverse than on the obverse. Generally, the reverse grades higher than the obverse, usually by a step, such as an AU-50 obverse and an AU-53 reverse (such a coin would be listed as the lower of the two, or AU-50).

AU-53

EF-40, 45 (Extremely Fine). ***Obverse:*** The center of the portrait is well worn, with the hair visible only in thick strands, although extensive detail remains in the hair tips at the left. No luster is seen. Contact marks are normal in the large expanse of open field, but should be mentioned if they are distracting. ***Reverse:*** The chain is bold and shows light wear. Other features show wear, as well—more extensive in appearance, as the relief is lower. The fields show some friction, but not as much as on the obverse.

EF-45

VF-20, 30 (Very Fine). ***Obverse:*** More wear is seen on the portrait, with perhaps half or slightly more of the hair detail showing, mostly near the left edge of the hair. The ear usually is visible (but might not be, depending on the sharpness of strike). The letters in LIBERTY show wear. The rim remains bold (more so than on the reverse). ***Reverse:*** The chain shows more wear than on the preceding, but is still bold. Other features show more wear and may be weak in areas. The rim may be weak in areas.

VF-30

F-12, 15 (Fine). ***Obverse:*** The hair details are mostly worn away, with about one-third visible, that being on the left. The rim is distinct on most examples. The bottoms of the date digits are weak or possibly worn away. ***Reverse:*** The chain is bold, as is the lettering within the chain. Lettering around the border shows extensive wear, but is complete. The rim may be flat in areas.

F-15

Illustrated coin: The surface is generally smooth and even under close scrutiny reveals only minor roughness. Note the shallow reverse rim bruise outside the letters AM in AMERICA and some mild encrustation around the letter C in CENT and the nearby chain links.

VG-8, 10 (Very Good). ***Obverse:*** The portrait is well worn, although Liberty's eye remains bold. Hair detail is gone at the center, but is evident at the left edge of the portrait. LIBERTY is always readable, but may be faded or partly missing on shallow strikes. The date is well worn, with the bottom of the numerals missing (published standards vary on this point, and it used to be the case that a full date was mandatory). ***Reverse:*** The chain remains bold, and the center letters are all readable. Border letters may be weak or incomplete. The rim is smooth in most areas.

VG-10

Illustrated coin: The coin is smooth in appearance with the worn areas showing lighter copper, while the fields have trace roughness and the classic black olive texture. Note the planchet flaw right of ONE, which appears as a void in the metal.

G-4, 6 (Good). ***Obverse:*** The portrait is worn smooth and is seen only in outline form, although the eye position can be discerned. LIBERTY may be weak. The date is weak, but the tops of the numerals can be discerned. ***Reverse:*** The chain is fully visible in outline form. Central lettering is mostly or completely readable, but light. Peripheral lettering is mostly worn away.

G-4

Illustrated coin: Natural obverse planchet flaws, as struck, can be seen both at 12 o'clock on the rim and above and to the left of the date, with other faint fissuring seen on the reverse under low magnification.

AG-3 (About Good). ***Obverse:*** The portrait is visible as an outline. LIBERTY and the date are mostly or even completely worn away. Contact marks may be extensive. ***Reverse:*** The chain is fully visible in outline form. Traces of the central letters—or, on better strikes, nearly all of the letters—can be seen. Around the border all letters are worn away.

AG-3

Circulation Strikes

	Mintage	GSID	AG-3	G-4	VG-8	F-12	VF-20	EF-40	AU-50	MS-60
Flowing Hair, Chain Reverse (1793)	**n/a**	**72308**	**$6,750**	**$8,500**	**$12,000**	**$18,000**	**$29,000**	**$57,500**	**$78,000**	**$210,000**
1793, Chain Reverse, AMERI. In Legend	36,103	1212	7,500	9,500	13,000	20,000	31,500	63,500	86,000	480,000
	Auctions: $108,000, PCGS AU-50 SBG 08/25; $440,625, PCGS MS-63 HA 08/25									
↳1793, Chain Reverse, AMERI. In Legend, S-1	*	76717	7,500	9,500	13,000	20,000	31,500	63,500	86,000	480,000
	Auctions: $348,000, PCGS AU-58 HA 01/24; $1,500,000, PCGS MS-64 HA 01/24									
1793, Chain Reverse, AMERICA, Without Periods	*	1213	6,750	8,500	12,000	18,000	29,000	57,500	78,000	210,000
	Auctions: $878,312, NGC MS-66 SBG 08/12									
↳1793, Chain Reverse, AMERICA, Without Periods, S-2	*	76718	6,750	8,500	12,000	18,000	29,000	57,500	78,000	210,000
	Auctions: $156,000, PCGS AU-53 HA 01/25; $528,000, PCGS MS-64 HA 01/25									
↳1793, Chain Reverse, AMERICA, Without Periods, S-3	*	76719	6,750	8,500	12,000	18,000	29,000	57,500	78,000	220,500
	Auctions: $150,000, PCGS AU-55 HA 09/24; $138,000, PCGS AU-55 HA 09/24									
↳1793, Chain Reverse, AMERICA, Without Periods, S-NC-1	*	76720	—	—	—	—	—	—	—	—
1793, Chain Reverse, AMERICA, With Periods	*	1217	6,750	8,500	12,000	18,000	29,000	57,500	78,000	210,000
	Auctions: $1,380,000, PCGS MS-65 HA 01/12									
↳1793, Chain Reverse, AMERICA, With Periods, S-4	*	76721	6,750	8,500	12,000	18,000	30,000	57,500	78,000	210,000
	Auctions: $119,400, PCGS AU-50 HA 01/25; $2,350,000, PCGS MS-66 HA 01/25									

* Included in number above.

FLOWING HAIR, WREATH REVERSE (1793)

Designer: *Henry Voigt.* **Weight:** *13.48 grams.* **Composition:** *Copper.* **Diameter:** *26 to 28 mm.* **Edge:** *Vine and bars design, or lettered ONE HUNDRED FOR A DOLLAR followed by either a single or a double leaf.* **Mint:** *Philadelphia.*

History. Between April 9 and July 17, 1793, the U.S. Mint struck and delivered 63,353 large copper cents. Most of these, and perhaps all, were of the Wreath type, although records do not specify when the design types were changed that year. The Wreath cent was named for the new reverse style. Both sides have raised beads at the border, similar to the style used on 1793 half cents.

Striking and Sharpness. These cents usually are fairly well struck, although high-grade pieces often exhibit some weakness on the highest hair tresses and on the leaf details. (On lower-grade pieces these areas are worn, so the point is moot.) Planchet quality varies widely, from smooth, glossy brown to dark and porous. The lettered-edge cents are often seen on defective planchets. Consult Sheldon's *Penny Whimsy (1793–1814)* and photographs to learn the characteristics of certain varieties. The borders have raised beads; on high-grade pieces these are usually very distinct, but they blend together on lower-grade coins and can sometimes be indistinct. The beads are not as prominent as those later used on the 1793 Liberty Cap cents.

Availability. At least several thousand examples exist of the different varieties of the type. Most are in lower grades, from AG-3 to VG-8, although Fine and VF pieces are encountered with regularity. Choice EF, AU, and finer coins see high demand. Some in MS have been billed as "specimen" or "presentation" coins, although this is supposition, as no records exist.

Grading Standards

MS-66

MS-60 to 70 (Mint State). ***Obverse:*** On MS-60 and 61 coins there are some traces of abrasion on the higher areas of the portrait, most particularly the hair. As this area can be lightly struck, careful inspection is needed for evaluation, not as much in Mint State (as other features come into play), but in higher circulated grades. Luster in the field is incomplete at lower Mint State levels, but should be in generous quantity. At MS-63, luster should be complete, and no abrasion evident. At higher levels, the luster is deeper, and some original mint color may be seen. At MS-65 there might be some scattered contact marks and possibly bare traces of fingerprints or discoloration. Above MS-65, a coin should approach perfection. A Mint State 1793 Wreath cent is an object of rare beauty. ***Reverse:*** In the lower Mint State grades some abrasion is seen on the higher areas of the leaves. Generally, luster is complete in all grades, as the open areas are protected by the lettering and wreath. In many ways, the grading guidelines for this type follow those of the 1793 half cent—also with sprays of berries (not seen elsewhere in the series).

Illustrated coin: Remarkably, this coin displays some original Mint orange.

AU-50

AU-50, 53, 55, 58 (About Uncirculated). ***Obverse:*** Friction is seen on the highest areas of the hair (which may also be lightly struck) and the cheek. Some scattered marks are normal in the field, ranging from more extensive at AU-50 to minimal at AU-58. ***Reverse:*** Friction is seen on the higher wreath leaves and (not as easy to discern) on the letters. The fields, protected by the designs (including sprays of berries at the center), show friction, but not as noticeably as on the obverse. At AU-55 and 58, little if any friction is seen. Border beads, if well struck, are separate and boldly defined.

Illustrated coin: Note the clash marks on the obverse indicative of a late die state. Significant portions of the reverse wreath are clashed in the field from Liberty's nose to the base of the throat, below the bust around the leaf cluster, and between some of the strands of hair at the back of Liberty's head. Additionally, the letters MERICA in the word AMERICA are clashed in the right-obverse field, the letters becoming bolder toward the end of that word.

EF-40

EF-40, 45 (Extremely Fine). ***Obverse:*** More extensive wear is seen on the high parts of the hair, creating mostly a solid mass (without detail of strands) of varying width in the area immediately to the left of the face. The cheek shows light wear. Luster is minimal or nonexistent at EF-40, and may survive in traces in protected areas (such as between the letters) at EF-45. ***Reverse:*** Wear is seen on the highest wreath and ribbon areas, and the letters. Luster is minimal, but likely more noticeable than on the obverse, as the fields are protected by the designs and lettering. Some of the beads blend together.

VF-25

VF-20, 30 (Very Fine). ***Obverse:*** Wear on the hair is more extensive, and varies depending on the die variety and sharpness of strike. The ANA grading standards suggest that two-thirds of the hair is visible, which in practice can be said to be "more or less." More beads are blended together, but the extent of this blending depends on the striking and variety. Certain parts of the rim are smooth, with beads scarcely visible at all. No luster is seen. The date, LIBERTY, and hair ends are bold. ***Reverse:*** The leaf details are nearly completely worn away at VF-20, with slight detail at VF-30. The border beads are blended together, with many indistinct. Some berries in the sprays are light, but nearly all remain distinct. No luster is seen.

Illustrated coin: The surfaces are a bit rough overall with a few areas also revealing slight verdigris.

F-12, 15 (Fine). ***Obverse:*** The hair details are mostly worn away, with about one-third visible, mainly at the edges. The ANA grading standards suggest that half of the details are visible, seemingly applying to the total area of the hair. However, the visible part, at the left, also includes intermittent areas of the field. Beads are weak or worn away in areas. F-15 shows slightly more detail. By this grade, scattered light scratches, noticeable contact marks, and the like are the rule, not the exception. These are not mentioned at all on holders and are often overlooked elsewhere, except in some auction catalogs and price lists. Such marks are implicit for coins in lower grades, and light porosity or granularity is common as well. ***Reverse:*** The wreath leaves are worn flat, but their edges are distinct. Border beads are weak or worn away in areas. F-15 shows slightly more detail.

F-12

Illustrated coin: Despite slight pock-marking on the obverse and scattered rim bruises, this coin features strong definition for an F-12 piece.

VG-8, 10 (Very Good). ***Obverse:*** The hair is well worn toward the face. Details at the left are mostly blended together in thick strands. The eye, nose, and lips often remain well defined. Border beads are completely gone, or just seen in traces, and part of the rim blends into the field. LIBERTY may be slightly weak. The 1793 date is fully visible, although there may be some lightness. Scattered marks are more common than on higher grades. ***Reverse:*** The wreath, bow, and lettering are seen in outline form, and some leaves and letters may be indistinct in parts. Most of the berries remain visible, but weak. Border beads are worn away, and the border blends into the field in most if not all of the periphery.

VG-8

G-4, 6 (Good). ***Obverse:*** The hair is worn smooth except for the thick tresses at the left. The eye, nose, and lips show some detail. LIBERTY is weak, with some letters missing. The date is discernible, although partially worn away. The sprig above the date is usually prominent. The border completely blends into the field. ***Reverse:*** Extensive overall wear. The wreath is seen in outline form, with some areas weak. Usually ONE CENT remains readable at the center. The border letters and fraction show extensive wear, with some letters very weak or even missing, although most should be discernible. Dark or porous coins may have more details on both sides in an effort to compensate for the roughness. Marks, edge bumps, and so on are normal.

G-4

Illustrated coin: Note minor surface roughness. Definition in the major devices is strong for this grade.

AG-3

AG-3 (About Good). ***Obverse:*** Wear is more extensive than on the preceding. The eye, nose, and lips may still be discernible, and the sprig above the date can usually be seen. LIBERTY may be very weak or even missing. The date is gone, or just a trace will remain. ***Reverse:*** Parts of the wreath are visible in outline form. ONE CENT might be readable, but this is not a requirement. Most border letters are gone. If a coin is dark or porous it may be graded AG-3 and may be sharper than just described, with the porosity accounting for the lower grade.

Vine-and-Bars Edge

Lettered Edge
(ONE HUNDRED FOR A DOLLAR)

Regular Sprig

Strawberry Leaf

Circulation Strikes

	Mintage	GSID	AG-3	G-4	VG-8	F-12	VF-20	EF-40	AU-50	MS-60
Flowing Hair, Wreath Reverse (1793)	**n/a**	**72309**	**$2,250**	**$3,250**	**$4,500**	**$6,500**	**$11,000**	**$23,000**	**$27,000**	**$54,000**
1793, Wreath Reverse, Vine-and-Bars Edge	63,353	1220	2,250	3,250	4,500	6,500	11,000	23,000	27,000	54,000
	Auctions: $566,056, PCGS MS-69 SBG 08/13									
↳1793, Wreath Reverse, Vine-and-Bars Edge, S-5	*	76722	2,250	3,250	4,500	6,500	11,000	23,000	27,000	54,000
	Auctions: $235,000, PCGS MS-66 SBG 02/16									
↳1793, Wreath Reverse, Vine-and-Bars Edge, S-6	*	76723	2,250	3,250	4,500	6,500	11,000	23,000	27,000	54,000
↳1793, Wreath Reverse, Vine-and-Bars Edge, S-7	*	76724	11,000	14,500	19,000	29,000	48,000	78,000	102,000	150,000
	Auctions: $120,000, NGC MS-61 HA 01/21									
↳1793, Wreath Reverse, Vine-and-Bars Edge, S-8	*	76725	2,250	3,250	4,500	6,500	11,000	23,000	27,000	54,000
	Auctions: $396,000, PCGS MS-67 HA 08/25									
↳1793, Wreath Reverse, Vine-and-Bars Edge, S-9	*	76726	2,250	3,250	4,500	6,500	11,000	23,000	27,000	54,000
	Auctions: $528,750, PCGS MS-66 HA 08/14									
↳1793, Wreath Reverse, Vine-and-Bars Edge, S-10	*	76727	2,250	3,250	4,500	6,500	11,000	23,000	27,000	54,000
	Auctions: $180,000, PCGS MS-65 HA 01/19									
↳1793, Wreath Reverse, Vine-and-Bars Edge, S-11a	*	76728	2,700	3,900	4,950	7,250	11,000	23,000	27,000	60,000
	Auctions: $217,375, PCGS MS-66 SBG 02/16									
1793, Wreath Reverse, Lettered Edge	*	1223	2,250	3,250	4,500	6,500	11,000	23,000	27,000	54,000
	Auctions: $276,000, PCGS MS-64 HA 01/08									
↳1793, Wreath Reverse, Lettered Edge, S-11b	*	76729	2,250	3,250	4,500	6,500	11,000	23,000	27,000	54,000
↳1793, Wreath Reverse, Lettered Edge, S-11c	*	76730	2,250	3,250	4,500	6,500	11,000	23,000	27,000	54,000
	Auctions: $102,000, PCGS MS-62 HA 02/22									
1793, Wreath Reverse, Strawberry Leaf	4 known	1226	—	374,500	540,000	864,000	—	—	—	—
	Auctions: $862,500, NGC F-12 SBG 01/09									
↳1793, Wreath Reverse, Strawberry Leaf, S-NC-2	*	76731	480,000	—	—	—	—	—	—	—
	Auctions: $352,500, PCGS AG2 HA 01/14									
↳1793, Wreath Reverse, Strawberry Leaf, S-NC-3	*	76732	—	374,500	540,000	864,000	—	—	—	—
	Auctions: $312,000, PCGS G-4 HA 04/25; $660,000, PCGS VG-10 SBG 04/25									

* Included in number above.

LIBERTY CAP (1793–1796)

Designer: *1793–1795, thick planchet—Probably Joseph Wright; 1795–1796, thin planchet—John Smith Gardner.* **Weight:** *1793–1795, thick planchet—13.48 grams; 1795–1796, thin planchet—10.89 grams.* **Composition:** *Copper.* **Diameter:** *Average 29 mm.* **Edge:** *1793–1795, thick planchet—Lettered ONE HUNDRED FOR A DOLLAR; 1795–1796, thin planchet—Plain.* **Mint:** *Philadelphia.*

Beaded Border (1793)

Denticle Border (1794–1796)

History. The Liberty Cap design was created in the summer of 1793 by artist and engraver Joseph Wright, who is also believed by some to have designed the 1793 half cent. On the cent, Liberty faces to the right, rather than to the left (as on the half cent). Liberty Cap cents of 1793 have raised beaded borders. Other issues have denticles. Cents of 1794 and some of 1795 are on thick planchets with the edge lettered ONE HUNDRED FOR A DOLLAR, while those made later in 1795, and in 1796, are on thinner planchets and have a plain edge.

Striking and Sharpness. The depth of relief and striking characteristics vary widely, depending on the variety. Points to check are the details of the hair on Liberty, the leaf details on the wreath, and the denticles on both sides. Generally, the earlier, thick-planchet issues are better strikes than are the thin-planchet coins. Plain-edge 1795 cents often have low or shallow rims. To determine the difference between lightness caused by shallow dies and lightness caused by wear, study the characteristics of the die variety involved (see in particular the reverses of 1793, BW-27, S-13, and 1793, BW-28/BW-29, S-15/S-12).

Availability. Cents of this type are readily available, although those of 1793 are rare and in great demand, and certain die varieties of the other dates are rare and can command high prices. Typical grades range from AG upward to Fine, VF, and, less often, EF. Attractive AU and MS coins are elusive, and when found are usually dated 1795, the thin planchet variety.

Grading Standards

MS-62BN

MS-60 to 70 (Mint State). ***Obverse:*** On MS-60 and 61 coins there are some traces of abrasion on the higher areas of the portrait. Luster is incomplete, particularly in the field. At MS-63, luster should be complete, and no abrasion evident. At higher levels, the luster is deeper, and some original mint color may be seen on some examples. At the MS-65 level there may be some scattered contact marks and possibly some traces of fingerprints or discoloration, but these should be very minimal and not at all distracting. Generally, Liberty Cap cents of 1793 (in particular) and 1794 are harder to find with strong eye appeal than are those of 1795 and 1796. Mint State coins of 1795 often have satiny luster. Above MS-65, a coin should approach perfection, especially if dated 1795 or 1796. Certified Mint State cents can vary in their strictness of interpretation. ***Reverse:*** In the lower Mint State grades some abrasion is seen on the higher areas of the leaves. Generally, luster is complete in all grades, as the open areas are protected by the lettering and wreath. Often on this type the reverse is shallower than the obverse and has a lower rim.

Illustrated coin: Boldly struck on both the obverse and reverse, with strong hair separation evident on Liberty and some evidence of a central vein on each leaf. Note the small toning speck under the L of LIBERTY.

AU-50, 53, 55, 58 (About Uncirculated). ***Obverse:*** Very light wear is evident on the highest parts of the hair above and to the left of the ear. Friction is seen on the cheek and the liberty cap. Coins at this level are usually on smooth planchets and have nice eye appeal. Color is very important. Dark and porous coins are relegated to lower grades, even if AU-level sharpness is present. ***Reverse:*** Very light wear is evident on the higher parts of the leaves and the ribbon, and, to a lesser extent, on the lettering. The reverse may have original luster, toned brown, varying from minimal (at lower About Uncirculated grades) to extensive. Grading at the About Uncirculated level is mainly done by viewing the obverse, as many reverses are inherently shallow due to lower-relief dies.

AU-50

Illustrated coin: Note the rough patch on and below Liberty's cap.

EF-40, 45 (Extremely Fine). ***Obverse:*** The center of the coin shows wear or a small, flat area, for most dies. Other hair details are strong. Luster is minimal or nonexistent at EF-40, and may survive in traces in protected areas (such as between the letters) at EF-45. ***Reverse:*** Wear is seen on the highest wreath and ribbon areas and the letters. Luster is minimal, but likely more noticeable than on the obverse, as the fields are protected by the designs and lettering. Sharpness varies depending on the die variety but is generally shallower than on the obverse, this being particularly true for many 1795 cents.

EF-40

VF-20, 30 (Very Fine). ***Obverse:*** Wear on the portrait has reduced the hair detail to indistinct or flat at the center, and on most varieties the individual strands at the left edge are blended together. One rule does not fit all. The ANA grading standards suggest that 75 percent of the hair shows, while PCGS suggests 30 percent to 70 percent on varieties struck from higher-relief dies, and less than 50 percent for others. Examples such as this reflect the artistic, rather than scientific, nature of grading. ***Reverse:*** The leaf details are nearly completely worn away at VF-20, and with slight detail at VF-30. Some border letters may be weak, and ditto for the central letters (on later varieties of this type). The border denticles are blended together with many indistinct. No luster is seen. The sharpness of details depends on the die variety.

VF-30

F-15

F-12, 15 (Fine). ***Obverse:*** The hair details are mostly worn away, with about one-third visible, mainly at the lower edges. Border denticles are weak or worn away in areas, depending on the height of the rim when the coin was struck. F-15 shows slightly more detail. ***Reverse:*** The wreath leaves are worn flat, but their edges are distinct. Border denticles are weak or worn away in areas. F-15 shows slightly more detail. At this level and lower, planchet darkness and light porosity are common, as are scattered marks.

VG-8

VG-8, 10 (Very Good). ***Obverse:*** The hair is more worn than on the preceding, with detail present only in the lower areas. Detail can differ, and widely, depending on the dies. Border denticles are worn away on some issues (not as much for 1793 and 1794 coins), and the border will blend into the field in areas in which the rim was low to begin with, or in areas struck slightly off center. LIBERTY and the date are bold. VG-10 is sometimes applied to especially nice Very Good coins. ***Reverse:*** The wreath, bow, and lettering are seen in outline form, and some leaves and letters may be indistinct in parts. Border denticles are worn away, and the border blends into the field in most if not all of the periphery. In certain die varieties and die states, especially of 1797, some letters may be very weak, or missing.

G-4

G-4, 6 (Good). ***Obverse:*** The portrait is worn smooth and is seen only in outline form, although the eye and nose can be discerned. LIBERTY and the date are complete, although the date may be weak. Denticles are gone on varieties struck with low or shallow rims. ***Reverse:*** Extensive wear is seen overall. From half to two-thirds of the letters in UNITED STATES OF AMERICA and the fraction numerals are worn away. Certain shallow-relief dies may have letters missing. G-6 is often assigned to finer examples in this category. Darkness, porosity, and marks characterize many coins.

Illustrated coin: This coin is an example of the highly sought 1794, Starred Reverse, variety.

AG-3 (About Good). ***Obverse:*** Wear is more extensive than on the preceding. The portrait is visible only in outline. LIBERTY will typically have some letters worn away. The date is weak, but discernible. ***Reverse:*** Parts of the wreath are visible in outline form, and all but a few letters are gone. Grading of AG-3 is usually done by the reverse, as the obverse typically appears to be in a slightly higher grade.

AG-3

Illustrated coin: This coin is closer to G-4 on the obverse, but weak on the reverse, prompting a more conservative grade. While the reverse is worn nearly smooth, almost a third of the stars at the denticles, which mark this cent as a 1794, Starred Reverse, are visible.

Head of 1793 (1793–1794)
Head in high, rounded relief.

Head of 1794 (1794)
Well-defined hair; hook on lowest curl.

Circulation Strikes

	Mintage	GSID	AG-3	G-4	VG-8	F-12	VF-20	EF-40	AU-50	MS-60
Liberty Cap (1793–1796)	**n/a**	**72312**	**$310**	**$490**	**$725**	**$1,100**	**$1,700**	**$3,750**	**$5,250**	**$7,750**
1793, Liberty Cap	11,056	711	6,000	7,500	10,000	19,000	38,500	114,000	168,000	1,080,000
	Auctions: $506,000, PCGS AU-53 GLDB 09/09									
↳**1793, Liberty Cap, S-12**	*	76796	8,750	21,500	24,000	30,000	72,000	—	—	—
↳**1793, Liberty Cap, S-13**	*	76733	6,000	7,500	10,000	19,000	38,500	114,000	168,000	1,080,000
	Auctions: $632,500, PCGS AU-55 HA 02/08									
↳**1793, Liberty Cap, S-14**	*	76734	6,500	8,250	11,000	21,000	42,000	114,000	168,000	—
	Auctions: $264,000, PCGS AU-53 HA 01/25; $144,000, PCGS AU-50 HA 01/25									
↳**1793, Liberty Cap, S-15**	*	76735	42,000	54,000	90,000	108,000	120,000	—	—	—
	Auctions: $102,000, NGC VG-10 HA 09/17									
↳**1793, Liberty Cap, S-16**	*	76736	6,000	7,500	21,500	60,000	78,000	—	—	—
	Auctions: $132,000, PCGS VF35 HA 01/22									
1794, Head of 1793	918,521	714	1,150	1,500	2,500	7,500	12,000	19,000	48,000	132,000
	Auctions: $276,000, PCGS MS-63 GLDB 02/13									
↳**1794, Head of 1793, S-17a**	*	76737	1,150	1,500	2,500	7,500	12,000	19,000	48,000	—
↳**1794, Head of 1793, S-18a**	*	76739	9,500	17,000	36,000	42,000	53,000	—	—	—
↳**1794, Head of 1793, S-18b**	*	76740	1,150	1,500	2,500	7,500	12,000	19,000	48,000	132,000
	Auctions: $432,000, PCGS MS-64 HA 01/24; $105,000, NGC MS-62 HA 01/24									
↳**1794, Head of 1793, S-19a**	*	76741	1,150	1,500	2,500	8,250	19,000	57,500	—	—
↳**1794, Head of 1793, S-19b**	*	76742	1,150	1,500	2,500	7,500	12,000	19,000	48,000	132,000
↳**1794, Head of 1793, S-20a**	*	76744	—	—	—	—	—	—	—	—
↳**1794, Head of 1793, S-20b**	*	76743	3,250	5,000	7,500	15,000	30,000	43,000	63,000	—
↳**1794, Head of 1793, S-NC-4**	*	76738	39,000	60,000	—	—	—	—	—	—

* Included in number above.

Circulation Strikes *(continued)*

	Mintage	GSID	AG-3	G-4	VG-8	F-12	VF-20	EF-40	AU-50	MS-60
1794, Head of 1794	*	723	$310	$490	$725	$1,100	$2,100	$4,000	$7,500	$18,000
	Auctions: $258,500, PCGS MS-67 LGND 10/20									
↳**1794, Head of 1794, S-21**	*	76745	345	550	850	1,200	2,200	4,250	7,750	18,000
↳**1794, Head of 1794, S-22**	*	76746	310	490	725	1,100	2,100	4,000	7,500	18,000
↳**1794, Head of 1794, S-23**	*	76747	345	550	850	2,000	4,000	12,000	21,500	—
↳**1794, Head of 1794, S-24**	*	76748	345	550	850	1,200	2,200	5,000	11,000	24,000
↳**1794, Head of 1794, S-25**	*	76749	310	490	775	1,600	2,250	10,000	18,000	—
↳**1794, Head of 1794, S-26**	*	76750	345	550	850	1,200	2,200	5,000	12,000	24,000
↳**1794, Head of 1794, S-27**	*	76751	650	1,400	2,250	4,400	9,500	24,000	48,000	—
↳**1794, Head of 1794, S-28**	*	76752	345	550	850	1,200	2,200	5,000	12,000	24,000
	Auctions: $588,000, NGC MS-66 HA 08/24									
↳**1794, Head of 1794, S-29**	*	76753	345	550	850	1,200	2,200	5,000	12,000	24,000
	Auctions: $102,000, PCGS MS-65 HA 01/24									
↳**1794, Head of 1794, S-30**	*	76754	310	490	725	1,100	2,100	4,000	7,500	18,000
↳**1794, Head of 1794, S-31**	*	76755	345	550	850	1,200	2,200	4,000	7,500	18,000
	Auctions: $264,000, PCGS MS-67 HA 01/22									
↳**1794, Head of 1794, S-32**	*	76756	310	490	725	1,100	2,100	4,000	7,500	18,000
↳**1794, Head of 1794, S-33**	*	76757	8,750	12,000	24,000	30,000	60,000	108,000	—	—
	Auctions: $103,500, PCGS VF35 HA 02/08									
↳**1794, Head of 1794, S-34**	*	76758	1,250	2,500	5,000	10,000	21,500	42,000	—	—
↳**1794, Head of 1794, S-35**	*	76759	1,500	1,750	2,500	3,750	7,500	26,500	57,500	—
↳**1794, Head of 1794, S-36**	*	76760	650	1,400	3,100	6,250	8,000	21,500	—	—
↳**1794, Head of 1794, S-37**	*	76761	18,000	30,000	38,500	66,000	114,000	—	—	—
	Auctions: $161,000, PCGS EF-45 HA 02/08									
↳**1794, Head of 1794, S-38**	*	76762	390	650	1,250	2,500	10,000	33,500	—	—
↳**1794, Head of 1794, S-39**	*	76763	2,500	4,400	6,250	10,000	19,000	33,500	55,000	—
↳**1794, Head of 1794, S-40**	*	76764	2,500	4,400	8,000	10,500	14,000	26,500	—	—
↳**1794, Head of 1794, S-41**	*	76765	345	550	850	1,200	2,200	8,000	14,500	—
↳**1794, Head of 1794, S-42**	*	76766	345	550	850	1,200	2,200	12,000	24,000	—
↳**1794, Head of 1794, S-43**	*	76767	345	550	850	1,200	2,200	4,500	11,000	26,500
↳**1794, Head of 1794, S-44**	*	76768	345	550	850	1,200	2,200	4,000	7,500	18,000
↳**1794, Head of 1794, S-45**	*	76769	950	2,250	3,400	5,500	9,000	24,000	—	—
↳**1794, Head of 1794, S-46**	*	76770	345	550	850	1,200	2,200	7,000	14,500	33,500
↳**1794, Head of 1794, S-47**	*	76771	325	525	900	1,500	4,400	18,000	29,000	—
↳**1794, Head of 1794, S-49**	*	76773	345	550	850	1,200	2,200	6,000	—	—
↳**1794, Head of 1794, S-50**	*	76774	775	1,150	2,000	2,750	9,500	18,000	—	—
↳**1794, Head of 1794, S-51**	*	76775	525	775	1,250	2,500	3,750	6,000	10,500	—
↳**1794, Head of 1794, S-52**	*	76776	1,250	2,500	4,400	12,000	19,000	33,500	41,000	—
↳**1794, Head of 1794, S-53**	*	76777	2,500	5,000	10,000	14,500	43,000	67,000	90,000	—
↳**1794, Head of 1794, S-54**	*	76778	390	650	1,000	2,250	5,250	8,750	18,000	—
↳**1794, Head of 1794, S-55**	*	76779	345	550	850	1,200	2,200	6,000	14,500	24,000
↳**1794, Head of 1794, S-56**	*	76780	345	550	850	1,200	3,100	10,500	17,000	—
↳**1794, Head of 1794, S-57**	*	76781	310	490	725	1,100	2,100	4,000	7,500	18,000
↳**1794, Head of 1794, S-58**	*	76782	345	550	850	1,200	2,500	9,000	17,000	—
↳**1794, Head of 1794, S-59**	*	76783	345	550	850	1,200	2,500	6,000	13,000	—
↳**1794, Head of 1794, S-60**	*	76784	345	550	850	1,200	2,500	6,000	13,000	27,500
↳**1794, Head of 1794, S-61**	*	76785	345	550	850	1,600	2,500	7,000	16,000	—
↳**1794, Head of 1794, S-62**	*	76786	345	550	850	1,700	3,250	7,500	—	—
↳**1794, Head of 1794, S-63**	*	76787	345	550	850	1,200	2,200	6,000	12,000	24,000
↳**1794, Head of 1794, S-65**	*	76789	310	490	725	1,100	2,100	4,000	7,500	18,000
↳**1794, Head of 1794, S-66**	*	76790	1,150	2,500	3,750	11,000	18,000	66,000	—	—

* Included in number above.

1794, Normal Reverse

1794, Starred Reverse

Lettered Edge (1793–1795)

Reeded Edge (1795)

Head of 1795 (1794–1796)
Head in low relief; no hook on lowest curl.

Circulation Strikes *(continued)*

	Mintage	GSID	AG-3	G-4	VG-8	F-12	VF-20	EF-40	AU-50	MS-60
1794, No Fraction Bar	*	726	—	$1,750	$2,500	$3,750	$9,500	$21,500	$33,500	$53,000
↳1794, No Fraction Bar, S-64	*	76788	—	1,750	2,500	3,750	9,500	21,500	33,500	53,000
	Auctions: $132,000, PCGS MS-65 HA 01/24									
1794, Starred Reverse	*	720	$17,000	29,000	48,000	66,000	120,000	342,000	600,000	—
	Auctions: $212,750, PCGS VF-30 GLDB 09/09									
↳1794, Starred Reverse, S-48	*	76772	17,000	29,000	48,000	66,000	120,000	342,000	600,000	—
	Auctions: $288,000, PCGS EF-40 HA 01/25; $632,500, PCGS AU-50 HA 01/25									
1794, Head of 1795 (a)	*	717	495	625	900	1,500	2,250	4,750	6,000	18,000
↳1794, Head of 1795, S-67	*	76791	525	700	1,000	1,600	2,400	6,250	14,500	—
↳1794, Head of 1795, S-68	*	76792	1,150	2,500	3,750	6,250	7,500	15,500	23,000	102,000
	Auctions: $235,000, NGC MS-62 HA 01/14									
↳1794, Head of 1795, S-69	*	76793	525	700	1,000	1,600	2,400	5,500	7,500	18,500
	Auctions: $109,250, PCGS MS-65 HA 02/08									
↳1794, Head of 1795, S-70	*	76794	525	700	1,000	1,600	2,400	6,000	8,500	21,500
↳1794, Head of 1795, S-71	*	76795	525	700	1,000	1,600	2,400	5,250	6,500	20,000
↳1794, Head of 1795, S-72	*	77487	495	625	900	1,500	2,250	4,750	6,000	18,000
1795, Lettered Edge	*	729	310	490	725	1,100	1,900	4,500	7,500	12,000
	Auctions: $155,250, PCGS MS-65 GLDB 09/09									
↳1795, Lettered Edge, S-73	*	77488	390	575	1,000	1,900	8,750	—	—	—
↳1795, Lettered Edge, S-74	*	77489	310	490	725	1,100	1,900	4,500	7,500	12,000
↳1795, Lettered Edge, S-75	*	77490	310	490	725	1,100	1,900	4,500	7,500	12,000
↳1795, Lettered Edge, S-76a	*	77491	390	650	1,050	2,250	4,000	8,000	18,000	—
1795, Plain Edge	*	732	310	490	725	1,100	1,700	3,750	5,250	7,750
↳1795, Plain Edge, S-76b	*	77492	310	490	725	1,100	1,700	3,750	5,250	7,750
↳1795, Plain Edge, S-77	*	77493	345	525	775	1,200	1,850	4,100	5,750	—
↳1795, Plain Edge, S-78	*	77494	310	490	725	1,100	1,700	3,750	5,250	7,750
1795, Reeded Edge	9 known	735	114,000	180,000	360,000	780,000	—	—	—	—
	Auctions: $1,265,000, PCGS VG-10 GLDB 09/09									
↳1795, Reeded Edge, S-79	9 known	77495	114,000	180,000	360,000	780,000	—	—	—	—
	Auctions: $646,250, PCGS VG-10 HA 01/14									

* Included in number above. **a.** The 1794 coin with Head of 1795 has a hooked curl but is in low relief.

1795, "Jefferson Head"

Circulation Strikes *(continued)*

	Mintage	GSID	AG-3	G-4	VG-8	F-12	VF-20	EF-40	AU-50	MS-60
1795, "Jefferson" Head, Plain Edge (b)	45–60 est. known	738	$18,000	$25,000	$36,000	$60,000	$102,000	$264,000	—	—
	Auctions: $184,000, NGC VF-25 HA 03/12									
↳**1795, "Jefferson" Head, Plain Edge, S-80** (b)	45 to 60 est. known	77496	18,000	25,000	36,000	60,000	102,000	264,000	—	—
	Auctions: $264,000, PCGS EF-40 HA 01/19									
1795, "Jefferson" Head, Lettered Edge (b)	3 known	741	—	—	—	300,000	420,000	—	—	—
	Auctions: $408,000, PCGS VF-30 SBG 08/20									
1796, Liberty Cap	109,825	744	345	525	1,000	1,750	3,000	7,000	$9,500	$21,500
	Auctions: $236,469, PCGS MS-65 SBG 08/12									
↳**1796, Liberty Cap, S-81**	*	77497	345	525	1,000	1,750	3,000	7,000	9,500	21,500
↳**1796, Liberty Cap, S-82**	*	77498	430	625	1,150	2,000	4,400	11,000	—	—
↳**1796, Liberty Cap, S-83**	*	77499	475	675	1,150	2,100	4,400	11,000	15,500	—
↳**1796, Liberty Cap, S-84**	*	77500	345	525	1,000	1,750	3,000	7,000	9,500	21,500
	Auctions: $115,000, PCGS MS-64 HA 02/08									
↳**1796, Liberty Cap, S-85**	*	77501	455	725	1,250	2,500	5,000	14,500	24,000	33,500
↳**1796, Liberty Cap, S-86**	*	77502	455	725	1,250	2,600	5,250	15,500	26,500	—
↳**1796, Liberty Cap, S-87**	*	77503	345	525	1,000	1,750	3,000	7,500	10,500	—
↳**1796, Liberty Cap, S-88**	*	77504	380	600	1,150	1,900	4,400	15,500	26,500	—
↳**1796, Liberty Cap, S-89**	*	77505	345	525	1,000	1,750	3,000	8,750	14,500	—
↳**1796, Liberty Cap, S-90**	*	77506	775	1,250	2,100	3,500	6,250	15,500	—	33,500
↳**1796, Liberty Cap, S-91**	*	77507	345	525	1,000	1,750	3,000	7,500	12,500	26,500

* Included in number above. **b.** The "Jefferson Head" is not a regular Mint issue, but a design struck privately in an attempt to win a federal coinage contract.

DRAPED BUST (1796–1807)

Designer: *Robert Scot.* **Weight:** *10.89 grams.* **Composition:** *Copper.*
Diameter: *Average 29 mm.* **Edge:** *Plain.* **Mint:** *Philadelphia.*

History. The Draped Bust cent made its debut in 1796, following a coinage of Liberty Cap cents the same year. The motif, from a drawing by Gilbert Stuart, was first employed on certain silver dollars of 1795. (Its use on half cents did not take place until later, in 1800.) In 1798 Liberty's head was slightly modified in design.

Striking and Sharpness. Most Draped Bust cents were struck on high-quality planchets. (This high planchet quality is less predictable for varieties of 1796, and almost never present for those of 1799 and 1800.) Detail sharpness differs by die variety. Weakness, when present, is usually on the hair behind the forehead, on the leaves in the upper part of the wreath, and among the denticles. However, a weak strike can show up in other areas as well. Many if not most Draped Bust cents are imperfectly centered, with the result that denticles can be bold on one side of a coin and light or even missing on the opposite side; this can occur on obverse as well as reverse. Typically this does not affect value. Certain Draped Bust cents of 1796 have semi-prooflike surfaces. Those of 1799 often have rough or porous surfaces and are found in lower grades.

Availability. As a type, Draped Bust cents are readily available, although the 1799, 9 Over 8, and 1799 are the keys to the series, and the 1804 is elusive. A different scenario evolves when considering engraving errors, repunched dates, and recut letters and numerals; many of these varieties are very difficult to locate. The eye appeal of these rarities usually is below par. Other years are generally available in high grades, VF and finer, well struck (except for some reverse leaves, in instances), on high-quality planchets, and with excellent eye appeal. Dark and porous coins are plentiful among coins graded below VF. True MS coins tend to be MS-60 to 63, when found.

GRADING STANDARDS

MS-60 to 70 (Mint State). ***Obverse:*** In the lower Mint State grades, MS-60 and 61, some slight abrasion can be seen on the higher areas of the portrait, especially the cheek, and the hair behind the forehead. Luster in the field is incomplete, particularly in the center of the open areas, which on this type are very open, especially at the right. At MS-63, luster should be nearly complete, and no abrasions evident. In higher levels, the luster is complete and deeper, and some original mint color should be seen. MS-64 coins may have some slight discoloration or scattered contact marks. A well-graded MS-65 or higher coin will have full, rich luster; no marks visible except under magnification; and a nice

MS-63BN

blend of brown toning or nicely mixed (not stained or blotchy) mint color and natural brown toning. ***Reverse:*** In the lower Mint State ranges some abrasions are seen on the higher areas of the leaves. Generally, luster is complete in all Mint State ranges, as the open areas are protected by the lettering and wreath. Sharpness of the leaves can vary by die variety, so check this aspect. Otherwise, the same comments apply as for the obverse.

Illustrated coin: This example is quite attractive despite the scratch on Liberty's bust and another through the D of UNITED. However, the left side of the reverse has toned differently from the rest of the coin's surfaces.

AU-50, 53, 55, 58 (About Uncirculated). ***Obverse:*** Friction is seen on the higher parts, particularly the hair of Liberty and the cheek. Friction and scattered marks are in the field, ranging from more extensive at AU-50 to minimal at AU-58. Luster may be seen in protected areas, minimal at AU-50, more visible at AU-58. At AU-58 the field may retain some luster, as well. In many instances, the luster is smaller in area and lesser in "depth" than on the reverse of this type. Cents of this type can be very beautiful in About Uncirculated. ***Reverse:*** Friction is seen on the higher wreath leaves and (not as easy to discern) on the letters. Again, the die variety should be checked. The fields, though protected by the designs, show friction, but not as noticeably as on the obverse. At AU-55 and 58, little if any friction is seen. The reverse may have original luster, toned brown, minimal on lower About Uncirculated grades, often extensive at the AU-58 level. General rules for cents follow the half cents of the same type.

AU-58

Illustrated coin: Note the die crack arcing through the lower-left obverse. This crack was also on the preceding coin, but is more noticeable here.

EF-40, 45 (Extremely Fine). ***Obverse:*** Wear is seen on the portrait overall, with reduction or elimination of some separation of hair strands on the highest part. By the standards of the Early American Coppers society, if the "spit curl" in front of Liberty's ear is missing, the coin is not EF. The cheek shows more wear than on higher grades, and the drapery covering the bosom is lightly worn on the higher areas. Often weakness in the separation of the drapery lines can be attributed to weakness in striking. Luster is minimal or nonexistent at EF-40, and may survive in amongst the letters of LIBERTY at EF-45. ***Reverse:*** Wear is seen on the highest wreath and ribbon areas, and on the letters. Luster is minimal, but likely more noticeable than on the obverse, as the fields are protected by the designs and lettering. The ANA grading standards state that at EF-45 nearly all of the "ribbing" (veins) in the leaves is visible, and that at EF-40 about 75 percent is sharp. In practice, striking plays a part as well, and some leaves may be weak even in higher grades.

EF-40

Illustrated coin: This coin features a few small patches of porosity.

VF-35

VF-20, 30 (Very Fine). ***Obverse:*** Wear on the portrait has reduced the hair detail further, especially to the left of the forehead. The rolling curls are solid or flat on their highest areas, as well as by the ribbon behind the hair. The border denticles are blended together, with many indistinct. No luster is seen. ***Reverse:*** The leaf details are nearly completely worn away at VF-20, and with slight detail at VF-30. The ANA grading standards are a bit stricter: 30 percent remaining at VF-20 and 50 percent at VF-30. In the marketplace, fewer details can be seen on most certified coins at these levels. The border denticles are blended together with many indistinct. No luster is seen.

F-12

F-12, 15 (Fine). ***Obverse:*** Many hair details are worn away, with perhaps one-half to one-third visible, mainly at the edges and behind the shoulder. Border denticles are weak or worn away in areas. F-15 shows slightly more detail. Porosity and scattered marks become increasingly common at this level and lower. ***Reverse:*** The wreath leaves are worn flat, but their edges are distinct. Little if anything remains of leaf vein details. Border denticles are weak or worn away in areas. F-15 shows slightly more detail.

Illustrated coin: There are several distracting contact marks on the obverse of this coin. Note the 6 visible under the 7 in the date.

VG-10

VG-8, 10 (Very Good). ***Obverse:*** The portrait is well worn, although the eye can be seen, as can hints of hair detail. Some hair at the left shows separation. Curls now appear as mostly solid blobs. Border denticles are worn away on most varieties, and the rim, although usually present, begins to blend into the field. LIBERTY and the date are bold in most areas, with some lightness toward the rim. VG-10 is sometimes applied to especially nice Very Good coins. ***Reverse:*** The wreath, bow, and lettering are seen in outline form, and some leaves and letters may be indistinct in parts. The border may blend into the field on some of the periphery. The strength of the letters is dependent to an extent on the specific die variety.

G-6

G-4, 6 (Good). ***Obverse:*** The portrait is worn smooth and is seen only in outline form, although the eye position can be discerned and some curls can be made out. LIBERTY is readable, but the tops of the letters may fade away. The date is clearly readable, but the lower part of the numerals may be very weak or worn away. The border will blend into the field more extensively than on the preceding, but significant areas will still be seen. ***Reverse:*** Extensive wear is seen overall. From one-half to two-thirds of the letters in UNITED STATES OF AMERICA and the fraction numerals are worn away. On most varieties, ONE CENT is fairly strong. G-6 is often assigned to finer examples in this category.

Illustrated coin: This coin shows evidence of a past cleaning, but it has retoned.

AG-3

AG-3 (About Good). ***Obverse:*** Wear is more extensive than on the preceding. The portrait is visible only in outline. LIBERTY is weak, partially worn away, but usually discernible. The date is weak, and the bottoms of the digits may be worn away, but must be identifiable. ***Reverse:*** Parts of the wreath are visible in outline form, and all but a few letters are gone. ONE CENT is usually mostly or completely discernible, depending on the variety.

Reverse of 1794 (1794–1796)
Note double leaf at top right;
14–16 leaves on left,
16–18 leaves on right.

Reverse of 1795 (1795–1798)
Note single leaf at top right;
17–21 leaves on left,
16–20 leaves on right.

Reverse of 1797 (1796–1807)
Note double leaf at top right;
16 leaves on left,
19 leaves on right.

1796, LIHERTY Error

Circulation Strikes

	Mintage	GSID	AG-3	G-4	VG-8	F-12	VF-20	EF-40	AU-50	MS-60
Draped Bust (1796–1807)	**n/a**	**72314**	**$75**	**$100**	**$130**	**$260**	**$500**	**$1,100**	**$1,750**	**$4,000**
1796, Draped Bust, Reverse of 1794	363,375	753	440	725	1,300	2,250	3,000	7,250	12,000	28,000
	Auctions: $178,250, PCGS MS-66 GLDB 09/09									
↳1796, Draped Bust, Reverse of 1794, S-101	*	77518	490	775	2,000	3,750	6,250	16,000	24,000	31,000
↳1796, Draped Bust, Reverse of 1794, S-102	*	77519	440	775	1,450	2,500	3,550	7,500	12,000	—
↳1796, Draped Bust, Reverse of 1794, S-106	*	77520	485	775	1,450	2,700	5,500	17,000	24,000	39,000
↳1796, Draped Bust, Reverse of 1794, S-107	*	77521	1,150	1,600	2,750	7,000	14,500	—	—	—
↳1796, Draped Bust, Reverse of 1794, S-108	*	77522	485	775	1,450	2,500	3,300	8,000	—	28,000
↳1796, Draped Bust, Reverse of 1794, S-109	*	77523	440	725	1,300	2,250	3,000	7,250	—	—
↳1796, Draped Bust, Reverse of 1794, S-110	*	77524	440	725	1,300	2,250	3,000	7,250	14,500	28,000
↳1796, Draped Bust, Reverse of 1794, S-111	*	77525	485	775	1,450	2,500	3,600	12,000	26,500	—
↳1796, Draped Bust, Reverse of 1794, S-112	*	77526	440	725	1,300	2,250	3,000	7,250	12,000	28,000
↳1796, Draped Bust, Reverse of 1794, S-NC-5	*	377596	9,000	—	—	—	—	—	—	—
1796, Draped Bust, Reverse of 1795	*	747	260	340	575	1,150	1,550	6,000	9,750	24,000
↳1796, Draped Bust, Reverse of 1795, S-92	*	77508	325	490	1,100	2,000	3,250	7,000	11,000	35,000
↳1796, Draped Bust, Reverse of 1795, S-93	*	77509	390	650	1,500	2,000	2,600	6,500	11,000	31,000
↳1796, Draped Bust, Reverse of 1795, S-95	*	77510	575	825	1,500	3,750	7,500	10,500	22,000	—
↳1796, Draped Bust, Reverse of 1795, S-96	*	77511	1,250	3,100	5,000	10,000	18,000	—	—	—
↳1796, Draped Bust, Reverse of 1795, S-97	*	77512	325	430	850	2,400	4,250	14,500	24,000	—
↳1796, Draped Bust, Reverse of 1795, S-98	*	77513	525	775	1,100	1,550	3,750	8,750	12,500	26,500
↳1796, Draped Bust, Reverse of 1795, S-99	*	77514	525	775	1,150	3,400	7,000	27,500	—	—
↳1796, Draped Bust, Reverse of 1795, S-116	*	77515	440	650	1,500	5,500	9,500	15,000	20,000	—
↳1796, Draped Bust, Reverse of 1795, S-NC-2	*	77516	—	—	—	—	—	—	—	—
↳1796, Draped Bust, Reverse of 1795, S-NC-4	*	77517	1,900	2,500	3,100	5,000	9,500	—	—	—
1796, Draped Bust, Reverse of 1797	*	756	195	260	455	1,250	1,600	4,400	6,250	12,000
↳1796, Draped Bust, Reverse of 1797, S-94	*	77527	390	650	1,000	3,100	5,000	—	—	—
↳1796, Draped Bust, Reverse of 1797, S-100	*	77528	525	775	1,150	3,100	6,250	12,000	21,500	—
↳1796, Draped Bust, Reverse of 1797, S-105	*	77529	340	650	2,250	3,750	7,000			
↳1796, Draped Bust, Reverse of 1797, S-113	*	77530	525	950	2,500	4,250	7,000	21,500	—	—
↳1796, Draped Bust, Reverse of 1797, S-114	*	77531	525	725	1,900	4,000	6,250	12,000	19,000	36,000
↳1796, Draped Bust, Reverse of 1797, S-115	*	77532	390	650	1,750	3,000	5,500	11,000	17,000	—
↳1796, Draped Bust, Reverse of 1797, S-117	*	77533	650	900	1,900	7,500	15,500	—	—	—
↳1796, Draped Bust, Reverse of 1797, S-118	*	77534	650	900	1,900	7,500	15,500	—	—	—
↳1796, Draped Bust, Reverse of 1797, S-119	*	77535	195	260	455	1,250	1,600	4,400	6,250	12,000
↳1796, Draped Bust, Reverse of 1797, S-NC-1	*	377651	2,250	2,750	3,750	6,500	10,000	19,000	—	—
↳1796, Draped Bust, Reverse of 1797, S-NC-3	*	377652	—	—	—	—	21,500	36,000	—	—
↳1796, Draped Bust, Reverse of 1797, S-NC-6	*	393281	—	—	—	—	—	—	—	—
1796, Draped Bust, LIHERTY Error	*	750	850	1,150	1,600	3,250	5,000	12,000	21,000	—
↳1796, Draped Bust, LIHERTY Error, S-103	*	74477	850	1,150	1,600	3,250	5,000	12,000	21,000	—
↳1796, Draped Bust, LIHERTY Error, S-104	*	74478	850	1,150	1,600	3,250	5,000	12,000	21,000	—
1796, Draped Bust, No Stems	4 known	393282	120,000	168,000	210,000	—	—	—	—	—
↳1796, Draped Bust, No Stems, S-NC-7	4 known	393283	120,000	168,000	210,000	—	—	—	—	—
1797, Reverse of 1795, Plain Edge	897,510	762	260	325	575	1,500	2,250	8,750	26,500	72,000
↳1797, Reverse of 1795, Plain Edge, S-120a	*	77536	260	325	575	1,500	2,250	8,750	26,500	72,000
↳1797, Reverse of 1795, Plain Edge, S-121a	*	77537	2,100	3,750	10,000	—	—	—	—	—

* Included in number above.

1797, Wreath With Stems

1797, Stemless Wreath

1798, 8 Over 7

Circulation Strikes *(continued)*

	Mintage	GSID	AG-3	G-4	VG-8	F-12	VF-20	EF-40	AU-50	MS-60
1797, Reverse of 1795, Plain Edge	897,510	762	$260	$325	$575	$1,500	$2,250	$8,750	$26,500	$72,000
↳1797, Reverse of 1795, Plain Edge, S-120a	*	77536	260	325	575	1,500	2,250	8,750	26,500	72,000
↳1797, Reverse of 1795, Plain Edge, S-121a	*	77537	2,100	3,750	10,000	—	—	—	—	—
1797, Reverse of 1795, Gripped Edge	*	759	195	365	455	975	1,600	4,400	10,500	29,000
↳1797, Reverse of 1795, Gripped Edge, S-120b	*	77538	195	365	455	975	1,600	4,400	10,500	29,000
↳1797, Reverse of 1795, Gripped Edge, S-121b	*	77539	195	365	455	975	1,600	4,400	10,500	29,000
1797, Reverse of 1797, Stems	*	765	130	235	390	775	1,300	2,750	5,000	8,000
↳1797, Reverse of 1797, Stems, S-122	*	77540	850	1,250	2,250	4,400	7,500	—	—	—
↳1797, Reverse of 1797, Stems, S-123	*	77541	145	255	430	850	1,450	3,000	5,500	8,750
↳1797, Reverse of 1797, Stems, S-124	*	77542	390	1,000	1,900	3,750	10,000	—	—	—
↳1797, Reverse of 1797, Stems, S-125	*	77543	290	650	1,400	3,100	6,250	14,500	—	—
↳1797, Reverse of 1797, Stems, S-126	*	77544	135	245	410	825	1,400	2,900	5,250	18,000
↳1797, Reverse of 1797, Stems, S-127	*	77545	260	340	525	1,150	3,050	9,250	12,000	—
↳1797, Reverse of 1797, Stems, S-128	*	77546	135	245	410	825	1,400	2,900	5,250	18,000
↳1797, Reverse of 1797, Stems, S-129	*	77547	340	525	1,500	3,250	10,500	18,000	—	—
↳1797, Reverse of 1797, Stems, S-130	*	77548	130	235	390	775	1,300	2,750	5,000	11,000
↳1797, Reverse of 1797, Stems, S-134	*	77549	145	255	430	850	1,450	6,250	7,500	—
↳1797, Reverse of 1797, Stems, S-135	*	77550	130	235	390	775	1,300	2,750	5,000	8,000
↳1797, Reverse of 1797, Stems, S-136	*	77551	135	245	430	850	1,900	3,750	5,750	10,500
↳1797, Reverse of 1797, Stems, S-137	*	77552	130	235	390	775	1,300	2,750	5,000	—
↳1797, Reverse of 1797, Stems, S-138	*	77553	130	235	390	775	1,300	2,750	5,000	8,000
↳1797, Reverse of 1797, Stems, S-139	*	77554	130	235	390	775	1,300	2,750	5,000	8,000
↳1797, Reverse of 1797, Stems, S-140	*	77555	130	235	390	775	1,300	2,750	5,000	12,000
↳1797, Reverse of 1797, Stems, S-141	*	77556	145	255	390	1,150	1,550	4,400	7,000	—
↳1797, Reverse of 1797, Stems, S-142	*	77557	775	1,250	2,750	4,250	5,000	—	—	—
↳1797, Reverse of 1797, Stems, S-NC-2	*	377653	—	—	—	—	—	—	—	—
↳1797, Reverse of 1797, Stems, S-NC-3	*	377654	—	1,600	—	—	—	—	—	—
↳1797, Reverse of 1797, Stems, S-NC-5	*	377655	1,250	1,750	3,750	—	—	—	—	—
↳1797, Reverse of 1797, Stems, S-NC-6	2 known	377656	50,500	—	—	—	—	—	—	—
1797, Reverse of 1797, Stemless	*	768	195	325	725	900	1,900	7,500	15,500	—
↳1797, Reverse of 1797, Stemless, S-131	*	77558	195	325	725	900	1,900	7,500	15,500	—
↳1797, Reverse of 1797, Stemless, S-132	*	77559	235	390	1,500	1,900	4,000	—	—	—
↳1797, Reverse of 1797, Stemless, S-133	*	77560	235	390	1,500	1,900	4,000	—	—	—
↳1797, Reverse of 1797, Stemless, S-143	*	77561	235	390	1,500	2,100	3,000	7,500	15,500	—
1798, 8 Over 7	1,841,745	1229	245	455	725	1,000	2,000	4,100	7,500	33,500
	Auctions: $103,500, PCGS MS-62 GLDB 09/09									
↳1798, 8 Over 7, S-150	*	79937	270	500	1,600	2,250	7,500	11,000	30,000	—
↳1798, 8 Over 7, S-151	*	79938	270	500	1,500	1,900	4,400	9,500	15,500	—
↳1798, 8 Over 7, S-152	*	79939	245	455	725	1,000	2,000	4,100	7,500	33,500

* Included in number above.

First Hair Style
Found on all coins of 1796 and 1797, many 1798 varieties, and 1800, 1800 Over 1798.

Second Hair Style
Found on coins of 1798–1807. Note the extra curl near shoulders.

Circulation Strikes *(continued)*

	Mintage	GSID	AG-3	G-4	VG-8	F-12	VF-20	EF-40	AU-50	MS-60
1798, Reverse of 1795	*	771	$260	$390	$650	$900	$2,750	$7,250	$10,000	$15,000
	Auctions: $114,562, PCGS MS-65 GLDB 01/16									
↳1798, Reverse of 1795, S-155	*	79942	260	390	650	900	2,750	7,250	10,000	15,000
↳1798, Reverse of 1795, S-156	*	79943	1,750	2,250	4,500	6,000	8,000	24,000	36,000	—
↳1798, Reverse of 1795, S-178	*	79964	1,200	2,500	7,000	11,000	21,500	48,000	—	—
1798, First Style Hair	*	774	100	145	290	550	950	1,750	3,750	12,000
↳1798, First Style Hair, S-144	*	79931	2,250	3,750	6,250	11,000	17,000	48,000	66,000	—
↳1798, First Style Hair, S-145	*	79932	155	235	455	725	1,250	4,500	8,250	—
↳1798, First Style Hair, S-146	*	79933	230	390	775	1,900	3,100	10,000	—	31,000
↳1798, First Style Hair, S-147	*	79934	230	365	775	2,000	3,000	7,000	11,000	—
↳1798, First Style Hair, S-148	*	79935	110	155	320	600	1,050	2,200	4,400	13,000
↳1798, First Style Hair, S-149	*	79936	360	650	2,250	4,400	6,250	—	—	—
↳1798, First Style Hair, S-153	*	79940	120	170	360	775	1,500	5,500	7,500	21,500
↳1798, First Style Hair, S-154	*	79941	180	260	430	750	1,550	6,250	9,750	21,500
↳1798, First Style Hair, S-157	*	79944	100	145	290	550	950	1,750	3,750	12,000
↳1798, First Style Hair, S-158	*	79945	120	170	290	550	950	1,750	3,750	12,000
↳1798, First Style Hair, S-159	*	79946	180	285	550	950	2,750	7,000	10,500	—
↳1798, First Style Hair, S-160	*	79947	120	170	490	725	1,250	5,000	7,500	—
↳1798, First Style Hair, S-161	*	79948	100	145	290	550	950	1,750	3,750	12,000
↳1798, First Style Hair, S-162	*	79949	120	195	575	850	1,750	5,500	7,500	—
↳1798, First Style Hair, S-163	*	79950	120	195	625	950	2,000	9,500	—	—
↳1798, First Style Hair, S-164	*	79951	160	230	490	800	1,750	4,750	8,000	13,000
↳1798, First Style Hair, S-NC-1	*	377630	—	—	12,000	—	—	—	—	—
↳1798, First Style Hair, S-NC-2	*	377631	—	11,000	—	—	—	—	—	—
1798, Second Style Hair	*	777	110	155	310	525	725	1,750	3,300	9,500
	Auctions: $207,000, PCGS MS-65 GLDB 09/08									
↳1798, Second Style Hair, S-165	*	79952	130	185	575	850	1,750	5,000	7,500	—
↳1798, Second Style Hair, S-166	*	79953	110	155	310	525	725	1,750	3,300	9,500
↳1798, Second Style Hair, S-167	*	79954	110	155	310	525	725	1,750	3,300	9,500
↳1798, Second Style Hair, S-168	*	79955	130	185	490	725	1,250	3,100	5,000	12,000
↳1798, Second Style Hair, S-169	*	79956	130	185	375	575	775	1,900	3,650	10,500
↳1798, Second Style Hair, S-170	*	79957	130	185	375	650	850	2,200	4,150	11,500
↳1798, Second Style Hair, S-171	*	79958	130	185	490	775	1,750	5,500	7,500	—
↳1798, Second Style Hair, S-172	*	79959	110	155	310	525	725	1,750	3,300	10,500
↳1798, Second Style Hair, S-173	*	79960	130	185	375	650	850	2,100	3,650	10,500
↳1798, Second Style Hair, S-174	*	70638	120	170	345	575	775	1,900	3,650	10,500

* Included in number above.

1799, 9 Over 8

1799, Normal Date

1800, 1800 Over 1798

1800, 80 Over 79

1800, Normal Date

1801, Normal Reverse

1801, 3 Errors: 1/000, One Stem, and IINITED

1801, Fraction 1/000

1801, 1/100 Over 1/000

Circulation Strikes *(continued)*

	Mintage	GSID	AG-3	G-4	VG-8	F-12	VF-20	EF-40	AU-50	MS-60
↳1798, Second Style Hair, S-175	*	79961	$130	$185	$490	$725	$1,250	$3,100	$5,500	—
↳1798, Second Style Hair, S-176	*	79962	130	185	550	850	1,900	6,250	8,750	$20,500
↳1798, Second Style Hair, S-177	*	79963	235	390	775	1,500	2,200	5,250	—	—
↳1798, Second Style Hair, S-179	*	79965	120	170	345	575	775	1,900	3,500	9,500
↳1798, Second Style Hair, S-180	*	79966	260	850	1,500	2,500	4,400	9,500	20,500	—
↳1798, Second Style Hair, S-181	*	79967	130	185	375	650	850	2,300	4,650	12,000
↳1798, Second Style Hair, S-182	*	79968	130	185	375	650	925	4,500	7,500	18,000
↳1798, Second Style Hair, S-183	*	79969	160	490	1,150	1,900	3,100	7,000	—	—
↳1798, Second Style Hair, S-184	*	79970	110	155	310	525	725	1,750	3,300	9,500
↳1798, Second Style Hair, S-185	*	79971	120	170	345	575	775	1,900	3,650	—
↳1798, Second Style Hair, S-186	*	79972	120	170	345	575	775	1,900	3,650	12,000
↳1798, Second Style Hair, S-187	*	79973	110	155	310	525	725	1,750	3,300	9,500
1799, Normal Date	904,565	780	3,300	5,500	11,000	20,500	31,000	150,000	240,000	480,000
	Auctions: $977,500, NGC MS-62 GLDB 09/09									
↳1799, Normal Date, S-189	*	79975	3,300	5,500	11,000	20,500	31,000	150,000	240,000	480,000
	Auctions: $210,000, PCGS EF-45 HA 01/25									
1799, 9 Over 8	**	1232	4,000	7,500	17,000	29,000	60,000	180,000	264,000	—
	Auctions: $368,000, PCGS EF-45 GLDB 09/09									
↳1799, 9 Over 8, S-188	**	79974	4,000	7,500	17,000	29,000	60,000	180,000	264,000	—
	Auctions: $150,000, PCGS EF-40 HA 01/25									
↳1799, 9 Over 8, S-NC-1	**	377663	—	—	—	—	—	—	—	—
1800, 1800 Over 1798, Head of 1797	2,822,175	1235	75	100	180	390	900	4,400	7,500	15,000
↳1800, 1800 Over 1798, Head of 1797, S-190	*	79976	75	100	180	390	900	4,400	7,500	15,000
↳1800, 1800 Over 1798, Head of 1797, S-191	*	79977	75	100	180	390	900	4,400	7,500	15,000
↳1800, 1800 Over 1798, Head of 1797, S-NC-6	13–15 known	377664	—	2,700	5,500	—	—	—	—	—
1800, 80 Over 79, Head of 1799	*	1238	75	100	130	290	650	3,100	6,000	12,000
↳1800, 80 Over 79, Head of 1799, S-192	*	79978	75	110	145	390	900	4,400	7,500	—
↳1800, 80 Over 79, Head of 1799, S-193	*	79979	100	130	325	775	1,250	5,000	8,750	—
↳1800, 80 Over 79, Head of 1799, S-194	*	79980	75	100	130	290	650	3,100	6,000	12,000
↳1800, 80 Over 79, Head of 1799, S-195	*	79981	195	340	775	1,600	3,000	7,500	12,000	—
↳1800, 80 Over 79, Head of 1799, S-196	*	79982	75	100	130	290	650	3,100	6,000	12,000
↳1800, 80 Over 79, Head of 1799, S-NC-1	3 known	377657	—	—	—	33,000	—	—	—	—
↳1800, 80 Over 79, Head of 1799, S-NC-2	*	377658	—	—	—	—	—	—	—	—

* Included in number above. ** Included in 1799, Normal Date, mintage figure. Most of this figure represents coinage from 1798 dies still in use.

Circulation Strikes *(continued)*

	Mintage	GSID	AG-3	G-4	VG-8	F-12	VF-20	EF-40	AU-50	MS-60
1800, Normal Date	*	783	$75	$110	$175	$360	$650	$2,900	$3,500	$9,500
↳**1800, Normal Date, S-197**	*	79983	75	110	175	360	650	2,900	3,500	9,500
↳**1800, Normal Date, S-198**	*	79984	325	650	1,900	11,000	15,500	—	—	—
↳**1800, Normal Date, S-199**	*	79985	75	110	260	775	1,250	8,000	14,500	—
↳**1800, Normal Date, S-200**	*	79986	100	130	210	490	1,000	4,250	7,500	—
↳**1800, Normal Date, S-201**	*	79987	130	195	1,600	5,500	7,500	—	—	—
↳**1800, Normal Date, S-202**	*	79988	160	260	1,900	6,250	8,000	8,750	12,000	—
↳**1800, Normal Date, S-203**	*	79989	75	110	195	360	650	3,750	5,500	14,000
↳**1800, Normal Date, S-204**	*	79990	75	110	195	395	725	5,000	6,250	14,500
↳**1800, Normal Date, S-205**	*	79991	75	110	195	395	725	3,450	3,850	9,500
↳**1800, Normal Date, S-206**	*	79992	75	110	175	360	650	2,900	3,500	—
↳**1800, Normal Date, S-207**	*	79993	75	110	195	395	725	3,150	4,900	—
↳**1800, Normal Date, S-208**	*	79994	75	110	195	360	650	5,000	9,500	—
↳**1800, Normal Date, S-209**	*	79995	75	110	195	360	650	3,500	5,250	11,000
↳**1800, Normal Date, S-210**	*	79996	260	575	1,750	6,250	7,500	—	—	—
↳**1800, Normal Date, S-211**	*	79997	75	110	195	360	650	3,750	6,250	—
↳**1800, Normal Date, S-212**	*	79998	75	110	195	395	775	3,000	4,600	12,000
↳**1800, Normal Date, S-NC-3**	*	377659	—	2,000	5,000	—	—	—	—	—
↳**1800, Normal Date, S-NC-4**	*	377660	7,500	11,000	—	—	—	—	30,000	—
1801, Normal Reverse	1,362,837	786	75	110	175	360	550	2,000	3,400	10,000
↳**1801, Normal Reverse, S-213**	*	79999	80	120	195	395	675	2,750	4,750	—
↳**1801, Normal Reverse, S-214**	*	80000	80	120	195	395	625	4,100	7,000	—
↳**1801, Normal Reverse, S-215**	*	80001	180	310	1,150	2,500	4,000	7,000	10,500	19,000
↳**1801, Normal Reverse, S-216**	*	80002	75	110	175	360	550	2,000	3,400	10,000
↳**1801, Normal Reverse, S-217**	*	80003	5,000	7,500	11,000	18,000	20,500	42,000	84,000	—
	Auctions: $103,500, PCGS AU-58 HA 02/08									
↳**1801, Normal Reverse, S-222**	*	80008	80	120	230	390	550	2,400	4,750	17,000
↳**1801, Normal Reverse, S-224**	*	80010	75	110	175	360	550	2,000	6,250	14,500
↳**1801, Normal Reverse, S-NC-1**	*	377665	950	1,250	2,000	3,100	—	—	—	—
↳**1801, Normal Reverse, S-NC-2**	*	377666	2,750	3,750	—	—	—	—	—	—
↳**1801, Normal Reverse, S-NC-4**	*	377667	—	2,250	—	—	—	—	—	—
1801, 3 Errors: 1/000, One Stem, and IINITED	*	789	145	360	775	1,600	3,750	12,500	26,500	48,000
	Auctions: $138,000, NGC MS-63 HA 01/05									
↳**1801, 3 Errors: 1/000, One Stem, and IINITED, S-218**	*	80004	2,100	3,100	5,000	8,000	11,000	—	—	—
↳**1801, 3 Errors: 1/000, One Stem, and IINITED, S-219**	*	80005	145	360	775	1,600	3,750	12,500	26,500	48,000
	Auctions: $108,000, PCGS MS-62 HA 01/22									
1801, Fraction 1/000	*	792	110	155	310	525	1,000	4,250	6,000	12,000
↳**1801, Fraction 1/000, S-220**	*	80006	110	155	310	525	1,000	4,250	6,000	12,000
↳**1801, Fraction 1/000, S-223**	*	80009	110	155	310	525	1,000	4,250	6,000	12,000
↳**1801, Fraction 1/000, S-NC-3**	*	377595	1,500	2,000	4,500	—	—	—	—	—
1801, 1/100 Over 1/000	*	795	130	195	390	725	1,500	5,500	12,000	31,000
↳**1801, 1/100 Over 1/000, S-221**	*	80007	130	195	390	725	1,500	5,500	12,000	31,000

* Included in number above.

1802, Normal Reverse

1802, Fraction 1/000

1802, Stemless Wreath

1803, Small Date

1803, Large Date

Note that Small Date varieties have a blunt 1 in the date, and Large Date varieties have a pointed 1 and noticeably larger 3.

1803, Small Fraction

1803, Large Fraction

1803, 1/100 Over 1/000

1803, Stemless Wreath

Circulation Strikes *(continued)*

	Mintage	GSID	AG-3	G-4	VG-8	F-12	VF-20	EF-40	AU-50	MS-60
1802, Normal Reverse	3,435,100	798	$90	$120	$155	$275	$500	$1,250	$2,100	$5,750
↳1802, Normal Reverse, S-225	*	80011	90	120	155	275	500	1,250	2,100	5,750
↳1802, Normal Reverse, S-226	*	80012	90	120	155	275	600	1,500	2,550	8,500
↳1802, Normal Reverse, S-227	*	80013	95	130	170	300	550	1,500	5,500	—
↳1802, Normal Reverse, S-229	*	80015	95	130	170	300	550	1,600	5,500	—
↳1802, Normal Reverse, S-230	*	80016	90	120	155	275	500	1,250	2,100	10,000
↳1802, Normal Reverse, S-232	*	80018	90	120	155	275	500	1,250	2,100	5,750
↳1802, Normal Reverse, S-233	*	80019	95	130	170	300	550	1,750	5,250	—
↳1802, Normal Reverse, S-234	*	80020	95	130	170	300	550	1,400	5,250	—
↳1802, Normal Reverse, S-235	*	80021	95	130	170	300	550	1,400	2,550	—
↳1802, Normal Reverse, S-236	*	80022	95	130	170	300	550	1,250	2,100	5,750
↳1802, Normal Reverse, S-237	*	80023	90	120	155	275	500	1,250	2,100	5,750
↳1802, Normal Reverse, S-238	*	80024	145	210	340	525	1,150	6,250	11,000	—
↳1802, Normal Reverse, S-239	*	80025	95	130	170	300	650	1,500	3,100	7,000
↳1802, Normal Reverse, S-240	*	80026	105	140	185	330	650	2,250	6,000	12,000
↳1802, Normal Reverse, S-242	*	80028	95	130	170	300	550	1,500	2,250	—
↳1802, Normal Reverse, S-NC-1	*	377661	525	725	1,150	1,750	6,000	—	—	—
↳1802, Normal Reverse, S-NC-2	*	377662	—	1,500	3,500	—	7,500	12,000	—	—
1802, Fraction 1/000	*	801	110	155	260	525	850	2,250	5,500	13,000
↳1802, Fraction 1/000, S-228	*	80014	110	155	260	525	850	2,250	5,500	13,000
1802, Stemless Wreath	*	804	100	155	260	420	650	1,400	3,000	14,500
↳1802, Stemless Wreath, S-231	*	80017	100	155	260	420	650	1,400	3,000	14,500
↳1802, Stemless Wreath, S-241	*	80027	100	155	260	420	650	1,400	3,000	14,500
1803, Small Date, Small Fraction	3,131,691	807	75	100	155	310	500	1,100	1,950	7,500
↳1803, Small Date, Small Fraction, S-244	*	80030	90	120	205	405	650	3,000	—	—
↳1803, Small Date, Small Fraction, S-245	*	80031	75	100	155	310	500	1,100	1,950	7,500
↳1803, Small Date, Small Fraction, S-246	*	80032	80	110	170	650	1,150	3,100	8,750	—
↳1803, Small Date, Small Fraction, S-247	*	80033	80	110	170	390	725	1,500	1,950	12,000
↳1803, Small Date, Small Fraction, S-248	*	80034	100	170	360	525	850	3,000	5,000	12,000
↳1803, Small Date, Small Fraction, S-250	*	80036	75	100	155	310	500	1,100	1,950	7,500
↳1803, Small Date, Small Fraction, S-251	*	80037	75	100	155	310	500	1,100	1,950	7,500
↳1803, Small Date, Small Fraction, S-252	*	80038	75	100	155	310	500	1,100	1,950	8,250
↳1803, Small Date, Small Fraction, S-253	*	80039	75	100	155	310	500	1,100	1,950	8,250
↳1803, Small Date, Small Fraction, S-254	*	80040	75	100	155	310	500	1,100	1,950	7,500
↳1803, Small Date, Small Fraction, S-255	*	80041	75	100	155	310	500	1,100	1,950	7,500
↳1803, Small Date, Small Fraction, S-256	*	80042	75	100	155	310	500	1,100	1,950	7,500
↳1803, Small Date, Small Fraction, S-262	*	80048	80	160	325	900	1,900	4,900	—	—
↳1803, Small Date, Small Fraction, S-263	*	80049	80	110	155	310	500	1,300	3,500	14,500

* Included in number above.

1804,
Broken Dies
S-266c

Unofficial
1804
"Restrike"

Circulation Strikes *(continued)*

	Mintage	GSID	AG-3	G-4	VG-8	F-12	VF-20	EF-40	AU-50	MS-60
1803, Small Date, Large Fraction	*	810	$75	$100	$150	$325	$575	$1,200	$1,750	$6,000
↳**1803, Small Date, Large Fraction, S-257**	*	80043	75	100	150	325	575	1,200	1,750	6,000
↳**1803, Small Date, Large Fraction, S-258**	*	80044	75	100	150	325	575	1,200	1,750	6,000
↳**1803, Small Date, Large Fraction, S-259**	*	80045	110	145	210	360	900	2,500	4,100	—
↳**1803, Small Date, Large Fraction, S-260**	*	80046	75	100	150	325	575	1,200	1,750	6,000
↳**1803, Small Date, Large Fraction, S-261**	*	80047	75	100	150	325	575	1,300	2,500	10,500
1803, Large Date, Small Fraction	*	813	4,400	9,750	15,500	18,000	42,000	120,000	—	—
	Auctions: $115,000, PCGS VF35 GLDB 06/13									
↳**1803, Large Date, Small Fraction, S-264**	*	80050	4,400	9,750	15,500	18,000	42,000	120,000	—	—
1803, Large Date, Large Fraction	*	816	195	325	525	1,250	2,750	9,500	14,500	—
↳**1803, Large Date, Large Fraction, S-265**	*	80051	195	325	525	1,250	2,750	9,500	14,500	—
1803, 1/100 Over 1/000	*	819	130	210	415	725	1,300	2,750	5,500	12,000
↳**1803, 1/100 Over 1/000, S-249**	*	80035	130	210	415	725	1,300	2,750	5,500	12,000
1803, Stemless Wreath	*	822	90	130	195	360	550	1,250	2,250	10,000
↳**1803, Stemless Wreath, S-243**	*	80029	90	130	195	360	550	1,250	2,250	10,000
1804 (a)	96,500	825	1,500	2,500	4,400	7,750	11,000	23,000	40,000	—
	Auctions: $661,250, PCGS MS-63 GLDB 09/09									
↳**1804, S-266** (a)	*	80052	1,500	2,500	4,400	7,750	11,000	23,000	48,000	—
	Auctions: $150,000, PCGS AU-55 HA 01/22									
1804, Unofficial Restrike of 1860 (b)		740	—	—	—	—	550	—	850	950
1805	941,116	828	75	100	145	285	550	1,100	2,500	5,500
	Auctions: $184,000, PCGS MS-66 GLDB 09/09									
↳**1805, S-267**	*	70637	75	100	145	285	550	1,100	2,500	5,500
↳**1805, S-268**	*	80053	90	120	170	455	775	5,000	—	—
↳**1805, S-269**	*	80054	75	100	145	285	550	1,100	2,500	5,500
1806	348,000	831	75	110	175	420	650	1,950	2,750	5,750
↳**1806, S-270**	*	80055	75	110	175	420	650	1,950	2,750	5,750

* Included in number above. **a.** All genuine 1804 cents have a crosslet 4 in the date and a large fraction. The 0 in the date is in line with the O in OF on the reverse. **b.** Discarded Mint dies were used, circa 1860, to create "restrikes" (actually novodels or fantasies) of the scarce 1804 cent for collectors. These combine two unrelated dies: an altered 1803 die was used for the obverse, and a die of the 1820 cent for the reverse. The resulting coins cannot be confused with genuine 1804 cents.

1807, Large Fraction

1807, "Comet" Variety
Note the die break behind Liberty's head.

Small 1807, 7 Over 6, Blunt 1

1807, Small Fraction

Large 1807, 7 Over 6, Pointed 1

Circulation Strikes *(continued)*

	Mintage	GSID	AG-3	G-4	VG-8	F-12	VF-20	EF-40	AU-50	MS-60
1807, Large Fraction	829,221	834	$75	$100	$135	$265	$575	$1,250	$2,500	$7,500
↳1807, Large Fraction, S-275	*	80060	75	100	155	305	675	1,450	3,100	12,000
↳1807, Large Fraction, S-276	*	80061	75	100	135	265	575	1,250	2,500	7,500
1807, "Comet" Variety	*	837	155	235	390	650	1,750	3,750	8,000	18,000
↳1807, "Comet" Variety, S-271	*	80056	155	235	390	650	1,750	3,750	8,000	18,000
1807, Small Fraction	*	840	130	210	390	1,150	3,100	10,000	26,500	42,000
↳1807, Small Fraction, S-274	*	80059	130	210	390	1,150	3,100	10,000	26,500	42,000
1807, Small 1807, 7 Over 6, Blunt 1	*	1241	2,400	3,000	4,500	10,000	24,000	72,000	120,000	—
	Auctions: $172,500, PCGS AU-53 GLDB 09/08									
↳1807, Small 1807, 7 Over 6, Blunt 1, S-272	*	80057	2,400	3,000	4,500	10,000	24,000	72,000	120,000	—
	Auctions: $126,000, PCGS AU-55 HA 01/24									
1807, Large 1807, 7 Over 6, Pointed 1	*	1244	100	195	275	490	900	1,600	3,500	8,750
↳1807, Large 1807, 7 Over 6, Pointed 1, S-273	*	80058	100	195	275	490	900	1,600	3,500	8,750

* Included in number above.

CLASSIC HEAD (1808–1814)

Designer: *John Reich.* **Weight:** *10.89 grams.* **Composition:** *Copper.* **Diameter:** *Average 29 mm.* **Edge:** *Plain.* **Mint:** *Philadelphia.*

History. The Classic Head design, by U.S. Mint assistant engraver John Reich, debuted in 1808. This cent type was minted through 1814. The quality of the coins' copper was poor during the War of 1812; the hostilities had ended the importation of high-quality planchets from England.

Striking and Sharpness. Striking sharpness varies, but often is poor. The cents of 1809 are notorious for having obverses much weaker than their reverses. Points to look for include sharpness of the denticles (which are often mushy, and in *most* instances inconsistent), star centers (a key area), hair details, and leaf details. Classic Head cents often are dark and porous due to the copper stock used.

Availability. Examples are readily available in grades from well worn to VF and EF, although overall quality often leaves much to be desired. AU and MS coins are elusive. Grading numbers do not mean much, as a connoisseur might prefer a high-quality EF-45 to a poorly struck MS-63. Overall eye appeal of obverse and reverse is often sub-par, a characteristic of this type.

Grading Standards

MS-64BN

MS-60 to 70 (Mint State). ***Obverse:*** In the lower Mint State grades, MS-60 and 61, some slight abrasions can be seen on the portrait, most evidently on the cheek, as the hair details are complex on this type. Luster in the field is complete or nearly complete; the field is not as open on this type as on the Draped Bust issues. At MS-63, luster should be complete, and no abrasion evident. In higher levels, the luster is complete and deeper, and some original mint color may be seen. MS-64 coins may have some slight discoloration or scattered contact marks. A well-graded MS-65 or higher coin will have full, rich luster; no marks visible except under magnification; and a nice blend of brown toning or nicely mixed (not stained or blotchy) mint color and natural brown toning. Incomplete striking of some details, especially the obverse stars, is the rule. ***Reverse:*** In the lower Mint State grades, some abrasion is seen on the higher areas of the leaves. Mint luster is complete in all Mint State grades, as the open areas are protected by the lettering and wreath. Sharpness of the leaves can vary by die variety, so check this aspect. Otherwise, the same comments apply as for the obverse.

Illustrated coin: The central devices are sharply struck and well preserved though obverse stars 1 through 5 are somewhat flat, as is virtually always seen on this type, and the reverse denticles from 8 o'clock to 11 o'clock are soft, which is also typical. This is one of the highest-graded Classic Head cents in existence.

AU-50, 53, 55, 58 (About Uncirculated). ***Obverse:*** Friction is seen on the higher parts, particularly the cheek. The hair will have friction and light wear, but will not be as obvious. Friction and scattered marks are in the field, ranging from more extensive at AU-50 to minimal at AU-58. Luster may be seen in protected areas, minimal at AU-50, but more visible at AU-58. At AU-58 the open field may retain some luster, as well. ***Reverse:*** Friction is seen on the higher wreath leaves and on the letters. Fields, protected by the designs, show less friction. At the AU-55 and 58 levels little if any friction is seen. The reverse may have original luster, toned brown, minimal on lower About Uncirculated grades, often extensive at AU-58.

AU-58

EF-40, 45 (Extremely Fine). ***Obverse:*** Wear is seen on the portrait overall, but most hair detail will still be present. The cheek shows light wear. Luster is minimal or nonexistent at EF-40, and may survive in among the letters of LIBERTY at EF-45. ***Reverse:*** Wear is seen on the highest wreath and ribbon areas and the letters. Leaf veins are visible except in the highest areas. Luster is minimal, but likely more noticeable than on the obverse, as the fields are protected by the designs and lettering.

EF-40

VF-20, 30 (Very Fine). ***Obverse:*** Wear on the portrait has reduced the hair detail, especially on the area to the right of the cheek and neck, but much can still be seen. ***Reverse:*** The wreath details, except for the edges of the leaves and certain of the tips (on leaves in lower relief), are worn away at VF-20, and with slightly more detail at VF-30.

VF-25

F-12, 15 (Fine). ***Obverse:*** The hair details are fewer than on the preceding, but many are still present. The central hair curl is visible. Stars have flat centers. F-15 shows slightly more detail. The portrait on this type held up well to wear. ***Reverse:*** The higher areas of wreath leaves are worn flat, but their edges are distinct. F-15 shows slightly more detail.

Illustrated coin: This is a dark and somewhat porous example of what is considered to be the key issue of the Classic Head type.

F-15

VG-10

VG-8, 10 (Very Good). ***Obverse:*** The portrait is well worn, although the eye and ear can be seen clearly. The hair is mostly blended, but some slight separation can be seen in areas. The border is raised in most or all areas. ***Reverse:*** The wreath is more worn than on the preceding grade, but there will still be some detail on the leaves. On most coins, ONE CENT is bold. Border letters are light or weak but are fully readable. The border is well defined in most areas.

G-6

G-4, 6 (Good). ***Obverse:*** The portrait is worn smooth and is seen only in outline form. Much or even all of LIBERTY on the headband is readable, but the letters are weak. The stars are weak, only in outline form, and several may be scarcely discernible. ***Reverse:*** Extensive wear is seen overall. Lettering in UNITED STATES OF AMERICA is weak, but completely discernible. The wreath is in outline, but still fairly bold, and ONE CENT is usually strong.

AG-3

AG-3 (About Good). ***Obverse:*** Wear is more extensive than on the preceding. The portrait is visible only in outline. Most letters of LIBERTY are discernible, as this feature is in low relief. The stars are weak or worn away on their outer edges, and the date is light. ***Reverse:*** The wreath is visible in outline form but remains fairly strong. Most or even all of UNITED STATES OF AMERICA is worn away. ONE CENT is usually easily readable.

1810, 10 Over 09

1810, Normal Date

1811, Last 1 Over 0

1811, Normal Date

1812, Small Date

1812, Large Date

1814, Plain 4

1814, Crosslet 4

Circulation Strikes

	Mintage	GSID	G-4	VG-8	F-12	VF-20	EF-40	AU-50	MS-60	MS-63
Classic Head (1808–1814), Brown	**n/a**	**72325**	**$145**	**$260**	**$525**	**$950**	**$1,700**	**$2,900**	**$8,500**	**$14,500**
Same, Red Brown	**n/a**	**72326**	**—**	**—**	**—**	**—**	**—**	**—**	**—**	**17,500**
1808	1,007,000	843	145	260	525	950	1,700	2,900	8,500	14,500
↳1808, S-277	*	80066	145	260	525	950	1,700	2,900	8,500	14,500
↳1808, S-278	*	80067	170	310	725	1,150	3,500	5,500	12,000	19,000
↳1808, S-279	*	80068	145	260	525	950	1,700	2,900	8,500	14,500
1809	222,867	846	310	700	1,400	1,900	3,750	5,250	15,500	30,000
	Auctions: $129,250, PCGS MS-64 GLDB 01/16									
↳1809, S-280	*	80069	310	700	1,400	1,900	3,750	5,250	15,500	30,000
1810, 10 Over 09	1,458,500	1247	165	310	675	1,150	3,000	6,500	13,000	19,000
↳1810, 10 Over 09, S-281	*	80070	165	310	675	1,150	3,000	6,500	13,000	19,000
1810, Normal Date	*	849	235	310	600	1,150	1,950	3,750	9,000	16,000
	Auctions: $149,500, PCGS MS-65 GLDB 09/09									
↳1810, Normal Date, S-282	*	80071	235	310	600	1,150	1,950	3,750	9,000	16,000
↳1810, Normal Date, S-283	*	80072	235	310	600	1,150	1,950	3,750	9,000	16,000
↳1810, Normal Date, S-284	*	80073	235	310	600	1,150	1,950	3,750	9,000	16,000
↳1810, Normal Date, S-285	*	80074	235	310	600	1,150	1,950	3,750	9,000	16,000
1811, Last 1 Over 0	218,025	1250	440	675	1,150	1,800	8,750	14,000	42,000	108,000
↳1811, Last 1 Over 0, S-286	*	80075	440	675	1,150	1,800	8,750	14,000	42,000	108,000
	Auctions: $102,000, NGC MS-63 SBG 08/18									
1811, Normal Date	*	852	260	440	725	1,500	3,000	4,750	9,500	17,000
↳1811, Normal Date, S-287	*	80076	260	440	725	1,500	3,000	4,750	9,500	17,000
1812, Small Date	1,075,500	855	145	260	525	950	1,700	2,900	8,500	14,500
↳1812, Small Date, S-290	*	80079	145	260	525	950	1,700	2,900	8,500	14,500
↳1812, Small Date, S-291	*	80080	145	260	525	950	1,700	2,900	8,500	14,500
1812, Large Date	*	858	145	260	525	950	1,700	2,900	8,500	14,500
↳1812, Large Date, S-288	*	80077	145	260	525	950	1,700	2,900	8,500	14,500
↳1812, Large Date, S-289	*	80078	145	260	525	950	1,700	2,900	8,500	14,500
1813	418,000	861	145	260	525	950	1,700	2,900	8,750	21,500
	Auctions: $207,000, PCGS MS-65 SBG 11/08									
↳1813, S-292	*	80081	145	260	525	950	1,700	2,900	8,750	21,500
↳1813, S-293	*	80082	145	260	525	950	1,700	2,900	8,750	21,500
1814, Crosslet 4	357,830	864	145	260	525	950	1,700	2,900	8,500	14,500
↳1814, Crosslet 4, S-294	*	80083	145	260	525	950	1,700	2,900	8,500	14,500
1814, Plain 4	*	867	145	260	525	950	1,700	2,900	8,500	14,500
↳1814, Plain 4, S-295	*	80084	145	260	525	950	1,700	2,900	8,500	14,500
	Auctions: $158,625, PCGS MS-67 HA 05/15									

* Included in number above.

CORONET HEAD (1816–1839)

Designer: *1816–1835, Coronet Head—Possibly Robert Scot or John Birch; 1835–1839, Coronet Head Modified (Young Head)—Christian Gobrecht.* **Weight:** *10.89 grams.* **Composition:** *Copper.* **Diameter:** *1816–1835, Coronet Head—28 to 29 mm; 1835–1839, Coronet Head Modified (Young Head)—27.5 mm.* **Edge:** *Plain.* **Mint:** *Philadelphia.*

Coronet Head (1816–1835), Circulation Strike

Coronet Head, Proof Strike

Coronet Head Modified (Young Head) (1835–1839), Circulation Strike

Coronet Head Modified (Young Head), Proof Strike

History. The term *Coronet Head* describes cents of 1816 to 1835 (none were struck in 1815). Engraver Christian Gobrecht experimented with various "Coronet Head Modified" portraits in the later 1830s.

Striking and Sharpness. Planchet quality is generally very good for Liberty Head cents. Color tends to be lighter on coins of the 1830s than on earlier dates. Striking can vary. Points to check include the obverse stars (in particular), the highest hair details, and the leaves on the reverse. Denticles can range from sharp to weak, and centering is often irregular. The reverse design is essentially the same as that used on the Classic Head of 1808 to 1814, and can be graded the same way. This motif stood up to circulation particularly well.

Availability. As a type, Liberty Head cents are easily available. The scarcest date by far is 1823 (and the related 1823, 3 Over 2, overdate). Cents of 1816 to 1820 (particularly 1818 and 1820) are readily available in MS. Other MS coins are generally scarce, although those of the 1830s are more easily obtainable than those of the teens and 1820s. Circulated examples exist in approximate relationship to their mintages. Planchet quality and striking sharpness vary in all grades.

Grading Standards

MS-63BN

MS-60 to 70 (Mint State). ***Obverse:*** In the lower Mint State grades, MS-60 and 61, some slight abrasions can be seen on the portrait, most evidently on the cheek, which on this type is very prominent. Higher areas of the hair can be checked, particularly the top and back of Liberty's head, but do not confuse with lightness of strike. Luster in the field is complete or nearly complete. At MS-63, luster should be complete, and no abrasion is evident. In higher levels, the luster is complete and deeper, and some original mint color may be seen. MS-64 coins may have some minimal discoloration or scattered contact marks. A well-graded MS-65 or higher coin will have full, rich luster; no marks visible except under magnification; and a nice blend of brown toning or nicely mixed mint color and natural brown toning. Randall Hoard coins of the 1816 to 1820 years usually have much mint red and some black spotting. ***Reverse:*** In the lower Mint State grades some abrasion is seen on the higher areas of the leaves. Mint luster is complete in all Mint State grades, as the open areas are protected by the lettering and wreath. Sharpness of the leaves can vary by die variety, so check this aspect. Otherwise, the same comments apply as for the obverse.

Illustrated coin: Note the reverse die break running from NI of UNITED to OF A in OF AMERICA.

AU-58

AU-50, 53, 55, 58 (About Uncirculated). ***Obverse:*** Friction is seen on the higher parts, particularly the cheek. The hair has friction and light wear, usually most notable in the general area above BER of LIBERTY. Friction and scattered marks are in the field, ranging from extensive at AU-50 to minimal at AU-58. Luster may be seen in protected areas, minimal at the AU-50 level, more visible at AU-58. At AU-58 the field may retain some luster as well. ***Reverse:*** Friction is seen on the higher wreath leaves and on the letters. Fields, protected by the designs, show friction. At the AU-55 and 58 levels little if any friction is seen. The reverse may have original luster, toned brown, minimal on lower About Uncirculated grades, often extensive at AU-58.

Illustrated coin: Flecks of darker patination spot both sides, but are particularly evident on the obverse.

EF-45

EF-40, 45 (Extremely Fine). ***Obverse:*** Wear is seen on the portrait overall, but most hair detail is still present, except in higher areas. The cheek shows light wear. Luster is minimal or nonexistent at EF-40, and may survive in among the letters of LIBERTY at EF-45. ***Reverse:*** Wear is seen on the highest wreath and ribbon areas, and on the letters. Leaf veins are visible except in the highest areas. Luster is minimal, but likely more noticeable than on the obverse, as the fields are protected by the designs and lettering.

VF-20

VF-20, 30 (Very Fine). ***Obverse:*** Wear on the portrait has reduced the hair detail, especially on the area to the right of the cheek and neck, but much can still be seen. ***Reverse:*** The wreath details, except for the edges of the leaves and certain of the tips (on leaves in lower relief), are worn away at VF-20, and with slightly more detail at VF-30.

F-12, 15 (Fine). ***Obverse:*** The hair details are fewer than on the preceding, but still many are present. Wear is extensive above and below the LIBERTY coronet, with the area from the forehead to the coronet worn flat. Stars have flat centers. F-15 shows slightly more detail. ***Reverse:*** The higher areas of wreath leaves are worn flat, but their edges are distinct. F-15 shows slightly more detail.

F-15

VG-8, 10 (Very Good). ***Obverse:*** The portrait is well worn, although the eye and ear can be seen clearly. The hair is mostly blended, but some slight separation can be seen in lower areas. The border is raised in most or all areas. ***Reverse:*** The wreath is more worn than on the preceding, but still there is some detail on the leaves. On most coins, ONE CENT is bold. Border letters are light or weak but are fully readable. The border is well defined in most areas.

VG-8

Illustrated coin: A die break caused the internal cud which connects stars 3 through 5, and that broken die would have been retired shortly after striking this piece.

G-4, 6 (Good). ***Obverse:*** The portrait is worn smooth and is seen only in outline form. Much or even all of LIBERTY on the headband is readable, but the letters are weak, and L may be missing. The stars are weak. The rim is usually discernible all around. ***Reverse:*** Extensive wear is seen overall. Lettering in UNITED STATES OF AMERICA is weak, but completely discernible. The wreath is in outline, but still fairly bold, and ONE CENT is usually strong. The rim is usually faded into the field in many areas (depending on the die variety).

G-4

Illustrated coin: Note the lovely golden brown and rose surfaces.

AG-3 (About Good). ***Obverse:*** Wear is more extensive than on the preceding. The portrait is visible only in outline. Most letters of LIBERTY remain discernible in the headband, as this feature is in low relief. The stars are weak or worn away on their outer edges, and the date is light. ***Reverse:*** The wreath is visible in outline form, but remains fairly strong. Most of UNITED STATES OF AMERICA is worn away. ONE CENT is usually readable, but light.

AG-3

PF-63BN

PF-60 to 70 (Proof). Proofs were made for cents from 1817 onward. Often, what are called "Proofs" are only partially mirrorlike, and sometimes the striking is casual, e.g., with weakness on certain of the stars. Complicating the situation is the fact that all but one of the same die pairs were also used to make circulation strikes. Many misattributions were made generations ago, some of which have been perpetuated. Except among large-cent specialists, debate is effectively ended when a certification service seals a coin as a Proof (logic aside). True Proofs with deeply mirrored surfaces are in the small minority. ***Obverse and Reverse:*** Proofs that are extensively hairlined or have dull surfaces, this being characteristic of many issues (exceptions, when found, are usually dated in the 1830s) are graded PF-60 to 62 or 63. Artificially toned and recolored coins may be graded lower. To qualify as PF-65 or higher, hairlines should be microscopic, and there should be no trace of friction. Surfaces should be prooflike or, better, fully mirrored and without dullness.

Illustrated coin: This coin shows high quality for the grade. The surfaces are a light, reddish brown with areas of deep tan and hints of blue, green, gold and violet as well as considerable faded mint red on the reverse. This is one of two known Proof examples for the year.

1817, 13 Stars

1817, 15 Stars

Circulation Strikes

	Mintage	GSID	G-4	VG-8	F-12	VF-20	EF-40	AU-50	MS-60	MS-63
Coronet Head (1816–1839), Brown	**n/a**	**72328**	**$24**	**$35**	**$46**	**$80**	**$150**	**$245**	**$375**	**$725**
Same, Red Brown	**n/a**	**72329**	**—**	**—**	**—**	**—**	**—**	**—**	**—**	**1,000**
Same, Red	**n/a**	**72330**	**—**	**—**	**—**	**—**	**—**	**—**	**—**	**2,900**
1816	2,820,982	870	34	40	55	115	310	455	850	1,100
↳1816, N-1	*	80091	—	—	—	—	—	—	—	—
↳1816, N-2	*	80094	34	40	55	115	310	455	850	1,100
↳1816, N-3	*	80097	—	—	—	—	—	—	—	—
↳1816, N-4	*	80100	34	40	55	115	310	455	850	1,100
↳1816, N-5	*	80103	34	40	55	115	310	455	850	1,100
↳1816, N-6	*	80106	34	40	55	115	310	455	850	1,100
↳1816, N-7	*	80109	34	40	55	115	310	455	850	1,100
↳1816, N-8	*	80112	34	40	55	115	310	455	850	1,100
↳1816, Large Center Dot, N-9	*	80115	34	40	55	115	310	455	850	1,100
1817, 13 Stars	3,948,400	873	35	47	75	145	310	550	850	1,250
↳1817, 13 Stars, N-1	*	80118	39	50	80	155	345	600	950	1,400
↳1817, 13 Stars, N-2	*	80121	35	47	75	145	310	550	850	1,250
↳1817, 13 Stars, N-3	*	80124	35	47	75	145	310	550	850	1,250
↳1817, 13 Stars, N-4	*	80127	35	47	75	145	310	550	850	1,250
↳1817, 13 Stars, N-5	*	80130	35	47	75	145	310	550	850	1,250
↳1817, 13 Stars, N-6	*	80133	35	47	75	145	310	550	850	1,250
↳1817, 13 Stars, N-7	*	80136	35	47	75	145	310	550	850	1,250
↳1817, 13 Stars, N-8	*	80139	35	47	75	145	310	550	850	1,250
↳1817, 13 Stars, N-9	*	80142	35	47	75	145	310	550	850	1,250
↳1817, 13 Stars, N-10	*	80145	35	47	75	145	310	550	850	1,250
↳1817, 13 Stars, N-11	*	80148	35	47	75	145	310	550	850	1,250
↳1817, 13 Stars, N-12	*	80151	35	47	75	145	310	550	850	1,250
↳1817, 13 Stars, N-13	*	80154	35	47	75	145	310	550	850	1,250
↳1817, 13 Stars, N-14	*	80157	35	47	75	145	310	550	850	1,250
↳1817, 13 Stars, N-15	*	80160	39	50	80	155	345	600	950	1,400
↳1817, 13 Stars, N-17	*	80166	155	325	725	1,400	3,450	5,000	—	—
1817, 15 Stars	*	876	43	55	90	195	775	1,250	3,000	6,250
↳1817, 15 Stars, N-16	*	80163	43	55	90	195	775	1,250	3,000	6,250

* Included in number above.

1819, Large Date

1819, Small Date

1819, 9 Over 8

1820, 20 Over 19
Note the 1 under the 2.

1820, Small Date
Note the curl-topped 2.

1820, Large Date
Note the plain-topped 2.

Circulation Strikes *(continued)*

	Mintage	GSID	G-4	VG-8	F-12	VF-20	EF-40	AU-50	MS-60	MS-63
1818	3,167,000	883	$24	$35	$46	$80	$195	$290	$525	$900
↳1818, N-1	*	80169	24	35	46	80	195	290	525	900
↳1818, N-2	*	80172	27	39	50	90	215	320	575	975
↳1818, N-3	*	80175	24	35	46	80	195	290	525	900
↳1818, N-4	*	80178	—	—	—	—	—	—	—	—
↳1818, N-5	*	80181	24	35	46	80	195	290	525	900
↳1818, N-6	*	80184	24	35	46	80	195	290	525	900
↳1818, N-7	*	80187	24	35	46	80	195	290	525	900
↳1818, N-8	*	80190	24	35	46	80	195	290	525	900
↳1818, N-9	*	80193	24	35	46	80	195	290	525	900
↳1818, N-10	*	80196	24	35	46	80	195	290	525	900
1819, Large Date (a)	2,671,000	889	24	35	46	80	195	390	775	1,100
↳1819, Large Date, N-2 (a)	*	80202	24	35	46	80	195	390	775	1,100
1819, Small Date	*	892	24	35	46	80	230	390	650	1,150
↳1819, Small Date, N-3	*	80205	24	35	46	80	230	390	650	1,150
↳1819, Small Date, N-4	*	80208	24	35	46	80	230	390	650	1,150
↳1819, Small Date, N-5	*	80211	24	35	46	80	230	390	650	1,150
↳1819, Small Date, N-6	*	80214	24	35	46	80	230	390	650	1,150
↳1819, Small Date, N-7	*	80217	27	39	50	90	250	430	725	1,250
↳1819, Small Date, N-8	*	80220	24	35	46	80	230	390	650	1,150
↳1819, Small Date, N-9	*	80223	24	35	46	80	230	390	650	1,150
↳1819, Small Date, N-10	*	80226	27	39	50	90	250	430	725	1,250
1819, 9 Over 8, Large Date	*	1253	24	35	55	110	360	650	1,450	2,500
↳1819, 9 Over 8, Large Date, N-1	*	80199	24	35	55	110	360	650	1,450	2,500
1820, 20 Over 19	4,407,500	1259	34	40	60	110	455	775	1,500	2,500
↳1820, 20 Over 19, N-1	*	80229	34	40	60	110	455	775	1,500	2,500
↳1820, 20 Over 19, N-2	*	80232	34	40	60	110	455	775	1,500	2,500
↳1820, 20 Over 19, N-3	*	80235	34	40	60	110	455	775	1,500	2,500
1820, Small Date	*	901	70	100	130	195	525	1,000	1,900	2,500
↳1820, Small Date, N-4	*	80238	—	—	—	—	—	—	—	—
↳1820, Small Date, N-5	*	80241	70	100	130	195	525	1,000	1,900	2,500
↳1820, Small Date, N-6	*	80244	—	—	—	—	—	—	—	—
↳1820, Small Date, N-7	*	80247	70	100	130	195	525	1,000	1,900	2,500
↳1820, Small Date, N-8	*	80250	70	100	130	195	525	1,000	1,900	2,500
↳1820, Small Date, N-15	*	80271	70	100	130	195	525	1,000	1,900	2,500

* Included in number above. **a.** The 1819, Large Date, is technically a 9 Over 8 similar to the listing below, but the underlying 8 is hardly visible.

1823, 3 Over 2

Unofficial 1823 "Restrike"

Circulation Strikes *(continued)*

	Mintage	GSID	G-4	VG-8	F-12	VF-20	EF-40	AU-50	MS-60	MS-63
1820, Large Date	*	898	$24	$35	$46	$80	$235	$340	$470	$775
↳1820, Large Date, N-9	*	80253	24	35	46	80	235	340	470	775
↳1820, Large Date, N-10	*	80256	24	35	46	80	235	340	470	775
↳1820, Large Date, N-11	*	80259	24	35	46	80	235	340	470	775
↳1820, Large Date, N-12	*	80262	24	35	46	80	235	340	470	775
↳1820, Large Date, N-13	*	80265	24	35	46	80	235	340	470	775
↳1820, Large Date, N-14	*	80268	—	—	—	—	—	—	—	—
1821	389,000	907	55	80	210	455	1,400	2,050	10,000	24,000
↳1821, N-1	*	80274	55	80	210	455	1,400	2,050	10,000	24,000
↳1821, N-2	*	80277	55	80	210	455	1,400	2,050	10,000	24,000
1822	2,072,339	913	34	46	80	160	390	725	1,250	2,500
↳1822, N-1	*	80280	34	46	80	160	390	725	1,250	2,500
↳1822, N-2	*	80283	34	46	80	160	390	725	1,250	2,500
↳1822, N-3	*	80286	34	46	80	160	390	725	1,250	2,500
↳1822, N-4	*	80289	34	46	80	160	390	725	1,250	2,500
↳1822, N-5	*	80292	34	46	80	160	390	725	1,250	2,500
↳1822, N-6	*	80295	34	46	80	160	390	725	1,250	2,500
↳1822, N-7	*	80298	34	46	80	160	390	725	1,250	2,500
↳1822, N-8	*	80301	37	50	90	180	430	775	1,400	2,750
↳1822, N-9	*	80304	—	—	—	—	—	—	—	—
↳1822, N-10	*	80307	34	46	80	160	390	725	1,250	2,500
↳1822, N-11	*	80310	34	46	80	160	390	725	1,250	2,500
↳1822, N-12	*	80313	37	50	90	180	430	775	1,400	2,750
↳1822, N-13	*	80316	—	—	—	—	—	—	—	—
↳1822, N-14	*	80319	—	—	—	—	—	—	—	—
1823, 3 Over 2	1,262,000	1262	130	285	550	1,000	2,500	7,000	21,000	—
↳1823, 3 Over 2, N-1	*	80322	130	285	550	1,000	2,500	7,000	21,000	—
1823, Normal Date, Original	*	919	160	260	575	950	3,000	6,250	19,000	27,500
	Auctions: $299,000, PCGS MS-66 GLDB 02/09									
↳1823, Normal Date, Original, N-2	*	80325	160	260	575	950	3,000	6,250	19,000	27,500
1823, Unofficial Restrike from broken obverse die, Copper (b)		200008	—	—	—	—	—	850	1,300	1,800
↳1823, Unofficial Restrike from broken obverse die, Copper, N-3	*	80328	—	—	—	—	—	850	1,300	1,800
1823, Unofficial Restrike from broken obverse die, Silver (b)		200010	—	—	—	—	—	—	—	21,500
↳1823, Unofficial Restrike from broken obverse die, Silver, N-3	*	80331	—	—	—	—	—	—	—	21,500

* Included in number above. **b.** The unofficial 1823 "restrikes" (actually novodels or fantasies) were made at the same time (around 1860) and by the same people as those of 1804. The coins were made from a discarded obverse die of 1823 and an 1813 reverse die—both heavily rusted, producing surface lumps. Most examples have both dies cracked.

1824, 4 Over 2

1826, 6 Over 5

Circulation Strikes *(continued)*

	Mintage	GSID	G-4	VG-8	F-12	VF-20	EF-40	AU-50	MS-60	MS-63
1824, 4 Over 2	1,262,000	1268	$130	$160	$230	$455	$950	$3,100	$6,250	$24,000
↳1824, 4 Over 2, N-1	*	80332	130	160	230	455	950	3,100	6,250	24,000
↳1824, 4 Over 2, N-5	*	80344	—	—	—	—	—	—	—	—
1824, Normal Date	*	922	70	130	195	325	575	775	3,100	5,500
↳1824, Normal Date, N-2	*	80335	70	130	195	325	575	775	3,100	5,500
↳1824, Normal Date, N-3	*	80338	70	130	195	325	575	775	3,100	5,500
↳1824, Normal Date, N-4	*	80341	70	130	195	325	575	775	3,100	5,500
1825	1,461,100	928	55	80	115	160	390	850	2,000	4,250
↳1825, N-1	*	80347	60	90	125	180	430	925	2,200	4,700
↳1825, N-2	*	80350	55	80	115	160	390	850	2,000	4,250
↳1825, N-3	*	80353	60	90	125	180	430	925	2,200	4,700
↳1825, N-4	*	80356	55	80	115	160	390	850	2,000	4,250
↳1825, N-5	*	226296	—	—	—	—	—	—	—	—
↳1825, N-6	*	80359	55	80	115	160	390	850	2,000	4,250
↳1825, N-7	*	80362	55	80	115	160	390	850	2,000	4,250
↳1825, N-8	*	80365	55	80	115	160	390	850	2,000	4,250
↳1825, N-9	*	80368	55	80	115	160	390	850	2,000	4,250
↳1825, N-10	*	80371	55	80	115	160	390	850	2,000	4,250
1826, Normal Date	1,517,425	934	55	80	130	160	310	600	1,150	2,100
↳1826, Normal Date, N-1	*	80374	55	80	130	160	310	600	1,150	2,100
↳1826, Normal Date, N-3	*	80377	55	80	130	160	310	600	1,150	2,100
↳1826, Normal Date, N-4	*	80380	55	80	130	160	310	600	1,150	2,100
↳1826, Normal Date, N-5	*	80383	55	80	130	160	310	600	1,150	2,100
↳1826, Normal Date, N-6	*	80386	55	80	130	160	310	600	1,150	2,100
↳1826, Normal Date, N-7	*	80389	55	80	130	160	310	600	1,150	2,100
↳1826, Normal Date, N-9	*	80395	55	80	130	160	310	600	1,150	2,100
1826, 6 Over 5	*	1271	130	160	260	455	1,100	1,900	4,000	8,250
↳1826, 6 Over 5, N-8	*	80392	130	160	260	455	1,100	1,900	4,000	8,250
1827	2,357,732	940	70	100	130	180	240	390	1,150	2,750
↳1827, N-1	*	80398	70	100	130	180	240	390	1,150	2,750
↳1827, N-2	*	80401	70	100	130	180	240	390	1,150	2,750
↳1827, N-3	*	80404	70	100	130	180	240	390	1,150	2,750
↳1827, N-4	*	80407	70	100	130	180	240	390	1,150	2,750
↳1827, N-5	*	80410	70	100	130	180	240	390	1,150	2,750
↳1827, N-6	*	80413	70	100	130	180	240	390	1,150	2,750
↳1827, N-7	*	80416	70	100	130	180	240	390	1,150	2,750
↳1827, N-8	*	80419	70	100	130	180	240	390	1,150	2,750
↳1827, N-9	*	80422	70	100	130	180	240	390	1,150	2,750
↳1827, N-10	*	80425	120	210	525	1,550	3,750	—	—	—
↳1827, N-11	*	80428	70	100	130	180	240	390	1,150	2,750
↳1827, N-12	*	80431	495	625	850	950	—	—	—	—

* Included in number above.

Large Letters (1808–1834)
Note individual letter size and proximity.

Medium Letters (1829–1837)
Note isolation of letters, especially STATES.

Small Letters (1837–1839)
Note letter spacing.

Date Size, Through 1828 (Large, Narrow Date)

Date Size, 1828 and Later (Small, Wide Date)

Circulation Strikes *(continued)*

	Mintage	GSID	G-4	VG-8	F-12	VF-20	EF-40	AU-50	MS-60	MS-63
1828, Large Narrow Date	2,260,264	946	$40	$60	$80	$110	$360	$525	$1,250	$2,500
↳1828, Large Narrow Date, N-1	*	80434	40	60	80	110	360	525	1,250	2,500
↳1828, Large Narrow Date, N-2	*	80437	40	60	80	110	360	525	1,250	2,500
↳1828, Large Narrow Date, N-3	*	80440	40	60	80	110	360	525	1,250	2,500
↳1828, Large Narrow Date, N-4	*	80443	45	65	90	120	395	575	1,400	2,750
↳1828, Large Narrow Date, N-5	*	80446	40	60	80	110	360	525	1,250	2,500
↳1828, Large Narrow Date, N-6	*	80449	40	60	80	110	360	525	1,250	2,500
↳1828, Large Narrow Date, N-7	*	80452	40	60	80	110	360	525	1,250	2,500
↳1828, Large Narrow Date, N-8	*	80455	40	60	80	110	360	525	1,250	2,500
↳1828, Large Narrow Date, N-9	*	80458	45	65	90	120	395	575	1,400	2,750
↳1828, Large Narrow Date, N-11	*	80464	40	60	80	110	360	525	1,250	2,500
↳1828, Large Narrow Date, N-12	*	80467	40	60	80	110	360	525	1,250	2,500
1828, Small Wide Date	*	949	115	160	230	325	525	775	2,500	3,750
↳1828, Small Wide Date, N-10	*	80461	115	160	230	325	525	775	2,500	3,750
1829, Large Letters	1,414,500	955	70	100	130	160	325	575	1,250	2,500
↳1829, Large Letters, N-1	*	80470	70	100	130	160	325	575	1,250	2,500
↳1829, Large Letters, N-2	*	80473	70	100	130	160	325	575	1,250	2,500
↳1829, Large Letters, N-4	*	80479	70	100	130	160	325	575	1,250	2,500
↳1829, Large Letters, N-6	*	80485	70	100	130	160	325	575	1,250	2,500
↳1829, Large Letters, N-7	*	80488	70	100	130	160	325	575	1,250	2,500
↳1829, Large Letters, N-8	*	80491	70	100	130	160	325	575	1,250	2,500
1829, Medium Letters	*	958	80	145	260	650	1,900	3,750	8,750	12,000
↳1829, Medium Letters, N-3	*	80476	80	145	260	650	1,900	3,750	8,750	12,000
↳1829, Medium Letters, N-5	*	80482	80	145	260	650	1,900	3,750	8,750	12,000
↳1829, Medium Letters, N-9	*	80494	90	155	285	725	2,050	4,100	9,500	13,000
1830, Large Letters	1,711,500	964	34	55	75	100	240	390	950	2,500
↳1830, Large Letters, N-1	*	80497	34	55	75	100	240	390	950	2,500
↳1830, Large Letters, N-2	*	80500	34	55	75	100	240	390	950	2,500
↳1830, Large Letters, N-3	*	80503	34	55	75	100	240	390	950	2,500
↳1830, Large Letters, N-4	*	80506	34	55	75	100	240	390	950	2,500
↳1830, Large Letters, N-5	*	80509	34	55	75	100	240	390	950	2,500
↳1830, Large Letters, N-7	*	80515	34	55	75	100	240	390	950	2,500
↳1830, Large Letters, N-8	*	80518	34	55	75	100	240	390	950	2,500
↳1830, Large Letters, N-9	*	80521	2,500	3,050	4,400	7,000	12,000	—	—	—
↳1830, Large Letters, N-10	*	80524	37	60	80	110	265	430	1,050	2,750
↳1830, Large Letters, N-11	*	80527	160	240	525	—	—	—	—	—
1830, Medium Letters	*	967	170	290	650	1,100	3,750	8,000	14,000	24,000
↳1830, Medium Letters, N-6	*	80512	170	290	650	1,100	3,750	8,000	14,000	24,000

* Included in number above.

Large 8 (1834–1835)

Small 8 (1834–1835)

Large Stars (1834–1835)

Small Stars (1834–1835)

Circulation Strikes *(continued)*

	Mintage	GSID	G-4	VG-8	F-12	VF-20	EF-40	AU-50	MS-60	MS-63
1831, Large Letters	3,359,260	973	$34	$55	$75	$100	$160	$290	$575	$1,000
↳1831, Large Letters, N-1	*	80530	34	55	75	100	160	290	575	1,000
↳1831, Large Letters, N-6	*	80545	34	55	75	100	160	290	575	1,000
↳1831, Large Letters, N-7	*	80548	34	55	75	100	160	290	575	1,000
↳1831, Large Letters, N-8	*	80551	34	55	75	100	160	290	575	1,000
↳1831, Large Letters, N-9	*	80554	34	55	75	100	160	290	575	1,000
↳1831, Large Letters, N-10	*	80557	34	55	75	100	160	290	575	1,000
↳1831, Large Letters, N-12	*	80563	34	55	75	100	160	290	575	1,000
↳1831, Large Letters, N-14	*	80566	37	60	80	110	180	320	650	1,150
1831, Medium Letters	*	976	38	49	60	95	175	345	950	1,400
↳1831, Medium Letters, N-2	*	80533	38	49	60	95	175	345	950	1,400
↳1831, Medium Letters, N-3	*	80536	38	49	60	95	175	345	950	1,400
↳1831, Medium Letters, N-4	*	80539	38	49	60	95	175	345	950	1,400
↳1831, Medium Letters, N-5	*	80542	42	55	65	105	195	380	1,050	1,500
↳1831, Medium Letters, N-11	*	80560	38	49	60	95	175	345	950	1,400
1832, Medium Letters	2,362,000	985	40	70	100	160	290	650	1,200	1,400
↳1832, Medium Letters, N-1	*	80569	40	70	100	160	290	650	1,200	1,400
↳1832, Medium Letters, N-2	*	80572	40	70	100	160	290	650	1,200	1,400
1832, Large Letters	*	982	34	55	75	100	160	290	650	1,550
↳1832, Large Letters, N-3	*	80575	34	55	75	100	160	290	650	1,550
1833	2,739,000	991	34	60	85	120	210	325	725	1,250
↳1833, N-1	*	80578	34	60	85	120	210	325	725	1,250
↳1833, N-2	*	80581	34	60	85	120	210	325	725	1,250
↳1833, N-3	*	80584	34	60	85	120	210	325	725	1,250
↳1833, N-4	*	80587	37	65	95	130	230	360	775	1,300
↳1833, N-5	*	80590	34	60	85	120	210	325	725	1,250
↳1833, N-6	*	80593	34	60	85	120	210	325	725	1,250
1834, Small 8, Large Stars, Medium Letters	1,855,100	1006	32	50	90	135	260	525	850	1,150
↳1834, Small 8, Large Stars, Medium Letters, N-1	*	80596	32	50	90	135	260	525	850	1,150
↳1834, Small 8, Large Stars, Medium Letters, N-2	*	80599	32	50	90	135	260	525	850	1,150
1834, Large 8, Small Stars, Medium Letters	*	997	47	70	100	130	230	390	850	2,300
↳1834, Large 8, Small Stars, Medium Letters, N-3	*	80602	47	70	100	130	230	390	850	2,300
↳1834, Large 8, Small Stars, Medium Letters, N-4	*	80605	47	70	100	130	230	390	850	2,300
1834, Large 8 and Stars, Medium Letters	*	1000	650	950	1,500	2,250	4,400	6,250	10,000	18,000
↳1834, Large 8 and Stars, Medium Letters, N-5	*	80608	650	950	1,500	2,250	4,400	6,250	10,000	18,000
1834, Large 8, Stars, and Letters	*	1003	100	160	230	455	1,150	1,800	2,750	5,500
↳1834, Large 8, Stars, and Letters, N-6	*	80611	100	160	230	455	1,150	1,800	2,750	5,500

* Included in number above.

1835, Coronet Head

1835, Head of 1836

Circulation Strikes *(continued)*

	Mintage	GSID	G-4	VG-8	F-12	VF-20	EF-40	AU-50	MS-60	MS-63
1835, Large 8 and Stars	3,878,400	1018	$47	$80	$115	$235	$360	$650	$1,250	$1,900
↳1835, Large 8 and Stars, N-1	*	80614	47	80	115	235	360	650	1,250	1,900
↳1835, Large 8 and Stars, N-9	*	80638	50	90	125	255	395	725	1,400	2,050
1835, Small 8 and Stars	*	1015	47	80	120	155	285	415	900	1,600
↳1835, Small 8 and Stars, N-2	*	80617	47	80	120	155	285	415	900	1,600
↳1835, Small 8 and Stars, N-3	*	80620	47	80	120	155	285	415	900	1,600
↳1835, Small 8 and Stars, N-4	*	80623	160	260	575	1,000	2,500	4,500	15,000	—
↳1835, Small 8 and Stars, N-5	*	80626	47	80	120	155	285	415	900	1,600
↳1835, Small 8 and Stars, N-6	*	80629	47	80	120	155	285	415	900	1,600
↳1835, Small 8 and Stars, N-10	*	80641	115	155	390	775	1,500	—	—	—
↳1835, Small 8 and Stars, N-11	*	80644	—	495	725	1,000	2,750	4,000	8,000	15,000
↳1835, Small 8 and Stars, N-12	*	80647	50	90	130	170	315	460	975	1,800
↳1835, Small 8 and Stars, N-13	*	80650	50	90	130	170	315	460	975	1,800
↳1835, Small 8 and Stars, N-18	*	80662	195	300	650	1,250	—	—	—	—
1835, Head of 1836	*	1012	34	55	80	95	180	285	1,000	1,400
↳1835, Head of 1836, N-7	*	80632	34	55	80	95	180	285	1,000	1,400
↳1835, Head of 1836, N-8	*	80635	37	60	90	105	200	315	1,150	1,500
↳1835, Head of 1836, N-14	*	80653	34	55	80	95	180	285	1,000	1,400
↳1835, Head of 1836, N-15	*	80656	34	55	80	95	180	285	1,000	1,400
↳1835, Head of 1836, N-16	*	80659	34	55	80	95	180	285	1,000	1,400
↳1835, Head of 1836, N-19	*	00005	160	245	525	1,600			—	—
1836	2,111,000	1024	34	55	75	100	160	455	650	1,100
↳1836, N-1	*	80668	34	55	75	100	160	455	650	1,100
↳1836, N-2	*	80671	34	55	75	100	160	455	650	1,100
↳1836, N-3	*	80674	34	55	75	100	160	455	650	1,100
↳1836, N-4	*	80677	34	55	75	100	160	455	650	1,100
↳1836, N-5	*	80680	34	55	75	100	160	455	650	1,100
↳1836, N-6	*	80683	34	55	75	100	160	455	650	1,100
↳1836, N-7	*	80686	37	60	80	110	180	500	725	1,200

* Included in number above.

1837
Note the plain hair cords.

1837, Head of 1838
Note the slim bust and the beaded hair cords.

Circulation Strikes *(continued)*

	Mintage	GSID	G-4	VG-8	F-12	VF-20	EF-40	AU-50	MS-60	MS-63
1837, Plain Cord, Medium Letters	5,558,300	1036	$24	$35	$46	$80	$150	$245	$525	$900
↳1837, Plain Cord, Medium Letters, N-1	*	80689	24	35	46	80	150	245	525	900
↳1837, Plain Cord, Medium Letters, N-2	*	80692	24	35	46	80	150	245	525	900
↳1837, Plain Cord, Medium Letters, N-3	*	80695	24	35	46	80	150	245	525	900
↳1837, Plain Cord, Medium Letters, N-4	*	80698	24	35	46	80	150	245	525	900
↳1837, Plain Cord, Medium Letters, N-6	*	80704	24	35	46	80	150	245	525	900
↳1837, Plain Cord, Medium Letters, N-7	*	80707	24	35	46	80	150	245	525	900
↳1837, Plain Cord, Medium Letters, N-13	*	80722	24	35	46	80	150	245	525	900
↳1837, Plain Cord, Medium Letters, N-14	*	80725	24	35	46	80	150	245	525	900
↳1837, Plain Cord, Medium Letters, N-15	*	80728	27	39	50	90	165	270	575	975
↳1837, Plain Cord, Medium Letters, N-16	*	80731	24	35	46	80	150	245	525	900
↳1837, Plain Cord, Medium Letters, N-17	*	80734	27	39	50	90	165	270	575	975
1837, Plain Cord, Small Letters	*	1033	34	40	60	100	160	285	525	1,000
↳1837, Plain Cord, Small Letters, N-5	*	80701	34	40	60	100	160	285	525	1,000
1837, Head of 1838	*	1030	24	35	55	95	195	275	525	875
↳1837, Head of 1838, N-9	*	80710	24	35	55	95	195	275	525	875
↳1837, Head of 1838, N-10	*	80713	24	35	55	95	195	275	525	875
↳1837, Head of 1838, N-11	*	80716	24	35	55	95	195	275	525	875
↳1837, Head of 1838, N-12	*	80719	24	35	55	95	195	275	525	875

* Included in number above.

1839, Silly Head
Note the prominent lock of hair at the forehead.

Circulation Strikes *(continued)*

	Mintage	GSID	G-4	VG-8	F-12	VF-20	EF-40	AU-50	MS-60	MS-63
1838	6,370,200	1042	$24	$35	$46	$80	$150	$245	$375	$775
↳1838, N-1	*	80737	24	35	46	80	150	245	375	775
↳1838, N-2	*	80740	24	35	46	80	150	245	375	775
↳1838, N-3	*	80743	24	35	46	80	150	245	375	775
↳1838, N-4	*	80746	24	35	46	80	150	245	375	775
↳1838, N-5	*	80749	24	35	46	80	150	245	375	775
↳1838, N-6	*	80752	24	35	46	80	150	245	375	775
↳1838, N-7	*	80755	24	35	46	80	150	245	375	775
↳1838, N-8	*	80758	24	35	46	80	150	245	375	775
↳1838, N-9	*	80761	24	35	46	80	150	245	375	775
↳1838, N-10	*	80764	24	35	46	80	150	245	375	775
↳1838, N-11	*	80767	24	35	46	80	150	245	375	775
↳1838, N-12	*	80770	24	35	46	80	150	245	375	775
↳1838, Heavy Rim Break Obverse, N-13	*	261928	40	70	100	195	390	650	1,500	2,500
↳1838, N-14	*	80773	27	39	50	90	165	270	415	850
↳1838, N-15	*	80776	—	360	525	650	—	—	—	—
↳1838, N-16	*	80779	—	—	—	—	—	—	—	—
1839, Coronet Head, Head of 1838, Beaded Cords	3,128,661	1048	40	55	80	110	195	325	525	850
↳1839, Coronet Head, Head of 1838, Beaded Cords, N-2	*	80785	40	55	80	110	195	325	525	850
↳1839, Coronet Head, Head of 1838, Beaded Cords, N-3	*	80788	40	55	80	110	195	325	525	850
1839, Coronet, Silly Head	*	1051	24	35	46	80	260	625	775	1,600
↳1839, Coronet, Silly Head, N-4	*	80791	24	35	46	80	260	625	775	1,600
↳1839, Coronet, Silly Head, N-9	*	80803	24	35	46	80	260	625	775	1,600

* Included in number above.

1839, Booby Head
Note the shoulder tip and the absence of a line under CENT.

1839, 1839 Over 1836
Note the closed 9 and the plain hair cords.

Circulation Strikes *(continued)*

	Mintage	GSID	G-4	VG-8	F-12	VF-20	EF-40	AU-50	MS-60	MS-63
1839, Coronet, Booby Head (a)	*	1054	$34	$47	$70	$95	$260	$525	$850	$1,750
↳1839, Coronet, Booby Head, N-5 (a)	*	80794	34	47	70	95	260	525	850	1,750
↳1839, Coronet, Booby Head, N-6 (a)	*	80797	34	47	70	95	260	525	850	1,750
↳1839, Coronet, Booby Head, N-7 (a)	*	80800	34	47	70	95	260	525	850	1,750
↳1839, Coronet, Booby Head, N-10 (a)	*	80806	34	47	70	95	260	525	850	1,750
↳1839, Coronet, Booby Head, N-11 (a)	*	80809	34	47	70	95	260	525	850	1,750
↳1839, Coronet, Booby Head, N-12 (a)	*	80812	37	50	75	105	285	575	925	1,900
↳1839, Coronet, Booby Head, N-13 (a)	*	80815	34	47	70	95	260	525	850	1,750
↳1839, Coronet, Booby Head, N-14 (a)	*	80818	34	47	70	95	260	525	850	1,750
↳1839, Coronet, Booby Head, N-15 (a)	*	80821	—	—	—	—	—	—	—	—
1839, Coronet, 9 Over 6, Plain Cords	*	1274	550	850	1,500	3,250	8,750	17,000	—	—
	Auctions: $264,500, PCGS MS-65 GLDB 02/09									
↳1839, Coronet, 9 Over 6, Plain Cords, N-1	*	80824	550	850	1,500	3,250	8,750	17,000	—	—

* Included in number above. **a.** The 1839 Booby Head variety has a modified reverse that omits the line under CENTS.

Proof Strikes

	GSID	PF-63	PF-64	PF-65
Coronet Head (1816–1839), Proof, Brown	**84872**	**$15,500**	**$23,000**	**$30,000**
1817	879	—	—	—
1819, 9 Over 8	1256	—	39,500	—
1820	904	—	—	—
1821	910	54,000	60,000	72,000
1822	916	39,000	48,000	—
1823	84873	—	—	—
1823, 3 Over 2	1265	39,500	54,000	—
1828	952	—	—	—
1829	213491	14,500	20,500	—
1829, Bronzed	961	—	37,000	48,000
1830	970	—	39,000	—
	Auctions: $184,000, PCGS PF-65 GLDB 02/09			
1831	979	15,500	23,000	30,000
1832	988	—	42,000	—
1833	994	—	—	—
1834	1009	66,000	72,000	86,500
1836 (a)	1027	50,000	—	—
1837	1039	26,500	36,000	54,000
1838	1045	15,500	23,000	30,000

* Included in number above. **a.** All are one-sided Proofs.

BRAIDED HAIR (1839–1857)

Designer: *Christian Gobrecht.* **Weight:** *10.89 grams.* **Composition:** *Copper.* **Diameter:** *27.5 mm.* **Edge:** *Plain.* **Mint:** *Philadelphia.*

Circulation Strike

Proof Strike

History. Christian Gobrecht's Braided Hair design was introduced in 1839. It loosely followed the design he had created for the 1838 gold eagle. On issues of 1839 through part of 1843, Liberty's portrait is tilted forward, with the left tip of her neck truncation over the 8 of the date. For most issues of 1843 and all later dates her head is larger and aligned in a more vertical position, and the tip of her neck is over the first digit of the date. The reverse lettering was made larger beginning in 1844. The net result is that cents after 1843 are less delicate in appearance than are those of earlier dates. These coins were made in large quantities, except for their final year. They remained in circulation in the United States until the late 1850s, not long enough to be worn down to very low grades. (Some circulated in the eastern part of Canada through the 1860s, accounting for many of the more worn examples seen today.)

Striking and Sharpness. Sharpness can vary. On the obverse, the star centers can be weak, especially for dates in the 1850s, and, less often, there can be lightness on the front of the coronet and the hair. On the reverse the leaves can be light, but most are well struck. The denticles can be mushy and indistinct on either side, this being particularly true of dates in the early and mid-1850s. Flaky or laminated planchets can be a problem, again among coins of the 1850s, in which tiny pieces of metal fall away from the surface, leaving areas in the field that interrupt the luster on MS coins.

Availability. All dates of Braided Hair cents are readily available, with the 1857 somewhat less so (it was minted in January 1857 in low quantity; seemingly not all were released). The delicate-featured issues of 1839 to 1843 are becoming more difficult to find in EF or finer grades without surface problems. Cents dated in the 1850s are usually seen in VF or higher grades. Certain die varieties attributed by Newcomb numbers can be scarce or rare. For issues in the 1850s the differences can be microscopic, thus limiting their numismatic appeal and making them unattributable unless in high grades. Hoards were found of some dates, particularly 1850 to 1856, making MS coins of these years more readily available than would otherwise be the case. MS-64RD or higher coins with *original* color range from scarce to very rare for dates prior to 1850, but those of the 1850s are seen regularly (except for 1857). Coins below VF-20 are not widely collected and, for many issues, are too worn to attribute by die variety.

Grading Standards

MS-60 to 70 (Mint State). ***Obverse:*** In the lower Mint State grades, MS-60 and 61, some slight abrasions can be seen on the portrait, most evidently on the cheek. Check the tip of the coronet and the hair above the ear, as well. Luster in the field is complete or nearly so. At MS-63, luster should be complete, and no abrasion evident. If there is weakness on the hair it is due to light striking, not to wear; this also applies for the stars. In higher levels, the luster is complete and deeper, and some original mint color may be seen. Mint frost on this type is usually deep, sometimes satiny, but hardly ever prooflike. MS-64 coins may have some slight discoloration or scattered contact marks. A well-graded MS-65 or higher coin will have full, rich luster; no marks visible except under magnification; and a nice blend of brown toning or nicely mixed (not stained or blotchy) mint color and natural brown toning. MS-64RD or higher coins with original color range from scarce to very rare for dates prior to 1850, but those of the 1850s are seen regularly (except for 1857). ***Reverse:*** In the lower Mint State grades some abrasion is seen on the higher areas of the leaves. Mint luster is complete in all Mint State ranges, as the open areas are protected by the lettering and wreath. The quality of the luster is the best way to grade both sides of this type.

MS-64BN

Illustrated coin: This coin is a light, golden olive with faint tints of pale green in places, with scattered red spotting on both the obverse and reverse. About half of the stars show their centers, but all of the stars are soft.

AU-50, 53, 55, 58 (About Uncirculated). ***Obverse:*** Wear is evident on the cheek, the hair above the ear, and the tip of the coronet. Friction is evident in the field. At AU-58, luster may be present except in the center of the fields. As the grade goes down to AU-50, wear becomes more evident on the cheek. Wear is seen on the stars, but is not as easy to discern as it is elsewhere and, in any event, many stars are weakly struck. At AU-50 there will be either no luster or only traces of luster close to the letters and devices. ***Reverse:*** Wear is most evident on the highest areas of the leaves and the ribbon bow. Luster is present in the fields. As grade goes down from AU-58 to 50, wear increases and luster decreases. At AU-50 there will be either no luster or just traces close to the letters and devices.

AU-58

EF-40, 45 (Extremely Fine). ***Obverse:*** Wear is more extensive on the portrait, including the cheek, the hair above the ear, and the coronet. The star centers are worn down slightly (if they were sharply struck to begin with). Traces of luster are minimal, if at all existent. ***Reverse:*** The centers of the leaves are well worn, with detail visible only near the edges of the leaves and nearby, with the higher parts worn flat. Letters show significant wear. Luster, if present, is minimal.

EF-45

VF-20, 30 (Very Fine). ***Obverse:*** Wear is more extensive than on the preceding. Some of the strands of hair are fused together at the top of the head, above the ear, and on the shoulder. The center radials of the stars are nearly completely worn away. ***Reverse:*** The leaves show more extensive wear. Details are visible at the leaves' edges only minimally and not on all the leaves. The lettering shows smooth, even wear.

VF-30

F-12, 15 (Fine). ***Obverse:*** About two-thirds of the hair detail is visible. Extensive wear is seen below the coronet. On the coronet the beginning of the word LIBERTY shows wear, with L sometimes only partially visible. The hair behind the neck is flat. The stars are flat. ***Reverse:*** The leaves show more wear and are flat except for the lower areas. The ribbon has very little detail.

F-12

PF-60 to 70 (Proof). Except for the Proof 1841 cent, Proof Braided Hair cents before 1855 range from rare to very rare. Those from 1855 to 1857 are seen with some frequency. Most later Proofs are well struck and of nice quality, but there are exceptions. Most pieces from this era that have been attributed as Proofs really are such, but beware of deeply toned "Proofs" that are actually prooflike, or circulation strikes with polished fields, and recolored. ***Obverse and Reverse:*** Superb gems PF-65 and 66 show hairlines only under high magnification, and at PF-67 none are seen. The fields usually are deeply mirrorlike on issues after 1843, sometimes less so on earlier dates of this type. Striking should be sharp, including the stars (unlike the situation for many Proofs of the Coronet Head type). There is no evidence of friction. In lower grades, hairlines are more numerous, with a profusion of them at the PF-60 to 62 levels, and there is also a general dullness of the fields. Typical color for an undipped coin ranges from light or iridescent brown to brown with some traces of mint color. Except for issues after 1854, Proofs are nearly always BN or, less often, RB. Prooflike pieces are sometimes offered as Proofs. Beware deeply toned "Proofs" and those that do not have full mirrorlike fields.

PF-64RB

Illustrated coin: Early Proofs from this period are scarce to extremely rare. This example retains some mint orange in protected areas, as well as exhibiting hints of lilac and electric blue on the obverse.

1840, Large Date

1840, Small Date

1840, Small Date Over Large 18

1842, Small Date

1842, Large Date

Circulation Strikes

	Mintage	GSID	G-4	VG-8	F-12	VF-20	EF-40	AU-50	MS-60	MS-63
Braided Hair (1839–1857), Brown	**n/a**	**72331**	**$26**	**$27**	**$34**	**$40**	**$60**	**$145**	**$210**	**$305**
Same, Red Brown	**n/a**	**72332**	**—**	**—**	**—**	**—**	**—**	**—**	**260**	**365**
Same, Red	**n/a**	**72333**	**—**	**—**	**—**	**—**	**—**	**—**	**415**	**975**
1839, Braided Hair, Type of 1840	3,128,661	1057	40	55	90	110	235	490	1,000	2,250
↳1839, Type of 1840, N-8	*	241131	40	55	90	110	235	490	1,000	2,250
1840, Large Date	2,462,700	1066	27	30	50	110	180	285	725	1,250
↳1840, Large Date, N-5	*	241341	27	30	50	110	180	285	725	1,250
↳1840, Large Date, N-6	*	241342	27	30	50	110	180	285	725	1,250
↳1840, Large Date, N-7	*	241343	27	30	50	110	180	285	725	1,250
↳1840, Large Date, N-8	*	241344	27	30	50	110	180	285	725	1,250
↳1840, Large Date, N-9	*	241345	27	30	50	110	180	285	725	1,250
↳1840, Large Date, N-10	*	241346	27	30	50	110	180	285	725	1,250
1840, Small Date	*	1069	26	34	60	95	155	415	900	1,400
↳1840, Small Date, N-1	*	241359	26	34	60	95	155	415	900	1,400
↳1840, Small Date, N-3	*	241360	—	—	—	—	—	—	900	1,400
↳1840, Small Date, N-4	*	241361	—	—	—	—	—	—	900	1,400
↳1840, Small Date, N-12	*	241362	26	34	60	95	155	415	900	1,400
1840, Small Date Over Large 18	*	1072	70	130	175	260	525	1,400	3,000	5,750
↳1840, Small Date Over Large 18, N-2	*	241371	70	130	175	260	525	1,400	3,000	5,750
1841	1,597,367	1078	34	70	100	145	180	260	900	1,450
↳1841, N-2	*	243739	34	70	100	145	180	260	900	1,450
↳1841, N-3	*	243740	34	70	100	145	180	260	900	1,450
↳1841, N-4	*	243741	34	70	100	145	180	260	900	1,450
↳1841, N-5	*	243742	34	70	100	145	180	260	900	1,450
↳1841, N-6	*	243743	34	70	100	145	180	260	900	1,450
↳1841, N-7	*	243744	34	70	100	145	180	260	900	1,450
1842, Large Date	2,383,390	1084	26	28	36	55	110	260	650	1,150
↳1842, Large Date, N-3	*	243757	26	28	36	55	110	260	650	1,150
↳1842, Large Date, N-4	*	243758	26	28	36	55	110	260	650	1,150
↳1842, Large Date, N-5	*	243759	26	28	36	55	110	260	650	1,150
↳1842, Large Date, N-6	*	243760	26	28	36	55	110	260	650	1,150
↳1842, Large Date, N-7	*	243761	26	28	36	55	110	260	650	1,150
↳1842, Large Date, N-8	*	243762	26	28	36	55	110	260	650	1,150
↳1842, Large Date, N-9	*	243763	26	28	36	55	110	260	650	1,150
1842, Small Date	*	1087	30	35	55	115	180	310	600	1,250
↳1842, Small Date, N-1	*	243778	30	35	55	115	180	310	600	1,250
↳1842, Small Date, N-2	*	243779	30	35	55	115	180	310	600	1,250

* Included in number above.

Petite Head (1839–1843)

Mature Head (1843–1857)

Small Letters (1839–1843)

Large Letters (1843–1857)

Circulation Strikes *(continued)*

	Mintage	GSID	G-4	VG-8	F-12	VF-20	EF-40	AU-50	MS-60	MS-63
1843, Petite Head, Small Letters	2,425,342	1093	$26	$28	$36	$55	$110	$235	$650	$1,100
↳1843, Petite Head, Small Letters, N-1	*	243784	26	28	36	55	110	235	650	1,100
↳1843, Petite Head, Small Letters, N-2	*	243785	26	28	36	55	110	235	650	1,100
↳1843, Petite Head, Small Letters, N-3	*	243786	26	28	36	55	110	235	650	1,100
↳1843, Petite Head, Small Letters, N-7	*	243787	26	28	36	55	110	235	650	1,100
↳1843, Petite Head, Small Letters, N-8	*	243788	26	28	36	55	110	235	650	1,100
↳1843, Petite Head, Small Letters, N-9	*	243789	26	28	36	55	110	235	650	1,100
↳1843, Petite Head, Small Letters, N-10	*	243790	26	28	36	55	110	235	650	1,100
↳1843, Petite Head, Small Letters, N-11	*	243791	26	28	36	55	110	235	650	1,100
↳1843, Petite Head, Small Letters, N-12	*	243792	26	28	36	55	110	235	650	1,100
↳1843, Petite Head, Small Letters, N-13	*	243793	26	28	36	55	110	235	650	1,100
↳1843, Petite Head, Small Letters, N-14	*	243794	26	28	36	55	110	235	650	1,100
↳1843, Petite Head, Small Letters, N-15	*	243795	26	28	36	55	110	235	650	1,100
1843, Petite Head, Large Letters	*	1096	38	47	70	100	285	440	750	1,250
↳1843, Petite Head, Large Letters, N-4	*	243820	38	47	70	100	285	440	750	1,250
1843, Mature Head, Large Letters	*	1099	38	46	60	95	455	575	775	1,900
↳1843, Mature Head, Large Letters, N-5	*	243823	38	46	60	95	455	575	775	1,900
↳1843, Mature Head, Large Letters, N-6	*	243824	38	46	60	95	455	575	775	1,900
↳1843, Mature Head, Large Letters, N-16	*	243825	38	46	60	95	455	575	775	1,900
↳1843, Mature Head, Large Letters, N-17, FS-301	*	243826	38	46	60	95	455	575	775	1,900

* Included in number above.

1844, 44 Over 81

1846, Small Date
Note the squat date and the closed 6.

1846, Medium Date
Note the medium date height and the ball-top 6.

1846, Tall Date
Note the vertically stretched date and the open-mouthed 6.

Circulation Strikes *(continued)*

	Mintage	GSID	G-4	VG-8	F-12	VF-20	EF-40	AU-50	MS-60	MS-63
1844	2,398,752	1105	$26	$28	$36	$55	$110	$260	$650	$1,500
↳1844, N-1	*	262103	26	28	36	55	110	260	650	1,500
↳1844, N-3	*	262104	26	28	36	55	110	260	650	1,500
↳1844, N-4	*	262105	26	28	36	55	110	260	650	1,500
↳1844, N-5	*	262106	26	28	36	55	110	260	650	1,500
↳1844, N-6	*	262107	26	28	36	55	110	260	650	1,500
↳1844, N-7	*	262108	26	28	36	55	110	260	650	1,500
1844, 44 Over 81 (a)	*	1277	100	130	160	260	525	950	1,900	3,750
↳1844, 44 Over 81, N-2 (a)	*	262121	100	130	160	260	525	950	1,900	3,750
1845	3,894,804	1111	26	27	34	40	60	145	310	525
↳1845, N-1	*	264469	26	27	34	40	60	145	310	525
↳1845, N-2	*	264470	26	27	34	40	60	145	310	525
↳1845, N-3	*	264471	26	27	34	40	60	145	310	525
↳1845, N-4	*	264472	26	27	34	40	60	145	310	525
↳1845, N-5	*	264473	26	27	34	40	60	145	310	525
↳1845, N-6	*	264474	26	27	34	40	60	145	310	525
↳1845, N-7	*	264475	26	27	34	40	60	145	310	525
↳1845, N-8	*	264476	26	27	34	40	60	145	310	525
↳1845, N-9	*	264477	26	27	34	40	60	145	310	525
↳1845, N-10	*	264478	26	27	34	40	60	145	310	525
↳1845, N-11	*	264479	26	27	34	40	60	145	310	525
↳1845, N-12	*	264480	26	27	34	40	60	145	310	525
↳1845, N-13	*	264481	26	27	34	40	60	145	310	525
↳1845, N-15	*	264482	26	27	34	40	60	145	310	525
1846, Small Date	4,120,800	1117	26	27	34	40	110	155	340	575
↳1846, Small Date, N-1	*	264511	26	27	34	40	110	155	340	575
↳1846, Small Date, N-2	*	264512	26	27	34	40	110	155	340	575
↳1846, Small Date, N-3	*	264513	26	27	34	40	110	155	340	575
↳1846, Small Date, N-4	*	264514	26	27	34	40	110	155	340	575
↳1846, Small Date, N-5	*	264515	26	27	34	40	110	155	340	575
↳1846, Small Date, N-6	*	264516	26	27	34	40	110	155	340	575
↳1846, Small Date, N-7	*	264517	26	27	34	40	110	155	340	575
↳1846, Small Date, N-8	*	264518	26	27	34	40	110	155	340	575
↳1846, Small Date, N-9	*	264519	26	27	34	40	110	155	340	575
↳1846, Small Date, N-10	*	264520	26	27	34	40	110	155	340	575
↳1846, Small Date, N-15	*	264521	26	27	34	40	110	155	340	575
↳1846, Small Date, N-17	*	264522	26	27	34	40	110	155	340	575
↳1846, Small Date, N-18	*	264523	26	27	34	40	110	155	340	575
↳1846, Small Date, N-19	*	264524	26	27	34	40	110	155	340	575
↳1846, Small Date, N-20	*	264525	26	27	34	40	110	155	340	575
↳1846, Small Date, N-21	*	264526	26	27	34	40	110	155	340	575
1846, Medium Date	*	1120	27	31	38	47	75	180	360	650
↳1846, Medium Date, N-11	*	264559	27	31	38	47	75	180	360	650

* Included in number above. **a.** See the discussion of date-punch blunders in the Braided Hair introductory text.

1847, 7 Over Small 7

Circulation Strikes *(continued)*

	Mintage	GSID	G-4	VG-8	F-12	VF-20	EF-40	AU-50	MS-60	MS-63
1846, Tall Date	*	1123	$40	$47	$60	$80	$120	$260	$725	$1,300
↳**1846, Tall Date, N-12**	*	264562	40	47	60	80	120	260	725	1,300
↳**1846, Tall Date, N-13**	*	264563	40	47	60	80	120	260	725	1,300
↳**1846, Tall Date, N-14**	*	264564	40	47	60	80	120	260	725	1,300
↳**1846, Tall Date, N-16**	*	264565	40	47	60	80	120	260	725	1,300
↳**1846, Tall Date, N-23, FS-301**	*	264566	40	47	60	80	120	260	725	1,300
↳**1846, Tall Date, N-25, FS-302**	*	264567	40	47	60	80	120	260	725	1,300
↳**1846, Tall Date, N-26**	*	264568	40	47	60	80	120	260	725	1,300
1847	6,183,669	1132	26	27	34	70	100	180	390	525
↳**1847, N-1**	*	258778	26	27	34	70	100	180	390	525
↳**1847, N-3**	*	258779	26	27	34	70	100	180	390	525
↳**1847, N-4**	*	258780	26	27	34	70	100	180	390	525
↳**1847, N-5**	*	258781	26	27	34	70	100	180	390	525
↳**1847, N-6**	*	258782	26	27	34	70	100	180	390	525
↳**1847, N-7**	*	258783	26	27	34	70	100	180	390	525
↳**1847, N-8**	*	258784	26	27	34	70	100	180	390	525
↳**1847, N-10**	*	258785	26	27	34	70	100	180	390	525
↳**1847, N-11**	*	258786	26	27	34	70	100	180	390	525
↳**1847, N-12**	*	258787	26	27	34	70	100	180	390	525
↳**1847, N-13**	*	258788	26	27	34	70	100	180	390	525
↳**1847, N-14**	*	258789	26	27	34	70	100	180	390	525
↳**1847, N-15**	*	258790	26	27	34	70	100	180	390	525
↳**1847, N-19**	*	258791	26	27	34	70	100	180	390	525
↳**1847, N-20**	*	258792	26	27	34	70	100	180	390	525
↳**1847, N-21**	*	258793	26	27	34	70	100	180	390	525
↳**1847, N-22**	*	258794	26	27	34	70	100	180	390	525
↳**1847, N-23**	*	258795	26	27	34	70	100	180	390	525
↳**1847, N-24**	*	258796	26	27	34	70	100	180	390	525
↳**1847, N-26**	*	258797	26	27	34	70	100	100	390	525
↳**1847, N-27**	*	258798	26	27	34	70	100	180	390	525
↳**1847, N-28**	*	258799	26	27	34	70	100	180	390	525
↳**1847, N-29**	*	258800	26	27	34	70	100	180	390	525
↳**1847, N-30**	*	258801	26	27	34	70	100	180	390	525
↳**1847, N-32**	*	258802	26	27	34	70	100	180	390	525
↳**1847, N-34**	*	258803	26	27	34	70	100	180	390	525
↳**1847, N-35**	*	258804	26	27	34	70	100	180	390	525
↳**1847, N-36, FS-301**	*	258805	26	27	34	70	100	180	390	525
↳**1847, N-37**	*	258806	26	27	34	70	100	180	390	525
↳**1847, N-38**	*	258807	26	27	34	70	100	180	390	525
↳**1847, N-39**	*	258808	26	27	34	70	100	180	390	525
↳**1847, N-41**	*	258809	26	27	34	70	100	180	390	525
↳**1847, N-43, FS-302**	*	258810	26	27	34	70	100	180	390	525
1847, Large Over Small 7 (a)	*	1283	70	100	130	160	325	455	1,400	2,300
↳**1847, Large Over Small 7, N-2** (a)	*	258877	70	100	130	160	325	455	1,400	2,300
↳**1847, Large Over Small 7, N-18** (a)	*	258878	70	100	130	160	325	455	1,400	2,300
↳**1847, Large Over Small 7, N-31** (a)	*	258879	70	100	130	160	325	455	1,400	2,300

* Included in number above. **a.** See the discussion of date-punch blunders in the Braided Hair introductory text.

Circulation Strikes *(continued)*

	Mintage	GSID	G-4	VG-8	F-12	VF-20	EF-40	AU-50	MS-60	MS-63
1848 (b)	6,415,799	1138	$26	$27	$34	$70	$100	$195	$350	$575
↳**1848, N-1**	*	264583	26	27	34	70	100	195	350	575
↳**1848, N-2**	*	264584	26	27	34	70	100	195	350	575
↳**1848, N-3**	*	264585	26	27	34	70	100	195	350	575
↳**1848, N-4**	*	264586	26	27	34	70	100	195	350	575
↳**1848, N-5**	*	264587	26	27	34	70	100	195	350	575
↳**1848, N-6**	*	264588	26	27	34	70	100	195	350	575
↳**1848, N-7**	*	264589	26	27	34	70	100	195	350	575
↳**1848, N-8**	*	264590	26	27	34	70	100	195	350	575
↳**1848, N-9**	*	264591	26	27	34	70	100	195	350	575
↳**1848, N-10**	*	264592	26	27	34	70	100	195	350	575
↳**1848, N-11**	*	264593	26	27	34	70	100	195	350	575
↳**1848, N-12**	*	264594	26	27	34	70	100	195	350	575
↳**1848, N-13**	*	264595	26	27	34	70	100	195	350	575
↳**1848, N-14**	*	264596	26	27	34	70	100	195	350	575
↳**1848, N-15**	*	264597	26	27	34	70	100	195	350	575
↳**1848, N-16**	*	264598	26	27	34	70	100	195	350	575
↳**1848, N-17**	*	264599	26	27	34	70	100	195	350	575
↳**1848, N-18**	*	264600	26	27	34	70	100	195	350	575
↳**1848, N-20**	*	264601	26	27	34	70	100	195	350	575
↳**1848, N-21**	*	264602	26	27	34	70	100	195	350	575
↳**1848, N-22**	*	264603	26	27	34	70	100	195	350	575
↳**1848, N-23**	*	264604	26	27	34	70	100	195	350	575
↳**1848, N-24**	*	264605	26	27	34	70	100	195	350	575
↳**1848, N-25**	*	264606	26	27	34	70	100	195	350	575
↳**1848, N-26**	*	264607	26	27	34	70	100	195	350	575
↳**1848, N-27**	*	264608	26	27	34	70	100	195	350	575
↳**1848, N-28**	*	264609	26	27	34	70	100	195	350	575
↳**1848, N-29**	*	264610	26	27	34	70	100	195	350	575
↳**1848, N-30**	*	264611	26	27	34	70	100	195	350	575
↳**1848, N-31**	*	264612	26	27	34	70	100	195	350	575
↳**1848, N-32**	*	264613	26	27	34	70	100	195	350	575
↳**1848, N-33**	*	264614	26	27	34	70	100	195	350	575
↳**1848, N-34**	*	264615	26	27	34	70	100	195	350	575
↳**1848, N-35**	*	264616	26	27	34	70	100	195	350	575
↳**1848, N-36**	*	264617	26	27	34	70	100	195	350	575
↳**1848, N-37**	*	264618	26	27	34	70	100	195	350	575
↳**1848, N-38**	*	264619	26	27	34	70	100	195	350	575
↳**1848, N-39**	*	264620	26	27	34	70	100	195	350	575
↳**1848, N-40**	*	264621	26	27	34	70	100	195	350	575
↳**1848, N-41**	*	264622	26	27	34	70	100	195	350	575
↳**1848, N-42**	*	264623	26	27	34	70	100	195	350	575
↳**1848, N-44**	*	264624	26	27	34	70	100	195	350	575

* Included in number above. **b.** The 1848, Small Date cent is a rare contemporary counterfeit.

Circulation Strikes *(continued)*

	Mintage	GSID	G-4	VG-8	F-12	VF-20	EF-40	AU-50	MS-60	MS-63
1849	4,178,500	1144	$26	$27	$34	$70	$100	$260	$420	$750
↳**1849, N-1**	*	264709	26	27	34	70	100	260	420	750
↳**1849, N-2**	*	264710	26	27	34	70	100	260	420	750
↳**1849, N-3**	*	264711	26	27	34	70	100	260	420	750
↳**1849, N-4**	*	264712	26	27	34	70	100	260	420	750
↳**1849, N-5**	*	264713	26	27	34	70	100	260	420	750
↳**1849, N-7**	*	264714	26	27	34	70	100	260	420	750
↳**1849, N-8**	*	264715	26	27	34	70	100	260	420	750
↳**1849, N-9**	*	264716	26	27	34	70	100	260	420	750
↳**1849, N-10**	*	264717	26	27	34	70	100	260	420	750
↳**1849, N-11**	*	264718	26	27	34	70	100	260	420	750
↳**1849, N-12**	*	264719	26	27	34	70	100	260	420	750
↳**1849, N-14**	*	264720	26	27	34	70	100	260	420	750
↳**1849, N-16**	*	264721	26	27	34	70	100	260	420	750
↳**1849, N-17**	*	264722	26	27	34	70	100	260	420	750
↳**1849, N-19**	*	264723	26	27	34	70	100	260	420	750
↳**1849, N-20**	*	264724	26	27	34	70	100	260	420	750
↳**1849, N-21**	*	264725	26	27	34	70	100	260	420	750
↳**1849, N-22**	*	264726	26	27	34	70	100	260	420	750
↳**1849, N-23**	*	264727	26	27	34	70	100	260	420	750
↳**1849, N-24**	*	264728	26	27	34	70	100	260	420	750
↳**1849, N-25, FS-301**	*	264729	26	27	34	70	100	260	420	750
↳**1849, N-26**	*	264730	26	27	34	70	100	260	420	750
↳**1849, N-27**	*	264731	26	27	34	70	100	260	420	750
↳**1849, N-28**	*	264732	26	27	34	70	100	260	420	750
↳**1849, N-29**	*	264733	26	27	34	70	100	260	420	750
↳**1849, N-30**	*	264734	26	27	34	70	100	260	420	750
1850	4,426,844	1150	26	27	34	40	60	145	220	360
↳**1850, N-1**	*	264787	26	27	34	40	60	145	220	360
↳**1850, N-2**	*	264788	26	27	34	40	60	145	220	360
↳**1850, N-3**	*	264789	26	27	34	40	60	145	220	360
↳**1850, N-4**	*	264790	26	27	34	40	60	145	220	360
↳**1850, N-5**	*	264791	26	27	34	40	60	145	220	360
↳**1850, N-6**	*	264792	26	27	34	40	60	145	220	360
↳**1850, N-7**	*	264793	26	27	34	40	60	145	220	360
↳**1850, N-9**	*	264794	26	27	34	40	60	145	220	360
↳**1850, N-11**	*	264795	26	27	34	40	60	145	220	360
↳**1850, N-12**	*	264796	26	27	34	40	60	145	220	360
↳**1850, N-13**	*	264797	26	27	34	40	60	145	220	360
↳**1850, N-14**	*	264798	26	27	34	40	60	145	220	360
↳**1850, N-15**	*	264799	26	27	34	40	60	145	220	360
↳**1850, N-17**	*	264800	26	27	34	40	60	145	220	360
↳**1850, N-18**	*	264801	26	27	34	40	60	145	220	360
↳**1850, N-19**	*	264802	26	27	34	40	60	145	220	360
↳**1850, N-20**	*	264803	26	27	34	40	60	145	220	360
↳**1850, N-21**	*	264804	26	27	34	40	60	145	220	360
↳**1850, N-22**	*	264805	26	27	34	40	60	145	220	360
↳**1850, N-23**	*	264806	26	27	34	40	60	145	220	360
↳**1850, Open 5, N-24, FS-301**	*	264807	26	27	34	40	60	145	220	360
↳**1850, N-25**	*	264808	26	27	34	40	60	145	220	360
↳**1850, N-26**	*	264809	26	27	34	40	60	145	220	360
↳**1850, N-27**	*	264810	26	27	34	40	60	145	220	360
↳**1850, N-28**	*	264811	26	27	34	40	60	145	220	360

* Included in number above.

1851, 51 Over 81

Circulation Strikes *(continued)*

	Mintage	GSID	G-4	VG-8	F-12	VF-20	EF-40	AU-50	MS-60	MS-63
1851	9,889,707	1156	$26	$27	$34	$40	$60	$145	$210	$305
↳1851, N-1	*	264862	26	27	34	40	60	145	210	305
↳1851, N-2	*	264863	26	27	34	40	60	145	210	305
↳1851, N-4	*	264864	26	27	34	40	60	145	210	305
↳1851, N-5	*	264865	26	27	34	40	60	145	210	305
↳1851, N-6	*	264866	26	27	34	40	60	145	210	305
↳1851, N-7	*	264867	26	27	34	40	60	145	210	305
↳1851, N-8	*	264868	26	27	34	40	60	145	210	305
↳1851, N-9	*	264869	26	27	34	40	60	145	210	305
↳1851, N-10	*	264870	26	27	34	40	60	145	210	305
↳1851, N-12	*	264871	26	27	34	40	60	145	210	305
↳1851, N-13	*	264872	26	27	34	40	60	145	210	305
↳1851, N-14	*	264873	26	27	34	40	60	145	210	305
↳1851, N-15	*	264874	26	27	34	40	60	145	210	305
↳1851, N-16	*	264875	26	27	34	40	60	145	210	305
↳1851, N-17	*	264876	26	27	34	40	60	145	210	305
↳1851, N-18	*	264877	26	27	34	40	60	145	210	305
↳1851, N-19	*	264878	26	27	34	40	60	145	210	305
↳1851, N-20	*	264879	26	27	34	40	60	145	210	305
↳1851, N-21	*	264880	26	27	34	40	60	145	210	305
↳1851, N-22	*	264881	26	27	34	40	60	145	210	305
↳1851, N-23	*	264882	26	27	34	40	60	145	210	305
↳1851, N-24	*	264883	26	27	34	40	60	145	210	305
↳1851, N-25	*	264884	26	27	34	40	60	145	210	305
↳1851, N-26	*	264885	26	27	34	40	60	145	210	305
↳1851, N-27	*	264886	26	27	34	40	60	145	210	305
↳1851, N-29	*	264887	26	27	34	40	60	145	210	305
↳1851, N-30	*	264888	26	27	34	40	60	145	210	305
↳1851, N-31	*	264889	26	27	34	40	60	145	210	305
↳1851, N-33	*	264890	26	27	34	40	60	145	210	305
↳1851, N-34	*	264891	26	27	34	40	60	145	210	305
↳1851, N-35	*	264892	26	27	34	40	60	145	210	305
↳1851, N-36	*	264893	26	27	34	40	60	145	210	305
↳1851, N-37	*	264894	26	27	34	40	60	145	210	305
↳1851, N-38	*	264895	26	27	34	40	60	145	210	305
↳1851, N-39	*	264896	26	27	34	40	60	145	210	305
↳1851, N-40	*	264897	26	27	34	40	60	145	210	305
↳1851, N-41	*	264898	26	27	34	40	60	145	210	305
↳1851, N-42, FS-301	unique	392835	—	—	—	—	—	—	—	—
↳1851, N-43	*	264899	26	27	34	40	60	145	210	305
↳1851, Repunched Date, N-44, FS-302	*	264900	26	27	34	40	60	145	210	305
↳1851, N-45	*	264901	26	27	34	40	60	145	210	305
1851, 51 Over 81 (a)	*	1286	70	100	130	160	230	470	700	1,400
↳1851, 51 Over 81, N-3 (a)	*	241239	70	100	130	160	230	470	700	1,400

* Included in number above. **a.** See the discussion of date-punch blunders in the Braided Hair introductory text.

Circulation Strikes *(continued)*

	Mintage	GSID	G-4	VG-8	F-12	VF-20	EF-40	AU-50	MS-60	MS-63
1852	5,063,094	1162	$26	$27	$34	$40	$60	$145	$210	$370
↳**1852, N-1**	*	240964	26	27	34	40	60	145	210	370
↳**1852, N-3**	*	240965	26	27	34	40	60	145	210	370
↳**1852, N-4**	*	240966	26	27	34	40	60	145	210	370
↳**1852, N-5**	*	240967	26	27	34	40	60	145	210	370
↳**1852, N-6**	*	240968	26	27	34	40	60	145	210	370
↳**1852, N-7**	*	240969	26	27	34	40	60	145	210	370
↳**1852, N-8**	*	240970	26	27	34	40	60	145	210	370
↳**1852, N-10**	*	240971	26	27	34	40	60	145	210	370
↳**1852, N-11**	*	240972	26	27	34	40	60	145	210	370
↳**1852, N-12**	*	240973	26	27	34	40	60	145	210	370
↳**1852, N-14**	*	240974	26	27	34	40	60	145	210	370
↳**1852, N-15**	*	240975	26	27	34	40	60	145	210	370
↳**1852, N-16**	*	240976	26	27	34	40	60	145	210	370
↳**1852, N-17**	*	240977	26	27	34	40	60	145	210	370
↳**1852, N-18**	*	240978	26	27	34	40	60	145	210	370
↳**1852, N-20**	*	240979	26	27	34	40	60	145	210	370
↳**1852, N-21**	*	240980	26	27	34	40	60	145	210	370
↳**1852, N-22/9**	*	240981	26	27	34	40	60	145	210	370
↳**1852, N-23**	*	240982	26	27	34	40	60	145	210	370
1853	6,641,131	1168	26	27	34	40	60	145	210	305
↳**1853, N-1**	*	241137	26	27	34	40	60	145	210	305
↳**1853, N-2**	*	241243	26	27	34	40	60	145	210	305
↳**1853, N-3**	*	241139	26	27	34	40	60	145	210	305
↳**1853, N-4**	*	241245	26	27	34	40	60	145	210	305
↳**1853, N-5**	*	241141	26	27	34	40	60	145	210	305
↳**1853, N-6**	*	241247	26	27	34	40	60	145	210	305
↳**1853, N-7**	*	241143	26	27	34	40	60	145	210	305
↳**1853, N-8**	*	241249	26	27	34	40	60	145	210	305
↳**1853, N-9**	*	241145	26	27	34	40	60	145	210	305
↳**1853, N-10**	*	241251	26	27	34	40	60	145	210	305
↳**1853, N-11**	*	241147	26	27	34	40	60	145	210	305
↳**1853, N-12**	*	241253	26	27	34	40	60	145	210	305
↳**1853, N-13**	*	241149	26	27	34	40	60	145	210	305
↳**1853, N-14**	*	241255	26	27	34	40	60	145	210	305
↳**1853, N-15**	*	241151	26	27	34	40	60	145	210	305
↳**1853, N-16**	*	241257	26	27	34	40	60	145	210	305
↳**1853, N-17**	*	241153	26	27	34	40	60	145	210	305
↳**1853, N-18**	*	241259	26	27	34	40	60	145	210	305
↳**1853, N-19**	*	241155	26	27	34	40	60	145	210	305
↳**1853, N-20**	*	241261	26	27	34	40	60	145	210	305
↳**1853, N-21**	*	241157	26	27	34	40	60	145	210	305
↳**1853, N-22**	*	241263	26	27	34	40	60	145	210	305
↳**1853, N-23**	*	241159	26	27	34	40	60	145	210	305
↳**1853, N-24**	*	241265	26	27	34	40	60	145	210	305
↳**1853, N-25**	*	241161	26	27	34	40	60	145	210	305
↳**1853, N-26**	*	241267	26	27	34	40	60	145	210	305
↳**1853, N-27**	*	241163	26	27	34	40	60	145	210	305
↳**1853, N-28**	*	241269	26	27	34	40	60	145	210	305
↳**1853, N-29**	*	241165	26	27	34	40	60	145	210	305
↳**1853, N-30**	*	241271	26	27	34	40	60	145	210	305
↳**1853, N-31**	*	241167	26	27	34	40	60	145	210	305
↳**1853, N-32**	*	241273	26	27	34	40	60	145	210	305
↳**1853, N-33**	*	241169	26	27	34	40	60	145	210	305

* Included in number above.

1855, Upright 5's

1855, Slanting 5's

1855, Knob on Ear

Circulation Strikes *(continued)*

	Mintage	GSID	G-4	VG-8	F-12	VF-20	EF-40	AU-50	MS-60	MS-63
1854	4,236,156	1174	$26	$27	$34	$40	$60	$145	$210	$305
↳1854, N-1	*	266557	26	27	34	40	60	145	210	305
↳1854, N-2	*	266558	26	27	34	40	60	145	210	305
↳1854, N-3	*	266559	26	27	34	40	60	145	210	305
↳1854, N-4	*	266560	26	27	34	40	60	145	210	305
↳1854, N-5	*	266561	26	27	34	40	60	145	210	305
↳1854, N-6	*	266562	26	27	34	40	60	145	210	305
↳1854, N-7	*	266563	26	27	34	40	60	145	210	305
↳1854, N-8	*	266564	26	27	34	40	60	145	210	305
↳1854, N-9	*	266565	26	27	34	40	60	145	210	305
↳1854, N-10	*	266566	26	27	34	40	60	145	210	305
↳1854, N-11	*	213883	26	27	34	40	60	145	210	305
↳1854, N-12	*	266567	26	27	34	40	60	145	210	305
↳1854, N-13	*	266568	26	27	34	40	60	145	210	305
↳1854, N-14	*	266569	26	27	34	40	60	145	210	305
↳1854, N-16	*	266570	26	27	34	40	60	145	210	305
↳1854, N-17	*	266571	26	27	34	40	60	145	210	305
↳1854, N-18	*	266572	26	27	34	40	60	145	210	305
↳1854, N-19	*	266573	26	27	34	40	60	145	210	305
↳1854, N-20	*	266574	26	27	34	40	60	145	210	305
↳1854, N-21	*	266575	26	27	34	40	60	145	210	305
↳1854, N-22	*	266576	26	27	34	40	60	145	210	305
↳1854, N-23	*	213932	26	27	34	40	60	145	210	305
↳1854, N-24	*	266577	26	27	34	40	60	145	210	305
↳1854, N-25	*	266578	26	27	34	40	60	145	210	305
↳1854, N-26	*	213933	26	27	34	40	60	145	210	305
↳1854, N-27	*	266579	26	27	34	40	60	145	210	305
↳1854, N-28	*	266580	26	27	34	40	60	145	210	305
↳1854, N-29	*	266581	26	27	34	40	60	145	210	305
↳1854, N-30	*	266582	26	27	34	40	60	145	210	305
1855, Upright 5's	1,574,829	1180	26	27	34	40	60	145	210	305
↳1855, Upright 5's, N-1	*	270451	26	27	34	40	60	145	210	305
↳1855, Upright 5's, N-2	*	270452	26	27	34	40	60	145	210	305
↳1855, Upright 5's, N-3	*	270453	26	27	34	40	60	145	210	305
↳1855, Upright 5's, N-4	*	270454	26	27	34	40	60	145	210	305
↳1855, Upright 5's, N-5	*	270455	26	27	34	40	60	145	210	305
↳1855, Upright 5's, N-6	*	270456	26	27	34	40	60	145	210	305
↳1855, Upright 5's, N-7	*	270457	26	27	34	40	60	145	210	305
↳1855, Upright 5's, N-8	*	270458	26	27	34	40	60	145	210	305
↳1855, Upright 5's, N-12	*	270459	26	27	34	40	60	145	210	305
↳1855, Upright 5's, N-13	*	270460	26	27	34	40	60	145	210	305
1855, Slanting 5's, Knob on Ear	*	1186	55	70	100	130	160	290	455	950
↳1855, Slanting 5's, Knob on Ear, N-9	*	270484	55	70	100	130	160	290	455	950

* Included in number above.

1856, Upright 5

1856, Slanting 5

1857, Large Date

1857, Small Date

Circulation Strikes *(continued)*

	Mintage	GSID	G-4	VG-8	F-12	VF-20	EF-40	AU-50	MS-60	MS-63
1855, Slanting 5's	*	1183	$26	$27	$34	$40	$60	$145	$210	$305
↳1855, Slanting 5's, N-10	*	270481	26	27	34	40	60	145	210	305
1856, Upright 5	2,690,463	1192	26	27	34	40	60	145	210	305
↳1856, Upright 5, N-6	*	275430	26	27	34	40	60	145	210	305
↳1856, Upright 5, N-7	*	275431	26	27	34	40	60	145	210	305
↳1856, Upright 5, N-8	*	275432	26	27	34	40	60	145	210	305
↳1856, Upright 5, N-9	*	275433	26	27	34	40	60	145	210	305
↳1856, Upright 5, N-10	*	275434	26	27	34	40	60	145	210	305
↳1856, Upright 5, N-11	*	275435	26	27	34	40	60	145	210	305
↳1856, Upright 5, N-12	*	275436	26	27	34	40	60	145	210	305
↳1856, Upright 5, N-20	*	275437	26	27	34	40	60	145	210	305
1856, Slanting 5	*	1195	26	27	34	40	60	145	210	305
↳1856, Slanted 5, N-1	*	275454	26	27	34	40	60	145	210	305
↳1856, Slanted 5, N-2	*	275455	26	27	34	40	60	145	210	305
↳1856, Slanted 5, N-3	*	275456	26	27	34	40	60	145	210	305
↳1856, Slanted 5, N-4	*	275457	26	27	34	40	60	145	210	305
↳1856, Slanted 5, N-13	*	275458	26	27	34	40	60	145	210	305
↳1856, Slanted 5, N-14	*	275459	26	27	34	40	60	145	210	305
↳1856, Slanted 5, N-16	*	275460	26	27	34	40	60	145	210	305
↳1856, Slanted 5, N-17	*	275461	26	27	34	40	60	145	210	305
↳1856, Slanted 5, N-18	*	275462	26	27	34	40	60	145	210	305
↳1856, Slanted 5, N-19	*	275463	26	27	34	40	60	145	210	305
↳1856, Slanted 5, N-21	*	275464	26	27	34	40	60	145	210	305
↳1856, Slanted 5, N-22, FS-301	*	275465	26	27	34	40	60	145	210	305
1857, Large Date	333,546	1201	70	130	170	195	240	290	455	725
↳1857, Large Date, N-1	*	275019	70	130	170	195	240	290	455	725
1857, Small Date	*	1204	70	135	180	260	360	420	550	850
↳1857, Small Date, N-2	*	275022	70	135	180	260	360	420	550	850
↳1857, Small Date, N-4	*	275023	70	135	180	260	360	420	550	850

Note: Numismatic anachronisms dated 1868 were struck in nickel and in copper, featuring the large cent design last used in 1857. These likely were quietly and unofficially sold by Mint employees to collectors. They are classified as Judd-610 and 611 in *United States Pattern Coins* (10th edition). * Included in number above.

Proof Strikes

		GSID	PF-63	PF-64	PF-65
Braided Hair (1839–1857), Proof, Brown		**84874**	**$4,400**	**$5,500**	**$8,750**
Same, Red Brown		**84875**	**5,000**	**6,250**	**9,500**
Same, Red		**84876**	**—**	**19,000**	**30,000**
1840, Small Date Over Large 18		1075	10,500	12,000	20,000
1841		1081	7,000	8,750	12,000
1842		1090	—	8,500	11,000
1843, Petite Head, Small Letters		1102	8,000	10,000	13,000
1844		1108	10,500	14,500	21,500
1845		1114	11,000	12,000	14,000
1846	10 est. known	1126	18,000	24,000	36,000
↳1846, Small Date	6 known	213489	18,000	24,000	36,000
↳1846, Tall Date	4 known	1129	21,500	29,000	43,000
1847		1135	8,750	11,000	13,000
1848		1141	7,500	10,500	15,500
1849		1147	8,250	11,000	14,500
1850		1153	8,750	11,000	18,000
1852		1165	—	54,000	78,000
1853		1171	—	33,500	—
1854	30 est. known	1177	5,250	8,000	10,000
1855, Slanting 5's	100 est. known	1189	4,400	5,500	8,750
1856, Slanting 5	100 est. known	1198	4,400	5,500	8,750
1857, Small Date		1207	4,400	5,500	8,750

THE PASSING OF THE LARGE CENT AND HALF CENT

By 1857 the U.S. Mint's costs for manufacturing and distributing its half cents and large cents had risen so high that Mint Director James Ross Snowden reported that the copper coins "barely paid expenses." Both denominations had become unpopular, and they rarely circulated outside the nation's larger cities. With this pressure, change was on the horizon. The Treasury Department had recent precedent to tinker with coinage sizes and compositions. For several years in the early 1850s the Mint had issued silver coins of reduced weight, as a way to discourage their melting and export (the coins' silver content had been greater than their face values). On the heels of this coinage reform, new legislation in 1857 replaced the large copper cent with a smaller copper-nickel coin of the same value, and terminated the half cent outright.

The coinage legislation of 1857 brought important benefits to the United States. Under its terms, Spanish coins were redeemed for melting at the Mint and exchanged for the new, small cents. The old-fashioned reckoning of business transactions in Spanish *reales* and *medios*, British shillings, and other currencies was (officially, at least) abandoned, and the American decimal system was popularized. Citizens found the new small cent to be convenient, and it quickly became a favored and useful means of retail trade. Tens of millions would be minted before the decade closed.

The hobby of coin collecting experienced a boom when the large cent and half cent passed away. Casual observers set aside the obsolete coins as mementoes of a time gone by, while more experienced collectors sought to assemble collections composed of one of each date. Over the ensuing decades the study and collecting of these old coppers has become more and more specialized while still attracting hobby newcomers. Their devoted enthusiasts appreciate the coins' historical connections and cultural significance.

Small Cents
1856–2025

AN OVERVIEW OF SMALL CENTS

On May 25, 1857, the U.S. Mint debuted its new small-diameter Flying Eagle cent. Designed by Chief Engraver James B. Longacre, the obverse featured a flying eagle, copied after Christian Gobrecht's silver dollar of 1836. The reverse showed an agricultural wreath enclosing the denomination. Problems developed with striking the pieces up properly, and in 1859 a new type, the Indian Head cent, was introduced. With several variations this design was continued through 1909. In that year the Lincoln cent with Wheat Ears reverse was introduced. The series was continued for many years, until 1959, when the Memorial Reverse type was introduced, continuing the same Lincoln portrait on the obverse. Then in 2009 four different reverses were introduced to commemorate the 200th anniversary of the birth of Abraham Lincoln. In 2010 a new reverse symbolized President Lincoln's preservation of the Union.

Scan for additional information.

Forming a type set of small cents is done easily enough, although the first two issues, the 1857 and 1858 Flying Eagles, as well as the 1859 Indian Head with laurel wreath reverse, can be expensive in higher grades. Striking quality is a consideration for all small cents from 1857 to the end of the Indian Head series in 1909, but enough exist that finding a needle-sharp piece is simply a matter of time. Lincoln cents are easy enough to find sharply struck, though some varieties are more difficult to find this way than others.

For the Collector and Investor: Small Cents as a Specialty

Flying Eagle and Indian Head cents often are collected together by specialists, who usually aspire to add the pattern 1856 Flying Eagle to the series. Proof Flying Eagle and Indian Head cents form a separate specialty and are widely collected. The Flying Eagle and Indian Cent Collectors Society (www.fly-inclub.org) welcomes aficionados of these series. Its journal, *Longacre's Ledger*, serves as a forum for new discoveries, market information, and the exchange of ideas and research.

This 1855 pattern large cent (J-167) depicts the flying eagle motif which would be adopted in 1856 on new small-cent planchets.

One of the foundations of modern American numismatics is the collecting of Lincoln cents, 1909 to date. Collectors have a wide variety of folders, albums, and holders to choose from; these have a tradition dating back to the 1930s, when R.K. Post of Neenah, Wisconsin, launched his "penny boards" (made for him by Whitman Publishing Co., which later acquired the rights), and Wayte Raymond marketed a series of "National" album pages. Today, a search through pocket change might yield coins dating back to 1959, the first year of the Lincoln Memorial reverse, before which date even high-mintage issues are hardly ever seen. A generation ago it was possible to find cents from 1909 onward. However, key issues such as 1909-S V.D.B. (the most famous of all "popular rarities" in the U.S. series), 1914-D, 1924-D, 1926-S, 1931-S, and 1955 Doubled Die Obverse eluded most enthusiasts.

Lincoln cents can be collected casually, or a specialty can be made of them. A dedicated enthusiast may want to secure one each in a grade such as MS-65, also taking care that each is sharply struck. There are quite a few issues, including Denver and San Francisco varieties from about 1916 to the late 1920s, that are plentiful *except* if sharply struck (with full hair detail on the Lincoln portrait, no tiny marks on Lincoln's shoulder, and sharp details and a smooth field on the reverse). Die-variety specialists have dozens of popular doubled dies, overmintmarks, and other varieties to hunt down, using the *Cherrypickers' Guide* as their standard reference. With the Mint's roll-out of four new reverse designs in 2009, and another in 2010, the Lincoln cent promises to intrigue another generation of Americans and continue to bring new collectors to the hobby.

EXPLORING VARIETIES

In volume 6 of the Red Book Series, Richard Snow guides collectors through the world of the Flying Eagle and Indian Head cents of 1856 to 1909. An unrivaled expert on the series, the author created the Snow numbering system used by collectors to identify varieties and die pairings. *Flying Eagle and Indian Head Cents* goes in-depth on regular issues and major varieties, and discusses Mint errors, toned Proofs, pattern coins, and other topics related to the series.

Snow, Richard. *Flying Eagle and Indian Cents*. 4th edition. Florence, AL: Whitman, 2025.

FLYING EAGLE (1856–1858)

Designer: *James B. Longacre.* **Weight:** *4.67 grams.*
Composition: *.880 copper, .120 nickel.*
Diameter: *19 mm.* **Edge:** *Plain.* **Mint:** *Philadelphia.*

Circulation Strike

Proof Strike

History. The nation's large copper cents became increasingly expensive to produce, leading the U.S. Mint to experiment with smaller versions during the 1850s. Finally a new design and format were chosen: the Flying Eagle cent, of smaller diameter and 4.67 grams' weight (compared to nearly 11). Many patterns were made of this design in 1856 (for distribution to interested congressmen), and later restrikes (bearing that same date) were extensive, with the result that many numismatists collect the 1856 cent along with the regular series. Distribution of the new 1857 Flying Eagle cents for circulation commenced on May 25 of that year. Problems resulted from striking the design properly, and the motif was discontinued in 1858. Although attempts were made to create a modified, thinner eagle, the unattractive results were scrapped in favor of an entirely new design. The coins remained in circulation until the early 1900s, by which time any found in pocket change were well worn.

Striking and Sharpness. The heavy wreath on the reverse was opposite in the dies (while in the press) from the head and tail of the eagle on the obverse, and, accordingly, many Flying Eagle cents were weakly struck in these areas. Today, this lightness of strike is most visible at each end of the eagle and on the wreath, particularly the higher areas, and on the vertical separation at the middle of the ribbon knot. Striking weakness is most obvious (especially for novice collectors) on the eagle's tail feathers. Many Flying Eagle cents, however, are quite well struck. A first-class Proof should have a fully and deeply mirrored field on both sides, except for those of 1856, which are usually a combination of mirror-like and grainy in character.

Availability. As a type the Flying Eagle cent is easy to find, although some varieties, such as 1856 and 1858, 8 Over 7, range from scarce to rare. Most are seen in worn grades. In MS, many are in the marketplace, although dipping, cleaning, and recoloring (causing staining and spotting) have eliminated the majority from consideration by connoisseurs. Proof Flying Eagle cents dated 1856 are plentiful, surviving from the quantity of perhaps 2,000 to 2,500 or more restruck in 1859 and later. (Today's collectors do not distinguish, price-wise, between the 1856 originals and restrikes dated 1856.) Proofs of 1857 are very rare. Proofs of 1858 are rare, but are significantly more readily available than for 1857. Some prooflike Mint State coins have been called Proofs. Quality is a challenge for Proofs, and problem-free examples are in the minority.

Grading Standards

Caveat: These grading standards do not take sharpness of strike into account.

MS-60 to 70 (Mint State). ***Obverse:*** Contact marks, most obvious in the field, are evident at MS-60, diminishing at MS-61, 62, and higher. The eagle, the feathers of which usually hide marks, shows some evidence of contact as well. At Gem MS-65 or finer there is no trace of friction or rubbing. A few tiny nicks or marks may be seen, but none are obvious. At MS-67 and higher levels the coin will approach perfection. A theoretically perfect MS-70 will have no marks at all evident, even under a strong magnifier. Although in practice this is not always consistent, at MS-66 and higher there should be no staining or other problems, and the coin should have good eye appeal overall. ***Reverse:*** Check the higher parts of the wreath for slight abrasions at MS-60 to 62. Otherwise, the above guidelines apply.

MS-64

Illustrated coin: The surfaces display a healthy satin luster, as well as an iridescent rose and golden-tan patina. The coin is sharply and evenly struck and offers razor-sharp definition.

AU-50, 53, 55, 58 (About Uncirculated). ***Obverse:*** At AU-50, light wear is seen on the breast of the eagle, the top edge of the closest wing, and, less so, on the head. As both the head and tail tip can be lightly struck, these are not reliable indicators of grade. Luster is present in traces among the letters. At higher About Uncirculated levels the evidence of wear diminishes. An AU-58 coin will have nearly full luster, but friction is seen in the fields, as are some marks. ***Reverse:*** At AU-50, light wear is seen on the ribbon bow and the highest areas of the leaves. Some luster is seen (more than on the obverse). Friction is evident, as are some marks, but these will not be as distracting as those on the obverse, as the heavy wreath and lettering are more protective of the reverse field. In higher grades, wear is less, and at AU-58 nearly full luster—or even completely full luster—is seen.

AU-53

Illustrated coin: The reverse features a large rim cud.

EF-40, 45 (Extremely Fine). ***Obverse:*** Wear is more extensive, especially on the eagle's breast and the top of the closest wing. Wear will also show on the other wing in the area below OF. Marks may be more extensive in the field. The wear is slightly greater at EF-40 than at EF-45, although in the marketplace these two grades are not clearly differentiated. ***Reverse:*** More wear shows on the higher areas of the wreath, but most detail will still be present. There may be tinges of luster in protected areas, more likely at EF-45 than at EF-40.

EF-40

VF-20

VF-20, 30 (Very Fine). ***Obverse:*** Wear is appreciable, with the breast feathers gone over a larger area and with more wear on the wings. The tail shows significant wear, negating the question as to whether it was well struck originally. Marks are more extensive, although across all grades the durable copper-nickel metal resisted heavy marks and cuts; any such should be separately described. Staining and spotting, not related to grade, is common. Cherrypicking (examining multiple coins, all slabbed at the same grade level, and selecting the finest of them) at this and lower grades will yield nice coins in any given category. ***Reverse:*** The wreath is worn flat in the higher and medium–relief areas, although some detail is seen in the lower areas close to the field. ONE / CENT may be slightly weak, depending on the quality of the original strike. Marks are fewer than on the obverse.

F-12

F-12, 15 (Fine). ***Obverse:*** The eagle shows extensive wear, with about half of the feathers gone. Some detail is still seen, especially on the underside of the closest wing, above the breast. ***Reverse:*** Wear is even more extensive, with the wreath nearing flatness, but still with some detail in the lower areas.

VG-10

VG-8, 10 (Very Good). ***Obverse:*** On the obverse the eagle is clear in outline form, but only a small number of feathers can be discerned, mostly above the breast. Letters and the date show extensive wear but are complete and clear. ***Reverse:*** The wreath is now mostly an outline, although some lower-relief features can be differentiated. ONE / CENT may be weak (depending on the strike).

G-4

G-4, 6 (Good). ***Obverse:*** The eagle is nearly completely flat, with just a few feathers, if any, discernible. The rim is worn down, making the outer parts of the letters and the lower part of the date slightly weak, but all are readable. ***Reverse:*** The wreath is basically in outline form, with hardly any detail. ONE / CENT is weak, usually with CENT weakest. The rim is worn down.

AG-3

AG-3 (About Good). ***Obverse:*** Wear is extensive, but most of the eagle is visible in outline form. The letters are mostly worn away, with vestiges remaining here and there. The date is partially worn away at the bottom, but is distinct and readable. ***Reverse:*** The wreath is so worn that it cannot be distinguished from the field in areas, usually toward the top. ONE / CENT is mostly gone, but much of CENT can be discerned (unless the coin was a weak strike to begin with).

PF-65

PF-60 to 70 (Proof). ***Obverse and Reverse:*** Gem PF-65 coins have very few hairlines, and these are visible only under a strong magnifying glass. At the PF-67 level or higher there should be no evidence of hairlines or friction at all. PF-60 coins can be dull from repeated dipping and cleaning (remember, hairlines on any Proof were caused by cleaning with an abrasive agent; they had no hairlines when struck). At PF-63 the mirrorlike fields should be attractive, and hairlines should be minimal, best seen when the coin is held at an angle to the light. No rubbing is seen. PF-64 coins are even nicer.

Illustrated coin: The fields of this coin are highly reflective for a nickel-alloy Proof cent.

1857, Obverse $20 Clash
FS-403

1857, Reverse 25¢ Clash
FS-901

1858, 8 Over 7
FS-301

1858, Large Letters

1858, Small Letters

Circulation Strikes

	Mintage	GSID	G-4	VG-8	F-12	VF-20	EF-40	AU-50	MS-60	MS-63
Flying Eagle (1856–1858)	**n/a**	**72334**	**$27**	**$40**	**$55**	**$90**	**$180**	**$350**	**$675**	**$1,250**
1856 (a)	2,000	15310	8,750	10,000	11,000	12,000	13,500	15,000	19,000	29,000
	Auctions: $172,500, PCGS MS-66 HA 01/04									
1857	17,450,000	15313	27	40	55	90	180	350	675	1,250
↳1857, Doubled Die Obverse	*	15321	—	95	130	170	265	440	825	1,500
↳1857, Repunched Date, Obverse of 1856, FS-401a, S-1	*	213011	—	—	—	—	—	—	—	4,500
↳1857, Repunched Date, Obverse of 1856, FS-401a, S-1	*	213012	—	—	—	—	—	—	—	—
↳1857, FS-104, S-5	*	212993	—	—	—	—	—	—	—	—
↳1857, FS-403, S-7	*	212995	—	—	—	—	—	—	—	—
↳1857, FS-901, S-8	*	212996	—	130	160	195	325	420	1,100	2,500
↳1857, Obverse Clash with Seated Half Dollar, FS-402, S-9	*	212997	60	80	115	145	290	440	775	1,400
1858, Small Letters	*	15316	27	40	55	90	180	350	750	1,400
1858, Large Letters	24,600,000	15315	27	40	55	90	180	350	675	1,250
1858, 8 Over 7, Strong Overdate	*	15322	130	195	310	525	950	1,750	4,250	8,250
↳1858, 8 Over 7, Large Letters, Strong Overdate, FS-301, S-1	*	213474	130	195	310	525	950	1,750	4,250	8,250
1858, 8 Over 7, Weak	*	213475	—	—	200	235	290	430	750	1,300
↳1858 Over (7), Large Letters, Weak Overdate, FS-302, S-7	*	213476	—	—	200	235	290	430	750	1,300

* Included in number above. **a.** Actually a pattern, but collected along with the regular issue since it shares the same design. See *United States Pattern Coins* (10th edition).

Proof Strikes

	Mintage	GSID	PF-60	PF-63	PF-65
Flying Eagle (1856–1858), Proof	**n/a**	**73857**	**$4,750**	**$6,250**	**$17,000**
1856 (a)	2,000	15311	16,500	19,000	33,500
1857	100	15314	4,750	6,250	31,000
1858, Large Letters	100	15317	4,750	6,250	17,000
1858, Small Letters	200	15318	5,250	8,750	26,500

a. Most of those seen are Proofs; a small number have been designated circulation strikes.

INDIAN HEAD (1859–1909)

Variety 1 (Copper-Nickel, Laurel Wreath Reverse, 1859):
Designer: *James B. Longacre.* **Weight:** *4.67 grams.* **Composition:** *.880 copper, .120 nickel.* **Diameter:** *19 mm.* **Edge:** *Plain.* **Mint:** *Philadelphia.*

Copper-Nickel, Laurel Wreath Reverse, Without Shield (1859), Circulation Strike

Copper-Nickel, Laurel Wreath Reverse, Without Shield, Proof Strike

Variety 2 (Copper-Nickel, Oak Wreath With Shield, 1860–1864):
Designer: *James B. Longacre.* **Weight:** *4.67 grams.* **Composition:** *.880 copper, .120 nickel.* **Diameter:** *19 mm.* **Edge:** *Plain.* **Mint:** *Philadelphia.*

Copper-Nickel, Oak Wreath Reverse, With Shield (1860–1864), Circulation Strike

Copper-Nickel, Oak Wreath Reverse, With Shield, Proof Strike

Variety 3 (Bronze, 1864–1909): **Designer:** *James B. Longacre.* **Weight:** *3.11 grams.* **Composition:** *.950 copper, .050 tin and zinc.* **Diameter:** *19 mm.* **Edge:** *Plain.* **Mints:** *Philadelphia and San Francisco.*

Bronze, Oak Wreath Reverse, With Shield (1864–1909), Circulation Strike

Bronze, Oak Wreath Reverse, With Shield, Proof Strike

History. After nearly a dozen varieties of patterns were made in 1858, in 1859 the Indian Head was adopted as the new motif for the cent. Observers of the time noted the incongruity of placing a Native American war bonnet on a bust which was meant to be both female and classically Greek; designer James B. Longacre's earlier use of a feathered tiara on the Indian Head three-dollar gold piece had been viewed as less strange. The reverse of the 1859 coin illustrates an olive (or laurel) wreath. In 1860 this was changed to a wreath of oak and other leaves with a shield at the apex, a design continued through the end of the series in 1909. From 1859 through spring 1864 cents were struck in copper-nickel, the alloy used earlier for Flying Eagle cents. In 1864 a new bronze alloy was adopted.

Indian Head cents remained in circulation through the 1940s, but by the early 1950s were rarely seen. In the 1930s, when Whitman and other coin boards and folders became widely available, collectors picked many key dates out of circulation. The typical grade for the scarce issues of the 1870s was Good or so, and the 1908-S and 1909-S could be found in VF.

Striking and Sharpness. The strike on Indian Head cents can vary widely. On the obverse the points to check include the details at the tips of the feathers and the diamonds on the ribbon. The diamonds *cannot* be used as a grading marker, and the feather tips can be used only if you have familiarity with how sharp the coin was struck to begin with. In general, the reverse is usually sharper, but check the leaf and shield details. On many bronze cents beginning in the 1870s the bottom of the N of ONE and the tops of the EN of CENT are light, as they were in the dies (this is not factored when grading). Check the denticles on both sides. Generally, copper-nickel cents of the early 1860s are candidates for light striking as are later issues in the bronze format, of the 1890s onward.

Availability. In worn grades Indian Head cents are available in proportion to their mintages, in combination with survival rates being higher for the later issues. (The low-mintage 1909-S was saved in larger quantities than the higher-mintage 1877, as an example.) MS coins survive as a matter of chance, with those of 1878 and before being much scarcer than those of 1879 and later, and some of the 1900s being readily available. Many if not most higher-grade MS coins have been dipped or recolored, unless they are a warm orange-red color with traces of natural brown. The search for quality among bronze cents is particularly challenging. Some tiny toning flecks are to be expected on many coins, and as long as they are microscopic they can often be ignored (except in grades on the far side of MS-65). A set of MS-65 coins in RB or RD can be formed quickly, but a collection with *original* color, sharp strike, and excellent eye appeal may take several years.

During the years these coins were in production, collectors who wanted single pieces each year often bought Proofs. In the late 1930s, many 1878–1909 Proof Indian Head cents began to be released from several estate hoards. These had vivid violet and blue iridescent toning from being stored for decades in tissue paper. They are highly sought-after today.

Proofs. Proof Indian Head cents were made of all dates 1859 to 1909. The 1864 bronze variety with a tiny L (for designer James B. Longacre) on the ribbon is a rarity, with only about two dozen known. Generally, Proofs are sharp strikes until the 1890s, when some can be weak. On bronze coins tiny carbon flecks are typical, but should be microscopic. If larger, avoid, and at PF-65 or higher, avoid as well. The majority of Proofs have been dipped, and many bronze pieces have been retoned. Most undipped coins are either rich brown (can be very attractive) or red and brown. The late John J. Pittman spent 50 years trying to find a Gem Proof 1907 Indian Head cent with brilliant original color! Cherrypicking is the order of the day. Extra value can be found in BN and RB, simply because investors won't buy them; instead, they are drawn to RD coins, most of which have been "improved" (dipped and retoned).

Proofs are generally designated BN if the surfaces are mainly brown or iridescent, or have up to perhaps 30 percent original mint red-orange color (there is little consistency, within the hobby community, in this determination). RB is the designation if the surface is a mixture of red-orange and brown, best if blended together nicely, but often with patches of mint color among brown areas. RD designates a coin with original (in theory) mint-red orange, always blending to slight natural brown toning unless the coin has been dipped. Likely, any RD coin with even a few hairlines has been cleaned (or at least mishandled) at one time; in most such cases, what appears to be mint-red color is not original. Certification services take no notice of this. For this reason, a connoisseur will prefer a gem BN coin with no hairlines to a PF-65 or 66, RD, coin with some hairlines. Proof copper-nickel Indian Head cents of 1859 to 1864 need no letter to indicate color, as their hue derives more from the nickel than the copper. As a general rule, these survive in higher grades and with greater eye appeal, as they stayed "brilliant" (the watchword for most collectors until recent decades) and did not need dipping. Moreover, when such pieces were cleaned and acquired hairlines, they tended to be fewer than on a bronze coin, due to the very hard nature of the copper-nickel alloy.

GRADING STANDARDS

Caveat: These grading standards do not take sharpness of strike into account.

MS-60 to 70 (Mint State). ***Obverse:*** Contact marks, most obvious in the field, are evident at MS-60, diminishing at MS-61, 62, and higher. This abrasion is most noticeable on copper-nickel cents, for it blends in with the background on bronze issues. The cheek of the Indian and the field show some evidence as well. Typical color is BN, occasionally RB at MS-63 and 64, unless dipped to be RD. At gem MS-65 or finer there is no trace of abrasion. A few tiny nicks or marks may be seen, but none are obvious. At MS-67 and finer the coin will approach perfection. Check "RD" coins for originality. A theoretically perfect MS-70 will have no marks at all, even under a strong magnifier. Although in practice this is not always consistent, at MS-66 and higher there should be no staining or other problems, and the coin should have good eye appeal overall. ***Reverse:*** Check the high parts of the wreath for abrasion. Otherwise the above comments apply.

MS-63

Illustrated coin: The surfaces display satin luster and a lovely pinkish-tan patina.

AU-50, 53, 55, 58 (About Uncirculated). ***Obverse:*** At AU-50, wear is most noticeable on the hair above the ear, on the central portion of the ribbon, on the curl to the right of the ribbon, and near the feather tips, although the last is not a reliable indicator due to striking. Luster is present, but mostly in protected areas. At AU-53 and 55, wear is less. At AU-58 friction is evident, rather than actual wear. Luster, toned brown, is nearly complete at AU-58, but may be incomplete in the field. ***Reverse:*** At AU-50, light wear is seen on the ribbon and the higher-relief areas of the leaves, while the lower areas retain their detail. Some luster may be present in protected areas. At AU 53 and 55, wear is less and luster is more extensive. An AU-58 coin will have nearly full luster and show only light friction.

AU-55

EF-40, 45 (Extremely Fine). ***Obverse:*** Wear is more extensive, but all of LIBERTY is very clear. Wear is seen on the hair above and below the ear, on the central portion of the ribbon, and on the feather tips. Overall the coin is bold. Scattered marks are normal for this and lower grades, most often seen on the cheek and in the field. ***Reverse:*** The higher-relief parts of the leaves and ribbon bow show light wear, but details are sharp in lower areas. Some tiny lines in the vertical stripes in the shield may be blended. Scattered marks may be present, but on all grades they are usually fewer on the reverse than on the obverse.

EF-45

VF-20, 30 (Very Fine). ***Obverse:*** Wear is more extensive. LIBERTY shows significant wear on BE, but it is sharp overall. Most hair detail is gone. The feather tips show greater wear (the extent of which will depend on the original strike). The ribbon and hair no longer show separation. ***Reverse:*** Wear is more extensive than at the preceding level, and many tiny vertical lines are fused together. Detail is still good on lower levels of the leaves.

VF-30

F-12, 15 (Fine). ***Obverse:*** Traditionally, the word LIBERTY should be fully readable, but weak on the higher letters of LIB. PCGS suggests this is true, but not if a coin was lightly struck. Full or incomplete, well-struck or lightly struck, no matter what the coin, most buyers still want the word to be discernible. Other areas have correspondingly more wear than on the next-higher grade. ***Reverse:*** The higher areas of the leaves and the bow show wear. The shield shows greater wear than at the preceding level. Overall, the reverse appears to be less worn than the obverse, this being generally true of all circulated grades.

F-15

VG-8, 10 (Very Good). ***Obverse:*** A total of at least three letters in LIBERTY must be visible. This can be a combination of several partial letters. PCGS does not adhere to this rule and suggests that wear on the feathers is a better indicator. The rim may blend into the field in areas, depending on striking. ***Reverse:*** Wear is even more extensive. Leaves on the left have hardly any detail, while those on the right may have limited detail. The rim is complete.

VG-10

G-4, 6 (Good). ***Obverse:*** The coin is worn flat, with the portrait visible mostly in outline form, with only slight indication of feathers. Lettering and date are complete. Part of the rim is usually gone. At G-6, the rim is clearer. ***Reverse:*** The wreath is nearly flat, although some hints of detail may be seen on the right side. All letters are readable, although the inscription is light at the center (on issues from the 1870s onward). The rim is discernible all around, but is light in areas. At G-6 the rim is clearly delineated.

Illustrated coin: The date is actually quite sharp for this grade.

G-6

AG-3 (About Good). ***Obverse:*** Most letters are worn away, as is the rim. The portrait is in outline form. The date is clearly readable, but may be weak or missing at the bottom. ***Reverse:*** Extensive wear prevails, although the rim will usually be more discernible than on the obverse. Most lettering, or sometimes all, is readable.

AG-3

PF-60 to 70 (Proof). ***Obverse and Reverse:*** Gem PF-65 coins will have very few hairlines, and these are visible only under a strong magnifying glass. At any level and color, a Proof with hairlines likely (though not necessarily) has been cleaned. At PF-67 or higher there should be no evidence of hairlines or friction at all. Such a coin is fully original. PF-60 coins can be dull from repeated dipping and cleaning and are often toned iridescent colors. At PF-63 the mirrorlike fields should be attractive, and hairlines should be minimal. These are easiest to see when the coin is held at an angle to the light. No rubbing is seen. PF-64 coins are even nicer.

PF-64RB

1860, Rounded Bust

1860, Pointed Bust

Circulation Strikes

	Mintage	GSID	G-4	VG-8	F-12	VF-20	EF-40	AU-50	MS-60	MS-63
Indian Head, Laurel Wreath Reverse (1859)	**n/a**	**72335**	**$13.50**	**$17.50**	**$24.00**	**$50.00**	**$145**	**$215**	**$430**	**$875**
Indian Head, Oak Wreath with Shield Reverse, Copper-Nickel (1860–1864)	**n/a**	**72336**	**11.50**	**13.00**	**16.00**	**32.00**	**60**	**95**	**210**	**440**
Indian Head, Oak Wreath with Shield Reverse, Bronze (1864–1909), Brown	**n/a**	**72337**	**1.60**	**2.20**	**2.60**	**4.10**	**8**	**24**	**47**	**95**
Same, Red Brown	**n/a**	**72338**	**—**	**—**	**—**	**—**	**—**	**—**	**60**	**115**
Same, Red	**n/a**	**72339**	**—**	**—**	**—**	**—**	**—**	**—**	**—**	**235**
1859	36,400,000	1289	13.50	17.50	24.00	50.00	145	215	430	875
↳**1859, Repunched Date, FS-301, S-1**	*	285502	16.00	21.00	29.00	60.00	310	650	1,550	2,400
1860, Rounded Bust	20,566,000	1291	12.00	17.50	22.00	49.00	70	110	240	500
1860, Pointed Bust	*	1290	20.00	34.00	40.00	75.00	110	210	375	725
↳**1860, Pointed Bust, FS-401**	*	285505	20.00	34.00	40.00	75.00	110	210	375	725
1861	10,100,000	1292	31.00	34.00	47.00	70.00	110	155	240	500
↳**1861, Repunched Date, FS-301, S-1**	*	285506	34.00	37.00	50.00	75.00	120	170	265	550

* Included in number above.

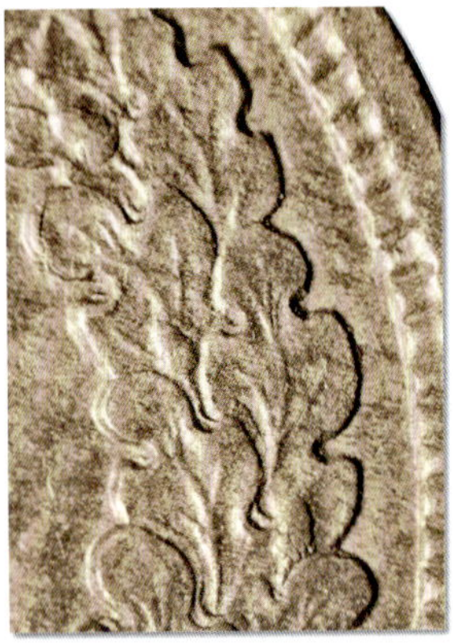

1863, Doubled Die Reverse FS-801.

1864, No L

1864, With L

1865, Die Gouge in Headdress
FS-1401

1865, Doubled Die Reverse
FS-1801

Circulation Strikes *(continued)*

	Mintage	GSID	G-4	VG-8	F-12	VF-20	EF-40	AU-50	MS-60	MS-63
1862	28,075,000	1293	$11.50	$13	$16	$32	$60	$95	$210	$440
↳1862, Misplaced Date, FS-301, S-2	*	285507	12.50	14	18	36	65	105	230	485
1863	49,840,000	1294	11.50	13	16	32	60	95	210	440
↳1863, Doubled Die Reverse, FS-801, S-10	*	285511	12.50	14	18	36	65	105	230	485
1864, Copper-Nickel	13,740,000	1295	24.00	32	39	45	90	130	260	495
1864, Bronze, No L, Brown	39,233,714	1296	16.00	24	30	55	75	90	130	190
1864, Bronze, No L, Red Brown	*	1297	—	—	—	—	—	—	—	290
1864, Bronze, No L, Red	*	1298	—	—	—	—	—	—	—	495
1864, Bronze, With L, Brown	*	1452	55.00	90	150	195	245	325	430	550
↳1864, Bronze, With L, Repunched Date, FS-2301, S-1, Brown	*	285523	60.00	100	165	215	270	360	470	600
↳1864, Bronze, With L, Repunched Date, FS-2305, S-2, Brown	*	285524	60.00	100	165	215	270	360	470	600
↳1864, Bronze, With L, Repunched Date, FS-2306, S-10, Brown	*	285528	60.00	100	165	215	270	360	470	600
1864, Bronze, With L, Red Brown	*	1453	—	—	—	—	—	—	625	825
1864, Bronze, With L, Red	*	1454	—	—	—	—	—	—	—	1,200
1865, Fancy 5, Brown	35,429,286	1299	16.00	20	32	40	55	80	110	210
↳1865, Fancy 5, Doubled Die Reverse, FS-1801, S-2, Brown	*	285542	18.00	22	36	45	60	90	120	230
↳1865, Fancy 5, Obverse Die Gouge, FS-1401, S-14, Brown	*	285544	18.00	22	36	45	60	90	120	230
1865, Fancy 5, Red Brown	*	1300	—	—	—	—	—	—	145	325
1865, Fancy 5, Red	*	1301	—	—	—	—	—	—	—	525
1865, Plain 5, Brown	*	1302	16.00	20	32	45	65	95	135	235
↳1865, Plain 5, Misplaced Date, FS-304, S-2, Brown	*	285554	18.00	22	36	49	70	105	150	255
1865, Plain 5, Red Brown	*	1303	—	—	—	—	—	—	—	390
1865, Plain 5, Red	*	1304	—	—	—	—	—	—	—	775

* Included in number above.

1867, 67 Over 67
FS-301

1869, 69 Over 69
FS-301

Shallow N

Bold N

1870, Doubled Die Reverse
FS-801

Circulation Strikes *(continued)*

	Mintage	GSID	G-4	VG-8	F-12	VF-20	EF-40	AU-50	MS-60	MS-63
1866, Brown	9,826,500	1305	$60	$75	$95	$135	$170	$245	$390	$525
↳1866, Doubled Die Obverse, FS-101, S-1, Brown	*	285565	65	85	105	165	390	455	675	1,500
↳1866, Repunched Date, FS-301, S-2, Brown	*	285566	65	85	105	150	185	270	430	575
↳1866, Repunched Date, FS-303, S-9, Brown	*	285568	65	85	105	150	185	270	430	575
1866, Red Brown	*	1306	—	—	—	—	—	—	—	650
1866, Red	*	1307	—	—	—	—	—	—	—	1,400
1867, Brown	9,821,000	1308	60	80	105	135	175	245	345	455
↳1867, Repunched Date, FS-303, S-2, Brown	*	285577	65	90	115	145	195	270	380	500
1867, Red Brown	*	1309	—	—	—	—	—	—	390	650
1867, Red	*	1310	—	—	—	—	—	—	—	950
1867, 67 Over 67, Brown	*	1455	100	180	235	360	725	950	1,550	2,400
↳1867, 67 Over 67, FS-301, S-1, Brown	*	285583	100	180	235	360	725	950	1,550	2,400
1867, 67 Over 67, Red Brown	*	1456	—	—	—	—	—	—	—	3,000
1867, 67 Over 67, Red	*	1457	—	—	—	—	—	—	—	—
1868, Brown	10,266,500	1311	60	80	105	135	195	260	330	440
↳1868, Doubled Die Obverse, FS-101, S-1, Brown	*	285586	65	90	115	150	215	285	365	485
↳1868, Misplaced Date, FS-301, S-8, Brown	*	285589	65	90	115	150	215	285	365	485
1868, Red Brown	*	1312	—	—	—	—	—	—	—	500
1868, Red	*	1313	—	—	—	—	—	—	—	1,300
1869, Brown	6,420,000	1314	95	130	230	290	455	550	775	900
1869, Red Brown	*	1315	—	—	—	—	—	—	—	1,150
1869, Red	*	1316	—	—	—	—	—	—	—	1,300
1869, 69 Over 69, Brown	*	331610	115	155	275	350	500	575	775	900
↳1869, 69 Over 69, FS-302, S-1, Brown	*	285601	115	155	275	350	500	575	775	900
↳1869, 69 Over 69, FS-301, S-3, Brown	*	70644	175	235	490	650	775	1,050	1,250	1,600
1869, 69 Over 69, Red Brown	*	331611	—	—	—	—	—	—	—	1,150
1869, 69 Over 69, Red	*	331612	—	—	—	—	—	—	—	1,300
1870, Brown	5,275,000	1317	70	135	195	260	435	500	675	850
↳1870, Doubled Die Obverse/Doubled Die Reverse, FS-101/801, S-2, Brown	*	285611	75	150	215	285	480	550	725	925
↳1870, Pick Axe, FS-303, Brown	*	285616	75	150	215	285	480	550	725	925
↳1870, Shallow N, FS-901, Brown	*	285617	75	150	215	285	480	550	725	925
1870, Red Brown	*	1318	—	—	—	—	—	—	—	1,000
1870, Red	*	1319	—	—	—	—	—	—	—	1,500

Note: Cents dated 1869 and earlier have a shallow N in ONE. Those dated 1870, 1871, or 1872 have either shallow N or bold N, except Proofs of 1872, which were struck only with the bold N, not the shallow N. Those dated 1873 to 1876 all have the bold N. Circulation strikes of 1877 have the shallow N, while Proofs have the bold N. * Included in number above.

1873, Close 3

1873, Open 3

1873, Doubled LIBERTY
FS-101

1875, Dot Reverse
FS-801

Circulation Strikes *(continued)*

	Mintage	GSID	G-4	VG-8	F-12	VF-20	EF-40	AU-50	MS-60	MS-63
1871, Brown	3,929,500	1320	$90	$130	$195	$235	$490	$575	$725	$850
↳1871, Date Variety, FS-301, S-2, Brown	*	285636	100	135	215	255	525	650	775	925
↳1871, Shallow N, FS-901, Brown	*	285634	100	135	215	255	575	775	1,000	1,900
1871, Red Brown	*	1321	—	—	—	—	—	—	—	1,000
1871, Red	*	1322	—	—	—	—	—	—	—	2,250
1872, Brown	4,042,000	1323	110	150	235	365	480	575	875	1,000
↳1872, Repunched Date, FS-301, S-1, Brown	*	285640	—	—	—	—	—	—	—	—
1872, Red Brown	*	1324	—	—	—	—	—	—	1,250	1,900
1872, Red	*	1325	—	—	—	—	—	—	—	3,250
	Auctions: $126,500, PCGS MS-66 HA 08/07									
1873, Open 3, Brown	11,676,500	1326	24	49	75	95	180	235	325	470
↳1873, Open 3, Repunched Date, FS-1301, S-1, Brown	*	285646	27	55	80	105	200	255	360	525
1873, Open 3, Red Brown	*	1327	—	—	—	—	—	—	—	625
1873, Open 3, Red	*	1328	—	—	—	—	—	—	—	1,000
1873, Closed 3, Brown	*	1329	30	60	85	105	210	285	420	550
↳1873, Closed 3, Doubled Die Obverse, FS-102, S-2, Brown	*	285653	—	—	—	285	360	450	850	1,450
1873, Closed 3, Red Brown	*	1330	—	—	—	—	—	—	—	775
1873, Closed 3, Red	*	1331	—	—	—	—	—	—	—	1,400
1873, Closed 3, Doubled LIBERTY, Brown	*	1332	260	360	650	1,200	2,750	3,450	4,750	7,750
↳1873, Closed 3, Doubled LIBERTY, FS-101, S-1, Brown	*	285652	260	360	650	1,200	2,750	3,450	4,750	7,750
1873, Closed 3, Doubled LIBERTY, Red Brown	*	1333	—	—	—	—	—	—	—	8,250
1873, Closed 3, Doubled LIBERTY, Red	*	1334	—	—	—	—	—	—	—	15,000
1874, Brown	14,187,500	1335	24	40	70	75	100	135	200	275
↳1874, Doubled Die Obverse, FS-101, S-1, Brown	*	285658	—	—	—	—	—	—	—	—
1874, Red Brown	*	1336	—	—	—	—	—	—	—	360
1874, Red	*	1337	—	—	—	—	—	—	—	625
1875, Brown	13,528,000	1338	24	40	70	75	130	175	240	305
↳1875, Repunched Date, FS-301, S-1, Brown	*	285661	24	40	70	75	130	175	240	305
↳1875, Possible Die Alteration, FS-801, S-16, Brown (a)	*	285664	—	—	—	—	—	—	—	850
1875, Red Brown	*	1339	—	—	—	—	—	—	—	405
1875, Red	*	1340	—	—	—	—	—	—	—	430

Note: Cents dated 1869 and earlier have a shallow N in ONE. Those dated 1870, 1871, or 1872 have either shallow N or bold N, except Proofs of 1872, which were struck only with the bold N, not the shallow N. Those dated 1873 to 1876 all have the bold N. Circulation strikes of 1877 have the shallow N, while Proofs have the bold N. * Included in number above. **a.** In 1875 Mint officials suspected a longtime employee was stealing Indian Head cents. They secretly modified a reverse die by making a small gouge in the N in ONE, and then put the die into production one morning. Later that morning the suspect employee was called aside. He was asked to empty his pockets, revealing 33 of the marked cents. At first he insisted his son gave him this pocket change, but when confronted with the secretly marked die, he admitted his guilt. He tendered his resignation, disgraced, after more than 50 years of service to the Mint. The market value for this variety is not yet reliably established.

1880, Doubled Die Obverse, Reverse Clash
FS-101

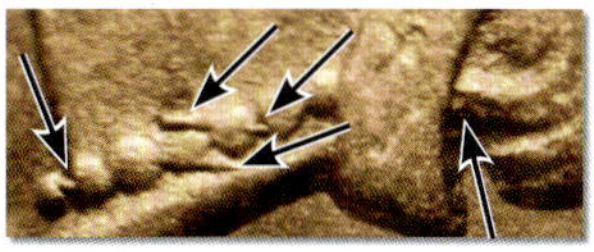

1882, Misplaced Date
FS-401

Circulation Strikes *(continued)*

	Mintage	GSID	G-4	VG-8	F-12	VF-20	EF-40	AU-50	MS-60	MS-63
1876, Brown	7,944,000	1341	$38.00	$50.00	$90.00	$145.00	$200	$275	$330	$365
1876, Red Brown	*	1342	—	—	—	—	—	—	—	455
1876, Red	*	1343	—	—	—	—	—	—	—	900
1877, Brown (b)	852,500	1344	575.00	950.00	1,150.00	1,550.00	2,700	3,450	5,250	7,750
1877, Red Brown (b)	*	1345	—	—	—	—	—	—	—	9,500
1877, Red (b)	*	1346	—	—	—	—	—	—	—	10,500
	Auctions: $149,500, PCGS MS-66 HA 08/07									
1878, Brown	5,797,500	1347	34.00	43.00	80.00	160.00	200	275	350	390
1878, Red Brown	*	1348	—	—	—	—	—	—	—	490
1878, Red	*	1349	—	—	—	—	—	—	—	775
1879, Brown	16,228,000	1350	8.00	11.00	20.00	40.00	70	80	95	170
1879, Red Brown	*	1351	—	—	—	—	—	—	135	235
1879, Red	*	1352	—	—	—	—	—	—	—	420
1880, Brown	38,961,000	1353	4.10	4.10	8.00	13.00	31	49	70	100
↳**1880, Doubled Die Obverse, Misaligned Die Clash Reverse, FS-101, S-1, Brown**	*	285676	—	—	—	—	—	—	—	—
1880, Red Brown	*	1354	—	—	—	—	—	—	—	180
1880, Red	*	1355	—	—	—	—	—	—	—	575
1881, Brown	39,208,000	1356	4.10	4.10	8.00	9.50	27	38	60	105
1881, Red Brown	*	1357	—	—	—	—	—	—	—	195
1881, Red	*	1358	—	—	—	—	—	—	—	430
1882, Brown	38,578,000	1359	4.10	4.10	8.00	11.00	27	38	60	115
↳**1882, Misplaced Date, FS-302, S-6, Brown**	*	285680	—	—	—	—	—	—	—	—
1882, Red Brown	*	1360	—	—	—	—	—	—	—	180
1882, Red	*	1361	—	—	—	—	—	—	—	440
1883, Brown	45,591,500	1362	4.10	4.10	6.75	9.50	23	34	60	120
↳**1883, Misplaced Date, FS-303, S-1, Brown**	*	285685	—	4.90	8.00	11.50	28	40	75	140
↳**1883, Doubled Die Reverse, FS-801, S-6, Brown**	*	285686	—	4.90	8.00	11.50	28	40	75	140
↳**1883, Misaligned Die Clash Obverse, FS-401, S-11, Brown**	*	285689	—	4.90	8.00	11.50	28	40	75	140
1883, Red Brown	*	1363	—	—	—	—	—	—	—	160
1883, Red	*	1364	—	—	—	—	—	—	—	325

Note: Cents dated 1869 and earlier have a shallow N in ONE. Those dated 1870, 1871, or 1872 have either shallow N or bold N, except Proofs of 1872, which were struck only with the bold N, not the shallow N. Those dated 1873 to 1876 all have the bold N. Circulation strikes of 1877 have the shallow N, while Proofs have the bold N. * Included in number above. **b.** Beware the numerous counterfeits and altered-date 1877 cents. The latter typically are altered from 1875- or 1879-dated cents.

1886, Variety 1
The last feather points between the I and the C in AMERICA.

1886, Variety 2
The last feather points between the C and the A in AMERICA.

1887, Doubled Die Obverse
FS-101

1888, Last 8 Over 7
FS-301

Circulation Strikes *(continued)*

	Mintage	GSID	G-4	VG-8	F-12	VF-20	EF-40	AU-50	MS-60	MS-63
1884, Brown	23,257,800	1365	$5.50	$8.00	$8.00	$17.50	$35	$49	$80	$130
1884, Red Brown	*	1366	—	—	—	—	—	—	—	170
1884, Red	*	1367	—	—	—	—	—	—	—	575
1885, Brown	11,761,594	1368	12.00	13.50	16.00	34.00	75	95	130	180
1885, Red Brown	*	1369	—	—	—	—	—	—	—	245
1885, Red	*	1370	—	—	—	—	—	—	—	455
1886, Variety 1, Brown	17,650,000	1371	6.75	12.00	22.00	70.00	170	195	220	280
1886, Variety 1, Red Brown	*	1372	—	—	—	—	—	—	—	420
1886, Variety 1, Red	*	1373	—	—	—	—	—	—	—	900
1886, Variety 2, Brown	*	1374	11.00	17.50	38.00	105.00	195	260	290	525
1886, Variety 2, Red Brown	*	1375	—	—	—	—	—	—	—	950
1886, Variety 2, Red	*	1376	—	—	—	—	—	—	—	2,200
1887, Brown	45,223,523	1377	3.40	3.40	4.70	6.50	23	35	55	115
↳1887, Doubled Die Obverse, FS-101, S-1, Brown	*	285703	—	—	—	—	—	—	—	—
1887, Red Brown	*	1378	—	—	—	—	—	—	—	180
1887, Red	*	1379	—	—	—	—	—	—	—	495
1888, Brown	37,489,832	1380	4.10	4.10	4.40	8.75	24	27	85	175
1888, Red Brown	*	1381	—	—	—	—	—	—	—	220
1888, Red	*	1382	—	—	—	—	—	—	—	440
1888, 8 Over 7, Brown	*	1458	1,250.00	2,000.00	3,600.00	5,250.00	7,750	12,000	34,000	45,500
↳1888, 8 Over 7, Overdate, FS-301, S-1, Brown	*	285715	1,250.00	2,000.00	3,600.00	5,250.00	7,750	12,000	34,000	45,500
1888, 8 Over 7, Red Brown	*	1459	—	—	—	—	—	—	—	53,000
1888, 8 Over 7, Red	*	285717	—	—	—	—	—	—	—	90,000
1889, Brown	48,866,025	1383	1.60	2.60	3.40	5.50	14	27	55	105
↳1889, Doubled Die Reverse, FS-801, S-1, Brown	*	285719	—	—	90.00	120.00	—	—	—	—
↳1889, Repunched Date, FS-302, S-4, Brown	*	285720	—	—	13.00	19.00	40	70	125	—
↳1889, Repunched Date, FS-301, S-12, Brown	*	285722	55.00	80.00	120.00	145.00	210	285	470	—
1889, Red Brown	*	1384	—	—	—	—	—	—	120	155
1889, Red	*	1385	—	—	—	—	—	—	—	340
1890, Brown	57,180,144	1386	1.60	2.60	3.40	4.40	11	32	75	110
↳1890, Quadrupled Die Obverse, FS-101, S-1, Brown	*	285734	—	—	—	—	—	—	—	—
↳1890, Misplaced Date, FS-301, S-3, Brown	*	285735	—	—	—	—	—	—	—	—
1890, Red Brown	*	1387	—	—	—	—	—	—	—	195
1890, Red	*	1388	—	—	—	—	—	—	—	235

* Included in number above.

1891, Doubled Die Obverse
FS-101

1894, Doubled Date
FS-301

Circulation Strikes *(continued)*

	Mintage	GSID	G-4	VG-8	F-12	VF-20	EF-40	AU-50	MS-60	MS-63
1891, Brown	47,070,000	1389	$1.60	$2.60	$3.40	$4.40	$12	$27	$60	$110
↳1891, Doubled Die Obverse, FS-101, S-1, Brown	*	285746	—	—	—	—	—	—	—	—
↳1891, Repunched Date, FS-301, S-3, Brown	*	285747	—	—	—	—	—	—	—	—
1891, Red Brown	*	1390	—	—	—	—	—	—	—	150
1891, Red	*	1391	—	—	—	—	—	—	—	310
1892, Brown	37,647,087	1392	2.60	3.00	4.10	5.50	14	27	60	130
↳1892, Repunched Date, Doubled Die Reverse, FS-302, S-1, Brown	*	285752	—	—	—	—	—	—	—	—
↳1892, "Scarface", FS-401, S-14, Brown	*	285754	—	—	—	—	—	—	—	—
1892, Red Brown	*	1393	—	—	—	—	—	—	—	150
1892, Red	*	1394	—	—	—	—	—	—	—	415
1893, Brown	46,640,000	1395	2.40	2.60	3.40	4.70	11	27	60	120
1893, Red Brown	*	1396	—	—	—	—	—	—	—	130
1893, Red	*	1397	—	—	—	—	—	—	—	365
1894, Brown	16,749,500	1398	6.50	8.00	16.00	22.00	50	70	100	155
1894, Red Brown	*	1399	—	—	—	—	—	—	—	180
1894, Red	*	1400	—	—	—	—	—	—	—	260
1894, Doubled Date, Brown	*	1401	80.00	100.00	130.00	195.00	455	1,000	1,500	2,400
↳1894, 1894 Over 1894, FS-301, S-1, Brown	*	285767	80.00	100.00	130.00	195.00	455	1,000	1,500	2,400
1894, Doubled Date, Red Brown	*	1402	—	—	—	—	—	—	—	2,500
1894, Doubled Date, Red	*	1403	—	—	—	—	—	—	—	—
1895, Brown	38,341,574	1404	1.60	2.20	2.60	4.10	8	30	55	115
↳1895, Repunched Date, FS-301, S-1, Brown	*	285770	—	—	—	—	—	—	—	—
1895, Red Brown	*	1405	—	—	—	—	—	—	—	125
1895, Red	*	1406	—	—	—	—	—	—	—	290
1896, Brown	39,055,431	1407	1.60	2.20	2.60	4.10	8	27	55	110
↳1896, Date Variety, FS-302, S-21, Brown	*	285780	—	—	—	—	—	—	—	—
1896, Red Brown	*	1408	—	—	—	—	—	—	—	125
1896, Red	*	1409	—	—	—	—	—	—	—	245
1897, Brown	50,464,392	1410	1.60	2.20	2.60	4.10	8	28	55	100
1897, Red Brown	*	1411	—	—	—	—	—	—	—	120
1897, Red	*	1412	—	—	—	—	—	—	—	265
1897, 1 in Neck, Brown	*	1413	47.00	75.00	110.00	160.00	260	325	725	1,400
↳1897, Misplaced Date, 1 in Neck, FS-401, S-1, Brown	*	234572	47.00	75.00	110.00	160.00	260	325	725	1,400
1897, 1 in Neck, Red Brown	*	1414	—	—	—	—	—	—	—	2,000
1897, 1 in Neck, Red	*	1415	—	—	—	—	—	—	—	3,100
1898, Brown	49,821,284	1416	1.60	2.20	2.60	4.10	8	24	47	100
1898, Red Brown	*	1417	—	—	—	—	—	—	115	160
1898, Red	*	1418	—	—	—	—	—	—	—	235

* Included in number above.

Circulation Strikes *(continued)*

	Mintage	GSID	G-4	VG-8	F-12	VF-20	EF-40	AU-50	MS-60	MS-63
1899, Brown	53,598,000	1419	$1.60	$2.20	$2.60	$4.10	$8	$24	$47	$95
↳1899, Repunched Date, FS-303, S-9, Brown	*	285795	—	—	—	—	—	—	—	—
1899, Red Brown	*	1420	—	—	—	—	—	—	—	115
1899, Red	*	1421	—	—	—	—	—	—	—	255
	Auctions: $108,000, PCGS MS-68 HA 08/19									
1900, Brown	66,831,502	1422	1.60	2.20	2.60	4.10	8	24	47	95
	Auctions: $141,000, PCGS MS-65 HA 04/15									
↳1900, 19 Over 19, Last 0 Over 0, FS-302, S-3, Brown	*	285804	—	—	—	—	—	—	—	—
1900, Red Brown	*	1423	—	—	—	—	—	—	—	115
1900, Red	*	1424	—	—	—	—	—	—	—	235
1901, Brown	79,609,158	1425	1.60	2.20	2.60	4.10	8	24	47	95
1901, Red Brown	*	1426	—	—	—	—	—	—	—	115
1901, Red	*	1427	—	—	—	—	—	—	—	235
1902, Brown	87,374,704	1428	1.60	2.20	2.60	4.10	8	24	47	95
↳1902, Die Gouge, FS-401, S-4, Brown	*	285812	—	—	—	—	—	—	—	—
1902, Red Brown	*	1429	—	—	—	—	—	—	—	115
1902, Red	*	1430	—	—	—	—	—	—	—	235
	Auctions: $144,000, PCGS MS-68 SBG 06/22									
1903, Brown	85,092,703	1431	1.60	2.20	2.60	4.10	8	24	47	95
1903, Red Brown	*	1432	—	—	—	—	—	—	—	115
1903, Red	*	1433	—	—	—	—	—	—	—	235
1904, Brown	61,326,198	1434	1.60	2.20	2.60	4.10	8	24	47	95
↳1904, Repunched Date, FS-301, S-10, Brown	*	285827	—	—	—	—	—	—	—	—
1904, Red Brown	*	1435	—	—	—	—	—	—	—	115
1904, Red	*	1436	—	—	—	—	—	—	—	235
1905, Brown	80,717,011	1437	1.60	2.20	2.60	4.10	8	24	47	95
	Auctions: $123,375, PCGS MS-64 HA 04/15									
1905, Red Brown	*	1438	—	—	—	—	—	—	—	115
1905, Red	*	1439	—	—	—	—	—	—	—	235
	Auctions: $253,000, PCGS MS-64 HA 01/10									
1906, Brown	96,020,530	1440	1.60	2.20	2.60	4.10	8	24	47	95
	Auctions: $276,000, NGC AU-58 SBG 09/09									
↳1906, Repunched Date, FS-303, S-20, Brown	*	285835	—	—	—	—	—	—	—	—
1906, Red Brown	*	1441	—	—	—	—	—	—	—	115
1906, Red	*	1442	—	—	—	—	—	—	—	235
1907, Brown	108,137,143	1443	1.60	2.20	2.60	4.10	8	24	47	95
↳1907, Repunched Date, FS-302, S-2, Brown	*	285843	—	—	—	—	—	—	—	—
1907, Red Brown	*	1444	—	—	—	—	—	—	—	115
1907, Red	*	1445	—	—	—	—	—	—	—	235
1908, Brown	32,326,367	1446	1.60	2.20	2.60	4.10	8	24	47	95
1908, Red Brown	*	1447	—	—	—	—	—	—	—	115
1908, Red	*	1448	—	—	—	—	—	—	—	235

* Included in number above.

Circulation Strikes *(continued)*

	Mintage	GSID	G-4	VG-8	F-12	VF-20	EF-40	AU-50	MS-60	MS-63
1908-S, Brown	1,115,000	1461	$80.00	$95.00	$110.00	$130	$175	$220	$325	$525
↳1908-S, Repunched Mintmark, FS-501, S-1, Brown	*	285859	—	—	—	—	—	—	—	—
1908-S, Red Brown	*	1462	—	—	—	—	—	—	410	700
1908-S, Red	*	1463	—	—	—	—	—	—	—	1,150
1909, Brown	14,368,470	1449	5.50	8.00	9.50	12	20	32	47	95
1909, Red Brown	*	1450	—	—	—	—	—	—	—	115
1909, Red	*	1451	—	—	—	—	—	—	—	235
1909-S, Brown	309,000	1464	305.00	325.00	410.00	455	625	775	1,200	1,600
1909-S, Red Brown	*	1465	—	—	—	—	—	—	—	1,750
1909-S, Red	*	1466	—	—	—	—	—	—	—	1,950

* Included in number above.

Proof Strikes

	Mintage	GSID	PF-60	PF-63	PF-65
Indian Head, Laurel Wreath Reverse (1859)	**n/a**	**73858**	**$1,100**	**$1,900**	**$4,250**
Same, Cameo (1859)	**n/a**	**80955**	**—**	**3,100**	**8,750**
Indian Head, Oak Wreath with Shield Reverse, Copper-Nickel (1860–1864)	**n/a**	**73859**	**525**	**875**	**2,000**
Same, Cameo (1860–1864)	**n/a**	**80957**	**—**	**1,250**	**2,900**
Same, Deep Cameo (1860–1864)	**n/a**	**80958**	**—**	**2,500**	**9,500**
Indian Head, Oak Wreath with Shield Reverse, Bronze (1864–1909), Brown	**n/a**	**73860**	**155**	**285**	**525**
Same, Red Brown	**n/a**	**73861**	**195**	**340**	**725**
Same, Red	**n/a**	**73862**	**285**	**390**	**1,100**
Same, Red Cameo	**n/a**	**80959**	**—**	**850**	**1,550**
1859	800	1467	1,100	1,900	4,250
↳1859, Cameo	*	1468	—	3,100	8,750
1860	1,000	1470	525	875	3,100
↳1860, Cameo	*	1471	—	—	5,500
1861	1,000	1473	850	1,900	5,750
↳1861, Cameo	*	1474	—	3,450	9,500
1862	550	1476	525	875	2,000
↳1862, Cameo	*	1477	—	1,250	2,900
1863	460	1479	525	875	2,400
↳1863, Cameo	*	1480	—	1,250	3,750
1864, Copper-Nickel	370	1482	525	875	2,500
↳1864, Copper-Nickel, Cameo	*	1489	—	1,250	3,750
1864, Bronze, No L, Brown	800	1486	420	950	1,700
1864, Bronze, No L, Red Brown	*	1484	—	$1,150	$2,250
1864, Bronze, No L, Red	*	1485	—	1,450	3,750
↳1864, Bronze, No L, Red Cameo	*	1487	—	—	14,500
1864, Bronze, With L, Brown	20	1718	$18,000	31,000	65,000
	Auctions: $129,250, PCGS PF-66 HA 09/13				
1864, Bronze, With L, Red Brown	*	1719	—	36,000	78,000
	Auctions: $161,000, PCGS PF-65 HA 10/11				
1864, Bronze, With L, Red	*	1720	—	78,000	144,000
	Auctions: $141,000, NGC PF-65 HA 09/13				
↳1864, Bronze, With L, Red Cameo	*	1491	—	84,000	120,000
	Auctions: $152,750, PCGS PF-65 HA 05/16				
1865, Brown	500	1493	195	390	775
1865, Red Brown	*	1494	—	650	1,750
1865, Red	*	1495	—	775	6,250
↳1865, Red Cameo	*	1496	—	—	17,500
1866, Brown	725	1498	170	300	525
1866, Red Brown	*	1499	—	525	1,250
1866, Red	*	1500	—	1,250	3,000
↳1866, Red Cameo	*	1501	—	—	4,000
1867, Brown	625	1503	170	300	650
1867, Red Brown	*	1504	—	525	1,200
1867, Red	*	1505	—	1,150	4,400
↳1867, Red Cameo	*	1506	—	1,750	8,000
1868, Brown	600	1508	210	350	775
1868, Red Brown	*	1509	—	405	1,000
1868, Red	*	1510	—	650	3,250
↳1868, Red Cameo	*	1511	—	—	4,500

* Included in number above.

Proof Strikes *(continued)*

	Mintage	GSID	PF-60	PF-63	PF-65
1869, Brown	600	1513	$455	$850	$1,250
1869, Red Brown	*	1514	—	950	1,600
1869, Red	*	1515	—	1,150	2,800
↳1869, Red Cameo	*	1516	—	—	3,750
1870, Brown	1000	1518	390	650	1,250
1870, Red Brown	*	1519	—	800	2,750
1870, Red	*	1520	—	1,000	3,250
↳1870, Red Cameo	*	1521	—	1,750	5,000
1871, Brown	960	1523	455	750	1,500
1871, Red Brown	*	1524	—	875	2,000
1871, Red	*	1525	—	1,100	2,700
↳1871, Red Cameo	*	1526	—	—	8,000
1872, Brown	850	1528	390	650	1,700
1872, Red Brown	*	1529	—	800	2,050
1872, Red	*	1530	—	950	4,400
↳1872, Red Cameo	*	1531	—	—	6,250
1873, Closed 3, Brown	*	1533	220	365	850
1873, Closed 3, Red Brown	*	1534	260	440	1,000
1873, Closed 3, Red	*	1535	—	775	2,750
↳1873, Closed 3, Red Cameo	*	1536	—	—	3,250
1874, Brown	700	1538	195	415	850
1874, Red Brown	*	1539	—	470	1,150
1874, Red	*	1540	—	575	3,250
↳1874, Red Cameo	*	1541	—	1,250	2,900
1875, Brown	700	1543	210	420	950
1875, Red Brown	*	1544	—	500	1,600
1875, Red	*	1545	—	650	5,500
↳1875, Red Cameo	*	1546	—	2,050	10,000
1876, Brown	1,150	1548	260	420	850
1876, Red Brown	*	1549	—	525	1,150
1876, Red	*	1550	—	625	2,050
↳1876, Red Cameo	*	1551	—	—	3,500
1877, Brown	900	1553	3,750	4,500	6,000
1877, Red Brown	*	1554	3,900	5,000	7,000
1877, Red	*	1555	—	4,750	11,500
↳1877, Red Cameo	*	1556	—	—	18,000
1878, Brown	2,350	1558	155	285	525
1878, Red Brown	*	1559	195	340	900
1878, Red	*	1560	340	470	1,300
↳1878, Red Cameo	*	1561	—	900	2,400
1879, Brown	3,200	1563	155	285	525
1879, Red Brown	*	1564	195	340	775
1879, Red	*	1565	285	390	1,100
↳1879, Red Cameo	*	1566	—	—	2,800
1880, Brown	3,955	1568	155	285	525
1880, Red Brown	*	1569	195	340	725
1880, Red	*	1570	285	390	1,100
↳1880, Red Cameo	*	1571	—	—	1,750

	Mintage	GSID	PF-60	PF-63	PF-65
1881, Brown	3,575	1573	$155	$285	$525
1881, Red Brown	*	1574	195	340	725
1881, Red	*	1575	285	390	1,250
↳1881, Red Cameo	*	1576	—	850	1,550
1882, Brown	3,100	1578	155	285	525
1882, Red Brown	*	1579	195	340	725
1882, Red	*	1580	285	390	1,100
↳1882, Red Cameo	*	1581	—	—	3,000
1883, Brown	6,609	1583	155	285	525
1883, Red Brown	*	1584	195	340	725
1883, Red	*	1585	285	390	1,100
↳1883, Red Cameo	*	1586	—	—	2,500
1884, Brown	3,942	1588	155	285	525
1884, Red Brown	*	1589	195	340	725
1884, Red	*	1590	285	390	1,100
↳1884, Red Cameo	*	1591	—	—	2,500
1885, Brown	3,790	1593	155	285	525
1885, Red Brown	*	1594	195	340	725
1885, Red	*	1595	285	390	1,100
↳1885, Red Cameo	*	1596	—	—	4,400
1886, Variety 1, Brown	4,290	1598	155	330	575
1886, Variety 1, Red Brown	*	1599	195	385	775
1886, Variety 1, Red	*	1600	390	575	1,750
1886, Variety 2, Brown	*	1601	290	455	1,250
1886, Variety 2, Red Brown	*	1602	390	625	1,800
1886, Variety 2, Red	*	1603	525	1,250	10,500
1887, Brown	2,960	1604	155	285	525
1887, Red Brown	*	1605	195	340	725
1887, Red	*	1606	285	525	3,100
↳1887, Red Cameo	*	1607	—	—	7,000
1888, Brown	4,582	1609	155	285	525
1888, Red Brown	*	1610	195	340	725
1888, Red	*	1611	285	390	3,750
↳1888, Red Cameo	*	1612	—	—	9,500
1889, Brown	3,336	1614	155	285	525
1889, Red Brown	*	1615	195	340	725
1889, Red	*	1616	340	525	2,400
↳1889, Red Cameo	*	1617	—	—	5,750
1890, Brown	2,740	1619	155	285	525
1890, Red Brown	*	1620	195	340	725
1890, Red	*	1621	285	390	1,100
↳1890, Red Cameo	*	1622	—	1,500	7,500
1891, Brown	2,350	1624	155	285	525
1891, Red Brown	*	1625	195	340	725
1891, Red	*	1626	285	390	1,600
↳1891, Red Cameo	*	1627	—	—	2,400
1892, Brown	2,745	1629	155	285	525

* Included in number above.

Proof Strikes *(continued)*

	Mintage	GSID	PF-60	PF-63	PF-65
1892, Red Brown	*	1630	$195	$340	$725
1892, Red	*	1631	285	390	1,100
↳1892, Red Cameo	*	1632	—	—	3,450
1893, Brown	2,195	1634	155	285	525
1893, Red Brown	*	1635	195	340	725
1893, Red	*	1636	285	390	1,100
↳1893, Red Cameo	*	1637	—	—	2,200
1894, Brown	2,632	1639	155	285	525
1894, Red Brown	*	1640	195	340	725
1894, Red	*	1641	285	390	1,100
↳1894, Red Cameo	*	1642	—	850	3,000
1895, Brown	2,065	1644	155	285	525
1895, Red Brown	*	1645	195	340	725
	Auctions: $141,000, NGC PF-64 HA 05/15				
1895, Red	*	1646	285	390	1,100
↳1895, Red Cameo	*	1647	—	850	3,000
1896, Brown	1,862	1649	155	285	525
1896, Red Brown	*	1650	195	340	725
1896, Red	*	1651	390	575	1,250
↳1896, Red Cameo	*	1652	—	850	1,550
1897, Brown	1,938	1654	155	285	525
1897, Red Brown	*	1655	195	340	725
1897, Red	*	1656	285	390	1,400
↳1897, Red Cameo	*	1657	—	850	2,500
1898, Brown	1,795	1659	155	285	525
1898, Red Brown	*	1660	195	340	725
1898, Red	*	1661	285	390	1,200
↳1898, Red Cameo	*	1662	—	—	2,200
1899, Brown	2,031	1664	155	285	525
1899, Red Brown	*	1665	195	340	750
1899, Red	*	1666	285	390	1,100
↳1899, Red Cameo	*	1667	—	—	4,400
1900, Brown	2,262	1669	155	285	525
1900, Red Brown	*	1670	195	340	725
1900, Red	*	1671	285	390	1,100
↳1900, Red Cameo	*	1672	—	—	4,700

	Mintage	GSID	PF-60	PF-63	PF-65
1901, Brown	1,985	1674	$155	$285	$525
1901, Red Brown	*	1675	195	340	725
1901, Red	*	1676	285	390	1,200
↳1901, Red Cameo	*	1677	—	—	4,400
1902, Brown	2,018	1679	155	285	525
1902, Red Brown	*	1680	195	340	725
1902, Red	*	1681	285	390	1,100
↳1902, Red Cameo	*	1682	—	—	3,000
1903, Brown	1,790	1684	155	285	525
1903, Red Brown	*	1685	195	340	725
1903, Red	*	1686	285	390	1,100
↳1903, Red Cameo	*	1687	—	—	3,000
1904, Brown	1,817	1689	155	285	525
1904, Red Brown	*	1690	195	340	725
1904, Red	*	1691	285	390	1,400
↳1904, Red Cameo	*	1692	—	850	1,550
1905, Brown	2,152	1694	155	285	525
1905, Red Brown	*	1695	195	340	725
1905, Red	*	1696	285	470	1,250
↳1905, Red Cameo	*	1697	—	—	5,000
1906, Brown	1,725	1699	155	285	525
1906, Red Brown	*	1700	195	340	725
1906, Red	*	1701	285	390	1,250
↳1906, Red Cameo	*	1702	—	—	2,500
1907, Brown	1,475	1704	155	285	525
1907, Red Brown	*	69463	195	340	725
1907, Red	*	1705	285	390	1,500
↳1907, Red Cameo	*	1706	—	—	—
1908, Brown	1,620	1708	155	285	525
1908, Red Brown	*	1709	195	340	725
1908, Red	*	1710	285	390	1,100
↳1908, Red Cameo	*	1711	—	—	3,750
1909, Brown	2,175	1713	155	285	525
1909, Red Brown	*	1714	195	340	725
1909, Red	*	1715	285	390	1,100
↳1909, Red Cameo	*	1716	—	—	5,000

* Included in number above.

LINCOLN, WHEAT EARS REVERSE (1909–1958)

Variety 1 (Bronze, 1909–1942): **Designer:** *Victor D. Brenner.* **Weight:** *3.11 grams.* **Composition:** *.950 copper, .050 tin and zinc.* **Diameter:** *19 mm.* **Edge:** *Plain.* **Mints:** *Philadelphia, Denver, and San Francisco.*

Variety 1, Bronze (1909–1942), Circulation Strike

Mintmark location, all varieties 1909 to date, is on the obverse below the date.

Variety 1, Bronze, Matte Proof Strike

Variety 2 (Steel, 1943): **Weight:** *2.7 grams.* **Composition:** *Steel, coated with zinc.* **Diameter:** *19 mm.* **Edge:** *Plain.* **Mints:** *Philadelphia, Denver, and San Francisco.*

Variety 2, Steel (1943)

Variety 1 Resumed (1944–1958): **Weight:** *3.11 grams.* **Composition:** *1944–1946—.950 copper and .050 zinc; 1947–1958—.950 copper and .050 tin and zinc.* **Diameter:** *19 mm.* **Edge:** *Plain.* **Mints:** *Philadelphia, Denver, and San Francisco.*

Variety 1 Resumed, Bronze (1944–1958), Circulation Strike

Variety 1 Resumed, Bronze, Mirror Proof Strike

History. The Lincoln cent debuted in 1909 in honor of the hundredth anniversary of the birth of Abraham Lincoln. Sculptor and engraver Victor David had been chosen to design the new cent because the artistry of Chief Engraver Charles Barber was under heavy criticism at the time. The new cent was released on August 2, 1909, and the earliest coins of the year's issue had Brenner's initials (V.D.B.) on the reverse; this was soon discontinued. (His initials would be restored in 1918, on the obverse, on Lincoln's shoulder.) This was the first U.S. cent to feature the motto IN GOD WE TRUST.

From 1909 to 1942 the coins were struck in bronze. In 1943, during World War II, zinc-coated steel was used for their planchets, as a way to reserve copper for the war effort. The bronze alloy would be resumed in 1944. (Although no bronze cents were officially issued in 1943, a few pieces struck on bronze or silver planchets are known to exist for that year; bronze examples have recently sold for more than $200,000. Such errors presumably occur when an older planchet is mixed in with the normal supply of planchets and goes through the minting process. Through a similar production error, a few 1944 cents were struck on steel planchets. Beware the many regular steel cents of 1943 that were later plated with copper, either as novelties or to deceive collectors; a magnet will reveal their true nature.) In 1944, 1945, and 1946, the Mint used salvaged gun-cartridge cases as its source metal for coining cents. In Mint State, the color of cents of these years can appear slightly different from other bronze Wheat Ears cents.

The Philadelphia, Denver, and San Francisco mints all produced Lincoln Wheat Ears cents, but not in all years. The Wheat Ears reverse design was used from 1909 until the coin's 50th anniversary in 1959, at which time it was replaced with a view of the Lincoln Memorial.

Striking and Sharpness. As a rule, Lincoln cents of 1909 through 1914 are fairly well struck. From 1915 through the end of the 1920s, many are weak, with Denver Mint coins particularly so. Issues of the 1930s onward are mostly well struck. With many different die pairs used over a long period of time, striking quality varies. On the obverse, check for details in Lincoln's hair and beard. Also check the lettering and the inner edge of the rim. Tiny marks on the shoulder of Lincoln indicate a weak strike there; this area cannot be used to determine wear on high-grade coins. (During striking, there was not enough die pressure to fill this, the deepest point of the obverse die; therefore, stray marks on the raw planchet remain evident in this spot.) On the reverse, check the wheat stalks, letters, and inner rim. A weak strike will usually manifest itself on the O of ONE (the area directly opposite Lincoln's shoulder). Coins struck from overused or "tired" dies can have grainy or even slightly wavy fields on either side.

Availability. Of the earlier Lincoln Wheat Ears cents, those of 1909 are easily found in MS; later early dates are scarcer, although Philadelphia varieties were made in higher quantities and are more often seen. Beginning in the early 1930s, collectors saved bank-wrapped rolls of Mint State cents in large quantities (starting mainly in 1934, though the low-mintage 1931-S was also hoarded). Dates after this time all are plentiful, although some more so than others, and there are a number of scarce and rare varieties. The collector demand for scarcer Lincoln cents and higher-grade issues is intense, resulting in a strong market. Many Mint State coins before the 1930s have been dipped and recolored, this being particularly true of pieces listed as RD. Others are stained and blotchy.

Proofs. Matte Proof Lincoln cents of a new style were made from 1909 to 1916. These have minutely matte or pebbled surfaces caused by special treatment of the dies. The rims are square and sharp. Such pieces cannot easily be told from certain circulation strikes with similar borders. Certified holders usually list these simply as "Proof," not "Matte Proof." Buy only coins that have been verified by an expert. Most are brown, or brown with tinges of red. Nearly all full "red" coins have been dipped or recolored.

Exceptional specimens dated 1917 are reported to exist, although no records exist to indicate they are true Proofs.

Mirror-finish Proofs were made from 1936 to 1942 and again from 1950 to 1958. Proofs of this era are mostly from dies polished overall (including the portrait), although some later issues have frosted ("cameo") portraits. Quality can be a problem for the 1936 to 1942 issues. Check for carbon spots and recoloring. Proofs of later dates are easy to find.

Generally, Proofs below 63 are unattractive and are not desired by most collectors.

Grading Standards

Caveat: These grading standards do not take sharpness of strike into account.

MS-64RB

MS-60 to 70 (Mint State). ***Obverse and Reverse:*** At MS-65 and higher, the luster is rich on all areas, except perhaps the shoulder (which may be grainy and show original planchet surface). There is no rubbing, and no contact marks are visible except under magnification. Coins with full or nearly full mint orange-red color can be designated RD; those with full or nearly full brown-toned surfaces can be designated BN; and those with a substantial percentage of red-orange and of brown can be called RB. Ideally, MS-65 or finer coins should have good eye appeal, which in the RB category means nicely blended colors, not stained or blotched. Below MS-65, full RD coins become scarce, and at MS-60 to 62 they are virtually non-existent, unless they have been dipped. Copper is a very active metal, and influences that define the grade—such as slight abrasions, contact marks, and so on—also affect the color. The ANA grading standards allow for "dull" and/or "spotted" coins at MS-60 and 61, as well as incomplete luster. In the marketplace, interpretations often vary widely. BN and RB coins at MS-60 and 61 are apt to be more attractive than (dipped) RD coins.

Illustrated coin: The rose-orange color of this cent is better than is usually expected for a coin graded Red Brown. Note some toning streaks on the obverse, lighter than the surrounding surfaces, across Lincoln's forehead and nose.

AU-50, 53, 55, 58 (About Uncirculated). ***Obverse:*** Slight wear shows on Lincoln's cheekbone to the left of his nose, and also on his beard. At AU-55 or 58 there may be some hints of mint red-orange. Most coins in About Uncirculated are BN, but they are seldom designated by color. ***Reverse:*** Slight wear is evident on the stalks of wheat to the left and right. Otherwise, the same standards apply as for the obverse.

AU-58

EF-40, 45 (Extremely Fine). ***Obverse:*** Light wear is seen on Lincoln's portrait, and hair detail is gone on the higher areas, especially above the ear. ***Reverse:*** Light wear is seen overall, but the parallel lines in the wheat stalks are clearly separated.

EF-45

VF-20, 30 (Very Fine). ***Obverse:*** Lincoln's portrait is worn all over, with most hair detail gone at the center. Hair separation is seen at the back and the top of the head, but hairs are blended together. The jaw outline is clear. The center of the ear is defined and the bowtie is clear. The date and lettering is sharp. ***Reverse:*** More wear is seen, but still the lines in the wheat stalks are separated. Lettering shows wear but is very clear.

VF-20

Illustrated coin: This coin features even wear and few marks.

F-12, 15 (Fine). ***Obverse:*** More wear is seen overall. Hair definition is less. The center of the ear is partially visible. The jaw outline and bowtie are clear. ***Reverse:*** Most lines in the wheat stalks are either weak or blended with others, but more than half of the separating lines are clear.

Illustrated coin: Other than one deep contact mark in the cheek, the surfaces are smooth.

F-15

VG-8, 10 (Very Good). ***Obverse:*** The portrait is more worn, with only slight hair strands visible (thick strands blended). The ear opening is visible. The bowtie and jacket show fewer details. ***Reverse:*** The lines in the wheat stalks are blended together in flat areas. Perhaps 40 percent to 50 percent of the separating lines can be seen. The rim may be weak in areas.

VG-10

G-4, 6 (Good). ***Obverse:*** The portrait is well worn. Some slight details are seen at the top of the head and the bottom of the coat. LIBERTY is weak. The rim may touch or blend with the tops of the letters forming IN GOD WE TRUST. The date and mintmark (if any) are very clear. ***Reverse:*** The wheat stalks are flat, with just a few scattered details visible.

G-6

AG-3 (About Good). ***Obverse:*** Wear is extensive. The portrait is mostly in outline form, with only scattered details visible. LIBERTY is weak and perhaps with some letters missing. IN GOD WE TRUST blends in with the rim, and several letters are very weak or missing. ***Reverse:*** The rim is worn down to blend with the outside of the wheat stalks in some areas, although some hints of the edge of the stalks can be seen. Lettering is weak, with up to several letters missing.

AG-3

PF-60 to 70 (Matte Proof). ***Obverse and Reverse:*** At the Matte PF-65 level or higher there are no traces of abrasion or contact marks. Color will range from brown (BN)—the most common—to brown with significant tinges of mint red-orange (RB), or with much mint color (RD). Most RD coins have been dipped. Some tiny flecks are normal on coins certified as PF-65 but should be microscopic or

PF-68RD

absent above that. Coins in the PF-60 to 63 range are BN or sometimes RB—almost impossible to be RD unless dipped. Lower-grade Proofs usually have poor eye appeal.

Illustrated coin: Most of the red tint is medium orange, but there is a faint pink tint to the upper-left obverse.

PF-60 to 70 (Mirror Proof). ***Obverse and Reverse:*** PF-65 and higher coins are usually RB (colors should be nicely blended) or RD, the latter with bright red-orange fading slightly to hints of brown. Some tiny flecks are normal on coins certified as PF-65 but should be microscopic or absent above that. PF-60 and 61 coins can be dull, stained, or spotted but still have some original mint color. Coins with fingerprints must be given a low numerical grade. Lower-grade Proofs usually have poor eye appeal.

PF-66RD

Illustrated coin: The mirrored surfaces are free of blemish.

Designer's initials, V.D.B. (1909 Reverse Only)

No V.D.B. on Reverse (1909–1958)

V.D.B. on Shoulder (Starting 1918)

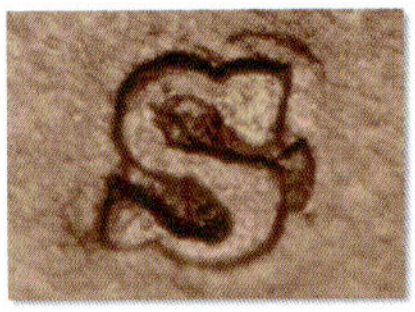

1909-S, S Over Horizontal S
FS-1502

Circulation Strikes

	Mintage	GSID	VG-8	F-12	VF-20	EF-40	AU-50	MS-60	MS-63	MS-65
Lincoln, Wheat Ears Reverse (1909–1958), Brown	**n/a**	**72340**	**$0.20**	**$0.20**	**$0.20**	**$0.20**	**$0.20**	**$0.20**	**$0.40**	**$2.20**
Same, Red Brown	**n/a**	**72341**	**—**	**—**	**—**	**—**	**—**	**0.40**	**0.60**	**4.10**
Same, Red	**n/a**	**72342**	**—**	**—**	**—**	**—**	**—**	**0.60**	**0.80**	**11.00**
Lincoln, Wheat Ears Reverse, Steel (1943), Steel, Wheat Reverse	**n/a**	**376180**	**0.30**	**0.30**	**0.30**	**0.30**	**0.40**	**1.50**	**2.60**	**13.50**
1909, V.D.B., Brown	27,995,000	1790	4.70	8.00	9.50	12.00	13.50	23.00	32.00	85.00
1909, V.D.B., Red Brown	*	1791	—	—	—	—	—	30.00	43.00	100.00
1909, V.D.B., Red	*	1792	—	—	—	—	—	—	75.00	195.00
1909, V.D.B., Doubled Die Obverse, Brown	*	1793	38.00	45.00	75.00	95.00	110.00	130.00	170.00	360.00
↳**1909, V.D.B., Doubled Die Obverse, FS-1101, Brown**	*	285297	38.00	45.00	75.00	95.00	110.00	130.00	170.00	360.00
1909, V.D.B., Doubled Die Obverse, Red Brown	27,995,000	285480	—	—	—	—	—	—	180.00	420.00
↳**1909, V.D.B., Doubled Die Obverse, FS-1101, Red Brown**	*	298952	—	—	—	—	—	—	180.00	420.00
1909, V.D.B., Doubled Die Obverse, Red	27,995,000	285481	—	—	—	—	—	—	260.00	850.00
↳**1909, V.D.B., Doubled Die Obverse, FS-1101, Red**	*	298953	—	—	—	—	—	—	260.00	850.00
1909-S, V.D.B., Brown (a)	484,000	1799	900.00	1,000.00	1,250.00	1,500.00	1,700.00	2,050.00	2,550.00	3,600.00
1909-S, V.D.B., Red Brown (a)	*	1800	—	—	—	—	—	—	2,900.00	4,750.00
1909-S, V.D.B., Red (a)	*	1801	—	—	—	—	—	2,500.00	3,500.00	7,500.00
	Auctions: $168,000, PCGS MS-67 SBG 04/22									

* Included in number above. **a.** Many counterfeits exist—some die struck, some made by adding an "S" to a Philadelphia coin.

Circulation Strikes *(continued)*

	Mintage	GSID	VG-8	F-12	VF-20	EF-40	AU-50	MS-60	MS-63	MS-65
1909, Brown	72,702,618	1721	$2.20	$2.60	$3.40	$6.75	$12.00	$17.50	$27.00	$60.00
1909, Red Brown	*	1722	—	—	—	—	—	—	38.00	120.00
1909, Red	*	1723	—	—	—	—	—	—	55.00	180.00
1909-S, Brown	1,825,000	1796	90.00	110.00	130.00	160.00	210.00	340.00	430.00	725.00
↳1909-S, S Over S, FS-1501, Brown	1,825,000	285299	90.00	110.00	130.00	160.00	210.00	340.00	475.00	850.00
1909-S, S Over Horizontal S, Brown	*	1802	100.00	120.00	160.00	190.00	275.00	340.00	415.00	650.00
↳1909-S, S Over Horizontal S, FS-1502, Brown	*	393271	100.00	120.00	160.00	190.00	275.00	340.00	415.00	650.00
1909-S, S Over Horizontal S, Red Brown	*	1797	—	—	—	—	—	—	450.00	850.00
↳1909-S, S Over Horizontal S, FS-1501, Red Brown	*	285300	—	—	—	—	—	—	495.00	975.00
1909-S, S Over Horizontal S, Red Brown	*	1803	—	—	—	—	—	—	450.00	775.00
↳1909-S, S Over Horizontal S, FS-1502, Red Brown	*	393272	—	—	—	—	—	—	450.00	775.00
1909-S, S Over Horizontal S, Red	*	1798	—	—	—	—	—	—	600.00	1,300.00
↳1909-S, S Over Horizontal S, FS-1501, Red	*	285301	—	—	—	—	—	—	650.00	1,750.00
1909-S, S Over Horizontal S, Red	*	1804	—	—	—	—	—	—	650.00	1,400.00
↳1909-S, S Over Horizontal S, FS-1502, Red	*	393273	—	—	—	—	—	—	650.00	1,400.00
1910, Brown	146,801,218	1724	0.60	0.60	0.80	4.40	10.00	19.00	27.00	95.00
1910, Red Brown	*	1725	—	—	—	—	—	—	31.00	115.00
1910, Red	*	1726	—	—	—	—	—	—	70.00	215.00
1910-S, Brown	6,045,000	1805	16.00	22.00	27.00	55.00	80.00	100.00	130.00	290.00
↳1910-S, S Over S, FS-502, Brown	*	285303	—	—	—	—	—	230.00	390.00	—
1910-S, Red Brown	*	1806	—	—	—	—	—	—	150.00	310.00
↳1910-S, S Over S, FS-502, Red Brown	*	285305	—	—	—	—	—	—	525.00	1,050.00
1910-S, Red	*	1807	—	—	—	—	—	—	230.00	725.00
↳1910-S, S Over S, FS-502, Red	*	285307	—	—	—	—	—	—	775.00	1,300.00
1911, Brown	101,177,787	1727	0.60	1.50	2.20	8.00	11.50	19.00	30.00	130.00
1911, Red Brown	*	1728	—	—	—	—	—	—	40.00	195.00
1911, Red	*	1729	—	—	—	—	—	—	130.00	525.00
1911-D, Brown	12,672,000	1808	7.50	11.50	27.00	60.00	75.00	95.00	145.00	420.00
↳1911-D, D Over D, FS-503, Brown	*	285310	—	—	—	—	—	—	—	—
↳1911-D, D Over D, FS-504, Brown	*	285311	—	—	—	—	—	—	—	—
1911-D, Red Brown	*	1809	—	—	—	—	—	—	155.00	625.00
↳1911-D, D Over D, FS-503, Red Brown	*	285314	—	—	—	—	—	—	—	—
↳1911-D, D Over D, FS-504, Red Brown	*	285315	—	—	—	—	—	—	—	—
1911-D, Red	*	1810	—	—	—	—	—	—	365.00	1,000.00
↳1911-D, D Over D, FS-503, Red	*	285318	—	—	—	—	—	—	—	—
↳1911-D, D Over D, FS-504, Red	*	285319	—	—	—	—	—	—	—	—
1911-S, Brown	4,026,000	1811	38.00	45.00	55.00	75.00	105.00	190.00	325.00	1,000.00
1911-S, Red Brown	*	1812	—	—	—	—	—	—	550.00	1,400.00
1911-S, Red	*	1813	—	—	—	—	—	—	550.00	2,500.00

* Included in number above.

Circulation Strikes *(continued)*

	Mintage	GSID	VG-8	F-12	VF-20	EF-40	AU-50	MS-60	MS-63	MS-65
1912, Brown	68,153,060	1730	$2.20	$2.60	$6.00	$15.00	$28.00	$34.00	$47	$115
1912, Red Brown	*	1731	—	—	—	—	—	—	55	290
1912, Red	*	1732	—	—	—	—	—	—	100	470
1912-D, Brown	10,411,000	1814	11.00	12.00	32.00	80.00	115.00	175.00	290	575
1912-D, Red Brown	*	1815	—	—	—	—	—	—	345	800
1912-D, Red	*	1816	—	—	—	—	—	—	390	1,500
1912-S, Brown	4,431,000	1817	19.00	23.00	40.00	70.00	110.00	180.00	260	850
1912-S, Red Brown	*	1818	—	—	—	—	—	—	390	1,150
1912-S, Red	*	1819	—	—	—	—	—	—	490	2,400
1913, Brown	76,532,352	1733	0.80	2.20	3.70	22.00	31.00	36.00	60	155
1913, Red Brown	*	1734	—	—	—	—	—	—	70	260
1913, Red	*	1735	—	—	—	—	—	—	155	525
1913-D, Brown	15,804,000	1820	2.60	3.40	8.75	55.00	70.00	110.00	210	575
1913-D, Red Brown	*	1821	—	—	—	—	—	—	260	650
1913-D, Red	*	1822	—	—	—	—	—	—	495	1,750
1913-S, Brown	6,101,000	1823	12.00	16.00	27.00	60.00	100.00	200.00	285	1,100
1913-S, Red Brown	*	1824	—	—	—	—	—	—	390	1,400
1913-S, Red	*	1825	—	—	—	—	—	—	650	4,600
1914, Brown	75,238,432	1736	1.10	2.20	6.75	20.00	43.00	55.00	75	160
1914, Red Brown	*	1737	—	—	—	—	—	—	90	260
1914, Red	*	1738	—	—	—	—	—	—	180	900
1914-D, Brown (b)	1,193,000	1826	220.00	280.00	360.00	825.00	1,400.00	2,750.00	3,750	6,500
1914-D, Red Brown (b)	*	1827	—	—	—	—	—	—	4,100	7,000
1914-D, Red (b)	*	1828	—	—	—	—	—	—	5,000	17,500
	Auctions: $158,625, PCGS MS-66 LGND 05/18									
1914-S, Brown	4,137,000	1829	20.00	24.00	31.00	90.00	150.00	345.00	575	1,750
1914-S, Red Brown	*	1830	—	—	—	—	—	—	775	3,250
1914-S, Red	*	1831	—	—	—	—	—	—	1,600	11,000
1915, Brown	29,092,120	1739	3.40	4.40	12.00	47.00	55.00	90.00	110	215
1915, Red Brown	*	1740	—	—	—	—	—	—	135	470
1915, Red	*	1741	—	—	—	—	—	—	230	725
1915-D, Brown	22,050,000	1832	3.70	6.75	12.00	34.00	49.00	80.00	110	260
1915-D, Red Brown	*	1833	—	—	—	—	—	—	130	725
1915-D, Red	*	1834	—	—	—	—	—	—	340	1,050
1915-S, Brown	4,833,000	1835	17.50	26.00	34.00	80.00	110.00	290.00	650	1,250
1915-S, Red Brown	*	1836	—	—	—	—	—	—	750	1,500
1915-S, Red	*	1837	—	—	—	—	—	—	—	7,500
1916, Brown	131,833,677	1742	0.50	0.80	2.60	8.75	15.00	20.00	27	110
1916, Red Brown	*	1743	—	—	—	—	—	—	50	170
1916, Red	*	1744	—	—	—	—	—	—	90	310
1916-D, Brown	35,956,000	1838	1.10	2.60	4.10	13.50	34.00	95.00	115	455
1916-D, Red Brown	*	1839	—	—	—	—	—	—	190	575
1916-D, Red	*	1840	—	—	—	—	—	—	260	1,400
1916-S, Brown	22,510,000	1841	2.20	3.40	13.50	30.00	50.00	115.00	200	700
1916-S, Red Brown	*	1842	—	—	—	—	—	—	210	850
1916-S, Red	*	1843	—	—	—	—	—	—	650	6,000
1917, Brown	196,429,785	1745	0.40	0.50	1.90	5.00	15.00	17.50	32	155
1917, Red Brown	*	1746	—	—	—	—	—	—	40	175
1917, Red	*	1747	—	—	—	—	—	—	130	470

* Included in number above. **b.** Many counterfeits exist, including crude fakes, sophisticated die-struck forgeries, and altered 1944-D cents (the latter, unlike an authentic 1914-D cent, will have the designer's initials, V.D.B., on the shoulder).

1917, Doubled Die Obverse
FS-101

Circulation Strikes *(continued)*

	Mintage	GSID	VG-8	F-12	VF-20	EF-40	AU-50	MS-60	MS-63	MS-65
1917, Doubled Die Obverse, Brown	*	1748	$195.00	$310.00	$455.00	$1,400.00	$2,300.00	$4,000	$7,500	$10,000
↳1917, Doubled Die Obverse, FS-101, Brown	*	310748	195.00	310.00	455.00	1,400.00	2,300.00	4,000	7,500	10,000
1917, Doubled Die Obverse, Red Brown	*	1749	—	—	—	—	—	—	8,500	12,000
↳1917, Doubled Die Obverse, FS-101, Red Brown	*	310749	—	—	—	—	—	—	8,500	12,000
1917, Doubled Die Obverse, Red	*	1750	—	—	—	—	—	—	10,000	18,000
	Auctions: $120,000, PCGS MS-67 SBG 02/19									
↳1917, Doubled Die Obverse, FS-101, Red	*	310750	—	—	—	—	—	—	10,000	18,000
1917-D, Brown	55,120,000	1844	1.50	3.40	5.50	40.00	49.00	80	130	390
1917-D, Red Brown	*	1845	—	—	—	—	—	—	215	575
1917-D, Red	*	1846	—	—	—	—	—	—	420	3,000
1917-S, Brown	32,620,000	1847	0.80	1.50	2.60	12.00	27.00	80	160	625
1917-S, Red Brown	*	1848	—	—	—	—	—	—	210	1,000
1917-S, Red	*	1849	—	—	—	—	—	—	775	8,000
1918, Brown	288,104,634	1751	0.40	0.50	0.80	4.70	9.75	13.50	22	230
1918, Red Brown	*	1752	—	—	—	—	—	—	27	260
1918, Red	*	1753	—	—	—	—	—	—	110	470
1918-D, Brown	47,830,000	1850	1.10	1.50	4.10	17.50	38.00	80	145	490
1918-D, Red Brown	*	1851	—	—	—	—	—	—	195	1,000
1918-D, Red	*	1852	—	—	—	—	—	—	430	4,000
1918-S, Brown	34,680,000	1853	0.80	1.50	3.40	11.50	35.00	75	195	725
1918-S, Red Brown	*	1854	—	—	—	—	—	—	260	1,250
1918-S, Red	*	1855	—	—	—	—	—	—	625	4,400
1919, Brown	392,021,000	1754	0.40	0.50	0.60	1.50	5.50	8	19	90
1919, Red Brown	*	1755	—	—	—	—	—	—	27	110
1919, Red	*	1756	—	—	—	—	—	—	55	300
1919-D, Brown	57,154,000	1856	1.50	2.00	4.10	11.00	28.00	70	116	325
1919-D, Red Brown	*	1857	—	—	—	—	—	—	150	975
1919-D, Red	*	1858	—	—	—	—	—	—	240	1,200
1919-S, Brown	139,760,000	1859	0.40	1.10	2.60	6.00	19.00	55	120	415
1919-S, Red Brown	*	1860	—	—	—	—	—	—	210	975
1919-S, Red	*	1861	—	—	—	—	—	—	490	5,500
1920, Brown	310,165,000	1757	0.30	0.60	1.10	2.60	8.00	16	23	80
1920, Red Brown	*	1758	—	—	—	—	—	—	27	130
1920, Red	*	1759	—	—	—	—	—	—	60	275
1920-D, Brown	49,280,000	1862	0.60	1.50	2.60	13.50	38.00	75	120	490
1920-D, Red Brown	*	1863	—	—	—	—	—	—	195	650
1920-D, Red	*	1864	—	—	—	—	—	—	310	1,800
1920-S, Brown	46,220,000	1865	0.60	1.50	2.60	13.50	38.00	115	180	750
1920-S, Red Brown	*	1866	—	—	—	—	—	—	325	1,600
1920-S, Red	*	1867	—	—	—	—	—	—	1,100	18,500

* Included in number above.

1922, Weak D

1922, No D
FS-401

Circulation Strikes *(continued)*

	Mintage	GSID	VG-8	F-12	VF-20	EF-40	AU-50	MS-60	MS-63	MS-65
1921, Brown	39,157,000	1760	$0.60	$0.80	$2.60	$11.50	$23	$46	$70	$180
1921, Red Brown	*	1761	—	—	—	—	—	—	80	195
1921, Red	*	1762	—	—	—	—	—	—	130	625
1921-S, Brown	15,274,000	1868	2.20	4.10	6.75	40.00	70	115	235	1,100
1921-S, Red Brown	*	1869	—	—	—	—	—	—	310	1,400
1921-S, Red	*	1870	—	—	—	—	—	—	525	12,000
1922-D, Brown	7,160,000	69742	23.00	24.00	30.00	45.00	75	110	235	525
1922-D, Red Brown	*	69743	—	—	—	—	—	—	340	900
1922-D, Red	*	69744	—	—	—	—	—	—	525	3,000
1922, Weak D, Weak Reverse, Brown (c)	*	393847	80.00	95.00	145.00	220.00	275	455	650	—
↳1922, Weak D, Weak Reverse, Die Pair 1, Brown (c)	7,160,000	310760	—	—	—	—	—	—	—	—
↳1922, Weak D, Weak Reverse, Die Pair 3, Brown (c)	7,160,000	310766	—	—	—	—	—	—	—	—
↳1922, Weak D, Weak Reverse, Die Pair 4, Brown (c)	7,160,000	1877	80.00	95.00	145.00	220.00	275	455	650	—
1922, Weak D, Weak Reverse, Red Brown (c)	*	393848	—	—	—	—	—	—	775	—
↳1922, Weak D, Weak Reverse, Die Pair 1, Red Brown (c)	*	310761	—	—	—	—	—	—	—	—
↳1922, Weak D, Weak Reverse, Die Pair 3, Red Brown (c)	*	310767	—	—	—	—	—	—	—	—
↳1922, Weak D, Weak Reverse, Die Pair 4, Red Brown (c)	*	1878	—	—	—	—	—	—	775	—
1922, Weak D, Weak Reverse, Red (c)	*	393849	—	—	—	—	—	—	2,750	—
↳1922, Weak D, Weak Reverse, Die Pair 1, Red (c)	*	310762	—	—	—	—	—	—	—	—
↳1922, Weak D, Weak Reverse, Die Pair 3, Red (c)	*	310768	—	—	—	—	—	—	—	—
↳1922, Weak D, Weak Reverse, Die Pair 4, Red (c)	*	1879	—	—	—	—	—	—	2,750	—
1922, Faint D, Die Pair ZeroB, Brown (c)	7,160,000	393497	—	—	—	—	—	—	—	—
1922, Faint D, Die Pair 5, Brown (c)	7,160,000	393498	—	—	—	—	—	—	—	—
1922, Faint D, Die Pair 6, Brown (c)	7,160,000	393499	—	—	—	—	—	—	—	—
1922, Well Worn D, Smear, Die Pair 8C, Brown (c)	7,160,000	393500	—	—	—	—	—	—	—	—
1922, Faint D, Die Pair 9, Brown (c)	7,160,000	393501	—	—	—	—	—	—	—	—
1922, Faint D, Die Pair 13B, Brown (c)	7,160,000	393502	—	—	—	—	—	—	—	—
1922, No D, Strong Reverse, Die Pair 2, Brown (c)	*	2330	750.00	850.00	1,100.00	2,050.00	3,900	11,000	21,500	81,500
↳1922, No D, Strong Reverse, Die Pair 2, FS-401, Brown (c)	*	376706	750.00	850.00	1,100.00	2,050.00	3,900	11,000	21,500	81,500

* Included in number above. **c.** Beware of fraudulently removed mintmark.

Circulation Strikes *(continued)*

	Mintage	GSID	VG-8	F-12	VF-20	EF-40	AU-50	MS-60	MS-63	MS-65
1922, No D, Strong Reverse, Die Pair 2, Red Brown (c)	*	2331	—	—	—	—	—	—	$36,000	$102,000
↳1922, No D, Strong Reverse, Die Pair 2, FS-401, Red Brown (c)	*	393201	—	—	—	—	—	—	36,000	102,000
1922, No D, Strong Reverse, Die Pair 2, Red (c)	*	2332	—	—	—	—	—	—	90,000	—
1922, No D, Strong Reverse, Die Pair 1, Brown (c)	7,160,000	1871	$155.00	$260.00	$340.00	$575.00	$900.00	$1,550.00	3,750	—
↳1922, No D, Weak Reverse, Die Pair 1, Red Brown (c)	*	1872	—	—	—	—	—	—	4,100	—
↳1922, No D, Weak Reverse, Die Pair 1, Red (c)	*	1873	—	—	—	—	—	—	5,250	—
1922, No D, Weak Reverse, Die Pair 3, Brown (c)	7,160,000	310763	—	—	—	—	—	—	—	—
↳1922, No D, Weak Reverse, Die Pair 3, Red Brown (c)	*	310764	—	—	—	—	—	—	—	—
↳1922, No D, Weak Reverse, Die Pair 3, Red (c)	*	310765	—	—	—	—	—	—	—	—
1922, No D, Weak Reverse, Die Pair 4, Brown (c)	7,160,000	310769	—	—	—	—	—	—	—	—
↳1922, No D, Weak Reverse, Die Pair 4, Red Brown (c)	*	310770	—	—	—	—	—	—	—	—
↳1922, No D, Weak Reverse, Die Pair 4, Red (c)	*	310771	—	—	—	—	—	—	—	—
1923, Brown	74,723,000	1763	0.40	0.40	1.20	6.75	11.50	15.00	22	130
1923, Red Brown	*	1764	—	—	—	—	—	—	47	180
1923, Red	*	1765	—	—	—	—	—	—	75	260
1923-S, Brown	8,700,000	1880	8.00	9.50	12.00	60.00	115.00	260.00	575	1,500
1923-S, Red Brown	*	1881	—	—	—	—	—	300.00	1,100	5,250
1923-S, Red	*	1882	—	—	—	—	—	—	1,300	30,000
1924, Brown	75,178,000	1766	0.40	0.40	0.80	5.50	11.00	19.00	40	95
1924, Red Brown	*	1767	—	—	—	—	—	—	55	245
1924, Red	*	1768	—	—	—	—	—	—	100	600
1924-D, Brown	2,520,000	1883	35.00	47.00	50.00	115.00	170.00	360.00	725	1,750
1924-D, Red Brown	*	1884	—	—	—	—	—	—	850	2,250
1924-D, Red	*	1885							1,250	12,000
1924-S, Brown	11,696,000	1886	1.50	2.60	5.50	35.00	90.00	120.00	340	1,750
1924-S, Red Brown	*	1887	—	—	—	—	—	—	575	2,100
1924-S, Red	*	1888	—	—	—	—	—	—	1,250	30,000
1925, Brown	139,949,000	1769	0.30	0.40	0.50	2.60	6.75	9.50	16	80
1925, Red Brown	*	1770	—	—	—	—	—	—	19	90
1925, Red	*	1771	—	—	—	—	—	—	47	130
1925-D, Brown	22,580,000	1889	0.80	2.20	2.60	16.00	32.00	70.00	130	340
1925-D, Red Brown	*	1890	—	—	—	—	—	—	170	850
1925-D, Red	*	1891	—	—	—	—	—	—	235	4,000
1925-S, Brown	26,380,000	1892	0.80	2.20	2.60	12.00	40.00	145.00	235	1,150
↳1925-S, S Over S, FS-501, Brown	*	199189	—	—	—	100.00	120.00	310.00	725	—
1925-S, Red Brown	*	1893	—	—	—	—	—	—	525	3,100
↳1925-S, S Over S, FS-501, Red Brown	*	199190	—	—	—	—	—	—	1,550	—
1925-S, Red	*	1894	—	—	—	—	—	—	1,750	31,000
↳1925-S, S Over S, FS-501, Red	*	199191	—	—	—	—	—	—	2,200	—

* Included in number above. **c.** Beware of fraudulently removed mintmark

Circulation Strikes *(continued)*

	Mintage	GSID	VG-8	F-12	VF-20	EF-40	AU-50	MS-60	MS-63	MS-65
1926, Brown	157,088,000	1772	$0.30	$0.40	$0.50	$1.50	$5.50	$8.00	$11.00	$27
1926, Red Brown	*	1773	—	—	—	—	—	—	12.00	40
1926, Red	*	1774	—	—	—	—	—	20.00	32.00	155
1926-D, Brown	28,020,000	1895	1.50	3.00	6.00	16.00	35.00	115.00	170.00	650
1926-D, Red Brown	*	1896	—	—	—	—	—	—	235.00	950
1926-D, Red	*	1897	—	—	—	—	—	—	435.00	3,750
1926-S, Brown	4,550,000	1898	12.00	13.50	17.50	40.00	80.00	260.00	550.00	3,450
1926-S, Red Brown	*	1899	—	—	—	—	—	—	925.00	9,750
1926-S, Red	*	1900	—	—	—	—	—	—	3,250.00	114,000
	Auctions: $149,500, PCGS MS-65 HA 01/06									
1927, Brown	144,440,000	1775	0.30	0.40	0.50	1.50	5.50	8.00	12.00	40
↳1927, Doubled Die Obverse, FS-101, Brown	*	285323	—	115.00	160.00	210.00	260.00	390.00	470.00	1,000
1927, Red Brown	*	1776	—	—	—	—	—	—	15.00	80
↳1927, Doubled Die Obverse, FS-101, Red Brown	*	285324	—	—	—	—	—	—	—	—
1927, Red	*	1777	—	—	—	—	—	—	34.00	155
↳1927, Doubled Die Obverse, FS-101, Red	*	285325	—	—	—	—	—	—	—	—
1927-D, Brown	27,170,000	1901	1.10	1.50	2.60	8.00	27.00	60.00	80.00	340
1927-D, Red Brown	*	1902	—	—	—	—	—	—	150.00	525
1927-D, Red	*	1903	—	—	—	—	—	—	260.00	1,750
1927-S, Brown	14,276,000	1904	1.10	1.50	2.60	16.00	45.00	115.00	215.00	1,700
1927-S, Red Brown	*	1905	—	—	—	—	—	—	365.00	3,000
1927-S, Red	*	1906	—	—	—	—	—	—	625.00	13,000
1928, Brown	134,116,000	1778	0.30	0.40	0.50	1.20	4.10	8.00	16.00	55
1928, Red Brown	*	1779	—	—	—	—	—	—	20.00	120
1928, Red	*	1780	—	—	—	—	—	—	40.00	155
1928-D, Brown	31,170,000	1907	0.80	1.50	2.40	6.75	20.00	47.00	80.00	260
1928-D, Red Brown	*	1908	—	—	—	—	—	—	110.00	470
1928-D, Red	*	1909	—	—	—	—	—	—	175.00	1,250
1928-S, Brown	17,266,000	1910	0.80	1.50	2.60	9.50	34.00	100.00	120.00	390
1928-S, Red Brown	*	1911	—	—	—	—	—	—	290.00	1,400
1928-S, Red	*	1912	—	—	—	—	—	—	650.00	6,250
1929, Brown	185,262,000	1781	0.30	0.40	0.40	2.60	5.50	6.75	9.50	27
1929, Red Brown	*	1782	—	—	—	—	—	—	12.00	55
1929, Red	*	1783	—	—	—	—	—	—	38.00	130
1929-D, Brown	41,730,000	1913	0.80	1.40	2.60	6.00	14.00	26.00	55.00	155
1929-D, Red Brown	*	1914	—	—	—	—	—	—	55.00	195
1929-D, Red	*	1915	—	—	—	—	—	—	95.00	575
1929-S, Brown	50,148,000	1916	0.80	2.00	2.60	6.75	15.50	20.00	27.00	80
1929-S, Red Brown	*	1917	—	—	—	—	—	—	35.00	195
1929-S, Red	*	1918	—	—	—	—	—	—	75.00	470
↳1929-S, S Over S, FS-501, Brown	*	199192	—	—	47.00	80.00	95.00	230.00	310.00	875
↳1929-S, S Over S, FS-501, Red Brown	*	199193	—	—	—	—	—	—	455.00	1,250
↳1929-S, S Over S, FS-501, Red	*	199194	—	—	—	—	—	—	525.00	1,500
1930, Brown	157,415,000	1784	0.20	0.30	0.50	1.20	2.60	4.10	5.50	23
1930, Red Brown	*	1785	—	—	—	—	—	—	6.75	27
1930, Red	*	1786	—	—	—	—	—	—	24.00	55

* Included in number above.

1934, Doubled Die Obverse
FS-101

Circulation Strikes *(continued)*

	Mintage	GSID	VG-8	F-12	VF-20	EF-40	AU-50	MS-60	MS-63	MS-65
1930-D, Brown	40,100,000	1919	$0.30	$0.40	$0.60	$2.20	$5.50	$11.00	$16.00	$38
↳1930-D, D Over D, FS-501, Brown	*	285332	—	—	—	—	—	—	—	—
1930-D, Red Brown	*	1920	—	—	—	—	—	—	23.00	60
↳1930-D, D Over D, FS-501, Red Brown	*	285334	—	—	—	—	—	—	—	—
1930-D, Red	*	1921	—	—	—	—	—	—	47.00	175
↳1930-D, D Over D, FS-501, Red	*	285336	—	—	—	—	—	—	—	—
1930-S, Brown	24,286,000	1922	0.20	0.50	1.20	1.50	6.75	9.50	11.00	27
1930-S, Red Brown	*	1923	—	—	—	—	—	—	12.00	70
1930-S, Red	*	1924	—	—	—	—	—	—	38.00	120
1931, Brown	19,396,000	1787	0.80	0.80	1.90	4.10	11.00	20.00	24.00	47
1931, Red Brown	*	1788	—	—	—	—	—	—	40.00	110
1931, Red	*	1789	—	—	—	—	—	—	65.00	130
1931-D, Brown	4,480,000	1925	6.00	6.75	8.00	16.00	38.00	55.00	90.00	220
1931-D, Red Brown	*	1926	—	—	—	—	—	—	120.00	415
1931-D, Red	*	1927	—	—	—	—	—	—	235.00	1,100
1931-S, Brown	866,000	1928	75.00	90.00	95.00	100.00	120.00	145.00	175.00	435
1931-S, Red Brown	*	1929	—	—	—	—	—	—	190.00	525
1931-S, Red	*	1930	—	—	—	—	—	—	275.00	675
1932, Brown	9,062,000	1931	1.90	2.60	3.40	6.75	13.50	19.00	23.00	34
1932, Red Brown	*	1932	—	—	—	—	—	—	26.00	60
1932, Red	*	1933	—	—	—	—	—	—	43.00	120
1932-D, Brown	10,500,000	2028	1.90	1.90	2.60	4.10	12.00	19.00	30.00	47
1932-D, Red Brown	*	2029	—	—	—	—	—	—	35.00	100
1932-D, Red	*	2030	—	—	—	—	—	—	60.00	310
1933, Brown	14,360,000	1934	1.90	2.40	2.60	6.75	12.00	17.50	22.00	30
1933, Red Brown	*	1935	—	—	—	—	—	—	24.00	60
1933, Red	*	1936	—	—	—	—	—	—	40.00	160
1933-D, Brown	6,200,000	2031	4.10	5.50	8.00	13.50	20.00	26.00	31.00	47
1933-D, Red Brown	*	2032	—	—	—	—	—	—	36.00	75
1933-D, Red	*	2033	—	—	—	—	—	—	47.00	145
1934, Brown	219,080,000	1937	0.20	0.20	0.20	0.20	0.30	1.50	5.50	11
↳1934, Doubled Die Obverse, FS-101, Brown	*	285338	—	—	—	—	—	—	—	—
1934, Red Brown	*	1938	—	—	—	—	—	—	9.50	24
↳1934, Doubled Die Obverse, FS-101, Red Brown	*	285339	—	—	—	—	—	—	—	—
1934, Red	*	1939	—	—	—	—	—	—	—	34
↳1934, Doubled Die Obverse, FS-101, Red	*	285340	—	—	—	—	—	—	—	—
1934-D, Brown	28,446,000	2034	0.60	0.80	0.80	1.00	1.50	4.10	11.00	20
↳1934-D, D Over D, FS-503, Brown	*	285342	—	—	—	—	—	—	—	—
1934-D, Red Brown	*	2035	—	—	—	—	—	—	19.00	46
↳1934-D, D Over D, FS-503, Red Brown	*	285345	—	—	—	—	—	—	—	—
1934-D, Red	*	2036	—	—	—	—	—	—	32.00	100
↳1934-D, D Over D, FS-503, Red	*	285348	—	—	—	—	—	—	—	—

* Included in number above.

1936, Doubled Die Obverse
FS-101

Circulation Strikes *(continued)*

	Mintage	GSID	VG-8	F-12	VF-20	EF-40	AU-50	MS-60	MS-63	MS-65
1935, Brown	245,388,000	1940	$0.20	$0.20	$0.20	$0.20	$0.30	$1.50	$5.50	$11.00
↳1935, Doubled Die Obverse, FS-101, Brown	*	69781	—	—	—	—	—	—	—	—
1935, Red Brown	*	1941	—	—	—	—	—	—	11.00	20.00
↳1935, Doubled Die Obverse, FS-101, Red Brown	*	69782	—	—	—	—	—	—	—	—
1935, Red	*	1942	—	—	—	—	—	—	—	30.00
↳1935, Doubled Die Obverse, FS-101, Red	*	69783	—	—	—	—	—	—	—	1,500.00
1935-D, Brown	47,000,000	2037	0.20	0.20	0.20	0.20	0.30	2.60	8.00	13.50
1935-D, Red Brown	*	2038	—	—	—	—	—	—	12.00	34.00
1935-D, Red	*	2039	—	—	—	—	—	—	22.00	55.00
1935-S, Brown	38,702,000	2040	0.20	0.30	0.40	0.60	0.80	5.50	11.00	27.00
1935-S, Red Brown	*	2041	—	—	—	—	—	—	16.00	55.00
1935-S, Red	*	2042	—	—	—	—	—	—	—	80.00
1936, Brown	309,632,000	1943	0.20	0.30	0.40	0.60	0.60	1.50	2.40	4.10
↳1936, Doubled Die Obverse, Variety 1, FS-101, Brown	*	285350	60.00	80.00	110.00	180.00	290.00	850.00	1,550.00	3,500.00
↳1936, Doubled Die Obverse, Variety 2, FS-102, Brown	*	285353	—	47.00	70.00	110.00	260.00	430.00	650.00	1,100.00
↳1936, Doubled Die Obverse, Variety 3, FS-103, Brown	*	285356	—	—	—	100.00	120.00	145.00	180.00	365.00
1936, Red Brown	*	1944	—	—	—	—	—	—	2.60	5.50
↳1936, Doubled Die Obverse, Variety 1, FS-101, Red Brown	*	285351	—	—	—	—	—	—	2,400.00	4,250.00
↳1936, Doubled Die Obverse, Variety 2, FS-102, Red Brown	*	285354	—	—	—	—	—	—	800.00	1,400.00
↳1936, Doubled Die Obverse, Variety 3, FS-103, Red Brown	*	285357	—	—	—	—	—	—	210.00	490.00
1936, Red	*	1945	—	—	—	—	—	—	4.10	11.00
↳1936, Doubled Die Obverse, Variety 1, FS-101, Red	*	285352	—	—	—	—	—	—	3,100.00	6,250.00
↳1936, Doubled Die Obverse, Variety 2, FS-102, Red	*	285355	—	—	—	—	—	—	875.00	1,450.00
↳1936, Doubled Die Obverse, Variety 3, FS-103, Red	*	285358	—	—	—	—	—	—	245.00	575.00
1936-D, Brown	40,620,000	2043	0.20	0.30	0.40	0.60	0.60	1.50	2.40	5.50
1936-D, Red Brown	*	2044	—	—	—	—	—	—	3.40	9.50
1936-D, Red	*	2045	—	—	—	—	—	—	5.50	13.50
1936-S, Brown	29,130,000	2046	0.20	0.30	0.40	0.60	0.80	2.20	2.60	6.75
1936-S, Red Brown	*	2047	—	—	—	—	—	—	4.10	11.00
1936-S, Red	*	2048	—	—	—	—	—	—	5.50	17.50
1937, Brown	309,170,000	1955	0.20	0.20	0.20	0.20	0.30	1.50	2.40	4.10
1937, Red Brown	*	1956	—	—	—	—	—	—	2.60	6.75
1937, Red	*	1957	—	—	—	—	—	—	4.10	13.50

* Included in number above.

Circulation Strikes *(continued)*

	Mintage	GSID	VG-8	F-12	VF-20	EF-40	AU-50	MS-60	MS-63	MS-65
1937-D, Brown	50,430,000	2049	$0.20	$0.20	$0.20	$0.20	$0.30	$1.50	$2.40	$4.10
1937-D, Red Brown	*	2050	—	—	—	—	—	—	2.60	6.75
1937-D, Red	*	2051	—	—	—	—	—	—	4.10	12.00
1937-S, Brown	34,500,000	2052	0.20	0.30	0.40	0.60	0.80	2.20	2.60	5.50
1937-S, Red Brown	*	2053	—	—	—	—	—	—	4.10	6.75
1937-S, Red	*	2054	—	—	—	—	—	—	5.50	13.50
1938, Brown	156,682,000	1958	0.20	0.20	0.20	0.20	0.30	1.50	2.40	4.10
1938, Red Brown	*	1959	—	—	—	—	—	—	2.60	8.00
1938, Red	*	1960	—	—	—	—	—	—	4.10	13.50
1938-D, Brown	20,010,000	2055	0.40	0.40	0.40	0.60	0.80	1.90	2.60	5.50
↳1938-D, D Over D, FS-501, Brown	*	285359	—	—	—	—	—	—	—	—
1938-D, Red Brown	*	2056	—	—	—	—	—	—	3.40	8.00
↳1938-D, D Over D, FS-501, Red Brown	*	285360	—	—	—	—	—	—	—	—
1938-D, Red	*	2057	—	—	—	—	—	—	4.10	16.00
↳1938-D, D Over D, FS-501, Red	*	285361	—	—	—	—	—	—	—	—
1938-S, Brown	15,180,000	2058	0.40	0.40	0.40	0.60	0.80	2.20	3.40	5.50
↳1938-S, S Over S, FS-501, Brown	*	285362	—	—	—	—	—	19.00	30.00	60.00
↳1938-S, S Over S, FS-502, Brown	*	285363	—	—	—	—	—	22.00	40.00	75.00
1938-S, Red Brown	*	2059	—	—	—	—	—	—	4.10	6.75
↳1938-S, S Over S, FS-501, Red Brown	*	285364	—	—	—	—	—	—	40.00	80.00
↳1938-S, S Over S, FS-502, Red Brown	*	285365	—	—	—	—	—	—	47.00	105.00
1938-S, Red	*	2060	—	—	—	—	—	—	4.10	11.00
↳1938-S, S Over S, FS-501, Red	*	285366	—	—	—	—	—	—	55.00	95.00
↳1938-S, S Over S, FS-502, Red	*	285367	—	—	—	—	—	—	60.00	130.00
1939, Brown	316,466,000	1961	0.20	0.20	0.20	0.20	0.30	1.50	2.40	4.10
1939, Red Brown	*	1962	—	—	—	—	—	—	2.60	5.50
1939, Red	*	1963	—	—	—	—	—	—	4.10	11.00
1939-D, Brown	15,160,000	2061	0.40	0.40	0.40	0.60	0.80	1.90	2.60	4.10
1939-D, Red Brown	*	2062	—	—	—	—	—	—	2.60	5.50
1939-D, Red	*	2063	—	—	—	—	—	—	5.50	11.00
1939-S, Brown	52,070,000	2064	0.20	0.30	0.40	0.60	0.80	2.20	2.60	5.50
1939-S, Red Brown	*	2065	—	—	—	—	—	—	4.10	8.00
1939-S, Red	*	2066	—	—	—	—	—	—	5.50	13.50
1940, Brown	586,810,000	1964	0.20	0.20	0.20	0.20	0.30	1.50	2.40	4.10
1940, Red Brown	*	1965	—	—	—	—	—	—	2.60	5.50
1940, Red	*	1966	—	—	—	—	—	—	3.40	13.50
1940-D, Brown	81,390,000	2067	0.20	0.20	0.30	0.40	0.60	1.50	2.40	4.10
1940-D, Red Brown	*	2068	—	—	—	—	—	—	2.60	5.50
1940-D, Red	*	2069	—	—	—	—	—	—	4.10	11.00
1940-S, Brown	112,940,000	2070	0.20	0.20	0.30	0.40	0.60	1.50	2.40	4.10
1940-S, Red Brown	*	2071	—	—	—	—	—	—	2.60	5.50
1940-S, Red	*	2072	—	—	—	—	—	—	4.10	11.00
1941, Brown	887,018,000	1967	0.20	0.20	0.20	0.20	0.30	1.50	2.40	4.10
1941, Red Brown	*	1968	—	—	—	—	—	—	2.60	5.50
1941, Red	*	1969	—	—	—	—	—	—	4.10	11.00

* Included in number above.

Circulation Strikes *(continued)*

	Mintage	GSID	VG-8	F-12	VF-20	EF-40	AU-50	MS-60	MS-63	MS-65
1941, Doubled Die Obverse, Brown	*	1970	—	—	$55.00	$110.00	$120.00	$260.00	$455.00	$850.00
↳1941, Doubled Die Obverse, FS-101, Brown	*	285371	—	—	55.00	110.00	120.00	260.00	455.00	850.00
1941, Doubled Die Obverse, Red Brown	*	1971	—	—	—	—	—	—	525.00	1,150.00
↳1941, Doubled Die Obverse, FS-101, Red Brown	*	285374	—	—	—	—	—	—	525.00	1,150.00
1941, Doubled Die Obverse, Red	*	1972	—	—	—	—	—	—	575.00	1,500.00
↳1941, Doubled Die Obverse, FS-101, Red	*	285377	—	—	—	—	—	—	575.00	1,500.00
1941-D, Brown	128,700,000	2073	$0.20	$0.20	0.30	0.40	0.60	1.50	2.40	4.10
1941-D, Red Brown	*	2074	—	—	—	—	—	—	2.60	5.50
1941-D, Red	*	2075	—	—	—	—	—	—	4.10	11.00
1941-S, Brown	92,360,000	2076	0.20	0.20	0.30	0.40	0.80	2.20	2.60	5.50
1941-S, Red Brown	*	2077	—	—	—	—	—	—	4.10	8.00
1941-S, Red	*	2078	—	—	—	—	—	—	5.50	12.00
1942, Brown	657,796,000	1973	0.20	0.20	0.20	0.20	0.30	1.50	2.40	4.10
↳1942, Doubled Die Obverse, FS-102, Brown	*	285381	—	—	—	775.00	—	—	—	—
1942, Red Brown	*	1974	—	—	—	—	—	—	2.60	5.50
↳1942, Doubled Die Obverse, FS-102, Red Brown	*	285385	—	—	—	—	—	—	—	—
1942, Red	*	1975	—	—	—	—	—	—	4.10	11.00
↳1942, Doubled Die Obverse, FS-102, Red	*	285389	—	—	—	—	—	—	—	—
1942-D, Brown	206,698,000	2079	0.20	0.20	0.20	0.20	0.30	1.50	2.40	4.10
↳1942-D, D Over D, FS-502, Brown	*	285392	—	—	—	—	—	—	—	—
1942-D, Red Brown	*	2080	—	—	—	—	—	—	2.60	5.50
↳1942-D, D Over D, FS-502, Red Brown	*	285394	—	—	—	—	—	—	—	—
1942-D, Red	*	2081	—	—	—	—	—	—	4.10	11.00
↳1942-D, D Over D, FS-502, Red	*	285396	—	—	—	—	—	—	—	455.00
1942-S, Brown	85,590,000	2082	0.20	0.20	0.30	0.40	0.80	2.20	4.70	8.00
↳1942-S, S Over S/Doubled Die Obverse, FS-101/301, Brown	*	285398	—	—	—	—	19.00	34.00	100.00	260.00
↳1942-S, S Over S, FS-512, Brown	*	285399	—	—	—	—	34.00	70.00	90.00	130.00
1942-S, Red Brown	*	2083	—	—	—	—	—	—	6.75	12.00
↳1942-S, S Over S/ Doubled Die Obverse, FS-101/301, Red Brown	*	285400	—	—	—	—	—	—	130.00	340.00
↳1942-S, S Over S, FS-512, Red Brown	*	285401	—	—	—	—	—	—	100.00	160.00
1942-S, Red	*	2084	—	—	—	—	—	—	9.50	19.00
↳1942-S, S Over S/ Doubled Die Obverse, FS-101/301, Red	*	285402	—	—	—	—	—	—	210.00	490.00
↳1942-S, S Over S, FS-512, Red	*	285403	—	—	—	—	—	—	145.00	235.00
1943, Steel (d)	684,628,670	1977	0.30	0.30	0.30	0.30	0.40	1.50	2.60	13.50
↳1943, Steel, FS-101 (d)	*	285404	—	—	—	—	—	—	525.00	900.00

* Included in number above. **d.** Due to a copper shortage in the critical war year 1943, the Treasury used zinc-coated steel for regular-issue cents. A handful were accidentally struck on old bronze and silver planchets, instead of the intended steel planchets. Today about a dozen are known to exist. Numerous regular steel cents have been plated with copper as novelties or with intent to deceive; their true nature is easily revealed with a magnet.

1943-D, Boldly Doubled Mintmark
FS-501

1944-D, D Over S
FS-511

Circulation Strikes *(continued)*

	Mintage	GSID	VG-8	F-12	VF-20	EF-40	AU-50	MS-60	MS-63	MS-65
1943-D, Steel (d)	217,660,000	2085	$0.30	$0.30	$0.30	$0.30	$0.40	$1.50	$2.60	$13.50
1943-D, D Over D, Steel (d)	*	2089	—	—	—	130.00	215.00	340.00	405.00	825.00
↳**1943-D, D Over D, Steel, FS-501** (d)	*	285406	—	—	—	—	—	340.00	405.00	825.00
1943-S, Steel (d)	191,550,000	2091	0.30	0.30	0.40	0.60	0.80	2.60	5.50	27.00
↳**1943-S, 3 Over 2, Doubled Die Obverse, Steel, FS-101** (d)	*	285407	—	—	—	—	—	—	—	1,250.00
1943, Bronze, Brown (d)	17+ est. known	1978	—	—	—	204,000.00	240,000.00	408,000.00	—	—
	Auctions: $312,000, PCGS AU-55 HA 04/25; $264,000, PCGS AU-55 HA 04/25									
1943, Bronze, Red Brown (d)	*	1979	—	—	—	—	—	—	—	—
1943-D, Bronze, Brown (d)	1 known	2086	—	—	—	—	—	—	—	—
	Auctions: $840,000, PCGS MS-64 HA 01/21									
1943-S, Bronze, Brown (d)	6 known	2092	—	—	—	198,000.00	252,000.00	—	600,000.00	—
	Auctions: $504,000, PCGS MS-63 HA 11/20									
1944, Bronze, Brown	1,435,400,000	1983	0.20	0.20	0.20	0.20	0.20	0.20	0.40	2.20
1944, Bronze, Red Brown	*	1984	—	—	—	—	—	—	0.60	4.10
1944, Bronze, Red	*	1981	—	—	—	—	—	—	0.80	11.00
1944-D, Bronze, Brown	430,578,000	2097	0.20	0.20	0.20	0.20	0.20	0.20	0.40	2.20
	Auctions: $115,000, NGC MS-63 HA 08/07									
1944-D, Bronze, Red Brown	*	2098	—	—	—	—	—	—	0.60	4.10
1944-D, Bronze, Red	*	2095	—	—	—	—	—	—	0.80	11.00
1944-D, D Over S, Bronze, Brown	*	2100	34.00	47.00	130.00	150.00	245.00	340.00	420.00	625.00
↳**1944-D, D Over S, Bronze, FS-511, Brown**	*	393202	34.00	47.00	130.00	150.00	245.00	340.00	420.00	625.00
1944-D, D Over S, Bronze, Red Brown	*	2101	—	—	—	—	—	—	490.00	900.00
↳**1944-D, D Over S, Bronze, FS-511, Red Brown**	*	393203	—	—	—	—	—	—	490.00	900.00
1944-D, D Over S, Bronze, Red	*	2099	—	—	—	—	—	—	550.00	1,900.00
↳**1944-D, D Over S, Bronze, FS-511, Red**	*	393204	—	—	—	—	—	—	550.00	1,900.00
1944-S, Brown	282,760,000	2103	0.20	0.20	0.20	0.20	0.20	0.40	0.80	3.40
	Auctions: $373,750, NGC MS-66 HA 08/08									
1944-S, Red Brown	*	2104	—	—	—	—	—	—	0.90	5.50
1944-S, Red	*	2102	—	—	—	—	—	—	1.40	11.00
1944, Steel	20–30 known	1982	—	—			33,500.00	60,000.00	108,000.00	—
	Auctions: $168,000, PCGS MS-64 HA 01/25; $108,000, PCGS MS-64 HA 01/25									
1944-D, Steel	7 known	2096	—	—	—	—	—	42,000.00	96,000.00	—
1944-S, Steel	2 known	373181	—	—	—	—	—	—	—	480,000.00
	Auctions: $408,000, PCGS MS-66 HA 08/21									

* Included in number above. **d.** Due to a copper shortage in the critical war year 1943, the Treasury used zinc-coated steel for regular-issue cents. A handful were accidentally struck on old bronze and silver planchets, instead of the intended steel planchets. Today about a dozen are known to exist. Numerous regular steel cents have been plated with copper as novelties or with intent to deceive; their true nature is easily revealed with a magnet.

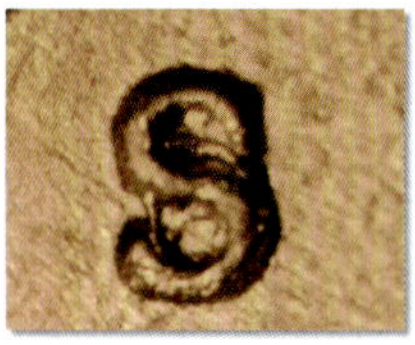

1946-S, S Over D
FS-511

Circulation Strikes *(continued)*

	Mintage	GSID	VG-8	F-12	VF-20	EF-40	AU-50	MS-60	MS-63	MS-65
1945, Brown	1,040,515,000	1986	$0.20	$0.20	$0.20	$0.20	$0.20	$0.20	$0.40	$2.20
1945, Red Brown	*	1987	—	—	—	—	—	—	0.60	4.10
1945, Red	*	1985	—	—	—	—	—	—	0.80	11.00
1945-D, Brown	266,268,000	2106	0.20	0.20	0.20	0.20	0.20	0.20	0.40	2.20
1945-D, Red Brown	*	2107	—	—	—	—	—	—	0.60	4.10
1945-D, Red	*	2105	—	—	—	—	—	—	0.80	11.00
1945-S, Brown	181,770,000	2109	0.20	0.20	0.20	0.20	0.20	0.40	0.80	3.40
1945-S, Red Brown	*	2110	—	—	—	—	—	—	0.90	5.50
1945-S, Red	*	2108	—	—	—	—	—	—	1.40	11.00
1946, Brown	991,655,000	1989	0.20	0.20	0.20	0.20	0.20	0.20	0.40	2.20
1946, Red Brown	*	1990	—	—	—	—	—	—	0.60	4.10
1946, Red	*	1988	—	—	—	—	—	—	0.80	11.00
1946-D, Brown	315,690,000	2112	0.20	0.20	0.30	0.30	0.40	0.40	0.80	3.40
1946-D, Red Brown	*	2113	—	—	—	—	—	—	0.90	4.10
1946-D, Red	*	2111	—	—	—	—	—	—	1.40	11.00
1946-S, Brown	198,100,000	2115	0.20	0.20	0.20	0.20	0.20	0.40	0.80	3.40
↳1946-S, S Over D, FS-511, Brown	*	285421	—	—	47.00	80.00	100.00	130.00	160.00	290.00
1946-S, Red Brown	*	2116	—	—	—	—	—	—	0.90	5.50
↳1946-S, S Over D, FS-511, Red Brown	*	285423	—	—	—	—	—	—	390.00	725.00
1946-S, Red	*	2114	—	—	—	—	—	—	1.40	11.00
↳1946-S, S Over D, FS-511, Red	*	285425	—	—	—	—	—	—	240.00	405.00
1947, Brown	190,555,000	1992	0.20	0.20	0.30	0.30	0.40	0.40	0.80	3.40
↳1947, Doubled Die Obverse, FS-101, Brown	*	285426	—	—	—	—	—	—	—	—
1947, Red Brown	*	1993	—	—	—	—	—	—	0.90	4.10
↳1947, Doubled Die Obverse, FS-101, Red Brown	*	285427	—	—	—	—	—	—	—	—
1947, Red	*	1991	—	—	—	—	—	—	1.40	11.00
↳1947, Doubled Die Obverse, FS-101, Red	*	285428	—	—	—	—	—	—	—	—
1947-D, Brown	194,750,000	2118	0.20	0.20	0.30	0.30	0.40	0.40	0.80	3.40
1947-D, Red Brown	*	2119	—	—	—	—	—	—	0.90	4.10
1947-D, Red	*	2117	—	—	—	—	—	—	1.40	11.00
1947-S, Brown	99,000,000	2121	0.20	0.20	0.30	0.30	0.40	0.40	0.80	3.40
1947-S, Red Brown	*	2122	—	—	—	—	—	—	0.90	4.10
1947-S, Red	*	2120	—	—	—	—	—	—	1.40	13.50
1948, Brown	317,570,000	1995	0.20	0.20	0.20	0.20	0.20	0.20	0.40	2.20
1948, Red Brown	*	1996	—	—	—	—	—	—	0.60	4.10
1948, Red	*	1994	—	—	—	—	—	—	0.80	11.00
1948-D, Brown	172,637,500	2124	0.20	0.20	0.30	0.30	0.40	0.40	0.80	3.40
1948-D, Red Brown	*	2125	—	—	—	—	—	—	0.90	4.10
1948-D, Red	*	2123	—	—	—	—	—	—	1.40	11.00

* Included in number above.

1951-D, D Over S
FS-512

Circulation Strikes *(continued)*

	Mintage	GSID	VG-8	F-12	VF-20	EF-40	AU-50	MS-60	MS-63	MS-65
1948-S, Brown	81,735,000	2127	$0.20	$0.20	$0.30	$0.30	$0.40	$0.40	$0.80	$3.40
1948-S, Red Brown	*	2128	—	—	—	—	—	—	0.90	4.10
1948-S, Red	*	2126	—	—	—	—	—	—	1.40	11.00
1949, Brown	217,775,000	1998	0.20	0.20	0.20	0.20	0.20	0.20	0.40	2.20
1949, Red Brown	*	1999	—	—	—	—	—	—	0.60	4.10
1949, Red	*	1997	—	—	—	—	—	—	0.80	11.00
1949-D, Brown	153,132,500	2130	0.20	0.20	0.30	0.30	0.40	0.40	0.80	3.40
↳1949-D, D Over D, FS-501, Brown	*	285432	—	—	—	—	—	—	—	—
1949-D, Red Brown	*	2131	—	—	—	—	—	—	0.90	4.10
↳1949-D, D Over D, FS-501, Red Brown	*	285433	—	—	—	—	—	—	—	—
1949-D, Red	*	2129	—	—	—	—	—	—	1.40	11.00
↳1949-D, D Over D, FS-501, Red	*	285434	—	—	—	—	—	—	—	—
1949-S, Brown	64,290,000	2133	0.20	0.20	0.30	0.30	0.40	0.40	0.80	3.40
1949-S, Red Brown	*	2134	—	—	—	—	—	—	0.90	4.10
1949-S, Red	*	2132	—	—	—	—	—	—	1.40	11.00
1950, Brown	272,635,000	2001	0.20	0.20	0.20	0.20	0.20	0.20	0.40	3.40
1950, Red Brown	*	2002	—	—	—	—	—	—	0.60	6.75
1950, Red	*	2000	—	—	—	—	—	—	2.60	20.00
1950-D, Brown	334,950,000	2136	0.20	0.20	0.20	0.20	0.20	0.20	0.40	2.20
1950-D, Red Brown	*	2137	—	—	—	—	—	—	0.60	5.50
1950-D, Red	*	2135	—	—	—	—	—	—	2.60	13.50
1950-S, Brown	118,505,000	2139	0.20	0.20	0.20	0.30	0.30	0.40	0.80	3.40
↳1950-S, S Over S, FS-504, Brown	*	285482	—	—	—	—	—	—	—	—
1950-S, Red Brown	*	2140	—	—	—	—	—	—	0.90	4.10
↳1950-S, S Over S, FS-504, Red Brown	*	285483	—	—	—	—	—	—	—	—
1950-S, Red	*	2138	—	—	—	—	—	—	1.50	13.50
↳1950-S, S Over S, FS-504, Red	*	285484	—	—	—	—	—	—	—	—
1951, Brown	284,576,000	2004	0.20	0.20	0.20	0.30	0.30	0.40	1.50	4.10
1951, Red Brown	*	2005	—	—	—	—	—	—	2.60	6.75
1951, Red	*	2003	—	—	—	—	—	—	8.00	23.00
1951-D, Brown	625,355,000	2142	0.20	0.20	0.20	0.20	0.20	0.20	0.40	2.20
↳1951-D, D Over S, FS-511, Brown	*	285439	—	—	—	—	—	24.00	34.00	70.00
↳1951-D, D Over D, FS-512, Brown	*	285440	—	—	—	—	—	34.00	47.00	90.00
1951-D, Red Brown	*	2143	—	—	—	—	—	—	0.60	5.50
↳1951-D, D Over S, FS-511, Red Brown	*	285442	—	—	—	—	—	—	47.00	90.00
↳1951-D, D Over D, FS-512, Red Brown	*	285443	—	—	—	—	—	—	60.00	110.00

* Included in number above.

Circulation Strikes *(continued)*

	Mintage	GSID	VG-8	F-12	VF-20	EF-40	AU-50	MS-60	MS-63	MS-65
1951-D, Red	*	2141	—	—	—	—	—	—	$0.80	$11.00
↳1951-D, D Over S, FS-511, Red	*	285445	—	—	—	—	—	—	—	120.00
↳1951-D, D Over D, FS-512, Red	*	285446	—	—	—	—	—	—	—	145.00
1951-S, Brown	136,010,000	2145	$0.20	$0.20	$0.20	$0.30	$0.30	$0.40	0.80	3.40
1951-S, Red Brown	*	2146	—	—	—	—	—	—	0.90	4.10
1951-S, Red	*	2144	—	—	—	—	—	—	1.40	11.00
1952, Brown	186,775,000	2007	0.20	0.20	0.20	0.30	0.30	0.40	0.80	3.40
1952, Red Brown	*	2008	—	—	—	—	—	—	0.90	4.10
1952, Red	*	2006	—	—	—	—	—	—	2.60	23.00
1952-D, Brown	746,130,000	2148	0.20	0.20	0.20	0.20	0.20	0.20	0.40	2.20
↳1952-D, D Over S, FS-511, Brown	*	285447	—	—	—	—	—	—	—	—
1952-D, Red Brown	*	2149	—	—	—	—	—	—	0.60	4.10
↳1952-D, D Over S, FS-511, Red Brown	*	285448	—	—	—	—	—	—	—	—
1952-D, Red	*	2147	—	—	—	—	—	—	0.80	11.00
↳1952-D, D Over S, FS-511, Red	*	285449	—	—	—	—	—	—	—	—
1952-S, Brown	137,800,004	2151	0.20	0.20	0.20	0.30	0.30	0.40	0.80	3.40
1952-S, Red Brown	*	2152	—	—	—	—	—	—	0.90	4.10
1952-S, Red	*	2150	—	—	—	—	—	—	1.40	11.00
1953, Brown	256,755,000	2010	0.20	0.20	0.20	0.30	0.30	0.40	0.80	3.40
1953, Red Brown	*	2011	—	—	—	—	—	—	0.90	4.10
1953, Red	*	2009	—	—	—	—	—	—	2.60	24.00
1953-D, Brown	700,515,000	2154	0.20	0.20	0.20	0.20	0.20	0.20	0.40	2.20
1953-D, Red Brown	*	2155	—	—	—	—	—	—	0.60	4.10
↳1953-D, D Over D, FS-501, Red Brown	*	285452	—	—	—	—	—	—	27.00	60.00
1953-D, Red	*	2153	—	—	—	—	—	—	2.60	13.50
↳1953-D, D Over D, FS-501, Red	*	285454	—	—	—	—	—	—	35.00	80.00
1953-S, Brown	181,835,000	2157	0.20	0.20	0.20	0.30	0.30	0.40	0.80	3.40
1953-S, Red Brown	*	2158	—	—	—	—	—	—	0.90	4.10
1953-S, Red	*	2156	—	—	—	—	—	—	1.40	11.00
1954, Brown	71,640,050	2013	0.20	0.20	0.20	0.20	0.20	0.20	0.40	2.20
1954, Red Brown	*	2014	—	—	—	—	—	—	2.60	6.75
1954, Red	*	2012	—	—	—	—	—	—	4.10	16.00
1954-D, Brown	251,552,500	2160	0.20	0.20	0.20	0.20	0.20	0.20	0.40	2.20
↳1954-D, D Over D Over D, FS-501, Brown	*	285456	—	—	2.60	4.10	6.75	13.50	27.00	40.00
1954-D, Red Brown	*	2161	—	—	—	—	—	—	0.60	4.10
↳1954-D, D Over D Over D, FS-501, Red Brown	*	285457	—	—	—	—	—	—	34.00	60.00
1954-D, Red	*	2159	—	—	—	—	—	—	0.80	11.00
↳1954-D, D Over D Over D, FS-501, Red	*	285458	—	—	—	—	—	—	43.00	80.00
1954-S, Brown	96,190,000	2163	0.20	0.20	0.20	0.30	0.30	0.40	0.80	3.40
1954-S, Red Brown	*	2164	—	—	—	—	—	—	0.90	4.10
1954-S, Red	*	2162	—	—	—	—	—	—	1.40	11.00

* Included in number above.

1955, Doubled Die Obverse
FS-101

1955, Doubled Die Obverse, Closeup of Date

Circulation Strikes *(continued)*

	Mintage	GSID	VG-8	F-12	VF-20	EF-40	AU-50	MS-60	MS-63	MS-65
1955, Brown	330,958,200	2016	$0.20	$0.20	$0.20	$0.20	$0.20	$0.20	$0.40	$2.20
↳1955, Doubled Die Obverse, FS-102, Brown	*	285459	—	55.00	70.00	90.00	115.00	160.00	210.00	290.00
1955, Red Brown	*	2017	—	—	—	—	—	—	0.60	4.10
↳1955, Doubled Die Obverse, FS-102, Red Brown	*	285460	—	—	—	—	—	—	235.00	370.00
1955, Red	*	2015	—	—	—	—	—	—	0.80	13.50
↳1955, Doubled Die Obverse, FS-102, Red (e)	*	285461	—	—	—	—	—	—	300.00	525.00
1955, Doubled Die Obverse, Brown (e)	*	2165	1,250.00	1,400.00	1,550.00	1,950.00	2,250.00	3,250.00	4,500.00	9,000.00
↳1955, Doubled Die Obverse, FS-101, Brown (e)	*	310752	1,250.00	1,400.00	1,550.00	1,950.00	2,250.00	3,250.00	4,500.00	9,000.00
1955, Doubled Die Obverse, Red Brown (e)	*	2166	—	—	—	—	—	3,750.00	5,750.00	17,000.00
↳1955, Doubled Die Obverse, FS-101, Red Brown (e)	*	310753	—	—	—	—	—	3,750.00	5,750.00	17,000.00
1955, Doubled Die Obverse, Red (e)	*	2167	—	—	—	—	—	—	9,000.00	60,000.00
	Auctions: $114,000, PCGS MS-65 SBG 03/18									
↳1955, Doubled Die Obverse, FS-101, Red (e)	*	310754	—	—	—	—	—	—	9,000.00	60,000.00
1955-D, Brown	563,257,500	2169	0.20	0.20	0.20	0.20	0.20	0.20	0.40	2.20
↳1955-D, Doubled Die Obverse, FS-101, Brown (e)	*	285462	—	—	—	—	—	—	—	—
1955-D, Red Brown	*	2170	—	—	—	—	—	—	0.60	4.10
↳1955-D, Doubled Die Obverse, FS-101, Red Brown	*	285464	—	—	—	—	—	—	—	—
1955-D, Red	*	2168	—	—	—	—	—	—	0.80	11.00
↳1955-D, Doubled Die Obverse, FS-101, Red	*	285466	—	—	—	—	—	—	100.00	175.00
1955-S, Brown	44,610,000	2172	0.20	0.20	0.20	0.20	0.20	0.40	0.80	3.40
↳1955-S, S Over S Over S, FS-501, Brown	*	285468	—	—	—	—	—	13.50	24.00	70.00
1955-S, Red Brown	*	2173	—	—	—	—	—	—	0.90	5.50
↳1955-S, S Over S Over S, FS-501, Red Brown	*	285479	—	—	—	—	—	—	32.00	100.00
1955-S, Red	*	2171	—	—	—	—	—	—	1.40	11.00
↳1955-S, S Over S Over S, FS-501, Red	*	285469	—	—	—	—	—	—	40.00	120.00

* Included in number above. **e.** Note that many counterfeit 1955 Doubled Die cents exist. On authentic pieces, there is a faint die scratch under the left horizontal bar of the T in CENT.

1956-D, D Above Shadow D
FS-508

1958, Doubled Die Obverse
FS-101

Circulation Strikes *(continued)*

	Mintage	GSID	VG-8	F-12	VF-20	EF-40	AU-50	MS-60	MS-63	MS-65
1956, Brown	420,745,000	2019	$0.20	$0.20	$0.20	$0.20	$0.20	$0.20	$0.40	$2.20
1956, Red Brown	*	2020	—	—	—	—	—	—	0.60	4.10
1956, Red	*	2018	—	—	—	—	—	—	0.80	16.00
1956-D, Brown	1,098,201,100	2175	0.20	0.20	0.20	0.20	0.20	0.20	0.40	2.20
↳1956-D, D Over D, FS-502, Brown	*	285471	5.50	9.50	12.00	16.00	27.00	43.00	55.00	95.00
↳1956-D, D Over D, FS-508, Brown	*	285472	5.50	9.50	12.00	16.00	27.00	43.00	55.00	95.00
1956-D, Red Brown	*	2176	—	—	—	—	—	—	0.60	4.10
↳1956-D, D Over D, FS-502, Red Brown	*	285474	—	—	—	—	—	—	55.00	120.00
↳1956-D, D Over D, FS-508, Red Brown	*	285475	—	—	—	—	—	—	55.00	120.00
1956-D, Red	*	2174	—	—	—	—	—	—	0.80	11.00
↳1956-D, D Over D, FS-502, Red	*	285477	—	—	—	—	—	—	75.00	155.00
↳1956-D, D Over D, FS-508, Red	*	285478	—	—	—	—	—	—	70.00	155.00
1957, Brown	282,540,000	2022	0.20	0.20	0.20	0.20	0.20	0.20	0.40	2.20
1957, Red Brown	*	2023	—	—	—	—	—	—	0.60	4.10
1957, Red	*	2021	—	—	—	—	—	—	0.80	11.00
1957-D, Brown	1,051,342,000	2178	0.20	0.20	0.20	0.20	0.20	0.20	0.40	2.20
1957-D, Red Brown	*	2179	—	—	—	—	—	—	0.60	4.10
1957-D, Red	*	2177	—	—	—	—	—	—	0.80	11.00
1958, Brown	252,525,000	2026	0.20	0.20	0.20	0.20	0.20	0.20	0.40	2.20
↳1958, Doubled Die Obverse, FS-101, Brown (f)	*	69894	—	—	—	—	—	—	—	—
1958, Red Brown	*	2027	—	—	—	—	—	—	0.60	4.10
↳1958, Doubled Die Obverse, FS-101, Red Brown (f)	*	69895	—	—	—	—	—	—	—	—
1958, Red	*	2024	—	—	—	—	—	—	0.80	11.00
1958, Doubled Die Obverse, Red (f)	3 known	2025	—	—	—	—	—	—	342,000.00	480,000.00
	Auctions: $336,000, PCGS MS-64 SBG 03/18									
↳1958, Doubled Die Obverse, FS-101, Red (f)	3 known	69896	—	—	—	—	—	—	—	—
1958-D, Brown	800,953,300	2181	0.20	0.20	0.20	0.20	0.20	0.20	0.40	2.20
1958-D, Red Brown	*	2182	—	—	—	—	—	—	0.60	4.10
1958-D, Red	*	2180	—	—	—	—	—	—	0.80	11.00

* Included in number above. **f.** No specimens have been reported being found in circulation, Wheat cent bags, Uncirculated rolls, "or other means that would lead to credibility of a true accidental release from the mint," as per the *Cherrypickers' Guide to Rare Die Varieties, Vol. I* (sixth edition).

Proof Strikes

	Mintage	GSID	PF-63	PF-65	PF-66
Lincoln, Wheat Ears Reverse (1909–1958), Brown	n/a	81378	$675	$1,100	$1,450
Same, Red Brown	n/a	81379	725	1,100	1,500
Same, Red	n/a	81380	875	1,250	3,000
1909, V.D.B., Brown (a)	1,194	2470	17,000	23,500	32,500
1909, V.D.B., Red Brown (a)	*	2471	19,000	27,000	38,000
	Auctions: $258,500, PCGS PF-67 HA 08/14				
1909, V.D.B., Red (a)	*	2472	22,000	43,000	60,500
1909, Brown	2,618	2473	750	1,250	1,550
1909, Red Brown	*	2474	825	1,250	1,700
1909, Red	*	2475	1,250	1,600	3,250
1910, Brown	4,118	2476	675	1,100	1,450
1910, Red Brown	*	2477	725	1,100	1,500
1910, Red	*	2478	875	1,250	3,000
1911, Brown	1,725	2479	675	1,150	1,550
1911, Red Brown	*	2480	725	1,250	2,750
1911, Red	*	2481	900	2,250	9,000
1912, Brown	2,172	2482	675	1,150	1,950
1912, Red Brown	*	2483	725	1,400	2,750
1912, Red	*	2484	875	2,700	17,000
1913, Brown	2,983	2485	675	1,100	1,450
1913, Red Brown	*	2486	725	1,100	1,500
1913, Red	*	2487	875	1,250	3,000
1914, Brown	1,365	2488	775	1,250	2,000
1914, Red Brown	*	2489	900	1,550	2,750
1914, Red	*	2490	1,100	2,200	4,050
	Auctions: $126,500, PCGS PF-68 HA 04/08				
1915, Brown	1,150	2491	850	1,750	2,100
1915, Red Brown	*	2492	950	2,250	3,750
1915, Red	*	2493	1,250	3,750	7,000
1916, Brown	1,050	2494	1,750	3,450	4,500
1916, Red Brown	*	2495	2,750	4,750	5,250
1916, Red	*	2496	3,750	7,500	18,000
1936, Satin Finish, Brown	5,569	2497	440	1,100	1,900
1936, Satin Finish, Red Brown	*	2498	550	1,300	2,200
1936, Satin Finish, Red	*	2499	775	3,750	4,250
1936, Brilliant Finish, Brown	*	2500	430	825	1,250
1936, Brilliant Finish, Red Brown	*	2501	470	925	1,600
1936, Brilliant Finish, Red	*	2502	$575	$1,750	$3,000
↳1936, Brilliant Finish, Red CAM	*	2503	1,250	6,250	8,750
1937, Brown	9,320	2506	60	120	260
1937, Red Brown	*	2509	80	160	390
1937, Red	*	2505	160	310	575
↳1937, Red CAM	*	2507	230	1,000	2,200
↳1937, Red DCAM	*	2508	—	1,550	3,450
1938, Brown	14,734	2511	47	110	130
1938, Red Brown	*	2514	60	120	155
1938, Red	*	2510	95	170	310
↳1938, Red CAM	*	2512	365	775	1,000
↳1938, Red DCAM	*	2513	—	1,250	2,250
1939, Brown	13,520	2516	47	90	155
1939, Red Brown	*	2519	60	100	195
1939, Red	*	2515	95	150	265
↳1939, Red CAM	*	2517	—	1,000	2,500
↳1939, Red DCAM	*	2518	—	—	—
1940, Brown	15,872	2521	40	90	160
1940, Red Brown	*	2524	47	100	195
1940, Red	*	2520	55	130	325
↳1940, Red CAM	*	2522	—	2,400	4,000
↳1940, Red DCAM	*	2523	—	—	—
1941, Brown	21,100	2526	40	90	160
1941, Red Brown	*	2529	47	90	160
1941, Red	*	2525	80	120	340
↳1941, Red CAM	*	2527	—	—	—
↳1941, Red DCAM	*	2528	—	—	—
1942, Brown	32,600	2532	32	100	195
1942, Red Brown	*	2535	40	120	260
1942, Red	*	2530	75	130	650
↳1942, Red CAM	*	2533	155	490	1,200
↳1942, Red DCAM	*	2534	—	1,500	5,000
1950, Brown	51,386	2536	43	55	70
1950, Red Brown	*	2537	50	65	75
1950, Red	*	2538	55	70	85
↳1950, Red CAM	*	2539	—	145	360
↳1950, Red DCAM	*	2540	—	650	1,250
1951, Brown	57,500	2541	40	49	55
↳1951, DDO, FS-101, Brown	*	315596	70	130	180
1951, Red Brown	*	2542	46	55	65
↳1951, DDO, FS-101, Red Brown	*	315597	100	180	235

Note: No early references (pre-1960s), Mint records, or reliable market listings have been found to confirm the existence of true 1917 Proofs. "Examples seen have had nice matte-like surfaces, sometimes on just one side, but have lacked the vital combination of broad, flat rims on both sides and a mirror Proof edge (when viewed edge-on from the side)" (*A Guide Book of Lincoln Cents*). The leading certification services do not recognize Proofs of this year. The editors of this book also do not believe that true Proofs of 1917 exist. * Included in number above. **a.** Of the 1,194 coins reported struck, an estimated 400 to 600 were issued.

Proof Strikes *(continued)*

	Mintage	GSID	PF-63	PF-65	PF-66
1951, Red	*	2543	$49.00	$60.00	$70.00
↳1951, DDO, FS-101, Red	*	315598	130.00	220.00	290.00
↳1951, Red CAM	*	2544	—	160.00	325.00
↳1951, DDO, FS-101, Red CAM	*	315599	—	390.00	725.00
1952, Brown	81,980	2546	15.00	24.00	34.00
1952, Red Brown	*	2547	20.00	30.00	47.00
1952, Red	*	2548	27.00	42.00	70.00
↳1952, Red CAM	*	2549	—	130.00	235.00
↳1952, Red DCAM	*	2550	—	1,250.00	2,200.00
1953, Brown	128,800	2551	11.00	19.00	27.00
1953, Red Brown	*	2552	16.00	24.00	40.00
1953, Red	*	2553	20.00	31.00	55.00
↳1953, Red CAM	*	2554	—	130.00	180.00
↳1953, Red DCAM	*	2555	—	575.00	950.00
1954, Brown	233,300	2556	5.50	8.00	13.50
1954, Red Brown	*	2557	8.00	12.00	20.00
1954, Red	*	2558	11.00	15.00	34.00
↳1954, Red CAM	*	2559	—	40.00	80.00
↳1954, Red DCAM	*	2560	—	390.00	575.00
1955, Brown	378,200	2561	5.50	8.00	13.50
↳1955, DDO/DDR, FS-103/801, Brown	*	315616	—	—	—
1955, Red Brown	*	2562	8.00	12.00	20.00
↳1955, DDO/DDR, FS-103/801, Red Brown	*	315617	—	195.00	—
1955, Red	*	2563	10.00	13.50	27.00
↳1955, DDO/DDR, FS-103/801, Red	*	315618	360.00	490.00	550.00

	Mintage	GSID	PF-63	PF-65	PF-66
↳1955, Red CAM	*	2564	—	$34.00	$55.00
↳1955, DDO/DDR, FS-103/801, Red CAM	*	315619	—	—	—
↳1955, Red DCAM	*	2565	—	260.00	390.00
↳1955, DDO/DDR, FS-103/801, Red DCAM	*	315620	—	—	—
1956, Brown	669,384	2566	$1.50	2.60	4.10
↳1956, DDO, FS-101, Brown	*	315621	—	—	—
1956, Red Brown	*	2567	1.90	3.00	9.50
↳1956, DDO, FS-101, Red Brown	*	315623	—	—	—
1956, Red	*	2568	2.20	4.10	20.00
↳1956, DDO, FS-101, Red	*	315625	—	—	—
↳1956, Red CAM	*	2569	—	20.00	40.00
↳1956, Red DCAM	*	2570	—	260.00	390.00
1957, Brown	1,247,952	2571	1.50	2.20	4.10
1957, Red Brown	*	2572	1.90	2.40	9.50
1957, Red	*	2573	2.20	2.90	20.00
↳1957, Red CAM	*	2574	—	20.00	40.00
↳1957, Red DCAM	*	2575	—	455.00	775.00
1958, Brown	875,652	2576	1.90	2.60	4.10
1958, Red Brown	*	2577	2.20	3.00	9.50
1958, Red	*	2578	2.20	3.70	17.50
↳1958, Red CAM	*	2579	—	20.00	40.00
↳1958, Red DCAM	*	2580	—	260.00	420.00

* Included in number above.

LINCOLN, MEMORIAL REVERSE (1959–2008)

Copper Alloy (1959–1982): **Designer:** *Victor D. Brenner (obverse), Frank Gasparro (reverse).* **Weight:** *3.11 grams.* **Composition:** *1959–1962—.950 copper, .050 tin and zinc; 1962–1982—.950 copper, .050 zinc.* **Diameter:** *19 mm.* **Edge:** *Plain.* **Mints:** *Philadelphia, Denver, and San Francisco.*

Copper Alloy (1959–1982), Circulation Strike

Copper Alloy, Proof Strike

Copper-Plated Zinc (1982–2008): **Designer:** *Victor D. Brenner (obverse), Frank Gasparro (reverse).* **Weight:** *2.5 grams.* **Composition:** *A core of .992 zinc, .008 copper, with a plating of pure copper; total content .975 zinc, .025 copper.* **Diameter:** *19 mm.* **Edge:** *Plain.* **Mints:** *Philadelphia, Denver, and San Francisco.*

Copper-Plated Zinc (1982–2008), Circulation Strike

Copper-Plated Zinc, Proof Strike

History. In 1959 a new cent design, by Frank Gasparro, was introduced to mark the 150th anniversary of Abraham Lincoln's birth. Victor Brenner's portrait of Lincoln was maintained on the obverse. The new reverse featured a view of the Lincoln Memorial in Washington, D.C., with Daniel Chester French's massive statue of the president faintly visible within. In 1969 the dies were modified to strengthen the design, and Lincoln's head on the obverse was made slightly smaller. In 1973 the dies were further modified, and the engraver's initials (FG) were enlarged. In 1974 the initials were reduced slightly. During 1982 the dies were modified again and the bust, lettering, and date were made slightly smaller. The Lincoln Memorial reverse was used until 2009, when a switch was made to four new reverse designs honoring the bicentennial of Lincoln's birth. Lincoln Memorial cents were struck for circulation at the Philadelphia, Denver, and San Francisco mints, with the latter in smaller numbers. Partway through 1982 the bronze alloy was discontinued in favor of copper-coated zinc. From 2005 to 2010, coins produced for Mint Sets were made with a Satin Finish instead of the traditional Uncirculated luster.

Striking and Sharpness. Striking varies and can range from "sloppy" to needle sharp. On the obverse, check Lincoln's hair and beard, although the sharpness of this feature varied in the dies; for more information see *A Guide Book of Lincoln Cents* (third edition). Tiny marks on the shoulder of Lincoln indicate a weak strike there. On the reverse the sharpness can vary, including on the tiny statue of Lincoln and the shrubbery. On the reverse there can be light striking on the steps of the Memorial, and at IBU and M of E PLURIBUS UNUM. The quality of the fields can vary, as well. Some early copper-coated zinc cents, particularly of 1982 and 1983, can have planchet blisters or other problems. All Proof Lincoln Memorial cents are of the mirror type, usually with cameo or frosted contrast between the devices and the fields. High quality is common. Special Mint Set (SMS) coins were struck in lieu of Proofs from 1965 to 1967, and in some instances these closely resemble Proofs.

Availability. Coins in this series are plentiful for standard dates and mintmarks. Collectible varieties exist, and are eagerly sought by specialists, who use the *Cherrypickers' Guide to Rare Die Varieties* as their standard reference. Some of the more popular varieties are illustrated and listed herein.

Grading Standards

Caveat: These grading standards do not take sharpness of strike into account.

MS-60 to 70 (Mint State). ***Obverse and Reverse:*** At MS-65 and higher, the luster is rich on all areas, except perhaps the shoulder (which may be grainy and show original planchet surface). There is no rubbing, and no contact marks are visible except under magnification. Coins with full or nearly full mint orange-red color can be designated RD; those with full or nearly full brown-toned surfaces can be designated BN; and those with a substantial percentage of red-orange and of brown can be called RB. Ideally, MS-65 or finer coins should have good eye appeal, which in the RB category means nicely blended colors, not stained or blotched. Below MS-65, full RD coins become scarce, and at MS-60 to 62 they are virtually non-existent, unless they have been dipped. Copper is a very active metal, and influences such as slight abrasions, contact marks, and so on that define the grade also affect the color. The ANA grading standards allow for "dull" and/or "spotted" coins at MS-60 and 61, as well as incomplete luster. In the marketplace, interpretations often vary widely. BN and RB coins at MS-60 and 61 are apt to be more attractive than (dipped) RD coins.

MS-68

AU-50, 53, 55, 58 (About Uncirculated). ***Obverse:*** Same guidelines as for the preceding type except that tinges of original mint-red are sometimes seen on coins that have not been cleaned. ***Reverse:*** Slight wear is seen on the Lincoln Memorial, particularly on the steps, the columns, and the horizontal architectural elements above.

Illustrated coin: The doubling of the obverse die of this popular variety is easily visible to the naked eye.

AU-58

EF-40, 45 (Extremely Fine). ***Obverse:*** Light wear is seen on Lincoln's portrait, and hair detail is gone on the higher areas, especially above the ear. ***Reverse:*** Most detail is gone from the steps of the Lincoln Memorial, and the columns and other higher-relief architectural elements show wear.

EF-40

PF-69RD Cameo

PF-60 to 70 (Proof). *Obverse and Reverse:* PF-65 and higher coins are usually RB (colors should be nicely blended) or RD, the latter with bright red-orange fading slightly to hints of brown. Some tiny flecks are normal on coins certified as PF-65 but should be microscopic or absent above that. PF-60 and 61 coins can be dull, stained, or spotted and still have some original mint color. Coins with fingerprints must be given a low numerical grade. Lower-grade Proofs usually have poor eye appeal. Generally, Proofs below PF-64 are not desired by most collectors.

1960, Large Date

1960, Small Date

1960-D, D Over D, Small Over Large Date
FS-101/501

1969-S, Doubled Die Obverse
FS-101

Circulation Strikes

	Mintage	GSID	MS-63	MS-65	MS-67
Lincoln, Memorial Reverse (1959–1982), Bronze, Brown	n/a	377845	$0.50	$2.60	—
Same, Red Brown	n/a	377846	0.60	3.40	—
Same, Red	n/a	377847	0.80	4.10	$12
Lincoln, Memorial Reverse (1982–2008), Zinc, Brown	n/a	374014	0.50	2.60	—
Same, Red Brown	n/a	374015	0.60	3.40	—
Same, Red	n/a	374016	0.80	4.10	12
1959	609,715,000	2183	5.50	13.50	525
1959-D	1,279,760,000	2333	4.10	8.00	170
↳**1959-D, D Over D, FS-501**	*	312796	34.00	70.00	—
1960, Lg Dt (a)	586,405,000	2186	4.10	11.00	495
1960, Sm Dt (a)	*	2187	4.10	6.75	340
1960-D, Lg Dt (a)	1,580,884,000	2336	4.10	9.50	490
↳**1960-D, D Over D, Lg Dt, FS-502** (a)	*	312799	—	65.00	1,150
1960-D, Sm Dt	*	2337	4.10	11.00	260
1960-D, D Over D/ Sm Dt Over Lg Dt (a)	1,580,884,000	2342	100.00	155.00	390
↳**1960-D, D Over D/ Sm Dt Over Lg Dt, FS-101/501** (a)	*	393276	145.00	235.00	950
1961	753,345,000	2192	4.10	9.50	490
1961-D	1,753,266,700	2345	2.60	11.00	575
↳**1961-D, D Over D, FS-501**	*	312802	50.00	95.00	—
1962	606,045,000	2195	4.10	9.50	310
1962-D	1,793,148,140	2348	2.60	8.00	1,150
1963	754,110,000	2198	2.60	8.00	525
1963-D	1,774,020,400	2351	2.60	11.00	6,250

	Mintage	GSID	MS-63	MS-65	MS-67
1964	2,648,575,000	2201	$2.60	$6.75	$1,250
↳**1964, DDR, FS-802**	*	312811	210.00	420.00	—
1964-D	3,799,071,500	2354	1.10	5.50	775
1965	1,497,224,900	2205	1.10	5.50	415
1966	2,188,147,783	2209	1.10	5.50	725
↳**1966, DDR, FS-801**	*	312817	—	—	—
1967	3,048,667,100	2213	0.90	4.10	470
1968	1,707,880,970	2217	1.10	5.50	290
1968-D	2,886,269,600	2357	1.10	5.75	215
1968-S	258,270,001	2360	0.90	4.10	120
1969	1,136,910,000	2220	1.10	5.75	775
1969-D	4,002,832,200	2363	0.90	4.10	195
1969-S	544,375,000	2365	4.10	6.75	455
1969-S, DDO (b)	*	2368	43,000.00	144,000.00	—
	Auctions: $126,500, PCGS MS-64 HA 01/08				
↳**1969-S, DDO, FS-101** (b)	*	312826	43,000.00	144,000.00	—
1970	1,898,315,000	2223	0.80	4.10	195
1970-D	2,891,438,900	2371	0.80	4.10	420
1970-S, Sm Dt	690,560,004	2374	47.00	90.00	650
↳**1970-S, Sm Dt, FS-1401**	*	315273	47.00	90.00	650
1970-S, Lg Dt	*	2375	0.80	8.00	195
1970-S, DDO	*	2378	2,250.00	3,600.00	—
↳**1970-S, DDO, FS-101**	*	315278	2,250.00	3,600.00	—
1971	1,919,490,000	2226	0.80	4.10	160
1971, DDO	*	2229	230.00	455.00	—
↳**1971, DDO, FS-101**	*	315282	230.00	455.00	—
1971-D	2,911,045,600	2383	0.80	4.10	290
1971-S	525,133,459	2386	0.80	8.00	170

Note: Values are for Red coins unless stated otherwise. * Included in number above. **a.** The alignment of the 1 and 9 in the date can be used for a quick determination of Large versus Small Date. Large Date: the top of the 1 is significantly lower than the top of the 9. Small Date: the tops of the 1 and 9 are at the same level. **b.** Beware of specimens that exhibit only strike doubling, as opposed to a true doubled die; these are worth only face value. See Appendix A of the *Cherrypickers' Guide to Rare Die Varieties, Vol. I* (sixth edition).

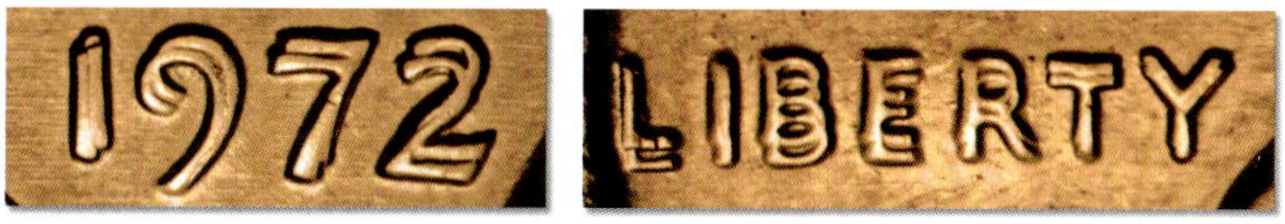

1972, Doubled Die Obverse
FS-101

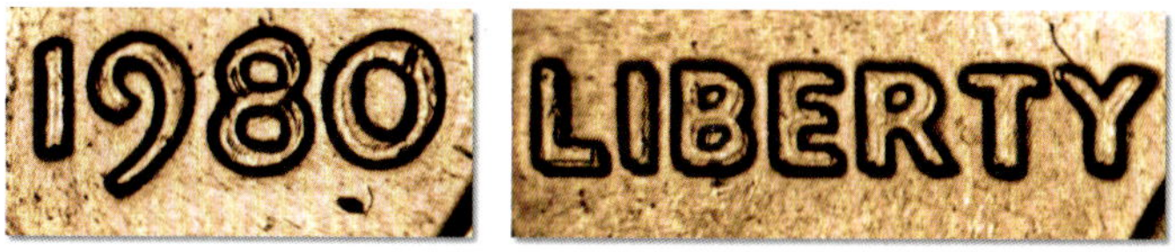

1980, Doubled Die Obverse
FS-101

1982, Large Date

1982, Small Date

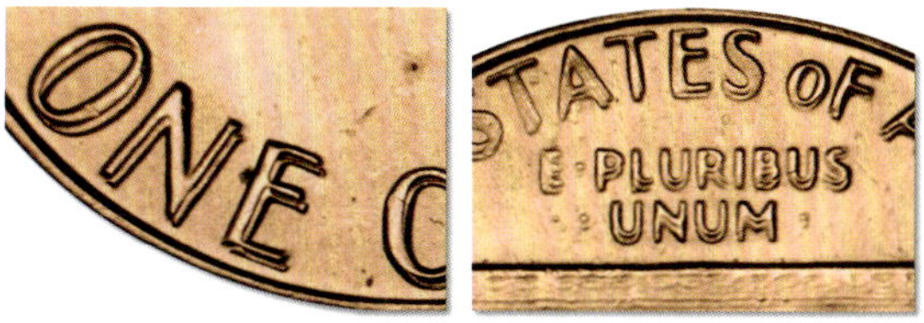

1983, Doubled Die Reverse
FS-801

1984, Doubled Ear
FS-101

Circulation Strikes *(continued)*

	Mintage	GSID	MS-63	MS-65	MS-67
1972	2,933,255,000	2234	$0.80	$4.10	$200
1972, DDO, Brown (c)	*	2231	360.00	455.00	—
↳1972, DDO, FS-101, Brown (c)	*	315283	360.00	455.00	—
↳1972, DDO, FS-104, Brown (c)	*	315286	—	—	—
1972, DDO, Red Brown (c)	*	2232	390.00	575.00	2,450
↳1972, DDO, FS-101, Red Brown (c)	*	315292	390.00	575.00	2,450
↳1972, DDO, FS 104, Red Brown (c)	*	315295			—
1972, DDO, Red (c)	*	2233	455.00	900.00	3,250
↳1972, DDO, FS-101, Red (c)	*	315301	455.00	900.00	3,250
↳1972, DDO, FS-104, Red (c)	*	315304	2,250.00	—	—
1972-D, Red	2,665,071,400	2388	0.80	4.10	525
1972-S, Red	376,939,108	2391	0.80	8.00	145
1973	3,728,245,000	2237	0.80	4.10	245
1973-D	3,549,576,588	2394	0.80	4.10	420
1973-S	317,177,295	2397	0.80	8.00	525
1974	4,232,140,523	2240	0.80	4.10	80
1974, Aluminum	1 known	374005	—	—	—
1974-D	4,235,098,000	2400	0.80	4.10	75
1974-D, Aluminum	1 known	374006	—	—	—

	Mintage	GSID	MS-63	MS-65	MS-67
1974-S	409,426,660	2405	$0.80	$8.00	$550
1975	5,451,476,142	2245	0.80	4.10	120
1975-D	4,505,275,300	2406	0.80	4.10	160
1976	4,674,292,426	2246	0.80	4.10	90
1976-D	4,221,592,455	2409	0.80	4.10	500
1977	4,469,930,000	2248	0.80	4.10	130
1977-D	4,194,062,300	2411	0.80	4.10	195
1978	5,558,605,000	2251	0.80	4.10	180
1978-D	4,280,233,400	2414	0.80	4.10	215
1979	6,018,515,000	2254	0.80	4.10	55
1979-D	4,139,357,254	2417	0.80	4.10	190
1980	7,414,705,000	2257	0.80	4.10	180
↳1980, DDO, FS-101	*	315312	325.00	725.00	—
1980-D	5,140,098,660	2418	0.80	4.10	120
1981	7,491,750,000	2260	0.80	4.10	130
1981-D	5,373,235,677	2419	0.80	4.10	170
1982, Bz, Lg Dt	10,712,525,000	71082	0.80	8.00	150
1982, Bz, Sm Dt	**	71083	5.50	16.00	210
1982-D, Bz, Lg Dt	6,012,979,368	2422	0.80	4.10	34
1982-D, Bz, Sm Dt	2–3 est. known	71080	24,000.00	—	—
1982, Zinc, Lg Dt	**	70034	0.80	4.10	38
1982, Zinc, Sm Dt	**	71111	1.50	8.00	55
↳1982, Zinc, Sm Dt, DDR, FS-1801	**	315318	—	20.00	80
1982-D, Zinc, Lg Dt	†	71081	0.80	4.10	47
1982-D, Zinc, Sm Dt	†	71084	0.80	4.10	47

Note: Values are for Red coins unless stated otherwise. * Included in number above. ** Included in 1982, Bz, Lg Dt, mintage figure. † Included in 1982-D, Bz, Lg Dt, mintage figure. **c.** Counterfeits of the 1972 doubled die are frequently encountered.

1997, Doubled Ear
FS-101

1999, Normal AM

1999, Wide AM

Circulation Strikes *(continued)*

	Mintage	GSID	MS-63	MS-65	MS-67
1983	7,752,355,000	2266	$0.80	$4.10	$46
↳**1983, DDO, FS-101**	*	315327	—	130.00	1,500
↳**1983, DDO, Counterclash, FS-401**	*	315330	—	—	—
1983, DDR	*	2269	$290.00	390.00	1,250
↳**1983, DDR, FS-801**	*	315335	310.00	420.00	1,400
1983-D	6,467,199,428	2426	0.80	4.10	30
1984	8,151,079,000	2271	0.80	4.10	27
1984, Doubled Ear	*	2274	215.00	260.00	575
↳**1984, Doubled Ear, FS-101**	*	315344	215.00	260.00	575
1984-D	5,569,238,906	2427	0.80	4.10	24
1985	5,648,489,887	2277	0.80	4.10	16
1985-D	5,287,339,926	2430	0.80	4.10	24
1986	4,491,395,493	2280	0.80	4.10	27
1986-D	4,442,866,698	2433	0.80	4.10	22
1987	4,682,466,931	2283	0.80	4.10	16
1987-D	4,879,389,514	2436	0.80	4.10	20
1988	6,092,810,000	2286	0.80	4.10	23
↳**1988, DDO, FS-101**	*	315356	—	2,500.00	—
↳**1988, Wide AM, FS-901** (d)	*	315357	180.00	325.00	—
1988-D	5,253,740,443	2439	0.80	4.10	15
↳**1988-D, Wide AM, FS-901** (d)	*	315360	—	—	—
1989	7,261,535,000	2288	0.80	4.10	15
1989-D	5,345,467,111	2441	0.80	4.10	16
1990	6,851,765,000	2291	0.80	4.10	20
1990-D	4,922,894,533	2442	0.80	4.10	15
1991	5,165,940,000	2294	0.80	4.10	16
1991-D	4,158,446,076	2445	0.80	4.10	15
1992	4,648,905,000	2297	0.80	4.10	15
1992, Close AM (d)	*	80831	21,000.00	30,000.00	51,000
↳**1992, Close AM, FS-901**(d)	*	393267	21,000.00	30,000.00	51,000

	Mintage	GSID	MS-63	MS-65	MS-67
1992-D	4,448,673,300	2448	$0.80	$4.10	$20.00
1992-D, Close AM (d)	15 est. known	70065	4,200.00	8,750.00	24,000.00
1993	5,684,705,000	2300	0.80	4.10	24.00
1993-D	6,426,650,571	2451	0.80	4.10	15.00
1994	6,500,850,000	70067	0.80	4.10	15.00
1994-D	7,131,765,000	2452	0.80	4.10	15.00
1995	6,411,440,000	2306	0.80	4.10	15.00
1995, DDO	*	2305	47.00	70.00	100.00
↳**1995, DDO, FS-101**	*	315372	47.00	70.00	100.00
1995-D	7,128,560,000	2455	0.80	4.10	20.00
↳**1995-D, DDO, FS-103**	*	315375	—	—	—
1996	6,612,465,000	2310	0.80	4.10	15.00
↳**1996, DDO, FS-101**	*	315378	—	—	—
1996-D	6,510,795,000	2458	0.80	4.10	15.00
1997	4,622,800,000	2311	0.80	4.10	27.00
1997-D	4,576,555,000	2459	0.80	4.10	22.00
1998	5,032,155,000	2314	0.80	4.10	17.50
↳**1998, Wide AM, FS-901** (d)	*	2317	34.00	70.00	525.00
1998-D	5,225,353,500	2460	0.80	4.10	20.00
1999	5,237,600,000	2319	0.80	4.10	19.00
	Auctions: $138,000, PCGS MS-66 HA 04/06				
1999, Wide AM (d)	*	2322	190.00	210.00	850.00
↳**1999, Wide AM, FS-901** (d)	*	392820	190.00	210.00	850.00
1999-D	6,360,065,000	2463	0.80	4.10	15.00
2000	5,503,200,000	2325	0.80	4.10	15.00
2000, Wide AM (d)	*	2326	11.00	20.00	170.00
↳**2000, Wide AM, FS-901** (d)	*	392823	11.00	20.00	170.00
2000, Cheerios	*	70092	47.00	55.00	100.00
2000-D	8,774,220,000	2464	0.80	4.10	15.00
2001	4,959,600,000	2327	0.80	4.10	12.00
2001-D	5,374,990,000	2465	0.80	4.10	12.00
2002	3,260,800,000	2328	0.80	4.10	12.00

Note: Values are for Red coins unless stated otherwise. * Included in number above. **d.** The reverse hub used for cents from 1974 to 1992 had the AM of AMERICA separated. A new reverse hub with the AM close together was used for all cents in 1993. At least one new reverse die of each type was used for 1992-P and -D cents made for circulation but it is not known if this usage was deliberate or accidental. Proof coinage reverted to the wide-AM design in 1994. In subsequent years a few dies from the circulation-strike hub were used for making Proof coins.

Circulation Strikes *(continued)*

	Mintage	GSID	MS-63	MS-65	MS-67
2002-D	4,028,055,000	2466	$0.80	$4.10	$12
2003	3,300,000,000	2468	0.80	4.10	12
2003-D	3,548,000,000	2467	0.80	4.10	12
2004	3,379,600,000	2329	0.80	4.10	20
↳2004, DDR, FS-801	*	315384	—	525.00	2,250
2004-D	3,456,400,000	2469	0.80	4.10	16
2005	3,935,600,000	24945	0.80	4.10	15
2005, Satin	1,160,000	24946	0.80	4.10	12
2005-D	3,764,450,500	24947	0.80	4.10	22
2005-D, Satin	1,160,000	76186	0.80	4.10	12
2006	4,290,000,000	65295	0.80	4.10	27
↳2006, DDO, FS-101	*	315389	—	—	—
2006, Satin	847,361	71085	$0.80	$4.10	$12
2006-D	3,944,000,000	68968	0.80	4.10	24
2006-D, Satin	847,361	68969	0.80	4.10	12
2007	3,762,400,000	68967	0.80	4.10	19
2007, Satin	895,628	71087	0.80	4.10	12
2007-D	3,638,800,000	68966	0.80	4.10	27
2007-D, Satin	895,628	71086	0.80	4.10	12
2008	2,558,800,000	69021	0.80	4.10	20
2008, Satin	745,464	76187	0.80	4.10	12
2008-D	2,849,600,000	69022	0.80	4.10	15
2008-D, Satin	745,464	71088	0.80	4.10	12

Note: Values are for Red coins unless stated otherwise. * Included in number above.

Special Mint Set Strikes

	Mintage	GSID	MS-65	MS-66	MS-67
1964	unknown	2202	$17,000.00	$19,000	$23,000
1965	2,360,000	2206	4.10	8	40
1966	2,261,583	2210	$4.10	$6.75	$19.00
1967	1,863,344	2214	4.10	6.75	13.50

Note: Values are for Red coins unless stated otherwise.

1970-S, Small Date (High 7)

1970-S, Large Date (Low 7)

1970-S, Proof, Doubled Die Obverse
FS-101

1999-S, Proof, Normal AM

1999-S, Proof, Close AM

Proof Strikes

	Mintage	GSID	PF-65	PF-66	PF-67
Lincoln, Memorial Reverse (1959–1982), Bronze, Proof	n/a	**395037**	**$4.10**	**$6.75**	**$8**
Lincoln, Memorial Reverse (1983–2008), Zinc, Proof	n/a	**395038**	**4.10**	**5.50**	**8**
1959	1,149,291	2583	3.00	13.50	27
1960, Lg Dt	1,691,602	2586	1.90	6.75	20
1960, Sm Dt	*	2587	13.50	20.00	27
1960, Lg Dt Over Sm Dt	*	2588	$175.00	$200.00	$220.00
↳1960, Lg Dt Over Sm Dt, FS-101	*	322161	175.00	200.00	220.00
1960, Sm Dt Over Lg Dt	*	2589	190.00	210.00	390.00
1961	3,028,244	2601	2.60	9.50	19.00
1962	3,218,019	2604	2.60	9.50	16.00
1963	3,075,645	2607	2.60	9.50	16.00
1964	3,950,762	2610	2.60	6.75	9.50

Note: Values are for Red Deep Cameo coins unless stated otherwise. * Included in number above.

Proof Strikes *(continued)*

	Mintage	GSID	PF-65	PF-66	PF-67
1968-S	3,041,506	2622	$4.10	$8.00	$8.00
1969-S	2,934,631	2625	4.10	8.00	12.00
1970-S, Sm Dt (High 7)	2,632,810	2631	100.00	130.00	195.00
↳1970-S, Sm Dt (High 7), FS-1402	*	322138	100.00	130.00	195.00
1970-S, Lg Dt (Low 7)	*	2629	4.10	8.00	34.00
↳1970-S, Lg Dt (Low 7) , FS-107	*	322152	—	—	—
1971-S	3,220,733	2638	4.10	8.00	12.00
1971-S, DDO	*	285489	525.00	650.00	1,000.00
↳1971-S, DDO, FS-101	*	2634	525.00	650.00	1,000.00
↳1971-S, DDO, FS-102	*	2637	575.00	725.00	1,100.00
1972-S	3,260,996	2639	4.10	8.00	12.00
1973-S	2,760,339	2640	4.10	8.00	12.00
1974-S	2,612,568	2641	4.10	8.00	12.00
1975-S	2,845,450	2642	4.10	6.75	9.50
1976-S	4,149,730	2643	4.10	6.75	9.50
1977-S	3,251,152	2644	4.10	6.75	8.00
1978-S	3,127,781	2645	4.10	6.75	8.00
1979-S, Var 1	3,677,175	2646	4.10	6.75	8.00
1979-S, Var 2	*	2647	4.10	6.75	8.00
↳1979-S, Var 2, FS-501	*	322113	4.10	6.75	8.00
1980-S	3,554,806	2648	4.10	6.75	8.00
1981-S, Var 1	4,063,083	2649	4.10	6.75	8.00
1981-S, Var 2	*	2650	11.00	16.00	35.00
↳1981-S, Var 2, FS-501	*	322118	11.00	16.00	35.00
1982-S	3,857,479	2651	4.10	6.75	8.00
1983-S	3,279,126	2652	4.10	6.75	8.00
1984-S	3,065,110	2653	4.10	6.75	8.00
1985-S	3,362,821	2654	$4.10	$6.75	$8
1986-S	3,010,497	2655	4.10	6.75	8
1987-S	4,227,728	2656	4.10	6.75	8
1988-S	3,262,948	2657	4.10	6.75	8
1989-S	3,220,194	2658	4.10	8.00	8
1990-S	3,299,559	2659	4.10	6.75	8
1990-(S), Missing Mintmark		2619	2,500.00	2,750.00	3,250
↳1990-(S), Missing Mintmark, FS-101 (a)	*	392824	2,500.00	2,750.00	3,250
1991-S	2,867,787	2660	4.10	6.75	8
1992-S	4,176,560	2661	4.10	6.75	8
1993-S	3,394,792	2662	4.10	6.75	8
1994-S	3,269,923	2663	4.10	6.75	8
1995-S	2,797,481	2664	4.10	6.75	8
1996-S	2,525,265	2665	4.10	6.75	8
1997-S	2,796,678	2666	4.10	6.75	8
1998-S	2,086,507	2667	4.10	6.75	8
1998-S, Close AM (b)	*	70860	95.00	130.00	175
↳1998-S, Close AM, FS-901 (b)	*	392827	95.00	130.00	175
1999-S	3,347,966	2668	4.10	8.00	8
1999-S, Close AM (b)	*	70086	55.00	60.00	70
↳1999-S, Close AM, FS-901 (b)	*	392830	55.00	60.00	70
2000-S	4,047,993	2669	4.10	5.50	8
2001-S	3,184,606	2670	4.10	5.50	8
2002-S	3,211,995	2671	4.10	5.50	8
2003-S	3,298,439	2672	4.10	5.50	8
2004-S	2,965,422	2673	4.10	5.50	8
2005-S	3,344,679	24920	4.10	5.50	8
2006-S	3,054,436	24921	4.10	5.50	8
2007-S	2,577,166	68772	4.10	5.50	8
2008-S	2,169,561	69240	4.10	5.50	8

Note: Values are for Red Deep Cameo coins unless stated otherwise. * Included in number above. **a.** An estimated 100 to 250 Proofs of 1990 were struck without the S mintmark (apparently from a circulation-strike die, without a mintmark, which had been given a mirror finish). This error escaped the notice of at least 14 people during die preparation and coining. **b.** Varieties were made in the circulation-strike style, with the A and the M in AMERICA nearly touching each other. On normal Proofs the two letters have a wide space between them.

LINCOLN, BIRTH BICENTENNIAL REVERSES (2009)

Designer: *Victor D. Brenner (obverse); see below for reverse designers.*
Weight: *Regular-issue coins—2.5 grams; special coins included in collector sets—3.1 grams.*
Composition: *Regular-issue coins—a core of .992 zinc, .008 copper, with a plating of pure copper; total content .975 zinc, .025 copper; special coins included in collector sets—.950 copper, .050 tin and zinc.* **Diameter:** *19 mm.* **Edge:** *Plain.* **Mints:** *Philadelphia, Denver, and San Francisco.*

Designers:

Obverse:. . . . . .Victor D. Brenner
Birth and Early Childhood Reverse: . . . . Richard Masters
Formative Years Reverse:. . . . . . . .Charles Vickers
Professional Life Reverse: . . . . Joel Iskowitz
Presidency Reverse: . . . . Susan Gamble

Circulation Strike

Birth and Early Childhood, Circulation Strike

Formative Years, Circulation Strike

Professional Life, Circulation Strike

Presidency, Circulation Strike

Proof Strike

Birth and Early Childhood, Proof Strike

Formative Years, Proof Strike

Professional Life, Proof Strike

Presidency, Proof Strike

History. The one-cent coins issued during 2009 pay unique tribute to President Abraham Lincoln, commemorating the bicentennial of his birth and the 100th anniversary of the first issuance of the Lincoln cent. Four different reverse designs were issued by the U.S. Mint, each representing a major aspect of Lincoln's life. The obverse retained the traditional profile portrait of previous years.

The reverse designs, released quarterly throughout 2009, are:

- Birth and Early Childhood (designer, Richard Masters; sculptor, Jim Licaretz), depicting a small log cabin like the one in which Lincoln was born in Kentucky.
- Formative Years (designer and sculptor, Charles Vickers), showing a youthful Abe Lincoln taking a break from rail-splitting to read a book, in Indiana.
- Professional Life (designer, Joel Iskowitz; sculptor, Don Everhart), with Lincoln standing in front of the Illinois state capitol in Springfield, symbolic of his pre-presidential career in law and politics.
- Presidency (designer, Susan Gamble; sculptor, Joseph Menna), depicting the partially completed U.S. Capitol dome in Washington, D.C., as it appeared when Lincoln held office.

The coins issued for general circulation were made of the exact same copper-plated composition used in the cent since 1982. Special versions struck for inclusion in collector sets were made of the same alloy as the first Lincoln cents of 1909—95 parts copper and 5 parts tin and zinc—and with a Satin finish.

Several die varieties (both circulation-strike and Proof) exist with minor doubling in the Formative Years reverse. Their values, which vary generally according to the severity of the doubling, are not yet firmly established with an active buy-and-sell market. These and other Lincoln cent die varieties are studied in greater depth in the *Cherrypickers' Guide to Rare Die Varieties.*

Striking and Sharpness. Striking is generally sharp. The quality of the fields can vary. Some 2009 cents, even from original rolls and bags, have surface marks that look like water spots. All Proof Lincoln Bicentennial cents are mirror Proofs, usually with cameo or frosted contrast between the devices and the fields.

Availability. Cents of this year were minted in quantities that, while large, were much smaller than for previous years (in the hundreds of millions, rather than multiple billions), if each of the four designs is considered individually. They are readily available in the numismatic marketplace, and are starting to be seen more frequently in circulation. High-quality Proofs (PF-69 and 70) are common in the secondary market.

Grading Standards

Caveat: These grading standards do not take sharpness of strike into account.

MS-60 to 70 (Mint State). ***Obverse and Reverse:*** At MS-65 and higher, luster is rich on all areas; there is no rubbing, and no contact marks are visible except under magnification. Coins with full or nearly full mint orange-red color can be designated RD; those with a substantial percentage of red-orange and of brown can be called RB; and those with full (or nearly full) brown-toned surfaces can be designated BN. Some 2009 cents, even from original rolls and bags, have surface marks that look like water spots.

MS-67RD

PF-60 to 70 (Proof). ***Obverse and Reverse:*** PF-65 and higher coins are RB (with colors nicely blended) or RD, the latter with bright red-orange color sometimes fading to hints of brown. Some tiny flecks are normal on coins certified as PF-65 but should be microscopic or absent above that level. PF-60 and 61 coins can be dull, stained, or spotted and still have some original mint luster. Proof coins with fingerprints are impaired and must be given a lower numerical grade. Lower-grade Proofs usually have poor eye appeal. Generally, Proofs of these types below PF-65 are not desired by most collectors.

PF-70RD
Deep Cameo

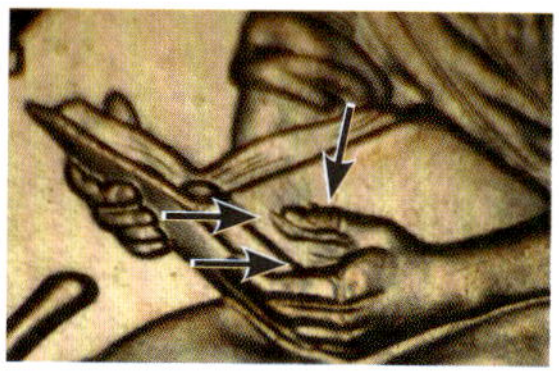

2009, Formative Years
FS-801: Seven Fingers.
Other varieties exist.

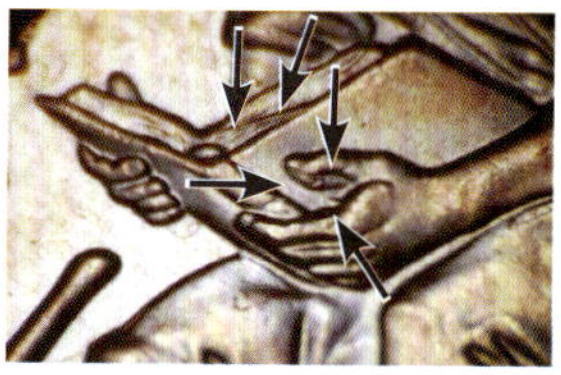

2009, Formative Years
FS-802: Seven Fingers.
Other varieties exist.

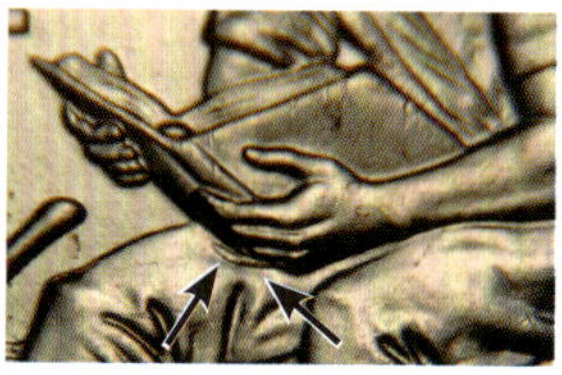

2009, Formative Years
FS-805: Doubled Pinky.
Other varieties exist.

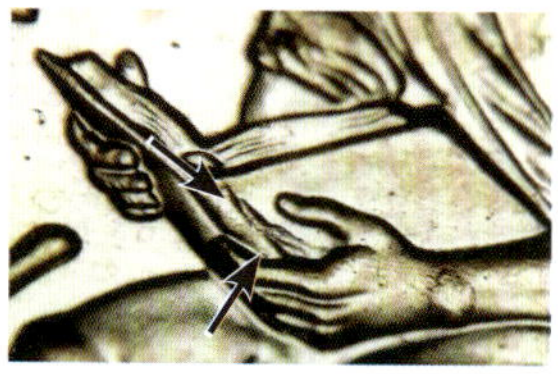

2009, Formative Years
FS-808: Skeleton Finger.
Other varieties exist.

Circulation Strikes

	Mintage	GSID	MS-65	MS-66	MS-67
Lincoln, Birth Bicentennial Reverse (2009)	**n/a**	**395039**	**$0.40**	**$6.75**	**$160.00**
Lincoln, Birth Bicentennial Reverse (2009), Satin Finish	**n/a**	**395040**	**2.40**	**5.50**	**6.75**
2009, Birth and Early Childhood	284,400,000	70560	0.40	8.00	195.00
2009, Birth and Early Childhood, Satin	784,614	71092	2.40	5.50	6.75
2009-D, Birth and Early Childhood	350,400,000	70961	0.40	6.75	260.00
2009-D, Birth and Early Childhood, Satin	784,614	71093	2.40	5.50	6.75
2009, Formative Years	376,000,000	70569	0.40	90.00	195.00
↳2009, Formative Years, DDR, FS-801	*	379403	—	—	—
↳2009, Formative Years, DDR, FS-802	*	379404	—	—	—
↳2009, Formative Years, DDR, FS-803	*	379405	—	—	—
↳2009, Formative Years, DDR, FS-804	*	379406	—	—	—
↳2009, Formative Years, DDR, FS-805	*	379407	—	—	—
↳2009, Formative Years, DDR, FS-806	*	379408	—	—	—
↳2009, Formative Years, DDR, FS-807	*	375869	—	—	—
↳2009, Formative Years, DDR, FS-808	*	379409	—	100.00	—
2009, Formative Years, Satin	784,614	71094	2.40	5.50	6.75
2009-D, Formative Years	363,600,000	70570	0.40	9.50	195.00
2009-D, Formative Years, Satin	784,614	71095	2.40	5.50	6.75
2009, Professional Life	316,000,000	70684	0.40	13.50	260.00
2009, Professional Life, Satin	784,614	71105	2.40	5.50	6.75
2009-D, Professional Life	336,000,000	70685	0.40	9.50	390.00
2009-D, Professional Life, Satin	784,614	71106	2.40	5.50	6.75
2009, Presidency	129,600,000	70958	0.40	8.00	160.00
2009, Presidency, Satin	784,614	71107	2.40	5.50	6.75
2009-D, Presidency	198,000,000	70959	0.40	6.75	260.00
2009-D, Presidency, Satin	784,614	71108	2.40	5.50	6.75

Note: Values are for Red coins unless stated otherwise.

Proof Strikes

	Mintage	GSID	PF-67	PF-68	PF-69
Lincoln, Birth Bicentennial Reverse (2009), Proof	**n/a**	**395041**	**$2.60**	**$4.10**	**$5.50**
Lincoln, Shield Reverse (2010–2025), Proof	**n/a**	**376182**	**2.60**	**5.50**	**8.00**
2009-S, Birth and Early Childhood	2,995,615	70818	2.60	4.10	5.50
2009-S, Formative Years	2,995,615	70819	2.60	4.10	5.50
2009-S, Professional Life	2,995,615	70820	2.60	4.10	5.50
2009-S, Presidency	2,995,615	70821	2.60	4.10	5.50

Note: Values are for Red Deep Cameo coins unless stated otherwise.

LINCOLN, SHIELD REVERSE (2010–2025)

Designer: *Victor D. Brenner (obverse) and Lyndall Bass (reverse).* **Weight:** *2.5 grams.* **Composition:** *A core of .992 zinc, .008 copper, with a plating of pure copper; total content .975 zinc, .025 copper.* **Diameter:** *19 mm.* **Edge:** *Plain.* **Mints:** *Philadelphia, Denver, San Francisco, and West Point.*

Circulation Strike

Proof Strike

History. Symbolically capping the life story told by the Lincoln Bicentennial cents of 2009, today's cents feature a reverse design "emblematic of President Lincoln's preservation of the United States as a single and united country." This is the seventh reverse used on the Lincoln type since 1909.

The shield motif was designed by U.S. Mint Artistic Infusion Program Associate Designer Lyndall Bass, and engraved by Mint Sculptor-Engraver Joseph Menna. It was unveiled during the launch ceremony for the fourth and final 2009 Bicentennial cent, held at the Ulysses S. Grant Memorial at the Capitol Building in Washington, D.C., November 12, 2009.

In addition to a new reverse design, the Shield Reverse cents feature a modern update of Victor David Brenner's original portrait for the 1909 Lincoln cent.

Striking and Sharpness. Striking is generally sharp. All Proof Lincoln, Shield Reverse, cents are mirror Proofs, usually with cameo or frosted contrast between the devices and the fields.

Availability. Cents of this design are minted in large quantities. They are readily available in the numismatic marketplace, and have successfully entered circulation through normal distribution channels. High-quality Proofs (PF-69 and 70) are common in the secondary market.

GRADING STANDARDS

Caveat: These grading standards do not take sharpness of strike into account.

MS-60 to 70 (Mint State). ***Obverse and Reverse:*** At MS-65 and higher, luster is rich on all areas; there is no rubbing, and no contact marks are visible except under magnification. Coins with full or nearly full mint orange-red color can be designated RD; those with a substantial percentage of red-orange and of brown can be called RB; and those with full (or nearly full) brown-toned surfaces can be designated BN. Some 2009 cents, even from original rolls and bags, have surface marks that look like water spots.

MS-67RD

PF-60 to 70 (Proof). ***Obverse and Reverse:*** PF-65 and higher coins are RB (with colors nicely blended) or RD, the latter with bright red-orange color sometimes fading to hints of brown. Some tiny flecks are normal on coins certified as PF-65 but should be microscopic or absent above that level. PF-60 and 61 coins can be dull, stained, or spotted and still have some original mint luster. Proof coins with fingerprints are impaired and must be given a lower numerical grade. Lower-grade Proofs usually have poor eye appeal. Generally, Proofs of this type below PF-65 are not desired by most collectors.

PF-70RD Deep Cameo

Circulation Strikes

	Mintage	GSID	MS-65	MS-66	MS-67
Lincoln, Shield Reverse (2010–2025), Red	**n/a**	**376181**	**$0.40**	**$5.50**	**$11.00**
2010	1,963,630,000	70960	0.40	34.00	1,000.00
2010, Satin	583,897	71103	2.40	5.50	6.75
2010-D	2,047,200,000	71100	5.50	40.00	1,100.00
2010-D, Satin	583,897	71104	2.40	5.50	6.75
2011	2,402,400,000	71101	0.40	6.75	16.00
2011-D	2,536,140,000	71102	0.40	8.00	17.50
2012	3,132,000,000	71568	0.40	8.00	30.00
2012-D	2,883,200,000	71591	0.40	8.00	27.00
2013	3,750,400,000	76188	0.40	9.50	30.00
2013-D	3,319,600,000	76189	0.40	5.50	16.00
2014	3,990,800,000	76190	0.40	11.00	22.00
2014-D	4,155,600,000	76191	0.40	11.00	23.00
2015	4,691,300,000	76192	0.40	8.00	32.00
2015-D	4,674,000,000	76193	0.40	6.75	27.00
2016	4,698,000,000	76194	0.40	9.50	40.00
2016-D	4,420,400,000	76195	0.40	6.75	22.00
2017-P (a)	4,361,220,000	76196	0.40	6.75	34.00
2017-D	4,272,800,000	76197	$0.40	$11.00	$34.00
2017-S, Enh Unc (b)	210,419	213470	2.60	4.10	6.75
2018-P	4,066,800,000	79375	0.40	5.50	20.00
2018-D	3,736,400,000	79376	0.40	5.50	20.00
2019-P	3,542,800,000	80832	0.40	5.50	27.00
2019-D	3,497,600,000	80833	0.40	5.50	16.00
2019-W (c)	346,257	80834	4.10	8.00	11.00
2020	3,560,800,000	81798	0.40	5.50	11.00
2020-D	4,035,600,000	81799	0.40	5.50	11.00
2021	3,925,820,000	85144	0.40	5.50	11.00
2021-D	3,982,800,000	85145	0.40	5.50	11.00
2022	3,129,200,000	193417	0.40	5.50	11.00
2022-D	3,230,400,000	193418	0.40	5.50	11.00
2023	2,262,000,000	199019	0.40	5.50	11.00
↳2023, Extra V	3,000 est.	375894	160.00	195.00	415.00
2023-D	2,260,800,000	199020	0.40	5.50	11.00
2024, Shield		347678	0.40	5.50	11.00
2024-D		347679	0.40	5.50	11.00
2025, Shield		376204	0.40	5.50	11.00
2025-D		376205	0.40	5.50	11.00

Note. Values are for Red coins unless stated otherwise. **a.** All 2017-dated cents struck at the Philadelphia Mint bear a P mintmark in honor of the 225th anniversary of U.S. coinage. **b.** Included n the special set of Enhanced Uncirculated coins issued in 2017 for the 225th anniversary of the San Francisco Mint. **c.** Included as a premium in the U.S. Mint 2019 Uncirculated Coin Set.

Proof Strikes

	Mintage	GSID	PF-67	PF-68	PF-69
Lincoln, Shield Reverse (2010–2025), Red	**n/a**	**376181**	**$0.40**	**$5.50**	**$11**
2010-S	1,689,216	71109	2.60	5.50	8
2011-S	1,673,010	70965	2.60	5.50	8
2012-S	1,239,148	79377	2.60	5.50	8
2013-S	1,274,505	79378	2.60	5.50	8
2014-S	1,193,699	71671	2.60	5.50	8
2014-S, DDO	*	392869	—	—	—
2015-S	1,099,182	79379	2.60	5.50	8
2016-S	1,011,624	79380	2.60	5.50	8
2017-S	979,475	79381	2.60	5.50	8
2018-S	901,072	79382	$2.60	$5.50	$8.00
2018-S, RevPf (a)	901,072	81802	15.00	16.00	17.50
2019-S	1,062,662	79383	2.60	5.50	8.00
2019-W (b)	601,327	79384	2.60	5.50	11.00
2019-W, RevPf (c)	412,708	81800	22.00	24.00	32.00
2020-S	823,909	81801	2.60	5.50	8.00
2021-S	868,644	85146	2.60	5.50	8.00
2022-S	699,097	193419	2.60	5.50	8.00
2023-S	593,245	213814	2.60	5.50	8.00
2024-S		347680	2.60	5.50	8.00
2025-S		376206	2.60	5.50	8.00

Note: Values are for Red Deep Cameo coins unless stated otherwise. * Included in number above. **a.** Included in the special set of Reverse Proof coins issued in 2018 for the 50th anniversary of the San Francisco Mint producing Proof coins. **b.** Included as a premium in the U.S. Mint 2019 Proof Set. **c.** Included as a premium in the 2019 U.S. Mint Silver Proof Set.

Two-Cent Pieces 1864–1873

AN OVERVIEW OF TWO-CENT PIECES

The two-cent piece was introduced in 1864. Made of bronze, it was designed by U.S. Mint chief engraver James B. Longacre, and was the first circulating U.S. coin to bear the motto IN GOD WE TRUST. At the time, coins were scarce in circulation because of the ongoing Civil War and the public's tendency to hoard hard currency, and silver and gold issues were entirely absent. Treasury officials felt that the two-cent piece would prove to be very popular as a companion to the Indian Head cent. However, the introduction of the nickel three-cent piece in 1865 negated much of this advantage, the production of two-cent pieces declined, and by 1873, when the denomination was discontinued, its only coinage consisted of Proofs for collectors.

A full "type set" of the two-cent piece consists of but a single coin. Most available in Mint State are the issues of 1864 and 1865, often seen with original mint orange color fading to natural brown. Proofs are available for all years.

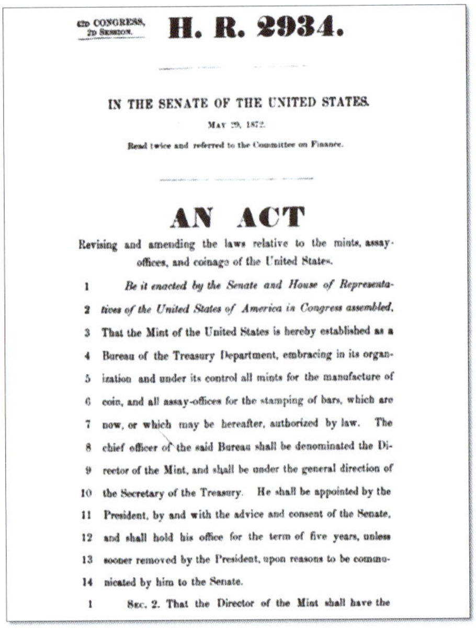
42D CONGRESS, 2D SESSION. **H. R. 2934.**

IN THE SENATE OF THE UNITED STATES.

MAY 29, 1872.

Read twice and referred to the Committee on Finance.

AN ACT

Revising and amending the laws relative to the mints, assay-offices, and coinage of the United States.

Be it enacted by the Senate and House of Representatives of the United States of America in Congress assembled, That the Mint of the United States is hereby established as a Bureau of the Treasury Department, embracing in its organization and under its control all mints for the manufacture of coin, and all assay-offices for the stamping of bars, which are now, or which may be hereafter, authorized by law. The chief officer of the said Bureau shall be denominated the Director of the Mint, and shall be under the general direction of the Secretary of the Treasury. He shall be appointed by the President, by and with the advice and consent of the Senate, and shall hold his office for the term of five years, unless sooner removed by the President, upon reasons to be communicated by him to the Senate.

SEC. 2. That the Director of the Mint shall have the

The Coinage Act of 1873 eliminated not only the two-cent piece but also the three-cent silver and half dime.

For the Collector and Investor: Two-Cent Pieces as a Specialty

Two-cent pieces can be collected by date and variety. A basic display consists of an 1864, Large Motto; 1864, Small Motto (rare); 1873, Close 3; and 1873, Open 3, the latter two being available only in Proof format. Some specialists opt to include just one of the 1873 varieties.

Collectors should select both circulation strikes and Proofs with care, for the number of truly choice *original* (unprocessed, undipped, not retoned) coins is but a small percentage of the whole. As a type, though, the two-cent piece is readily available for collecting.

Several specialized studies of two-cent pieces have been published over a long span of years, the first of significance being "Two-Cent Pieces of the United States," by S.W. Freeman, published in the *Numismatist*, June 1954.

SHIELD (1864–1873)

Designer: *James B. Longacre.* **Weight:** *6.22 grams.* **Composition:** *.950 copper, .050 tin and zinc.* **Diameter:** *23 mm.* **Edge:** *Plain.* **Mint:** *Philadelphia.*

Circulation Strike

Proof Strike

History. The two-cent piece, struck in bronze like the new Indian Head cents, made its debut under the Mint Act of April 22, 1864. Coins of all kinds were scarce in circulation at the time, due to hoarding. The outcome of the Civil War was uncertain, and Americans desired "hard money." Many millions of two-cent pieces were struck in 1864, after which the mintage declined, due to once-hoarded Indian Head cents becoming available again and to the new nickel three-cent coins being introduced in 1865. Continually decreasing quantities were made through 1872, and only Proofs were struck in the coin's final year, 1873.

Scan for additional information.

Striking and Sharpness. Points to check for sharpness on the obverse include WE in the motto, the leaves, and the horizontal shield lines. On the reverse check the wreath details and the border letters. Check the denticles on both sides. Most coins are quite well struck.

Availability. Most MS coins are dated 1864 or 1865, after which the availability declines sharply, especially for the issue of 1872. Among 1864 coins most seen are of the Large Motto variety. Small Motto coins are elusive. Coins with much or nearly all *original* mint red-orange color are rare for the later years, with most in the marketplace being recolored. The 1864, Small Motto, Proof, is a great rarity, with fewer than two dozen estimated to exist. Coins of 1873 were made only in Proof format, of the Close 3 and Open 3 styles. Proofs of most dates are easily enough acquired. Very few have original color. Do not overlook the many nice brown and red-and-brown pieces on the market (some investors acquire only "red" copper coins, leaving many great values among others). Refer to the comments under Proof Indian Head cents.

Grading Standards

MS-66RD

MS-60 to 70 (Mint State). ***Obverse and Reverse:*** At MS-65 and higher, the luster is rich on all areas. There is no rubbing, and no contact marks are visible except under magnification. Coins with full or nearly full mint orange-red color can be designated RD (the color on this is often more orange than red), those with full or nearly full brown-toned surfaces can be designated BN, and those with a substantial percentage of red-orange and of brown can be called RB. Ideally, MS-65 or finer coins should have good eye appeal, which in the RB category means nicely blended colors, not stained or blotched, the latter problem mostly with dipped and irregularly retoned coins. Below MS-65, full RD coins become scarce, although MS-64RD coins can be attractive. These usually have more flecks and tiny spots, while the color remains bright. At MS-60 to 62, RD coins are virtually nonexistent, unless they have been dipped. The ANA standards allow for "dull" and/or "spotted" coins at MS-60 and 61 as well as incomplete luster. As a rule, MS-60 to 63BN coins can be fairly attractive if not spotted or blotched, but those with hints of color usually lack eye appeal.

AU-50, 53, 55, 58 (About Uncirculated). ***Obverse:*** WE shows light wear, this being the prime place to check. The arrowheads and leaves also show light wear. At AU-50, level wear is more noticeable. At AU-53 and 55, wear is less. At AU-58, friction is evident, rather than actual wear. Luster, toned brown, is nearly complete at AU-58, but may be incomplete in the field. ***Reverse:*** At AU-50, light wear is seen on the ribbon and the higher-relief areas of the leaves and grains, while the lower areas retain their detail. Some luster may be present in protected areas. At AU-53 and 55, wear is lesser and luster is more extensive. An AU-58 coin will have nearly full luster and show only light friction.

AU-58

EF-40, 45 (Extremely Fine). ***Obverse:*** Wear is more extensive. WE shows wear extensively, but still is clear. The leaves lack detail on their highest points. Some scattered marks are normal at this and lower grades. ***Reverse:*** The higher-relief parts of the leaves and ribbon bow show further wear, as do other areas.

EF-45

VF-20, 30 (Very Fine). ***Obverse:*** WE is clear, but not strong. Leaves show more wear, as do all other areas. ***Reverse:*** Still more wear is seen, but the leaves still are separately defined. The wheat grains are very clear.

VF-20

F-12, 15 (Fine). ***Obverse:*** WE is the defining factor and is very weak, but readable, if only barely. Other areas show more wear. The edges of some leaves are gone, blending them into adjacent leaves. ***Reverse:*** Wear is more extensive. Near the apex of the wreath the edges of some leaves are gone, blending them into adjacent leaves. The grains of wheat are clear, but some are slightly weak.

Illustrated coin: WE is very weak.

F-15

VG-8, 10 (Very Good). ***Obverse:*** WE is gone, although the ANA grading standards and *Photograde* suggest "very weak." IN GOD and TRUST are readable, but some areas may be weak. The inner edges of most leaves are gone. ***Reverse:*** The wear appears to be less extensive than on the obverse. All lettering is bold. A few grains of wheat may be well worn or even missing.

VG-8

G-4, 6 (Good). ***Obverse:*** Wear is more extensive, and the leaf bunches are in flat clumps. IN GOD and TRUST are very worn, with a letter or two not visible. ***Reverse:*** All letters are clear. The wreath is mostly in outline on G-4. On G-6, perhaps half the grains are visible.

G-4

AG-3 (About Good). ***Obverse:*** The motto only shows only a few letters. The leaves are flat. Only a few horizontal shield stripes can be seen. ***Reverse:*** The wreath is in outline form. The letters are weak, with 20% to 40% worn away entirely.

AG-3

PF-60 to 70 (Proof). ***Obverse and Reverse:*** Gem PF-65 two-cent pieces will have very few hairlines, and these visible only under a strong magnifying glass. At any level and color, a Proof with hairlines has likely been cleaned, a fact usually overlooked. At PF-67 or higher there should be no evidence of hairlines or friction at all. Such a coin is fully original. PF-60 coins can be dull from repeated dipping and cleaning and are often toned iridescent colors or have mottled surfaces. At PF-63, the mirrorlike fields should be attractive, and hairlines should be minimal, most easily seen when the coin is held at an angle to the light. No rubbing is seen. PF-64 coins are even nicer. As a general rule, Proofs of 1873 are of very high quality but, unless dipped or cleaned, are nearly always toned light brown.

PF-64RD

1864, Small Motto

1864, Large Motto

1865, Plain 5

1865, Fancy 5

Circulation Strikes

	Mintage	GSID	VG-8	F-12	VF-20	EF-40	AU-50	MS-60	MS-63	MS-65
Shield Obverse (1864–1873), Brown	n/a	72347	$22	$24	$32	$55	$85	$130	$220	$455
Same, Red Brown	n/a	72348	—	—	—	—	—	—	260	600
Same, Red	n/a	72349	—	—	—	—	—	—	550	1,450
1864, Small Motto, Brown (a)	19,822,500	2677	245	390	525	750	1,050	1,300	1,500	2,600
↳1864, Small Motto, FS-401, Brown (a)	*	377848	245	390	525	750	1,050	1,300	1,500	2,600
1864, Small Motto, Red Brown (a)	*	2678	—	—	—	—	—	—	1,750	3,900
↳1864, Small Motto, FS-401, Red Brown (a)	*	377849	—	—	—	—	—	—	1,750	3,900
1864, Small Motto, Red (a)	*	2679	—	—	—	—	—	—	3,750	11,000
↳1864, Small Motto, FS-401, Red (a)	*	377850	—	—	—	—	—	—	3,750	11,000
1864, Large Motto, Brown (b)	*	2674	22	24	32	55	85	130	220	455
↳1864, Large Motto, Repunched Date, FS-1302, Brown (b)	*	329318	—	—	—	60	90	145	245	525
↳1864, Large Motto, Repunched Date, FS-1303, Brown (b)	*	329319	—	—	—	60	90	145	245	525
↳1864, Large Motto, Clashed with Indian Cent, FS-1901, Brown (b)	*	329322	—	—	—	—	345	440	650	1,000
1864, Large Motto, Red Brown (b)	*	2675	—	—	—	—	—	—	260	600
↳1864, Large Motto, Repunched Date, FS-1302, Red Brown (b)	*	329324	—	—	—	—	—	—	285	725
↳1864, Large Motto, Repunched Date, FS-1303, Red Brown (b)	*	329325	—	—	—	—	—	—	285	725
↳1864, Large Motto, Clashed with Indian Cent, FS-1901, Red Brown (b)	*	329328	—	—	—	—	—	—	775	1,200
1864, Large Motto, Red Brown	*	2676	—	—	—	—	—	—	550	1,450
1865, Brown (c)	13,640,000	2680	22	24	32	55	85	130	220	455
1865, Red Brown (c)	*	2681	—	—	—	—	—	—	260	600
1865, Red (c)	*	2682	—	—	—	—	—	—	550	1,450
1865, Plain 5, Brown	*	213353	26	29	39	65	100	155	265	550
↳1865, Plain 5, Repunched Date, FS-301, Brown (c)	*	377767	29	32	43	70	110	170	290	600
1865, Plain 5, Red Brown (c)	*	213354	—	—	—	—	—	—	310	725
↳1865, Plain 5, Repunched Date, FS-301, Red Brown (c)	*	377771	—	—	—	—	—	—	345	800
1865, Plain 5, Red (c)	*	213355	—	—	—	—	—	—	675	1,750
↳1865, Plain 5, Repunched Date, FS-301, Red (c)	*	377775	—	—	—	—	—	—	725	1,950
1865, Fancy 5, Brown (c)	*	213356	22	24	32	55	85	130	220	455
↳1865, Fancy 5, Repunched Date, FS-1302, Brown (c)	*	373813	24	27	36	60	90	145	245	525
↳1865, Fancy 5, Misplaced Date, FS-1305, Brown (c)	*	377777	24	27	36	60	90	145	245	525

* Included in number above. **a.** The circulated Small Motto is distinguished by a wider D in GOD, and the first T in TRUST nearly touching the ribbon crease at left. **b.** The circulated Large Motto is distinguished by a narrow D in GOD, and a 1 mm gap between the first T in TRUST and the ribbon crease. **c.** Circulated varieties show the tip of the 5 either plain or fancy (curved).

1867, Doubled Die Obverse
FS-101

Circulation Strikes *(continued)*

	Mintage	GSID	VG-8	F-12	VF-20	EF-40	AU-50	MS-60	MS-63	MS-65
1865, Fancy 5, Red Brown (c)	*	213357	—	—	—	—	—	—	$260	$600
↳**1865, Fancy 5, Repunched Date, FS-1302, Red Brown** (c)	*	373816	—	—	—	—	—	—	—	1,400
↳**1865, Fancy 5, Misplaced Date, FS-1305, Red Brown** (c)	*	377779	—	—	—	—	—	—	—	950
1865, Fancy 5, Red (c)	*	213358	—	—	—	—	—	—	550	1,450
1866, Brown	3,177,000	2683	$23	$40	$55	$65	$105	$150	240	500
1866, Red Brown	*	2684	—	—	—	—	—	—	290	750
1866, Red	*	2685	—	—	—	—	—	—	575	1,600
1867, Brown	2,938,750	2686	23	40	55	65	100	150	235	575
1867, Red Brown	*	2687	—	—	—	—	—	—	275	775
1867, Red	*	2688	—	—	—	—	—	—	725	3,100
1867, Doubled Die Obverse, Brown (d)	*	2689	160	290	390	750	1,000	2,250	4,000	7,500
↳**1867, Doubled Die Obverse, FS-101, Brown** (d)	*	351921	160	290	390	750	1,000	2,250	4,000	7,500
1867, Doubled Die Obverse, Red Brown (d)	*	2690	—	—	—	—	—	—	5,500	11,000
↳**1867, Doubled Die Obverse, FS-101, Red Brown** (d)	*	351922	—	—	—	—	—	—	5,500	11,000
1867, Doubled Die Obverse, Red (d)	*	2691	—	—	—	—	—	—	—	18,000
1868, Brown	2,803,750	2692	24	40	55	70	110	200	260	650
↳**1868, Repunched Date, FS-303, Brown**	*	351925	27	45	60	75	120	220	285	725
1868, Red Brown	*	2693	—	—	—	—	—	—	390	1,200
↳**1868, Repunched Date, FS-303, Red Brown**	*	351927	—	—	—	—	—	—	430	1,300
1868, Red	*	2694	—	—	—	—	—	—	625	2,500
1869, Brown	1,546,500	2695	31	49	60	100	130	175	260	575
↳**1869, Repunched Date, FS-302, Brown**	*	285494	—	—	70	120	155	210	340	—
1869, Red Brown	*	2696	—	—	—	—	—	—	490	950
↳**1869, Repunched Date, FS-302, Red Brown**	*	285496	—	—	—	—	—	—	625	—
1869, Red	*	2697	—	—	—	—	—	—	775	2,500
↳**1869, Repunched Date, FS-302, Red**	*	285498	—	—	—	—	—	—	1,000	—
1870, Brown	861,250	2698	47	70	95	145	200	290	415	850
↳**1870, Doubled Die Obverse, FS-101, Brown**	*	392848	—	—	—	—	—	—	—	—
1870, Red Brown	*	2699	—	—	—	—	—	—	470	1,550
↳**1870, Doubled Die Obverse, FS-101, Red Brown**	*	392849	—	—	—	—	—	—	—	—

* Included in number above. **c.** Circulated varieties show the tip of the 5 either plain or fancy (curved). **d.** This variety is somewhat common in low-end circulated grades, but is considered rare in EF and AU, and very rare in MS.

Circulation Strikes *(continued)*

	Mintage	GSID	VG-8	F-12	VF-20	EF-40	AU-50	MS-60	MS-63	MS-65
1870, Red	*	2700	—	—	—	—	—	—	$950	$3,450
↳1870, Doubled Die Obverse, FS-101, Red	*	392850	—	—	—	—	—	—	—	—
1871, Brown	721,250	2701	$55	$75	$115	$170	$210	$325	420	950
↳1871, Repunched Date, FS-301, Brown	*	373679	60	80	125	185	230	360	465	1,050
1871, Red Brown	*	2702	—	—	—	—	—	—	675	1,400
↳1871, Repunched Date, FS-301, Red Brown	*	373682	—	—	—	—	—	—	750	1,500
1871, Red	*	2703	—	—	—	—	—	—	850	3,500
↳1871, Repunched Date, FS-301, Red	*	373685	—	—	—	—	—	—	925	3,850
1872, Brown	65,000	2704	420	550	725	1,100	1,450	2,800	3,500	4,500
1872, Red Brown	*	2705	—	—	—	—	—	3,250	4,000	7,000
1872, Red	*	2706	—	—	—	—	—	—	8,750	18,000
1872, Red Brown	*	2705	—	—	—	—	—	—	—	3,550
1872, Red	*	2706	—	—	—	—	—	—	—	—

* Included in number above.

Proof Strikes

	Mintage	GSID	PF-60	PF-63	PF-65
Shield Obverse (1864–1873), Brown	**n/a**	**73777**	**$365**	**$575**	**$1,000**
Same, Red Brown	**n/a**	**73778**	**—**	**600**	**1,250**
Same, Red	**n/a**	**73779**	**—**	**900**	**2,050**
1864, Small Motto, Brown	20	2710	32,000	45,500	66,000
1864, Small Motto, Red Brown	*	2711	43,000	66,000	144,000
	Auctions: $132,000, PCGS PF-65 HA 01/25				
1864, Small Motto, Red	*	2712	—	90,000	144,000
	Auctions: $105,750, PCGS PF-66 HA 06/14				
1864, Large Motto, Brown	100	2707	575	1,100	2,250
1864, Large Motto, Red Brown	*	2708	—	1,450	3,050
1864, Large Motto, Red	*	2709	—	2,000	8,750
1865, Brown	500	2717	365	575	1,200
1865, Red Brown	*	2718	—	600	1,600
1865, Red	*	2719	—	1,000	3,450
1866, Brown	725	2722	365	575	1,000
1866, Red Brown	*	2723	—	725	1,400
1866, Red	*	2724	—	900	3,100
1867, Brown	625	2727	365	575	1,000
1867, Red Brown	*	2728	—	600	1,250

	Mintage	GSID	PF-60	PF-63	PF-65
1867, Red	*	2729	—	$1,000	$3,500
1868, Brown	600	2732	$365	575	1,000
1868, Red Brown	*	2733	—	600	1,250
1868, Red	*	2734	—	900	3,100
1869, Brown	600	2737	365	575	1,000
1869, Red Brown	*	2738	—	600	1,500
1869, Red	*	2739	—	900	2,050
1870, Brown	1,000	2742	365	575	1,000
1870, Red Brown	*	2743	—	600	1,250
1870, Red	*	2744	—	1,000	3,250
1871, Brown	960	2747	365	575	1,000
1871, Red Brown	*	2748	—	600	1,250
1871, Red	*	2749	—	950	2,300
1872, Brown	950	2752	625	875	1,200
1872, Red Brown	*	2753	—	725	1,900
1872, Red	*	2754	—	950	2,700
1873, Closed 3, Brown	600	2757	2,600	2,800	3,100
1873, Closed 3, Red Brown	*	2758	—	2,950	3,750
1873, Closed 3, Red	*	2759	—	3,750	5,500
1873, Open 3, Brown	*	2760	2,900	3,300	4,200
1873, Open 3, Red Brown	*	2761	—	3,550	4,500
1873, Open 3, Red	*	2762	—	4,100	5,750

* Included in number above.

Three-Cent Pieces 1851–1889

AN OVERVIEW OF THREE-CENT PIECES

Silver Three-Cent Pieces

The silver three-cent piece or *trime* is one of the more curious coins in American numismatics. The rising price of silver in 1850 created a situation in which silver coins cost more to produce than their face value. Mintages dropped sharply and older pieces disappeared from circulation. In 1851 a solution was provided by the three-cent piece. Instead of being made with 90 percent silver content, the fineness was set at 75 percent. Accordingly, the coins were worth less intrinsically, and there was no advantage in melting them. Large quantities were made through 1853. In that year, the standards for regular silver coins were changed, and other denominations reappeared on the marketplace, making the trime unnecessary. Mintages dropped beginning in 1854, until 1873, when production amounted to just 600 Proofs for collectors.

Scan for additional information.

Of the three varieties of trimes, Variety 2 (1854–1858) is at once the scarcest and, by far, the most difficult to find with a sharp strike. In fact, not one in fifty Variety 2 coins is needle sharp. Curiously, when such pieces are found they are likely to be dated 1855, the lowest-mintage issue of the type. Trimes of the Variety 1 design (1851–1853) vary widely in striking, but can be found sharp. Variety 3 coins (1859–1873) often are sharp.

Mint State coins are readily found for Variety 1 and are usually in grades from MS-60 to 63 or so, although quite a few gems are around with attractive luster. Sharply struck gems are another matter and require some searching to find. Mint State Variety 2 trimes are all rare, and when seen are apt to be miserably struck and in lower grades. Variety 3 coins are readily found in Mint State, including in MS-65 and higher grades.

The term *trime* was first used by the director of the United States Mint, James Ross Snowden, at the time of the coins' production.

Proofs were made of all years, but not in quantity until 1858, when an estimated 210 were struck. For all dates after 1862, high-grade Proofs are much more readily available today than are Mint State coins. Circulated examples are available of all three varieties. While extensively worn coins of Variety 1 are available, most Variety 2 coins are Fine or better and most Variety 3 pieces are VF or better.

For the Collector and Investor: Silver Three-Cent Pieces as a Specialty

Trimes cover a fairly long span of years and embrace several design types, but comprise no "impossible" rarities. Accordingly, it is realistic to collect one of each Philadelphia Mint coin from 1851 to 1873 plus the 1851-O. There are two overdates in the series, 1862, 2 Over 1 (which is distinct and occurs only in circulation-strike format) and 1863, 3 Over 2 (only Proofs, and not boldly defined), which some specialists collect and others ignore. A curious variety of 1852 has the first digit of the date over an inverted 2.

Typically, a high-grade set includes Mint State examples of all issues 1851 through 1857 and Proofs after that date. As noted, Variety 2 trimes usually are very poorly struck, save the occasionally encountered sharp 1855. As an example, a specialist in the series who found an 1856 with needle-sharp details, at three times the regular market price, might be well advised to buy it. After 1862, Mint State coins are rare for most dates. The formation of a choice Mint State set 1851 through 1872 plus a Proof 1873 would be a formidable challenge.

A set of circulated coins can be gathered through and including 1862, after which such pieces become very rare. Most later dates will have to be acquired on a catch-as-catch-can basis, perhaps by acquiring impaired Proofs for certain of the years.

Nickel Three-Cent Pieces

Nickel three-cent pieces were introduced in 1865 to help fill the need for coins in circulation. At the time, silver and gold issues were hoarded, and were available only at a premium. The nickel three-cent piece joined the Indian Head cent and the new (as of 1864) two-cent piece. The coin proved to be very popular in its time, and millions were struck. In 1866 the nickel five-cent piece was introduced, after which time the demand for the nickel three-cent piece diminished somewhat. However, pieces were made in quantity until 1876. In that year silver coins again returned to circulation, and mintages for the nickel three-cent piece dropped sharply. Only Proofs were made in 1877 and 1878. In later years, mintages ranged from small to modest, except for 1881.

Mint State coins are readily available for the early years, although many if not most have weak striking in areas or are from clashed dies. Pristine, sharp Mint State coins on the market are mostly of later years, in the 1880s, where such pieces are the rule, not the exception.

For the Collector and Investor: Nickel Three-Cent Pieces as a Specialty

Nickel three-cent coins are interesting to collect by date sequence from 1865 to 1889. Varieties are provided by the 1873, Close 3, and 1873, Open 3, and the 1887, 7 Over 6, overdate. A set of Mint State coins is considerably more difficult to form than a run of Proofs. A hand-selected set of well-struck coins MS-65 or finer could take several years to complete.

Among Proofs, the rarest year is 1865, probably followed by the "perfect date" (not overdate) 1887. Proofs of the 1860s and early 1870s are scarce in PF-65 with excellent strike and eye appeal. Proofs of the latter decade of coinage are much more readily available and usually are choice.

SILVER THREE-CENT PIECES (TRIMES) (1851–1873)

Variety 1: No Border on Star (1851–1853): **Designer:** *James B. Longacre.* **Weight:** *0.80 gram.* **Composition:** *.750 silver, .250 copper.* **Diameter:** *14 mm.* **Edge:** *Plain.* **Mints:** *Philadelphia and New Orleans.*

No Border on Star (1851–1853), Circulation Strike

No Border on Star (1851–1853), Proof Strike

Variety 2: Double Border on Star (1854–1858): **Designer:** *James B. Longacre.* **Weight:** *0.75 gram.* **Composition:** *.900 silver, .100 copper.* **Diameter:** *14 mm.* **Edge:** *Plain.* **Mint:** *Philadelphia.*

Double Border on Star (1854–1858), Circulation Strike

Double Border on Star (1854–1858), Proof Strike

Variety 3: Single Border on Star (1859–1873): **Designer:** *James B. Longacre.* **Weight:** *0.75 gram.* **Composition:** *.900 silver, .100 copper.* **Diameter:** *14 mm.* **Edge:** *Plain.* **Mint:** *Philadelphia.*

Single Border on Star (1859–1873), Circulation Strike

Single Border on Star (1859–1873), Proof Strike

History. In 1850 Americans began hoarding their silver coins, as the flood of gold from California made silver disproportionately valuable. To provide a small coin for commerce, the Mint introduced the silver three-cent piece, or *trime*. These were .750 fine (as opposed to the standard .900 fineness), and contained less than 3¢ of metal, so there was no incentive to hoard or melt them. Three different designs were made, Variety 1 of which was struck from 1851 to 1853. These coins were popular in their time and circulated widely. These are distinguished from the other two designs by having no outline or frame around the obverse star. The Act of February 21, 1853, reduced the amount of silver in other denominations (from the half dime to the half dollar, but not the dollar), which discouraged people from hoarding them. The tiny trime lost the public's favor, and mintages decreased.

In 1854 the design was changed considerably, creating Variety 2, which was made through 1858. The alloy was modified to the standard for other issues and the weight was lightened. A raised border was added to the obverse star plus two line frames around it. On the reverse an olive branch was placed above the III and a bundle of arrows below it. This new motif proved to be very difficult to strike up properly.

In 1859 the design was modified again, creating Variety 3. Demand for the denomination continued to be small, and after 1862 very few were made for circulation, as silver coins were hoarded by the war-weary public and began to trade at a premium. Under the Coinage Act of 1873 the trime was discontinued, and that year only Proofs were struck. Also in that year, nearly the entire production of non-Proof coins of 1863 to 1872 was melted.

Striking and Sharpness. On the Variety 1 obverse the tiny shield at the center of the star often lacks certain details. On the reverse check the details and strength of the III. On both sides check the rims. Needle-sharp coins are in the minority. Sharpness of strike has been nearly completely overlooked in the marketplace.

Trimes of Variety 2 are usually poorly struck, with some or all of these characteristics: obverse lettering weak in places; frames around the star of inconsistent strength or missing in certain areas; shield weak in places; reverse stars irregular and poorly formed; olive branch and arrows weak in areas; weak or irregular rims. Now and then a sharp 1855 is found.

Most Variety 3 trimes are sharply struck. Points to look for include full outlines around the star, full shield on the star, and full leaf details and sharp stars.

Most Proofs are needle sharp and have mirrored surfaces, although some of the late 1860s and early 1870s can have slightly grainy or satiny lustrous surfaces. Striking quality varies. Lint marks and surface problems are not unusual. Careful examination is recommended.

Availability. Circulated examples of the Variety 1 trimes are plentiful. MS coins are often seen, although the 1851-O is scarce in MS and high circulated grades. Most MS coins are lustrous and attractive, especially at 63 and above. Circulated Variety 2 coins are scarce in all grades, particularly so at MS-64 and higher. With a needle-sharp strike, MS-65 and higher are *rarities*. Among Variety 3 trimes, circulated coins of the years 1859 to 1862 are easy to find. All later dates range from scarce to rare in circulation-strike format. MS-63 and better coins 1865 and later are very rare. A few Proofs were made in the early 1850s and are great rarities today. After 1857, production increased to an estimated 210 or so in 1858, through 500 to 700 or so as a yearly average in the 1860s to 1873.

Grading Standards

MS-60 to 70 (Mint State). ***Obverse and Reverse:*** At MS-60, some abrasion and very minor contact marks are evident, most noticeably on the obverse star and the C ornament on the reverse. At MS-63, abrasion is hard to detect except under magnification. An MS-65 coin will have no abrasion. Luster should be full and rich (not grainy). Grades above MS-65 are defined by having fewer marks as perfection is approached. Most high-grade Mint State coins are of the Variety 3 design.

MS-66

AU-50, 53, 55, 58 (About Uncirculated). ***Obverse:*** Light wear is most obvious on the star arms and shield on Variety 1, and on the points of the frames on Variety 2 and Variety 3. At AU-50, luster is evident, but only on part of the field. At AU-58 luster is nearly complete. ***Reverse:*** Light wear is seen on the C ornament and III. On Variety 2 and 3, light wear is seen on the leaves and arrows.

AU-50

Illustrated coin: This is sharply struck, as are most Variety 3 trimes.

EF-40, 45 (Extremely Fine). ***Obverse:*** More wear is seen, most noticeable on the ridges of the star arms, this in addition to more wear on the frames (Variety 2 and Variety 3). Luster is absent, or seen only in traces. ***Reverse:*** More wear is seen on the C ornament and III. On Variety 2 and Variety 3 more wear is seen on the leaves and arrows.

EF-45

VF-20, 30 (Very Fine). ***Obverse:*** Further wear reduced the relief of the star. On Variety 2 and Variety 3 the frames show further wear and begin to blend together. The center shield shows wear, and its border is indistinct in areas, but its horizontal and vertical stripes are fully delineated (unless the coin was weakly struck). ***Reverse:*** Still more wear is seen on the C ornament and III. On Variety 2 and Variety 3 the high-relief areas of the leaves and the feathers of the arrow are partially worn away. Stars are flat at their centers (on sharply struck coins in addition to, as expected, on weak strikes).

VF-30

F-12, 15 (Fine). ***Obverse:*** The star is worn so as to have lost most of its relief. On Variety 2 and Variety 3 the frames are mostly blended together. The center shield shows wear, and its border is flat (or else showing only slight separation of its two outlines), but its horizontal and vertical stripes still are delineated (unless the coin was weakly struck). ***Reverse:*** Still more wear is seen on the C ornament and III. On Variety 2 and Variety 3 the high-relief areas of the leaves, and the feathers of the arrow, have slight if any detail. Stars are flat. The designs within the C ornament are missing much detail.

F-12

VG-8, 10 (Very Good). ***Obverse:*** The border is incomplete in places, but all lettering is bold. The horizontal and vertical stripes within the shield begin to blend together, but most remain well delineated. ***Reverse:*** Still more wear is seen on all areas. The designs within the C ornament have more detail gone.

Illustrated coin: The obverse of this coin shows VG wear, but if the dent in the star was considered it would grade lower.

VG-10

G-4, 6 (Good). ***Obverse:*** The border is worn into the tops of the letters and the bottom of the date. The shield is blended into the star, and only traces of the shield outline remain. In this grade most coins seen are Variety 1. ***Reverse:*** The border is worn into the outer parts of the stars. Additional wear is seen in all other areas.

G-6

AG-3 (About Good). ***Obverse:*** The star is flat. Strong elements of the shield are seen, but the tiny lines are mostly or completely blended together. Lettering and date are weak and partially missing, but the date must be identifiable. In this grade most coins seen are Variety 1. ***Reverse:*** The border is worn into the stars, with outer elements of the stars now gone. Additional wear is seen in all other areas. The designs within the C ornament are only in outline form.

AG-3

PF-60 to 70 (Proof). ***Obverse and Reverse:*** Proofs that are extensively cleaned and have many hairlines, or that are dull and grainy, are lower level, such as PF-60 to 62. These are difficult to verify as Proofs. For a trime with medium hairlines and good reflectivity, an assigned grade of PF-64 is indicated, and with relatively few hairlines, gem PF-65. PF-66 should have hairlines so delicate that magnification is needed to see them. Above that, a Proof should be free of such lines.

PF-66

Illustrated coin: Note the remarkable sharpness of strike, particularly evident on the obverse.

1853, Repunched Date
FS-301

1854, Repunched Date
FS-301

1862, 2 Over 1
FS-301

Circulation Strikes

	Mintage	GSID	G-4	VG-8	F-12	VF-20	EF-40	AU-50	MS-60	MS-63
Silver, Star Obverse Without Border, Variety 1 (1851–1853)	**n/a**	**73773**	**$47**	**$55**	**$65**	**$80**	**$115**	**$170**	**$230**	**$325**
Silver, Star Obverse With Double Border, Variety 2 (1854–1858)	n/a	**73774**	**55**	**60**	**75**	**90**	**155**	**230**	**430**	**900**
Silver, Star Obverse With Single Border, Variety 3 (1859–1873)	n/a	**73775**	**55**	**60**	**70**	**75**	**130**	**195**	**310**	**470**
1851	5,447,400	3617	47	55	70	85	130	190	260	385
↳1851, Repunched Date, FS-302	*	226434	—	—	—	—	—	275	675	1,000
1851-O	720,000	3640	75	85	110	135	260	490	925	1,400
1852	18,663,500	3618	47	55	65	80	115	170	230	325
↳1852, Doubled Die Reverse, FS-801	*	374623	50	60	70	85	125	185	250	360
1853	11,400,000	3620	47	55	65	80	115	170	230	325
↳1853, Repunched Date, FS-301	*	374624	—	60	70	85	125	185	250	360
1854	671,000	3621	65	70	75	100	155	230	430	900
↳1854, Repunched Date, FS-301	*	226435	—	75	85	110	170	250	470	975
1855	139,000	3622	90	110	130	170	265	490	775	1,600
1856	1,458,000	3623	60	65	75	95	155	230	430	950
1857	1,042,000	3624	55	60	75	95	155	240	495	900
1858	1,603,700	3625	55	60	75	90	155	240	470	950
1859	364,200	3626	55	60	70	75	130	195	310	500
1860	286,000	3627	55	60	70	75	130	195	310	470
1861	497,000	3628	55	60	70	75	130	195	310	470
1862	343,000	3629	55	60	70	75	130	195	310	470
1862, 2 Over 1	*	3641	60	65	70	95	130	235	525	675
↳1862, 2 Over 1, Overdate, FS-301	*	374625	60	65	70	95	130	235	525	675
1863	21,000	3630	525	575	650	725	775	900	1,150	2,000
1864	12,000	3631	525	575	650	725	775	900	1,250	1,500
1865	8,000	3632	525	575	650	725	775	900	1,900	2,750
	Auctions: $180,000, PCGS MS-69 SBG 08/24									
1866	22,000	3633	575	650	750	800	950	1,050	1,400	2,250
1867	4,000	3634	525	575	650	725	850	1,400	2,250	3,750
1868	*3,500*	3635	850	950	1,150	1,500	2,000	2,900	5,250	7,500
1869, 9 Over 9	4,500	3636	525	575	650	725	850	1,200	1,600	2,400
1870	3,000	3637	525	575	725	775	950	1,200	1,900	2,300
1871	3,400	3638	525	575	650	725	850	900	1,050	1,250
1872	1,000	3639	725	900	1,150	1,500	2,000	2,500	3,900	4,900

* Included in number above.

Proof Strikes

	Mintage	GSID	PF-60	PF-63	PF-65
Silver, Star Obverse Without Border, Variety 1 (1851–1853), Proof	**n/a**	**73780**	**—**	**—**	**—**
Silver, Star Obverse With Double Border, Variety 2 (1854–1858), Proof	**n/a**	**73781**	**$1,900**	**$2,400**	**$5,500**
Silver, Star Obverse With Single Border, Variety 3 (1859–1873), Proof	**n/a**	**73782**	**650**	**1,100**	**1,500**
Same, Proof Cameo	**n/a**	**79404**	**—**	**1,200**	**1,750**
Same, Proof Deep Cameo	**n/a**	**79405**	**—**	**—**	**5,500**
1855		3652	3,750	6,250	15,500
1856		3655	2,500	5,000	12,000
1857		3658	2,250	3,450	11,000
1858	210	3661	1,900	2,400	5,500
1859	800	3664	650	1,100	2,000
1860	1,000	3667	675	1,200	3,750
1861	1,000	3670	650	1,100	2,500
1862	550	3673	650	1,100	1,500
1863	460	3676	650	1,100	1,500
1863, 3 Over 2	*	3709	2,250	3,300	7,500
1864	470	3679	675	1,200	2,250
1865	500	3682	775	1,150	1,800
1866	725	3685	650	1,100	1,500
1867	625	3688	650	1,100	1,500
1868	600	3691	650	1,100	1,500
1869, Wide Date	600	3712	2,000	2,750	4,900
1869, 9 Over "8," Narrow Date	*	3694	650	1,100	1,750
1870	1,000	3697	650	1,100	1,500
1871	960	3700	650	1,100	1,500
1872	950	3703	650	1,100	1,500
1873, Closed 3	600	3706	1,400	1,800	2,550

* Included in number above.

NICKEL THREE-CENT PIECES (1865–1889)

Designer: *James B. Longacre.* **Weight:** *1.94 grams.*
Composition: *.750 copper, .250 nickel.*
Diameter: *17.9 mm.* **Edge:** *Plain.* **Mint:** *Philadelphia.*

Circulation Strike

Proof Strike

History. The copper-nickel three-cent coin debuted in the final year of the Civil War, 1865. The American public was still hoarding silver coins (a situation that would continue until 1876), including the silver three-cent piece. The highest-denomination coin remaining in circulation at the time was the recently introduced two-cent piece. After 1875, when silver coins circulated once again, the three-cent denomination became redundant and mintages dropped. The last pieces were coined in 1889.

Striking and Sharpness. On the obverse check the hair and other portrait details. On the reverse the tiny vertical lines in the Roman numeral III can be weak. Check the denticles on both sides of the coin. Among circulation strikes, clashed dies are common, particularly for the earlier high-mintage years. Generally, coins of the 1860s and 1870s have weakness in one area or another. Many if not most of the 1880s are well struck. Proofs from 1878 onward often have satiny or frosty fields, rather than mirrored surfaces, and resemble circulation strikes.

Availability. Circulated examples of dates from 1865 to the mid-1870s are readily available. MS coins, particularly from the 1860s, are easily found, but often have areas of weakness or lack aesthetic appeal. MS coins of the 1880s are readily found for most dates (except for 1883, 1884, 1885, and 1887), some of them probably sold as Proofs. Many Proofs of the era had slight to extensive mint luster. Proofs were struck of all dates and can be found easily enough in the marketplace. The rarest is the first year of issue, 1865, of which only an estimated 500 or so were made. The vast majority of 1865s have a repunched date. Second rarest (not counting PF-only date of 1877) is the 1887 (perfect date, not the overdate) with a production of about 1,000 coins. Proofs of the years 1865 to 1876 can be difficult to find as true gems, while later Proofs are nearly all gems.

Grading Standards

MS-61

MS-60 to 70 (Mint State). ***Obverse and Reverse:*** Mint luster is complete in the obverse and reverse fields. Lower grades such as MS-60, 61, and 62 can show some evidence of abrasion. This is usually on the area of the hair to the right of the face (on the obverse), and on the highest parts of the wreath (on the reverse). Abrasion can appear as scattered contact marks elsewhere. At MS-63, these marks are few, and on MS-65 they are fewer yet. In grades above MS-65, marks can only be seen under magnification.

AU-50, 53, 55, 58 (About Uncirculated). ***Obverse:*** Light wear is seen on the portrait, most notably on the upper cheek and on the hair to the right of the face. Mint luster is present in the fields, ranging from partial at AU-50 to nearly complete at AU-58. All details are sharp, unless lightly struck. ***Reverse:*** Light wear is seen on the top and bottom horizontal edges of the III and the wreath. Luster is partial at AU-50, increasing to nearly full at AU-58. All details are sharp, unless lightly struck.

AU-55

EF-40, 45 (Extremely Fine). ***Obverse:*** More wear is seen on the cheek and the hair to the right of the face and neck. The hair to the right of the coronet beads shows light wear. ***Reverse:*** The wreath still shows most detail on the leaves. Some wear is seen on the vertical lines within III (but striking can also cause weakness). Overall the reverse appears to be very bold.

EF-40

VF-20, 30 (Very Fine). ***Obverse:*** Most hair detail is gone, with a continuous flat area to the right of the face and neck, where the higher hair strands have blended together. The hair to the right of the coronet beads shows about half of the strands. ***Reverse:*** Higher details of the leaves are worn away; the central ridges are seen on some. Wear on the vertical lines in III has caused some to merge, but most are separate.

VF-25

F-12, 15 (Fine). ***Obverse:*** Wear is more extensive. The forehead blends into the hair above it. About 10 percent to 29 percent of the hair detail to the right of the coronet remains, and much detail is seen lower, at the right edge opposite the ear and neck. Denticles are distinct. ***Reverse:*** The top (highest-relief) part of most leaves is flat. Many vertical lines in III are fused. Denticles are distinct.

F-15

VG-8, 10 (Very Good). ***Obverse:*** Less hair detail shows. Denticles all are clear. ***Reverse:*** The leaves show more wear. The inner edges of some leaves are worn away, causing leaves to merge. Only about half, or slightly fewer, of the lines in III are discernible.

VG-10

G-4, 6 (Good). ***Obverse:*** Most hair details are gone, but some remain at the lower right. The rim is worn smooth in areas, and many denticles are missing. The lettering is weak, but readable. ***Reverse:*** The leaves mostly are worn flat. Very few lines remain in III. The rim is worn smooth in areas, and many denticles are missing.

G-4

AG-3 (About Good). ***Obverse:*** The rim is worn away and into the tops of most of the letters. The date remains bold. ***Reverse:*** The rim is worn away and into some of the leaves.

AG-3

PF-60 to 70 (Proof). ***Obverse and Reverse:*** PF-60, 61, and 62 coins show varying amounts of hairlines in the field, decreasing as the grade increases. Fields may be dull or cloudy on lower-level pieces. At PF-65, hairlines are visible only under magnification and are very light; the cheek of Liberty does not show any friction or "album slide marks." Above PF-65, hairlines become fewer, and in ultra-high grades are nonexistent, this meaning that the coins have never been subject to wiping or abrasive cleaning. At PF-65 or better, expect excellent aesthetic appeal. Blotched, deeply toned, or recolored coins are sometimes seen at Proof levels from PF-60 through 65 or even 66 and should be avoided, but these are less often seen than on contemporary Proof nickel five-cent pieces.

PF-65

1866, Doubled Die Obverse
FS-101

Circulation Strikes

	Mintage	GSID	G-4	VG-8	F-12	VF-20	EF-40	AU-50	MS-60	MS-63
Nickel (1865–1889)	**n/a**	**72350**	**$16.00**	**$17.50**	**$19**	**$26**	**$43**	**$70**	**$145**	**$220**
1865	11,382,000	2767	19.00	20.00	22	28	46	70	145	220
↳1865, Repunched Date, FS-304	*	226436	25.00	26.00	28	37	60	90	185	285
1866	4,801,000	2768	16.00	17.50	19	26	43	70	145	220
↳1866, Doubled Die Obverse, FS-101	*	377268	—	—	—	—	—	—	—	—
1867	3,915,000	2769	19.00	20.00	34	49	70	100	160	245
1868	3,252,000	2770	16.00	17.50	19	26	43	70	145	220
1869	1,604,000	2771	16.00	17.50	19	28	46	75	150	235
↳1869, Repunched Date, FS-301	*	392861	—	—	—	—	—	—	—	—
↳1869, Repunched Date, FS-302	*	392862	—	—	—	—	—	—	—	—
1870	1,335,000	2772	19.00	20.00	22	28	46	75	150	240
1871	604,000	2773	19.00	22.00	24	32	50	110	170	235
↳1871, Tripled Die Obverse, FS-101	*	226438	—	—	36	49	75	155	255	525
1872	862,000	2774	19.00	20.00	24	31	50	115	180	290
1873, Closed 3	390,000	2775	24.00	27.00	31	40	70	85	170	290
1873, Open 3	783,000	2776	24.00	27.00	32	40	70	100	195	325
1874	790,000	2777	19.00	20.00	24	31	47	80	155	260
1875	228,000	2778	26.00	30.00	34	47	75	95	180	245
↳1875, Misplaced Date, FS-301	*	226439	—	—	—	—	110	155	235	345
1876	162,000	2779	35.00	40.00	49	65	100	130	260	390
1879	38,000	2780	80.00	100.00	130	135	155	210	305	390
1880	21,000	2781	125.00	140.00	170	180	215	240	360	525
1881	1,077,000	2782	19.00	20.00	26	32	46	70	145	235
1882	22,200	2783	155.00	180.00	215	240	290	365	410	650
1883	4,000	2784	350.00	420.00	490	550	775	1,150	1,750	3,450
1884	1,700	2785	825.00	1,000.00	1,350	1,600	2,200	4,050	5,250	7,750
1885	1,000	2786	950.00	1,250.00	1,600	1,900	2,500	3,250	4,250	6,500
1887	5,001	2787	305.00	360.00	390	525	650	750	900	950
1888	36,501	2788	65.00	70.00	80	90	115	170	290	365
1889	18,125	2789	110.00	140.00	185	210	245	275	300	420

* Included in number above.

1887, 7 Over 6, Proof
FS-302

Proof Strikes

	Mintage	GSID	PF-60	PF-63	PF-65
Nickel (1865–1889), Proof	**n/a**	**73783**	**$280**	**$405**	**$550**
Same, Proof Cameo	**n/a**	**79406**	**—**	**440**	**550**
Same, Proof Deep Cameo	**n/a**	**79407**	**—**	**725**	**1,300**
1865	500	2790	725	1,600	3,100
1866	725	2793	280	405	950
1867	625	2796	280	405	850
1868	600	2799	280	405	750
1869	600	2802	310	430	775
1870	1,000	2805	280	405	575
1871	960	2808	280	405	575
1872	950	2811	280	405	575
1873, Closed 3	1,100	2814	280	405	575
1874	700	2817	280	405	625
1875	700	2820	280	405	750
1876	1,150	2823	280	405	575
1877	900	2826	1,800	2,100	2,750
1878	2,350	2829	800	825	850
1879	3,200	2832	280	405	550
1880	3,955	2835	280	405	550
1881	3,575	2838	280	405	550
1882	3,100	2841	280	405	550
1883	6,609	2844	280	405	550
1884	3,942	2847	280	405	550
1885	3,790	2850	280	405	625
1886	4,290	2853	415	420	625
1887	2,960	2856	305	480	750
1887, 7 Over 6, Strong Overdate	*	2865	525	550	725
↳1887, 7 Over 6, Strong Overdate, FS-302	*	392815	525	550	725
1887, 7 Over 6, Weak Overdate	*	375974	340	525	825
1888	4,582	2859	280	405	550
1889	3,436	2862	280	405	550

* Included in number above.

Nickel Five-Cent Pieces 1866 to Date

AN OVERVIEW OF NICKEL FIVE-CENT PIECES

Five-cent pieces made of nickel were introduced in 1866, in an era in which the silver half dime as well as other silver denominations were not seen in circulation. More than a dozen designs and their variations have graced the "nickel" in the past 140-plus years.

Scan for additional information.

While Shield nickels of both varieties are slightly scarce in upper Mint State levels, they are within the financial reach of most collectors. Proofs are available of each variety, but the 1866–1867, With Rays, and the 1913 Buffalo, Variety 1, issues are rare.

The quality of strike presents a challenge across the various types of nickel five-cent pieces, most particularly with the 1866–1867, With Rays, for there are fewer possibilities from which to choose. Although 1913–1938 Buffalo, Variety 2, nickels are often poorly struck, there are enough sharp ones that finding a choice example should present no great challenge for the collector.

For the Collector and Investor: Five-Cent Pieces as a Specialty

Shield nickels of the 1866–1883 era are often collected by date sequence. A full set includes 1866 and 1867, With Rays, plus 1867 to 1883, Without Rays. In addition, there is the 1879, 9 Over 8, overdate, which is found only in Proof format but is readily available (constituting perhaps a third or so of the Proof mintage of 3,200 for the 1879 year) and the 1883, 3 Over 2 (scarce, and available only as a circulation strike).

Circulation strikes are available of all Shield nickel dates, 1866 to 1883, except 1877 and 1878, which were made only in Proof format. A set of Proofs can be completed except for the 1867, With Rays, which is exceedingly rare in Proof, with an estimated population of fewer than two dozen coins. Most 1878 Proofs are frosty and appear not much different from Mint State, but only Proofs were made this year.

In circulated grades, Shield nickels are available in proportion to their mintage figures. The dates 1879 to 1881 had high Proof mintages (in the context of Proof figures), but low circulation-strike mintages, and thus they are key dates in the latter format. In other words, a gem MS-65 1880 Shield nickel (16,000 coined, but few were saved, as collectors acquired Proofs instead) is exceedingly rare today. In the same year 3,955 Proofs were struck, all were preserved by collectors and dealers, and today the Proof 1880 is one of the most plentiful dates.

Liberty Head nickels of the 1883, Without CENTS (or "No CENTS"), variety are plentiful in Mint State and also in Proof. Later dates With CENTS, through 1912, are generally available in proportion to their mintages. The 1885 and 1886 are considered to be key dates. Proofs are readily collectible, although pristine high-quality examples can be hard to find. The 1912-D and 1912-S are scarce. In 1913 an estimated five Liberty Head nickels were made, and today stand as famous rarities.

Among Buffalo nickels, 1913 to 1938, the different dates and mints can be collected easily enough in circulated grades, although certain issues such as 1913-S, Variety 2; 1921-S; and 1926-S are on the scarce side. An overdate, 1918-D, 8 Over 7, is a rarity at all grade levels. Curious varieties are provided by the very rare 1916, Doubled Date; the scarce 1937-D, 3-Legged (the die was heavily polished, resulting in some loss of detail); and the fascinating and readily available 1938-D, D Over S, overmintmark.

Popularized in the 1890s and throughout the beginning of the 1900s, coin-operated machines took cents and other denominations, but the coin of choice was the nickel. Pictured is a postcard for Horn & Hardart restaurants, 1930s, where patrons would serve themselves with such coin-operated devices.

In choice or gem Mint State most branch-mint Buffalo nickels, 1914–1927, are fairly scarce, and some are quite rare. Most branch-mint coins of the 1920s are lightly struck in one area or another, with the 1926-D being particularly infamous in this regard. Sharply struck examples of such varieties are worth much more than lightly struck ones, although the grading services take no particular note of such differences. Matte Proofs of dates 1913 to 1916 were struck, and mirror-finish Proofs were made in 1936 and 1937. These exist today in proportion to their mintages.

Jefferson nickels from 1938 to date are readily collectible in Mint State and Proof format. Many otherwise common varieties can be very rare if sharply struck.

SHIELD (1866–1883)

Designer: *James B. Longacre.* **Weight:** *5 grams.* **Composition:** *.750 copper, .250 nickel.* **Diameter:** *20.5 mm.* **Edge:** *Plain.* **Mint:** *Philadelphia.*

Variety 1, With Rays (1866–1867), Circulation Strike

Variety 1, With Rays, Proof Strike

Variety 2, Without Rays (1867–1883), Circulation Strike

Variety 2, Without Rays, Proof Strike

History. The nickel five-cent piece was introduced in 1866. At the time, silver coins (except the trime) did not circulate in the East or Midwest. The new denomination proved popular, and "nickels" of the Shield variety were made continuously from 1866 to 1883. All 1866 nickels have rays between the stars on the reverse, as do a minority of 1867 issues, after which this feature was dropped. In 1877 and 1878 only Proofs were made, with no circulation strikes. The design, by Chief Engraver James B. Longacre, is somewhat similar to the obverse of the two-cent piece. Some Shield nickels were still seen in circulation in the 1930s, by which time most had been worn nearly smooth.

Striking and Sharpness. Sharpness can be a problem for Shield nickels in the 1860s through 1876, much less so for later years. On the obverse the horizontal shield stripes, vertical stripes, and leaves should be checked. The horizontal stripes in particular can be blended together. On the reverse the star centers can be weak. Check all other areas as well. Die cracks are seen on *most* circulation-strike Shield nickels, and do not affect value. Proof Shield nickels were struck of all dates 1866 to 1883, including two varieties of 1867 (With Rays, a great rarity, and the usually seen Without Rays). Fields range from deeply mirrorlike to somewhat grainy in character to mirror-surface, depending on a given year. Many of 1878, a date struck only in Proof format, have *lustrous* surfaces or prooflike surfaces combined with some luster, resembling a circulation strike. While most Proofs are sharp, some have weakness on the shield on the obverse and/or the star centers on the reverse. Lint marks or tiny recessed marks from scattered debris on the die faces are sometimes encountered, especially on issues of the 1870s, but not factored into the grade in commercial certification unless excessive.

Availability. Circulated coins generally are available in proportion to their mintage quantities (exceptions being the 1873, Open 3, and 1873, Close 3, varieties, which tend to be elusive in all grades despite their relatively high mintage). MS coins are similarly available, except that 1880 is a rarity. Those dated 1882 and 1883 are plentiful.

Grading Standards

MS-60 to 70 (Mint State). ***Obverse and Reverse:*** At MS-60 some abrasion and very minor contact marks are evident, most noticeably on high points of the shield on the obverse and the field on the reverse. Sometimes light striking on the shield and stars can be mistaken for light wear, and marks on the numeral 5 on the reverse can be from the original planchet surface not struck up fully. At MS-63 abrasions are hard to detect except under magnification. An MS-65 coin will have no abrasion. Luster should be full and rich (not grainy). Grades above MS-65 are defined by having no marks that can be seen by the naked eye. Higher-grade coins display deeper luster or virtually perfect prooflike surfaces, depending on the dies used.

MS-66

Illustrated coin: Note the faint golden toning along the obverse border.

AU-50, 53, 55, 58 (About Uncirculated). ***Obverse:*** Light wear is on the outside edges of the leaves, the frame of the shield, and the horizontal stripes (although the stripes can also be weakly struck). Mint luster is present in the fields, ranging from partial at AU-50 to nearly complete at AU-58. All details are sharp, unless lightly struck. ***Reverse:*** Light wear is seen on the numeral 5, and friction is seen in the field, identifiable as a change of color (loss of luster). Luster is partial at AU-50, increasing to nearly full at AU-58. All details are sharp, unless lightly struck.

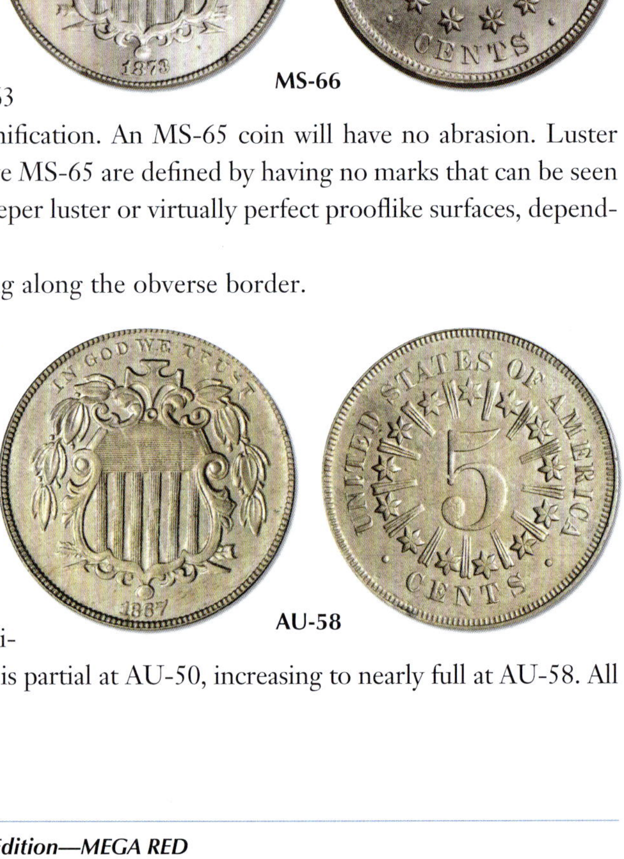

AU-58

EF-40, 45 (Extremely Fine). ***Obverse:*** Nearly all shield border and leaf detail is visible. Light wear is seen on the shield stripes (but the horizontal stripes can be weakly struck). ***Reverse:*** More wear is seen on the numeral 5. The radial lines in the stars (if sharply struck to begin with) show slight wear. The field shows more wear.

EF-40

VF-20, 30 (Very Fine). ***Obverse:*** The frame details and leaves show more wear, with much leaf detail gone. The shield stripes show more wear, and some of the vertical lines will begin to blend together. ***Reverse:*** More wear is seen overall, but some radial detail can still be seen on the stars.

VF-20

F-12, 15 (Fine). ***Obverse:*** Most leaves are flat and have little detail, but will remain outlined. The shield frame is mostly flat. Most horizontal lines are blended together, regardless of original strike. Many vertical lines in the stripes are blended together. IN GOD WE TRUST is slightly weak. ***Reverse:*** All areas are in outline form except for slight traces of the star radials. Lettering is bold.

F-12

VG-8, 10 (Very Good). ***Obverse:*** Many leaves are flat and blended with adjacent leaves. The frame is blended and has no details. Only a few horizontal lines may show. Vertical lines in the stripes are mostly blended. IN GOD WE TRUST is weak. ***Reverse:*** All elements are visible only in outline form. The rim is complete.

VG-10

G-4, 6 (Good). ***Obverse:*** The shield and elements are seen in outline form except the vertical stripe separations. IN GOD WE TRUST is weak, and a few letters may be missing. ***Reverse:*** The rim is mostly if not completely worn away and into the tops of the letters.

Illustrated coin: Overall this coin is slightly better than G-4, but the 5 in the date is weak, making G-4 an appropriate attribution.

G-4

AG-3 (About Good). ***Obverse:*** The rim is worn down and blended with the wreath. Only traces of IN GOD WE TRUST can be seen. The date is fully readable. ***Reverse:*** The rim is worn down and blended with the letters, some of which may be missing.

AG-3

PF-60 to 70 (Proof). ***Obverse and Reverse:*** PF-60, 61, and 62 coins show varying amounts of hairlines in the reverse field in particular, decreasing as the grade increases. Fields may be dull or cloudy on lower-level pieces. At PF-65, hairlines are visible only under magnification and are very light and usually only on the reverse. Above PF-65, hairlines become fewer, and in ultra-high grades are nonexistent, this meaning that the coins have never been subject to wiping or abrasive cleaning. At PF-65 or better, expect excellent aesthetic appeal.

PF-66

1866, Repunched Date
Several varieties exist.

Circulation Strikes

	Mintage	GSID	G-4	VG-8	F-12	VF-20	EF-40	AU-50	MS-60	MS-63	MS-63
Shield Obverse, With Rays Reverse (1866–1867)	**n/a**	**72351**	**$32**	**$45**	**$70**	**$115**	**$180**	**$230**	**$415**	**$625**	**$1,700**
Shield Obverse, Without Rays Reverse (1867–1883)	**n/a**	**72352**	**31**	**34**	**38**	**47**	**85**	**115**	**155**	**245**	**575**
1866	14,742,500	2868	32	45	70	115	180	230	415	625	1,700
↳**1866, With Rays, Doubled Die Obverse, FS-101**	*	376253	—	49	75	125	215	250	460	675	1,850
1866, With Rays, 1866 Over 1866 Repunched Date	*	2887	195	285	455	850	1,100	1,400	2,300	4,100	14,500
↳**1866, With Rays, 1866 Over 1866 Repunched Date, FS-301**	*	376255	195	285	455	850	1,100	1,400	2,300	4,100	14,500
↳**1866, With Rays, 1866 Over 1866 Repunched Date, FS-302**	*	376256	195	285	455	850	1,100	1,400	2,300	4,100	14,500
↳**1866, With Rays, 1866 Over 1866 Repunched Date, FS-307**	*	376260	195	285	455	850	1,100	1,400	2,300	4,100	14,500

* Included in number above.

1873, Close 3

1873, Open 3

1873, Close 3, Doubled Die Obverse
FS-102

1873, Open 3, Large Over Small 3
FS-1301

Circulation Strikes *(continued)*

	Mintage	GSID	G-4	VG-8	F-12	VF-20	EF-40	AU-50	MS-60	MS-63	MS-63
1867, With Rays	2,019,000	2869	$36	$49	$75	$130	$210	$275	$495	$725	$3,250
↳1867, With Rays, Repunched Date, FS-301	2,019,000	376263	—	—	—	775	1,300	2,300	4,050	7,000	—
↳1867, With Rays, Doubled Die Obverse/ Repunched Date, FS-302	2,019,000	376264	—	—	—	260	—	—	—	—	—
↳1867, With Rays, Mis-aligned Die Clash, FS-1401	2,019,000	376268	—	—	—	—	—	1,900	24,000	—	—
↳1867, With Rays, Obverse/Reverse Die Clash, FS-1402/1901	2,019,000	376269	—	—	—	—	—	—	—	—	—
1867, No Rays	28,890,500	2870	31	34	38	47	85	115	170	265	875
↳1867, No Rays, Doubled Die Obverse/ Repunched Date, FS-1102	28,890,500	379390	—	—	—	95	175	275	390	575	2,000
↳1867, No Rays, Repunched Date, FS-1301	28,890,500	391422	—	—	—	—	—	—	—	—	—
1868	28,817,000	2871	31	34	38	47	85	115	175	260	850
↳1868, Tripled Die Obverse, FS-102	*	392763	—	—	—	—	—	—	—	—	—
↳1868, Doubled Die Obverse, FS-111	*	392767	—	—	—	—	—	—	—	—	—
↳1868, Repunched Date, FS-301	*	377786	—	—	—	—	—	—	—	—	—
↳1868, Repunched Date, FS-310	*	379397	—	—	—	—	—	—	—	—	—
↳1868, Repunched Date, FS-314	*	392776	—	—	—	—	—	—	—	—	—
↳1868, Missing Leaf, Scribe Mark, FS-401	*	379392	—	—	—	—	—	—	—	—	—
1869	16,395,000	2872	31	34	38	47	85	115	155	280	775
↳1869, Wide Date, Doubled Die Obverse, FS-1102	*	392777	—	—	—	—	—	—	—	—	—
↳1869, Wide Date, Repunched Date, FS-1303	*	392781	—	—	—	—	—	—	—	—	—
1870	4,806,000	2873	35	40	65	85	110	155	245	455	1,300
↳1870, Doubled Die Obverse, FS-101	*	392789	—	—	—	—	—	—	—	—	—
↳1870, Doubled Die Reverse, FS-802	*	392792	—	—	—	—	—	—	—	—	—
1871	561,000	2874	90	115	160	235	340	470	675	1,000	2,250
↳1871, Repunched Date, FS-301	*	375222	—	—	—	—	—	—	—	—	—
1872	6,036,000	2875	47	60	100	120	130	155	220	275	1,300
↳1872, Doubled Die Obverse, FS-103	*	377272	—	—	—	—	—	—	—	—	—
↳1872, Doubled Die Obverse, FS-106	*	392797	—	—	—	—	—	—	—	—	—
↳1872, Repunched Date, FS-301	*	392799	—	—	—	—	—	—	—	—	—
1873, Closed 3	436,050	2877	55	70	95	145	180	260	455	850	2,300
1873, Open 3	4,113,950	2876	35	49	65	80	100	190	310	650	1,700
1873, Open 3, Large Over Small 3, FS-1301	*	2878	—	—	—	—	7,500	11,000	14,500	16,000	19,000
1873, Doubled Die Obverse	*	326616	95	120	155	195	290	470	650	1,100	3,100
↳1873, Doubled Die Obverse, Closed 3, FS-101	*	326617	—	—	—	—	290	470	650	1,100	3,100
↳1873, Doubled Die Obverse, Closed 3, FS-102	*	326618	—	—	—	—	390	650	2,050	2,600	—
↳1873, Doubled Die Obverse, Open 3, FS-1101	*	326621	—	—	—	—	—	—	—	—	—
↳1873, Doubled Die Obverse, Open 3, FS-1103	*	326623	—	—	—	—	—	—	—	—	5,000
1874	3,538,000	2879	38	55	90	110	130	145	230	325	1,100
↳1874, Doubled Die Obverse, FS-103	*	373964	—	—	—	—	—	—	—	—	—
1875	2,097,000	2880	55	75	110	145	215	260	360	575	1,400
↳1875, Doubled Die Obverse, FS-101	*	377274	—	—	—	—	—	490	725	1,250	3,750

* Included in number above.

1883, 3 Over 2
Several varieties exist, as well as pieces with a recut 3. Pictured are FS-301 (left) and FS-305 (right).

Circulation Strikes *(continued)*

	Mintage	GSID	G-4	VG-8	F-12	VF-20	EF-40	AU-50	MS-60	MS-63	MS-63
1876	2,530,000	2881	$49	$65	$100	$145	$195	$215	$285	$360	$950
↳1876, Tripled Die Obverse, FS-101	*	379396	—	—	—	—	—	—	—	—	—
↳1876, Doubled Die Obverse/ Repunched Date, FS-104/301	*	392810	—	—	—	—	—	—	—	—	—
1879	25,900	2882	575	775	875	1,000	1,750	2,050	3,250	4,000	5,000
1880	16,000	2883	2,600	3,400	4,250	5,500	8,000	12,000	18,000	36,000	62,000
1881	68,800	2884	275	390	470	525	675	850	1,200	1,500	3,250
1882	11,472,900	2885	31	34	38	47	85	115	155	245	575
↳1882, Doubled Die Obverse, FS-101	*	392811	—	—	—	—	—	—	—	—	—
↳1882, Repunched Date, FS-301	*	392812	—	—	—	—	—	—	—	—	—
↳1882, Repunched Date, FS-302	*	392813	—	—	—	—	—	—	—	—	—
1883	1,451,500	2886	31	34	38	47	85	115	155	245	575
↳1883, Repunched Date, FS-312	*	226467	—	—	—	—	—	180	390	525	950
1883, 3 Over 2 (a)	*	2888	260	360	550	675	775	900	1,100	1,500	3,750
↳1883, 3 Over 2, FS-301 (a)	*	226468	260	360	550	675	775	900	1,100	1,500	3,750
↳1883, 3 Over 2, FS-302 (a)	*	226469	260	360	550	675	775	900	1,100	1,500	3,750
↳1883, 3 Over 2, FS-303 (a)	*	226470	260	360	550	675	775	900	1,100	1,500	3,750
↳1883, 3 Over 2, FS-304 (a)	*	226471	260	360	550	675	775	900	1,100	1,500	3,750
↳1883, 3 Over 2, FS-305 (a)	*	226472	260	360	550	675	775	900	1,100	1,500	3,750

* Included in number above. **a.** Several varieties exist. For more information, see the *Cherrypickers' Guide to Rare Die Varieties, Vol. I* (sixth edition): "Beware of 1882 Shield nickels with a filled-in, blobby 2, as these are very frequently offered as 1883, 3 Over 2. This is possibly the single most misunderstood coin in all U.S. coinage." (Howard Spindel, communication to Q. David Bowers, quoted in *A Guide Book of Shield and Liberty Head Nickels*.)

Proof Strikes

	Mintage	GSID	PF-60	PF-63	PF-65
Shield Obverse, With Rays Reverse (1866–1867), Proof	n/a	72353	$1,250	$1,750	$2,750
Same, Proof Cameo	n/a	72354	1,450	2,000	3,500
Same, Proof Deep Cameo	n/a	72355	—	—	8,000
Shield Obverse, Without Rays Reverse (1867–1883), Proof	n/a	72356	275	495	625
Same, Proof Cameo	n/a	72357	—	550	700
Same, Proof Deep Cameo	n/a	72358	—	950	2,000
1866	600	2889	1,250	1,750	2,750
1867, With Rays	25	2892	21,500	28,000	36,000
	Auctions: $132,250, NGC PF-66 HA 01/04				
1867, Without Rays	600	2893	290	600	1,150
1867, Without Rays, Pattern Reverse (a)	*	81149	2,250	3,750	10,500

	Mintage	GSID	PF-60	PF-63	PF-65
1868	600	2898	$275	$525	$850
1869	600	2901	275	500	725
1870	1,000	2904	275	525	725
1871	960	2907	275	525	900
1872	950	2910	275	525	700
1873, Closed 3	1,100	2913	275	525	700
1874	700	2916	275	525	800
1875	700	2919	305	550	1,150
1876	1,150	2922	275	495	725
1877	900	2925	2,400	3,000	3,750
1878	2,350	2928	950	1,400	1,450
1879	3,200	2931	275	495	725
1879, 9 Over 8	*	2944	470	650	950
1880	3,955	2934	275	495	625
1881	3,575	2937	275	495	625
1882	3,100	2940	275	495	625
1883	5,419	2943	275	495	625

* Included in number above. **a.** On the pattern reverse, the star points between the T and the S in CENTS; on the regular Proof reverse, the star is centered above the T.

LIBERTY HEAD (1883–1913)

Designer: *Charles E. Barber.* **Weight:** *5 grams.* **Composition:** *.750 copper, .250 nickel.* **Diameter:** *21.2 mm.* **Edge:** *Plain.* **Mints:** *Philadelphia, Denver, and San Francisco.*

Variety 1, Without CENTS (1883), Circulation Strike

Variety 1, Without CENTS, Proof Strike

Variety 2, With CENTS (1883–1912) Circulation Strike

Mintmark locations is on the reverse, to the left of CENTS.

Variety 2, With CENTS, Proof Strike

History. Liberty Head nickels were popular in their time, minted in large quantities most years, and remained in circulation through the 1940s, by which time most were worn down to grades such as AG-3 and G-4. Stray coins could still be found in the early 1950s. Serious numismatic interest in circulated examples began in the 1930s with the popularity of Whitman and other coin boards, folders, and albums. Many of the scarcer dates were picked from circulation at that time. The five known 1913 Liberty Head nickels were not an authorized Mint issue, and were never placed into circulation.

Striking and Sharpness. Many Liberty Head nickels have areas of light striking. On the obverse, this is often seen at the star centers, particularly near the top border. The hair above the forehead can be light as well, and always is thus on 1912-S (the obverse die on this San Francisco issue is slightly bulged). On the reverse, E PLURIBUS UNUM can vary in sharpness of strike. Weakness is often seen at the wreath bow and on the ear of corn to the left (the kernels in the ear can range from indistinct to bold). Even Proofs can be weakly struck in areas. Mint luster can range from minutely pebbly or grainy (but still attractive) to a deep, rich frost. Some later Philadelphia coins show stress marks in the field, particularly the obverse, from the use of "tired" dies. This can be determined only by observation, as "slabbed" grades for MS coins do not indicate the quality of the luster or surfaces. Proof Liberty Head nickels were struck of all dates 1883 to 1912, plus both varieties of 1883 (with and without CENTS). The fields range from deeply mirrorlike to somewhat grainy character to mirror-surface, depending on a given year. While most Proofs are sharp, some have weakness at the star centers and/or the kernels on the ear of corn to the left of the ribbon bow. These weaknesses are overlooked by the certification services. Generally, later issues are more deeply mirrored than are earlier ones. Some years in the 1880s and 1890s can show graininess, a combination of mint luster and mirror quality. Lint marks or tiny recessed marks from scattered debris on the die faces are sometimes encountered, but not factored into third-party–certified grades unless excessive.

Availability. All issues from 1883 to 1912 are readily collectible, although the 1885 (in particular), 1886, and 1912-S are considered to be key dates. Most readily available are well-worn coins in AG-3 and G-4. As a class, VF, EF, and AU pieces are very scarce in relation to demand. MS coins are generally scarce in the 1880s, except for the 1883, Without CENTS, which is plentiful in all grades. MS pieces are less scarce in the 1890s and are easily found for most twentieth-century years, save for 1909, 1912-D, and 1912-S, all of which are elusive.

Grading Standards

MS-60 to 70 (Mint State). ***Obverse and Reverse:*** Mint luster is complete in the obverse and reverse fields. Lower grades such as MS-60, 61, and 62 can show some evidence of abrasion, usually on the portrait on the obverse and highest parts of the wreath on the reverse, and scattered contact marks elsewhere. At MS-63 these marks are few, and at MS-65 they are fewer yet. In grades above MS-65, marks can only be seen under magnification.

MS-65

AU-50, 53, 55, 58 (About Uncirculated). ***Obverse:*** Light wear is seen on the portrait and on the hair under LIB. Mint luster is present in the fields, ranging from partial at AU-50 to nearly complete at AU-58. All details are sharp, unless lightly struck. ***Reverse:*** Light wear is seen on the V, the other letters, and the wreath. Luster is partial at AU-50, increasing to nearly full at AU-58. All details are sharp, unless lightly struck.

AU-58

EF-40, 45 (Extremely Fine). ***Obverse:*** Nearly all hair detail is visible, save for some lightness above the forehead. Stars show radial lines (except for those that may have been lightly struck). Overall bold appearance. ***Reverse:*** The wreath still shows most detail on the leaves. Denticles are bold inside the rim.

EF-40

VF-20, 30 (Very Fine). ***Obverse:*** Letters in LIBERTY are all well defined. Hair detail is seen on the back of the head and some between the ear and the coronet. Denticles are bold. Some stars show radial lines. ***Reverse:*** Detail is seen in the wreath leaves. Lettering and denticles are bold, although E PLURIBUS UNUM may range from medium-light to bold (depending on the strike).

VF-20

F-12, 15 (Fine). ***Obverse:*** All of the letters in LIBERTY are readable, although the I may be quite weak. The detail beginning at the front of hair is visible. Denticles are well defined. ***Reverse:*** Detail of the leaves begins to fade in the wreath. Denticles are well defined all around the border. E PLURIBUS UNUM has medium definition, and is complete.

F-15

VG-8, 10 (Very Good). ***Obverse:*** Three or more letters in LIBERTY can be discerned. This can be a combination of two full letters and two or more partial letters. Some hair detail shows at the back of the head. The rim is well outlined and shows traces of most or even all denticles. ***Reverse:*** The wreath and lettering are bold, but in outline form. E PLURIBUS UNUM is readable, but may be weak. The rim is complete all around, with traces of most denticles present.

VG-8

G-4, 6 (Good). ***Obverse:*** The rim is complete all around. Some denticles show on the inside of the rim. The date, Liberty head, and stars are in outline form. No letters of LIBERTY are visible in the coronet. ***Reverse:*** V and the wreath are visible in outline form. Most letters are complete, but may be faint. E PLURIBUS UNUM is very weak (this feature can vary, and on some G-4 coins it is better defined). The rim is complete in most areas, but may blend with the field in some parts.

G-6

AG-3 (About Good). ***Obverse:*** The head is outlined, with only the ear hole as a detail. The date is well worn; the bottom of the digits can be weak or incomplete. The stars are solid, without detail; some may be incomplete. The rim is indistinct or incomplete in some areas. ***Reverse:*** Details are nearly all worn away, showing greater effects of wear than does the obverse. V is in outline form. The wreath is in outline form, and may be indistinct in areas. Lettering ranges from faint to missing, but with some letters readable. The rim is usually worn down into the letters.

AG-3

PF-66
Deep Cameo

PF-60 to 70 (Proof). ***Obverse and Reverse:*** PF-60, 61, and 62 coins show varying amounts of hairlines in the field, decreasing as the grade increases. Fields may be dull or cloudy on lower-level pieces. At PF-65, hairlines are visible only under magnification and are very light; the cheek of Liberty does not show any abrasion or "album slide marks." Above PF-65, hairlines become fewer, and in ultra-high grades are nonexistent, this meaning that the coins have never been subject to wiping or abrasive cleaning. At PF-65 or better, expect excellent aesthetic appeal. Blotched, deeply toned, or recolored coins can be found at most Proof levels from PF-60 through 65 or even 66, and should be avoided. Watch for artificially toned lower-grade Proofs colored to mask the true nature of the fields.

Illustrated coin: This Proof shows spotting in the fields.

1899, Repunched Date, Early Die State

1899, Repunched Date, Late Die State

FS-301

1900, Doubled Die Reverse
FS-801

1913, Liberty Head

Circulation Strikes

	Mintage	GSID	G-4	VG-8	F-12	VF-20	EF-40	AU-50	MS-60	MS-63	MS-65
Liberty Head, Without CENTS (1883)	**n/a**	**72815**	**$6.75**	**$8.00**	**$9.50**	**$11.00**	**$15**	**$20**	**$55**	**$95**	**$260**
Liberty Head, With CENTS (1883–1913)	**n/a**	**72359**	**1.60**	**2.20**	**4.10**	**9.50**	**32**	**60**	**95**	**160**	**470**
1883, Without CENTS	5,474,300	2947	6.75	8.00	9.50	11.00	15	20	55	95	260
↳**1883, Without CENTS, Repunched Date, FS-1301**	*	346843	—	—	—	40.00	70	100	195	325	—
1883, With CENTS	16,026,200	2948	20.00	31.00	40.00	55.00	90	120	160	215	525
1884	11,270,000	2949	21.00	35.00	40.00	60.00	90	135	195	300	1,150
↳**1884, Repunched Date, FS-301**	*	346845	—	—	—	—	—	—	—	—	—
1885	1,472,700	2950	340.00	625.00	775.00	1,150.00	1,250	1,500	2,400	4,100	7,500
1886	3,326,000	2951	170.00	235.00	365.00	450.00	650	800	1,300	2,200	4,250
1887	15,260,692	2952	13.50	20.00	32.00	45.00	80	100	155	285	775
1888	10,167,901	2953	28.00	45.00	70.00	130.00	175	235	310	390	950
1889	15,878,025	2954	13.50	16.00	32.00	55.00	90	130	180	245	625
1890	16,256,532	2955	8.00	16.00	27.00	40.00	70	115	160	230	675
↳**1890, Repunched Date, FS-301**	*	346850	—	—	—	—	—	—	—	—	—
1891	16,832,000	2956	5.50	8.00	22.00	38.00	60	120	150	210	550
1892	11,696,897	2957	5.50	8.00	22.00	40.00	70	120	160	245	850
1893	13,368,000	2958	5.50	8.00	22.00	38.00	60	110	150	215	650
1894	5,410,500	2959	13.50	31.00	100.00	160.00	255	325	430	575	1,450
1895	9,977,822	2960	4.70	6.75	17.50	40.00	70	120	170	290	1,000
1896	8,841,058	2961	6.00	22.00	40.00	70.00	130	170	220	365	1,100
1897	20,426,797	2962	2.20	3.70	8.00	20.00	47	80	110	190	750
↳**1897, Repunched Date, FS-301**	*	346851	—	—	—	—	—	—	—	—	—
1898	12,530,292	2963	2.20	3.70	8.00	17.50	60	95	150	230	650
↳**1898, Repunched Date, FS-301**	*	346852	—	—	—	—	—	—	—	—	—
↳**1898, Repunched Date, FS-302**	*	346853	—	—	—	—	—	—	—	—	—
1899	26,027,000	2964	1.60	2.20	4.10	9.50	32	60	110	180	500
↳**1899, Repunched Date, FS-301**	*	346854	—	—	—	—	—	—	—	—	—
1900	27,253,733	2965	1.60	2.20	4.10	9.50	32	60	95	160	500
↳**1900, Doubled Die Reverse, FS-801**	*	346855	—	—	—	—	—	—	—	—	—
1901	26,478,228	2966	1.60	2.20	4.10	9.50	32	60	95	175	500
1902	31,480,579	2967	1.60	2.20	4.10	9.50	32	60	95	160	525
1903	28,004,935	2968	1.60	2.20	4.10	9.50	32	60	95	160	470
1904	21,403,167	2969	1.60	2.20	4.10	9.50	32	60	95	160	470
1905	29,825,124	2970	1.60	2.20	4.10	9.50	32	60	95	160	470
1906	38,612,000	2971	1.60	2.20	4.10	9.50	32	60	95	160	470
↳**1906, Doubled Die Reverse, FS-801**	*	346856	—	—	5.25	12.50	39	70	115	195	550
1907	39,213,325	2972	1.60	2.20	4.10	9.50	32	60	95	160	625
1908	22,684,557	2973	1.60	2.20	4.10	9.50	32	60	95	160	550
1909	11,585,763	2974	1.60	2.20	4.10	9.50	32	60	95	160	550
1910	30,166,948	2975	1.60	2.20	4.10	9.50	32	60	95	160	480
1911	39,557,639	2976	1.60	2.20	4.10	9.50	32	60	95	160	470
1912	26,234,569	2977	1.60	2.20	4.10	9.50	32	60	95	160	470
1912-D	8,474,000	2978	2.60	3.70	11.00	38.00	100	180	330	525	1,150
1912-S	238,000	2979	120.00	135.00	195.00	470.00	1,000	1,450	1,750	2,000	2,600

* Included in number above.

Proof Strikes

	Mintage	GSID	PF-60	PF-63	PF-65	PF-66
Liberty Head, Without CENTS (1883), Proof	**n/a**	**76198**	**$260**	**$310**	**$625**	**$800**
Same, Proof Cameo	**n/a**	**76199**	**—**	**415**	**675**	**900**
Same, Proof Deep Cameo	**n/a**	**76200**	**—**	**—**	**1,900**	**2,500**
Liberty Head, With CENTS (1883–1913), Proof	**n/a**	**73863**	**230**	**310**	**525**	**775**
Same, Proof Cameo	**n/a**	**73864**	**—**	**345**	**600**	**850**
Same, Proof Deep Cameo	**n/a**	**73865**	**—**	**900**	**1,550**	**2,000**
1883, Without CENTS	5,219	2980	260	310	625	800
1883, With CENTS	6,783	2981	230	310	525	775
1884	3,942	2988	230	310	550	825
↳1884, Repunched Date, FS-301	*	346858	275	375	675	975
1885	3,790	2991	950	1,200	1,300	1,500
1886	4,290	2994	490	575	900	1,150
1887	2,960	2997	230	310	525	775
1888	4,582	3000	230	310	525	850
1889	3,336	3003	230	310	525	775
1890	2,740	3006	230	310	525	775
1891	2,350	3009	230	310	525	775
1892	2,745	3012	230	310	550	825
1893	2,195	3015	230	310	525	775
1894	2,632	3018	230	310	525	775
1895	2,062	3021	230	310	525	775
1896	1,862	3024	230	310	525	775
1897	1,938	3027	230	310	525	775
1898	1,795	3030	230	310	525	775
1899	2,031	3033	230	310	525	775
1900	2,262	3036	230	310	525	775
1901	1,985	3039	230	310	525	775
1902	2,018	3042	230	310	525	775
1903	1,790	3045	230	310	525	775
1904	1,817	3048	230	310	525	775
1905	2,152	3051	230	310	525	775
1906	1,725	3054	230	310	525	775
1907	1,475	70787	230	310	525	775
1908	1,620	3059	230	310	525	775
1909	4,763	3062	230	310	525	775
1910	2,405	3065	230	310	525	775
1911	1,733	3068	230	310	525	775
1912	2,145	3071	230	310	525	775
1913, Liberty Head (a)	5 known	3074	1,200,000	3,000,000	4,800,000	5,400,000
	Auctions: $4,560,000, PCGS PF-66 SBG 08/18					

* Included in number above. **a.** An estimated five 1913 Liberty Head nickels were struck under uncertain circumstances at the Mint. Some researchers consider them all to be Proofs. Research published by John Dannreuther in 2021 suggests the 1913 nickels were executed with circulation-strike dies on regular unpolished planchets, leading Dannreuther to conclude that the coins should be classified as Specimens or other special strikes. They were dispersed and are now held in various public and private collections.

INDIAN HEAD OR BUFFALO (1913–1938)

Designer: *James Earle Fraser.* **Weight:** *5 grams.* **Composition:** *.750 copper, .250 nickel.* **Diameter:** *21.2 mm.* **Edge:** *Plain.* **Mints:** *Philadelphia, Denver, and San Francisco.*

Variety 1, FIVE CENTS on Raised Ground (1913), Circulation Strike

Mintmark location for all varieties is on the reverse, below FIVE CENTS.

Variety 1, FIVE CENTS on Raised Ground, Proof Strike

Variety 2, FIVE CENTS in Recess (1913–1938), Circulation Strike

Variety 2, FIVE CENTS in Recess, Matte Proof Strike (1913–1916)

Variety 2, FIVE CENTS in Recess, Satin Proof Strike (1936)

Variety 2, FIVE CENTS in Recess, Mirror Proof Strike (1936–1937)

History. The Indian Head nickel five-cent piece today is almost universally known as the "Buffalo" nickel, after the American bison on the reverse. The design made its debut in 1913. James Earle Fraser, a sculptor well known in the private sector, was its creator. The obverse features an authentic portrait of a Native American, modeled as a composite from life, with three subjects posing. Unlike any preceding coin made for circulation, the Buffalo nickel had little in the way of open, smooth field surfaces. Instead, most areas on the obverse and reverse were filled with design elements or, especially on the reverse, an irregular background, as on a bas-relief plaque. Soon after the first coins were released, it was thought that the inscription FIVE CENTS, on a high area of the motif, would wear too quickly. The Mint modified the design to lower the ground under the bison, which had been arranged in the form of a mound (on what became known as Variety 1). The flat-ground design is called Variety 2.

Striking and Sharpness. Most circulation-strike Buffalo nickels are poorly struck in one or more areas, and for many Denver and San Francisco issues of the 1920s the striking is very poor. However, enough sharp strikes exist among common dates of the 1930s that one can be found with some patience. Certification services do not reflect the quality of strike on their labels, so examine carefully. The matter of striking sharpness on Buffalo nickels is an exceedingly important aspect for the connoisseur (who might prefer, for example, a sharply struck coin in AU-58 over a fully lustrous MS example with much shallower detail). Points to check on the obverse include the center of the coin, especially the area immediately above the tie on the braid. On the reverse check the fur on the head of the bison, and the fur "line" above the bison's shoulder on its back. On both sides, examine the overall striking of letters and other details.

Availability. Among circulated varieties of standard dates and mintmarks, availability is in proportion to their mintages. Among early issues the 1913-S, Variety 2, is the scarcest. The date wore away more quickly on the Variety 1 coins than on the modified design used from later 1913 through the end of the series. In the 1920s the 1926-S is the hardest to find. Collectors sought Buffalo nickels from circulation until the 1960s, after which most were gone. By that time the dates in the teens were apt to have their dates completely worn away, or be AG-3 or G-4. Among MS nickels, the issues of 1913 were saved in quantity as novelties, although 1913-S, Variety 2, is slightly scarce. Philadelphia Mint issues are readily available through the 1920s, while MS-63 and finer mintmarked issues from 1914 to 1927 can range from scarce to rare. From 1931 to 1938, all dates and mintmarks were saved in roll quantities, and all are plentiful today. Many Buffalo nickels in MS are very rare if with Full Details, this being especially true for mintmarked issues after 1913, into the early 1930s. Sharpness of strike is not noted on certification holders, but a connoisseur would probably rather own a Full Details coin in MS-65 than an MS-66 or higher with a flat strike.

Proofs. Proof Buffalo nickels are of two main styles. Matte Proofs were made from 1913 to 1916 and are rare. These have minutely granular or matte surfaces, are sharply struck with Full Details of the design on both sides, and have edges (as viewed edge-on) that are mirrored, a distinctive figure. These are easily confused with circulation strikes except for the features noted. Certified holders usually list these simply as "Proof," not "Matte Proof." Some early Proofs of 1936 have satiny rather than mirror-like fields. Later Proofs of 1936 and all of 1937 have a mirror surface in the fields. The motifs of the 1936 and 1937 mirror Proofs are lightly polished in the die (not frosty or matte).

Grading Standards

MS-67

MS-60 to 70 (Mint State). ***Obverse and Reverse:*** Mint luster is complete in the obverse and reverse fields, except in areas not fully struck up, in which graininess or marks from the *original planchet surface* can be seen. Lower grades such as MS-60, 61, and 62 can show some evidence of abrasion, usually on the center of the obverse above the braid, and on the reverse at the highest parts of the bison. These two checkpoints are often areas of light striking, so abrasion must be differentiated from original planchet marks. At MS-63 evidences of abrasion are few, and at MS-65 they are fewer yet. In grades above MS-65, a Buffalo nickel should be mark-free.

AU-53

AU-50, 53, 55, 58 (About Uncirculated). ***Obverse:*** Light wear is seen on the highest area of the cheek, to the left of the nose, this being the most obvious checkpoint. Light wear is also seen on the highest-relief areas of the hair. Luster is less extensive, and wear more extensive, at AU-50 than at higher grades. An AU-58 coin will have only slight wear and will retain the majority of luster. ***Reverse:*** Light wear is seen on the shoulder and hip, these being the key checkpoints. Light wear is also seen on the flank of the bison and on the horn and top of the head. Luster is less extensive, and wear more extensive, at AU-50 than at higher grades. An AU-58 coin will have only slight wear and will retain the majority of luster.

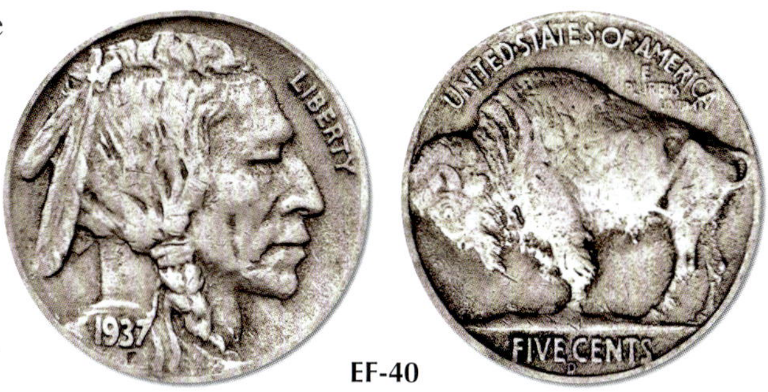

EF-40

EF-40, 45 (Extremely Fine). ***Obverse:*** More wear is seen on the cheek (in particular) and the rest of the face. The center of the coin above the braid is mostly smooth. Other details are sharp. ***Reverse:*** More wear is evident. The tip of the horn is well defined on better strikes. The shoulder, flank, and hip show more wear. The tip of the tail may be discernible, but is mostly worn away.

VF-20

VF-20, 30 (Very Fine). ***Obverse:*** The hair above the braid is mostly flat, but with some details visible. The braid is discernible. The feathers lack most details. On Variety 1 coins the date is light. ***Reverse:*** Wear is more extensive, with most fur detail on the high area of the shoulder gone, the tip of the tail gone, and the horn flat. Ideally the tip of the horn should show, but in the marketplace many certified coins do not show this. On some coins this is due to a shallow strike.

Illustrated coin: On this highly desirable variety one of the buffalo's forelegs has been polished off of the die, probably as the result of an attempt to remove clash marks.

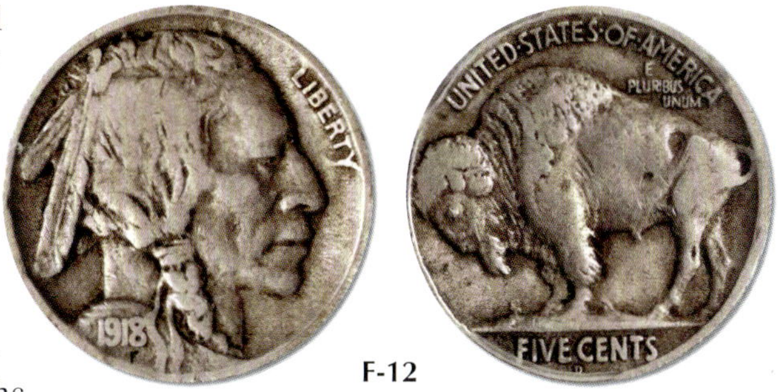

F-12

F-12, 15 (Fine). ***Obverse:*** Only slight detail remains in the hair above the braid. Some of the braid twists are blended together. LIBERTY is weak, and on some coins the upper part of the letters is faint. The rim still is separate. On all coins, the date shows extensive wear. On Variety 1 coins it is weak. ***Reverse:*** The horn is half to two-thirds visible. Fur details are gone except on the neck at the highest part of the back.

VG-8

VG-8, 10 (Very Good). ***Obverse:*** Hair details above the braid are further worn, as is the hair at the top of the head. Most braid twists are blended together. The rim is worn down to the tops of the letters in LIBERTY. The date is light on all coins and very weak on those of Variety 1. ***Reverse:*** The base of the horn is slightly visible. Fur details are worn more, but details can still be seen on the neck and top of the back. The hip and flank beneath are worn flat.

G-4, 6 (Good). ***Obverse:*** Scarcely any hair details are seen at the center, and the braid is flat. The rim and tops of the letters in LIBERTY are blended. The date is weak but readable, with at least the last two numerals showing on earlier issues. ***Reverse:*** The rim is worn to blend into the tops of some or all letters in UNITED STATES OF AMERICA (except for Variety 1). E PLURIBUS UNUM and FIVE CENTS are full, and the mintmark, if any, is clear. The front part of the bison's head blends into the rim.

G-4

AG-3 (About Good). ***Obverse:*** The head is mostly flat, but the facial features remain clear. LIBERTY is weak and partly missing. The date may be incomplete but must be identifiable. ***Reverse:*** Further wear is seen. On Variety 1 coins, UNITED STATES OF AMERICA is full and readable. On the Variety 2 the rim is worn further into the letters. The reverse of the Variety 1 nickels is bolder as the overall grade is defined by the date, which wore away more quickly than on the Variety 2.

AG-3

PF-60 to 70 (Matte Proof). ***Obverse and Reverse:*** Most Matte Proofs are in higher grades. Those with abrasion or contact marks can be graded PF-60 to 62; these are not widely desired. PF-64 can have some abrasion. Tiny flecks are not common, but are sometimes seen. At the Matte PF-65 level or higher there will no traces of abrasion or flecks. Differences between higher-grade Proofs are highly subjective, and one certified at PF-65 can be similar to another at PF-67, and vice-versa.

Matte PF-67

PF-60 to 70 (Mirror Proof). ***Obverse and Reverse:*** Most mirror Proofs are in higher grades. PF-60 to 62 coins can have abrasion or minor handling marks, but are usually assigned such grades because of staining or blotches resulting from poor cleaning. PF-63 and 64 can have minor abrasion and staining. Tiny flecks are not common, but are sometimes seen, as are dark stripe lines from the glued seams in the cellophane envelopes used by the Mint. PF-65 and higher coins should be free of stains, flecks, and abrasion of any kind. Differences between higher-grade Proofs are highly subjective, and one certified PF-65 can be similar to another at PF-67, and vice-versa.

Mirror PF-66

1913, Variety 1, 3-1/2 Legged
FS-901

1914, 4 Over 3
FS-101

1916, Missing Designer's Initial
FS-401

1916, Doubled Die Obverse
FS-101

Circulation Strikes

	Mintage	GSID	G-4	VG-8	F-12	VF-20	EF-40	AU-50	MS-60	MS-63	MS-65
Buffalo, Variety 1: FIVE CENTS on Raised Ground (1913)	n/a	72360	$9.50	$12.00	$13.50	$16.00	$23.00	$26	$40	$80	$180
Buffalo, Variety 2: FIVE CENTS in Recess, (1913–1938)	n/a	72361	0.70	0.90	1.20	1.50	2.60	8	24	30	40
1913, Variety 1	30,992,000	3077	9.50	12.00	13.50	16.00	23.00	26	40	80	180
↳1913, Variety 1, 3-1/2 Legged, FS-901	*	322089	—	—	—	—	—	—	—	3,750	9,500
1913-D, Variety 1	5,337,000	3101	16.00	20.00	22.00	34.00	40.00	60	90	120	340
↳1913-D, Variety 1, 2 Feathers, FS-401	*	392874	—	—	75.00	100.00	135.00	170	305	405	1,750
1913-S, Variety 1	2,105,000	3103	47.00	50.00	60.00	70.00	90.00	120	180	290	850
↳1913-S, Variety 1, 2 Feathers, FS-401	*	392875	—	—	—	—	—	285	725	1,600	—
1913, Variety 2	29,857,186	3078	9.50	13.50	17.50	19.00	22.00	24	34	70	440
↳1913, Variety 2, Doubled Die Obverse, FS-1101	*	326579	—	—	—	—	—	—	415	725	1,300
1913-D, Variety 2	4,156,000	3102	130.00	155.00	160.00	170.00	210.00	235	310	440	1,250
1913-S, Variety 2	1,209,000	3104	200.00	275.00	360.00	420.00	495.00	600	875	1,250	2,750
1914	20,664,463	3079	16.00	19.00	22.00	24.00	28.00	38	60	130	435
1914, 4 Over 3	*	3105	325.00	390.00	525.00	575.00	675.00	1,000	2,250	4,500	19,000
↳1914, 4 Over 3, FS-101	*	392876	325.00	390.00	525.00	575.00	675.00	1,000	2,250	4,500	19,000
1914-D	3,912,000	3106	95.00	110.00	130.00	160.00	240.00	320	430	525	1,200
1914-S	3,470,000	3107	27.00	36.00	45.00	60.00	100.00	160	260	470	2,500
↳1914-S, Overdate, FS-101	*	392877	—	—	—	—	—	—	—	—	—
1915	20,986,220	3080	4.10	5.50	6.75	11.00	16.00	39	50	105	525
↳1915, Doubled Die Obverse, FS-101	*	156400	195.00	—	—	—	—	—	—	—	—
1915-D	7,569,000	3108	20.00	30.00	43.00	75.00	125.00	150	275	365	1,450
↳1915-D, D Over D, FS-501	*	317325	—	100.00	120.00	155.00	215.00	260	1,550	3,450	—
1915-S	1,505,000	3109	40.00	60.00	85.00	180.00	390.00	600	925	1,550	2,900
↳1915-S, S Over S, FS-501	*	326582	—	—	290.00	370.00	495.00	—	—	—	—
↳1915-S, S Over S, FS-502	*	392878	—	—	—	—	—	—	—	—	—
1916	63,497,466	3081	4.10	5.50	6.75	8.00	11.00	24	60	95	325
↳1916, No F, FS-401 (a)	*	199046	—	70.00	90.00	120.00	155.00	235	420	550	725
1916, Doubled Die Obverse (b)	*	3110	5,000.00	7,000.00	9,750.00	12,000.00	18,000.00	25,000	60,000	126,000	—
	Auctions: $264,500, PCGS MS-64 HA 09/05										
↳1916, Doubled Die Obverse, FS-101 (b)	*	390392	5,000.00	7,000.00	9,750.00	12,000.00	18,000.00	25,000	60,000	126,000	—
	Auctions: $138,000, PCGS MS-63 HA 08/22										

* Included in number above. **a.** The initial F, for Fraser—normally below the date—is clearly absent. Some dies exist with a partially missing or weak initial; these do not command the premium of the variety with a completely missing initial **b.** The date, chin, throat, feathers, and the tie on the braid are all doubled. From the *Cherrypickers' Guide to Rare Die Varieties, Vol. I* (sixth edition): "Beware of 1916 nickels with strike doubling on the date offered as this variety. . . . The true doubled die must look like the coin shown here.'

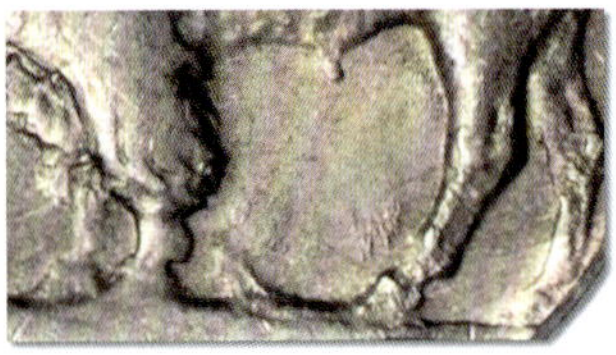

1917-D, 3-1/2 Legged
FS-901

1918, Doubled Die Reverse
FS-801

1918-D, 8 Over 7
FS-101

Circulation Strikes *(continued)*

	Mintage	GSID	G-4	VG-8	F-12	VF-20	EF-40	AU-50	MS-60	MS-63	MS-65
1916-D	13,333,000	3111	$18.00	$24.00	$28.00	$35.00	$80.00	$100	$175	$310	$1,500
↳1916-D, 3-1/2 Legged, FS-901	*	199048	—	—	—	—	—	525	—	—	—
1916-S	11,860,000	3112	11.00	15.00	22.00	35.00	80.00	120	235	390	2,500
1917	51,424,019	3082	4.10	5.50	6.75	8.00	13.50	34	70	210	525
↳1917, Doubled Die Reverse, FS-801	*	326584	290.00	340.00	405.00	450.00	650.00	—	—	—	—
1917-D	9,910,000	3113	20.00	32.00	50.00	85.00	170.00	310	495	825	2,250
↳1917-D, 3-1/2 Legged, FS-901	*	85078	180.00	260.00	415.00	470.00	575.00	750	2,200	3,500	—
1917-S	4,193,000	3114	24.00	43.00	95.00	130.00	215.00	390	1,150	1,700	4,000
	Auctions: $138,000, NGC MS-67 HA 08/08										
1918	32,086,314	3083	4.70	5.50	6.75	8.00	24.00	65	180	415	1,100
↳1918, Doubled Die Reverse, FS-801	*	326588	—	190.00	220.00	260.00	360.00	725	—	—	—
1918-D	8,362,000	3116	23.00	36.00	60.00	120.00	235.00	360	600	1,100	3,750
1918-D, 8 Over 7	*	3115	850.00	1,200.00	2,400.00	3,250.00	8,750.00	11,000	29,000	43,000	258,000
	Auctions: $264,500, PCGS MS-65 HA 01/10										
↳1918-D, 8 Over 7, FS-101	*	390393	850.00	1,200.00	2,400.00	3,250.00	8,750.00	11,000	29,000	43,000	258,000
1918-S	4,882,000	3117	13.50	27.00	55.00	100.00	200.00	390	975	2,100	12,000
1919	60,868,000	3084	2.20	3.40	4.10	6.75	13.50	35	70	155	405
1919-D (c)	8,006,000	3118	17.00	30.00	70.00	110.00	245.00	390	950	1,600	4,200
1919-S (c)	7,521,000	3119	8.00	20.00	50.00	110.00	245.00	430	875	1,750	7,500
	Auctions: $109,250, PCGS MS-66 HA 10/06										
1920	63,093,000	3085	1.10	1.90	2.60	5.50	16.00	38	90	170	650
1920-D (c)	9,418,000	3120	8.75	19.50	36.00	110.00	265.00	390	750	1,500	5,250
↳1920-D, D Over D, FS-502	*	326596	—	—	—	—	—	1,250	2,250	—	—
1920-S	9,689,000	3121	4.10	9.50	22.00	80.00	195.00	280	725	1,450	9,000
1921	10,663,000	3086	3.40	5.50	6.75	20.00	60.00	90	150	390	950
1921-S	1,557,000	3122	60.00	95.00	120.00	245.00	750.00	1,200	2,000	3,600	9,500
1923	35,715,000	3087	1.90	3.00	4.10	6.75	13.50	40	75	180	500
1923-S (c)	6,142,000	3123	6.75	10.00	24.00	100.00	235.00	340	600	1,100	4,900
1924	21,620,000	3088	1.10	1.50	2.60	6.75	22.00	46	115	235	850
1924-D	5,258,000	3124	7.75	11.00	30.00	80.00	245.00	390	575	1,200	3,750
1924-S	1,437,000	3125	16.00	40.00	90.00	260.00	775.00	1,500	2,750	4,300	12,000
	Auctions: $105,750, PCGS MS-66 SBG 11/16										
1925	35,565,100	3089	2.20	3.40	4.10	6.75	20.00	31	50	135	405
1925-D (c)	4,450,000	3126	9.75	21.00	43.00	90.00	180.00	390	550	1,000	3,500
1925-S	6,256,000	3127	3.70	9.00	20.00	75.00	195.00	310	725	1,300	8,500
↳1925-S, S Over S, FS-501	*	317328	—	—	—	—	—	—	—	—	—
1926	44,693,000	3090	0.70	0.90	2.60	5.50	11.50	22	30	80	195
↳1926, Doubled Die Obverse/ Doubled Die Reverse, FS-101/801	*	326601	—	—	—	—	—	—	—	—	—

* Included in number above. **c.** Uncirculated pieces with full, sharp details are worth considerable more.

1935, Doubled Die Reverse
FS-801

1936-D, 3-1/2 Legged
FS-901

Circulation Strikes *(continued)*

	Mintage	GSID	G-4	VG-8	F-12	VF-20	EF-40	AU-50	MS-60	MS-63	MS-65
1926-S	970,000	3129	$24.00	$55.00	$80.00	$175.00	$875.00	$2,050	$5,250	$9,250	$72,000
	Auctions: $246,750, PCGS MS-65 LGND 09/19										
1927	37,981,000	3091	0.70	0.90	2.20	4.10	12.00	22	40	95	325
1927-D	5,730,000	3130	2.60	6.75	9.50	34.00	85.00	130	195	430	3,500
↳1927-D, D Over D, FS-501	*	326603	—	—	—	—	—	—	—	—	—
↳1927-D, 3-1/2 Legged, FS-901	*	78043	110.00	130.00	210.00	260.00	575.00	900	3,100	—	—
1927-S	3,430,000	3131	1.90	2.20	6.75	40.00	120.00	260	1,000	2,250	12,000
↳1927-S, Doubled Die Obverse, FS-101	*	326604	—	—	—	—	—	—	—	—	—
1928	23,411,000	3093	0.70	0.90	2.20	4.10	12.00	24	40	90	300
1928-D	6,436,000	3132	0.70	0.90	3.40	15.00	43.00	50	70	130	525
1928-S	6,936,000	3133	0.70	0.90	2.60	11.50	30.00	95	305	700	2,600
1929	36,446,000	3094	0.70	0.90	2.20	4.10	12.00	22	34	80	245
1929-D	8,370,000	3134	0.70	0.90	1.90	6.75	35.00	47	60	130	850
1929-S	7,754,000	3135	0.70	0.90	1.90	2.60	12.00	27	60	150	405
1930	22,849,000	3095	0.70	0.90	2.20	4.10	11.50	22	32	70	190
↳1930, Doubled Die Obverse, FS-101	*	329297	—	—	—	—	—	160	290	420	725
↳1930, Doubled Die Reverse, FS-802	*	326609	—	—	—	—	—	—	—	—	—
1930-S	5,435,000	3136	0.70	0.90	2.60	4.10	16.00	43	95	170	495
↳1930-S, S Over S, FS-501	*	329301	—	—	—	—	—	—	—	—	—
1931-S	1,200,000	3137	12.00	15.00	16.00	19.00	35.00	50	80	135	280
↳1931-S, Doubled Die Reverse, FS-801	*	329302	—	—	—	—	—	—	—	—	—
↳1931-S, Doubled Die Reverse, FS-802	*	329303	—	—	—	—	—	—	—	—	—
1934	20,213,003	3096	0.70	0.90	2.20	4.10	10.00	26	49	65	195
1934-D	7,480,000	3138	0.70	0.90	4.10	9.50	22.00	49	80	130	420
1935	58,264,000	3097	0.70	0.90	1.20	1.50	2.60	8	24	38	115
1935, Doubled Die Reverse (d)	*	3098	55.00	70.00	90.00	120.00	450.00	1,050	4,750	8,750	36,000
↳1935, Doubled Die Reverse, FS-801 (d)	*	373547	55.00	70.00	100.00	160.00	625.00	1,300	5,000	9,500	—
1935-D	12,092,000	3139	0.70	0.90	2.20	5.50	20.00	49	70	90	275
↳1935-D, D Over D, FS-502	*	329305	55.00	90.00	120.00	160.00	230.00	260	440	950	—
1935-S	10,300,000	3140	0.70	0.90	1.20	1.90	2.60	22	50	65	180
↳1935-S, Doubled Die Reverse, FS-801	*	329306	—	—	—	—	—	—	—	—	—
1936	118,997,000	3099	0.70	0.90	1.20	1.50	4.10	10	30	49	80
1936-D	24,814,000	3141	0.70	0.90	1.20	1.90	2.60	23	39	55	80
↳1936-D, D Over D, FS-502	*	199160	—	—	—	—	—	—	—	130	190
↳1936-D, D Over D Over D, FS-511	*	199161	—	—	—	—	—	—	390	470	725
1936-D, 3-1/2 Legged	*	3142	675.00	1,000.00	1,250.00	1,750.00	4,500.00	7,250	14,500	24,000	—

* Included in number above. **d.** Strong doubling is evident on FIVE CENTS, E PLURIBUS UNUM, and the eye, horn, and mane of the bison. This variety (FS-801) is extremely rare above VF, and fewer than a dozen are known in MS. Do not mistake it for the more moderately doubled FS-803, which commands much lower premiums.

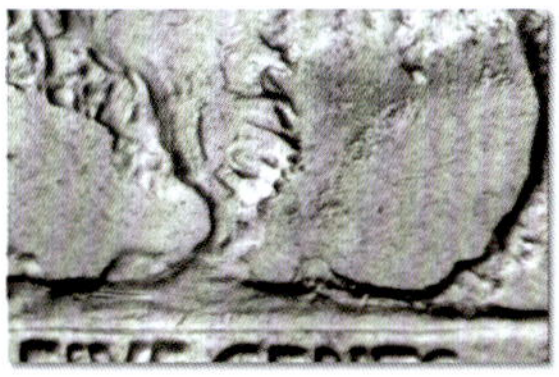

1937-D, 3-Legged
FS-901

1938-D, D Over S
FS-511

Circulation Strikes *(continued)*

	Mintage	GSID	G-4	VG-8	F-12	VF-20	EF-40	AU-50	MS-60	MS-63	MS-65
1936-S	14,930,000	3143	$0.70	$0.90	$1.20	$2.20	$2.60	$11	$35	$43	$105
↳1936-S, S Over S, FS-501	*	70604	—	—	—	34.00	55.00	100	180	290	750
1937	79,480,000	3100	0.70	0.90	1.20	1.50	2.60	8	24	32	60
1937-D	17,826,000	3144	0.70	0.90	1.20	1.90	2.60	8	31	40	65
1937-D, 3-Legged (e)	*	3145	500.00	550.00	650.00	850.00	1,100.00	1,400	2,750	6,000	31,000
↳1937-D, 3-Legged, FS-901 (e)	*	376679	500.00	550.00	650.00	850.00	1,100.00	1,400	2,750	6,000	31,000
1937-S	5,635,000	3146	0.70	0.90	1.20	1.50	2.60	8	24	38	75
1938-D	7,020,000	3147	2.20	2.40	2.60	3.40	4.40	8	24	30	40
1938-D, D Over S	*	3149	9.50	11.00	12.00	13.50	19.00	36	55	75	95
↳1938-D, D Over S, FS-511	*	199181	9.50	11.00	12.00	13.50	19.00	36	55	75	95
↳1938-D, D Over S, FS-513	*	199183	9.50	11.00	12.00	13.50	19.00	36	55	75	95
↳1938-D, D Over S, FS-514	*	199184	9.50	11.00	12.00	13.50	19.00	36	55	75	95
↳1938-D, D Over S, FS-515	*	199185	9.50	11.00	12.00	13.50	19.00	36	55	75	95

* Included in number above. **e.** Beware altered examples fraudulently passed as genuine. From the *Cherrypickers' Guide to Rare Die Varieties, Vol. I* (sixth edition): "Look for a line of raised dots from the middle of the bison's belly to the ground as one of the diagnostics on the genuine specimen."

Proof Strikes

	Mintage	GSID	PF-60	PF-63	PF-65
Buffalo, Variety 1: FIVE CENTS on Raised Ground, (1913), Proof, Matte Finish	**n/a**	**72362**	**$1,500**	**$3,900**	**$4,600**
Buffalo, Variety 2: FIVE CENTS in Recess, (1913–1938), Proof, Matte Finish	**n/a**	**72363**	**900**	**1,800**	**2,400**
Same, Proof, Satin Finish	**n/a**	**74212**	**1,000**	**1,300**	**1,550**
Same, Proof, Brilliant Finish	**n/a**	**74213**	**925**	**1,250**	**1,350**
1913, Variety 1, Matte Finish	1,520	3150	1,500	3,900	4,600
1913, Variety 2, Matte Finish	1,514	3151	1,000	1,800	2,400
1914, Matte Finish	1,275	3152	900	1,800	2,400
1915, Matte Finish	1,050	3153	1,100	1,950	2,800
1916, Matte Finish	600	3154	1,500	3,000	4,500
1927, Special Strike (a)	6 known	377439	—	78,000	—
1936, Satin Finish	4,420	3155	1,000	1,300	1,550
1936, Brilliant Finish	*	3156	1,050	1,300	1,700
1937, Brilliant Finish	5,769	3159	925	1,250	1,350

* Included in number above. **a.** Some experts believe that certain 1927 nickels were carefully made circulation strikes; such pieces are sometimes certified as "Examples" or "Presentation Strikes." Professional numismatic opinions vary. See Bowers, *A Guide Book of Buffalo and Jefferson Nickels* (second edition).

JEFFERSON (1938–2003)

Designer: *Felix Schlag.* **Weight:** *5 grams.* **Composition:** *1938–1942, 1946–2003—.750 copper, .250 nickel; 1942–1945—.560 copper, .350 silver, .090 manganese, with net weight .05626 oz. pure silver.* **Diameter:** *21.2 mm.* **Edge:** *Plain.* **Mints:** *Philadelphia, Denver, and San Francisco.*

Circulation Strike

Mintmark location, 1938–1941 and 1946–1964, is on the reverse, to the right of Monticello.

Mintmark location, 1942–1945, is on the reverse, above Monticello.

Proof Strike

Wartime Silver Alloy (1942–1945), Circulation Strike

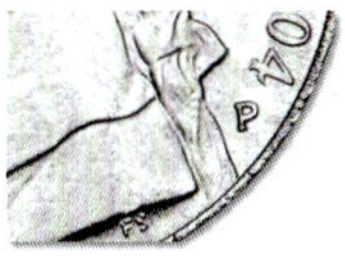

Mintmark location, 1968–2004, is on the obverse, near the date.

Wartime Silver Alloy, Proof Strike

History. The Jefferson nickel, designed by Felix Schlag in a public competition, made its debut in 1938, and has been a numismatic favorite since. The obverse features a portrait of Thomas Jefferson after the famous bust by Jean Antoine Houdon, and the reverse a front view of Jefferson's home, Monticello. From partway through 1942 to the end of 1945 a copper-silver-manganese alloy replaced the traditional 75 percent copper and 25 percent nickel composition. This was to help save nickel for the war effort. These silver-content coins bear a distinctive P, D, or S mintmark above the dome of Monticello. Starting in 1966, Felix Schlag's initials, FS, were added below the presidential bust. The coinage dies were remodeled to strengthen the design in 1971, 1972, 1977, and 1982. The mintmark position, originally on the reverse to the right of Monticello, was moved to the obverse starting in 1968.

Striking and Sharpness. On the obverse, check for weakness on the portrait, especially in the lower jaw area. On the reverse, most circulation strikes have weak details on the six steps of Monticello, especially under the third pillar from the left, as this section on the reverse was opposite in the dies (in the press) from the high parts of the Jefferson portrait, and metal could not effectively flow in both directions at once. Planchet weight allowance was another cause, the dies being spaced slightly too far apart. Jefferson nickels can be classified as "Full Steps" (FS) if either five or six of Monticello's porch steps (with the top step counting as one) are clear. Notations of 5FS or 6FS can indicate the number of visible steps. It is easier to count the incuse lines than the raised steps. If there are four complete, unbroken lines, the coin qualifies as Full Steps (with five steps); five complete, unbroken lines indicate six full steps. There must be no nicks, cuts, or scratches interrupting the incuse lines. It is difficult to determine a full five-step count on the 1938 and some 1939 issues, as the steps are wavy and ill-defined; a great deal of subjectivity is common for these dates. Even if the steps are mostly or fully defined, check other areas to determine if a coin has Full Details overall. Interestingly, nickels of the 1950s and 1960s are among the most weakly struck. The silver-content coins of the 1940s usually are well struck. Some nickels of the 1950s to 1970s discolored easily, perhaps due to some impurities in the alloy. Proofs were struck from 1938 to 1942, 1950 to 1964, and 1968 to 2003. All have mirror fields. Striking is usually with Full Details, although there are scattered exceptions. Most survivors are in high grade, PF-64 and upward. Most since the 1970s have frosted or cameo contrast on the higher features. Special Mint Set (SMS) coins were struck in lieu of Proofs from 1965 to 1967; these in some instances closely resemble Proofs.

Availability. All basic dates and mintmarks were saved in roll quantities. Scarce issues in MS include 1939-D and 1942-D. The low-mintage 1950-D was a popular speculation in its time, and most of the mintage went into numismatic hands, making MS coins common today. Many different dates and mints are rare if with 5FS or 6FS; consult *A Guide Book of Buffalo and Jefferson Nickels* for details.

Grading Standards

MS-60 to 70 (Mint State). ***Obverse and Reverse:*** Mint luster is complete in the obverse and reverse fields, except in areas not fully struck up, in which graininess or marks from the *original planchet surface* can be seen. This may include the jaw, the back of Jefferson's head, and the higher-relief central features of Monticello. The highest parts of the design may have evidence of abrasion and/or contact marks in lower MS grades. Lower grades such as MS-60, 61, and 62 can show some evidence of abrasion, usually on the same areas that display weak striking. At MS-63, evidences of abrasion are few, and at MS-65 they are fewer yet. In grades above MS-65, a Jefferson nickel should be mark-free.

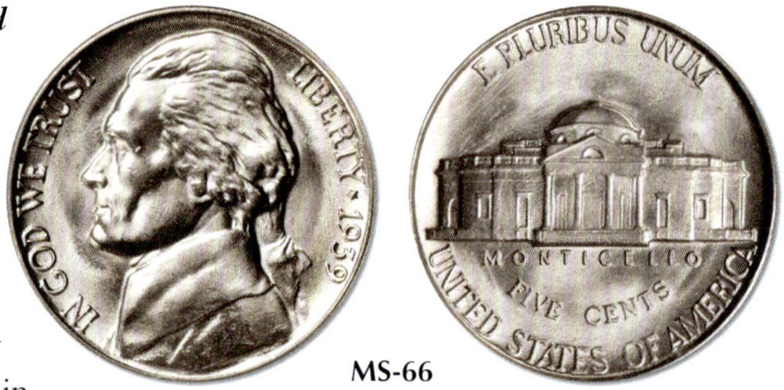

MS-66

AU-50, 53, 55, 58 (About Uncirculated). ***Obverse:*** The cheekbone and the higher points of the hair show light wear, more at AU-50 than at AU-58. Some mint luster will remain on some AU-55 and most AU-58 coins. ***Reverse:*** The central part of Monticello shows light wear, but is difficult to evaluate as this area often shows weakness of strike. Some mint luster will remain on some AU-55 and most AU-58 coins.

AU-58

EF-40, 45 (Extremely Fine). ***Obverse:*** More wear is evident on the cheekbone. The higher parts of the hair are without detail. ***Reverse:*** Monticello shows wear overall. The bottom edge of the triangular area above the columns at the center are worn away.

EF-40

VF-20, 30 (Very Fine). ***Obverse:*** Most hair detail is lost, except for the back of the head and lower area. The cheekbone is flat and mostly blended into the hair at the right. ***Reverse:*** Many shallow-relief architectural features are worn away. The windows remain clear and the four columns are distinct.

VF-20

PF-60 to 70 (Proof). ***Obverse and Reverse:*** Most Proof Jefferson nickels are in higher grades. Those with abrasion or contact marks can be graded PF-60 to 62 or even 63; these are not widely desired by collectors. PF-64 can have some abrasion. Tiny flecks are sometimes seen on coins of 1938 to 1942, as are discolorations (even to the extent of black streaks); these flaws are from cellophane holders. You should avoid such coins. Undipped Proofs of the early era often have a slight bluish or yellowish tint. At PF-65 or higher there are no traces of abrasion or flecks. Evaluation of differences between higher-grade Jefferson Proofs is highly subjective; one certified at PF-65 might be similar to another at PF-67, and vice-versa. Striking is typically with full details, although there are scattered exceptions. At PF-69 and 70 there are no traces of abrasion, contact marks, or other flaws.

PF-70
Deep Cameo

Five Steps

Six Steps

Circulation Strikes

	Mintage	GSID	EF-40	AU-50	MS-60	MS-63	MS-64	MS-65	MS-66	MS-67
Jefferson, Memorial Reverse (1938–1942, 1946–2003)	**n/a**	**374526**	**$0.20**	**$0.20**	**$0.20**	**$0.20**	**$0.20**	**$0.80**	**$2.60**	**$8**
Same, Wartime Silver Alloy (1942–1945)	**n/a**	**85088**	**3.20**	**3.60**	**5.00**	**8.75**	**11.50**	**16.00**	**32.00**	**60**
1938	19,496,000	3162	0.40	0.80	4.10	8.00	12.00	16.00	47.00	160
↳1938, Doubled Die Obverse, FS-101	*	376606	—	130.00	195.00	260.00	285.00	360.00	—	—
↳1938, Quadruple Die Obverse, FS-105	*	376607	—	35.00	70.00	100.00	115.00	130.00	290.00	—
↳1938, Doubled Die Obverse, FS-106	*	376427	—	34.00	55.00	80.00	100.00	155.00	290.00	—
1938, Full Steps	*	3163	—	—	—	—	55.00	95.00	155.00	455
↳1938, Doubled Die Obverse, FS-101, Full Steps	*	376608	—	—	—	—	—	—	—	—
↳1938, Quadruple Die Obverse, FS-105, Full Steps	*	376609	—	—	—	—	—	—	—	—
↳1938, Doubled Die Obverse, FS-106, Full Steps	*	376428	—	—	—	—	—	—	—	—
1938-D	5,376,000	3214	1.50	2.20	4.10	6.75	8.00	11.00	27.00	95
1938-D, Full Steps	*	3215	—	—	—	—	20.00	47.00	95.00	370
1938-S	4,105,000	3216	2.60	3.00	5.50	9.50	12.00	16.00	30.00	220
1938-S, Full Steps	*	3217	—	—	—	—	110.00	180.00	525.00	1,000
1939, Reverse of 1938	120,615,000	3164	0.80	1.10	2.60	9.50	12.00	27.00	55.00	155
1939, Reverse of 1938, Full Steps	*	3167	—	—	—	—	115.00	210.00	390.00	1,500
1939, Reverse of 1940	120,615,000	3169	0.80	1.10	2.40	7.50	8.00	24.00	47.00	150

* Included in number above.

1939, Doubled Die Reverse
FS-801

Circulation Strikes *(continued)*

	Mintage	GSID	EF-40	AU-50	MS-60	MS-63	MS-64	MS-65	MS-66	MS-67
1939, Doubled MONTICELLO, FIVE CENTS	*	3165	$160.00	$195.00	$390.00	$750.00	$925.00	$1,400.00	$1,750	$3,000
↳1939, Reverse of 1940, Doubled Die Reverse, FS-801	*	375862	160.00	195.00	390.00	750.00	925.00	1,400.00	1,750	3,000
↳1939, Reverse of 1940, Doubled Die Reverse, FS-802	*	378702	—	—	155.00	245.00	310.00	525.00	775	—
1939, Doubled MONTICELLO, FIVE CENTS, Full Steps	*	3168	—	—	—	—	16.00	40.00	130	390
↳1939, Reverse of 1940, Doubled Die Reverse, FS-801, Full Steps	*	375863	—	—	—	900.00	1,750.00	3,000.00	6,250	10,500
↳1939, Reverse of 1940, Doubled Die Reverse, FS-802, Full Steps	*	378703	—	—	—	—	—	—	—	—
1939-D, Reverse of 1938	3,514,000	3218	5.50	16.00	40.00	50.00	55.00	60.00	90	135
1939-D, Reverse of 1938, Full Steps	*	3219	—	—	—	—	195.00	415.00	625	975
1939-D, Reverse of 1940	3,514,000	3221	5.50	16.00	47.00	65.00	70.00	80.00	110	340
1939-D, Reverse of 1940, Full Steps	*	3220	—	—	—	—	170.00	260.00	525	2,000
1939-S, Reverse of 1938	6,630,000	3222	0.60	2.60	27.00	35.00	40.00	50.00	80	210
1939-S, Reverse of 1938, Full Steps	*	3223	—	—	—	—	115.00	215.00	525	2,500
1939-S, Reverse of 1940	6,630,000	3225	2.60	5.50	30.00	40.00	47.00	80.00	215	950
1939-S, Reverse of 1940, Full Steps	*	3224	—	—	—	115.00	155.00	235.00	775	6,000
1940	176,485,000	3170	0.30	0.30	1.50	4.10	5.50	9.50	12	120
1940, Full Steps	*	3171	—	—	—	—	13.50	30.00	60	290
1940-D	43,540,000	3226	0.30	0.30	2.60	4.70	5.50	9.50	13.50	100
1940-D, Full Steps	*	3227	—	—	—	13.50	16.00	22.00	38	175
1940-S	39,690,000	3228	0.80	1.10	5.50	8.00	11.00	15.00	34	195
↳1940-S, S Over S, FS-501	*	392879	—	—	—	—	—	—	—	—
1940-S, Full Steps	*	3229	—	—	—	19.00	27.00	40.00	105	675
↳1940-S, S Over S, FS-501, Full Steps	*	392880	—	—	—	—	—	—	—	—
1941	203,265,000	3172	0.70	0.90	2.20	4.10	6.75	12.00	16	75
1941, Full Steps	*	3173	—	—	—	—	13.50	34.00	80	350
1941-D	53,432,000	3230	1.90	3.00	4.10	6.75	8.00	9.50	19	55
1941-D, Full Steps	*	3231	—	—	—	—	11.00	20.00	40	135
1941-S	43,445,000	3232	2.20	3.40	5.50	9.50	11.00	16.00	40	390
↳1941-S, S Over S, Large S, FS-501	*	376484	—	—	—	—	100.00	130.00	235	—
↳1941-S, S Over S, Large S, FS-502	*	374087	—	—	—	—	—	—	—	—

* Included in number above.

1942-D, D Over Horizontal D
FS-501

1943-P, 3 Over 2
FS-101

1943-P, Doubled Die Obverse
FS-106: the "Doubled Eye" variety.

Circulation Strikes *(continued)*

	Mintage	GSID	EF-40	AU-50	MS-60	MS-63	MS-64	MS-65	MS-66	MS-67
1941-S, Full Steps	*	3233	—	—	—	—	$38.00	$70.00	$175	$2,500
↳1941-S, S Over S, Large S, FS-501, Full Steps	*	376485	—	—	—	—	—	—	—	—
↳1941-S, S Over S, Large S, FS-502, Full Steps	*	374088	—	—	—	—	—	—	—	—
1942	49,789,000	3174	$1.50	$2.60	$4.10	$11.00	12.00	13.50	32	160
↳1942, Variety 1, Doubled Die Obverse, FS-101	*	392883	—	—	—	—	—	—	—	—
1942, Full Steps	*	3175	—	—	—	—	38.00	75.00	415	950
↳1942, Variety 1, Doubled Die Obverse, FS-101, Full Steps	*	392885	—	—	—	—	—	—	—	—
1942-D	13,938,000	3234	6.75	8.00	30.00	38.00	40.00	47.00	70	180
1942-D, D Over Horizontal D	*	3236	175.00	325.00	1,500.00	3,250.00	3,750.00	4,600.00	7,250	—
↳1942-D, D Over Horizontal D, FS-501	*	393206	175.00	325.00	1,500.00	3,250.00	3,750.00	4,600.00	7,250	—
1942-D, Full Steps	*	3235	—	—	—	40.00	50.00	65.00	90	405
↳1942-D, D Over Horizontal D, FS-501, Full Steps	*	393207	—	—	—	—	—	—	—	—
1942-P, Silver	57,873,000	3240	3.40	4.10	10.50	14.00	18.50	26.00	35	80
↳1942-P, Silver, P Over P, Variety 2, FS-501	*	374089	—	—	—	—	—	—	—	—
1942-P, Silver, Full Steps	*	3241	—	—	—	27.00	35.00	70.00	110	455
↳1942-P, Silver, P Over P, Variety 2, FS-501, Full Steps	*	374090	—	—	—	—	—	—	2,250	—
1942-S	32,900,000	3242	3.40	4.10	9.75	14.00	18.50	24.00	35	70
↳1942-S, Silver, Mintmark Right of Monticello, FS-502	unique	392887	—	—	—	—	—	—	—	—
1942-S, Full Steps	*	3243	—	—	—	—	27.00	60.00	155	625
1943-P	271,165,000	3248	3.20	3.60	5.00	8.75	11.50	16.00	32	60
1943-P, Full Steps	*	3250	—	—	—	—	13.50	38.00	95	285
1943-P, 3 Over 2	*	3244	110.00	160.00	325.00	470.00	525.00	575.00	950	1,900
↳1943-P, 3 Over 2, Doubled Die Obverse, FS-101	*	378704	110.00	160.00	325.00	470.00	525.00	575.00	950	1,900
1943-P, 3 Over 2, Full Steps	*	3245	—	—	—	775.00	1,050.00	1,400.00	2,400	5,000
↳1943-P, 3 Over 2, Doubled Die Obverse, FS-101, Full Steps	*	378705	—	—	—	775.00	1,050.00	1,400.00	2,400	5,000
1943-P, Doubled Eye	*	3353	47.00	60.00	130.00	195.00	235.00	360.00	575	1,000
↳1943-P, Doubled Eye, FS-106	*	392892	—	—	—	—	—	—	—	—
1943-P, Doubled Eye, Full Steps	*	3249	—	—	—	340.00	440.00	775.00	1,250	8,000
↳1943-P, Doubled Eye, FS-106, Full Steps	*	392893	—	—	—	340.00	440.00	775.00	1,250	8,000

* Included in number above.

1945-P, Doubled Die Reverse
FS-803

Circulation Strikes *(continued)*

	Mintage	GSID	EF-40	AU-50	MS-60	MS-63	MS-64	MS-65	MS-66	MS-67
1943-D	15,294,000	3246	$3.20	$3.60	$5.00	$8.75	$11.50	$16	$32	$65
↳1943-D, D Over D, FS-501	*	331687	—	—	—	—	70.00	130	235	—
1943-D, Full Steps	*	3247	—	—	—	—	12.00	20	40	120
↳1943-D, D Over D, FS-501, Full Steps	*	331688	—	—	—	—	110.00	220	340	2,000
1943-S	104,060,000	3251	3.20	3.60	5.00	8.75	11.50	16	43	100
1943-S, Full Steps	*	3252	—	—	—	—	13.50	27	90	310
1944-P	119,150,000	3255	3.20	3.60	10.50	14.00	18.50	26	43	100
1944-P, Full Steps	*	3256	—	—	—	—	20.00	55	130	495
1944-D	32,309,000	3253	3.40	4.10	10.50	14.00	18.50	23	35	80
↳1944-D, D Over D, FS-501	*	392894	—	—	—	—	—	—	—	—
1944-D, Full Steps	*	3254	—	—	—	—	20.00	27	55	155
↳1944-D, D Over D, FS-501, Full Steps	*	392895	—	—	—	—	—	—	—	—
1944-S	21,640,000	3257	3.40	4.10	10.50	14.00	18.50	23	40	90
1944-S, Full Steps	*	3258	—	—	—	—	100.00	170	360	800
1945-P	119,408,100	3261	3.40	4.10	6.50	11.00	15.50	22	47	190
↳1945-P, Tripled Die Reverse, FS-803	*	378706	—	—	120.00	145.00	160.00	195	365	525
↳1945-P, Tripled Die Reverse, FS-501/804	*	378707	—	40.00	80.00	145.00	160.00	180	775	1,500
1945-P, Full Steps	*	3263	—	—	—	—	40.00	75	290	3,450
↳1945-P, Tripled Die Reverse, FS-803, Full Steps	*	378708	—	—	—	—	—	—	—	—
↳1945-P, Tripled Die Reverse, FS-501/804, Full Steps	*	378709	—	—	—	—	—	—	—	—
1945-P, Doubled Die Reverse	*	3354	27.00	47.00	160.00	245.00	290.00	345	550	1,400
↳1945-P, Doubled Die Reverse, FS-801	*	378710	27.00	47.00	160.00	245.00	290.00	345	550	1,400
1945-P, Doubled Die Reverse, Full Steps	*	3262	—	—	—	1,000.00	1,900.00	4,400	8,750	—
↳1945-P, Doubled Die Reverse, FS-801, Full Steps	*	378711	—	—	—	1,000.00	1,900.00	4,400	8,750	—
1945-D	37,158,000	3259	3.20	3.60	5.00	8.75	11.50	19	40	90
1945-D, Full Steps	*	3260	—	—	—	—	13.50	30	70	275
1945-S	58,939,000	3264	3.20	3.60	5.00	8.75	11.50	16	32	155
1945-S, Full Steps	*	3265	—	—	—	80.00	235.00	310	850	2,500
1946	161,116,000	3176	0.50	0.80	1.60	2.60	5.50	11	27	405
1946, Full Steps	*	3177	—	—	—	—	47.00	90	725	2,700
1946-D	45,292,200	3266	0.50	0.80	1.80	2.40	4.10	11	20	170
↳1946-D, D Over Inverted D, FS-501	*	393208	—	—	—	390.00	490.00	750	1,550	2,050
1946-D, Full Steps	*	3267	—	—	—	—	11.00	20	47	525
↳1946-D, D Over Inverted D, FS-501, Full Steps	*	393209	—	—	—	—	575.00	1,700	2,250	3,450

Note: 1944 nickels without mintmarks are counterfeits. Genuine examples of some wartime dates were struck in nickel, in error.
* Included in number above.

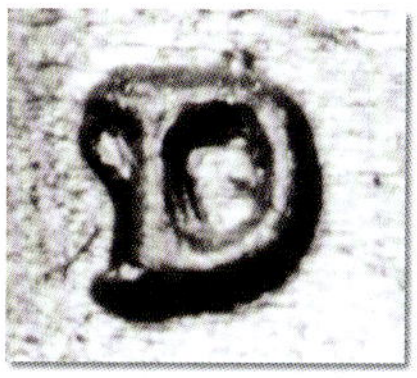

1949-D, D Over S
FS-501

Circulation Strikes *(continued)*

	Mintage	GSID	EF-40	AU-50	MS-60	MS-63	MS-64	MS-65	MS-66	MS-67
1946-S	13,560,000	3270	$0.50	$0.80	$1.00	$1.50	$5.50	$11.00	$34	$370
↳**1946-S, Doubled Die Obverse, FS-101**	*	392900	—	—	—	—	—	—	—	—
1946-S, Full Steps	*	3271	—	—	—	22.00	27.00	40.00	160	3,600
↳**1946-S, Doubled Die Obverse, FS-101, Full Steps**	*	392901	—	—	—	—	—	—	—	—
1947	95,000,000	3178	0.50	0.80	1.40	2.60	4.10	11.00	40	195
1947, Full Steps	*	3179	—	—	—	—	13.50	27.00	195	1,550
1947-D	37,822,000	3272	0.50	0.80	1.40	2.60	4.10	11.00	30	260
1947-D, Full Steps	*	3273	—	—	—	—	11.00	19.00	85	490
1947-S	24,720,000	3274	0.50	0.80	1.50	2.60	5.50	12.00	40	750
1947-S, Full Steps	*	3275	—	—	—	40.00	55.00	80.00	195	2,400
1948	89,348,000	3180	0.50	0.80	1.10	4.10	11.00	13.50	90	1,000
1948, Full Steps	*	3181	—	—	—	30.00	40.00	90.00	390	2,500
1948-D	44,734,000	3276	0.60	1.50	2.60	4.10	5.50	11.00	30	245
1948-D, Full Steps	*	3277	—	—	—	—	15.00	34.00	55	625
1948-S	11,300,000	3278	0.40	0.80	1.90	4.10	5.50	9.50	24	160
1948-S, Full Steps	*	3279	—	—	—	22.00	32.00	60.00	195	1,150
1949	60,652,000	3182	0.80	3.00	5.50	9.50	12.00	15.00	60	850
1949, Full Steps	*	3183	—	—	—	—	950.00	2,500.00	4,750	—
1949-D	36,498,000	3280	0.60	1.50	3.70	6.75	9.50	12.00	30	525
1949-D, Full Steps	*	3281	—	—	—	—	13.50	34.00	155	2,200
1949-D, D Over S	*	3282	75.00	130.00	195.00	260.00	325.00	405.00	675	1,750
↳**1949-D, D Over S, FS-501**	*	392902	75.00	130.00	195.00	260.00	325.00	405.00	675	1,750
1949-D, D Over S, Full Steps	*	3283	—	—	—	—	1,000.00	1,750.00	2,800	21,500
↳**1949-D, D Over S, FS-501, Full Steps**	*	392903					1,000.00	1,750.00	2,000	21,500
1949-S	9,716,000	3284	0.50	1.50	3.00	5.50	11.00	24.00	70	650
1949-S, Full Steps	*	3285	—	—	—	145.00	195.00	310.00	525	4,000
1950	9,796,000	3184	0.40	0.80	1.80	2.60	11.00	19.00	55	575
1950, Full Steps	*	3185	—	—	—	—	75.00	95.00	310	2,050
1950-D	2,630,030	3286	5.50	6.75	8.00	13.50	17.50	26.00	40	170
1950-D, Full Steps	*	3287	—	—	—	19.00	24.00	35.00	115	525
1951	28,552,000	3186	0.50	0.80	4.10	8.00	11.00	16.00	40	155
1951, Full Steps	*	3187	—	—	—	—	70.00	340.00	525	3,900
1951-D	20,460,000	3288	0.50	0.80	4.10	6.75	9.50	15.00	24	200
1951-D, Full Steps	*	3289	—	—	—	—	34.00	80.00	280	1,600
1951-S	7,776,000	3290	0.60	1.10	4.10	8.00	9.50	16.00	47	290
1951-S, Full Steps	*	3291	—	—	—	—	115.00	170.00	1,000	4,900
1952	63,988,000	3188	0.40	0.60	2.20	5.50	15.00	26.00	75	1,000
1952, Full Steps	*	3189	—	—	—	—	650.00	1,150.00	2,700	—
1952-D	30,638,000	3292	0.40	1.10	3.70	8.00	12.00	19.00	75	390
1952-D, Full Steps	*	3293	—	—	—	—	70.00	95.00	405	5,250

* Included in number above.

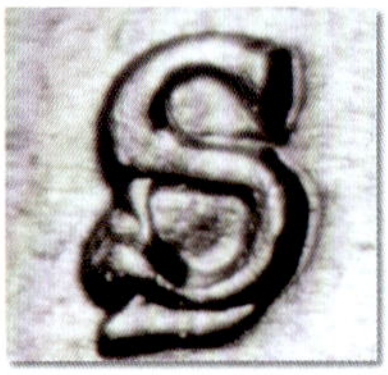

1954-S, S Over D
FS-501

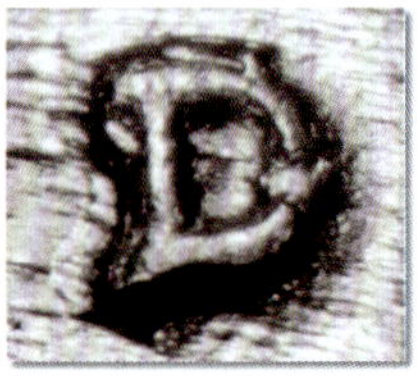

1955-D, D Over S
FS-501

Circulation Strikes *(continued)*

	Mintage	GSID	EF-40	AU-50	MS-60	MS-63	MS-64	MS-65	MS-66	MS-67
1952-S	20,572,000	3294	$0.30	$0.40	$1.00	$4.10	$9.50	$16	$34	$575
1952-S, Full Steps	*	3295	—	—	—	95.00	120.00	155	775	8,000
1953	46,644,000	3190	0.30	0.40	0.60	2.60	8.00	23	60	2,800
1953, Full Steps	*	3191	—	—	—	—	1,600.00	2,750	4,700	7,500
1953-D	59,878,600	3296	0.30	0.40	0.40	2.60	6.75	16	60	1,150
↳1953-D, D Over D, FS-501	*	378712	—	—	—	—	—	245	850	—
1953-D, Full Steps	*	3297	—	—	—	70.00	100.00	155	775	6,000
1953-S	19,210,900	3298	0.30	0.40	0.80	4.10	11.00	27	60	1,900
1953-S, Full Steps	*	3299	—	—	—	—	2,000.00	4,750	19,000	—
1954	47,684,050	3192	0.40	0.50	1.10	5.50	12.00	23	70	525
1954, Full Steps	*	3193	—	—	—	95.00	130.00	435	1,000	—
1954-D	117,183,060	3300	0.20	0.30	0.50	5.50	13.50	50	175	—
↳1954-D, D Over D, FS-501	*	392905	—	—	—	—	—	—	—	—
1954-D, Full Steps	*	3301	—	—	—	—	80.00	900	2,500	—
↳1954-D, D Over D, FS-501, Full Steps	*	392906	—	—	—	—	—	—	—	—
1954-S	29,384,000	3302	0.20	0.30	0.40	4.10	11.00	27	55	375
↳1954-S, Doubled Die Reverse, FS-801	*	376431	—	—	—	43.00	55.00	90	430	—
↳1954-S, S Over S, FS-502	*	392907	—	—	—	—	—	—	—	—
1954-S, Full Steps	*	3303	—	—	—	—	1,250.00	4,750	8,750	11,000
1954-S, S Over D (a)	*	3304	13.50	15.50	30.00	80.00	95.00	215	875	—
↳1954-S, S Over D, FS-501 (a)	*	392908	13.50	15.50	30.00	80.00	95.00	215	875	—
1955	7,888,000	3194	0.20	0.20	0.50	2.60	11.00	19	40	210
1955, Full Steps	*	3195	—	—	—	—	230.00	495	1,500	6,250
1955-D	74,464,100	3306	0.20	0.20	0.30	2.60	11.00	15	100	260
1955-D, Full Steps	*	3307	—	—	—	575.00	850.00	2,250	7,000	—
1955-D, D Over S	*	3308	14.00	26.00	55.00	90.00	130.00	215	775	—
↳1955-D, D Over S, FS-501	*	392816	14.00	26.00	55.00	90.00	130.00	215	775	—
1956	35,216,000	3196	0.20	0.20	0.20	1.50	4.10	11	31	390
↳1956, Tripled Die Reverse, FS-802	*	392817	—	—	—	—	—	—	—	—
1956, Full Steps	*	3197	—	—	—	—	19.00	47	155	2,250
1956-D	67,222,940	3310	0.20	0.20	0.30	1.50	5.50	12	34	245
1956-D, Full Steps	*	3311	—	—	—	—	260.00	900	1,300	3,750
1957	38,408,000	3198	0.20	0.20	0.40	1.50	6.75	22	60	525
1957, Full Steps	*	3199	—	—	—	—	47.00	90	470	3,100
1957-D	136,828,900	3312	0.20	0.20	0.20	0.80	2.60	12	47	235
1957-D, Full Steps	*	3313	—	—	—	—	45.00	100	525	2,000
1958	17,088,000	3200	0.20	0.20	0.20	2.60	9.50	50	455	—
1958, Full Steps	*	3201	—	—	—	20.00	75.00	195	3,000	—

* Included in number above. **a.** The overall strength of the strike is the important factor in this overmintmark's value.

Circulation Strikes *(continued)*

	Mintage	GSID	EF-40	AU-50	MS-60	MS-63	MS-64	MS-65	MS-66	MS-67
1958-D	168,249,120	3314	$0.20	$0.20	$0.20	$0.80	$1.50	$6.75	$38	$480
↳1958-D, D Over Inverted D, FS-501	*	392909	—	—	—	—	—	—	—	—
1958-D, Full Steps	*	3315	—	—	—	—	13.50	30.00	43	775
↳1958-D, D Over Inverted D, FS-501, Full Steps	*	392910	—	—	—	—	—	—	—	—
1959	27,248,000	3202	0.20	0.20	0.20	0.80	5.50	24.00	110	230
1959, Full Steps	*	3203	—	—	—	16.00	24.00	38.00	170	1,900
1959-D	160,738,240	3316	0.20	0.20	0.20	0.80	6.75	16.00	49	950
1959-D, Full Steps	*	3317	—	—	—	—	60.00	100.00	1,250	2,500
1960	55,416,000	3204	0.20	0.20	0.20	0.80	5.50	13.50	47	215
1960, Full Steps	*	3205	—	—	—	415.00	775.00	1,250.00	6,000	—
1960-D	192,582,180	3318	0.20	0.20	0.20	0.80	5.50	16.00	47	1,250
1960-D, Full Steps	*	240960	—	—	—	—	—	—	—	—
1961	73,640,100	3206	0.20	0.20	0.20	0.80	1.50	8.00	40	775
1961, Full Steps	*	3207	—	—	—	—	1,600.00	3,750.00	11,000	—
1961-D	229,342,760	3320	0.20	0.20	0.20	0.80	2.60	17.50	100	4,400
1961-D, Full Steps	*	3321	—	—	—	—	6,000.00	15,000.00	—	—
1962	97,384,000	3208	0.20	0.20	0.20	0.80	2.60	9.50	40	360
1962, Full Steps	*	3209	—	—	—	—	16.00	43.00	145	3,000
1962-D	280,195,720	3322	0.20	0.20	0.20	0.80	12.00	55.00	260	—
1962-D, Full Steps	*	3323	—	—	—	130.00	525.00	3,000.00	5,000	—
1963	175,776,000	3210	0.20	0.20	0.20	0.80	4.10	8.00	27	575
↳1963, Tripled Die Reverse, FS-801	*	374091	—	—	—	—	—	—	—	—
1963, Full Steps	*	3211	—	—	—	—	38.00	80.00	325	2,700
↳1963, Tripled Die Reverse, FS-801, Full Steps	*	374092	—	—	—	—	—	—	—	—
1963-D	276,829,460	3324	0.20	0.20	0.20	2.60	13.50	55.00	155	—
1963-D, Full Steps	*	3325	—	—	—	1,250.00	3,750.00	7,000.00	10,500	—
1964	1,024,672,000	3212	0.20	0.20	0.20	2.20	2.60	5.50	34	455
1964, Full Steps	*	3213	—	—	—	—	55.00	195.00	900	2,500
1964-D	1,787,297,160	3326	0.20	0.20	0.20	0.80	1.50	5.50	34	725
↳1964-D, D Over D, FS-501	*	375267	—	—	—	—	—	—	—	—
1964-D, Full Steps	*	3327	—	—	—	—	230.00	650.00	1,250	2,500
1965	136,131,380	3328	0.20	0.20	0.50	2.60	5.50	13.50	55	1,250
1965, Full Steps	*	3329	—	—	—	—	—	12,000.00	19,000	—
1966	156,208,283	3330	0.20	0.20	1.50	5.50	13.50	27.00	100	1,000
1966, Full Steps	*	3331	—	—	—	—	1,700.00	7,500.00	12,000	—
1967	107,325,800	3332	0.20	0.20	0.50	0.80	1.90	12.00	55	3,750
1967, Full Steps	*	240961	—	—	—	—	—	—	—	—
1968-D	91,227,880	3355	0.20	0.20	0.80	2.40	4.10	11.00	55	725
1968-D, Full Steps	*	3356	—	—	—	—	3,750.00	18,000.00	—	—
1968-S	100,396,004	3357	0.20	0.20	0.80	2.20	2.60	6.75	23	290
1968-S, Full Steps	*	3358	—	—	—	—	390.00	650.00	3,750	—
1969-D	202,807,500	3359	0.20	0.20	0.80	2.60	6.75	15.00	60	145
1969-D, Full Steps	*	3360	—	—	—	—	—	30,000.00	—	—
1969-S	120,165,000	3361	0.20	0.20	0.70	0.80	2.40	5.50	115	3,750
1969-S, Full Steps	*	240962	—	—	—	—	—	—	—	—
1970-D	515,485,380	3363	0.20	0.20	0.50	0.80	2.40	16.00	60	—
1970-D, Full Steps	*	3364	—	—	—	—	—	5,500.00	10,000	—

* Included in number above.

Circulation Strikes *(continued)*

	Mintage	GSID	EF-40	AU-50	MS-60	MS-63	MS-64	MS-65	MS-66	MS-67
1970-S	238,832,004	3365	$0.20	$0.20	$0.50	$1.50	$3.70	$16.00	$60.00	—
1970-S, Full Steps	*	3366	—	—	—	—	110.00	525.00	1,750.00	$3,750
1971	106,884,000	3334	0.20	0.20	0.50	1.10	4.10	9.50	50.00	—
1971, Full Steps	*	3335	—	—	—	—	5.00	23.00	65.00	1,150
1971-D	316,144,800	3367	0.20	0.20	0.20	0.80	1.90	4.10	12.00	—
1971-D, Full Steps	*	3368	—	—	—	—	5.50	13.50	40.00	455
1972	202,036,000	3336	0.20	0.20	0.20	1.90	4.10	11.00	60.00	—
1972, Full Steps	*	3337	—	—	—	—	16.00	40.00	170.00	3,750
1972-D	351,694,600	3369	0.20	0.20	0.20	1.50	2.60	9.50	47.00	—
1972-D, Full Steps	*	3370	—	—	—	—	8.00	24.00	100.00	3,100
1973	384,396,000	3338	0.20	0.20	0.20	0.80	1.90	5.50	9.50	390
1973, Full Steps	*	3339	—	—	—	—	4.10	12.00	60.00	2,300
1973-D	261,405,000	3371	0.20	0.20	0.20	0.80	4.10	4.10	13.50	260
1973-D, Full Steps	*	3372	—	—	—	—	4.10	19.00	55.00	2,500
1974	601,752,000	3340	0.20	0.20	0.20	1.50	5.50	12.00	75.00	—
1974, Full Steps	*	3341	—	—	—	—	27.00	80.00	650.00	3,750
1974-D	277,373,000	3373	0.20	0.20	0.20	0.80	1.90	5.50	47.00	—
1974-D, Full Steps	*	3374	—	—	—	—	6.75	16.00	47.00	1,700
1975	181,772,000	3342	0.20	0.20	0.20	0.80	2.40	5.50	24.00	180
1975, Full Steps	*	3343	—	—	—	—	8.00	24.00	160.00	2,600
1975-D	401,875,300	3375	0.20	0.20	0.20	0.80	2.40	5.50	31.00	—
1975-D, Full Steps	*	3376	—	—	—	—	16.00	38.00	115.00	—
1976	367,124,000	3344	0.20	0.20	0.20	1.50	3.70	6.75	36.00	—
1976, Full Steps	*	3345	—	—	—	—	65.00	130.00	775.00	2,700
1976-D	563,964,147	3377	0.20	0.20	0.20	1.10	4.10	12.00	60.00	—
1976-D, Full Steps	*	3378	—	—	—	—	19.00	46.00	260.00	2,500
1977	585,376,000	3346	0.20	0.20	0.20	1.50	3.40	6.75	40.00	—
1977, Full Steps	*	3347	—	—	—	—	27.00	80.00	575.00	—
1977-D	297,313,422	3379	0.20	0.20	0.20	0.80	2.20	5.50	47.00	—
1977-D, Full Steps	*	3380	—	—	—	—	16.00	47.00	180.00	4,250
1978	391,308,000	3348	0.20	0.20	0.20	1.50	11.00	20.00	80.00	—
1978, Full Steps	*	3349	—	—	—	27.00	40.00	90.00	650.00	3,000
1978-D	313,092,780	3381	0.20	0.20	0.20	0.80	1.90	6.75	23.00	—
1978-D, Full Steps	*	3382	—	—	—	—	8.00	16.00	47.00	2,000
1979	463,188,000	3350	0.20	0.20	0.20	0.80	4.10	13.50	75.00	—
1979, Full Steps	*	3351	—	—	—	55.00	100.00	230.00	1,150.00	—
1979-D	325,867,672	3383	0.20	0.20	0.20	0.80	2.60	11.00	60.00	—
1979-D, Full Steps	*	3384	—	—	—	19.00	24.00	55.00	260.00	1,500
1980-P	593,004,000	3387	0.20	0.20	0.20	0.80	1.90	5.50	27.00	—
1980-P, Full Steps	*	3388	—	—	—	—	16.00	40.00	155.00	1,250
1980-D	502,323,448	3385	0.20	0.20	0.20	0.80	2.40	6.75	55.00	—
1980-D, Full Steps	*	3386	—	—	—	32.00	55.00	100.00	310.00	1,900
1981-P	657,504,000	3391	0.20	0.20	0.20	0.80	2.40	6.75	70.00	—
1981-P, Full Steps	*	3392	—	—	—	—	130.00	455.00	1,000.00	4,400
1981-D	364,801,843	3389	0.20	0.20	0.20	1.50	3.70	5.50	30.00	—
1981-D, Full Steps	*	3390	—	—	—	—	5.50	13.50	60.00	1,150
1982-P	292,355,000	3395	0.20	0.20	5.50	8.00	11.00	16.00	95.00	290
1982-P, Full Steps	*	3396	—	—	—	49.00	70.00	115.00	365.00	3,900
1982-D	373,726,544	3393	0.20	0.20	1.50	2.60	4.10	9.50	40.00	215
1982-D, Full Steps	*	3394	—	—	—	30.00	50.00	100.00	525.00	2,500

* Included in number above.

Circulation Strikes *(continued)*

	Mintage	GSID	EF-40	AU-50	MS-60	MS-63	MS-64	MS-65	MS-66	MS-67
1983-P	561,615,000	3399	$0.20	$0.20	$2.20	$3.50	$6.75	$27.00	$155.00	—
1983-P, Full Steps	*	3400	—	—	—	—	235.00	525.00	2,500.00	—
1983-D	536,726,276	3397	0.20	0.20	2.20	3.50	5.50	20.00	60.00	$455
1983-D, Full Steps	*	3398	—	—	—	90.00	130.00	310.00	1,250.00	3,250
1984-P	746,769,000	3403	0.20	0.20	0.20	0.80	1.90	4.10	6.75	—
1984-P, Full Steps	*	3404	—	—	—	19.00	24.00	40.00	100.00	850
1984-D	517,675,146	3401	0.20	0.20	0.20	0.80	2.20	5.50	47.00	455
1984-D, Full Steps	*	3402	—	—	—	13.50	19.00	27.00	130.00	3,750
1985-P	647,114,962	3407	0.20	0.20	0.20	0.80	2.20	5.50	47.00	—
1985-P, Full Steps	*	3408	—	—	—	—	8.00	20.00	110.00	3,750
1985-D	459,747,446	3405	0.20	0.20	0.20	0.80	2.20	5.50	47.00	—
1985-D, Full Steps	*	3406	—	—	—	—	8.00	16.00	155.00	2,500
1986-P	536,883,483	3411	0.20	0.20	0.20	0.80	1.90	4.10	40.00	—
1986-P, Full Steps	*	3412	—	—	—	—	11.00	27.00	80.00	5,000
1986-D	361,819,140	3409	0.20	0.20	0.20	0.80	1.90	4.10	34.00	—
1986-D, Full Steps	*	3410	—	—	—	22.00	32.00	55.00	260.00	3,100
1987-P	371,499,481	3415	0.20	0.20	0.20	0.80	1.50	2.60	13.50	—
1987-P, Full Steps	*	3416	—	—	—	—	2.60	5.50	19.00	210
1987-D	410,590,604	3413	0.20	0.20	0.20	0.80	1.90	4.10	6.75	—
1987-D, Full Steps	*	3414	—	—	—	—	6.75	16.00	40.00	2,150
1988-P	771,360,000	3419	0.20	0.20	0.20	0.80	1.90	4.10	23.00	—
1988-P, Full Steps	*	3420	—	—	—	—	8.00	20.00	75.00	1,150
1988-D	663,771,652	3417	0.20	0.20	0.20	0.80	1.90	4.10	11.00	215
1988-D, Full Steps	*	3418	—	—	—	13.50	19.00	32.00	80.00	1,300
1989-P	898,812,000	3423	0.20	0.20	0.20	0.80	1.50	2.60	6.75	90
1989-P, Full Steps	*	3424	—	—	—	—	6.75	16.00	40.00	775
1989-D	570,842,474	3421	0.20	0.20	0.20	0.80	2.20	5.50	27.00	—
1989-D, Full Steps	*	3422	—	—	—	—	6.75	16.00	80.00	—
1990-P	661,636,000	3427	0.20	0.20	0.20	0.80	2.20	5.50	9.50	—
1990-P, Full Steps	*	3428	—	—	—	16.00	22.00	38.00	80.00	675
1990-D	663,938,503	3425	0.20	0.20	0.20	0.80	1.90	8.00	34.00	—
1990-D, Full Steps	*	3426	—	—	—	—	6.75	16.00	80.00	1,500
1991-P	614,104,000	3431	0.20	0.20	0.20	0.80	1.90	7.50	30.00	—
1991-P, Full Steps	*	3432	—	—	—	—	4.10	9.50	90.00	1,500
1991-D	436,496,678	3429	0.20	0.20	0.20	0.80	1.90	4.10	20.00	—
1991-D, Full Steps	*	3430	—	—	—	—	6.75	16.00	55.00	2,500
1992-P	399,552,000	3435	0.20	0.20	0.20	0.80	1.50	2.60	6.75	—
1992-P, Full Steps	*	3436	—	—	—	—	6.75	13.50	40.00	1,150
1992-D	450,565,113	3433	0.20	0.20	0.20	0.80	1.90	4.10	6.75	—
1992-D, Full Steps	*	3434	—	—	—	—	2.60	9.50	40.00	3,550
1993-P	412,076,000	3439	0.20	0.20	0.20	0.80	1.90	4.10	11.00	—
1993-P, Full Steps	*	3440	—	—	—	—	2.60	6.75	70.00	2,750
1993-D	406,084,135	3437	0.20	0.20	0.20	0.80	1.90	4.10	6.75	80
1993-D, Full Steps	*	3438	—	—	—	—	2.60	6.75	27.00	340
1994-P	722,160,000	3443	0.20	0.20	0.20	0.80	1.90	4.10	6.75	13.50
1994-P, Full Steps	*	3444	—	—	—	—	2.60	9.50	80.00	260
1994-P	167,703	376897	4.70	5.50	9.50	11.00	13.50	15.00	19.00	24
1994-P, Matte Finish (b)	167,703	3602	4.70	5.50	9.50	11.00	13.50	15.00	19.00	24

* Included in number above. **b.** Special "frosted" Uncirculated nickels were included in Thomas Jefferson 250th Anniversary of Birth (1993) commemorative sets sold in 1994 and in Botanic Garden commemorative sets of 1997 (see separate set listings at the end of the commemorative coin listings for each respective issue). They resemble Matte Proof coins.

Circulation Strikes *(continued)*

	Mintage	GSID	EF-40	AU-50	MS-60	MS-63	MS-64	MS-65	MS-66	MS-67
1994-D	715,762,110	3441	$0.20	$0.20	$0.20	$0.80	$1.90	$4.10	$20.00	—
1994-D, Full Steps	*	3442	—	—	—	—	11.00	24.00	115.00	$1,750.00
1995-P	774,156,000	3447	0.20	0.20	0.20	0.80	1.90	4.10	13.50	—
1995-P, Full Steps	*	3448	—	—	—	—	2.60	6.75	30.00	370.00
1995-D	888,112,000	3445	0.20	0.20	0.20	0.80	1.90	4.10	16.00	—
1995-D, Full Steps	*	3446	—	—	—	—	2.60	6.75	34.00	1,250.00
1996-P	829,332,000	3451	0.20	0.20	0.20	0.80	1.90	4.10	6.75	34.00
1996-P, Full Steps	*	3452	—	—	—	2.60	8.00	16.00	40.00	145.00
1996-D	817,736,000	3449	0.20	0.20	0.20	0.80	1.90	4.10	8.00	—
1996-D, Full Steps	*	3450	—	—	—	8.00	13.50	19.00	30.00	210.00
1997-P	470,972,000	3455	0.20	0.20	0.20	0.80	1.90	4.10	6.75	90.00
1997-P, Full Steps	*	3456	—	—	—	—	4.10	9.50	75.00	525.00
1997-P, Matte Finish (b)	*	377517	—	—	—	—	—	—	—	—
1997-P, Matte Finish (b)	25,000	3606	15.00	16.00	27.00	32.00	35.00	40.00	47.00	90.00
1997-D	466,640,000	3453	0.20	0.20	0.20	0.80	1.90	4.10	12.00	—
1997-D, Full Steps	*	3454	—	—	—	—	13.50	30.00	60.00	2,750.00
1998-P	688,272,000	3459	0.20	0.20	0.20	0.80	1.90	4.10	9.50	210.00
1998-P, Full Steps	*	3460	—	—	—	—	5.50	13.50	70.00	455.00
1998-D	635,360,000	3457	0.20	0.20	0.20	0.80	2.20	5.50	100.00	—
↳**1998-D**	*	346882	—	—	—	—	—	—	—	—
1998-D, Full Steps	*	3458	—	—	—	—	24.00	55.00	470.00	—
1999-P	1,212,000,000	3463	0.20	0.20	0.20	0.80	1.90	4.10	6.75	34.00
1999-P, Full Steps	*	3464	—	—	—	—	2.60	11.00	47.00	650.00
1999-D	1,066,720,000	3461	0.20	0.20	0.20	0.80	1.90	6.75	9.50	195.00
1999-D, Full Steps	*	3462	—	—	—	—	4.10	11.00	60.00	390.00
2000-P	846,240,000	3467	0.20	0.20	0.20	0.80	1.90	4.10	8.00	55.00
2000-P, Full Steps	*	3468	—	—	—	—	2.60	6.75	47.00	725.00
2000-D	1,509,520,000	3465	0.20	0.20	0.20	0.80	1.90	4.10	6.75	—
2000-D, Full Steps	*	3466	—	—	—	—	2.60	6.75	34.00	325.00
2001-P	675,704,000	3471	0.20	0.20	0.20	0.80	1.90	4.10	6.75	20.00
2001-P, Full Steps	*	3472	—	—	—	—	5.50	11.00	24.00	80.00
2001-D	627,680,000	3469	0.20	0.20	0.20	0.80	1.90	4.10	6.75	13.50
2001-D, Full Steps	*	3470	—	—	—	—	2.60	6.75	20.00	325.00
2002-P	539,280,000	3475	0.20	0.20	0.20	0.80	1.90	4.10	6.75	—
2002-P, Full Steps	*	3476	—	—	—	—	11.00	16.00	47.00	160.00
2002-D	691,200,000	3473	0.20	0.20	0.20	0.80	1.90	4.10	20.00	—
2002-D, Full Steps	*	3474	—	—	—	—	2.60	6.75	60.00	3,100.00
2003-P	441,840,000	3480	0.20	0.20	0.20	0.80	1.90	4.10	6.75	20.00
2003-P, Full Steps	*	3479	—	—	—	—	2.60	6.75	15.00	60.00
2003-D	383,040,000	3478	0.20	0.20	0.20	0.80	1.90	4.10	6.75	—
2003-D, Full Steps	*	3477	—	—	—	—	4.10	12.00	70.00	1,900.00

* Included in number above. **b.** Special "frosted" Uncirculated nickels were included in Thomas Jefferson 250th Anniversary of Birth (1993) commemorative sets sold in 1994 and in Botanic Garden commemorative sets of 1997 (see separate set listings at the end of the commemorative coin listings for each respective issue). They resemble Matte Proof coins.

Special Mint Set Strikes

	Mintage	GSID	MS-63	MS-65	MS-66
1964	unknown	82044	$7,500.00	$8,750.00	$10,000
1965	2,360,000	3553	6.75	9.50	11
1966	2,261,583	3556	6.75	9.50	11
1967	1,863,344	3559	6.75	9.50	11

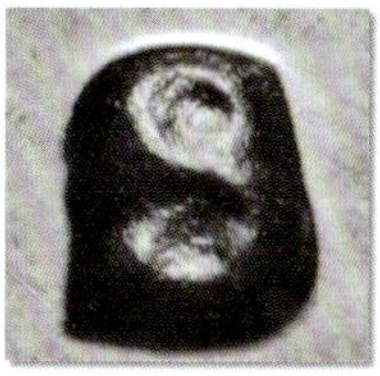

1979-S, Filled S (Variety 1), Proof

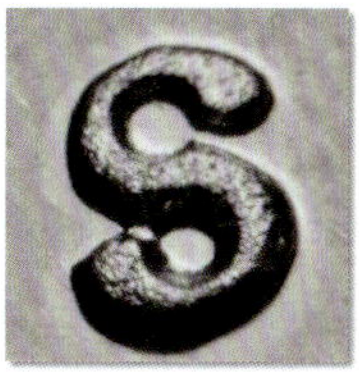

1979-S, Clear S (Variety 2), Proof

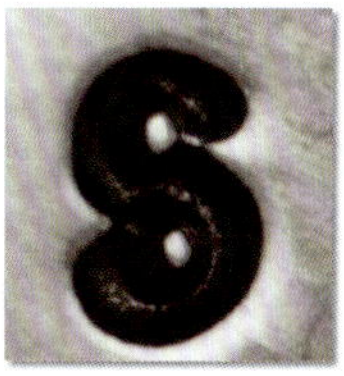

1981-S, Rounded S (Variety 1), Proof

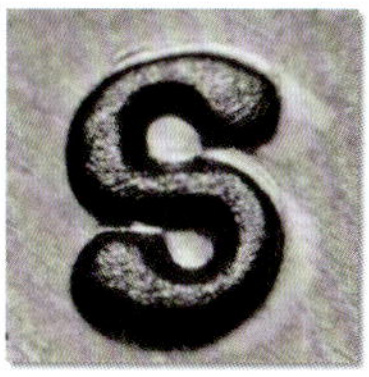

1981-S, Flat S (Variety 2), Proof

Proof Strikes

	Mintage	GSID	PF-65	PF-67	PF-69
Jefferson, Memorial Reverse (1938–1942, 1946–2003), Proof	**n/a**	**394035**	**$1.50**	**$4.10**	**$8**
Same, Wartime Silver Alloy (1942), Proof	n/a	394036	75.00	260.00	—
1939	12,535	3494	100.00	360.00	—
1940	14,158	3497	85.00	340.00	14,500
↳**1940, Reverse of 1938, FS-901**	*	297867	310.00	1,250.00	—
1941	18,720	3500	60.00	195.00	—
1942	29,600	3503	70.00	155.00	—
1942-P	27,600	3565	75.00	260.00	—
1950	51,386	3506	55.00	80.00	1,250
1951	57,500	3509	47.00	65.00	455
1952	81,980	3512	38.00	75.00	285
1953	128,800	3515	34.00	70.00	210
1954	233,300	3518	19.00	30.00	130
1955	378,200	3521	13.50	30.00	120
1956	669,384	3524	2.60	20.00	130
1957	1,247,952	3527	6.75	20.00	155
1958	875,652	3530	2.60	24.00	100
1959	1,149,291	3533	1.50	24.00	100
1960	1,691,602	3536	1.50	11.00	130
1961	3,028,144	3539	1.50	13.50	75
1962	3,218,019	3542	1.50	11.00	55
1963	3,075,645	3545	1.50	11.00	30
1964	3,950,762	3550	1.50	11.00	27
↳**1964, TDR, FS-801**	*	375133	—	—	—
1968-S	3,041,506	3570	1.50	8.00	130
↳**1968-S, S Over S, FS-501**	*	392928	—	—	—
1969-S	2,934,631	3573	1.50	8.00	310
1970-S	2,632,810	3576	1.50	4.10	260
1971-S	3,220,733	3577	1.50	4.10	80
↳**1971, No S** (a)	*	3564	1,100.00	1,400.00	4,200
↳**1971, No S, FS-501** (a)		392937	1,100.00	1,400.00	4,200
1972-S	3,220,733	3578	1.50	4.10	8
1973-S	2,760,339	3579	$1.50	$4.10	$8
1974-S	2,612,568	3580	1.50	4.10	8
1975-S	2,845,450	3581	1.50	4.10	8
1976-S	4,149,730	3582	1.50	4.10	8
1977-S	3,251,152	3583	1.50	4.10	8
1978-S	3,127,781	3584	1.50	4.10	8
1979-S, Variety 1	3,677,175	3585	1.50	4.10	8
1979-S, Variety 2	*	3586	1.50	6.75	16
↳**1979-S, Variety 2, FS-501**	3,677,175	392938	1.50	6.75	16
1980-S	3,554,806	3587	1.50	4.10	8
1981-S, Variety 1	4,063,083	3588	1.50	4.10	8
1981-S, Variety 2	*	3589	1.50	4.10	8
↳**1981-S, Variety 2, FS-501**	4,063,083	392941	1.50	4.10	8
1982-S	3,857,479	3590	1.50	4.10	8
1983-S	3,279,126	3591	1.50	4.10	8
1984-S	3,065,110	3592	1.50	4.10	8
1985-S	3,362,821	3593	1.50	4.10	8
1986-S	3,010,497	3594	1.50	4.10	8
1987-S	4,227,728	3595	1.50	4.10	8
1988-S	3,262,948	3596	1.50	4.10	8
1989-S	3,220,194	3597	1.50	4.10	8
1990-S	3,299,559	3598	1.50	4.10	8
↳**1990-S, DDO, FS-101**	*	375895	210.00	260.00	390
1991-S	2,867,787	3599	1.50	4.10	8
1992-S	4,176,560	3600	1.50	4.10	8
1993-S	3,394,792	3601	1.50	4.10	8
1994-S	3,269,923	3603	1.50	4.10	8
1995-S	2,797,481	3604	1.50	4.10	8
1996-S	2,525,265	3605	1.50	4.10	8
1997-S	2,796,678	3607	1.50	4.10	8
1998-S	2,086,507	3608	1.50	4.10	8
1999-S	3,347,966	3609	1.50	4.10	8
2000-S	4,047,993	3611	1.50	4.10	8
2001-S	3,184,606	3612	1.50	4.10	8
2002-S	3,211,995	3613	1.50	4.10	8
2003-S	3,298,439	3614	1.50	4.10	8

* Included in number above. **a.** 1971-S, Proof, nickels without the S mintmark were made in error after an assistant engraver forgot to punch a mintmark into a die. The U.S. Mint estimates that 1,655 such error coins were struck.

WESTWARD JOURNEY (2004–2005)

Designers: *See image captions for designers.* **Weight:** *5 grams.* **Composition:** *.750 copper, .250 nickel.* **Diameter:** *21.2 mm.* **Edge:** *Plain.* **Mints:** *Philadelphia, Denver, and San Francisco.*

Designers:

2004, Obverse: .... Felix Schlag
2004, Peace Medal Obverse: . Norman E. Nemeth
2004, Keelboat Reverse:............ Al Maletsky
2005, Obverse: .... Joe Fitzgerald
2005, Amerian Bison Reverse:...... Jamie Franki
2005, Ocean in View Reverse:..... Joe Fitzgerald
(based on a photograph by Andrew Cier)

Circulation Strikes

Obverse (2004)

Peace Medal Reverse (2004)

Keelboat Reverse (2004)

Obverse (2005)

American Bison Reverse (2005)

Ocean in View Reverse (2005)

Proof Strikes

Obverse

Peace Medal Reverse

Keelboat Reverse

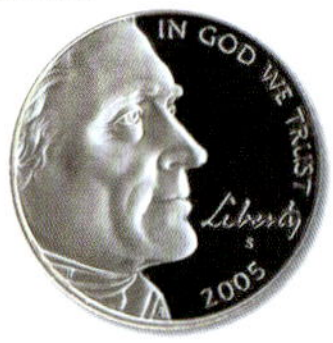
Obverse (2005)

American Bison Reverse

Ocean in View Reverse

Mintmark location, 2005, is on the obverse, near the date (2004 location is the same as previous years).

History. In 2004 special designs commemorating the Westward Journey (Lewis and Clark expedition) were introduced. They utilized the previous obverse design paired with two different reverse designs, one representing the Peace Medals given out by Lewis and Clark, the other showing the keelboat that provided much of their transportation. Two new reverse designs were introduced for 2005, showing the American Bison and a representation of Clark's journal entry upon spotting what he thought was the Pacific Ocean (in actuality, they were still approximately 20 miles from the coast). They were paired with a new obverse, a tightly cropped profile of Jefferson facing right.

Striking and Sharpness. On the obverse, check for weakness on the portrait. Proofs were struck for each design. All have mirror fields. Most have frosted or cameo contrast on the higher features.

Availability. All basic dates and mintmarks were saved in roll quantities.

Grading Standards

MS-60 to 70 (Mint State). ***Obverse and Reverse:*** Mint luster is complete in the obverse and reverse fields. Check the higher parts of the obverse and reverse for abrasion and contact marks.

MS-66

PF-60 to 70 (Proof). ***Obverse and Reverse:*** Evaluation of differences between higher-grade Jefferson Proofs is highly subjective; one certified at PF-65 might be similar to another at PF-67, and vice-versa. All Proof Westward Journey nickels have mirror fields. Striking is typically with full details, although there are scattered exceptions. Nearly all Westward Journey nickel Proofs are as issued, in PF-69 or 70.

PF-70
Ultra Cameo

Circulation Strikes

	Mintage	GSID	EF-40	AU-50	MS-60	MS-63	MS-64	MS-65	MS-66	MS-67
Jefferson, Westward Journey (2004–2005)	**n/a**	**394033**	**$0.20**	**$0.20**	**$0.20**	**$0.40**	**$1.10**	**$1.50**	**$2.60**	**$16**
Same, Satin Finish (2005)	**n/a**	**394034**	**0.30**	**0.40**	**0.80**	**1.90**	**4.10**	**5.50**	**6.75**	**8**
2004-P, Peace Medal	361,440,000	3486	0.20	0.20	0.20	0.80	1.90	5.50	16.00	210
↳2004-P, Peace Medal, Doubled Die Obverse, FS-101	*	392911	—	8.00	13.50	22.00	50.00	80.00	195.00	—
2004-D, Peace Medal	372,000,000	3483	0.20	0.20	0.20	0.40	1.10	1.50	2.60	16
2004-P, Keelboat	366,720,000	3485	0.20	0.20	0.20	0.40	1.10	2.60	8.00	27
2004-D, Keelboat	344,880,000	3482	0.20	0.20	0.20	0.40	1.10	1.50	2.60	20
2005-P, American Bison	448,320,000	24949	0.20	0.20	0.20	0.40	1.10	6.75	40.00	1,250
2005-P, American Bison, Satin	1,160,000	24950	0.30	0.40	0.80	1.90	4.10	5.50	6.75	8
↳2005-P, American Bison, Satin, Doubled Die Obverse, FS-101	*	392912	—	8.00	13.50	22.00	50.00	80.00	195.00	—
2005-D, American Bison	487,680,000	24951	0.20	0.20	0.20	0.80	1.90	6.75	47.00	—
2005-D, American Bison, Speared Bison	*	24953	40.00	70.00	120.00	210.00	340.00	525.00	900.00	—
2005-D, American Bison, Satin	1,160,000	24952	0.30	0.40	0.80	1.90	4.10	6.75	11.00	27
2005-P, Ocean in View	394,080,000	24954	0.20	0.20	0.20	0.80	1.90	6.75	55.00	1,250
2005-P, Ocean in View, Satin	1,160,000	24955	0.30	0.40	0.80	1.90	4.10	5.50	6.75	8
2005-D, Ocean in View	411,120,000	24956	0.20	0.20	0.50	2.20	4.40	6.75	40.00	1,150
2005-D, Ocean in View, Satin	1,160,000	24957	0.30	0.40	0.80	1.90	4.10	5.50	6.75	8

* Included in number above.

Proof Strikes

	Mintage	GSID	PF-65	PF-67	PF-69
Jefferson, Westward Journey (2004–2005), Proof	**n/a**	**394037**	**$1.50**	**$4.10**	**$6.75**
2004-S, Peace Medal	2,992,069	3616	1.50	4.10	6.75
2004-S, Keelboat	2,965,422	3615	1.50	4.10	6.75
2005-S, American Bison	3,344,679	15323	1.50	4.10	6.75
2005-S, Ocean in View	3,344,679	15324	1.50	4.10	6.75

JEFFERSON, MODIFIED PORTRAIT (2006 TO DATE)

Designers: *Jamie Franki (obverse) and Felix Schlag (reverse).* **Weight:** *5 grams.* **Composition:** *.750 copper, .250 nickel.* **Diameter:** *21.2 mm.* **Edge:** *Plain.* **Mints:** *Philadelphia, Denver, San Francisco, and West Point.*

Circulation Strike

Mintmark location, 2006 to date, is on the obverse, below the date.

Proof Strike

History. 2006 saw the return of Felix Schlag's reverse design showing a front view of Jefferson's home, Monticello. It also featured the debut of another new Jefferson portrait on the obverse, this time in three-quarters profile.

Striking and Sharpness. On the obverse, check for weakness on the portrait. Jefferson nickels can be classified as "Full Steps" (FS) if either five or six of Monticello's porch steps (with the top step counting as one) are clear. Notations of 5FS or 6FS can indicate the number of visible steps. It is easier to count the incuse lines than the raised steps. If there are four complete, unbroken lines, the coin qualifies as Full Steps (with five steps); five complete, unbroken lines indicate six full steps. There must be no nicks, cuts, or scratches interrupting the incuse lines. Even if the steps are mostly or fully defined, check other areas to determine if a coin has Full Details overall. Proofs were struck; all have mirror fields. Striking is usually with Full Details, although there are scattered exceptions. Most survivors are in high grade, PF-64 and upward. Most have frosted or cameo contrast on the higher features.

Availability. All basic dates and mintmarks were saved in roll quantities.

Grading Standards

MS-60 to 70 (Mint State). ***Obverse and Reverse:*** Mint luster is complete in the obverse and reverse fields. Check the higher parts of the obverse and reverse for abrasion and contact marks.

MS-65
Full Steps

PF-60 to 70 (Proof). ***Obverse and Reverse:*** Evaluation of differences between higher-grade Jefferson Proofs is highly subjective; one certified at PF-65 might be similar to another at PF-67, and vice-versa. All Proof Jefferson Modified nickels have mirror fields. Striking is typically with full details, although there are scattered exceptions. Nearly all Jefferson Modified nickel Proofs are as issued, in PF-69 or 70.

PF-70
Deep Cameo

Circulation Strikes

	Mintage	GSID	EF-40	AU-50	MS-60	MS-63	MS-64	MS-65	MS-66	MS-67
Jefferson, Modified Portrait (2006 to Date)	n/a	376183	$0.20	$0.20	$0.20	$0.20	$0.20	$0.80	$2.60	$11.00
Same, Satin Finish (2006–2010)	n/a	376861	—	2.60	3.40	3.70	4.10	5.50	8.00	9.50
2006-P	693,120,000	65320	0.20	0.20	0.20	0.20	0.20	0.80	2.60	11.00
2006-P, Full Steps	*	76229	—	—	—	0.20	0.20	1.50	70.00	875.00
2006-P, Satin	847,361	76230	—	2.60	3.40	3.70	4.10	5.50	8.00	9.50
2006-D	809,280,000	65321	0.20	0.20	0.20	0.40	1.10	2.60	2.60	47.00
2006-D, Full Steps	*	76231	—	—	—	—	1.50	4.10	12.00	155.00
2006-D, Satin	847,361	70500	—	2.60	3.40	3.70	4.10	5.50	8.00	9.50
2007-P	571,680,000	76207	0.20	0.20	0.20	0.40	1.10	2.60	4.10	11.00
2007-P, Full Steps	*	68970	—	—	—	—	1.50	4.10	27.00	—
2007-P, Satin	895,628	68971	—	2.60	3.40	3.70	4.10	5.50	8.00	9.50
2007-D	626,160,000	76208	0.20	0.20	0.20	0.40	1.10	2.60	4.10	11.00
2007-D, Full Steps	*	68972	—	—	—	—	5.50	19.00	130.00	455.00
2007-D, Satin	895,628	68973	—	2.60	3.40	3.70	4.10	5.50	8.00	9.50
2008-P	279,840,000	76209	0.20	0.20	0.20	0.40	1.10	2.60	2.60	11.00
2008-P, Full Steps	*	69703	—	—	—	—	1.50	4.10	40.00	900.00
2008-P, Satin	745,464	69348	—	2.60	3.40	3.70	4.10	5.50	8.00	9.50
2008-D	345,600,000	76210	0.20	0.20	0.20	0.40	1.10	2.60	4.10	11.00
2008-D, Full Steps	*	69704	—	—	—	—	1.50	4.10	245.00	—
2008-D, Satin	745,464	69349	—	2.60	3.40	3.70	4.10	5.50	8.00	9.50
2009-P	39,840,000	76211	0.20	0.20	0.20	0.40	1.10	2.60	4.10	11.00
2009-P, Full Steps	*	71424	—	—	—	—	1.50	4.10	70.00	—
2009-P, Satin	784,614	76232	—	2.60	3.40	3.70	4.10	5.50	8.00	9.50
2009-D	46,800,000	76212	0.20	0.20	0.20	0.40	1.10	2.60	4.10	11.00
2009-D, Full Steps	*	71204	—	—	—	—	1.50	4.10	38.00	—
2009-D, Satin	784,614	76233	—	2.60	3.40	3.70	4.10	5.50	8.00	9.50
2010-P	260,640,000	76213	0.20	0.20	0.20	0.40	1.10	2.60	4.10	11.00
2010-P, Full Steps	*	71205	—	—	—	—	1.50	2.60	6.75	60.00
2010-P, Satin	583,897	76234	—	2.60	3.40	3.70	4.10	5.50	8.00	9.50
2010-D	229,920,000	76214	0.20	0.20	0.20	0.20	0.20	0.80	2.60	11.00
2010-D, Full Steps	*	71208	—	—	—	0.20	0.20	0.80	6.75	60.00
2010-D, Satin	583,897	76235	—	2.60	3.40	3.70	4.10	5.50	8.00	9.50
2011-P	450,000,000	76215	0.20	0.20	0.20	0.20	0.20	0.80	2.60	11.00
2011-P, Full Steps	*	71209	—	—	—	0.20	0.20	0.80	2.60	11.00
2011-D	540,240,000	76216	0.20	0.20	0.20	0.20	0.20	0.80	2.60	11.00
2011-D, Full Steps	*	71210	—	—	—	0.20	0.20	0.80	2.60	11.00
2012-P	464,640,000	76217	0.20	0.20	0.20	0.20	0.20	0.80	2.60	11.00
2012-P, Full Steps	*	71211	—	—	—	0.20	0.20	0.80	2.60	11.00
2012-D	558,960,000	76218	0.20	0.20	0.20	0.20	0.20	0.80	2.60	11.00
2012-D, Full Steps	*	71212	—	—	—	0.20	0.20	0.80	2.60	11.00
2013-P	607,440,000	76219	0.20	0.20	0.20	0.20	0.20	0.80	2.60	11.00
2013-P, Full Steps	*	76236	—	—	—	0.20	0.20	0.80	2.60	11.00
2013-D	615,600,000	76220	0.20	0.20	0.20	0.20	0.20	0.80	2.60	11.00
2013-D, Full Steps	*	76237	—	—	—	0.20	0.20	0.80	2.60	11.00
2014-P	635,520,000	76221	0.20	0.20	0.20	0.20	0.20	0.80	2.60	11.00
2014-P, Full Steps	*	76238	—	—	—	0.20	0.20	0.80	2.60	11.00
2014-D	570,720,000	76222	0.20	0.20	0.20	0.20	0.20	0.80	2.60	11.00
2014-D, Full Steps	*	76239	—	—	—	0.20	0.20	0.80	2.60	11.00

* Included in number above.

Circulation Strikes

	Mintage	GSID	EF-40	AU-50	MS-60	MS-63	MS-64	MS-65	MS-66	MS-67
2015-P	752,880,000	76223	$0.20	$0.20	$0.20	$0.20	$0.20	$0.80	$2.60	$11.00
2015-P, Full Steps	*	76240	—	—	—	0.20	0.20	0.80	2.60	11.00
2015-D	846,720,000	76224	0.20	0.20	0.20	0.20	0.20	0.80	2.60	11.00
2015-D, Full Steps	*	76241	—	—	—	0.20	0.20	0.80	2.60	11.00
2016-P	786,960,000	76225	0.20	0.20	0.20	0.20	0.20	0.80	2.60	11.00
2016-P, Full Steps	*	76242	—	—	—	0.20	0.20	0.80	2.60	11.00
2016-D	759,600,000	76226	0.20	0.20	0.20	0.20	0.20	0.80	2.60	11.00
2016-D, Full Steps	*	76243	—	—	—	0.20	0.20	0.80	2.60	11.00
2017-P	710,160,000	76227	0.20	0.20	0.20	0.20	0.20	0.80	2.60	11.00
2017-P, Full Steps	*	76244	—	—	—	0.20	0.20	0.80	2.60	11.00
2017-D	663,120,000	76228	0.20	0.20	0.20	0.20	0.20	0.80	2.60	11.00
2017-D , Full Steps	*	76245	—	—	—	0.20	0.20	0.80	2.60	11.00
2017-S, Enh Unc (a)	210,419	393454	2.50	2.60	3.40	3.70	4.10	5.50	6.75	8.00
2017-S, Enh Unc (a)	210,419	82046	2.50	2.60	3.40	3.70	4.10	5.50	6.75	8.00
2018-P	629,520,000	79344	0.20	0.20	0.20	0.20	0.20	0.80	2.60	11.00
2018-P, Full Steps	*	79342	—	—	—	0.20	0.20	2.60	20.00	100.00
2018-D	626,880,000	79345	0.20	0.20	0.20	0.20	0.20	0.80	2.60	11.00
2018-D, Full Steps	*	79343	—	—	—	0.20	0.20	0.80	2.60	11.00
2019-P	567,854,400	81807	0.20	0.20	0.20	0.20	0.20	0.80	2.60	11.00
2019-P, Full Steps	*	81804	—	—	—	0.20	0.20	0.80	2.60	11.00
2019-D	527,040,000	81808	0.20	0.20	0.20	0.20	0.20	0.80	2.60	11.00
2019-D, Full Steps	*	79408	—	—	—	0.20	0.20	0.80	2.60	11.00
2020-P	772,780,000	84300	0.20	0.20	0.20	0.20	0.20	0.80	2.60	11.00
2020-P, Full Steps	*	81805	—	—	—	0.20	0.20	0.80	2.60	11.00
2020-D	798,000,000	84301	0.20	0.20	0.20	0.20	0.20	0.80	2.60	11.00
2020-D, Full Steps	*	81806	—	—	—	0.20	0.20	0.80	2.60	11.00
2021-P	772,780,000	85141	0.20	0.20	0.20	0.20	0.20	0.80	2.60	11.00
2021-P, Full Steps	*	85139	—	—	—	0.20	0.20	0.80	2.60	11.00
2021-D	798,000,000	85142	0.20	0.20	0.20	0.20	0.20	0.80	2.60	11.00
2021-D, Full Steps	*	85140	—	—	—	0.20	0.20	0.80	2.60	11.00
2022-P	769,920,000	193420	0.20	0.20	0.20	0.20	0.20	0.80	2.60	11.00
2022-P, Full Steps	*	193423	—	—	—	0.20	0.20	0.80	2.60	11.00
2022-D	777,600,000	193421	0.20	0.20	0.20	0.20	0.20	0.80	2.60	11.00
2022-D, Full Steps	*	193424	—	—	—	0.20	0.20	0.80	2.60	11.00
2023-P	692,600,000	199015	0.20	0.20	0.20	0.20	0.20	0.80	2.60	11.00
2023-P, Full Steps	*	199017	—	—	—	0.20	0.20	0.80	2.60	11.00
2023-D	734,800,000	199016	0.20	0.20	0.20	0.20	0.20	0.80	2.60	11.00
2023-D, Full Steps	*	199018	—	—	—	0.20	0.20	0.80	2.60	11.00
2024-P		347683	0.20	0.20	0.20	0.20	0.20	0.80	2.60	11.00
2024-P, Full Steps	*	347684	—	—	—	0.20	0.20	0.80	2.60	11.00
2024-D		347685	0.20	0.20	0.20	0.20	0.20	0.80	2.60	11.00
2024-D, Full Steps	*	347686	—	—	—	0.20	0.20	0.80	2.60	11.00
2025-P		376271	0.20	0.20	0.20	0.20	0.20	0.80	2.60	11.00
2025-P, Full Steps	*	376272	—	—	—	0.20	0.20	0.80	2.60	11.00
2025-D		376273	0.20	0.20	0.20	0.20	0.20	0.80	2.60	11.00
2025-D, Full Steps	*	376274	—	—	—	0.20	0.20	0.80	2.60	11.00

* Included in number above. **a.** Included in the special set of Enhanced Uncirculated coins issued in 2017 for the 225th anniversary of the San Francisco Mint.

Proof Strikes

	Mintage	GSID	PF-65	PF-67	PF-69
Jefferson, Modified Portrait (2006 to Date), Proof	**n/a**	**376184**	**$1.50**	**$4.10**	**$6.75**
2006-S	3,054,436	65351	1.50	4.10	6.75
2007-S	2,577,166	68773	1.50	4.10	6.75
2008-S	2,169,561	69239	1.50	4.10	6.75
2009-S	2,179,867	71569	1.50	4.10	6.75
2010-S	1,689,216	71213	1.50	4.10	6.75
2011-S	1,673,010	71558	1.50	4.10	6.75
2012-S	1,239,148	71661	1.50	4.10	6.75
2013-S	1,274,505	76571	1.50	4.10	6.75
2014-S	1,190,369	76572	1.50	4.10	6.75
2015-S	1,099,182	76573	1.50	4.10	6.75
2016-S	1,011,624	76574	1.50	4.10	6.75
2017-S	979,475	76575	1.50	4.10	6.75
2018-S	901,072	79346	1.50	4.10	6.75
2018-S, Reverse Proof (a)	844,220	213808	6.75	9.50	16.00
2019-S	1,061,558	79347	1.50	4.10	6.75
2020-S	824,332	81803	1.50	4.10	6.75
2020-W (b)	465,080	84806	1.50	4.10	6.75
2020-W, Reverse Proof (c)	313,184	84807	9.50	12.00	16.00
2021-S	792,612	85143	1.50	4.10	6.75
2022-S	646,177	193422	1.50	4.10	6.75
2023-S		213809	1.50	4.10	6.75
2024-S		347687	1.50	4.10	6.75
2025-S		376275	1.50	4.10	6.75

a. Included in the special silver Reverse Proof set issued in 2018 in honor of the 50th anniversary of the San Francisco Mint's first production of Proof coins. **b.** Included as a premium in the 2020 U.S. Mint Proof Set. **c.** Included as a premium in the 2020 U.S. Mint Silver Proof Set.

Half Dismes
1792

AN OVERVIEW OF HALF DISMES

Half dimes or five-cent silver coins were provided for in the Mint Act of April 2, 1792. The spelling was stated as *half disme*. The latter word (likely pronounced "dime," as in modern usage, but perhaps in some places as "deem," in the French mode) was used intermittently in government correspondence for years afterward, but on coins dated 1794 and beyond it appeared only as *dime*.

President George Washington, in his fourth annual message to the House of Representatives, November 6, 1792, referred to the half disme:

> In execution of the authority given by the Legislature, measures have been taken for engaging some artists from abroad to aid in the establishment of our Mint; others have been employed at home. Provision has been made of the requisite buildings, and these are now putting into proper condition for the purposes of the establishment.
>
> There has also been a small beginning in the coinage of half-dismes; the want of small coins in circulation calling the first attention to them. The regulation of foreign coins, in correspondence with the principles of our national Coinage, as being essential to their due operation, and to order in our money-concerns, will, I doubt not, be resumed and completed.

The 1792 half dismes used to be considered patterns by some numismatists. However, the coins circulated as currency.

The 1792 half dismes are studied in *United States Pattern Coins* (the hobby's standard reference on pattern coins and experimental and trial pieces), and some numismatists have traditionally referred to them as patterns. It is true that they were struck at a private shop in Philadelphia while the official Mint buildings were still in planning. However, several factors point to their status as regular circulating coins. The half disme was authorized as a federal issue by congressional legislation. Its mintage was considerable—some 1,500 or so pieces—and, as noted by President Washington, the coins were meant to alleviate the national need for small change. Furthermore, nearly all surviving examples show signs of extensive wear.

The 1792 half dismes are not commonly collected, simply because they are not common coins; only 200 to 250 are estimated to still exist. However, their rarity, the romance of their connection to the nation's founding, and the mysteries and legends surrounding their creation make them a perennial favorite among numismatists.

HALF DISME (1792)

Designer: *Unknown (possibly Robert Birch).* **Weight:** *1.35 grams.*
Composition: *.8924 silver, .1076 copper.* **Diameter:** *16.5 mm.* **Edge:** *Reeded.*
Mint: *John Harper's shop, Philadelphia, and possibly at the Philadelphia Mint.*

History. Rumors and legends are par for the course with the 1792 half disme. Martha Washington was sometimes said to have posed for the portrait of Liberty, despite the profile's dissimilarity to life images of the First Lady. Longstanding numismatic tradition said that President George Washington had his own silver tableware taken to the mint factory to be melted down, with these little coins being the result. That legend has been proven fanciful, most authoritatively by researchers Pete Smith, Joel J. Orosz, and Leonard Augsburger in *1792: Birth of a Nation's Coinage*. While the Philadelphia Mint was in the planning stage (its cornerstone would be laid on July 31, 1792), dies were being cut for the first federal coinage of that year. The designer may have been Robert Birch, a Mint engraver who created (or helped create) the dies for the half disme, the disme, and other coins. The half dismes were struck in a private facility owned by saw-maker John Harper, in mid-July and in October. It is believed, from Thomas Jefferson's records, that 1,500 were made. Most were placed into circulation. The coin's designs, with a unique head of Liberty and an outstretched eagle, would not be revived when normal production of the half dime denomination started at the Mint's official facilities in 1795.

Striking and Sharpness. These coins usually are fairly strongly struck, but with some lightness on Liberty's hair above her ear, and on the eagle's breast. Most were struck off center to some degree. Some have what appear to be adjustment marks (which come from a planchet being manually filed to adjust its weight prior to striking); these striations might actually be roller marks from the planchet-production process.

Availability. Most of the estimated 200 to 250 surviving coins show extensive wear. Some AU and MS coins exist, several in choice and gem state, perhaps from among the eight or nine examples that Mint Director David Rittenhouse is said to have reserved for himself.

Grading Standards

MS-60 to 70 (Mint State). ***Obverse:*** No wear is visible. Luster ranges from nearly full at MS-60 to frosty at MS-65 or higher. Toning often masks the surface, so careful inspection is required. ***Reverse:*** No wear is visible. The field around the eagle is lustrous, ranging from not completely full at MS-60 to deep and frosty at MS-65 and higher.

MS-64

AU-50, 53, 55, 58 (About Uncirculated). ***Obverse:*** Light wear is seen on the cheek and on the hair (not as easily observable, as certain areas of the hair may be lightly struck). Luster ranges from light and mostly in protected areas at AU-50, to extensive at AU-58. Friction is evident in the field, less so in the higher ranges. ***Reverse:*** Light wear is seen on the eagle, but is less noticeable on the letters. Luster ranges from light and mostly in protected areas at AU-50, to extensive at AU-58. Friction is evident in the field, less in the higher ranges.

AU-55

EF-40, 45 (Extremely Fine). ***Obverse:*** The hair shows medium wear to the right of the face and on the bust end. The fields have no luster. Some luster may be seen among the hair strands and letters. ***Reverse:*** The eagle shows medium wear on its breast and the right wing, less so on the left wing. HALF DISME shows wear. The fields have no luster. Some luster may be seen among the design elements and letters.

EF-40

VF-20, 30 (Very Fine). ***Obverse:*** More wear is seen on the hair, including to the right of the forehead and face, where only a few strands may be seen. The hair tips at the right are well detailed. The bust end is flat on its high area. Letters all show light wear. ***Reverse:*** The eagle displays significant wear, with its central part flat and most of the detail missing from the right wing. Letters all show light wear.

VF-30

F-12, 15 (Fine). ***Obverse:*** The portrait, above the neck, is essentially flat, but details of the eye, the nose, and, to a lesser extent, the lips can be seen. The bust end and neck truncation are flat. Some hair detail can be seen to the right of the neck and behind the head, with individual strands blended into heavy groups. Both obverse and reverse at this grade and lower are apt to show marks, minor digs, and other evidence of handling. ***Reverse:*** Wear is more advanced than on a Very Fine coin, with significant reduction of the height of the lettering, and with some letters weak in areas, especially if the rim nearby is flat.

F-12

VG-8, 10 (Very Good). ***Obverse:*** The head has less detail than a Fine coin and is essentially flat except at the neck. Some hair, in thick strands, can be seen. The letters show extensive wear, but are readable. ***Reverse:*** The eagle is mostly flat, and the letters are well worn, some of them incomplete at the borders. Detail overall is weaker than on the obverse.

VG-10

G-4, 6 (Good). ***Obverse:*** There is hardly any detail on the portrait, except that the eye can be seen, as well as some thick hair tips. The date is clear. Around the border the edges of the letters are worn away, and some are weak overall. ***Reverse:*** The eagle is only in outline form. The letters are very worn, with some missing.

G-6

AG-3 (About Good). ***Obverse:*** Extreme wear has reduced the portrait to an even shallower state. Around the border some letters are worn away completely, some partially. The 1792 date can be seen but is weak and may be partly missing. ***Reverse:*** Traces of the eagle will remain and there are scattered letters and fragments of letters. Most of the coin is worn flat.

AG-3

Illustrated coin: The scratches on the obverse should be noted.

Circulation Strikes

	Mintage	GSID	AG-3	G-4	VG-8	F-12	VF-20	EF-40	AU-50	MS-60	MS-63
Half Disme (1792)	**n/a**	**3715**	**$44,500**	**$53,000**	**$66,000**	**$84,000**	**$114,000**	**$156,000**	**$180,000**	**$240,000**	**$360,000**
1792, Half Disme	1,500	240963	44,500	53,000	66,000	84,000	114,000	156,000	180,000	240,000	360,000
	Auctions: $432,000, PCGS MS-64 HA 04/25; $931,922, PCGS MS-66 SBG 04/25										
1792, Half Disme, Special Strike	1–2 known	3716	—	—	—	—	—	—	—	—	720,000
	Auctions: $1,410,000, PCGS MS-67 HA 01/13										

100 GREATEST™ UNITED STATES COINS

No. 14 1792 HALF DISME

Half Dimes
1794–1873

AN OVERVIEW OF HALF DIMES

Scan for additional information.

The first half dimes, dated 1794 and of the Flowing Hair type, were not actually struck until 1795. In that year additional half dimes with the 1795 date were made. In 1796 and 1797 the short-lived Draped Bust obverse combined with the Small Eagle reverse was used, after which no half dimes were struck until 1801. From that year through 1805, excepting 1804, the Draped Bust obverse was used in combination with the Heraldic Eagle reverse. Then followed a long span of years without any coinage of the denomination. In 1829 the laying of the cornerstone for the second Philadelphia Mint precipitated a new issue, the Capped Bust design, some examples of which were made for the ceremony. Production was resumed for circulation, and half dimes of this motif were made through 1837. In that year the Liberty Seated motif, by Christian Gobrecht, was introduced, to be continued without interruption through 1873, although there were a number of design modifications and changes during that span.

Assembling a set of the different half-dime types is a challenge for the collector. The 1794 and 1795, Flowing Hair, half dimes are fairly scarce at all levels and are quite rare in choice Mint State. Then come the Draped Bust obverse, Small Eagle reverse half dimes of 1796 and 1797. In the late 1960s, researcher Jim Ruddy found that of the various silver types (including the more famous 1796–1797 half dollars), half dimes of this type were the hardest to complete a photographic set of, from the lowest grades to the highest.

Draped Bust obverse, Heraldic Eagle reverse half dimes of the 1800–1805 years are scarce in all grades, more so than generally realized. In Mint State they are very rare, although on occasion some dated 1800 turn up (not often for the others). Finding a *sharply struck* example is next to impossible, and a collector may have to give up on this aspect and settle for one that has some weakness in areas.

Capped Bust half dimes and the several variations of Liberty Seated half dimes will pose no problem at all, and with some small amount of patience a collector will be able to find a sharply struck example in nearly any grade desired.

For the Collector and Investor: Half Dimes as a Specialty

Collecting half dimes by early die varieties of 1794–1837, and/or by dates and mintmarks (beginning with the 1838-O), has captured the fancy of many numismatists over the years. As these coins are so small it is necessary to have a magnifying glass when studying the series—something the collector of silver dollars and double eagles does not need.

The new design upon the resumption of the denomination in 1829 was created by Chief Engraver William Kneass. It is thought to have been based upon an earlier design by John Reich.

One of the earlier enthusiasts in the field was Philadelphia attorney and numismatist Harold P. Newlin, who in 1883 issued *A Classification of the Early Half Dimes of the United States.* Newlin's two favorite varieties were the 1792 half disme and the rare 1802, and after reading his enticing prose about the desirability of each, no doubt some collectors in 1883 put both coins on their "must have" lists.

Among early half dimes the rarest and most expensive is the 1802. In 1883 Newlin listed just 16 examples known to him. Although no one has compiled an up-to-date registry, it is likely that fewer than 30 exist. Most are well worn. Other early half dimes range from rare to very rare.

Capped Bust half dimes of the 1829–1837 years are all easily available as dates, but some of the die varieties are very rare. Today, most half dimes on the market are not attributed by varieties, making the search for such things rewarding when a rarity is found for the price of a regular coin.

In 1978 the numismatic world was startled to learn that Chicago dealer Edward Milas had located an 1870-S half dime, a variety not earlier known to exist and not listed in the annual Mint reports. Other than this coin, still unique today, the dates and mints in the Liberty Seated series 1837 to 1873-S are readily collectible by date and mint, with no great rarities. There are several very curious varieties within that span, the most interesting of which may be the 1858, Over Inverted Date. The date was first punched into the die upside down, the error was noted, and then it was corrected.

EXPLORING VARIETIES

This book is the standard work for early half dime die varieties. Its LM numbers, which identify each variety, are cited in auction catalogs and references. These numbers give collectors a framework to organize and study this long-running but often overlooked denomination.

Logan, Russell, and John McCloskey. *Federal Half Dimes 1792–1837.* Manchester, MI: 1998.

FLOWING HAIR (1794–1795)

Designer: *Unknown.* **Engraver:** *Robert Scot.*
Weight: *1.35 grams.* **Composition:** *.8924 silver, .1076 copper.*
Diameter: *Approximately 16.5 mm.* **Edge:** *Reeded.* **Mint:** *Philadelphia.*

History. Half dimes dated 1794 and 1795, of the Flowing Hair type, were all struck in the calendar year 1795, although dies were ready by the end of 1794. The Flowing Hair motif was also used on half dollars and silver dollars of the same years, but not on other denominations.

Striking and Sharpness. Many Flowing Hair half dimes have problems of one sort or another, including adjustment marks (from the planchet being filed down to proper weight) and/or light striking in some areas. On the obverse, check the hair and stars, and on the reverse the breast of the eagle. It may not be possible to find a *needle-sharp* example, but with some extensive searching a fairly decent strike can be obtained. Sharp striking and excellent eye appeal add dramatically to the value.

Availability. Examples appear on the market with frequency, typically in lower circulated grades. Probably 250 to 500 could be classified as MS, most of these dated 1795. Some searching is needed to locate choice examples in any grade. As a rule, half dimes are more readily available than are half dollars and dollars of the same design, and when found are usually more attractive and have fewer problems.

Grading Standards

MS-63

MS-60 to 70 (Mint State). ***Obverse:*** At MS-60 some abrasion and contact marks are evident, most noticeably on the cheek and in the fields. Luster is present, but may be dull or lifeless, and interrupted in patches. At MS-63, contact marks are very few, and abrasion is hard to detect except under magnification. An MS-65 coin has no abrasion, and contact marks are so minute as to require magnification. Luster should be full and rich. Coins graded above MS-65 are more theoretical than actual for this type—but they do exist, and are defined by having fewer marks as perfection is approached. ***Reverse:*** Comments apply as for the obverse, except that abrasion and contact marks are most noticeable on the eagle at the center. The field area is small and is protected by lettering and the wreath, and in any given grade shows fewer marks than on the obverse.

Illustrated coin: This coin reveals increased olive and blue iridescence under bright light. The central weakness is typical for the striking of this die marriage.

AU-50, 53, 55, 58 (About Uncirculated). ***Obverse:*** Light wear is seen on the hair area immediately to the left of the face and neck, on the cheek, and on the top of the neck truncation, more so at AU-50 than at AU-53 or 55. An AU-58 coin will have minimal traces of wear. An AU-50 will have luster in protected areas among the stars and letters, with little in the open fields or on the portrait. At AU-58, most luster is present in the fields, but is worn away on the highest parts of the motifs. ***Reverse:*** Light wear is seen on the eagle's body and right wing. At AU-50, detail is lost in most feathers in this area. However, striking can play a part, and some coins are weak to begin with. Light wear is seen on the wreath and lettering. Luster is the best key to actual wear. This will range from perhaps 20 percent remaining in protected areas at AU-50 to nearly full mint bloom at AU-58.

AU-55

Illustrated coin: Liberty's hair displays impressive detail for this grade.

EF-40, 45 (Extremely Fine). ***Obverse:*** More wear is evident on the portrait, especially on the hair to the left of the face and neck; the cheek; and the tip of the neck truncation. Excellent detail remains in low-relief areas of the hair. The stars show wear, as do the date and letters. Luster, if present at all, is minimal and in protected areas. ***Reverse:*** The eagle, this being the focal point to check, shows more wear. Observe in combination with a knowledge of the die variety, to determine the sharpness of the coin when it was first struck. Some were flat at the center at the time they were made. Additional wear is on the wreath and letters, but many details are present. Some luster may be seen in protected areas, and if present is slightly more abundant than on the obverse.

EF-40

VF-20, 30 (Very Fine). ***Obverse:*** The hair is well worn at the VF-20 level, less so at VF-30. The strands are blended so as to be heavy. The cheek shows only slight relief, and the tip of the neck truncation is flat. The stars have more wear, making them appear larger (an optical illusion). ***Reverse:*** The body of the eagle shows few if any feathers, while the wings have about half of the feathers visible, depending on the strike. The leaves lack detail and are in outline form. Scattered, non-disfiguring marks are normal for this and lower grades. Any major defects should be noted separately.

VF-30

F-12

F-12, 15 (Fine). ***Obverse:*** Wear is more extensive than on a Very Fine coin, reducing the definition of the thick strands of hair. The cheek has less detail, and the stars appear larger. The rim is distinct and many denticles remain visible. ***Reverse:*** Wear is more extensive. Now, feather details are reduced, mostly remaining on the right wing. The wreath and lettering are more worn, and the rim is usually weak in areas, although some denticles can be seen.

Illustrated coin: Two light adjustment marks on the lower left of the portrait date from the time of striking.

VG-8

VG-8, 10 (Very Good). ***Obverse:*** The portrait is mostly seen in outline form, with most hair strands gone, although the tips at the lower left are clear. The ear is discernible, as is the eye. The stars appear larger still, again an illusion. The rim is weak in areas. LIBERTY and the date are readable and usually full, although some letters may be weak at their tops. ***Reverse:*** The eagle is mostly an outline, although some traces of feathers may be seen in the tail and the lower part of the inside of the right wing. The rim is worn, as are the letters, with some weak, but the motto is readable.

G-6

G-4, 6 (Good). ***Obverse:*** Wear is more extensive, and some stars may be missing or only partially visible. The head is an outline, although a few elements of thick hair strands may be seen. The eye is visible only in outline form. The rim is well worn or even missing. LIBERTY is worn, and parts of some letters may be missing, but elements of all are readable. The date is readable, but worn. ***Reverse:*** The eagle is flat and discernible in outline form. The wreath is well worn. Some of the letters may be partly missing. At this level some "averaging" can be done. If the letters are stronger than usual in one area, but some are missing in another area, the coin can still qualify as G-4.

Illustrated coin: There are several adjustment marks on the obverse, but this coin lacks the bisecting obverse die crack typical of later issues struck from this die pair. The reverse die on this coin was rotated 20 degrees out of the normal alignment.

AG-3 (About Good). ***Obverse:*** Wear is so extensive that the coin is barely identifiable. The head is in outline form, LIBERTY is mostly gone, and the date, while readable, may be partially missing. ***Reverse:*** The reverse is well worn with parts of the wreath and lettering missing.

AG-3

Circulation Strikes

	Mintage	GSID	AG-3	G-4	VG-8	F-12	VF-20	EF-40	AU-50	MS-60	MS-63
Flowing Hair (1794–1795)	**n/a**	**72449**	**$1,150**	**$1,550**	**$2,250**	**$2,900**	**$3,900**	**$6,500**	**$7,500**	**$11,000**	**$15,500**
1794	7,756	3717	1,900	2,250	3,250	4,400	5,250	9,500	12,000	20,500	33,000
	Auctions: $152,088, NGC MS-67 SBG 08/10										
↳1794, LM-1	*	198138	2,050	2,500	3,600	4,800	5,750	10,500	13,000	22,500	36,500
↳1794, LM-2	*	198139	2,050	2,500	3,600	4,800	5,750	10,500	13,000	22,500	36,500
↳1794, LM-3	*	198140	1,900	2,250	3,250	4,400	5,250	9,500	12,000	20,500	33,000
	Auctions: $132,000, PCGS MS-66 HA 01/21										
↳1794, LM-4	*	198141	1,900	2,250	3,250	4,400	5,250	9,500	12,000	20,500	33,000
1794, Specimen Strike	3	3838	—	—	—	—	—	—	—	—	210,000
	Auctions: $367,775, PCGS MS-67 HA 10/12										
1795	78,660	3718	1,150	1,550	2,250	2,900	3,900	6,500	7,500	11,000	15,500
	Auctions: $161,000, PCGS MS-67 ANR 11/04										
↳1795, LM-1	*	198142	—	—	—	—	—	8,250	10,500	17,500	—
↳1795, LM-2	*	198143	—	—	—	—	5,500	9,500	11,000	15,000	45,500
↳1795, LM-3	*	198144	1,250	1,700	2,500	3,150	4,250	7,250	8,000	12,000	17,000
↳1795, LM-4	*	198145	—	—	—	—	—	—	9,500	14,500	22,000
↳1795, LM-5	*	198146	1,250	1,700	2,500	3,150	4,250	7,250	8,750	13,000	18,500
↳1795, LM-6	*	198147	—	—	—	4,500	5,500	7,500	9,500	—	—
↳1795, LM-7	*	198148	1,450	2,050	2,900	3,750	5,000	8,500	9,500	14,000	20,500
↳1795, LM-8	*	198149	1,150	1,550	2,250	2,900	3,900	6,500	7,500	11,000	15,500
	Auctions: $152,750, NGC MS-67 HA 08/14										
↳1795, LM-9	*	198150	1,150	1,550	2,250	2,900	3,900	6,500	7,500	11,000	15,500
	Auctions: $132,000, PCGS MS-67 HA 09/20										
↳1795, LM-10	*	198151	1,150	1,550	2,250	2,900	3,900	6,500	7,500	11,000	17,000
	Auctions: $176,250, PCGS MS-67 SBG 05/15										

* Included in number above.

DRAPED BUST, SMALL EAGLE REVERSE (1796–1797)

Designer: *Probably Gilbert Stuart.* **Engraver:** *Robert Scot.*
Weight: *1.35 grams.* **Composition:** *.8924 silver, .1076 copper.*
Diameter: *Approximately 16.5 mm.* **Edge:** *Reeded.* **Mint:** *Philadelphia.*

History. Although the Draped Bust obverse design was used on various copper and silver coins circa 1795 to 1808, it was employed in combination with the *Small Eagle* reverse only on silver coins of 1795 to 1798—for the half dime series, only in 1796 and 1797.

Striking and Sharpness. Most 1796–1797 half dimes are weak in at least one area. Points to check for sharpness include the hair of Liberty, the centers of the stars, the bust line, and, on the reverse, the center of the eagle. Check for planchet adjustment marks (these are infrequent). Denticles around the border are usually decent, but may vary in strength from one part of the border to another. Sharp striking and excellent eye appeal add to the value dramatically.

Availability. This type is fairly scarce in *any* grade; in MS-63 and finer, no more than a few dozen examples have been traced. As is advisable for other early silver types, beware of deeply toned or vividly iridescent-toned pieces whose flawed surface characters are obscured by the toning, but which are offered as MS; in truth some of these are barely better than EF.

Grading Standards

MS-62

MS-60 to 70 (Mint State). ***Obverse:*** At MS-60 some abrasion and contact marks are evident, most noticeably on the cheek, on the drapery, and in the right field. Luster is present, but may be dull or lifeless, and interrupted in patches. At MS-63, contact marks are very few, and abrasion is hard to detect except under magnification, although this type is sometimes graded liberally due to its rarity. An MS-65 coin has no abrasion, and contact marks are so minute as to require magnification. Luster should be full and rich. Coins graded above MS-65 are more theoretical than actual for this type—but they do exist, and are defined by having fewer marks as perfection is approached. ***Reverse:*** Comments apply as for the obverse, except that abrasion and marks are most noticeable on the eagle at the center, a situation complicated by the fact that this area was often flatly struck. Grading is best done by the obverse, then verified by the reverse. The field area is small and is protected by lettering and the wreath, and in any given grade shows fewer marks than on the obverse.

Illustrated coin: Note the clash marks in the right obverse field, which are typical for this die variety.

AU-50

AU-50, 53, 55, 58 (About Uncirculated). ***Obverse:*** Light wear is seen on the hair area above the ear and extending to left of the forehead, on the ribbon, and on the bosom—more so at AU-50 than at AU-53 or 55. An AU-58 coin has minimal traces of wear. An AU-50 coin has luster in protected areas among the stars and letters, with little in the open fields or on the portrait. At AU-58, most luster is present in the fields, but is worn away on the highest parts of the motifs. ***Reverse:*** Light wear is seen on the eagle's body (keep in mind this area might be lightly struck) and edges of the wings. Light wear is seen on the wreath and lettering. Luster is the best key to actual wear. This ranges from perhaps 20 percent remaining in protected areas at AU-50 to nearly full mint bloom at AU-58.

Illustrated coin: This is the LIKERTY variety, its fanciful name derived from the top and bottom lines of the B being defective.

EF-40

EF-40, 45 (Extremely Fine). ***Obverse:*** More wear is evident on the upper hair area and the ribbon and on the drapery and bosom. Excellent detail will remain in low relief areas of the hair. The stars show wear as will the date and letters. Luster, if present at all, is minimal and in protected areas. ***Reverse:*** The eagle shows more wear, this being the focal point to check. On most examples, many feathers remain on the interior areas of the wings. Check the eagle in combination with a knowledge of the die variety to determine the sharpness of the coin when it was first struck. Additional wear is evident on the wreath and letters, but many details are present. Some luster may be seen in protected areas and, if present, is slightly more abundant than on the obverse.

VF-30

VF-20, 30 (Very Fine). ***Obverse:*** The higher-relief areas of hair are well worn at VF-20, less so at VF-30. The drapery and bosom show extensive wear. The stars have more wear, making them appear larger (an optical illusion seen on most worn silver coins of this era). ***Reverse:*** The body of the eagle shows few if any feathers, while the wings have about half of the feathers visible, depending on the strike. The leaves lack most detail and are in outline form. Scattered, non-disfiguring marks are normal for this and lower grades; any major distractions should be noted separately.

F-15

F-12, 15 (Fine). ***Obverse:*** Wear is more extensive than on a Very Fine coin. Wear is particularly noticeable on the hair, face, and bosom, and the stars appear larger. About half the hair detail remains, most noticeably behind the neck and shoulder. The rim may be partially worn away and may blend into the field. ***Reverse:*** Wear is more extensive. Feather details are diminished, with fewer than half remaining on the wings. The wreath and lettering are worn further, and the rim is usually weak in areas, although some denticles can be seen.

VG-8

VG-8, 10 (Very Good). ***Obverse:*** The portrait is mostly seen in outline form, with most hair strands gone, although there is some definition at the back of the hair and behind the shoulder. The ear is discernible, as is the eye. The stars appear larger still, again an illusion. The rim is weak in areas. LIBERTY and the date are readable and usually full, although some letters may be weak at their tops. ***Reverse:*** The eagle is mostly an outline, with parts blending into the field (on lighter strikes). The rim is worn, as are the letters, with some weak, but the motto is readable.

G-4

G-4, 6 (Good). ***Obverse:*** Wear is more extensive, and some stars may be partly missing. The head is an outline. The eye is visible only in outline form. The rim is well worn or even missing in areas. LIBERTY is worn, and parts of some letters may be missing, but elements of all should be readable. The date is readable, but worn. ***Reverse:*** The eagle is flat and discernible in outline form, and may be blending into the field. The wreath is well worn. Some of the letters may be partly missing. At this level some "averaging" can be done. If the letters are stronger than usual in one area, but some are missing in another area, the coin can still qualify as G-4.

AG-3

AG-3 (About Good). ***Obverse:*** Wear is so extensive that the coin is barely identifiable. The head is in outline form. LIBERTY is mostly gone, as are some of the stars. The date, while readable, may be partially worn away. ***Reverse:*** The reverse is well worn, with parts of the wreath and lettering missing.

1796, 6 Over 5
LM-2

1796, LIKERTY
LM-1

1797, 15 Stars
LM-1

1797, 16 Stars
LM-3

1797, 13 Stars
LM-4

Circulation Strikes

	Mintage	GSID	AG-3	G-4	VG-8	F-12	VF-20	EF-40	AU-50	MS-60	MS-63
Draped Bust, Small Eagle Reverse (1796–1797)	**n/a**	**72450**	**$1,250**	**$1,600**	**$2,000**	**$3,450**	**$4,800**	**$5,750**	**$8,750**	**$17,000**	**$23,000**
1796, LIKERTY (a,b)	10,230	3720	1,300	1,700	2,200	3,750	4,800	7,750	10,500	22,000	36,000
↳1796, LIKERTY, LM-1 (a,b)	*	393194	1,300	1,700	2,200	3,750	4,800	7,750	10,500	22,000	36,000
	Auctions: $411,250, PCGS MS-67 SBG 05/15										
1796, 6 Over 5 (a)	*	3757	2,000	2,500	3,100	4,400	5,500	9,500	14,500	28,000	36,000
	Auctions: $345,000, PCGS MS-66 HA 01/08										
↳1796, 6 Over 5, LM-2 (a)	*	393195	2,000	2,500	3,100	4,400	5,500	9,500	14,500	28,000	36,000
	Auctions: $188,000, PCGS MS-66 SBG 05/15										
1797, 15 Stars	44,527	3721	1,250	1,600	2,000	3,450	4,800	5,750	8,750	17,000	23,000
↳1797, 15 Stars, LM-1	*	393196	1,250	1,600	2,000	3,450	4,800	5,750	8,750	17,000	23,000
	Auctions: $164,500, PCGS MS-67 SBG 05/15										
1797, 16 Stars	*	3722	1,250	1,600	2,000	3,450	4,800	5,750	8,750	17,000	23,000
	Auctions: $115,000, NGC MS-66 ANR 01/05										
↳1797, 16 Stars, LM-2	*	198152	1,250	1,600	2,000	3,450	4,800	5,750	8,750	17,000	23,000
	Auctions: $141,000, PCGS MS-66 HA 08/14										
↳1797, 16 Stars, LM-3	*	198153	1,250	1,600	2,000	3,450	4,800	5,750	8,750	17,000	23,000
	Auctions: $129,250, PCGS MS-66 SBG 05/15										
1797, 13 Stars	*	3723	3,500	4,750	5,500	6,750	8,250	14,500	31,000	84,000	144,000
↳1797, 13 Stars, LM-4	*	393197	3,500	4,750	5,500	6,750	8,250	14,500	31,000	84,000	144,000

* Included in number above. **a.** Some certified examples may be labeled "1796" only, with no mention of the variety. **b.** A die imperfection makes the B in LIBERTY somewhat resemble a K.

DRAPED BUST, HERALDIC EAGLE REVERSE (1800–1805)

Designer: *Robert Scot.* **Weight:** *1.35 grams.* **Composition:** *.8924 silver, .1076 copper.* **Diameter:** *Approximately 16.5 mm.* **Edge:** *Reeded.* **Mint:** *Philadelphia.*

History. The combination of Draped Bust obverse / Heraldic Eagle reverse was used in the silver half dime series from 1800 to 1805. The obverse style, standardized with 13 stars, is the same as used in 1796 and 1797. During this span the rare 1802 was produced, and none were minted with the date 1804.

Striking and Sharpness. Most 1800–1805 half dimes are lightly struck in one area or another. The obverse stars usually show some weakness. On many coins the central details of Liberty are not sharp. On the reverse the upper right of the shield and the adjacent part of the eagle's wing are often soft, and several or even most stars may be lightly defined (sharp stars show sharply peaked centers); high parts of the clouds are often weak. The area on the reverse opposite the bosom of Liberty may be flat or weak, due to the metal having to flow in both directions when the coins were struck. (The area curving obliquely up and to the right of the eagle's head—exactly mirroring the curvature of the bust on the obverse—is especially prone to weakness of strike.) Denticles are likely to be weak or missing in areas. Many have Mint-caused adjustment marks, from overweight planchets being filed down to proper specifications. In summary, *a sharply struck coin is a goal, not necessarily a reality*. In this series, sharp striking and excellent eye appeal will add to a coin's value dramatically, this being particularly true for all issues from 1801 to 1805.

Availability. This is a challenging type to find with nice eye appeal. Many toned pieces have been recolored to hide flaws or to improve eye appeal. Some are porous or have other problems. The majority of pieces surviving today are dated 1800, and nearly all of the AU or finer coins are of this date.

Grading Standards

MS-63

MS-60 to 70 (Mint State). ***Obverse:*** At MS-60 some abrasion and contact marks are evident, most noticeably on the cheek, on the drapery, and in the right field. Luster is present, but may be dull or lifeless, and interrupted in patches. At MS-63, contact marks are very few, and abrasion is hard to detect except under magnification, although this type is sometimes graded liberally due to its rarity. An MS-65 coin will have no abrasion, and contact marks are so minute as to require magnification. Luster should be full and rich. Coins graded above MS-65 are more theoretical than actual for this type—but they do exist, and are defined by having fewer marks as perfection is approached. ***Reverse:*** Comments apply as for the obverse, except that abrasion and contact marks are most noticeable on the eagle's neck, the tips of the wing, and the tail. The field area is complex—with stars above the eagle, the arrows and olive branch, and other features, there is not much open space. Accordingly, marks will not be as noticeable as on the obverse.

AU-58

AU-50, 53, 55, 58 (About Uncirculated). ***Obverse:*** Light wear is seen on the hair area above the ear and extending to left of the forehead, on the ribbon, and on the bosom, more so at AU-50 than at AU-53 or 55. An AU-58 coin will have minimal traces of wear. An AU-50 coin will have luster in protected areas among the stars and letters, with little in the open fields or on the portrait. At AU-58, most luster is present in the fields, but is worn away on the highest parts of the motifs. ***Reverse:*** Comments as for Mint State coins, except that the eagle's neck, the tips and top of the wings, the clouds, and the tail show noticeable wear, as do other features. Luster ranges from perhaps 20 percent remaining in protected areas at AU-50 to nearly full mint bloom at AU-58. Often the reverse of this type retains much more luster than the obverse.

Illustrated coin: Note the areas of rich, blue toning.

EF-45

EF-40, 45 (Extremely Fine). ***Obverse:*** More wear is evident on the upper hair area and the ribbon, and on the drapery and bosom. Excellent detail remains in low-relief areas of the hair. The stars show wear, as do the date and letters. Luster, if present at all, is minimal and only in protected areas. ***Reverse:*** Wear is greater than on an About Uncirculated coin, overall. The neck lacks feather detail on its highest points. Feathers lose some detail near the edges of the wings, and some areas of the horizontal lines in the shield may be blended together. Some traces of luster may be seen, more so at EF-45 than at EF-40.

Illustrated coin: The obverse cud break is as struck.

VF-20

VF-20, 30 (Very Fine). ***Obverse:*** The higher-relief areas of hair are well worn at VF-20, less so at VF-30. The drapery and bosom show extensive wear. The stars have more wear, making them appear larger (an optical illusion seen on most worn silver coins of this era). ***Reverse:*** Wear is greater, including on the shield and wing feathers. Star centers are flat. Other areas have lost detail as well.

F-15

F-12, 15 (Fine). ***Obverse:*** Wear is more extensive than on a Very Fine coin, particularly noticeable on the hair, face, and bosom, and the stars appear larger. About half the hair detail remains, most noticeably behind the neck and shoulder. The rim may be partially worn away and may blend into the field. ***Reverse:*** Wear is even more extensive, with the shield and wing feathers being points to observe. The incuse E PLURIBUS UNUM may have a few letters worn away. The clouds all seem to be connected. The stars are weak. Parts of the border and lettering may be weak.

VG-8

VG-8, 10 (Very Good). ***Obverse:*** The portrait is mostly seen in outline form, with most hair strands gone, although there is some definition at the back of the hair and behind the shoulder. The ear is discernible, as is the eye. The stars appear larger still, again an illusion. The rim is weak in areas. LIBERTY and the date are readable and usually full, although some letters may be weak at their tops. ***Reverse:*** Half or so of the letters in the motto are worn away. Most feather details are worn away, although separation of some of the lower feathers may be seen. Some stars are faint. The border blends into the field in areas, and some letters are weak.

G-6

G-4, 6 (Good). ***Obverse:*** Some stars may be partly missing. The head is an outline. The eye is visible only in outline form. The rim is well worn or even missing in areas. LIBERTY is worn, and parts of some letters may be missing, but elements of all should be readable. The date is readable, but worn. ***Reverse:*** The upper part of the eagle is flat, and feathers are noticeable only at the lower edge of the wings and do not have detail. The upper part of the shield is flat. Only a few letters of the motto can be seen. The rim is worn extensively, and a few letters may be missing.

AG-3

AG-3 (About Good). ***Obverse:*** Wear is so extensive that the coin is barely identifiable. The head is in outline form. LIBERTY is mostly gone; same for the stars. The date, while readable, may be partially worn away. ***Reverse:*** Extensive wear is seen overall, with the rim worn away and some areas worn smooth. The eagle can be discerned in outline form, but not necessarily completely. A few stray motto letters may remain.

1800, LIBEKTY

1803, Large 8

1803, Small 8

Circulation Strikes

	Mintage	GSID	AG-3	G-4	VG-8	F-12	VF-20	EF-40	AU-50	MS-60	MS-63
Draped Bust, Heraldic Eagle Reverse (1800–1805)	**n/a**	**72451**	**$1,150**	**$1,700**	**$1,950**	**$2,400**	**$3,250**	**$5,500**	**$7,750**	**$12,500**	**$18,500**
1800	24,000	3724	1,150	1,700	1,950	2,400	3,250	5,500	7,750	12,500	18,500
↳**1800, LM-1**	*	198154	1,150	1,700	1,950	2,400	3,250	5,500	7,750	12,500	18,500
	Auctions: $381,875, PCGS MS-68 SBG 05/15										
↳**1800, LM-2**	*	198155	—	—	—	—	7,000	12,000	20,000	42,000	—
1800, LIBEKTY (a)	16,000	3725	1,400	1,750	2,050	2,500	3,750	6,250	8,750	14,500	21,000
↳**1800, LIBEKTY, LM-3** (a)	*	198156	1,400	1,750	2,050	2,500	3,750	6,250	8,750	14,500	21,000
	Auctions: $152,750, PCGS MS-66 SBG 05/15										
↳**1800, LIBEKTY, LM-4** (a)	*	198157	—	—	—	—	—	—	—	—	—
↳**1800, LIBEKTY, LM-5** (a)	1 known	198162	18,000	—	—	—	—	—	—	—	—
1801	27,760	3726	1,250	1,800	2,100	2,550	3,550	6,000	8,250	18,500	26,500
↳**1801, LM-1**	2–3 est. known	198158	—	—	—	9,500	—	15,000	—	—	—
↳**1801, LM-2**	*	198159	1,250	1,800	2,100	2,550	3,550	6,000	8,250	18,500	26,500
	Auctions: $164,500, NGC MS-67 HA 10/14										
1802†	3,060	3727	84,000	93,500	120,000	156,000	180,000	240,000	384,000	—	—
	Auctions: $352,500, PCGS AU-50 HA 06/14										
↳**1802, LM-1**	*	393198	84,000	93,500	120,000	156,000	180,000	240,000	384,000	—	—
	Auctions: $324,000, PCGS AU-50 SBG 03/24; $114,000, PCGS VG-8 HA 03/24										
1803, Large 8	37,850	3728	1,150	1,700	1,950	2,400	3,250	5,500	7,750	13,500	36,000
	Auctions: $164,500, PCGS MS-65 SBG 07/15										
↳**1803, Large 8, LM-2**	*	198160	1,150	1,700	1,950	2,400	3,250	5,500	7,750	13,500	36,000
↳**1803, Large 8, LM-3**	*	198161	1,150	1,700	1,950	2,400	3,250	5,500	7,750	13,500	36,000
	Auctions: $170,375, PCGS MS-65 HA 08/14										
1803, Small 8	*	3729	1,900	2,750	3,750	5,000	7,250	11,000	15,500	72,000	108,000
↳**1803, Small 8, LM-1**	*	393199	1,900	2,750	3,750	5,000	7,250	11,000	15,500	72,000	108,000
1805	15,000	3730	1,700	2,050	2,750	3,500	5,000	13,000	26,500	—	—
↳**1805, LM-1**	*	393200	1,700	2,050	2,750	3,500	5,000	13,000	26,500	—	—

* Included in number above. **a.** A defective die punch gives the R in LIBERTY the appearance of a K.

CAPPED BUST (1829–1837)

Engraver: *William Kneass, after a design by John Reich.* **Weight:** *1.35 grams (changed to 1.34 grams in 1837).* **Composition:** *.8924 silver, .1076 copper (changed to .900 silver, .100 copper in 1837).* **Diameter:** *Approximately 15.5 mm.* **Edge:** *Reeded.* **Mint:** *Philadelphia.*

Circulation Strike

Proof Strike

History. Half dimes of the Capped Bust design were first struck the morning of July 4, 1829, to be included in the cornerstone time capsule of the new (second) Philadelphia Mint building and, presumably, to have some inexpensive coins on hand for distribution as souvenirs. Engraver John Reich's design was not new; it had been used on half dollars as early as 1807. It was logical to employ it on the new half dime, a coin that had not been made since 1805. The new half dimes proved popular and remained in circulation for many years.

Striking and Sharpness. Striking varies among Capped Bust half dimes, and most show lightness in one area or another. On the obverse, check the hair details to the left of the eye, as well as the star centers. On the reverse, check the eagle's feathers and neck. The motto, which can be a problem on certain other coins of this design (notably half dollars), is usually bold on the half dimes. Denticles range from well defined to somewhat indistinct, and, in general, are sharper on the obverse than on the reverse.

Proofs. Proofs were struck in small quantities, generally as part of silver Proof sets, although perhaps some were made to mark the Mint cornerstone event mentioned above; facts are scarce. True Proofs have fully mirrored fields. Scrutinize deeply toned pieces (deep toning often masks the true nature of a coin, e.g., if it is not a true Proof, or if it has been cleaned or repaired). Some pieces attributed as "Proofs" are not Proofs. This advice applies across the entire Capped Bust silver series.

Availability. Finding an example in any desired grade should not be a challenge. Finding one with Full Details will take more time. Connoisseurship is required at the MS level, given the high value of these coins.

Grading Standards

MS-65

MS-60 to 70 (Mint State). ***Obverse:*** At MS-60 some abrasion and contact marks are evident, most noticeably on the cheek, on the hair below the left part of LIBERTY, and on the area near the drapery clasp. Luster is present, but may be dull or lifeless, and interrupted in patches. At MS-63, contact marks are very few, and abrasion is hard to detect except under magnification. An MS-65 coin has no abrasion, and has contact marks so minute as to require magnification. Luster should be full and rich, usually more so on half dimes than larger coins of the Capped Bust type. Grades above MS-65 are seen now and again, and are defined by having fewer marks as perfection is approached. ***Reverse:*** Comments apply as for the obverse, except that abrasion and contact marks are most noticeable on the eagle's neck, the top of the wings, the claws, and the flat band that surrounds the incuse motto. The field is mainly protected by design elements and does not show abrasion as much as does the obverse.

AU-58

AU-50, 53, 55, 58 (About Uncirculated). ***Obverse:*** Light wear is seen on the cap, the hair below LIBERTY, the hair near the clasp, and the drapery at the bosom. At AU-58, the luster is extensive except in the open area of the field, especially to the right. At AU-50 and 53, luster remains only in protected areas. ***Reverse:*** Wear is visible on the eagle's neck, the top of the wings, the claws, and the flat band above the eagle. An AU-58 coin will have nearly full luster. At AU-50 and 53, there will still be significant luster, more than on the obverse.

Illustrated coin: Note the rings of toning on the obverse, displaying russet, cobalt, and rosy iridescence.

EF-40

EF-40, 45 (Extremely Fine). ***Obverse:*** Wear is most noticeable on the higher areas of the hair. The cap shows more wear, as does the cheek. Stars, usually protected by the rim, still show their centers (unless lightly struck). Luster, if present, is in protected areas among the star points and close to the portrait. ***Reverse:*** The wings show wear on the higher areas of the feathers, and some details are lost. Feathers in the neck are light. The eagle's claws and the leaves show wear. Luster may be present in protected areas, even if there is little or none on the obverse.

VF-30

VF-20, 30 (Very Fine). ***Obverse:*** Wear has caused most of the hair to be combined into thick tresses without delicate features. The curl on the neck is flat. Most stars, unless they were weakly struck, retain their interior lines. ***Reverse:*** Wear is most evident on the eagle's neck, to the left of the shield, and on the leaves and claws. Most feathers in the wing remain distinct.

F-12

F-12, 15 (Fine). ***Obverse:*** Wear is more extensive, with much of the hair blended together. The drapery is indistinct at its upper edge. Stars have lost some detail at the centers, but still have relief (are not flat). ***Reverse:*** Wear is more extensive, now with only about half of the feathers remaining on the wings. Some of the horizontal lines in the shield may be worn away.

VG-8, 10 (Very Good). ***Obverse:*** The hair is less distinct, with the area surrounding the face blended into the facial features. LIBERTY is complete, but weak in areas. The stars are nearly flat, although some interior detail can be seen on certain strikings. ***Reverse:*** Feathers are fewer and mostly appear on the right wing. Other details are weaker. All lettering remains easily visible.

VG-8

G-4, 6 (Good). ***Obverse:*** The portrait is mostly in outline, with few interior details discernible. LIBERTY may still be readable or may be partially worn away, depending on the variety. Stars are flat at their centers. ***Reverse:*** The eagle mostly is in outline form, although some feathers can be seen in the right wing. All letters around the border are clear. E PLURIBUS UNUM may be weak, sometimes with a few letters worn away.

G-6

AG-3 (About Good). ***Obverse:*** The portrait is an outline, although traces of LIBERTY can still be seen. The rim is worn down, and some stars are weak. The date remains clear. ***Reverse:*** The reverse shows more wear overall than the obverse, with the rim indistinct in areas and many letters worn away.

AG-3

PF-60 to 70 (Proof). ***Obverse and Reverse:*** Proofs that are extensively cleaned and have many hairlines, or that are dull and grainy, are lower level, such as PF-60 to 62. These are not of great interest to specialists unless they are of rare die varieties (such as 1829, LM-1 to 3, described in the image caption). With medium hairlines, an assigned grade of PF-64 may be in order, and with relatively few hairlines, gem PF-65. PF-66 should have hairlines so delicate that magnification is needed to see them. Above that, a Proof should be free of such lines. Grading is highly subjective with early Proofs, and eye appeal also is a factor.

PF-67+

Illustrated coin: Stunning in sharpness of strike and attractiveness of toning, this coin is the finest-known Proof of this type.

Circulation Strikes

	Mintage	GSID	G-4	VG-8	F-12	VF-20	EF-40	AU-50	MS-60	MS-63
Capped Bust (1829–1837)	n/a	72452	$75	$95	$115	$145	$205	$285	$550	$1,000
1829	1,230,000	3731	75	95	115	145	205	285	550	1,000
↳1829, LM-1	*	212533	75	95	115	145	205	285	550	1,000
↳1829, LM-2	*	212534	75	95	115	145	205	285	550	1,000
↳1829, LM-3	*	212535	75	95	115	145	205	285	550	1,000
↳1829, LM-4	*	212536	75	95	115	145	205	285	550	1,000
↳1829, LM-5	*	212537	75	95	115	145	205	285	550	1,000
↳1829, LM-6.1	*	212538	85	110	130	165	235	330	625	1,150
↳1829, LM-6.2	*	212539	85	110	130	165	235	330	625	1,150
↳1829, LM-6.3	*	212540	85	110	130	165	235	330	625	1,150
↳1829, LM-7.1	*	212541	80	105	125	160	225	315	600	1,100
↳1829, LM-7.2	*	212542	80	105	125	160	225	315	600	1,100
↳1829, LM-7.3	*	212543	80	105	125	160	225	315	600	1,100
↳1829, LM-8	*	212544	—	—	—	—	—	—	—	—
↳1829, LM-9	*	212545	80	105	125	160	225	315	600	1,100
↳1829, LM-10	*	212546	80	105	125	160	225	315	600	1,100
↳1829, LM-11	*	212547	—	—	—	390	575	850	1,500	—
↳1829, LM-12	*	212548	—	—	—	—	—	—	—	—
↳1829, LM-13.1	*	212549	75	95	115	145	205	285	550	1,000
↳1829, LM-13.2	*	212550	75	95	115	145	205	285	550	1,000
↳1829, LM-14	*	212551	80	105	125	160	225	315	600	1,100
↳1829, LM-15.1	*	212552	80	105	125	160	225	315	600	1,100
↳1829, LM-15.2	*	212553	80	105	125	160	225	315	600	1,100
↳1829, LM-16.1	*	212554	75	95	115	145	205	285	550	1,000
↳1829, LM-16.2	*	212555	75	95	115	145	205	285	550	1,000
↳1829, LM-17	*	212556	80	105	125	160	225	315	600	1,100
↳1829, LM-18	*	212557	80	105	125	160	225	315	600	1,100
1830	1,240,000	3733	75	95	115	145	205	285	550	1,000
↳1830, LM-1.1	*	212559	80	105	125	160	225	315	600	1,100
↳1830, LM-1.2	*	212560	80	105	125	160	225	315	600	1,100
↳1830, LM-2	*	212561	75	95	115	145	205	285	550	1,000
↳1830, LM-3	*	212562	75	95	115	145	205	285	550	1,000
↳1830, LM-4.1	*	212563	75	95	115	145	205	285	550	1,000
↳1830, LM-4.2	*	212564	75	95	115	145	205	285	550	1,000
↳1830, LM-5	*	212565	—	—	325	490	775	1,150	—	—
↳1830, LM-6	*	212566	80	105	125	160	225	315	600	1,100
↳1830, LM-7	*	212567	75	95	115	145	205	285	550	1,000
↳1830, LM-8	*	212568	75	95	115	145	205	285	550	1,000
↳1830, LM-9.1	*	212569	80	105	125	160	225	315	600	1,100
↳1830, LM-9.2	*	212570	80	105	125	160	225	315	600	1,100
↳1830, LM-9.3	*	212657	—	—	—	—	—	—	—	—
↳1830, LM-10	*	212571	—	—	—	1,550	3,100	5,000	20,000	—
↳1830, LM-11	*	212572	—	—	—	—	—	—	—	—
↳1830, LM-12	*	212573	80	105	125	160	225	315	600	1,100
↳1830, LM-13	*	212574	75	95	115	145	205	285	550	1,000
↳1830, LM-14	*	212575	75	95	115	145	205	285	550	1,000

* Included in number above.

Circulation Strikes *(continued)*

	Mintage	GSID	G-4	VG-8	F-12	VF-20	EF-40	AU-50	MS-60	MS-63
1831	1,242,700	3735	$75	$95	$115	$145	$205	$285	$550	$1,000
↳1831, LM-1.1	*	212576	75	95	115	145	205	285	550	1,000
↳1831, LM-1.2	*	212577	75	95	115	145	205	285	550	1,000
↳1831, LM-1.3	*	212578	75	95	115	145	205	285	550	1,000
↳1831, LM-2	*	212579	75	95	115	145	205	285	550	1,000
↳1831, LM-3	*	212580	80	105	125	160	225	315	600	1,100
↳1831, LM-4	*	212581	75	95	115	145	205	285	550	1,000
↳1831, LM-5	*	212582	75	95	115	145	205	285	550	1,000
↳1831, LM-6	*	212583	75	95	115	145	205	285	550	1,000
↳1831, LM-7	*	212584	75	95	115	145	205	285	550	1,000
1832	965,000	3737	75	95	115	145	205	285	550	1,000
↳1832, LM-1	*	212585	80	105	125	160	225	315	600	1,100
↳1832, LM-2	*	212586	75	95	115	145	205	285	550	1,000
↳1832, LM-3	*	212587	75	95	115	145	205	285	550	1,000
↳1832, LM-4	*	212588	80	105	125	160	225	315	600	1,100
↳1832, LM-5	*	212589	75	95	115	145	205	285	550	1,000
↳1832, LM-6	*	212590	80	105	125	160	225	315	600	1,100
↳1832, LM-7	*	212591	75	95	115	145	205	285	550	1,000
↳1832, LM-8.1	*	212592	75	95	115	145	205	285	550	1,000
↳1832, LM-8.2	*	212593	75	95	115	145	205	285	550	1,000
↳1832, LM-8.3	*	212594	75	95	115	145	205	285	550	1,000
↳1832, LM-8.4	*	212595	75	95	115	145	205	285	550	1,000
↳1832, LM-8.5	*	212596	75	95	115	145	205	285	550	1,000
↳1832, LM-9.1	*	212597	75	95	115	145	205	285	550	1,000
↳1832, LM-9.2	*	212598	75	95	115	145	205	285	550	1,000
↳1832, LM-10.1	*	212599	75	95	115	145	205	285	550	1,000
↳1832, LM-10.2	*	212600	75	95	115	145	205	285	550	1,000
↳1832, LM-10.3	*	212601	75	95	115	145	205	285	550	1,000
↳1832, LM-10.4	*	212602	75	95	115	145	205	285	550	1,000
↳1832, LM-11.1	*	212603	80	105	125	160	225	315	600	1,100
↳1832, LM-11.2	*	212604	80	105	125	160	225	315	600	1,100
↳1832, LM-12	*	212605	75	95	115	145	205	285	550	1,000
↳1832, LM-13	*	212606	75	95	115	145	205	285	550	1,000
↳1832, LM-14	*	212607	80	105	125	160	225	315	600	1,100
1833	1,370,000	3739	75	95	115	145	205	285	550	1,000
↳1833, LM-1	*	212608	75	95	115	145	205	285	550	1,000
↳1833, LM-2	*	212609	—	950	1,500	2,500	4,050	6,250	—	—
↳1833, LM-3.1	*	212610	75	95	115	145	205	285	550	1,000
↳1833, LM-3.2	*	212611	75	95	115	145	205	285	550	1,000
↳1833, LM-3.3	*	212612	75	95	115	145	205	285	550	1,000
↳1833, LM-3.4	*	212613	75	95	115	145	205	285	550	1,000
↳1833, LM-3.5	*	212614	75	95	115	145	205	285	550	1,000
↳1833, LM-4.1	*	212615	75	95	115	145	205	285	550	1,000
↳1833, LM-4.2	*	212616	75	95	115	145	205	285	550	1,000
↳1833, LM-4.3	*	212617	75	95	115	145	205	285	550	1,000
↳1833, LM-5	*	212618	—	—	—	—	—	—	—	—
↳1833, LM-6	*	212619	—	—	—	—	—	1,550	3,100	5,000
↳1833, LM-7	*	212620	75	95	115	145	205	285	550	1,000
↳1833, LM-8	*	212621	75	95	115	145	205	285	550	1,000
↳1833, LM-9	*	212622	75	95	115	145	205	285	550	1,000
↳1833, LM-9.1	*	395017	75	95	115	145	205	285	550	1,000
↳1833, LM-9.2	*	395018	75	95	115	145	205	285	550	1,000
↳1833, LM-10	*	212623	75	95	115	145	205	285	550	1,000

* Included in number above.

1834, 3 Over Inverted 3
FS-301

1835, Large Date

1835, Small Date

Large 5 C.

Small 5 C.

Circulation Strikes *(continued)*

	Mintage	GSID	G-4	VG-8	F-12	VF-20	EF-40	AU-50	MS-60	MS-63
1834	1,480,000	3741	$75	$95	$115	$145	$205	$285	$550	$1,000
↳1834, LM-2	*	212624	75	95	115	145	205	285	550	1,000
↳1834, LM-4	*	212625	75	95	115	145	205	285	550	1,000
↳1834, LM-5	*	212626	75	95	115	145	205	285	550	1,000
↳1834, 3 Over Inverted 3	*	3742	80	115	135	160	290	525	750	1,250
↳1834, 3 Over Inverted 3, LM-1, FS-301	*	212627	80	115	135	160	290	525	750	1,250
↳1834, 3 Over Inverted 3, LM-3, FS-301	*	212628	80	115	135	160	290	525	750	1,250
1835, All Varieties	2,760,000	395014	75	95	115	145	205	285	550	1,000
1835, Large Date, Large 5 C.	*	3744	75	95	115	145	205	285	550	1,000
↳1835, Large Date, Large 5 C., LM-1	*	212629	75	95	115	145	205	285	550	1,000
↳1835, Large Date, Large 5 C., LM-2	*	212630	80	105	125	160	225	315	600	1,100
↳1835, Large Date, Large 5 C., LM-3	*	212631	75	95	115	145	205	285	550	1,000
↳1835, Large Date, Large 5 C., LM-4	*	212632	75	95	115	145	205	285	550	1,000
↳1835, Large Date, Large 5 C., LM-7	*	212633	75	95	115	145	205	285	550	1,000
1835, Large Date, Small 5 C.	*	3745	75	95	115	145	205	285	550	1,000
↳1835, Large Date, Small 5 C., LM-5.1	*	212634	75	95	115	145	205	285	550	1,000
↳1835, Large Date, Small 5 C., LM-5.2	*	212635	75	95	115	145	205	285	550	1,000
↳1835, Large Date, Small 5 C., LM-6	*	212636	75	95	115	145	205	285	550	1,000
1835, Small Date, Large 5 C.	*	3746	75	95	115	145	205	285	550	1,050
↳1835, Small Date, Large 5 C., LM-8.1	*	212637	75	95	115	145	205	285	550	1,050
↳1835, Small Date, Large 5 C., LM-8.2	*	212638	75	95	115	145	205	285	550	1,050
↳1835, Small Date, Large 5 C., LM-9.1	*	212639	75	95	115	145	205	285	550	1,050
↳1835, Small Date, Large 5 C., LM-9.2	*	212640	75	95	115	145	205	285	550	1,050
↳1835, Small Date, Large 5 C., LM-12	*	212641	2,750	4,000	—	8,000	15,000	21,000	36,000	48,000
1835, Small Date, Small 5 C.	*	3747	75	95	115	145	205	285	550	1,000
↳1835, Small Date, Small 5 C., LM-10	*	212642	75	95	115	145	205	285	550	1,000
↳1835, Small Date, Small 5 C., LM-11	*	212643	80	105	125	160	225	315	600	1,100

* Included in number above.

Circulation Strikes *(continued)*

	Mintage	GSID	G-4	VG-8	F-12	VF-20	EF-40	AU-50	MS-60	MS-63
1836, All Varieties	1,900,000	395015	$75	$95	$115	$145	$205	$285	$550	$1,000
1836, 3 Over Inverted 3	*	3750	75	95	115	145	205	285	550	1,000
↳1836, Small 5 C., LM-2	*	212648	75	95	115	145	205	285	550	1,000
↳1836, Small 5 C., LM-4	*	212649	75	95	115	145	205	285	550	1,000
↳1836, Small 5 C., LM-5	*	212650	75	95	115	145	205	285	550	1,000
1836, Large 5 C.	*	3749	75	95	115	145	205	285	550	1,000
↳1836, Large 5 C., LM-1.1	*	212644	75	95	115	145	205	285	550	1,000
↳1836, Large 5 C., LM-1.2	*	212645	75	95	115	145	205	285	550	1,000
↳1836, Large 5 C., LM-6	*	212646	75	95	115	145	205	285	550	1,000
↳1836, Large 5 C., LM-7	*	212647	75	95	115	145	205	285	550	1,000
1836, 3 Over Inverted 3	*	3751	95	120	160	230	330	440	675	1,500
↳1836, 3 Over Inverted 3, LM-3, FS-301	*	374052	95	120	160	230	330	440	675	1,500
1837, All Varieties	871,000	395016	75	95	115	145	205	285	550	1,000
1837, Large 5 C.	*	3753	75	95	115	145	205	285	550	1,000
↳1837, Large 5 C., LM-1	*	212652	75	95	115	145	205	285	550	1,000
↳1837, Large 5 C., LM-2	*	212653	80	105	125	160	225	315	600	1,100
↳1837, Large 5 C., LM-3	*	212654	85	110	130	165	235	330	625	1,150
↳1837, Large 5 C., LM-5	*	212655	75	95	115	145	205	285	550	1,000
1837, Small 5 C.	*	3754	130	160	195	260	390	775	2,050	2,800
↳1837, Small 5 C., LM-4	*	212656	130	160	195	260	390	775	2,050	2,800

* Included in number above.

Proof Strikes

		GSID	PF-60	PF-63	PF-65
Capped Bust Half Dime, Proof	**n/a**	**73784**	**$3,750**	**$9,500**	**$27,000**
1829	20–30 est. known	3732	5,000	10,000	30,000
	Auctions: $103,500, PCGS PF-67 HA 01/12				
1830	5–6 est. known	3734	—	12,000	36,000
1831	10–20 est. known	3736	—	12,000	30,000
1832	1–2 est. known	3738	—	—	—
1834	20–30 est. known	3743	3,750	9,500	27,000
1836	2–3 est. known	3752	—	—	36,000
1837		226299	—	—	—

LIBERTY SEATED (1837–1873)

No Stars on Obverse (1837–1838): **Designer:** *Christian Gobrecht.* **Weight:** *1.34 grams.* **Composition:** *.900 silver, .100 copper.* **Diameter:** *15.5 mm.* **Edge:** *Reeded.* **Mints:** *Philadelphia and New Orleans.*

No Stars on Obverse (1837–1838), Circulation Strike

No Stars on Obverse (1837–1838), Proof Strike

Stars on Obverse (1838–1853): **Designer:** *Christian Gobrecht.* **Weight:** *1.34 grams.* **Composition:** *.900 silver, .100 copper.* **Diameter:** *15.5 mm.* **Edge:** *Reeded.* **Mints:** *Philadelphia and New Orleans.*

Stars on Obverse (1838–1853), Circulation Strike

Stars on Obverse (1838–1853), Proof Strike

Stars on Obverse, Arrows at Date, Reduced Weight (1853–1855): **Designer:** *Christian Gobrecht.* **Weight:** *1.24 grams.* **Composition:** *.900 silver, .100 copper.* **Diameter:** *15.5 mm.* **Edge:** *Reeded.* **Mints:** *Philadelphia and New Orleans.*

Stars on Obverse, Arrows at Date, Reduced Weight (1853–1855), Circulation Strike

Stars on Obverse, Arrows at Date, Reduced Weight (1853–1855), Proof Strike

Stars on Obverse, Arrows Removed, Reduced Weight (1856–1859): **Designer:** *Christian Gobrecht.* **Weight:** *1.24 grams.* **Composition:** *.900 silver, .100 copper.* **Diameter:** *15.5 mm.* **Edge:** *Reeded.* **Mints:** *Philadelphia and New Orleans.*

Stars on Obverse, Arrows Removed, Reduced Weight (1856–1859), Circulation Strike

Stars on Obverse, Arrows Removed, Reduced Weight (1856–1859), Proof Strike

Legend on Obverse (1860–1873): **Designer:** *Christian Gobrecht.* **Weight:** *1.24 grams.* **Composition:** *.900 silver, .100 copper.* **Diameter:** *15.5 mm.* **Edge:** *Reeded.* **Mints:** *Philadelphia, New Orleans, and San Francisco.*

Legend on Obverse (1860–1873), Circulation Strike

Mintmark location, 1860–1869 and 1872–1873, is on the reverse, below the bow.

Mintmark location, 1870–1872, is on the reverse, above the bow.

Legend on Obverse (1860–1873), Proof Strike

History. The Liberty Seated design without obverse stars, known as Variety 1, was used in the half dime and dime series only at the Philadelphia Mint in 1837 and the New Orleans Mint in 1838 (1838-O). The motif, by Christian Gobrecht, follows the obverse inaugurated on the 1836 silver dollar. Liberty has no drapery at her elbow. In 1838 13 obverse stars were added, and in 1840 a restyling (drapery added to the elbow) by Robert Ball Hughes appeared. Arrows were added to the sides of the date starting in 1853, through 1855; these denoted the reduction of weight under the terms of the Act of February 21, 1853. The earlier design resumed in 1856. The reverse design stayed the same during these changes. In 1860 on the half dime the legend UNITED STATES OF AMERICA was moved to the obverse, in place of the stars. The reverse displayed a "cereal wreath" (as it was called in Mint records) enclosing the words HALF DIME.

Striking and Sharpness. For half dimes dated 1837 to 1838, check the highest parts of the Liberty Seated figure (especially the head and horizontal shield stripes) and, on the reverse, the leaves. Check the denticles on both sides. These coins are very attractive, and the starless obverse gives them a cameo-like appearance. For half dimes dated 1838 to 1859, strike quality varies widely. Most from 1838 to 1852 are sharper than later ones, but there are exceptions. (Coins with "mushy" details are especially common among the high-mintage dates of the mid- to late 1850s.) On the obverse, check the star centers, the head and center of Liberty, and the denticles. On the reverse, check the wreath leaves and denticles. Excellent strike and deeply mirrored fields characterized nearly all Proofs. Points to check on coins dated 1860 to 1873 include the head of Liberty on the obverse, the wreath details on the reverse (particularly at the inside upper left, above the H of HALF) and the denticles on both sides. Generally, MS coins have excellent luster, although some struck from relapped dies tend to be prooflike and with many striae. The word LIBERTY is not an infallible guide to grading at lower levels, as on some dies the shield was in lower relief, and the letters wore away less quickly. This guideline should be used in combination with other features. Generally, Proofs are well made, with deeply mirrored fields, although some of the late 1860s and early 1870s can have weak areas. Average quality in the marketplace is higher than for larger Liberty Seated denominations.

Availability. Liberty Seated half dimes are easily available as a type, but with many scarce varieties. The Philadelphia coins are easily available in all grades. The 1838-O is a rarity in true Mint State, often is over-graded, and typically has low eye appeal. Such issues as 1849-O and 1846 are extreme rarities at the true MS level. San Francisco coins, first made in 1863, are rare in MS for the first several years. Grades above MS-65 are seen with regularity, more often than the related No Stars dimes. Quality varies widely, and many MS coins are artificially toned.

Proofs. It is likely that at least several dozen Proofs were made of the 1837 half dime, although perhaps more were made of the related dime. Today, attractive examples exist and are rare. Nearly all designated as Proofs are, indeed, Proofs. If you aspire to acquire one, select an example with deep mirror surfaces. 1858 was the first year Proofs were widely sold to collectors, and an estimated 210 silver sets were distributed. (Proofs were made of earlier dates, but in much smaller numbers.) It is believed that 800 Proofs were struck of 1859, of which slightly more than 400 found buyers. From 1860 to 1873, Proof coins were made in fair quantities each year and are readily available today. The quality of Proofs on the market varies widely, mainly due to cleaning and dipping. Patience and care are needed to find a choice example.

Grading Standards

MS-64

MS-60 to 70 (Mint State). ***Obverse:*** At MS-60 some abrasion and contact marks are evident, most noticeably on the bosom, thighs, and knees. Luster is present, but may be dull or lifeless, and interrupted in patches in the large open field. At MS-63, contact marks are very few, and abrasion is hard to detect except under magnification. An MS-65 coin has no abrasion, and contact marks are so minute as to require magnification. Luster should be full and rich, except for Philadelphia (but not San Francisco) half dimes of the early and mid-1860s. Most Mint State coins of 1861 to 1865, Philadelphia issues, will have extensive die striae (from the dies being incompletely finished). Some low-mintage Philadelphia issues may be prooflike (and some may even be mislabeled as Proofs). Clashmarks are common in this era. Half dimes of this type can be very beautiful at this level. ***Reverse:*** Comments apply as for the obverse except that in lower Mint State grades abrasion and contact marks are most noticeable on the highest parts of the leaves and the ribbon, less so on HALF DIME. The field is mainly protected by design elements and does not show abrasion as much as does the open-field obverse on a given coin.

Illustrated coin: This coin was struck in medallic alignment, as is seen with multiple examples of 1844-O, V-2.

AU-50

AU-50, 53, 55, 58 (About Uncirculated). ***Obverse:*** Light wear is seen on the thighs and knees, bosom, and head. At AU-58, the luster is extensive, but incomplete. Friction is seen in the large open field. At AU-50 and 53, luster is less. ***Reverse:*** Wear is noticeable on the leaves and ribbon. An AU-58 coin has nearly full luster—more so than on the obverse, as the design elements protect the small field areas. At AU-50 and 53, there still is significant luster, more than on the obverse.

EF-40

EF-40, 45 (Extremely Fine). ***Obverse:*** Further wear is seen on all areas, especially the thighs and knees, bosom, and head. Little or no luster is seen. ***Reverse:*** Further wear is seen on all areas, most noticeably at the leaves to each side of the wreath apex, and on the ribbon bow knot. Leaves retain details except on the higher areas.

VF-35

VF-20, 30 (Very Fine). ***Obverse:*** Further wear is seen. Most details of the gown are worn away, except in the lower-relief areas above and to the right of the shield. Hair detail is gone on the higher points. ***Reverse:*** Wear is more extensive. The highest leaves are flat, particularly the larger leaves at the top of the wreath.

F-15

F-12, 15 (Fine). ***Obverse:*** The seated figure is well worn, but with some detail above and to the right of the shield. LIBERTY on the shield is fully readable, but weak in areas. ***Reverse:*** Most detail of the leaves is gone. The rim is worn but remains bold, and most if not all denticles are visible.

VG-10

VG-8, 10 (Very Good). ***Obverse:*** The seated figure is more worn, but some detail can be seen above and to the right of the shield. The shield is discernible. In LIBERTY at least three letters are readable but very weak at VG-8; a few more appear at VG-10. ***Reverse:*** Further wear has combined the details of most leaves. The rim is complete, but weak in areas. On most coins the reverse appears to be in a slightly higher grade than the obverse.

G-4

G-4, 6 (Good). ***Obverse:*** The seated figure is worn smooth. At G-4 there are no letters in LIBERTY remaining. At G-6, traces of one or two can be seen. ***Reverse:*** Wear is more extensive. The leaves are all combined and in outline form. The rim is clear but well worn and missing in some areas, causing the outer parts of the peripheral letters to be worn away in some instances. On most coins the reverse appears to be in a slightly higher grade than the obverse.

Illustrated coin: This is a No Stars variety.

AG-3 (About Good). ***Obverse:*** The seated figure is mostly visible in outline form, with no detail. The rim is worn away. The date remains clear. ***Reverse:*** Many if not most letters are worn away, as are parts of the wreath, though this and the interior letters are discernible. The rim can usually be seen, but is weak.

Illustrated coin: This is a No Stars variety.

AG-3

PF-60 to 70 (Proof). ***Obverse and Reverse:*** Proofs that are extensively cleaned and have many hairlines, or that are dull and grainy, are lower level, such as PF-60 to 62. These are not widely desired, save for the rare (in any grade) date of 1846. Both the half dime and dime Proofs of 1837 were often cleaned, resulting in coins which have lost much of their mirror surface. With medium hairlines and good reflectivity, a grade of PF-64 is assigned, and with relatively few hairlines, gem PF-65. In various grades hairlines are most easily seen in the obverse field. PF-66 should have hairlines so delicate that magnification is needed to see them. Above that, a Proof should be free of such lines.

PF-66
Ultra Cameo

1837, Small Date
Note the flat-topped 1.

1837, Large Date
Note the pointed-top 1.

No Drapery From Elbow (1837–1840)

Drapery From Elbow (Starting 1840)

Circulation Strikes

	Mintage	GSID	G-4	VG-8	F-12	VF-20	EF-40	AU-50	MS-60	MS-63
Liberty Seated, No Stars on Obverse (1837–1838)	**n/a**	**72444**	**$49**	**$90**	**$130**	**$210**	**$340**	**$550**	**$850**	**$1,400**
Liberty Seated, Stars on Obverse (1838–1853, 1856–1859)	**n/a**	**72446**	**32**	**36**	**43**	**49**	**80**	**145**	**195**	**325**
Liberty Seated, Stars on Obverse, Arrows at Date (1853–1855)	**n/a**	**72447**	**32**	**36**	**43**	**49**	**100**	**150**	**220**	**365**
Liberty Seated, Legend on Obverse (1860–1873)	**n/a**	**72448**	**30**	**35**	**38**	**40**	**55**	**95**	**195**	**325**
1837, Large Date	1,405,000	3758	49	90	130	210	340	550	850	1,400
1837, Small Date	*	3759	49	90	130	210	340	550	900	1,500

* Included in number above.

1838, Large Stars

1838, Small Stars

1840-O, No Drapery, Normal Reverse
Note four-leaf cluster next to DIME.

1840-O, No Drapery, Transitional Reverse
FS-901. Note three-leaf cluster next to DIME.

Circulation Strikes *(continued)*

	Mintage	GSID	G-4	VG-8	F-12	VF-20	EF-40	AU-50	MS-60	MS-63
1838-O, No Stars	70,000	3802	$195	$290	$575	$1,100	$2,700	$4,400	$6,500	$12,000
1838, No Drapery, Large Stars	2,225,000	3760	38	43	50	75	120	210	360	600
↳1838, No Drapery, Large Stars, Rusted Reverse Die, FS-901	*	213524	—	—	—	—	—	—	—	—
1838, No Drapery, Small Stars	*	3761	45	60	95	140	260	325	725	950
1839, No Drapery	1,069,150	3762	38	43	50	75	120	210	390	675
1839-O, No Drapery	1,291,000	3803	40	46	55	85	160	420	1,000	2,000
↳1839-O, No Drapery, Large O, FS-501	*	392946	—	—	—	—	—	—	—	—
1840, No Drapery	1,034,000	3763	38	43	50	75	120	210	360	600
1840-O, No Drapery	695,000	3804	135	180	255	340	625	775	2,000	5,500
↳1840-O, No Drapery, Huge O, FS-501	*	392980	150	195	280	370	675	850	2,200	6,000
↳1840-O, No Drapery, Transitional Reverse, FS-901	*	227324	—	—	—	—	—	—	—	—
1840, With Drapery	310,085	3764	60	90	135	190	260	345	525	1,000
1840-O, With Drapery	240,000	3805	125	185	285	450	875	1,600	7,000	22,000
1841	1,150,000	3765	32	36	43	49	80	145	195	325
1841-O	815,000	3806	90	125	170	230	340	455	1,250	2,600
1842	815,000	3766	32	36	43	49	80	145	285	390
1842-O	350,000	3807	90	145	230	465	725	1,100	1,550	2,250
1843	815,000	3767	32	36	43	49	80	145	210	390
↳1843, Repunched Date, FS-301	*	392947	—	—	—	—	—	—	—	—
1844	430,000	3768	35	39	46	60	120	210	370	550
↳1844, Repunched Date, FS-301	*	199176	39	43	50	65	130	230	410	600
1844-O	220,000	3808	150	235	370	775	1,500	2,500	7,500	11,000
1845	1,564,000	3769	32	36	43	49	80	145	215	390
↳1845, Repunched Date, FS-301	*	199177	—	—	—	—	—	—	—	—
↳1845, Repunched Date, FS-302	*	199178	—	—	—	—	—	—	—	—
1846	27,000	3770	850	1,350	2,000	3,000	4,750	9,000	21,500	50,500
1847	1,274,000	3771	32	36	43	49	80	145	195	340

* Included in number above.

1848, Medium Date

1848, Large Date

1849, 9 Over 6
FS-301

1849, 9 Over Widely Spaced 6
FS-302

Circulation Strikes *(continued)*

	Mintage	GSID	G-4	VG-8	F-12	VF-20	EF-40	AU-50	MS-60	MS-63
1848, Medium Date	668,000	3772	$32	$36	$43	$49	$80	$145	$360	$575
↳1848, Medium Date, Repunched Date, FS-302	*	227325	—	—	—	—	—	—	—	—
1848, Large Date	*	3773	43	60	90	130	230	525	950	2,200
↳1848, Large Date, FS-301	*	392948	—	—	—	—	—	—	—	—
1848-O	600,000	3809	39	50	65	115	230	390	650	1,000
1849, Normal Date	1,309,000	3774	32	36	43	49	80	145	260	525
1849, 9 Over 6 (a)	*	3811	55	85	130	145	215	390	775	1,200
↳1849, 9 Over 6, FS-301 (a)	*	297894	—	—	—	—	—	—	—	—
↳1849, 9 Over Widely Placed 6, FS-302	*	3810	55	85	130	150	215	390	900	1,550
↳1849, 9 Over So-Called 8, FS-303	*	297896	—	—	—	—	—	—	—	—
1849-O	140,000	3812	95	155	260	375	650	1,150	2,250	3,900
1850	955,000	3775	32	36	43	49	80	145	195	360
1850-O	690,000	3813	35	39	46	75	145	290	725	1,550
1851	781,000	3776	32	36	43	49	80	145	235	390
1851-O	860,000	3814	35	43	50	75	150	290	525	1,000
1852	1,000,500	3777	32	36	43	49	80	145	195	370
1852-O	260,000	3815	47	80	130	180	325	575	1,200	3,000
1853, No Arrows	135,000	3778	50	90	140	210	340	625	775	1,100
1853-O, No Arrows	160,000	3816	335	575	950	1,550	3,000	4,050	12,000	15,500
1853, With Arrows	13,210,020	3779	32	36	43	49	100	150	220	365
↳1853, With Arrows, Misplaced Date, FS-301	*	392949	—	—	—	—	—	—	—	—
1853-O, With Arrows	2,200,000	3817	34	39	46	55	120	195	470	1,150
1854	5,740,000	3780	32	36	43	49	100	150	220	365
1854-O	1,560,000	3818	32	36	46	55	100	215	390	900
1855	1,750,000	3781	32	36	43	49	100	150	220	365
1855-O	600,000	3819	32	39	46	70	135	210	650	1,100
1856	4,880,000	3782	32	36	43	49	80	145	195	325
↳1856, Misplaced Date, FS-301	*	392950	—	—	—	—	—	—	—	—
1856-O	1,100,000	3820	32	36	46	60	115	260	525	975
1857	7,280,000	3783	32	36	43	49	80	145	195	325
1857-O	1,380,000	3821	40	42	49	60	100	210	390	625
1858	3,500,000	3784	32	36	43	49	80	145	195	325

* Included in number above. **a.** As noted in the *Cherrypickers' Guide to Rare Die Varieties, Vol. II* (sixth edition), Fivaz and Stanton contend that this is actually a 9 Over 8 overdate.

1858, Repunched High Date
FS-301

1858, Over Inverted Date
FS-302

1861, 1 Over 0
FS-301

Circulation Strikes *(continued)*

	Mintage	GSID	G-4	VG-8	F-12	VF-20	EF-40	AU-50	MS-60	MS-63
1858, Over Inverted Date	*	3785	$90	$115	$150	$180	$365	$410	$950	$1,600
↳1858, Over Inverted Date, FS-302	*	377366	90	115	150	180	365	410	950	1,600
1858, Repunched High Date	*	3756	70	110	130	155	260	390	850	1,900
↳1858, Repunched High Date, FS-301	*	377367	—	—	—	—	—	—	—	—
1858-O	1,660,000	3822	36	42	49	55	95	145	290	455
1859	340,000	3786	32	36	46	50	90	155	235	390
1859-O	560,000	3823	35	42	70	100	160	235	390	525
1860, Obverse of 1859 (With Stars), Reverse of 1860 (b)	100	3787	—	—	—	—	—	—	3,000	4,500
1860	798,000	3788	30	35	38	40	55	95	195	325
1860-O	1,060,000	3824	32	40	46	50	90	145	325	525
1861	3,360,000	3789	38	40	43	46	55	95	195	325
1861, 1 Over 0	*	3825	43	55	90	135	260	320	575	775
↳1861, 1 Over 0, FS-301	*	375399	43	55	90	135	260	320	575	775
1862	1,492,000	3790	30	35	38	40	55	95	195	325
1863	18,000	3791	210	270	385	435	550	675	850	950
1863-S	100,000	3826	40	75	130	170	260	455	850	1,100
↳1863-S, Misplaced Date, FS-301	*	375400	—	—	—	—	—	—	—	—
1864	48,000	3792	365	575	875	975	1,250	1,300	1,400	1,500
1864-S	90,000	3827	115	155	215	305	525	725	1,000	1,500
1865	13,000	3793	325	490	725	825	1,000	1,100	1,200	1,400
1865-S	120,000	3828	55	85	130	185	325	650	1,200	2,500
↳1865-S, Repunched Date, FS-301	*	227326	—	—	—	—	—	—	—	—
1866	10,000	3794	575	675	750	850	1,000	1,150	1,500	2,050
1866-S	120,000	3829	36	55	75	125	230	390	575	1,200
1867	8,000	3795	490	600	825	875	950	1,100	1,250	1,700
1867-S	120,000	3830	55	85	130	160	230	305	650	1,150
1868	88,600	3796	60	100	155	200	310	455	650	900
1868-S	280,000	3831	30	35	40	50	80	150	375	600
1869	208,000	3797	30	35	40	60	95	130	230	325
1869-S	230,000	3832	30	35	40	65	120	145	365	950
1870	535,000	3798	30	35	38	40	55	95	195	325
1870-S	unique	3833	—	—	—	—	—	—	—	3,600,000
	Auctions: $3,120,000, PCGS MS-64 HA 01/23									
1871	1,873,000	3799	30	35	38	40	55	95	195	325
↳1871, Misplaced Date, FS-301	*	227327	—	—	—	—	—	—	—	—
1871-S	161,000	3834	32	38	45	65	95	180	275	430

* Included in number above. **b.** Classified as Judd-232 in *United States Pattern Coins* (10th edition), this features the obverse design of 1859 and the reverse of 1860.

1872, Doubled Die Obverse
FS-101

Circulation Strikes *(continued)*

	Mintage	GSID	G-4	VG-8	F-12	VF-20	EF-40	AU-50	MS-60	MS-63
1872	2,947,000	3800	$30	$35	$38	$40	$55	$95	$195	$325
↳**1872, Doubled Die Obverse, FS-101**	*	227328	—	—	—	—	—	—	—	—
1872-S, Mintmark Below Bow	837,000	3835	30	35	38	40	55	95	195	325
↳**1872-S, Mintmark Below Bow, FS-301**	*	392951	—	—	—	—	—	—	—	—
↳**1872-S, Mintmark Below Bow, FS-302**	*	227329	30	35	38	40	55	95	195	325
1872-S, Mintmark Above Bow	*	3836	30	35	38	40	55	95	195	325
1873	712,000	3801	30	35	38	40	55	95	195	325
1873-S	324,000	3837	30	35	40	47	60	95	195	325

* Included in number above.

Proof Strikes

	Mintage	GSID	PF-60	PF-63	PF-65
Liberty Seated, No Stars on Obverse (1837–1838), Proof	**n/a**	**76283**	**$8,000**	**$17,000**	**$38,500**
Liberty Seated, No Drapery (1838–1840), Proof	**n/a**	**76284**	**14,500**	**21,000**	**38,500**
Liberty Seated, Stars on Obverse (1838–1853, 1856–1859), Proof	**n/a**	**74192**	**525**	**900**	**2,400**
Same, Proof Cameo	**n/a**	**74193**	**—**	**1,250**	**2,900**
Same, Proof Deep Cameo	**n/a**	**74194**	**—**	**—**	**4,750**
Liberty Seated, Stars, Arrows at Date (1853–1855), Proof	**n/a**	**74195**	**4,400**	**7,500**	**10,000**
Liberty Seated, Legend on Obverse (1860–1873), Proof	**n/a**	**74198**	**325**	**550**	**1,000**
Same, Proof Cameo	**n/a**	**74199**	**—**	**750**	**1,250**
Same, Proof Deep Cameo	**n/a**	**74200**	**—**	**—**	**2,250**
1837	20 est. known	3839	8,000	17,000	38,500
	Auctions: $105,750, PCGS PF-67 HA 06/14				
1838, No Drapery	2–3 est. known	3842	—	42,000	—
	Auctions: $182,125, NGC PF-66 HA 01/14				
1839, No Drapery	5–7 est. known	3845	14,500	21,000	38,500
1840, No Drapery	5 est. known	3848	14,500	21,000	38,500
1840, With Drapery	5–10 est. known	3849	14,500	21,000	38,500
1841	7–10 est. known	3854	—	17,000	29,000
1842	5–10 est. known	3857	—	—	21,000
1843	10–15 est. known	3860	—	12,500	24,000
1844	10–15 est. known	3863	7,500	12,000	18,000
1845	10–15 est. known	3866	—	14,000	30,000
1846	10–12 est. known	3869	—	12,500	26,500
1847	8–12 est. known	3872	—	12,500	21,500
1848	6 known	3875	—	14,000	29,000
1849	10–15 est. known	3878	—	14,000	26,500
1850	4–6 est. known	3881	—	14,000	29,000

* Included in number above.

1860, Obverse of 1859, Reverse of 1860
Transitional pattern, with stars (Judd-267).

Proof Strikes *(continued)*

	Mintage	GSID	PF-60	PF-63	PF-65
1852	5–10 est. known	3887	$7,000	$9,500	$20,000
1853, With Arrows	3–5 est. known	3890	—	79,000	—
1854, With Arrows	12–16 est. known	3893	4,400	7,500	10,000
1855, With Arrows	15–20 est. known	3896	4,400	7,500	10,000
1856	40–50 est. known	3899	2,500	4,000	7,250
1857	50–75 est. known	3902	2,050	3,000	4,250
1858	300	3905	775	1,150	3,100
1859	800	3908	525	900	2,400
1859, Obverse of 1859 (With Stars), Reverse of 1860 (a)	20	3909	26,500	42,000	90,000
1860	1,000	3912	325	550	1,000
1861	1,000	3915	340	550	1,000
1862	550	3918	325	550	1,000
1863	460	3921	325	550	1,000
1864	470	3924	325	550	1,000
1865	500	3927	390	650	1,500
1866	725	3930	325	550	1,000
1867	625	3933	325	550	1,000
1868	600	3936	325	550	1,000
1869	600	3939	325	550	1,000
1870	1,000	3942	325	550	1,000
1871	960	3945	325	550	1,000
1872	950	3948	325	550	1,000
1873	600	3951	325	550	1,000

a. This transitional issue, made surreptitiously at the Mint for a private collector, has the new Liberty Seated die made in the old style of 1859, but with the date of 1860. The reverse is the regular die of 1860, with a cereal wreath. Classified as Judd-267 in *United States Pattern Coins* (10th edition).

Dimes
1796 to Date

AN OVERVIEW OF DIMES

A collection of dimes ranging from 1796 to date includes many interesting issues. As a type, none are super-rare, but earlier types, combining low mintages with commonly weak striking, can be a challenge for the collector.

Scan for additional information.

The 1796–1797 dime with Draped Bust obverse, Small Eagle reverse, is the rarest of the dime types by far, with fewer than 50,000 pieces minted. These hail from an era in which there was no numismatic interest in saving such coins. Finding a choice example in whatever grade desired will require time and effort.

Then comes the Draped Bust obverse, Heraldic Eagle reverse type, made from 1798 through 1807 (except for 1799). Today these are available easily enough in circulated grades, but are elusive in Mint State. Nearly all are lightly struck—another challenge. Capped Bust dimes of the 1809–1828 years also require connoisseurship to locate a sharply struck specimen. For all of these early types some compromise with perfection is required.

Later Capped Bust dimes of 1828 to 1837 can be found well struck, as can be the later variations within the Liberty Seated type. Barber, Mercury, and Roosevelt dimes are easy to find in just about any grade desired.

Proofs are most readily available from the Liberty Seated era to the present and are sometimes included in type sets, usually answering the call for sharply struck pieces, as most (but not all) were made with care.

Controversy over Chief Engraver John R. Sinnock's design arose after claims that Sinnock had borrowed his design from Selma Burke's bas relief, as seen at the Recorder of Deeds building in Washington, D.C.

For the Collector and Investor: Dimes as a Specialty

Dimes have been a very popular denomination to collect on a systematic basis. Generally, interest is separated into different eras. Those of the early years, the Draped Bust and Capped Bust issues, 1796 to 1837, are enthusiastically sought not only for dates and major varieties (as, for example, those listed in the charts to follow), but also by more rarefied die varieties. Aficionados use the book *Early United States Dimes, 1796–1837*, whose listings are by JR numbers, for John

Reich, the designer of the Capped Bust silver issues. The John Reich Collectors Society (www.jrcs.org), publisher of the *John Reich Journal*, serves as a forum for the exchange of ideas and new information.

Among early varieties, the 1796; 1797, 16 Stars; and 1797, 13 Stars, are each rare in all grades. Dimes with the Heraldic Eagle reverse, 1798–1807, are generally scarce, but not prohibitively rare, although Mint State coins are elusive. Among the reverse dies some were shared with contemporary quarter eagles of like design and diameter—feasible as there is no indication of denomination on them. Indeed, there was no mark of value on any dime until 1809.

Among Classic Head dimes of the 1809–1828 years, the 1822 is the key date and is especially rare in high grades. Among the modified Classic Head dimes of 1829–1837, all varieties listed in this book are available without difficulty. An example of how a newly discovered variety can be considered unique or exceedingly rare, and later be recognized as plentiful, is provided by the 1830, 30 Over 29, overdate, first publicized by Don Taxay in 1970 in *Scott's Comprehensive Catalogue of United States Coinage* (cover-dated 1971). The overdate was then considered one of a kind, but since then dozens more have been identified.

Liberty Seated dimes of the various varieties have been a popular specialty over a long period of time. There are no impossible rarities except for the unique 1873-CC, Without Arrows, but certain other varieties are very hard to find, including the Carson City issues of the early 1870s.

Barber dimes can be collected by date and mint from 1892 to 1916, except for the 1894-S, of which only 24 are believed to have been struck, with only about 10 accounted for today. The other Barber varieties range from common to scarce. Mercury dimes, 1916–1945, have an enthusiastic following. The key issues are 1916-D (in particular); 1921; 1921-D; 1942, 2 Over 1; and 1942-D, 2 Over 1. Roosevelt dimes from 1946 to date can easily be collected by date and mint and are very popular.

EXPLORING VARIETIES

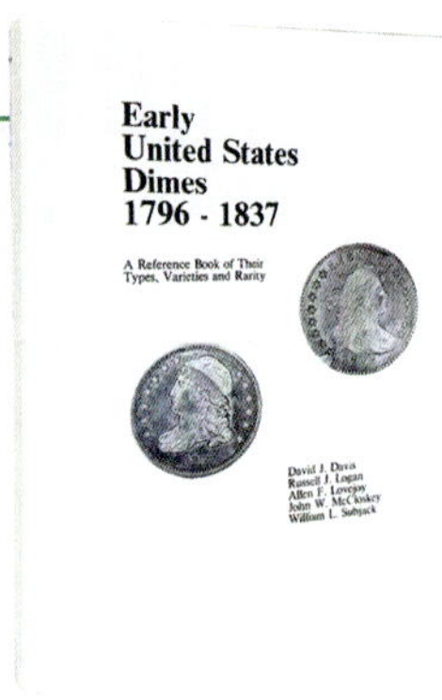

This book is the standard reference for early U.S. dimes and introduces a system of JR (John Reich) numbers for cataloging die varieties date by date. This system enables collectors and dealers to communicate about specific die marriages.

Davis, David J.; Russell J. Logan; Allen F. Lovejoy; John W. McCloskey; William L. Subjack. *Early United States Dimes, 1796-1837: A Reference Book of Their Types, Varieties, and Rarity.* Ypsilanti, MI: John Reich Collectors Society, 1984.

DRAPED BUST, SMALL EAGLE REVERSE (1796–1797)

Designer: *Probably Gilbert Stuart.* **Engraver:** *Robert Scot.*
Weight: *2.7 grams.* **Composition:** *.8924 silver, .1076 copper.*
Diameter: *Approximately 19 mm.* **Edge:** *Reeded.* **Mint:** *Philadelphia.*

History. Dimes were first minted for circulation in 1796. There are no records of publicity surrounding their debut. The coins featured the Draped Bust obverse, as used on cents and other silver coins, combined with the Small Eagle reverse. Some 1796 dimes exhibit prooflike surfaces, suggesting that they may have been "presentation pieces," but no records exist to confirm this possibility.

Striking and Sharpness. Most dimes of this type have weakness or problems in one area or another, usually more so on those dated 1797. Points to check for sharpness include the hair of Liberty, the drapery lines on the bust, the centers of the stars, and, on the reverse, the breast and wing feathers of the eagle. Also check for adjustment marks. A sharply struck coin is a goal, not necessarily a reality. Sharp striking and excellent eye appeal add dramatically to the value.

Availability. This is the rarest and most expensive type in the dime series. Within any desired grade, examples should be selected with great care, as many have problems of one sort or another. MS coins are especially rare; when seen they are usually dated 1796. Dimes of 1797 are much rarer in all grades, and nearly impossible to find in MS-63 or finer.

Grading Standards

MS-63

MS-60 to 70 (Mint State). ***Obverse:*** At MS-60, some abrasion and contact marks are evident, most noticeably on the cheek, the drapery, and the right field. Luster is present, but may be dull or lifeless, and interrupted in patches. At MS-63, contact marks are very few, and abrasion is hard to detect except under magnification, although this type is sometimes graded liberally due to its rarity. An MS-65 coin has no abrasion, and contact marks are so minute as to require magnification. Luster should be full and rich. Coins graded above MS-65 are more theoretical than actual for this type—but they do exist, and are defined by having fewer marks as perfection is approached. ***Reverse:*** Comments apply as for the obverse, except that abrasion and marks are most noticeable on the eagle at the center, a situation complicated by the fact that this area was sometimes lightly struck. The field area is small and is protected by lettering and the wreath, and in any given grade shows fewer marks than on the obverse.

Illustrated coin: This coin is one of only two known with this triangular rim break on the reverse. The dies were likely discarded shortly after the break occurred. Also note the die break from the rim break to the eagle's left wing.

AU-55

AU-50, 53, 55, 58 (About Uncirculated). ***Obverse:*** Light wear is seen on the hair area above the ear and extending to left of the forehead, on the ribbon, and on the bosom, more so at AU-50 than at AU-53 or 55. An AU-58 coin has minimal traces of wear. An AU-50 coin has luster in protected areas among the stars and letters, with little in the open fields or on the portrait. At AU-58, most luster is present in the fields, but is worn away on the highest parts of the motifs. Generally, grading guidelines for this dime type follow those of the related half dimes. ***Reverse:*** Light wear is seen on the eagle's body (keep in mind that the higher parts of this area might be lightly struck) and the edges of the wings. Light wear is seen on the wreath and lettering. Luster is the best key to actual wear. This ranges from perhaps 20 percent remaining in protected areas (at AU-50) to nearly full mint bloom (at AU-58).

EF-45

EF-40, 45 (Extremely Fine). ***Obverse:*** More wear is evident on the upper hair area and the ribbon, and on the drapery and bosom. Excellent detail remains in low-relief areas of the hair. The stars show wear as do the date and letters. Luster, if present at all, is minimal and in protected areas. ***Reverse:*** The eagle shows more wear, this being the focal point to check. Many feathers remain on the interior areas of the wings. Additional wear is on the wreath and letters, but many details are present. Some luster may be seen in protected areas, and if present is slightly more abundant than on the obverse.

Illustrated coin: Note the single adjustment mark running across the eagle's chest. Most examples of this die variety bear similar adjustment marks at varying angles.

VF-30

VF-20, 30 (Very Fine). ***Obverse:*** The higher-relief areas of hair are well worn at VF-20, less so at VF-30. The drapery and bosom show extensive wear. The stars have more wear, making them appear larger (an optical illusion seen on most worn silver coins of this era). ***Reverse:*** The body of the eagle shows few if any feathers, while the wings have about half of the feathers visible, depending on the strike. At VF-30 more than half of the feathers may show. The leaves lack most detail and are in outline form. Scattered, non-disfiguring marks are normal for this and lower grades. Any major defects should be noted separately.

F-12, 15 (Fine). ***Obverse:*** Wear is more extensive than on a Very Fine coin, particularly noticeable on the hair, face, and bosom, and the stars appear larger. About half the hair detail remains, most noticeably behind the neck and shoulder. The rim may be partially worn away and blend into the field. ***Reverse:*** Wear is more extensive. Now, feather details are diminished, with fewer than half remaining on the wings. The wreath and lettering are worn further, and the rim is usually weak in areas, although some denticles can be seen.

F-12

Illustrated coin: This coin falls at the low end of the Fine range.

VG-8, 10 (Very Good). ***Obverse:*** The portrait is mostly seen in outline form, with most hair strands gone, although there is some definition at the back of the hair and behind the shoulder. The ear is discernible, as is the eye. The stars appear larger still, again an illusion. The rim is weak in areas. LIBERTY and the date are readable and usually full, although some letters may be weak at their tops. ***Reverse:*** The eagle is mostly an outline with parts blending into the field (on lighter strikes). The rim is worn, as are the letters, with some weak, but the motto is readable.

VG-8

G-4, 6 (Good). ***Obverse:*** Wear is more extensive, and some stars may be partly missing. The head is an outline. The eye is visible only in outline form. The rim is well worn or even missing in areas. LIBERTY is worn, and parts of some letters may be missing, but elements of all should be readable. The date is readable, but worn. ***Reverse:*** The eagle is flat and discernible in outline form, and may be blending into the field. The wreath is well worn. Some of the letters may be partly missing. At this level some "averaging" can be done. If the letters are stronger than usual in one area, but some are missing in another area, the coin can still qualify as G-4.

G-4

AG-3 (About Good). ***Obverse:*** Wear is so extensive that the coin is barely identifiable. The head is in outline form. LIBERTY is mostly gone, same for the stars. The date, while readable, may be partially worn away. ***Reverse:*** The reverse is well worn with parts of the wreath and lettering missing.

AG-3

1797, 16 Stars

1797, 13 Stars

Circulation Strikes

	Mintage	GSID	AG-3	G-4	VG-8	F-12	VF-20	EF-40	AU-50	MS-60	MS-63
Draped Bust, Small Eagle Reverse (1796–1797)	**n/a**	**72453**	**$3,500**	**$4,400**	**$5,000**	**$6,250**	**$8,000**	**$11,000**	**$15,000**	**$25,000**	**$43,000**
1796	22,135	3957	3,500	4,400	5,000	6,250	8,000	11,000	15,000	25,000	43,000
	Auctions: $881,250, PCGS MS-67 HA 06/14										
↳1796, JR-1	*	213014	3,500	4,400	5,000	6,250	8,000	11,000	15,000	25,000	43,000
	Auctions: $144,000, PCGS MS-66 HA 04/25; $750,000, PCGS MS-67 HA 04/25										
↳1796, JR-2	*	213015	3,500	4,400	5,000	6,250	8,000	11,000	15,000	25,000	43,000
	Auctions: $141,000, PCGS MS-66 HA 08/15										
↳1796, JR-3	*	213016	3,850	4,800	5,500	7,000	9,000	12,000	16,500	27,500	47,500
↳1796, JR-4	*	213017	3,500	4,400	5,000	6,250	8,000	11,000	15,000	25,000	43,000
	Auctions: $372,000, PCGS MS-66 HA 01/23										
↳1796, JR-5	*	213018	3,850	4,800	5,500	7,000	9,000	12,000	16,500	27,500	47,500
↳1796, JR-6	*	241023	3,500	4,400	5,000	6,250	8,000	11,000	15,000	25,000	43,000
	Auctions: $793,125, PCGS MS-68 HA 08/14										
↳1796, JR-7	*	213019	—	—	—	—	—	—	—	—	—
1797, 16 Stars	25,261	3958	3,500	4,400	5,000	6,250	8,000	12,000	17,500	38,500	57,500
↳1797, 16 Stars, JR-1	*	374671	3,500	4,400	5,000	6,250	8,000	12,000	17,500	38,500	57,500
	Auctions: $199,750, PCGS MS-66 SBG 05/15										
1797, 13 Stars	*	3959	3,850	4,800	5,500	7,000	8,500	15,500	22,000	57,500	90,000
	Auctions: $402,500, NGC MS-65 HA 08/08										
↳1797, 13 Stars, JR-2	*	374672	3,850	4,800	5,500	7,000	8,500	15,500	22,000	57,500	90,000
	Auctions: $176,250, PCGS MS-64 SBG 05/15										

* Included in number above.

DRAPED BUST, HERALDIC EAGLE REVERSE (1798–1807)

Designer: *Robert Scot.* **Weight:** *2.7 grams.* **Composition:** *.8924 silver, .1076 copper.* **Diameter:** *Approximately 19 mm.* **Edge:** *Reeded.* **Mint:** *Philadelphia.*

History. Dimes of this style were minted each year from 1798 to 1807 (with the exception of 1799 and 1805). The designs follow those of other silver coins of the era.

Striking and Sharpness. Nearly all have one area or another of light striking. On the obverse, check the hair details and drapery lines, and the star centers. On the reverse, the upper right of the shield and the adjacent part of the eagle's wing often are soft, and several or even most stars may be lightly defined (sharp stars show sharply peaked centers); high parts of the clouds are often weak. Denticles are likely to be weak or missing in areas on either side. Expect to compromise on the strike; a sharply struck coin is a goal, not necessarily a reality. Certain reverse dies of this type were also used to coin quarter eagles. Sharp striking and excellent eye appeal dramatically add to a Draped Bust dime's value, this being particularly true for the dates most often seen in MS: 1805 and 1807 (which are usually weakly struck, especially 1807).

Availability. Although certain die varieties are rare, the basic years are available, with 1805 and 1807 being the most often seen. As a class, MS coins are rare. Again, when seen they are usually dated 1805 or 1807, and have areas of striking weakness. Coins of 1801 through 1804 are scarce in VF and higher grades, very scarce in AU and better.

Grading Standards

MS-62

MS-60 to 70 (Mint State). ***Obverse:*** At MS-60 some abrasion and contact marks are evident, most noticeably on the cheek, the drapery at the shoulder, and the right field. Luster is present, but may be dull or lifeless, and interrupted in patches. At MS-63, contact marks are very few, and abrasion is hard to detect except under magnification. An MS-65 coin has no abrasion, and contact marks are so minute as to require magnification. Luster should be full and rich. Coins graded above MS-65 are more theoretical than actual for this type—but they do exist, and are defined by having fewer marks as perfection is approached. ***Reverse:*** Comments apply as for the obverse, except that abrasion and marks are most noticeable on the eagle's neck, the tips of the wing, and the tail. The field area is complex, without much open space, given the stars above the eagle, the arrows and olive branch, and other features. Accordingly, marks are not as noticeable as on the obverse.

Illustrated coin: Attractive luster and toning increase the eye appeal and desirability of this coin, despite softer-than-average striking. More than one important twentieth-century collector has called this the finest dime of its kind.

AU-50

AU-50, 53, 55, 58 (About Uncirculated). ***Obverse:*** Light wear is seen on the hair area above the ear and extending to left of the forehead, on the ribbon, and on the drapery at the shoulder, more so at AU-50 than at AU-53 or 55. An AU-58 coin has minimal traces of wear. An AU-50 coin has luster in protected areas among the stars and letters, with little in the open fields or on the portrait. At AU-58, most luster is present in the fields, but is worn away on the highest parts of the motifs. ***Reverse:*** Comments as preceding, except that the eagle's neck, the tips and top of the wings, the clouds, and the tail now show noticeable wear, as do other features. As always, a familiarity with a given die variety will help differentiate striking weakness from actual wear. Luster ranges from perhaps 20 percent remaining in protected areas (at AU-50) to nearly full mint bloom (at AU-58). Often the reverse of this type will retain much more luster than the obverse.

EF-45

EF-40, 45 (Extremely Fine). ***Obverse:*** More wear is evident on the upper hair area and the ribbon and on the drapery and bosom. Excellent detail remains in low-relief areas of the hair. The stars show wear, as do the date and letters. Luster, if present at all, is minimal and in protected areas. ***Reverse:*** The neck lacks feather detail on its highest points. Feathers have lost some detail near the edges of the wings, and some areas of the horizontal lines in the shield may be blended together, particularly at the right (an area that is also susceptible to weak striking). Some traces of luster may be seen, more so at EF-45 than at EF-40.

Illustrated coin: Note the die crack on the reverse from above OF to below the eagle's left foot. There is also some die clashing evident in the field behind the eagle. This reverse was used to coin dimes long after it was damaged.

VF-20

VF-20, 30 (Very Fine). ***Obverse:*** The higher-relief areas of hair are well worn at VF-20, less so at VF-30. The drapery and bosom show extensive wear. The stars have more wear, making them appear larger (an optical illusion seen on most worn silver coins of this era). ***Reverse:*** Wear is greater, including on the shield and wing feathers. Star centers are flat. Other areas have lost detail, as well. E PLURIBUS UNUM is complete (this incuse feature tended to wear away slowly).

Illustrated coin: Here is a problem-free example with normal wear for this grade.

F-15

F-12, 15 (Fine). ***Obverse:*** Wear is more extensive than on a Very Fine coin, particularly noticeable on the hair, face, and bosom, and the stars appear larger. About half the hair detail remains, most noticeably behind the neck and shoulder. The rim may be partially worn away and blend into the field. ***Reverse:*** Wear is even more extensive, with the shield and wing feathers being points to observe. About half of the feathers are visible (depending on striking). E PLURIBUS UNUM may have a few letters worn away. The clouds all seem to be connected. The stars are weak. Parts of the border and lettering may be weak.

Illustrated coin: There are some digs in the fields of both the obverse and reverse.

VG-8

VG-8, 10 (Very Good). ***Obverse:*** The portrait is mostly seen in outline form, with most hair strands gone, although there is some definition at the back of the hair and behind the shoulder. The ear may be discernible. The eye is evident. The stars appear larger still, again an illusion. The rim is weak in areas. LIBERTY and the date are readable and usually full, although some letters may be weak at their tops. ***Reverse:*** Half or so of the letters in the motto are worn away. Most feathers are worn away, although separation of some may be seen. Some stars are faint. The border blends into the field in areas, and some letters are weak. Sharpness can vary widely depending on the die variety. At this level, grading by the obverse first, then checking the reverse, is recommended.

G-4

G-4, 6 (Good). ***Obverse:*** Some stars may be partly missing. The head is an outline. The eye is visible only in outline form. The rim is well worn or even missing in areas. LIBERTY is worn, and parts of some letters may be missing, but elements of all should be readable. The date is readable, but worn. ***Reverse:*** The upper part of the eagle is flat, and feathers are noticeable at the lower edge of the wing. Some scattered feather detail may or may not be seen. The upper part of the shield is flat or nearly so, depending on the variety. Only a few letters of the motto can be seen, although this depends on the variety. The rim is worn extensively, and a few letters may be missing.

AG-3 (About Good). ***Obverse:*** Wear is very extensive, and some stars and letters are extremely weak or missing entirely. The date is readable. ***Reverse:*** Extensive wear is seen overall, with the rim worn away and some areas worn smooth. The eagle can be discerned in outline form, but not necessarily completely. A few stray motto letters may remain. Sometimes the obverse can be exceedingly worn (but the date must be readable) and the reverse with more detail, or vice-versa.

AG-3

1798, 8 Over 7

1798, 8 Over 7, 16-Star Reverse

1798, 8 Over 7, 13-Star Reverse

1798, Large 8

1798, Small 8

Circulation Strikes

	Mintage	GSID	AG-3	G-4	VG-8	F-12	VF-20	EF-40	AU-50	MS-60	MS-63
Draped Bust, Heraldic Eagle Reverse (1798–1807)	**n/a**	**72454**	**$625**	**$875**	**$1,200**	**$1,500**	**$2,300**	**$3,800**	**$5,000**	**$7,000**	**$10,000**
1798, 8 Over 7, 16-Star Reverse	27,550	4014	1,000	1,250	1,750	2,250	2,750	4,100	5,250	8,750	21,000
	Auctions: $117,500, PCGS MS-65 SBG 10/15										
↳1798, 8 Over 7, 16-Star Reverse, JR-1	*	374673	1,000	1,250	1,750	2,250	2,750	4,100	5,250	8,750	21,000
1798, 8 Over 7, 13-Star Reverse	*	4015	3,500	4,750	7,500	10,000	12,000	18,000	30,000	42,000	216,000
	Auctions: $103,500, PCGS MS-63 HA 08/08										
↳1798, 8 Over 7, 13-Star Reverse, JR-2	*	374674	3,500	4,750	7,500	10,000	12,000	18,000	30,000	42,000	216,000
	Auctions: $199,750, PCGS MS-63 SBG 05/15										
1798, Large 8	*	3960	850	1,250	1,600	2,750	3,250	4,500	5,250	13,000	39,000
↳1798, Large 8, JR-4	*	374675	850	1,250	1,600	2,750	3,250	4,500	5,250	13,000	39,000
1798, Small 8	*	3961	1,250	2,250	3,000	4,000	7,500	12,000	18,000	57,000	72,000
	Auctions: $253,000, NGC MS-66 HA 08/08										
↳1798, Small 8, JR-3	*	374676	1,250	2,250	3,000	4,000	7,500	12,000	18,000	57,000	72,000
	Auctions: $141,000, PCGS MS-65 SBG 05/15										

* Included in number above.

1804, 13-Star Reverse

1804, 14-Star Reverse

1805, 4 Berries

1805, 5 Berries

Circulation Strikes *(continued)*

	Mintage	GSID	AG-3	G-4	VG-8	F-12	VF-20	EF-40	AU-50	MS-60	MS-63
1800	21,760	3962	$950	$1,150	$1,500	$2,500	$3,450	$4,800	$8,750	$17,000	$36,000
	Auctions: $352,500, PCGS MS-66 HA 06/14										
↳1800, JR-1	*	213020	950	1,150	1,500	2,500	3,450	4,800	8,750	17,000	36,000
↳1800, JR-2	*	213021	950	1,150	1,500	2,500	3,450	4,800	8,750	17,000	36,000
	Auctions: $192,000, PCGS MS-66 HA 08/22										
1801	34,640	3963	1,200	1,500	2,500	3,450	4,400	7,500	12,500	49,000	75,000
↳1801, JR-1	*	213022	1,200	1,500	2,500	3,450	4,400	7,500	12,500	49,000	75,000
	Auctions: $111,625, NGC MS-65 HA 10/14										
↳1801, JR-2	*	213023	1,200	1,500	2,500	3,450	4,400	7,500	12,500	49,000	75,000
1802	10,975	3964	1,700	2,250	3,200	4,200	6,500	10,000	18,000	36,000	114,000
	Auctions: $138,000, NGC MS-62 HA 08/08										
↳1802, JR-1	*	213024	—	—	—	—	—	—	—	—	—
↳1802, JR-2	*	213025	1,700	2,250	3,200	4,200	6,500	10,000	18,000	36,000	114,000
↳1802, JR-3	*	213026	1,850	2,500	3,500	4,600	7,250	11,000	20,000	39,500	125,500
↳1802, JR-4	*	213027	1,700	2,250	3,200	4,200	6,500	10,000	18,000	36,000	114,000
1803	33,040	3965	950	1,400	1,800	2,500	3,450	5,500	8,250	60,000	120,000
	Auctions: $322,000, NGC MS-64 HA 08/08										
↳1803, JR-1	*	213028	—	—	—	—	—	19,000	—	—	—
↳1803, JR-2	*	213029	1,050	1,500	2,000	2,750	3,800	6,000	9,000	66,000	132,000
↳1803, JR-3	*	213030	950	1,400	1,800	2,500	3,450	5,500	8,250	60,000	120,000
	Auctions: $216,000 PCGS MS-64 HA 01/25										
↳1803, JR-4	*	213031	950	1,400	1,800	2,500	3,450	5,500	8,250	60,000	120,000
↳1803, JR-5	*	213032	—	—	—	—	—	—	—	—	—
1804, 13-Star Reverse	8,265	3966	5,250	6,500	10,000	16,000	21,000	33,000	66,000	—	—
	Auctions: $149,500, NGC AU-55 HA 08/08										
↳1804, 13-Star Reverse, JR-1	*	374666	5,250	6,500	10,000	16,000	21,000	33,000	66,000	—	—
	Auctions: $164,500, PCGS AU-55 SBG 05/15										
1804, 14-Star Reverse	*	3967	7,000	8,750	13,000	18,000	24,000	43,000	90,000	390,000	480,000
	Auctions: $632,500, NGC AU-58 HA 08/08										
↳1804, 14-Star Reverse, JR-2	*	374667	7,000	8,750	13,000	18,000	24,000	43,000	90,000	390,000	480,000
	Auctions: $329,000, PCGS AU-58 SBG 05/15										
1805, 4 Berries	120,780	3968	625	875	1,200	1,500	2,300	3,800	5,000	7,000	10,000
	Auctions: $149,500, PCGS MS-67 ANR 07/04										
↳1805, 4 Berries, JR-2	*	374668	625	875	1,200	1,500	2,300	3,800	5,000	7,000	10,000
	Auctions: $188,000, PCGS MS-67 HA 08/14										
1805, 5 Berries	*	3969	675	950	1,250	1,800	2,800	4,200	6,000	8,250	14,500
↳1805, 5 Berries, JR-1	*	374669	675	950	1,250	1,800	2,800	4,200	6,000	8,250	14,500
1807	165,000	3970	625	875	1,200	1,500	2,300	3,800	5,000	7,000	10,000
↳1807, JR-1	*	374670	625	875	1,200	1,500	2,300	3,800	5,000	7,000	10,000

* Included in number above.

CAPPED BUST (1809–1837)

Variety 1, Large Planchet (1809–1828): **Designer:** *John Reich.*
Weight: *2.7 grams.* **Composition:** *.8924 silver, .1076 copper.*
Diameter: *Approximately 18.8 mm.* **Edge:** *Reeded.* **Mint:** *Philadelphia.*

Variety 1, Large Planchet (1809–1828), Circulation Strike

Variety 1, Large Planchet, Proof Strike

Variety 2, Small Planchet (1828–1837): **Designer:** *John Reich.*
Weight: *2.7 grams (changed to 2.67 grams, .900 fine in 1837).* **Composition:** *.8924 silver, .1076 copper.*
Diameter: *Approximately 18.5 mm.* **Edge:** *Reeded.* **Mint:** *Philadelphia.*

Variety 2, Small Planchet (1828–1837), Circulation Strike

Variety 2, Small Planchet, Proof Strike

History. The large-planchet dimes were struck intermittently from 1809 to 1828. The design, by John Reich, closely follows that inaugurated with the Capped Bust half dollars of 1807. New equipment at the U.S. Mint was used to make the 1828, Small Date, dimes, and those subsequent. The slightly modified design on a smaller planchet includes smaller denticles or beads in the border and other minor differences, and they are of uniform diameter. The 2 in the 1828, Small Date, dime has a square (not curled) base.

Striking and Sharpness. Many if not most Large Planchet dimes have areas of light striking. On the obverse, check the star centers, the hair details, and the drapery at the bosom. On the reverse, check the eagle, especially the area in and around the upper right of the shield. Denticles are sometimes weak, but are usually better defined on the reverse than on the obverse. The height of the rims on both sides can vary, and coins with a low rim or rims tend to show wear more quickly. Most dimes of the modified design (Variety 2) are fairly well struck, with fewer irregularities of strike than those of 1809 to 1828. On the obverse, check the hair and the brooch. The stars usually are sharp, but don't overlook them. On the reverse, check the details of the eagle. The denticles usually are sharp.

Availability. There are no extremely rare dates in this series, so all are available to collectors, but certain die varieties range from rare to extremely rare. In MS, most are scarce and some rare. The dates of the early 1830s to 1835 are the most readily available. Those exhibiting a strong strike, with Full Details, command a premium, especially the earlier dates. Most have nice eye appeal.

Proofs. Proof Capped Bust dimes of 1809 to 1828 were struck in small numbers, likely mostly as part of presentation sets. As is the case with any and all early Proofs, you should insist on a coin with deeply and fully (not partially) mirrored surfaces, well struck, and with good contrast. Carefully examine deeply toned pieces (deep toning can mask the true nature of a coin, e.g., if it is not a true Proof, or if it has been cleaned or repaired). More than just a few pieces attributed as "Proofs" are not Proofs at all. Proofs were made of each year from 1828 to 1837 and are rare. Beware of "Proofs" that have deeply toned surfaces or fields that show patches of mint frost. Buy slowly and carefully.

Grading Standards

MS-64

MS-60 to 70 (Mint State). ***Obverse:*** The rims are more uniform for the 1828–1837 variety than for the 1809–1828 variety, striking is usually very sharp, and any abrasion occurs evenly on both sides. At MS-60 some abrasion and contact marks are evident, most noticeably on the cheek and on the area near the drapery clasp. Luster is present, but may be dull or lifeless, and interrupted in patches. At MS-63, contact marks are very few, and abrasion is hard to detect except under magnification. An MS-65 coin has no abrasion, and contact marks are so minute as to require magnification. Luster should be full and rich. Grades above MS-65 are seen now and again, and are defined by having fewer marks as perfection is approached. ***Reverse:*** Comments apply as for the obverse, except that abrasion and contact marks are most noticeable on the eagle's neck, the top of the wings, the claws, and the flat band that surrounds the incuse motto. The field is mainly protected by design elements and does not show abrasion as much as does the obverse.

AU-55

AU-50, 53, 55, 58 (About Uncirculated). ***Obverse:*** The rims are more uniform for the 1828–1837 variety than for the 1809–1828 variety, striking is usually very sharp, and any abrasion occurs evenly on both sides. Light wear is seen on the cap, the hair below LIBERTY, the hair near the clasp, and the drapery at the bosom. At AU-58, the luster is extensive except in the open area of the field, especially to the right. At AU-50 and 53, luster remains only in protected areas. As is true of all high grades, sharpness of strike can affect the perception of wear. ***Reverse:*** Wear is evident on the eagle's neck, the top of the wings, and the claws. An AU-58 has nearly full luster. At AU-50 and 53, there still is significant luster, more than on the obverse.

Illustrated coin: The stars on this coin are weakly struck.

EF-40

EF-40, 45 (Extremely Fine). ***Obverse:*** The rims are more uniform for the 1828–1837 variety than for the 1809–1828 variety, striking is usually very sharp, and the wear occurs evenly on both sides. Wear is more extensive, most noticeable on the higher areas of the hair. The cap shows more wear, as does the cheek. Stars still show their centers (unless lightly struck, and *many* are). Luster, if present, is in protected areas among the star points and close to the portrait. ***Reverse:*** The wings show wear on the higher areas of the feathers (particularly on the right wing), and some details are lost. Feathers in the neck are light. The eagle's claws show wear. Luster may be present in protected areas, even if there is little or none on the obverse.

VF-20, 30 (Very Fine). ***Obverse:*** The rims are more uniform for the 1828–1837 variety than for the 1809–1828 variety, striking is usually very sharp, and wear occurs evenly on both sides. Wear is more extensive, and most of the hair is combined into thick tresses without delicate features. The curl on the neck is flat. Unless they were weakly struck to begin with, most stars retain their interior lines. ***Reverse:*** Wear is most evident on the eagle's neck, to the left of the shield, and on the leaves and claws. Most feathers in the wing remain distinct.

VF-30

F-12, 15 (Fine). ***Obverse:*** The rims are more uniform for the 1828–1837 variety than for the 1809–1828 variety, striking is usually very sharp, and wear occurs evenly on both sides. (For both varieties the striking is not as important at this and lower grades.) Wear is more extensive, with much of the hair blended together. The drapery is indistinct along part of its upper edge. Stars have lost detail at the center and some may be flat. The height of obverse rim is important in the amount of wear the coin has received. ***Reverse:*** Wear is more extensive, now with only about a third to half of the feathers remaining on the wings, more on the wing to the left. Some of the horizontal lines in the shield may be worn away.

F-15

VG-8, 10 (Very Good). ***Obverse:*** The hair is less distinct, with the area surrounding the face blended into the facial features. LIBERTY is complete, but weak in areas. Stars are nearly flat. ***Reverse:*** Feathers are fewer and mostly visible on the eagle's left wing. Other details are weaker. All lettering remains easily readable, although some letters may be faint.

VG-8

G-4, 6 (Good). ***Obverse:*** The portrait is mostly in outline, with few interior details discernible. LIBERTY may still be readable or may be partially worn away, depending on the variety (this varies due to the strike characteristics of some die marriages). Stars are flat at their centers. ***Reverse:*** The eagle is mostly in outline form, although some feathers can be seen in the right wing. All letters around the border are clear on a sharp strike; some letters are light or missing on a coin with low rims. E PLURIBUS UNUM may be weak, often with some letters worn away.

Illustrated coin: This is an attractive, problem-free coin at this grade.

G-4

AG-3 (About Good). ***Obverse:*** The portrait is an outline, although traces of LIBERTY can still be seen. The rim is worn down, and some stars are weak. The date remains clear although weak toward the rim. ***Reverse:*** The reverse shows more wear overall than the obverse, with the rim indistinct in areas and many if not most letters worn away.

AG-3

PF-60 to 70 (Proof). ***Obverse and Reverse:*** Generally, Proof dimes of the 1828–1837 variety are of better quality than the 1809–1828 variety and have Full Details in almost all areas. Proofs of this type can have areas of light striking, such as at the star centers. Proofs that are extensively cleaned and have many hairlines, or that are dull and grainy, are lower level, such as PF-60 to 62. These are not of great interest to specialists unless they are of rare die varieties. A PF-64 has fewer hairlines, but they are obvious, perhaps slightly distracting. A Gem PF-65 should have fewer still and full mirrored surfaces (no trace of cloudiness or dullness). PF-66 should have hairlines so delicate that magnification is needed to see them. Above that, a Proof should be free of such lines. Grading is highly subjective with early Proofs; eye appeal also is a major factor.

PF-65 Cameo

Illustrated coin: Note the awkward mix of numerals in the date. Punches of different sizes were used, and the 3 in particular looks clumsy and large in comparison to the 8 and the 5.

1811, 11 Over 09

1814, Small Date

1814, Large Date

Circulation Strikes

	Mintage	GSID	G-4	VG-8	F-12	VF-20	EF-40	AU-50	MS-60	MS-63
Capped Bust, Large Planchet (1809–1828)	n/a	72455	$85	$130	$175	$285	$625	$775	$1,500	$2,400
Capped Bust, Small Planchet (1828–1837)	n/a	72456	40	60	85	130	290	525	900	1,900
Variety 1: Large Planchet										
1809	51,065	3971	950	1,250	1,750	2,500	4,000	5,000	6,500	11,000
↳**1809, JR-1**	*	375312	950	1,250	1,750	2,500	4,000	5,000	6,500	11,000
1811, 11 Over 09	65,180	4016	260	390	950	1,300	1,900	2,500	3,750	8,000
↳**1811, 11 Over 09, JR-1**	*	375313	260	390	950	1,300	1,900	2,500	3,750	8,000
1814, Large Date	421,500	3972	85	130	175	285	625	775	1,500	2,400
↳**1814, Large Date, JR-2**	*	213033	85	130	175	285	625	775	1,500	2,400
↳**1814, Large Date, JR-3**	*	213034	85	130	175	285	625	775	1,500	2,400
↳**1814, Large Date, JR-4**	*	213035	85	130	175	285	625	775	1,500	2,400
1814, Small Date	*	3973	110	155	220	390	775	1,100	2,100	4,050
↳**1814, Small Date, JR-1**	*	375314	110	155	220	390	775	1,100	2,100	4,050

* Included in number above.

1814, STATESOFAMERICA

1820, Large 0

1820, Small 0

1820, STATESOFAMERICA

1821, Large Date

1821, Small Date

Circulation Strikes *(continued)*

	Mintage	GSID	G-4	VG-8	F-12	VF-20	EF-40	AU-50	MS-60	MS-63
1814, STATESOFAMERICA	*	3974	$390	$650	$1,000	$1,250	$1,900	$4,400	$8,750	$18,000
↳1814, STATESOFAMERICA, JR-5, FS-901	*	375315	390	650	1,000	1,250	1,900	4,400	8,750	18,000
1820, Small 0	942,587	3976	85	130	175	285	650	900	1,900	2,900
↳1820, Small 0, JR-2	*	213036	85	130	175	285	650	900	1,900	2,900
	Auctions: $152,750, PCGS MS-67 HA 08/14									
↳1820, Small 0, JR-3	*	213037	85	130	175	285	650	900	1,900	2,900
↳1820, Small 0, JR-4	*	213038	90	135	195	315	725	975	2,050	3,150
↳1820, Small 0, JR-5	*	213039	90	135	195	315	725	975	2,050	3,150
↳1820, Small 0, JR-6	*	213040	85	130	175	285	650	900	1,900	2,900
↳1820, Small 0, JR-7	*	213041	85	130	175	285	650	900	1,900	2,900
↳1820, Small 0, JR-10	*	213042	85	130	175	285	650	900	1,900	2,900
↳1820, Small 0, JR-11	*	213043	85	130	175	285	650	900	1,900	2,900
↳1820, Small 0, JR-12	*	213044	230	455	900	2,050	—	—	—	—
1820, Large 0	*	3975	85	130	175	285	625	1,000	2,250	4,050
↳1820, Large 0, JR-8	*	213045	85	130	175	285	625	1,000	2,250	4,050
↳1820, Large 0, JR-9	*	213046	90	135	195	315	675	1,150	2,500	4,450
↳1820, Large 0, JR-13	*	213047	85	130	175	285	625	1,000	2,250	4,050
1820, STATESOFAMERICA (a)	*	3977	180	260	420	575	1,250	2,250	5,000	10,000
↳1820, STATESOFAMERICA, JR-1, FS-901 (a)	*	375316	180	260	420	575	1,250	2,250	5,000	10,000
1821, Small Date	1,186,512	3980	85	130	175	285	650	950	2,750	4,750
↳1821, Small Date, JR-8	*	213058	85	130	175	285	650	950	2,750	4,750
↳1821, Small Date, JR-9	*	213059	85	130	175	285	650	950	2,750	4,750
↳1821, Small Date, JR-10	*	213060	90	135	195	315	725	1,050	3,000	5,250
1821, Large Date	*	3979	85	130	175	285	625	850	1,700	2,400
↳1821, Large Date, JR-1	*	213051	85	130	175	285	625	850	1,700	2,400
↳1821, Large Date, JR-2	*	213052	525	—	—	—	—	—	—	—
↳1821, Large Date, JR-3	*	213053	90	135	195	315	675	925	1,850	2,600
↳1821, Large Date, JR-4	*	213054	85	130	175	285	625	850	1,700	2,400
↳1821, Large Date, JR-5	*	213055	85	130	175	285	625	850	1,700	2,400
↳1821, Large Date, JR-6	*	213056	85	130	175	285	625	850	1,700	2,400
↳1821, Large Date, JR-7	*	213057	85	130	175	285	625	850	1,700	2,400

* Included in number above. **a.** This is identical to the die used in 1814.

1823, 3 Over 2

1823, 3 Over 2, Small E's

1823, 3 Over 2, Large E's

1824, 4 Over 2

1824 and 1827, Flat Top 1

1824 and 1827, Pointed Top 1

Circulation Strikes *(continued)*

	Mintage	GSID	G-4	VG-8	F-12	VF-20	EF-40	AU-50	MS-60	MS-63
1822	100,000	3982	$2,000	$3,000	$5,250	$7,750	$10,500	$13,000	$20,500	$29,000
↳1822, JR-1	*	375317	2,000	3,000	5,250	7,750	10,500	13,000	20,500	29,000
	Auctions: $129,250, PCGS MS-66 SBG 02/16									
1823, 3 Over 2, Small E's	440,000	4017	110	160	260	455	775	950	1,600	3,750
↳1823, 3 Over 2, Small E's, JR-1	*	375318	110	160	260	455	775	950	1,600	3,750
1823, 3 Over 2, Large E's	*	4018	110	195	260	365	725	850	2,500	4,400
↳1823, 3 Over 2, Large E's, JR-2	*	213061	120	215	285	435	850	1,000	3,000	7,500
↳1823, 3 Over 2, Large E's, JR-3	*	213062	110	195	260	365	725	850	2,500	4,400
↳1824, 4 Over 2, Flat Top 1, JR-1	*	213063	115	145	260	575	875	1,000	1,750	2,700
↳1824, 4 Over 2, Pointed Top 1, JR-2	*	213064	340	575	1,550	4,400	7,000	—	—	—
1825	510,000	3984	85	130	175	285	625	775	1,800	2,550
↳1825, JR-1	*	213065	90	135	195	315	675	850	2,000	2,800
↳1825, JR-2	*	213066	85	130	175	285	625	775	1,800	2,550
↳1825, JR-3	*	213067	90	135	195	315	675	850	2,000	2,800
↳1825, JR-4	*	213068	85	130	175	285	625	775	1,800	2,550
↳1825, JR-5	*	213069	90	135	195	315	675	850	—	—
1827, Pointed Top 1 in 10 C.	1,215,000	3986	85	130	175	285	625	775	1,500	2,400
↳1827, Pointed Top 1 in 10 C., JR-1	*	4021	90	135	195	315	675	850	1,650	2,600
↳1827, Pointed Top 1 in 10 C., JR-3	*	213071	85	130	175	285	625	775	1,500	2,400
↳1827, Pointed Top 1 in 10 C., JR-4	*	213072	85	130	175	285	625	775	1,500	2,400
↳1827, Pointed Top 1 in 10 C., JR-5	*	213073	85	130	175	285	625	775	1,500	2,400
↳1827, Pointed Top 1 in 10 C., JR-6	*	71809	85	130	175	285	625	775	1,500	2,400
↳1827, Pointed Top 1 in 10 C., JR-7	*	213074	85	130	175	285	625	775	1,500	2,400
↳1827, Pointed Top 1 in 10 C., JR-8	*	213075	90	135	195	315	675	850	1,650	2,600
↳1827, Pointed Top 1 in 10 C., JR-9	*	213076	90	135	195	315	675	850	1,650	2,600
↳1827, Pointed Top 1 in 10 C., JR-10	*	213077	—	—	—	—	—	—	—	—
↳1827, Pointed Top 1 in 10 C., JR-11	*	213078	85	130	175	285	625	775	1,500	2,400
↳1827, Pointed Top 1 in 10 C., JR-12	*	213079	85	130	175	285	625	775	1,500	2,400
↳1827, Pointed Top 1 in 10 C., JR-13	*	213080	85	130	175	285	625	775	1,500	2,400
1827, Flat Top 1 in 10 C.	*	322095	210	290	360	525	1,250	9,500	—	—
↳1827, Flat Top 1 in 10 C., JR-2	*	213070	210	290	360	525	1,250	9,500	—	—
↳1827, Flat Top 1 in 10 C., JR-14	1 known	213081	—	9,500	—	—	—	—	—	—

* Included in number above.

1828, Large Date, Curl Base 2 (Variety 1)

1828, Small Date, Square Base 2 (Variety 2)

1829, Curl Base 2

1829, Small 10 C.

1829, Medium 10 C.

1829, Large 10 C.

1830, 30 Over 29

1830, Large 10 C.

1830, Small 10 C.

Circulation Strikes *(continued)*

	Mintage	GSID	G-4	VG-8	F-12	VF-20	EF-40	AU-50	MS-60	MS-63
1828, Large Date, Curl Base 2	125,000	3988	$155	$215	$310	$600	$1,400	$2,250	$5,250	$12,000
↳1828, Large Date, Curl Base 2, JR-2	*	375319	155	215	310	600	1,400	2,250	5,250	12,000
Variety 2: Small Planchet										
1828, Small Date, Square Base 2	*	3989	90	145	195	260	575	950	2,050	3,750
↳1828, Small Date, Square Base 2, JR-1	*	375320	90	145	195	260	575	950	2,050	3,750
1829	770,000	226504	40	60	85	130	290	525	900	1,900
1829, Extra Large 10 C.	*	193384	90	130	190	265	650	1,000	2,050	4,400
↳1829, Extra Large 10 C., JR-1, FS-902	*	375321	90	130	190	265	650	1,000	2,050	4,400
1829, Large 10 C.	*	3993	70	90	155	235	525	800	1,500	3,750
↳1829, Large 10 C., JR-2	*	375322	70	90	155	235	525	800	1,500	3,750
1829, Small 10 C.	*	226505	40	60	85	130	290	525	900	1,900
↳1829, Small 10 C., JR-3	*	226506	40	60	85	130	290	525	900	1,900
↳1829, Small 10 C., JR-4	*	226507	40	60	85	130	290	525	900	1,900
↳1829, Small 10 C., JR-5	*	226508	40	60	85	130	290	525	900	1,900
↳1829, Small 10 C., JR-6	*	226509	40	60	85	130	290	525	900	1,900
↳1829, Small 10 C., JR-7	*	70884	40	60	85	130	290	525	900	1,900
↳1829, Small 10 C., JR-8	*	226510	40	60	85	130	290	525	900	1,900
↳1829, Small 10 C., JR-9, FS-901	*	3991	40	60	85	130	290	525	900	1,900
1829, Curl Base 2	40 known	3992	5,500	8,750	11,000	14,500	27,000	—	—	—
↳1829, Curl Base 2, JR-10, FS-301	40 known	375323	5,500	8,750	11,000	14,500	27,000	—	—	—
1829, Medium 10 C.	*	3994	55	70	90	130	390	575	1,550	2,800
↳1829, Medium 10 C., JR-11	*	213082	60	75	100	145	430	650	1,700	3,100
↳1829, Medium 10 C., JR-12	*	213083	55	70	90	130	390	575	1,550	2,800
1830, 30 Over 29	510,000	4022	55	70	100	160	390	650	1,550	3,500
↳1830, 30 Over 29, JR-4, FS-301	*	213089	55	70	100	160	390	650	1,550	3,500
↳1830, 30 Over 29, JR-5, FS-301	*	213090	55	70	100	160	390	650	1,550	3,500
1830, Medium 10 C.	*	3996	40	60	85	130	290	525	900	1,900
↳1830, Medium 10 C., JR-1	*	213084	40	60	85	130	290	525	900	1,900
↳1830, Medium 10 C., JR-3	*	213085	40	60	85	130	290	525	900	1,900
↳1830, Medium 10 C., JR-6	*	213086	40	60	85	130	290	525	900	1,900
↳1830, Medium 10 C., JR-7	*	213087	45	65	90	145	320	575	975	2,050
↳1830, Medium 10 C., JR-8	*	213088	40	60	85	130	290	525	900	1,900
1830, Small 10 C.	*	3997	40	60	85	130	290	550	1,250	2,400
↳1830, Small 10 C., JR-2	*	373912	40	60	85	130	290	550	1,250	2,400

* Included in number above.

1833, Last 3 Normal

1833, Last 3 High

1834, Small 4

1834, Large 4

Circulation Strikes *(continued)*

	Mintage	GSID	G-4	VG-8	F-12	VF-20	EF-40	AU-50	MS-60	MS-63
1831	771,350	3999	$40	$60	$85	$130	$290	$525	$900	$1,900
↳1831, JR-1	*	213091	40	60	85	130	290	525	900	1,900
↳1831, JR-2	*	213092	40	60	85	130	290	525	900	1,900
↳1831, JR-3	*	213093	40	60	85	130	290	525	900	1,900
↳1831, JR-4	*	213094	40	60	85	130	290	525	900	1,900
↳1831, JR-5	*	213095	40	60	85	130	290	525	900	1,900
↳1831, JR-6	*	213096	40	60	85	130	290	525	900	1,900
1832	522,500	4001	40	60	85	130	290	525	950	1,900
↳1832, JR-1	*	213097	40	60	85	130	290	525	950	1,900
↳1832, JR-2	*	213098	40	60	85	130	290	525	950	1,900
↳1832, JR-3	*	213099	45	65	90	145	320	575	1,050	2,050
↳1832, JR-4	*	213100	40	60	85	130	290	525	950	1,900
↳1832, JR-5	*	213101	40	60	85	130	290	525	950	1,900
↳1832, JR-6	*	213102	40	60	85	130	290	525	950	1,900
↳1832, JR-7	*	213103	40	60	85	130	290	525	950	1,900
1833	485,000	4003	40	60	85	130	290	525	900	1,900
↳1833, JR-1	*	213104	40	60	85	130	290	525	900	1,900
↳1833, JR-2	*	213105	45	65	90	145	320	575	975	2,050
↳1833, JR-3	*	213106	325	525	—	—	—	1,900	—	—
↳1833, JR-4	*	213107	40	60	85	130	290	525	900	1,900
↳1833, JR-6	*	213108	40	60	85	130	290	525	900	1,900
↳1833, JR-8	*	213109	—	—	—	—	—	—	—	—
↳1833, JR-9	*	213110	40	60	85	130	290	525	900	1,900
↳1833, JR-10	*	213111	40	60	85	130	290	525	900	1,900
1833, Last 3 High	*	4004	40	60	85	130	290	525	950	2,100
↳1833, Last 3 High, JR-5	*	213112	40	60	85	130	290	525	950	2,100
↳1833, Last 3 High, JR-7	*	213113	90	130	—	—	—	1,150	—	—
1834, Large 4	635,000	4007	40	60	85	130	290	525	900	1,900
↳1834, Large 4, JR-1	*	213114	40	60	85	130	290	525	900	1,900
↳1834, Large 4, JR-2	*	213115	40	60	85	130	290	525	900	1,900
↳1834, Large 4, JR-3	*	213116	—	—	—	175	390	—	—	—
↳1834, Large 4, JR-4	*	213117	40	60	85	130	290	525	900	1,900
↳1834, Large 4, JR-5	*	213118	40	60	85	130	290	525	900	1,900
↳1834, Large 4, JR-6	*	213119	40	60	85	130	290	525	900	1,900
1834, Small 4	*	4006	40	60	85	130	290	525	900	1,900
↳1834, Small 4, JR-7	*	374434	40	60	85	130	290	525	900	1,900

* Included in number above.

Circulation Strikes *(continued)*

	Mintage	GSID	G-4	VG-8	F-12	VF-20	EF-40	AU-50	MS-60	MS-63
1835	1,410,000	4009	$40	$60	$85	$130	$290	$525	$900	$1,900
↳1835, JR-1	*	213120	40	60	85	130	290	525	900	1,900
↳1835, JR-2	*	213121	45	65	90	145	320	575	975	2,050
↳1835, JR-3	*	213122	40	60	85	130	290	525	900	1,900
↳1835, JR-4	*	213123	40	60	85	130	290	525	900	1,900
↳1835, JR-5	*	213124	40	60	85	130	290	525	900	1,900
↳1835, JR-6	*	213125	45	65	90	145	320	575	975	2,050
↳1835, JR-7	*	213126	45	65	90	145	320	575	975	2,050
↳1835, JR-8	*	213127	40	60	85	130	290	525	900	1,900
↳1835, JR-9	*	213128	40	60	85	130	290	525	900	1,900
1836	1,190,000	4011	40	60	85	130	290	525	900	1,900
↳1836, JR-1	*	213129	40	60	85	130	290	525	900	1,900
↳1836, JR-2	*	213130	40	60	85	130	290	525	900	1,900
↳1836, JR-3	*	213131	40	60	85	130	290	525	900	1,900
1837	359,500	4013	40	60	85	130	290	525	900	1,900
↳1837, JR-1	*	213132	45	65	90	145	320	575	975	2,050
↳1837, JR-2	*	213133	40	60	85	130	290	525	900	1,900
↳1837, JR-3	*	213134	40	60	85	130	290	525	900	1,900
↳1837, JR-4	*	213135	40	60	85	130	290	525	900	1,900

* Included in number above.

Proof Strikes

		GSID	PF-63	PF-65
Capped Bust, Large Planchet (1809–1827), Proof	**n/a**	**74190**	**$29,000**	**$63,000**
Capped Bust, Small Planchet (1828–1837), Proof	**n/a**	**74191**	**27,000**	**57,500**
Variety 1: Large Planchet				
1820	1–3 known	213136	—	—
	Auctions: $156,000, NGC PF-66 HA 01/19			
1821	3–5 known	3981	—	168,000
	Auctions: $204,000, NGC PF-65 HA 08/24			
1822	3 known	3983	—	—
1824, 4 Over 2		4020	29,000	63,000
	Auctions: $108,000, NGC PF-67 HA 01/19			
1825	6 known	3985	29,000	63,000
1827	5–10 known	3987	29,000	63,000
	Auctions: $120,750, NGC PF-67 SU 02/08			
1827, JR-10		213139	29,000	63,000
Variety 2: Small Planchet				
1828, Small Planchet, Small Date, JR-1	5 known	3990	27,000	57,500
1829	5–8 known	3995	29,500	63,500
1830		3998	27,000	57,500
1831	15–20 known	4000	27,000	57,500
1832, JR-2	2–4 known	4002	33,000	66,500
1833, JR-2	3–5 known	4005	33,000	66,500
	Auctions: $149,500, PCGS PF-66 HA 08/08			
1834	8–10 known	4008	27,000	57,500
1835	10–12 known	4010	27,000	57,500
	Auctions: $143,750, PCGS PF-67 HA 01/07			
↳1835, JR-1	unique	393994	—	—
↳1835, JR-4	10–12 known	393995	27,000	57,500
1836	1–3 known	213143	29,500	63,500

LIBERTY SEATED (1837–1891)

Variety 1, No Stars on Obverse (1837–1838): **Designer:** *Christian Gobrecht.* **Weight:** *2.67 grams.* **Composition:** *.900 silver, .100 copper.* **Diameter:** *17.9 mm.* **Edge:** *Reeded.* **Mints:** *Philadelphia and New Orleans.*

Variety 1, No Stars on Obverse (1837–1838), Circulation Strike

Variety 1, No Stars on Obverse, Proof, Strike

Variety 2, Stars on Obverse (1838–1853): **Designer:** *Christian Gobrecht.* **Weight:** *2.67 grams.* **Composition:** *.900 silver, .100 copper.* **Diameter:** *17.9 mm.* **Edge:** *Reeded.* **Mints:** *Philadelphia, New Orleans, and San Francisco.*

Variety 2, Stars on Obverse (1838–1853), Circulation Strike

Mintmark location, 1837–1860 (Variety 2), is on the reverse, above the bow.

Variety 2, Stars on Obverse, Proof Strike

Variety 3, Stars on Obverse, Arrows at Date, Reduced Weight (1853–1855): **Designer:** *Christian Gobrecht.* **Weight:** *2.49 grams.* **Composition:** *.900 silver, .100 copper.* **Diameter:** *17.9 mm.* **Edge:** *Reeded.* **Mints:** *Philadelphia, New Orleans, and San Francisco.*

Variety 3, Stars on Obverse, Arrows at Date, Reduced Weight (1853–1855), Circulation Strike

Variety 3, Stars on Obverse, Arrows at Date, Reduced Weight, Proof Strike

Variety 2 Resumed, With Weight Standard of Variety 3 (1856–1860): **Designer:** *Christian Gobrecht.* **Weight:** *2.49 grams.* **Composition:** *.900 silver, .100 copper.* **Diameter:** *17.9 mm.* **Edge:** *Reeded.* **Mints:** *Philadelphia, New Orleans, and San Francisco.*

Variety 2 Resumed, Weight Standard of Variety 3 (1856–1860), Circulation Strike

Variety 2 Resumed, Weight Standard of Variety 3, Proof Strike

Variety 4, Legend on Obverse (1860–1873): **Designer:** *Christian Gobrecht.* **Weight:** *2.49 grams.* **Composition:** *.900 silver, .100 copper.* **Diameter:** *17.9 mm.* **Edge:** *Reeded.* **Mints:** *Philadelphia, New Orleans, San Francisco, and Carson City.*

Variety 4, Legend on Obverse (1860–1873), Circulation Strike

Mintmark location, 1860 (Variety 4)–1891, is on the reverse, below the bow.

Variety 4, Legend on Obverse, Proof Strike

Variety 5, Legend on Obverse, Arrows at Date, Increased Weight (1873–1874): **Designer:** *Christian Gobrecht.* **Weight:** *2.5 grams.* **Composition:** *.900 silver, .100 copper.* **Diameter:** *17.9 mm.* **Edge:** *Reeded.* **Mints:** *Philadelphia, New Orleans, San Francisco, and Carson City.*

Variety 5, Legend on Obverse, Arrows at Date, Increased Weight (1873–1874), Circulation Strike

Variety 5, Legend on Obverse, Increased Weight, Proof Strike

Variety 4 Resumed, With Weight Standard Variety of 5 (1875–1891): **Designer:** *Christian Gobrecht.* **Weight:** *2.5 grams.* **Composition:** *.900 silver, .100 copper.* **Diameter:** *17.9 mm.* **Edge:** *Reeded.* **Mints:** *Philadelphia, New Orleans, San Francisco, and Carson City.*

Variety 4 Resumed, Weight Standard Variety of 5 (1875–1891), Circulation Strike

Variety 4 Resumed, Weight Standard Variety of 5, Proof Strike

History. The first of the Liberty Seated designs, with no stars on the obverse, was inspired by Christian Gobrecht's silver dollar of 1836. The reverse features a different motif, with a wreath and inscription. This variety was made only at the Philadelphia Mint in 1837 and at the New Orleans Mint in 1838. Liberty Seated dimes of the Stars on Obverse varieties were first made without drapery at Liberty's elbow. These early issues have the shield tilted sharply to the left. Drapery was added in 1840, and the shield reoriented, this being the style of the 1840s onward. Variety 3 coins (minted in part of 1853, and all of 1854 and 1855) have arrows at the date, signifying the reduction in weight brought on by the Coinage Act of February 21, 1853. The earlier design resumed in 1856 at the new weight standard. Liberty Seated dimes were made in large quantities, and circulated widely. In 1860 the Liberty Seated design continued with UNITED STATES OF AMERICA replacing the stars on the obverse. A new reverse featured what the Mint called a "cereal wreath," encircling ONE DIME in two lines. In 1873 the dime was increased in weight to 2.5 grams (from 2.49); arrows at the date in 1873 and 1874 indicate this change, making Variety 5. Variety 4 (without the arrows) resumed from 1875 and continued to the end of the series in 1891.

Striking and Sharpness. Coins of these varieties usually are fairly well struck for the earlier years, somewhat erratic in the 1870s, and better from the 1880s to 1891. Many Civil War dimes of Philadelphia, 1861 to 1865, have parallel die striae from the dies not being finished (this being so for virtually all silver and gold issues of that period). Some dimes, especially dates from 1879 to 1881, are found prooflike. Check the highest parts of the Liberty Seated figure (especially the head and horizontal shield stripes), the star centers, and, on the reverse, the leaves. Check the denticles on both sides. Avoid coins struck from "tired" or overused dies, as evidenced by grainy rather than lustrous fields (on higher-grade coins). Issues of the Carson City Mint in the early 1870s, particularly 1873-CC, With Arrows, are often seen with porous surfaces (a post-striking effect).

Note that the word LIBERTY on the shield is not an infallible key to attributing lower grades. On some dies such as those of the early 1870s the shield was in low relief on the coins and wore away slowly, with the result that part or all of the word can be readable in grades below F-12.

Availability. The 1837 is readily available in all grades, including MS-65 and higher. The 1838-O is usually seen with wear and is a rarity if truly MS-63 or above. Beware coins with deep or vivid iridescent toning, which often masks friction or evidence of wear. Coins with uniformly grainy etching on both sides have been processed and should be avoided. The 1838 to 1860 dimes are plentiful as a rule, although certain dates and varieties are rare. Most MS coins on the market are dated in the 1850s and are often found MS-63 to 65. While certain issues of the 1860s through 1881 range from scarce to very rare, those from 1882 to 1891 are for the most part very common, even in MS-63 and finer.

Proofs. Examples of Proofs have deep-mirror surfaces and are mostly quite attractive. Proofs of 1837 (but not 1838-O) were struck in an unknown small quantity, but seemingly more than the related 1837 half dime. Proofs were made of most years and are mostly available from 1854 onward, with 1858 and especially 1859 being those often seen. Some Proofs of the 1860s and early 1870s can be carelessly struck, with areas of lightness and sometimes with lint marks. Those of the mid-1870s onward are usually sharply struck and without problems. Proof Liberty Seated dimes of this variety were made continuously from 1860 to 1891. They exist today in proportion to their mintages. Carefully examine deeply toned pieces to ensure the toning does not hide flaws.

Grading Standards

MS-64

MS-60 to 70 (Mint State). ***Obverse:*** At MS-60, some abrasion and contact marks are evident, most noticeably on the bosom and thighs and knees. Luster is present, but may be dull or lifeless, and interrupted in patches in the large open field. At MS-63, contact marks are very few, and abrasion is hard to detect except under magnification. An MS-65 coin has no abrasion, and contact marks are so minute as to require magnification. Luster should be full and rich, except for Philadelphia (but not San Francisco) dimes of the early and mid-1860s. Most Mint State coins of the 1861 to 1865 years, Philadelphia issues, have extensive die striae (from not completely finishing the die). Some low-mintage Philadelphia issues may be prooflike. Clashmarks are common in this era. This is true of contemporary half dimes as well. Half dimes of this type can be very beautiful at this level. Grades above MS-65 are seen with regularity, more so than for the related No Stars dimes. ***Reverse:*** Comments apply as for the obverse, except that in lower Mint State grades abrasion and contact marks are most noticeable on the highest parts of the leaves and the ribbon, less so on ONE DIME. At MS-65 or higher there are no marks visible to the unaided eye. The field is mainly protected by design elements and does not show abrasion as much as does the open-field obverse on a given coin.

Illustrated coin: Note the blend of pink, lilac, and gold tones.

AU-58

AU-50, 53, 55, 58 (About Uncirculated). ***Obverse:*** Light wear is seen on the thighs and knees, bosom, and head. At AU-58, the luster is extensive, but incomplete. Friction is seen in the large open field. At AU-50 and 53, luster is less. ***Reverse:*** Wear is evident on the leaves (especially at the top of the wreath) and ribbon. An AU-58 coin has nearly full luster, more so than on the obverse, as the design elements protect the small field areas. At AU-50 and 53, there still is significant luster, more than on the obverse.

EF-45

EF-40, 45 (Extremely Fine). ***Obverse:*** Further wear is seen on all areas, especially the thighs and knees, bosom, and head. Little or no luster is seen. ***Reverse:*** Further wear is seen on all areas, most noticeably at the leaves to each side of the wreath apex and on the ribbon bow knot. Leaves retain details except on the higher areas.

VF-30

VF-20, 30 (Very Fine). ***Obverse:*** Further wear is seen. Most details of the gown are worn away, except in the lower-relief areas above and to the right of the shield. Hair detail is mostly or completely gone. ***Reverse:*** Wear is more extensive. The highest leaves are flat.

F-15

F-12, 15 (Fine). ***Obverse:*** The seated figure is well worn, with little detail remaining. LIBERTY on the shield is fully readable but weak in areas. On the 1838–1840 subtype Without Drapery, LIBERTY is in higher relief and will wear more quickly; ER may be missing, but other details are at the Fine level. ***Reverse:*** Most detail of the leaves is gone. The rim is worn but bold, and most if not all denticles are visible.

VG-8, 10 (Very Good). ***Obverse:*** The seated figure is more worn, but some detail can be seen above and to the right of the shield. The shield is discernible. In LIBERTY at least three letters are readable but very weak at VG-8; a few more visible at VG-10. On the 1838–1840 subtype Without Drapery, LIBERTY is in higher relief, and at Very Good only one or two letters may be readable. However, LIBERTY is not an infallible way to grade this type, as some varieties have the word in low relief on the die, so it wore away slowly. ***Reverse:*** Further wear has combined the details of most leaves. The rim is complete, but weak in areas. The reverse appears to be in a slightly higher grade than the obverse.

VG-8

G-4, 6 (Good). ***Obverse:*** The seated figure is worn smooth. At G-4 there are no letters in LIBERTY remaining on most (but not all) coins. At G-6, traces of one or two can be seen (except on the early No Drapery coins). ***Reverse:*** Wear is more extensive. The leaves are all combined and in outline form. The rim is well worn and missing in some areas, causing the outer parts of the peripheral letters to be worn away in some instances. On most coins the reverse appears to be in a slightly higher grade than the obverse.

Illustrated coin: The scratch on the obverse lessens the desirability of this coin.

G-4

AG-3 (About Good). ***Obverse:*** The seated figure is mostly visible in outline form, with no detail. The rim is worn away. The date remains clear. ***Reverse:*** Many if not most letters are worn away, at least in part. The wreath and interior letters are discernible. The rim is weak.

AG-3

PF-60 to 70 (Proof). ***Obverse and Reverse:*** Proofs that are extensively cleaned and have many hairlines, or that are dull and grainy, are lower level, such as PF-60 to 62. These command less attention than more visually appealing pieces, save for the scarce (in any grade) dates of 1844 and 1846, and 1863 through 1867. Both the half dime and dime Proofs of 1837 were often cleaned, resulting in coins that have lost much of their mirror surface. With medium hairlines and good reflectivity, an assigned grade of PF-64 is indicated, and with relatively few hairlines, Gem PF-65. In various grades hairlines are most easily seen in the obverse field. PF-66 should have hairlines so delicate that magnification is needed to see them. Above that, a Proof should be free of such lines.

PF-66 Cameo

1837, Large Date

1837, Small Date

No Drapery From Elbow, Tilted Shield (1838–1840)

Drapery From Elbow, Upright Shield (1840–1891)

1838, Small Stars

1838, Large Stars

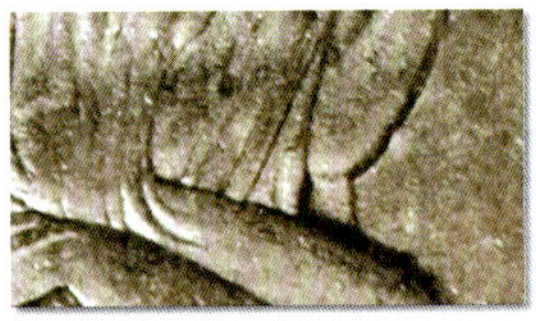
1838, So-Called Partial Drapery

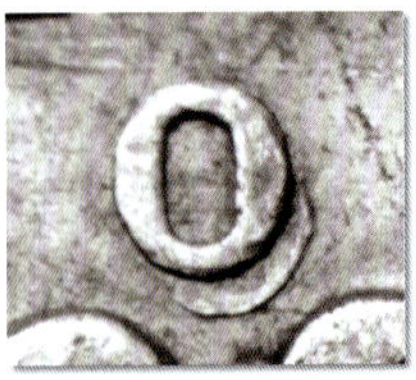
1839-O, Repunched Mintmark

1841-O, Transitional Reverse, Small O

1841-O, Transitional Reverse, Large O

Regular Reverse Style of 1841-O

Circulation Strikes

	Mintage	GSID	G-4	VG-8	F-12	VF-20	EF-40	AU-50	MS-60	MS-63
Liberty Seated, No Stars on Obverse (1837–1838)	**n/a**	**72457**	**$65.00**	**$105**	**$170**	**$260**	**$575**	**$850**	**$1,300**	**$2,200**
Liberty Seated, Stars on Obverse (1838–1853, 1856–1860)	**n/a**	**72459**	**17.50**	**19**	**22**	**32**	**80**	**195**	**340**	**550**
Liberty Seated, Stars, Arrows at Date (1853–1855)	**n/a**	**72460**	**19.00**	**20**	**22**	**38**	**90**	**180**	**365**	**675**
Liberty Seated, Legend on Obverse (1860–1873, 1875–1891)	**n/a**	**72461**	**15.00**	**16**	**19**	**24**	**34**	**90**	**175**	**340**
Liberty Seated, Legend, Arrows at Date (1873–1874)	**n/a**	**72462**	**19.00**	**26**	**40**	**80**	**195**	**350**	**550**	**900**
1837, Large Date	682,500	4023	65.00	105	170	260	575	850	1,300	2,200
1837, Small Date	*	4024	110.00	170	235	300	650	850	1,300	2,200
1838-O	489,034	4088	120.00	180	275	470	875	1,400	4,000	6,750
1838, Large Stars	1,992,500	4026	22.00	27	38	95	230	325	600	1,000
1838, Small Stars	*	4027	36.00	55	90	180	410	455	775	1,500
1838, Partial Drapery (a)	*	4028	35.00	55	75	195	390	725	1,200	1,750
1839, No Drapery	1,053,115	4029	22.00	27	38	95	230	325	600	1,000
1839-O, No Drapery	1,291,600	4089	34.00	55	95	155	260	455	850	2,200
↳1839-O, No Drapery, Repunched Mintmark, Cracked Reverse, FS-501	*	213194	37.00	60	105	170	285	500	925	2,400
1840, No Drapery	981,500	4030	22.00	27	38	95	240	325	600	1,000
1840-O, No Drapery	1,175,000	4090	80.00	115	160	260	625	1,250	5,750	11,000
1840, With Drapery	377,500	4031	100.00	130	180	360	850	1,400	3,500	12,000
1841, With Drapery	1,622,500	4032	17.50	20	24	38	100	195	390	775
1841-O	2,007,500	4091	27.00	40	55	90	160	290	900	1,450
↳1841-O, Transitional Reverse, Small O, FS-901	*	213201	27.00	40	55	90	160	290	900	1,450
↳1841-O, Transitional Reverse, Large O, Small Letters, FS-902	*	199165	27.00	40	55	90	160	290	900	1,450

* Included in number above. **a.** The so-called "partial drapery" is not a design variation; rather, it is evidence of die clashing from the E in DIME on the reverse.

Circulation Strikes *(continued)*

	Mintage	GSID	G-4	VG-8	F-12	VF-20	EF-40	AU-50	MS-60	MS-63
1842	1,887,500	4033	$17.50	$20.00	$24	$38	$100	$195	$340	$550
1842-O	2,020,000	4092	47.00	70.00	100	235	550	1,000	3,000	5,000
1843	1,370,000	4034	17.50	20.00	24	38	100	195	455	850
1843-O	150,000	4093	195.00	325.00	600	1,400	3,100	11,000	72,000	150,000
	Auctions: $141,000, PCGS MS-62 HA 06/14									
1844	72,500	4035	195.00	275.00	340	495	950	1,900	4,500	10,000
1845	1,755,000	4036	19.00	22.00	24	38	100	195	420	675
1845-O	230,000	4094	75.00	130.00	260	625	1,400	3,450	13,000	33,500
	Auctions: $123,376, PCGS MS-69 HA 05/15									
1846	31,300	4037	450.00	600.00	925	2,000	2,700	7,500	24,000	54,000
1847	245,000	4038	40.00	47.00	60	100	195	420	1,500	3,400
1848	451,500	4039	34.00	47.00	60	90	130	260	775	1,100
1849	839,000	4040	27.00	34.00	40	55	110	260	525	875
1849-O	300,000	4095	34.00	47.00	80	170	415	775	2,500	4,500
1850	1,931,500	4041	20.00	27.00	34	43	95	215	390	725
1850-O	510,000	4096	46.00	70.00	95	130	360	875	2,250	5,000
1851	1,026,500	4042	20.00	23.00	26	42	90	230	455	750
1851-O	400,000	4097	34.00	55.00	80	135	325	1,150	2,800	3,750
1852	1,535,500	4043	17.50	19.00	22	34	90	195	340	550
1852-O	430,000	4098	47.00	80.00	130	260	455	675	1,900	3,100
1853, No Arrows	95,000	4044	215.00	290.00	440	550	950	1,150	1,500	2,200
1853, With Arrows	12,078,010	4045	19.00	20.00	22	38	90	180	365	675
	Auctions: $102,000, PCGS MS-68 HA 01/22									
↳**1853, With Arrows, Repunched Date, FS-301**	*	285499	19.00	20.00	22	38	90	180	365	675
1853-O	1,100,000	4099	24.00	47.00	95	120	290	675	2,250	5,000
1854	4,470,000	4046	19.00	20.00	22	38	90	180	365	675
1854-O	1,770,000	4100	40.00	70.00	100	130	160	260	455	900
1855	2,075,000	4047	19.00	20.00	22	38	90	180	365	675
1856, Small Date	5,780,000	4048	17.50	19.00	22	32	80	195	340	550
1856, Large Date	*	4049	47.00	70.00	100	130	195	305	725	2,200
1856-O	1,180,000	4101	34.00	47.00	75	115	160	420	800	1,250
1856-S	70,000	4102	420.00	675.00	950	1,500	2,100	2,750	7,500	14,500
1857	5,580,000	4050	17.50	19.00	22	32	80	195	340	550
1857-O	1,540,000	4103	22.00	27.00	32	49	85	210	430	650
1858	1,540,000	4051	17.50	19.00	22	32	80	195	365	600
1858-O	290,000	4104	30.00	40.00	60	125	215	390	950	2,200
1858-S	60,000	4105	285.00	390.00	525	1,000	1,900	2,400	8,750	17,000
1859	429,200	4052	17.50	19.00	22	40	85	195	340	550
1859-O	480,000	4106	27.00	34.00	40	70	150	260	455	750
1859-S	60,000	4107	415.00	675.00	950	1,600	4,500	8,250	19,000	33,500
1860-S	140,000	4109	110.00	170.00	260	390	725	1,100	2,500	8,750
1860	606,000	4053	15.00	16.00	19	24	65	95	240	455
1860-O	40,000	4108	1,100.00	1,800.00	2,500	3,500	6,000	11,000	20,500	43,000
1861	1,883,000	4054	16.00	17.50	22	27	42	95	190	370

* Included in number above.

1872, Doubled Die Reverse
FS-801

1873, With Arrows, Doubled Die Obverse
FS-101

1873, Close 3

1873, Open 3

Circulation Strikes *(continued)*

	Mintage	GSID	G-4	VG-8	F-12	VF-20	EF-40	AU-50	MS-60	MS-63
1861-S	172,500	4110	$195.00	$285.00	$455	$725	$1,000	$1,250	$5,000	$18,000
1862	847,000	4055	19.00	20.00	23	30	47	90	180	390
1862-S	180,750	4111	230.00	325.00	455	725	1,250	2,750	4,700	11,000
1863	14,000	4056	950.00	1,150.00	1,500	1,800	2,250	2,800	3,450	4,100
1863-S	157,500	4112	150.00	210.00	325	575	1,000	1,250	3,750	8,750
1864	11,000	4057	750.00	925.00	1,200	1,500	2,000	2,250	3,000	3,750
1864-S	230,000	4113	145.00	190.00	260	435	850	1,100	1,600	2,200
1865	10,000	4058	1,150.00	1,300.00	1,750	2,250	3,250	4,000	5,500	7,500
1865-S	175,000	4114	145.00	235.00	390	650	1,150	2,950	8,000	14,500
1866	8,000	4059	850.00	1,100.00	1,500	1,700	2,100	2,500	3,100	3,500
1866-S	135,000	4115	145.00	235.00	390	500	775	1,500	3,750	7,500
1867	6,000	4060	1,050.00	1,400.00	1,650	1,750	2,000	2,250	3,250	4,400
1867-S	140,000	4116	155.00	230.00	300	430	1,100	1,800	3,250	5,250
1868	464,000	4061	23.00	27.00	32	50	90	155	290	725
1868-S	260,000	4117	70.00	100.00	160	290	575	700	1,500	2,500
1869	256,000	4062	32.00	39.00	47	105	230	290	650	1,100
1869-S	450,000	4118	40.00	60.00	90	145	290	405	900	1,400
1870	470,500	4063	23.00	26.00	31	45	110	155	340	575
1870-S	50,000	4119	390.00	550.00	675	900	1,150	1,250	2,250	3,100
1871	906,750	4064	17.50	19.00	22	32	65	170	365	625
1871-CC	20,100	4120	4,250.00	7,500.00	9,250	11,000	18,000	24,000	45,000	138,000
	Auctions: $270,250, NGC MS-65 HA 10/14									
1871-S	320,000	4121	40.00	80.00	130	195	420	900	1,600	3,750
1872	2,395,500	4065	16.00	17.50	20	26	40	90	175	365
↳1872, Doubled Die Reverse, FS-801	*	213236	24.00	38.00	55	100	235	440	1,500	4,100
1872-CC	35,480	4122	1,750.00	2,500.00	3,250	4,400	11,000	24,000	108,000	408,000
	Auctions: $216,200, PCGS MS-63 SBG 08/12									
1872-S	190,000	4123	70.00	110.00	155	235	430	725	2,000	3,500
1873, No Arrows, Closed 3	1,506,900	4066	17.50	24.00	34	55	80	130	285	525
↳1873, No Arrows, Closed 3, Repunched Date, FS-301	*	213238	—	—	—	—	95	155	345	625
1873, No Arrows, Open 3	*	4067	22.00	32.00	60	80	130	260	850	1,200
1873-CC, No Arrows (b)	unique	4124	—	—	—	—	—	—	—	—
	Auctions: $3,600,000, PCGS MS-65 HA 01/23									

* Included in number above. **b.** Most of the mintage of 1873-CC, No Arrows, was melted after the law of 1873, affecting the statuses and physical properties of U.S. coinage, was passed.

1875-CC, Mintmark Above Bow

1875-CC, Mintmark Below Bow

1876-CC, Variety 1 Reverse

1876-CC, Variety 2 Reverse
FS-901

Circulation Strikes *(continued)*

	Mintage	GSID	G-4	VG-8	F-12	VF-20	EF-40	AU-50	MS-60	MS-63
1873, With Arrows	2,337,000	4068	$19	$26	$40	$80	$195	$350	$550	$900
↳1873, With Arrows, Doubled Die Obverse, FS-101	*	4069	775	1,250	1,600	2,500	4,400	8,750	15,000	—
1873-CC, With Arrows	18,791	4125	3,250	4,250	7,000	10,000	24,000	54,000	108,000	168,000
	Auctions: $324,300, PCGS MS-65 SBG 08/12									
1873-S	455,000	4126	27	32	40	90	200	525	950	1,650
1874	2,940,000	4070	19	26	40	80	195	350	550	900
1874-CC	10,817	4127	12,500	16,000	20,000	25,000	36,000	60,000	132,000	288,000
	Auctions: $152,750, PCGS MS-63 HA 10/14									
1874-S	240,000	4128	55	80	130	170	390	850	1,250	2,250
1875	10,350,000	4071	15	16	19	24	34	90	175	340
↳1875, Misplaced Date, FS-301	*	213241	—	—	—	—	—	—	—	—
1875-CC, Mintmark Above Bow	4,465,000	4129	35	43	60	90	130	365	850	1,300
1875-CC, Mintmark Below Bow	*	4130	32	35	60	120	235	470	1,000	1,900
1875-S, Mintmark Above Bow	9,070,000	4132	15	16	19	24	34	130	260	390
1875-S, Mintmark Below Bow	*	4131	15	16	19	24	34	90	175	340
1876	11,450,000	4072	15	16	19	24	34	90	175	340
1876-CC	8,270,000	4133	40	49	60	85	155	260	525	850
↳1876-CC, Doubled Die Obverse, Right C Low, FS-103	*	213247	—	—	—	—	—	—	—	—
↳1876-CC, Doubled Die Reverse, FS-801	*	392982	—	—	—	—	—	—	—	—
1876-S	10,420,000	4134	19	20	27	34	50	95	195	390
↳1876-S, Repunched Date, Variety 1 Reverse, FS-301	*	213253	—	—	—	—	—	—	—	—
↳1876-S, Repunched Date, FS-301	*	392983	—	—	—	—	—	—	—	—
1877	7,310,000	4073	15	16	19	24	34	90	175	340
1877-CC	7,700,000	4135	32	35	38	60	145	245	360	850
1877-S	2,340,000	4136	26	30	32	40	60	115	325	950
1878	1,677,200	4074	15	16	19	24	34	90	190	430
1878-CC	200,000	4137	285	350	440	725	950	1,600	2,450	3,500
1879	14,000	4075	195	235	280	390	525	625	675	775
1880	36,000	4076	145	210	260	325	415	470	575	650
1881	24,000	4077	210	260	310	375	495	650	900	1,250
1882	3,910,000	4078	15	16	19	24	34	90	175	340
1883	7,674,673	4079	15	16	19	24	34	90	175	340

* Included in number above.

1891-O, Medium O Over Horizontal O
FS-501

1891-S, Medium S Over Small S
FS-501

Circulation Strikes *(continued)*

	Mintage	GSID	G-4	VG-8	F-12	VF-20	EF-40	AU-50	MS-60	MS-63
1884	3,365,505	4080	$15.00	$16	$19	$24	$34	$90	$175	$340
1884-S	564,969	4138	40.00	60	80	145	285	420	775	1,250
1885	2,532,497	4081	15.00	16	19	24	34	90	175	340
1885-S	43,690	4139	1,000.00	1,450	2,000	2,500	4,400	5,750	8,750	14,500
1886	6,376,684	4082	15.00	16	19	24	34	90	175	340
1886-S	206,524	4140	47.00	60	80	115	160	230	550	1,150
1887	11,283,229	4083	15.00	16	19	24	34	90	175	340
1887-S	4,454,450	4141	15.00	16	19	24	34	95	195	370
1888	5,495,655	4084	15.00	16	19	24	34	90	175	340
1888-S	1,720,000	4142	19.00	22	24	34	49	100	360	675
1889	7,380,000	4085	15.00	16	19	24	34	90	175	340
↳1889, Doubled Die Reverse, FS-801	*	213266	—	—	—	—	—	—	—	—
1889-S	972,678	4143	27.00	32	40	60	90	145	360	875
↳1889-S, Repunched 1	972,678	377762	—	—	—	—	—	—	—	—
1890	9,910,951	4086	15.00	16	19	24	34	90	175	340
1890-S	1,423,076	4144	16.00	19	24	45	75	145	260	575
1891	15,310,000	4087	15.00	16	19	24	34	90	175	340
1891-O	4,540,000	4145	20.00	23	27	30	49	95	195	390
↳1891-O, Medium O Over Horizontal O, FS-501	*	213275	70.00	110	160	260	650	1,100	3,100	—
1891-S	3,196,116	4146	15.00	16	19	24	34	90	175	390
↳1891-S, Medium S Over Small S, FS-501	*	213277	19.50	21	25	32	44	115	230	500

* Included in number above.

100 GREATEST™ UNITED STATES COINS

No. 26 1873-CC "NO ARROWS" LIBERTY SEATED DIME

11859 Transitional Pattern Dime:
Obverse of 1859, Reverse of 1860, Proof
Judd-233

Proof Strikes

	Mintage	GSID	PF-60	PF-63	PF-65
Liberty Seated, No Stars on Obverse (1837–1838), Proof	**n/a**	**74052**	**$6,250**	**$14,000**	**$42,000**
Same, Proof Cameo	**n/a**	**79427**	**—**	**15,500**	**—**
Same, Proof Deep Cameo	**n/a**	**79433**	**—**	**—**	**—**
Liberty Seated, Stars on Obverse (1838–1853, 1856–1860), Proof	**n/a**	**74054**	**675**	**1,100**	**2,250**
Same, Proof Cameo	**n/a**	**79429**	**—**	**1,600**	**3,000**
Same, Proof Deep Cameo	**n/a**	**79435**	**—**	**2,500**	**6,750**
Liberty Seated, Stars, Arrows at Date (1853–1855), Proof	**n/a**	**74055**	**8,750**	**13,000**	**22,000**
Same, Proof Cameo	**n/a**	**79430**	**—**	**15,000**	**33,500**
Liberty Seated, Legend on Obverse (1860–1873, 1875–1891), Proof	**n/a**	**74056**	**415**	**600**	**875**
Same, Proof Cameo	**n/a**	**79431**	**—**	**725**	**1,200**
Same, Proof Deep Cameo	**n/a**	**79437**	**—**	**1,150**	**3,100**
Liberty Seated, Legend, Arrows at Date (1873–1874), Proof	**n/a**	**74057**	**550**	**850**	**2,750**
Same, Proof Cameo	**n/a**	**79432**	**—**	**950**	**3,000**
1858	300	4213	850	1,450	3,750
1859	800	4216	675	1,100	2,250
1859, Obverse of 1859 (With Stars), Reverse of 1860 (a)	20+	4217	12,000	16,000	21,500

	Mintage	GSID	PF-60	PF-63	PF-65
1860	1,000	4220	$430	$725	$1,050
1861	1,000	4223	525	875	2,900
1862	550	4226	650	1,050	2,250
1863	460	4229	650	1,050	2,250
1864	470	4232	650	1,050	2,250
1865	500	4235	650	1,050	2,250
1866	725	4238	650	925	1,600
1867	625	4241	525	775	1,150
1868	600	4244	495	725	1,200
1869	600	4247	415	600	875
1870	1,000	4250	415	600	875
1871	960	4253	415	600	875
1872	950	4256	415	600	875
1873, Closed 3	600	4259	415	600	950
1873	800	4260	550	850	2,750
1874	700	4265	550	850	2,750
1875	700	4268	415	600	875
1876	1,150	4271	415	600	875
1877	510	4274	415	600	875
1878	800	4277	415	600	875
1879	1,100	4280	415	600	875
1880	1,355	4283	415	600	875
1881	975	4286	415	600	875
1882	1,100	4289	415	600	875
1883	1,039	4292	415	600	875
1884	875	4295	415	600	875
1885	930	4298	415	600	875
1886	886	4301	415	600	875
1887	710	4304	415	600	875
1888	832	4307	415	600	875
1889	711	4310	415	600	875
1890	590	4313	415	600	875
1891	600	4316	415	600	875

a. In 1859 the Mint made a dime pattern, of which some 13 to 20 examples are known. These "coins without a country" do not bear the nation's identity (UNITED STATES OF AMERICA). They are transitional pieces, not made for circulation, but struck at the time that the dime's legend was being transferred from the reverse to the obverse (see Variety 4). For more information, consult *United States Pattern Coins* (10th edition).

BARBER (1892–1916)

Designer: *Charles E. Barber.* **Weight:** *2.5 grams.* **Composition:** *.900 silver, .100 copper (net weight: .07234 oz. pure silver).* **Diameter:** *17.9 mm.* **Edge:** *Reeded.* **Mints:** *Philadelphia, Denver, New Orleans, and San Francisco.*

Circulation Strike

Mintmark location is on the reverse, below the bow.

Proof Strike

History. This dime belongs to a suite of silver coins (including the quarter and half dollar) designed by U.S. Mint chief engraver Charles E. Barber. It features a large Liberty Head styled similarly to contemporary French coinage. The reverse of the dime continues the "cereal wreath" motif of the late Liberty Seated era.

Striking and Sharpness. Check the details of the hair on the obverse. The reverse usually is sharp. If weakness is seen, it is typically in the wreath details. The denticles usually are sharp on the obverse and reverse. The Proofs of 1892 to 1901 usually have cameo contrast between the designs and the mirror fields. Later Proofs vary in contrast.

Availability. With the exception of the rare 1894-S, of which fewer than a dozen are known, all dates and mintmarks are collectible. Probably 90 percent or more of the survivors are in lower grades such as AG-3 and G-4. The word LIBERTY in the headband, a key to grading, tended to wear away quickly. Relatively few are in grades from Fine upward. MS coins are somewhat scarce, this being especially true of the branch-mint issues. MS-63 and finer Barber dimes usually are from the Philadelphia Mint or, if from a branch mint, are dated after 1905. Proof Barber dimes survive in proportion to their mintages. Choice and Gem examples are more easily found among dimes than among quarters and half dollars of this type. All were originally sold in silver-coin sets.

Grading Standards

MS-65

MS-60 to 70 (Mint State). ***Obverse:*** At MS-60, some abrasion and contact marks are evident, most noticeably on the cheek and the obverse field to the right. Luster is present, but may be dull or lifeless. Many Barber coins have been cleaned, especially of the earlier dates. At MS-63, contact marks are very few; abrasion still is evident, but less than at lower levels. An MS-65 coin may have minor abrasion on the cheek, but contact marks are so minute as to require magnification. Luster should be full and rich. ***Reverse:*** Comments apply as for the obverse, except that in lower Mint State grades abrasion and contact marks are most noticeable on the highest parts of the leaves and the ribbon, less so on ONE DIME. At MS-65 or higher, there are no marks visible to the unaided eye. The field is mainly protected by design elements and does not show abrasion as much as does the obverse on a given coin.

Illustrated coin: The striking on this example is razor sharp.

AU-53

AU-50, 53, 55, 58 (About Uncirculated). ***Obverse:*** Light wear is seen on the head, especially on the forward hair under LIBERTY. At AU-58, the luster is extensive, but incomplete, especially on the higher parts and in the right field. At AU-50 and 53, luster is less. ***Reverse:*** Wear is seen on the leaves and ribbon. An AU-58 coin will have nearly full luster, more so than on the obverse, as the design elements protect the small field areas. At AU-50 and 53, there still is significant luster.

EF-40

EF-40, 45 (Extremely Fine). ***Obverse:*** Further wear is seen on the head. The hair above the forehead lacks most detail. LIBERTY shows wear but still is strong. ***Reverse:*** Further wear is seen on all areas, most noticeably at the wreath and ribbon. Leaves retain excellent details except on the higher areas.

VF-30

VF-20, 30 (Very Fine). ***Obverse:*** The head shows more wear, now with nearly all detail gone in the hair above the forehead. LIBERTY shows wear, but is complete. The leaves on the head all show wear, as does the upper part of the cap. ***Reverse:*** Wear is more extensive. The details in the highest leaves are weak or missing, but in lower levels the leaf details remain strong.

F-12

F-12, 15 (Fine). ***Obverse:*** The head shows extensive wear. LIBERTY, the key place to check, is weak, especially at ER, but is fully readable. The ANA grading standards and *Photograde* adhere to this. PCGS suggests that lightly struck coins "may have letters partially missing." Traditionally, collectors insist on full LIBERTY. ***Reverse:*** Much detail of the leaves in the higher areas is gone. The rim remains bold.

Illustrated coin: LIBERTY is readable, but letters ER are light.

VG-8, 10 (Very Good). ***Obverse:*** A net of three letters in LIBERTY must be readable. Traditionally LI is clear, and after that there is a partial letter or two. ***Reverse:*** Further wear has made the wreath flat; now only in outline form with only a few traces of details. The rim is complete.

VG-10

G-4, 6 (Good). ***Obverse:*** The head is in outline form, with the center flat. Most of the rim is there. All letters and the date are full. ***Reverse:*** The leaves are all combined and in outline form. The rim is weak in areas.

G-6

AG-3 (About Good). ***Obverse:*** The lettering is readable, but the parts near the border may be worn away. The date is clear. ***Reverse:*** The wreath and interior letters are partially worn away. The rim is weak.

AG-3

PF-60 to 70 (Proof). ***Obverse and Reverse:*** Proofs that are extensively cleaned and have many hairlines, or that are dull and grainy, are lower level, such as PF-60 to 62. These are not widely desired, save for the rare (in any grade) year of 1895, and even so most collectors would rather have a lustrous MS-60 than a dull PF-60. With medium hairlines and good reflectivity, an assigned grade of PF-64 is indicated. Tiny horizontal lines on Liberty's cheek, known as *slide marks*, from National and other album slides scuffing the relief of the cheek, are endemic among Barber silver coins. With noticeable marks of this type, the highest grade assignable is PF-64. With relatively few hairlines, a rating of PF-65 can be given. PF-66 should have hairlines so delicate that magnification is needed to see them. Above that, a Proof should be free of any hairlines or other problems.

PF-67
Deep Cameo

Illustrated coin: Proof dimes of 1911 are rare (only 543 minted), but one with a Deep Cameo finish, as displayed by this coin, is *extremely* rare. The coin is fully struck on both sides, and has neither a blemish nor a trace of toning.

1893, 3 Over 2

Circulation Strikes

	Mintage	GSID	G-4	VG-8	F-12	VF-20	EF-40	AU-50	MS-60	MS-63
Barber (1892–1916)	**n/a**	**72463**	**$7.75**	**$8.00**	**$8.75**	**$15.50**	**$35**	**$75**	**$145**	**$200**
1892	12,120,000	4321	9.00	12.00	19.50	29.00	46	75	145	200
1892-O	3,841,700	4346	11.00	19.00	38.00	60.00	85	115	235	440
1892-S	990,710	4347	80.00	155.00	240.00	285.00	340	390	575	975
1893	3,339,940	4322	10.50	13.50	22.00	32.00	60	80	155	340
1893, 3 Over 2	*	4348	170.00	235.00	310.00	365.00	575	800	1,550	2,200
↳**1893, 3 Over 2, FS-301**	*	377737	170.00	235.00	310.00	365.00	575	800	1,550	2,200
1893-O	1,760,000	4349	31.00	47.00	100.00	120.00	160	260	340	650
1893-S	2,491,401	4350	13.50	24.00	43.00	60.00	100	155	365	850
↳**1893-S, S Over S, FS-501**	*	199162	—	27.00	48.00	70.00	110	170	400	1,000
1894	1,330,000	4323	24.00	47.00	130.00	155.00	195	230	300	470
1894-O	720,000	4351	55.00	90.00	220.00	290.00	525	900	2,200	5,000
1895	690,000	4324	95.00	170.00	365.00	490.00	550	625	775	950
1895-O	440,000	4353	550.00	700.00	1,100.00	1,550.00	2,600	3,600	6,000	14,000
1895-S	1,120,000	4354	43.00	60.00	145.00	210.00	235	340	575	1,200
1896	2,000,000	4325	14.50	25.00	60.00	90.00	110	120	155	405
1896-O	610,000	4355	90.00	160.00	285.00	375.00	525	1,000	1,500	3,000
1896-S	575,056	4356	115.00	215.00	310.00	390.00	550	750	1,100	2,000
1897	10,868,533	4326	8.00	8.50	10.00	19.00	42	75	145	200
1897-O	666,000	4357	80.00	145.00	325.00	415.00	525	775	1,500	2,900
1897-S	1,342,844	4358	20.00	40.00	110.00	135.00	235	325	775	1,150
1898	16,320,000	4327	7.75	8.25	10.00	17.50	38	75	145	200
1898-O	2,130,000	4359	12.00	39.00	100.00	155.00	200	300	490	1,100
1898-S	1,702,507	4360	8.00	15.00	38.00	55.00	120	180	575	1,500
1899	19,580,000	4328	7.75	8.00	10.00	18.00	35	75	145	200
1899-O	2,650,000	4361	14.50	30.00	80.00	115.00	195	245	430	1,000
1899-S	1,867,493	4362	13.00	19.00	38.00	43.00	65	110	340	675
1900	17,600,000	4329	7.75	8.00	8.75	15.50	35	75	145	200
1900-O	2,010,000	4363	17.50	40.00	130.00	170.00	220	285	600	1,250
1900-S	5,168,270	4364	11.00	16.00	22.00	34.00	60	100	285	525
1901	18,859,665	4330	7.75	8.00	8.75	15.50	35	75	145	200
1901-O	5,620,000	4365	9.50	13.50	22.00	43.00	90	175	725	1,100
↳**1901-O, O Over Horizontal O, FS-501**	*	227332	40.00	55.00	80.00	130.00	290	455	775	1,150
1901-S	593,022	4366	100.00	195.00	415.00	500.00	600	850	1,750	2,600
1902	21,380,000	4331	7.75	8.00	8.75	15.50	35	75	145	235
1902-O	4,500,000	4367	10.50	14.50	24.00	39.00	85	160	390	750
1902-S	2,070,000	4368	13.50	28.00	60.00	100.00	135	200	390	875
1903	19,500,000	4332	7.75	8.00	8.75	18.00	35	75	145	200
1903-O	8,180,000	4369	9.00	10.50	17.50	34.00	80	130	260	750
1903-S	613,300	4370	80.00	145.00	470.00	550.00	775	1,100	1,500	1,900
1904	14,600,357	4333	7.75	8.00	8.75	16.50	35	75	145	210
1904-S	800,000	4371	40.00	80.00	155.00	240.00	325	490	900	1,600
1905	14,551,623	4334	7.75	8.00	8.75	15.50	35	75	145	200

* Included in number above.

1905-O, Normal O

1905-O, Micro O

Circulation Strikes

	Mintage	GSID	G-4	VG-8	F-12	VF-20	EF-40	AU-50	MS-60	MS-63
1905-O	3,400,000	4372	$9.00	$16.00	$38.00	$60.00	$130	$155	$325	$490
1905-O, Micro O	*	4373	100.00	145.00	210.00	260.00	600	950	3,000	6,250
↳1905-O, Micro O, FS-501	*	391420	100.00	145.00	210.00	260.00	600	950	3,000	6,250
1905-S	6,855,199	4374	9.75	13.50	20.00	40.00	70	115	200	280
1906	19,957,731	4335	7.75	8.00	8.75	15.50	35	75	145	200
↳1906, Repunched Date, FS-302	*	376683	8.25	8.75	9.75	17.00	39	80	155	220
1906-D	4,060,000	4375	9.00	10.50	14.00	22.00	45	80	155	360
↳1906-D, D Over O, FS-501	*	392984	—	—	—	—	—	—	—	—
1906-O	2,610,000	4376	13.00	24.00	55.00	90.00	130	145	195	420
↳1906-O, Repunched Date/Misplaced Date, FS-301	*	329264	14.50	27.00	60.00	95.00	145	155	215	465
1906-S	3,136,640	4377	9.00	10.50	16.00	31.00	70	145	290	495
1907	22,220,000	4336	7.75	8.00	8.75	15.50	35	75	145	200
↳1907, Repunched Date, FS-301	*	329266	8.25	8.75	9.75	17.00	39	80	155	220
1907-D	4,080,000	4378	9.00	10.50	15.50	27.00	55	115	260	750
1907-O	5,058,000	4379	10.50	15.00	36.00	55.00	85	110	200	320
↳1907-O, O Over O, FS-501	*	329268	11.50	16.50	40.00	60.00	90	120	220	350
1907-S	3,178,470	4380	10.50	14.50	22.00	43.00	90	150	360	725
1908	10,600,000	4337	7.75	8.00	8.75	15.50	35	75	145	200
1908-D	7,490,000	4381	7.75	8.00	8.75	16.00	40	75	145	235
1908-O	1,789,000	4382	11.50	19.00	50.00	70.00	130	190	440	775
1908-S	3,220,000	4383	8.75	10.50	16.00	23.00	70	175	365	775
1909	10,240,000	4338	7.75	8.00	8.75	15.50	35	75	145	200
1909-D	954,000	4384	16.00	28.00	70.00	110.00	135	220	525	875
1909-O	2,287,000	4385	9.00	12.00	16.00	31.00	70	155	310	725
1909-S	1,000,000	4386	21.00	39.00	100.00	135.00	190	305	525	1,250
1910	11,520,000	4339	7.75	8.00	8.75	15.50	35	75	145	230
1910-D	3,490,000	4387	10.50	13.50	17.00	27.00	65	100	210	390
1910-S	1,240,000	4388	13.00	24.00	55.00	80.00	135	195	415	650
1911	18,870,000	4340	7.75	8.00	8.75	15.50	35	75	145	215
1911-D	11,209,000	4389	7.75	8.00	8.75	18.00	38	75	145	200
1911-S	3,520,000	4390	10.50	13.50	17.00	27.00	60	110	195	360
1912	19,349,300	4341	7.75	8.00	8.75	15.50	35	75	145	200
1912-D	11,760,000	4391	7.75	8.00	8.75	15.50	35	75	145	200
↳1912-D, D Over D, FS-501	*	392964	—	—	—	—	—	—	—	—
1912-S	3,420,000	4392	10.50	13.50	17.00	31.00	60	95	180	310
↳1912-S, Doubled Die Obverse, FS-101	*	392965	—	—	—	—	—	—	—	—
↳1912-S, Die Chips, FS-401	*	392985	—	—	—	—	—	—	—	—
1913	19,760,000	4342	7.75	8.00	8.75	15.50	35	75	145	200
1913-S	510,000	4393	47.00	80.00	155.00	215.00	365	650	1,250	2,000
1914	17,360,230	4343	7.75	8.00	8.75	15.50	35	75	145	200
1914-D	11,908,000	4394	7.75	8.00	8.75	15.50	35	75	145	220
1914-S	2,100,000	4395	8.25	9.50	12.00	23.00	55	95	170	325
1915	5,620,000	4344	7.75	8.00	8.75	15.50	35	75	145	200
1915-S	960,000	4396	13.00	20.00	38.00	55.00	90	130	235	365
1916	18,490,000	4345	7.75	8.00	8.75	15.50	35	75	145	200
1916-S	5,820,000	4397	7.75	8.00	8.75	15.50	35	75	145	220

* Included in number above.

Proof Strikes

	Mintage	GSID	PF-60	PF-63	PF-65	PF-66
Barber (1892–1916), Proof	**n/a**	**73853**	**$330**	**$490**	**$875**	**$1,200**
Same, Proof Cameo	**n/a**	**73854**	**—**	**575**	**950**	**1,250**
Same, Proof Deep Cameo	**n/a**	**73855**	**—**	**900**	**1,600**	**2,500**
1892	1,245	4398	330	490	875	1,200
1893	792	4401	330	490	875	1,200
1893, 3 Over 2	*	84861	7,000	10,500	—	—
1894	972	4404	330	490	875	1,200
1894-S (a)	9 known	4352	1,110,000	1,380,000	1,800,000	2,100,000
	Auctions: $2,160,000 PCGS PF-66 HA 01/25					
1895	880	4407	330	490	875	1,200
1896	762	4410	330	490	875	1,200
1897	731	4413	330	490	875	1,200
1898	735	4416	330	490	875	1,200
1899	846	4419	330	490	875	1,200
1900	912	4422	330	490	875	1,200
1901	813	4425	330	490	875	1,200
1902	777	4428	330	490	875	1,200
1903	755	4431	330	490	875	1,200
1904	670	4434	330	490	875	1,200
1905	727	4437	330	490	875	1,200
1906	675	4440	330	490	875	1,200
1907	575	70950	330	490	875	1,200
1908	545	4445	330	490	875	1,200
1909	650	4448	330	490	875	1,200
1910	551	4451	330	490	875	1,200
1911	543	4454	330	490	875	1,200
1912	700	4457	330	490	875	1,200
1913	622	4460	330	490	875	1,200
1914	425	4463	330	490	1,000	1,300
1915	450	4466	330	490	1,150	1,750

* Included in number above. **a.** The reason for the low mintage of the Proof 1894-S dime is unknown. Popular theories, among others, include a rounding out of the Mint's record books, or a special presentation to bankers visiting the San Francisco Mint. Fewer than a dozen examples are known to exist. Five of these coins were reserved for assay.

MERCURY (WINGED LIBERTY HEAD) (1916–1945)

Designer: *Adolph A. Weinman.* **Weight:** *2.5 grams.* **Composition:** *.900 silver, .100 copper (net weight .07234 oz. pure silver).* **Diameter:** *17.9 mm.* **Edge:** *Reeded.* **Mints:** *Philadelphia, Denver, and San Francisco.*

Circulation Strike

Mintmark location is on the reverse, at the base of the branch.

Proof Strike

History. In 1916 a new dime, designed by sculptor Adolph A. Weinman (who also created the half dollar that debuted that year), replaced Charles Barber's Liberty Head type. Officially Weinman's design was known as the Winged Liberty Head, but numismatists commonly call the coin the *Mercury* dime, from Liberty's wing-capped resemblance to the Roman god. The reverse depicts a fasces (symbolic of strength in unity) and an olive branch (symbolic of peaceful intentions). Production was continuous from 1916 to 1945, except for 1922, 1932, and 1933. The Mint also created a 2016 gold Mercury dime at a smaller dimension. See page 448.

Striking and Sharpness. Many Mercury dimes exhibit areas of light striking, most notably in the center horizontal band across the fasces, less so in the lower horizontal band. The bands are composed of two parallel lines with a separation or "split" between. The term Full Bands, abbreviated FB, describes coins with both parallel lines in the center band distinctly separated. *In addition*, some dimes may display weak striking in other areas (not noted by certification services or others), including at areas of Liberty's hair, the rim, and the date. Dimes of 1921 in particular can have FB but poorly struck dates. Proof dies were completely polished, including the portrait.

Availability. Certain coins, such as 1916-D; 1921-P; 1921-D; 1942, 2 Over 1; and 1942-D, 2 Over 1, are elusive in any grade. Others are generally available in lower circulated grades, although some are scarce. In MS many of the issues before 1931 range from scarce to rare. If with FB and also sharply struck in other areas, some are rare. MS coins usually are very lustrous. In the marketplace certain scarce early issues such as 1916-D, 1921, and 1921-D are often graded slightly more liberally than are later varieties. Proofs were minted from 1936 to 1942 and are available in proportion to their mintages.

Grading Standards

MS-66 Full Bands

MS-60 to 70 (Mint State). ***Obverse:*** At MS-60, some abrasion and contact marks are evident on the highest part of the portrait, including the hair immediately to the right of the face and the upper left part of the wing. At MS-63, abrasion is slight at best, less so for MS-64. Album slide marks on the cheek, if present, should not be at any grade above MS-64. An MS-65 coin should display no abrasion or contact marks except under magnification, and MS-66 and higher coins should have none at all. Luster should be full and rich. ***Reverse:*** Comments apply as for the obverse, except that the highest parts of the fasces, these being the horizontal bands, are the places to check. The field is mainly protected by design elements and does not show contact marks readily.

AU-50, 53, 55, 58 (About Uncirculated). ***Obverse:*** Light wear is seen on the cheek, the hair immediately to the right of the face, the left edge of the wing, and the upper right of the wing. At AU-58, the luster is extensive, but incomplete, especially on the higher parts and in the field. At AU-50 and 53, luster is less. ***Reverse:*** Light wear is seen on the higher parts of the fasces. An AU-58 coin has nearly full luster, more so than on the obverse, as the design elements protect the field areas. At AU-50 and 53, there still is significant luster. Generally, the reverse appears to be in a slightly higher grade than the obverse.

AU-50

EF-40, 45 (Extremely Fine). ***Obverse:*** Further wear is seen on the head. Many of the hair details are blended together, as are some feather details at the left side of the wing. ***Reverse:*** The horizontal bands on the fasces may be fused together. The diagonal bands remain in slight relief against the vertical lines (sticks).

EF-45

VF-20, 30 (Very Fine). ***Obverse:*** The head shows more wear, now with the forehead and cheek mostly blending into the hair. More feather details are gone. ***Reverse:*** Wear is more extensive, but the diagonal and horizontal bands on the fasces still are separated from the thin vertical sticks.

VF-20

F-12, 15 (Fine). ***Obverse:*** The head shows more wear, the hair has only slight detail, and most of the feathers are gone. In the marketplace a coin in F-12 grade usually has slightly less detail than stated by the ANA grading standards or *Photograde*, from modern interpretations. ***Reverse:*** Many of the tiny vertical sticks in the fasces are blended together. The bands can be barely discerned and may be worn away at the highest-relief parts.

F-12

VG-8

VG-8, 10 (Very Good). ***Obverse:*** Wear is more extensive on the portrait, and only a few feathers are seen on the wing. The outlines between the hair and cap and of the wing are distinct. Lettering is clear, but light in areas. ***Reverse:*** The rim is complete, or it may be slightly worn away in areas. Only a few traces of the vertical sticks remain in the fasces. Current interpretations in the marketplace are given here and are less strict than those listed by the ANA grading standards and *Photograde*. Often, earlier issues are graded more liberally than are later dates.

G-4

G-4, 6 (Good). ***Obverse:*** Wear is more extensive, with not all of the outline between the hair and the wing visible. The rim is worn into the edges of the letters and often into the bottom of the last numeral in the date. ***Reverse:*** The rim is worn away, as are the outer parts of the letters. The fasces is flat or may show a hint of a vertical stick or two. The leaves are thick from wear. The mintmark, if any, is easily seen.

AG-3

AG-3 (About Good). ***Obverse:*** The rim is worn further into the letters. The head is mostly outline all over, except for a few indicates of edges. Folds remain at the top of the cap. The date is clearly visible. ***Reverse:*** The rim is worn further into the letters. The mintmark, if any, is clear but may be worn away slightly at the bottom. The apparent wear is slightly greater on the reverse than on the obverse.

PF-67

PF-60 to 70 (Proof). ***Obverse and Reverse:*** Proofs that are extensively cleaned and have many hairlines, or that are dull and grainy, are lower level, such as PF-60 to 62. These are not widely desired, and represent coins that have been mistreated. With medium hairlines and good reflectivity, assigned grades of PF-63 or 64 are appropriate. Tiny horizontal lines on Liberty's cheek, known as *slide marks*, from National and other album slides scuffing the relief of the cheek, are common; coins with such marks should not be graded higher than PF-64, but sometimes are. With relatively few hairlines and no noticeable slide marks, a rating of PF-65 can be given. PF-66 should have hairlines so delicate that magnification is needed to see them. Above that, a Proof should be free of any hairlines or other problems.

Full Bands

Circulation Strikes

	Mintage	GSID	VG-8	F-12	VF-20	EF-40	AU-50	MS-60	MS-63	MS-65	MS-66	MS-67
Mercury (1916–1945)	n/a	72464	$4.80	$4.90	$5.50	$6.50	$6.50	$9.75	$13.50	$26	$40	$80
Same, Full Bands	n/a	72465	—	—	—	—	—	16.00	23.00	43	60	130
1916	22,180,080	4469	8.75	10.50	12.50	16.00	20.00	55.00	100.00	180	340	900
1916, Full Bands	*	4470	—	—	—	—	—	70.00	130.00	245	495	1,000
1916-D (a)	264,000	4523	2,200.00	3,600.00	4,950.00	7,250.00	11,000.00	14,000.00	18,500.00	29,000	45,500	—
1916-D, Full Bands (a)	*	4524	—	—	—	—	11,000	19,000.00	30,000.00	66,000	86,500	192,000
	Auctions: $204,000, PCGS MS-67 SBG 03/20											
1916-S	10,450,000	4525	8.75	13.00	18.00	27.00	32.00	49.00	115.00	310	415	1,500
1916-S, Full Bands	*	4526	—	—	—	—	—	115.00	210.00	925	1,500	3,750
1917	55,230,000	4471	5.00	5.50	6.25	7.75	12.00	28.00	60.00	195	390	925
1917, Full Bands	*	4472	—	—	—	—	—	80.00	155.00	470	850	2,000
1917-D	9,402,000	4527	10.00	16.00	30.00	75.00	110.00	170.00	290.00	850	1,500	5,500
1917-D, Full Bands	*	4528	—	—	—	—	—	340.00	725.00	4,200	5,750	36,500
1917-S	27,330,000	4529	8.25	9.75	11.50	18.50	34.00	125.00	215.00	405	850	1,900
1917-S, Full Bands	*	4530	—	—	—	—	—	235.00	390.00	1,600	2,200	8,000
1918	26,680,000	4473	5.25	6.50	12.00	35.00	45.00	90.00	155.00	470	1,250	—
1918, Full Bands	*	4474	—	—	—	—	—	245.00	390.00	1,000	3,400	14,500
1918-D	22,674,800	4531	5.25	6.00	13.50	35.00	75.00	195.00	365.00	900	1,700	3,500
1918-D, Full Bands	*	4532	—	—	—	—	—	1,200.00	2,500.00	14,000	53,000	180,000
	Auctions: $182,125, PCGS MS-67 LGND 09/15											
1918-S	19,300,000	4533	9.50	11.50	13.50	27.00	70.00	160.00	390.00	925	1,100	2,400
1918-S, Full Bands	*	4534	—	—	—	—	—	2,000.00	3,500.00	11,000	20,500	108,000
	Auctions: $144,000, PCGS MS-67 HA 01/19											
1919	35,740,000	4475	5.25	5.75	7.00	11.00	30.00	70.00	180.00	440	850	1,750
↳1919, Doubled Die Obverse, FS-101	*	234556	3,750.00	4,250.00	5,250.00	10,000.00	—	—	—	—	—	—
1919, Full Bands	*	4476	—	—	—	—	—	170.00	260.00	900	1,700	8,000
1919-D	9,939,000	4535	10.00	15.50	24.00	60.00	120.00	345.00	725.00	1,450	3,600	6,000
1919-D, Full Bands	*	4536	—	—	—	—	—	1,300.00	3,000.00	32,000	108,000	—
	Auctions: $218,500, PCGS MS-66 HA 08/00											
1919-S	8,850,000	4537	5.50	13.50	22.00	43.00	115.00	390.00	900.00	2,000	2,500	3,400
1919-S, Full Bands	*	4538	—	—	—	—	—	1,950.00	5,750.00	21,500	72,000	132,000
	Auctions: $132,000, PCGS MS-66 HA 05/24											
1920	59,030,000	4477	5.00	5.50	6.25	7.75	12.00	35.00	95.00	245	495	1,450
1920, Full Bands	*	4478	—	—	—	—	—	80.00	155.00	470	625	2,100
1920-D	19,171,000	4539	7.50	10.50	13.50	27.00	75.00	210.00	495.00	725	1,450	3,750
1920-D, Full Bands	*	4540	—	—	—	—	—	600.00	1,150.00	3,100	4,050	45,500
1920-S	13,820,000	4541	7.50	11.50	16.50	46.00	135.00	340.00	575.00	1,500	2,400	—
1920-S, Full Bands	*	4542	—	—	—	—	—	850.00	1,750.00	7,500	12,000	74,500
1921	1,230,000	4479	95.00	130.00	260.00	575.00	1,000.00	1,800.00	2,750.00	4,000	5,000	—
1921, Full Bands	*	4480	—	—	—	—	—	2,300.00	3,600.00	5,500	11,000	26,500

* Included in number above. **a.** Beware of altered or otherwise spurious mintmarks.

1928-S, Small S

1928-S, Large S
FS-501

Circulation Strikes *(continued)*

	Mintage	GSID	VG-8	F-12	VF-20	EF-40	AU-50	MS-60	MS-63	MS-65	MS-66	MS-67
1921-D	1,080,000	4543	$135.00	$195.00	$360.00	$675.00	$1,300.00	$2,000	$2,750	$3,750	$4,750	$14,500
1921-D, Full Bands	*	4544	—	—	—	—	—	2,600	4,200	8,500	11,000	33,500
1923 (b)	50,130,000	4481	4.80	4.90	6.00	7.75	11.50	32	55	195	260	850
1923, Full Bands	*	4482	—	—	—	—	—	49	95	310	430	925
1923-S	6,440,000	4545	7.50	14.50	25.00	110.00	170.00	415	650	1,400	2,250	3,250
1923-S, Full Bands	*	4546	—	—	—	—	—	650	1,600	8,250	48,000	—
	Auctions: $105,750, PCGS MS-66 LGND 09/18											
1924	24,010,000	4483	5.25	5.75	7.00	16.00	32.00	75	130	235	415	1,200
1924, Full Bands	*	4484	—	—	—	—	—	115	210	550	1,250	3,250
1924-D	6,810,000	4547	7.50	14.50	27.00	70.00	115.00	310	525	1,150	1,900	3,250
1924-D, Full Bands	*	4548	—	—	—	—	—	550	900	2,250	3,250	14,500
1924-S	7,120,000	4549	7.50	11.50	27.00	95.00	160.00	390	575	1,950	3,450	7,000
1924-S, Full Bands	*	4550	—	—	—	—	—	650	1,600	21,500	54,000	—
1925	25,610,000	4485	4.80	4.90	6.00	9.00	13.50	49	115	290	575	1,200
1925, Full Bands	*	4486	—	—	—	—	—	90	210	900	1,250	2,750
1925-D	5,117,000	4551	13.00	21.00	60.00	155.00	245.00	525	900	1,750	2,900	—
1925-D, Full Bands	*	4552	—	—	—	—	—	675	1,700	5,000	8,500	20,500
1925-S	5,850,000	4553	11.50	18.50	35.00	120.00	210.00	405	775	1,450	2,250	—
1925-S, Full Bands	*	4554	—	—	—	—	—	675	1,400	3,750	5,250	30,000
1926	32,160,000	4487	4.80	4.90	6.00	8.50	13.50	43	80	260	455	1,000
↳1926, Doubled Die Obverse, FS-101	*	390491	—	—	—	—	—	—	—	—	—	—
1926, Full Bands	*	4488	—	—	—	—	—	65	120	405	825	2,800
↳1926, Doubled Die Obverse, FS-101, Full Bands	*	390492	—	—	—	—	—	—	—	—	—	—
1926-D	6,828,000	4555	6.25	10.50	19.00	40.00	80.00	215	310	650	1,550	2,750
1926-D, Full Bands	*	4556	—	—	—	—	—	365	725	3,000	4,750	36,000
1926-S	1,520,000	4557	20.00	43.00	95.00	310.00	525.00	1,800	3,000	4,750	5,500	11,500
1926-S, Full Bands	*	4558	—	—	—	—	—	2,500	4,500	9,500	29,000	66,000
1927	28,080,000	4489	4.80	4.90	6.00	9.00	14.50	43	85	155	325	1,000
1927, Full Bands	*	4490	—	—	—	—	—	70	145	600	825	1,250
1927-D	4,812,000	4559	8.75	15.50	35.00	115.00	160.00	440	775	1,700	2,100	—
1927-D, Full Bands	*	4560	—	—	—	—	—	850	2,000	8,250	15,500	—
1927-S	4,770,000	4561	8.75	11.50	19.00	49.00	120.00	475	850	1,550	3,000	7,500
1927-S, Full Bands	*	4562	—	—	—	—	—	1,900	2,900	5,250	15,000	79,000
1928	19,480,000	4491	4.80	4.90	6.00	7.75	11.50	35	70	145	340	725
1928, Full Bands	*	4492	—	—	—	—	—	65	150	365	550	1,550
1928-D	4,161,000	4563	8.75	22.00	36.00	90.00	155.00	235	500	1,100	2,000	2,750
1928-D, Full Bands	*	4564	—	—	—	—	—	600	1,250	3,100	7,000	43,000
1928-S (b)	7,400,000	4565	8.75	10.50	12.50	22.00	40.00	170	340	550	775	1,750
1928-S, Full Bands (b)	*	4566	—	—	—	—	—	575	975	2,500	5,500	14,500

* Included in number above. **b.** Two mintmark styles exist: Large S (scarce) and Small S (common). About 80% of 1928-S dimes are of the Small S style. The scarcer Large S is worth about two to three times the values listed (which are for the Small S).

1929-S, Doubled Die Obverse
FS-101

Circulation Strikes *(continued)*

	Mintage	GSID	VG-8	F-12	VF-20	EF-40	AU-50	MS-60	MS-63	MS-65	MS-66	MS-67
1929	25,970,000	4493	$4.80	$4.90	$6.00	$7.75	$10.50	$27	$38	$90	$180	$415
1929, Full Bands	*	4494	—	—	—	—	—	—	80	310	405	1,200
1929-D	5,034,000	4567	4.80	4.90	6.00	7.75	10.50	30	43	130	235	575
1929-D, Full Bands	*	4568	—	—	—	—	—	—	120	285	625	1,400
1929-S	4,730,000	4569	5.50	5.75	6.50	8.50	12.00	40	75	235	365	750
↳1929-S, Doubled Die Obverse, FS-101	*	392966	—	—	—	—	—	—	—	—	—	—
1929-S, Full Bands	*	4570	—	—	—	—	—	—	210	675	1,200	1,900
↳1929-S, Doubled Die Obverse, FS-101, Full Bands	*	213567	—	—	—	—	—	—	—	1,500	—	—
1930 (b)	6,770,000	4495	4.80	4.90	6.00	8.50	10.50	34	60	130	240	2,000
1930, Full Bands	*	4496	—	—	—	—	—	—	155	575	1,200	3,100
1930-S	1,843,000	4571	5.25	5.75	8.25	23.00	55.00	110	160	375	550	1,600
1930-S, Full Bands	*	4572	—	—	—	—	—	—	310	1,250	1,750	3,750
1931	3,150,000	4497	5.00	6.25	9.75	13.00	22.00	55	110	195	340	1,500
1931, Full Bands	*	4498	—	—	—	—	—	130	285	650	1,450	3,750
1931-D	1,260,000	4573	13.00	20.00	28.00	55.00	70.00	130	175	430	575	1,200
1931-D, Full Bands	*	4574	—	—	—	—	—	—	390	650	850	2,300
↳1931-D, Doubled Die Obverse, FS-101, Full Bands	*	213568	—	—	—	—	—	—	430	725	950	2,550
↳1931-D, Doubled Die Obverse, FS-101	*	234558	—	—	—	60.00	75.00	135	190	470	650	1,250
1931-S	1,800,000	4575	6.75	8.25	13.50	32.00	70.00	130	195	405	650	1,100
1931-S, Full Bands	*	4576	—	—	—	—	—	325	775	2,550	3,250	12,000
	Auctions: $270,250, PCGS MS-67 LGND 06/19											
1934	24,080,000	4499	4.80	4.90	6.00	10.50	14.50	30	38	49	80	260
1934-D	6,772,000	4577	5.25	5.25	7.00	17.50	31.00	60	70	95	175	650
↳1934-D, D Over D, FS-501	*	234559	—	—	—	—	—	—	—	—	—	—
1934-D, Full Bands	*	4578	—	—	—	—	—	—	130	350	725	1,550
↳1934-D, D Over D, FS-501, Full Bands	*	213570	—	—	—	—	—	—	—	—	—	—
1935	58,830,000	4501	4.80	4.90	6.00	7.00	7.00	15	23	43	70	180
1935, Full Bands	*	4502	—	—	—	—	—	—	43	110	175	430
1935-D	10,477,000	4579	5.25	5.25	6.00	12.00	27.00	40	55	85	180	725
1935-D, Full Bands	*	4580	—	—	—	—	—	—	130	405	575	1,350
1935-S	15,840,000	4581	5.25	5.25	6.00	7.75	11.50	27	32	40	80	310
1935-S, Full Bands	*	4582	—	—	—	—	—	—	130	405	575	1,250
1936	87,500,000	4503	4.80	4.90	6.00	7.00	7.00	11	15	30	60	110
1936, Full Bands	*	4504	—	—	—	—	—	—	35	95	145	455

* Included in number above.

1936-S, Overdate
FS-110

Circulation Strikes *(continued)*

	Mintage	GSID	VG-8	F-12	VF-20	EF-40	AU-50	MS-60	MS-63	MS-65	MS-66	MS-67
1936-D	16,132,000	4583	$5.25	$5.25	$6.00	$9.50	$13.50	$32.00	$46.00	$80	$115	$415
↳1936-D, D Over D, FS-501	*	392968	—	—	—	—	—	—	—	—	—	—
1936-D, Full Bands	*	4584	—	—	—	—	—	—	95.00	260	340	525
↳1936-D, D Over D, FS-501, Full Bands	*	392969	—	—	—	—	—	—	—	—	—	—
1936-S	9,210,000	4585	5.25	5.25	6.00	7.75	12.00	30.00	38.00	46	90	340
↳1936-S, Overdate, FS-110	*	392987	—	—	—	—	—	—	—	—	—	—
1936-S, Full Bands	*	4586	—	—	—	—	—	—	55.00	135	190	550
↳1936-S, Overdate, FS-110, Full Bands	*	213572	—	—	—	—	—	—	—	—	—	—
1937	56,860,000	4505	4.80	4.90	6.00	7.00	7.00	9.75	13.50	26	47	100
1937, Full Bands	*	4506	—	—	—	—	—	—	31.00	50	90	200
1937-D	14,146,000	4587	4.80	4.90	6.00	7.75	9.25	26.00	34.00	55	80	150
1937-D, Full Bands	*	4588	—	—	—	—	—	—	39.00	120	145	405
1937-S	9,740,000	4589	4.80	4.90	6.00	7.75	10.50	24.00	30.00	50	100	140
1937-S, Full Bands	*	4590	—	—	—	—	—	—	75.00	275	310	725
1938	22,190,000	4507	4.80	4.90	6.00	7.00	7.00	9.75	16.00	34	55	105
1938, Full Bands	*	4508	—	—	—	—	—	—	35.00	105	120	280
1938-D	5,537,000	4591	4.80	4.90	6.00	7.75	10.50	24.00	30.00	43	75	195
1938-D, Full Bands	*	4592	—	—	—	—	—	—	35.00	85	130	325
1938-S	8,090,000	4593	4.80	4.90	6.00	7.75	10.50	24.00	32.00	46	70	195
1938-S, Full Bands	*	4594	—	—	—	—	—	—	55.00	190	340	825
	Auctions: $364,250, PCGS MS-68 LGND 06/19											
1939	67,740,000	4509	4.80	4.90	6.00	7.00	7.00	9.75	13.50	26	47	95
1939, Full Bands	*	4510	—	—	—	—	—	—	50.00	175	290	825
1939-D	24,394,000	4595	4.80	4.90	6.00	7.75	10.00	24.00	30.00	42	55	95
1939-D, Full Bands	*	4596	—	—	—	—	—	—	34.00	60	80	195
1939-S	10,540,000	4597	4.80	4.90	6.00	7.75	10.00	24.00	30.00	40	70	260
1939-S, Full Bands	*	4598	—	—	—	—	—	—	155.00	550	1,150	2,500
1940	65,350,000	4511	4.80	4.90	6.00	7.00	7.25	9.75	13.50	26	40	80
1940, Full Bands	*	4512	—	—	—	—	—	—	23.00	50	70	235
1940-D	21,198,000	4599	4.80	4.90	6.00	7.00	7.25	9.75	13.50	39	55	100
1940-D, Full Bands	*	4600	—	—	—	—	—	—	23.00	50	95	200
1940-S	21,560,000	4601	4.80	4.90	6.00	7.00	7.25	9.75	17.50	39	47	110
↳1940-S, S Over S, FS-501	*	234563	—	—	—	—	—	—	—	—	—	—
↳1940-S, Doubled Die Obverse/Doubled Die Reverse, FS-101/801	*	234564	—	—	—	—	—	—	—	—	—	—
1940-S, Full Bands	*	4602	—	—	—	—	—	—	28.00	105	130	470
↳1940-S, FS-501, Full Bands	*	213578	—	—	—	—	—	—	—	—	—	—
↳1940-S, Doubled Die Obverse/Doubled Die Reverse, FS-101/801, Full Bands	*	213577	—	—	—	—	—	—	—	—	—	—

* Included in number above.

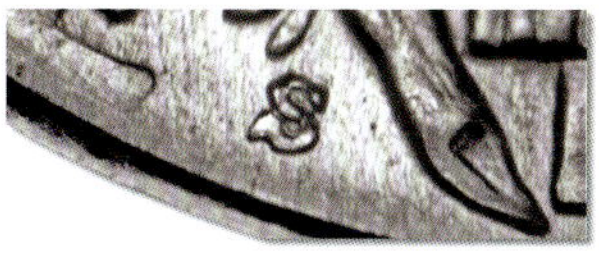

1941-S, Small S

1941-S, Large S
FS-511

1942, 42 Over 41
FS-101

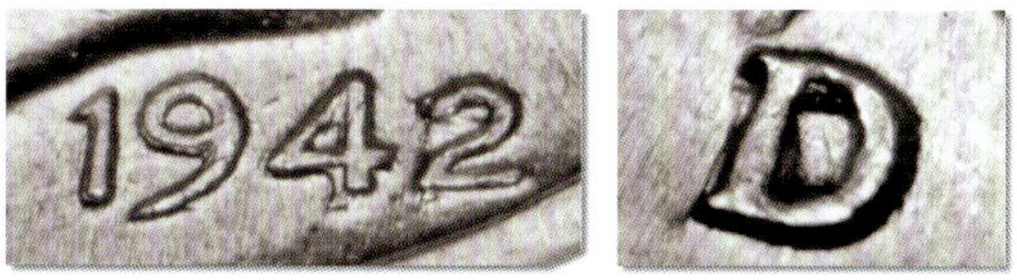

1942-D, 42 Over 41, Repunched Mintmark
FS-101

Circulation Strikes *(continued)*

	Mintage	GSID	VG-8	F-12	VF-20	EF-40	AU-50	MS-60	MS-63	MS-65	MS-66	MS-67
1941	175,090,000	4513	$4.80	$4.90	$5.50	$6.50	$6.50	$9.75	$13.50	$26	$40	$80
1941, Full Bands	*	4514	—	—	—	—	—	—	23.00	46	80	175
1941-D	45,634,000	4603	4.80	4.90	5.50	6.50	6.50	9.75	17.50	30	55	90
1941-D, Full Bands	*	4604	—	—	—	—	—	—	23.00	55	70	135
1941-S	43,090,000	4605	4.80	4.90	5.50	6.50	6.50	9.75	13.50	39	55	95
↳1941-S, S Over S, FS-501	*	375857	9.50	12.00	16.00	22.00	27.00	49.00	85.00	145	260	—
↳1941-S, S Over S, FS-502	*	375858	—	—	—	—	—	—	—	—	—	—
↳1941-S, Large S, FS-511	*	375859	—	17.50	22.00	30.00	49.00	90.00	130.00	180	280	—
1941-S, Full Bands	*	4606	—	—	—	—	—	—	28.00	50	75	235
↳1941-S, S Over S, FS-501, Full Bands	*	213581	—	—	—	—	—	55	110.00	210	285	—
↳1941-S, S Over S, FS-502, Full Bands	*	213582	—	—	—	—	—	—	—	—	—	—
↳1941-S, Large S, FS-511, Full Bands	*	213583	—	—	—	—	—	—	260.00	415	625	950
1942	205,410,000	4515	4.80	4.90	5.50	6.50	6.50	9.75	13.50	26	40	80
1942, Full Bands	*	4516	—	—	—	—	—	—	23.00	43	75	260
1942, 42 Over 41	*	4607	430.00	500.00	625.00	775.00	1,200.00	3,450.00	5,500.00	10,500	15,000	36,000
↳1942, 42 Over 41, FS-101	*	390394	430.00	500.00	625.00	775.00	1,200.00	3,450.00	5,500.00	10,500	15,000	36,000
1942, 42 Over 41, Full Bands	*	4608	—	—	—	—	1,500	5,500	17,500.00	50,500	120,000	—
↳1942, 42 Over 41, FS-101, Full Bands	*	390395	—	—	—	—	1,500	5,500	17,500.00	50,500	120,000	—
	Auctions: $102,000, PCGS MS-66 HA 05/24											
1942-D	60,740,000	4611	4.80	4.90	5.50	6.50	6.50	9.75	17.50	30	47	90
1942-D, Full Bands	*	4612	—	—	—	—	—	—	23.00	55	75	160
1942-D, 42 Over 41	*	4609	470.00	525.00	575.00	750.00	1,250.00	3,250.00	6,250.00	10,500	24,000	—
↳1942-D, 42 Over 41, FS-101	*	390396	470.00	525.00	575.00	750.00	1,250.00	3,250.00	6,250.00	10,500	24,000	—
1942-D, 42 Over 41, Full Bands	*	4610	—	—	—	—	2,450	4,250	8,000.00	11,000	31,000	66,000
↳1942-D, 42 Over 41, FS-101, Full Bands	*	390397	—	—	—	—	2,450	4,250	8,000.00	11,000	31,000	66,000

* Included in number above.

1945-D, D Over Horizontal D
FS-502

Circulation Strikes *(continued)*

	Mintage	GSID	VG-8	F-12	VF-20	EF-40	AU-50	MS-60	MS-63	MS-65	MS-66	MS-67
1942-S	49,300,000	4613	$4.80	$4.90	$5.50	$6.50	$6.50	$9.75	$13.50	$30	$50	$110
↳**1942-S, Inverted Mintmark, FS-501**	*	234566	—	—	—	—	—	—	—	—	—	—
↳**1942-S, S Over S, FS-502**	*	392972	—	—	—	—	—	—	—	—	—	—
1942-S, Full Bands	*	4614	—	—	—	—	—	—	40.00	130	180	470
↳**1942-S, Inverted Mintmark, FS-501, Full Bands**	*	213585	—	—	—	—	—	—	—	—	—	—
↳**1942-S, S Over S, FS-502, Full Bands**	*	392973	—	—	—	—	—	—	—	—	—	—
1943	191,710,000	4517	4.80	4.90	5.50	6.50	6.50	9.75	13.50	26	40	80
1943, Full Bands	*	4518	—	—	—	—	—	—	23.00	46	90	245
1943-D	71,949,000	4615	4.80	4.90	5.50	6.50	6.50	9.75	16.00	26	40	90
↳**1943-D, D Over D, FS-501**	*	377829	—	—	—	—	—	—	—	—	—	—
1943-D, Full Bands	*	4616	—	—	—	—	—	—	26.00	50	65	160
↳**1943-D, D Over D, FS-501, Full Bands**	*	377830	—	—	—	—	—	—	—	—	—	—
1943-S	60,400,000	4617	4.80	4.90	5.50	6.50	6.50	9.75	16.00	26	40	90
↳**1943-S, S Over S, FS-501**	*	234567	—	—	—	—	—	—	—	—	—	—
1943-S, Full Bands	*	4618	—	—	—	—	—	—	28.00	75	95	310
↳**1943-S, S Over S, FS-501, Full Bands**	*	213587	—	—	—	—	—	—	—	—	—	—
1944	231,410,000	4519	4.80	4.90	5.50	6.50	6.50	9.75	13.50	26	40	80
1944, Full Bands	*	4520	—	—	—	—	—	—	32.00	80	180	550
1944-D	62,224,000	4619	4.80	4.90	5.50	6.50	6.50	9.75	16.00	26	40	85
↳**1944-D, D Over D, FS-501**	*	374000	—	—	—	—	—	—	—	—	—	—
1944-D, Full Bands	*	4620	—	—	—	—	—	—	26.00	55	65	130
↳**1944-D, D Over D, FS-501, Full Bands**	*	213589	—	—	—	—	—	—	—	120	155	235
1944-S	49,490,000	4621	4.80	4.90	5.50	6.50	6.50	11.00	17.50	30	47	90
1944-S, Full Bands	*	4622	—	—	—	—	—	—	28.00	50	80	160
1945	159,130,000	4521	4.80	4.90	5.50	6.50	6.50	9.75	13.50	26	40	95
1945, Full Bands	*	4522	—	—	—	—	—	5,000.00	8,500.00	12,000	20,500	60,000
1945-D	40,245,000	4623	4.80	4.90	5.50	6.50	6.50	9.75	13.50	26	40	80
↳**1945-D, D Over D, FS-501**	*	392974	—	—	—	—	—	—	—	—	—	—
↳**1945-D, D Over Horizontal D, FS-502**	*	234569	—	—	—	—	—	—	—	—	—	—

* Included in number above.

1945-S, S Over Horizontal S
FS-503

1945-S, Normal S

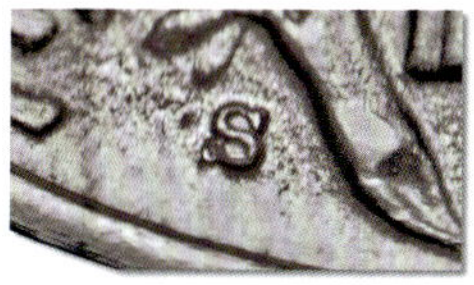

1945-S, Micro S
FS-512

Circulation Strikes *(continued)*

	Mintage	GSID	VG-8	F-12	VF-20	EF-40	AU-50	MS-60	MS-63	MS-65	MS-66	MS-67
1945-D, Full Bands	*	4624	—	—	—	—	—	—	$26	$50	$65	$155
↳1945-D, D Over D, FS-501, Full Bands	*	213590	—	—	—	—	—	—	—	—	—	—
↳1945-D, D Over Horizontal D, FS-502, Full Bands	*	213591	—	—	—	—	—	—	—	—	—	—
1945-S	41,920,000	4625	$4.80	$4.90	$5.50	$6.50	$6.50	$9.75	16	26	40	145
↳1945-S, S Over Horizontal S, FS-503	*	234570	—	—	—	—	—	—	—	—	—	—
↳1945-S, Inverted Mintmark, FS-504	*	392977	—	—	—	—	—	—	—	—	—	—
1945-S, Full Bands	*	4626	—	—	—	—	—	—	43	115	235	525
↳1945-S, S Over Horizontal S, FS-503, Full Bands	*	392978	—	—	—	—	—	—	—	—	—	—
↳1945-S, Inverted Mintmark, FS-504, Full Bands	*	392979	—	—	—	—	—	—	—	—	—	—
1945-S, Micro S (c)	*	4627	5.50	6.25	7.25	9.00	12.00	34.00	55	120	160	420
1945-S, Micro S, Full Bands (c)	*	4628	—	—	—	—	—	—	275	625	1,150	2,800

* Included in number above. **c.** The S mintmark is significantly smaller than that of the normal S punch. This variety has the only mintmark punch of this type and size known to have been used during the 1940s. It was originally used for Philippine coins of 1907 through 1920.

Proof Strikes

	Mintage	GSID	PF-60	PF-63	PF-65	PF-66
Mercury (1936–1942), Proof	**n/a**	**76248**	**$130**	**$145**	**$175**	**$200**
1936	4,130	4629	625	750	1,150	1,500
1937	5,756	4632	260	375	455	575
1938	8,728	4635	155	200	285	345
1939	9,321	4638	130	170	215	280
1940	11,827	4641	130	145	190	230
1941	16,557	4644	130	145	175	215
1942	22,329	4647	130	145	175	200

ROOSEVELT (1946 TO DATE)

Designer: *John R. Sinnock.* **Weight:** *Silver issue (1946–1964) and silver Proofs (1968–2018)—2.5 grams; clad issue (1965 to date)—2.27 grams; silver Proofs (2019 to date)—2.537 grams.* **Composition:** *Silver issue (1946–1964) and silver Proofs (1968–2018)—.900 silver, .100 copper (net weight: .07234 oz. pure silver); clad issue (1965 to date)—a core of pure copper, clad in outer layers of copper-nickel (.750 copper, .250 nickel); silver Proofs (2019 to date)—.999 silver, .001 copper (net weight: .0728 oz. pure silver).* **Diameter:** *17.9 mm.* **Edge:** *Reeded.* **Mints:** *Philadelphia, Denver, San Francisco, and West Point.*

Circulation Strike

Mintmark location, 1946–1964, is on the reverse, to the left of the fasces.

Mintmark location, 1968 to date, is on the obverse, above the date.

Proof Strike

History. After President Franklin D. Roosevelt died in 1945, the Treasury rushed to create a coin in his honor. The ten-cent denomination was particularly appropriate, given the president's active support of the March of Dimes' fundraising efforts to cure polio. The obverse of the coin bears Roosevelt's profile portrait, while the reverse features a torch flanked by branches of olive and oak.

Striking and Sharpness. Compared to earlier coinage series, collectors and dealers have paid relatively little attention to the sharpness of Roosevelt dimes. The obverse portrait is such that lightness of strike on the higher points is difficult to detect. On the reverse, check the leaves and the details of the torch. Some with complete separation on the lower two bands have been called Full Torch (FT) or Full Bands (FB), but interest in this distinction seems to be minimal in today's marketplace.

Availability. All are common, although some are more common than others. MS coins in higher grades are usually very lustrous.

Note: Values of common-date silver coins have been based on a silver current bullion price of $27.50 per ounce, and may vary with the prevailing spot price.

Grading Standards

MS-60 to 70 (Mint State). ***Obverse:*** At MS-60, some abrasion and contact marks are evident on the cheek, the hair above the ear, and the neck. At MS-63, abrasion is slight at best, less so for MS-64. An MS-65 coin should display no abrasion or contact marks except under magnification, and MS-66 and higher coins should have none at all. Luster should be full and rich. ***Reverse:*** Comments apply as for the obverse, except that the highest parts of the torch, flame, and leaves are the places to check. On both sides the fields are protected by design elements and do not show contact marks readily.

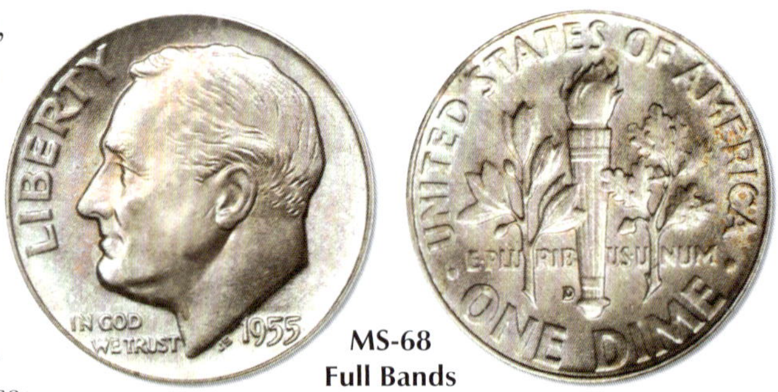

MS-68
Full Bands

AU-50, 53, 55, 58 (About Uncirculated). ***Obverse:*** Light wear is seen on the cheek and higher-relief part of the hair. At AU-58, the luster is extensive, but incomplete, especially on the higher parts and in the field. At AU-50 and 53, luster is less. ***Reverse:*** Light wear is seen on the higher parts of the torch and leaves. An AU-58 coin has nearly full luster. At AU-50 and 53, there still is significant luster.

AU-58

EF-40, 45 (Extremely Fine). ***Obverse:*** Further wear is seen on the head. Some details are gone in the hair to the right of the forehead. ***Reverse:*** Further wear is seen on the torch, but the vertical lines are visible, some just barely. The higher-relief details in the leaves, never strong to begin with, are worn away.

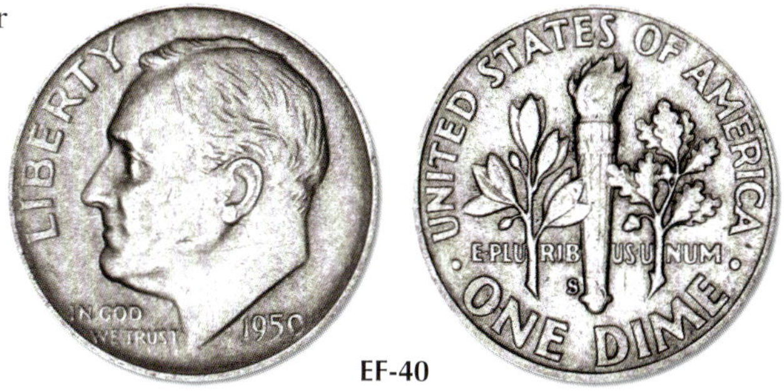

EF-40

PF-60 to 70 (Proof). ***Obverse and Reverse:*** Proofs that are extensively cleaned and have many hairlines, or that are dull and grainy, are lower level, such as PF-60 to 62. These are not widely desired, and represent coins that have been mistreated. Fortunately, only a few Proof Roosevelt dimes are in this category. With medium hairlines and good reflectivity, assigned grades of PF-63 or 64 are appropriate. PF-65 may have hairlines so delicate that magnification is needed to see them. Above that, a Proof should be free of any hairlines or other problems.

PF-69
Deep Cameo

Illustrated coin: The S mintmark is missing from this popular variety.

Circulation Strikes

	Mintage	GSID	MS-63	MS-65	MS-66
Roosevelt, Silver (1946–1964)	**n/a**	**76246**	**$5.00**	**$9.50**	**$17.50**
Same, Clad (1965 to Date)	**n/a**	**374760**	**0.30**	**1.50**	**4.10**
Same, Clad, Satin Finish (1965 to Date)	**n/a**	**376862**	**2.60**	**4.10**	**5.50**
Roosevelt, Silver (1946–1964), Full Bands	**n/a**	**84310**	**—**	**15.00**	**20.00**
Same, Clad (1965 to Date), Full Bands	**n/a**	**374761**	**0.40**	**2.20**	**5.50**
1946	255,250,000	4650	6.50	12.00	20.00
↳1946, Doubled Die Obverse/Doubled Die Reverse, FS-101/803	*	392990	—	—	—
↳1946, Doubled Die Obverse, FS-104	*	392992	—	—	—
↳1946, Doubled Die Reverse, FS-802	*	392994	—	—	—
1946, Full Bands	*	4651	—	27.00	34.00
↳1946, Doubled Die Obverse, FS-104, Full Bands	*	392997	—	—	—
↳1946, Doubled Die Reverse, FS-802, Full Bands	*	392999	—	—	—
1946-D	61,043,500	4689	6.50	15.00	26.00
↳1946-D, D Over D, FS-501	*	393000	—	—	—
↳1946-D, D Over D, FS-503	*	393001	—	—	—
1946-D, Full Bands	*	4690	—	—	34.00
↳1946-D, D Over D, FS-501, Full Bands	*	393002	—	—	—
↳1946-D, D Over D, FS-502, Full Bands	*	376597	—	—	—
1946-S	27,900,000	4691	6.50	16.00	31.00
↳1946-S, S Over S, Doubled Die Reverse, FS-501/801	*	376598	30.00	50.00	80.00
↳1946-S, S Over S, Doubled Die Reverse, FS-502/802	*	376599	49.00	70.00	95.00
↳1946-S, Sans Serif Mint Mark, FS-504	*	376434	375.00	440.00	550.00
1946-S, Full Bands	*	4692	24.00	40.00	70.00
↳1946-S, S Over S/Doubled Die Reverse, FS-501/801, Full Bands	*	376600	40.00	75.00	100.00
↳1946-S, S Over S/Doubled Die Reverse, FS-502/802, Full Bands	*	376601	55.00	80.00	115.00
↳1946-S, Sans Serif Mint Mark, FS-504, Full Bands	*	376435	415.00	490.00	575.00
1947	121,520,000	4652	5.75	13.50	22.00
1947, Full Bands	*	4653	—	—	36.00
1947-D	46,835,000	4693	6.75	12.00	27.00
↳1947-D, Doubled Die Obverse, FS-101	*	393055	—	—	—
1947-D, Full Bands	*	4694	—	47.00	70.00
↳1947-D, Doubled Die Obverse, FS-101, Full Bands	*	393056	—	—	—
1947-S	34,840,000	4695	7.25	13.50	24.00
↳1947-S, S Over D, FS-501	*	70265	—	—	—
↳1947-S, S Over S, FS-503	*	70269	—	—	—
↳1947-S, S Over S, FS-504	*	70271	—	—	—
↳1947-S, Doubled Die Reverse, FS-801	*	70273	—	—	—
1947-S, Full Bands	*	4696	—	24.00	40.00
↳1947-S, S Over D, FS-501, Full Bands	*	393057	—	—	—
↳1947-S, S Over S, FS-503, Full Bands	*	393058	—	—	—
↳1947-S, S Over S, FS-504, Full Bands	*	393059	—	—	—
1948	74,950,000	4654	6.50	16.00	27.00
1948, Full Bands	*	4655	—	20.00	34.00
1948-D	52,841,000	4697	6.75	13.50	24.00
1948-D, Full Bands	*	4698	—	24.00	43.00
1948-S	35,520,000	4699	5.75	11.00	19.00
1948-S, Full Bands	*	4700	—	27.00	43.00
1949	30,940,000	4656	23.00	30.00	40.00
1949, Full Bands	*	4657	24.00	40.00	55.00

* Included in number above.

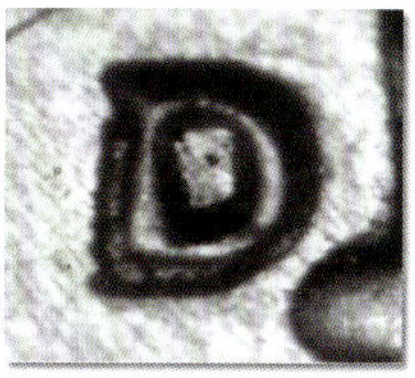

1950-D, D Over D
FS-502

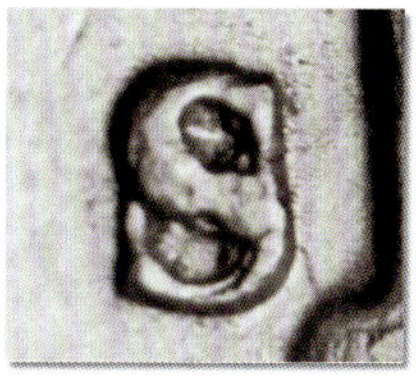

1950-S, S Over Inverted S
FS-501

Full Bands

Circulation Strikes

	Mintage	GSID	MS-63	MS-65	MS-66
1949-D	26,034,000	4701	$11.00	$16.00	$20
1949-D, Full Bands	*	4702	12.00	19.00	27
1949-S	13,510,000	4703	35.00	46.00	50
↳**1949-S, Bugs Bunny, FS-401**	*	393063	—	—	—
1949-S, Full Bands	*	4704	—	90.00	180
↳**1949-S, Bugs Bunny, FS-401, Full Bands**	*	393064	—	—	—
1950	50,130,114	4658	11.00	16.00	23
1950, Full Bands	*	4659	—	30.00	47
1950-D	46,803,000	4705	6.50	12.00	20
↳**1950-D, D Over D, FS-501**	*	393065	—	—	—
↳**1950-D, D Over D, FS-502**	*	393066	—	—	—
↳**1950-D, Doubled Die Reverse, FS-801**	*	393067	—	—	—
1950-D, Full Bands	*	4706	—	22.00	30
↳**1950-D, D Over D, FS-501, Full Bands**	*	393068	—	—	—
↳**1950-D, D Over D, FS-502, Full Bands**	*	393069	—	—	—
↳**1950-D, Doubled Die Reverse, FS-801, Full Bands**	*	393070	—	—	—
1950-S	20,440,000	4707	35.00	40.00	47
↳**1950-S, S Over Inverted S, FS-501**	*	199163	—	80.00	170
1950-S, Full Bands	*	4708	—	90.00	130
1951	103,880,102	4660	5.50	13.50	27
1951, Full Bands	*	4661	13.50	24.00	40
1951-D	56,529,000	4709	5.50	13.50	24
1951-D, Full Bands	*	4710	—	16.00	26
1951-S	31,630,000	4711	17.50	22.00	30
1951-S, Full Bands	*	4712	—	22.00	30
1952	99,040,093	4662	5.75	12.00	26
1952, Full Bands	*	4663	—	—	47
1952-D	122,100,000	4713	5.75	13.50	24
1952-D, Full Bands	*	4714	—	—	26
1952-S	44,419,500	4715	6.50	16.00	26
↳**1952-S, S Over S, FS-501**	*	376602	—	—	—
1952-S, Full Bands	*	4716	—	30.00	47
↳**1952-S, S Over S, FS-501, Full Bands**	*	376603	—	—	—
1953	53,490,120	4664	5.75	12.00	30
1953, Full Bands	*	4665	—	38.00	60
1953-D	136,433,000	4717	5.50	11.00	22
↳**1953-D, D Over Horizontal D, FS-501**	*	393073	—	—	—
1953-D, Full Bands	*	4718	—	16.00	24
↳**1953-D, D Over Horizontal D, FS-501, Full Bands**	*	393074	—	—	—

* Included in number above.

Circulation Strikes *(continued)*

	Mintage	GSID	MS-63	MS-65	MS-66
1953-S	39,180,000	4719	$6.50	$22.00	$40.00
↳1953-S, Bugs Bunny, FS-401	*	377831	—	—	—
↳1953-S, S Over S, FS-501	*	198970	—	90.00	180.00
↳1953-S, Acorn, FS-901	*	377832	—	—	—
1953-S, Full Bands	*	4720	—	32.00	43.00
↳1953-S, Bugs Bunny, FS-401, Full Bands	*	377833	—	—	—
↳1953-S, S Over S, FS-501, Full Bands	*	377834	—	—	—
↳1953-S, Acorn, FS-901, Full Bands	*	377835	—	—	—
1954	114,010,203	4666	5.00	12.00	20.00
↳1954, Doubled Die Reverse, FS-801	*	393075	—	—	—
1954, Full Bands	*	4667	—	32.00	50.00
↳1954, Doubled Die Reverse, FS-801, Full Bands	*	393076	—	—	—
1954-D	106,397,000	4721	5.00	9.50	19.00
1954-D, Full Bands	*	4722	—	19.00	24.00
1954-S	22,860,000	4723	5.50	12.00	22.00
↳1954-S, Missing Designer's Initials, FS-401	*	376604	—	—	—
↳1954-S, S Over S, FS-501	*	393077	—	—	—
1954-S, Full Bands	*	4724	—	22.00	32.00
↳1954-S, Missing Designer's Initials, FS-401, Full Bands	*	376605	—	—	—
↳1954-S, S Over S, FS-501, Full Bands	*	393078	—	—	—
1955	12,450,181	4668	5.25	9.50	23.00
1955, Full Bands	*	4669	—	38.00	100.00
1955-D	13,959,000	4725	5.25	9.50	20.00
1955-D, Full Bands	*	4726	—	16.00	30.00
1955-S	18,510,000	4727	5.25	9.50	19.00
↳1955-S, Bugs Bunny, FS-401	18,510,000	377836	—	—	—
1955-S, Full Bands	*	4728	—	38.00	55.00
1956	108,640,000	4670	5.00	9.50	20.00
1956, Full Bands	*	4671	—	43.00	75.00
1956-D	108,015,100	4729	5.00	9.50	19.00
1956-D, Full Bands	*	4730	—	16.00	27.00
1957	160,160,000	4672	5.00	9.50	20.00
1957, Full Bands	*	4673	12.00	50.00	100.00
1957-D	113,354,330	4731	5.25	9.50	19.00
1957-D, Full Bands	*	4732	6.75	19.00	43.00
1958	31,910,000	4674	5.00	9.50	20.00
1958, Full Bands	*	4675	—	55.00	155.00
1958-D	136,564,600	4733	5.00	9.50	17.50
1958-D, Full Bands	*	4734	—	16.00	22.00
1959	85,780,000	4676	5.00	9.50	23.00
1959, Full Bands	*	4677	—	22.00	30.00
1959-D	164,919,790	4735	5.00	9.50	17.50
↳1959-D, D Over Inverted D, FS-501	*	393079	—	80.00	130.00
↳1959-D, D Over D, FS-504	*	393082	—	—	—
1959-D, Full Bands	*	4736	—	16.00	24.00
↳1959-D, D Over Inverted D, FS-501, Full Bands	*	393083	—	—	—
↳1959-D, D Over D, FS-504, Full Bands	*	393086	—	34.00	—
1960	70,390,000	4678	5.00	9.50	17.50
1960, Full Bands	*	4679	16.00	46.00	75.00

* Included in number above.

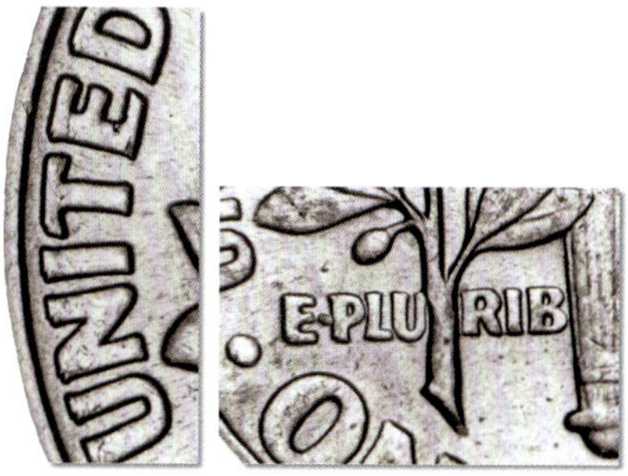

1963, Doubled Die Reverse
FS-805

1963-D, Doubled Die Reverse
FS-801

1964-D, Doubled Die Reverse
FS-801. Other varieties exist.

Circulation Strikes *(continued)*

	Mintage	GSID	MS-63	MS-65	MS-66
1960-D	200,160,400	4737	$5.00	$9.50	$17.50
1960-D, Full Bands	*	4738	—	30.00	50.00
1961	93,730,000	4680	5.00	9.50	19.00
1961, Full Bands	*	4681	—	85.00	110.00
1961-D	209,146,550	4739	5.00	9.50	17.50
1961-D, Full Bands	*	4740	—	—	70.00
1962	72,450,000	4683	5.00	9.50	17.50
1962, Full Bands	*	4682	13.50	24.00	34.00
1962-D	334,948,380	4742	5.00	9.50	17.50
↳1962-D, D Over D, FS-501	*	393087	—	—	—
1962-D, Full Bands	*	4741	—	—	34.00
↳1962-D, D Over D, FS-501, Full Bands	*	393088	—	—	—
1963	123,650,000	4685	5.00	12.00	20.00
↳1963, Doubled Die Obverse, FS-101	*	374585	27.00	40.00	—
1963, Doubled Die Reverse, FS-805	*	374586	90.00	230.00	325.00
1963, Full Bands	*	4684	—	49.00	95.00
↳1963, Doubled Die Obverse, FS-101, Full Bands	*	374587	—	—	—
1963-D	421,476,530	4744	5.00	9.50	17.50
↳1963-D, Doubled Die Reverse, FS-801	*	393089	—	—	—
1963-D, Full Bands	*	4743	—	—	80.00
↳1963-D, Doubled Die Reverse, FS-801, Full Bands	*	393090	—	—	—
1964	929,360,000	4687	5.00	9.50	17.50
1964, Full Bands	*	4686	—	20.00	60.00
1964-D	1,357,517,180	4748	5.00	9.50	17.50
↳1964-D, D Over D, FS-501	*	374098	—	100.00	210.00
↳1964-D, D Over D, FS-502	*	393095	—	—	—
1964-D, Full Bands	*	4747	—	30.00	46.00
↳1964-D, D Over D, FS-501, Full Bands	*	374099	—	130.00	310.00
↳1964-D, D Over D, FS-502, Full Bands	*	393096	—	—	—
1964-D, Doubled Die Reverse	*	329230	260.00	525.00	725.00
↳1964-D, Doubled Die Reverse, FS-801	*	329232	—	—	—
↳1964-D, Doubled Die Reverse, FS-802	*	329233	—	—	—
↳1964-D, Doubled Die Reverse, FS-803	*	329234	—	—	—
1964-D, Doubled Die Reverse, Full Bands	*	329231	—	—	—
↳1964-D, Doubled Die Reverse, FS-801, Full Bands	*	329235	—	—	—
↳1964-D, Doubled Die Reverse, FS-802, Full Bands	*	329236	—	—	—
↳1964-D, Doubled Die Reverse, FS-803, Full Bands	*	329237	—	—	—

* Included in number above.

1967, Doubled Die Obverse
FS-101

1970, Doubled Die Reverse
FS-801

Circulation Strikes *(continued)*

	Mintage	GSID	MS-63	MS-65	MS-66
1965	1,652,140,570	4750	$0.80	$3.00	$12.00
1965, Full Bands	*	4749	—	30.00	46.00
1966	1,382,734,540	4752	0.30	1.50	4.10
1966, Full Bands	*	4751	—	27.00	43.00
1967	2,244,007,320	4754	0.30	1.50	4.10
1967, Full Bands	*	4753	—	—	32.00
1968	424,470,400	4756	0.30	1.50	6.75
↳1968, Doubled Die Obverse, FS-101	*	198972	32.00	60.00	95.00
1968, Full Bands	*	4755	—	43.00	65.00
1968-D	480,748,280	4784	0.40	2.60	16.00
1968-D, Full Bands	*	4783	—	12.00	16.00
1969	145,790,000	4758	0.60	2.60	34.00
↳1969, Reverse of 1968, FS-901	*	347658	—	—	—
1969, Full Bands	*	4757	—	325.00	950.00
↳1969, Reverse of 1968, FS-901, Full Bands	*	347659	—	—	—
1969-D	563,323,870	4786	0.60	2.60	9.50
↳1969-D, D Over D, FS-501	*	393097	19.00	27.00	34.00
1969-D, Full Bands	*	4785	—	70.00	160.00
↳1969-D, D Over D, FS-501, Full Bands	*	393098	—	120.00	230.00
1970	345,570,000	374590	0.50	2.20	34.00
1970, Full Bands	*	374591	—	—	—
1970-D	754,942,100	4788	0.30	1.50	4.10
↳1970-D, Doubled Die Reverse, FS-801	*	393101	—	—	—
↳1970-D, Doubled Die Reverse, FS-802	*	393102	—	—	—
↳1970-D, Reverse of 1968, FS-901	*	393103	—	—	—
1970-D, Full Bands	*	4787	16.00	55.00	575.00
↳1970-D, Doubled Die Reverse, FS-801, Full Bands	*	393104	—	—	—
↳1970-D, Doubled Die Reverse, FS-802, Full Bands	*	393105	—	—	—
↳1970-D, Reverse of 1968, FS-901, Full Bands	*	393106	—	—	—
1971	162,690,000	4762	0.30	1.50	23.00
1971, Full Bands	*	4761	—	210.00	360.00
1971-D	377,914,240	4790	0.30	1.50	4.10
↳1971-D, D Over D, FS-501	*	393107	—	—	—
1971-D, Full Bands	*	4789	—	—	55.00
↳1971-D, D Over D, FS-501, Full Bands	*	393108	—	—	—
1972	431,540,000	4764	0.30	1.50	12.00
1972, Full Bands	*	4763	—	80.00	455.00
1972-D	330,290,000	4792	0.30	1.50	4.10
1972-D, Full Bands	*	4791	—	30.00	90.00
1973	315,670,000	4766	0.30	1.50	8.00
1973, Full Bands	*	4765	—	90.00	145.00
1973-D	455,032,426	4794	0.30	1.50	6.75
1973-D, Full Bands	*	4793	—	16.00	27.00

* Included in number above.

1982, No P, Strong Rims
FS-501

1982, No P, Weak Rims
FS-502

Circulation Strikes *(continued)*

	Mintage	GSID	MS-63	MS-65	MS-66
1974	470,248,000	4768	$0.30	$1.50	$32.00
1974, Full Bands	*	4767	—	525.00	1,250.00
1974-D	571,083,000	4796	0.30	1.50	6.75
1974-D, Full Bands	*	4795	—	20.00	100.00
1975	585,673,900	4770	0.30	1.50	11.00
1975, Full Bands	*	4769	—	47.00	130.00
1975-D	313,705,300	4798	0.30	1.50	4.10
1975-D, Full Bands	*	4797	—	43.00	110.00
1976	568,760,000	4772	0.30	1.50	15.00
1976, Full Bands	*	4771	—	525.00	1,250.00
1976-D	695,222,774	4800	0.30	1.50	4.10
1976-D, Full Bands	*	4799	—	60.00	130.00
1977	796,930,000	4774	0.30	1.50	13.50
1977, Full Bands	*	4773	—	195.00	455.00
1977-D	376,607,228	4802	0.30	1.50	4.10
1977-D, Full Bands	*	4801	—	60.00	115.00
1978	663,980,000	4776	0.30	1.50	4.10
1978, Full Bands	*	4775	—	525.00	1,250.00
1978-D	282,847,540	4804	0.30	1.50	4.10
1978-D, Full Bands	*	4803	70.00	360.00	650.00
1979	315,440,000	4778	0.30	1.50	4.10
1979, Full Bands	*	4777	—	850.00	2,200.00
1979-D	390,921,184	4806	0.30	1.50	4.10
1979-D, Full Bands	*	4805	—	70.00	455.00
1980-P	735,170,000	4810	0.30	1.50	4.10
1980-P, Full Bands	*	4809	—	850.00	2,200.00
1980-D	719,354,321	4808	0.30	1.50	11.00
1980-D, Full Bands	*	4807	—	1,500.00	3,000.00
1981-P	676,650,000	4814	0.30	1.50	4.10
1981-P, Full Bands	*	4813	—	4.10	11.00
1981-D	712,284,143	4812	0.30	1.50	4.10
1981-D, Full Bands	*	4811	—	4.10	8.00
1982-P	519,475,000	4818	9.50	19.00	80.00
1982-P, Full Bands	*	4817	—	27.00	90.00
1982 No P, Strong Rims, FS-501	*	4779	170.00	220.00	360.00
1982 No P, Weak Rims, FS-502	*	4782	110.00	180.00	290.00
1982-D	542,713,584	4816	5.50	15.00	55.00
1982-D, Full Bands	*	4815	—	49.00	60.00
1983-P	647,025,000	4822	2.40	8.00	24.00
1983-P, Full Bands	*	4821	—	100.00	390.00

	Mintage	GSID	MS-63	MS-65	MS-66
1983-D	730,129,224	4820	$2.40	$8.00	$24.00
↳1983-D, D/D, FS-501	*	393109	—	—	—
1983-D, Full Bands	*	4819	—	195.00	525.00
↳1983-D, D/D, FS-501, Full Bands	*	393110	—	—	—
1984-P	856,669,000	4826	0.30	1.50	4.10
1984-P, Full Bands	*	4825	—	4.10	12.00
1984-D	704,803,976	4824	0.30	1.50	6.75
1984-D, Full Bands	*	4823	—	4.10	30.00
1985-P	705,200,962	4830	0.30	1.50	4.10
1985-P, Full Bands	*	4829	—	4.10	40.00
1985-D	587,979,970	4828	0.30	1.50	4.10
1985-D, Full Bands	*	4827	—	4.10	16.00
1986-P	682,649,693	4834	0.30	1.50	4.10
1986-P, Full Bands	*	4833	—	24.00	100.00
1986-D	473,326,970	4832	0.30	1.50	6.75
1986-D, Full Bands	*	4831	—	80.00	235.00
1987-P	762,709,481	4838	0.30	1.50	5.50
1987-P, Full Bands	*	4837	—	32.00	80.00
1987-D	653,203,402	4836	0.30	1.50	4.10
1987-D, Full Bands	*	4835	—	47.00	130.00
1988-P	1,030,550,000	4842	0.30	1.50	4.10
1988-P, Full Bands	*	4841	—	27.00	47.00
1988-D	962,385,489	4840	0.30	1.50	4.10
1988-D, Full Bands	*	4839	—	16.00	24.00
1989-P	1,298,400,000	4846	0.30	1.50	4.10
1989-P, Full Bands	*	4845	—	16.00	27.00
1989-D	896,535,597	4844	0.30	1.50	4.10
1989-D, Full Bands	*	4843	—	12.00	24.00
1990-P	1,034,340,000	4850	0.30	1.50	4.10
1990-P, Full Bands	*	4849	—	415.00	650.00
1990-D	839,995,824	4848	0.30	1.50	4.10
1990-D, Full Bands	*	4847	—	525.00	1,400.00
1991-P	927,220,000	4854	0.30	1.50	4.10
1991-P, Full Bands	*	4853	—	155.00	260.00
1991-D	601,241,114	4852	0.30	1.50	4.10
1991-D, Full Bands	*	4851	—	1,250.00	2,000.00
1992-P	593,500,000	4858	0.30	1.50	4.10
1992-P, Full Bands	*	4857	—	60.00	110.00
1992-D	616,273,932	4856	0.30	1.50	4.10
1992-D, Full Bands	*	4855	—	4.10	24.00

* Included in number above.

Circulation Strikes *(continued)*

	Mintage	GSID	MS-63	MS-65	MS-66
1993-P	766,180,000	4862	$0.30	$1.50	$4.10
1993-P, Full Bands	*	4861	—	32.00	70.00
1993-D	750,110,166	4860	0.30	1.50	4.10
1993-D, Full Bands	*	4859	—	100.00	415.00
1994-P	1,189,000,000	4866	0.30	1.50	4.10
1994-P, Full Bands	*	4865	—	4.10	20.00
1994-D	1,303,268,110	4864	0.30	1.50	4.10
1994-D, Full Bands	*	4863	—	30.00	55.00
1995-P	1,125,500,000	4870	0.30	1.50	4.10
1995-P, Full Bands	*	4869	—	16.00	35.00
1995-D	1,274,890,000	4868	0.30	1.50	4.10
1995-D, Full Bands	*	4867	—	180.00	360.00
1996-P	1,421,163,000	4874	0.30	1.50	4.10
1996-P, Full Bands	*	4873	—	12.00	22.00
1996-D	1,400,300,000	4872	0.30	1.50	4.10
1996-D, Full Bands	*	4871	—	16.00	43.00
1996-W (a)	1,457,000	4876	13.50	15.00	20.00
1996-W, Full Bands (a)	*	4875	—	22.00	30.00
1997-P	991,640,000	4880	0.30	1.50	4.10
1997-P, Full Bands	*	4879	—	4.10	30.00
1997-D	979,810,000	4878	0.30	1.50	4.10
1997-D, Full Bands	*	4877	—	19.00	49.00
1998-P	1,163,000,000	4884	0.30	1.50	5.50
1998-P, Full Bands	*	4883	—	8.00	16.00
1998-D	1,172,250,000	4882	0.30	1.50	4.10
1998-D, Full Bands	*	4881	—	4.10	47.00
1999-P	2,164,000,000	4888	0.30	1.50	4.10
1999-P, Full Bands	*	4887	—	2.20	5.50
1999-D	1,397,750,000	4886	0.30	1.50	4.10
1999-D, Full Bands	*	4885	—	2.20	5.50
2000-P	1,842,500,000	4892	0.30	1.50	4.10
2000-P, Full Bands	*	4891	—	2.20	5.50
2000-D	1,818,700,000	4890	0.30	1.50	4.10
2000-D, Full Bands	*	4889	—	2.20	5.50
2001-P	1,369,590,000	4896	0.30	1.50	4.10
2001-P, Full Bands	*	4895	—	4.10	16.00
2001-D	1,412,800,000	4894	0.30	1.50	4.10
2001-D, Full Bands	*	4893	—	2.20	5.50
2002-P	1,187,500,000	4900	0.30	1.50	4.10
2002-P, Full Bands	*	4899	—	2.20	5.50
2002-D	1,379,500,000	4898	0.30	1.50	4.10
2002-D, Full Bands	*	4897	—	4.10	16.00
2003-P	1,085,500,000	4904	0.30	1.50	4.10
2003-P, Full Bands	*	4903	—	2.20	5.50
2003-D	986,500,000	4902	0.30	1.50	4.10
2003-D, Full Bands	*	4901	—	3.40	8.00
2004-P	1,328,000,000	4908	0.30	1.50	4.10
2004-P, Full Bands	*	4907	—	6.00	11.00
2004-D	1,159,500,000	4906	$0.30	$1.50	$4.10
↳2004-D, Curved Image, FS-401	*	393111	—	—	—
2004-D, Full Bands	*	4905	—	2.20	13.50
↳2004-D, Curved Image, FS-401, Full Bands	*	393112	—	—	—
2005-P	1,412,000,000	15325	0.30	1.50	4.10
2005-P, Full Bands	*	15326	—	13.50	34.00
2005-P, Satin	1,160,000	82047	2.60	4.10	5.50
2005-D	1,423,500,000	15327	0.30	1.50	4.10
2005-D, Full Bands	*	15328	—	16.00	27.00
2005-D, Satin	1,160,000	82048	2.60	4.10	5.50
2006-P	1,381,000,000	15329	0.30	1.50	4.10
2006-P, Full Bands	*	15330	—	12.00	30.00
2006-P, Satin	847,361	82049	2.60	4.10	5.50
2006-D	1,447,000,000	15331	0.30	1.50	4.10
2006-D, Full Bands	*	15332	—	12.00	20.00
2006-D, Satin	847,361	82050	2.60	4.10	5.50
2007-P	1,047,500,000	77864	0.30	1.50	4.10
2007-P, Full Bands	*	68974	—	16.00	40.00
2007-P, Satin	895,628	82051	2.60	4.10	5.50
2007-D	1,042,000,000	77865	0.30	1.50	4.10
2007-D, Full Bands	*	68976	—	4.10	16.00
2007-D, Satin	895,628	82052	2.60	4.10	5.50
2008-P	391,000,000	70395	0.30	1.50	8.00
2008-P, Full Bands	*	77888	0.40	6.00	40.00
2008-P, Satin	745,464	82053	2.60	4.10	5.50
2008-D	624,500,000	69705	0.30	1.50	4.10
2008-D, Full Bands	*	77889	0.40	6.00	24.00
2008-D, Satin	745,464	82054	2.60	4.10	5.50
2009-P	96,500,000	77866	0.30	1.50	4.10
2009-P, Full Bands	*	71319	0.40	7.50	40.00
2009-P, Satin	784,614	82055	2.60	4.10	5.50
2009-D	49,500,000	77867	0.30	1.50	4.10
2009-D, Full Bands	*	71320	0.40	6.00	30.00
2009-D, Satin	784,614	82056	2.60	4.10	5.50
2010-P	557,000,000	77868	0.30	1.50	4.10
2010-P, Full Bands	*	77890	0.40	4.10	11.00
2010-P, Satin	583,897	82057	2.60	4.10	5.50
2010-D	562,000,000	77869	0.30	1.50	4.10
2010-D, Full Bands	*	77891	0.40	4.10	11.00
2010-D, Satin	583,897	82058	2.60	4.10	5.50
2011-P	748,000,000	77870	0.30	1.50	4.10
2011-P, Full Bands	*	77892	0.40	4.10	11.00
2011-D	754,000,000	77871	0.30	1.50	4.10
2011-D, Full Bands	*	77893	0.40	2.20	5.50
2012-P	808,000,000	77872	0.30	1.50	4.10

* Included in number above. **a.** Issued in Mint sets only, to mark the 50th anniversary of the design.

Circulation Strikes *(continued)*

	Mintage	GSID	MS-63	MS-65	MS-66
2012-P, Full Bands	*	77894	$0.40	$2.20	$5.50
2012-D	868,000,000	77873	0.30	1.50	4.10
2012-D, Full Bands	*	77895	0.40	2.20	5.50
2013-P	1,086,500,000	77874	0.30	1.50	4.10
2013-P, Full Bands	*	77896	0.40	2.20	5.50
2013-D	1,025,500,000	77875	0.30	1.50	4.10
2013-D, Full Bands	*	77897	0.40	4.10	11.00
2014-P	1,125,500,000	77876	0.30	1.50	4.10
2014-P, Full Bands	*	77898	0.40	4.10	11.00
2014-D	1,177,000,000	77877	0.30	1.50	4.10
2014-D, Full Bands	*	77899	0.40	4.10	11.00
2015-P	1,497,510,000	77878	0.30	1.50	4.10
↳2015-P, DDR, FS-801	*	393113	—	—	—
2015-P, Full Bands	*	77900	0.40	2.20	5.50
↳2015-P, DDR, FS-801, Full Bands	*	393114	—	—	—
2015-D	1,543,500,000	77879	0.30	1.50	4.10
2015-D, Full Bands	*	77901	0.40	2.20	5.50
2016-P	1,517,000,000	77880	0.30	1.50	4.10
2016-P, Full Bands	*	77902	0.40	2.20	5.50
2016-D	1,437,000,000	77881	0.30	1.50	4.10
2016-D, Full Bands	*	77903	0.40	2.20	5.50
2017-P	1,437,500,000	77882	0.30	1.50	4.10
2017-P, Full Bands	*	77904	0.40	2.20	5.50
2017-D	1,290,500,000	77883	0.30	1.50	4.10
2017-D, Full Bands	*	77905	0.40	2.20	5.50
2017-S, Enh Unc	210,419	393455	2.60	4.10	5.50
2017-S, Enh Unc, Full Bands	*	82059	2.60	4.10	5.50
2018-P	1,193,000,000	79348	0.30	1.50	4.10
2018-P, Full Bands	*	79350	$0.40	$2.20	$5.50
2018-D	1,006,000,000	79349	0.30	1.50	4.10
2018-D, Full Bands	*	79351	0.40	2.20	5.50
2019-P	1,147,500,000	81891	0.30	1.50	4.10
2019-P, Full Bands	*	81887	0.40	2.20	5.50
2019-D	1,001,500,000	81892	0.30	1.50	4.10
2019-D, Full Bands	*	81888	0.40	4.10	11.00
2020-P	1,349,250,000	81893	0.30	1.50	4.10
2020-P, Full Bands	*	81889	0.40	2.20	5.50
2020-D	1,481,000,000	81894	0.30	1.50	4.10
2020-D, Full Bands	*	81890	0.40	2.20	5.50
2021-P	1,333,500,000	85148	0.30	1.50	4.10
2021-P, Full Bands	*	85149	0.40	2.20	5.50
2021-D	1,445,000,000	85147	0.30	1.50	4.10
2021-D, Full Bands	*	85150	0.40	2.20	5.50
2022-P		193426	0.30	1.50	4.10
2022-P, Full Bands	*	193427	0.40	2.20	5.50
2022-D		193425	0.30	1.50	4.10
2022-D, Full Bands	*	193428	0.40	2.20	5.50
2023-P		199011	0.30	1.50	4.10
2023-P, Full Bands	*	199013	0.40	2.20	5.50
2023-D		199012	0.30	1.50	4.10
2023-D, Full Bands	*	199014	0.40	2.20	5.50
2024-P		347688	0.30	1.50	4.10
2024-P, Full Bands		347689	0.40	2.20	5.50
2024-D		347690	0.30	1.50	4.10
2024-D, Full Bands		347691	0.40	2.20	5.50
2025-P, Full Bands		376277	0.40	2.20	5.50
2025-P		376276	0.30	1.50	4.10
2025-D		376278	0.30	1.50	4.10
2025-D, Full Bands		376279	0.40	2.20	5.50

* Included in number above.

Special Mint Set Strikes

	Mintage	GSID	MS-63	MS-65	MS-66
1964	unknown	4959	$5,500.00	$7,000.00	$7,500.00
1965	2,360,000	4963	2.60	4.10	5.50
1966	2,261,583	4966	2.60	4.10	5.50
↳1966, 5 on Cheek, FS-401	*	346887	170.00	210.00	230.00
1967	1,863,344	4969	2.60	4.10	5.50
↳1967, Doubled Die Obverse, FS-101	*	347661	—	—	—

* Included in number above.

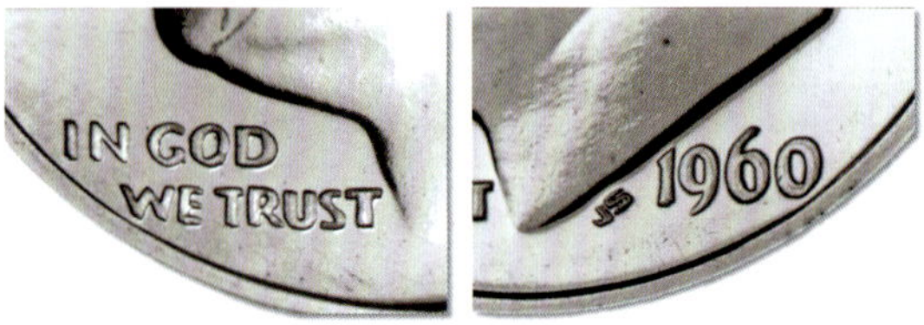

1960, Doubled Die Obverse, Proof
FS-102. Various die states exist.

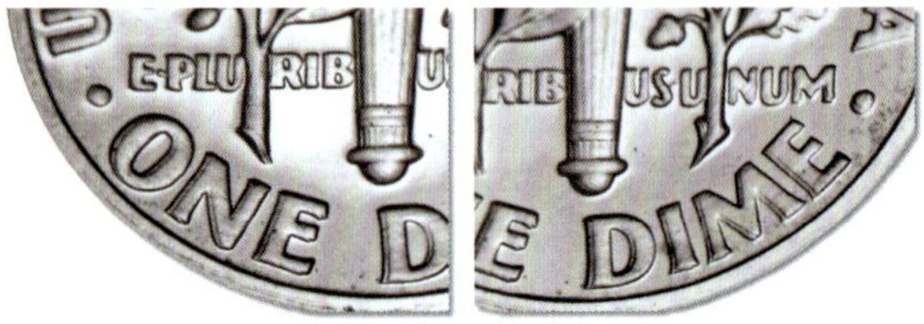

1963, Doubled Die Reverse, Proof
FS-802. Other varieties exist.

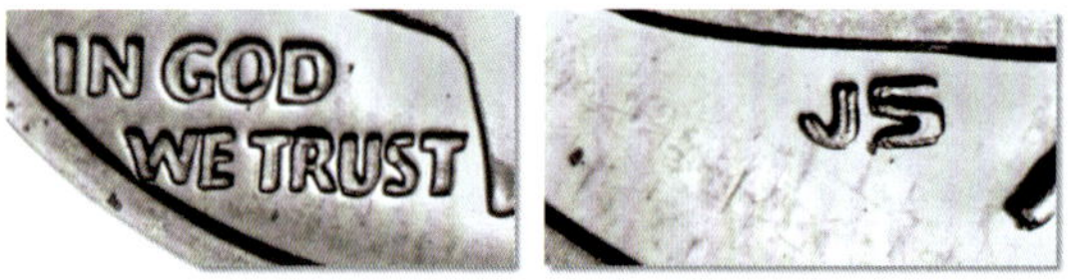

1968-S, Doubled Die Obverse, Proof
FS-102

1968-S, No S, Proof
FS-501

Proof Strikes

	Mintage	GSID	PF-65	PF-67	PF-69
Roosevelt, Silver (1950–1964), Proof	**n/a**	**393668**	**$8.00**	**$17.50**	**$26.00**
Same, Silver, Proof Deep Cameo	**n/a**	**393679**	**7.00**	**9.75**	**12.00**
Same, Clad, Proof Deep Cameo (1960 to Date)	**n/a**	**393669**	**1.50**	**5.50**	**8.00**
1950	51,386	4911	55.00	70.00	950.00
1951	57,500	4914	47.00	70.00	310.00
1952	81,980	4917	32.00	70.00	290.00
1953	128,800	4920	27.00	40.00	160.00
1954	233,300	4923	17.50	40.00	260.00
1955	378,200	4926	15.00	30.00	155.00
1956	669,384	4929	11.00	24.00	110.00
1957	1,247,952	4932	9.50	22.00	36.00
1958	875,652	4935	9.50	24.00	100.00
1959	1,149,291	4938	9.50	23.00	80.00
1960	1,691,602	4941	8.00	17.50	30.00
1960, Doubled Die Obverse	*	4944	115.00	195.00	850.00
↳1960, Doubled Die Obverse, Early Die State, FS-102a	*	390478	115.00	195.00	850.00
↳1960, Doubled Die Obverse, Late Die State, FS-102b	*	393015	—	—	—
↳1960, Doubled Die Reverse, FS-801	*	393016	115.00	195.00	850.00
1961	3,028,244	4947	8.00	17.50	28.00
1962	3,218,019	4950	8.00	17.50	28.00
1963	3,075,645	4953	8.00	17.50	27.00
1963, Doubled Die Reverse	*	4956	115.00	155.00	260.00
↳1963, Doubled Die Reverse, FS-802	*	376680	115.00	155.00	260.00
↳1963, Doubled Die Reverse, FS-803	*	393022	115.00	155.00	260.00
1964	3,950,762	4960	8.00	17.50	26.00
↳1964, Doubled Die Obverse, FS-101	*	393027	290.00	575.00	—
1968-S	3,041,506	4983	1.50	5.50	8.00
↳1968-S, Doubled Die Obverse, FS-102	*	393041	120.00	230.00	—
↳1968-S, S Over S, FS-502	*	393042	190.00	575.00	—
↳1968-S, Doubled Die Reverse, FS-801	*	393043	130.00	290.00	575.00
1968, No S (a)	24 est. known	4972	14,500.00	20,000.00	48,000.00
↳1968, No S, FS-501 (a)	*	393045	14,500.00	20,000.00	48,000.00
↳1968, No S, FS-501, Cameo (a)	*	393046	15,500.00	21,500.00	54,000.00
↳1968, No S, FS-501, Deep Cameo (a)	*	393346	19,000.00	26,500.00	66,000.00

* Included in number above. **a.** The S mintmark was inadvertently left off the coinage die; this defect was probably discovered before the end of the die's life.

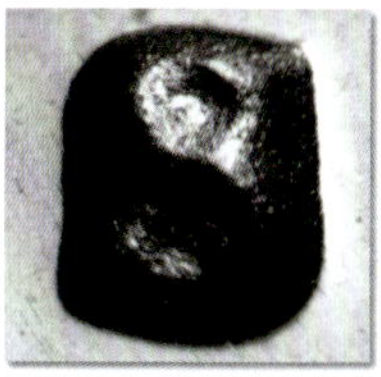

1979-S, Filled S (Variety 1), Proof

1979-S, Clear S (Variety 2), Proof

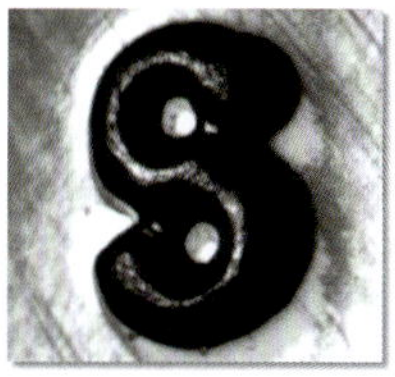

1981-S, Rounded S (Variety 1), Proof

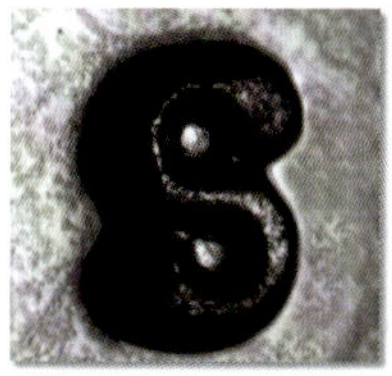

1981-S, Flat S (Variety 2), Proof

Proof Strikes *(continued)*

	Mintage	GSID	PF-65	PF-67	PF-69
1969-S	2,394,631	4986	$1.50	$5.50	$16.00
1970-S	2,632,810	4987	1.50	5.50	8.00
1970, No S (a)	*	71685	525.00	675.00	1,100.00
↳**1970, No S, FS-501** (a)	*	393047	525.00	675.00	1,100.00
↳**1970, No S, FS-501, Cameo** (a)	*	393048	575.00	750.00	3,000.00
↳**1970, No S, FS-501, Deep Cameo** (a)	*	393049	850.00	1,100.00	3,750.00
1971-S	3,220,733	4988	1.50	5.50	8.00
1972-S	3,260,996	4989	1.50	5.50	8.00
1973-S	2,760,339	4990	1.50	5.50	12.00
1974-S	2,612,568	4991	1.50	5.50	8.00
1975-S	2,845,450	4992	1.50	5.50	8.00
↳**1975-S, S Over S, FS-501**	*	393050	—	—	—
1975, No S (a)	*	81056	—	540,000.00	—
	Auctions: $456,000, PCGS PF-68 HA 09/19				
↳**1975, No S, FS-502** (a)	*	393051	—	540,000.00	—
1976-S	4,149,730	4993	1.50	5.50	8.00
1977-S	3,251,152	4994	1.50	5.50	8.00
1978-S	3,127,781	4995	1.50	5.50	8.00
1979-S, Variety 1 (a)	3,677,175	4996	1.50	5.50	8.00
1979-S, Variety 2 (a)	*	4997	1.50	5.50	8.00
1980-S	3,554,806	4998	1.50	5.50	8.00
1981-S, Variety 1 (a)	4,063,083	4999	1.50	5.50	8.00
1981-S, Variety 2 (a)	*	5000	5.50	16.00	24.00
1982-S	3,857,479	5001	1.50	5.50	8.00
1983-S	3,279,126	5002	1.50	5.50	8.00
1983, No S (a)	*	4980	490.00	625.00	925.00
↳**1983, No S, FS-501, Deep Cameo** (a)	*	393052	490.00	625.00	925.00
1984-S	3,065,110	5003	1.50	5.50	8.00
1985-S	3,362,821	5004	1.50	5.50	8.00
1986-S	3,010,497	5005	1.60	5.50	9.50
1987-S	4,227,728	5006	1.50	5.50	8.00
1988-S	3,262,948	5007	1.50	5.50	8.00
1989-S	3,220,194	5008	1.50	5.50	8.00
1990-S	3,299,559	5009	1.50	5.50	8.00
1991-S	2,867,787	5010	1.50	5.50	8.00
1992-S	2,858,981	5012	1.90	5.75	9.50
1992-S, Silver	1,317,579	5011	7.00	9.75	12.00
1993-S	2,633,439	5014	4.10	6.75	11.00
1993-S, Silver	761,353	5013	7.50	10.00	13.50
1994-S	2,484,594	5016	2.60	5.50	8.00
1994-S, Silver	785,329	5015	7.00	9.75	12.00

* Included in number above. **a.** The S mintmark was inadvertently left off the coinage die; this defect was probably discovered before the end of the die's life.

Proof Strikes *(continued)*

	Mintage	GSID	PF-65	PF-67	PF-69
1995-S	2,117,496	5018	$5.50	$8.00	$13.50
1995-S, Silver	679,985	5017	7.50	10.50	15.00
1996-S	1,750,244	5020	1.90	5.75	9.50
1996-S, Silver	775,021	5019	7.50	10.50	15.00
1997-S	2,055,000	5022	4.10	6.75	11.00
1997-S, Silver	741,678	5021	7.50	10.50	15.00
1998-S	2,086,507	5024	1.90	5.75	9.50
1998-S, Silver	878,792	5023	7.00	9.75	12.00
1999-S	2,543,401	5026	1.90	5.75	9.50
1999-S, Silver	804,565	5025	7.00	9.75	12.00
2000-S	3,082,572	5028	1.60	5.50	9.50
2000-S, Silver	965,421	5027	7.00	9.75	12.00
2001-S	2,294,909	5030	1.60	5.50	9.50
2001-S, Silver	889,697	5029	7.00	9.75	12.00
2002-S	2,319,766	5032	1.60	5.50	9.50
2002-S, Silver	892,229	5031	7.00	9.75	12.00
2003-S	2,172,684	5034	1.60	5.50	9.50
2003-S, Silver	1,125,755	5033	7.00	9.75	12.00
2004-S	1,789,488	5036	1.90	5.75	9.50
2004-S, Silver	1,175,934	5035	7.00	9.75	12.00
2005-S	2,275,000	15333	1.60	5.50	9.50
2005-S, Silver	1,069,679	15334	7.00	9.75	12.00
2006-S	2,000,428	15335	1.60	5.50	9.50
2006-S, Silver	1,054,008	15336	7.00	9.75	12.00
2007-S	1,384,797	68774	1.60	5.50	9.50
2007-S, Silver	1,054,008	81881	7.00	9.75	12.00
2008-S	1,377,424	69241	1.90	5.75	9.50
2008-S, Silver	620,664	69242	7.00	9.75	12.00
2009-S	1,377,424	81882	1.90	5.75	9.50
2009-S, Silver	697,365	70823	7.00	9.75	12.00
2010-S	1,103,815	71321	5.50	8.00	11.00
2010-S, Silver	585,401	71322	7.00	9.75	12.00
2011-S	1,098,835	71324	5.50	8.00	11.00
2011-S, Silver	574,175	71325	7.00	9.75	12.00

	Mintage	GSID	PF-65	PF-67	PF-69
2012-S	843,705	79352	$5.50	$8.00	$11.00
2012-S, Silver	445,612	79353	7.00	9.75	12.00
2013-S	856,953	79354	5.50	8.00	11.00
2013-S, Silver	467,691	79355	7.00	9.75	12.00
2014-S	784,206	79356	5.50	13.50	22.00
2014-S, Silver	472,107	79357	7.00	9.75	12.00
2015-P, RevPf, Silver (b)	74,430	79367	23.00	34.00	47.00
2015-S	711,872	79358	5.50	13.50	22.00
2015-S, Silver	387,310	79359	7.00	9.75	12.00
2015-W, Silver	74,430	79368	13.50	20.00	55.00
2016-S	641,775	79360	5.50	13.50	22.00
2016-S, Silver	419,496	79361	7.00	9.75	12.00
2017-S	621,390	79362	5.50	13.50	22.00
2017-S, Silver	406,986	79363	7.00	9.75	12.00
2018-S	568,804	79364	5.50	13.50	22.00
2018-S, Silver	381,748	79365	7.00	9.75	12.00
2018-S, RevPf, Silver (c)	350,820	79443	23.00	34.00	47.00
2019-S	649,050	79366	5.50	13.50	22.00
2019-S, Silver	460,925	81878	7.00	9.75	12.00
2020-S	511,148	81879	5.50	13.50	22.00
2020-S, Silver	363,179	81880	7.00	9.75	12.00
2021-S	521,826	85151	5.50	13.50	22.00
2021-S, Silver	319,317	85152	7.00	9.75	12.00
2022-S		193431	5.50	13.50	22.00
2022-S, Silver		193432	7.50	10.00	13.50
2023-S		213810	5.50	13.50	22.00
2023-S, Silver		213811	7.00	9.75	12.00
2024-S		347692	5.50	13.50	22.00
2024-S, Silver		347693	7.00	9.75	12.00
2025-S		376280	5.50	13.50	22.00
2025-S, Silver		376281	7.00	9.75	12.00

b. Included in the March of Dimes commemorative Proof set. **c.** Included in the special silver Reverse Proof set issued in 2018 in honor of the 50th anniversary of the San Francisco Mint's first production of Proof coins.

Twenty-Cent Pieces
1875–1878

AN OVERVIEW OF TWENTY-CENT PIECES

The twenty-cent piece, made in silver, proved to be the shortest-lived denomination in American coinage history. The coins were struck in quantity in their first year of issue, 1875, after which it was learned that the public confused them with quarter dollars. Mintages dropped sharply, and in 1877 and 1878 coinage was limited to just Proofs for collectors.

Scan for additional information.

Both sides of the twenty-cent piece were designed by U.S. Mint chief engraver William Barber. The obverse is simply an adaptation of the Liberty Seated motif earlier used on other denominations. The reverse is new and depicts a perched eagle (of the same general appearance as introduced by Barber on the 1873 silver trade dollar).

Only one twenty-cent piece is needed for inclusion in a type set. By far the most readily available in Mint State is the 1875-S, followed by the 1875-CC. These are often somewhat lightly struck on the reverse, particularly near the top of the eagle's wings. The 1875 and 1876 Philadelphia coins are occasionally encountered in Mint State and are usually well struck.

Proofs are readily available for all years, 1875 through 1878.

Senator John P. Jones was involved with the minting of the twenty-cent piece silver coin.

For the Collector and Investor: Twenty-Cent Pieces as a Specialty

A full date-and-mintmark set of twenty-cent pieces consists of the 1875, 1875-CC, 1875-S, 1876, 1876-CC, 1877, and 1878, the latter two years being available only in Proof format. The great challenge in forming a set is the 1876 CC, of which 10,000 were minted, but, seemingly, all but about two dozen were melted. Those that do survive are typically encountered in Mint State and are widely heralded when they are offered at auction.

LIBERTY SEATED (1875–1878)

Designer: *William Barber.* **Weight:** *5 grams.* **Composition:** *.900 silver, .100 copper.* **Diameter:** *22 mm.* **Edge:** *Plain.* **Mints:** *Philadelphia, Carson City, and San Francisco.*

Circulation Strike

Mintmark location is on the reverse, below the eagle.

Proof Strike

History. The twenty-cent coin debuted in 1875 as a convenient denomination to make change in the West (at the time silver coins did not circulate in the East or Midwest). The coins sometimes were confused with quarter dollars, given their similar Liberty Seated design on the obverse, and their similar size. The quantity minted dropped considerably in 1876, and in 1877 and 1878 only Proofs were struck. Despite the brief time of their production, these coins were still seen in circulation through the early 1900s, by which time they were often casually used as quarters. Proof coins were made of all years 1875 to 1878.

Striking and Sharpness. Areas of weakness are common. On the obverse, check the head of Liberty and the stars. The word LIBERTY is *raised* on this coin, a curious departure from other Liberty Seated coins of the era, on which it is recessed or incuse (the Gobrecht silver dollars of 1836 and 1839 being exceptions). On the reverse, check the eagle's feathers, especially the top of the wing on the left, but other areas can be weak as well. Some 1875-S coins are highly prooflike. The 1877 and 1878 are Proof-only issues with no related circulation strikes. Most have been cleaned or even lightly polished. Many Proofs in the marketplace have been convincingly retoned to mask problems. Proofs are usually well struck, but more than just a few are somewhat flat on the hair details of Liberty.

Availability. Most often seen is the high-mintage 1875-S, although the 1875 and 1875-CC are encountered with frequency. The 1876 is quite scarce and when seen is usually in high grades and well struck. The 1876-CC is a rarity, and only about two dozen are known, nearly all of which are MS. The eye appeal of MS coins can vary widely. The number of letters in LIBERTY on certain coins graded from VG through VF can vary widely in the marketplace. Proofs most often seen are those of 1875 and 1876. For some unexplained reason, high-quality Proofs of the series' final two years are very hard to find.

GRADING STANDARDS

MS-64

MS-60 to 70 (Mint State). ***Obverse:*** At MS-60, some abrasion and contact marks are evident, most noticeably on the bosom and thighs and knees. Luster is present, but may be dull or lifeless. At MS-63, contact marks are very few, and abrasion is hard to detect except under magnification. An MS-65 coin has no abrasion, and contact marks are sufficiently minute as to require magnification. Check the knees of Liberty and the right field. Luster should be full and rich. ***Reverse:*** Comments apply as for the obverse, except that in lower Mint State grades abrasion and contact marks are most noticeable on the eagle's breast and the top of the wing to the left. At MS-65 or higher, there are no marks visible to the unaided eye. The field is mainly protected by design elements and does not show abrasion as much as does the obverse on a given coin.

Illustrated coin: Semi-Proof surfaces contrast nicely against the frosted devices of this well-struck piece.

AU-50, 53, 55, 58 (About Uncirculated). ***Obverse:*** Light wear is seen on the thighs and knees, bosom, and head. At AU-58, the luster is extensive but incomplete, especially in the right field. At AU-50 and 53, luster is less. ***Reverse:*** Very light wear is evident on the eagle's breast (the prime focal point) and at the top of the wings. An AU-58 coin will have nearly full luster, more so than on the obverse, as the design elements protect the small field areas. At AU-50 and 53, there still are traces of luster.

AU-55

EF-40, 45 (Extremely Fine). ***Obverse:*** Further wear is seen on all areas, especially the thighs and knees, bosom, and head. Little or no luster is seen on most coins. From this grade downward, sharpness of strike of the stars and the head does not matter to connoisseurs. ***Reverse:*** More wear is evident on the eagle's breast and the top of the wings. Some feathers may be blended together, but most details are defined.

EF-45

VF-20, 30 (Very Fine). ***Obverse:*** Further wear is seen. Most details of the gown are worn away, except in the lower-relief areas above and to the right of the shield. Hair detail is mostly or completely gone. As to whether LIBERTY should be completely readable, this seems to be a matter of debate. On many coins in the marketplace the word is weak or missing one to several letters. ANA grading standards and PCGS require full LIBERTY. ***Reverse:*** Wear is more extensive, but at least three-quarters of the feathers in the breast and wings are distinct. At VF-30 the head is flat with distinct details; head details are less distinct at VF-20.

VF-30

F-12, 15 (Fine). ***Obverse:*** The seated figure is well worn, but with some detail above and to the right of the shield. LIBERTY has at least three letters visible (per ANA grading standards). In the marketplace, some have more letters missing. ***Reverse:*** Wear is extensive, with about half of the feathers flat or blended with others and head details are indistinct except for the eye.

F-15

VG-8, 10 (Very Good). ***Obverse:*** The seated figure is more worn, but some detail can be seen above and to the right of the shield. The shield is discernible. In LIBERTY a letter or two may be visible per ANA grading standards. In the marketplace, many have no letters. ***Reverse:*** Further wear has flattened about half of the feathers. Those remaining are on the inside of the wings. The rim is full and shows many if not most denticles.

VG-10

G-4, 6 (Good). ***Obverse:*** The seated figure is worn nearly smooth, but with some slight detail above and to the right of the shield. At G-4, there are no letters in LIBERTY remaining. On some at the G-6 level, there may be a trace of letters. ***Reverse:*** Most feathers in the eagle are gone. The border lettering is weak. The rim is visible partially or completely (depending on the strike).

G-6

AG-3 (About Good). ***Obverse:*** The seated figure is mostly visible in outline form, with only a hint of detail. Much of the rim is worn away. The date remains clear. ***Reverse:*** The border letters are partially worn away. The eagle is mostly in outline form, but with a few details discernible. The rim is weak or missing.

AG-3

PF-60 to 70 (Proof). ***Obverse and Reverse:*** Proofs that are extensively cleaned and have many hairlines, or that are dull and grainy, are lower level, such as PF-60 to 62. These are not widely desired. With medium hairlines and good reflectivity, an assigned grade of PF-64 is indicated, and with relatively few hairlines, Gem PF-65. In various grades hairlines are most easily seen in the obverse field. PF-66 should have hairlines so delicate that magnification is needed to see them. Above that, a Proof should be free of such lines.

PF-61

Illustrated coin: Lovely frosted devices are complemented by indigo toning in the peripheries of the fields.

Circulation Strikes

	Mintage	GSID	G-4	VG-8	F-12	VF-20	EF-40	AU-50	MS-60	MS-63
Liberty Seated (1875–1878)	**n/a**	**72420**	**$130**	**$150**	**$195**	**$230**	**$280**	**$390**	**$875**	**$1,250**
1875	38,500	5037	220	245	280	325	440	625	950	1,750
1875-CC	133,290	5039	245	300	440	525	900	1,150	2,100	3,600
1875-S	1,155,000	5040	130	150	195	230	280	390	875	1,250
↳1875-S, Misplaced Date, FS-301	*	213842	—	—	—	—	305	430	950	1,400
↳1875-S, Misplaced Date, FS-302	*	213843	—	—	—	—	305	430	950	1,400
1876	14,750	5038	260	365	455	550	650	800	1,500	2,250
↳1876, Doubled Die Reverse, FS-801	*	392945	—	—	—	—	—	900	1,650	2,500
1876-CC	15+ est. known	5041	—	—	—	—	168,000	198,000	258,000	384,000
	Auctions: $690,000, PCGS MS-65 HA 08/24									
↳1876-CC, Doubled Die Obverse, FS-101	*	392989	—	—	—	—	168,000	198,000	258,000	384,000
	Auctions: $444,000, PCGS MS-64 HA 04/25									

Proof Strikes

	Mintage	GSID	PF-60	PF-63	PF-65
Liberty Seated (1875–1878), Proof	**n/a**	**72421**	**$1,600**	**$3,250**	**$5,750**
Same, Proof Cameo	**n/a**	**72422**	**—**	**4,100**	**8,500**
Same, Proof Deep Cameo	**n/a**	**72423**	**—**	**7,500**	**17,000**
1875	1,200	5042	1,600	3,250	5,750
1875-S, Branch Mint	10–20 est. known	5055	15,000	36,000	—
1876	1,150	5045	1,600	3,400	5,750
1877	510	5048	5,750	8,250	10,500
1878	600	5051	3,100	4,200	8,750
1876	1,150	5045	1,600	3,400	5,750
1877	510	5048	5,750	8,250	10,500
1878	600	5051	3,100	4,200	8,750

Quarter Dollars
1796 to Date

AN OVERVIEW OF QUARTER DOLLARS

In 1796 the first silver quarters were struck at the Philadelphia Mint. The Draped Bust obverse in combination with the Small Eagle reverse was produced only in this year, after which no pieces of this denomination were produced until 1804. At that time the Draped Bust obverse was continued, but now with the Heraldic Eagle reverse. The coinage proved to be brief and lasted only through 1807, after which no quarters were struck until 1815. The new quarters dated 1815 were of the Capped Bust style, by John Reich. These were produced intermittently through 1838. The Liberty Seated motif, by Christian Gobrecht, made its debut in 1838 and was produced continuously through 1891, with several modifications in design and metallic content over the years. The Liberty Head quarter, today called the Barber quarter after its designer, was introduced in 1892 and minted continuously through 1916. The obverse features the head of Liberty, and the reverse a heraldic eagle. In late 1916 the Standing Liberty by Hermon A. MacNeil became the new design. This was produced through 1930, except for 1922. Some changes to both the obverse and reverse were made partway through 1917.

The Washington quarter dollar was struck in 1932 to observe the 200th anniversary of the birth of our first president. Washington quarters have been struck continuously since then, except for 1933, and with none dated 1975. In 1976 a special Bicentennial motif was introduced. Beginning in 1999 the State quarters were launched, issued at the rate of five per year, covering all 50 states, each coin having its own distinctive design. After this successful and popular program came quarter dollars with motifs celebrating the District of Columbia and U.S. territories. A similar program commemorating national parks started in 2010 and is slated to run through 2021.

While there are no super-rarities among the different *types* of quarter dollars, the first one, the 1796 with Draped Bust obverse and Small Eagle reverse, is hard to find and expensive in all grades. The values are, of course, justified by the great demand for this single-year type.

Quarter-dollar designers Hermon A. MacNeil and John Flanagan.

The collector's greatest challenge in finding a decent strike is in the short-lived 1804–1807 type with the Heraldic Eagle reverse. Sufficient quantities were made that examples from these years are not rarities, but nearly all are weakly struck. Quarters of the 1815–1828 Capped Bust, large planchet, type are available easily enough in worn grades but are scarce to rare in Mint State. Some cherrypicking (close examination for high quality within a given grade) is needed to find a sharp strike.

Respite from the sharp-strike difficulty is at last found with the 1831–1838 type, Capped Bust, small diameter, and without E PLURIBUS UNUM. Most are quite nicely struck. Also, for the first time Mint State coins are generally available with frequency in the marketplace, although those with good eye appeal are in the distinct minority.

The Liberty Seated quarters of the several types made from 1838 to 1891 are generally available in proportion to their mintages, with an allowance for the earlier dates being scarcer than the later ones—as they had a longer time to become worn or lost. Many quarters of earlier dates were melted circa 1850 to 1853, when the price of silver rose on international markets, making such coins worth slightly more than 25 cents in melt-down value.

Barber quarters, 1892–1916, present no difficulty for the collector, except that there is a challenge to find an example with sharp striking overall, including in the telltale area on the reverse at and near the eagle's leg to the right. MS-65 and better Barber quarters are scarcer than generally known (the same can be said for Barber half dollars). Proofs were sold to collectors and saved, and thus they are available in proportion to their mintages, with probably 70 percent to 80 percent surviving today.

The Variety 1 Standing Liberty quarter is a rarity if dated 1916, for only 52,000 were struck, and not many were saved. The feasible alternative is the 1917, Variety 1, which is often seen in Mint State, sharply struck, and very beautiful. Standing Liberty quarters of the Variety 2 design, minted from partway through 1917 to 1930, often are weakly struck on the head of Liberty and on the shield rivets, and sometimes other places as well. Diligent searching is needed to locate a nice example.

Washington quarters also present no difficulty for collectors. The State, D.C./Territorial, and America the Beautiful (National Park) reverses are appealing in their diversity and make a fascinating study in themselves.

For the Collector and Investor: Quarter Dollars as a Specialty

The formation of a specialized collection of quarter dollars from 1796 to date, by dates, mints, and major varieties, is a considerable challenge. As a class, quarters are considerably more difficult to acquire than are either dimes or half dollars. Relatively few numismatists have ever concentrated on the entire series.

The 1796 is rare and popular both as a date and a type. The 1804, although elusive in worn grades, is of commanding importance if in AU or Mint State. The 1823, 3 Over 2, is a classic rarity and is nearly always encountered well worn. From the same decade the 1827 is famous. Although Mint records indicate that 4,000 circulation strikes were produced in calendar-year 1827, they were probably struck from 1825-dated or earlier dies, as no unequivocal circulation strike has ever been located. There are, however, a dozen or so Proofs. Originals are distinguished by the 2 (in the 25 C. denomination) having a curved base, while restrikes, also very rare, have a square-base 2.

One of the unsolved mysteries in numismatics involves certain quarter dollars dated 1815 (the die variety known as Browning-1) and 1825, 5 Over 3 (Browning-2), which are often seen counterstamped, above the cap, with either an E or an L. Hundreds exist. As other quarter-dollar die varieties were made during this period, but only these two bear counterstamps, it may be that this was done either at the Mint or elsewhere before they were generally distributed.

Ard W. Browning's 1925 text, *The Early Quarter Dollars of the United States, 1796–1838*, remains the standard reference on the series, together with new information added here and there, including in issues of the *John Reich Journal*, the magazine of the John Reich Collectors Society, and in more recently published books.

The panorama of Liberty Seated quarters from 1838 to 1891 is highlighted by several rarities, notably the 1842, Small Date (known only in Proof format), and the 1873-CC, Without Arrows (of which only five are known, at least three being Mint State). The others are generally available, but some can be almost impossible to find in Mint State, the 1849-O, certain early San Francisco issues, and Carson City coins of the early 1870s being well known in this regard. From the mid-1870s onward Mint State coins are generally available, including choice and gem pieces. Proofs from 1858 onward can be found in proportion to their mintages, with later dates often being seen with higher numerical designations than are earlier ones.

Barber quarters are collectible by date and mint, although the "big three" rarities, the 1896-S, 1901-S, and 1913-S, are expensive and hard to find.

Standing Liberty quarters, 1916–1930, represent a short-lived series, one easy enough to collect in grades up to MS-63, except for the rare 1918-S, 8 Over 7, overdate. Finding higher-grade coins that are sharply struck is another matter entirely, and over the years few sets of this nature have been assembled.

Washington quarters are all collectible, with no great rarities. However, in relation to the demand for them, certain early issues are elusive, the 1932-D being a well-known example. Modern issues, including the Bicentennial, State, District of Columbia and U.S. Territories, America the Beautiful, Crossing the Delaware, and American Women coins, are at once plentiful, inexpensive, and interesting.

EXPLORING VARIETIES

Ard W. Browning's book was the first to catalog all the die marriages of early quarters, covering Draped Bust through Capped Bust designs. Each unique obverse-reverse pairing was assigned a B-number, which collectors still use today. These numbers remain the standard language for identifying Bust quarters in auctions, references, and grading-service attributions.

Browning, Ard W. *The Early Quarter Dollars of the United States, 1796–1838*. 1925 (reprinted 1980).

DRAPED BUST, SMALL EAGLE REVERSE (1796)

Designer: *Probably Gilbert Stuart.* **Engraver:** *Robert Scot.* **Weight:** *6.74 grams.* **Composition:** *.8924 silver, .1076 copper.* **Diameter:** *Approximately 27.5 mm.* **Edge:** *Reeded.* **Mint:** *Philadelphia.*

History. The Philadelphia Mint coined its first quarter dollar in 1796. Its design followed that of other silver U.S. coins. Only 6,146 were made, followed by a production hiatus until 1804, by which time a new reverse was used. Thus the 1796 was isolated as a single-year type.

Striking and Sharpness. On the obverse, check the hair details and the star centers. Most are well struck. On the reverse, most are well struck except for the head of the eagle, which can be shallow or flat, especially on the Browning-2 variety (there are two known die varieties for this year, Browning-1 being the rarer). Rarely is a Full Details coin encountered. The denticles are unusually bold and serve to frame the motifs. Check for planchet adjustment marks (from overweight planchets being filed down at the Mint to achieve proper weight). A few pieces have carbon streaks, which lower their value. Sharp striking (as on Browning-2) will add to the value. Most MS examples have excellent eye appeal.

Availability. Examples are available in all grades from well worn to superb MS. Nearly all of the latter are highly prooflike, but there are some exceptions. Although hundreds of circulated examples exist, demand for this famous coin exceeds supply in the marketplace, making public offerings a scene of excitement and strong bidding. Hundreds of higher-grade examples also survive, many of them prooflike and attractive. They attract great attention when offered for sale.

Grading Standards

MS-62

MS-60 to 70 (Mint State). ***Obverse:*** At MS-60, some abrasion and contact marks are evident, most noticeably on the cheek, the drapery, and the right field. Luster is present, but may be dull or lifeless, and interrupted in patches. On prooflike coins the contact marks are more prominent. At MS-63, contact marks are very few, and abrasion is hard to detect except under magnification, although this type is sometimes graded liberally due to its rarity. An MS-65 coin has no abrasion, and contact marks are so minute as to require magnification. Luster should be full and rich. Grades above MS-65 are defined by having fewer marks as perfection is approached. ***Reverse:*** Comments apply as for the obverse, except that abrasion and contact marks are most noticeable on the eagle at the center, a situation complicated by the fact that this area is typically flatly struck (except on the Browning-2 variety). Grading is best done by the obverse, then verified by the reverse. The field area is small and is protected by lettering and the wreath and in any given grade shows fewer marks than on the obverse.

Illustrated coin: This coin is well struck on the obverse, and the weak striking on the eagle's breast and head is typical of this issue.

AU-58

AU-50, 53, 55, 58 (About Uncirculated). ***Obverse:*** Light wear is seen on the hair area above the ear and extending to left of the forehead, on the ribbon, on the drapery at the shoulder, and on the high points of the bust line, more so at AU-50 than at AU-53 or 55. An AU-58 coin has minimal traces of wear. An AU-50 coin has luster in protected areas among the stars and letters, with little in the open fields or on the portrait. At AU-58, most luster remains in the fields, but is worn away on the highest parts of the motifs. ***Reverse:*** Light wear is seen on the eagle's body (keep in mind this area is nearly always lightly struck) and the edges of the wings. Light wear is seen on the wreath and lettering. Luster is the best key to actual wear. This ranges from perhaps 20 percent remaining in protected areas (at AU-50) to nearly full mint bloom (at AU-58).

EF-40

EF-40, 45 (Extremely Fine). ***Obverse:*** More wear is evident on the upper hair area and the ribbon, and on the drapery and bosom. Excellent detail remains in low-relief areas of the hair. The stars show wear as do the date and letters. Luster, if present at all, is minimal and in protected areas. ***Reverse:*** The eagle shows more wear, this being the focal point to check. Most feathers remain on the interior areas of the wings. Additional wear is on the wreath and letters, but many details are present. Some luster may be seen in protected areas and if present is slightly more abundant than on the obverse.

VF-30

VF-20, 30 (Very Fine). ***Obverse:*** The higher-relief areas of hair are well worn at VF-20, less so at VF-30, although much detail remains on the areas below the ear. The drapery and bosom show extensive wear. The stars have more wear, making them appear larger (an optical illusion seen on most worn silver coins of this era). ***Reverse:*** The body of the eagle shows few if any feathers, while the wings have about half of the feathers visible, mostly on the right wing, depending on the strike. The leaves lack most detail and are in outline form. Scattered, non-disfiguring marks are normal for this and lower grades. Any major defects should be noted separately.

F-12, 15 (Fine). ***Obverse:*** Wear is more extensive than on a Very Fine coin, particularly noticeable on the hair, face, and bosom. The stars appear larger. About half the hair detail remains, most noticeably behind the neck and shoulder. The denticles remain strong (while on most other silver denominations of this design they become weak at this grade level). ***Reverse:*** Wear is more extensive. Now feather details are diminished, with fewer than half remaining on the wings. The wreath and lettering are worn further, and the rim is slightly weak in areas, although most denticles can be seen.

F-12

VG-8, 10 (Very Good). ***Obverse:*** The portrait is mostly seen in outline form, with most hair strands gone, although there is some definition at the back of the hair and behind the shoulder. The ear is discernible, as is the eye. The stars appear larger still, again an illusion. The rim is weak in areas. Most denticles are seen, some of them even bold. LIBERTY and the date are readable and usually full, although some letters may be weak at their tops (the high rim and denticles protect the design more on the quarter dollar than on other silver coins of this type). ***Reverse:*** The eagle is mostly an outline, with parts blending into the field (on lighter strikes), although some slight feather detail can be seen on the right wing. The rim is worn, as are the letters, with some weak, but the motto is readable. Most denticles remain clear.

VG-10

G-4, 6 (Good). ***Obverse:*** Wear is more extensive. The head is an outline. The rim still is present, as are most of the denticles, most well defined. LIBERTY is worn, but complete. The date is bold. ***Reverse:*** The eagle is flat and discernible in outline form, blending into the field in areas. The wreath is well worn. Some of the letters may be partly missing. Some rim areas and denticles are discernible. At this level some "averaging" can be done. If the letters are stronger than usual in one area, but some are missing in another area, the coin can still qualify as G-4.

G-4

100 GREATEST™ UNITED STATES COINS

No. 69 1796 DRAPED BUST QUARTER DOLLAR

G-3 (About Good). ***Obverse:*** Wear is so extensive that the coin is barely identifiable. The head is in outline form, LIBERTY is mostly gone, same for the stars, and the date, while readable, may be partially worn away. ***Reverse:*** The reverse is well worn, with parts of the wreath and lettering missing.

AG-3

Circulation Strikes

	Mintage	GSID	G-4	VG-8	F-12	VF-20	EF-40	AU-50	MS-60	MS-63
Draped Bust, Small Eagle Reverse (1796)	**n/a**	**74207**	**$15,000**	**$26,500**	**$36,000**	**$45,500**	**$59,000**	**$79,000**	**$144,000**	**$228,000**
1796	6,146	5056	15,000	26,500	36,000	45,500	59,000	79,000	144,000	228,000
	Auctions: $144,000, NGC MS-62 SBG 08/24; $1,527,500, NGC MS-67 HA 08/24									
↳1796, B-1	*	212662	16,500	29,000	39,500	50,000	64,500	87,000	158,500	251,000
	Auctions: $168,000, PCGS MS-61 HA 04/25									
↳1796, B-2	*	212663	15,000	26,500	36,000	45,500	59,000	79,000	144,000	228,000
	Auctions: $156,000, NGC MS-62 HA 08/24; $1,740,000, PCGS MS-66 HA 08/24									

* Included in number above.

DRAPED BUST, HERALDIC EAGLE REVERSE (1804–1807)

Designer: *Robert Scot.* **Weight:** *6.74 grams.* **Composition:** *.8924 silver, .1076 copper.* **Diameter:** *Approximately 27.5 mm.* **Edge:** *Reeded.* **Mint:** *Philadelphia.*

History. Early on, the U.S. Mint's production of silver coins in any given year depended on requests made by depositors of silver; they were not made for the Mint's own account. After 1796 no quarters were struck until 1804. When production started up again, the Draped Bust obverse was used, but with the new Heraldic Eagle reverse—similar to that on other silver (and gold) denominations of the time. The Heraldic Eagle design was patterned after the Great Seal of the United States.

Striking and Sharpness. Virtually all examples are lightly struck in one area or another. On the obverse, check the hair details and the star centers. On the reverse, check the shield, stars, feathers, and other design elements. The denticles and rims on both sides often have problems. Quarters of 1807 are usually the lightest struck. Also check for planchet adjustment marks (where an overweight planchet was filed down by a Mint worker to reach acceptable standards). Sharp striking and excellent eye appeal add to a coin's value. This series often is misgraded due to lack of understanding of its strike anomalies.

Availability. All dates are collectible, with 1804 being scarcer than the others and a rarity in MS. Those of 1805, 1806, and 1807 are readily available in the marketplace, usually in circulated grades although MS examples are sometimes seen. Some die varieties are rare. High-grade coins with Full Details are very rare.

Grading Standards

MS-66

MS-60 to 70 (Mint State). ***Obverse:*** At MS-60, some abrasion and contact marks are evident, most noticeably on the cheek, the drapery, and the right field. Luster is present, but may be dull or lifeless, and interrupted in patches. At MS-63, contact marks are very few, and abrasion is hard to detect except under magnification. An MS-65 coin will have no abrasion, and contact marks are so minute as to require magnification. Luster should be full and rich. Coins graded above MS-65 are more theoretical than actual for this type—but they do exist, and are defined by having fewer marks as perfection is approached. As noted in the introduction, expect weakness in some areas. ***Reverse:*** Comments apply as for the obverse, except that abrasion and contact marks are most noticeable on the eagle's neck, the tips of the wing, and the tail. The field area is complex, without much open space, given the stars above the eagle, the arrows and olive branch, and other features. Accordingly, marks are not as noticeable as on the obverse.

Illustrated coin: This coin is lightly struck on the right obverse stars and at the center of the reverse. Some planchet adjustment marks are mostly hidden. Some tiny carbon streaks are on the obverse (seemingly typical for Browning-9).

AU-58

AU-50, 53, 55, 58 (About Uncirculated). ***Obverse:*** Light wear is seen on the hair area above the ear and extending to left of the forehead, on the ribbon, and on the drapery at the shoulder, more so at AU-50 than at AU-53 or 55. An AU-58 coin has minimal traces of wear. An AU-50 coin has luster in protected areas among the stars and letters, with little in the open fields or on the portrait. At AU-58, most luster is present in the fields, but is worn away on the highest parts of the motifs. ***Reverse:*** Comments as preceding, except that the eagle's neck, the tips and top of the wings, the clouds, and the tail now show noticeable wear, as do other features. Luster ranges from perhaps 20 percent remaining in protected areas (at AU-50) to nearly full mint bloom (at AU-58). Often the reverse retains much more luster than the obverse, more so on quarter dollars than on other denominations of this design.

Illustrated coin: Lightly struck on the obverse stars. The reverse has some light areas but is sharp overall. A few planchet adjustment marks are visible. Abundant luster and good eye appeal rank this as an exceptional example of this date, the most difficult of the type to find in high grades.

EF-45

EF-40, 45 (Extremely Fine). ***Obverse:*** More wear is evident on the upper hair area and the ribbon, and on the drapery at the shoulder and the bosom. Excellent detail remains in low-relief areas of the hair. The stars show wear, as do the date and letters (note: on most coins of this type the stars are softly struck). Luster, if present at all, is minimal and in protected areas. ***Reverse:*** Wear is greater than on an About Uncirculated coin, overall. The neck lacks feather detail on its highest points. Feathers have lost some detail near the edges of the wings, and some areas of the horizontal lines in the shield may be blended together. Some traces of luster may be seen, more so at EF-45 than at EF-40.

VF-30

VF-20, 30 (Very Fine). ***Obverse:*** The higher-relief areas of hair are well worn at VF-20, less so at VF-30. The drapery and bosom show extensive wear. The stars have more wear, making them appear larger (an optical illusion seen on most worn silver coins of this era). ***Reverse:*** Wear is greater, including on the shield and wing feathers, although more than half of the feathers are defined. Star centers are flat. Other areas have lost detail as well. Some letters in the motto may be missing, depending on the strike.

F-12, 15 (Fine). ***Obverse:*** Wear is more extensive than on a Very Fine coin, particularly noticeable on the hair, face, and bosom. The stars appear larger. About half the hair detail remains with the tresses fused so as to appear thick, most noticeably behind the neck and shoulder. The rim may be partially worn away and blend into the field. ***Reverse:*** Wear is even more extensive, with the shield and wing feathers being points to observe. About half of the feathers can be seen. The incuse E PLURIBUS UNUM may have a few letters worn away. The clouds all seem to be connected. The stars are weak. Parts of the border and lettering may be weak. As with most quarters of this type, peculiarities of striking can account for some weakness.

F-12

VG-8, 10 (Very Good). ***Obverse:*** The portrait is mostly seen in outline form, with most hair strands gone, although there is slight definition at the back of the hair and behind the shoulder. The ear is discernible, as is the eye. The stars appear larger still, again an illusion. The rim is weak in areas. LIBERTY and the date are readable and usually full, although some letters may be weak at their tops. ***Reverse:*** Wear is more extensive. Half or so of the letters in the motto are worn away. Most feathers are worn away, although separation of some of the lower feathers may be seen. Some stars are faint. The border blends into the field in areas (depending on striking), and some letters are weak.

VG-8

G-4, 6 (Good). ***Obverse:*** Wear is more extensive, and some stars may be partly missing. The head is an outline. The eye is visible only in outline form. The rim is well worn or even missing in areas. LIBERTY is worn, and parts of some letters may be missing, but elements of all should be readable. The date is readable, but worn. ***Reverse:*** Wear is more extensive. The upper part of the eagle is flat, and feathers are noticeable only at some (but not necessarily all) of the lower edge of the wings, and do not have detail. The shield lacks most of its detail. Only a few letters of the motto can be seen (depending on striking). The rim is worn extensively, and a few letters may be missing.

G-4

AG-3

AG-3 (About Good). ***Obverse:*** Wear is so extensive that the coin is barely identifiable. The head is in outline form, LIBERTY is mostly gone. Same for the stars. The date, while readable, may be partially worn away. ***Reverse:*** Extensive wear is seen overall, with the rim worn away and some areas worn smooth. The eagle can be discerned in outline form, but not necessarily completely. A few stray motto letters may remain. Sometimes the obverse appears to be more worn than the reverse, or vice-versa.

1806, 6 Over 5

Circulation Strikes

	Mintage	GSID	G-4	VG-8	F-12	VF-20	EF-40	AU-50	MS-60	MS-63
Draped Bust, Heraldic Eagle Reverse (1804–1807)	**n/a**	**72424**	**$430**	**$575**	**$1,100**	**$1,600**	**$3,250**	**$4,800**	**$10,000**	**$14,500**
1804	6,738	5057	3,750	5,500	8,250	11,500	30,000	54,000	108,000	186,000
	Auctions: $345,000, NGC MS-65 HA 01/11									
↳1804, B-1	*	212664	3,750	5,500	8,250	11,500	30,000	54,000	108,000	186,000
	Auctions: $336,000, NGC MS-65 HA 06/18									
↳1804, B-2	*	212665	4,100	6,250	9,000	12,500	33,000	59,500	119,000	204,500
1805	121,394	5058	430	575	1,100	1,700	3,500	5,500	10,000	14,500
	Auctions: $402,500, NGC MS-66 HA 01/08									
↳1805, B-1	*	212666	470	650	1,200	1,850	3,850	6,000	11,000	16,000
↳1805, B-2	*	212667	430	575	1,100	1,700	3,500	5,500	10,000	14,500
↳1805, B-3	*	212668	430	575	1,100	1,700	3,500	5,500	10,000	14,500
↳1805, B-4	*	212669	430	575	1,100	1,700	3,500	5,500	10,000	14,500
↳1805, B-5	*	212670	—	—	—	—	—	—	—	—
1806	206,124	5059	430	575	1,100	1,600	3,250	4,800	10,000	14,500
↳1806, B-2	*	212671	430	575	1,100	1,600	3,250	4,800	10,000	14,500
↳1806, B-3	*	212672	430	575	1,100	1,600	3,250	4,800	10,000	14,500
↳1806, B-4	*	212673	470	650	1,200	1,800	3,600	5,250	11,000	16,000
↳1806, B-5	*	212674	470	650	1,200	1,800	3,600	5,250	11,000	16,000
↳1806, B-6	*	212675	—	—	—	—	—	—	—	—
↳1806, B-7	*	212676	—	—	—	—	—	—	—	—
↳1806, B-8	*	212677	3,000	6,250	12,000	19,000	—	—	—	—
↳1806, B-9	*	212678	430	575	1,100	1,600	3,250	4,800	10,000	14,500
	Auctions: $102,000, PCGS MS-65 HA 01/18									
↳1806, B-10	*	212679	—	—	—	—	—	—	—	—
1806, 6 Over 5	*	5098	550	800	1,200	1,750	4,000	7,500	13,000	29,000
	Auctions: $152,750, NGC MS-66 HA 11/13									
↳1806, 6 Over 5, B-1	*	212680	550	800	1,200	1,750	4,000	7,500	13,000	29,000
	Auctions: $188,000, PCGS MS-66 SBG 05/15									
1807	220,643	5060	430	575	1,100	1,600	3,250	4,800	10,000	14,500
	Auctions: $411,250, NGC MS-66 HA 11/13									
↳1807, B-1	*	212681	430	575	1,100	1,600	3,250	4,800	10,000	14,500
	Auctions: $630,000, PCGS MS-67 HA 11/20									
↳1807, B-2	*	212682	430	575	1,100	1,600	3,250	4,800	10,000	14,500
	Auctions: $252,000, NGC MS-66 HA 08/23									

* Included in number above.

CAPPED BUST (1815–1838)

Variety 1, Large Diameter (1815–1828): **Designer:** *John Reich.* **Weight:** *6.74 grams.* **Composition:** *.8924 silver, .1076 copper.* **Diameter:** *Approximately 27 mm.* **Edge:** *Reeded.* **Mint:** *Philadelphia.*

Variety 1, Large Diameter (1815–1828), Circulation Strike

Variety 1, Large Diameter, Proof Strike

Variety 2, Reduced Diameter, Motto Removed (1831–1838): **Designer:** *William Kneass.* **Weight:** *6.74 grams (changed to 6.68 grams, .900 fine, in 1837).* **Composition:** *.8924 silver, .1076 copper.* **Diameter:** *24.3 mm.* **Edge:** *Reeded.* **Mint:** *Philadelphia.*

Variety 2, Reduced Diameter, Motto Removed (1831–1838), Circulation Strike

Variety 2, Reduced Diameter, Motto Removed, Proof Strike

History. The Capped Bust design, by John Reich, was introduced on the half dollar of 1807 but was not used on the quarter until 1815. The difference between the Large Diameter and the Reduced Diameter types resulted from the introduction of the close collar in 1828. Capped Bust, Reduced Diameter, quarter dollars are similar in overall appearance to the preceding type, but with important differences. The diameter is smaller, E PLURIBUS UNUM no longer appears on the reverse, and the denticles are smaller and restyled using a close collar.

Striking and Sharpness. Striking sharpness of Capped Bust, Large Diameter, quarters varies. On the obverse, check the hair of Liberty, the broach clasp (a particular point of observation), and the star centers. On this type the stars are often well defined (in contrast with half dollars of the same design). On the reverse, check the neck of the eagle and its wings, and the letters. The details of the eagle often are superbly defined. Check the scroll or ribbon above the eagle's head for weak or light areas. Examine the denticles on both sides. When weakness occurs it is usually in the center. Proofs were struck for inclusion in sets and for numismatists. Some deeply toned coins, and coins with patches of mint luster, have been described as Proofs but are mostly impostors, some of which have been certified or have "papers" signed by Walter Breen. Be careful! Nearly all coins of the Capped Bust, Reduced Diameter, Motto Removed, variety are very well struck. Check all areas for sharpness. Some quarters of 1833 and 1834 are struck from rusted or otherwise imperfect dies and can be less attractive than coins from undamaged dies. Avoid any Proofs that show patches of mint frost or that are darkly toned.

Availability. Most quarters of the Large Diameter variety range from slightly scarce to rare, with the 1823, 3 Over 2, and the 1827 being famous rarities. Typical coins range from well worn to Fine and VF. AU and MS coins are elusive (and are usually dated before the 1820s), and gems are particularly rare. All authentic Proofs are rarities. Examples of the Reduced Diameter, Motto Removed, variety are readily available of all dates, including many of the first year of issue. Mint frost ranges from satiny (usual) to deeply frosty. Proofs were struck of all dates for inclusion in sets and for sale or trade to numismatists; avoid deeply toned pieces, and seek those with deep and full (not partial) mirror surfaces and good contrast.

Grading Standards

MS-62

MS-60 to 70 (Mint State). ***Obverse:*** At MS-60, some abrasion and contact marks are evident, most noticeably on the cheek, the hair below LIBERTY, and the area near the drapery clasp. Luster is present, but may be dull or lifeless, and interrupted in patches. At MS-63, contact marks are very few, and abrasion is hard to detect except under magnification. An MS-65 coin has no abrasion, and contact marks are so minute as to require magnification. Luster should be full and rich. Grades above MS-65 are seen now and again and are defined by having fewer marks as perfection is approached. Grading for Reduced Diameter, Motto Removed, examples is similar, except the rims are more uniform, striking is usually very sharp, and the wear occurs evenly on both sides. ***Reverse:*** Comments apply as for the obverse, except that abrasion and contact marks are most noticeable on the eagle's neck, the top of the wings, the claws, and the flat band that surrounds the incuse motto. The field is mainly protected by design elements and does not show abrasion as much as does the obverse on a given coin.

AU-55

AU-50, 53, 55, 58 (About Uncirculated). ***Obverse:*** Light wear is seen on the cap, the hair below LIBERTY, the curl on the neck, the hair near the clasp, and the drapery. At AU-58, the luster is extensive except in the open area of the field, especially to the right. At AU-50 and 53, luster remains only in protected areas. Grading for Reduced Diameter, Motto Removed, examples is similar, except the rims are more uniform, striking is usually very sharp, and the wear occurs evenly on both sides. ***Reverse:*** Wear is evident on the eagle's neck, the top of the wings, the claws, and the flat band above the eagle. An AU-58 coin has nearly full luster. At AU-50 and 53, there still is significant luster, more than on the obverse. Generally, light wear is most obvious on the obverse.

EF-40, 45 (Extremely Fine). ***Obverse:*** Wear is more extensive, most noticeably on the higher areas of the hair. The cap shows more wear, as does the cheek. Most or all stars have some radial lines visible (unless lightly struck, as many are). Luster, if present, is in protected areas among the star points and close to the portrait. Grading for Reduced Diameter, Motto Removed, examples is similar, except the rims are more uniform, striking is usually very sharp, and the wear occurs evenly on both sides. ***Reverse:*** The wings show wear on the higher areas of the feathers, and some details are lost. Feathers in the neck are light on some (but not on especially sharp strikes). The eagle's claws and the leaves show wear. Luster may be present in protected areas, even if there is little or none on the obverse.

EF-40

VF-20, 30 (Very Fine). ***Obverse:*** Wear is more extensive, and most of the hair is combined into thick tresses without delicate features. The curl on the neck is flat. Details of the drapery are well defined at the lower edge. Unless they were weakly struck, the stars are mostly flat although a few may retain radial lines. Grading for Reduced Diameter, Motto Removed, examples is similar, except the rims are more uniform, striking is usually very sharp, and the wear occurs evenly on both sides. ***Reverse:*** Wear is most evident on the eagle's neck, to the left of the shield, and on the leaves and claws. Most feathers in the wing remain distinct, but some show light wear. Overall, the reverse on most quarters at this level shows less wear than the obverse.

VF-20

F-12, 15 (Fine). ***Obverse:*** Wear is more extensive, with much of the hair blended together. The drapery is indistinct at its upper edge. The stars are flat. Grading for Reduced Diameter, Motto Removed, examples is similar, except the rims are more uniform, striking is usually very sharp, and the wear occurs evenly on both sides. ***Reverse:*** Wear is more extensive, now with only about half of the feathers remaining on the wings. The claws on the right are fused at their upper parts.

F-15

VG-10

VG-8, 10 (Very Good). ***Obverse:*** The hair is less distinct, with the area above the face blended into the facial features. LIBERTY is complete, but can be weak in areas. At the left the drapery and bosom are blended together in a flat area. The rim is worn away in areas, and blends into the field. ***Reverse:*** Feathers are fewer and mostly on the eagle's wing to the left. Other details are weaker. E PLURIBUS UNUM is weak, perhaps with some letters missing. All border lettering remains easily readable.

Illustrated coin: Gunmetal toning in the fields contrasts nicely with the lighter devices. The over-punched denomination shows signs of the 50 punched first into the die to the left of both 2 and 5.

G-4

G-4, 6 (Good). ***Obverse:*** The portrait is mostly in outline, with few interior details discernible. LIBERTY may still be readable or may be partially worn away, depending on the variety. Most or all of the border is worn away, and the outer parts of the stars are weak. ***Reverse:*** The eagle mostly is in outline form, although some feathers can be seen in the wing to the left. All letters around the border are clear. E PLURIBUS UNUM is mostly or completely worn away.

AG-3

AG-3 (About Good). ***Obverse:*** The portrait is an outline. Most of LIBERTY can still be seen. Stars are weak or missing toward what used to be the rim. The date remains clear, but may be weak at the bottom. ***Reverse:*** The reverse shows more wear than at G-4, but parts of the rim may remain clear.

PF-64 Cameo

PF-60 to 70 (Proof). ***Obverse and Reverse:*** Proofs that are extensively cleaned and have many hairlines, or that are dull and grainy, are lower level, such as PF-60 to 62. While any early Proof coin will attract attention, lower-level examples are not of great interest to specialists unless they are of rare die varieties. With medium hairlines, an assigned grade of PF-64 may be in order and with relatively few, Gem PF-65. PF-66 should have hairlines so delicate that magnification is needed to see them. Above that, a Proof should be free of such lines. Grading is highly subjective with early Proofs, and eye appeal also is a factor.

Illustrated coin: This coin features frosted devices and reflective fields, though the fields are marred by some light scratches.

1818, 8 Over 5

1818, Normal Date

1819, Small 9

1819, Large 9

1820, Small 0

1820, Large 0

Circulation Strikes

	Mintage	GSID	G-4	VG-8	F-12	VF-20	EF-40	AU-50	MS-60	MS-63
Capped Bust, Large Diameter (1815–1828)	**n/a**	**72425**	**$150**	**$210**	**$340**	**$525**	**$1,300**	**$2,050**	**$3,900**	**$6,250**
Capped Bust, Reduced Diameter, Motto Removed (1831–1838)	**n/a**	**72426**	**110**	**130**	**145**	**180**	**405**	**725**	**2,050**	**3,750**
Variety 1: Large Diameter										
1815	89,235	5061	260	390	525	775	2,400	2,750	3,900	6,250
	Auctions: $282,000, NGC MS-67 HA 11/13									
↳1815, B-1	89,235	393311	260	390	525	775	2,400	2,750	3,900	6,250
	Auctions: $126,000, CAC MS-67 HA 12/23									
↳1815, Counterstamp "L," B-1	*	212686	—	—	—	—	—	—	4,500	12,000
↳1815, Counterstamp "E," B-1	*	212687	—	—	—	—	—	—	4,500	12,000
1818	361,174	5062	150	210	340	525	1,300	2,050	3,900	6,250
↳1818, B-2	*	212688	150	210	340	525	1,300	2,050	3,900	6,250
↳1818, B-4	*	212689	150	210	340	525	1,300	2,050	3,900	6,250
↳1818, B-5	*	212690	165	230	370	575	1,450	2,250	4,250	7,000
↳1818, B-6	*	212691	165	230	370	575	1,450	2,250	4,250	7,000
↳1818, B-7	*	212692	165	230	370	575	1,450	2,250	4,250	7,000
↳1818, B-8	*	212693	150	210	340	525	1,300	2,050	3,900	6,250
↳1818, B-9	*	212694	165	230	370	575	1,450	2,250	4,250	7,000
↳1818, B-10	*	212695	150	210	340	525	1,300	2,050	3,900	6,250
1818, 8 Over 5	*	5099	150	210	340	525	1,300	2,050	3,900	6,250
	Auctions: $176,250, NGC MS-67 HA 11/13									
↳1818, 8 Over 5, B-1	*	212696	150	210	340	525	1,300	2,050	3,900	6,250
	Auctions: $182,125, NGC MS-67 HA 08/14									
↳1818, 8 Over 5, B-3	*	212697	150	210	340	525	1,300	2,050	3,900	6,250
1819, Small 9	144,000	5063	150	210	340	525	1,300	2,050	4,400	9,500
↳1819, Small 9, B-3	*	212698	150	210	340	525	1,300	2,050	4,400	9,500
↳1819, Small 9, B-4	*	212699	165	230	370	575	1,450	2,250	4,800	10,500
1819, Large 9	*	5064	150	210	340	525	1,300	2,500	5,250	10,500
↳1819, Large 9, B-1	*	212700	165	230	370	575	1,450	2,750	5,750	11,500
↳1819, Large 9, B-2	*	212701	150	210	340	525	1,300	2,500	5,250	10,500
1820, Small 0	127,444	5065	150	210	340	525	1,300	2,050	4,400	10,500
↳1820, Small 0, B-4	*	212702	150	210	340	525	1,300	2,050	4,400	10,500
↳1820, Small 0, B-5	*	212703	195	340	525	—	2,000	3,250	—	—
1820, Medium 0	127,444	212704	165	230	370	575	1,450	2,250	4,800	11,500
↳1820, Medium 0, B-3	127,444	390407	165	230	370	575	1,450	2,250	4,800	11,500
1820, Large 0	*	5066	150	210	340	525	1,300	2,500	6,250	11,500
↳1820, Large 0, B-1	*	212705	165	230	405	775	1,550	2,500	6,250	11,500
↳1820, Large 0, B-2	*	212706	150	210	340	525	1,300	2,500	6,250	11,500

* Included in number above.

1822, 25 Over 50 C.

1823, 3 Over 2

1824, 4 Over 2

1825, 5 Over 2

1825, 5 Over 4

1828, 25 Over 50 C.

Circulation Strikes *(continued)*

	Mintage	GSID	G-4	VG-8	F-12	VF-20	EF-40	AU-50	MS-60	MS-63
1821	216,851	5068	$150	$210	$340	$525	$1,300	$2,050	$3,900	$6,250
↳1821, B-1	*	212707	150	210	340	525	1,300	2,050	3,900	6,250
↳1821, B-2	*	212708	165	230	370	575	1,450	2,250	4,250	—
↳1821, B-3	*	212709	150	210	340	525	1,300	2,050	3,900	6,250
↳1821, B-4	*	212710	150	210	340	525	1,300	2,050	3,900	6,250
↳1821, B-5	*	212711	165	230	370	575	1,450	2,250	4,250	7,000
↳1821, B-6	*	212712	—	—	—	—	—	—	—	—
1822	64,080	5070	230	360	575	1,000	1,900	3,100	6,500	10,500
↳1822, B-1	*	378716	230	360	575	1,000	1,900	3,100	6,500	10,500
	Auctions: $164,500, PCGS MS-67 HA 06/15									
1822, 25 Over 50 C.	*	5071	5,500	8,000	17,000	22,000	36,000	46,000	60,000	90,000
	Auctions: $195,500, NGC MS-66 HA 03/06									
↳1822, 25 Over 50 C., FS-901, B-2	*	378717	5,500	8,000	17,000	22,000	36,000	46,000	60,000	90,000
	Auctions: $188,000, PCGS MS-65 SBG 05/15									
1823, 3 Over 2	17,800	5100	46,000	53,000	72,000	84,000	96,000	126,000	276,000	—
	Auctions: $146,875, PCGS AU-55 LGND 09/22									
↳1823, 3 Over 2, B-1	*	375301	46,000	53,000	72,000	84,000	96,000	126,000	276,000	—
	Auctions: $246,750, PCGS AU-58 SBG 05/15									
1824, 4 Over 2	168,000	5102	575	950	1,400	1,900	4,000	6,500	24,000	54,000
	Auctions: $115,000, PCGS MS-64 HA 01/09									
↳1824, 4 Over 2, B-1	*	375302	575	950	1,400	1,900	4,000	6,500	24,000	54,000
	Auctions: $141,000, PCGS MS-64 SBG 05/15									
1825, 5 Over 4 Over 2	144,000	5104	195	245	455	650	1,500	2,500	5,000	7,000
↳1825, 5 Over 4 Over 2, FS-301, B-1	*	212713	215	270	500	725	1,650	2,750	5,500	7,750
↳1825, 5 Over 4 Over 2, FS-302, B-2	*	188565	195	245	455	650	1,500	2,500	5,000	7,000
↳1825, 5 Over 4 Over 2, Counterstamp "E," B-2	*	393563	—	—	—	—	—	—	—	—
↳1825, 5 Over 4 Over 2, Counterstamp "L," B-2	*	393564	—	—	—	—	—	—	—	—
↳1825, 5 Over 4 Over 2, FS-303, B-3	*	212714	195	245	455	650	1,500	2,500	5,000	7,000

Note: Although 4,000 1827 quarters were reported to have been made for circulation, their rarity today (only one worn piece is known, and it could be a circulated Proof) suggests that this quantity was for coins struck in calendar-year 1827 but bearing an earlier date, probably 1825. * Included in number above.

1828, 25 Over 50 C.

1831, Small Letters
Browning-2

1831, Large Letters
Browning-6

1834, O Over F in OF
FS-901

Circulation Strikes *(continued)*

	Mintage	GSID	G-4	VG-8	F-12	VF-20	EF-40	AU-50	MS-60	MS-63
1828	102,000	5077	$150	$210	$340	$525	$1,300	$2,050	$3,900	$6,250
	Auctions: $111,625, PCGS MS-66 SBG 07/15									
↳1828, B-1	*	212715	150	210	340	525	1,300	2,050	3,900	6,250
↳1828, B-2	*	212716	150	210	340	525	1,300	2,050	3,900	6,250
↳1828, B-4	*	212717	150	210	340	525	1,300	2,050	3,900	6,250
	Auctions: $108,688, NGC MS-67 HA 06/15									
1828, 25 Over 50 C.	*	5078	1,150	1,550	2,500	3,250	7,500	11,000	18,000	60,000
	Auctions: $352,500, NGC MS-67 HA 11/13									
↳1828, 25 Over 50 C., FS-901, B-3	*	393249	1,150	1,550	2,500	3,250	7,500	11,000	18,000	60,000
	Auctions: $282,000, NGC MS-67 HA 05/15									
Variety 2: Reduced Diameter, Motto Removed										
1831, Small Letters	398,000	5080	110	130	145	180	405	725	2,050	3,750
	Auctions: $117,500, NGC MS-67 HA 11/13									
↳1831, Small Letters, B-1	*	212954	110	130	145	180	405	725	2,050	3,750
↳1831, Small Letters, B-2	*	212955	110	130	145	180	405	725	2,050	3,750
↳1831, Small Letters, B-3	*	212956	120	135	155	200	445	800	2,250	4,100
↳1831, Small Letters, B-4	*	212957	110	130	145	180	405	725	2,050	3,750
1831, Large Letters	*	5081	110	130	145	180	405	725	2,500	5,000
↳1831, Large Letters, FS-301, B-5	*	212958	110	130	145	180	405	725	2,500	5,000
↳1831, Large Letters, B-6	*	212959	110	130	145	180	405	725	2,500	5,000
↳1831, Large Letters, FS-301, B-7	*	212960	120	135	155	200	445	800	2,750	5,500
1832	320,000	5084	110	130	145	180	405	725	2,050	3,750
↳1832, B-1	*	212961	110	130	145	180	405	725	2,050	3,750
↳1832, B-2	*	212962	110	130	145	180	405	725	2,050	3,750
1833	156,000	5086	110	130	145	195	490	775	2,500	4,500
↳1833, B-1	*	212963	110	130	145	195	490	775	2,500	4,500
↳1833, Recut Legend Reverse, FS-901, B-2	*	212964	120	135	155	215	525	850	2,750	4,950
1834	286,000	5088	110	130	145	180	405	725	2,050	3,750
↳1834, B-2	*	212966	120	135	155	200	445	800	2,250	4,100
↳1834, B-3	*	212967	110	130	145	180	405	725	2,050	3,750
↳1834, B-4	*	212968	110	130	145	180	405	725	2,050	3,750
↳1834, B-5	*	212969	120	135	155	200	445	800	2,250	4,100
1834, O Over F in OF	*	212965	110	130	145	180	405	725	2,050	3,750
↳1834, O Over F in OF, FS-901, B-1	*	393248	110	130	145	180	405	725	2,050	3,750

* Included in number above.

Circulation Strikes *(continued)*

	Mintage	GSID	G-4	VG-8	F-12	VF-20	EF-40	AU-50	MS-60	MS-63
1835	1,952,000	5090	$110	$130	$145	$180	$405	$725	$2,050	$3,750
↳1835, B-1	*	212970	110	130	145	180	405	725	2,050	3,750
↳1835, B-2	*	212971	110	130	145	180	405	725	2,050	3,750
↳1835, B-3	*	212972	120	135	155	200	445	800	2,250	4,100
↳1835, B-4	*	212973	120	135	155	200	445	800	2,250	4,100
↳1835, B-5	*	212974	110	130	145	180	405	725	2,050	3,750
↳1835, B-6	*	212975	110	130	145	180	405	725	2,050	3,750
↳1835, B-7	*	212976	110	130	145	180	405	725	2,050	3,750
↳1835, B-8	*	212977	120	135	155	200	445	800	2,250	4,100
1836	472,000	5092	110	130	145	180	405	725	2,250	5,500
↳1836, B-1	*	212978	110	130	145	180	405	725	2,250	5,500
↳1836, B-2	*	212979	110	130	145	180	405	725	2,250	5,500
↳1836, B-3	*	212980	110	130	145	180	405	725	2,250	5,500
↳1836, B-4	*	212981	120	135	155	200	445	800	2,500	6,000
↳1836, B-5	*	212982	—	3,500	4,250	6,250	7,750	—	—	—
1837	252,400	5094	110	130	145	180	405	725	2,050	3,750
↳1837, B-1	*	212983	120	135	155	200	445	800	2,250	4,100
↳1837, B-2	*	212984	110	130	145	180	405	725	2,050	3,750
	Auctions: $152,750, PCGS MS-67 SBG 05/15									
↳1837, B-3	*	212985	120	135	155	200	445	800	2,250	4,100
↳1837, B-4	*	212986	110	130	145	180	405	725	2,050	3,750
↳1837, B-5	*	212987	120	135	155	200	445	800	2,250	4,100
↳1837, B-6	*	212988	—	—	—	—	—	—	—	—
1838	366,000	5096	110	130	145	180	405	725	2,050	3,750
↳1838, B-1	*	393250	110	130	145	180	405	725	2,050	3,750

* Included in number above.

1827, Original, Proof
Curl-Base 2 in 25 C.

1827, Restrike, Proof
Square-Base 2 in 25 C.

Proof Strikes

		GSID	PF-63	PF-64	PF-65
Capped Bust, Large Diameter (1815–1828), Proof	**n/a**	**74171**	**$42,000**	**$66,000**	**$90,000**
Capped Bust, Reduced Diameter, Motto Removed (1831–1838), Proof	**n/a**	**74172**	**27,500**	**54,000**	**81,500**
Variety 1: Large Diameter					
1818	1 or 2 known	213013	—	—	—
1820	4 known	5067	—	90,000	132,000
	Auctions: $218,500, NGC PF-67 HA 09/05				
1821	4 or 5 known	5069	—	210,000	270,000
	Auctions: $252,000, PCGS PF-64 SBG 08/23				
1822	3 known	5073	48,000	66,000	90,000
	Auctions: $246,750, PCGS PF-67 SBG 05/15				
1822	3 known	5072	—	—	270,000
	Auctions: $229,125, PCGS PF-65 HA 01/14				
1823, 3 Over 2	unique	5101	—	660,000	—
	Auctions: $396,562, PCGS PF-64 HA 06/14				
1824, 4 Over 2, B-1	unique	5103	240,000	—	—
1825, 5 Over 4 Over 2		226353	—	—	—
1827, Original (Curl-Base 2 in 25 C.) (a)	9 known	5075	228,000	420,000	570,000
	Auctions: $180,000 PCGS PF-63 HA 01/25; $444,000, PCGS PF-65 HA 01/25				
1827, Restrike (Square-Base 2 in 25 C.)	11 known	5076	108,000	132,000	162,000
	Auctions: $114,000, PCGS PF-64 SBG 08/24				
1818	1 or 2 known	213013	—	—	—
Variety 2: Reduced Diameter, Motto Removed					
1831, Large Letters, B-5	<15 known	5082	27,500	54,000	81,500
	Auctions: $218,500, NGC PF-66 HA 01/09				
1831, Small Letters, B-1	1–2 known	374469	—	—	81,500
	Auctions: $230,000, PCGS PF-64 GLDB 05/09				
1833	5 known	5087	54,000	96,000	180,000
	Auctions: $149,500, PCGS PF-65 HA 06/08				
1834	<10 known	5089	27,500	54,000	81,500
	Auctions: $235,000, NGC PF-66 HA 11/13				
1835	6-8 known	5091	27,500	54,000	81,500
	Auctions: $135,125, NGC PF-64 SBG 08/12				
1836	<6 known	5093	27,500	54,000	81,500
	Auctions: $132,000, NGC PF-67 HA 01/19				
1837	1 known	5095	—	—	210,000
1838	3 known	5097	33,000	65,000	98,000
	Auctions: $184,000, PCGS PF-66 HA 01/07				

* Included in number above. **a.** The 7 is punched over a 3, which is punched over an earlier 2.

LIBERTY SEATED (1838–1891)

Variety 1, No Motto Above Eagle (1838–1853): **Designer:** *Christian Gobrecht.* **Weight:** *6.68 grams.* **Composition:** *.900 silver, .100 copper.* **Diameter:** *24.3 mm.* **Edge:** *Reeded.* **Mints:** *Philadelphia and New Orleans.*

Variety 1 (1838–1853), Circulation Strike

Mintmark location is on the reverse, below the eagle, for all varieties.

Variety 1, Proof Strike

Variety 2, Arrows at Date, Rays Around Eagle (1853): **Designer:** *Christian Gobrecht.* **Weight:** *6.22 grams.* **Composition:** *.900 silver, .100 copper.* **Diameter:** *24.3 mm.* **Edge:** *Reeded.* **Mints:** *Philadelphia and New Orleans.*

Variety 2 (1853), Circulation Strike

Variety 2, Proof Strike

Variety 3, Arrows at Date, No Rays (1854–1855): **Designer:** *Christian Gobrecht.* **Weight:** *6.22 grams.* **Composition:** *.900 silver, .100 copper.* **Diameter:** *24.3 mm.* **Edge:** *Reeded.* **Mints:** *Philadelphia, New Orleans, and San Francisco.*

Variety 3 (1854–1855), Circulation Strike

Variety 3, Proof Strike

Variety 1 Resumed, With Weight Standard of Variety 2 (1856–1865): **Designer:** *Christian Gobrecht.* **Weight:** *6.22 grams.* **Composition:** *.900 silver, .100 copper.* **Diameter:** *24.3 mm.* **Edge:** *Reeded.* **Mints:** *Philadelphia, New Orleans, and San Francisco.*

Variety 1 Resumed, Weight Standard of Variety 2 (1856–1865), Circulation Strike

Variety 1 Resumed, Weight Standard of Variety 2, Proof Strike

Variety 4, Motto Above Eagle (1866–1873): **Designer:** *Christian Gobrecht.* **Weight:** *6.22 grams.* **Composition:** *.900 silver, .100 copper.* **Diameter:** *24.3 mm.* **Edge:** *Reeded.* **Mints:** *Philadelphia, San Francisco, and Carson City.*

Variety 4 (1866–1873), Circulation Strike

Variety 4, Proof Strike

Variety 5, Arrows at Date (1873–1874): **Designer:** *Christian Gobrecht.* **Weight:** *6.25 grams.* **Composition:** *.900 silver, .100 copper.* **Diameter:** *24.3 mm.* **Edge:** *Reeded.* **Mints:** *Philadelphia, San Francisco, and Carson City.*

Variety 5 (1873–1874), Circulation Strike

Variety 5, Proof Strike

Variety 4 Resumed, With Weight Standard of Variety 5 (1875–1891): **Designer:** *Christian Gobrecht.* **Weight:** *6.25 grams.* **Composition:** *.900 silver, .100 copper.* **Diameter:** *24.3 mm.* **Edge:** *Reeded.* **Mints:** *Philadelphia, New Orleans, and San Francisco.*

Variety 4 Resumed, Weight Standard of Variety 5 (1875–1891), Circulation Strike

Variety 4 Resumed, Weight Standard of Variety 5, Proof Strike

History. The long-running Liberty Seated design was introduced on the quarter dollar in 1838. Early issues lack drapery at Liberty's elbow and have small lettering on the reverse. Drapery was added in 1840 and continued afterward. In 1853 a reduction in the coin's weight was indicated with the addition of arrows at the date and rays on the reverse (in the field around the eagle). The rays were omitted after 1853, but the arrows were retained through 1855. The motto IN GOD WE TRUST was added to the reverse in 1866. Arrows were placed at the date in the years 1873 and 1874 to denote the change of weight from 6.22 to 6.25 grams. The new weight, without the arrows, continued through 1891.

Striking and Sharpness. On the obverse, check the head of Liberty and the star centers. If these are sharp, then check the central part of the seated figure. On the reverse, check the eagle, particularly the area to the lower left of the shield. Check the denticles on both sides. Generally, the earliest issues are well struck, as are those of the 1880s onward. The word LIBERTY is not an infallible guide to grading at lower levels, as on some dies the shield was in lower relief, and the letters wore away less quickly. This guideline should be used in combination with examining other features. Some Proofs (1858 is an example) have lint marks, and others can have light striking (particularly in the 1870s and 1880s). Avoid "problem" coins and those with deep or artificial (and often colorful) toning.

Availability. Coins of this type are available in proportion to their mintages. MS coins can range from rare to exceedingly rare, as they were mostly ignored by numismatists until the series ended. Quality can vary widely, especially among branch-mint coins. Proofs of the earlier years are very rare. Beginning with 1856, they were made in larger numbers, and from 1859 onward the yearly production was in the multiple hundreds. Proofs of the later era are readily available today; truly choice and gem pieces with no distracting hairlines are in the minority and will require diligent searching.

Grading Standards

MS-67

MS-60 to 70 (Mint State). ***Obverse:*** At MS-60, some abrasion and contact marks are evident, most noticeably on the bosom and thighs and knees. Luster is present, but may be dull or lifeless. At MS-63, contact marks are very few, and abrasion is hard to detect except under magnification. An MS-65 coin has no abrasion, and contact marks are sufficiently minute as to require magnification. Check the knees of Liberty and the right field. Luster should be full and rich. Most Mint State coins of the 1861 to 1865 years, Philadelphia issues, have extensive die striae (from not completely finishing the die). ***Reverse:*** Comments apply as for the obverse, except that in lower Mint State grades abrasion and contact marks are most noticeable on the eagle's neck, the claws, and the top of the wings (harder to see there, however). At MS-65 or higher there are no marks visible to the unaided eye. The field is mainly protected by design elements and does not show abrasion as much as does the obverse on a given coin.

Illustrated coin: Note the delicate toning in the fields. In addition to hints of green, rose, and teal there is a good deal of luster as well.

AU-53

AU-50, 53, 55, 58 (About Uncirculated). ***Obverse:*** Light wear is seen on the thighs and knees, bosom, and head. At AU-58, the luster is extensive, but incomplete, especially in the right field. At AU-50 and 53, luster is less. ***Reverse:*** Wear is evident on the eagle's neck, claws, and top of the wings. An AU-58 coin has nearly full luster, more so than on the obverse, as the design elements protect the small field areas. At AU-50 and 53, there still are traces of luster.

EF-40, 45 (Extremely Fine). ***Obverse:*** Further wear is seen on all areas, especially the thighs and knees, bosom, and head. Little or no luster is seen on most coins. From this grade downward, sharpness of strike of the stars and the head does not matter to connoisseurs. ***Reverse:*** Further wear is evident on the eagle's neck, claws, and wings. Some feathers in the right wing may be blended together.

EF-40

VF-20, 30 (Very Fine). ***Obverse:*** Further wear is seen. Most details of the gown are worn away, except in the lower-relief areas above and to the right of the shield. Hair detail is mostly or completely gone. ***Reverse:*** Wear is more extensive, with more feathers blended together, especially in the right wing. The area below the shield shows more wear.

Illustrated coin: The surfaces of this coin are unusually smooth and problem free for the issue.

VF-20

F-12, 15 (Fine). ***Obverse:*** The seated figure is well worn, but with some detail above and to the right of the shield. LIBERTY is readable but weak in areas. ***Reverse:*** Wear is extensive, with about half of the feathers flat or blended with others.

F-12

VG-8, 10 (Very Good). ***Obverse:*** The seated figure is more worn, but some detail can be seen above and to the right of the shield. The shield is discernible. In LIBERTY at least the equivalent of two or three letters (can be a combination of partial letters) must be readable but can be very weak at VG-8, with a few more visible at VG-10. However, LIBERTY is not an infallible guide to grade this type, as some varieties had the word in low relief on the die, so it wore away slowly. ***Reverse:*** Further wear has flattened all but a few feathers, and the horizontal lines of the shield are indistinct. The leaves are only in outline form. The rim is visible all around, as are the ends of most denticles.

VG-10

Illustrated coin: Note the faint red toning evident in areas of this otherwise pleasingly gray coin.

G-6

G-4, 6 (Good). ***Obverse:*** The seated figure is worn smooth. At G-4 there are no letters in LIBERTY remaining on most (but not all) coins; some coins, especially of the early 1870s, are exceptions. At G-6, traces of one or two can barely be seen. ***Reverse:*** The designs are only in outline form, although some vertical shield stripes can be seen on some. The rim is worn down, and tops of the border letters are weak or worn away, although the inscription can still be read.

AG-3

AG-3 (About Good). ***Obverse:*** The seated figure is mostly visible in outline form, with only a hint of detail. Much of the rim is worn away. The date remains clear. ***Reverse:*** The border letters are partially worn away. The eagle is mostly in outline form, but with a few details discernible. The rim is weak or missing.

PF-65

PF-60 to 70 (Proof). ***Obverse and Reverse:*** Proofs that are extensively cleaned and have many hairlines, or that are dull and grainy, are lower level, such as PF-60 to 62. These are not widely desired by connoisseurs. With medium hairlines and good reflectivity, an assigned grade of PF-64 is appropriate and with relatively few hairlines, Gem PF-65. In various grades hairlines are most easily seen in the obverse field. PF-66 should have hairlines so delicate that magnification is needed to see them. Above that, a Proof should be free of such lines.

100 GREATEST UNITED STATES COINS

No. 74 1873-CC "NO ARROWS" LIBERTY SEATED QUARTER DOLLAR

1839, No Drapery

1840-O, Drapery

1840-O, Drapery, Normal O

1840-O, Drapery, Large O

1842, Small Date
Philadelphia Small Date is Proof only.

1842, Large Date

1842-O, Small Date

1842-O, Large Date

Circulation Strikes

	Mintage	GSID	G-4	VG-8	F-12	VF-20	EF-40	AU-50	MS-60	MS-63
Liberty Seated, No Drapery, No Motto Above Eagle (1838–1840)	n/a	72427	$49	$80	$130	$310	$650	$1,200	$2,050	$5,250
Liberty Seated, No Motto Above Eagle (1838–1865)	n/a	72433	32	36	43	55	120	245	430	725
Liberty Seated, No Motto, Arrows at Date, With Rays Around Eagle (1853)	n/a	72434	38	45	60	95	220	430	1,150	2,050
Liberty Seated, No Motto, Arrows at Date, No Rays Around Eagle (1854–1855)	n/a	72435	32	35	43	47	115	260	725	1,200
Liberty Seated, With Motto Above Eagle (1866–1891)	n/a	72436	32	35	38	46	120	170	290	550
Liberty Seated, Arrows at Date, With Motto Above Eagle (1873–1874)	n/a	72437	32	35	50	100	210	500	900	1,500
1838, No Drapery	466,000	5108	49	80	130	310	650	1,200	2,050	5,250
	Auctions: $195,500, PCGS MS-68 HA 05/09									
1839, No Drapery	491,146	5109	49	80	130	310	650	1,200	2,050	5,250
↳1839, No Drapery, Reverse of 1838	*	213176	49	80	130	310	650	1,200	2,050	5,250
↳1839, No Drapery, Reverse of 1839	*	213177	49	80	130	310	650	1,200	2,050	5,250
1840-O, No Drapery	382,200	5165	60	100	170	310	650	1,200	2,050	5,250
	Auctions: $329,000, NGC MS-67 HA 11/13									
1840, With Drapery	188,127	5110	32	36	70	170	360	650	1,900	5,500
1840-O, With Drapery	43,000	5166	70	115	180	310	650	900	2,250	5,750
1840-O, With Drapery, Large O, FS-501	*	200097	1,500	1,950	2,750	3,300	7,250	10,000	13,000	19,000
1841	120,000	5111	70	100	130	260	495	850	1,300	1,800
1841-O	452,000	5167	49	75	130	360	470	575	1,100	1,950
1842, Large Date	88,000	5112	70	90	145	260	525	900	1,700	4,700
1842-O, Large Date	769,000	5168	50	55	75	130	290	575	1,750	3,750
1842-O, Small Date	*	5169	650	1,250	1,600	3,000	8,000	12,000	35,000	69,500
1843	645,600	5113	32	36	43	80	220	360	725	1,500
1843-O	968,000	5170	50	80	160	365	1,000	1,600	2,750	6,250
↳1843-O, Repunched Date, FS-301	*	393357	55	90	180	400	1,150	1,800	3,000	7,000
↳1843-O, Large O, FS-501	*	227316	55	90	180	400	1,150	1,800	3,000	7,000

* Included in number above.

1853, Recut Date, No Arrows or Rays
FS-301

1853, 3 Over 4 (Arrows at Date, Rays Around Eagle)
FS-301

1854-O, Normal O

1854-O, Huge O

Circulation Strikes *(continued)*

	Mintage	GSID	G-4	VG-8	F-12	VF-20	EF-40	AU-50	MS-60	MS-63
1844	421,200	5114	$35	$45	$70	$120	$230	$370	$950	$2,250
1844-O	740,000	5171	55	70	80	120	260	455	1,400	1,600
1845	922,000	5115	43	55	90	130	230	370	675	1,400
1846	510,000	5116	55	80	110	130	290	440	1,000	2,000
1847	734,000	5117	32	36	43	55	120	260	725	1,750
1847-O	368,000	5172	115	160	325	575	950	1,600	7,500	14,500
1848	146,000	5118	55	80	115	155	390	550	1,250	5,000
1849	340,000	5119	32	36	43	80	120	325	1,000	1,500
1849-O	*	5173	1,450	2,050	3,000	3,500	7,000	8,000	18,000	30,000
1850	190,800	5120	50	115	210	305	495	850	1,900	3,250
↳1850, Misplaced Date, FS-301	*	377796	55	125	230	335	550	925	2,050	3,600
1850-O	412,000	5174	75	135	180	245	725	950	2,000	5,000
1851	160,000	5121	175	290	455	675	950	1,250	2,200	3,500
1851-O	88,000	5175	490	725	950	1,400	3,000	4,000	11,000	38,500
1852	177,060	5122	155	235	310	390	775	950	1,300	2,250
	Auctions: $105,750, NGC MS-68 HA 11/13									
1852-O	96,000	5176	490	675	950	1,500	3,750	7,000	12,000	29,000
	Auctions: $126,500, PCGS MS-63 HA 11/07									
1853, Recut Date, No Arrows or Rays	44,200	5123	1,300	1,900	2,750	3,450	4,250	4,950	7,000	7,500
↳1853, Recut Date, No Arrows or Rays, FS-301	*	373209	1,300	1,900	2,750	3,450	4,250	4,950	7,000	7,500
1853	15,210,020	5124	38	45	60	95	220	430	1,150	2,050
1853, 3 Over 4	*	5177	95	130	220	340	675	1,000	2,750	5,750
↳1853, 3 Over 4, FS-301	*	390390	95	130	220	340	675	1,000	2,750	5,750
1853-O	1,332,000	5178	50	70	100	160	420	1,000	4,400	10,000
↳1853-O, O Over Horizontal O, FS-501	*	390391	55	75	110	180	465	1,150	4,800	11,000
1854	12,380,000	5125	32	35	43	47	115	260	725	1,200
1854-O	1,484,000	5179	50	55	70	90	130	325	1,000	1,750
1854-O, Huge O	*	5180	825	1,150	1,400	1,900	3,750	5,000	15,000	—
↳1854-O, Huge O, FS-501	*	393115	825	1,150	1,400	1,900	3,750	5,000	15,000	—
1855	2,857,000	5126	32	35	43	47	115	260	725	1,200
↳1855, Doubled Die Obverse, FS-101	*	393116	36	39	48	50	125	285	800	1,300
1855-O	176,000	5181	160	235	390	775	1,900	3,100	7,000	15,500
1855-S	396,400	5182	195	290	455	725	1,150	1,750	3,750	9,500
1856	7,264,000	5127	32	36	43	55	120	245	430	725
↳1856, Mark in Shield, FS-401	*	393117	36	40	48	60	130	270	470	775
1856-O	968,000	5183	50	60	90	155	290	625	1,400	2,600

* Included in number above.

1856-S, S Over Small S
FS-501

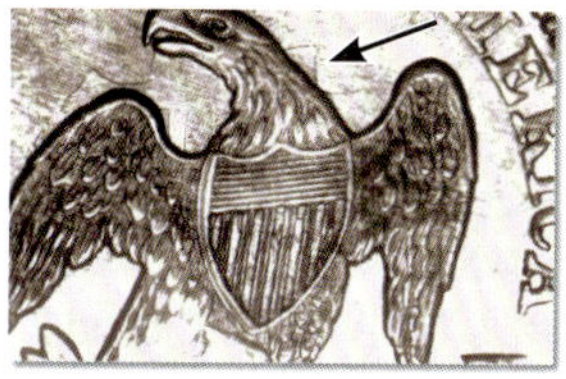

1857, Reverse Die Clash
FS-901

Circulation Strikes *(continued)*

	Mintage	GSID	G-4	VG-8	F-12	VF-20	EF-40	AU-50	MS-60	MS-63
1856-S	286,000	5184	$405	$575	$775	$950	$2,000	$3,750	$9,500	$18,000
1856-S, S Over Small S	*	5185	525	950	1,250	2,000	6,250	11,000	21,500	—
↳1856-S, S Over Small S, FS-501	*	393118	525	950	1,250	2,000	6,250	11,000	21,500	—
1857	9,644,000	5128	32	36	43	55	120	245	430	725
↳1857, Reverse Die Clash with Flying Eagle Cent, FS-901	*	374084	36	40	48	60	130	270	470	775
1857-O	1,180,000	5186	55	75	110	180	310	575	1,300	4,000
↳1857-O, Misplaced Date, FS-302	*	393119	60	85	120	200	345	650	1,450	4,400
1857-S	82,000	5187	340	525	650	850	1,250	2,100	4,750	9,500
1858	7,368,000	5129	32	36	43	55	120	245	430	725
↳1858, Reverse Die Clash with Flying Eagle Cent, FS-901	*	227319	36	40	48	60	130	270	470	775
1858-O	520,000	5188	50	60	90	130	290	650	4,400	10,000
1858-S	121,000	5189	285	440	650	1,100	2,750	4,750	21,500	—
1859	1,343,200	5130	32	36	43	55	120	245	455	900
1859-O	260,000	5190	60	90	115	170	325	1,150	2,750	7,500
1859-S	80,000	5191	455	625	1,000	1,400	4,750	10,500	—	—
1860	804,400	5131	32	36	43	55	155	290	575	1,100
1860-O	388,000	5192	50	60	90	115	260	490	1,150	2,000
1860-S	56,000	5193	1,050	1,600	3,000	5,500	8,750	15,000	42,000	—
1861	4,853,600	5132	32	36	43	55	120	245	550	900
↳1861, Doubled Die Obverse, FS-101	*	393121	36	40	48	60	130	270	625	975
↳1861, Variety 1 Reverse, FS-901	*	393122	36	40	48	60	130	270	625	975
1861-S	96,000	5194	725	950	1,250	2,500	4,700	10,000	—	—
1862	932,000	5133	35	40	55	80	145	260	600	950
1862-S	67,000	5195	195	325	455	650	1,400	2,500	4,400	8,000
1863	191,600	5134	40	55	70	130	525	725	1,150	1,750
↳1863, Repunched Date, FS-301	*	393123	45	60	75	135	575	775	1,250	1,900
1864	93,600	5135	215	290	360	495	775	925	1,750	3,100
1864-S	20,000	5196	1,100	1,250	1,500	2,200	5,250	7,500	14,500	21,000
1865	58,800	5136	100	130	230	405	550	950	1,900	3,000
1865-S	41,000	5197	290	390	575	925	1,250	1,900	6,000	11,000
1866	16,800	5137	775	1,100	1,250	1,450	1,600	1,900	2,450	2,850
1866-S	28,000	5198	575	950	1,450	1,600	2,500	3,100	6,250	15,000
1867	20,000	5138	525	775	1,000	1,250	1,700	2,050	3,250	5,500
1867-S	48,000	5199	650	1,000	1,250	1,550	3,000	8,750	11,000	14,500

* Included in number above.

1873, No Arrows, Closed 3

1873, No Arrows, Open 3

Circulation Strikes *(continued)*

	Mintage	GSID	G-4	VG-8	F-12	VF-20	EF-40	AU-50	MS-60	MS-63
1868	29,400	5139	$260	$360	$455	$525	$800	$1,100	$1,900	$3,750
1868-S	96,000	5200	130	195	325	775	900	1,900	5,000	8,750
1869	16,000	5140	550	725	900	1,100	1,300	1,700	2,250	5,000
1869-S	76,000	5201	200	325	550	775	1,250	2,000	5,250	8,000
1870	86,400	5141	130	210	285	360	495	950	1,700	3,100
1870-CC	8,340	5202	9,750	14,500	21,500	26,500	78,000	129,500	—	—
	Auctions: $108,000 PCGS AU-50 HA 04/25; $216,200, PCGS AU-55 SBG 04/25									
1871	118,200	5142	55	80	115	160	325	470	775	1,600
1871-CC	10,890	5203	10,500	15,500	21,500	34,000	62,500	86,500	138,000	228,000
	Auctions: $456,000, PCGS MS-65 HA 08/22									
1871-S	30,900	5204	1,150	1,600	2,500	3,450	4,500	5,500	8,250	11,000
1872	182,000	5143	70	100	175	235	420	575	1,500	2,500
↳1872, Repunched Date, FS-301	*	393124	75	110	195	255	465	650	1,650	2,750
↳1872, Misplaced Date, FS-302	*	393125	75	110	195	255	465	650	1,650	2,750
1872-CC	22,850	5205	2,250	2,800	5,000	11,000	16,000	21,500	69,500	—
1872-S	83,000	5206	2,200	2,500	3,000	4,500	7,500	11,000	18,000	27,000
1873, No Arrows, Closed 3	40,000	5144	525	775	1,000	1,400	2,050	3,750	24,000	36,000
1873, No Arrows, Open 3	*	5145	100	130	195	290	390	575	1,250	2,300
1873-CC, No Arrows	5 known	5207	—	—	—	72,000	96,000	126,000	180,000	432,000
	Auctions: $360,000 PCGS MS-63 HA 01/25									
1873, With Arrows	1,271,160	5146	32	35	50	100	210	500	900	1,500
1873-CC, With Arrows	12,462	5208	8,750	14,500	19,000	26,500	37,000	66,000	114,000	180,000
	Auctions: $336,000, PCGS MS-64 HA 08/22									
1873-S	156,000	5209	110	145	210	310	675	1,000	3,500	8,000
1874	471,200	5147	32	35	50	100	210	500	900	1,500
1874-S	392,000	5210	32	35	50	100	210	500	900	1,500
1875	4,292,800	5148	32	35	38	46	120	170	290	550
1875-CC	140,000	5211	260	390	575	900	1,900	2,500	5,500	8,000
1875-S	680,000	5212	35	49	70	115	195	290	675	850
1876	17,816,000	5149	32	35	38	46	120	170	290	550
↳1876, Misplaced Date, FS-301	*	393127	36	39	42	50	130	185	320	600
↳1876, Repunched/Misplaced Date, FS-302	*	393128	36	39	42	50	130	185	320	600
↳1876, Repunched Date, FS-304	*	227321	—	—	—	—	140	205	350	650
↳1876, Misplaced Date, FS-306	*	393131	36	39	42	50	130	185	320	600
↳1876, Misplaced Date, FS-307	*	393132	36	39	42	50	130	185	320	600
1876-CC	4,944,000	5213	60	90	120	145	210	310	750	1,200
↳1876-CC, Doubled Die Obverse, FS-101	*	393133	65	95	130	155	230	345	825	1,300
1876-S	8,596,000	5214	32	35	40	46	120	170	290	550

* Included in number above.

1877-S, S Over Horizontal S
FS-501

Circulation Strikes *(continued)*

	Mintage	GSID	G-4	VG-8	F-12	VF-20	EF-40	AU-50	MS-60	MS-63
1877	10,911,200	5150	$32	$35	$38	$46	$120	$170	$290	$550
1877-CC (a)	4,192,000	5215	60	90	120	145	195	340	600	1,500
↳**1877-CC, Repunched Date, FS-301** (a)	*	227322	65	95	130	155	215	370	650	1,650
1877-S	8,996,000	5216	32	35	38	46	120	170	290	550
↳**1877-S, S Over Horizontal S**	*	5217	36	50	90	195	325	575	1,150	1,600
↳**1877-S, S Over Horizontal S, FS-501**	*	393137	36	50	90	195	325	575	1,150	1,600
1878	2,260,000	5151	32	35	38	46	120	170	290	550
1878-CC	996,000	5218	60	75	90	130	275	390	900	1,450
1878-S	140,000	5219	455	575	775	1,250	2,000	3,100	5,250	7,000
1879	13,600	5152	160	210	290	390	525	575	725	900
1880	13,600	5153	160	210	290	415	550	625	750	900
1881	12,000	5154	160	210	290	390	575	650	800	1,100
1882	15,200	5155	160	210	290	390	525	575	725	900
1883	14,400	5156	160	210	290	390	525	575	725	900
1884	8,000	5157	230	260	360	390	525	575	725	900
1885	13,600	5158	160	195	260	390	525	575	725	950
1886	5,000	5159	340	440	550	650	950	1,000	1,400	1,900
1887	10,000	5160	195	260	325	420	625	725	950	1,200
1888	10,001	5161	235	290	340	430	575	675	1,000	1,450
1888-S	1,216,000	5220	32	35	38	46	120	210	390	775
1889	12,000	5162	160	210	290	360	420	525	800	1,200
1890	80,000	5163	130	160	195	260	290	360	700	850
1891	3,920,000	5164	32	35	38	46	120	170	290	550
1891-O	68,000	5221	390	775	1,200	1,750	2,750	3,750	8,000	13,000
	Auctions: $161,000, NGC MS-65 HA 06/08									
1891-S	2,216,000	5222	32	35	38	46	120	195	390	575

* Included in number above. **a.** The 1877-CC quarter with fine edge-reeding is scarcer than that with normally spaced reeding; in the marketplace, there is no price differential.

Proof Strikes

	Mintage	GSID	PF-60	PF-63	PF-65
Liberty Seated, No Drapery, No Motto Above Eagle (1838–1839), Proof	n/a	74179	—	$300,000	$420,000
Liberty Seated, With Drapery, No Motto Above Eagle (1840–1865), Proof	n/a	74180	$650	1,250	3,500
Same, Proof Cameo	n/a	74181	—	1,300	3,900
Same, Proof Deep Cameo	n/a	74182	—	2,250	6,250
Liberty Seated, Arrows at Date, With Rays Around Eagle (1853), Proof	n/a	76285	24,000	36,000	102,000
Liberty Seated, Arrows at Date, No Rays Around Eagle (1854–1855), Proof	n/a	74183	6,250	12,000	24,000
Liberty Seated, With Motto Above Eagle (1866–1891), Proof	n/a	74184	495	800	1,350
Same, Proof Cameo	n/a	74185	600	950	1,700
Same, Proof Deep Cameo	n/a	74186	—	1,550	3,000
Liberty Seated, Arrows at Date, With Motto Above Eagle (1873–1874), Proof	n/a	74187	950	1,750	4,200
Same, Proof Cameo	n/a	74188	—	1,950	5,500
Same, Proof Deep Cameo	n/a	74189	—	4,500	—
1838, No Drapery		5224	—	300,000	420,000
	Auctions: $381,875, PCGS PF-63 HA 01/13				
1839, No Drapery		5227	—	300,000	420,000
	Auctions: $517,500, NGC PF-65 HA 04/08				
1840		5230	—	—	96,000
	Auctions: $149,500, NGC PF-65 HA 08/07				
1841		5231	60,000	86,500	114,000
	Auctions: $345,000, NGC PF-66 HA 01/08				
1842, Small Date	5 known	5234	—	90,000	264,000
	Auctions: $222,000, PCGS PF-65 HA 04/25				
1843		5237	—	21,500	84,000
1844		5242	—	—	204,000
	Auctions: $322,000, NGC PF-66 HA 01/08				
1845		5243	—	30,000	53,000
	Auctions: $195,500, NGC PF-66 HA 01/08				
1846		5246	—	18,000	38,500
1847		5249	—	10,000	26,500
1848		5254	—	15,000	26,500
1849		5257	—	10,000	27,500

	Mintage	GSID	PF-60	PF-63	PF-65
1850		5258	$17,000	$26,500	$72,000
	Auctions: $460,000, NGC PF-68 HA 01/08				
1852		5266	—	—	84,000
	Auctions: $138,000, NGC PF-65 HA 08/08				
1853		5267	24,000	36,000	102,000
	Auctions: $276,000, NGC PF-66 HA 08/07				
1854		5270	6,250	12,000	24,000
	Auctions: $138,000, NGC PF-66 HA 08/07				
1855		5273	7,500	12,000	24,000
1855-S, Branch Mint		5387	—	—	—
	Auctions: $276,000, NGC PF-64 HA 08/11				
1856		5276	3,450	4,200	12,000
1857		5279	2,100	2,750	7,500
1858	300	5282	1,200	1,600	5,000
1859	800	5285	725	1,300	3,750
1860	1,000	5288	725	1,300	3,750
1861	1,000	5291	725	1,250	3,750
1862	550	5294	650	1,250	3,500
1863	460	5297	650	1,250	3,500
1864	470	5300	650	1,250	3,500
1865	500	5303	650	1,250	3,750
1866	725	5306	650	1,050	2,250
1867	625	5309	550	900	1,600
1868	600	5312	525	875	2,250
1869	600	5315	525	875	1,750
1870	1,000	5318	525	875	2,450
1871	960	5321	525	875	2,250
1872	950	5324	525	875	1,700
1873, Closed 3	540	5327	525	875	1,350
1873, With Arrows	500	5328	950	1,750	4,200
1874	700	5333	950	1,750	4,200
1875	700	5336	495	800	1,350
1876	1,150	5339	495	800	1,350
1877	510	5342	495	800	1,350
1878	800	5345	495	925	1,550
1879	1,100	5348	495	800	1,350
1880	1,355	5351	675	1,000	1,350
1881	975	5354	495	800	1,350
1882	1,100	5357	495	800	1,350
1883	1,039	5360	495	800	1,350
1884	875	5363	495	800	1,350
1885	930	5366	495	800	1,350
1886	886	5369	495	800	1,350
1887	710	5372	495	800	1,450
1888	832	5375	495	800	1,350
1889	711	5378	495	800	1,350
1890	590	5381	495	800	1,350
1891	600	5384	495	800	1,350

Note: The 1866 Proof quarter, half, and dollar without motto are not mentioned in the Mint director's report and were not issued for circulation. * Included in number above.

BARBER (1892–1916)

Designer: *Charles E. Barber.* **Weight:** *6.25 grams.*
Composition: *.900 silver, .100 copper (net weight .18084 oz. pure silver).*
Diameter: *24.3 mm.* **Edge:** *Reeded.* **Mints:** *Philadelphia, Denver, New Orleans, and San Francisco.*

Circulation Strike

Mintmark location is on the reverse, below the eagle.

Proof Strike

History. The Liberty Head design was by Charles E. Barber, chief engraver of the U.S. Mint. Barber quarters feature the same obverse motif used on dimes and half dollars of the era, with the designer's initial, B, found at the truncation of the neck of Liberty. The reverse depicts a heraldic eagle holding an olive branch in one talon and arrows in the other, along with a ribbon reading E PLURIBUS UNUM.

Striking and Sharpness. On the obverse, check the hair details and other features. On the reverse, the eagle's leg at the lower right and the arrows can be weak. Also check the upper-right portion of the shield and the nearby wing. Once these coins entered circulation and acquired wear, the word LIBERTY on the headband tended to disappear quickly. Most Proofs are sharply struck, although more than just a few are weak on the eagle's leg at the lower right and on certain parts of the arrows. The Proofs of 1892 to 1901 usually have cameo contrast between the designs and the mirror fields. Later Proofs vary in their contrast.

Availability. Barber quarters in Fine or better grade are scarce. Today, among circulation strikes, 90 percent or more in existence are G-4 or below. MS coins are available of all dates and mints, but some are very elusive. The 1896-S, 1901-S, and 1913-S are the key dates in all grades. Proofs exist in proportion to their mintages. Choicer examples tend to be of later dates.

Grading Standards

MS-60 to 70 (Mint State). ***Obverse:*** At MS-60, some abrasion and contact marks are evident, most noticeably on the cheek and the obverse field to the right. Luster is present, but may be dull or lifeless. Many Barber coins have been cleaned, especially of the earlier dates. At MS-63, contact marks are very few. Abrasion still is evident, but less than at lower levels. Indeed, the cheek of Liberty virtually showcases abrasion. An MS-65 coin may have minor abrasion, but contact marks are so minute as to require magnification. Luster should be full and rich. ***Reverse:*** Comments apply as for the obverse, except that in lower Mint State grades abrasion and contact marks are most noticeable on the head and tail of the eagle and on the tips of the wings. At MS-65 or higher, there are no marks visible to the unaided eye. The field is mainly protected by design elements, and often appears to grade a point or two higher than the obverse.

MS-67

Illustrated coin: This brilliant coin shows full satin luster.

AU-50

AU-50, 53, 55, 58 (About Uncirculated). ***Obverse:*** Light wear is seen on the head, especially on the forward hair under LIBERTY. At AU-58, the luster is extensive but incomplete, especially on the higher parts and in the right field. At AU-50 and 53, luster is less. ***Reverse:*** Wear is evident on the head and tail of the eagle and on the tips of the wings. At AU-50 and 53, there still is significant luster. An AU-58 coin (as determined by the obverse) can have the reverse appear to be full Mint State.

EF-40

EF-40, 45 (Extremely Fine). ***Obverse:*** Further wear is seen on the head. The hair above the forehead lacks most detail. LIBERTY shows wear, but still is strong. ***Reverse:*** Further wear is seen on the head and tail of the eagle and on the tips of the wings, most evident at the left and right extremes of the wings. At this level and below, sharpness of strike on the reverse is not important.

Illustrated coin: Note the subtle lilac and gold toning.

VF-20

VF-20, 30 (Very Fine). ***Obverse:*** The head shows more wear, now with nearly all detail gone in the hair above the forehead. LIBERTY shows wear, but is complete. The leaves on the head all show wear, as does the upper part of the cap. ***Reverse:*** Wear is more extensive, particularly noticeable on the outer parts of the wings, the head, the shield, and the tail.

Illustrated coin: The dig and discoloration in Liberty's cheek decrease the appeal of this example.

F-15

F-12, 15 (Fine). ***Obverse:*** The head shows extensive wear. LIBERTY, the key place to check, is weak, especially at ER, but is fully readable. The ANA grading standards and *Photograde* adhere to this. PCGS suggests that lightly struck coins "may have letters partially missing." Traditionally, collectors insist on full LIBERTY. ***Reverse:*** More wear is seen on the reverse in the places as above. E PLURIBUS UNUM is light, with one to several letters worn away.

VG-8, 10 (Very Good). ***Obverse:*** A net of three letters in LIBERTY must be readable. Traditionally, LI is clear, and after that there is a partial letter or two. ***Reverse:*** Further wear has smoothed more than half of the feathers in the wing. The shield is indistinct except for a few traces of interior lines. The motto is partially worn away. The rim is full, and many if not most denticles can be seen.

VG-10

G-4, 6 (Good). ***Obverse:*** The head is in outline form, with the center flat. Most of the rim is there. All letters and the date are full. ***Reverse:*** The eagle shows only a few feathers, and only a few scattered letters remain in the motto. The rim may be worn flat in some or all of the area, but the peripheral lettering is clear.

G-4

AG-3 (About Good). ***Obverse:*** The stars and motto are worn, and the border may be indistinct. Distinctness varies at this level. The date is clear. Grading is usually determined by the reverse. ***Reverse:*** The rim is gone and the letters are partially worn away. The eagle is mostly flat, perhaps with a few hints of feathers.

AG-3

PF-60 to 70 (Proof). ***Obverse and Reverse:*** Proofs that are extensively cleaned and have many hairlines, or that are dull and grainy, are lower level, such as PF-60 to 62. These are not widely desired by collectors. With medium hairlines and good reflectivity, an assigned grade of PF-64 is appropriate. Tiny horizontal lines on Liberty's cheek, known as slide marks, from National and other album slides scuffing the relief of the cheek, are endemic on all Barber silver coins. With noticeable marks of this type, the highest grade assignable is PF-64. With relatively few hairlines, a rating of PF-65 can be given. PF-66 should have hairlines so delicate that magnification is needed to see them. Above that, a Proof should be free of any hairlines or other problems.

PF-68 Cameo

Illustrated coin: Exceptional fields offset the bright devices.

Circulation Strikes

	Mintage	GSID	G-4	VG-8	F-12	VF-20	EF-40	AU-50	MS-60	MS-63
Barber (1892–1916)	**n/a**	**72438**	**$16.00**	**$19**	**$24**	**$32**	**$65**	**$140**	**$275**	**$365**
1892	8,236,000	5388	16.00	19	24	32	65	140	275	365
↳1892, Doubled Die Obverse, FS-101	*	226473	—	—	—	39	80	160	325	495
↳1892, Repunched Date, Tripled Die Obverse, FS-301	*	393358	—	—	—	—	—	—	—	—
1892-O	2,460,000	5413	16.00	23	47	70	110	195	345	525
↳1892-O, Doubled Die Obverse, FS-101	*	226475	—	—	—	—	130	215	380	575
↳1892-O, Repunched Date, FS-301	*	330038	—	—	—	—	130	215	380	575
↳1892-O, Clashed Dies/ Covered E Reverse, FS-401/901	*	213526	—	—	—	—	130	215	380	575
1892-S	964,079	5414	34.00	65	100	150	240	490	725	1,100
↳1892-S, S Over S, FS-501	*	330039	—	—	—	—	290	525	775	1,200
1893	5,444,023	5389	16.00	19	24	40	80	155	290	550
1893-O	3,396,000	5415	19.00	23	40	70	130	195	325	525
1893-S	1,454,535	5416	27.00	46	90	160	310	430	675	1,600
1894	3,432,000	5390	17.50	21	38	55	115	175	340	575
1894-O	2,852,000	5417	23.00	34	80	130	200	285	495	800
1894-S	2,648,821	5418	18.00	24	40	75	160	230	365	650
1895	4,440,000	5391	17.50	20	31	40	80	140	290	455
1895-O	2,816,000	5419	17.50	32	60	110	235	325	470	1,150
1895-S	1,764,681	5420	30.00	60	100	150	210	360	625	1,400
1896	3,874,000	5392	16.00	19	24	32	65	140	275	365
1896-O	1,484,000	5421	70.00	110	210	325	650	1,000	1,200	2,100
1896-S	188,039	5422	675.00	1,400	2,400	3,750	5,250	7,500	14,500	18,500
1897	8,140,000	5393	16.00	19	24	32	65	140	275	375
1897-O	1,414,800	5423	47.00	95	230	415	650	950	1,600	2,500
1897-S	542,229	5424	130.00	195	375	775	1,000	1,450	2,500	3,750
1898	11,100,000	5394	16.00	19	24	32	65	140	275	365
1898-O	1,868,000	5425	16.00	34	95	155	360	525	950	1,250
1898-S	1,020,592	5426	18.00	24	55	100	235	470	1,300	2,750
1899	12,624,000	5395	16.00	19	24	32	65	140	305	410
1899-O	2,644,000	5427	19.00	30	60	115	180	260	550	825
1899-S	708,000	5428	32.00	90	150	200	340	495	1,500	2,750
1900	10,016,000	5396	16.00	19	24	39	90	160	310	470
1900-O	3,416,000	5429	24.00	38	90	135	245	470	875	1,450
1900-S	1,858,585	5430	19.00	24	34	55	130	285	725	1,450
1901	8,892,000	5397	16.00	19	24	32	65	140	285	390
1901-O	1,612,000	5431	60.00	100	220	430	875	1,300	2,000	2,750
1901-S	72,664	5432	4,700.00	10,000	16,000	22,000	31,000	34,000	53,000	62,500
	Auctions: $376,912, PCGS MS-68 SBG 03/10									
1902	12,196,967	5398	16.00	19	24	32	65	140	275	395
1902-O	4,748,000	5433	21.00	30	46	90	190	310	725	1,050
↳1902-O, Misplaced Date, FS-301	*	393008	—	—	—	—	—	—	—	—
1902-S	1,524,612	5434	20.00	38	70	145	260	455	950	1,250
1903	9,759,309	5399	16.00	19	24	32	65	140	285	490
1903-O	3,500,000	5435	20.00	27	40	70	130	245	525	1,000

* Included in number above.

Circulation Strikes *(continued)*

	Mintage	GSID	G-4	VG-8	F-12	VF-20	EF-40	AU-50	MS-60	MS-63
1903-S	1,036,000	5436	$19.50	$26	$46	$95	$150	$275	$650	$1,200
1904	9,588,143	5400	16.00	19	24	32	65	140	275	525
1904-O	2,456,000	5437	32.00	60	115	195	275	525	1,000	1,250
1905	4,967,523	5401	20.00	30	50	70	75	145	300	405
1905-O	1,230,000	5438	49.00	75	145	245	340	420	1,000	1,450
1905-S	1,884,000	5439	27.00	40	90	120	150	235	650	1,300
1906	3,655,760	5402	16.00	19	24	32	65	140	275	365
1906-D	3,280,000	5440	16.00	19	24	32	65	140	275	415
1906-O	2,056,000	5441	19.00	27	43	70	145	245	420	775
1907	7,132,000	5403	16.00	19	24	32	65	140	275	365
1907-D	2,484,000	5442	16.00	19	27	50	80	210	410	775
↳1907-D, Doubled Die Obverse/Repunched Date, FS-301	*	226477	—	—	—	—	95	230	450	850
1907-O	4,560,000	5443	19.00	26	35	60	130	195	340	575
1907-S	1,360,000	5444	18.00	27	60	120	340	500	1,000	2,000
↳1907-S, S Over S, FS-501	*	330040	—	—	—	260	575	—	—	—
1908	4,232,000	5404	16.00	19	24	32	65	140	275	365
1908-D	5,788,000	5445	16.00	19	24	32	65	140	275	365
↳1908-D, Misplaced Date, FS-301	*	377838	—	—	—	—	—	—	—	—
1908-O	6,244,000	5446	16.00	19	24	32	65	140	275	390
1908-S	784,000	5447	50.00	95	160	215	440	725	1,400	1,900
1909	9,268,000	5405	16.00	19	24	32	65	140	275	365
1909-D	5,114,000	5448	16.00	19	24	32	65	140	275	365
1909-O	712,000	5449	75.00	210	600	1,000	2,750	4,000	5,250	6,000
1909-S	1,348,000	5450	19.00	26	44	110	180	285	575	1,150
↳1909-S, Inverted Mintmark, FS-501	*	393009	—	—	—	—	—	—	—	—
1910	2,244,000	5406	16.00	19	24	32	65	140	275	365
1910-D	1,500,000	5451	19.00	26	49	75	130	260	455	775
1911	3,720,000	5407	16.00	19	24	32	65	140	275	365
1911-D	933,600	5452	24.00	47	170	325	490	675	1,000	1,400
1911-S	988,000	5453	19.00	26	43	80	195	310	525	725
1912	4,400,000	5408	16.00	19	24	32	65	140	275	365
1912-S	708,000	5454	23.00	38	75	120	155	300	650	1,200
1913	484,000	5409	40.00	70	130	210	430	575	800	950
1913-D	1,450,800	5455	17.50	20	38	60	95	175	390	650
1913-S	40,000	5456	1,350.00	2,450	4,900	7,500	11,000	12,500	15,500	20,000
	Auctions: $172,500, PCGS MS-68 HA 01/05									
1914	6,244,230	5410	16.00	19	24	32	65	140	275	365
1914-D	3,046,000	5457	16.00	19	24	32	65	140	275	365
↳1914-D, Doubled Die Obverse, FS-101	*	226478	—	—	—	—	80	155	300	400
1914-S	264,000	5458	100.00	180	390	625	1,100	1,450	2,100	3,250
1915	3,480,000	5411	16.00	19	24	32	65	140	275	365
1915-D	3,694,000	5459	16.00	19	24	32	65	140	275	365
1915-S	704,000	5460	30.00	46	70	95	115	210	300	495
1916	1,788,000	5412	16.00	19	24	32	65	140	275	365
1916-D	6,540,800	5461	16.00	19	24	32	65	140	275	365

* Included in number above.

Proof Strikes

	Mintage	GSID	PF-60	PF-63	PF-65
Barber (1892–1915), Proof	**n/a**	**73850**	**$440**	**$650**	**$1,250**
Same, Proof Cameo	**n/a**	**73851**	**—**	**825**	**1,600**
Same, Proof Deep Cameo	**n/a**	**73852**	**—**	**1,250**	**3,250**
1892	1,245	5462	440	650	1,250
1893	792	5465	440	650	1,250
1894	972	5468	440	650	1,250
1895	880	5471	440	650	1,250
1896	762	5474	440	650	1,250
1897	731	5477	440	650	1,250
1898	735	5480	440	650	1,250
1899	846	5483	440	650	1,250
1900	912	5486	440	650	1,250
1901	813	5489	440	650	1,250
1902	777	5492	440	650	1,250
1903	755	5495	440	650	1,250
1904	670	5498	440	650	1,250
1905	727	5501	440	650	1,250
1906	675	5504	440	650	1,250
1907	575	5507	440	650	1,250
1908	545	5509	440	650	1,250
1909	650	5512	440	650	1,250
1910	551	5515	440	650	1,250
1911	543	5518	440	650	1,250
1912	700	5521	440	650	1,400
1913	613	5524	440	650	1,250
1914	380	5527	470	775	1,550
1915	450	5530	440	650	1,250

STANDING LIBERTY (1916–1930)

Variety 1, No Stars Below Eagle (1916–1917): **Designer:** *Hermon A. MacNeil.* **Weight:** *6.25 grams.* **Composition:** *.900 silver, .100 copper (net weight .18084 oz. pure silver).* **Diameter:** *24.3 mm.* **Edge:** *Reeded.* **Mints:** *Philadelphia, Denver, and San Francisco.*

Variety 1, No Stars Below Eagle (1916–1917)

Mintmark location is on the obverse, at the top left of the date, for both varieties.

Variety 2, Stars Below Eagle (1917–1930): **Designer:** *Hermon A. MacNeil.* **Weight:** *6.25 grams.* **Composition:** *.900 silver, .100 copper (net weight .18084 oz. pure silver).* **Diameter:** *24.3 mm.* **Edge:** *Reeded.* **Mints:** *Philadelphia, Denver, and San Francisco.*

Variety 2, Stars Below Eagle (1917–1930)

History. The Standing Liberty quarter dollar, designed by sculptor Hermon A. MacNeil (whose initial, M, is located above and to the right of the date), was greeted with wide acclaimed from its first appearance. All of 1916 and many of 1917 are of the Variety 1 design, with the right breast of Liberty exposed on the obverse and with no stars below the eagle on the reverse. Variety 2 of the Standing Liberty design was introduced in 1917 and continued to the end of the series. Liberty is clothed in a jacket of chainmail armor, and the reverse is slightly redesigned, with stars below the eagle. These changes came at the suggestion of the designer, Hermon A. MacNeil. The Mint also created a 2016 gold Standing Liberty quarter at a smaller dimension. See page 529.

Striking and Sharpness. Many if not most 1916 quarters are somewhat lightly struck on the head and body of Liberty. The 1917, Variety 1, quarters usually are quite well struck. When light striking is found, it is usually on the higher-relief parts of the head, the right knee (not as obvious), and the rivets on the left side of the shield. The 1917 Philadelphia Mint coins are usually sharper than the other varieties of this type. Most coins of the Variety 2 design have areas of light striking. On the obverse these are most notable on the head of Liberty and on the shield, the latter often with the two lower-left rivets weak or missing and with the center emblem on the shield weak. The center of the standing figure can be weak as well, as can the upper-left area at and near the date. After 1924 the date was slightly recessed, eliminating that problem. On the reverse, check the eagle's breast. A misleading term, Full Head (FH), is widely used to describe quarters that have only *partial* head details; such coins often actually have the two lower-left shield rivets poorly struck or not visible at all. Most third-party grading services define these criteria for "Full Head" designation (in order of importance): a full, unbroken hairline from Liberty's brow down to the jawline; all three leaves on the head showing; and a visible ear hole.

Availability. The 1916 quarter is the key to the series. Examples tend to be liberally graded in the real-life marketplace, especially in EF and AU, this in contrast to more careful grading for the less valuable 1917 issues. Circulated coins of 1916 and 1917 often have the date worn partly away, due to the high position of this feature in the design. Among Variety 2 coins, the 1918-S, 8 Over 7, is recognized as the key issue, and the 1919-D, 1921, 1923-S, and 1927-S as quite scarce. MS coins are readily available for most issues, but Full Details coins can be *extreme* rarities. Circulated coins dated from 1917 through 1924 often have the date worn partly away, due to the high position of this feature in the design. On MS coins the luster usually is rich and attractive. No Proof coins of this type were officially issued, but specimen strikings dated 1917 are known to exist.

Grading Standards

MS-65
Full Head

MS-60 to 70 (Mint State). ***Obverse:*** At MS-60 some abrasion and contact marks are evident on the higher areas, which are also the areas most likely to be weakly struck. This includes the rivets on the shield to the left and the central escutcheon on the shield, the head, and the right leg of Liberty. The luster may not be complete in those areas on weakly struck coins, even those certified above MS-65—the *original planchet surface* may be revealed as it was not smoothed out by striking. Accordingly, grading is best done by evaluating abrasion and mint luster as it is observed. Luster may be dull or lifeless at MS-60 to 62 but should have deep frost at MS-63 or better, particularly in the lower-relief areas. At MS-65 or better, it should be full and rich. ***Reverse:*** Striking is usually quite good, permitting observation of luster in all areas. Check the eagle's breast and the surface of the right wing. Luster may be dull or lifeless at MS-60 to 62 but should have deep frost at MS-63 or better, particularly in the lower-relief areas. At MS-65 or better, it should be full and rich.

Illustrated coin: See the subtle notes of gold, blue, and pink on this lustrous example.

AU-53

AU-50, 53, 55, 58 (About Uncirculated). ***Obverse:*** Light wear is seen on the figure of Liberty, especially noticeable around her midriff and right knee. The shield shows wear, as does the highest part of the sash where it crosses Liberty's waist. At AU-58 the luster is extensive, but incomplete on the higher areas, although it should be nearly full in the panels of the parapet to the left and right, and in the upper field. At AU-50 and 53, luster is less. ***Reverse:*** Wear is most evident on the eagle's breast, the edges of both wings, and the interior area of the right wing. Luster is nearly complete at AU-58, but at AU-50, half or more is gone.

EF-40

EF-40, 45 (Extremely Fine). ***Obverse:*** Wear is more extensive, with the higher parts of Liberty now without detail and the front of the right leg flat. The shield is worn. On coins dated from 1917 to 1924 the date shows wear at the top (on those of 1925 to 1930, with the date recessed, the numbers are bold). Little or no luster is seen, except perhaps among the letters. ***Reverse:*** The eagle shows more wear, with the surface of the right wing being mostly flat. Little or no luster is evident.

VF-20

VF-20, 30 (Very Fine). ***Obverse:*** Wear is more extensive. The higher-relief areas of Liberty are flat, and the sash crossing her waist is mostly blended into it (some sharply struck pieces being exceptions). The left side of the shield is mostly flat, although its outline can be seen. On quarters dated 1917 to 1924 the top of the date shows more wear. ***Reverse:*** The eagle shows further wear, with the body blending into the wing above it. Much feather detail is gone from the wing to the left (on quarters dated 1925 to 1930; less so for those dated 1917 to 1924). Most detail is gone from the right wing.

F-12

F-12, 15 (Fine). ***Obverse:*** Liberty is worn nearly flat. Most detail in her gown is gone, except to the left of her leg and below her knee to the right. The stars on the parapet are well worn, with some indistinct. The top of the date is weak. Quarters of the rare 1916 date are slightly weaker than those of 1917 in this and lower grades. On quarters of 1917 to 1924 the top of the date is weak. On those dated 1925 to 1930 the date remains strong. ***Reverse:*** The eagle shows further wear, this being greater on 1925 to 1930 issues than on the earlier dates.

VG-10

VG-8, 10 (Very Good). ***Obverse:*** The obverse is worn further, with fewer details in the skirt, and part of the shield border to the left blended into the standing figure. The date is partially worn away at the top, and quarters from 1917 to 1924 have less detail. Those from 1925 to 1930 retain more detail, and the date is full. ***Reverse:*** The eagle is worn further, with only about a third of the feathers now discernible, these mostly on the wing to the left.

G-6

G-4, 6 (Good). ***Obverse:*** The wear is more extensive. Most coins have the stars missing, the standing figure flat, and much of the date worn away, although still clearly identifiable. Quarters of 1925 to 1930 show more detail and the date is clear. ***Reverse:*** The eagle is mostly in outline form, with only a few feather details visible. The rim is worn into the letters, and on quarters of 1916 to 1924, E PLURIBUS UNUM is very faint; it is clear on quarters of later dates.

AG-3

AG-3 (About Good). ***Obverse:*** The obverse is worn nearly smooth, and the date is mostly gone. On some coins just one or two digits are seen. Fortunately, those digits are usually on the right, such as a trace of just a 6, which will identify the coin as a 1916. On quarters of 1925 to 1930 the wear is more extensive than for G-4, but most features are discernible and the date is clear. ***Reverse:*** The eagle is flat, and the border is worn down further. On quarters of 1916 to 1924, E PLURIBUS UNUM is extremely faint or even missing in areas; it remains readable on quarters of later dates.

Full Head Details, Variety 1
Note the excellently defined cheek, facial features, and wreath.

Full Head Details, Variety 2
Note the full unbroken hairline from brow to neck, all three leaves clearly visible in Liberty's cap, and a visible ear hole.

Pedestal Date (1917–1924)

Recessed Date (1925–1930)

Circulation Strikes

	Mintage	GSID	VG-8	F-12	VF-20	EF-40	AU-50	MS-60	MS-63	MS-65	MS-66
Standing Liberty, Variety 1: No Stars Below Eagle (1916–1917)	**n/a**	**72439**	**$50.00**	**$70.00**	**$100**	**$150**	**$180**	**$260**	**$375**	**$750**	**$1,100**
Same, Full Head	**n/a**	**72440**	**—**	**—**	**—**	**—**	**—**	**420**	**575**	**1,250**	**2,400**
Standing Liberty, Variety 2: With Stars Below Eagle (1917–1930)	**n/a**	**72441**	**13.50**	**14.50**	**20**	**46**	**95**	**195**	**280**	**500**	**675**
Same, Full Head	**n/a**	**72442**	**—**	**—**	**—**	**—**	**180**	**345**	**500**	**925**	**1,200**
Variety 1: No Stars Below Eagle											
1916	52,000	5533	6,000.00	6,750.00	8,500	11,000	12,000	14,500	18,000	22,000	35,000
1916, Full Head	*	5534	—	—	—	—	—	17,500	20,500	37,000	53,000
	Auctions: $312,000, NGC MS-65 HA 01/04										
1917, Variety 1	8,740,000	5535	50.00	70.00	100	150	180	260	375	750	1,100
1917, Variety 1, Full Head	*	5536	—	—	—	—	—	420	575	1,250	2,400
1917-D, Variety 1	1,509,200	5563	75.00	95.00	120	155	245	325	440	850	1,200
↳1917-D, Variety 1, Doubled Die Reverse, FS-801	*	226411	—	—	—	—	—	—	—	—	—
1917-D, Variety 1, Full Head	*	5564	—	—	—	—	—	475	625	1,450	2,900
↳1917-D, Variety 1, Doubled Die Reverse, FS-801, Full Head	*	226418	—	—	—	—	—	—	—	—	—
1917-S, Variety 1	1,952,000	5567	85.00	115.00	155	195	290	360	440	1,150	1,950
↳1917-S, Variety 1, "Shish Kebab", FS-401	*	374762	—	130.00	325	—	—	—	—	—	—
1917-S, Variety 1, Full Head	*	5568	—	—	—	—	—	675	1,250	2,400	4,100
↳1917-S, Variety 1, "Shish Kebab", FS-401, Full Head	*	374763	—	—	—	—	—	—	—	—	—
Variety 2: With Stars Below Eagle											
1917, Variety 2	13,880,000	5537	47.00	55.00	70	110	135	220	310	625	900
1917, Variety 2, Full Head	*	5538	—	—	—	—	—	345	525	1,750	2,450
	Auctions: $114,000, PCGS MS-68 SBG 08/22										
1917-D, Variety 2	6,224,400	5565	70.00	110.00	140	160	215	280	375	1,300	2,000
1917-D, Variety 2, Full Head	*	5566	—	—	—	—	—	490	950	2,300	5,000
1917-S, Variety 2	5,552,000	5569	70.00	105.00	130	165	210	285	415	1,250	1,550
1917-S, Variety 2, Full Head	*	5570	—	—	—	—	—	550	1,150	2,750	5,500
1918	14,240,000	5539	27.00	32.00	40	55	95	195	305	650	1,150
1918, Full Head	*	5540	—	—	—	—	—	380	650	2,250	4,500
1918-D	7,380,000	5573	43.00	75.00	105	145	195	285	410	1,500	2,500
1918-D, Full Head	*	5574	—	—	—	—	290	470	900	4,500	7,250

* Included in number above.

1918-S, 8 Over 7
FS-101

Circulation Strikes *(continued)*

	Mintage	GSID	VG-8	F-12	VF-20	EF-40	AU-50	MS-60	MS-63	MS-65	MS-66
1918-S, Normal Date	11,072,000	5575	$20	$31	$39	$100	$155	$260	$430	$1,600	$2,500
1918-S, Normal Date, Full Head	*	5576	—	—	—	—	525	1,000	1,900	11,500	14,000
1918-S, 8 Over 7	*	5571	2,500	3,300	3,900	7,500	11,000	20,000	29,000	90,000	120,000
	Auctions: $109,250, PCGS MS-65 HA 05/11										
↳1918-S, 8 Over 7, Overdate, FS-101	*	392833	2,500	3,300	3,900	7,500	11,000	20,000	29,000	90,000	120,000
	Auctions: $108,000, NGC MS-67 HA 08/24										
1918-S, 8 Over 7, Full Head	*	5572	—	—	—	—	13,000	45,500	108,000	—	—
	Auctions: $297,275, PCGS MS-64 SBG 08/12										
↳1918-S, 8 Over 7, Overdate, FS-101, Full Head	*	392834	—	—	—	—	13,000	45,500	108,000	—	—
	Auctions: $336,000, PCGS MS-64 HA 09/20										
1919	11,324,000	5541	55	65	75	90	130	230	340	650	1,200
1919, Full Head	*	5542	—	—	—	—	180	390	725	2,400	3,250
1919-D	1,944,000	5577	145	230	440	675	950	1,950	3,250	5,500	7,500
1919-D, Full Head	*	5578	—	—	—	—	—	5,000	8,500	41,000	150,000
	Auctions: $132,000, PCGS MS-66 HA 01/25; $132,000, PCGS MS-66 HA 01/25										
1919-S	1,836,000	5579	130	210	420	725	1,000	2,400	3,250	10,000	12,000
1919-S, Full Head	*	5580	—	—	—	—	3,550	6,500	13,000	50,500	115,000
	Auctions: $258,500, PCGS MS-67 HA 04/14										
1920	27,860,000	5543	20	24	38	55	110	215	310	550	750
↳1920, Clashed Dies, FS-401	*	226412	—	—	—	—	—	—	—	—	—
1920, Full Head	*	5544	—	—	—	—	—	380	550	1,250	2,400
↳1920, Clashed Dies, FS-401, Full Head	*	226419	—	—	—	—	—	—	—	—	—
1920-D	3,586,400	5581	130	160	195	245	345	675	1,200	2,250	3,250
1920-D, Full Head	*	5582	—	—	—	—	1,250	1,900	3,750	12,000	18,500
	Auctions: $372,000, PCGS MS-68 HA 08/21										
1920-S	6,380,000	5583	24	28	36	80	215	455	1,150	3,000	5,500
↳1920-S, Clashed Dies, FS-401	*	226413	—	—	—	—	—	—	—	—	—
1920-S, Full Head	*	5584	—	—	—	—	—	3,750	5,750	27,000	120,000
	Auctions: $105,000, PCGS MS-66 HA 01/25										
↳1920-S, Clashed Dies, FS-401, Full Head	*	226420	—	—	—	—	—	—	—	—	—
1921	1,916,000	5545	195	345	550	800	1,100	1,750	2,200	2,750	4,100
1921, Full Head	*	5546	—	—	—	—	—	1,800	3,250	7,500	14,500
1923	9,716,000	5547	23	34	40	55	110	215	310	500	675
1923, Full Head	*	5548	—	—	—	—	—	380	550	2,400	4,400
1923-S	1,360,000	5585	470	650	850	1,500	1,950	2,900	3,900	4,400	5,500
1923-S, Full Head	*	5586	—	—	—	—	2,400	3,500	5,000	9,750	18,000

* Included in number above.

Circulation Strikes *(continued)*

	Mintage	GSID	VG-8	F-12	VF-20	EF-40	AU-50	MS-60	MS-63	MS-65	MS-66
1924	10,920,000	5549	$23.00	$27.00	$36	$49	$115	$215	$310	$500	$1,000
1924, Full Head	*	5550	—	—	—	—	—	380	550	1,900	3,100
1924-D	3,112,000	5587	70.00	110.00	135	200	240	285	390	525	675
1924-D, Full Head	*	5588	—	—	—	—	—	775	1,100	2,750	8,750
1924-S	2,860,000	5589	34.00	46.00	75	160	285	525	1,050	2,300	3,000
1924-S, Full Head	*	5590	—	—	—	—	1,000	1,800	3,250	7,500	33,500
1925	12,280,000	5551	13.50	16.00	24	65	120	220	310	550	725
1925, Full Head	*	5552	—	—	—	—	—	345	500	1,200	1,750
1926	11,316,000	5553	13.50	14.50	20	46	95	195	280	500	675
1926, Full Head	*	5554	—	—	—	—	—	430	625	1,550	3,750
1926-D	1,716,000	5591	19.00	27.00	49	100	135	215	310	500	900
1926-D, Full Head	*	5592	—	—	—	—	—	4,250	10,000	23,000	47,000
	Auctions: $105,750, PCGS MS-67 HA 04/14										
1926-S	2,700,000	5593	16.50	24.00	55	145	260	575	1,300	2,900	4,400
1926-S, Full Head	*	5594	—	—	—	—	—	7,000	11,000	36,000	48,000
1927	11,912,000	5555	13.50	14.50	20	46	95	195	280	550	850
1927, Full Head	*	5556	—	—	—	—	—	420	600	1,150	1,700
1927-D	976,000	5595	24.00	34.00	80	180	275	365	430	650	1,000
1927-D, Full Head	*	5596	—	—	—	—	—	525	850	2,750	5,000
1927-S	396,000	5597	90.00	150.00	290	1,150	2,600	7,750	14,000	19,000	20,000
1927-S, Full Head	*	5598	—	—	—	—	—	18,000	42,000	180,000	300,000
	Auctions: $258,500, PCGS MS-66 HA 08/14										
1928	6,336,000	5557	13.50	14.50	20	46	95	195	280	500	675
1928, Full Head	*	5558	—	—	—	—	—	380	550	1,400	2,300
	Auctions: $120,000, PCGS MS-67 HA 08/21										
1928-D	1,627,600	5599	13.50	14.50	20	46	95	195	280	500	675
1928-D, Full Head	*	5600	—	—	—	—	—	1,250	2,200	4,750	15,500
1928-S (a)	2,644,000	5601	13.50	14.50	20	46	95	195	280	500	675
↳1928-S, Inverted Mintmark, FS-501	*	226415	—	—	—	—	—	—	—	—	—
↳1928-S, Repunched Mintmark, FS-502	*	226416	—	—	—	—	—	—	—	—	—
1928-S, Full Head	*	5602	—	—	—	—	—	380	550	1,150	1,600
↳1928-S, Inverted Mintmark, FS-501, Full Head	*	226423	—	—	—	—	—	—	—	—	—
↳1928-S, Repunched Mintmark, FS-502, Full Head	*	226424			—	—	—	—	—	—	—
1929	11,140,000	5559	13.50	14.50	20	46	95	195	280	500	675
1929, Full Head	*	5560	—	—	—	—	—	380	550	1,000	1,300
1929-D	1,358,000	5603	13.50	14.50	20	46	95	195	280	500	675
1929-D, Full Head	*	5604	—	—	—	—	—	725	1,350	5,500	11,000
1929-S	1,764,000	5605	13.50	14.50	20	46	95	215	310	500	675
1929-S, Full Head	*	5606	—	—	—	—	—	345	500	925	1,250
1930	5,632,000	5561	13.50	14.50	20	46	95	195	280	500	675
↳1930, Incomplete Shield, FS-401	*	374764	55.00	—	—	—	—	—	—	—	—
1930, Full Head	*	5562	—	—	—	—	—	345	500	925	1,200
↳1930, Incomplete Shield, FS-401, Full Head	*	374765	—	—	—	—	—	—	—	—	—
1930-S	1,556,000	5607	13.50	14.50	20	46	95	195	280	500	675
1930-S, Full Head	*	5608	—	—	—	—	—	380	550	1,000	1,250

* Included in number above. **a.** Large and small mintmarks exist; their values are the same.

WASHINGTON, EAGLE REVERSE (1932–1998)

Designer: *John Flanagan.* **Weight:** *Silver issue—6.25 grams; clad issue—5.67 grams; silver Proofs—6.25 grams.* **Composition:** *Silver issue—.900 silver, .100 copper (net weight .18084 oz. pure silver); clad issue—a core of pure copper, clad in outer layers of copper-nickel (.750 copper, .250 nickel); silver Proofs—.900 silver, .100 copper (net weight .18084 oz. pure silver).* **Diameter:** *24.3 mm.* **Edge:** *Reeded.* **Mints:** *Philadelphia, Denver, and San Francisco.*

Circulation Strike

Proof Strike

Mintmark location, 1932–1964, is on the reverse, below the eagle.

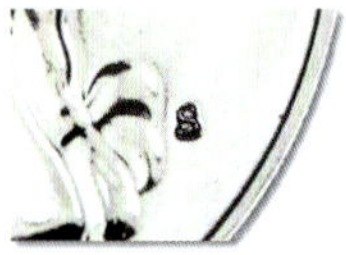

Mintmark location, 1965–2021, is on the obverse, to the right of the hair ribbon.

Mintmark location, 2022 to date, is on the obverse, below the date.

Bicentennial variety: **Designers:** *John Flanagan and Jack L. Ahr.* **Weight:** *Silver issue—5.75 grams; copper-nickel issue—5.67 grams.* **Composition:** *Silver issue—a core of .209 silver and .791 copper, clad in outer layers of .800 silver, .200 copper (net weight .0739 oz. pure silver); copper-nickel issue—a core of pure copper, clad in outer layers of copper-nickel (.750 copper, .250 nickel).* **Diameter:** *24.3 mm.* **Edge:** *Reeded.* **Mints:** *Philadelphia, Denver, and San Francisco.*

Bicentennial Variety, Circulation Strike

Bicentennial Variety, Proof Strike

History. The Washington quarter, designed by New York sculptor John Flanagan, originally was intended to be a commemorative coin, but it ultimately was produced as a regular circulation issue. The obverse is inspired by a famous bust by Jean Antoine Houdon. Flanagan's initials, JF, are at the base of Washington's neck. The reverse features a modernistic eagle perched on a quiver of arrows, with wings unfolding. In October 1973, the Treasury Department announced an open contest for the selection of suitable designs for the Bicentennial reverses of the quarter, half dollar, and dollar, with $5,000 to be awarded to each winner. Twelve semifinalists were chosen, and from these the symbolic entry of Jack L. Ahr was selected for the quarter reverse. It features a military drummer facing left, with a victory torch encircled by 13 stars at the upper left. Except for the dual dating, "1776–1976," the obverse remained unchanged. Pieces with this dual dating were coined during 1975 and 1976. They were struck for general circulation and included in all the U.S. Mint's offerings of Proof and Uncirculated coin sets. (The grading instructions below are for the regular Eagle Reverse variety.)

Striking and Sharpness. The relief of both sides of the Washington quarter issues from 1932 to 1998 is shallow. Accordingly, any lightness of strike is not easily seen. Nearly all are well struck. On all quarters of 1932 and some of 1934, the motto IN GOD WE TRUST is light, as per the design. It was strengthened in 1934.

Availability. The 1932-D and -S are key issues but not rarities. All others are readily available in high grades, but some are scarcer than others. Proof dates available are 1936 to 1942 and 1950 to 1964 (from the Philadelphia Mint) and 1968 to 1998 (from San Francisco). Certain later Proofs are available in clad metal as well as silver strikings. Special Mint Set (SMS) coins were struck in lieu of Proofs from 1965 to 1967; these in some instances closely resemble Proofs. The majority of Proofs made in recent decades are in high levels, PF-66 to 68 or higher.

Note: Values of common-date silver coins have been based on the current bullion price of silver, $45 per ounce, and may vary with the prevailing spot price.

Grading Standards

MS-60 to 70 (Mint State). ***Obverse:*** At MS-60, some abrasion and contact marks are evident on the hair above the ear and at the top of the head below the E of LIBERTY. At MS-63, abrasion is slight at best, less so for MS-64. An MS-65 coin should display no abrasion or contact marks except under magnification, and MS-66 and higher coins should have none at all. Luster should be full and rich. ***Reverse:*** Comments apply as for the obverse, except that the eagle's breast and legs are the places to check. On both sides the fields are protected by design elements and do not show contact marks readily.

MS-64

AU-50, 53, 55, 58 (About Uncirculated). ***Obverse:*** Light wear is seen on the cheek, the high areas of the hair, and the neck. At AU-58, the luster is extensive but incomplete, especially on the higher parts and in the field. At AU-50 and 53, luster is less. ***Reverse:*** Light wear is seen on the breast, legs, and upper edges of the wings of the eagle. An AU-58 coin has nearly full luster. At AU-50 and 53, there still is significant luster.

AU-55

EF-40, 45 (Extremely Fine). ***Obverse:*** Further wear is seen on the head. Higher-relief details are gone in the hair. The higher-relief parts of the neck show wear, most noticeably just above the date. ***Reverse:*** Further wear is seen on the eagle. Most breast feathers, not strong to begin with, are worn away.

EF-40

VF-20, 30 (Very Fine). ***Obverse:*** Most hair detail is worn away, except above the curls. The delineation between the temple and the edge of the hair is faint. The curl by the ear is worn flat. Tips of the letters in LIBERTY and the date digits touch the rim in some instances. ***Reverse:*** More details of the eagle are worn away, and the outlines of the feathers in the wing, while nearly all present, are faint. Tips of the letters touch the rim in some instances on this and lower grades, but this can vary from coin to coin depending on the strength of the rim.

VF-30

F-12, 15 (Fine). ***Obverse:*** Most of the hair is worn flat, with no distinction between the face and the beginning of the hair. There is some detail remaining just above and below the curls. ***Reverse:*** More feathers are worn away. The end of the branch at the left is worn so as to blend into the wing. The edge of the rim is barely visible and in some areas is worn away. (In this and the Very Good grade, opinions concerning the rim vary in the ANA grading standards and in *Photograde*; PCGS is silent on the matter.)

F-12

VG-8, 10 (Very Good). ***Obverse:*** Further wear is seen on the head, with most of the upper part of the curls now blending into the hair above. ***Reverse:*** The rim is worn into the tops of the letters. There is no detail on the leaves. About half of the feathers are outlined, but only faintly.

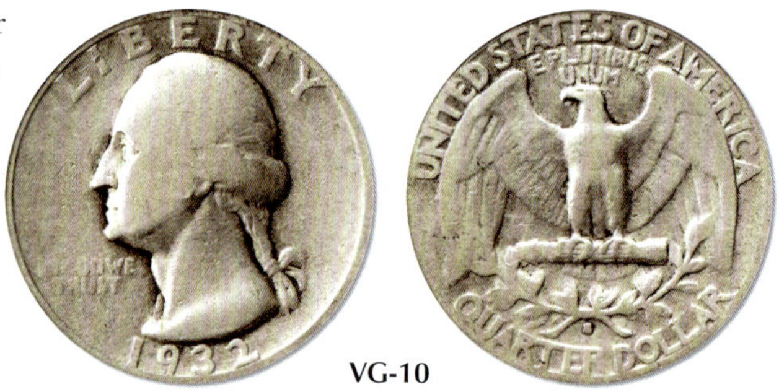

VG-10

G-4, 6 (Good). ***Obverse:*** Further wear is seen in all areas. On 1932 and some 1934 coins the IN GOD WE TRUST motto is so worn that some letters are missing. ***Reverse:*** The rim is worn further into the letters. Fewer details are seen on the eagle's wing. On both sides the coin appears to be "worn flat," with little in relief.

G-4

AG-3 (About Good). ***Obverse:*** Wear is more extensive, with about half of the letters gone. ***Reverse:*** Wear is more extensive, with about half of the letters gone. Slight detail remains in the eagle's wings. The mintmark, if any, is very clear.

AG-3

PF-60 to 70 (Proof). ***Obverse and Reverse:*** Proofs that are extensively cleaned and have many hairlines, or that are dull and grainy, are lower level, such as PF-60 to 62. These are not widely desired, and represent coins that have been mistreated. Most low-level Proofs are of the 1936 to 1942 dates. With medium hairlines and good reflectivity, assigned grades of PF-63 or 64 are appropriate. PF-66 should have hairlines so delicate that magnification is needed to see them. Above that, a Proof should be free of any hairlines or other problems.

PF-70
Deep Cameo

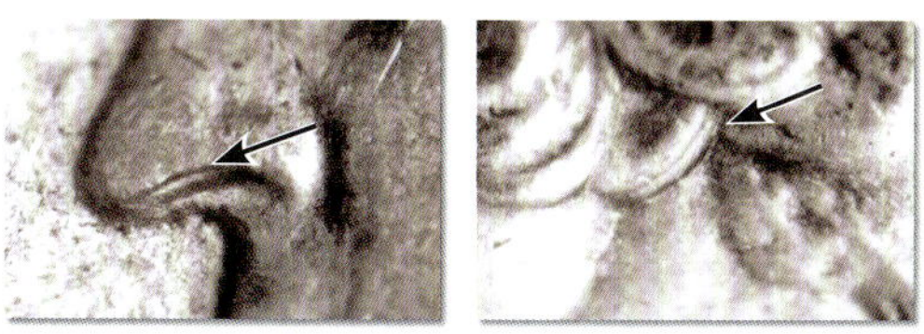

1932, Doubled Die Obverse
FS-101

1934, Light Motto
FS-401

1934, Medium Motto
FS-402

1934, Heavy Motto
FS-403

Circulation Strikes

	Mintage	GSID	F-12	VF-20	EF-40	AU-50	MS-60	MS-63	MS-65	MS-66	MS-67
Washington, Silver (1932–1964)	**n/a**	**72443**	**$12.00**	**$12.00**	**$12.00**	**$12.00**	**$12.00**	**$12.00**	**$16.00**	**$30**	**$70**
Washington, Clad (1965–1998)	**n/a**	**376587**	**—**	**—**	**—**	**0.40**	**0.60**	**0.80**	**2.60**	**11**	**20**
1932	5,404,000	5609	13.00	14.00	14.50	17.50	38.00	60.00	245.00	650	5,500
↳**1932, Doubled Die Obverse, FS-101**	*	199166	—	—	—	120.00	155.00	210.00	1,000.00	3,100	—
1932-D	436,800	5646	100.00	135.00	220.00	340.00	975.00	1,600.00	7,500.00	90,000	—
1932-S	408,000	5647	95.00	100.00	120.00	160.00	420.00	550.00	2,400.00	31,000	—
1934, Light Motto	*	5611	12.50	13.50	17.50	23.00	47.00	60.00	210.00	430	2,000
↳**1934, Light Motto, FS-401**	*	374321	12.50	13.50	17.50	23.00	47.00	60.00	210.00	430	2,000
1934, Medium Motto	31,912,052	5610	13.00	13.50	14.00	15.50	27.00	40.00	70.00	170	525
↳**1934, Medium Motto, FS-402**	*	374322	13.00	13.50	14.00	15.50	27.00	40.00	70.00	170	525
1934, Heavy Motto	*	5613	13.00	16.00	21.00	31.00	50.00	60.00	155.00	365	2,600
↳**1934, Heavy Motto, FS-403**	*	374323	13.00	16.00	21.00	31.00	50.00	60.00	155.00	365	2,600

* Included in number above.

1934, Doubled Die Obverse
FS-101

1937, Doubled Die Obverse
FS-101

Circulation Strikes *(continued)*

	Mintage	GSID	F-12	VF-20	EF-40	AU-50	MS-60	MS-63	MS-65	MS-66	MS-67
1934, Doubled Die Obverse	*	5612	$95.00	$130.00	$235.00	$390.00	$850	$1,250	$2,750	$4,000	—
↳1934, Doubled Die Obverse, FS-101	*	374324	95.00	130.00	235.00	390.00	850	1,250	2,750	4,000	—
1934-D	3,527,200	5648	12.00	20.00	34.00	110.00	195	310	455	900	$5,500
1934-D, Heavy Motto	*	5649	18.50	28.00	49.00	120.00	195	245	575	1,000	10,500
↳1934-D, Small D	*	374325	—	75.00	130.00	160.00	260	310	950	1,750	13,000
1935	32,484,000	5614	12.50	13.50	14.00	16.00	23	32	60	80	360
1935-D	5,780,000	5650	14.50	20.00	43.00	130.00	220	285	320	470	1,550
1935-S	5,660,000	5651	13.50	15.00	23.00	38.00	80	95	155	220	650
1936	41,300,000	5615	12.50	14.00	16.50	18.50	30	40	90	110	345
↳1936, Doubled Die Obverse, FS-101	*	69491	—	—	—	—	725	950	1,250	2,500	—
1936-D	5,374,000	5652	17.50	30.00	70.00	160.00	500	600	875	1,100	3,250
1936-S	3,828,000	5653	12.50	15.50	19.00	50.00	95	115	215	245	700
1937	19,696,000	5616	13.00	16.00	23.00	30.00	40	43	90	130	480
1937, Doubled Die Obverse	*	5617	195.00	325.00	500.00	775.00	1,900	2,800	7,500	12,000	—
↳1937, Doubled Die Obverse, FS-101	*	374326	195.00	325.00	500.00	775.00	1,900	2,800	7,500	12,000	—
1937-D	7,189,600	5654	12.50	14.50	23.00	32.00	75	95	130	220	575
↳1937-D, D Over D, FS-501	*	374327	—	—	—	—	—	—	—	—	—
1937-S	1,652,000	5655	14.50	21.00	46.00	100.00	155	200	275	375	1,550
1938	9,472,000	5618	12.50	14.50	27.00	47.00	95	110	120	180	375
1938-S	2,832,000	5656	12.50	16.00	32.00	55.00	80	105	155	195	600
1939	33,540,000	5619	12.50	13.50	14.00	14.50	24	30	60	75	160
1939-D	7,092,000	5657	12.50	13.50	16.00	23.00	45	55	80	100	470
↳1939-D, D Over S, FS-501	*	374317	—	—	—	—	—	—	650	850	1,250
1939-S	2,628,000	5658	12.50	16.00	27.00	60.00	95	150	195	280	525
1940	35,704,000	5620	12.50	13.50	16.00	18.50	32	34	46	75	130
1940-D	2,797,600	5659	13.50	16.00	40.00	90.00	130	155	235	260	550
↳1940-D, Doubled Die Obverse, FS-101	*	374328	—	—	—	—	—	—	—	—	—
↳1940-D, D Over D, FS-501	*	227302	—	—	—	—	—	285	490	950	—
↳1940-D, D Over D, FS-502	*	374329	—	—	—	—	—	—	—	—	—
1940-S	8,244,000	5660	12.50	13.50	16.00	23.00	36	50	65	95	365
1941	79,032,000	5621	12.00	12.00	12.00	12.00	15	19	43	70	180
↳1941, Doubled Die Obverse, FS-101	*	374330	—	—	—	—	—	—	—	—	—
↳1941, Doubled Die Reverse, FS-801	*	227304	—	60.00	—	130.00	175	200	240	360	—
1941-D	16,714,800	5661	12.00	12.00	12.50	18.50	47	60	75	110	470
↳1941-D, Doubled Die Obverse, FS-101	*	374319	—	—	—	—	—	115.00	525	1,600	3,250
↳1941-D, Doubled Die Reverse, FS-801	*	227305	—	—	—	—	—	—	200	220	—

* Included in number above.

1942-D, Doubled Die Obverse
FS-101

1942-D, Doubled Die Reverse
FS-801

1943, Doubled Die Obverse
FS-103. Other varieties exist.

1943-S, Doubled Die Obverse
FS-101

Circulation Strikes *(continued)*

	Mintage	GSID	F-12	VF-20	EF-40	AU-50	MS-60	MS-63	MS-65	MS-66	MS-67
1941-S	16,080,000	5662	$12.00	$12.00	$13.50	$16.00	$40.00	$49.00	$65	$80	$325
↳**1941-S, Doubled Die Reverse, FS-801**	*	393181	—	—	—	—	—	—	—	—	—
1942	102,096,000	5622	12.00	12.00	12.00	12.50	15.00	17.50	30	80	325
↳**1942, Doubled Die Reverse, FS-801**	*	199168	—	—	—	—	525.00	775.00	1,750	4,400	—
↳**1942, Doubled Die Reverse, FS-802**	*	199169	—	—	—	—	1,250.00	1,900.00	—	—	—
1942-D	17,487,200	5663	12.00	12.00	12.00	12.00	22.00	24.00	43	70	430
1942-D, Doubled Die Obverse	*	5664	100.00	145.00	260.00	360.00	1,150.00	2,500.00	7,500	—	—
↳**1942-D, Doubled Die Obverse, FS-101**	*	374316	100.00	145.00	260.00	360.00	1,150.00	2,500.00	7,500	—	—
1942-D, Doubled Die Reverse,	*	5665	—	—	—	230.00	390.00	525.00	1,100	5,500	—
1942-S	19,384,000	5666	12.50	14.00	16.00	22.00	40.00	55.00	65	80	310
↳**1942-S, S Over S, FS-501**	*	374332	—	—	—	—	—	—	—	—	—
1943	99,700,000	5623	12.00	12.00	12.00	12.00	13.50	16.50	46	70	275
1943, Doubled Die Obverse	*	326571	575.00	1,250.00	2,800.00	3,550.00	6,250.00	9,500.00	14,000	17,000	24,000
↳**1943, Doubled Die Obverse, FS-101**	*	326572	—	—							
↳**1943, Doubled Die Obverse, FS-103**	*	5624	575.00	1,250.00	2,800.00	3,550.00	6,250.00	9,500.00	14,000	17,000	24,000
1943-D	16,095,600	5667	12.00	12.00	15.50	17.50	31.00	46.00	60	90	240
1943-S	21,700,000	5668	12.00	12.00	13.50	18.50	40.00	49.00	110	155	405
↳**1943-S, Goiter, FS-401**	*	374333	70.00	—	—	—	—	525.00	950	1,900	5,000
↳**1943-S, S Over S, FS-503**	*	374336	—	—	—	—	—	—	—	285	—
↳**1943-S, S Over S, FS-504**	*	374337	—	—	—	—	—	—	—	210	—
1943-S, Doubled Die Obverse	*	5669	80.00	100.00	145.00	180.00	455.00	650.00	1,200	1,900	12,000
1944	104,956,000	5625	12.00	12.00	12.00	12.00	13.50	16.50	30	55	235
1944-D	14,600,800	5670	12.00	12.00	12.00	12.00	17.50	23.00	42	70	130
1944-S	12,560,000	5671	12.00	12.00	12.00	12.50	19.00	26.00	32	60	145
1945	74,372,000	5626	12.00	12.00	12.00	12.00	13.00	14.50	40	80	290
↳**1945, Doubled Die Obverse, FS-101**	*	326576	—	—	—	—	—	195.00	650	—	—
1945-D	12,341,600	5672	12.00	12.00	12.00	12.00	13.50	27.00	35	60	325

* Included in number above.

1950-D, D Over S
FS-601. Other varieties exist.

1950-S, S Over D
FS-601

Circulation Strikes *(continued)*

	Mintage	GSID	F-12	VF-20	EF-40	AU-50	MS-60	MS-63	MS-65	MS-66	MS-67
1945-S	17,004,001	5673	$12.00	$12.00	$12.00	$12.00	$13.50	$20.00	$34	$70	$285
↳1945-S, Doubled Die Obverse, FS-101	*	326577	—	—	—	—	—	—	—	950	—
↳1945-S, S Over S, FS-501	*	374339	—	—	—	—	—	—	—	—	—
1946	53,436,000	5627	12.00	12.00	12.00	12.50	15.00	17.50	38	90	455
↳1946, Doubled Die Obverse/Doubled Die Reverse, FS-102/802	*	393184	—	—	—	—	—	—	—	—	—
1946-D	9,072,800	5674	12.00	12.00	12.00	12.50	15.00	19.00	35	55	175
↳1946-D, D Over D, FS-501	*	374320	—	—	—	—	—	—	—	—	—
1946-S	4,204,000	5675	12.00	12.00	12.00	12.50	15.00	19.00	32	80	215
1947	22,556,000	5628	12.00	12.00	12.00	12.00	13.50	20.00	32	50	195
↳1947, Doubled Die Obverse, FS-101	*	374340	—	—	—	—	—	—	—	—	—
↳1947, Spitting Eagle, FS-901	*	393185	—	—	—	—	—	—	—	—	—
1947-D	15,338,400	5676	12.00	12.00	12.00	12.00	13.00	17.50	38	47	155
1947-S	5,532,000	5677	12.00	12.00	12.00	12.00	13.00	16.00	27	50	175
↳1947-S, S Over S, FS-502	*	374342	—	—	—	—	—	—	—	—	325
1948	35,196,000	5629	12.00	12.00	12.00	12.00	13.00	15.50	24	55	155
1948-D	16,766,800	5678	12.00	12.00	12.00	12.00	14.00	19.00	35	55	340
1948-S	15,960,000	5679	12.00	12.00	12.00	12.00	13.00	16.50	45	75	195
↳1948-S, S Over S, FS-501	*	285898	—	—	—	—	—	—	—	—	—
1949	9,312,000	5630	12.00	12.50	14.50	21.00	38.00	46.00	60	80	245
1949-D	10,068,400	5680	12.00	12.00	14.50	17.50	26.00	35.00	43	80	195
↳1949-D, D Over D, FS-501	*	374343	—	—	—	—	—	120.00	—	—	—
↳1949-D, D Over S, FS-601	*	374344	—	—	—	—	—	120.00	275	650	—
1950	24,920,126	5631	12.00	12.00	12.00	12.00	13.00	17.50	35	55	310
1950-D	21,075,600	5681	12.00	12.00	12.00	12.00	13.50	23.00	40	90	285
1950-D, D Over S	*	5682	60.00	90.00	120.00	160.00	245.00	775.00	2,250	3,000	17,000
↳1950-D, D Over S, FS-601	*	374348	60.00	90.00	120.00	160.00	245.00	775.00	2,250	3,000	17,000
1950-S	10,284,004	5683	12.00	12.00	12.00	12.00	13.50	19.00	36	60	310
↳1950-S, S Over S, FS-501	*	374349	—	—	—	—	—	—	—	235	—
1950-S, S Over D	*	5684	70.00	120.00	215.00	290.00	365.00	455.00	1,200	1,600	7,500
↳1950-S, S Over D, FS-601	*	374351	70.00	120.00	215.00	290.00	365.00	455.00	1,200	1,600	7,500
1951	43,448,102	5632	12.00	12.00	12.00	12.00	13.50	17.50	27	40	160
1951-D	35,354,800	5685	12.00	12.00	12.00	12.00	13.50	17.50	32	46	210
↳1951-D, D Over D, FS-501	*	374353	—	—	—	—	—	100.00	—	—	—
1951-S	9,048,000	5686	12.00	12.00	12.00	12.00	15.00	28.00	40	65	110
↳1951-S, S Over S, FS-501	*	393186	—	—	—	—	—	—	—	—	—
1952	38,780,093	5633	12.00	12.00	12.00	12.00	14.00	19.00	36	55	115
1952-D	49,795,200	5687	12.00	12.00	12.00	12.00	13.50	16.50	35	55	625
↳1952-D, Large D, FS-501	*	374354	—	—	—	—	—	—	—	—	—

* Included in number above.

Circulation Strikes *(continued)*

	Mintage	GSID	F-12	VF-20	EF-40	AU-50	MS-60	MS-63	MS-65	MS-66	MS-67
1952-S	13,707,800	5688	$12.00	$12.00	$12.00	$12.00	$13.50	$20.00	$40.00	$75.00	$160
↳**1952-S, S Over S, FS-502**	*	374355	—	—	—	—	—	—	—	—	—
1953	18,536,120	5634	12.00	12.00	12.00	12.00	13.50	16.50	26.00	39.00	195
1953-D	56,112,400	5689	12.00	12.00	12.00	12.00	13.50	17.50	35.00	60.00	495
↳**1953-D, D Over Inverted D, FS-501**	*	374356	—	—	—	—	—	—	—	—	—
↳**1953-D, D Over S, FS-601**	*	374357	—	—	—	—	—	—	290.00	—	—
↳**1953-D, Doubled Die Reverse, FS-801**	*	285865	—	—	—	—	—	75.00	160.00	—	—
1953-S	14,016,000	5690	12.00	12.00	12.00	12.00	13.50	15.00	30.00	60.00	130
1954	54,412,203	5635	12.00	12.00	12.00	12.00	12.00	12.00	16.00	38.00	155
1954-D	42,305,500	5691	12.00	12.00	12.00	12.00	12.00	14.50	24.00	60.00	470
1954-S	11,834,722	5692	12.00	12.00	12.00	12.00	12.50	15.00	20.00	32.00	195
1955	18,180,181	5636	12.00	12.00	12.00	12.00	12.00	12.00	30.00	50.00	420
1955-D	3,182,400	5693	12.00	12.00	12.00	12.00	12.00	12.00	34.00	80.00	9,000
1956	44,144,000	5637	12.00	12.00	12.00	12.00	12.00	12.00	16.00	30.00	70
↳**1956, Type B Reverse, FS-901**	*	329316	—	—	—	—	—	50.00	95.00	470.00	—
1956-D	32,334,500	5694	12.00	12.00	12.00	12.00	12.00	12.00	20.00	43.00	310
↳**1956-D, D Over D, FS-501**	*	285866	—	—	—	—	50.00	70.00	130.00	260.00	—
1957	46,532,000	5638	12.00	12.00	12.00	12.00	12.00	12.00	16.00	30.00	70
1957, Type B Reverse, FS-901	46,532,000	374358	12.00	12.00	12.00	13.50	15.00	17.50	30.00	40.00	325
1957-D	77,924,160	5695	12.00	12.00	12.00	12.00	12.00	12.00	30.00	47.00	115
↳**1957-D, Separated Mintmark, FS-902**	77,924,160	374359	—	—	—	—	—	55.00	115.00	260.00	—
1958	6,360,000	5639	12.00	12.00	12.00	12.00	12.00	12.00	16.00	30.00	70
↳**1958, Type B Reverse, FS-901**	*	227310	—	—	—	—	16.00	30.00	55.00	100.00	—
1958-D	78,124,900	5696	12.00	12.00	12.00	12.00	12.00	12.00	30.00	49.00	70
1959	24,384,000	5640	12.00	12.00	12.00	12.00	12.00	12.00	16.00	43.00	850
↳**1959, Type B Reverse, FS-901**	*	374361	—	—	—	—	—	19.00	75.00	130.00	1,400
1959-D	62,054,232	5697	12.00	12.00	12.00	12.00	12.00	12.00	19.00	75.00	725
↳**1959-D, D Over D, FS-501**	*	374362	—	—	—	—	—	—	—	—	—
1960	29,164,000	5641	12.00	12.00	12.00	12.00	12.00	12.00	16.00	47.00	390
↳**1960, Type B Reverse, FS-901**	*	227311	—	—	—	—	—	40.00	80.00	130.00	—
1960-D	63,000,324	5698	12.00	12.00	12.00	12.00	12.00	12.00	22.00	50.00	2,000
1961	37,036,000	5642	12.00	12.00	12.00	12.00	12.00	12.00	24.00	60.00	2,000
↳**1961, Type B Reverse, FS-901**	*	374363	—	—	17.00	17.50	20.00	24.00	47.00	220.00	1,250
1961-D	83,656,928	5699	12.00	12.00	12.00	12.00	12.00	12.00	30.00	80.00	2,250
↳**1961-D, D Over D, FS-503**	*	393188	—	—	—	—	—	—	—	—	—
1962	36,156,000	5643	12.00	12.00	12.00	12.00	12.00	12.00	30.00	47.00	1,150
↳**1962, Type B Reverse, FS-901**	*	227312	—	—	—	—	—	—	100.00	340.00	—
1962-D	127,554,756	5700	12.00	12.00	12.00	12.00	12.00	12.00	22.00	70.00	2,250

* Included in number above.

1966, Doubled Die Reverse
FS-801

1970-D, Doubled Die Obverse
FS-101

Circulation Strikes *(continued)*

	Mintage	GSID	F-12	VF-20	EF-40	AU-50	MS-60	MS-63	MS-65	MS-66	MS-67
1963	74,316,000	5644	$12.00	$12.00	$12.00	$12.00	$12.00	$12.00	$27.00	$47.00	$550
↳1963, Doubled Die Obverse, FS-101	*	317332	—	—	—	—	43.00	55.00	130.00	155.00	850
↳1963, Type B Reverse, FS-901	*	317335	—	—	—	—	—	55.00	95.00	130.00	850
↳1963, Type B Reverse, Space Between Arrow and Leaf, FS-901a	*	374368	—	—	—	—	—	60.00	—	—	—
1963-D	135,288,184	5701	12.00	12.00	12.00	12.00	12.00	12.00	27.00	60.00	650
1964	560,390,585	5645	12.00	12.00	12.00	12.00	12.00	12.00	22.00	40.00	430
↳1964, Doubled Die Obverse, FS-101	*	374370	—	—	—	—	—	—	—	—	—
↳1964, Doubled Die Reverse, FS-801	*	374371	—	—	—	—	—	—	—	—	—
↳1964, Doubled Die Reverse, FS-804	*	374374	—	—	—	—	—	—	—	—	—
↳1964, Type B Reverse, FS-901	*	227313	—	—	—	—	—	—	70.00	325.00	775
1964-D	704,135,528	5702	12.00	12.00	12.00	12.00	12.00	12.00	24.00	55.00	290
↳1964-D, Doubled Die Obverse, FS-101	*	227314	—	—	—	—	—	—	290.00	—	—
↳1964-D, D Over D, FS-503	*	393189	—	—	—	—	—	—	—	—	—
↳1964-D, Doubled Die Reverse, FS-801	*	374377	—	—	—	—	—	—	—	—	—
↳1964-D, Reverse of 1965	*	374378	—	34.00	47.00	75.00	130.00	195.00	420.00	650.00	—
↳1964-D, Misplaced Mintmark, FS-902	*	393190	—	—	—	—	—	—	—	—	—
1965	1,819,717,540	5703	0.40	0.40	0.40	0.40	1.50	4.10	6.75	34.00	345
↳1965, Doubled Die Obverse, FS-101	*	374379	—	—	—	—	—	—	—	—	—
↳1965, Doubled Die Reverse, FS-801	*	374381	—	—	—	—	—	—	—	—	—
1966	821,101,500	5704	0.40	0.40	0.40	0.40	1.50	1.50	9.50	24.00	215
↳1966, Doubled Die Reverse, FS-801	*	374382	—	—	—	—	—	—	—	—	—
1967	1,524,031,848	5705	0.40	0.40	0.40	0.40	5.50	5.50	11.00	20.00	80
1968	220,731,500	5706	0.40	0.40	0.40	0.40	1.50	1.50	8.00	27.00	60
1968-D	101,534,000	5720	0.40	0.40	0.40	0.40	1.50	1.50	5.50	16.00	55
↳1968-D, Doubled Die Reverse, FS-801	*	374383	—	—	—	—	—	—	—	3,250.00	—
1969	176,212,000	5707	0.40	0.40	0.40	0.40	1.50	1.50	16.00	80.00	2,400
1969-D	114,372,000	5721	0.40	0.40	0.40	0.40	1.50	2.60	8.00	13.50	90
↳1969-D, D Over D, FS-501	*	374384	—	—	—	—	—	—	—	80.00	—
1970	136,420,000	5708	0.40	0.40	0.40	0.40	1.50	1.50	12.00	34.00	340
1970-D (a)	417,341,364	5722	0.40	0.40	0.40	0.40	1.50	1.50	5.50	11.00	47
↳1970-D, Doubled Die Obverse, FS-102	*	374387	—	—	—	—	—	—	—	—	—
↳1970-D, Doubled Die Reverse, FS-801	*	374388	—	—	—	—	—	—	—	—	360
↳1970-D, Doubled Die Reverse, FS-802	*	374389	—	—	—	—	—	—	—	—	—
1971	109,284,000	5709	0.40	0.40	0.40	0.40	1.50	1.50	6.75	120.00	3,100
1971-D	258,634,428	5723	0.40	0.40	0.40	0.40	1.50	1.50	6.75	19.00	100
↳1971-D, Doubled Die Reverse, FS-801	*	374391	—	—	—	—	—	—	—	—	—
1972	215,048,000	5710	0.40	0.40	0.40	0.40	1.50	1.50	5.50	36.00	525
1972-D	311,067,732	5724	0.40	0.40	0.40	0.40	1.50	1.50	9.50	13.50	60
1973	346,924,000	5711	0.40	0.40	0.40	0.40	1.50	1.50	5.50	55.00	390
1973-D	232,977,400	5725	0.40	0.40	0.40	0.40	1.50	1.50	4.10	27.00	120
1974	801,456,000	5712	0.40	0.40	0.40	0.40	0.60	0.80	4.10	20.00	235
1974-D	353,160,300	5726	0.40	0.40	0.40	0.40	0.60	0.80	4.10	34.00	150

* Included in number above.

1989-D, Repunched Mintmark
FS-501

Circulation Strikes *(continued)*

	Mintage	GSID	F-12	VF-20	EF-40	AU-50	MS-60	MS-63	MS-65	MS-66	MS-67
1776–1976, Copper-Nickel Clad	809,784,016	5714	$0.40	$0.40	$0.40	$0.40	$0.60	$0.80	$4.10	$20.00	$70
1776–1976-D, Copper-Nickel Clad	860,118,839	5727	0.40	0.40	0.40	0.40	0.60	0.80	4.10	20.00	110
↳**1976-D, Clad, Doubled Die Obverse, FS-101**	*	374392	—	—	—	145.00	575.00	—	4,050.00	9,500.00	—
1776–1976-S, Silver Clad (b)	11,000,000	5728	4.50	4.50	4.50	4.50	4.50	4.50	4.80	13.50	19
1977	468,556,000	5715	0.40	0.40	0.40	0.40	0.60	0.80	4.10	20.00	70
1977-D	256,524,978	5729	0.40	0.40	0.40	0.40	0.60	0.80	4.10	24.00	130
1978	521,452,000	5716	0.40	0.40	0.40	0.40	0.60	0.80	4.10	27.00	130
1978-D	287,373,152	5730	0.40	0.40	0.40	0.40	0.60	0.80	4.10	27.00	390
1979	515,708,000	5717	0.40	0.40	0.40	0.40	0.60	0.80	4.10	27.00	145
1979-D	489,789,780	5731	0.40	0.40	0.40	0.40	0.60	0.80	4.10	24.00	325
1980-P	635,832,000	5718	0.40	0.40	0.40	0.40	0.60	0.80	4.10	19.00	115
1980-D	518,327,487	5732	0.40	0.40	0.40	0.40	0.60	0.80	4.10	20.00	180
1981-P	601,716,000	5734	0.40	0.40	0.40	0.40	0.60	0.80	4.10	27.00	195
1981-D	575,722,833	5733	0.40	0.40	0.40	0.40	0.60	0.80	4.10	20.00	115
1982-P	500,931,000	5736	0.40	0.40	0.40	0.40	2.60	5.50	38.00	145.00	365
1982-D	480,042,788	5735	0.40	0.40	0.40	0.40	2.60	5.50	27.00	90.00	210
1983-P	673,535,000	5719	0.40	0.40	0.40	0.40	9.50	18.50	55.00	90.00	650
↳**1983-P, Spitting Eagle, FS-901**	*	374394	—	—	—	—	—	—	230.00	390.00	—
1983-D	617,806,446	5737	0.40	0.40	0.40	0.40	5.50	10.00	34.00	70.00	650
1984-P	676,545,000	5739	0.40	0.40	0.40	0.40	0.60	0.80	4.10	34.00	525
1984-D	546,483,064	5738	0.40	0.40	0.40	0.40	0.60	0.80	4.10	38.00	405
1985-P	775,818,962	5741	0.40	0.40	0.40	0.40	0.60	0.80	4.10	30.00	575
1985-D	519,962,888	5740	0.40	0.40	0.40	0.40	0.60	0.80	4.10	30.00	245
1986-P	551,199,333	5743	0.40	0.40	0.40	0.40	0.60	0.80	4.10	40.00	1,600
1986-D	504,298,660	5742	0.40	0.40	0.40	0.40	0.60	0.80	4.10	24.00	390
1987-P	582,499,481	5745	0.40	0.40	0.40	0.40	0.60	0.80	4.10	40.00	260
1987-D	655,594,696	5744	0.40	0.40	0.40	0.40	0.60	0.80	4.10	20.00	260
1988-P	562,052,000	5747	0.40	0.40	0.40	0.40	0.60	0.80	4.10	75.00	1,550
1988-D	596,810,688	5746	0.40	0.40	0.40	0.40	0.60	0.80	4.10	55.00	725
1989-P	512,868,000	5749	0.40	0.40	0.40	0.40	0.60	0.80	11.00	90.00	1,500
↳**1989, No P, FS-501**	*	393191	—	—	—	—	—	—	—	—	—
1989-D	896,535,597	5748	0.40	0.40	0.40	0.40	0.60	0.80	4.10	24.00	280
↳**1989-D, D Over D, FS-501**	*	393192	—	—	—	—	—	—	—	—	—
1990-P	613,792,000	5751	0.40	0.40	0.40	0.40	0.60	0.80	4.10	27.00	1,250
1990-D	927,638,181	5750	0.40	0.40	0.40	0.40	0.60	0.80	2.60	13.50	135
1991-P	570,968,000	5753	0.40	0.40	0.40	0.40	0.60	0.80	4.10	43.00	260
1991-D	630,966,693	5752	0.40	0.40	0.40	0.40	0.60	0.80	4.10	55.00	1,800
1992-P	384,764,000	5755	0.40	0.40	0.40	0.40	0.60	0.80	4.10	70.00	265
1992-D	389,777,107	5754	0.40	0.40	0.40	0.40	0.60	0.80	4.10	60.00	650
1993-P	639,276,000	5757	0.40	0.40	0.40	0.40	0.60	0.80	4.10	24.00	120
1993-D	645,476,128	5756	0.40	0.40	0.40	0.40	0.60	0.80	4.10	47.00	235

* Included in number above.

Circulation Strikes *(continued)*

	Mintage	GSID	F-12	VF-20	EF-40	AU-50	MS-60	MS-63	MS-65	MS-66	MS-67
1994-P	825,600,000	5759	$0.40	$0.40	$0.40	$0.40	$0.60	$0.80	$4.10	$36.00	$525
↳**1994, No P, FS-501**	*	393193	—	—	—	—	—	—	—	—	—
1994-D	880,034,110	5758	0.40	0.40	0.40	0.40	0.60	0.80	4.10	60.00	1,150
1995-P	1,004,336,000	5761	0.40	0.40	0.40	0.40	0.60	0.80	4.10	20.00	70
1995-D	1,103,216,000	5760	0.40	0.40	0.40	0.40	0.60	0.80	4.10	24.00	80
1996-P	925,040,000	5763	0.40	0.40	0.40	0.40	0.60	0.80	2.60	11.00	27
1996-D	906,868,000	5762	0.40	0.40	0.40	0.40	0.60	0.80	2.60	11.00	20
1997-P	595,740,000	5765	0.40	0.40	0.40	0.40	0.60	0.80	2.60	20.00	70
1997-D	599,680,000	5764	0.40	0.40	0.40	0.40	0.60	0.80	2.60	16.00	60
1998-P	896,268,000	24989	0.40	0.40	0.40	0.40	0.60	0.80	2.60	11.00	22
1998-D	821,000,000	24990	0.40	0.40	0.40	0.40	0.60	0.80	2.60	40.00	180

* Included in number above.

Special Mint Set Strikes

	Mintage	GSID	MS-63	MS-65	MS-66	MS-67	MS-68
1964	unknown	5910	$4,400.00	$8,000.00	$11,000.00	$24,000	$38,500
1965	2,360,000	5914	1.50	5.50	9.50	12	34
1966	2,261,583	5917	1.50	5.50	9.50	11	47
1967	1,863,344	5920	1.50	5.50	11.00	16	30
↳**1967, Doubled Die Obverse, FS-101**	*	71459	—	—	90.00	110	325

* Included in number above.

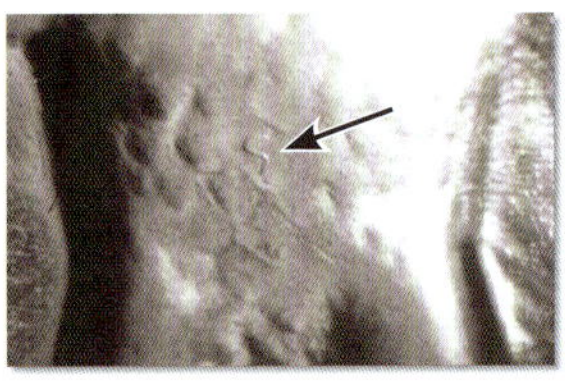

1952, Superbird, Proof
FS-901

Proof Strikes

	Mintage	GSID	PF-63	PF-65	PF-67	PF-68
Washington, Silver (1932–1964), Proof	**n/a**	**81455**	**$75.00**	**$95.00**	**$195**	**$2,250**
Washington, Clad (1968–1998), Proof	**n/a**	**393670**	**2.80**	**3.40**	**3.70**	**—**
1936	3,837	5847	525.00	825.00	6,250	—
1937	5,542	5850	170.00	245.00	850	7,000
1938	8,045	5853	110.00	155.00	900	7,750
1939	8,795	5856	130.00	135.00	405	7,000
1940	11,246	5859	80.00	110.00	340	2,600
1941	15,287	5862	75.00	95.00	195	2,250
1942	21,123	5865	75.00	95.00	195	2,250
1950	51,386	5868	47.00	65.00	110	650
1951	57,500	5871	40.00	55.00	100	340
1952	81,980	5874	38.00	47.00	80	290
↳**1952, Superbird, FS-901**	*	69542	80.00	170.00	290	525
↳**1952, Hand-Engraved Tail Feathers, Superbird, FS-902**	*	315361	—	—	—	—
1953	128,800	5877	22.00	45.00	60	95
↳**1953, Doubled Die Obverse, FS-101**	*	315364	70.00	80.00	145	235
1954	233,300	5880	15.00	20.00	55	70

* Included in number above.

1968-S, Doubled Die Reverse, Proof
FS-801

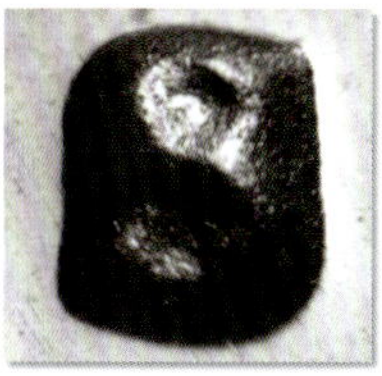

1979-S, Filled S (Variety 1), Proof

1979-S, Clear S (Variety 2), Proof

1981-S, Rounded S (Variety 1), Proof

1981-S, Flat S (Variety 2), Proof

Proof Strikes *(continued)*

	Mintage	GSID	PF-63	PF-65	PF-67	PF-68
1955	378,200	5883	$15.00	$19.00	$40.00	$75.00
1956	669,384	5886	12.50	13.50	30.00	47.00
↳1956, Doubled Die Obverse, FS-101	*	393138	—	—	—	—
1957	1,247,952	5889	12.50	13.50	27.00	45.00
1958	875,652	5892	12.50	13.50	27.00	55.00
1959	1,149,291	5895	11.50	13.50	40.00	55.00
↳1959, Doubled Die Obverse, FS-101	*	69566	—	—	—	—
1960	1,691,602	5898	11.50	14.50	22.00	29.00
↳1960, Doubled Die Reverse, FS-801	1,691,602	393144	—	—	—	—
1961	3,028,244	5901	11.50	14.50	22.00	29.00
↳1961, Doubled Die Obverse, FS-101	*	69573	—	—	—	—
1962	3,218,019	5904	11.50	14.50	17.00	22.00
1963	3,075,645	5907	11.50	14.50	24.00	31.00
↳1963, Doubled Die Obverse, FS-101	3,075,645	393149	50.00	90.00	525.00	—
1964	3,950,762	5911	11.50	14.50	17.00	24.00
1968-S	3,041,506	5923	5.50	6.75	8.00	9.50
↳1968-S, Repunched Mintmark, FS-501	*	393153	—	—	—	245.00
↳1968-S, Type F Reverse, FS-902	*	375977	—	—	—	—
1969-S	2,934,631	5926	5.50	6.75	8.75	11.00
↳1969-S, Doubled Die Obverse, FS-101	2,934,631	393164	—	—	340.00	390.00
↳1969-S, Repunched Mintmark/Doubled Die Obverse, FS-501/102	2,934,631	393165	—	—	—	—
1970-S	2,632,810	5929	5.50	6.75	9.50	12.00
↳1970-S, Doubled Die Reverse, FS-801	2,632,810	393170	—	—	—	—
1971-S	3,220,733	5934	—	47.00	130.00	260.00
1972-S	3,260,996	5937	6.00	9.50	13.50	19.00
1973-S	2,760,339	5940	5.50	6.75	9.50	12.00
1974-S	2,612,568	5943	5.50	6.75	8.00	9.50
1776–1976-S, Copper-Nickel Clad	7,059,099	5947	2.20	3.40	5.50	13.50
1776–1976-S, Silver Clad (a)	4,000,000	5949	6.25	8.00	11.00	15.00
1977-S	3,251,152	5952	4.10	4.70	5.50	6.75
1978-S	3,127,781	5955	4.10	4.70	5.50	6.75
1979-S, Variety 1	3,677,175	5959	4.10	4.70	5.50	8.00
1979-S, Variety 2	*	5961	4.40	5.00	6.75	8.00
1980-S	3,554,806	5964	4.10	4.70	5.50	9.50
1981-S, Variety 1	4,063,083	5968	4.10	4.70	5.50	9.50
1981-S, Variety 2	*	5970	5.50	6.75	9.50	13.50
1982-S	3,857,479	5973	4.40	5.00	6.75	9.50
↳1982-S, Doubled Die Obverse, FS-101	3,857,479	393713	—	—	—	—
1983-S	3,279,126	5976	4.40	5.00	6.75	12.00
1984-S	3,065,110	5979	4.40	5.00	6.75	9.50

* Included in number above. **a.** Mintages are approximate. Several million were melted in 1982.

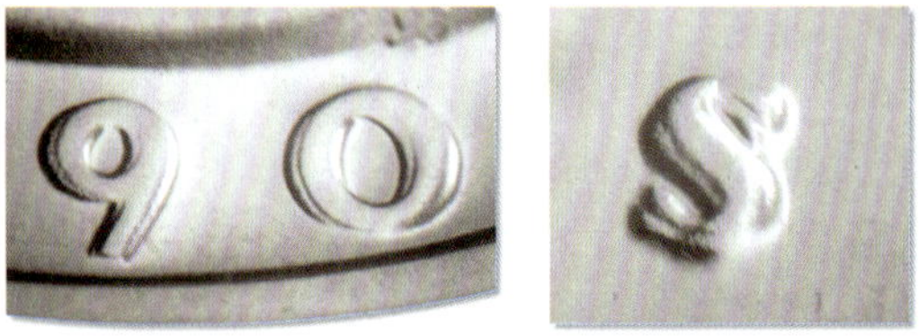

1990-S, Doubled Die Obverse, Proof
FS-101

Proof Strikes *(continued)*

	Mintage	GSID	PF-63	PF-65	PF-67	PF-68
1985-S	3,362,821	5982	$4.40	$5.00	$6.75	$9.50
1986-S	3,010,497	5985	4.10	4.70	5.50	8.00
1987-S	4,227,728	5988	4.10	4.70	5.50	6.75
1988-S	3,262,948	5991	4.10	4.70	5.50	8.00
1989-S	3,220,194	5994	4.10	4.70	5.50	6.75
1990-S	3,299,559	5997	3.00	3.50	4.10	5.50
↳1990-S, Doubled Die Obverse, FS-101	*	375896	160.00	240.00	285.00	310.00
1991-S	2,867,787	6000	3.00	3.50	4.10	5.50
1992-S	2,858,981	6006	3.00	3.50	4.10	5.50
1992-S, Silver	1,317,579	6004	11.50	12.50	14.50	15.50
1993-S	2,633,439	6012	3.00	3.50	4.10	5.50
1993-S, Silver	761,353	6010	11.50	12.50	14.50	15.50
1994-S	2,484,594	6018	3.00	3.50	4.10	5.50
1994-S, Silver	785,329	6016	11.50	12.50	14.50	15.50
1995-S	2,117,496	6024	3.00	3.50	4.10	5.50
↳1995-S, Doubled Die Obverse, FS-101	2,117,496	393173	24.00	35.00	60.00	—
1995-S, Silver	679,985	6022	11.50	12.50	14.50	15.50
1996-S	1,750,244	6030	3.00	3.50	4.10	5.50
1996-S, Silver	775,021	6028	11.50	12.50	14.50	15.50
1997-S	2,055,000	6036	3.00	3.50	4.10	5.50
1997-S, Silver	741,678	6034	11.50	12.50	14.50	15.50
1998-S	2,086,507	6042	3.00	3.50	4.10	5.50
1998-S, Silver	878,792	6040	11.50	12.50	14.50	15.50

* Included in number above.

WASHINGTON, STATE (1999–2008)

Designers: *John Flanagan (obverse); see below for reverse designers.*
Weight: *Clad issue—5.67 grams; silver Proofs—6.25 grams.*
Composition: *Clad issue—a core of pure copper, clad in outer layers of copper-nickel (.750 copper, .250 nickel); silver Proofs—.900 silver, .100 copper (net weight .18084 oz. pure silver).* **Diameter:** *24.3 mm.* **Edge:** *Reeded.*
Mints: *Clad issue—Philadelphia, Denver, and San Francisco.*

Reverse Designers:

1999, Delaware	William Cousins
1999, Pennsylvania	John Mercanti
1999, New Jersey	Alfred Maletsky
1999, Georgia	T. James Ferrell
1999, Connecticut	T. James Ferrell
2000, Massachussets	Thomas D. Rodgers
2000, Maryland	Thomas D. Rodgers
2000, South Carolina	Thomas D. Rodgers
2000, New Hampshire	William Cousins
2000, Virginia	Edgar Z. Steever
2001, New York	Alfred Maletsky
2001, North Carolina	John Mercanti
2001, Rhode Island	Thomas D. Rodgers
2001, Vermont	T. James Ferrell
2001, Kentucky	T. James Ferrell
2002, Tennessee	Donna Weaver
2002, Ohio	Donna Weaver
2002, Louisiana	John Mercanti
2002, Indiana	Donna Weaver
2002, Mississippi	Donna Weaver
2003, Illinois	Donna Weaver
2003, Alabama	Norman E. Nemeth
2003, Maine	Donna Weaver
2003, Missouri	Alfred Maletsky
2003, Arkansas	John Mercanti
2004, Michigan	Donna Weaver
2004, Florida	T. James Ferrell
2004, Texas	Norman E. Nemeth
2004, Iowa	John Mercanti
2004, Wisconsin	Alfred Maletsky
2005, California	Don Everhart
2005, Minnesota	Charles L. Vickers
2005, Oregon	Donna Weaver
2005, Kansas	Norman E. Nemeth
2005, West Virginia	John Mercanti
2006, Nevada	Don Everhart
2006, Nebraska	Charles L. Vickers
2006, Colorado	Norman E. Nemeth
2006, North Dakota	Donna Weaver
2006, South Dakota	John Mercanti
2007, Montana	Don Everhart
2007, Washington	Charles L. Vickers
2007, Idaho	Don Everhart
2007, Wyoming	Norman E. Nemeth
2007, Utah	Joseph F. Menna
2008, Oklahoma	Phebe Hemphill
2008, New Mexico	Don Everhart
2008, Arizona	Joseph F. Menna
2008, Alaska	Charles L. Vickers
2008, Hawaii	Don Everhartl

Circulation Strike

Proof Strike

History. In 1999 the U.S. Mint introduced a new program of State quarters (officially called the United States Mint 50 State Quarters® Program). These were released at the rate of five new reverse designs each year, in combination with a restyled obverse, through 2008. Each design honored the state the coin was issued for, and they were released in public celebrations in the order in which the states joined the Union. The coins became very popular, adding millions of Americans to the ranks of everyday coin collectors, and are still widely collected with enthusiasm. In 2009 the Mint released a similar program of quarter dollars for Washington, D.C., and the five U.S. territories. Circulation strikes were made at the Philadelphia and Denver mints, and special silver-content and Proof issues at San Francisco. Each coin combines a modified obverse depicting George Washington, without a date. The reverses are distinctive and bear the date of issue, the date of statehood (for the State quarters), and other design elements. Each state or district/territory selected its own design.

Some State quarters were accidentally made with "disoriented" dies and are valued higher than ordinary pieces. Normal U.S. coins have dies oriented in coin alignment, such that the reverse appears upside down when the coin is flipped from right to left. Values for the rotated-die quarters vary according to the amount of shifting. The most valuable are those that are shifted 180 degrees, so that both sides appear upright when the coin is turned over (called *medal alignment*).

Striking and Sharpness. State quarters can have light striking on the highest area of the obverse. On the reverse there can be weak areas, depending on the design, seemingly more often seen on Denver Mint coins. Some in the State quarter series were struck through grease, obliterating portions of both the obverse (usually) and reverse designs.

Availability. All modern quarters are readily available in high grades. Typical MS coins are MS-63 and 64 with light abrasion. MS-65 and higher coins are in the minority, but enough exist that finding them is no problem. Around MS-68 many issues are scarce, and higher grades are scarcer yet.

Proofs. State quarter dollar Proofs are made in San Francisco. For certain later issues of Washington quarters as well as State issues, Proofs are available in copper-nickel–clad metal as well as silver strikings. On some Proofs over-polishing of dies eliminated some details, as on part of the WC (for William Cousins) initials on certain 1999 Delaware pieces.

Grading Standards

MS-60 to 70 (Mint State). ***Obverse:*** At MS-60, some abrasion and contact marks are evident on the highest-relief parts of the hair and the cheek. At MS-63, abrasion is slight at best, less so at MS-64. An MS-65 coin should display no abrasion or contact marks except under magnification, and MS-66 and higher coins should have none at all. Luster should be full. ***Reverse:*** Check the highest-relief areas of the design (these differ from coin to coin). Otherwise, comments are as for the obverse.

MS-66

AU-50, 53, 55, 58 (About Uncirculated). ***Obverse:*** Light wear is seen on the cheek, the high areas of the hair, and the neck. At AU-58, the luster is extensive, but incomplete, especially on the higher parts and in the field. At AU-50 and 53, luster is less. About Uncirculated coins usually lack eye appeal. ***Reverse:*** Light wear is seen on the higher-relief areas. Otherwise, comments are as for the obverse.

AU-58

PF-60 to 70 (Proof). *Obverse and Reverse:* These coins are so recent, and as only a few have been cleaned, most approach perfection and can be designated PF-68 to 70, the latter only if no contact marks or other problems can be seen under magnification. A cleaned coin with extensive hairlines would not be collectible for most numismatists and would be classified at a lower level such as PF-60 to 63. Those with lighter hairlines qualify for PF-64 or 65.

PF-70
Ultra Cameo

1999,
Delaware

1999,
Pennsylvania

1999,
New Jersey

1999,
Georgia

1999,
Connecticut

2000,
Massachusetts

2000,
Maryland

2000,
South Carolina

2000,
New Hampshire

2000,
Virginia

2001,
New York

2001,
North Carolina

2001,
Rhode Island

2001,
Vermont

2001,
Kentucky

2002,
Tennessee

2002,
Ohio

2002,
Louisiana

2002,
Indiana

2002,
Mississippi

2003,
Illinois

2003,
Alabama

2003,
Maine

2003,
Missouri

2003,
Arkansas

2004, Michigan

2004, Florida

2004, Texas

2004, Iowa

2004, Wisconsin

2004-D, Wisconsin, Normal Reverse

2004-D, Wisconsin, Extra Leaf High
FS-5901

2004-D, Wisconsin, Extra Leaf Low
FS-5902

2005, California

2005, Minnesota

2005, Oregon

2005, Kansas

2005, West Virginia

2006, Nevada

2006, Nebraska

2006, Colorado

2006, North Dakota

2006, South Dakota

2007, Montana

2007, Washington

2007, Idaho

2007, Wyoming

2007, Utah

2008, Oklahoma

2008, New Mexico

2008, Arizona

2008, Alaska

2008, Hawaii

Circulation Strikes

	Mintage	GSID	MS-65	MS-66	MS-67
State Quarters, (1999–2008)	n/a	393968	—	—	—
State Quarters, (2005–2008), Satin Finish	n/a	84877	$2.60	$4.10	$11.00
1999-P, DE	373,400,000	5772	0.80	4.10	11.00
1999-D, DE	401,424,000	5767	0.80	4.10	11.00
1999-P, PA	349,000,000	5775	0.80	4.10	11.00
1999-D, PA	358,332,000	5770	0.80	4.10	55.00
1999-P, NJ	363,200,000	5774	0.80	4.10	11.00
1999-D, NJ	299,028,000	5769	0.80	4.10	40.00
1999-P, GA	451,188,000	5773	0.80	4.10	11.00
1999-D, GA	488,744,000	5768	0.80	4.10	11.00
1999-P, CT	688,744,000	5771	0.80	4.10	11.00
1999-D, CT	657,880,000	5766	0.80	4.10	11.00
2000-P, MA	628,600,000	5792	0.80	4.10	11.00
2000-D, MA	535,184,000	5786	0.80	4.10	11.00
2000-P, MD	678,200,000	5791	0.80	4.10	11.00
2000-D, MD	556,532,000	5785	0.80	4.10	11.00
2000-P, SC	742,576,000	5794	0.80	4.10	11.00
2000-D, SC	566,208,000	5788	0.80	4.10	11.00
2000-P, NH	673,040,000	5793	0.80	4.10	11.00
2000-D, NH	495,976,000	5787	0.80	4.10	11.00
2000-P, VA	943,000,000	5796	0.80	4.10	11.00
2000-D, VA	651,616,000	5790	0.80	4.10	11.00
2001-P, NY	655,400,000	5804	0.80	4.10	11.00
2001-D, NY	619,640,000	5798	0.80	4.10	11.00
2001-P, NC	627,600,000	5805	0.80	4.10	11.00
2001-D, NC	427,876,000	5799	0.80	4.10	11.00
2001-P, RI	423,000,000	5806	0.80	4.10	11.00
2001-D, RI	447,100,000	5800	0.80	4.10	24.00
2001-P, VT	423,400,000	5808	0.80	4.10	11.00
2001-D, VT	459,404,000	5802	0.80	4.10	11.00
2001-P, KY	353,000,000	5803	0.80	4.10	11.00
2001-D, KY	370,564,000	5797	0.80	4.10	30.00
2002-P, TN	361,600,000	5820	0.80	4.10	11.00
2002-D, TN	286,468,000	5814	0.80	4.10	11.00
2002-P, OH	217,200,000	5818	0.80	4.10	11.00
2002-D, OH	414,832,000	5812	0.80	4.10	11.00
2002-P, LA	362,000,000	5816	0.80	4.10	11.00
2002-D, LA	402,204,000	5810	0.80	4.10	11.00
2002-P, IN	362,600,000	5815	0.80	4.10	11.00
2002-D, IN	327,200,000	5809	0.80	4.10	13.50
2002-P, MS	290,000,000	5817	0.80	4.10	11.00
2002-D, MS	289,600,000	5811	0.80	4.10	16.00
2003-P, IL	225,800,000	5829	0.80	4.10	16.00
2003-D, IL	237,400,000	5823	0.80	4.10	22.00
2003-P, AL	225,000,000	5827	0.80	11.00	30.00
2003-D, AL	232,400,000	5821	0.80	11.00	30.00
2003-P, ME	217,400,000	5830	0.80	11.00	38.00
2003-D, ME	231,400,000	5824	$0.80	$11.00	$24.00
2003-P, MO	225,000,000	5831	0.80	11.00	24.00
2003-D, MO	228,200,000	5825	0.80	4.10	11.00
2003-P, AR	228,000,000	5828	0.80	4.10	11.00
2003-D, AR	229,800,000	5822	0.80	4.10	16.00
2004-P, MI	233,800,000	5841	0.80	4.10	11.00
2004-D, MI	225,800,000	5835	0.80	4.10	11.00
2004-P, FL	240,200,000	5839	0.80	4.10	11.00
2004-D, FL	241,600,000	5833	0.80	4.10	11.00
2004-P, TX	278,800,000	5843	0.80	4.10	11.00
2004-D, TX	263,000,000	5837	0.80	4.10	11.00
2004-P, IA	213,800,000	5840	0.80	11.00	38.00
2004-D, IA	251,400,000	5834	0.80	4.10	11.00
2004-P, WI	226,400,000	5844	0.80	8.00	30.00
2004-D, WI	226,800,000	5838	0.80	4.10	11.00
2004-D, WI, Extra Leaf Low, FS-5902	*	15340	160.00	235.00	575.00
2004-D, WI, Extra Leaf High, FS-5901	*	15341	285.00	340.00	775.00
2005-P, CA	257,200,000	15342	0.80	4.10	11.00
2005-P, CA, Satin	1,160,000	15343	2.60	4.10	11.00
2005-D, CA	263,200,000	15352	0.80	8.00	24.00
2005-D, CA, Satin	1,160,000	15353	2.60	4.10	11.00
2005-P, MN	239,600,000	15344	0.80	4.10	11.00
2005-P, MN, Extra Tree, FS-805	*	198973	30.00	75.00	115.00
2005-P, MN, Satin	1,160,000	15345	2.60	4.10	11.00
2005-P, MN, Extra Tree, Satin, FS-803	*	82069	30.00	43.00	60.00
2005-D, MN	248,400,000	15354	0.80	4.10	11.00
2005-D, MN, Extra Tree	*	198974	55.00	80.00	130.00
2005-D, MN, Satin	1,160,000	15355	2.60	4.10	11.00
2005-D, MN, Extra Tree, Satin	*	82070	34.00	55.00	100.00
2005-P, OR	316,200,000	15346	0.80	4.10	11.00
2005-P, OR, Satin	1,160,000	15347	2.60	4.10	100.00
2005-D, OR	404,000,000	15356	0.80	4.10	11.00
2005-D, OR, Satin	1,160,000	15357	2.60	4.10	11.00
2005-P, KS	263,400,000	15348	0.80	4.10	11.00
2005-P, KS, Satin	1,160,000	15349	2.60	4.10	11.00
2005-D, KS	300,000,000	15358	0.80	4.10	11.00
2005-D, KS, Satin	1,160,000	15359	2.60	4.10	11.00
2005-P, WV	365,400,000	15350	0.80	4.10	11.00
2005-P, WV, Satin	1,160,000	15351	2.60	4.10	11.00
2005-D, WV	356,200,000	15360	0.80	4.10	24.00
2005-D, WV, Satin	1,160,000	15361	2.60	4.10	11.00
2006-P, NV	277,000,000	77565	0.80	4.10	11.00
2006-P, NV, Satin	847,361	70498	2.60	4.10	11.00
2006-D, NV	312,800,000	77566	0.80	8.00	19.00

* Included in number above.

Circulation Strikes *(continued)*

	Mintage	GSID	MS-65	MS-66	MS-67
2006-D, NV, Satin	847,361	70499	$2.60	$4.10	$11.00
2006-P, NE	318,000,000	70793	0.80	8.00	34.00
2006-P, NE, Satin	847,361	285875	2.60	4.10	11.00
2006-D, NE	273,000,000	70794	0.80	8.00	34.00
2006-D, NE, Satin	*	285876	2.60	4.10	11.00
2006-P, CO	274,800,000	68433	0.80	8.00	27.00
2006-P, CO, Satin	847,361	82071	2.60	4.10	11.00
2006-D, CO	294,200,000	77567	0.80	4.10	34.00
2006-D, CO, Satin	847,361	68407	2.60	4.10	11.00
2006-P, ND	305,800,000	69116	0.80	13.50	47.00
2006-P, ND, Satin	847,361	69117	2.60	4.10	11.00
2006-D, ND	359,000,000	69118	0.80	8.00	24.00
2006-D, ND, Satin	847,361	82072	2.60	4.10	11.00
2006-P, SD	245,000,000	65267	0.80	4.10	47.00
2006-P, SD, Satin	847,361	65268	2.60	4.10	11.00
2006-D, SD	265,800,000	65269	0.80	4.10	13.50
2006-D, SD, Satin	847,361	65270	2.60	4.10	11.00
2007-P, MT	257,000,000	69652	0.80	12.00	24.00
2007-P, MT, Satin	895,628	82073	2.60	4.10	11.00
2007-D, MT	256,240,000	68978	0.80	11.00	40.00
2007-D, MT, Satin	895,628	82074	2.60	4.10	11.00
2007-P, WA	265,200,000	77584	0.80	4.10	38.00
2007-P, WA, Satin	895,628	82075	2.60	4.10	11.00
2007-D, WA	280,000,000	68979	0.80	4.10	47.00
2007-D, WA, Satin	895,628	82076	2.60	4.10	11.00
2007-P, ID	294,600,000	77585	0.80	16.00	80.00
2007-P, ID, Satin	895,628	82077	2.60	4.10	11.00
2007-D, ID	286,800,000	68980	0.80	4.10	19.00
2007-D, ID, Satin	895,628	82078	2.60	4.10	11.00
2007-P, WY	243,600,000	68962	$16.00	$70.00	$235.00
↳2007-P, WY, DDR, FS-802	*	198976	145.00	310.00	—
2007-P, WY, Satin	895,628	82079	2.60	4.10	11.00
2007-D, WY	320,800,000	68963	0.80	16.00	43.00
2007-D, WY, Satin	895,628	82080	2.60	4.10	11.00
2007-P, UT	255,000,000	68961	2.60	16.00	195.00
2007-P, UT, Satin	895,628	82081	2.60	4.10	11.00
2007-D, UT	253,200,000	68960	0.80	13.50	80.00
2007-D, UT, Satin	895,628	82082	2.60	4.10	11.00
2008-P, OK	222,000,000	69023	0.80	4.10	19.00
2008-P, OK, Satin	745,464	70547	2.60	4.10	11.00
2008-D, OK	194,600,000	69024	0.80	5.50	38.00
2008-D, OK, Satin	745,464	70551	2.60	4.10	11.00
2008-P, NM	244,200,000	69025	0.80	5.50	38.00
2008-P, NM, Satin	745,464	70549	2.60	4.10	11.00
2008-D, NM	244,400,000	69026	0.80	24.00	70.00
2008-D, NM, Satin	745,464	70552	2.60	4.10	11.00
2008-P, AZ	244,600,000	69706	0.80	5.50	38.00
2008-P, AZ, Satin	745,464	70548	2.60	4.10	11.00
2008-D, AZ	265,000,000	69707	0.80	16.00	47.00
2008-D, AZ, Satin	745,464	82083	2.60	4.10	11.00
2008-P, AK	251,800,000	69648	0.80	5.50	38.00
2008-P, AK, Satin	745,464	69650	2.60	4.10	11.00
2008-D, AK	254,000,000	69649	0.80	5.50	38.00
2008-D, AK, Satin	745,464	69651	2.60	4.10	11.00
2008-P, HI	254,000,000	69708	0.80	5.50	38.00
2008-P, HI, Satin	745,464	70550	2.60	4.10	11.00
2008-D, HI	263,600,000	69709	0.80	5.50	38.00
2008-D, HI, Satin	745,464	70553	2.60	4.10	11.00

* Included in number above.

Proof Strikes

	Mintage	GSID	PF-68	PF-69	PF-70
States Quarters, Clad (1999–2008)	n/a	393969	$4.10	$9.50	$30
State Quarters, Silver (1999–2008)	n/a	393970	12.50	14.00	34
1999-S, DE	3,713,359	6045	4.10	9.50	90
1999-S, DE, Silver	804,565	6046	19.50	40.00	405
1999-S, PA	3,713,359	6051	4.10	9.50	30
1999-S, PA, Silver	804,565	6052	12.50	14.00	90
1999-S, NJ	3,713,359	6049	4.10	9.50	95
1999-S, NJ, Silver	804,565	6050	12.50	14.00	115
1999-S, GA	3,713,359	6047	4.10	9.50	70
1999-S, GA, Silver	804,565	6048	12.50	14.00	80
1999-S, CT	3,713,359	6043	4.10	9.50	70
1999-S, CT, Silver	804,565	6044	12.50	14.00	70
2000-S, MA	4,020,172	6057	4.10	9.50	40
2000-S, MA, Silver	965,421	6058	12.50	14.00	70
2000-S, MD	4,020,172	6055	4.10	9.50	34
2000-S, MD, Silver	965,421	6056	$12.50	$14.00	$75
2000-S, SC	4,020,172	6062	4.10	9.50	30
2000-S, SC, Silver	965,421	6061	12.50	14.00	70
2000-S, NH	4,020,172	6059	4.10	9.50	34
2000-S, NH, Silver	965,421	6060	12.50	14.00	90
2000-S, VA	4,020,172	6065	4.10	9.50	34
2000-S, VA, Silver	965,421	6066	12.50	14.00	75
2001-S, NY	3,094,140	6070	4.10	9.50	34
2001-S, NY, Silver	889,697	6071	12.50	14.00	70
2001-S, NC	3,094,140	6072	4.10	9.50	38
2001-S, NC, Silver	889,697	6069	12.50	14.00	60
2001-S, RI	3,094,140	6073	4.10	9.50	34
2001-S, RI, Silver	889,697	6074	12.50	14.00	60
2001-S, VT	3,094,140	6077	4.10	9.50	34
2001-S, VT, Silver	889,697	6078	12.50	14.00	40
2001-S, KY	3,094,140	6067	4.10	9.50	38
2001-S, KY, Silver	889,697	6068	12.50	14.00	60

Proof Strikes *(continued)*

	Mintage	GSID	PF-68	PF-69	PF-70
2002-S, TN	3,084,245	6089	$4.10	$9.50	$40
2002-S, TN, Silver	892,229	6090	12.50	14.00	70
2002-S, Ohio	3,084,245	6085	4.10	9.50	38
2002-S, Ohio, Silver	892,229	6086	12.50	14.00	55
2002-S, LA	3,084,245	6081	4.10	9.50	40
2002-S, LA, Silver	892,229	6082	12.50	14.00	70
2002-S, IN	3,084,245	6079	4.10	9.50	34
2002-S, IN, Silver	892,229	6080	12.50	14.00	75
2002-S, MS	3,084,245	6083	4.10	9.50	38
2002-S, MS, Silver	892,229	6084	12.50	14.00	55
2003-S, IL	3,408,516	6095	4.10	9.50	34
2003-S, IL, Silver	1,125,755	6096	12.50	14.00	40
2003-S, AL	3,408,516	6091	4.10	9.50	34
2003-S, AL, Silver	1,125,755	6092	12.50	14.00	47
2003-S, ME	3,408,516	6098	4.10	9.50	34
2003-S, ME, Silver	1,125,755	6099	12.50	14.00	55
2003-S, MO	3,408,516	6100	4.10	9.50	34
2003-S, MO, Silver	1,125,755	6101	12.50	14.00	40
2003-S, AR	3,408,516	6093	4.10	9.50	34
2003-S, AR, Silver	1,125,755	6094	12.50	14.00	38
2004-S, MI	2,740,684	6108	4.10	9.50	34
2004-S, MI, Silver	1,769,786	6109	12.50	14.00	55
2004-S, FL	2,740,684	6104	4.10	9.50	34
2004-S, FL, Silver	1,769,786	6105	12.50	14.00	60
2004-S, TX	2,740,684	6110	4.10	9.50	34
2004-S, TX, Silver	1,769,786	6111	12.50	14.00	75
2004-S, IA	2,740,684	6106	4.10	9.50	40
2004-S, IA, Silver	1,769,786	6107	12.50	14.00	70
2004-S, WI	2,740,684	6112	4.10	9.50	47
2004-S, WI, Silver	1,769,786	6113	12.50	14.00	60
2005-S, CA	3,262,960	15362	4.10	9.50	30
2005-S, CA, Silver	1,678,649	15363	12.50	14.00	55
2005-S, MN	3,262,960	15364	4.10	9.50	30
2005-S, MN, Silver	1,678,649	15365	12.50	14.00	38
2005-S, OR	3,262,960	15366	4.10	9.50	30
2005-S, OR, Silver	1,678,649	15367	12.50	14.00	34
2005-S, KS	3,262,960	15368	4.10	9.50	30
2005-S, KS, Silver	1,678,649	15369	$12.50	$14.00	$36
↳2005-S, KS, Silver, Large Dent Reverse, FS-901	1,678,649	393174	19.50	21.00	40
2005-S, WV	3,262,960	15370	4.10	9.50	30
2005-S, WV, Silver	1,678,649	15371	12.50	14.00	34
2006-S, NV	2,882,428	65099	4.10	9.50	30
2006-S, NV, Silver	1,585,008	65104	12.50	14.00	34
2006-S, NE	2,882,428	65096	4.10	9.50	30
2006-S, NE, Silver	1,585,008	65101	12.50	14.00	34
2006-S, CO	2,882,428	65100	4.10	9.50	30
2006-S, CO, Silver	1,585,008	65105	12.50	14.00	34
2006-S, ND	2,882,428	65098	4.10	9.50	30
2006-S, ND, Silver	1,585,008	65103	12.50	14.00	34
2006-S, SD	2,882,428	65097	4.10	9.50	30
2006-S, SD, Silver	1,585,008	65102	12.50	14.00	34
2007-S, MT	2,002,812	68617	4.10	9.50	34
2007-S, MT, Silver	1,094,993	68618	12.50	14.00	40
2007-S, WA	2,002,812	68621	4.10	9.50	34
2007-S, WA, Silver	1,094,993	68622	12.50	14.00	55
2007-S, ID	2,002,812	68615	4.10	9.50	30
2007-S, ID, Silver	1,094,993	68616	12.50	14.00	43
2007-S, WY	2,002,812	68623	4.10	9.50	34
2007-S, WY, Silver	1,094,993	68624	12.50	14.00	160
2007-S, UT	2,002,812	68619	4.10	9.50	30
2007-S, UT, Silver	1,094,993	68620	12.50	14.00	40
2008-S, OK	2,047,284	69060	4.10	9.50	30
2008-S, OK, Silver	1,020,768	69061	12.50	14.00	34
2008-S, NM	2,047,284	69062	4.10	9.50	30
2008-S, NM, Silver	1,020,768	69063	12.50	14.00	34
2008-S, AZ	2,047,284	69064	4.10	9.50	30
2008-S, AZ, Silver	1,020,768	69065	12.50	14.00	34
2008-S, AK	2,047,284	69066	4.10	9.50	30
2008-S, AK, Silver	1,020,768	69067	12.50	14.00	34
2008-S, HI	2,047,284	69068	4.10	9.50	30
2008-S, HI, Silver	1,020,768	69069	12.50	14.00	34

WASHINGTON, D.C. AND U.S. TERRITORIES (2009)

Designers: *John Flanagan (obverse); see below for reverse designers.* **Weight:** *Clad issue—5.67 grams; silver Proofs—6.25 grams.* **Composition:** *Clad issue—a core of pure copper, clad in outer layers of copper-nickel (.750 copper, .250 nickel); silver Proofs—.900 silver, .100 copper (net weight .18084 oz. pure silver).* **Diameter:** *24.3 mm.* **Edge:** *Reeded.* **Mints:** *Clad issue—Philadelphia, Denver, and San Francisco.*

Reverse Designers:

2009, District of Columbia . . . . Don Everhart
2009, Puerto Rico. . . . . .Joseph F. Menna
2009, Guam. . . . . .Jim Licaretz
2009, American Samoa. . . . . .Charles L. Vickers
2009, U.S. Virgin Islands. . . . . .Joseph F. Menna
2009, Northern Mariana Islands . . . . Phebe Hemphill

Circulation Strike

Proof Strike

History. In 1999 the U.S. Mint introduced a new program of State quarters (officially called the United States Mint 50 State Quarters® Program). These were released at the rate of five new reverse designs each year, in combination with a restyled obverse, through 2008. Each design honored the state the coin was issued for, and they were released in public celebrations in the order in which the states joined the Union. The coins became very popular, adding millions of Americans to the ranks of everyday coin collectors, and are still widely collected with enthusiasm. In 2009 the Mint released a similar program of quarter dollars for Washington, D.C., and the five U.S. territories. Circulation strikes were made at the Philadelphia and Denver mints, and special silver-content and Proof issues at San Francisco. Each coin combines a modified obverse depicting George Washington, without a date. The reverses are distinctive and bear the date of issue, the date of statehood (for the State quarters), and other design elements. Each state or district/territory selected its own design.

Some State quarters were accidentally made with "disoriented" dies and are valued higher than ordinary pieces. Normal U.S. coins have dies oriented in coin alignment, such that the reverse appears upside down when the coin is flipped from right to left. Values for the rotated-die quarters vary according to the amount of shifting. The most valuable are those that are shifted 180 degrees, so that both sides appear upright when the coin is turned over (called *medal alignment*).

Striking and Sharpness. D.C./U.S. Territories quarters can have light striking on the highest area of the obverse. On the reverse there can be weak areas, depending on the design, seemingly more often seen on Denver Mint coins.

Availability. All modern quarters are readily available in high grades. Typical MS coins are MS-63 and 64 with light abrasion. MS-65 and higher coins are in the minority, but enough exist that finding them is no problem. Around MS-68 many issues are scarce, and higher grades are scarcer yet.

Proofs. D.C./U.S. Territories quarter dollar Proofs are made in San Francisco. For certain later issues of Washington quarters as well as D.C., and Territorial issues, Proofs are available in copper-nickel–clad metal as well as silver strikings. On some Proofs over-polishing of dies eliminated some details, as on part of the WC (for William Cousins) initials on certain 1999 Delaware pieces.

Grading Standards

MS-60 to 70 (Mint State). ***Obverse:*** At MS-60, some abrasion and contact marks are evident on the highest-relief parts of the hair and the cheek. At MS-63, abrasion is slight at best, less so at MS-64. An MS-65 coin should display no abrasion or contact marks except under magnification, and MS-66 and higher coins should have none at all. Luster should be full. ***Reverse:*** Check the highest-relief areas of the design (these differ from coin to coin). Otherwise, comments are as for the obverse.

MS-66

AU-50, 53, 55, 58 (About Uncirculated). ***Obverse:*** Light wear is seen on the cheek, the high areas of the hair, and the neck. At AU-58, the luster is extensive, but incomplete, especially on the higher parts and in the field. At AU-50 and 53, luster is less. About Uncirculated coins usually lack eye appeal. ***Reverse:*** Light wear is seen on the higher-relief areas. Otherwise, comments are as for the obverse.

AU-58

PF-60 to 70 (Proof). ***Obverse and Reverse:*** These coins are so recent, and as only a few have been cleaned, most approach perfection and can be designated PF-68 to 70, the latter only if no contact marks or other problems can be seen under magnification. A cleaned coin with extensive hairlines would not be collectible for most numismatists and would be classified at a lower level such as PF-60 to 63. Those with lighter hairlines qualify for PF-64 or 65.

PF-70
Ultra Cameo

2009, District of Columbia

2009, American Samoa

2009, Puerto Rico

2009, U.S. Virgin Islands

2009, Guam

2009, Northern Mariana Islands

Circulation Strikes

	Mintage	GSID	MS-65	MS-66	MS-67
DC and US Territories Quarter, (2009)	**n/a**	**393971**	**$0.80**	**$2.60**	**$9.50**
DC and US Territories Quarter (2009), Satin	**n/a**	**393972**	**2.60**	**4.10**	**8.00**
2009-P, DC	83,600,000	70027	0.80	2.60	9.50
2009-P, DC, Satin	784,614	82084	2.60	4.10	8.00
2009-D, DC	88,800,000	70028	0.80	2.60	9.50
↳2009-D, DC, Doubled Die Reverse, FS-801	88,800,000	393179	2,000.00	3,250.00	—
2009-D, DC, Satin	784,614	82085	2.60	4.10	8.00
2009-P, PR	53,200,000	71268	0.80	2.60	9.50
2009-P, PR, Satin	784,614	82086	2.60	4.10	8.00
2009-D, PR	86,000,000	71269	0.80	2.60	9.50
2009-D, PR, Satin	784,614	82087	2.60	4.10	8.00
2009-P, Guam	45,000,000	70796	0.80	2.60	9.50
2009-P, Guam, Satin	784,614	82088	$2.60	$4.10	$8.00
2009-D, Guam	42,600,000	70797	0.80	2.60	9.50
2009-D, Guam, Satin	784,614	82089	2.60	4.10	8.00
2009-P, AmSam	42,600,000	71270	0.80	2.60	9.50
2009-P, AmSam, Satin	784,614	82090	2.60	4.10	8.00
2009-D, AmSam	39,600,000	71271	0.80	2.60	9.50
2009-D, AmSam, Satin	784,614	82091	2.60	4.10	8.00
2009-P, USVI	41,000,000	71272	0.80	2.60	9.50
2009-P, USVI, Satin	784,614	82092	2.60	4.10	8.00
2009-D, USVI	41,000,000	71273	0.80	2.60	9.50
2009-D, USVI, Satin	784,614	82093	2.60	4.10	8.00
2009-P, NMI	35,200,000	71274	0.80	2.60	9.50
2009-P, NMI, Satin	784,614	82094	2.60	4.10	8.00
2009-D, NMI	37,600,000	71275	0.80	2.60	9.50
2009-D, NMI, Satin	784,614	82095	2.60	4.10	8.00

Proof Strikes

	Mintage	GSID	PF-68	PF-69	PF-70
DC and US Territories Quarter (2009), Proof	**n/a**	**393973**	**$4.10**	**$9.50**	**$30**
DC and US Territories Quarter, Silver (2009), Proof	**n/a**	**393974**	**12.50**	**14.00**	**34**
2009-S, DC	2,113,478	70666	4.10	9.50	30
2009-S, DC, Silver	996,548	70667	12.50	14.00	39
2009-S, PR	2,113,478	71265	4.10	9.50	32
2009-S, PR, Silver	996,548	70670	12.50	14.00	36
2009-S, Guam	2,113,478	71266	$4.10	$9.50	$30
2009-S, Guam, Silver	996,548	70668	12.50	14.00	40
2009-S, AmSam	2,113,478	71262	4.10	9.50	30
2009-S, AmSam, Silver	996,548	71263	12.50	14.00	34
2009-S, USVI	2,113,478	71264	4.10	9.50	30
2009-S, USVI, Silver	996,548	70671	12.50	14.00	40
2009-S, NMI	2,113,478	71267	4.10	9.50	32
2009-S, NMI, Silver	996,548	70669	12.50	14.00	34

WASHINGTON, AMERICA THE BEAUTIFUL (2010–2021)

Designers: *John Flanagan (obverse); see below for reverse designers.* **Weight:** *Clad issue—5.67 grams; silver Proofs (2010–2018)—6.25 grams; silver Proofs (2019 to date)—6.343 grams.* **Composition:** *Clad issue—a core of pure copper, clad in outer layers of copper-nickel (.750 copper, .250 nickel); silver Proofs (2010–2018)—.900 silver, .100 copper (net weight .18084 oz. pure silver); silver Proofs (2019 to date)—.999 silver, .001 copper (net weight .182 oz. pure silver).* **Diameter:** *24.3 mm.* **Edge:** *Reeded.* **Mints:** *Clad issue—Philadelphia, Denver, San Francisco, and West Point.*

Reverse Designers:

2010, Hot Springs .... Don Everhart
2010, Yellowstone............... Don Everhart
2010, Yosemite ....Joseph Menna
2010, Grand Canyon .... Phebe Hemphill
2010, Mount Hood .... Phebe Hemphill
2011, Gettysburg .... Joel Iskowitz
2011, Glacier.....................Barbara Fox
2011, Olympic.................. Susan Gamble
2011, VIcksburg .... Thomas Cleveland
2011, Chickasaw .... Donna Weaver
2012, El Yunque................. Gary Whitley
2012, Chaco Culture .... Donna Weaver
2012, Acadia ....Barbara Fox
2012, Hawai'i .... Charles L. Vickers
2012, Denali .... Susan Gamble
2013, White Mountain .... Phebe Hemphill
2013, Perry's Victory .... Don Everhart
2013, Great Basin........... Ronald D. Sanders
2013, Ft. McHenry..............Joseph Menna
2013, Mount Rushmore..........Joseph Menna
2014, Great Smoky Mts..........Chris Costello
2014, Shenandoah .... Phebe Hemphill
2014, Arches .... Donna Weaver
2014, Great Sand Dunes .... Don Everhart
2014, Everglades................ Joel Iskowitz
2015, Homestead .... Ronald D. Sanders
2015, Kisatchie .... Susan Gamble
2015, Blue Ridge Pkwy ....Frank Morris
2015, Bombay Hook .... Joel Iskowitz
2015, Saratoga...................Barbara Fox
2016, Shawnee ....Justin Kunz
2016, Cumberland Gap ....Barbara Fox
2016, Harpers Ferry......... Thomas Hipschen
2016, T. Roosevelt............... Joel Iskowitz
2016, Ft. Moultrie/ Ft. Sumter.................Richard Scott
2017, Effigy Mounds .... Richard Masters
2017, F. Douglass........... Thomas Hipschen
2017, Ozark Riverways....... Ronald D. Sanders
2017, Ellis Island..................Barbara Fox
2017, George Rogers Clark........Frank Morris
2018, Pictured Rocks .... Paul C. Balan
2018, Apostle Islands .... Richard Masters
2018, Voyageurs ....Patricia Lucas-Morris
2018, Cumberland Island........ Donna Weaver
2018, Block Island ....Chris Costello
2019, Lowell .... Joel Iskowitz
2019, Am. Memorial .... Donna Weaver
2019, War in the Pacific ....Chris Costello
2019, San Antonio Missions .... Joel Iskowitz
2019, Frank Church River of No Return .... Emily Damstra
2020, Nat'l Park of American Samoa......... Richard Masters
2020, Weir Farm ....Justin Kunz
2020, Salt River Bay........... Richard Masters
2020, Marsh-Billings-Rockefeller .... Donna Weaver
2020, Tallgrass Prairie.......... Emily Damstra
2021, Tuskegee Airmen..........Chris Costello

Circulation Strike

Proof Strike

History. In 2010 the U.S. Mint introduced a new program of quarters honoring national parks and historic sites in each state, the District of Columbia, and the five U.S. territories. They were released at the rate of five new reverse designs each year, in combination with the obverse found on the State and D.C./ Territorial quarters of previous years; the program concluded in 2021 with the Tuskegee Airmen National Historic Site (Alabama) quarter. Circulation strikes were made at the Philadelphia and Denver mints, and special silver content and Proof issues at San Francisco. Each coin features a modified obverse depicting George Washington, without a date. The reverses are distinctive and bear the date of issue and a special design showcasing a national park in the state, district, or territory. The official title of the series was the America the Beautiful™ Quarters Program; popularly, they are known as National Park quarters.

In 2012, the U.S. Mint introduced a new innovation in the National Park quarters program. For the first time since the 1950s, the San Francisco Mint is being used to produce quarters in a non-Proof format. These Uncirculated coins are made in limited quantities for collectors. They can be purchased directly from the Mint for a premium above their face value, as opposed to being released into circulation like normal quarters. Unlike the Uncirculated S-mintmark Bicentennial quarters dated 1976, which were 40 percent silver and sold only in sets, the S-mintmark National Park quarters are of normal copper-nickel–clad composition and are sold in bags of 100 and rolls of 40 coins. Thus the 2012-S coins are considered the first circulation-strike quarters made at San Francisco since 1954. The S-mintmark coins have been made of each National Park design from 2012 to date.

Striking and Sharpness. These quarters can have light striking on the highest area of the obverse. On the reverse there can be weak areas, depending on the design, seemingly more often seen on Denver Mint coins.

Availability. All modern quarters are readily available in high grades. Typical MS coins are MS-63 and 64 with light abrasion. MS-65 and higher coins are in the minority, but enough exist that finding them is easy. Around MS-68 many issues are scarce; higher grades are scarcer yet. The S-mintmark coins are proportionally scarce compared to Philadelphia and Denver issues, and are not seen in circulation. They are available for direct purchase from the U.S. Mint in their year of issue, and from the secondary market after that.

Proofs. National Park quarter dollar Proofs are made in San Francisco. Through 2018, silver Proofs were .900 fine silver; as of 2019, all regular silver Mint products are .999 fine silver. Proofs are available in clad metal as well as silver strikings. On some Proofs over-polishing of dies has eliminated some details.

Grading Standards

MS-68

MS-60 to 70 (Mint State). ***Obverse:*** At MS-60, some abrasion and contact marks are evident on the highest-relief parts of the hair and the cheek. At MS-63, abrasion is slight at best, less so at MS-64. An MS-65 coin should display no abrasion or contact marks except under magnification, and MS-66 and higher coins should have none at all. Luster should be full. ***Reverse:*** Check the highest-relief areas of the design (these differ from coin to coin). Otherwise, comments are as for the obverse.

PF-60 to 70 (Proof). ***Obverse and Reverse:*** These coins are so recent, and as only a few have been cleaned, most approach perfection and can be designated PF-68 to 70, the latter only if no contact marks or other problems can be seen under magnification. A cleaned coin with extensive hairlines would not be collectible for most numismatists and would be classified at a lower level such as PF-60 to 63. Those with lighter hairlines qualify for PF-64 or 65.

PF-69
Ultra Cameo

2010, Hot Springs National Park (AR)

2010, Yellowstone National Park (WY)

2010, Yosemite National Park (CA)

2010, Grand Canyon National Park (AZ)

2010, Mt. Hood National Forest (OR)

2011, Gettysburg National Military Park (PA)

2011, Glacier National Park (MT)

2011, Olympic National Park (WA)

2011, Vicksburg National Military Park (MS)

2011, Chickasaw National Recreation Area (OK)

2012, El Yunque National Forest (PR)

2012, Chaco Culture National Historical Park (NM)

2012, Acadia National Park (ME)

2012, Hawai'i Volcanoes National Park (HI)

2012, Denali National Park and Preserve (AK)

2013, White Mountain National Forest (NH)

2013, Perry's Victory and International Peace Memorial (OH)

2013, Great Basin National Park (NV)

2013, Fort McHenry National Monument and Historic Shrine (MD)

2013, Mount Rushmore National Memorial (SD)

2014, Great Smoky Mountains National Park (TN)

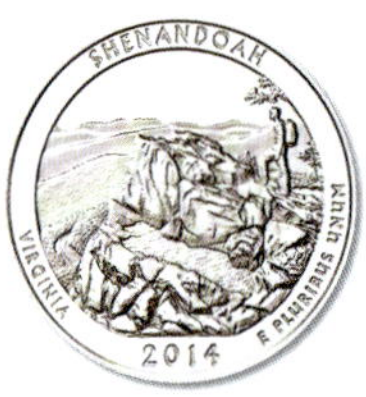

2014, Shenandoah National Park (VA)

2014, Arches National Park (UT)

2014, Great Sand Dunes National Park (CO)

2014, Everglades National Park (FL)

2015, Homestead National Monument of America (NE)

2015, Kisatchie National Forest (LA)

2015, Blue Ridge Parkway (NC)

2015, Bombay Hook National Wildlife Refuge (DE)

2015, Saratoga National Historical Park (NY)

2016, Shawnee National Forest (IL)

2016, Cumberland Gap National Historical Park (KY)

2016, Harpers Ferry National Historical Park (WV)

2016, Theodore Roosevelt National Park (ND)

2010, Mt. Hood National Forest (OR)

2017, Effigy Mounds National Monument (IA)

2017, Frederick Douglass National Historic Site (DC)

2017, Ozark National Scenic Riverways (MO)

2017, Ellis Island (Statue of Liberty National Monument) (NJ)

2017, George Rogers Clark National Historical Park (IN)

2018, Pictured Rocks National Lakeshore (MI)

2018, Apostle Islands National Lakeshore (WI)

2018, Voyageurs National Park (MN)

2018, Cumberland Island National Seashore (GA)

2018, Block Island National Wildlife Refuge (RI)

2019,
Lowell National Historical Park (MA)

2019,
American Memorial Park (Northern Mariana Islands)

2019,
San Antonio Missions National Historical Park (TX)

2019,
War in the Pacific National Historical Park (Guam)

2019,
Frank Church River of No Return Wilderness (ID)

2020,
National Park of American Samoa (AS)

2020,
Weir Farm National Historic Site (CT)

2020,
Salt River Bay National Historical Park and Ecological Preserve (USVI)

2020,
Marsh-Billings-Rockefeller National Historical Park (VT)

2020,
Tallgrass Prairie National Preserve (KS)

2021,
Tuskegee Airmen National Historic Site (AL)

2020 Obverse Privy Mark

Circulation Strikes

	Mintage	GSID	MS-65	MS-66	MS-67
American the Beautiful Quarter (2010–2021)	**n/a**	**393975**	**$0.80**	**$2.60**	**$16.00**
American the Beautiful Quarter (2010), Satin Finish	**n/a**	**393976**	**4.10**	**4.70**	**5.50**
American the Beautiful Quarter (2017), Enhanced Uncirculated	**n/a**	**393977**	**4.10**	**4.70**	**5.50**
American the Beautiful Quarter (2020), V75 Privy Mark	**n/a**	**393978**	**22.00**	**30.00**	**100.00**
2010-P, Hot Springs National Park (AR)	35,600,000	70924	0.80	2.60	16.00
2010-P, Hot Springs National Park (AR), Satin	583,897	82096	4.10	4.70	6.75
2010-D, Hot Springs National Park (AR)	34,000,000	70925	0.80	2.60	16.00
2010-D, Hot Springs National Park (AR), Satin	583,897	82097	4.10	4.70	6.75
2010-P, Yellowstone National Park (WY)	33,600,000	70926	0.80	2.60	16.00
2010-P, Yellowstone National Park (WY), Satin	583,897	82098	4.10	4.70	6.75
2010-D, Yellowstone National Park (WY)	34,800,000	70927	0.80	2.60	16.00
2010-D, Yellowstone National Park (WY), Satin	583,897	82099	4.10	4.70	6.75
2010-P, Yosemite National Park (CA)	35,200,000	70928	0.80	2.60	16.00
2010-P, Yosemite National Park (CA), Satin	583,897	82100	4.10	4.70	6.75
2010-D, Yosemite National Park (CA)	34,800,000	70929	0.80	2.60	16.00
2010-D, Yosemite National Park (CA), Satin	583,897	82101	4.10	4.70	6.75
2010-P, Grand Canyon National Park (AZ)	34,800,000	70930	0.80	2.60	16.00
2010-P, Grand Canyon National Park (AZ), Satin	583,897	82102	4.10	4.70	5.50
2010-D, Grand Canyon National Park (AZ)	35,400,000	70931	0.80	2.60	16.00
2010-D, Grand Canyon National Park (AZ), Satin	583,897	82103	4.10	4.70	5.50

Circulation Strikes *(continued)*

	Mintage	GSID	MS-65	MS-66	MS-67
2010-P, Mount Hood National Forest (OR)	34,400,000	70932	$0.80	$2.60	$16.00
2010-P, Mount Hood National Forest (OR), Satin	583,897	82104	4.10	4.70	6.75
2010-D, Mount Hood National Forest (OR)	34,400,000	70933	0.80	2.60	16.00
2010-D, Mount Hood National Forest (OR), Satin	583,897	82105	4.10	4.70	5.50
2011-P, Gettysburg National Military Park (PA)	30,800,000	77700	0.80	2.60	16.00
2011-D, Gettysburg National Military Park (PA)	30,400,000	70935	0.80	2.60	16.00
2011-P, Glacier National Park (MT)	30,400,000	70936	0.80	2.60	49.00
2011-D, Glacier National Park (MT)	31,200,000	70937	0.80	2.60	40.00
2011-P, Olympic National Park (WA)	30,400,000	77701	0.80	2.60	16.00
2011-D, Olympic National Park (WA)	30,600,000	70939	0.80	2.60	16.00
2011-P, Vicksburg National Military Park (MS)	30,800,000	77702	0.80	2.60	16.00
2011-D, Vicksburg National Military Park (MS)	33,400,000	70941	0.80	2.60	16.00
2011-P, Chickasaw National Recreation Area (OK)	73,800,000	77703	0.80	2.60	16.00
2011-D, Chickasaw National Recreation Area (OK)	69,400,000	70943	0.80	2.60	16.00
2012-P, El Yunque National Forest (PR)	25,800,000	77704	0.80	2.60	16.00
2012-D, El Yunque National Forest (PR)	25,000,000	71560	0.80	2.60	40.00
2012-S, El Yunque National Forest (PR) (a)	1,680,140	77705	0.80	2.60	30.00
2012-P, Chaco Culture National Historical Park (NM)	22,000,000	71559	0.80	2.60	16.00
2012-D, Chaco Culture National Historical Park (NM)	22,000,000	77706	0.80	2.60	16.00
2012-S, Chaco Culture National Historical Park (NM) (a)	1,389,020	77707	0.80	2.60	27.00
2012-P, Acadia National Park (ME)	24,800,000	77709	0.80	2.60	40.00
2012-D, Acadia National Park (ME)	21,606,000	77710	0.80	2.60	195.00
2012-S, Acadia National Park (ME) (a)	1,409,120	77711	0.80	2.60	16.00
2012-P, Hawai'i Volcanoes National Park (HI)	46,200,000	77712	0.80	2.60	22.00
2012-D, Hawai'i Volcanoes National Park (HI)	78,600,000	77713	0.80	2.60	22.00
2012-S, Hawai'i Volcanoes National Park (HI) (a)	1,409,120	77714	0.80	2.60	16.00
2012-P, Denali National Park and Preserve (AK)	135,400,000	77715	0.80	2.60	16.00
2012-D, Denali National Park and Preserve (AK)	166,600,000	77716	0.80	2.60	16.00
2012-S, Denali National Park and Preserve (AK) (a)	1,409,220	77717	0.80	2.60	16.00
2013-P, White Mountain National Forest (NH)	68,800,000	77718	0.80	2.60	16.00
2013-D, White Mountain National Forest (NH)	107,600,000	77719	0.80	2.60	19.00
2013-S, White Mountain National Forest (NH) (a)	1,606,900	77720	0.80	2.60	16.00
2013-P, Perry's Victory and International Peace Memorial (OH)	107,800,000	77721	0.80	2.60	16.00
2013-D, Perry's Victory and International Peace Memorial (OH)	131,600,000	77722	0.80	2.60	19.00
2013-S, Perry's Victory and International Peace Memorial (OH) (a)	1,425,860	77723	0.80	2.60	16.00
2013-P, Great Basin National Park (NV)	122,400,000	77724	0.80	2.60	16.00
2013-D, Great Basin National Park (NV)	141,400,000	77725	0.80	2.60	16.00
2013-S, Great Basin National Park (NV) (a)	1,316,500	77726	0.80	2.60	16.00
2013-P, Fort McHenry National Monument and Historical Shrine (MD)	120,000,000	77727	0.80	2.60	16.00
2013-D, Fort McHenry National Monument and Historical Shrine (MD)	151,400,000	77728	0.80	2.60	19.00
2013-S, Fort McHenry National Monument and Historical Shrine (MD) (a)	1,313,680	77729	0.80	2.60	27.00
2013-P, Mount Rushmore National Memorial (SD)	231,800,000	77730	0.80	2.60	16.00
2013-D, Mount Rushmore National Memorial (SD)	272,400,000	77731	0.80	2.60	16.00
2013-S, Mount Rushmore National Memorial (SD) (a)	1,373,260	77732	0.80	2.60	16.00
2014-P, Great Smoky Mountains National Park (TN)	73,200,000	77733	0.80	2.60	16.00
2014-D, Great Smoky Mountains National Park (TN)	99,400,000	77734	0.80	2.60	16.00
2014-S, Great Smoky Mountains National Park (TN) (a)	1,360,780	77735	0.80	2.60	16.00

a. Not issued for circulation. From 2012–2021, the San Francisco Mint made Uncirculated S-mintmark quarters of each design in the National Park series. These could be purchased by collectors directly from the U.S. Mint, in bags of 100 or rolls of 40 coins, for a premium above face value.

Circulation Strikes *(continued)*

	Mintage	GSID	MS-65	MS-66	MS-67
2014-P, Shenandoah National Park (VA)	112,800,000	77736	$0.80	$2.60	$16.00
2014-D, Shenandoah National Park (VA)	197,800,000	77737	0.80	2.60	27.00
2014-S, Shenandoah National Park (VA) (a)	1,266,720	77738	0.80	2.60	16.00
2014-P, Arches National Park (UT)	214,200,000	77739	0.80	2.60	16.00
2014-D, Arches National Park (UT)	251,400,000	77740	0.80	2.60	22.00
2014-S, Arches National Park (UT) (a)	1,235,940	77741	0.80	2.60	16.00
2014-P, Great Sand Dunes National Park (CO)	159,600,000	77742	0.80	2.60	16.00
2014-D, Great Sand Dunes National Park (CO)	171,800,000	77743	0.80	2.60	16.00
2014-S, Great Sand Dunes National Park (CO) (a)	1,176,760	77744	0.80	2.60	16.00
2014-P, Everglades National Park (FL)	157,601,200	77745	0.80	2.60	16.00
2014-D, Everglades National Park (FL)	142,400,000	77746	0.80	2.60	16.00
2014-S, Everglades National Park (FL) (a)	1,180,900	77747	0.80	2.60	16.00
2015-P, Homestead National Monument of America (NE)	214,400,000	77748	0.80	2.60	16.00
2015-D, Homestead National Monument of America (NE)	248,600,000	77749	0.80	2.60	16.00
2015-S, Homestead National Monument of America (NE) (a)	1,153,840	77750	0.80	2.60	16.00
2015-P, Kisatchie National Forest (LA)	397,200,000	77751	0.80	2.60	22.00
2015-D, Kisatchie National Forest (LA)	379,600,000	77752	0.80	2.60	16.00
2015-S, Kisatchie National Forest (LA) (a)	1,099,380	77753	0.80	2.60	16.00
2015-P, Blue Ridge Parkway (NC)	325,616,000	77754	0.80	2.60	16.00
2015-D, Blue Ridge Parkway (NC)	505,200,000	77755	0.80	2.60	16.00
2015-S, Blue Ridge Parkway (NC) (a)	1,096,620	77756	0.80	2.60	16.00
2015-P, Bombay Hook National Wildlife Refugee (DE)	275,000,000	77757	0.80	2.60	16.00
2015-D, Bombay Hook National Wildlife Refugee (DE)	206,400,000	77758	0.80	2.60	22.00
2015-S, Bombay Hook National Wildlife Refugee (DE) (a)	1,013,920	77759	0.80	2.60	16.00
2015-P, Saratoga National Historical Park (NY)	223,000,000	77760	0.80	2.60	16.00
2015-D, Saratoga National Historical Park (NY)	215,800,000	77761	0.80	2.60	16.00
2015-S, Saratoga National Historical Park (NY) (a)	1,045,500	77762	0.80	2.60	16.00
2016-P, Shawnee National Forest (IL)	155,600,000	77763	0.80	2.60	16.00
2016-D, Shawnee National Forest (IL)	151,800,000	77764	0.80	2.60	16.00
2016-S, Shawnee National Forest (IL) (a)	1,081,914	77765	0.80	2.60	16.00
2016-P, Cumberland Gap National Historical Park (KY)	215,400,000	77766	0.80	2.60	34.00
2016-D, Cumberland Gap National Historical Park (KY)	223,200,000	77767	0.80	2.60	16.00
2016-S, Cumberland Gap National Historical Park (KY) (a)	1,036,093	77768	0.80	2.60	16.00
2016-P, Harpers Ferry National Historical Park (WV)	434,630,000	77769	0.80	2.60	16.00
2016-D, Harpers Ferry National Historical Park (WV)	424,000,000	77770	0.80	2.60	16.00
2016-S, Harpers Ferry National Historical Park (WV) (a)	1,050,185	77771	0.80	2.60	16.00
2016-P, Theodore Roosevelt National Park (ND)	231,600,000	81977	0.80	2.60	16.00
2016-D, Theodore Roosevelt National Park (ND)	223,200,000	81978	0.80	2.60	16.00
2016-S, Theodore Roosevelt National Park (ND) (a)	1,073,092	81979	0.80	2.60	16.00
2016-P, Fort Moultrie at Fort Sumter National Monument (SC)	154,400,000	77772	0.80	2.60	16.00
2016-D, Fort Moultrie at Fort Sumter National Monument (SC)	142,200,000	77773	0.80	2.60	16.00
2016-S, Fort Moultrie at Fort Sumter National Monument (SC) (a)	979,566	77774	0.80	2.60	16.00
2017-P, Effigy Mounds National Monument (IA)	271,200,000	77775	0.80	2.60	19.00
2017-D, Effigy Mounds National Monument (IA)	210,800,000	77776	0.80	2.60	16.00
2017-S, Effigy Mounds National Monument (IA) (a)	945,853	77777	0.80	2.60	16.00
2017-S, Effigy Mounds National Monument (IA), Enhanced Uncirculated (b)	210,419	82106	4.10	4.70	5.50

a. Not issued for circulation. From 2012–2021, the San Francisco Mint made Uncirculated S-mintmark quarters of each design in the National Park series. These could be purchased by collectors directly from the U.S. Mint, in bags of 100 or rolls of 40 coins, for a premium above face value. **b.** Coinciding with National Coin Week (April 21–27, 2019), the United States Mint released into circulation 10 million 2019 quarters struck at the West Point Mint, each bearing a W mintmark. The coins were mixed into bulk bags of quarters at the Philadelphia and Denver mints and shipped and distributed to banks and financial institutions by the Federal Reserve starting in early April.

Circulation Strikes *(continued)*

	Mintage	GSID	MS-65	MS-66	MS-67
2017-P, Frederick Douglass National Historic Site (DC)	184,800,000	81986	$0.80	$2.60	$16.00
2017-D, Frederick Douglass National Historic Site (DC)	185,800,000	81987	0.80	2.60	16.00
2017-S, Frederick Douglass National Historic Site (DC) (a)	950,503	81988	0.80	2.60	16.00
2017-S, Frederick Douglass National Historic Site (DC), Enhanced Uncirculated (b)	210,419	82109	4.10	4.70	5.50
2017-P, Ozark National Scenic Riverways (MO)	203,000,000	81983	0.80	2.60	16.00
2017-D, Ozark National Scenic Riverways (MO)	200,000,000	81984	0.80	2.60	16.00
2017-S, Ozark National Scenic Riverways (MO) (a)	921,747	81985	0.80	2.60	16.00
2017-S, Ozark National Scenic Riverways (MO), Enhanced Uncirculated (b)	210,419	82108	4.10	4.70	5.50
2017-P, Ellis Island (Statue of Liberty National Monument) (NJ)	234,000,000	81980	0.80	2.60	16.00
2017-D, Ellis Island (Statue of Liberty National Monument) (NJ)	254,000,000	81981	0.80	2.60	16.00
2017-S, Ellis Island (Statue of Liberty National Monument) (NJ) (a)	973,147	81982	0.80	2.60	16.00
2017-S, Ellis Island (Statue of Liberty National Monument) (NJ), Enhanced Uncirculated (b)	210,419	82107	4.10	4.70	5.50
2017-P, George Rogers Clark National Historical Park (IN)	191,600,000	81989	0.80	2.60	16.00
2017-D, George Rogers Clark National Historical Park (IN)	180,800,000	81990	0.80	2.60	16.00
2017-S, George Rogers Clark National Historical Park (IN) (a)	933,150	81991	0.80	2.60	16.00
2017-S, George Rogers Clark National Historical Park (IN), Enhanced Uncirculated (b)	210,419	82110	4.10	4.70	5.50
2018-P, Pictured Rocks National Lakeshore (MI)	186,714,000	77778	0.80	2.60	16.00
2018-D, Pictured Rocks National Lakeshore (MI)	182,600,000	77779	0.80	2.60	16.00
2018-S, Pictured Rocks National Lakeshore (MI) (a)	931,220	77780	0.80	2.60	16.00
2018-P, Apostle Islands National Lakeshore (WI)	223,200,000	77781	0.80	2.60	22.00
2018-D, Apostle Islands National Lakeshore (WI)	216,600,000	77782	0.80	2.60	16.00
2018-S, Apostle Islands National Lakeshore (WI) (a)	889,080	77783	0.80	2.60	16.00
2018-P, Voyageurs National Park (MN)	237,400,000	77784	0.80	2.60	16.00
2018-D, Voyageurs National Park (MN)	197,800,000	77785	0.80	2.60	16.00
2018-S, Voyageurs National Park (MN) (a)	867,400	77786	0.80	2.60	16.00
2018-P, Cumberland Island National Seashore (GA)	138,000,000	77787	0.80	2.60	16.00
2018-D, Cumberland Island National Seashore (GA)	151,600,000	77788	0.80	2.60	16.00
2018-S, Cumberland Island National Seashore (GA) (a)	880,940	77789	0.80	2.60	40.00
2018-P, Block Island National Wildlife Refuge (RI)	159,600,000	77790	0.80	2.60	16.00
2018-D, Block Island National Wildlife Refuge (RI)	159,600,000	77791	0.80	2.60	16.00
2018-S, Block Island National Wildlife Refuge (RI) (a)	854,940	77792	0.80	2.60	47.00
2019-P, Lowell National Historical Park (MA)	165,800,000	81992	0.80	2.60	16.00
2019-D, Lowell National Historical Park (MA)	182,200,000	81993	0.80	2.60	16.00
2019-S, Lowell National Historical Park (MA) (a)	909,080	81994	0.80	2.60	16.00
2019-W, Lowell National Historical Park (MA) (b)	2,000,000	81700	110.00	155.00	405.00
2019-P, American Memorial Park (NMI)	142,800,000	81995	0.80	2.60	16.00
2019-D, American Memorial Park (NMI)	182,600,000	81996	0.80	2.60	16.00
2019-S, American Memorial Park (NMI) (a)	904,880	81997	0.80	2.60	16.00
2019-W, American Memorial Park (NMI) (b)	2,000,000	81701	110.00	155.00	405.00
2019-P, San Antonio Missions National Historical Park (TX)	142,800,000	82001	0.80	2.60	16.00
2019-D, San Antonio Missions National Historical Park (TX)	129,400,000	82002	0.80	2.60	16.00
2019-S, San Antonio Missions National Historical Park (TX) (a)	931,580	82003	0.80	2.60	16.00
2019-W, San Antonio Missions National Historical Park (TX) (b)	2,000,000	81703	110.00	155.00	405.00

a. Not issued for circulation. From 2012–2021, the San Francisco Mint made Uncirculated S-mintmark quarters of each design in the National Park series. These could be purchased by collectors directly from the U.S. Mint, in bags of 100 or rolls of 40 coins, for a premium above face value. **b.** Coinciding with National Coin Week (April 21–27, 2019), the United States Mint released into circulation 10 million 2019 quarters struck at the West Point Mint, each bearing a W mintmark. The coins were mixed into bulk bags of quarters at the Philadelphia and Denver mints and shipped and distributed to banks and financial institutions by the Federal Reserve starting in early April.

Circulation Strikes *(continued)*

	Mintage	GSID	MS-65	MS-66	MS-67
2019-P, War in the Pacific National Historical Park (Guam)	116,600,000	81998	$0.80	$2.60	$16.00
2019-D, War in the Pacific National Historical Park (Guam)	114,400,000	81999	0.80	2.60	16.00
2019-S, War in the Pacific National Historical Park (Guam) (a)	924,380	82000	0.80	2.60	16.00
2019-W, War in the Pacific National Historical Park (Guam) (b)	2,000,000	81702	20.00	34.00	325.00
2019-P, Frank Church River of No Return Wilderness (IA)	223,400,000	82004	0.80	2.60	16.00
2019-D, Frank Church River of No Return Wilderness (IA)	251,600,000	82005	0.80	2.60	16.00
2019-S, Frank Church River of No Return Wilderness (IA) (a)	901,920	82006	0.80	2.60	16.00
2019-W, Frank Church River of No Return Wilderness (IA) (b)	2,000,000	81704	47.00	110.00	405.00
2020-P, National Park of American Samoa (AmSam)	286,000,000	82007	0.80	2.60	19.00
2020-D, National Park of American Samoa (AmSam)	212,200,000	82008	0.80	2.60	19.00
2020-S, National Park of American Samoa (AmSam) (a)	939,760	82009	0.80	2.60	16.00
2020-W, National Park of American Samoa (AmSam), V75 Privy Mark (c)	2,000,000	82010	22.00	35.00	160.00
2020-P, Weir Farm National Historic Site (CT)	125,600,000	82014	0.80	2.60	17.50
2020-D, Weir Farm National Historic Site (CT)	155,000,000	82015	0.80	2.60	16.00
2020-S, Weir Farm National Historic Site (CT) (a)	945,820	82016	0.80	2.60	16.00
2020-W, Weir Farm National Historic Site (CT), V75 Privy Mark (c)	2,000,000	82017	22.00	30.00	100.00
2020-P, Salt River Bay National Historical Park and Ecological Preserve (USVI)	580,200,000	82018	0.80	2.60	16.00
2020-D, Salt River Bay National Historical Park and Ecological Preserve (USVI)	515,000,000	82019	0.80	2.60	16.00
2020-S, Salt River Bay National Historical Park and Ecological Preserve (USVI) (a)	930,960	82020	0.80	2.60	30.00
2020-W, Salt River Bay National Historical Park and Ecological Preserve (USVI), V75 Privy Mark (c)	2,000,000	85050	22.00	55.00	390.00
2020-P, Marsh-Billings-Rockefeller National Historical Park (VT)	304,600,000	82021	0.80	2.60	16.00
2020-D, Marsh-Billings-Rockefeller National Historical Park (VT)	345,800,000	82022	0.80	2.60	16.00
2020-S, Marsh-Billings-Rockefeller National Historical Park (VT) (a)	928,940	82023	0.80	2.60	16.00
2020-W, Marsh-Billings-Rockefeller National Historical Park (VT), V75 Privy Mark (c)	2,000,000	85051	55.00	145.00	1,000.00
2020-P, Tallgrass Prairie National Preserve (KS)	101,200,000	82011	0.80	2.60	17.50
2020-D, Tallgrass Prairie National Preserve (KS)	142,400,000	82012	0.80	2.60	16.00
2020-S, Tallgrass Prairie National Preserve (KS) (a)	931,060	82013	0.80	2.60	16.00
2020-W, Tallgrass Prairie National Preserve (KS), V75 Privy Mark (c)	2,000,000	85049	55.00	130.00	405.00
2021-P, Tuskegee Airmen National Historic Site (AL)	160,400,000	85129	0.80	2.60	22.00
2021-D, Tuskegee Airmen National Historic Site (AL)	304,000,000	85130	0.80	2.60	16.00
2021-S, Tuskegee Airmen National Historic Site (AL) (a)		85131	0.80	2.60	34.00

a. Not issued for circulation. From 2012–2021, the San Francisco Mint made Uncirculated S-mintmark quarters of each design in the National Park series. These could be purchased by collectors directly from the U.S. Mint, in bags of 100 or rolls of 40 coins, for a premium above face value. **b.** Coinciding with National Coin Week (April 21–27, 2019), the United States Mint released into circulation 10 million 2019 quarters struck at the West Point Mint, each bearing a W mintmark. The coins were mixed into bulk bags of quarters at the Philadelphia and Denver mints and shipped and distributed to banks and financial institutions by the Federal Reserve starting in early April. **c.** To recognize the 75th anniversary of the conclusion of World War II, the United States Mint released into circulation 2020 quarters struck at the West Point Mint, each bearing a W mintmark and a privy mark. The mark has the text "V75," signifying the allied victory in World War II, placed inside an outline representing the Rainbow Pool of the World War II Memorial in Washington, D.C., as seen from the air. The coins were mixed into bulk bags of quarters at the Philadelphia and Denver mints and shipped and distributed to banks and financial institutions by the Federal Reserve starting in early April.

Proof Strikes

	Mintage	GSID	PF-68	PF-69	PF-70
American the Beautiful Quarter, Clad (2010–2021), Proof	**n/a**	**393979**	**$4.10**	**$9.50**	**$27**
American the Beautiful Quarter, Silver (2010–2021), Proof	**n/a**	**393980**	**12.50**	**14.00**	**30**
2010-S, Hot Springs National Park (AR)	1,402,889	71179	4.10	9.50	27
2010-S, Hot Springs National Park (AR), Silver	859,417	71180	12.50	14.00	30
2010-S, Yellowstone National Park (WY)	1,404,259	71181	4.10	9.50	27
2010-S, Yellowstone National Park (WY), Silver	859,417	71182	12.50	14.00	30
2010-S, Yosemite National Park (CA)	1,401,522	71183	4.10	9.50	27
2010-S, Yosemite National Park (CA), Silver	859,417	71184	12.50	14.00	30
2010-S, Grand Canyon National Park (AZ)	1,401,462	71185	4.10	9.50	27
2010-S, Grand Canyon National Park (AZ), Silver	859,417	71186	12.50	14.00	30
2010-S, Mount Hood National Forest (OR)	1,398,106	71187	4.10	9.50	27
2010-S, Mount Hood National Forest (OR), Silver	859,417	71188	12.50	14.00	30
2011-S, Gettysburg National Military Park (PA)	1,273,068	71189	4.10	9.50	27
2011-S, Gettysburg National Military Park (PA), Silver	722,076	71190	12.50	14.00	30
2011-S, Glacier National Park (MT)	1,269,422	71191	4.10	9.50	27
2011-S, Glacier National Park (MT), Silver	722,076	71192	12.50	14.00	30
2011-S, Olympic National Park (WA)	1,268,231	71193	4.10	9.50	27
2011-S, Olympic National Park (WA), Silver	722,076	71194	12.50	14.00	30
2011-S, Vicksburg National Military Park (MS)	1,268,623	71195	4.10	9.50	27
2011-S, Vicksburg National Military Park (MS), Silver	722,076	71196	12.50	14.00	30
2011-S, Chickasaw National Recreation Area (OK)	1,266,825	71197	4.10	9.50	27
2011-S, Chickasaw National Recreation Area (OK), Silver	722,076	71198	12.50	14.00	30
2012-S, El Yunque National Forest (PR)	1,012,094	77793	4.10	9.50	27
2012-S, El Yunque National Forest (PR), Silver	608,060	77794	12.50	14.00	30
2012-S, Chaco Culture National Historical Park (NM)	961,464	77795	4.10	9.50	27
2012-S, Chaco Culture National Historical Park (NM), Silver	608,060	77796	12.50	14.00	30
2012-S, Acadia National Park (ME)	962,038	77797	4.10	9.50	27
2012-S, Acadia National Park (ME), Silver	608,060	77798	12.50	14.00	30
2012-S, Hawai'i Volcanoes National Park (HI)	962,447	77799	4.10	9.50	27
2012-S, Hawai'i Volcanoes National Park (HI), Silver	608,060	77800	12.50	14.00	30
2012-S, Denali National Park and Preserve (AK)	959,602	77801	4.10	9.50	27
2012-S, Denali National Park and Preserve (AK), Silver	608,060	77802	12.50	14.00	30
2013-S, White Mountain National Forest (NH)	989,803	77803	4.10	9.50	27
2013-S, White Mountain National Forest (NH), Silver	467,691	77804	12.50	14.00	30
2013-S, Perry's Victory and International Peace Memorial (OH)	947,815	77805	4.10	9.50	27
2013-S, Perry's Victory and International Peace Memorial (OH), Silver	467,691	77806	12.50	14.00	30
2013-S, Great Basin National Park (NV)	945,777	77807	4.10	9.50	27
2013-S, Great Basin National Park (NV), Silver	467,691	77808	12.50	14.00	30
2013-S, Fort McHenry National Monument and Historical Shrine (MD)	946,380	77809	4.10	9.50	27
2013-S, Fort McHenry National Monument and Historical Shrine (MD), Silver	467,691	77810	12.50	14.00	30
2013-S, Mount Rushmore National Memorial (SD)	958,853	77811	4.10	9.50	27
2013-S, Mount Rushmore National Memorial (SD), Silver	467,691	77812	12.50	14.00	30
2014-S, Great Smoky Mountains National Park (TN)	881,896	77813	4.10	9.50	27
2014-S, Great Smoky Mountains National Park (TN), Silver	472,107	77814	12.50	14.00	30
2014-S, Shenandoah National Park (VA)	846,441	77815	4.10	9.50	27
2014-S, Shenandoah National Park (VA), Silver	472,107	77816	12.50	14.00	30
2014-S, Arches National Park (UT)	844,775	77817	4.10	9.50	27
2014-S, Arches National Park (UT), Silver	472,107	77818	12.50	14.00	30
2014-S, Great Sand Dunes National Park (CO)	843,238	77819	4.10	9.50	27
2014-S, Great Sand Dunes National Park (CO), Silver	472,107	77820	12.50	14.00	30

Proof Strikes *(continued)*

	Mintage	GSID	PF-68	PF-69	PF-70
2014-S, Everglades National Park (FL)	856,139	77821	$4.10	$9.50	$27
2014-S, Everglades National Park (FL), Silver	472,107	77822	12.50	14.00	30
2015-S, Homestead National Monument of America (NE)	831,503	77823	4.10	9.50	27
2015-S, Homestead National Monument of America (NE), Silver	490,829	77824	12.50	14.00	30
2015-S, Kisatchie National Forest (LA)	762,407	77825	4.10	9.50	27
2015-S, Kisatchie National Forest (LA), Silver	490,829	77826	12.50	14.00	30
2015-S, Blue Ridge Parkway	762,407	77827	4.10	9.50	27
2015-S, Blue Ridge Parkway, Silver	490,829	77828	12.50	14.00	30
2015-S, Bombay Hook National Wildlife Refugee (DE)	762,407	77829	4.10	9.50	27
2015-S, Bombay Hook National Wildlife Refugee (DE), Silver	490,829	77830	12.50	14.00	30
2015-S, Saratoga National Historical Park (NY)	791,347	77831	4.10	9.50	27
2015-S, Saratoga National Historical Park (NY), Silver	490,829	77832	12.50	14.00	30
2016-S, Shawnee National Forest (IL)	696,564	77833	4.10	9.50	27
2016-S, Shawnee National Forest (IL), Silver	502,039	77834	12.50	14.00	30
2016-S, Cumberland Gap National Historical Park (KY)	666,857	77837	4.10	9.50	27
2016-S, Cumberland Gap National Historical Park (KY), Silver	502,039	77838	12.50	14.00	30
2016-S, Harpers Ferry National Historical Park (WV)	666,857	77839	4.10	9.50	27
2016-S, Harpers Ferry National Historical Park (WV), Silver	502,039	77840	12.50	14.00	30
2016-S, Theodore Roosevelt National Park (ND)	666,857	77841	4.10	9.50	27
2016-S, Theodore Roosevelt National Park (ND), Silver	502,039	77842	12.50	14.00	30
2016-S, Fort Moultrie at Fort Sumter National Monument (SC)	683,741	77835	4.10	9.50	27
2016-S, Fort Moultrie at Fort Sumter National Monument (SC), Silver	502,039	77836	12.50	14.00	30
2017-S, Effigy Mounds National Monument (IA)	692,129	77843	4.10	9.50	27
2017-S, Effigy Mounds National Monument (IA), Silver	496,618	77844	12.50	14.00	30
2017-S, Frederick Douglass National Historic Site (DC)	657,587	77845	4.10	9.50	27
2017-S, Frederick Douglass National Historic Site (DC), Silver	496,618	77846	12.50	14.00	30
2017-S, Ozark National Scenic Riverways (MO)	657,587	77847	4.10	9.50	27
2017-S, Ozark National Scenic Riverways (MO), Silver	496,618	77848	12.50	14.00	30
2017-S, Ellis Island (Statue of Liberty National Monument) (NJ)	657,587	77849	4.10	9.50	27
2017-S, Ellis Island (Statue of Liberty National Monument) (NJ), Silver	496,618	77850	12.50	14.00	30
2017-S, George Rogers Clark National Historical Park (IN)	675,757	77851	4.10	9.50	27
2017-S, George Rogers Clark National Historical Park (IN), Silver	496,618	77852	12.50	14.00	30
2018-S, Pictured Rocks National Lakeshore (MI)	653,176	77853	4.10	9.50	27
2018-S, Pictured Rocks National Lakeshore (MI), Silver	461,048	77854	12.50	14.00	30
2018-S, Pictured Rocks National Lakeshore (MI), Silver, Reverse Proof (a)	199,116	285284	12.50	14.00	30
2018-S, Apostle Islands National Lakeshore (WI)	618,988	77857	4.10	9.50	27
2018-S, Apostle Islands National Lakeshore (WI), Silver	461,048	77858	12.50	14.00	30
2018-S, Apostle Islands National Lakeshore (WI), Silver, Reverse Proof (a)	199,116	285286	12.50	14.00	30
2018-S, Voyageurs National Park (MN)	619,013	77861	4.10	9.50	27
2018-S, Voyageurs National Park (MN), Silver	461,048	77862	12.50	14.00	30
2018-S, Voyageurs National Park (MN), Silver, Reverse Proof (a)	199,116	285288	12.50	14.00	30
2018-S, Cumberland Island National Seashore (GA)	618,725	77859	4.10	9.50	27
2018-S, Cumberland Island National Seashore (GA), Silver	461,048	77860	12.50	14.00	30
2018-S, Cumberland Island National Seashore (GA), Silver, Reverse Proof (a)	199,116	285287	12.50	14.00	30
2018-S, Block Island National Wildlife Refuge (RI)	636,372	77855	4.10	9.50	27
2018-S, Block Island National Wildlife Refuge (RI), Silver	461,048	77856	12.50	14.00	30
2018-S, Block Island National Wildlife Refuge (RI), Silver, Reverse Proof (a)	199,116	285285	12.50	14.00	30

a. Included in the special silver Reverse Proof set issued in 2018 in honor of the 50th anniversary of the San Francisco Mint's first production of Proof coins.

Proof Strikes *(continued)*

	Mintage	GSID	PF-68	PF-69	PF-70
2019-S, Lowell National Historical Park (MA)	780,732	82024	$4.10	$9.50	$27
2019-S, Lowell National Historical Park (MA), Silver	539,510	82025	12.50	14.00	30
2019-S, American Memorial Park (NMI)	712,674	82026	4.10	9.50	27
2019-S, American Memorial Park (NMI), Silver	539,510	82027	12.50	14.00	30
2019-S, San Antonio Missions National Historical Park (TX)	712,743	82030	4.10	9.50	27
2019-S, San Antonio Missions National Historical Park (TX), Silver	539,510	82031	12.50	14.00	30
2019-S, War in the Pacific National Historical Park (Guam)	712,768	82028	4.10	9.50	27
2019-S, War in the Pacific National Historical Park (Guam), Silver	539,510	82029	12.50	14.00	30
2019-S, Frank Church River of No Return Wilderness (IA)	730,874	82032	4.10	9.50	27
2019-S, Frank Church River of No Return Wilderness (IA), Silver	539,510	82033	12.50	14.00	30
2020-S, National Park of American Samoa (AmSam)	574,037	82034	4.10	9.50	27
2020-S, National Park of American Samoa (AmSam) Silver	427,191	82035	12.50	14.00	30
2020-S, Weir Farm National Historic Site (CT)	544,660	82038	4.10	9.50	27
2020-S, Weir Farm National Historic Site (CT), Silver	427,191	82039	12.50	14.00	30
2020-S, Salt River Bay National Historical Park and Ecological Preserve (USVI)	544,515	82040	4.10	9.50	27
2020-S, Salt River Bay National Historical Park and Ecological Preserve (USVI), Silver	427,191	82041	12.50	14.00	30
2020-S, Marsh-Billings-Rockefeller National Historical Park (VT)	544,589	82042	4.10	9.50	27
2020-S, Marsh-Billings-Rockefeller National Historical Park (VT), Silver	427,191	82043	12.50	14.00	30
2020-S, Tallgrass Prairie National Preserve (KS)	561,452	82036	4.10	9.50	27
2020-S, Tallgrass Prairie National Preserve (KS), Silver	427,191	82037	12.50	14.00	30
2021-S, Tuskegee Airmen National Historic Site (AL)		85135	4.10	9.50	27
2021-S, Tuskegee Airmen National Historic Site (AL), Silver		85136	12.50	14.00	30

WASHINGTON, CROSSING THE DELAWARE (2021)

Designers: *John Flanagan and Benjamin Sowards.* **Weight:** *Clad issue—5.67 grams; silver Proofs—6.343 grams.* **Composition:** *Clad issue—a core of pure copper, clad in outer layers of copper-nickel (.750 copper, .250 nickel); silver Proofs—.999 silver, .001 copper (net weight .182 oz. pure silver).* **Diameter:** *24.3 mm.* **Edge:** *Reeded.* **Mints:** *Clad issue—Philadelphia, Denver, and San Francisco.*

Circulation Strike

Proof Strike

History. The America's Beautiful National Parks Quarter Dollar Coin Act of 2008 specified what would happen to the coin after that program ended in 2021: "The reverse of the quarter dollar shall contain an image of General Washington crossing the Delaware River prior to the Battle of Trenton," and the obverse would "revert to the same design containing an image of President Washington" that was used before the State quarters program started in 1999.

Grading Standards

MS-60 to 70 (Mint State). ***Obverse:*** At MS-60, some abrasion and contact marks are evident on the highest-relief areas. At MS-63, abrasion is slight at best, less so at MS-64. An MS-65 coin should display no abrasion or contact marks except under magnification, and MS-66 and higher coins should have none at all. Luster should be full. ***Reverse:*** Check the highest-relief areas of the design. Otherwise, comments are as for the obverse.

MS-67

PF-60 to 70 (Proof). ***Obverse and Reverse:*** These coins are so recent, and as only a few have been cleaned, most approach perfection and can be designated PF-68 to 70, the latter only if no contact marks or other problems can be seen under magnification. A cleaned coin with extensive hairlines would not be collectible for most numismatists and would be classified at a lower level such as PF-60 to 63. Those with lighter hairlines qualify for PF-64 or 65.

PF-70
Deep Cameo

Circulation Strikes

	Mintage	GSID	MS-65	MS-66	MS-67
2021-P, Crossing the Delaware	998,800,000	85132	$0.80	$2.60	$16
2021-D, Crossing the Delaware	1,169,400,000	85133	0.80	2.60	16

Proof Strikes

	Mintage	GSID	PF-68	PF-69	PF-70
2021-S, Crossing the Delaware	512,729	85134	$4.10	$11	$30
2021-S, Crossing the Delaware, Silver	350,323	198054	12.50	14	32

WASHINGTON, AMERICAN WOMEN (2022–2025)

Designers: *Laura Gardin Fraser (obverse); see below for reverse designers.* **Weight:** *Clad issue—5.67 grams; silver Proofs—6.343 grams.* **Composition:** *Clad issue—a core of pure copper, clad in outer layers of copper-nickel (.750 copper, .250 nickel); silver Proofs—.999 silver, .001 copper (net weight .182 oz. pure silver).* **Diameter:** *24.3 mm.* **Edge:** *Reeded.* **Mints:** *Clad issue—Philadelphia, Denver, and San Francisco.*

Reverse Designers:

2022, Maya Angelou. . . . . Emily Damstra
2022, Wilma Mankiller . . . . . . Benjamin Sowards
2022, Nina Otero-Warren. . . . . Chris Costello
2022, Sally Ride . . . . .Elana Hagler
2022, Ali May Wong . . . . Emily Damstra
2023, Bessie Coleman . . . . Chris Costello
2023, Jovita Idar . . . . .John P. McGraw
2023, Edith Kanaka'ole . . . . Emily Damstra
2023, Eleanor Roosevelt . . . . Don Everhart
2023, Maria Tallchief. . . . . Benjamin Sowards
2024, Celia Cruz. . . . . Phebe Hemphill
2024, Mary Edwards Walker. . . . Phebe Hemphill
2024, Patsy Takemoto Mink . . . . .Beth Zaiken
2024, Pauli Murray. . . . . Emily Damstra
2024, Zitkala-Ša . . . . Don Everhart
2025, Ida B. Wells . . . . .Elana Hagler
2025, Juliette Gordon Low . . . . . . Tom Hipschen
2025, Dr. Vera Rubin. . . . . .Christina Hess
2025, Stacey Park Milbern. . . . . .Elana Hagler
2025, Althea Gibson. . . . . Don Everhart

Circulation Strike

Proof Strike

History. The Circulating Collectible Coin Redesign Act of 2020 was signed into law on January 13, 2021, and brought wide-ranging changes to all of America's circulating coins. In particular, it scheduled the quarter dollar as the venue for several new educational coin programs, including the American Women Quarters program. From 2022 to 2025, the quarter commemorates prominent American women and the ratification of the Nineteenth Amendment granting women the right to vote. Five coins are being issued per year, each featuring a new reverse design honoring a woman selected from fields and accomplishments such as "suffrage, civil rights, abolition, government, humanities, science, space, and arts." Circulation strikes are produced at Philadelphia, Denver, and San Francisco, which also produces the clad and silver Proof strikes. For the first year of issue, the subjects are poet Maya Angelou; Dr. Sally Ride, the first American woman in space; Wilma Mankiller, the first woman elected chief of the Cherokee Nation; suffragist and educator Nina Otero-Warren; and Anna May Wong, the first Chinese American film star in Hollywood.

The subject of the obverse design remains a bust of George Washington, but for the duration of the program features a likeness by sculptor Laura Gardin Fraser. In 1932, Fraser submitted her design as a candidate for the new Washington quarter, but John Flanagan's design was chosen instead. Fraser's design, which depicts Washington in profile to the right (as opposed to Flanagan's, which faces left), was later used on the 1999 commemorative for the bicentennial of Washington's death.

Striking and Sharpness. These coins are generally sharply struck on both the obverse and the reverse.

Availability. All modern quarters are readily available in high grades. Typical Mint State coins are MS-63 and 64 with light abrasion. MS-65 and higher coins are in the minority, but enough exist that finding them is easy. Around MS-68 many issues are scarce; higher grades are scarcer still. The S-mintmark coins are proportionally scarce compared to Philadelphia and Denver issues and are not seen in circulation. They are available for direct purchase from the U.S. Mint in their year of issue, and from the secondary market after that.

Proofs. National Park quarter dollar Proofs are made in San Francisco. Through 2018, silver Proofs were .900 fine silver; as of 2019, all regular silver Mint products are .999 fine silver. Proofs are available in clad metal as well as silver strikings. On some Proofs over-polishing of dies has eliminated some details.

Grading Standards

MS-60 to 70 (Mint State). ***Obverse:*** At MS-60, some abrasion and contact marks are evident on the cheek and the high parts of the hair and neck. At MS-63, abrasion is slight at best, and at MS-64 slighter still. At MS-65, the coin should display no abrasion or contact marks except under magnification, and at MS-66 and higher, none at all. Luster should be full. ***Reverse:*** Check the highest-relief areas of the design (these differ from coin to coin). Otherwise, comments are as for the obverse.

MS-67

PF-60 to 70 (Proof). ***Obverse and Reverse:*** These coins are so recent, with so very few having been cleaned, most approach perfection and can be designated PF-68 to 70, the latter only if no contact marks or other problems can be seen under magnification. A cleaned coin with extensive hairlines would not be collectible for most numismatists and would be classified at a lower level such as PF-60 to 63. Those with lighter hairlines qualify for PF-64 or 65.

PF-70
Deep Cameo

2022, Maya Angelou

2022, Dr. Sally Ride

2022, Wilma Mankiller

2022, Nina Otero-Warren

2022, Anna May Wong

2023, Bessie Coleman

2023, Edith Kanaka'ole

2023, Eleanor Roosevelt

2023, Jovita Idar

2023, Maria Tallchief

2024, Dr. Rev. Pauli Murray

2024, Hon. Patsy Takemoto Mink

2024, Dr. Mary Edwards Walker

2024, Celia Cruz

2024, Zitkala-Ša

2025, Ida B. Wells

2025, Juliette Gordon Low

2025, Dr. Vera Rubin

2025, Stacey Park Milbern

2025, Althea Gibson

Circulation Strikes

	Mintage	GSID	MS-65	MS-66	MS-67
American Women Quarter (2022–2025)	**n/a**	**393981**	**$0.60**	**$5.50**	**$27**
2022-P, Maya Angelou	237,600,000	193257	0.60	5.50	27
2022-D, Maya Angelou	258,200,000	193258	0.60	5.50	27
2022-S, Maya Angelou (a)	303,520	198055	4.10	8.00	32
2022-P, Dr. Sally Ride	275,200,000	193260	0.60	5.50	27
2022-D, Dr. Sally Ride	278,000,000	193261	0.60	5.50	27
2022-S, Dr. Sally Ride (a)	304,120	198056	4.10	8.00	32
2022-P, Wilma Mankiller	310,000,000	193262	0.60	5.50	27
2022-D, Wilma Mankiller	296,800,000	193263	0.60	5.50	27
2022-S, Wilma Mankiller (a)	304,640	198057	4.10	8.00	32
2022-P, Nina Otero-Warren	225,000,000	193264	0.60	5.50	27
2022-D, Nina Otero-Warren	219,200,000	193265	0.60	5.50	27
2022-S, Nina Otero-Warren (a)	305,560	198058	4.10	8.00	32

a. Not issued for circulation. From 2012–2021, the San Francisco Mint made Uncirculated S-mintmark quarters of each design in the National Park series. These could be purchased by collectors directly from the U.S. Mint, in bags of 100 or rolls of 40 coins, for a premium above face value.

Circulation Strikes *(continued)*

	Mintage	GSID	MS-65	MS-66	MS-67
2022-P, Anna May Wong	226,800,000	193266	$0.60	$5.50	$27
2022-D, Anna May Wong	240,800,000	193267	0.60	5.50	27
2022-S, Anna May Wong (a)	304,680	198059	4.10	8.00	32
2023-P, Bessie Coleman	302,000,000	199021	0.60	5.50	27
2023-D, Bessie Coleman	317,200,000	199022	0.60	5.50	27
2023-S, Bessie Coleman (a)	500,360	199023	4.10	8.00	32
2023-P, Edith Kanaka'ole	372,800,000	199024	0.60	5.50	27
2023-D, Edith Kanaka'ole	368,600,000	199025	0.60	5.50	27
2023-S, Edith Kanaka'ole (a)	503,400	199026	4.10	8.00	32
2023-P, Eleanor Roosevelt	284,000,000	199027	0.60	5.50	27
2023-D, Eleanor Roosevelt	271,800,000	199028	0.60	5.50	27
2023-S, Eleanor Roosevelt (a)	507,120	199029	4.10	8.00	32
2023-P, Jovita Idar	190,600,000	199030	0.60	5.50	27
2023-D, Jovita Idar	188,000,000	199031	0.60	5.50	27
2023-S, Jovita Idar (a)	503,840	199032	4.10	8.00	32
2023-P, Maria Tallchief	185,800,000	199033	0.60	5.50	27
2023-D, Maria Tallchief	184,800,000	199034	0.60	5.50	27
2023-S, Maria Tallchief (a)	502,200	199035	4.10	8.00	32
2024-P, Reverend Dr. Pauli Murray		346868	0.60	5.50	27
2024-D, Reverend Dr. Pauli Murray		346869	0.60	5.50	27
2024-S, Reverend Dr. Pauli Murray (a)		346870	4.10	8.00	32
2024-P, Hon. Patsy Takemoto Mink		374280	0.60	5.50	27
2024-D, Hon. Patsy Takemoto Mink		374281	0.60	5.50	27
2024-S, Hon. Patsy Takemoto Mink (a)		374282	4.10	8.00	32
2024-P, Dr. Mary Edwards Walker		374283	0.60	5.50	27
2024-D, Dr. Mary Edwards Walker		374284	0.60	5.50	27
2024-S, Dr. Mary Edwards Walker (a)		374285	4.10	8.00	32
2024-P, Celia Cruz		374286	0.60	5.50	27
2024-D, Celia Cruz		374287	0.60	5.50	27
2024-S, Celia Cruz (a)		374288	4.10	8.00	32
2024-P, Zitkala-Ša		374289	0.60	5.50	27
2024-D, Zitkala-Ša		374290	0.60	5.50	27
2024-S, Zitkala-Ša (a)		374291	4.10	8.00	32
2025-P, Ida B. Wells		376293	$0.60	$5.50	$27
2025-D, Ida B. Wells		376294	0.60	5.50	27
2025-S, Ida B. Wells (a)		376295	4.10	8.00	32
2025-P, Juliette Gordon Low		376296	0.60	5.50	27
2025-D, Juliette Gordon Low		376297	0.60	5.50	27
2025-S, Juliette Gordon Low (a)		376298	4.10	8.00	32
2025-P, Dr. Vera Rubin		376299	0.60	5.50	27
2025-D, Dr. Vera Rubin		376300	0.60	5.50	27
2025-S, Dr. Vera Rubin (a)		376301	4.10	8.00	32
2025-P, Stacey Park Milbern		376302	0.60	5.50	27
2025-D, Stacey Park Milbern		376303	0.60	5.50	27
2025-S, Stacey Park Milbern (a)		376304	4.10	8.00	32
2025-P, Althea Gibson		376305	0.60	5.50	27
2025-D, Althea Gibson		376306	0.60	5.50	27
2025-S, Althea Gibson (a)		376307	4.10	8.00	32

a. Not issued for circulation. From 2012–2021, the San Francisco Mint made Uncirculated S-mintmark quarters of each design in the National Park series. These could be purchased by collectors directly from the U.S. Mint, in bags of 100 or rolls of 40 coins, for a premium above face value.

Proof Strikes

	Mintage	GSID	PF-68	PF-69	PF-70
American Women Quarter, Clad (2022–2025), Proof	**n/a**	**393982**	**$5.50**	**$11**	**$30**
American Women Quarter, Silver (2022–2025), Proof	**n/a**	**393983**	**12.50**	**14**	**32**
2022-S, Maya Angelou	442,828	193259	5.50	11	30
2022-S, Maya Angelou, Silver	352,834	198060	12.50	14	32
2022-S, Dr. Sally Ride	442,828	193268	5.50	11	30
2022-S, Dr. Sally Ride, Silver	352,834	198061	12.50	14	32
2022-S, Wilma Mankiller	442,828	193269	5.50	11	30
2022-S, Wilma Mankiller, Silver	352,834	198062	12.50	14	32
2022-S, Nina Otero-Warren	442,828	193270	5.50	11	30
2022-S, Nina Otero-Warren, Silver	352,834	198063	12.50	14	32
2022-S, Anna May Wong	442,828	193271	5.50	11	30
2022-S, Anna May Wong, Silver	352,834	198064	12.50	14	32
2023-S, Bessie Coleman	593,245	199036	5.50	11	30
2023-S, Bessie Coleman, Silver	269,709	199037	12.50	14	32
2023-S, Edith Kanaka'ole	593,245	199038	5.50	11	30
2023-S, Edith Kanaka'ole, Silver	269,709	199039	12.50	14	32
2023-S, Eleanor Roosevelt	593,245	199040	5.50	11	30
2023-S, Eleanor Roosevelt, Silver	269,709	199041	12.50	14	32
2023-S, Jovita Idar	593,245	199042	5.50	11	30
2023-S, Jovita Idar, Silver	269,709	199043	12.50	14	32
2023-S, Maria Tallchief	593,245	199044	5.50	11	30
2023-S, Maria Tallchief, Silver	269,709	199045	12.50	14	32
2024-S, Reverend Dr. Pauli Murray		346871	5.50	11	30
2024-S, Reverend Dr. Pauli Murray, Silver		346872	12.50	14	32
2024-S, Hon. Patsy Takemoto Mink		346873	5.50	11	30
2024-S, Hon. Patsy Takemoto Mink, Silver		346874	12.50	14	32
2024-S, Dr. Mary Edwards Walker		346875	5.50	11	30
2024-S, Dr. Mary Edwards Walker, Silver		346876	12.50	14	32
2024-S, Celia Cruz		346877	5.50	11	30
2024-S, Celia Cruz, Silver		346878	12.50	14	32
2024-S, Zitkala-Ša		346879	5.50	11	30
2024-S, Zitkala-Ša, Silver		346880	12.50	14	32
2025-S, Ida B. Wells		376308	5.50	11	30
2025-S, Ida B. Wells, Silver		376309	12.50	14	32
2025-S, Juliette Gordon Low		370310	5.50	11	30
2025-S, Juliette Gordon Low, Silver		376311	12.50	14	32
2025-S, Dr. Vera Rubin		376312	5.50	11	30
2025-S, Dr. Vera Rubin, Silver		376313	12.50	14	32
2025-S, Stacey Park Milbern		376314	5.50	11	30
2025-S, Stacey Park Milbern, Silver		376315	12.50	14	32
2025-S, Althea Gibson		376316	5.50	11	30
2025-S, Althea Gibson, Silver		376317	12.50	14	32

Half Dollars
1794 to Date

AN OVERVIEW OF HALF DOLLARS

Many hobbyists consider a collection of half dollars to be one of the most satisfying in the American series. The panorama of designs is extensive, ranging from the early Flowing Hair issues of 1794 and 1795 down to classic twentieth-century motifs and the presidential portrait of the present day. The large size of half dollar coins makes them convenient to view and easy to enjoy.

Scan for additional information.

Among the types, the 1794–1795 Flowing Hair half dollar is readily available in circulated grades and rare in Mint State, but at any level is hard to find well struck and without adjustment marks (evidence of where a Mint worker filed an overweight planchet down to proper weight). Most on the market are dated 1795. Careful selection for quality is advised.

The next type, dated 1796–1797 with a Draped Bust obverse and Small Eagle reverse, is the scarcest in the American silver series excepting the 1839 Gobrecht dollar. (However, the latter is available in Proof restrike form, yielding choice and gem examples, so it can be considered in a different category from the circulation-strike 1796–1797 half dollar type.) It might not be possible to be particular, but, finances permitting, a collector should take some time and endeavor to find an example that is sharply struck on both sides. Needle-sharp striking is more of a theory than a practicality, and some compromise in this regard may be necessary.

Half dollars of the 1801–1807 type, with the obverse as preceding but now with the Heraldic Eagle reverse, are plentiful enough in worn grades but somewhat scarce in Mint State. Striking is seldom needle-sharp and ranges from average to very poor. However, there are enough coins in the marketplace that collectors can afford to take their time and seek a sharp strike.

Capped Bust half dollars with a lettered edge, 1807–1836, abound in just about any grade desired. Again, striking is a consideration, and some searching is needed for a high-quality strike. Generally, those in the late 1820s and the 1830s are better struck than are those of earlier dates, the earlier coins being scarcer and more expensive in any event.

THE NUMISMATIST

June 1948

VOLUME LXI • NO. 6

Published Monthly at 1051 N. Broadway, Wichita, Kansas

SIXTY-FIRST YEAR OF CONTINUOUS PUBLICATION

FRANKLIN INSTITUTE CELEBRATES DEBUT OF THE BENJAMIN FRANKLIN HALF-DOLLAR

By ARTHUR SIPE, Philadelphia, Pennsylvania

Philadelphia was paid a high honor on the evening of April 29, 1948, when the new Franklin half-dollar was given its debut at the Franklin Institute.

Mrs. Nellie Tayloe Ross, Director of the United States Mint, is seen here as she presented The Franklin Institute with President Truman's gift of two Benjamin Franklin half-dollars, embedded in plastic. The happy recipient is Dr. Henry Butler Allen, Executive Vice President and Secretary of The Institute. The presentation was made at a commemorative dinner on the eve of the nationwide distribution of the new coin

Members of the Association receive the magazine without additional cost beyond their annual dues of $3.00. Yearly subscription $3.00. Single copy, 25 cents.

Entered as Second Class Matter at the Wichita, Kansas, Post Office under the Act of March 3, 1879.

The release of the Franklin half dollar was announced to the coin-collecting world on the front page of the *Numismatist*, June 1948.

The short-lived type of 1836–1837, Capped Bust with a reeded edge and with the denomination spelled as 50 CENTS, is available easily enough through the high-mintage 1837, but most have problems with the quality of striking. Then comes the 1838–1839 type of the same obverse style, its reverse modified with a slightly different eagle and with the denomination as HALF DOL. Generally these are fairly well struck.

Liberty Seated half dollars of the several styles within the series, 1839–1891, admit of no great rarities for the type collector, save for the 1839, No Drapery, in levels of MS-63 and finer. However, among the earlier types in particular, sharply struck pieces are in the minority. Curiously, the most readily available Mint State Liberty Seated half dollars also are the lowest-mintage issues, the dates 1879 and later, as these were recognized as desirable at the time of issue and were widely saved.

Barber half dollars were not popular in their time, and while Proofs exist in proportion to their production figures, few circulation-strike coins were saved by collectors and Mint State examples are quite scarce today. In fact, as a type, a Barber half dollar dated 1900 or later in Mint State is the scarcest of all silver issues of that century. Well-struck MS-63 and better Barber half dollars, with the upper-right corner of the shield and the leg at lower right showing full details, are significantly scarcer than generally realized.

Liberty Walking half dollars, minted from 1916 to 1947, are plentiful in all grades. Again, some attention should be made to striking sharpness, which makes the search become more intense. Fortunately there are countless thousands of MS-63 and finer coins of the 1940s on the market, giving collectors a wide choice. Then come Franklin half dollars, made only from 1948 to 1963, with representative coins easy enough to acquire in about any grade desired. Kennedy half dollars exist in several varieties, all of which are available without any problem. Among these and other modern coins care needs to be taken for value received versus price paid. Modern issues in, for example, MS-65 and 66, selected for quality, are for many collectors preferable to MS-69 or 70 coins offered at a much higher price.

For the Collector and Investor: Half Dollars as a Specialty

Many collectors over the years have pursued half dollars by date, mint, and variety. Except for the series of copper cents, half dollars are the most generally available coins over a nearly continuous span, making them possible to collect for reasonable cost. Also, enough die varieties exist that this can form another focus of interest and importance.

In general, the half dollars of the early era form a concentration in themselves. Die varieties can be attributed by Overton numbers, as listed by Al C. Overton in his immensely popular *Early Half Dollar Die Varieties 1794–1836*. Glenn R. Peterson's book, *The Ultimate Guide to Attributing Bust Half Dollars*, is also useful in this regard. The John Reich Collectors Society (www.jrcs.org) publishes the *John Reich Journal* and serves as a forum for the exchange of information, updates, news about die varieties, and the like.

Among rarities in the early years, the 1796 and 1797 half dollars with the Draped Bust obverse and Small Eagle reverse are perhaps the most famous, needed for variety collections as well as one example for a type set. Variety enthusiasts aspire to get two of 1796—one with 15 stars on the obverse and the other with 16 stars—plus the 1797.

Draped Bust half dollars from 1801 through 1807 have a number of rare die varieties (as listed by Overton), but the basic varieties are easy enough to find. The 1805, 5 Over 4, overdate is particularly popular, as there was no "perfect date" 1804, and this is the closest collectors can come to it.

A vast and interesting field in early American numismatics is that of the Capped Bust half dollar, 1807–1836, with a lettered edge. Several hundred different die combinations exist, and many collectors are active in their pursuit, using the Overton book as a road map. All the major varieties are readily collectible except the 1817, 7 Over 4, overdate, of which only about a half dozen exist. The 1815, 5 Over 2, is considered the key issue among the specific dates (rather than varieties of dates). The majority of these survive in VF grade, not often lower and not often higher either—an interesting situation. During the 1820s vast quantities of these were transferred among banks, not wearing down from as much hand-to-hand circulation as they might have otherwise. While many if not most of the varieties listed herein can be obtained in Mint State, most collectors opt for VF or EF, these grades showing the necessary details but also permitting a budget to be stretched to include more varieties, rather than just a few high-grade pieces. Choice and gem examples can be found here and there, and are most plentiful among the later dates.

Among the Capped Bust half dollars of reduced size, 1836–1837, the 1836 is a key date, with fewer than 5,000 believed to have been minted. The next type, 1838 and 1839, Capped Bust, reeded edge, with a modified eagle on the reverse, includes the famous 1838-O rarity, of which only 20 are said to have been struck (per a note published in 1894 in the catalog of the Friesner Collection). These have a proof-like surface. Interestingly, they were not struck until 1839. In the same year, 1839-O half dollars were also struck, to the extensive quantity of 178,976 pieces; they are unusual as the mintmark is on the obverse, an odd placement for the era.

Within the series of Liberty Seated half dollars, collectors generally seek the varieties listed herein, although certain dedicated specialists will consult the *Complete Guide to Liberty Seated Half Dollars*, by Randy Wiley and Bill Bugert—a volume that delineates many interesting features, including the number of different reeds on the edges of certain coins.

Among Liberty Seated half dollars there is just one "impossible" rarity, that being the 1853-O coin without arrows at the date. Only three exist, and each shows extensive wear. At the San Francisco Mint, half dollars were first struck in 1855, and at the Carson City Mint in 1870. Generally, large quantities were minted of most dates and mintmark varieties of Liberty Seated half dollars, making them readily obtainable today. Except for the later dates, 1879 to 1891, Mint State pieces are generally scarce, gems especially so. Many specialists in half dollars belong to the Liberty Seated Collectors Club (LSCC, at www.lsccweb.org) and receive its magazine, *The Gobrecht Journal*.

Proof Liberty Seated halves can be collected by date sequence from 1858 onward. Survivors exist in proportion to their mintage quantities. Generally those before the mid-1870s often are found cleaned or hairlined, and more care is needed in selecting choice examples than is necessary for the later dates.

Barber half dollars were made continuously from 1892 through 1915, in such quantities that today there are no great rarities in the series. However, a number of issues are quite scarce, even in well-worn grades, and in MS-63 and better many are difficult to find. These coins had little honor in the era in which they were issued, and few numismatists saved them. Proofs were made each year from 1892 to 1915 and today can be obtained in proportion to their mintages. However, those of 1914 and 1915 are hard to find with choice, original surfaces—decades ago a collector hoarded these two dates and polished the ones in his possession.

Liberty Walking half dollars are popular to collect by date and mint. Scarce varieties include the 1917-S with obverse mintmark, the three issues of 1921, and the low mintage 1938-D, although the latter is not inordinately expensive. Mint State pieces are most readily available for 1916 and 1917, and then especially so in the 1930s and 1940s. Striking quality can be a problem, particularly for issues of the mid-1920s and also the later dates. For example, with a needle-sharp strike the 1923-S is an extreme rarity. Among later coins the 1940-S and 1941-S often are weakly struck.

Franklin half dollars minted from 1948 through 1963 have been very popular in recent decades. The complete series of dates and mintmarks is short and contains no scarce or rare pieces in higher grades such as MS-63 and 64. However, if you consider the element of sharp striking, usually defined as Full Bell Lines (FBL) on the reverse, certain otherwise common dates become elusive. Proofs of most years can also be readily collected.

Kennedy half dollars are easily enough collected, and so many have been made by this time that nearly 200 date-and-mintmark combinations extend from 1964 to present, including a gold version that marks the design's 50th anniversary. The wise collector will select coins that have a meeting point between a high grade such as MS-65 or 66 (or equivalent Proofs) and a reasonable price.

EXPLORING VARIETIES

The early editions of this catalog, by Al C. Overton, introduced Overton numbers, which are the core attribution system for Bust half dollars. Each number marks a die marriage, and collectors, dealers, and grading services all use these designations. Overton numbers are among the most widely used variety references in U.S. numismatics.

Parsley, Donald L. *Early Half Dollar Die Varieties 1794–1836.* Fifth edition. Murietta, CA: 2014.

EXPLORING VARIETIES

This is the main reference for Liberty Seated half dollars, covering issues by date and mintmark along with major varieties. Its WB numbers are assigned for the most significant varieties. Later publications by Bill Bugert (lsccweb.org/Bill-Bugert-Books) provide a near-complete die-variety analysis of the entire Liberty Seated half dollar series.

Wiley, Randy, and Bill Bugert. *The Complete Guide to Liberty Seated Half Dollars.* Virginia Beach, VA: 1993.

FLOWING HAIR (1794–1795)

Designer: *Robert Scot.* **Weight:** *13.48 grams.*
Composition: *.8924 silver, .1076 copper.* **Diameter:** *Approximately 32.5 mm.*
Edge: *FIFTY CENTS OR HALF A DOLLAR with decorations between the words.* **Mint:** *Philadelphia.*

History. The Flowing Hair design inaugurated the half-dollar denomination. They were immediately popular, as was evident in 1795, when many depositors of silver at the Philadelphia Mint asked for half dollars in return. The same motif was used on half dimes and silver dollars of the same years. Early half dollars have been extensively collected by die varieties, of which many exist for most dates. Valuations given below are in each case for the most readily available variety; scarcer ones, as listed by Overton, generally command higher prices.

Striking and Sharpness. Many have problems of one sort or another, including adjustment marks from the planchet being filed down to proper weight and mushy denticles. On the obverse, check the hair details and the stars. On the reverse, check the breast of the eagle in particular. As with other silver coins of this design, it may not be possible to find a *needle-sharp* example, but with some extensive searching a fairly decent strike can be obtained. Sharp striking and excellent eye appeal add to the value dramatically. However, very few 1794 and 1795 halves are uniformly sharp on both sides.

Availability. Probably 3,500 to 6,000 circulated Flowing Hair half dollars exist. Most are dated 1795, the 1794 being considered a rare date (though not among the great U.S. coin rarities). Typical grades are Good to Fine. EF and AU grades are elusive in regard to the total population. Probably 100 or so could be graded MS (nearly all of them 1795). Unlike half dollars of the 1796–1797 type, none of these are known to have been made with prooflike surfaces.

Grading Standards

MS-63

MS-60 to 70 (Mint State). ***Obverse:*** At MS-60, some abrasion and contact marks are evident, most noticeably on the cheek and in the fields. This denomination, heavier than the half dime of the same design, was more susceptible to contact and other outside influences. A typical half dollar certified at MS-60 or 61 today might well have been designated as About Uncirculated a generation ago. Luster is present, but may be dull or lifeless, and interrupted in patches, perhaps as much from old cleaning as from contact the coin may have received. At MS-63, contact marks are very few, and abrasion is present, but not as noticeable. An MS-65 coin has no abrasion, and contact marks are very few. Luster should be full and rich. Higher grades are seldom seen in this type, but are defined in theory by having fewer marks as perfection is approached. ***Reverse:*** Comments apply as for the obverse, except that abrasion and contact marks are most noticeable on the eagle at the center. This area is often lightly struck, so in all grades do not mistake weak striking for actual wear. Knowledge of specific die varieties is helpful in this regard. The field area is small and is protected by lettering and the wreath, and in any given grade shows fewer marks than on the obverse.

Illustrated coin: This is a well-struck example with superb eye appeal.

AU-50, 53, 55, 58 (About Uncirculated). ***Obverse:*** Light wear is seen on the hair area immediately to the left of the face and above the forehead, on the cheek, and, to a lesser extent, on the top of the neck truncation, more so at AU-50 than at AU-53 or 55. An AU-58 coin has minimal traces of wear. An AU-50 coin has luster in protected areas among the stars and letters, with little in the open fields or on the portrait. At AU-58, much luster is present in the fields but is worn away on the highest parts of the motifs. ***Reverse:*** Light wear is seen on the eagle's body and the upper part of both wings. On well-struck pieces the details of the wing features are excellent. At AU-50, detail is lost in some feathers in this area. However, striking can play a part, as some coins were weakly struck to begin with. Light wear is seen on the wreath and lettering, but is harder to discern. Luster is the best key to actual wear. This will range from perhaps 20 percent remaining in protected areas (at AU-50) to nearly full mint bloom (at AU-58), although among certified coins the amounts of luster can vary widely.

AU-55

Illustrated coin: Significant luster remains in protected areas on this attractive early half dollar.

EF-40, 45 (Extremely Fine). ***Obverse:*** More wear is evident on the portrait, especially on the hair to the left of and above the forehead, and in the back below the LI of LIBERTY. The tip of the neck truncation shows flatness, and the cheek is worn. Excellent detail remains in low-relief areas of the hair. The stars show wear, as do the date and letters. Luster, if present at all, is minimal and in protected areas. ***Reverse:*** The eagle shows more wear on the body and on the tops of the wings. Interior wing detail is good on most coins (depending on the variety and the striking), and the tail feathers can be discerned. Additional wear is on the wreath and letters, but many details are present. Some luster may be seen in protected areas and if present is slightly more abundant than on the obverse.

EF-40

Illustrated coin: Note some lightness of the stars at the right and at the reverse center, as struck. The scrape on the reverse below the ribbon knot was mentioned by the cataloger in an auction offering.

VF-20

VF-20, 30 (Very Fine). ***Obverse:*** The hair is well worn at VF-20, less so at VF-30, and is most noticeable in the upper part of the head, the area above the level of the eye, and extending to the back. The strands are blended as to be heavy. The cheek shows only slight relief, and the tip of the neck truncation is flat. The stars have more wear, making them appear larger (an optical illusion). Scattered marks are common on half dollars at this level and below, and should be mentioned if particularly serious. ***Reverse:*** The body of the eagle shows few if any feathers, while the wings have perhaps a quarter or a third of the feathers visible depending on the strike, with sharper strikes having up to half visible (as PCGS suggests). *Photograde* and the ANA grading standards suggest half of the feathers on all, which may be the case on coins that were well struck to begin with. The leaves lack detail and are in outline form. Scattered, non-disfiguring marks are normal for this and lower grades. Any major defects should be noted separately.

Illustrated coin: On this variety in this grade, the denticles are especially prominent on each side. Such aspects vary from coin to coin.

F-12

F-12, 15 (Fine). ***Obverse:*** Wear is more extensive than on the preceding, with less hair visible. The ear position can be seen, as can the eye. The cheek is nearly flat, and the stars appear larger. The rim is distinct and most denticles remain visible. ***Reverse:*** Wear is more extensive. Now, feather details are fewer, mostly remaining on the wing to the left. The wreath and lettering are more worn, and the rim is usually weak in areas, although most denticles can be seen.

VG-8

VG-8, 10 (Very Good). ***Obverse:*** The portrait is mostly seen in outline form, with most hair strands gone save for an area centered behind the neck. The hair tips at the lower left are clear. The eye location is barely discernible. The stars appear larger still and often quite bold, again an illusion. The rim is weak in areas. LIBERTY and the date are readable and usually full, although some letters may be weak at their tops. ***Reverse:*** The eagle is mostly an outline, although traces of the separation between the body and the right wing can sometimes be seen. The rim is worn, as are the letters, with some weak, but the motto is readable. On many coins the rim remains fairly prominent.

Illustrated coin: Note a spot, a tiny edge bruise, and some adjustment marks. A cataloger mentioned that "the top of the obverse is slightly soft due to axial misalignment"—a technical note. On any half dollar of this era, knowledge of the varieties and peculiarities of striking is useful.

G-6

G-4, 6 (Good). ***Obverse:*** Wear is more extensive, and some stars may be missing or only partially visible. The head is an outline, although a few elements of thick hair strands may be seen. The rim is well worn or even missing. LIBERTY is worn, and parts of some letters may be missing, but elements of all should be readable. The date is readable, but worn. ***Reverse:*** The eagle is flat and discernible in outline form. The wreath is well worn. Some of the letters may be partly missing. At this level some "averaging" can be done. If the letters are stronger than usual in one area, but some are missing in another area, the coin can still qualify as G-4. Often on this type in lower grades the reverse is more detailed than the obverse.

AG-3

AG-3 (About Good). ***Obverse:*** Wear is very extensive. The head is in outline form (perhaps partly blended into the field). LIBERTY is mostly gone. The date, while readable, may be partially worn away. Some stars are missing. ***Reverse:*** The reverse is well worn, with parts of the wreath and lettering very weak or even missing. The details that remain and those that do not are often dependent on the particular die variety.

Circulation Strikes

	Mintage	GSID	AG-3	G-4	VG-8	F-12	VF-20	EF-40	AU-50	MS-60	MS-63
Flowing Hair (1794–1795)	**n/a**	**72408**	**$1,000**	**$1,600**	**$2,250**	**$2,900**	**$4,000**	**$7,000**	**$13,000**	**$42,000**	**$138,000**
1794	23,464	6118	2,750	3,500	4,750	8,000	13,000	31,000	69,500	240,000	420,000
	Auctions: $120,000, PCGS AU-58 SBG 08/24; $287,500, PCGS AU-58 SBG 08/24										
↳1794, O-101	*	193693	2,750	3,500	4,750	8,000	13,000	31,000	69,500	240,000	420,000
	Auctions: $264,000, PCGS MS-61 SBG 08/25										
↳1794, O-101a	*	193694	2,750	3,500	4,750	8,000	13,000	31,000	69,500	240,000	420,000
	Auctions: $1,800,000, PCGS MS-64 HA 01/23										
↳1794, O-102	*	193695	—	—	14,500	21,500	36,000	—	—	—	—
↳1794, O-103	*	193696	3,300	4,200	5,750	9,500	15,500	37,500	83,500	288,000	504,000
↳1794, O-104	*	193697	3,000	3,850	5,250	8,750	14,500	34,500	76,500	264,000	462,000
↳1794, O-104a	*	193698	3,300	4,200	5,750	9,500	15,500	37,500	83,500	288,000	504,000
↳1794, O-105	*	193699	3,000	3,850	5,250	8,750	14,500	34,500	76,500	264,000	462,000
	Auctions: $192,000, PCGS AU-58 HA 08/18										
↳1794, O-105a	*	193700	3,300	4,200	5,750	9,500	15,500	37,500	83,500	288,000	504,000
↳1794, O-106	*	193701	3,300	4,200	5,750	9,500	15,500	37,500	83,500	288,000	504,000
↳1794, O-106a	*	193702	—	—	—	—	—	—	—	—	—
↳1794, O-107	*	193703	3,300	4,200	5,750	9,500	15,500	37,500	83,500	288,000	504,000
↳1794, O-108	*	193704	—	10,000	—	—	—	48,000	—	—	—
↳1794, O-109	*	193705	—	—	—	—	—	—	—	—	—
	Auctions: $705,000, NGC VF-25 HA 04/15										
↳1794, O-110	*	193706	—	12,500	—	—	24,000	—	76,500	—	—
↳1794, O-111	*	193707	—	—	—	—	—	—	—	—	—

* Included in number above.

1795, Two Leaves Under Each Wing

1795, Three Leaves Under Each Wing

Circulation Strikes

	Mintage	GSID	AG-3	G-4	VG-8	F-12	VF-20	EF-40	AU-50	MS-60	MS-63
1795, 2 Leaves Under Each Wing	299,680	6119	$1,000	$1,600	$2,250	$2,900	$4,000	$7,000	$13,000	$42,000	$138,000
	Auctions: $176,250, PCGS MS-63 LGND 09/16										
↳1795, 2 Leaves Under Each Wing, O-101	*	194037	—	—	12,500	15,000	18,000	—	—	—	—
↳1795, 2 Leaves Under Each Wing, O-102	*	194038	1,000	1,600	2,250	2,900	4,000	7,000	13,000	42,000	138,000
	Auctions: $102,000, PCGS MS-62 HA 01/24										
↳1795, 2 Leaves Under Each Wing, O-102a	*	194039	—	—	—	3,750	5,250	9,000	—	—	—
↳1795, 2 Leaves Under Each Wing, O-103	*	194040	1,200	1,950	2,700	3,450	4,800	8,500	16,000	50,500	165,500
↳1795, 2 Leaves Under Each Wing, O-103a	*	194041	1,200	1,950	2,700	3,450	4,800	8,500	16,000	50,500	165,500
↳1795, 2 Leaves Under Each Wing, O-104	*	194042	1,100	1,800	2,500	3,150	4,400	7,750	14,500	46,000	152,000
↳1795, 2 Leaves Under Each Wing, O-105	*	194043	1,000	1,600	2,250	2,900	4,000	7,000	13,000	42,000	138,000
↳1795, 2 Leaves Under Each Wing, O-105a	*	194044	1,100	1,800	2,500	3,150	4,400	7,750	14,500	46,000	152,000
↳1795, 2 Leaves Under Each Wing, O-106	*	194045	1,200	1,950	2,700	3,450	4,800	8,500	16,000	50,500	165,500
↳1795, 2 Leaves Under Each Wing, O-107	*	194046	1,250	2,100	2,900	3,750	5,250	9,000	17,000	54,500	179,500
↳1795, 2 Leaves Under Each Wing, O-107a	*	194047	1,200	1,950	2,700	3,450	4,800	8,500	16,000	50,500	165,500
↳1795, 2 Leaves Under Each Wing, O-108	*	194048	1,100	1,800	2,500	3,150	4,400	7,750	14,500	46,000	152,000
↳1795, 2 Leaves Under Each Wing, O-108a	*	194049	1,100	1,800	2,500	3,150	4,400	7,750	14,500	46,000	138,000
	Auctions: $114,000, PCGS MS-63 HA 04/25										
↳1795, 2 Leaves Under Each Wing, O-109	*	194050	1,100	1,800	2,500	3,150	4,400	7,750	14,500	46,000	152,000
↳1795, 2 Leaves Under Each Wing, O-110	*	194051	1,000	1,600	2,250	2,900	4,000	7,000	13,000	42,000	138,000
↳1795, 2 Leaves Under Each Wing, O-110a	*	194052	1,100	1,800	2,500	3,150	4,400	7,750	14,500	46,000	152,000
	Auctions: $129,250, PCGS MS-63 HA 08/14										
↳1795, 2 Leaves Under Each Wing, O-114	*	194057	1,250	2,100	2,900	3,750	5,250	9,000	17,000	54,500	179,500
↳1795, 2 Leaves Under Each Wing, O-115	*	194058	1,100	1,800	2,500	3,150	4,400	7,750	14,500	46,000	152,000
↳1795, 2 Leaves Under Each Wing, O-116	*	194059	1,000	1,600	2,250	2,900	4,000	7,000	13,000	42,000	138,000
↳1795, 2 Leaves Under Each Wing, O-117	*	194060	1,000	1,600	2,250	2,900	4,000	7,000	13,000	42,000	138,000
	Auctions: $552,000, PCGS MS-65 HA 02/21										
↳1795, 2 Leaves Under Each Wing, O-117a	*	194061	1,000	1,600	2,250	2,900	4,000	7,000	13,000	42,000	138,000
↳1795, 2 Leaves Under Each Wing, O-119	*	194063	1,000	1,600	2,250	2,900	4,000	7,000	13,000	42,000	138,000
	Auctions: $240,000, PCGS MS-64 SBG 08/24										
↳1795, 2 Leaves Under Each Wing, O-120	*	194064	1,250	2,100	2,900	3,750	5,250	9,000	17,000	54,500	179,500
↳1795, 2 Leaves, Y Over Star, O-121	*	194065	1,100	1,800	2,500	3,150	4,400	7,750	14,500	46,000	152,000
	Auctions: $234,000, PCGS MS-64 HA 08/23										
↳1795, 2 Leaves, Y Over Star, O-121a	*	194066	1,200	1,950	2,700	3,450	4,800	8,500	16,000	50,500	165,500
	Auctions: $199,750, PCGS MS-64 SBG 05/15										
↳1795, 2 Leaves Under Each Wing, O-122	*	194067	1,200	1,950	2,700	3,450	4,800	8,500	16,000	50,500	165,500
↳1795, 2 Leaves Under Each Wing, O-123	*	194068	—	—	—	—	—	—	—	—	—
↳1795, 2 Leaves Under Each Wing, O-123a	*	194479	—	—	—	—	—	—	—	—	—
↳1795, 2 Leaves Under Each Wing, O-124	*	194069	1,200	1,950	2,700	3,450	4,800	8,500	16,000	50,500	165,500
↳1795, 2 Leaves Under Each Wing, O-125	*	194070	1,100	1,800	2,500	3,150	4,400	7,750	14,500	46,000	152,000
↳1795, 2 Leaves, Second S Over D, O-129	*	194076	1,200	1,950	2,700	3,450	4,800	8,500	16,000	50,500	165,500
	Auctions: $141,000, PCGS MS-63 HA 04/15										
↳1795, 2 Leaves, Second S Over D, O-129a	*	194077	1,250	2,100	2,900	3,750	5,250	9,000	17,000	54,500	179,500

* Included in number above.

1795, Normal Date

1795, Recut Date

Circulation Strikes

	Mintage	GSID	AG-3	G-4	VG-8	F-12	VF-20	EF-40	AU-50	MS-60	MS-63
↳1795, 2 Leaves Under Each Wing, O-130	*	194078	$1,200	$1,950	$2,700	$3,450	$4,800	$8,500	$16,000	$50,500	$165,500
↳1795, 2 Leaves, Silver Plug, O-130	*	194079	—	39,000	—	—	—	—	—	—	—
↳1795, 2 Leaves Under Each Wing, O-131	*	194080	1,100	1,800	2,500	3,150	4,400	7,750	14,500	46,000	152,000
	Auctions: $348,000, PCGS MS-64 HA 01/23										
↳1795, 2 Leaves Under Each Wing, O-132	*	194081	—	—	—	—	—	—	—	—	—
↳1795, 2 Leaves Under Each Wing, O-133	*	194082	—	—	—	—	—	—	—	—	—
1795, 3 Leaves Under Each Wing, 3 Leaves	*	6120	1,600	2,000	2,600	5,000	7,500	20,000	36,000	63,000	—
↳1795, Recut Date, 3 Leaves, O-111	*	194053	1,600	2,000	2,600	5,000	7,500	20,000	36,000	63,000	—
1795, Small Head	*	6123	1,100	1,800	2,500	4,700	8,000	15,500	29,000	—	240,000
↳1795, Small Head, Silver Plug	*	6122	—	—	—	—	—	—	—	—	—
↳1795, Small Head, O-126	*	194071	1,100	1,800	2,500	4,700	8,000	15,500	29,000	—	240,000
↳1795, Small Head, O-126a	*	194072	1,100	1,800	2,500	4,700	8,000	15,500	29,000	—	240,000
	Auctions: $528,000, PCGS MS-63 HA 11/20										
↳1795, Small Head, O-127	*	194073	1,250	2,050	2,850	5,500	9,250	18,000	33,000	—	—
↳1795, Small Head, O-127a	*	194074	1,250	2,050	2,850	5,500	9,250	18,000	33,000	—	—
↳1795, Small Head, O-128	*	194075	1,200	1,950	2,700	5,250	9,000	17,000	31,500	—	—
↳1795, Small Head, Silver Plug, O-128 (a)	*	193708	—	—	—	—	—	—	—	—	—
1795, Silver Plug	*	6121	—	36,000	45,000	55,000	—	—	—	—	—
1795, Recut Date, 2 Leaves	*	6226	1,000	1,600	2,250	2,900	4,700	12,500	20,500	—	—
↳1795, Recut Date, 2 Leaves, O-112	*	194054	1,000	1,600	2,250	2,900	4,700	12,500	20,500	—	—
1795, A Over E in STATES	*	81055	1,100	1,600	2,700	3,450	4,400	8,500	16,000	48,500	138,000
↳1795, 2 Leaves, A Over E in STATES, O-113	*	194055	1,200	1,800	2,950	3,800	4,850	9,250	17,500	53,000	152,000
↳1795, 2 Leaves, A Over E in STATES, O-113a	*	194056	1,100	1,600	2,700	3,450	4,400	8,500	16,000	48,500	138,000

* Included in number above. **a.** Varieties of 1795 are known with the final S in STATES over a D; with the A in STATES over an E; and with the Y in LIBERTY over a star. All are scarce. Some 1794 and 1795 half dollars were weight-adjusted by insertion of a silver plug in the center of the blank planchet before the coin was struck.

DRAPED BUST, SMALL EAGLE REVERSE (1796–1797)

Designer: *Robert Scot.* **Weight:** *13.48 grams.*
Composition: *.8924 silver, .1076 copper.* **Diameter:** *Approximately 32.5 mm.*
Edge: *FIFTY CENTS OR HALF A DOLLAR with decorations between words.* **Mint:** *Philadelphia.*

History. Robert Scot's Draped Bust design is similar to that used on the half dime, dime, quarter, and silver dollar of this era. In 1796 and 1797 there was little demand for half dollars and the combined mintage for the two years was therefore low. Among design types of U.S. silver coins made in circulation-strike format this is the Holy Grail—a classic rarity, with no common date in the series.

Striking and Sharpness. On the obverse, check the hair details and the stars. On the reverse, first check the breast of the eagle, but examine other areas as well. Also check the denticles on both sides. Look especially for coins that do not have significant adjustment marks (from an overweight planchet being filed down to correct specifications). Coins of this denomination are on average better struck than are half dimes, dimes, quarters (which have reverse problems), and dollars in the Draped Bust suite.

Availability. Examples are rare in any grade—survivors likely number only in the hundreds of coins. MS examples are particularly rare, and when seen are nearly always dated 1796. Some of these have partially prooflike surfaces. Any half dollar of this type has strong market demand.

Grading Standards

MS-66

MS-60 to 70 (Mint State). ***Obverse:*** At MS-60, some abrasion and contact marks are evident, most noticeably on the cheek, the drapery at the shoulder, and the right field. Also check the hair to the left of the forehead. Luster is present, but may be dull or lifeless, and interrupted in patches. At MS-63, contact marks are few, and abrasion is hard to detect, although this type is sometimes graded liberally due to its rarity. An MS-65 coin has no abrasion, and contact marks are so minute as to require magnification. Luster should be full and rich. Coins graded above MS-65 are more theoretical than actual for this type, although some notable pieces have crossed the auction block. These are defined by having fewer marks as perfection is approached. ***Reverse:*** Comments apply as for the obverse, except that abrasion and contact marks are most noticeable on the eagle at the center, a situation that should be evaluated by considering the original striking (which can be quite sharp, but with many exceptions). The field area is small and is protected by lettering and the wreath, and in any given grade shows fewer marks than on the obverse.

Illustrated coin: This superb gem has prooflike surfaces.

AU-50, 53, 55, 58 (About Uncirculated). ***Obverse:*** Light wear is seen on the hair area above the ear and extending to the left of the forehead, on the ribbon, and on the drapery at the shoulder, more so at AU-50 than at AU-53 or 55. An AU-58 coin has minimal traces of wear. An AU-50 coin has luster in protected areas among the stars and letters, with little in the open fields or on the portrait. At AU-58, most luster is present in the fields, but is worn away on the highest parts of the motifs. ***Reverse:*** Light wear is seen on the eagle's body and the edges of the wings. Light wear is seen on the wreath and lettering. Luster is the best key to actual wear. This ranges from perhaps 20 percent remaining in protected areas (at AU-50) to nearly full mint bloom (at AU-58).

AU-50

EF-40, 45 (Extremely Fine). ***Obverse:*** More wear is evident on the upper hair area, particularly to the left of the forehead and also below the LI of LIBERTY, in the ribbon, and on the drapery and bosom. Excellent detail remains in low-relief areas of the hair. The stars show wear as do the date and letters. Luster, if present at all, is minimal and in protected areas. ***Reverse:*** The eagle shows more wear, this being the focal point to check. Many feathers remain on the interior areas of the wings. Additional wear is on the wreath and letters, but many details are present. Some luster may be seen in protected areas and if present is slightly more abundant than on the obverse.

EF-40

VF-20, 30 (Very Fine). ***Obverse:*** The higher-relief areas of hair are well worn at VF-20, less so at VF-30. The drapery and bosom show extensive wear. The stars have more wear. ***Reverse:*** The body of the eagle shows few if any feathers, while the wings have about half or more of the feathers visible, depending on the strike. The leaves lack most detail and are outlined. Scattered, non-disfiguring marks are normal for this and lower grades; major defects should be noted separately.

VF-20

F-12, 15 (Fine). ***Obverse:*** Wear is more extensive than on a Very Fine coin, particularly noticeable on the hair, face, and bosom. The stars appear larger (an optical illusion). About half the hair detail remains, most noticeably behind the neck and shoulder. The rim may be partially worn away and blend into the field, but on many coins it remains intact. ***Reverse:*** Wear is more extensive. Now, feather details are diminished, with fewer than half remaining on the wings. The wreath and lettering are worn further, and the rim is usually weak in areas, but most denticles can be seen.

F-15

VG-8, 10 (Very Good). ***Obverse:*** The portrait is mostly seen in outline form, with most hair strands gone, although there is some definition at the back of the hair and behind the shoulder. The ear is barely discernible and the eye is fairly distinct. The stars appear larger still, again an illusion. The rim is weak in areas, but shows most denticles. LIBERTY and the date are readable and usually full, although some letters may be weak at their tops. ***Reverse:*** The eagle is mostly an outline, with parts blending into the field (on lighter strikes). The rim is worn, as are the letters, with some weak, but the motto is readable.

VG-10

G-4, 6 (Good). ***Obverse:*** Wear is more extensive, and some stars may be partly missing. The head is an outline. The eye is visible only in outline form. The rim is well worn or even missing in areas, but many denticles remain. LIBERTY is worn. The letters and date are weak but fully readable. ***Reverse:*** The eagle is flat and discernible in outline form, and may be blending into the field. The wreath is well worn. Some of the letters may be partly missing. At this level some "averaging" can be done. If the letters are stronger than usual in one area, but some are missing in another area, the coin can still qualify as G-4.

G-4

AG-3 (About Good). ***Obverse:*** Wear is so extensive that the coin is barely identifiable. The head is in outline form. LIBERTY is mostly gone; same for the stars. The date, while readable, may be partially worn away. ***Reverse:*** The reverse is well worn, with parts of the wreath and lettering missing. On most coins the reverse shows more wear than the obverse.

AG-3

1796, 15 Stars

1796, 16 Stars

Circulation Strikes

	Mintage	GSID	AG-3	G-4	VG-8	F-12	VF-20	EF-40	AU-50	MS-60	MS-63
Draped Bust, Small Eagle Reverse (1796–1797)	**n/a**	**72409**	**$29,000**	**$33,500**	**$41,000**	**$47,000**	**$57,500**	**$103,000**	**$150,000**	**$288,000**	**$384,000**
1796, 15 Stars	3,918	6124	29,000	33,500	41,000	47,000	57,500	103,000	150,000	288,000	384,000
	Auctions: $373,750, NGC MS-63 HA 02/08										
↳1796, 15 Stars, O-101	*	194083	29,000	33,500	41,000	47,000	57,500	103,000	150,000	288,000	384,000
	Auctions: $108,000, PCGS VF-30 HA 01/25; $312,000, PCGS MS-62 SBG 01/25										
1796, 16 Stars	*	6125	29,000	33,500	41,000	47,000	57,500	103,000	150,000	288,000	384,000
	Auctions: $470,000, NGC MS-63 HA 11/13										
↳1796, 16 Stars, O-102	*	194084	29,000	33,500	41,000	47,000	57,500	103,000	150,000	288,000	384,000
	Auctions: $102,000, PCGS VF35 HA 01/25; $1,800,000, PCGS MS-66 HA 01/25										
1797, 15 Stars	*	6127	29,000	33,500	41,000	47,000	57,500	103,000	150,000	288,000	384,000
	Auctions: $282,000, PCGS MS-63 HA 06/14										
↳1797, 15 Stars, O-101	*	193709	29,000	33,500	41,000	47,000	57,500	103,000	150,000	288,000	384,000
↳1797, 15 Stars, O-101a	*	193710	29,000	33,500	41,000	47,000	57,500	103,000	150,000	288,000	384,000
	Auctions: $144,000, PCGS AU-50 HA 09/24; $1,680,000, PCGS MS-66 SBG 09/24										
↳1797, 15 Stars, O-102	*	193711	29,000	33,500	41,000	47,000	57,500	103,000	150,000	288,000	384,000
	Auctions: $162,000, PCGS AU-55 HA 01/25										

* Included in number above.

100 GREATEST™ UNITED STATES COINS

No. 66 1796 AND 1797 DRAPED BUST HALF DOLLARS

DRAPED BUST, HERALDIC EAGLE REVERSE (1801–1807)

Designer: *Robert Scot.* **Weight:** *13.48 grams.*
Composition: *.8924 silver, .1076 copper.* **Diameter:** *Approximately 32.5 mm.*
Edge: *FIFTY CENTS OR HALF A DOLLAR with decorations between words.* **Mint:** *Philadelphia.*

History. The half dollar's Draped Bust, Heraldic Eagle design is similar to that of other silver coins of the era. While dies were prepared for the 1804 half dollar, none were minted in that year, despite Mint reports that state otherwise.

Striking and Sharpness. Most have light striking in one area or another. On the obverse, check the hair details and, in particular, the star centers. On the reverse, check the stars above the eagle, the clouds, the details of the shield, and the eagle's wings. Check the denticles on both sides. Adjustment marks are sometimes seen, from overweight planchets being filed down to correct weight, but not as often as on earlier half dollar types. Typically, the earlier years are better struck; many of 1806 and nearly all of 1807 are poorly struck. Sharp striking and excellent eye appeal add to the value dramatically, this being particularly true for those of 1805 to 1807, which are often weak (particularly 1807).

Availability. Earlier years are scarce in the marketplace, beginning with the elusive 1801 and including the 1802, after which they are more readily available. Some die varieties are scarce. Most MS coins are dated 1806 and 1807, but all are scarce. Finding sharply struck high-grade coins is almost impossible, a goal more than a reality.

Grading Standards

MS-63

MS-60 to 70 (Mint State). ***Obverse:*** At MS-60, some abrasion and contact marks are evident, most noticeably on the cheek, the drapery at the shoulder, and the right field. Luster is present, but may be dull or lifeless, and interrupted in patches. At MS-63, contact marks are very few, and abrasion is hard to detect except under magnification. An MS-65 coin has no abrasion, and contact marks are so minute as to require magnification. Luster should be full and rich. Coins grading above MS-65 are more theoretical than actual for this type—but they do exist and are defined by having fewer marks as perfection is approached. Later years usually have areas of flat striking. ***Reverse:*** Comments apply as for the obverse, except that abrasion and contact marks are most noticeable on the eagle's neck, the tips of the wing, and the tail. The field area is complex, without much open space, given the stars above the eagle, the arrows and olive branch, and other features. Accordingly, marks are not as noticeable as on the obverse.

Illustrated coin: This is an extraordinary strike with superb eye appeal. A connoisseur might prefer this coin to an MS-65 example with flat striking.

AU-50

AU-50, 53, 55, 58 (About Uncirculated). ***Obverse:*** Light wear is seen on the hair area above the ear and extending to left of the forehead, on the ribbon, and on the bosom, more so at AU-50 than at AU-53 or 55. An AU-58 coin has minimal traces of wear. An AU-50 coin has luster in protected areas among the stars and letters, with little in the open fields or on the portrait. At AU-58, most luster is present in the fields, but is worn away on the highest parts of the motifs. ***Reverse:*** Comments as preceding, except that the eagle's neck, the tips and top of the wings, the clouds, and the tail now show noticeable wear, as do other features. Luster ranges from perhaps 20 percent remaining in protected areas (at AU-50) to nearly full mint bloom (at AU-58). Often the reverse of this type retains much more luster than the obverse.

Illustrated coin: This example has gray and lilac toning.

EF-40

EF-40, 45 (Extremely Fine). ***Obverse:*** More wear is evident on the upper hair area and the ribbon, and on the drapery and bosom. Excellent detail remains in low-relief areas of the hair. The stars show wear, as do the date and letters. Luster, if present at all, is minimal and in protected areas. ***Reverse:*** Wear is greater than on an About Uncirculated coin, overall. The neck lacks feather detail on its highest points. Feathers have lost some detail near the edges of the wings, and some areas of the horizontal lines in the shield may be blended together. Some traces of luster may be seen, more so at EF-45 than at EF-40.

Illustrated coin: Light striking at the obverse center is normal for this die variety.

VF-30

VF-20, 30 (Very Fine). ***Obverse:*** The higher-relief areas of hair are well worn at VF-20, less so at VF-30. The drapery on the shoulder and the bosom show extensive wear. The stars have more wear, making them appear larger (an optical illusion seen on most worn silver coins of this era). ***Reverse:*** Wear is greater, including on the shield and wing feathers. Half to two-thirds of the feathers are visible. Star centers are flat. Other areas have lost detail as well.

Illustrated coin: Note the cud break on the reverse rim over the E in UNITED.

F-15

F-12, 15 (Fine). ***Obverse:*** Wear is more extensive than on a Very Fine coin, particularly noticeable on the hair, face, and bosom. The stars appear larger. About half the hair detail remains, most noticeably behind the neck and shoulder, but the fine hair is now combined into thicker tresses. The rim may be partially worn away and blend into the field. ***Reverse:*** Wear is even more extensive, with the shield and wing feathers being points to observe. The incuse E PLURIBUS UNUM may have half or more of the letters worn away (depending on striking). The clouds all appear connected. The stars are weak. Parts of the border and lettering may be weak.

VG-8

VG-8, 10 (Very Good). ***Obverse:*** The portrait is mostly seen in outline form, with most hair strands gone, although there is some definition at the back of the hair and behind the shoulder. The ear is discernible as is the eye. The stars appear larger still, again an illusion. The rim is weak in areas. LIBERTY and the date are readable and usually full, although some letters may be weak at their tops. ***Reverse:*** Wear is more extensive. Half or more of the letters in the motto are worn away. Most feathers are worn away, although separation of some of the lower feathers may be seen. Some stars are faint (depending on the strike). The border blends into the field in areas and some letters are weak.

G-4

G-4, 6 (Good). ***Obverse:*** Wear is more extensive, and some stars may be partly missing. The head is mostly an outline, although some hair strand outlines may be visible on some strikings. The rim is well worn or even missing in areas. LIBERTY is worn, and parts of some letters may be missing, but elements should be readable. The date is readable, but worn. ***Reverse:*** Wear is more extensive. The upper part of the eagle is flat. Feathers are noticeable only at the lower edge of the wings, and do not have detail. The upper part of the shield is flat or mostly so (depending on the strike). Only a few letters of the motto can be seen. The rim is worn extensively, and a few letters may be missing.

AG-3 (About Good). ***Obverse:*** Wear is so extensive that the coin is barely identifiable. The head is in outline form. LIBERTY is mostly gone; same for the stars. The date, while readable, may be partially worn away. ***Reverse:*** Extensive wear is seen overall, with the rim worn away and some areas worn smooth. The eagle can be discerned in outline form, but not necessarily completely. A few stray motto letters may remain.

AG-3

1803, Small 3

1803, Large 3

1805, 5 Over 4

Circulation Strikes

	Mintage	GSID	AG-3	G-4	VG-8	F-12	VF-20	EF-40	AU-50	MS-60	MS-63
Draped Bust, Heraldic Eagle Reverse (1801–1807)	n/a	72410	$210	$285	$365	$575	$850	$1,750	$2,500	$7,500	$11,000
1801	30,289	6128	775	1,000	1,600	2,300	2,750	6,500	12,000	84,000	192,000
	Auctions: $329,000, NGC MS-64 HA 11/13										
↳**1801, O-101**	*	193712	775	1,000	1,600	2,300	2,750	6,500	12,000	84,000	192,000
	Auctions: $210,000, PCGS MS-63 HA 01/23										
↳**1801, O-102**	*	193713	925	1,250	1,950	2,800	3,300	7,750	14,000	101,000	230,500
	Auctions: $420,000, NGC MS-64 HA 05/23										
1802	29,890	6129	1,250	1,750	2,200	3,000	4,500	7,500	15,500	79,000	—
↳**1802, O-101**	*	193714	1,250	1,750	2,200	3,000	4,500	7,500	15,500	79,000	—
	Auctions: $126,000, PCGS MS-62 HA 01/23										
1803, Large 3	188,234	6130	340	415	495	700	1,100	2,400	3,900	19,000	66,000
	Auctions: $120,000, PCGS MS-63 SBG 08/25										
↳**1803, Large 3, 12 Arrows, O-101**	*	194087	355	435	525	725	1,150	2,500	4,050	19,000	66,000
	Auctions: $186,000, PCGS MS-64 HA 01/23										
↳**1803, Large 3, O-102**	*	194088	440	550	650	925	1,350	3,100	5,000	25,000	86,000
↳**1803, Large 3, O-102a**	*	194089	370	460	550	775	1,200	2,600	4,250	21,000	72,500
↳**1803, Large 3, O-103**	*	194090	340	415	495	700	1,100	2,400	3,900	19,000	66,000
1803, Small 3	*	6131	310	390	525	725	1,150	3,000	4,600	30,000	81,500
	Auctions: $195,500, PCGS MS-64 SBG 01/09										
↳**1803, Small 3, O-104**	*	194091	345	430	575	775	1,250	3,300	5,000	33,000	81,500
	Auctions: $188,000, PCGS MS-64 SBG 05/15										
1805, 5 Over 4	*	6227	390	525	900	1,400	2,000	3,750	7,000	36,000	90,000
	Auctions: $152,750, NGC MS-65 HA 11/13										
↳**1805, 5 Over 4, O-101**	*	193715	390	525	900	1,400	2,000	3,750	7,000	36,000	90,000
	Auctions: $192,000, PCGS MS-65 HA 01/23										
↳**1805, 5 Over 4, O-101a**	*	193716	525	700	1,200	1,850	2,700	5,000	9,250	48,500	121,500
↳**1805, 5 Over 4, O-102**	*	193717	390	525	900	1,400	2,000	3,750	7,000	36,000	90,000
↳**1805, 5 Over 4, O-103**	*	193718	490	650	1,100	1,700	2,500	4,700	8,500	45,000	112,500
↳**1805, 5 Over 4, O-103a**	*	193719	490	650	1,100	1,700	2,500	4,700	8,500	45,000	112,500
↳**1805, 5 Over 4, O-103b**	*	193720	500	675	1,150	1,800	2,600	4,900	9,000	47,000	117,000

* Included in number above.

1806, Knob 6, Large Stars. *With traces of overdate.*

1806, Knob 6, Small Stars

1806, 6 Over 5

1806, 6 Over Inverted 6

1806, No Stem Through Claw

1806, Stem Through Claw

Circulation Strikes *(continued)*

	Mintage	GSID	AG-3	G-4	VG-8	F-12	VF-20	EF-40	AU-50	MS-60	MS-63
1805	211,722	6132	$310	$390	$575	$775	$1,200	$2,250	$4,250	$21,500	$48,000
↳1805, O-104	*	193721	405	500	750	1,000	1,550	2,900	5,500	28,000	62,500
↳1805, O-104a	*	193722	—	—	2,500	3,100	4,000	5,000	6,000	—	—
↳1805, O-105	*	193723	—	495	700	950	1,400	2,550	4,900	—	—
↳1805, O-105a	*	193724	—	—	1,750	2,200	2,700	4,050	—	—	—
↳1805, O-106	*	193725	375	470	675	925	1,400	2,700	5,000	26,000	57,500
↳1805, O-107	*	193726	405	500	750	1,000	1,550	2,900	5,500	28,000	62,500
↳1805, O-108	*	193727	405	500	750	1,000	1,550	2,900	5,500	28,000	62,500
↳1805, O-109	*	193728	375	470	675	925	1,400	2,700	5,000	26,000	57,500
↳1805, O-109a	*	193729	375	470	675	925	1,400	2,700	5,000	26,000	57,500
↳1805, O-110	*	193730	405	500	750	1,000	1,550	2,900	5,500	28,000	62,500
↳1805, O-111	*	193731	345	430	625	850	1,300	2,500	4,700	24,000	53,000
↳1805, O-112	*	193732	310	390	575	775	1,200	2,250	4,250	21,500	48,000
↳1805, O-112a	*	194086	—	—	675	925	1,400	2,700	5,000	—	—
↳1805, O-113	*	193733	375	470	675	925	1,400	2,700	5,000	26,000	57,500
↳1805, O-113a	*	193734	310	390	575	775	1,200	2,250	4,250	21,500	48,000
↳1805, O-114	*	193735	—	—	64,000	—	—	—	—	—	—
1806, 6 Over 5, Large Stars	*	6228	340	415	495	700	1,100	2,400	4,000	13,000	48,000
	Auctions: $193,875, PCGS MS-66 SBG 07/15										
↳1806, 6 Over 5, Large Stars, O-101	*	193736	340	415	495	700	1,100	2,400	4,000	13,000	48,000
↳1806, 6 Over 5, Large Stars, O-101a	*	193737	—	—	—	—	—	—	—	—	—
↳1806, 6 Over 5, Large Stars, O-102	*	193738	340	415	495	700	1,100	2,400	4,000	13,000	48,000
↳1806, 6 Over 5, Large Stars, O-103	*	193739	340	415	495	700	1,100	2,400	4,000	13,000	48,000
↳1806, 6 Over 5, Large Stars, O-103a	*	193740	—	—	550	775	1,200	2,400	4,000	—	—
↳1806, 6 Over 5, Large Stars, O-104	*	193741	—	—	—	—	—	—	—	—	—
↳1806, 6 Over 5, Large Stars, O-104a	*	193742	—	—	—	—	—	—	—	—	—
↳1806, 6 Over 5, Large Stars, O-104b	*	193743	—	—	—	—	—	9,500	—	—	—
1806, Knob 6, Small Stars	839,576	6137	210	285	390	600	875	1,750	2,500	12,500	48,000
↳1806, Knob 6, Small Stars, O-105	*	194092	210	285	390	600	875	1,750	2,500	12,500	48,000
↳1806, Knob 6, Small Stars, O-105a	*	194093	210	285	390	600	875	1,750	2,500	12,500	48,000
↳1806, Knob 6, Small Stars, O-106	*	194094	230	315	430	675	950	1,900	2,750	14,000	53,000
↳1806, Knob 6, Small Stars, O-107	*	194095	270	370	500	800	1,100	2,300	3,250	16,500	62,500
↳1806, Knob 6, Small Stars, O-107a	*	194096	250	345	470	725	1,050	2,100	3,000	15,000	57,500

* Included in number above.

Circulation Strikes *(continued)*

	Mintage	GSID	AG-3	G-4	VG-8	F-12	VF-20	EF-40	AU-50	MS-60	MS-63
1806, Knob 6, No Stem Through Claw	*	6134	$43,000	$48,000	$57,500	$72,000	$93,500	$126,000	—	—	—
	Auctions: $126,500, PCGS EF-40 SBG 01/09										
↳1806, Knob 6, No Stem, O-108	*	194097	43,000	48,000	57,500	72,000	93,500	126,000	—	—	—
	Auctions: $105,750, PCGS EF-40 SBG 05/15										
1806, 6 Over Inverted 6	*	6135	260	360	455	925	1,450	4,400	$8,000	$30,000	$54,000
↳1806, 6 Over Inverted 6, O-111	*	194101	285	395	500	1,000	1,600	4,800	9,000	33,000	59,500
↳1806, 6 Over Inverted 6, O-111a	*	194102	260	360	455	925	1,450	4,400	8,000	30,000	54,000
↳1806, 6 Over Inverted 6, O-111b	*	194103	—	—	—	—	—	—	—	—	—
↳1806, 6 Over Inverted 6, O-112	*	194104	285	395	500	1,000	1,600	4,800	9,000	33,000	59,500
1806, Pointed 6, No Stem Through Claw	*	6138	210	285	365	575	850	1,750	2,500	10,000	17,000
↳1806, Pointed 6, No Stem, O-109	*	194098	210	285	365	575	850	1,750	2,500	10,000	17,000
	Auctions: $129,250, PCGS MS-65 SBG 05/15										
↳1806, Pointed 6, No Stem, O-109a	*	194099	230	315	400	625	950	1,900	2,750	11,000	18,500
1806, Pointed 6, Stem Through Claw	*	6133	210	285	365	575	850	1,750	2,500	7,500	11,000
↳1806, Pointed 6, Stem, O-110	*	194100	375	495	1,750	2,750	3,750	—	—	—	—
↳1806, Pointed 6, Stem, O-113	*	194105	270	370	475	750	1,100	2,300	3,250	9,750	14,000
↳1806, Pointed 6, Stem, O-114	*	194106	270	370	475	750	1,100	2,300	3,250	9,750	14,000
↳1806, Pointed 6, Stem, O-114a	*	194107	250	345	435	675	1,000	2,100	3,000	9,000	13,000
↳1806, Pointed 6, Stem, O-115	*	194108	210	285	365	575	850	1,750	2,500	7,500	11,000
↳1806, Pointed 6, Stem, O-115a	*	194109	210	285	365	575	850	1,750	2,500	7,500	11,000
↳1806, Pointed 6, Stem, O-116	*	194110	230	315	400	625	950	1,900	2,750	8,250	12,000
	Auctions: $117,500, PCGS MS-65 HA 01/15										
↳1806, Pointed 6, Stem, O-117	*	194111	270	370	475	750	1,100	2,300	3,250	9,750	14,000
↳1806, Pointed 6, Stem, O-117a	*	194112	—	—	—	—	—	—	—	—	—
↳1806, Pointed 6, Stem, O-118	*	194113	250	345	435	675	1,000	2,100	3,000	9,000	13,000
↳1806, Pointed 6, Stem, O-118a	*	194114	230	315	400	625	950	1,900	2,750	8,250	12,000
↳1806, Pointed 6, Stem, O-119	*	194115	230	315	400	625	950	1,900	2,750	8,250	12,000
↳1806, Pointed 6, Stem, O-119a	*	194116	270	370	475	750	1,100	2,300	3,250	9,750	14,000
↳1806, Pointed 6, Stem, O-120	*	194117	230	315	400	625	950	1,900	2,750	8,250	12,000
	Auctions: $204,000, PCGS MS-66 HA 01/23										
↳1806, Pointed 6, Stem, O-120a	*	194118	250	345	435	675	1,000	2,000	2,750	7,500	11,000
↳1806, Pointed 6, Stem, O-120b	*	194480	270	370	475	750	1,100	2,300	3,250	9,750	14,000
↳1806, Pointed 6, Stem, O-121	*	194119	250	345	435	675	1,000	1,900	2,900	9,000	13,000
↳1806, Pointed 6, Stem, O-122	*	194120	—	—	2,750	3,500	4,000	7,500	—	—	—
↳1806, Pointed 6, Stem, O-123	*	194121	270	370	475	750	1,100	2,300	3,250	9,750	14,000
↳1806, Pointed 6, Stem, E Over A in STATES, O-124	*	194122	270	370	475	750	1,100	2,300	3,250	9,750	14,000
↳1806, Pointed 6, Stem, O-125	*	194123	270	370	475	750	1,100	2,300	3,250	9,750	14,000
↳1806, Pointed 6, Stem, O-125a	*	194124	—	—	—	—	—	—	—	—	—
↳1806, Pointed 6, Stem, O-126	*	194125	—	—	3,750	4,750	—	—	9,500	—	—
↳1806, Pointed 6, Stem, O-127	*	194481	—	—	—	—	—	—	—	—	—
↳1806, Pointed 6, Stem, O-127a	*	194126	—	—	—	—	—	—	—	—	—
↳1806, Pointed 6, Stem, O-128	*	194468	—	—	—	—	—	—	—	—	—
↳1806, Pointed 6, Stem, O-129	*	194469	—	—	—	—	—	—	—	—	—
↳1806, Pointed 6, Stem, O-130	*	194470	—	—	—	—	—	—	—	—	—
1806, Knob 6, Large Stars	*	6136	210	285	365	575	850	1,750	2,500	—	—

* Included in number above.

Circulation Strikes *(continued)*

	Mintage	GSID	AG-3	G-4	VG-8	F-12	VF-20	EF-40	AU-50	MS-60	MS-63
1807	301,076	6139	$210	$285	$365	$575	$850	$1,750	$2,500	$7,500	$11,000
↳1807, O-101	*	194127	270	370	475	750	1,100	2,300	3,250	9,750	14,000
↳1807, O-102	*	194128	210	285	365	575	850	1,750	2,500	7,500	17,000
↳1807, O-103	*	194129	230	315	400	625	950	1,900	2,750	8,250	12,000
↳1807, O-103a	*	194130	230	315	400	625	950	1,900	2,750	8,250	12,000
↳1807, O-104	*	194131	270	370	475	750	1,100	2,300	3,250	9,750	14,000
↳1807, O-104a	*	194482	—	—	—	—	—	—	—	—	—
↳1807, O-105	*	194132	210	285	365	575	850	1,750	2,500	7,500	11,000
	Auctions: $144,000, PCGS MS-66 HA 05/24										
↳1807, O-105a	*	194133	230	315	400	625	950	1,900	2,750	8,250	12,000
↳1807, O-106	*	194134	230	315	400	625	950	1,900	2,750	8,250	12,000
↳1807, O-107	*	194135	270	370	475	750	1,100	2,300	3,250	9,750	14,000
↳1807, O-107a	*	194136	270	370	475	750	1,100	2,300	3,250	9,750	14,000
↳1807, O-108	*	194137	250	345	435	675	1,000	2,100	3,000	9,000	13,000
↳1807, O-109	*	194138	—	495	600	1,250	—	—	—	—	—
↳1807, O-109a	*	194139	250	345	435	675	1,000	2,100	3,000	9,000	13,000
↳1807, O-110	*	194140	210	285	365	575	850	1,750	2,500	7,500	11,000
↳1807, O-110a	*	194141	210	285	365	575	850	1,750	2,500	7,500	11,000
↳1807, O-115	*	194142	—	—	—	—	21,000	—	—	—	—

* Included in number above.

CAPPED BUST, LETTERED EDGE (1807–1836)

Designer: *John Reich.* **Weight:** *13.48 grams.*
Composition: *.8924 silver, .1076 copper.* **Diameter:** *Approximately 32.5 mm.*
Edge: *1807–1814—FIFTY CENTS OR HALF A DOLLAR; 1814–1831—star added between DOLLAR and FIFTY; 1832–1836—vertical lines added between words.* **Mint:** *Philadelphia.*

First Style (1807–1808)

Remodeled Portrait and Eagle (1809–1836), Circulation Strike

Remodeled Portrait and Eagle, Proof Strike

History. The Capped Bust design was created by Mint assistant engraver John Reich; the motif was widely used, in several variations, on much of the era's coinage. Reich was the first artist to consistently include the denomination in his designs for U.S. gold and silver coins. The half dollar, minted continuously from 1807 to 1836, except 1816, was the largest silver coin of the realm at the time (silver dollars had not been struck since 1804).

Striking and Sharpness. On the obverse, check the hair and broach details. The stars are often flatly struck on Capped Bust half dollars, much more so than on other denominations. On the reverse, check the motto band and the eagle's head, and the wing to the left, as well as other areas (the neck feathers, often lightly struck on other denominations of Capped Bust silver, are usually fairly sharp on half dollars). The E PLURIBUS UNUM band is often weak in the area left of its center; this does not normally occur on other Capped Bust silver coins. Inspect the denticles on both sides. Generally, later dates are better struck than are earlier ones. Many half dollars have semi-prooflike surfaces, or patches of mirrorlike character interspersed with luster. Others can have nearly full prooflike surfaces, with patches of luster being in the minority (and often in the left obverse field); some of these have been mischaracterized as "Proofs." Some issues from the early 1830s have little digs or "bite marks" on the portrait, possibly from some sort of a gadget used to eject them from the press. Unlike the Capped Bust half dime, dime, and quarter dollar, the half dollar is particularly subject to very wide variations in striking quality.

True Proofs have deeply mirrored surfaces. Impostors are often seen, with deeply toned surfaces or with patches of mint luster. This situation is more prevalent with half dollars than with any other Capped

Bust denomination. Proceed slowly, and be careful. There are some crushed-lettered-edge ("CLE") Proofs of the 1833 to 1835 era that are especially beautiful and are more deeply mirrorlike than original issues. Some of these are restrikes (not necessarily an important consideration, but worth mentioning), believed to have been made at the Mint beginning in the spring of 1859.

Availability. Examples of most dates and overdates are easily found in just about any grade desired, from Fine and VF to MS. (As the largest silver coin struck between 1803 and 1836, these half dollars spent much of their time in bags, transferred from bank to bank, rather than wearing down in circulation.) The later years are the most readily available and are also seen in higher average grades. Many die varieties range from scarce to rare. Proofs were made in limited numbers for presentation purposes and for distribution to numismatists.

Grading Standards

MS-60

MS-60 to 70 (Mint State). ***Obverse:*** At MS-60, some abrasion and contact marks are evident, most noticeably on the cheek, the hair below the left part of LIBERTY, the cap, and the front part of the bosom and drapery. These areas also coincide with the highest parts of the coin and are thus susceptible to lightness of strike. Complicating matters is that when an area is lightly struck, and the planchet is not forced into the deepest parts of the die, the *original planchet surface* (which may exhibit scuffing and nicks) is visible. A lightly struck coin can have virtually perfect luster in the fields, deep and rich, and yet appear to be "worn" on the higher parts, due to the lightness of strike. This is a very sophisticated concept and is hard to quantify. In practice, the original planchet surface will usually be considered as wear on the finished coin, which of course is not true. Such grades as high About Uncirculated and low Mint State levels are often assigned to pieces that, if well struck, would be MS-64 and 65. As a matter of practicality, but not of logic, you will need to do the same. If a coin has original planchet abrasions, but otherwise is a Gem, those abrasions must be taken into consideration. Apart from this, on well-struck coins in lower Mint State grades, luster is present, but may be dull or lifeless, and interrupted in patches. At MS-63, on a well-struck coin, contact marks are very few, and abrasion is hard to detect except under magnification. A well-struck MS-65 coin has no abrasion, and contact marks are so minute as to require magnification. Luster should be full and rich. Grades above MS-65 are seen now and again and are defined by having fewer marks as perfection is approached. ***Reverse:*** Comments apply as for the obverse, except that nearly all coins with weak striking on the obverse (so as to reveal original planchet surface) do not show such original surface on the reverse, except perhaps on the motto ribbon. Accordingly, market grading is usually by the obverse only, even if the reverse seems to be in much better preservation. On well-struck coins, abrasion and contact marks are most noticeable on the eagle's head, the top of the wings, the claws, and the flat band that surrounds the incuse motto. The field is mainly protected by design elements and does not show abrasion as much as does the obverse on a given coin.

Illustrated coin: This is an exceptional coin at the low Mint State level.

AU-50, 53, 55, 58 (About Uncirculated). ***Obverse:*** Light wear is seen on the cheek, the hair below the left part of LIBERTY, the cap, and the front part of the bosom and drapery. Some of this apparent "wear" may be related to the original planchet surface (as noted under Mint State, above), but at the About Uncirculated level the distinction is less important. On a well-struck coin, at AU-58 the luster is extensive except in the open area of the field, especially to the right. At AU-50 and 53, luster remains only in protected areas. ***Reverse:*** Wear is evident on the eagle's head, the top of the wings, the claws, and the flat band above the eagle. An AU-58 coin has nearly full luster. At AU-50 and 53, there still is significant luster, more than on the obverse.

AU-55

Illustrated coin: An attractive coin by any measure, this has light toning and ample areas of original luster.

EF-40, 45 (Extremely Fine). ***Obverse:*** Wear is more extensive, most noticeably on the higher areas of the hair. The cap shows more wear, as does the cheek. Luster, if present, is in protected areas among the star points and close to the portrait. ***Reverse:*** The wings show wear on the higher areas of the feathers, and some details are lost. The top of the head and the beak are flat. The eagle's claws and the leaves show wear. Luster may be present in protected areas, even if there is little or none on the obverse.

EF-45

Illustrated coin: This coin probably was lightly cleaned years ago so as to give a light silver color, which added some hairlines, but now it has halo toning around the borders that adds attractiveness.

VF-20, 30 (Very Fine). ***Obverse:*** Wear is more extensive, and most of the hair is combined into thick tresses without delicate features. The curl on the neck is flat. The cap shows significant wear at its top, and the left part of the drapery and bosom is nearly flat. Stars are flat at their centers (even if sharply struck to begin with). ***Reverse:*** Wear is most evident on the eagle's head, the tops of the wings, and the leaves and claws. Nearly all feathers in the wing remain distinct.

VF-30

Illustrated coin: The areas of wear appear exaggerated due to the light toning, a feature often observed on half dollars of this date but not as often among other years.

F-12, 15 (Fine). ***Obverse:*** Wear is more extensive, with much of the hair blended together. The drapery is indistinct on most of its upper edge. The stars are flat at their centers. LIBERTY remains bold. ***Reverse:*** Wear is more extensive, now with only about half of the feathers remaining on the wings, more on the right wing. The head shows the eye, nostril, and beak but no details. The claws show more wear. Other features are worn as well, but not as noticeable as the key points mentioned.

F-12

VG-8, 10 (Very Good). ***Obverse:*** The hair is less distinct, with the forehead blended into the hair above. LIBERTY is complete, but may be slightly weak in areas. The stars are flat. The rim is distinct, with most if not all denticles visible. ***Reverse:*** Feathers are fewer and mostly on the right wing, although sharp strikes can show detail in both wings. Other details are weaker. All lettering remains easily readable.

Illustrated coin: This coin was cleaned and partially retoned. It is sharply struck on the reverse.

VG-8

G-4, 6 (Good). ***Obverse:*** The portrait is mostly in outline, with few interior details discernible. LIBERTY may still be readable or may be partially worn away, depending on the variety. The rim is weak, but distinct in most areas. ***Reverse:*** The eagle is mostly in outline form, although some feathers can be seen in the right wing. All letters around the border are clear. E PLURIBUS UNUM may be weak. Overall, a typical coin has the reverse in a slightly higher grade than the obverse.

G-4

AG-3 (About Good). ***Obverse:*** The portrait is an outline, although some of LIBERTY can still be seen. The rim is worn down, and some stars are blended into it. The date remains clear, but is weak at the bottom (on most but not all). ***Reverse:*** At this level the reverse shows more wear overall than the obverse, with the rim indistinct in areas and many letters worn away. This is an interesting turnabout from the situation of most G-4 coins.

AG-3

PF-60 to 70 (Proof). ***Obverse and Reverse:*** Proofs of this type have confused experts for a long time (as have large copper cents of the same era). Proofs that were extensively cleaned and therefore have many hairlines, or that are dull and grainy, are lower level, such as PF-60 to 62. While any early Proof half dollar will generate interest among collectors, lower levels are not of great interest to specialists unless they are of rare die varieties. With medium hairlines, an assigned grade of PF-64 may be in order and with relatively few, Gem PF-65. PF-66 should have hairlines so delicate that magnification is needed to see them. Above that, a Proof should be free of such lines. Grading is highly subjective with early Proofs, with eye appeal being a major factor.

PF-64 Cameo

1807, Small Stars

1807, Large Stars

1807, Large Stars, 50 Over 20

1807, Bearded Goddess

1808, 8 Over 7

Circulation Strikes

	Mintage	GSID	G-4	VG-8	F-12	VF-20	EF-40	AU-50	MS-60	MS-63
Capped Bust, Lettered Edge (1807–1836)	**n/a**	**72411**	**$70**	**$85**	**$95**	**$130**	**$210**	**$330**	**$1,000**	**$1,700**
1807, Large Stars, 50 Over 20	750,500	6140	170	285	525	725	1,250	2,500	7,500	12,000
↳1807, Large Stars, 50 Over 20, O-111	*	194143	—	—	4,550	—	15,500	—	—	—
↳1807, Large Stars, 50 Over 20, Light Beard, O-111a	*	81391	525	775	1,250	2,250	3,250	15,000	—	—
↳1807, Large Stars, 50 Over 20, O-112	*	194144	170	285	525	725	1,250	2,500	7,500	12,000
	Auctions: $129,250, PCGS MS-65 SBG 09/15									
1807, Bearded Goddess, 50 Over 20	*	213928	3,000	4,000	5,000	6,000	9,000	41,000	—	—
↳1807, Bearded Goddess, 50 Over 20, O-111b	*	71370	3,000	4,000	5,000	6,000	9,000	41,000	—	—
1807, Small Stars	*	6142	195	365	800	1,000	1,900	3,600	13,500	27,500
↳1807, Small Stars, O-113	*	194146	195	365	800	1,000	1,900	3,600	13,500	27,500
	Auctions: $129,250, PCGS MS-65 SBG 07/15									
↳1807, Small Stars, O-113a	*	194147	195	365	800	1,000	1,900	3,600	13,500	27,500
	Auctions: $108,688, PCGS MS-65 LGND 09/21									
1807, Large Stars	*	6141	195	290	625	775	2,100	3,000	13,000	30,000
	Auctions: $188,000, PCGS MS-65 LGND 09/18									
↳1807, Large Stars, O-114	*	194148	195	290	625	775	2,100	3,000	13,000	30,000
	Auctions: $192,000, PCGS MS-65 HA 08/24									
1808, 8 Over 7	*	6229	115	175	275	375	850	1,500	5,000	8,500
↳1808, 8 Over 7, O-101	*	193744	115	175	275	375	850	1,500	5,000	8,500

* Included in number above.

1809, XXX Edge
Experimental edge has "XXX" between the words.

1809, III Edge
Experimental edge has "III" between the words.

Circulation Strikes *(continued)*

	Mintage	GSID	G-4	VG-8	F-12	VF-20	EF-40	AU-50	MS-60	MS-63
1808	1,368,600	6144	$90	$120	$155	$290	$525	$1,300	$4,250	$6,500
↳1808, O-102	*	193745	110	140	185	350	625	1,600	5,000	8,000
↳1808, O-102a	*	193746	90	120	155	290	525	1,300	4,250	6,500
↳1808, O-103	*	193747	90	120	155	290	525	1,300	4,250	6,500
↳1808, O-104	*	193748	90	120	155	290	525	1,300	4,250	6,500
↳1808, O-104a	*	193749	110	140	185	350	625	1,600	5,000	8,000
↳1808, O-105	*	193750	90	120	155	290	525	1,300	4,250	6,500
↳1808, O-106	*	193751	90	120	155	290	525	1,300	4,250	6,500
↳1808, O-106a	*	193752	90	120	155	290	525	1,300	4,250	6,500
↳1808, O-107	*	193753	90	120	155	290	525	1,300	4,250	6,500
↳1808, O-107a	*	193754	90	120	155	290	525	1,300	4,250	6,500
↳1808, O-108	*	193755	90	120	155	290	525	1,300	4,250	6,500
↳1808, O-108a	*	193756	90	120	155	290	525	1,300	4,250	6,500
↳1808, O-109	*	193757	90	120	155	290	525	1,300	4,250	6,500
↳1808, O-109a	*	193758	90	120	155	290	525	1,300	4,250	6,500
↳1808, O-110	*	193759	100	130	170	320	575	1,450	4,700	7,250
↳1808, O-110a	*	193760	100	130	170	320	575	1,450	4,700	7,250
1809, XXX Edge	*	6146	180	260	345	525	950	1,800	7,000	21,500
↳1809, XXX Edge, O-101	*	194149	235	340	450	675	1,250	2,350	9,000	28,000
↳1809, XXX Edge, O-102 EDS	*	194150	180	260	345	525	950	1,800	7,000	21,500
↳1809, XXX Edge, O-102a	*	375979	—	—	—	—	—	—	—	—
↳1809, XXX Edge, O-108a	*	194159	220	310	415	625	1,150	2,200	8,250	26,000
↳1809, XXX Edge, O-110	*	194163	220	310	415	625	1,150	2,200	8,250	26,000
1809, Normal Edge	1,405,810	6145	120	155	230	310	600	1,150	2,750	5,500
↳1809, Normal Edge, O-102	*	195836	120	155	230	310	600	1,150	2,750	5,500
↳1809, Normal Edge, O-102a	*	194151	120	155	230	310	600	1,150	2,750	5,500
↳1809, Normal Edge, O-103	*	194152	120	155	230	310	600	1,150	2,750	5,500
↳1809, Normal Edge, O-104	*	194153	140	185	275	375	725	1,350	3,300	6,500
↳1809, Normal Edge, O-105	*	194154	120	155	230	310	600	1,150	2,750	5,500
↳1809, Normal Edge, O-106	*	194155	120	155	230	310	600	1,150	2,750	5,500
↳1809, Normal Edge, O-112	*	194166	140	185	275	375	725	1,350	3,300	6,500
↳1809, Normal Edge, O-113	*	194167	140	185	275	375	725	1,350	3,300	6,500
↳1809, Normal Edge, O-113a	*	194168	140	185	275	375	725	1,350	3,300	6,500
↳1809, Normal Edge, O-114	*	194169	140	185	275	375	725	1,350	3,300	6,500
↳1809, Normal Edge, O-114a	*	194170	140	185	275	375	725	1,350	3,300	6,500
↳1809, Normal Edge, O-115	*	194171	120	155	230	310	600	1,150	2,750	5,500
↳1809, Normal Edge, O-115a	*	194172	120	155	230	310	600	1,150	2,750	5,500
1809, III Edge	*	6147	130	195	285	365	725	1,300	6,250	12,500
↳1809, III Edge, O-107	*	194156	130	195	285	365	725	1,300	6,250	12,500
↳1809, III Edge, O-107a	*	194157	155	235	345	435	850	1,600	7,500	15,000
↳1809, III Edge, O-108	*	194158	155	235	345	435	850	1,600	7,500	15,000
↳1809, III Edge, O-109	*	194160	145	215	315	400	775	1,450	7,000	14,000
↳1809, III Edge, O-109a	*	194161	130	195	285	365	725	1,300	6,250	12,500
↳1809, III Edge, O-109b	*	194162	145	215	315	400	775	1,450	7,000	14,000
↳1809, III Edge, O-111	*	194164	145	215	315	400	775	1,450	7,000	14,000
↳1809, III Edge, O-111a	*	194165	145	215	315	400	775	1,450	7,000	14,000

* Included in number above.

1811, (18.11), 11 Over 10
The date is "punctuated" with a period.

1811, Large 8

1811, Small 8

Circulation Strikes *(continued)*

	Mintage	GSID	G-4	VG-8	F-12	VF-20	EF-40	AU-50	MS-60	MS-63
1810	1,276,276	6148	$95	$130	$180	$275	$575	$900	$2,750	$5,750
↳1810, O-101	*	193761	95	130	180	275	575	900	2,750	5,750
↳1810, O-101a	*	193762	95	130	180	275	575	900	2,750	5,750
↳1810, O-102	*	193763	95	130	180	275	575	900	2,750	5,750
↳1810, O-102a	*	193764	95	130	180	275	575	900	2,750	5,750
↳1810, O-103	*	193765	105	145	200	300	650	975	3,000	6,250
↳1810, O-104	*	193766	105	145	200	300	650	975	3,000	6,250
↳1810, O-104a	*	193767	105	145	200	300	650	975	3,000	6,000
↳1810, O-105	*	193768	95	130	180	275	575	900	2,750	5,750
↳1810, O-106	*	193769	105	145	200	300	650	975	3,000	6,250
↳1810, O-106a	*	193770	105	145	200	300	650	975	3,000	6,250
↳1810, O-107	*	193771	115	155	220	330	700	1,100	3,300	7,000
↳1810, O-107a	*	193772	115	155	220	330	700	1,100	3,300	7,000
↳1810, O-108	*	193773	105	145	200	300	650	975	3,000	6,250
↳1810, O-108a	*	193774	115	155	220	330	700	1,100	3,300	7,000
↳1810, O-109	*	193775	105	145	200	300	650	975	3,000	6,250
↳1810, O-109a	*	193776	115	155	220	330	700	1,100	3,300	7,000
↳1810, O-110	*	193777	95	130	180	275	575	900	2,750	5,750
1811, (18.11), 11 Over 10, Punctuated Date	1,203,644	6230	130	160	275	420	725	1,400	4,700	7,500
↳1811, (18.11), 11 Over 10, O-101	*	193778	130	160	275	420	725	1,400	4,700	7,500
↳1811, (18.11), 11 Over 10, O-102	*	193779	130	160	275	420	725	1,550	5,250	8,750
1811, Large 8	*	6149	90	130	180	285	675	1,250	2,750	7,500
↳1811, Large 8, O-103	*	194173	100	145	200	315	725	1,400	3,000	8,250
↳1811, Large 8, O-103a	*	194174	100	145	200	315	725	1,400	3,000	8,250
↳1811, Large 8, O-104	*	194175	—	—	—	—	—	—	—	—
↳1811, Large 8, O-104a	*	194176	90	130	180	285	675	1,250	2,750	7,500
1811, Small 8	*	6150	90	120	145	290	495	950	2,100	4,400
↳1811, Small 8, O-105	*	194177	100	130	160	320	550	1,050	2,350	4,800
↳1811, Small 8, O-105a	*	194178	90	120	145	290	495	950	2,250	4,750
	Auctions: $156,000, NGC MS-68 HA 08/21									
↳1811, Small 8, O-106	*	194179	90	120	145	290	495	950	2,100	4,400
↳1811, Small 8, O-107	*	194180	100	130	160	320	550	1,050	2,350	4,600
↳1811, Small 8, O-108	*	194181	90	120	145	290	495	950	2,100	4,400
	Auctions: $132,000, PCGS MS-67 HA 01/23									
↳1811, Small 8, O-108a	*	194182	90	120	145	290	495	950	2,100	4,400
↳1811, Small 8, O-109	*	194183	95	130	155	305	525	1,000	2,250	4,600
↳1811, Small 8, O-110	*	194184	90	120	145	290	495	950	2,100	4,400
↳1811, Small 8, O-110a	*	194185	90	120	145	290	495	950	2,100	4,400
↳1811, Small 8, O-111	*	194186	90	120	145	290	495	950	2,100	4,400
↳1811, Small 8, O-111a	*	194187	95	130	155	305	525	1,000	2,250	4,600
↳1811, Small 8, O-112	*	194188	100	130	160	320	550	1,050	2,350	4,800
↳1811, Small 8, O-112a	*	194189	110	140	175	350	600	1,150	2,550	5,250
↳1811, Small 8, O-113	*	194190	195	260	360	525	1,400	2,200	—	—

* Included in number above.

1812, 2 Over 1, Small 8

1812, 2 Over 1, Large 8

1812, Single Leaf Below Wing

1813, 50 C. Over UNI.

Circulation Strikes *(continued)*

	Mintage	GSID	G-4	VG-8	F-12	VF-20	EF-40	AU-50	MS-60	MS-63
1812, 2 Over 1, Large 8	*	6232	$2,000	$3,250	$5,000	$8,750	$17,000	$27,000	—	—
↳1812, 2 Over 1, Large 8, O-101	*	194191	2,000	3,250	5,000	8,750	17,000	27,000	—	—
↳1812, 2 Over 1, Large 8, O-101a	*	194192	2,000	3,250	5,000	8,750	17,000	27,000	—	—
1812, 2 Over 1, Small 8	*	6231	130	160	230	325	600	1,400	$4,050	$9,500
↳1812, 2 Over 1, Small 8, O-102	*	194193	130	160	230	325	600	1,400	4,050	9,500
↳1812, 2 Over 1, Small 8, O-102a	*	194194	130	160	230	325	600	1,400	4,050	9,500
1812	1,628,059	6151	90	120	140	195	575	750	1,900	3,250
↳1812, O-103	*	194195	90	120	140	195	575	750	1,900	3,250
↳1812, O-104	*	194196	90	120	140	195	575	750	1,900	3,250
↳1812, O-104a	*	194197	90	120	140	195	575	750	1,900	3,250
↳1812, O-105	*	194198	90	120	140	195	575	750	1,900	3,250
↳1812, O-105a	*	194199	90	120	140	195	575	750	1,900	3,250
↳1812, O-106	*	194200	95	130	145	205	600	775	1,950	3,400
↳1812, O-107	*	194201	90	120	140	195	575	750	1,900	3,250
↳1812, O-108	*	194202	95	130	145	205	600	775	1,950	3,400
↳1812, O-108a	*	194203	95	130	145	205	600	775	1,950	3,400
↳1812, O-109	*	194204	100	130	155	215	625	825	2,050	3,600
↳1812, O-109a	*	194205	90	120	140	195	575	750	1,900	3,250
↳1812, O-110	*	194206	90	120	140	195	575	750	1,900	3,250
↳1812, O-110a	*	194207	90	120	140	195	575	750	1,900	3,250
↳1812, Single Leaf Below Wing, O-110b	*	194208	3,000	4,500	7,500	12,000	18,000	29,000	—	—
1813, 50 C. Over UNI	*	6153	130	180	290	495	900	1,600	3,500	8,500
↳1813, 50 C. Over UNI, O-101	*	194209	130	180	290	495	900	1,600	3,500	8,500
↳1813, 50 C. Over UNI, O-101a	*	194210	130	180	290	495	900	1,600	3,500	8,500
1813	1,241,903	6152	105	130	155	235	575	1,000	2,500	4,750
	Auctions: $141,000, NGC MS-67 HA 11/13									
↳1813, O-102	*	193780	110	135	165	245	600	1,100	2,600	5,000
↳1813, O-103	*	193781	105	130	155	235	575	1,000	2,500	4,750
↳1813, O-104	*	193782	115	145	170	255	625	1,150	2,750	5,250
↳1813, O-105	*	193783	105	130	155	235	575	1,000	2,500	4,750
↳1813, O-105a	*	193784	115	145	170	255	625	1,150	2,750	5,250
↳1813, O-106	*	193785	110	135	165	245	600	1,100	2,600	5,000
↳1813, O-106a	*	193786	110	135	165	245	600	1,100	2,600	5,000
↳1813, O-107	*	193787	110	135	165	245	600	1,100	2,600	5,000
↳1813, O-107a	*	193788	105	130	155	235	575	1,000	2,500	4,750
↳1813, O-108	*	193789	110	135	165	245	600	1,100	2,600	5,000
↳1813, O-108a	*	193790	115	145	170	255	625	1,150	2,750	5,250
↳1813, O-109	*	193791	110	135	165	245	600	1,100	2,600	5,000
↳1813, Single Leaf Below Wing, O-109a	*	194211	115	145	170	255	625	1,150	2,750	5,250
↳1813, O-110	*	193792	110	135	165	245	600	1,100	2,600	5,000

* Included in number above.

1814, 4 Over 3

1814, Single Leaf Below Wing

1814, E Over A in STATES

1817, Dated 181.7
The date is "punctuated" with a period between the second 1 and the 7.

1815, 5 Over 2

1817, 7 Over 3

1817, 7 Over 4

Circulation Strikes *(continued)*

	Mintage	GSID	G-4	VG-8	F-12	VF-20	EF-40	AU-50	MS-60	MS-63
1814, 4 Over 3	*	6233	$175	$240	$360	$525	$1,100	$1,800	$5,000	$12,000
↳1814, 4 Over 3, O-101	*	193793	—	—	—	—	—	—	—	—
↳1814, 4 Over 3, O-101a	*	193794	175	240	360	525	1,100	1,800	5,000	12,000
1814	1,039,075	6154	120	150	190	275	750	1,050	2,200	4,750
↳1814, O-102	*	193795	120	150	190	275	750	1,050	2,200	4,750
↳1814, O-102a	*	193796	120	150	190	275	750	1,050	2,200	4,750
↳1814, O-103	*	193797	120	150	190	275	750	1,050	2,200	4,750
↳1814, O-104	*	193798	130	165	205	300	825	1,150	2,400	5,250
↳1814, O-104a	*	193799	120	150	190	275	750	1,050	2,200	4,750
↳1814, O-105	*	193800	120	150	190	275	750	1,050	2,200	4,750
↳1814, Single Leaf Below Wing, O-105a	*	194212	150	260	390	650	1,500	4,000	7,750	14,500
↳1814, O-106	*	193801	140	180	225	330	900	1,250	2,600	5,750
↳1814, O-106a	*	193802	130	165	205	300	825	1,150	2,400	5,250
↳1814, O-107	*	193803	120	150	190	275	750	1,050	2,200	4,750
↳1814, O-107a	*	193804	140	180	225	330	900	1,250	2,600	5,750
↳1814, O-109	*	193805	130	155	200	285	775	1,100	2,300	4,750
1814, E Over A in STATES	*	6155	180	290	420	575	1,400	1,950	12,000	24,000
↳1814, E Over A in STATES, O-108	*	194213	180	290	420	575	1,400	1,950	12,000	24,000
↳1814, E Over A in STATES, O-108a	*	194214	180	290	420	575	1,400	1,950	12,000	24,000
1815, 5 Over 2	47,150	6234	2,250	3,000	3,600	4,400	6,750	8,750	20,000	41,000
	Auctions: $182,125, NGC MS-66 HA 08/12									
↳1815, 5 Over 2, O-101	*	193806	2,250	3,000	3,600	4,400	6,750	8,750	20,000	41,000
	Auctions: $126,000, PCGS MS-65 HA 01/23									
↳1815, 5 Over 2, O-101a	*	193807	2,250	3,000	3,600	4,400	6,750	8,750	20,000	41,000
1817, 7 Over 3	*	6235	195	290	525	675	1,250	2,750	5,250	15,000
↳1817, 7 Over 3, O-101	*	193808	195	290	525	675	1,250	2,750	5,250	15,000
↳1817, 7 Over 3, O-101a	*	193809	195	290	525	675	1,250	2,750	5,250	15,000
1817, 7 Over 4	11 known	6236	108,000	150,000	204,000	330,000	420,000	504,000	—	—
	Auctions: $356,500, PCGS AU-50 SBG 07/09									
↳1817, 7 Over 4, O-102	11 known	193810	108,000	150,000	204,000	330,000	420,000	504,000	—	—
	Auctions: $282,000, PCGS VF35 SBG 09/15									
↳1817, 7 Over 4, O-102a	11 known	193811	108,000	150,000	204,000	330,000	420,000	504,000	—	—
	Auctions: $288,000, PCGS VF-20 HA 08/24									
1817, Dated 181.7	*	6157	130	195	260	325	850	2,800	11,000	26,500
↳1817, Dated 181.7, O-103	*	194215	130	195	260	325	850	2,800	11,000	26,500
↳1817, Dated 181.7, O-103b	*	374395	—	—	—	—	—	—	—	—

* Included in number above.

1817, Single Leaf Below Wing

1818, First 8 Small, Second 8 Over 7

1818, First 8 Large, Second 8 Over 7

1819, Small 9 Over 8

1819, Large 9 Over 8

1820, 20 Over 19, Square-Base 2

1820, 20 Over 19, Curl-Base 2

1820, Curl-Base, No Knob 2, Small Date

1820, Square-Base, Knob 2, Large Date

1820, Square-Base, No Knob 2, Large Date

Circulation Strikes *(continued)*

	Mintage	GSID	G-4	VG-8	F-12	VF-20	EF-40	AU-50	MS-60	MS-63
1817	1,215,567	6156	$115	$145	$170	$260	$480	$1,050	$2,500	$6,250
↳1817, O-103a	*	193812	125	150	175	275	500	1,100	2,600	6,500
↳1817, O-104	*	193813	—	—	—	8,000	—	—	—	—
↳1817, O-104a	*	193814	—	—	—	—	—	—	—	—
↳1817, O-105	*	193815	—	1,000	1,150	1,250	1,750	3,100	—	—
↳1817, O-105a	*	193816	130	155	185	285	525	1,150	2,750	7,000
↳1817, O-106	*	193817	125	150	175	275	500	1,100	2,600	6,500
↳1817, Single Leaf Below Wing, O-106a	*	194216	115	145	170	260	480	1,050	2,500	6,250
↳1817, O-107	*	193818	130	155	185	285	525	1,150	2,750	7,000
↳1817, O-108	*	193819	—	—	900	1,900	3,750	5,500	—	—
↳1817, O-108a	*	193820	130	155	185	285	525	1,150	2,750	7,000
↳1817, O-109	*	193821	125	150	175	275	500	1,100	2,600	6,500
↳1817, O-110	*	193822	115	145	170	260	480	1,050	2,500	6,250
↳1817, O-110a	*	193823	115	145	170	260	480	1,050	2,500	6,250
↳1817, O-111	*	193824	115	145	170	260	480	1,050	2,500	6,250
↳1817, O-111a	*	193825	115	145	170	260	480	1,050	2,500	6,250
↳1817, O-112	*	193826	125	150	175	275	500	1,100	2,600	6,500
↳1817, O-112a	*	193827	115	145	170	260	480	1,050	2,500	6,250
↳1817, O-113	*	193828	115	145	170	260	480	1,050	2,500	6,250
↳1817, O-113a	*	193829	115	145	170	260	480	1,050	2,500	6,250
1818, 8 Over 7, Large 8	*	6238	110	135	160	240	650	1,400	3,550	6,750
↳1818, 8 Over 7, Large 8, O-101	*	194217	110	135	160	240	650	1,400	3,550	6,750
↳1818, 8 Over 7, Large 8, O-101a	*	194218	110	135	160	240	650	1,400	3,550	6,750
↳1818, 8 Over 7, Large 8, O-103	*	194221	120	150	180	265	725	1,500	3,900	7,500
↳1818, 8 Over 7, Large 8, O-103a	*	194222	130	165	195	290	775	1,650	3,550	6,750
1818, 8 Over 7, Small 8	*	6237	105	130	175	260	550	1,500	3,100	11,000
↳1818, 8 Over 7, Small 8, O-102	*	194219	105	130	175	260	550	1,500	3,100	11,000
↳1818, 8 Over 7, Small 8, O-102a	*	194220	105	130	175	260	550	1,500	3,100	11,000

* Included in number above.

Circulation Strikes *(continued)*

	Mintage	GSID	G-4	VG-8	F-12	VF-20	EF-40	AU-50	MS-60	MS-63
1818	1,960,322	6159	$95	$130	$145	$200	$440	$950	$2,100	$4,500
↳1818, O-104	*	193830	—	—	—	650	—	—	—	—
↳1818, O-104a	*	193831	100	130	150	210	465	1,000	2,250	4,700
↳1818, O-104b	*	376867	—	—	—	—	—	—	—	—
↳1818, O-105	*	193832	105	135	155	220	485	1,050	2,350	4,950
↳1818, O-105a	*	193833	115	150	170	240	525	1,150	2,550	5,500
↳1818, O-106	*	193834	115	150	170	240	525	1,150	2,550	5,500
↳1818, O-106a	*	193835	105	135	155	220	485	1,050	2,350	4,950
↳1818, O-107	*	193836	95	130	145	200	440	950	2,100	4,500
↳1818, O-107a	*	226354	95	130	145	200	440	950	2,100	4,500
↳1818, Pincher 8's, O-108	*	193838	95	130	145	200	440	950	2,100	4,500
↳1818, O-109	*	193839	100	130	150	210	465	1,000	2,250	4,700
↳1818, O-109a	*	193840	95	130	145	200	440	950	2,100	4,500
↳1818, O-110	*	193841	105	135	155	220	485	1,050	2,350	4,950
↳1818, O-111	*	193842	95	130	145	200	440	950	2,100	4,500
↳1818, O-112	*	193843	95	130	145	200	440	950	2,100	4,500
↳1818, O-112a	*	193844	115	150	170	240	525	1,150	2,550	5,500
↳1818, O-113	*	193845	105	135	155	220	485	1,050	2,350	4,950
↳1818, O-114	*	193846	105	135	155	220	485	1,050	2,350	4,950
↳1818, O-114a	*	193847	100	130	150	210	465	1,000	2,250	4,700
↳1818, O-115	*	193848	115	150	170	240	525	1,150	2,550	5,500
↳1818, O-115a	*	193849	105	135	155	220	485	1,050	2,350	4,950
1819, Small 9 Over 8	*	6239	85	100	135	255	455	750	2,500	7,000
↳1819, Small 9 Over 8, O-101	*	194223	85	100	135	255	455	750	2,500	7,000
1819, Large 9 Over 8	*	6240	85	115	175	285	525	725	3,250	7,250
↳1819, Large 9 Over 8, O-102	*	194224	85	115	175	285	525	725	3,250	7,250
↳1819, Large 9 Over 8, O-103	*	194225	110	145	230	370	675	850	3,900	8,000
↳1819, Large 9 Over 8, O-103a	*	194226	95	125	195	315	575	775	3,600	8,000
↳1819, Large 9 Over 8, O-104	*	194227	85	115	175	285	525	725	3,250	7,250
↳1819, Large 9 Over 8, O-104a	*	194228	110	145	230	370	675	925	4,200	9,250
↳1819, Large 9 Over 8, O-105	*	194229	105	135	210	345	625	850	3,900	8,500
↳1819, Large 9 Over 8, O-106	*	194230	105	135	210	345	625	850	3,900	8,500
1819	2,208,000	6161	75	105	155	235	430	775	2,250	4,500
↳1819, O-107	*	193850	85	115	170	255	470	850	2,500	4,950
↳1819, O-107a	*	193851	85	115	170	255	470	850	2,500	4,950
↳1819, O-108	*	193852	80	110	165	245	450	825	2,350	4,700
↳1819, O-109	*	193853	80	110	165	245	450	825	2,350	4,700
↳1819, O-109a	*	193854	85	115	170	255	470	850	2,500	4,950
↳1819, O-110	*	193855	85	115	170	255	470	850	2,500	4,950
↳1819, O-110a	*	193856	80	110	165	245	450	825	2,350	4,700
↳1819, O-111	*	193857	80	110	165	245	450	825	2,350	4,700
↳1819, O-112	*	193858	85	115	170	255	470	850	2,500	4,950
↳1819, O-112a	*	193859	90	125	185	280	525	925	2,700	5,500
↳1819, O-113	*	193860	75	105	155	235	430	775	2,250	4,500
↳1819, O-114	*	193861	75	105	155	235	430	775	2,250	4,500
↳1819, O-115	*	193862	80	110	165	245	450	825	2,350	4,700
1820, 20 Over 19, Square-Base 2	751,122	6241	105	135	160	260	900	1,250	6,000	12,500
↳1820, 20 Over 19, Square-Base 2, O-101	*	194231	105	135	160	260	900	1,250	6,000	12,500
↳1820, 20 Over 19, Square-Base 2, O-101a	*	194232	105	135	160	260	900	1,250	6,000	12,500

* Included in number above.

1820, Broken Serifs on E's
Compare with normal serifs on 1834, Large Letters, reverse.

1822, So-Called 2 Over 1

1823, Broken 3

1823, Broken 3

1823, Patched 3

1823, Normal 3

1823, Ugly 3

1824, 4 Over 1

Circulation Strikes *(continued)*

	Mintage	GSID	G-4	VG-8	F-12	VF-20	EF-40	AU-50	MS-60	MS-63
1820, 20 Over 19, Curl-Base 2	*	6242	$105	$135	$160	$260	$775	$1,150	$4,000	$9,500
↳1820, 20 Over 19, Curl-Base 2, O-102	*	194233	105	135	160	260	775	1,150	4,000	9,500
1820, Curl-Base 2, Small Date	*	6163	105	160	230	325	575	900	5,000	11,000
↳1820, Curl-Base 2, Small Date, O-103	*	194234	105	160	230	325	575	900	5,000	11,000
↳1820, Curl-Base 2, Small Date, O-103a	*	194235	105	160	230	325	575	900	5,000	11,000
1820, Square-Base 2, Knob 2	*	6166	105	160	195	260	575	1,250	4,750	10,500
↳1820, Square-Base 2, Knob 2, O-104	*	194236	110	170	205	275	625	1,300	5,000	11,000
↳1820, Square-Base 2, Knob 2, O-104a	*	194237	1,600	1,950	2,200	2,500	3,750	—	—	—
↳1820, Square-Base 2, Knob 2, O-105	*	194238	105	160	195	260	575	1,250	4,750	10,500
↳1820, Square-Base 2, Knob 2, O-105a	*	194239	110	170	205	275	625	1,300	5,000	11,000
1820, Square-Base 2, No Knob	*	6165	90	130	160	230	550	950	3,500	8,750
↳1820, Square-Base 2, No Knob, O-106	*	194240	90	130	160	230	550	950	3,500	8,750
↳1820, Square-Base 2, No Knob, O-108	*	194242	90	130	160	230	550	950	3,500	8,750
1820, No Serif on E's	*	6164	900	1,500	2,250	5,000	9,500	15,000	60,000	—
↳1820, No Serif on E's, O-107	*	194241	900	1,500	2,250	5,000	9,500	15,000	60,000	—
1821	1,305,797	6168	85	95	120	195	405	575	1,450	3,900
	Auctions: $115,000, NGC MS-67 HA 03/08									
↳1821, O-101	*	193863	90	100	130	205	425	625	1,500	4,050
↳1821, O-101a	*	193864	85	95	120	195	405	575	1,450	3,900
↳1821, O-102	*	193865	90	100	130	205	425	625	1,500	4,050
↳1821, O-103	*	193866	85	95	120	195	405	575	1,450	3,900
↳1821, O-103a	*	193867	90	105	130	215	445	650	1,600	4,250
↳1821, O-104	*	193868	85	95	120	195	405	575	1,450	3,900
↳1821, O-104a	*	193869	85	95	120	195	405	575	1,450	3,900
↳1821, O-105	*	193870	85	95	120	195	405	575	1,450	3,900
↳1821, O-105a	*	193871	85	95	120	195	405	575	1,450	3,900
↳1821, O-106	*	193872	85	95	120	195	405	575	1,450	3,900
↳1821, O-106a	*	193873	85	95	120	195	405	575	1,450	3,900
↳1821, O-107	*	193874	85	95	120	195	405	575	1,450	3,900
1822, So-Called 2 Over 1	*	6243	90	115	135	195	575	1,150	2,800	5,000
↳1822, So-Called 2 Over 1, O-101	*	193875	90	115	135	195	575	1,150	2,800	5,000
↳1822, So-Called 2 Over 1, O-102	*	193876	110	130	160	235	700	1,350	3,400	6,000

* Included in number above.

Circulation Strikes *(continued)*

	Mintage	GSID	G-4	VG-8	F-12	VF-20	EF-40	AU-50	MS-60	MS-63
1822	1,559,573	6170	$70	$95	$110	$195	$390	$495	$1,500	$2,100
↳1822, O-103	*	193877	75	105	125	215	430	550	1,650	2,350
↳1822, O-103a	*	193878	75	105	125	215	430	550	1,650	2,350
↳1822, O-104	*	193879	70	95	110	195	390	495	1,500	2,100
↳1822, O-105	*	193880	70	95	110	195	390	495	1,500	2,100
↳1822, O-105a	*	194483	85	115	130	235	470	600	1,800	2,550
↳1822, O-106	*	193881	70	95	110	195	390	495	1,500	2,100
↳1822, O-106a	*	193882	75	100	120	205	410	525	1,600	2,250
↳1822, O-107	*	193883	75	100	120	205	410	525	1,600	2,250
↳1822, O-108	*	193884	75	100	120	205	410	525	1,600	2,250
↳1822, O-108a	*	193885	75	100	120	205	410	525	1,600	2,250
↳1822, O-109	*	193886	75	100	120	205	410	525	1,600	2,250
↳1822, O-109a	*	194484	85	115	130	235	470	600	1,800	2,550
↳1822, O-110	*	193887	70	95	110	195	390	495	1,500	2,100
↳1822, O-110a	*	193888	70	95	110	195	390	495	1,500	2,100
↳1822, O-111	*	193889	75	100	120	205	410	525	1,600	2,250
↳1822, O-112	*	193890	75	105	125	215	430	550	1,650	2,350
↳1822, O-113	*	193891	75	100	120	205	410	525	1,600	2,250
↳1822, O-114	*	193892	75	100	120	205	410	525	1,600	2,250
↳1822, O-115	*	193893	75	100	120	205	410	525	1,600	2,250
1823, Broken 3	*	6173	130	160	260	455	1,000	1,900	8,500	13,000
↳1823, Broken 3, O-101	*	194243	130	160	260	455	1,000	1,900	8,500	13,000
1823, Patched 3	*	6174	105	135	195	325	900	1,600	4,400	9,500
↳1823, Patched 3, O-101a	*	194244	105	135	195	325	900	1,600	4,400	9,500
↳1823, Patched 3, O-102	*	194245	115	150	215	360	975	1,800	4,800	10,500
1823, Normal 3	1,694,200	6172	70	95	110	175	325	600	1,500	3,250
↳1823, Normal 3, O-103	*	193894	70	95	110	175	325	600	1,500	3,250
↳1823, Normal 3, O-104	*	193895	70	95	110	175	325	600	1,500	3,250
↳1823, Normal 3, O-105	*	193896	70	95	110	175	325	600	1,500	3,250
↳1823, Normal 3, O-106	*	193897	75	100	120	185	340	625	1,600	3,400
↳1823, Normal 3, O-106a	*	193898	70	95	110	175	325	600	1,500	3,250
↳1823, Normal 3, O-107	*	193899	75	100	120	185	340	625	1,600	3,400
↳1823, Normal 3, O-108	*	193900	75	100	120	185	340	625	1,600	3,400
	Auctions: $102,000, NGC MS-67 HA 02/23									
↳1823, Normal 3, O-108a	*	193901	75	100	120	185	340	625	1,600	3,400
↳1823, Normal 3, O-109	*	193902	1,250	1,550	2,000	2,300	2,750	3,250	—	—
↳1823, Normal 3, O-110	*	193903	70	95	110	175	325	600	1,500	3,250
↳1823, Normal 3, O-111	*	193904	75	100	120	185	340	625	1,600	3,400
↳1823, Normal 3, O-111a	*	193905	70	95	110	175	325	600	1,500	3,250
↳1823, Normal 3, O-112	*	193906	70	95	110	175	325	600	1,500	3,250
↳1823, Normal 3, O-113	*	193907	—	11,500	—	—	—	—	—	—
1823, Ugly 3	*	6175	105	160	235	390	850	2,500	7,500	13,000
↳1823, Ugly 3, O-110a	*	194246	105	160	235	390	850	2,500	7,500	13,000
1824, 4 Over 1	*	6244	105	135	160	195	390	650	3,000	7,000
↳1824, 4 Over 1, O-101	*	193908	105	135	160	195	390	650	3,000	7,000
↳1824, 4 Over 1, O-101a	*	193909	105	135	160	195	390	650	3,000	7,000
↳1824, 4 Over 1, O-102	*	193910	575	750	1,000	1,500	3,000	4,500	14,500	43,000

* Included in number above.

1824, 4 Over Various Dates
Probably 4 Over 2 Over 0.

1824, Normal Date

1824, 4 Over 4
4 Over 4 varieties are easily mistaken for the scarcer 4 Over 1. Note the distance between the 2 and 4 in each.

Circulation Strikes *(continued)*

	Mintage	GSID	G-4	VG-8	F-12	VF-20	EF-40	AU-50	MS-60	MS-63
1824, 4 Over Various Dates	*	6178	$85	$110	$135	$200	$490	$1,250	$3,450	$6,000
↳1824, 4 Over Various Dates, O-103	*	194247	85	110	135	200	490	1,250	3,450	6,000
1824, Normal Date	3,504,954	6177	70	85	95	130	210	330	1,250	2,250
↳1824, Normal Date, O-104	*	193911	75	90	100	135	220	350	1,300	2,350
↳1824, Normal Date, O-105	*	193912	70	85	95	130	210	330	1,250	2,250
↳1824, Normal Date, O-106	*	193913	75	90	105	145	230	365	1,400	2,500
↳1824, Normal Date, O-106a	*	193914	—	—	285	390	575	1,100	—	—
↳1824, Normal Date, O-107	*	193915	75	90	100	135	220	350	1,300	2,350
↳1824, Normal Date, O-108	*	193916	75	90	100	135	220	350	1,300	2,350
↳1824, Normal Date, O-108a	*	193917	75	90	105	145	230	365	1,400	2,500
↳1824, Normal Date, O-111	*	193921	75	90	100	135	220	350	1,300	2,350
↳1824, Normal Date, O-112	*	193922	75	90	105	145	230	365	1,400	2,500
↳1824, Normal Date, O-112a	*	193923	75	90	105	145	230	365	1,400	2,500
↳1824, Normal Date, O-113	*	193924	70	85	95	130	210	330	1,250	2,250
↳1824, Normal Date, O-113a	*	226355	—	—	—	—	—	—	—	—
↳1824, Normal Date, O-114	*	193925	—	—	—	325	850	1,500	—	—
↳1824, Normal Date, O-115	*	193926	70	85	95	130	210	330	1,250	2,250
↳1824, Normal Date, O-116	*	193927	75	90	100	135	220	350	1,300	2,350
↳1824, Normal Date, O-117	*	193928	70	85	95	130	210	330	1,250	2,250
1824, 4 Over 4	*	6245	85	110	135	200	390	675	2,400	4,050
↳1824, 4 Over 4, O-109	*	193918	85	110	135	200	390	675	2,400	4,050
↳1824, 4 Over 4, O-110	*	193919	85	110	135	200	390	675	2,400	4,050
↳1824, 4 Over 4, O-110a	*	193920	90	120	145	220	430	750	2,600	4,250
1825	2,943,166	6180	70	85	95	130	210	330	1,000	1,800
↳1825, O-101	*	193929	70	85	95	130	210	330	1,000	1,800
↳1825, O-102	*	193930	70	85	95	130	210	330	1,000	1,800
↳1825, O-103	*	193931	85	100	115	155	250	400	1,250	2,150
↳1825, O-104	*	193932	85	100	115	155	250	400	1,250	2,150
↳1825, O-105	*	193933	75	90	105	145	230	365	1,150	1,950
↳1825, O-106	*	193934	70	85	95	130	210	330	1,000	1,800
↳1825, O-106a	*	193935	70	85	95	130	210	330	1,000	1,800
↳1825, O-107	*	193936	75	90	105	145	230	365	1,150	1,950
↳1825, O-108	*	193937	85	100	115	155	250	400	1,250	2,150
↳1825, O-109	*	193938	85	100	115	155	250	400	1,250	2,150
↳1825, O-110	*	193939	70	85	95	130	210	330	1,000	1,800
↳1825, O-111	*	193940	70	85	95	130	210	330	1,000	1,800
↳1825, O-112	*	193941	70	85	95	130	210	330	1,000	1,800
↳1825, O-113	*	193942	70	85	95	130	210	330	1,000	1,800
↳1825, O-114	*	193943	70	85	95	130	210	330	1,000	1,800
↳1825, O-115	*	193944	70	85	95	130	210	330	1,000	1,800
↳1825, O-116	*	193945	70	85	95	130	210	330	1,000	1,800
↳1825, O-117	*	193946	85	100	115	155	250	400	1,250	2,150
↳1825, O-118	*	193947	—	—	—	—	—	—	—	—

* Included in number above.

1827, 7 Over 6

Circulation Strikes *(continued)*

	Mintage	GSID	G-4	VG-8	F-12	VF-20	EF-40	AU-50	MS-60	MS-63
1826	4,004,180	6182	$70	$85	$95	$130	$210	$330	$1,000	$1,850
↳1826, O-101	*	193948	70	85	95	130	210	330	1,000	1,850
↳1826, O-101a	*	193949	70	85	95	130	210	330	1,000	1,850
↳1826, O-102	*	193950	70	85	95	130	210	330	1,000	1,850
↳1826, O-103	*	193951	100	155	260	360	575	775	1,550	4,400
↳1826, O-104	*	193952	75	90	105	145	230	365	1,150	2,050
↳1826, O-104a	*	193953	75	90	105	145	230	365	1,150	2,050
↳1826, O-105	*	193954	75	90	105	145	230	365	1,150	2,050
↳1826, O-106	*	193955	75	90	105	145	230	365	1,150	2,050
↳1826, O-106a	*	193956	70	85	95	130	210	330	1,000	1,850
↳1826, O-107	*	193957	75	90	105	145	230	365	1,150	2,050
↳1826, O-108	*	193958	85	100	115	155	250	400	1,250	2,200
↳1826, O-108a	*	193959	70	85	95	130	210	330	1,000	1,850
↳1826, O-109	*	193960	70	85	95	130	210	330	1,250	3,000
↳1826, O-110	*	193961	70	85	95	130	210	330	1,000	1,850
↳1826, O-111	*	193962	70	85	95	130	210	330	1,000	1,850
↳1826, O-111a	*	226356	—	—	—	—	—	—	—	—
↳1826, O-112	*	193964	85	100	115	155	250	400	1,250	2,200
↳1826, O-112a	*	193965	70	85	95	130	210	330	1,000	1,850
↳1826, O-113	*	193966	85	100	115	155	250	400	1,250	2,200
↳1826, O-113a	*	193967	85	100	115	155	250	400	1,250	2,200
↳1826, O-114	*	193968	85	100	115	155	250	400	1,250	2,200
↳1826, O-115	*	193969	85	100	115	155	250	400	1,250	2,200
↳1826, O-116	*	193970	—	—	—	—	—	—	—	—
↳1826, O-116a	*	193971	70	85	95	130	210	330	1,000	1,850
↳1826, O-117	*	193972	70	85	95	130	210	330	1,000	1,850
↳1826, O-117a	*	193973	75	90	105	145	230	365	1,150	2,050
↳1826, O-118	*	193974	75	90	105	145	230	365	1,150	2,050
↳1826, O-118a	*	193975	70	85	95	130	210	330	1,000	1,850
↳1826, O-119	*	193976	85	100	115	155	250	400	1,250	2,200
↳1826, O-120	*	193977	85	100	115	155	250	400	1,250	2,200
↳1826, O-120a	*	193978	85	100	115	155	250	400	1,250	2,200
1827, 7 Over 6	5,493,400	6246	110	135	160	200	455	725	2,000	4,200
↳1827, 7 Over 6, O-101	*	193979	110	135	160	200	455	725	2,000	4,200
↳1827, 7 Over 6, O-102	*	193980	110	135	160	200	455	725	2,000	4,200
↳1827, 7 Over 6, O-103	*	193981	130	165	195	240	550	850	2,400	4,600

* Included in number above.

1827, Square-Base 2

1827, Curl-Base 2

1828, Curl-Base 2, No Knob

1828, Curl-Base 2, With Knob

1828, Square-Base 2, Large 8's

1828, Square-Base 2, Small 8's

1828, Large Letters

1828, Small Letters

Circulation Strikes *(continued)*

	Mintage	GSID	G-4	VG-8	F-12	VF-20	EF-40	AU-50	MS-60	MS-63
1827, Square-Base 2	*	6184	$70	$85	$95	$130	$210	$365	$1,150	$1,900
↳1827, Square-Base 2, O-104	*	194249	70	85	95	130	210	365	1,150	1,900
↳1827, Square-Base 2, O-105	*	194250	75	90	105	145	230	400	1,250	2,100
↳1827, Square-Base 2, O-106	*	194251	70	85	95	130	210	365	1,150	1,900
↳1827, Square-Base 2, O-107	*	194252	75	90	105	145	230	400	1,250	2,100
↳1827, Square-Base 2, O-108	*	194253	85	100	115	155	250	440	1,350	2,300
↳1827, Square-Base 2, O-108a	*	194254	85	100	115	155	250	440	1,350	2,300
↳1827, Square-Base 2, O-109	*	194255	85	100	115	155	250	440	1,350	2,300
↳1827, Square-Base 2, O-110	*	194256	85	100	115	155	250	440	1,350	2,300
↳1827, Square-Base 2, O-111	*	194257	85	100	115	155	250	440	1,350	2,300
↳1827, Square-Base 2, O-112	*	194258	75	90	105	145	230	400	1,250	2,100
↳1827, Square-Base 2, O-112a	*	194259	85	100	115	155	250	440	1,350	2,300
↳1827, Square-Base 2, O-113	*	194260	85	100	115	155	250	440	1,350	2,300
↳1827, Square-Base 2, O-113a	*	194261	85	100	115	155	250	440	1,350	2,300
↳1827, Square-Base 2, O-114	*	194262	75	90	105	145	230	400	1,250	2,100
↳1827, Square-Base 2, O-115	*	194263	75	90	105	145	230	400	1,250	2,100
↳1827, Square-Base 2, O-116	*	194264	85	100	115	155	250	440	1,350	2,300
↳1827, Square-Base 2, O-116a	*	194265	90	110	125	170	270	475	1,450	2,500
↳1827, Square-Base 2, O-117	*	194266	75	90	105	145	230	400	1,250	2,100
↳1827, Square-Base 2, O-117a	*	194267	85	100	115	155	250	440	1,350	2,300
↳1827, Square-Base 2, O-118	*	194268	85	100	115	155	250	440	1,350	2,300
↳1827, Square-Base 2, O-118a	*	194269	75	90	105	145	230	400	1,250	2,100
↳1827, Square-Base 2, O-119	*	194270	85	100	115	155	250	440	1,350	2,300
↳1827, Square-Base 2, O-120	*	194271	—	—	—	495	625	725	1,400	4,400
↳1827, Square-Base 2, O-120a	*	194272	70	85	95	130	210	365	1,150	1,900
↳1827, Square-Base 2, O-121	*	194273	85	100	115	155	250	440	1,350	2,300
↳1827, Square-Base 2, O-122	*	194274	—	—	290	390	575	1,100	—	—
↳1827, Square-Base 2, O-123	*	194275	85	100	115	155	250	440	1,350	2,300

* Included in number above.

Circulation Strikes *(continued)*

	Mintage	GSID	G-4	VG-8	F-12	VF-20	EF-40	AU-50	MS-60	MS-63
↳1827, Square-Base 2, O-124	*	194276	—	—	—	—	—	—	—	—
↳1827, Square-Base 2, O-124a	*	226357	—	—	$650	$850	$1,300	$2,250	$6,250	—
↳1827, Square-Base 2, O-125	*	194278	$75	$90	105	145	230	400	1,250	—
↳1827, Square-Base 2, O-126	*	194279	75	90	105	145	230	400	1,250	2,100
↳1827, Square-Base 2, O-127	*	194280	—	—	470	725	2,000	3,500	—	—
↳1827, Square-Base 2, O-128	*	194281	85	100	115	155	250	440	1,250	2,100
↳1827, Square-Base 2, O-129	*	194282	85	100	115	155	250	440	1,350	2,300
↳1827, Square-Base 2, O-130	*	194283	85	100	115	155	250	440	1,350	2,300
↳1827, Square-Base 2, O-131	*	194284	70	85	95	130	210	365	1,150	1,900
↳1827, Square-Base 2, O-132	*	194285	75	90	105	145	230	400	1,250	2,100
↳1827, Square-Base 2, O-133	*	194286	85	100	115	155	250	440	1,350	2,300
↳1827, Square-Base 2, O-134	*	194287	85	100	115	155	250	440	1,350	2,300
↳1827, Square-Base 2, O-135	*	194288	75	90	105	145	230	400	1,250	1,900
↳1827, Square-Base 2, O-136	*	194289	85	100	115	155	250	440	1,350	2,300
↳1827, Square-Base 2, O-137	*	194290	—	—	4,000	5,500	7,500	—	—	—
↳1827, Square-Base 2, O-138	*	194291	85	100	115	155	250	440	1,350	2,300
↳1827, Square-Base 2, O-139	*	194292	85	100	115	155	250	440	1,350	2,300
↳1827, Square-Base 2, O-140	*	194293	85	100	115	155	250	440	1,350	2,300
↳1827, Square-Base 2, O-140a	*	194294	—	235	285	390	—	3,750	—	—
↳1827, Square-Base 2, O-141	*	194295	75	90	105	145	230	400	1,250	2,100
↳1827, Square-Base 2, O-142	*	194296	70	85	95	130	210	365	1,150	1,900
↳1827, Square-Base 2, O-143	*	194297	85	100	115	155	250	440	1,350	2,300
↳1827, Square-Base 2, O-144	*	194298	240	360	725	950	1,500	3,500	—	—
↳1827, Square-Base 2, O-145	*	194299	130	195	245	340	850	1,550	5,250	8,750
↳1827, Square-Base 2, O-148	*	194302	—	—	14,000	15,500	20,000	—	—	—
↳1827, Square-Base 2, O-148a	*	226268	—	—	—	—	—	—	—	—
↳1827, Square-Base 2, O-149	*	194304	—	43,000	—	—	—	—	—	—
1827, Curl-Base 2	*	6185	85	100	110	150	470	650	2,000	4,100
↳1827, Curl-Base 2, O-146	*	194300	85	100	110	150	470	650	2,000	4,100
↳1827, Curl-Base 2, O-147	*	194301	100	120	130	180	550	775	2,400	4,950
1828, Curl-Base 2, No Knob	3,075,200	6187	70	85	95	130	210	360	1,250	2,500
↳1828, Curl-Base 2, No Knob, O-101	*	194305	70	85	95	130	210	360	1,250	2,500
↳1828, Curl-Base 2, No Knob, O-102	*	194306	70	85	95	130	210	360	1,250	2,500
↳1828, Curl-Base 2, No Knob, O-103	*	194307	70	85	95	130	210	360	1,250	2,500
↳1828, Curl-Base 2, No Knob, O-104	*	194308	85	100	115	155	250	430	1,500	3,000
↳1828, Curl-Base 2, No Knob, O-105	*	194309	—	210	360	675	900	1,750	3,100	—
1828, Curl-Base 2, With Knob	*	6188	85	100	130	210	365	775	2,500	4,400
↳1828, Curl-Base 2, With Knob, O-106	*	194310	100	120	155	250	435	925	3,000	5,250
↳1828, Curl-Base 2, With Knob, O-107	*	194311	85	100	130	210	365	775	2,500	4,400
↳1828, Curl-Base 2, With Knob, O-107a	*	194312	—	—	—	—	—	900	—	—
1828, Square-Base 2, Large 8's	*	6191	70	85	105	160	300	470	1,250	2,500
↳1828, Square-Base 2, Large 8's, O-108	*	194313	70	85	105	160	300	470	1,250	2,500
↳1828, Square-Base 2, Large 8's, O-109	*	194314	75	90	115	180	330	525	1,400	2,750

* Included in number above.

1829, 9 Over 7

1830, Small 0

1830, Large 0

Circulation Strikes *(continued)*

	Mintage	GSID	G-4	VG-8	F-12	VF-20	EF-40	AU-50	MS-60	MS-63
1828, Square-Base 2, Small 8's, Large Letters	*	6189	$70	$85	$95	$130	$210	$390	$1,100	$1,700
↳1828, Square-Base 2, Small 8's, Large Letters, O-110	*	194315	70	85	95	130	210	390	1,100	1,700
↳1828, Square-Base 2, Small 8's, Large Letters, O-111	*	194316	85	100	115	155	250	470	1,300	2,050
↳1828, Square-Base 2, Small 8's, Large Letters, O-112	*	194317	75	90	105	145	230	430	1,200	1,900
↳1828, Square-Base 2, Small 8's, Large Letters, O-113	*	194318	75	90	105	145	230	430	1,200	1,900
↳1828, Square-Base 2, Small 8's, Large Letters, O-114	*	194319	75	90	105	145	230	430	1,200	1,900
↳1828, Square-Base 2, Small 8's, Large Letters, O-114a	*	194320	75	90	105	145	230	430	1,200	1,900
↳1828, Square-Base 2, Small 8's, Large Letters, O-115	*	194321	70	85	95	130	210	390	1,100	1,700
↳1828, Square-Base 2, Small 8's, Large Letters, O-116	*	194322	70	85	95	130	210	390	1,100	1,700
↳1828, Square-Base 2, Small 8's, Large Letters, O-117	*	194323	70	85	95	130	210	390	1,100	1,700
↳1828, Square-Base 2, Small 8's, Large Letters, O-117a	*	194324	70	85	95	130	210	390	1,100	1,700
↳1828, Square-Base 2, Small 8's, Large Letters, O-118	*	194325	75	90	105	145	230	430	1,200	1,900
↳1828, Square-Base 2, Small 8's, Large Letters, O-118a	*	194326	85	100	115	155	250	470	1,300	2,050
↳1828, Square-Base 2, Small 8's, Large Letters, O-120	*	194328	70	85	95	130	210	390	1,100	1,700
↳1828, Square-Base 2, Small 8's, Large Letters, O-121	*	194329	85	100	115	155	250	470	1,300	2,050
↳1828, Square-Base 2, Small 8's, Large Letters, O-121a	*	194330	85	100	115	155	250	470	1,300	2,050
↳1828, Square-Base 2, Small 8's, Large Letters, O-122	*	194331	75	90	105	145	230	430	1,200	1,900
↳1828, Square-Base 2, Small 8's, Large Letters, O-123	*	194332	—	—	—	—	—	—	—	—
↳1828, Square-Base 2, Small 8's, Large Letters, O-123a	*	194333	—	—	725	775	1,150	3,750	—	—
1828, Square-Base 2, Small 8's, Small Letters	*	6190	130	160	195	290	455	950	3,200	8,500
↳1828, Square-Base 2, Small 8's, Small Letters, O-119	*	194327	130	160	195	290	455	950	3,200	8,500
1829, 9 Over 7	*	6247	100	130	180	260	405	800	1,950	3,500
↳1829, 9 Over 7, O-101	*	193982	100	130	180	260	405	800	1,950	3,500
↳1829, 9 Over 7, O-101a	*	193983	100	130	180	260	405	800	1,950	3,500
↳1829, 9 Over 7, O-102	*	193984	100	130	180	260	405	800	1,950	3,500
↳1829, 9 Over 7, O-102a	*	193985	130	160	235	340	525	1,050	2,500	4,550

* Included in number above.

Circulation Strikes *(continued)*

	Mintage	GSID	G-4	VG-8	F-12	VF-20	EF-40	AU-50	MS-60	MS-63
1829, Small Letters	3,712,156	6193	$70	$85	$95	$130	$210	$330	$1,000	$1,700
↳1829, Small Letters, O-103	*	194334	70	85	95	130	210	330	1,000	1,700
↳1829, Small Letters, O-104	*	194335	—	—	—	390	550	675	—	—
↳1829, Small Letters, O-104a	*	194336	85	100	115	155	250	400	1,250	2,050
↳1829, Small Letters, O-105	*	194337	70	85	95	130	210	330	1,000	1,700
↳1829, Small Letters, O-105a	*	193986	70	85	95	130	210	330	1,000	1,700
↳1829, Small Letters, O-106	*	194338	120	155	210	260	415	775	—	—
↳1829, Small Letters, O-107	*	194339	75	90	105	145	230	365	1,150	1,900
↳1829, Small Letters, O-108	*	194340	85	100	115	155	250	400	1,250	2,050
↳1829, Small Letters, O-108a	*	194341	75	90	105	145	230	365	1,150	1,900
↳1829, Small Letters, O-109	*	194342	—	—	—	260	390	—	1,300	—
↳1829, Small Letters, O-109a	*	194343	85	100	115	155	250	400	1,250	2,050
↳1829, Small Letters, O-111	*	194346	70	85	95	130	210	330	1,000	1,700
↳1829, Small Letters, O-111a	*	194347	75	90	105	145	230	365	1,150	1,900
↳1829, Small Letters, O-112	*	194348	70	85	95	130	210	330	1,000	1,700
↳1829, Small Letters, O-112a	*	194349	70	85	95	130	210	330	1,000	1,700
↳1829, Small Letters, O-113	*	194350	85	100	115	155	250	400	1,250	2,050
↳1829, Small Letters, O-113a	*	194351	75	90	105	145	230	365	1,150	1,900
↳1829, Small Letters, O-114	*	194352	75	90	105	145	230	365	1,150	1,900
↳1829, Small Letters, O-115	*	194353	70	85	95	130	210	330	1,000	1,700
↳1829, Medium Letters, O-116	*	194354	85	100	115	155	250	400	1,250	2,050
↳1829, Medium Letters, O-116a	*	194355	85	100	115	155	270	950	1,500	2,250
↳1829, Small Letters, O-117	*	194356	75	90	105	145	230	365	1,150	1,900
↳1829, Small Letters, O-118	*	194357	—	—	—	575	850	2,500	—	—
↳1829, Small Letters, O-119	*	194358	75	90	105	145	230	365	1,150	1,900
↳1829, Small Letters, O-120	*	194359	—	—	—	—	—	—	—	—
1829, Large Letters	*	297891	75	90	105	145	230	365	1,150	1,900
↳1829, Large Letters, O-110	*	194344	75	90	105	145	230	365	1,150	1,900
↳1829, Large Letters, O-110a	*	194345	75	90	105	145	230	365	1,150	1,900
1830, Small 0	4,764,800	6195	70	85	95	130	210	330	1,000	1,900
↳1830, Small 0, O-101	*	194360	70	85	95	130	210	330	1,000	1,900
↳1830, Small 0, O-102	*	194361	70	85	95	130	210	330	1,000	1,900
↳1830, Small 0, O-103	*	194362	70	85	95	130	210	330	1,000	1,900
↳1830, Small 0, O-104	*	194363	85	100	115	155	250	400	1,250	2,300
↳1830, Small 0, O-105	*	194364	85	100	115	155	250	400	1,250	2,300
↳1830, Small 0, O-106	*	194365	75	90	105	145	230	365	1,150	2,100
↳1830, Small 0, O-106a	*	194366	95	115	130	175	280	450	1,350	2,600
↳1830, Small 0, O-107	*	194367	70	85	95	130	210	330	1,000	1,900
↳1830, Small 0, O-107a	*	194368	70	85	95	130	210	330	1,000	1,900
↳1830, Small 0, O-108	*	194369	75	90	105	145	230	365	1,150	2,100
↳1830, Small 0, O-109	*	194370	85	100	115	155	250	400	1,250	2,300
↳1830, Small 0, O-110	*	194371	75	90	105	145	230	365	1,150	2,100
↳1830, Small 0, O-111	*	194372	70	85	95	130	210	330	1,000	1,900
↳1830, Small 0, O-112	*	194373	85	100	115	155	250	400	1,250	2,300
↳1830, Small 0, O-112a	*	194374	85	100	115	155	250	400	1,250	2,300
↳1830, Small 0, O-113	*	194375	70	85	95	130	210	330	1,000	1,900
↳1830, Small 0, O-115	*	194377	70	85	95	130	210	330	1,000	1,900
↳1830, Small 0, O-116	*	194378	70	85	95	130	210	330	1,000	1,900
↳1830, Small 0, O-117	*	194379	70	85	95	130	210	330	1,000	1,900
↳1830, Small 0, O-118	*	194380	85	100	115	155	250	400	1,250	2,300

* Included in number above.

1830, Large Letters

Experimental Edge of 1830
Raised segment lines angled to the right.

Experimental Edge of 1830–1831
Raised segment lines angled to the left.

Edge Adopted for Coinage, 1830–1836
Straight vertical lines.

Circulation Strikes *(continued)*

	Mintage	GSID	G-4	VG-8	F-12	VF-20	EF-40	AU-50	MS-60	MS-63
1830, Large Letters, Small 0	*	81148	$900	$1,900	$2,500	$3,100	$5,000	$8,750	$18,000	$30,000
↳1830, Large Letters, Small 0, O-114	*	194376	900	1,900	2,500	3,100	5,000	8,750	18,000	30,000
1830, Medium 0, O-119	4,764,800	194381	70	85	95	130	210	330	1,000	1,700
1830, Large 0	*	6196	70	85	95	130	210	330	1,000	1,700
↳1830, Large 0, O-120	*	194382	75	90	105	145	230	365	1,150	1,900
↳1830, Large 0, O-121	*	194383	75	90	105	145	230	365	1,150	1,900
↳1830, Large 0, O-122	*	194384	70	85	95	130	210	330	1,000	1,700
↳1830, Large 0, O-123	*	194385	70	85	95	130	210	330	1,000	1,700
1831	5,873,660	6198	70	85	95	130	210	330	1,000	1,700
↳1831, O-101	*	193987	75	90	105	145	230	365	1,150	1,900
↳1831, O-102	*	193988	70	85	95	130	210	330	1,000	1,700
↳1831, O-103	*	193989	70	85	95	130	210	330	1,000	1,700
↳1831, O-104	*	193990	70	85	95	130	210	330	1,000	1,700
↳1831, O-105	*	193991	75	90	105	145	230	365	1,150	1,900
↳1831, O-106	*	193992	75	90	105	145	230	365	1,150	1,900
↳1831, O-107	*	193993	75	90	105	145	230	365	1,150	1,900
↳1831, O-108	*	193994	70	85	95	130	210	330	1,000	1,700
↳1831, O-109	*	193995	70	85	95	130	210	330	1,000	1,700
↳1831, O-110	*	193996	70	85	95	130	210	330	1,000	1,700
↳1831, O-110a	*	226358	—	—	—	—	—	—	—	—
↳1831, O-111	*	193998	70	85	95	130	210	330	1,000	1,700
↳1831, O-112	*	193999	85	100	115	155	250	400	1,250	2,050
↳1831, O-113	*	194000	85	100	115	155	250	400	1,250	2,050
↳1831, O-114	*	194001	75	90	105	145	230	365	1,150	1,900
↳1831, O-115	*	194002	85	100	115	155	250	400	1,250	2,050
↳1831, O-116	*	194003	85	100	115	155	250	400	1,250	2,050
↳1831, O-117	*	194004	85	100	115	155	250	400	1,250	2,050
↳1831, O-118	*	194005	75	90	105	145	230	365	1,150	1,900
↳1831, O-119	*	194006	75	90	105	145	230	365	1,150	1,900
↳1831, O-120	*	194007	—	2,100	3,550	6,250	—	—	—	—

* Included in number above.

1832, Large Letters Reverse
O-101a. Note the prominent die crack.

Circulation Strikes *(continued)*

	Mintage	GSID	G-4	VG-8	F-12	VF-20	EF-40	AU-50	MS-60	MS-63
1832, Large Letters (a)	4,797,000	6201	$70	$85	$95	$145	$245	$435	$1,600	$4,000
↳1832, Large Letters, O-101	*	194386	70	85	95	145	245	435	1,600	4,000
↳1832, Large Letters, O-101a	*	194387	70	85	95	145	245	435	1,600	4,000
1832, Small Letters	*	6200	70	85	95	130	210	330	1,000	1,700
↳1832, Small Letters, O-102	*	194388	70	85	95	130	210	330	1,000	1,700
↳1832, Small Letters, O-102a	*	194389	75	90	105	145	230	365	1,150	1,900
↳1832, Small Letters, O-103	*	194390	70	85	95	130	260	440	1,150	2,050
↳1832, Small Letters, O-104	*	194391	85	100	115	155	250	400	1,250	2,050
↳1832, Small Letters, O-105	*	194392	75	90	105	145	230	365	1,150	1,900
↳1832, Small Letters, O-105a	*	226359	—	—	—	—	—	—	—	—
↳1832, Small Letters, O-106	*	194394	70	85	95	130	210	330	1,000	1,700
↳1832, Small Letters, O-107	*	194395	70	85	95	130	210	330	1,000	1,700
↳1832, Small Letters, O-108	*	194396	85	100	115	155	250	400	1,250	2,050
↳1832, Small Letters, O-108a	*	390400	—	—	—	—	—	—	—	—
↳1832, Small Letters, O-109	*	194397	85	100	115	155	250	400	1,250	2,050
↳1832, Small Letters, O-110	*	194398	70	85	95	130	210	330	1,000	1,700
↳1832, Small Letters, O-111	*	194399	70	85	95	130	210	330	1,000	1,700
↳1832, Small Letters, O-112	*	194400	70	85	95	130	210	330	1,000	1,700
↳1832, Small Letters, O-113	*	194401	70	85	95	130	210	330	1,000	1,700
↳1832, Small Letters, O-113a	*	226360	—	—	—	—	—	—	—	—
↳1832, Small Letters, O-114	*	194403	85	100	115	155	250	400	1,250	2,050
↳1832, Small Letters, O-115	*	194404	70	85	95	130	210	330	1,000	1,700
↳1832, Small Letters, O-116	*	194405	75	90	105	145	230	365	1,150	1,900
↳1832, Small Letters, O-117	*	194406	85	100	115	155	250	400	1,250	2,050
↳1832, Small Letters, O-118	*	194407	70	85	95	130	210	330	1,000	1,700
↳1832, Small Letters, O-119	*	194408	85	100	115	155	250	400	1,250	2,050
↳1832, Small Letters, O-120	*	194409	85	100	115	155	250	400	1,250	2,050
↳1832, Small Letters, O-120a	*	194410	75	90	105	145	230	365	1,150	1,900
↳1832, Small Letters, O-121	*	194411	75	90	105	145	230	365	1,150	1,900
↳1832, Small Letters, O-121a	*	194412	75	90	105	145	230	365	1,150	1,900
↳1832, Small Letters, O-122	*	194413	70	85	95	130	210	330	1,000	1,700

* Included in number above. **a.** All 1832, Large Letters, examples have a heavy die break on the eagles' left wing.

1834, Large Date

1834, Small Date

1834, Large Letters

1834, Small Letters

Circulation Strikes *(continued)*

	Mintage	GSID	G-4	VG-8	F-12	VF-20	EF-40	AU-50	MS-60	MS-63
1833	5,206,000	6203	$70	$85	$95	$130	$210	$330	$1,000	$1,700
↳1833, O-101	*	194008	70	85	95	130	210	330	1,000	1,700
↳1833, O-102	*	194009	70	85	95	130	210	330	1,000	1,700
↳1833, O-103	*	194010	70	85	95	130	210	330	1,000	1,700
↳1833, O-103a	*	226361	70	85	95	130	210	330	1,000	1,700
↳1833, O-104	*	194012	70	85	95	130	210	330	1,000	1,700
↳1833, O-105	*	194013	70	85	95	130	210	330	1,000	1,700
↳1833, O-105a	*	226362	—	—	—	—	—	—	—	—
↳1833, O-106	*	194015	70	85	95	130	210	330	1,000	1,700
↳1833, O-107	*	194016	75	90	105	145	230	365	1,150	1,900
↳1833, O-108	*	194017	70	85	95	130	210	330	1,000	1,700
↳1833, O-109	*	194018	70	85	95	130	210	330	1,000	1,700
↳1833, O-110	*	194019	70	85	95	130	210	330	1,000	1,700
↳1833, O-110a	*	194020	75	90	105	145	230	365	1,150	1,900
↳1833, O-111	*	194021	85	100	115	155	250	400	1,250	2,050
↳1833, O-112	*	194022	70	85	95	130	210	330	1,000	1,700
↳1833, O-113	*	194023	75	90	105	145	230	365	1,150	1,900
↳1833, O-114	*	194024	70	85	95	130	210	330	1,000	1,700
↳1833, O-115	*	194025	—	310	900	1,100	1,750	—	—	—
1834, Large Date, Large Letters	6,412,004	6205	70	85	95	130	210	330	1,000	1,700
↳1834, Large Date, Large Letters, O-101	*	194414	70	85	95	130	210	330	1,000	1,700
↳1834, Large Date, Large Letters, O-102	*	194415	70	85	95	130	210	330	1,000	1,700
↳1834, Large Date, Large Letters, O-103	*	194416	70	85	95	130	210	330	1,000	1,700
1834, Large Date, Small Letters	*	6206	70	85	95	130	210	330	1,000	1,700
↳1834, Large Date, Small Letters, O-104	*	194417	70	85	95	130	210	330	1,000	1,700
↳1834, Large Date, Small Letters, O-105	*	194418	70	85	95	130	210	330	1,000	1,700
↳1834, Large Date, Small Letters, O-106	*	194419	70	85	95	130	210	330	1,000	1,700
↳1834, Large Date, Small Letters, O-107	*	194420	70	85	95	130	210	330	1,000	1,700
↳1834, Large Date, Small Letters, O-108	*	194421	70	85	95	130	210	330	1,000	1,700
1834, Small Date, Small Letters	*	6207	70	85	95	130	210	330	1,000	1,700
↳1834, Small Date, Small Letters, O-109	*	194422	70	85	95	130	210	330	1,000	1,700
↳1834, Small Date, Small Letters, O-110	*	194423	85	100	115	155	250	400	1,250	2,050
↳1834, Small Date, Small Letters, O-111	*	194424	70	85	95	130	210	330	1,000	1,700
↳1834, Small Date, Small Letters, O-112	*	194425	75	90	105	145	230	365	1,150	1,900
↳1834, Small Date, Small Letters, O-113	*	194426	70	85	95	130	210	330	1,000	1,700
↳1834, Small Date, Small Letters, O-114	*	194427	70	85	95	130	210	330	1,000	1,700
↳1834, Small Date, Small Letters, O-115	*	194428	70	85	95	130	210	330	1,000	1,700
↳1834, Small Date, Small Letters, O-115a	*	194429	85	100	115	155	250	400	1,250	2,050
↳1834, Small Date, Small Letters, O-116	*	194430	70	85	95	130	210	330	1,000	1,700
↳1834, Small Date, Small Letters, O-117	*	194431	70	85	95	130	210	330	1,000	1,700
↳1834, Small Date, Small Letters, O-118	*	194432	85	100	115	155	250	400	1,250	2,050
↳1834, Small Date, Small Letters, O-119	*	194433	85	100	115	155	250	400	1,250	2,050
↳1834, Small Date, Small Letters, O-120	*	194434	75	90	105	145	230	365	1,150	1,900
↳1834, Small Date, Small Letters, O-121	*	194435	75	90	105	145	230	365	1,150	1,900

* Included in number above.

1836, Over 1336

Circulation Strikes *(continued)*

	Mintage	GSID	G-4	VG-8	F-12	VF-20	EF-40	AU-50	MS-60	MS-63
1835	5,352,006	6210	$70	$85	$95	$130	$210	$330	$1,000	$1,700
↳1835, O-101	*	194026	70	85	95	130	210	330	1,000	1,700
↳1835, O-102	*	194027	75	90	105	145	230	365	1,150	1,900
↳1835, O-103	*	194028	70	85	95	130	210	330	1,000	1,700
↳1835, O-104	*	194029	85	100	115	155	250	400	1,250	2,050
↳1835, O-105	*	194030	70	85	95	130	210	330	1,000	1,700
↳1835, O-106	*	194031	70	85	95	130	210	330	1,000	1,700
↳1835, O-107	*	194032	70	85	95	130	210	330	1,000	1,700
↳1835, O-108	*	194033	75	90	105	145	230	365	1,150	1,900
↳1835, O-109	*	194034	70	85	95	130	210	330	1,000	1,700
↳1835, O-110	*	194035	75	90	105	145	230	365	1,150	1,900
1836, Lettered Edge	6,545,000	6213	70	85	95	130	210	330	1,000	1,700
↳1836, Lettered Edge, O-101	*	194436	70	85	95	130	210	330	1,000	1,700
↳1836, Lettered Edge, O-101a	*	194437	70	85	95	130	210	330	1,000	1,700
↳1836, Lettered Edge, O-102	*	194438	85	100	115	155	250	400	1,250	2,050
↳1836, Lettered Edge, O-103	*	194439	85	100	115	155	250	400	1,250	2,050
↳1836, Lettered Edge, O-104	*	194440	85	100	115	155	250	400	1,250	2,050
↳1836, Lettered Edge, O-104a	*	194441	75	90	105	145	230	365	1,150	1,900
↳1836, Lettered Edge, O-105	*	194442	85	100	115	155	250	400	1,250	2,050
↳1836, Lettered Edge, O-107	*	194445	85	100	115	155	250	400	1,250	2,050
↳1836, Lettered Edge, O-109	*	194448	85	100	115	155	250	400	1,250	2,050
↳1836, Lettered Edge, O-110	*	194449	70	85	95	130	210	330	1,000	1,700
↳1836, Lettered Edge, O-111	*	194450	85	100	115	155	250	400	1,250	2,050
↳1836, Lettered Edge, O-113	*	194452	70	85	95	130	210	330	1,000	1,700
↳1836, Lettered Edge, O-113a	*	194453	75	110	155	200	470	775	1,600	3,100
↳1836, Lettered Edge, O-114	*	194454	70	85	95	130	210	330	1,000	1,700
↳1836, Lettered Edge, O-115	*	194455	75	90	105	145	230	365	1,150	1,900
↳1836, Lettered Edge, O-116a	*	194457	90	110	125	170	270	430	1,300	2,250
↳1836, Lettered Edge, O-117	*	194458	75	90	105	145	230	365	1,150	1,900
↳1836, Lettered Edge, O-119	*	194460	85	100	115	155	250	400	1,250	2,050
↳1836, Lettered Edge, O-123	*	194464	85	100	115	155	250	400	1,250	2,050
1836, Lettered Edge, Beaded Border on Reverse	*	226428	70	85	95	130	210	330	1,000	1,700
↳1836, Lettered Edge, Beaded Reverse, O-106	*	194443	70	85	95	130	210	330	1,000	1,700
↳1836, Lettered Edge, Beaded Reverse, O-106a	*	194444	80	105	130	170	310	420	1,250	3,750
1836, Lettered Edge, Bar Dot	*	194466	70	85	95	130	210	330	1,000	1,700
↳1836, Lettered Edge, Bar Dot, O-112	*	194451	70	85	95	130	210	330	1,000	1,700
↳1836, Lettered Edge, Bar Dot, O-118	*	194459	75	90	105	145	230	365	1,150	1,900
↳1836, Lettered Edge, Bar Dot, O-120	*	194461	85	100	115	155	250	400	1,250	2,050
↳1836, Lettered Edge, Bar Dot, O-121	*	194462	260	415	675	1,750	2,500	3,750	—	—
↳1836, Lettered Edge, Bar Dot, O-122	*	194463	70	85	95	130	210	330	1,000	1,700
1836, Lettered Edge, 50 Over 00	*	6214	130	160	230	360	490	850	2,750	5,250
↳1836, Lettered Edge, 50 Over 00, O-116	*	194456	130	160	230	360	490	850	2,750	5,250
1836, Lettered Edge, 1836 Over 1336, Lettered Edge	*	68641	105	135	195	290	455	725	1,550	3,450
↳1836, Lettered Edge, 1836 Over 1336, O-108	*	194446	105	135	195	290	455	725	1,550	3,450
↳1836, Lettered Edge, 1836 Over 1336, O-108a	*	194447	105	135	195	290	455	725	1,550	3,450

* Included in number above.

Proof Strikes

		GSID	PF-60	PF-63	PF-65
1818	3–5 known	6160	$29,000	—	$108,000
	Auctions: $126,500, NGC PF-66 HA 01/08				
1820		6167	—	$72,000	—
1821		6169	—	—	78,000
1822	3–5 known	6171	—	—	—
1823		6176	—	90,000	—
1825	4–6 known	6181	—	—	—
1826	5–8 known	6183	—	36,000	102,000
1827	4–6 known	6186	—	66,000	102,000
	Auctions: $258,500, PCGS PF-67 SBG 02/16				
1829	6–8 known	6194	—	54,000	96,000
	Auctions: $102,812, PCGS PF-64 HA 01/14				
1830	4–6 known	6197	—	50,500	96,000
1831	4–6 known	6199	—	—	102,000
1832, Small Letters	4–6 known	6202	—	66,000	96,000
1833, Crushed Lettered Edge	4–6 known	6204	—	—	216,000
	Auctions: $141,000, PCGS PF-65 SBG 02/16				
1834	5–8 known	6208	—	26,500	72,000
	Auctions: $103,500, NGC PF-67 HA 01/07				
1834, Crushed Lettered Edge	5–8 known	6209	—	—	—
1835	4–6 known	6212	—	—	—
1835, Crushed Lettered Edge	2 known	6211	—	72,000	—
1836, Lettered Edge	6–10 known	6216	—	48,000	90,000
	Auctions: $109,250, NGC PF-67 HA 01/06				
1836, Lettered Edge, 50 Over 00	6–10 known	193561	—	54,000	—
	Auctions: $373,750, NGC PF-65 GLDB 02/08				

CAPPED BUST, REEDED EDGE (1836–1839)

Designer: *Christian Gobrecht.* **Weight:** *13.36 grams.* **Composition:** *.900 silver, .100 copper.* **Diameter:** *30 mm.* **Edge:** *Reeded.* **Mint:** *Philadelphia and New Orleans.*

Reverse 50 CENTS (1836–1837), Circulation Strike

Reverse 50 CENTS, Proof Strike

Reverse HALF DOL. (1838–1839), Circulation Strike

Mintmark location is on the obverse, above the date.

Reverse HALF DOL., Proof Strike

History. This half dollar type features a slight restyling of John Reich's Capped Bust design, modified by Christian Gobrecht. It is of smaller diameter than the preceding type, and made with a reeded edge. The reverse is of two variations: the 1836–1837, with 50 CENTS; and the 1838–1839, with HALF DOL.

Striking and Sharpness. The key points for observation are the stars on the obverse. On the reverse, check the border letters and the details of the eagle. The 1839-O nearly always shows die cracks, often extensive (these have no effect on desirability or market value).

Availability. The 1836 is rare. The 1838-O is a famous rarity, and the 1839-O is scarce. The others are easily available in nearly any grade desired, with 1837 being the most common. Proofs are occasionally encountered of the year 1836 and are quite rare. Authentic Proofs of 1837 exist but for all practical purposes are unobtainable. Most 1838-O (a rarity) and a few 1839-O coins have been called branch-mint Proofs.

Grading Standards

MS-60 to 70 (Mint State). ***Obverse and Reverse:*** Grading guidelines are the same as for the 1807–1836 type, except on this type the rims are more uniform. On the 1836–1837 dates the reverse rim is generally lower than the obverse, causing the reverse to wear slightly more quickly. On the 1838–1839 type (with slightly different lettering) the wear occurs evenly on both sides, and light striking showing areas of the original planchet on the obverse does not occur here.

MS-62

Illustrated coin: This example displays light gray toning with a sprinkling of gold over fully lustrous surfaces.

AU-50, 53, 55, 58 (About Uncirculated). ***Obverse and Reverse:*** Grading guidelines are the same as for the 1807–1836 type, except on this type the rims are more uniform. On the 1836–1837 dates the reverse rim is generally lower than the obverse, causing the reverse to wear slightly more quickly. On the 1838–1839 type (with slightly different lettering) the wear occurs evenly on both sides.

AU-53

EF-40, 45 (Extremely Fine). ***Obverse and Reverse:*** Grading guidelines are the same as for the 1807–1836 type, except on this type the rims are more uniform. On the 1836–1837 dates the reverse rim is generally lower than the obverse, causing the reverse to wear slightly more quickly. On the 1838–1839 type (with slightly different lettering) the wear occurs evenly on both sides.

EF-40

VF-20, 30 (Very Fine). ***Obverse and Reverse:*** Grading guidelines are the same as for the 1807–1836 type, except on this type the rims are more uniform. On the 1836–1837 dates the reverse rim is generally lower than the obverse, causing the reverse to wear slightly more quickly. On the 1838–1839 type (with slightly different lettering) the wear occurs evenly on both sides.

VF-20

F-12, 15 (Fine). ***Obverse and Reverse:*** Grading guidelines are the same as for the 1807–1836 type, except on this type the rims are more uniform. On the 1836–1837 dates the reverse rim is generally lower than the obverse, causing the reverse to wear slightly more quickly. On the 1838–1839 type (with slightly different lettering) the wear occurs evenly on both sides.

F-15

VG-8, 10 (Very Good). ***Obverse and Reverse:*** Grading guidelines are the same as for the 1807–1836 type, except on this type the rims are more uniform. On the 1836–1837 dates the reverse rim is generally lower than the obverse, causing the reverse to wear slightly more quickly. On the 1838–1839 type (with slightly different lettering) the wear occurs evenly on both sides.

VG-10

G-4, 6 (Good). ***Obverse and Reverse:*** Grading guidelines are the same as for the 1807–1836 type, except on this type the rims are more uniform. On the 1836–1837 dates the reverse rim is generally lower than the obverse, causing the reverse to wear slightly more quickly. On the 1838–1839 type (with slightly different lettering) the wear occurs evenly on both sides.

G-4

AG-3 (About Good). ***Obverse and Reverse:*** Grading guidelines are the same as for the 1807–1836 type, except on this type the rims are more uniform. On the 1836–1837 dates the reverse rim is generally lower than the obverse, causing the reverse to wear slightly more quickly. On the 1838–1839 type (with slightly different lettering) the wear occurs evenly on both sides.

AG-3

PF-60 to 70 (Proof). ***Obverse and Reverse:*** Proofs in grades of PF-60 to 62 show extensive hairlines and cloudiness. At PF-63, hairlines are obvious, but the mirrored fields are attractive. PF-64 and 65 coins have fewer hairlines, but they still are obvious when the coin is slowly turned while held at an angle to the light. PF-66 coins require a magnifier to discern hairlines, and higher grades should have no hairlines.

PF-64
Cameo

Circulation Strikes

	Mintage	GSID	G-4	VG-8	F-12	VF-20	EF-40	AU-50	MS-60	MS-63
Capped Bust, Reeded Edge (1836–1839)	n/a	72412	$80	$100	$130	$170	$390	$600	$1,500	$3,250
1836, Reeded Edge	1,200+	6215	1,100	1,400	2,000	2,500	3,750	4,750	9,500	19,500
↳1836, Reeded Edge, GR-1	*	377687	1,100	1,400	2,000	2,500	3,750	4,750	9,500	19,500
1837	3,629,820	6219	80	100	130	170	390	600	1,500	3,250
	Auctions: $103,500, PCGS MS-67 HA 08/06									
↳1837, GR-1	*	377688	80	100	130	170	390	600	1,500	3,250
↳1837, GR-3	*	377689	80	100	130	170	390	600	1,500	3,250
↳1837, GR-5	*	377690	80	100	130	170	390	600	1,500	3,250
↳1837, GR-6	*	377691	80	100	130	170	390	600	1,500	3,250
↳1837, GR-7	*	377692	80	100	130	170	390	600	1,500	3,250
↳1837, GR-8	*	377693	80	100	130	170	390	600	1,500	3,250
↳1837, GR-9	*	377694	80	100	130	170	390	600	1,500	3,250
	Auctions: $111,625, PCGS MS-67 SBG 05/16									
↳1837, GR-11	*	377695	80	100	130	170	390	600	1,500	3,250
↳1837, GR-12	*	377696	80	100	130	170	390	600	1,500	3,250
↳1837, GR-13	*	377697	80	100	130	170	390	600	1,500	3,250
↳1837, GR-14	*	377681	80	100	130	170	390	600	1,500	3,250
↳1837, GR-15	*	377698	80	100	130	170	390	600	1,500	3,250
↳1837, GR-16	*	377699	80	100	130	170	390	600	1,500	3,250
↳1837, GR-17	*	375303	80	100	130	170	390	600	1,500	3,250
	Auctions: $180,000, PCGS MS-67 HA 01/23									
↳1837, GR-20	*	377700	80	100	130	170	390	600	1,500	3,250
↳1837, GR-21	*	377701	80	100	130	170	390	600	1,500	3,250
↳1837, GR-23	*	377702	80	100	130	170	390	600	1,500	3,250
↳1837, GR-24	*	377703	80	100	130	170	390	600	1,500	3,250
↳1837, GR-25	*	377704	80	100	130	170	390	600	1,500	3,250
1838	3,546,000	6221	80	100	130	170	390	600	1,500	3,250
↳1838, GR-3	*	377705	80	100	130	170	390	600	1,500	3,250
↳1838, GR-4	*	377706	80	100	130	170	390	600	1,500	3,250
↳1838, GR-5	*	377707	80	100	130	170	390	600	1,500	3,250
↳1838, GR-6	*	377708	80	100	130	170	390	600	1,500	3,250
↳1838, GR-8	*	377709	80	100	130	170	390	600	1,500	3,250
↳1838, GR-9	*	377710	80	100	130	170	390	600	1,500	3,250
↳1838, GR-10	*	377711	80	100	130	170	390	600	1,500	3,250
↳1838, GR-11	*	377712	80	100	130	170	390	600	1,500	3,250
↳1838, GR-12	*	377713	80	100	130	170	390	600	1,500	3,250
↳1838, GR-13	*	377714	80	100	130	170	390	600	1,500	3,250
↳1838, GR-14	*	377715	80	100	130	170	390	600	1,500	3,250
↳1838, GR-15	*	377716	80	100	130	170	390	600	1,500	3,250
1839	1,392,976	6223	80	100	130	175	420	700	1,750	4,250
↳1839, GR-2	*	377717	80	100	130	175	420	700	1,750	4,250
↳1839, GR-3	*	377718	80	100	130	175	420	700	1,750	4,250
↳1839, GR-4	*	377719	80	100	130	175	420	700	1,750	4,250
↳1839, GR-5	*	377720	80	100	130	175	420	700	1,750	4,250
↳1839, GR-6	*	377721	80	100	130	175	420	700	1,750	4,250
↳1839, GR-7	*	377722	80	100	130	175	420	700	1,750	4,250
↳1839, GR-8	*	377723	80	100	130	175	420	700	1,750	4,250

* Included in number above.

1839, Regular Letters Reverse

1839, Small Letters Reverse

Circulation Strikes *(continued)*

	Mintage	GSID	G-4	VG-8	F-12	VF-20	EF-40	AU-50	MS-60	MS-63
1839, Small Letters Reverse	*	6224	$20,500	$26,500	$31,000	$48,000	$84,000	$114,000	—	—
1839-O	116,000	6250	725	950	1,400	1,900	2,750	3,750	$9,750	$17,000
	Auctions: $195,500, NGC MS-64 HA 08/08									
↳1839-O, GR-1	*	377724	725	950	1,400	1,900	2,750	3,750	9,750	17,000
	Auctions: $211,500, PCGS MS-67 SBG 05/16									
↳1839-O, GR-2	*	377725	725	950	1,400	1,900	2,750	3,750	9,750	17,000
↳1839-O, GR-3	*	377726	725	950	1,400	1,900	2,750	3,750	9,750	17,000
↳1839-O, GR-4	*	377727	725	950	1,400	1,900	2,750	3,750	9,750	17,000
↳1839-O, GR-5	*	377728	725	950	1,400	1,900	2,750	3,750	9,750	17,000

* Included in number above.

Proof Strikes

	Mintage	GSID	PF-60	PF-63	PF-65
1836, Reeded Edge	10–15 known	6217	$21,500	$31,000	$66,000
1837, Reeded Edge	3–5 known	6220	—	—	—
1838 (a)	5 est. known	6222	—	—	—
	Auctions: $336,000, PCGS PF-66 HA 08/18				
1838-O, Branch Mint	10 known	6248	450,000	540,000	—
	Auctions: $763,750, NGC PF-64 HA 01/14				
1839	1 or 2 known	6225	—	—	—
1839-O, Branch Mint	5	81393	—	150,000	264,000
	Auctions: $299,000, NGC PF-65 HA 02/12				

a. The 1838-O, Proof, was the first branch-mint half dollar, though it was not mentioned in the Mint director's report. The New Orleans chief coiner stated that only 20 were struck. All were struck as presentation pieces.

LIBERTY SEATED (1839–1891)

Variety 1, No Motto Above Eagle (1839–1853): **Designer:** *Christian Gobrecht.* **Weight:** *13.36 grams.* **Composition:** *.900 silver, .100 copper.* **Diameter:** *30.6 mm.* **Edge:** *Reeded.* **Mints:** *Philadelphia and New Orleans.*

Variety 1 (1839–1853), Circulation Strike

Mintmark location is on the reverse, below the eagle, for all varieties.

Variety 1, Proof Strike

Variety 2, Arrows at Date, Rays Around Eagle (1853): **Designer:** *Christian Gobrecht.* **Weight:** *12.44 grams.* **Composition:** *.900 silver, .100 copper.* **Diameter:** *30.6 mm.* **Edge:** *Reeded.* **Mints:** *Philadelphia and New Orleans.*

Variety 2 (1853), Circulation Strike

Variety 2, Proof Strike

Variety 3, Arrows at Date, No Rays (1854–1855): **Designer:** *Christian Gobrecht.* **Weight:** *12.44 grams.* **Composition:** *.900 silver, .100 copper.* **Diameter:** *30.6 mm.* **Edge:** *Reeded.* **Mints:** *Philadelphia, New Orleans, and San Francisco.*

Variety 3 (1854–1855), Circulation Strike

Variety 3, Proof Strike

Variety 1 Resumed, With Weight Standard of Variety 2 (1856–1866): **Designer:** *Christian Gobrecht.* **Weight:** *12.44 grams.* **Composition:** *.900 silver, .100 copper.* **Diameter:** *30.6 mm.* **Edge:** *Reeded.* **Mints:** *Philadelphia, New Orleans, and San Francisco.*

Variety 1 Resumed, Weight Standard of Variety 2 (1856–1866), Circulation Strike

Variety 1 Resumed, Weight Standard of Variety 2, Proof Strike

Variety 4, Motto Above Eagle (1866–1873): **Designer:** *Christian Gobrecht.*
Weight: *12.44 grams.* **Composition:** *.900 silver, .100 copper.* **Diameter:** *30.6 mm.*
Edge: *Reeded.* **Mints:** *Philadelphia, San Francisco, and Carson City.*

Variety 4 (1866–1873), Circulation Strike

Variety 4, Proof Strike

Variety 5, Arrows at Date (1873–1874): **Designer:** *Christian Gobrecht.*
Weight: *12.5 grams.* **Composition:** *.900 silver, .100 copper.* **Diameter:** *30.6 mm.*
Edge: *Reeded.* **Mints:** *Philadelphia, San Francisco, and Carson City.*

Variety 5 (1873–1874), Circulation Strike

Variety 5, Proof Strike

Variety 4 Resumed, With Weight Standard of Variety 5 (1875–1891): **Designer:** *Christian Gobrecht.*
Weight: *12.5 grams.* **Composition:** *.900 silver, .100 copper.* **Diameter:** *30.6 mm.*
Edge: *Reeded.* **Mints:** *Philadelphia, San Francisco, and Carson City.*

Variety 4 Resumed, Weight Standard of Variety 5 (1875–1891), Circulation Strike

Variety 4 Resumed, Weight Standard of Variety 5, Proof Strike

History. Half dollars of the Liberty Seated type were struck every year from 1839 to 1891. The designs varied slightly over the years, but with the basic obverse and reverse motifs remaining the same (e.g., from 1842 to 1853 the coins bore a modified reverse with large letters in the legend, and in 1846 the date size was enlarged). Large quantities were made until 1879, at which time there was a glut of silver coins in commerce. After that mintages were reduced. The earliest Liberty Seated half dollars, dated 1839, lacked drapery at Liberty's elbow. In that year Robert Ball Hughes modified Christian Gobrecht's design by adding drapery, a feature that continued for the rest of the series.

Striking and Sharpness. On the obverse, first check the head of Liberty and the star centers. On coins of the Arrows at Date variety, especially 1855, the word LIBERTY tends to wear faster compared to earlier and later varieties. On the reverse, check the eagle at the lower left. Afterward, check all other features. Generally, the higher-mintage issues are the least well struck, and many New Orleans Mint coins can be lightly struck, particularly those of the 1850s. The luster on MS coins usually is very attractive. Resurfaced dies often are prooflike, some with the drapery polished away (as with 1877-S, in particular). Above and beyond issues of strike, the Small Letters coins of 1839 to 1842 have narrower, lower rims that afforded less protection to the central devices of the reverse. In contrast, the No Motto, Large Letters, coins have wider, higher rims that tend to better protect the central devices. Many pre–Civil War dates, particularly of the 1840s, show evidence of extensive die polishing in the fields (especially evident in the open expanses of the obverse). From grades of EF downward, sharpness of strike of the stars and the head does not matter to connoisseurs. Quality is often lacking, with lint marks seen on some issues of the late 1850s and early 1860s. Light striking is occasionally seen on the star centers and the head of Liberty; connoisseurs avoid coins with this detraction, but most buyers will not be aware. Slide marks (usually seen on the right knee) from coin albums can be a problem, more so on Liberty Seated halves than on lower denominations of this design.

Availability. Collecting these coins is a popular pursuit with many enthusiasts. Examples of the higher-mintage dates are readily available, with earlier years being much scarcer than later ones. Most often seen among MS coins are issues from the mid-1870s onward. Circulated coins from well worn through AU can be found of most dates and mintmarks; these are avidly sought. Proofs were made in most years, with production beginning in a particularly significant way in 1858, when an estimated 210 silver sets were sold. Today, Proofs from 1858 through 1891 are readily available.

Grading Standards

MS-63

MS-60 to 70 (Mint State). ***Obverse:*** At MS-60, some abrasion and contact marks are evident, most noticeably on the bosom and thighs and knees. Luster is present, but may be dull or lifeless. At MS-63, contact marks are very few, and abrasion is hard to detect except under magnification. An MS-65 coin has no abrasion, and contact marks are sufficiently minute as to require magnification. Check the knees of Liberty and the right field. Luster should be full and rich. Most Mint State coins of the 1861 to 1865 years, Philadelphia issues, have extensive die striae (from dies not being completely finished); note that these are *raised* (whereas cleaning hairlines are incuse). ***Reverse:*** Comments as preceding, except that in lower Mint State grades abrasion and contact marks are most noticeable on the eagle's head, neck, and claws, and the top of the wings (harder to see there, however). At MS-65 or higher there are no marks visible to the unaided eye. The field is mainly protected by design elements and does not show abrasion as much as does the obverse on a given coin.

AU-50, 53, 55, 58 (About Uncirculated). ***Obverse:*** Light wear is seen on the thighs and knees, bosom, and head. At AU-58, the luster is extensive, but incomplete, especially in the right field. At AU-50 and 53, luster is less. ***Reverse:*** Wear is evident on the eagle's neck, the claws, and the top of the wings. An AU-58 coin has nearly full luster, more so than on the obverse, as the design elements protect the small field areas. At AU-50 and 53, there still are traces of luster.

AU-55

Illustrated coin: Gray toning is evident on this coin. The reverse is lightly struck, a characteristic that should not be mistaken for wear.

EF-40, 45 (Extremely Fine). ***Obverse:*** Further wear is seen on all areas, especially the thighs and knees, bosom, and head. Little or no luster is seen on most coins. From this grade downward, sharpness of strike of stars and the head does not matter to connoisseurs. ***Reverse:*** Further wear is evident on the eagle's neck, claws, and wings.

EF-40

VF-20, 30 (Very Fine). ***Obverse:*** Further wear is seen. Most details of the gown are worn away, except in the lower-relief areas above and to the right of the shield. Hair detail is mostly or completely gone. ***Reverse:*** Wear is more extensive, with some of the feathers blended together.

VF-20

F-12, 15 (Fine). ***Obverse:*** The seated figure is well worn, but with some detail above and to the right of the shield. LIBERTY is readable but weak in areas, perhaps with a letter missing (a slightly looser interpretation than the demand for full LIBERTY a generation ago). ***Reverse:*** Wear is extensive, with about a third to half of the feathers flat or blended with others.

F-12

VG-8, 10 (Very Good). ***Obverse:*** The seated figure is more worn, but some detail can be seen above and to the right of the shield. The shield is discernible, but the upper-right section may be flat and blended into the seated figure. In LIBERTY at least the equivalent of two or three letters (can be a combination of partial letters) must be readable, possibly very weak at VG-8, with a few more visible at VG-10. In the marketplace and among certified coins, parts of *two* letters seem to be allowed. Per PCGS, "localized weakness may obscure some letters." LIBERTY is *not* an infallible guide: some varieties have the word in low relief on the die, so it wore away slowly. ***Reverse:*** Further wear has flattened all but a few feathers, and many if not most horizontal lines of the shield are indistinct. The leaves are only in outline form. The rim is visible all around, as are the ends of most denticles.

VG-8

G-4, 6 (Good). ***Obverse:*** The seated figure is worn nearly smooth. At G-4 there are no letters in LIBERTY remaining on most (but not all) coins; some coins, especially of the early 1870s, are exceptions. At G-6, traces of one or two can barely be seen and more details can be seen in the figure. ***Reverse:*** The eagle shows only a few details of the shield and feathers. The rim is worn down, and the tops of the border letters are weak or worn away, although the inscription can still be read.

G-6

AG-3 (About Good). ***Obverse:*** The seated figure is visible in outline form. Much or all of the rim is worn away. The date remains clear. ***Reverse:*** The border letters are partially worn away. The eagle is mostly in outline form, but with a few details discernible. The rim is weak or missing.

AG-3

PF-60 to 70 (Proof). ***Obverse and Reverse:*** Proofs that are extensively cleaned and have many hairlines, or that are dull and grainy, are lower level, such as PF-60 to 62. These are not widely desired, save for the low mintage (in circulation-strike format) years from 1879 to 1891. With medium hairlines and good reflectivity, an assigned grade of PF-64 is appropriate, and with relatively few hairlines, Gem PF-65. In various grades hairlines are most easily seen in the obverse field. PF-66 should have hairlines so delicate that magnification is needed to see them. Above that, a Proof should be free of such lines.

PF-65

No Drapery From Elbow (1839)

Drapery From Elbow (Starting 1839)

Small Letters in Legend (1839–1841)

1840 (Only), Medium Letters, Large Eagle

Large Letters in Legend (1842–1853)

Circulation Strikes

	Mintage	GSID	G-4	VG-8	F-12	VF-20	EF-40	AU-50	MS-60	MS-63
Liberty Seated, No Drapery From Elbow, No Motto Above Eagle (1839)	**n/a**	**74466**	**$390**	**$470**	**$625**	**$1,150**	**$2,500**	**$4,100**	**$10,000**	**$25,000**
Liberty Seated, No Motto Above Eagle (1839–1853, 1856–1866)	**n/a**	**72415**	**55**	**70**	**85**	**110**	**210**	**340**	**825**	**1,550**
Liberty Seated, No Motto Above Eagle, Arrows at Date, Rays Around Eagle (1853)	**n/a**	**72416**	**70**	**95**	**130**	**170**	**365**	**700**	**1,550**	**3,750**
Liberty Seated, No Motto Above Eagle, Arrows at Date, No Rays Around Eagle (1854–1855)	**n/a**	**72417**	**55**	**65**	**80**	**100**	**175**	**280**	**575**	**1,250**
Liberty Seated, Motto Above Eagle (1866–1873, 1875–1891)	**n/a**	**72418**	**55**	**70**	**85**	**130**	**180**	**215**	**455**	**825**
Liberty Seated, Motto Above Eagle, Arrows at Date (1873–1874)	**n/a**	**72419**	**55**	**65**	**85**	**110**	**310**	**495**	**1,000**	**2,100**
1839, No Drapery From Elbow	*	6251	390	470	625	1,150	2,500	4,100	10,000	25,000
	Auctions: $172,500, NGC MS-67 HA 01/11									
1839, Drapery From Elbow	1,972,400	6252	60	90	110	155	430	775	2,250	5,000
1840, Small Letters	1,435,008	6254	95	130	145	195	390	525	1,000	2,000
1840, Medium Letters (a)	*	6253	325	455	775	1,000	2,000	2,600	6,750	11,000
1840-O	855,100	6312	60	75	110	180	325	490	2,250	5,500
1841	310,000	6255	75	100	130	195	390	725	1,500	2,900
1841-O	401,000	6313	75	100	130	170	455	850	1,500	3,550
↳1841-O, Medium O, Baseball Die Crack, FS-901, WB-2	*	226482	455	750	1,000	1,800	2,800	4,500	7,500	19,000

* Included in number above. **a.** Struck at the New Orleans Mint from a reverse die of the previous style without mintmark.

1842, Small Date

1842, Medium Date

1844-O, Doubled Date
FS-301

1847, 7 Over 6
FS-301

1846, Medium Date

1846, Tall Date

1846-O, Medium Date

1846-O, Tall Date

Circulation Strikes *(continued)*

	Mintage	GSID	G-4	VG-8	F-12	VF-20	EF-40	AU-50	MS-60	MS-63
1842, Small Date, Small Letters	*	6257	$10,000	$15,000	$21,000	$36,000	—	—	—	—
1842, Small Date, Large Letters	*	6258	90	130	155	210	$325	$725	$1,750	$4,250
1842, Medium Date	401,000	6256	60	80	100	130	220	455	1,150	2,250
1842-O, Small Date, Small Letters	4 known	6314	875	1,200	1,600	2,250	3,750	7,250	15,500	30,000
1842-O, Medium Date	203,000	6315	70	90	145	260	525	1,250	3,500	6,250
1843	3,844,000	6259	55	70	85	110	265	495	1,000	2,250
1843-O	2,268,000	6316	75	95	115	150	275	525	2,050	4,000
1844	1,766,000	6260	55	70	90	145	260	440	925	2,000
1844-O	2,005,000	6317	55	70	100	175	345	550	1,750	3,750
↳1844-O, Doubled Date	*	6318	850	1,100	1,300	2,000	3,400	5,500	7,000	18,000
1845	589,000	6261	70	90	120	180	470	775	1,500	4,400
1845-O	2,094,000	6319	55	90	95	130	255	490	1,000	3,400
↳1845-O, Repunched Date, FS-302, WB-18	*	373152	—	180	275	440	625	850	2,050	—
↳1845-O, Repunched Date, FS-303, WB-1	*	226483	70	105	115	155	305	575	1,250	4,050
↳1845-O, O Over Horizontal O, FS-501, WB-3	*	226484	145	195	340	575	800	1,100	1,500	—
1845-O, No Drapery (b)	*	6320	100	130	160	195	525	875	1,300	4,400
1846, Medium Date	2,210,000	6262	55	70	85	110	240	470	1,050	2,100
↳1846, Tall Date	*	6264	100	130	195	290	390	490	1,300	2,500
↳1846, 6 Over Horizontal 6	*	6263	325	470	850	1,250	2,100	3,250	6,250	9,500
1846-O, Medium Date	2,304,000	6321	55	80	130	170	310	525	2,000	5,000
↳1846-O, Tall Date	*	6322	230	325	525	900	2,000	2,250	10,500	18,000
1847	1,156,000	6265	60	85	110	145	245	390	900	2,250
1847, 7 Over 6, Early Die State	*	310733	2,500	3,100	3,750	4,500	10,500	13,000	24,000	—
↳1847, 7 Over 6, Early Die State, FS-301, WB-9	*	6323	2,500	3,100	3,750	4,500	10,500	13,000	24,000	—
1847, 7 Over 6, Late Die State	*	310734	80	110	135	185	320	500	1,150	2,900
↳1847, 7 Over 6, Late Die State, FS-301A, WB-10	*	226485	80	110	135	185	320	500	1,150	2,900
1847-O	2,584,000	6324	55	70	85	120	240	525	1,450	5,000
1848	580,000	6266	55	70	130	210	360	725	1,250	3,000
1848-O	3,180,000	6325	55	70	85	155	310	575	1,550	2,500

* Included in number above. **b.** Drapery is missing because of excessive die polishing.

1849, Dramatically Doubled Date

1855, 1855 Over 854
FS-301

Circulation Strikes *(continued)*

	Mintage	GSID	G-4	VG-8	F-12	VF-20	EF-40	AU-50	MS-60	MS-63
1849	1,252,000	6267	$55	$80	$90	$130	$240	$420	$1,150	$2,750
↳1849, Dramatically Doubled Date	*	331689	950	1,250	1,900	3,000	4,000	5,000	—	—
1849-O	2,310,000	6326	65	80	110	150	405	850	1,600	3,500
1850	227,000	6268	455	575	725	850	1,000	1,300	2,100	4,500
	Auctions: $117,500, PCGS MS-67 HA 05/15									
1850-O	2,456,000	6327	55	70	85	120	230	390	1,000	2,000
1851	200,750	6269	900	950	1,150	1,400	2,100	2,500	3,750	4,750
1851-O	402,000	6328	120	180	260	390	650	1,000	1,600	4,500
1852	77,130	6270	525	650	775	1,150	1,900	2,400	3,500	5,000
1852-O	144,000	6329	470	600	775	950	1,400	2,250	4,500	13,000
1853-O	4 known	6330	198,000	222,000	300,000	432,000	780,000	—	—	—
	Auctions: $288,000, PCGS G6 HA 01/25; $228,000, PCGS F-12 SBG 01/25									
1853	3,532,708	6271	70	95	130	170	365	700	1,550	3,750
1853-O	1,328,000	6331	70	95	130	170	470	950	3,100	7,000
1854	2,982,000	6272	55	65	80	100	175	280	575	1,250
1854-O	5,240,000	6332	55	65	80	100	175	280	575	1,250
1855, Normal Date	759,500	6273	55	65	80	100	195	420	1,100	2,000
1855, 1855 Over 1854	*	6333	100	160	230	390	550	1,000	2,100	4,000
1855-O	3,688,000	6334	55	65	80	100	175	280	575	1,400
1855-S	129,950	6335	525	1,200	1,400	1,750	3,750	6,250	24,000	60,000
	Auctions: $132,250, NGC MS-67 SBG 08/11									
1856	938,000	6274	55	70	85	110	210	340	900	1,700
1856-O	2,658,000	6336	60	75	95	130	255	405	950	1,950
1856-S	211,000	6337	170	260	455	625	1,250	2,100	5,500	11,000
1857	1,988,000	6275	55	70	85	110	210	340	825	1,550
1857-O	818,000	6338	55	70	85	120	260	525	1,750	4,400
1857-S	158,000	6339	210	260	390	525	1,250	2,000	3,750	9,750
1858	4,225,700	6276	55	70	85	110	210	340	825	1,550
1858-O	7,294,000	6340	55	70	85	110	210	340	900	1,900
1858-S	476,000	6341	60	95	130	230	360	650	2,000	4,700
1859	747,200	6277	55	70	85	110	210	340	825	1,700
1859-O	2,834,000	6342	55	80	95	120	220	370	900	2,000
1859-S	566,000	6343	70	95	125	180	290	650	1,450	3,750
1860	302,700	6278	55	70	85	110	230	385	975	1,750
1860-O	1,290,000	6344	55	70	85	130	245	385	1,000	1,800
1860-S	472,000	6345	75	110	145	180	390	575	2,000	5,500
1861	2,887,400	6279	65	75	95	130	285	470	1,000	1,750

* Included in number above.

1861-O, CSA Obverse, Cracked Die
FS-401

Circulation Strikes *(continued)*

	Mintage	GSID	G-4	VG-8	F-12	VF-20	EF-40	AU-50	MS-60	MS-63
1861-O (c)	2,532,633	6346	$90	$130	$180	$260	$575	$850	$1,800	$3,750
↳**1861-O, Bisected Date, Speared Olive Bud**	*	226497	95	145	220	390	1,500	3,750	—	—
1861-O, CSA Obverse (d)	*	76266	90	130	180	260	650	1,250	2,200	4,050
↳**861-O, CSA Obverse, Cracked Die, FS-401** (d)	*	226495	390	650	900	1,250	3,600	5,750	19,000	26,500
↳**1861-O, CSA Obverse, Bisected Date, FS-402**	*	226496	90	130	180	260	650	1,250	2,200	4,050
↳**1861-O, CSA Obverse, Speared Olive, FS-901**	*	226498	160	260	390	525	1,000	2,000	4,400	7,000
1861-S	939,500	6347	60	75	110	130	420	775	1,250	3,500
1862	253,000	6280	80	115	155	230	390	650	1,200	1,900
1862-S	1,352,000	6348	70	90	95	160	260	455	1,300	2,600
1863	503,200	6281	145	210	285	390	725	950	1,300	2,050
1863-S	916,000	6349	100	130	160	245	415	625	1,600	3,100
1864	379,100	6282	100	150	285	490	725	1,050	2,200	3,250
1864-S	658,000	6350	100	145	215	260	575	1,000	2,500	6,250
1865	511,400	6283	120	135	170	290	725	1,250	2,400	2,900
↳**1865, Repunched Date, FS-301**	*	373156	140	165	205	350	850	1,500	2,850	3,500
1865-S	675,000	6351	130	170	210	275	625	900	2,500	4,400
1866-S, No Motto	60,000	6352	725	850	950	1,200	1,900	2,750	10,000	15,500
	Auctions: $164,500, NGC MS-67 HA 11/13									
1866	744,900	6284	70	80	90	130	210	325	775	2,050
1866-S	994,000	6353	75	90	115	180	275	455	1,400	3,000
1867	449,300	6285	80	100	155	245	360	625	1,150	2,000
1867-S	1,196,000	6354	70	80	115	155	260	575	1,900	3,550
1868	417,600	6286	90	115	130	210	325	575	1,000	2,000
1868-S	1,160,000	6355	55	75	115	190	325	440	1,500	3,750
1869	795,300	6287	70	80	95	130	215	405	900	1,700
1869-S	656,000	6356	75	90	100	135	260	525	1,250	3,100
1870	633,900	6288	55	75	100	155	260	495	875	2,000
1870-CC	54,617	6357	2,100	3,750	5,500	6,750	12,000	29,000	74,500	192,000
	Auctions: $198,375, NGC MS-62 SBG 08/11									
1870-S	1,004,000	6358	80	100	130	195	550	850	2,750	4,750

* Included in number above. **c.** The 1861-O mintage includes 330,000 half dollars struck by the United States government; 1,240,000 struck for the State of Louisiana after it seceded from the Union; and 962,633 struck after Louisiana joined the Confederate States of America. All of these coins were made from federal dies, rendering it impossible to distinguish one from another with but one exception. **d.** In 1861, the New Orleans Mint used a federal obverse die and a Confederate reverse die to strike a handful of Confederate half dollars. That particular obverse die was also paired with a regular federal reverse die to strike some 1861-O half dollars, which today are popular among collectors, especially in higher grades. Their identifying feature is a die crack running from the denticles to the right of the sixth star down to Liberty's nose (and to her shoulder below her jaw).

1873, Close 3

1873, Open 3

1877, 7 Over 6
FS-301

Circulation Strikes *(continued)*

	Mintage	GSID	G-4	VG-8	F-12	VF-20	EF-40	AU-50	MS-60	MS-63
1871	1,203,600	6289	$55	$70	$85	$130	$180	$285	$775	$1,400
1871-CC	153,950	6359	725	1,000	1,400	2,250	4,000	6,500	31,000	78,000
1871-S	2,178,000	6360	55	70	85	130	195	290	1,000	2,400
1872	880,600	6290	55	70	85	130	180	290	850	1,400
1872-CC	257,000	6361	525	675	1,200	1,500	3,250	5,750	24,000	60,000
	Auctions: $100,625, PCGS MS-62 SU 09/08									
1872-S	580,000	6362	55	70	115	195	325	650	2,000	3,900
1873, No Arrows, Closed 3	587,000	6291	55	70	85	145	215	430	1,150	2,250
1873, No Arrows, Open 3	*	6292	3,450	4,750	5,000	6,000	8,750	13,000	42,000	78,000
1873-CC, No Arrows	214,200	6363	390	650	1,150	2,000	3,500	6,250	12,500	32,500
1873, With Arrows	1,815,200	6293	55	65	85	110	310	495	1,000	2,100
↳1873, Small Arrows, Doubled Die Obverse, Quadruple Stripes, FS-101, WB-109	*	285908	65	80	100	130	375	600	1,250	2,550
1873-CC, With Arrows	214,560	6364	275	525	650	1,000	2,000	3,300	9,500	18,000
1873-S	228,000	6365	80	160	230	260	650	850	3,250	8,750
1874	2,359,600	6294	55	65	85	110	310	495	1,000	2,100
1874-CC	59,000	6366	1,200	1,900	3,000	4,250	6,250	8,250	16,000	31,000
1874-S	394,000	6367	100	195	235	260	390	750	1,700	2,900
1875	6,026,800	6295	55	70	85	130	180	215	455	825
1875-CC	1,008,000	6368	110	155	285	440	900	1,250	2,250	4,100
1875-S	3,200,000	6369	55	70	85	130	180	215	455	825
1876	8,418,000	6296	55	70	85	130	180	215	455	825
↳1876, Large Over Small Date, FS-301, WB-106	*	373160	160	290	525	800	1,100	1,250	1,700	—
1876-CC	1,956,000	6370	115	175	325	430	875	1,300	2,500	4,000
↳1876-CC, Misplaced Date, FS-301, WB-23	*	373164	125	195	360	470	950	1,450	2,750	4,400
1876-S	4,528,000	6371	55	70	85	130	180	215	525	1,100
1877	8,304,000	6297	55	70	85	130	180	215	455	825
1877, 7 Over 6	*	6372	—	285	390	625	1,250	2,750	5,000	7,500
↳1877, 7 Over 6, FS-301	*	377729	—	285	390	625	1,250	2,750	5,000	7,500
1877-CC	1,420,000	6373	100	130	210	390	575	825	1,550	2,800
1877-S	5,356,000	6374	55	70	85	130	180	215	455	825
1878	1,377,600	6298	70	100	130	135	210	290	525	1,250
1878-CC	62,000	6375	1,550	2,000	2,600	3,250	4,500	5,750	12,000	20,000
1878-S	12,000	6376	31,000	45,500	53,000	60,000	75,500	81,500	102,000	156,000
	Auctions: $288,000, PCGS MS-66 SBG 03/20									
1879	4,800	6299	415	525	650	775	950	1,100	1,400	1,800
1880	8,400	6300	325	525	625	725	950	1,050	1,400	2,000
1881	10,000	6301	430	525	725	850	950	1,250	1,700	2,200
1882	4,400	6302	325	360	490	575	850	950	1,200	1,600
1883	8,000	6303	365	415	575	650	900	1,050	1,400	2,400

* Included in number above.

Circulation Strikes *(continued)*

	Mintage	GSID	G-4	VG-8	F-12	VF-20	EF-40	AU-50	MS-60	MS-63
1884	4,400	6304	$390	$470	$650	$850	$1,150	$1,250	$1,550	$2,100
1885	5,200	6305	360	390	490	575	850	950	1,200	2,000
1886	5,000	6306	390	490	525	575	850	1,000	1,250	1,900
1887	5,000	6307	490	550	625	675	850	950	1,200	2,000
1888	12,001	6308	390	455	600	800	950	1,100	1,400	2,050
1889	12,000	6309	260	360	455	550	900	1,000	1,250	2,400
1890	12,000	6310	275	360	455	550	750	950	1,300	1,900
	Auctions: $120,000, PCGS MS-68 SBG 03/20									
1891	200,000	6311	60	90	145	160	230	360	550	1,250

Proof Strikes

		GSID	PF-60	PF-63	PF-65
Liberty Seated, No Drapery, No Motto Above Eagle (1839), Proof	**n/a**	**76201**	**$60,000**	**$108,000**	**$210,000**
Liberty Seated, No Motto Above Eagle (1839–1866), Proof	**n/a**	**74065**	**1,150**	**2,000**	**4,000**
Same, Proof Cameo	**n/a**	**74066**	**1,750**	**2,750**	**6,000**
Same, Proof Deep Cameo	**n/a**	**74067**	**—**	**5,000**	**13,000**
Liberty Seated, Arrows at Date, Rays Around Eagle (1853), Proof	**n/a**	**76202**	**39,000**	**90,000**	**192,000**
Liberty Seated, Arrows at Date, (1854–1855), Proof	**n/a**	**76203**	**9,000**	**14,500**	**36,000**
Same, Proof Cameo	**n/a**	**76204**	**—**	**—**	**42,000**
Liberty Seated, Motto Above Eagle (1866–1891), Proof	**n/a**	**74068**	**775**	**1,250**	**2,200**
Same, Proof Cameo	**n/a**	**74069**	**—**	**1,300**	**2,750**
Same, Proof Deep Cameo	**n/a**	**74070**	**—**	**2,400**	**5,500**
Liberty Seated, Arrows at Date (1873–1874), Proof	**n/a**	**74071**	**1,100**	**2,000**	**7,500**
Same, Proof Cameo	**n/a**	**74072**	**—**	**2,200**	**8,250**
Same, Proof Deep Cameo	**n/a**	**74073**	**—**	**—**	**—**
1839, No Drapery	4–6 known	6382	60,000	108,000	210,000
	Auctions: $241,500, NGC PF-65 HA 05/09				
1839, With Drapery	1–2 known	6379	—	—	—
	Auctions: $102,000, NGC PF-64 SBG 03/24				
1840	4–8 known	6383	15,000	36,000	72,000
	Auctions: $109,250, NGC PF-65 HA 08/07				
1841	4–8 known	6386	14,000	27,000	37,000
1842	4–8 known	6389	12,500	29,000	60,000
1843	4–8 known	6392	12,000	30,000	54,000
1844	3-6 known	6397	14,500	33,500	66,000
1845	3-6 known	6400	11,000	24,000	42,000
1846	15–20 known	6401	11,000	18,000	45,500
1847	15–20 known	6404	11,000	20,500	36,000
1848	4–8 known	6409	—	—	72,000
1849	4–8 known	6410	11,000	20,500	42,000
1850	4–8 known	6415	11,000	20,500	42,000
	Auctions: $161,000, NGC PF-66 HA 01/08				
1852	3–6 known	6419	14,500	29,500	51,500
1852-O, Branch Mint		6548	—	—	—
1853	5–6 est. known	6422	39,000	90,000	192,000
	Auctions: $228,000, PCGS PF-65 HA 08/18				
1854	15–20 known	6425	9,000	16,000	38,500
1855	9 est. known	6428	9,000	14,500	36,000
	Auctions: $112,125, NGC PF-63 DLRC 03/05				

Proof Strikes

	Mintage	GSID	PF-60	PF-63	PF-65
1855-S, Branch Mint	2–3 est. known	6552	—	$186,000	—
	Auctions: $276,000, NGC PF-65 HA 08/11				
1855, 55 Over 54	*	6549	$9,500	18,000	$55,000
1856	20–30 known	6431	4,250	8,000	21,000
1857	30–50 known	6434	2,500	3,500	20,000
1858	300	6437	1,250	2,250	6,250
1859	800	6440	1,250	2,600	4,900
1860	1,000	6443	1,150	2,000	5,750
1861	1,000	6446	1,250	2,250	4,600
1861-O, Special Strike	4 known	376129	—	90,000	—
1862	550	6449	1,200	2,150	4,250
1863	460	6452	1,400	2,400	4,600
1864	470	6455	1,150	2,000	4,000
1865	500	6458	1,150	2,000	4,000
1866, Motto Above Eagle	725	6462	775	1,250	3,100
1867	625	6467	775	1,300	2,900
1868	600	6470	775	1,300	3,250
1869	600	6473	950	1,500	3,750
1870	1,000	6476	775	1,600	2,750
1871	960	6479	775	1,300	3,100
1872	950	6482	850	1,250	2,400
1873, No Arrows, Closed 3	600	6485	775	1,250	2,500
1873, With Arrows	500	6486	1,100	2,000	7,500
1874	700	6494	1,100	2,000	7,500
1875	700	6497	775	1,250	2,200
1876	1,150	6500	775	1,250	2,200
1877	510	6503	775	1,250	3,000
1878	800	6506	775	1,250	2,200
1879	1,100	6509	775	1,250	2,200
1880	1,355	6512	775	1,250	2,200
1881	975	6515	775	1,250	2,200
1882	1,100	6518	775	1,250	2,200
1883	1,039	6521	775	1,250	2,200
1884	875	6524	775	1,250	2,200
1885	930	6527	775	1,250	2,200
1886	886	6530	775	1,250	2,200
1887	710	6533	775	1,250	2,200
1888	832	6536	775	1,250	2,200
1889	711	6539	775	1,250	2,200
1890	590	6542	775	1,250	2,200
1891	600	6545	775	1,250	2,200

BARBER (1892–1915)

Designer: *Charles E. Barber.* **Weight:** *12.5 grams.* **Composition:** *.900 silver, .100 copper.* **Diameter:** *30.6 mm.* **Edge:** *Reeded.* **Mints:** *Philadelphia, Denver, New Orleans, and San Francisco.*

Circulation Strike

Mintmark location is on the reverse, below the eagle.

Proof Strike

History. Charles E. Barber, chief engraver of the U.S. Mint, crafted the eponymous "Barber" or Liberty Head half dollars along with similarly designed dimes and quarters of the same era. His initial, B, is at the truncation of Liberty's neck. Production of the coins was continuous from 1892 to 1915, stopping a year before the dime and quarter of the same design.

Striking and Sharpness. On the obverse, check Liberty's hair details and other features. On the reverse, the eagle's leg at the lower right and the arrows often are weak, and there can be weakness at the upper right of the shield and the nearby wing area. At EF and below, sharpness of strike on the reverse is not important. Most Proofs are sharply struck, although many are weak on the eagle's leg at the lower right and on certain parts of the arrows and/or the upper-right area of the shield and the nearby wing. The Proofs of 1892 to 1901 usually have cameo contrast between the designs and the mirror fields. Those of 1914 and 1915 are often with extensive hairlines or other problems.

Availability. Most examples seen in the marketplace are well worn. There are no rarities in the Barber half dollar series, although some are scarcer than others. Coins that are Fine or better are much scarcer—in particular the San Francisco Mint issues of 1901, 1904, and 1907. MS coins are available of all dates and mints, but some are very elusive. Proofs exist in proportion to their mintages. Choicer examples tend to be of later dates, similar to other Barber coins.

Grading Standards

MS-60 to 70 (Mint State). ***Obverse:*** At MS-60, some abrasion and contact marks are evident, most noticeably on the cheek and the obverse field to the right. Luster is present, but may be dull or lifeless. Many Barber coins have been cleaned, especially of the earlier dates. At MS-63, contact marks are very few; abrasion still is evident but less than at lower levels. Indeed, the cheek of Liberty virtually showcases abrasion. This is even more evident on a half dollar than on lower denominations. An MS-65 coin may have minor abrasions, but contact marks are so minute as to require magnification. Luster should be full and rich. ***Reverse:*** Comments apply as for the obverse, except that in lower Mint State grades abrasion and contact marks are most noticeable on the head and tail of the eagle and on the tips of the wings. At MS-65 or higher there are no marks visible to the unaided eye. The field is mainly protected by design elements, so the reverse often appears to grade a point or two higher than the obverse.

MS-62

Illustrated coin: On this example, mottled light-brown toning appears over lustrous surfaces.

AU-53

AU-50, 53, 55, 58 (About Uncirculated). ***Obverse:*** Light wear is seen on the head, especially on the forward hair under LIBERTY. At AU-58, the luster is extensive but incomplete, especially on the higher parts and in the right field. At AU-50 and 53, luster is less. ***Reverse:*** Wear is seen on the head and tail of the eagle and on the tips of the wings. At AU-50 and 53, there still is significant luster. An AU-58 coin (as determined by the obverse) can have the reverse appear to be full Mint State.

Illustrated coin: Areas of original Mint luster can be seen on this coin, more so on the reverse than on the obverse.

EF-45

EF-40, 45 (Extremely Fine). ***Obverse:*** Further wear is seen on the head. The hair above the forehead lacks most detail. LIBERTY shows wear but still is strong. ***Reverse:*** Further wear is seen on the head and tail of the eagle and on the tips of the wings, most evident at the left and right extremes of the wings At this level and below, sharpness of strike on the reverse is not important.

VF-30

VF-20, 30 (Very Fine). ***Obverse:*** The head shows more wear, now with nearly all detail gone in the hair above the forehead. LIBERTY shows wear, but is complete. The leaves on the head all show wear, as does the upper part of the cap. ***Reverse:*** Wear is more extensive, particularly noticeable on the outer parts of the wings, the head, the shield, and the tail.

Illustrated coin: This coin is seemingly lightly cleaned.

F-12

F-12, 15 (Fine). ***Obverse:*** The head shows extensive wear. LIBERTY, the key place to check, is weak, especially at ER, but is fully readable. The ANA grading standards and *Photograde* adhere to this. PCGS suggests that lightly struck coins "may have letters partially missing." Traditionally, collectors insist on full LIBERTY. ***Reverse:*** More wear is seen on the reverse, in the places as above. E PLURIBUS UNUM is light, with one to several letters worn away.

VG-8, 10 (Very Good). ***Obverse:*** A net of three letters in LIBERTY must be readable. Traditionally LI is clear, and after that there is a partial letter or two. ***Reverse:*** Further wear has smoothed more than half of the feathers in the wing. The shield is indistinct except for a few traces of interior lines. The motto is partially worn away. The rim is full, and many if not most denticles can be seen.

VG-8

G-4, 6 (Good). ***Obverse:*** The head is in outline form, with the center flat. Most of the rim is there and all letters and the date are full. ***Reverse:*** The eagle shows only a few feathers, and only a few scattered letters remain in the motto. The rim may be worn flat in some or all of the area, but the peripheral lettering is clear.

Illustrated coin: On this coin the obverse is perhaps G-6 and the reverse AG-3. The grade might be averaged as G-4.

G-4

AG-3 (About Good). ***Obverse:*** The stars and motto are worn, and the border may be indistinct. Distinctness varies at this level. The date is clear. Grading is usually determined by the reverse. ***Reverse:*** The rim is gone and the letters are partially worn away. The eagle is mostly flat, perhaps with a few hints of feathers. Usually, the obverse appears to be in a slightly higher grade than the reverse.

AG-3

PF-60 to 70 (Proof). ***Obverse and Reverse:*** Proofs that are extensively cleaned and have many hairlines, or that are dull and grainy, are lower level, such as PF-60 to 62; these are not widely desired. With medium hairlines and good reflectivity, an assigned grade of PF-64 is appropriate. Tiny horizontal lines on Liberty's cheek, known as slide marks, from National and other album slides scuffing the relief of the cheek, are endemic on all Barber silver coins. With noticeable marks of this type, the highest grade assignable is PF-64. With relatively few hairlines, a rating of PF-65 can be given. PF-66 should have hairlines so delicate that magnification is needed to see them. Above that, a Proof should be free of any hairlines or other problems.

Illustrated coin: This is an attractive coin at the relatively low PF-61 grade.

PF-61

1892-O, Normal O

1892-O, Micro O
FS-501

Circulation Strikes

	Mintage	GSID	G-4	VG-8	F-12	VF-20	EF-40	AU-50	MS-60	MS-63
Barber (1892–1915)	**n/a**	**72413**	**$26**	**$31**	**$60**	**$160**	**$215**	**$340**	**$625**	**$925**
1892	934,000	6553	70	80	95	180	240	365	650	925
↳1892, Tripled Die Reverse, FS-801	*	226406	80	95	115	210	340	650	1,300	1,800
1892-O	390,000	6577	285	600	650	775	950	1,100	1,300	2,000
	Auctions: $108,688, NGC MS-66 HA 04/13									
↳1892-O, Micro O	<100 known	6578	6,250	7,750	11,000	13,500	17,000	19,000	33,500	43,000
	Auctions: $199,750, PCGS MS-68 LGND 05/22									
↳1892-O, Micro O, FS-501	<100 known	351943	6,250	7,750	11,000	13,500	17,000	19,000	33,500	43,000
1892-S	1,029,028	6579	310	390	470	675	900	1,200	1,700	2,600
1893	1,826,000	6554	37	48	85	180	240	405	675	1,100
1893-O	1,389,000	6580	47	90	150	260	420	575	900	1,250
1893-S	740,000	6581	155	390	725	950	1,500	1,950	2,850	4,750
1894	1,148,000	6555	42	55	120	210	260	410	675	1,000
1894-O	2,138,000	6582	35	47	100	180	255	495	800	1,300
1894-S	4,048,690	6583	30	47	95	180	310	470	750	1,550
1895	1,834,338	6556	30	44	75	180	240	375	675	1,050
1895-O	1,766,000	6584	43	75	155	195	255	410	850	1,600
1895-S	1,108,086	6585	90	180	310	495	725	775	1,200	2,400
1896	950,000	6557	39	50	85	180	240	470	775	1,250
1896-O	924,000	6586	100	220	390	950	2,500	4,750	11,000	19,000
	Auctions: $123,375, PCGS MS-67 LGND 01/19									
1896-S	1,140,948	6587	145	210	415	800	1,500	1,900	2,950	3,750
1897	2,480,000	6558	30	39	70	175	240	375	675	1,150
1897-O	632,000	6588	160	240	525	1,200	2,050	2,600	3,750	6,600
1897-S	933,900	6589	155	235	365	575	1,400	1,900	3,000	3,450
1898	2,956,000	6559	29	36	70	160	215	340	625	950
1898-O	874,000	6590	45	105	220	525	725	875	1,700	2,600
1898-S	2,358,550	6591	42	65	120	195	430	675	1,900	2,700
↳1898-S, Inverted Mintmark, FS-501	*	351945	46	70	130	215	470	750	2,050	2,950
1899	5,538,000	6560	29	33	60	160	215	340	625	925
1899-O	1,724,000	6592	30	43	95	180	255	405	1,150	1,950
1899-S	1,686,411	6593	30	45	95	180	260	455	1,000	2,400
↳1899-S, Inverted Mintmark, FS-501	*	351946	33	49	105	200	285	500	1,150	2,600
1900	4,762,000	6561	29	33	60	180	240	375	675	1,000
1900-O	2,744,000	6594	37	60	110	200	415	625	2,200	4,750
1900-S	2,560,322	6595	34	47	95	210	390	550	1,100	2,600
1901	4,268,000	6562	26	31	60	160	215	340	625	925
1901-O	1,124,000	6596	45	90	180	340	1,300	1,900	2,450	4,400
1901-S	847,044	6597	85	130	340	550	1,550	2,400	4,400	7,250

* Included in number above.

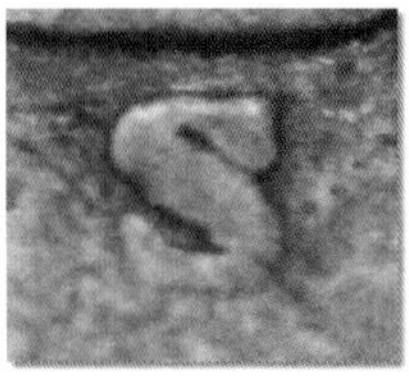

1906-S, Inverted Mintmark
FS-501

1911-S, Repunched/Inverted Mintmark
FS-501

Circulation Strikes *(continued)*

	Mintage	GSID	G-4	VG-8	F-12	VF-20	EF-40	AU-50	MS-60	MS-63
1902	4,922,000	6563	$26	$33	$60	$160	$215	$340	$625	$925
1902-O	2,526,000	6598	29	34	70	180	255	470	1,000	2,000
1902-S	1,460,670	6599	30	40	120	260	470	650	1,550	2,500
1903	2,278,000	6564	29	37	75	180	240	375	725	1,250
1903-O	2,100,000	6600	29	35	65	180	240	475	950	1,500
1903-S	1,920,772	6601	29	39	90	215	390	650	1,250	2,250
1904	2,992,000	6565	26	31	60	160	215	340	625	925
1904-O	1,117,600	6602	39	55	130	290	650	1,150	2,000	4,100
1904-S	553,038	6603	70	155	455	1,000	2,100	6,500	12,000	18,000
	Auctions: $138,000, PCGS MS-67 HA 08/10									
1905	662,000	6566	30	47	110	185	240	490	775	1,300
	Auctions: $132,250, PCGS MS-68 HA 08/10									
1905-O	505,000	6604	37	60	175	260	415	775	1,250	1,900
1905-S	2,494,000	6605	30	37	80	180	255	470	850	1,350
1906	2,638,000	6567	26	31	60	160	215	340	625	925
1906-D	4,028,000	6606	26	31	60	160	215	340	625	925
1906-O	2,446,000	6607	29	33	65	175	340	575	1,100	1,900
1906-S	1,740,154	6608	30	41	130	230	280	475	1,250	1,950
↳**1906-S, Inverted Mintmark, FS-501**	*	351947	33	46	145	250	305	525	1,400	2,150
1907	2,598,000	6568	26	33	60	160	215	340	625	925
1907-D	3,856,000	6609	29	31	60	160	215	340	625	975
1907-O	3,946,600	6610	30	41	70	160	215	340	625	975
1907-S	1,250,000	6611	37	75	170	220	525	1,150	3,250	4,800
1908	1,354,000	6569	26	33	60	160	215	340	625	925
1908-D	3,280,000	6612	26	31	60	160	215	340	625	925
1908-O	5,360,000	6613	26	33	60	160	230	340	650	950
1908-S	1,644,828	6614	34	45	80	195	495	875	1,450	2,600
1909	2,368,000	6570	26	33	60	160	215	340	625	925
1909-O	925,400	6615	34	50	110	230	650	850	1,550	2,400
1909-S	1,764,000	6616	29	35	60	160	360	625	1,000	1,550
1910	418,000	6571	30	55	95	180	350	440	700	1,250
1910-S	1,948,000	6617	29	37	70	170	325	525	875	1,700
1911	1,406,000	6572	29	33	60	160	215	340	625	925
1911-D	695,080	6618	29	35	70	180	240	370	625	925
1911-S	1,272,000	6619	29	33	70	180	340	650	1,500	2,250
↳**1911-S, Repunched/ Inverted Mintmark, FS-501**	*	226410	34	40	75	200	370	725	1,650	2,500
1912	1,550,000	6573	26	33	60	160	215	340	625	925
1912-D	2,300,800	6620	26	33	60	160	215	340	625	925
1912-S	1,370,000	6621	29	33	70	175	245	420	775	1,200

* Included in number above.

Circulation Strikes *(continued)*

	Mintage	GSID	G-4	VG-8	F-12	VF-20	EF-40	AU-50	MS-60	MS-63
1913	188,000	6574	$75	$115	$220	$430	$900	$1,500	$2,200	$2,750
1913-D	534,000	6622	39	60	110	220	310	435	750	1,200
1913-S	604,000	6623	37	60	130	235	420	800	1,250	2,050
1914	124,230	6575	120	175	340	550	1,050	1,250	2,050	2,900
1914-S	992,000	6624	29	47	105	205	290	575	800	1,450
1915	138,000	6576	95	145	290	455	750	1,150	1,550	2,900
1915-D	1,170,400	6625	26	33	60	160	215	340	625	925
1915-S	1,604,000	6626	26	33	60	160	215	340	625	925

Proof Strikes

	Mintage	GSID	PF-60	PF-63	PF-65
Barber Half Dollar (1892–1915), Proof	**n/a**	**74062**	**$675**	**$1,050**	**$1,650**
Same, Proof Cameo	**n/a**	**74063**	**850**	**1,500**	**2,600**
Same, Proof Deep Cameo	**n/a**	**74064**	**—**	**2,400**	**4,900**
1892	1,245	6627	675	1,050	1,650
1893	792	6630	675	1,050	1,650
1894	972	6633	675	1,050	1,650
1895	880	6636	675	1,050	1,650
1896	762	6639	675	1,050	1,650
1897	731	6642	675	1,050	1,650
1898	735	6645	675	1,050	1,650
1899	846	6648	675	1,050	1,650
1900	912	6651	675	1,050	1,650
1901	813	6654	675	1,050	1,650
1902	777	6657	$675	$1,050	$1,650
1903	755	6660	675	1,050	1,650
1904	670	6663	675	1,050	1,650
1905	727	6666	675	1,050	1,650
1906	675	6669	675	1,050	1,650
1907	575	68834	675	1,050	1,650
1908	545	6674	675	1,050	1,650
1909	650	6677	675	1,050	1,650
1910	551	6680	675	1,050	1,650
1911	543	6683	675	1,050	1,650
1912	700	6686	675	1,050	1,650
1913	627	6689	675	1,050	1,650
1914	380	6692	675	1,200	2,750
1915	450	6695	675	1,050	1,900

LIBERTY WALKING (1916–1947)

Designer: *Adolph A. Weinman.* **Weight:** *12.5 grams.*
Composition: *.900 silver, .100 copper (net weight .36169 oz. pure silver).*
Diameter: *30.6 mm.* **Edge:** *Reeded.* **Mints:** *Philadelphia, Denver, and San Francisco.*

Circulation Strike

Proof Strike

Mintmark location, 1916–1917, is on the obverse, below the motto.

Mintmark location, 1917–1947, is on the reverse, below the branch.

History. The Liberty Walking half dollar was designed by Adolph A. Weinman, the sculptor who also created the Mercury or Winged Liberty Head dime. His monogram appears under the tips of the eagle's wing feathers. Mintage was intermittent from 1916 to 1947, with none struck in 1922, 1924, 1925, 1926, 1930, 1931, and 1932. On the 1916 coins and some of the 1917 coins, the mintmark is located on the obverse, below IN GOD WE TRUST. Other coins of 1917, and those through 1947, have the mintmark on the reverse, under the pine branch. The Mint also created a 2016 gold Liberty Walking half dollar at a smaller dimension. See page 617.

Striking and Sharpness. Most circulation-strike Liberty Walking half dollars are lightly struck. In this respect they are similar to Standing Liberty quarters of the same era. On the obverse, the key points to check are Liberty's left hand, the higher parts and lines in the skirt, and her head; after that, check all other areas. *Very few* coins are sharply struck in these areas, and for some issues sharp strikes might not exist at all. On the reverse, check the breast of the eagle.

Proofs were made beginning in 1936 and continuing through 1942. The entire die was polished (including the figure of Liberty and the eagle), generating coins of low contrast. Proofs are usually fairly well struck. Most Proofs of 1941 are from over-polished dies, with the AW monogram of the designer no longer present. Striking sharpness can vary. Seek coins with full head and left-hand details.

Availability. All dates and mintmarks are readily collectible, although some, such as 1917-S (obverse mintmark), 1919-D, the three issues of 1921, and 1938-D, are scarce. Earlier years are often seen with extensive wear. MS coins are most often seen of the three issues of 1916, the 1917, and those of 1933 to 1947. Collectors saved the issues of the 1940s in large quantities, making the coins common today. As noted, coins with Full Details can range from scarce to extremely rare for certain dates. Half dollars dated 1928-D are counterfeit.

Note: Values of common-date silver coins have been based on the current bullion price of silver, $45 per ounce, and may vary with the prevailing spot price.

Grading Standards

MS-60 to 70 (Mint State). ***Obverse:*** At MS-60, some abrasion and contact marks are evident on the higher areas, which are also the areas most likely to be weakly struck. This includes Liberty's left arm, her hand, and the areas of the skirt covering her left leg. The luster may not be complete in those areas on weakly struck coins (even those certified above MS-65)—the *original planchet surface* may be revealed, as it was not smoothed out by striking. Accordingly, grading is best done by evaluating abrasion as it is observed *in the right field*, plus evaluating the mint luster. Luster may be dull or lifeless at MS-60 to 62, but should have deep frost at MS-63 or better, particularly in the lower-relief areas. At MS-65 or better, it should be full and rich. Sometimes, to compensate for flat striking, certified coins with virtually flawless luster in the fields, evocative of an MS-65 or 66 grade, are called MS-63 or a lower grade. Such coins would seem to offer a lot of value for the money, if the variety is one that is not found with Full Details (1923-S is one of many examples). ***Reverse:*** Striking is usually better, permitting observation of luster in all areas except the eagle's body, which may be lightly struck. Luster may be dull or lifeless at MS-60 to 62, but should have deep frost at MS-63 or better, particularly in the lower-relief areas. At MS-65 or better, it should be full and rich.

MS-65

Illustrated coin: This is a lustrous gem example.

AU-50, 53, 55, 58 (About Uncirculated). ***Obverse:*** Light wear is seen on the higher-relief areas of Liberty, the vertical area from her head down to the date. At AU-58, the luster in the field is extensive, but is interrupted by friction and light wear. At AU-50 and 53, luster is less. ***Reverse:*** Wear is most evident on the eagle's breast immediately under the neck feathers, the left leg, and the top of the left wing. Luster is nearly complete at AU-58, but at AU-50 half or more is gone.

AU-50

EF-40, 45 (Extremely Fine). ***Obverse:*** Wear is more extensive, with the higher parts of Liberty now without detail, and with no skirt lines visible directly over her left leg. Little or no luster is seen. ***Reverse:*** The eagle shows more wear overall, with the highest parts of the body and left leg worn flat.

EF-40

VF-20, 30 (Very Fine). ***Obverse:*** Wear is more extensive, and Liberty is worn mostly flat in the line from her head to her left foot. Her skirt is worn, but most lines are seen, except over the leg and to the left and right. The lower part of her cape (to the left of her waist) is worn. ***Reverse:*** The eagle is worn smooth from the head to the left leg, and the right leg is flat at the top. Most feathers in the wings are delineated, but weak.

VF-20

F-12, 15 (Fine). ***Obverse:*** Wear is more extensive, now with only a few light lines visible in the skirt. The rays of the sun are weak below the cape, and may be worn away at their tips. ***Reverse:*** Wear is more extensive, with most details now gone on the eagle's right leg. Delineation of the feathers is less, and most in the upper area and right edge of the left wing are blended together.

F-12

VG-8, 10 (Very Good). ***Obverse:*** Wear is slightly more extensive, but the rim still is defined all around. The tops of the date numerals are worn and blend slightly into the ground above. ***Reverse:*** Wear is more extensive. On the left wing only a few feathers are delineated, and on the shoulder of the right wing most detail is gone. Detail in the pine branch is lost and it appears as a clump.

VG-8

G-4, 6 (Good). ***Obverse:*** Liberty is worn flat, with her head, neck, and arms all blended together. Folds can be seen at the bottom of the skirt, and nearly all gown lines are visible. The rim is worn done into the tops of some of the letters. ***Reverse:*** All areas show more wear. The rim is worn down into the tops of some of the letters, particularly at the top border.

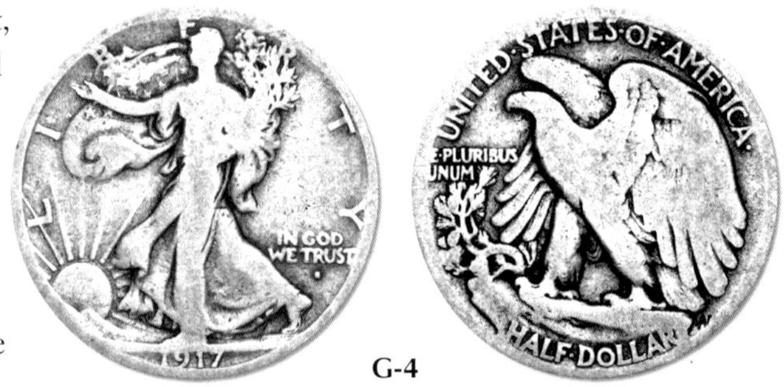

G-4

AG-3 (About Good). ***Obverse:*** Wear is more extensive. The sun's rays are nearly all gone, the motto is very light and sometimes incomplete, and the rim is worn down into more of the letters. ***Reverse:*** Wear is more extensive, with the eagle essentially worn flat. The rim is worn down into more of the letters.

AG-3

PF-65

PF-60 to 70 (Proof). ***Obverse and Reverse:*** Proofs that are extensively cleaned and have many hairlines, or that are dull and grainy, are lower level, such as PF-60 to 62. These are not widely desired, and represent coins that have been mistreated. With medium hairlines and good reflectivity, assigned grades of PF-63 or 64 are appropriate. Tiny horizontal lines on Liberty's leg, known as slide marks, from National and other album slides scuffing the relief of the cheek, are common; coins with such marks should not be graded higher than PF-64, but sometimes are. With relatively few hairlines and no noticeable slide marks, a rating of PF-65 can be given. PF-66 should have hairlines so delicate that magnification is needed to see them. Above that, a Proof should be free of any hairlines or other problems.

Illustrated coin: This example is a brilliant gem Proof.

Circulation Strikes

	Mintage	GSID	VG-8	F-12	VF-20	EF-40	AU-50	MS-60	MS-63	MS-65
Liberty Walking (1916–1947)	**n/a**	**72414**	**$25**	**$25**	**$25**	**$26**	**$27**	**$38**	**$60**	**$110**
1916	608,000	6698	60	100	175	245	390	850	1,200	2,400
1916-D, Obverse Mintmark	1,014,400	6711	70	100	160	260	390	775	1,050	2,100
↳1916-D, D Over D, FS-501	*	351929	75	110	180	285	430	850	1,150	2,300
1916-S, Obverse Mintmark	508,000	6712	170	340	575	925	1,400	2,750	3,750	8,000
1917	12,292,000	6699	27	28	31	43	100	245	415	1,000
1917-D, Obverse Mintmark	765,400	6713	55	100	155	340	525	1,000	1,550	5,000
1917-D, Reverse Mintmark	1,940,000	6714	41	60	130	300	575	1,400	2,200	10,000
1917-S, Obverse Mintmark	952,000	6715	70	175	455	1,150	1,900	4,600	6,250	19,000
	Auctions: $152,750, PCGS MS-67 HA 08/15									
1917-S, Reverse Mintmark	5,554,000	6716	35	50	90	235	365	1,000	1,750	10,000
1918	6,634,000	6700	29	38	90	155	325	800	1,250	3,600
1918-D	3,853,040	6717	35	75	180	360	675	1,750	2,750	24,000
	Auctions: $340,750, PCGS MS-66 LGND 04/21									
1918-S	10,282,000	6718	29	41	70	155	310	825	1,650	11,500
1919	962,000	6701	55	100	325	725	1,250	2,500	3,250	9,000
1919-D	1,165,000	6719	105	235	415	1,400	2,400	6,250	10,500	144,000
	Auctions: $270,250, PCGS MS-66 HA 11/04									
1919-S	1,552,000	6720	55	145	430	1,200	2,500	7,500	10,000	21,000
1920	6,372,000	6702	27	33	43	95	260	675	1,150	3,100
1920-D	1,551,000	6721	50	110	360	925	1,800	4,500	8,000	23,000
1920-S	4,624,000	6722	33	55	130	290	775	1,600	3,400	15,000
1921	246,000	6703	220	525	1,000	2,600	4,500	8,000	9,750	29,000
1921-D	208,000	6723	470	850	1,500	4,600	6,000	9,750	12,000	38,500
	Auctions: $168,000, PCGS MS-66 HA 01/18									
1921-S	548,000	6724	130	390	950	4,000	11,000	26,500	39,000	93,500
	Auctions: $138,000 NGC MS-66 HA 01/25									
1923-S	2,178,000	6725	47	90	310	1,150	2,050	4,100	5,000	13,000
1927-S	2,392,000	6726	30	45	80	440	950	1,900	2,900	6,500
1928-S (a,b)	1,940,000	6727	31	46	110	360	1,150	2,600	3,750	7,250
1929-D	1,001,200	6728	27	31	49	115	260	675	1,000	2,250
1929-S	1,902,000	6729	29	38	45	155	340	725	1,300	3,000

* Included in number above. **a.** Large and small mintmark varieties exist. **b.** Half dollars dated 1928-D are counterfeit.

1936, Doubled Die Obverse
FS-101

Circulation Strikes *(continued)*

	Mintage	GSID	VG-8	F-12	VF-20	EF-40	AU-50	MS-60	MS-63	MS-65
1933-S	1,786,000	6730	$27	$33	$43	$100	$310	$900	$1,400	$3,100
1934	6,964,000	6704	25	25	26	30	38	105	150	370
1934-D (a)	2,361,000	6731	25	26	29	47	110	195	340	1,000
1934-S	3,652,000	6732	25	25	29	47	100	390	950	2,000
1935	9,162,000	6705	25	25	26	31	37	75	100	310
1935-D	3,003,800	6733	25	25	27	34	80	180	375	1,100
1935-S	3,854,000	6734	25	25	29	49	130	390	675	1,550
1936	12,614,000	6706	25	26	27	31	34	70	115	245
↳1936, Doubled Die Obverse, FS-101	*	351932	28	29	30	35	37	75	125	270
1936-D	4,252,400	6735	25	25	26	30	43	120	180	470
1936-S	3,884,000	6736	25	25	27	45	90	210	310	750
1937	9,522,000	6707	25	25	25	30	33	75	120	220
1937-D	1,676,000	6737	25	26	27	47	110	275	370	675
1937-S	2,090,000	6738	25	25	27	40	75	210	310	750
1938	4,110,000	6708	25	25	27	33	40	95	175	360
1938-D	491,600	6739	55	90	110	155	220	650	850	1,250
1939	6,812,000	6709	25	25	25	29	34	70	100	215
1939-D	4,267,800	6740	25	25	26	30	34	70	110	235
↳1939-D, D Over D, FS-501	*	351933	30	30	31	36	41	80	130	280
1939-S	2,552,000	6741	25	25	26	30	80	145	210	310
1940	9,156,000	6710	25	25	25	27	29	42	70	170
1940-S	4,550,000	6742	25	25	26	29	40	55	105	395
1941	24,192,000	6743	25	25	25	26	27	38	60	110
1941-D	11,248,400	6751	25	25	25	27	28	43	90	150
1941-S	8,098,000	6752	25	25	25	29	35	90	130	435
↳1941-S, S Over S, FS-501	*	199155	27	27	27	32	39	100	140	480
↳1941-S, Missing Wing Feather, FS-901	*	199156	27	27	27	32	39	100	140	480
1942	47,818,000	6744	25	25	25	26	27	38	60	110
↳1942, Doubled Die Reverse, FS-801	*	226461	27	30	35	50	70	170	260	525
1942-D	10,973,800	6753	25	25	25	27	28	39	70	150
1942-S (a)	12,708,000	6754	25	25	25	27	34	47	95	245
1943	53,190,000	6745	25	25	25	26	27	38	60	110
	Auctions: $120,000, PCGS MS-68 SBG 06/21									
1943-D	11,346,000	6755	25	25	25	27	29	50	80	170
1943-S	13,450,000	6756	25	25	25	27	33	55	95	180
1944	28,206,000	6746	25	25	25	26	27	38	60	110
	Auctions: $109,250, PCGS MS-68 HA 08/10									
1944-D	9,769,000	6757	25	25	25	27	30	46	70	120
↳1944-D, Hand-Engraved Initials, FS-901	*	226462	27	30	35	50	60	95	130	210
1944-S	8,904,000	6758	25	25	25	27	30	55	85	235

* Included in number above. **a.** Large and small mintmark varieties exist.

1946, Doubled Die Reverse
FS-801

Circulation Strikes *(continued)*

	Mintage	GSID	VG-8	F-12	VF-20	EF-40	AU-50	MS-60	MS-63	MS-65
1945	31,502,000	6747	$25	$25	$25	$26	$27	$38	$60	$110
↳1945, Sunburst, FS-401	*	351938	27	27	27	29	30	42	70	120
1945-D	9,966,800	6759	25	25	25	27	29	39	60	110
1945-S	10,156,000	6760	25	25	25	27	33	50	70	110
1946	12,118,000	6748	25	25	25	26	27	38	60	110
↳1946, Doubled Die Obverse, FS-101	12,118,000	226465	29	33	38	55	80	155	310	850
1946, Doubled Die Reverse		6749	$9	70	90	130	180	470	1,000	2,600
↳1946, Doubled Die Reverse, FS-801		377686	49	70	90	130	180	470	1,000	2,600
1946-D	2,151,000	6761	25	26	28	31	35	46	70	115
1946-S	3,724,000	6762	25	25	26	30	40	60	70	120
1947	4,094,000	6750	25	25	26	29	37	50	80	115
1947-D	3,900,600	6763	25	25	26	28	35	50	80	110

* Included in number above.

1945, Missing Designer's Initials, Proof
FS-901

Proof Strikes

	Mintage	GSID	PF-63	PF-65	PF-66
Liberty Walking (1916–1947), Proof	**n/a**	**77708**	**$365**	**$430**	**$575**
1936	3,901	6764	1,800	3,250	4,750
1937	5,728	6767	550	850	1,150
1938	8,152	6770	525	750	925
1939	8,808	6773	500	675	900
1940	11,279	6776	390	495	625
1941 (a)	15,412	6780	365	430	575
1942	21,120	6783	365	430	575

a. Struck with and without designer's initials. The variety without the designer's initials was created by the over-polishing of dies.

FRANKLIN (1948–1963)

Designer: *John R. Sinnock.* **Weight:** *12.5 grams.*
Composition: *.900 silver, .100 copper (net weight .36169 oz. pure silver).*
Diameter: *30.6 mm.* **Edge:** *Reeded.* **Mints:** *Philadelphia, Denver, and San Francisco.*

Circulation Strike

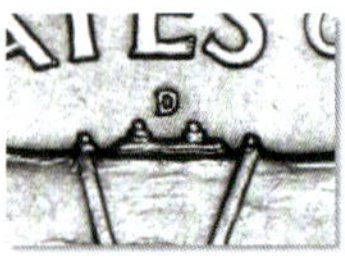

Mintmark location is on the reverse, above the beam.

Proof Strike

History. U.S. Mint chief engraver John R. Sinnock developed a motif for a silver half dime in 1942; it was proposed but never adopted for regular coinage. In 1948, the year after Sinnock died, his Franklin half dollar was introduced, its design an adaptation of his earlier half dime motif. The Liberty Bell is similar to that used by Sinnock on the 1926 Sesquicentennial commemorative half dollar modeled from a sketch by John Frederick Lewis. The designs were finished by Sinnock's successor, chief engraver Gilroy Roberts. The coin-collecting community paid little attention to the Franklin half dollar at the time, but today the coins are widely collected.

Striking and Sharpness. Given the indistinct details of the obverse, sharpness of strike usually is ignored. On the reverse, if the bottom lines of the Liberty Bell are complete the coin may be designated as Full Bell Lines (FBL). Virtually all Proofs are well struck.

Availability. All dates and mintmarks are easily available in grades from VF upward. Lower-level MS coins can be unattractive due to contact marks and abrasion, particularly noticeable on the obverse. High-quality gems are generally inexpensive, although varieties that are rare with FBL can be costly amid much competition in the marketplace. Most collectors seek MS coins. Grades below EF are not widely desired. Proofs were made from 1950 to 1963 and are available today in proportion to their mintages. Those with cameo-frosted devices are in the minority and often sell for strong premiums.

Note: Values of common-date silver coins have been based on the current bullion price of silver, $45 per ounce, and may vary with the prevailing spot price.

Grading Standards

MS-65

MS-60 to 70 (Mint State). ***Obverse:*** At MS-60, some abrasion and contact marks are evident on the cheek, on the hair left of the ear, and the neck. At MS-63, abrasion is slight at best, less so for MS-64. An MS-65 coin should display no abrasion or contact marks except under magnification, and MS-66 and higher coins should have none at all. Luster should be full and rich. As details are shallow on this design, the amount and "depth" of luster is important to grading. ***Reverse:*** General comments apply as for the obverse. The points to check are the bell harness, the words PASS AND STOW on the upper area of the Liberty Bell, and the bottom of the bell.

Illustrated coin: Satiny brilliance is seen on the obverse of this coin, light golden toning on the reverse.

AU-50, 53, 55, 58 (About Uncirculated). ***Obverse:*** At AU-50, medium wear is evident on the portrait, and most of the luster in the field is gone. At AU-53, wear is less and luster is more extensive. AU-55 and 58 coins show much luster. Wear is noticeable on the portrait and, to a lesser extent, in the field. ***Reverse:*** At AU-50, medium wear is evident on most of the Liberty Bell, and most of the luster in the field is gone. At AU-53, wear is slightly less. AU-55 and 58 coins show much luster. Light wear is seen on the higher areas of the bell.

AU-50

EF-40, 45 (Extremely Fine). ***Obverse:*** Wear is more extensive, and some hair detail (never strong to begin with) is lost. There is no luster. ***Reverse:*** Wear is seen overall. The inscription on the bell is weak, and the highest parts of the bottom horizontal lines are worn away. There is no luster.

EF-40

PF-60 to 70 (Proof). ***Obverse and Reverse:*** Proofs that are extensively cleaned and have many hairlines, or that are dull and grainy, are lower level, such as PF-60 to 62. These are not widely desired, and represent coins that have been mistreated. Fortunately, only a few Proof Franklin half dollars are in this category. With medium hairlines and good reflectivity, assigned grades of PF-63 or 64 are appropriate. PF-66 should have hairlines so delicate that magnification is needed to see them. Above that, a Proof should be free of any hairlines or other problems.

PF-65
Cameo

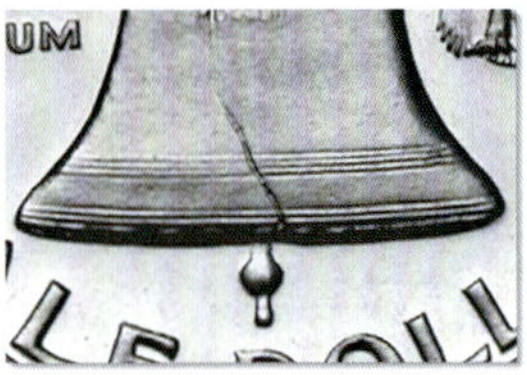

Full Bell Lines

1948, Doubled Die Reverse
FS-801

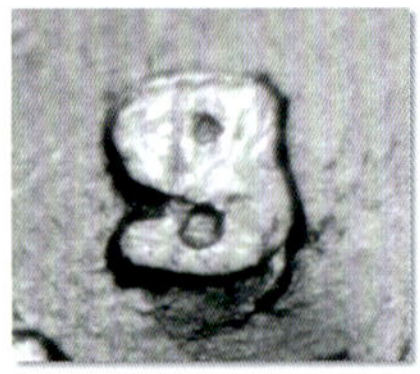

1949-S, Repunched Mintmark
FS-501

Circulation Strikes

	Mintage	GSID	AU-50	MS-60	MS-63	MS-65	MS-66	MS-67
Franklin (1948–1963)	**n/a**	**76527**	**$26**	**$26**	**$29**	**$39**	**$65**	**$285**
Same, Full Bell Lines	**n/a**	**76528**	**—**	**28**	**29**	**55**	**120**	**850**
1948	3,006,814	6788	26	30	36	80	215	1,200
↳1948, Doubled Die Reverse, FS-801	*	351950	—	—	—	—	—	—
1948, Full Bell Lines	*	6789	—	44	55	95	235	1,400
↳1948, Doubled Die Reverse, FS-801, Full Bell Lines	*	261891	—	—	—	160	775	—
1948-D	4,028,600	6820	26	28	33	80	195	3,750
1948-D, Full Bell Lines	*	6821	—	—	50	95	210	3,750
1949	5,614,000	6790	26	34	40	80	235	5,000
↳1949, Bugs Bunny Die Clash, FS-401	*	351952	—	—	110	195	340	—
1949, Full Bell Lines	*	6791	—	—	65	95	290	5,500
↳1949, Bugs Bunny Die Clash, FS-401, Full Bell Lines	*	261893	—	—	130	285	525	—
1949-D	4,120,600	6822	30	50	55	180	775	—
1949-D, Full Bell Lines	*	6823	—	—	60	210	775	24,000
1949-S	3,744,000	6824	43	70	80	100	155	575
↳1949-S, S Over S, FS-501	*	351954	55	90	100	125	195	725
1949-S, Full Bell Lines	*	6825	—	—	160	340	525	3,250
↳1949-S, S Over S, FS-501, Full Bell Lines	*	375943	—	—	—	—	—	—
1950	7,742,123	6792	26	34	35	100	300	2,500
↳1950, Booger, FS-402a	*	351956	575	—	—	—	—	—
↳1950, Scar Face, FS-403	*	394994	—	—	—	—	—	—
1950, Full Bell Lines	*	6793	—	—	60	130	405	3,250
↳1950, Booger, FS-402a, Full Bell Lines	*	261895	—	—	—	—	—	—
↳1950, Scar Face, FS-403, Full Bell Lines	*	394995	—	—	—	—	—	—
1950-D	8,031,600	6826	26	33	39	150	575	4,400
↳1950-D, D Over D, FS-501	*	351957	31	39	46	180	700	—
1950-D, Full Bell Lines	*	6827	—	—	60	190	750	14,500
↳1950-D, D Over D, FS-501, Full Bell Lines	*	261896	—	—	75	225	900	—
1951	16,802,102	6794	26	27	31	80	195	1,000
↳1951, Doubled Die Reverse, FS-802	*	351958	—	—	—	—	—	—
1951, Full Bell Lines	*	6795	—	28	29	160	365	4,400
↳1951, Doubled Die Reverse, FS-802, Full Bell Lines	*	375946	—	—	—	—	—	—
1951-D	9,475,200	6828	26	35	38	95	310	—
1951-D, Full Bell Lines	*	6829	—	—	55	130	405	10,000

* Included in number above.

1951-S, Doubled Die Reverse
FS-801

Circulation Strikes

	Mintage	GSID	AU-50	MS-60	MS-63	MS-65	MS-66	MS-67
1951-S	13,696,000	6830	$26	$28	$32	$50	$155	$950
↳1951-S, S Over S, FS-501	*	310738	—	—	80	130	360	2,000
↳1951-S, Doubled Die Reverse, FS-801	*	6832	—	—	—	130	310	—
1951-S, Full Bell Lines	*	6833	—	—	—	310	650	4,250
↳1951-S, S Over S, FS-501, Full Bell Lines	*	310739	—	—	210	430	1,150	—
1952	21,192,093	6796	26	27	31	70	170	850
↳1952, Cracked Die, FS-402	*	351959	—	—	—	—	—	—
1952, Full Bell Lines	*	6797	—	—	—	95	200	1,100
↳1952, Cracked Die, FS-402, Full Bell Lines	*	375901	—	—	—	—	—	—
1952-D	25,395,600	6834	26	27	30	100	260	2,000
↳1952-D, Booger, FS-401	*	351960	—	—	—	—	—	—
↳1952-D, Booger, FS-402	*	351961	—	—	—	—	—	—
1952-D, Full Bell Lines	*	6835	—	—	31	100	405	8,250
↳1952-D, Booger, FS-401, Full Bell Lines	*	261899	—	—	—	—	—	—
↳1952-D, Booger, FS-402, Full Bell Lines	*	375947	—	—	—	—	—	—
1952-S	5,526,000	6836	43	55	65	95	145	650
↳1952-S, S Over S, FS-501	*	310740	50	70	110	325	—	—
1952-S, Full Bell Lines	*	6837	—	—	215	775	1,150	9,500
↳1952-S, S Over S, FS-501, Full Bell Lines	*	310741	—	—	—	—	—	—
1953	2,668,120	6798	26	27	31	65	180	1,450
1953, Full Bell Lines	*	6799	—	—	75	625	1,250	23,000
1953-D	20,900,400	6838	26	27	30	80	260	10,500
1953-D, Full Bell Lines	*	6839	—	—	29	65	310	7,500
1953-S	4,148,000	6840	26	31	34	50	150	1,150
↳1953-S, Bugs Bunny Die Clash, FS-401	*	261903	30	38	47	70	180	1,250
↳1953-S, S Over S, FS-501	*	351963	55	110	175	285	490	1,750
1953-S, Full Bell Lines	*	6841	—	—	12,000	31,000	50,500	84,000
1954	13,188,202	6800	26	27	31	44	145	1,250
1954, Full Bell Lines	*	6801	—	—	29	55	310	6,250
1954-D	25,445,580	6842	26	27	30	49	235	4,400
1954-D, Full Bell Lines	*	6843	—	—	29	75	340	8,250
1954-S	4,993,400	6844	26	27	31	43	75	1,100
1954-S, Full Bell Lines	*	6845	—	—	50	155	650	4,750
1955	2,498,181	6802	26	27	31	49	120	775
1955, Full Bell Lines	*	6803	—	—	33	85	195	4,100
1956	4,032,000	6804	26	27	31	39	65	285
1956, Full Bell Lines	*	6805	—	—	29	55	120	850
1957	5,114,000	6806	26	27	31	39	65	285
1957, Full Bell Lines	*	6807	—	—	29	95	155	850

* Included in number above.

Circulation Strikes

	Mintage	GSID	AU-50	MS-60	MS-63	MS-65	MS-66	MS-67
1957-D	19,966,850	6846	$26	$27	$30	$41	$105	$575
↳1957-D, D Over D, Clashed Die, Repunched Mintmark, FS-402	*	351965	—	—	—	—	—	—
↳1957-D, D Over D, FS-501	*	351966	—	—	—	—	—	—
↳1957-D, D Over D, FS-502	*	351967	—	—	—	—	—	—
1957-D, Full Bell Lines	*	6847	—	—	29	55	120	1,100
↳1957-D, D Over D, Clashed Die, Repunched Mintmark, FS-402, Full Bell Lines	*	375953	—	—	—	—	—	—
↳1957-D, D Over D, FS-501, Full Bell Lines	*	261910	—	—	—	—	—	—
↳1957-D, D Over D, FS-502, Full Bell Lines	*	375954	—	—	—	—	—	—
1958	4,042,000	6808	26	27	31	39	65	285
1958, Full Bell Lines	*	6809	—	—	29	85	120	1,250
	Auctions: $129,250, PCGS MS-67 LGND 09/18							
1958-D	23,962,412	6848	26	27	31	39	65	285
1958-D, Full Bell Lines	*	6849	—	—	29	55	120	850
1959	6,200,000	6810	26	27	31	44	300	2,250
↳1959, Goiter, FS-402	*	315454	—	95	130	340	775	—
1959, Full Bell Lines	*	6811	—	—	29	80	575	9,500
↳1959, Goiter, FS-402, Full Bell Lines	*	261911	—	—	—	—	—	—
1959-D	13,053,750	6850	26	27	30	41	285	1,600
1959-D, Full Bell Lines	*	6851	—	—	29	70	345	5,000
1960	6,024,000	6812	26	27	31	55	300	3,900
1960, Full Bell Lines	*	6813	—	—	29	120	500	15,500
1960-D	18,215,812	6852	26	27	30	60	310	—
1960-D, Full Bell Lines	*	6853	—	—	32	175	1,000	24,000
1961	8,290,000	6814	26	27	31	41	285	2,000
1961, Full Bell Lines	*	6815	—	30	50	675	4,750	30,000
1961-D	20,276,442	6854	26	27	30	60	275	2,500
↳1961-D, D Over D, FS-501	*	351970	—	—	—	—	—	—
1961-D, Full Bell Lines	*	6855	—	—	38	435	2,000	30,000
1962	9,714,000	6816	26	28	31	46	260	2,500
1962, Full Bell Lines	*	6817	—	—	90	650	5,000	30,000
1962-D	35,473,281	6856	26	28	31	45	415	9,500
1962-D, Full Bell Lines	*	6857	—	—	32	285	1,500	30,000
1963	22,164,000	6818	26	26	29	39	275	3,100
1963, Full Bell Lines	*	6819	—	—	215	1,000	7,000	24,000
1963-D	67,069,292	6858	26	26	29	39	215	3,750
1963-D, Full Bell Lines	*	6859	—	—	29	130	775	15,000

* Included in number above.

1957, Tripled Die Reverse, Proof
FS-801

Proof Strikes

	Mintage	GSID	PF-63	PF-65	PF-66	PF-67	PF-68
Franklin (1948–1963), Proof	**n/a**	**213894**	**$23**	**$27**	**$30**	**$38**	**$60**
Same, Proof Cameo	**n/a**	**213895**	**24**	**36**	**45**	**60**	**120**
Same, Proof Deep Cameo	**n/a**	**213896**	**27**	**55**	**90**	**155**	**345**
1950	51,386	6860	375	455	675	2,500	16,000
↳1950, Quadrupled Die Obverse, FS-101	*	226446	415	500	725	3,000	18,000
↳1950, Re-engraved Wing Feathers, FS-901	*	351971	415	500	725	2,750	18,000
1950, Cameo	*	6861	650	1,700	3,400	7,000	48,000
1950, Deep Cameo	*	6863	8,750	31,000	72,000	108,000	—
1951	57,500	6864	260	305	435	1,100	5,500
1951, Cameo	*	6865	370	675	1,600	3,000	15,000
1951, Deep Cameo	*	6866	725	2,000	7,000	14,000	72,000
1952	81,980	6867	130	170	215	575	2,250
↳1952, Bugs Bunny Die Clash, FS-403	*	285893	—	1,150	1,400	1,750	—
1952, Cameo	*	6868	285	390	525	1,400	5,500
1952, Deep Cameo	*	6869	1,250	3,750	7,500	18,000	—
1953	128,800	6870	90	100	130	220	1,150
↳1953, Re-engraved Wing Feathers, FS-901	*	351972	—	—	—	—	—
1953, Cameo	*	6871	110	215	245	650	2,600
1953, Deep Cameo	*	6872	850	1,500	2,500	6,250	21,500
1954	233,300	6873	55	70	80	130	470
↳1954, Doubled Die Obverse, FS-101	*	351973	850	—	—	—	—
1954, Cameo	*	6874	75	120	145	260	1,000
1954, Deep Cameo	*	6875	130	575	900	1,750	6,000
1955	378,200	6876	50	60	70	75	190
1955, Cameo	*	6877	55	70	150	195	360
1955, Deep Cameo	*	6878	—	470	550	1,000	3,450
1956, Variety 1	669,384	6882	55	70	145	180	470
1956, Variety 1, Cameo	*	6880	230	310	390	725	1,750
1956, Variety 1, Deep Cameo	*	6881	—	1,250	2,400	4,400	17,500
1956, Variety 2	*	6879	27	40	50	60	75
↳1956, Variety 2, Doubled Die Reverse, FS-803	*	351974	—	—	—	—	—
1956, Cameo	*	6883	47	70	80	115	170
↳1956, Variety 2, Doubled Die Reverse, FS-802	*	310737	—	—	290	490	775
1956, Deep Cameo	*	6884	90	160	195	230	390
↳1956, Variety 2, Doubled Die Reverse, FS-802	*	377350	—	—	—	—	—
1957	1,247,952	6885	26	31	34	47	85
↳1957, Tripled Die Reverse, FS-801	*	226450	—	—	325	390	525
1957, Cameo	*	6886	28	60	95	145	275
1957, Deep Cameo	*	6887	—	360	390	700	1,000
1958	875,652	6888	31	35	40	55	75
1958, Cameo	*	6889	35	80	100	195	420
1958, Deep Cameo	*	6890	—	525	725	1,100	5,000

* Included in number above.

1961, Doubled Die Reverse, Proof
FS-801

Proof Strikes *(continued)*

	Mintage	GSID	PF-63	PF-65	PF-66	PF-67	PF-68
1959	1,149,291	6891	$23	$27	$32	$47	$75
1959, Cameo	*	6892	34	100	230	455	2,000
1959, Deep Cameo	*	6893	—	2,500	6,250	14,500	20,500
1960	1,691,602	6894	23	27	30	40	70
↳1960, Doubled Die Obverse, FS-101	*	226451	55	80	115	155	210
↳1960, Doubled Die Reverse, FS-801	*	351975	—	—	—	—	—
1960, Cameo	*	6895	27	40	60	90	150
1960, Deep Cameo	*	6896	70	130	180	470	650
1961	3,028,244	6897	23	27	30	38	60
↳1961, Cameo	*	6901	24	36	45	60	260
↳1961, Deep Cameo	*	6902	40	100	130	230	900
1961, Doubled Die Reverse	*	6900	1,400	2,750	4,000	6,000	14,500
↳1961, Doubled Die Reverse, FS-801	*	226452	1,500	3,000	4,400	7,250	16,000
1962	3,218,019	6903	23	27	30	38	60
↳1962, Doubled Die Obverse, FS-101	*	226455	—	180	215	310	430
1962, Cameo	*	6904	24	36	45	60	120
↳1962, Doubled Die Obverse, FS-101	*	226457	—	215	245	390	525
1962, Deep Cameo	*	6905	27	55	90	155	360
1963	3,075,645	6906	23	27	30	38	60
1963, Cameo	*	6907	24	36	45	60	120
1963, Deep Cameo	*	6908	27	55	90	235	455

* Included in number above.

KENNEDY (1964 TO DATE)

Designers: *Gilroy Roberts and Frank Gasparro.* **Weight:** *1964, modern silver Proofs, and 2014 silver—12.5 grams; 1965–1970—11.5 grams; 1971 to date—11.34 grams.* **Composition:** *1964 and modern silver Proofs—.900 silver, .100 copper (net weight .36169 oz. pure silver); 1965–1970—a core of .209 silver and .791 copper, clad in outer layers of .800 silver, .200 copper (net weight .1479 oz. pure silver); 1971 to date—a core of pure copper, clad in outer layers of copper-nickel (.750 copper, .250 nickel).* **Diameter:** *30.6 mm.* **Edge:** *Reeded.* **Mints:** *Philadelphia, Denver, and San Francisco.*

Circulation Strike

Proof Strike

Mintmark location, 1964, is on the reverse, below the claw holding the branch.

Mintmark location, 1968 to date, is on the obverse, above the date.

Bicentennial variety: **Designers:** *Gilroy Roberts and Seth Huntington.* **Weight:** *Silver clad—11.5 grams; copper-nickel clad—11.34 grams.* **Composition:** *Silver clad—a core of .209 silver and .791 copper, clad in outer layers of .800 silver, .200 copper (net weight .14792 oz. pure silver); copper-nickel clad—a core of pure copper, clad in outer layers of copper-nickel (.750 copper, .250 nickel).* **Diameter:** *30.6 mm.* **Edge:** *Reeded.* **Mints:** *Philadelphia, Denver, and San Francisco.*

Bicentennial Variety, Circulation Strike

Bicentennial Variety, Proof Strike

History. Kennedy half dollars, minted from 1964 to date, were struck in 90 percent silver the first year, then with 40 percent silver content through 1970, and in later years in copper-nickel (except for special silver issues made for collectors and a gold issue in 2014). The obverse, by Chief Engraver Gilroy Roberts, features a portrait of President John F. Kennedy, while the reverse, by Frank Gasparro, displays a modern version of a heraldic eagle.

The 1976 Bicentennial coin shows Philadelphia's Independence Hall, a design by Seth G. Huntington. The obverse was unchanged except for the dual dating 1776–1976. The Bicentennial half dollars were struck during 1975 and 1976 and were used for general circulation as well as being included in Proof and Uncirculated sets for 1975 and 1976.

The year 2014 brought several special issues to mark the 50th year of the Kennedy half dollar: a .9999 fine gold version containing three-quarters of an ounce of pure gold; a Proof in silver; a Reverse Proof in silver; an Enhanced Uncirculated in silver; and an Uncirculated in silver. These coins are dual-dated 1964–2014 on the obverse. They were offered for sale by the U.S. Mint in a number of packages and options.

Striking and Sharpness. Nearly all are well struck. Check the highest points of the hair on the obverse and the highest details on the reverse.

Availability. All issues are common in high circulated grades as well as MS and Proof.

Proofs and Special Mint Set Coins. Proofs of 1964 were struck at the Philadelphia Mint. Those from 1968 to date have been made in San Francisco. All are easily obtained. Most from the 1970s to date have cameo contrast. Special Mint Set (SMS) coins were struck in lieu of Proofs from 1965 to 1967; in some instances, these closely resemble Proofs. Silver Proofs have been struck in recent years, for Silver Proof sets and for the 2014 50th Anniversary issue (which also includes a Reverse Proof). In 1998, a special Matte Proof silver Kennedy half dollar was struck for inclusion in the Robert F. Kennedy commemorative coin set.

Note: Values of common-date silver coins have been based on the current bullion price of silver, $45 per ounce, and may vary with the prevailing spot price.

Grading Standards

MS-60 to 70 (Mint State). ***Obverse:*** At MS-60, some abrasion and contact marks are evident on the cheek, and on the hair to the right of the forehead and temple. At MS-63, abrasion is slight at most, and less so for MS-64. An MS-65 coin should display no abrasion or contact marks except under magnification, and MS-66 and higher coins should have none at all. Luster should be full and rich. ***Reverse:*** Comments apply as for the obverse, except that the highest parts of the eagle at the center are the key places to check.

MS-66

AU-50, 53, 55, 58 (About Uncirculated). ***Obverse:*** Light wear is seen on the cheek and higher-relief area of the hair below the part, high above the ear. At AU-58, the luster is extensive but incomplete, especially on the higher parts and in the field. At AU-50 and 53, luster is less. ***Reverse:*** Light wear is seen on the higher parts of the eagle. At AU-50 and 53, there still is significant luster.

AU-55

EF-40, 45 (Extremely Fine). ***Obverse:*** Further wear is seen on the head. More details are gone on the higher parts of the hair. ***Reverse:*** Further wear is seen on the eagle in particular, but also on other areas in high relief (including the leaves, arrowheads, and clouds).

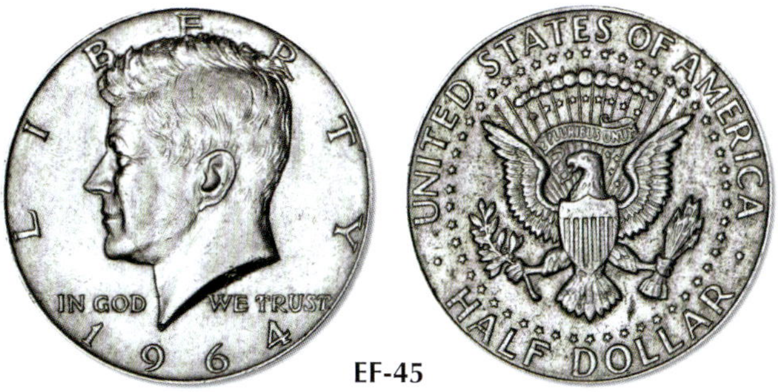

EF-45

PF-60 to 70 (Proof). ***Obverse and Reverse:***, Proofs that are extensively cleaned and have many hairlines, or that are dull and grainy, are lower level, such as PF-60 to 62. There are not many of these in the marketplace. With medium hairlines and good reflectivity, assigned grades of PF-63 or 64 are appropriate. With relatively few hairlines a rating of PF-65 can be given. PF-66 should have hairlines so delicate that magnification is needed to see them. Above that, a Proof should be free of any hairlines or other problems.

PF-66

1964, Doubled Die Obverse
FS-102

1964-D, Doubled Die Obverse
FS-101

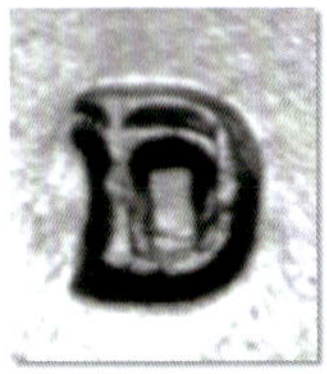

1964-D, Repunched Mintmark
FS-502

1972, Doubled Die Obverse
FS-101

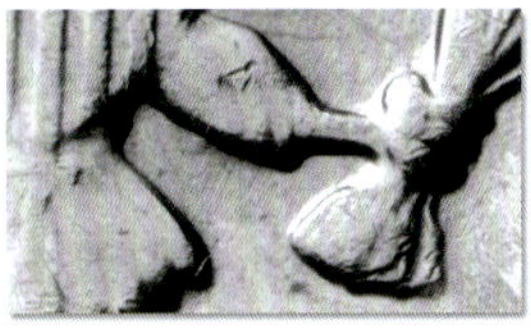

1972-D, Missing Designer's Initials
FS-901

Circulation Strikes

	Mintage	GSID	MS-63	MS-65	MS-66	MS-67
Kennedy, Silver (1964)	**n/a**	**24983**	**$26.00**	**$35.00**	**$70.00**	**$470.00**
Kennedy, Silver Clad (1965–1970)	**n/a**	**24984**	**9.75**	**27.00**	**70.00**	**495.00**
Kennedy, Clad (1971 to Date)	**n/a**	**24985**	**1.50**	**8.00**	**11.00**	**16.00**
Kennedy, Satin (2005–2010)	**n/a**	**394038**	**4.10**	**8.00**	**9.50**	**13.50**
1964	273,304,004	6909	26.00	35.00	70.00	470.00
↳1964, Doubled Die Obverse, FS-102	*	213500	70.00	160.00	390.00	—
1964-D	156,205,446	6921	26.00	39.00	70.00	525.00
↳1964-D, Doubled Die Obverse, FS-101	*	6922	80.00	195.00	650.00	2,250.00
↳1964-D, D Over D, FS-502	*	351996	30.00	46.00	100.00	—
↳1964-D, Tripled Die Obverse	*	6923	100.00	235.00	455.00	—
↳1964-D, Tripled Die Obverse, FS-103	*	393342	100.00	235.00	455.00	—
↳1964-D, Quadrupled Die Obverse	*	213504	75.00	260.00	775.00	—
↳1964-D, Quadrupled Die Obverse, FS-105	*	393343	75.00	260.00	775.00	—
1965	65,879,366	6910	9.75	27.00	120.00	1,900.00
↳1965, Doubled Die Reverse, FS-802	*	213506	120.00	325.00	725.00	—
1966	108,984,932	6911	9.75	27.00	155.00	1,900.00
1967	295,046,978	6912	9.75	27.00	70.00	1,000.00
↳1967, Doubled Die Obverse, FS-102	*	213508	1,250.00	2,500.00	—	—
↳1967, Doubled Die Obverse, FS-103	*	213509	195.00	275.00	325.00	—
1968-D	246,951,930	6924	9.75	27.00	70.00	495.00
1969-D	129,881,800	6925	9.75	27.00	120.00	1,600.00
1970-D (a)	2,150,000	6926	19.50	47.00	260.00	4,750.00
1971	155,164,000	6913	1.50	27.00	70.00	1,500.00
1971-D	302,097,424	6927	1.50	8.00	13.50	70.00
↳1971-D, Doubled Die Obverse, FS-102	*	213514	70.00	100.00	340.00	—
1972	153,180,000	6914	1.50	13.50	40.00	1,150.00
1972-D	141,890,000	6928	1.50	8.00	20.00	120.00
↳1972-D, Missing Designer's Initials, FS-901	*	213516	775.00	—	—	—
1973	64,964,000	6915	1.50	20.00	50.00	290.00
1973-D	83,171,400	6929	1.50	8.00	27.00	230.00
↳1973-D, Doubled Die Obverse, FS-101	*	213517	285.00	—	—	—
1974	201,596,000	6916	1.50	8.00	70.00	925.00
1974-D	79,066,300	6931	1.50	8.00	55.00	290.00
1974-D, Doubled Die Obverse	*	6930	40.00	80.00	775.00	—
↳1974-D, Doubled Die Obverse, FS-101	*	393344	—	—	—	—

* Included in number above. **a.** Issued only in Mint sets.

Circulation Strikes *(continued)*

	Mintage	GSID	MS-63	MS-65	MS-66	MS-67
1776–1976	234,308,000	6917	$1.50	$13.50	$95.00	$1,600
1776–1976-D	287,565,248	6932	1.50	27.00	34.00	650
1776–1976-S, Silver Clad	11,000,000	6933	9.75	20.00	27.00	38
1977	43,598,000	6918	1.50	8.00	36.00	100
1977-D	31,449,106	6934	1.50	8.00	47.00	360
1978	14,350,000	6919	1.50	8.00	31.00	155
1978-D	13,765,799	6935	1.50	8.00	40.00	360
1979	68,312,000	6920	1.50	8.00	31.00	275
1979-D	15,815,422	6936	1.50	8.00	27.00	470
1980-P	44,134,000	6938	1.50	11.00	20.00	110
1980-D	33,456,449	6937	1.90	20.00	95.00	155
1981-P	29,544,000	6940	1.50	12.00	70.00	525
1981-D	27,839,533	6939	1.50	8.00	60.00	725
1982-P	10,819,000	6942	1.50	60.00	100.00	925
1982-D	13,140,102	6941	6.75	13.50	40.00	260
1983-P	34,139,000	6944	6.00	20.00	75.00	365
1983-D	32,472,244	6943	1.50	20.00	55.00	390
1984-P	26,029,000	6946	1.50	8.00	22.00	340
1984-D	26,262,158	6945	1.50	8.00	55.00	850
1985-P	18,706,962	6948	1.50	8.00	19.00	135
1985-D	19,814,034	6947	1.50	8.00	17.50	70
1986-P	13,107,633	6950	2.20	8.00	20.00	115
1986-D	15,336,145	6949	1.50	8.00	16.00	43
1987-P (b)	2,890,758	6952	1.50	8.00	27.00	180
1987-D (b)	2,890,758	6951	1.50	8.00	16.00	60
1988-P	13,626,000	6954	1.50	8.00	22.00	95
1988-D	12,000,096	6953	1.50	8.00	19.00	60
1989-P	24,542,000	6956	1.50	8.00	17.50	200
1989-D	23,000,216	6955	1.50	8.00	20.00	130
1990-P	22,278,000	6958	1.50	8.00	22.00	290
1990-D	20,096,242	6957	1.50	8.00	32.00	575
1991-P	14,874,000	6960	1.50	8.00	22.00	95
1991-D	15,054,678	6959	1.50	8.00	27.00	130
1992-P	17,628,000	6962	1.50	8.00	16.00	70
1992-D	17,000,106	6961	1.50	8.00	17.50	75
1993-P	15,510,000	6964	2.00	8.00	19.00	55
1993-D	15,000,006	6963	2.00	8.00	16.00	70
1994-P	23,718,000	6966	1.50	8.00	17.50	47
1994-D	23,828,110	6965	1.50	8.00	20.00	150
1995-P	26,496,000	6968	1.50	8.00	17.50	55
1995-D	26,288,000	6967	1.50	8.00	16.00	55
1996-P	24,442,000	6970	1.50	8.00	11.00	22
1996-D	24,744,000	6969	1.50	8.00	11.00	27
1997-P	20,882,000	6972	1.50	8.00	13.50	90
1997-D	19,876,000	6971	1.50	8.00	19.00	195
1998-P	15,646,000	6974	1.50	8.00	19.00	47
1998-D	15,064,000	6973	1.50	8.00	19.00	90
1998-S, Silver, Matte Finish (c)	62,000	6975	80.00	90.00	90.00	95

b. Not issued for circulation; included with Mint and Souvenir sets. **c.** Minted for inclusion in the Robert F. Kennedy commemorative set (along with an RFK commemorative dollar).

Circulation Strikes *(continued)*

	Mintage	GSID	MS-63	MS-65	MS-66	MS-67
1999-P	8,900,000	6977	$1.50	$8.00	$11.00	$16.00
1999-D	10,682,000	6976	1.50	8.00	12.00	34.00
2000-P	22,600,000	6979	1.50	8.00	11.00	34.00
2000-D	19,466,000	6978	1.50	8.00	12.00	155.00
2001-P	21,200,000	6981	1.50	8.00	11.00	16.00
2001-D	19,504,000	6980	1.50	8.00	11.00	32.00
2002-P (d)	3,100,000	6983	1.50	8.00	11.00	27.00
2002-D (d)	2,500,000	6982	1.50	8.00	11.00	24.00
2003-P (d)	2,500,000	6985	1.50	8.00	11.00	47.00
2003-D (d)	2,500,000	6984	1.50	8.00	13.50	55.00
2004-P (d)	2,900,000	6987	1.50	8.00	12.00	55.00
2004-D (d)	2,900,000	6986	1.50	8.00	11.00	34.00
2005-P (d)	3,800,000	15373	1.50	8.00	40.00	210.00
2005-P, Satin	1,160,000	15375	4.10	8.00	9.50	13.50
2005-D (d)	3,500,000	15374	1.50	8.00	15.00	120.00
2005-D, Satin	1,160,000	15376	4.10	8.00	9.50	13.50
2006-P (d)	2,400,000	65271	1.50	8.00	11.00	27.00
2006-P, Satin	847,361	65272	4.10	8.00	9.50	13.50
2006-D (d)	2,000,000	65273	1.50	8.00	11.00	60.00
2006-D, Satin	847,361	65274	4.10	8.00	9.50	13.50
2007-P (d)	2,400,000	77863	1.80	8.00	11.00	27.00
2007-P, Satin	895,628	68859	4.10	8.00	9.50	13.50
2007-D (d)	2,400,000	68981	1.50	8.00	11.00	34.00
2007-D, Satin	895,628	69346	4.10	8.00	9.50	16.00
2008-P (d)	1,700,000	69027	1.50	8.00	11.00	70.00
2008-P, Satin	745,464	70485	4.10	8.00	9.50	13.50
2008-D (d)	1,700,000	69028	1.50	8.00	13.50	390.00
2008-D, Satin	745,464	81793	4.10	8.00	9.50	13.50
2009-P (d)	1,900,000	70728	1.50	8.00	12.00	60.00
2009-P, Satin	784,614	81794	4.10	8.00	9.50	13.50
2009-D (d)	1,900,000	70729	1.50	8.00	24.00	180.00
2009-D, Satin	784,614	81795	4.10	8.00	9.50	13.50
2010-P (d)	1,800,000	74088	1.50	8.00	11.00	27.00
2010-P, Satin	583,897	81796	4.10	8.00	9.50	13.50
2010-D (d)	1,700,000	74089	1.50	8.00	15.00	55.00
2010-D, Satin	583,897	81797	4.10	8.00	9.50	13.50
2011-P (d)	1,750,000	74090	1.50	8.00	11.00	24.00
2011-D (d)	1,700,000	74091	1.50	8.00	11.00	16.00
2012-P (d)	1,800,000	74092	1.50	8.00	11.00	20.00
2012-D (d)	1,700,000	71562	1.50	8.00	11.00	55.00
2013-P (d)	5,000,000	74093	1.50	8.00	11.00	23.00
2013-D (d)	4,600,000	74094	1.50	8.00	11.00	16.00
2014-P (d)	2,500,000	74095	2.60	8.00	11.00	27.00
2014-P, High Relief (e)	197,608	82061	20.00	24.00	30.00	34.00
2014-D (d)	2,100,000	74096	2.60	8.00	11.00	16.00
2014-D, Silver (f)	219,173	198230	25.00	26.00	26.00	27.00
2014-D, High Relief (e)	197,608	82062	8.00	11.00	12.00	22.00
2014-S, Silver Enhanced Uncirculated (f)	219,173	84799	26.00	26.00	26.00	27.00

d. Not issued for circulation. Sold directly to the public in rolls and small bags. **e.** For the 50th anniversary of the Kennedy half dollar, in 2014 the U.S. Mint issued an Uncirculated two-coin set featuring a Kennedy half dollar from Philadelphia and one from Denver. **f.** Included in the 2014 half dollar silver-coin collection released by the U.S. Mint for the 50th anniversary of the Kennedy half dollar.

Circulation Strikes *(continued)*

	Mintage	GSID	MS-63	MS-65	MS-66	MS-67
2015-P (d)	2,300,000	74097	$1.50	$8.00	$11.00	$16.00
2015-D (d)	2,300,000	74098	1.50	8.00	11.00	47.00
2016-P (d)	2,100,000	74099	1.50	8.00	11.00	34.00
2016-D (d)	2,100,000	74100	1.50	8.00	11.00	24.00
2017-P (d)	1,800,000	74101	1.50	8.00	11.00	27.00
2017-D (d)	2,900,000	74102	1.50	8.00	11.00	16.00
2017-S, Enhanced Uncirculated (e)	210,419	82060	6.75	8.00	8.00	9.50
2018-P (d)	4,800,000	79372	1.50	8.00	11.00	16.00
2018-D (d)	6,100,000	79373	1.50	8.00	11.00	16.00
2019-P (d)	1,700,000	81395	1.50	8.00	11.00	16.00
2019-D (d)	1,700,000	79374	1.50	8.00	11.00	16.00
2020-P (d)	2,300,000	84802	1.50	8.00	11.00	16.00
2020-D (d)	3,400,000	84803	1.50	8.00	11.00	16.00
2021-P	5,400,000	85153	1.50	8.00	11.00	16.00
2021-D	7,700,000	85154	1.50	8.00	11.00	16.00
2022-P	4,800,000	193435	1.50	8.00	11.00	16.00
2022-D	4,900,000	193438	1.50	8.00	11.00	16.00
2023-P	30,200,000	199009	1.50	8.00	11.00	16.00
2023-D	27,800,000	199010	1.50	8.00	11.00	16.00
2024-P (d)		349855	1.50	8.00	11.00	16.00
2024-D (d)		349856	1.50	8.00	11.00	16.00
2025-P (d)		376282	1.50	8.00	11.00	16.00
2025-D (d)		376283	1.50	8.00	11.00	16.00

d. Not issued for circulation. Sold directly to the public in rolls and small bags. **e.** Included in the 2017-S set of Enhanced Uncirculated coins issued in honor of the 225th anniversary of the San Francisco Mint.

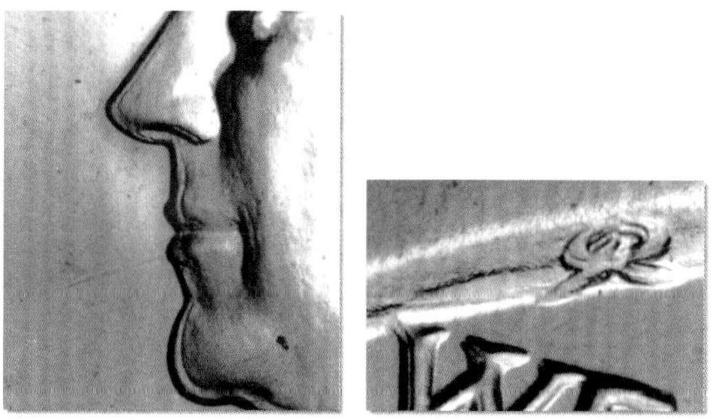

1966, Doubled Die Obverse, Special Mint Set
FS-103

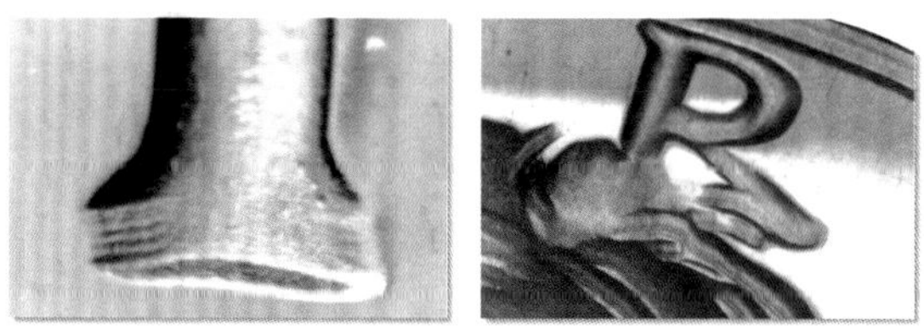

1967, Quintupled Die Obverse, Special Mint Set
FS-101

Special Mint Set Strikes

	Mintage	GSID	MS-63	MS-65	MS-66
1964	unknown	6988	$30,000.00	$38,500.00	$48,000.00
	Auctions: $108,000 PCGS MS-68 HA 08/25				
1965	2,360,000	6998	9.75	14.00	17.50
1966	2,261,583	7001	9.75	14.00	22.00
↳**1966, Doubled Die Obverse, FS-104**	*	352001	—	75.00	130.00
↳**1966, Tripled Die Obverse, FS-106**	*	352003	—	50.00	100.00
↳**1966, Missing Designer's Initials, Doubl, FS-901**	*	352004	100.00	195.00	410.00
1967	1,863,344	7004	9.75	14.00	22.00
↳**1967, Quintupled Die Obverse, FS-101**	*	352005	—	55.00	110.00

* Included in number above.

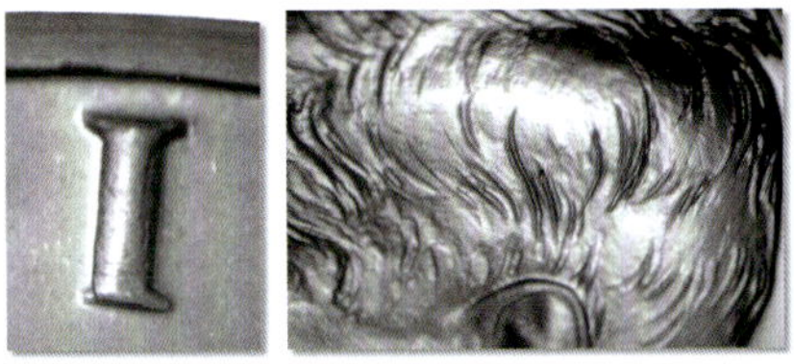

1964, Heavily Accented Hair, Proof

Proof Strikes

	Mintage	GSID	PF-66	PF-67	PF-68
Kennedy, Silver (1964), Proof	**n/a**	**376570**	**$24.00**	**$32.00**	**$49.00**
Kennedy, Silver Clad (1965–1970), Proof	**n/a**	**376571**	**17.00**	**19.00**	**22.00**
Kennedy, Clad (1971 to Date), Proof	**n/a**	**376572**	**8.00**	**9.50**	**12.00**
1964	3,950,762	6989	24.00	32.00	49.00
↳1964, Doubled Die Obverse, FS-101	*	352006	75.00	100.00	145.00
↳1964, Quadrupled Die Obverse, FS-105	*	352008	175.00	260.00	—
1964, Accented Hair (a)	3,950,762	6993	115.00	150.00	245.00
↳1964, Accented Hair, Doubled Die Obverse, FS-103	*	352012	260.00	455.00	775.00
↳1964, Accented Hair, Quadrupled Die Obverse, FS-802	*	352013	230.00	390.00	675.00
↳1964, Accented Hair, Cameo (a)	*	6994	155.00	275.00	850.00
↳1964, Accented Hair, Doubled Die Obverse, FS-103, Cameo	*	352015	525.00	950.00	2,250.00
↳1964, Accented Hair, Quadrupled Die Obverse, FS-802, Cameo	*	352016	455.00	725.00	1,900.00
↳1964, Accented Hair, Deep Cameo (a)	*	6995	1,150.00	2,750.00	8,500.00
1968-S	3,041,506	7007	17.00	19.00	22.00
↳1968-S, Inverted Mintmark, FS-511	*	352019	575.00	775.00	—
↳1968-S, Inverted Serif S Over Knob S, FS-512	*	352020	—	—	—
↳1968-S, Cameo	*	7008	17.00	19.00	24.00
↳1968-S, Inverted Mintmark, FS-511, Cameo	*	352023	550.00	650.00	—
↳1968-S, Inverted Serif S Over Knob S, FS-512, Cameo	*	352024	—	—	—
↳1968-S, Deep Cameo	*	7009	20.00	30.00	90.00
↳1968-S, Inverted Mintmark, FS-511, Deep Cameo	*	352027	875.00	—	—
↳1968-S, Inverted Serif S Over Knob S, FS-512, Deep Cameo	*	352028	—	—	—
1969-S	2,934,631	7010	17.00	19.00	22.00
↳1969-S, Cameo	*	7011	17.00	19.00	24.00
↳1969-S, Deep Cameo	*	7012	20.00	23.00	32.00
1970-S	2,632,810	7013	17.00	19.00	22.00
↳1970-S, Cameo	*	7014	17.00	19.00	22.00
↳1970-S, Deep Cameo	*	7015	20.00	23.00	35.00
↳1970-S, Doubled Die Obverse, FS-102	*	352035	155.00	195.00	290.00
1971-S	3,220,733	7016	8.00	9.50	13.50
↳1971-S, Doubled Die Obverse, FS-101	*	352036	70.00	90.00	260.00
↳1971-S, Cameo	*	7017	11.00	15.00	27.00
↳1971-S, Doubled Die Obverse, FS-102	*	352040	90.00	120.00	325.00
↳1971-S, Doubled Die Obverse, FS-103	*	352041	1,200.00	1,500.00	—
↳1971-S, Deep Cameo	*	7018	12.00	17.50	115.00
1972-S	3,260,996	7019	8.00	9.50	13.50
↳1972-S, Cameo	*	7020	8.00	9.50	15.00
↳1972-S, Deep Cameo	*	7021	11.00	12.00	17.50
1973-S	2,760,339	7022	8.00	9.50	13.50
↳1973-S, Cameo	*	7023	8.00	9.50	15.00
↳1973-S, Deep Cameo	*	7024	11.00	12.00	17.50

* Included in number above. **a.** First Lady Jacqueline Kennedy participated in the coin's design process. After the first year of production, the hair lines above the ear were lightened at her request.

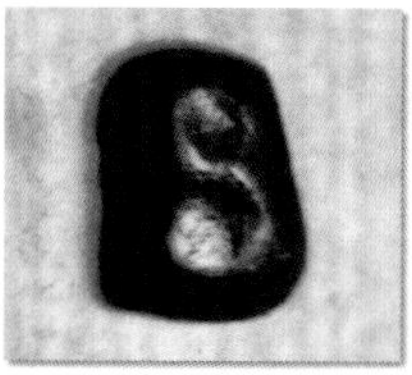

1979-S, Filled S (Variety 1), Proof

1979-S, Clear S (Variety 2), Proof

1981-S, Rounded S (Variety 1), Proof

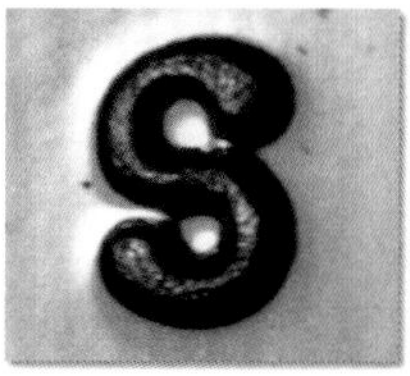

1981-S, Flat S (Variety 2), Proof

1988-S, Doubled Die Obverse, Proof
FS-101

Proof Strikes *(continued)*

	Mintage	GSID	PF-66	PF-67	PF-68
1974-S	2,612,568	7025	$8.00	$9.50	$13.50
↳**1974-S, Cameo**	*	7026	8.00	9.50	15.00
↳**1974-S, Deep Cameo**	*	7027	11.00	12.00	17.50
1776–1976-S	7,059,099	7031	11.00	12.00	17.50
↳**1776–1976-S, DDR, FS-801**	*	352044	470.00	725.00	1,100.00
↳**1776–1976-S, Silver Clad**	4,000,000	7033	17.00	19.00	24.00
1977-S	3,251,152	7036	11.00	12.00	17.50
1978-S	3,127,781	7039	11.00	12.00	17.50
1979-S, Variety 1	3,677,175	7043	11.00	12.00	17.50
1979-S, Variety 2	*	7045	17.50	22.00	27.00
1980-S	3,554,806	7048	8.00	9.50	12.00
1981-S, Variety 1	4,063,083	7052	8.00	9.50	12.00
1981-S, Variety 2	*	7054	24.00	30.00	43.00
1982-S	3,857,479	7057	8.00	9.50	12.00
1983-S	3,279,126	7060	8.00	9.50	12.00
1984-S	3,065,110	7063	8.00	9.50	12.00
1985-S	3,362,821	7066	8.00	9.50	12.00
1986-S	3,010,497	7069	8.00	9.50	12.00
1987-S	4,227,728	7072	8.00	9.50	12.00
1988-S	3,262,948	7075	8.00	9.50	12.00
↳**1988-S, DDO, FS-101**	*	352047	360.00	390.00	440.00
1989-S	3,220,194	7078	8.00	9.50	12.00
1990-S	3,299,559	7081	8.00	9.50	12.00
1991-S	2,867,787	7084	8.00	9.50	12.00
1992-S	2,858,981	7090	8.00	9.50	12.00
1992-S, Silver	1,317,579	7088	29.00	30.00	33.00
↳**1992-S, Silver, DDO, FS-101**	*	352048	—	—	2,500.00
1993-S	2,633,439	7095	8.00	9.50	12.00
1993-S, Silver	761,353	7092	29.00	30.00	33.00
1994-S	2,484,594	7101	8.00	9.50	12.00
1994-S, Silver	785,329	7098	29.00	30.00	33.00

	Mintage	GSID	PF-66	PF-67	PF-68
1995-S	2,117,496	7107	$8.00	$9.50	$12.00
1995-S, Silver	679,985	7104	38.00	40.00	43.00
1996-S	1,750,244	7113	8.00	9.50	12.00
1996-S, Silver	775,021	7110	29.00	30.00	33.00
1997-S	2,055,000	7119	8.00	9.50	12.00
1997-S, Silver	741,678	7116	29.00	30.00	33.00
1998-S	2,086,507	7125	8.00	9.50	12.00
1998-S, Silver	878,792	7122	29.00	30.00	33.00
1999-S	2,543,401	7131	8.00	9.50	12.00
1999-S, Silver	804,565	7128	29.00	30.00	33.00
2000-S	3,082,483	7134	8.00	9.50	12.00
2000-S, Silver	965,421	7133	29.00	30.00	33.00
2001-S	2,294,909	7136	8.00	9.50	12.00
2001-S, Silver	889,697	7135	29.00	30.00	33.00
2002-S	2,319,766	7138	8.00	9.50	12.00
2002-S, Silver	892,229	7137	29.00	30.00	33.00
2003-S	2,172,684	7140	8.00	9.50	12.00
2003-S, Silver	1,125,755	7139	29.00	30.00	33.00
2004-S	1,789,488	7141	8.00	9.50	12.00
2004-S, Silver	1,175,934	7142	29.00	30.00	33.00
2005-S	2,275,000	15377	8.00	9.50	12.00
2005-S, Silver	1,069,679	15378	29.00	30.00	33.00
2006-S	2,000,428	65340	8.00	9.50	12.00
2006-S, Silver	1,054,008	65352	29.00	30.00	33.00
2007-S	1,384,797	68775	8.00	9.50	12.00
2007-S, Silver	875,050	69016	29.00	30.00	33.00
2008-S	1,377,424	69088	16.00	22.00	27.00
2008-S, Silver	763,887	76250	29.00	30.00	33.00
2009-S	1,482,502	70730	19.00	22.00	27.00
2009-S, Silver	697,365	70731	29.00	30.00	33.00
2010-S	1,482,502	76251	20.00	27.00	38.00
2010-S, Silver	585,401	71557	29.00	30.00	33.00
2011-S	1,098,835	71561	16.00	22.00	27.00
2011-S, Silver	574,175	76252	29.00	30.00	33.00

Note: All values from 1976 to date are in Deep Cameo condition. * Included in number above.

Proof Strikes *(continued)*

	Mintage	GSID	PF-66	PF-67	PF-68
2012-S	843,705	76253	$22.00	$30.00	$35.00
2012-S, Silver	445,612	76254	95.00	105.00	115.00
2013-S	854,785	76255	16.00	22.00	27.00
2013-S, Silver	467,691	76256	29.00	30.00	33.00
2014-P, Silver	219,173	84797	17.50	19.00	26.00
2014-W, RevPf, Silver (a)	219,173	84798	43.00	46.00	49.00
2014-S	767,977	76257	16.00	22.00	27.00
2014-S, Silver	472,107	76258	29.00	30.00	33.00
2015-S	711,872	76259	20.00	27.00	34.00
2015-S, Silver	387,310	76260	29.00	30.00	33.00
2016-S	621,774	76261	22.00	28.00	35.00
2016-S, Silver	406,330	76267	29.00	30.00	33.00
2017-S	621,390	76262	24.00	32.00	38.00
2017-S, Silver	406,986	76268	29.00	30.00	33.00
2018-S	567,856	79369	22.00	28.00	35.00
2018-S, Silver	381,356	79370	29.00	30.00	33.00
2018-S, RevPf, Silver (b)	199,116	84474	$38.00	$40.00	$47.00
2019-S	642,309	79371	13.50	19.00	24.00
2019-S, Silver	460,925	81394	29.00	30.00	33.00
2019-S, Enh RevPf (c)	99,998	84473	27.00	30.00	32.00
2020-S	510,726	81735	32.00	38.00	43.00
2020-S, Silver	363,244	81736	80.00	85.00	90.00
2021-S	512,729	85155	20.00	27.00	35.00
2021-S, Silver	350,323	85156	90.00	95.00	105.00
2022-S	400,007	193441	24.00	30.00	35.00
2022-S, Silver	295,153	193442	75.00	80.00	90.00
2023-S		213812	24.00	30.00	35.00
2023-S, Silver		213813	75.00	80.00	90.00
2024-S		349857	24.00	30.00	35.00
2024-S, Silver		349858	65.00	75.00	80.00
2025-S		376284	24.00	30.00	35.00
2025-S, Silver		376285	65.00	75.00	80.00

Note: All values from 1976 to date are in Deep Cameo condition. **a.** Featured in the 2014 half dollar silver-coin collection released by the U.S. Mint to commemorate the 50th anniversary of the Kennedy half dollar. **b.** Included in the 50th Anniversary Silver Reverse Proof Set. **c.** Included in the Apollo 11 50th Anniversary Proof Half Dollar Set.

Silver Dollars
1794–1935

AN OVERVIEW OF SILVER DOLLARS

The silver dollar was authorized by Congress on April 2, 1792, and first coined in 1794. This denomination includes some of the most popular series in American numismatics.

Scan for additional information.

The first coin of the denomination, the Flowing Hair dollar, is easy enough to obtain (given the proper budget) in grades from VF through low Mint State. Striking usually ranges from poor to barely acceptable, and adjustment marks (from an overweight planchet being filed down to correct weight) are often seen. Accordingly, careful examination is needed to find a good example.

The silver dollar with the Draped Bust obverse in combination with the Small Eagle reverse was made from 1795 through 1798, with most examples being dated 1796 or 1797. Today both the 1796 and 1797 exist in about the same numbers. Although mintage figures refer to the quantities produced in the given calendar year, these do not necessarily refer to the dates on the coins themselves, as Mint workers would use coinage dies into the next calendar year. Silver dollars of this type are fairly scarce. Sharpness of strike presents a challenge to the collector, and usually there are weaknesses in details, particularly on the reverse eagle.

The 1798 to 1804 type features a Draped Bust obverse and Heraldic Eagle reverse. Many such coins exist, mostly in grades from VF through lower Mint State levels. Striking can be indifferent, but the population of surviving coins is such that collectors have more to choose from, and can select for quality.

The Gobrecht silver dollars of 1836 (starless obverse, stars on reverse, plain edge) and 1839 (stars on obverse, starless reverse, reeded edge) present a special challenge in the formation of a type set. For quite a few years these were considered by numismatists to be *patterns*, and thus anyone forming a type set of regular-issue U.S. coins did not have to notice them. However, in recent decades, research by R.W. Julian (in particular), Walter Breen, and others, has revealed that the vast majority of 1836 and 1839 silver dollars originally produced were put into circulation at face value. Accordingly, they were coins of the realm at the time, were spent as currency, and are deserving of a place among regular coinage types.

The 1836 Gobrecht dollar is easy enough to find in today's marketplace, although expensive. The original production amounted to 1,600 coins, to which an unknown number of restrikes can be added. The main problem arises with the 1839, made only to the extent of 300 pieces. Those that exist today nearly always have abundant signs of circulation. This is the rarest of all major U.S. coin design types, even outclassing the 1796–1797 half dollar and the 1808 quarter eagle.

In 1840 the regular Liberty Seated dollar made its appearance, with the reverse depicting a perched eagle holding an olive branch and arrows. This style was continued through 1873, with minor modifications over the years; for example, in 1866 the motto IN GOD WE TRUST was added to the reverse.

Generally, Liberty Seated dollars can be easily enough found in circulated grades from VF up, as well as low Mint State levels. MS-63 and higher pieces are in the minority, particularly of the 1840–1865 type.

The Coinage Act of 1873 authorized a new series: a .900-fine silver dollar, weighing 420 grains, for use in the export trade. Circulation strikes were produced from 1873 through 1878, when the passage of the Bland-Allison Act authorized the government to buy millions of ounces of silver each year and resume the production of standard silver dollars (which had not been minted since 1873). Proof trade dollars continued to be struck for numismatists through 1883, with a few more being quietly struck and distributed in 1884 and 1885. Coins of these last two issues are great rarities today.

Choosing a trade dollar for a type set is easy enough to do, the choices being a circulation strike, which requires some connoisseurship, or a Proof, most of which are sharply struck and attractive. Enough exist in both formats that collectors will easily find a nice example, except that MS-65 and better pieces are elusive.

Morgan silver dollars, made by the hundreds of millions from 1878 through 1921, are easily found, with the 1881-S being at once the most common of all varieties existing today in gem condition and also usually seen with sharp strike and nice appearance.

Peace silver dollars of 1921 through 1935 exist in large quantities. Some collectors select the first year of issue, 1921, as a separate type, as the design is in high relief. The 1921 is plentiful in Mint State, but rarely is found sharply struck at the obverse and reverse center. Later Peace dollars with shallow relief abound in MS-63 and finer grades, although strike quality can be a problem.

The Peace dollar was the last of the United States' circulating .900 fine silver dollars. One final type of dollar coin was produced in the large 38.1 mm format—the Eisenhower dollar, often colloquially called a "silver dollar" even though its regular issues were made of copper and nickel. Since the Eisenhower dollar, U.S. coins of this denomination have been produced in smaller diameters and in base metals. These modern dollars are explored in detail in the next chapter. The U.S. Mint has also produced various *commemorative* silver dollars from 1900 to date, and the one-ounce American Silver Eagle bullion coin has a denomination of one dollar. These coins are covered in the Commemoratives and Bullion sections, respectively.

Anthony de Francisci, designer of the Peace dollar, used his wife Teresa as the model for his Liberty.

For the Collector and Investor: Silver Dollars as a Specialty

Generally, silver dollars of the 1794–1803 years are collected by dates and major types.

Although the 1794, of which an estimated 135 or so exist today, is famous and expensive, other varieties are eminently affordable in such grades as VF and EF. Beyond the listings herein there is a rich panorama of die varieties, most extensively delineated in the 1993 two-volume study *Silver Dollars and Trade Dollars of the United States: A Complete Encyclopedia*. This built upon earlier works, including J.W. Haseltine's *Type Table of United States Dollars, Half Dollars and Quarter Dollars*, and, especially, the long-term standard work by M.H. Bolender, *The United States Early Silver Dollars from 1794 to 1803*. In many instances among early dollars the number of aficionados desiring a particularly rare die combination may be even smaller than the population of coins available—with the result that not much premium has to be paid.

The 1804 silver dollar is a study in itself. None were actually produced in the year 1804. Several were made in 1834 as presentation pieces for foreign dignitaries, and even later examples were made for private collectors. Only a handful exist of this classic rarity, the "King of American Coins."

After 1803 it is a long jump to 1836, when silver dollars (of the Gobrecht design) were again struck for circulation. In 1839 more Gobrecht dollars were struck, with the design modified. In addition to the listings in this book are a number of other die combinations, edge and metal varieties, etc., including pieces of the year 1838, most of which are pattern restrikes (studied in *United States Pattern Coins*). These are avidly desired and collected.

Forming a specialized collection of Liberty Seated dollars from 1840 through 1873 has been a pursuit of many collectors over the years. Generally, the Philadelphia Mint dates are available without difficulty, although the 1851 and 1852 are typically acquired as Proof restrikes—originals of both years being prohibitively rare. Most difficult to find in higher grades are coins of the branch mints, including the famous 1870-S, of which only 10 are known to exist and for which no mintage quantity figure was ever listed in official reports. Branch-mint pieces, starting with the 1846-O, were placed into circulation and used extensively. Beginning in 1870, dollars of this type were struck at Carson City; these also are seen with evidence of circulation. The only exceptions to this are certain dollars of 1859-O and 1860-O which turned up in very "baggy" Mint State preservation (showing contact marks from other coins) among Treasury hoards, to the extent of several thousand pieces of both dates combined.

Among trade dollars, there are two great rarities: the Proof-only 1884, of which just ten are known, and the Proof-only 1885, of which only five are known. Not counting those two, one can with some effort form a complete collection of trade dollars. Circulation strikes were not made after 1878, but Proofs—which had greater appeal to collectors of the era—were made each year of the denomination. Very few circulation strikes were saved by numismatists, finding a choice or gem Mint State example today can be a great challenge. The key issue is the 1878-CC. With the lowest mintage by far among circulation strikes in the series, it is scarce in any and all grades. As trade dollars became numismatically popular in the United States, thousands were repatriated from China, often bearing Chinese characters called chopmarks, which were applied by bankers and merchants. More often than not the imported coins had been harshly cleaned in China, where shiny coins were more desirable. However, many choice and undamaged pieces were imported as well. Chopmarked coins are collectible in their own right in view of their historical significance.

Collectors are warned that many modern counterfeit trade dollars lurk in the marketplace.

Morgan silver dollars from 1878 through 1921 are one of the most active and popular series in American numismatics. Approximately 100 different major varieties can be collected, although certain unusual varieties (not basic dates and mintmarks) can be dropped from a collection or added as desired. The vast majority of Morgan dollars can be found in Mint State. When these coins were first minted there was little need for them in circulation, and hundreds of millions of coins piled up in Treasury and other vaults. Although many were melted in 1918, enough remained that untold millions exist today in the hands of the public.

Varieties such as the 1881-S are common and are normally seen in high grades with sharp strike, but others with high mintages, the 1886-O and 1896-O being examples, are quite rare in MS-63 and finer, and when seen usually have rather poor eye appeal. Accordingly, quite a bit of discernment is recommended for the savvy collector.

Peace silver dollars, minted from 1921 to 1935, include the High Relief style of 1921, and the shallow-relief motif of 1922 to 1935. A basic set of 24 different dates and mintmarks is easily enough obtained, including in Mint State. The most elusive is the 1934-S.

EXPLORING VARIETIES

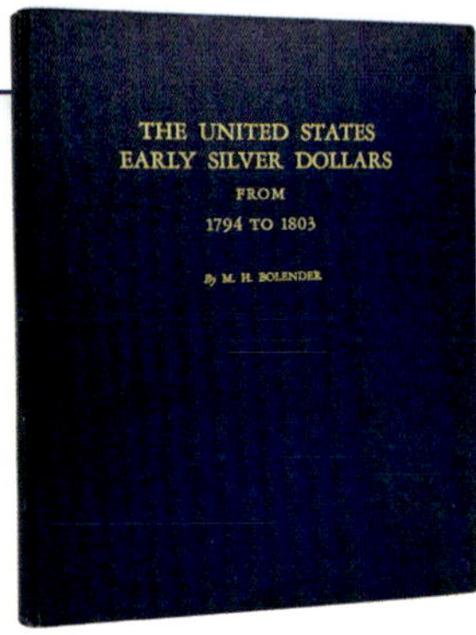

M.H. Bolender's catalog established the Bolender numbers for die marriages of early dollars. These are still in use, although later researchers refined rarity ratings and die states. Collectors use B-numbers for early dollars the same way they use Overton or Browning numbers for other Bust coinage.

Bolender, M.H. *The United States Early Silver Dollars from 1794 to 1803*. Fifth edition. Iola, WI: 1987.

EXPLORING VARIETIES

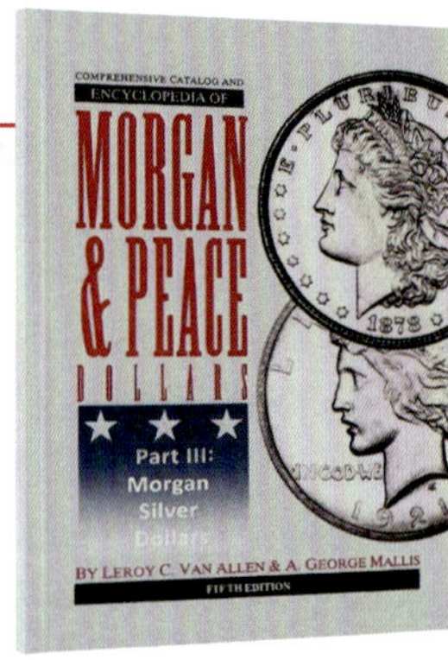

This book created the VAM (Van Allen–Mallis) system, assigning numbers to varieties of Morgan and Peace dollars. VAM collecting has grown into its own specialty, with a large community (vamworld.com) and detailed study of even minor varieties. VAM numbers are now standard references in auction listings and grading-service labels.

Van Allen, Leroy C., and A. George Mallis. *Comprehensive Catalogue and Encyclopedia of U.S. Morgan and Peace Silver Dollars.* New York, NY: 1997.

100 GREATEST™ UNITED STATES COINS

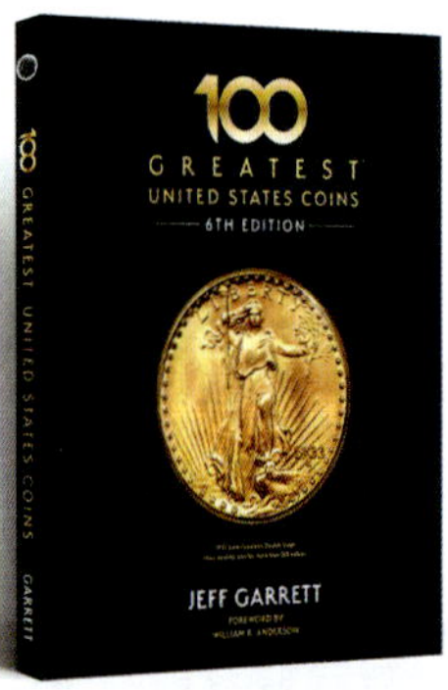

No. 6

1794 FLOWING HAIR SILVER DOLLAR

FLOWING HAIR (1794–1795)

Engraver: *Robert Scot.* **Weight:** *26.96 grams.* **Composition:** *.900 silver, .100 copper (net weight 0.78011 oz. pure silver).* **Diameter:** *Approximately 39–40 mm.* **Edge:** *HUNDRED CENTS ONE DOLLAR OR UNIT with decorations between words.* **Mint:** *Philadelphia.*

History. The first U.S. silver dollars were of the Flowing Hair design. In 1794 only 1,758 were released for circulation (slightly fewer than were struck), and the next year nearly 100 times that amount. These coins were popular in their time and circulated for decades afterward. Many were used in international trade, particularly in the Caribbean.

Striking and Sharpness. On the obverse, check the hair details. It is essential to check the die variety, as certain varieties were struck with very little detail at the center. Accordingly, high-grade examples can appear to be well worn on the hair. Check the star centers, as well. On the reverse, check the breast and wings of the eagle. All 1794 dollars are lightly struck at the lower left of the obverse (often at portions of the date) and to a lesser extent the corresponding part of the reverse. Many coins of both dates have planchet adjustment marks (from overweight blanks being filed down to proper weight before striking), often heavy and sometimes even disfiguring; these are not noted by the certification services. Expect weakness in some areas on dollars of this type; a coin with Full Details on both sides is virtually unheard of. Sharp striking and excellent eye appeal add to the value dramatically. These coins are very difficult to find problem-free, even in MS.

Availability. The 1794 is rare in all grades, with an estimated 125 to 135 known, including a handful in MS. The 1795 is easily available, with an estimated 4,000 to 7,500 still existing, although some die varieties range from scarce to rare. Many if not most have been dipped at one time or another, and many have been retoned, often satisfactorily. The existence of *any* luster is an exception between EF-40 and AU-58. MS coins are quite scarce (perhaps 150 to 250 existing, most dated 1795), especially at MS-63 or above.

Varieties listed herein are those most significant to collectors, but numerous minor variations may be found because each of the early dies was made individually. (Values of varieties not listed in this guide depend on collector interest and demand.) Blanks were weighed before the dollars were struck and overweight pieces were filed to remove excess silver. Coins with old adjustment marks from this filing process may be worth less than the values shown here. Some Flowing Hair dollars were weight-adjusted through insertion of a small (8 mm) silver plug in the center of the blank planchet before the coin was struck.

Grading Standards

MS-64

MS-60 to 70 (Mint State). ***Obverse:*** At MS-60, some abrasion and contact marks are evident, most noticeably on the cheek and in the fields. Luster is present, but may be dull or lifeless, and interrupted in patches. At MS-63, contact marks are very few, and abrasion is light and not obvious. An MS-65 coin has little or, better yet, no abrasion, and contact marks are minute. Luster should be full and rich. Coins graded above MS-65 are more theoretical than actual for this type—but they do exist, and are defined by having fewer marks as perfection is approached. ***Reverse:*** Comments apply as for the obverse, except that abrasion and contact marks are most noticeable on the eagle at the center, although most dollars of this type are lightly struck in the higher points of that area. The field area is small and is protected by lettering and the wreath and in any given grade shows fewer marks than on the obverse.

Illustrated coin: Like all 1794 dollars, this coin is weak at the left obverse and the corresponding part of the reverse. Planchet flaws are seen at stars 3 and 5. The center obverse is very well struck.

AU-58

AU-50, 53, 55, 58 (About Uncirculated). ***Obverse:*** Light wear is seen on the hair area immediately to the left of the face and neck (except for those flatly struck there), on the cheek, and on the top of the neck truncation, more so at AU-50 than at AU-53 or 55. An AU-58 coin has minimal traces of wear. An AU-50 coin has luster in protected areas among the stars and letters, with little luster in the open fields or the portrait. Some certified coins have virtually no luster, but are considered high quality in other aspects. At AU-58, most luster is partially present in the fields. On any high-grade dollar, luster is often a better key to grading than is the appearance of wear. ***Reverse:*** Light wear is seen on the eagle's body and the upper edges of the wings. At AU-50, detail is lost for some of the feathers in this area. However, some coins are weak to begin with. Light wear is seen on the wreath and lettering. Again, luster is the best key to actual wear. This ranges from perhaps 20 percent remaining in protected areas (at AU-50) to two-thirds or more (at AU-58). Generally, the reverse has more luster than the obverse.

Illustrated coin: This coin shows above-average striking sharpness on the obverse.

EF-40

EF-40, 45 (Extremely Fine). ***Obverse:*** More wear is evident on the portrait, especially on the hair to the left of the face and neck (again, remember that some varieties were struck with flatness in this area), the cheek, and the tip of the neck truncation. Excellent detail remains in low-relief areas of the hair. The stars show wear, as do the date and letters. Luster, if present at all, is minimal and in protected areas. ***Reverse:*** The eagle shows more wear, this being the focal point to check. Most or nearly all detail is well defined. These aspects should be reviewed in combination with knowledge of the die variety, to determine the sharpness of the coin when it was first struck. Most silver dollars of this type were flat at the highest area of the center at the time they were made, as this was opposite the highest point of the hair in the press when the coins were struck. Additional wear is on the wreath and letters, but many details are present. Some luster may be seen in protected areas, and if present is slightly more abundant than on the obverse.

Illustrated coin: On the obverse, a massive die crack extends upward through the 7 of the date.

VF-20, 30 (Very Fine). ***Obverse:*** The hair is well worn at VF-20, less so at VF-30. On well-struck varieties the weakness is in the area left of the temple and cheek. The strands are blended as to be heavy. The cheek shows only slight relief. The stars have more wear, making them appear larger (an optical illusion). ***Reverse:*** The body of the eagle shows few if any feathers, while the wings have a third to half of the feathers visible, depending on the strike. The leaves lack most detail, but veins can be seen on a few. Scattered, non-disfiguring marks are normal for this and lower grades. Any major defects should be noted separately.

VF-20

Illustrated coin: Light rim bumps should be noted. This coin features attractive medium toning.

F-12, 15 (Fine). ***Obverse:*** Wear is more extensive than on the preceding, reducing the definition of the thick strands of hair. The cheek has less detail, but the eye is usually well defined. On most coins, the stars appear larger. The rim is distinct in most areas, and many denticles remain visible. ***Reverse:*** Wear is more extensive. Now, feather details are fewer, mostly remaining on the wing to the left and at the extreme tip of the wing on the right. As always, the die variety in question can have an influence on this. The wreath and lettering are worn further. The rim is usually complete, with most denticles visible.

F-12

Illustrated coin: This variety is flatly struck on the head, and examples in higher grades show no detail at the center. Note the smooth, even wear with some marks.

VG-8, 10 (Very Good). ***Obverse:*** The portrait is mostly seen in outline form, with most hair strands gone, although some are visible left of the neck, and the tips at the lower left are clear. The eye is distinct. The stars appear larger still, again an illusion. LIBERTY and the date are readable and usually full, although some letters may be weak at their tops. The rim is usually complete, and many denticles can be seen. ***Reverse:*** The eagle is mostly an outline, although some traces of feathers may be seen in the tail and the lower part of the inside of the right wing. The rim is worn, as are the letters, with some weak, but the motto is readable.

VG-10

Illustrated coin: This coin shows some microscopic granularity overall. It is an interesting variety with a silver plug inserted at the center of the planchet prior to minting, to slightly increase the weight; this feature can barely be seen in outline form.

G-6

G-4, 6 (Good). ***Obverse:*** Wear is more extensive. LIBERTY and the stars are all there, but weak. The head is an outline, although the eye can still be seen. The rim is well worn or even missing. LIBERTY is worn, and parts of some letters may be missing, but elements of all should be readable. The date is readable, but worn. ***Reverse:*** The eagle is flat and discernible in outline form. The wreath is well worn. Some of the letters may be partly missing. At this level some "averaging" can be done. If the letters are stronger than usual in one area, but some are missing in another area, the coin can still qualify as G-4.

Illustrated coin: This is an attractive example with smooth, even wear and a few defects.

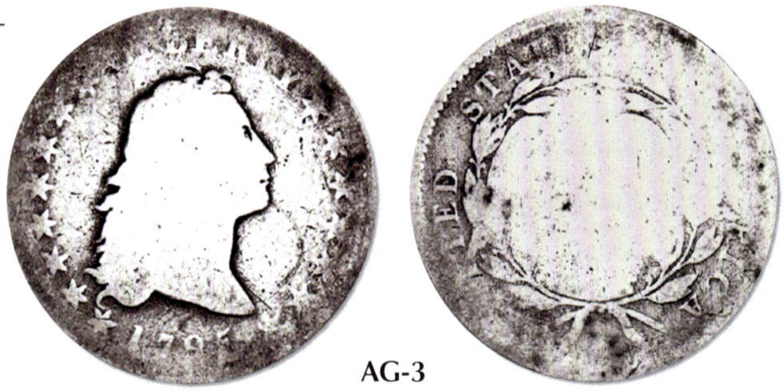

AG-3

AG-3 (About Good). ***Obverse:*** Wear is extensive, but some stars and letters can usually be discerned. The head is in outline form. The date, while readable, may be partially worn away. ***Reverse:*** The reverse is well worn, with parts of the wreath and lettering missing.

1795, Two Leaves Beneath Each Wing

1795, Three Leaves Beneath Each Wing

Circulation Strikes

	Mintage	GSID	AG-3	G-4	VG-8	F-12	VF-20	EF-40	AU-50	MS-60
Flowing Hair (1794–1795)	**n/a**	**72398**	**$2,750**	**$3,500**	**$4,250**	**$5,750**	**$7,750**	**$13,000**	**$21,500**	**$62,500**
1794	1,758	7143	50,500	66,000	108,000	132,000	192,000	372,000	600,000	1,140,000
	Auctions: $2,820,000, PCGS MS-64 SBG 08/17									
↳1794, B-1, BB-1	*	393251	50,500	66,000	108,000	132,000	192,000	372,000	600,000	1,140,000
	Auctions: $528,000, PCGS EF-45 HA 11/23; $6,600,000, PCGS MS-66 HA 11/23									
1794, Silver Plug, Specimen (a)	unique	7144	—	—	—	—	—	—	—	—
1795, Two Leaves	160,295	7147	2,850	3,600	4,550	6,250	8,500	16,000	23,000	77,000
	Auctions: $576,000, PCGS MS-65 SBG 12/20									
↳1795, Two Leaves, B-3, BB-11	*	199057	3,150	4,000	5,000	7,000	9,250	18,000	25,000	84,500
↳1795, Two Leaves, B-11, BB-12	*	199058	—	—	—	—	—	18,000	—	—
↳1795, Two Leaves, B-9, BB-13	*	199059	2,850	3,600	4,550	6,250	8,500	16,000	23,000	77,000
↳1795, Two Leaves, B-4, BB-14	*	199060	2,850	3,600	4,550	6,250	8,500	16,000	23,000	77,000
↳1795, Two Leaves, B-8, BB-15	*	199061	—	—	—	—	—	—	—	—
↳1795, Two Leaves, B-20, BB-16	4 known	199062	—	—	—	—	14,500	—	—	—
↳1795, Two Leaves, B-18, BB-17	unique	199063	—	—	—	—	—	—	—	—
↳1795, Two Leaves, B-2, BB-20	*	199064	2,850	3,600	4,550	6,250	8,500	16,000	23,000	77,000
	Auctions: $253,000, NGC MS-65 HA 06/11									

* Included in number above. **a.** This unique piece, graded SP-66, shows evidence of planchet adjustment marks, as well as traces of a silver plug that was added to bring the coin's weight up to specification.

1795, Silver Plug
Three Leaves, B-7, BB-18

Circulation Strikes *(continued)*

	Mintage	GSID	AG-3	G-4	VG-8	F-12	VF-20	EF-40	AU-50	MS-60
↳1795, Two Leaves, B-1, BB-21	*	199065	$2,850	$3,600	$4,550	$6,250	$8,500	$16,000	$23,000	$77,000
	Auctions: $600,000, PCGS MS-65 HA 06/21									
↳1795, Two Leaves, B-10, BB-22	*	199066	—	—	—	—	—	—	—	—
↳1795, Two Leaves, B-16, BB-23	*	199067	—	—	—	—	—	—	—	—
↳1795, Two Leaves, B-13, BB-24	*	199068	3,150	4,000	5,000	7,000	9,250	18,000	25,000	84,500
	Auctions: $258,500, PCGS MS-65 SBG 09/15									
↳1795, Two Leaves, B-22, BB-29	2 known	199142	—	—	—	—	—	—	—	—
1795, Three Leaves	*	7145	2,750	3,500	4,250	5,750	7,750	13,000	21,500	62,500
	Auctions: $204,000, NGC MS-64 SBG 02/25; $646,250, NGC MS-65 HA 02/25									
↳1795, Three Leaves, B-7, BB-18	*	199070	2,750	3,500	4,250	5,750	7,750	13,000	21,500	62,500
	Auctions: $822,500, PCGS MS-66 SBG 09/15									
↳1795, Three Leaves, B-6, BB-25	*	199071	2,750	3,500	4,250	5,750	7,750	13,000	21,500	62,500
↳1795, Three Leaves, Missing Leaf, B-6, BB-25	*	199072	—	—	—	—	—	—	—	—
↳1795, Three Leaves, B-12, BB-26	*	199073	3,300	4,200	5,000	7,000	9,500	14,500	24,000	—
↳1795, Three Leaves, B-5, BB-27	*	199074	2,750	3,500	4,250	5,750	7,750	13,000	21,500	62,500
	Auctions: $132,000, NGC MS-63 HA 06/24; $282,000, PCGS MS-64 LGND 06/24									
↳1795, Three Leaves, B-21, BB-28	unique	199069	—	—	—	—	—	—	—	—
1795, Silver Plug	*	7149	3,750	5,750	8,750	12,000	15,000	27,500	79,000	210,000
	Auctions: $210,000, PCGS MS-61 SBG 11/23									
↳1795, Silver Plug, Two Leaves, B-3, BB-11	*	199075	—	—	—	—	—	43,000	79,000	—
↳1795, Silver Plug, Two Leaves, B-9, BB-13	*	199076	—	—	—	—	—	—	—	—
↳1795, Silver Plug, Two Leaves, B-4, BB-14	*	199077	3,750	5,750	8,750	12,000	15,000	27,500	79,000	210,000
↳1795, Silver Plug, Three Leaves, B-7, BB-18	*	199078	3,750	5,750	8,750	12,000	15,000	27,500	79,000	210,000
	Auctions: $105,000, PCGS AU-55 HA 01/25; $705,000, PCGS MS-65 SBG 01/25									
↳1795, Silver Plug, Three Leaves, B-19, BB-19	unique	199143	—	—	—	90,000	—	—	—	—
↳1795, Silver Plug, Two Leaves, B-1, BB-21	*	199079	3,750	5,750	8,750	12,000	15,000	27,500	79,000	210,000
	Auctions: $102,000, PCGS AU-53 HA 08/24									
↳1795, Silver Plug, Two Leaves, B-5, BB-27	*	199080	—	—	—	13,000	—	—	—	—

* Included in number above.

DRAPED BUST, SMALL EAGLE REVERSE (1795–1798)

Designer: *Robert Scot.* **Weight:** *26.96 grams.* **Composition:** *.8924 silver, .1076 copper (net weight .77352 oz. pure silver).* **Diameter:** *Approximately 39–40 mm.* **Edge:** *HUNDRED CENTS ONE DOLLAR OR UNIT with decorations between words.* **Mint:** *Philadelphia.*

History. The Draped Bust silver dollar with the Small Eagle reverse, inaugurated in 1795, brought the first appearance of this popular obverse portrait—a depiction of Liberty that later was used on other silver denominations as well as copper half cents and cents. The motif was continued into 1798. Production of the Draped Bust silver dollars started at the end of the year on a new mint press that was first used for striking Flowing Hair dollars that summer. Draped Bust dollars circulated widely, especially outside the United States, and in the Caribbean in particular.

Striking and Sharpness. On the obverse, check the highest areas of the hair, the bust line, and the centers of the stars. On the reverse, check the feathers on the eagle's breast and wings. Examine the denticles. Planchet adjustment marks (from the filing down of overweight blanks) are common and should be avoided. Studying die varieties can be helpful for accurate grading. For example, the Small Letters reverse, a long-lived die design used from 1795 to 1798, has shallow relief and is usually seen with a low rim, with the result that its grade is lower than that of the obverse. On some reverse dies the eagle has very little detail. Fairly sharp striking (not necessarily Full Details) and excellent eye appeal add to the value dramatically.

Availability. These silver dollars are readily available as a type, although certain varieties range from scarce to very rare. MS coins are elusive and when seen are usually of the 1795 date, sometimes with prooflike surfaces. Most coins have been dipped and/or retoned, some successfully. These coins acquired marks more readily than did smaller denominations, and such are to be expected (but should be noted along with the grade, if distracting). Careful buying is needed to obtain coins with good eye appeal. Many AU examples are deeply toned and recolored.

The Smithsonian's National Numismatic Collection includes a unique Specimen 1794 dollar, plugged, and a unique Specimen 1797 10 Stars Left, 6 Stars Right, dollar.

Grading Standards

MS-60 to 70 (Mint State). ***Obverse:*** At MS-60, some abrasion and contact marks are evident, most noticeably on the cheek, the drapery at the shoulder, and the right field. Luster is present, but may be dull or lifeless, and interrupted in patches. At MS-63, contact marks are few, and abrasion is harder to detect. Many coins listed as Mint State are deeply toned, making it impossible to evaluate abrasion and even light wear; these are best avoided completely. An MS-65 coin has no abrasion, and contact marks are so minute as to require magnification. Luster should be full and rich. Coins grading above MS-65 are more theoretical than actual for this type—but they do exist, and are defined by having fewer marks as perfection is approached. ***Reverse:*** Comments apply as for the obverse, except that abrasion and contact marks are most noticeable on the eagle at the center, a situation complicated by the fact that this area was often flatly struck, not only on the famous Small Letters dies used from 1795 to 1798, but on some others as well. Grading is best done by the obverse, then verified by the reverse. In the Mint State category the amount of luster is usually a good key to grading. The field area is small and is protected by lettering and the wreath, and in any given grade shows fewer marks than on the obverse.

MS-60

Illustrated coin: Note the tiny dig near Liberty's ear. This coin is fairly well struck overall, but with some lightness on the eagle's body and leg on the right. It has excellent eye appeal.

AU-50, 53, 55, 58 (About Uncirculated). ***Obverse:*** Light wear is seen on the hair area above the ear and extending to left of the forehead, on the ribbon, and on the drapery at the shoulder, more so at AU-50 than at AU-53 or 55. An AU-58 coin has minimal traces of wear. An AU-50 coin has luster in protected areas among the stars and letters, with little in the open fields or on the portrait. At AU-58, most luster is present in the fields, but is worn away on the highest parts of the motifs. At this level there are many deeply toned and recolored coins, necessitating caution when buying. ***Reverse:*** Light wear is seen on the eagle's body (keep in mind this area might be lightly struck) and edges of the wings. Light wear is seen on the wreath and lettering. Luster is the best key to actual wear. This ranges from perhaps 20 percent remaining in protected areas (at AU-50) to nearly full mint bloom (at AU-58).

AU-50

Illustrated coin: This coin has some lightness of strike, but is better than average. It has some dings and marks, but these are not immediately obvious; without them, the coin might grade higher. This illustrates the many variables on these large, heavy coins. No single rule fits all.

EF-40

EF-40, 45 (Extremely Fine). ***Obverse:*** More wear is evident on the upper hair area and the ribbon, and on the drapery and bosom. Excellent detail remains in low-relief areas of the hair. The stars show wear, as do the date and letters. Luster, if present at all, is minimal and in protected areas. For any and all dollars of this type, knowledge of die variety characteristics is essential to grading. Once again, one rule does not fit all. ***Reverse:*** The eagle, this being the focal point to check, shows more wear. On most strikings, the majority of feathers remain on the interior areas of the wings. Additional wear is on the wreath and letters, but many details are present. Some luster may be seen in protected areas and if present is slightly more abundant than on the obverse.

Illustrated coin: Some marks are on the neck and a small pit is above the eagle's beak.

VF-20

VF-20, 30 (Very Fine). ***Obverse:*** The higher-relief areas of hair are well worn at VF-20, less so at VF-30. The drapery and bosom show extensive wear, usually resulting in loss of most detail below the neck. The stars have more wear, making them appear larger. ***Reverse:*** The body of the eagle shows few if any feathers, while the wings have about half of the feathers visible, depending on the strike. The leaves lack most detail and are in outline form. Scattered, non-disfiguring marks are normal for this and lower grades. Any major defects should be noted separately.

Illustrated coin: This is the particularly famous Small Letters die (one of three Small Letters dies used for this type) first used in 1795 and last used in 1798. Used on 1795 BB-51, later 1796 BB-62, BB-63, and BB-66 now relapped, 1797 BB-72, and 1798 BB-81. The rims are low, and the eagle is in low relief. For coins struck from this particular reverse die, grading must be done by the obverse only.

F-12

F-12, 15 (Fine). ***Obverse:*** Wear is more extensive than on a Very Fine coin, particularly noticeable on the hair, face, and bosom. The stars appear larger. About half the hair detail remains, most noticeably behind the neck and shoulder. The rim shows wear but is complete or nearly so, with most denticles visible. ***Reverse:*** Wear is more extensive. Now, feather details are diminished, with relatively few remaining on the wings. The wreath and lettering are worn further, and the rim is usually weak in areas, although most denticles can be seen.

Illustrated coin: This is not the long-lived Small Letters die discussed above; this Small Letters die was used only in 1796. It is distinguished by a piece out of the die at the lower right of the reverse.

VG-8, 10 (Very Good). ***Obverse:*** The portrait is worn further, with much detail lost in the area above the level of the ear, although the curl over the forehead is delineated. There is some definition at the back of the hair and behind the shoulder, with the hair now combined to form thick strands. The ear is discernible, as is the eye. The stars appear larger still, again an illusion. The rim is weak in areas. LIBERTY and the date are readable and usually full. The rim is worn away in areas, although many denticles can still be discerned. ***Reverse:*** The eagle is mostly an outline, with parts blending into the field (on lighter strikes). The rim is worn, as are the letters, with some weak, but the motto is readable.

VG-10

Illustrated coin: Note the vertical scratches on the cheek.

G-4, 6 (Good). ***Obverse:*** Wear is more extensive, and some stars may be partly missing. The head is an outline. The eye is visible only in outline form. The rim is well worn or even missing in areas. LIBERTY is worn, and parts of some letters may be missing, but elements of all should be readable. The date is readable, but worn. Usually the date is rather bold. ***Reverse:*** The eagle is flat and discernible in outline form, and may be blending into the field. The wreath is well worn. Some of the letters may be partly missing (for some shallow-relief dies with low rims). At this level some "averaging" can be done. If the letters are stronger than usual in one area, but some are missing in another area, the coin can still qualify as G-4. This general rule is applicable to most other series as well.

G-4

Illustrated coin: This is a well-circulated coin with several edge bumps.

AG-3 (About Good). ***Obverse:*** Wear is very extensive, but most letters and stars should be discernible. The head is in outline form. The date, while readable, may be partially worn away. ***Reverse:*** The reverse is well worn, with parts of the wreath and lettering missing. At this level, the reverse usually gives much less information than does the obverse.

AG-3

1795, Off-Center Bust

1795, Centered Bust

1796, Small Date

1796, Large Date

Small Letters

Large Letters

Circulation Strikes

	Mintage	GSID	AG-3	G-4	VG-8	F-12	VF-20	EF-40	AU-50	MS-60
Draped Bust, Small Eagle (1795–1798)	**n/a**	**72399**	**$1,900**	**$2,500**	**$3,000**	**$4,050**	**$5,000**	**$8,250**	**$12,500**	**$50,500**
1795, Centered Bust	42,738	7146	1,900	2,500	3,000	4,050	5,000	8,250	12,500	50,500
	Auctions: $373,750, PCGS MS-65 HA 01/07									
↳1795, Centered Bust, B-15, BB-52	*	315634	1,900	2,500	3,000	4,050	5,000	8,250	12,500	50,500
	Auctions: $204,000, NGC MS-65 SBG 02/25; $646,250, PCGS MS-66 SBG 02/25									
1795, Off-Center Bust	*	7148	1,900	2,500	3,000	4,050	5,000	8,250	12,500	62,500
	Auctions: $168,000, PCGS MS-64 SBG 04/25; $910,625, NGC MS-66 HA 04/25									
↳1795, Off-Center Bust, B-14, BB-51	*	315635	1,900	2,500	3,000	4,050	5,000	8,250	12,500	62,500
	Auctions: $186,000, NGC MS-64 HA 09/20									
1796, Small Date, Small Letters	79,920	7150	1,900	2,500	3,000	4,050	5,000	8,250	12,500	144,000
	Auctions: $1,175,000, NGC MS-65 HA 04/13									
↳1796, Small Date, Small Letters, B-3, BB-62	4 known	199114	—	—	—	42,000	53,000	66,000	81,500	—
↳1796, Small Date, Small Letters, B-2, BB-63	*	199115	1,900	2,500	3,000	4,050	5,000	8,250	12,500	144,000
↳1796, Small Date, Small Letters, B-1, BB-66	*	199116	1,900	2,500	3,000	4,050	5,000	8,250	12,500	144,000
	Auctions: $456,000, NGC MS-64 SBG 08/21									
1796, Small Date, Large Letters	*	7151	1,900	2,500	3,000	4,050	5,000	9,000	15,000	132,000
	Auctions: $352,500, NGC MS-63 HA 11/13									
↳1796, Small Date, Large Letters, B-4, BB-61	*	70412	1,900	2,500	3,000	4,050	5,000	9,000	15,000	132,000
	Auctions: $180,000, PCGS MS-61 HA 04/25									
↳1796, Small Date, Large Letters, B-6, BB-64	*	199081	—	—	—	—	—	—	—	—
1796, Large Date, Small Letters	*	7152	2,000	2,700	3,200	4,300	5,250	9,750	12,500	89,000
	Auctions: $123,375, PCGS MS-62 LGND 09/21									
↳1796, Large Date, Small Letters, B-5, BB-65	*	70411	2,000	2,700	3,200	4,300	5,250	9,750	12,500	89,000
	Auctions: $246,750, PCGS MS-64 SBG 05/16									

* Included in number above.

1797, 10 Stars Left, 6 Stars Right

1797, 9 Stars Left, 7 Stars Right

1798, 15-Star Obverse

1798, 13-Star Obverse

Circulation Strikes *(continued)*

	Mintage	GSID	AG-3	G-4	VG-8	F-12	VF-20	EF-40	AU-50	MS-60
1797, 9 Stars Left, 7 Stars Right, Small Letters	7,776	7155	$2,000	$2,600	$3,300	$6,250	$12,000	$24,000	$79,000	$132,000
	Auctions: $381,875, NGC MS-64 HA 11/13									
↳1797, 9 Stars Left, 7 Stars Right, Small Letters, B-2, BB-72, FS-901	*	315636	2,000	2,600	3,300	6,250	12,000	24,000	79,000	132,000
1797, 9 Stars Left, 7 Stars Right, Large Letters	*	7153	1,900	2,500	3,000	4,050	5,500	9,000	12,500	57,500
	Auctions: $164,500, NGC MS-62 HA 11/13									
↳1797, 9 Stars Left, 7 Stars Right, Large Letters, B-1, BB-73	*	70414	1,900	2,500	3,000	4,050	5,500	9,000	12,500	57,500
1797, 10 Stars Left, 6 Stars Right	*	7154	1,900	2,500	3,000	4,050	5,000	8,250	12,500	50,500
	Auctions: $440,625, NGC MS-64 HA 11/13									
↳1797, 10 Stars Left, 6 Stars Right, B-3, BB-71	*	70413	1,900	2,500	3,000	4,050	5,000	8,250	12,500	50,500
	Auctions: $223,250, NGC MS-65 HA 04/15									
1798, Small Eagle, 13-Star Obverse (a)	327,536	7156	2,000	2,600	3,100	4,200	6,000	12,000	26,500	138,000
	Auctions: $356,500, PCGS AU-58 GLDB 05/11									
↳1798, Small Eagle, 13-Star Obverse, B-1, BB-82	*	70415	2,000	2,600	3,100	4,200	6,000	12,000	26,500	138,000
	Auctions: $132,000, PCGS AU-58 HA 02/24; $111,000, NGC AU 58 HA 02/24									
1798, Small Eagle, 15-Star Obverse	*	7157	1,900	2,500	3,500	4,700	7,000	12,500	33,500	132,000
	Auctions: $129,250, NGC AU-58 HA 11/13									
↳1798, Small Eagle, 15-Star Obverse, B-2, BB-81	*	199082	1,900	2,500	3,500	4,700	7,000	12,500	33,500	132,000
	Auctions: $360,000, PCGS MS-62 HA 04/25; $216,000, PCGS MS-61 HA 04/25									

* Included in number above. **a.** The Mint struck 327,536 silver dollars in 1798, but did not record how many of each type (Small Eagle reverse and Heraldic Eagle reverse).

DRAPED BUST, HERALDIC EAGLE REVERSE (1798–1804)

Designer: *Robert Scot.* **Weight:** *26.96 grams.* **Composition:** *.8924 silver, .1076 copper (net weight .77352 oz. pure silver).* **Diameter:** *Approximately 39–40 mm.* **Edge:** *HUNDRED CENTS ONE DOLLAR OR UNIT with decorations between words.* **Mint:** *Philadelphia.*

Circulation Strike

Proof Strike, Restrike

History. The design of the silver dollar closely follows that of other silver coinvs of the era. The two earliest reverse dies of 1798 have five vertical lines in the stripes in the shield. All dollar dies thereafter have four vertical lines. Production of the Draped Bust dollar continued through early 1804, but in that year the coins were struck from earlier-dated dies.

1804 silver dollars were first struck in 1834 from 1804-dated dies prepared at that time. (As a class these can be called *novodels*, rather than *restrikes*, as no originals were ever made in 1804.) The 1804 dollars were produced in Proof format. Later, probably circa 1859, a new reverse die was made up and combined with the earlier 1804 obverse (made in 1834). Those coins made in 1834 and around that time are today known as Class I dollars, whereas those made with a different reverse, beginning in 1859 and continuing perhaps through the 1870s, are known as Class III. An intermediate variety, from the Class III die combination but with a plain instead of lettered edge, is in the Smithsonian Institution's National Numismatic Collection and is known as Class II. All varieties combined comprise 15 different specimens. The 1804 dollar has been called the "King of American Coins" for well over a century and has achieved great fame. Interested numismatists are directed to *The Fantastic 1804 Dollar, Tribute Edition* (2009).

Striking and Sharpness. Very few of these coins have Full Details. On the obverse, check the highest points of the hair, the details of the drapery, and the centers of the stars. On the reverse, check the shield, the eagle, the stars above the eagle, and the clouds. Examine the denticles on both sides. Planchet adjustment marks are often seen, from overweight blanks being filed down to proper specifications, but they usually are lighter than on the earlier silver dollar types. The relief of the dies and the height of the rims can vary, affecting sharpness. Sharp striking and excellent eye appeal add to the value dramatically. Top-grade MS coins, when found, usually are dated 1800.

Availability. This is the most readily available type among the early silver dollars. Most often seen are the dates 1798 and 1799. Many varieties are available in any grade desired, although MS-63 and 65 coins are elusive. Other die varieties are rare at any level. As with other early dollars, connoisseurship is needed to acquire high-quality coins. These silver dollars usually have problems. To evaluate one for the market it is necessary to grade it, determine its quality of striking, and examine the characteristics of its surface. Nearly all have been dipped or cleaned.

Proofs. There were no Proofs coined in the era this type was issued. Years later, in 1834, the U.S. Mint made up new dies with the 1804 date and struck an unknown number of Proofs, perhaps a dozen or so, for inclusion in presentation Proof sets for foreign dignitaries. Today these are called Class I 1804 dollars. Eight examples are known, one of which shows circulation. The finest by far is the Sultan of Muscat coin, which approaches perfection. Circa 1858 or 1859 the Mint prepared a new obverse die dated 1804 and struck an unknown number of examples for private sale to collectors and dealers—the Class III dollars. No records were kept. These were artificially worn to give them the appearance of original dollars struck in 1804.

Sometime between circa 1858 and the 1870s, the Mint prepared new obverse dies dated 1801, 1802, and 1803, and struck Proof dollars for secret sale to the numismatic market. Many if not most were distributed through J.W. Haseltine, a Philadelphia dealer who had close connections with Mint officials. Today these are known as "Proof restrikes." All are rare, the 1801 being particularly so.

Class I 1804 dollars typically show hairlines and light abrasion. Grading is usually very liberal, in view of the fame of this rarity (not that this is logical). Circulated examples of Class I and Class III 1804 dollars have been graded using prefixes such as EF and AU. Proof restrikes of 1801 to 1803 generally survive in much higher grades, PF-64 or finer.

Grading Standards

MS-60 to 70 (Mint State). ***Obverse:*** At MS-60, some abrasion and contact marks are evident, most noticeably on the cheek, the drapery, and the right field. Luster is present, but may be dull or lifeless, and interrupted in patches. At MS-63, contact marks are very few, and abrasion is hard to detect except under magnification. Knowledge of the die variety is desirable, but on balance the portraits on this type are usually quite well struck. An MS-65 coin has no abrasion, and contact marks are so minute as to require magnification. Luster should be full and rich. Coins grading above MS-65 are more theoretical than actual for this type—but they do exist and are defined by having fewer marks as perfection is approached. ***Reverse:*** Comments apply as for the obverse, except that abrasion and contact marks are most noticeable on the eagle's neck, the tips of the wing, and the tail. The field area is complex, without much open space, given the stars above the eagle, the arrows and olive branch, and other features. Accordingly, marks will not be as noticeable as on the obverse.

MS-63

Illustrated coin: This coin is well struck, essentially problem free, and with superb eye appeal.

AU-50, 53, 55, 58 (About Uncirculated). ***Obverse:*** Light wear is seen on the hair area above the ear and extending to left of the forehead, on the ribbon, and on the drapery and bosom, more so at AU-50 than AU-53 or 55. An AU-58 coin has minimal traces of wear. An AU-50 coin has luster in protected areas among the stars and letters, with little in the open fields or on the portrait. At AU-58, much luster is present in the fields, but is worn away on the highest parts of the motifs. ***Reverse:*** Comments as preceding, except that the eagle's neck, the tips and top of the wings, the clouds, and the tail now show noticeable wear, as do other features. Luster ranges from perhaps 20 percent remaining in protected areas (at AU-50) to nearly full mint bloom (at AU-58). Sometimes the reverse of this type retains much more luster than the obverse, this being dependent on the height of the rim and the depth of the strike (particularly at the center).

AU-50

Illustrated coin: This is an attractive and problem-free coin.

EF-40, 45 (Extremely Fine). ***Obverse:*** More wear is evident on the upper hair area and the ribbon, and on the drapery and bosom. The shoulder is a key spot to check for wear. Excellent detail remains in low-relief areas of the hair. The stars show wear, as do the date and letters. Luster, if present at all, is minimal and in protected areas. ***Reverse:*** Wear is greater than on an AU coin, overall. The neck has lost its feather detail on the highest points. Feathers have lost some detail near the edges of the wings. Some traces of luster may be seen, more so at EF-45 than at EF-40.

EF-45

Illustrated coin: This is an attractive example retaining some mint luster. It has above-average striking sharpness.

VF-20, 30 (Very Fine). ***Obverse:*** The higher-relief areas of hair are well worn at VF-20, less so at VF-30. The drapery at the shoulder and the bosom show extensive wear. The stars have more wear, making them appear larger (an optical illusion seen on most worn silver coins of this era). ***Reverse:*** Wear is greater, including on the shield and the wing feathers. Most of the feathers on the wings are clear. The star centers are flat. Other areas have lost detail as well.

VF-20

Illustrated coin: Some scratches appear on the portrait. This coin was cleaned long ago and now is retoned. It is a typical early dollar at this grade.

F-12, 15 (Fine). ***Obverse:*** Wear is more extensive than on a Very Fine coin, particularly on the hair, face, and bosom. The stars appear larger. About half the hair detail remains, most noticeably behind the neck and shoulder. The rim may be partially worn away and blend into the field. ***Reverse:*** Wear is even more extensive, with the shield and wing feathers being points to observe. Half or slightly more of the feathers will remain clear. The incuse E PLURIBUS UNUM may have a few letters worn away. The clouds all seem to be connected except on varieties in which they are spaced apart. The stars are weak. Parts of the border and lettering may be weak.

F-12

Illustrated coin: This coin was cleaned long ago. Cleaning and retoning is common on dollars of this era, but often is not noted by the grading services.

VG-8, 10 (Very Good). ***Obverse:*** The portrait is mostly seen in outline form, with most hair strands gone, although there is some definition at the back of the hair and behind the shoulder. The ear is discernible, as is the eye. The stars appear larger still, again an illusion. The rim is weak in areas. LIBERTY and the date are readable and usually full, although some letters may be weak at their tops. ***Reverse:*** Wear is more extensive. Half or more of the letters in the motto are worn away. Most feathers are worn away, although separation of some of the lower feathers may be seen at the edges of the wings. Some stars are faint or missing. The border blends into the field in areas and some letters are weak. As always, a particular die variety can vary in areas of weakness.

VG-8

G-4, 6 (Good). ***Obverse:*** Wear is more extensive, and some stars may be partly missing. The head is an outline. The eye is visible only in outline form. The rim is well worn or even missing in areas. LIBERTY is worn, and parts of some letters may be missing, but elements of all should be readable. The date is readable, but worn. ***Reverse:*** Wear is more extensive. The upper part of the eagle is flat. The feathers are noticeable only at the lower edge of the wings, sometimes incompletely, and do not have detail. The upper part of the shield is mostly flat. Only a few letters of the motto can be seen, if any at all. The rim is worn extensively, and the letters are well worn, but the inscription should be readable.

G-4

Illustrated coin: This coin has some marks, but is respectable for the grade.

AG-3 (About Good). ***Obverse:*** Wear is so extensive that the coin is barely identifiable. The head is in outline form. LIBERTY is mostly gone; same for the stars. The date, while readable, may be partially worn away. ***Reverse:*** Extensive wear is seen overall, with the rim worn away and some areas worn smooth. The eagle can be discerned in outline form, but not necessarily completely. A few stray motto letters may remain.

AG-3

PF-60 to 70 (Proof). ***Obverse and Reverse:*** For lower Proof levels, extensive abrasion is seen in the fields, or even evidence of circulation (the Mickley example of the 1804 Class I, earlier graded as AU-50, was certified as PF-62 by a leading certification service in 2008). Numbers assigned by grading services have been erratic. No rules are known, and grading has not been consistent.

PF-66

1798, Pointed 9

1798, Pointed 9, Close Date

1798, Pointed 9, 4 Berries

1798, Knob 9

Four Vertical Lines in Shield's Stripes

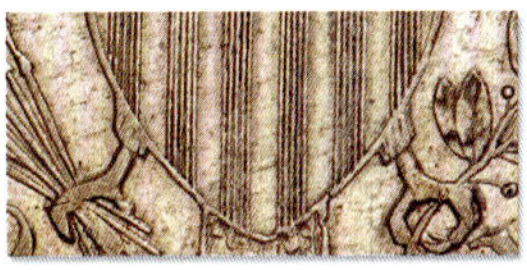

Five Vertical Lines in Shield's Stripes

1798, Pointed 9, 10 Arrows

1798, Pointed 9, Wide Date

Circulation Strikes

	Mintage	GSID	AG-3	G-4	VG-8	F-12	VF-20	EF-40	AU-50	MS-60
Draped Bust, Heraldic Eagle (1798–1804)	**n/a**	**72400**	**$1,000**	**$1,250**	**$1,550**	**$2,100**	**$2,750**	**$4,050**	**$6,500**	**$22,000**
1798, Pointed 9	327,536	7158	1,000	1,250	1,550	2,100	2,750	4,050	6,500	22,000
	Auctions: $115,000, PCGS MS-64 HA 04/08									
↳1798, Pointed 9, 5 Berries, B-18, BB-103	*	199094	—	8,500	14,500	24,000	—	—	—	—
↳1798, Pointed 9, 5 Berries, B-10, BB-109	*	70416	1,150	1,400	1,700	2,350	3,000	4,450	7,250	24,500
↳1798, Pointed 9, 5 Berries, B-11, BB-111	*	199101	1,000	1,250	1,550	2,100	2,750	4,050	6,500	22,000
↳1798, Pointed 9, Close Date, B-27, BB-113	*	199102	1,000	1,250	1,550	2,100	2,750	4,050	6,500	22,000
	Auctions: $204,000, PCGS MS-65 HA 02/24									
↳1798, Pointed 9, Close Date, B-26, BB-114	*	199103	1,150	1,400	1,700	2,350	3,000	4,450	7,250	24,500
↳1798, Pointed 9, Close Date, B-31, BB-115	*	199104	1,000	1,250	1,550	2,100	2,750	4,050	6,500	22,000

* Included in number above.

Circulation Strikes *(continued)*

	Mintage	GSID	AG-3	G-4	VG-8	F-12	VF-20	EF-40	AU-50	MS-60
↳1798, Pointed 9, Close Date, B-30, BB-116	*	199105	$1,150	$1,400	$1,700	$2,350	$3,000	$4,450	$7,250	$24,500
↳1798, Pointed 9, Close Date, B-33, BB-117	*	199106	—	—	—	—	—	—	—	—
↳1798, Pointed 9, Close Date, B-28, BB-118	*	199107	1,000	1,250	1,550	2,100	2,750	4,050	6,500	22,000
↳1798, Pointed 9, Close Date, B-29, BB-119	*	199108	1,000	1,250	1,550	2,100	2,750	4,050	6,500	22,000
↳1798, Pointed 9, Close Date, B-9, BB-121	*	199110	1,000	1,250	1,550	2,100	2,750	4,050	6,500	22,000
↳1798, Pointed 9, 5 Berries, B-14, BB-122	*	71452	1,000	1,250	1,550	2,100	2,750	4,050	6,500	22,000
↳1798, Pointed 9, Close Date, B-25, BB-123	*	199111	1,000	1,250	1,550	2,100	2,750	4,050	6,500	22,000
↳1798, Pointed 9, 5 Berries, B-24, BB-124	*	199112	1,000	1,250	1,550	2,100	2,750	4,050	6,500	22,000
↳1798, Pointed 9, 4 Berries, B-8, BB-125	*	70417	1,000	1,250	1,550	2,100	2,750	4,050	6,500	22,000
↳1798, Pointed 9, 5 Berries, B-34, BB-126	*	199113	—	—	—	—	—	—	—	—
1798, Knob 9	*	7161	1,250	1,500	1,900	2,550	3,300	4,900	7,750	26,500
↳1798, Knob 9, 4 Vertical Lines, B-3, BB-94	*	199089	1,250	1,500	1,900	2,550	3,300	4,900	7,750	26,500
↳1798, Knob 9, 4 Vertical Lines, B-7, BB-95	*	199090	1,250	1,500	1,900	2,550	3,300	4,900	7,750	26,500
1798, 5 Vertical Lines	*	7160	1,250	1,500	1,900	2,550	3,300	4,900	7,750	26,500
	Auctions: $126,500, PCGS MS-63 HA 01/06									
↳1798, Knob 9, 5 Vertical Lines, B-32, BB-91	*	199084	1,300	1,650	2,050	2,800	3,650	5,250	8,500	29,500
↳1798, Knob 9, 5 Vertical Lines, B-4, BB-92	*	199085	1,250	1,500	1,900	2,550	3,300	4,900	7,750	26,500
↳1798, Pointed 9, 10 Arrows, 5 Vertical Lines, B-17, BB-101	*	199091	1,250	1,500	1,900	2,550	3,300	4,900	7,750	26,500
1798, 10 Arrows	*	7159	1,250	1,500	1,900	2,550	3,300	4,900	7,750	26,500
↳1798, Knob 9, 10 Arrows, 4 Vertical Lines, B-5, BB-93	*	199088	—	—	—	—	—	—	—	—
↳1798, Knob 9, 10 Arrows, 5 Vertical Lines, B-6, BB-96	*	199086	1,250	1,500	1,900	2,550	3,300	4,900	7,750	26,500
↳1798, Pointed 9, 10 Arrows, B-21, BB-107	*	199098	1,300	1,650	2,050	2,800	3,650	5,250	8,500	29,500
↳1798, Pointed 9, 10 Arrows, B-13, BB-108	*	199099	1,250	1,500	1,900	2,550	3,300	4,900	7,750	26,500
1798, Pointed 9, Wide Date	*	7162	1,150	1,400	1,700	2,350	3,000	4,900	7,250	22,000
	Auctions: $270,250, PCGS MS-65 LGND 10/20									
↳1798, Pointed 9, Wide Date, B-15, BB-112	*	70418	1,150	1,400	1,700	2,350	3,000	4,900	7,250	22,000
↳1798, Pointed 9, Wide Date, B-20, BB-102	*	199093	1,250	1,500	1,900	2,550	3,350	5,250	7,750	24,500
↳1798, Pointed 9, Wide Date, B-22, BB-104	*	199095	1,150	1,400	1,700	2,350	3,000	4,900	7,250	22,000
↳1798, Pointed 9, Wide Date, B-23, BB-105	*	199096	1,150	1,400	1,700	2,350	3,000	4,900	7,250	22,000
↳1798, Pointed 9, Wide Date, B-19, BB-106	*	199097	1,250	1,500	1,900	2,550	3,350	5,250	7,750	24,500
↳1798, Pointed 9, Wide Date, B-16, BB-110	*	199100	1,150	1,400	1,700	2,350	3,000	4,900	7,250	22,000
↳1798, Pointed 9, Wide Date, B-12, BB-120	*	199109	1,150	1,400	1,700	2,350	3,000	4,900	7,250	22,000

* Included in number above.

1799, Normal Date

1799, Irregular Date

1799, Irregular Date, 13-Star Reverse

1799, Irregular Date, 15-Star Reverse

Circulation Strikes *(continued)*

	Mintage	GSID	AG-3	G-4	VG-8	F-12	VF-20	EF-40	AU-50	MS-60
1799, 7 Stars Left, 6 Right	423,515	7163	$1,000	$1,250	$1,550	$2,100	$2,750	$4,050	$6,500	$22,000
	Auctions: $822,500, NGC MS-67 HA 11/13									
↳1799, 7 Stars Left, 6 Stars Right, B-18, BB-154	*	199144	1,150	1,400	1,700	2,350	3,000	4,450	7,250	24,500
↳1799, 7 Stars Left, 6 Stars Right, B-19, BB-155	*	70422	1,150	1,400	1,700	2,350	3,000	4,450	7,250	24,500
↳1799, 7 Stars Left, 6 Stars Right, B-7, BB-156	*	199145	1,150	1,400	1,700	2,350	3,000	4,450	7,250	24,500
↳1799, 7 Stars Left, 6 Stars Right, B-5, BB-157	*	70420	1,000	1,250	1,550	2,100	2,750	4,050	6,500	22,000
↳1799, 7 Stars Left, 6 Stars Right, B-16, BB-158	*	199146	1,000	1,250	1,550	2,100	2,750	4,050	6,500	22,000
↳1799, 7 Stars Left, 6 Stars Right, B-12, BB-160	*	199147	1,000	1,250	1,550	2,100	2,750	4,050	6,500	22,000
	Auctions: $152,750, NGC MS-65 HA 09/15									
↳1799, 7 Stars Left, 6 Right, B-11, BB-161	*	199137	1,000	1,250	1,550	2,100	2,750	4,050	6,500	22,000
↳1799, 7 Stars Left, 6 Stars Right, B-6, BB-162	*	199138	1,000	1,250	1,550	2,100	2,750	4,050	6,500	22,000
↳1799, 7 Stars Left, 6 Stars Right, B-10, BB-163	*	199148	1,000	1,250	1,550	2,100	2,750	4,050	6,500	22,000
↳1799, 7 Stars Left, 6 Stars Right, B-17, BB-164	*	70419	1,000	1,250	1,550	2,100	2,750	4,050	6,500	22,000
↳1799, 7 Stars Left, 6 Stars Right, B-8, BB-165	*	199139	1,000	1,250	1,550	2,100	2,750	4,050	6,500	22,000
↳1799, 7 Stars Left, 6 Stars Right, B-9, BB-166	*	70504	1,000	1,250	1,550	2,100	2,750	4,050	6,500	22,000
	Auctions: $114,000, NGC MS-65 HA 08/20									
↳1799, 7 Stars Left, 6 Stars Right, B-14, BB-167	*	70421	1,000	1,250	1,550	2,100	2,750	4,050	6,500	22,000
↳1799, 7 Stars Left, 6 Stars Right, B-22, BB-168	*	213684	1,000	1,250	1,550	2,100	2,750	4,050	6,500	22,000
↳1799, 7 Stars Left, 6 Stars Right, B-21, BB-169	*	213685	1,150	1,400	1,700	2,350	3,000	5,000	10,500	—
1799, Irregular Date, 13-Star Reverse	*	7165	1,150	1,400	1,700	2,350	3,000	4,450	10,000	24,000
	Auctions: $115,000, PCGS MS-64 GLDB 05/11									
↳1799, Irregular Date, 13-Star Reverse, B-13, BB-151	*	199149	1,250	1,500	1,900	2,550	3,350	4,900	11,000	26,500
↳1799, Irregular Date, 13-Star Reverse, B-15, BB-152	*	199150	1,150	1,400	1,700	2,350	3,000	4,450	10,000	24,000
	Auctions: $129,250, NGC MS-65 HA 01/15									
1799, Irregular Date, 15-Star Reverse	*	7166	1,150	1,400	1,700	2,350	3,100	6,250	13,000	30,000
↳1799, Irregular Date, 15-Star Reverse, B-4, BB-153	*	199151	1,150	1,400	1,700	2,350	3,100	6,250	13,000	30,000

* Included in number above.

1799, 8 Stars Left, 5 Stars Right

1799, 99 Over 98, 15-Star Reverse

1799, 99 Over 98, 13-Star Reverse

Circulation Strikes *(continued)*

	Mintage	GSID	AG-3	G-4	VG-8	F-12	VF-20	EF-40	AU-50	MS-60
1799, 8 Stars Left, 5 Stars Right	*	7164	$1,150	$1,400	$1,700	$2,350	$3,100	$4,950	$10,500	$39,000
	Auctions: $143,750, PCGS MS-64 ANR 06/05									
↪1799, 8 Stars Left, 5 Stars Right, B-23, BB-159	*	351779	1,150	1,400	1,700	2,350	3,100	4,950	10,500	39,000
1799, 99 Over 98, 15-Star Reverse	423,515	7185	1,150	1,400	1,700	2,550	3,300	4,900	7,250	24,500
	Auctions: $141,881, PCGS MS-64 SBG 11/12									
↪1799, 99 Over 98, 15-Star Reverse, B-3, BB-141	*	70423	1,150	1,400	1,700	2,550	3,300	4,900	7,250	24,500
	Auctions: $168,000, PCGS MS-65 HA 06/21									
1799, 99 Over 98, 13-Star Reverse	423,515	7186	1,150	1,400	1,700	2,550	3,300	4,900	7,250	23,000
↪1799, 99 Over 98, 13-Star Reverse, B-1, BB-142	*	199140	1,150	1,400	1,700	2,550	3,300	4,900	7,250	23,000
↪1799, 99 Over 98, 13-Star Reverse, B-2, BB-143	*	199141	1,150	1,400	1,700	2,550	3,300	4,900	7,250	23,000
1800, Normal Dies	220,920	7167	1,050	1,300	1,600	2,200	2,900	4,300	7,000	24,000
	Auctions: $246,750, PCGS MS-65 LGND 10/20									
↪1800, Normal Dies, B-1, BB-181	*	199129	1,150	1,400	1,800	2,450	3,150	4,750	7,500	26,500
↪1800, Normal Dies, B-2, BB-182	*	199130	1,250	1,550	1,950	2,650	3,450	5,250	8,250	29,000
↪1800, Normal Dies, B-3, BB-183	*	199131	1,150	1,400	1,800	2,450	3,150	4,750	7,500	26,500
↪1800, Normal Dies, B-12, BB-184	*	70425	1,050	1,300	1,600	2,200	2,900	4,300	7,000	24,000
↪1800, Normal Dies, B-20, BB-185	*	199132	1,250	1,550	1,950	2,650	3,450	5,250	8,250	29,000
↪1800, Normal Dies, B-4, BB-186	*	199133	1,050	1,300	1,600	2,200	2,900	4,300	7,000	24,000
↪1800, Normal Dies, B-16, BB-187	*	70426	1,050	1,300	1,600	2,200	2,900	4,300	7,000	24,000
↪1800, Normal Dies, B-8, BB-188	*	199134	1,050	1,300	1,600	2,200	2,900	4,300	7,000	24,000
↪1800, Normal Dies, B-5, BB-189	*	199135	1,150	1,400	1,800	2,450	3,150	4,750	7,500	26,500
↪1800, Normal Dies, B-13, BB-193	*	199136	1,050	1,300	1,600	2,200	2,900	4,300	7,000	24,000

* Included in number above.

1800, "Dotted Date"

1800, 12 Arrows

1800, AMERICAI

1800, Very Wide Date, Low 8

1802, Narrow Normal Date

1802, Wide Normal Date

Circulation Strikes *(continued)*

	Mintage	GSID	AG-3	G-4	VG-8	F-12	VF-20	EF-40	AU-50	MS-60
1800, Dotted Date	*	7171	$1,150	$1,400	$1,800	$2,450	$3,150	$4,750	$7,500	$24,000
↳1800, Dotted Date, B-14, BB-194	*	377839	1,150	1,400	1,800	2,450	3,150	4,750	7,500	24,000
1800, 12 Arrows	*	7169	1,150	1,400	1,800	2,200	2,900	4,300	7,000	24,000
↳1800, 12 Arrows, B-17, BB-196	*	377840	1,150	1,400	1,800	2,200	2,900	4,300	7,000	24,000
1800, 10 Arrows	*	7168	1,150	1,400	1,800	2,650	3,450	5,250	9,500	43,000
↳1800, 10 Arrows, B-15, BB-195	*	377841	1,150	1,400	1,800	2,650	3,450	5,250	9,500	43,000
1800, AMERICAI	*	7170	1,150	1,400	1,800	2,650	3,150	5,000	8,000	30,000
	Auctions: $223,250, NGC MS-65 HA 11/13									
↳1800, AMERICAI, B-19, BB-192	*	199152	1,150	1,400	1,800	2,650	3,150	5,000	8,000	30,000
	Auctions: $156,000, NGC MS-65 HA 01/20									
1800, Wide Date, Low 8	*	7172	1,050	1,300	1,600	2,200	2,900	4,300	7,000	24,000
	Auctions: $115,000, PCGS MS-64 ANR 06/05									
↳1800, Wide Date, Low 8, B-10, BB-190	*	70424	1,050	1,300	1,600	2,200	2,900	4,300	7,000	24,000
1800, Wide Date, Low 8, AMERICAI	*	377448	1,250	1,550	1,950	2,950	3,500	5,500	9,000	33,000
↳1800, Wide Date, Low 8, AMERICAI, B-11, BB-191	*	7173	1,250	1,550	1,950	2,950	3,500	5,500	9,000	33,000
1801	54,454	7174	1,150	1,400	1,700	2,550	2,900	5,250	7,250	23,500
	Auctions: $329,000, NGC MS-65 HA 11/13									
↳1801, B-1, BB-211	*	199127	1,150	1,400	1,700	2,550	2,900	5,250	7,250	23,500
↳1801, B-2, BB-212	*	70427	1,150	1,400	1,700	2,550	2,900	5,250	7,250	23,500
↳1801, B-3, BB-213	*	199128	1,150	1,400	1,700	2,550	2,900	5,250	7,250	23,500
↳1801, B-4, BB-214	*	70432	1,200	1,450	1,800	2,700	3,000	5,500	7,500	24,500
1802	41,650	199117	1,150	1,400	1,700	2,550	3,300	4,900	7,250	22,000
	Auctions: $300,000, PCGS MS-65 HA 11/20									
1802, Narrow Date	41,650	7176	1,150	1,400	1,700	2,550	3,300	4,900	7,250	22,000
	Auctions: $188,000, PCGS MS-65 LGND 04/23									
↳1802, Narrow Date, B-6, BB-241	*	70433	1,150	1,400	1,700	2,550	3,300	4,900	7,250	22,000
	Auctions: $270,250, PCGS MS-65 LGND 10/20									
1802, Wide Date	*	7177	1,250	1,500	1,900	2,800	3,650	5,250	7,750	24,500
	Auctions: $247,250, PCGS MS-65 ANR 06/05									
↳1802, Wide Date, B-5, BB-242	*	393252	1,250	1,500	1,900	2,800	3,650	5,250	7,750	24,500

* Included in number above.

1802, 2 Over 1, Narrow Date

1802, 2 Over 1, Wide Date

1803, Small 3

1803, Large 3

Circulation Strikes *(continued)*

	Mintage	GSID	AG-3	G-4	VG-8	F-12	VF-20	EF-40	AU-50	MS-60
1802, 2 Over 1	*	226405	$1,150	$1,400	$1,700	$2,550	$3,300	$4,900	$7,250	$22,000
1802, 2 Over 1, Narrow Date	*	7187	1,150	1,400	1,700	2,550	3,300	4,900	7,250	22,000
↳1802, 2 Over 1, Narrow Date, B-1, BB-231	*	199118	1,200	1,450	1,800	2,700	3,450	5,000	7,500	23,500
↳1802, 2 Over 1, Narrow Date, B-4, BB-232	*	199119	1,150	1,400	1,700	2,550	3,300	4,900	7,250	22,000
1802, 2 Over 1, Wide Date	*	7188	1,150	1,400	1,700	2,550	3,300	4,900	8,750	26,500
	Auctions: $199,750, NGC MS-64 HA 11/13									
↳1802, 2 Over 1, Wide Date, B-2, BB-233	*	199120	1,150	1,400	1,700	2,550	3,300	4,900	8,750	26,500
↳1802, 2 Over 1, Wide Date, B-3, BB-234	*	199121	1,150	1,400	1,700	2,550	3,300	4,900	8,750	26,500
↳1802, 2 Over 1, Wide Date, B-9, BB-235	*	199122	1,250	1,500	1,900	2,800	3,650	5,250	9,500	29,000
1803, Small 3	85,634	7180	1,150	1,400	1,700	2,350	3,050	5,250	7,750	33,000
	Auctions: $117,500, NGC MS-63 HA 11/13									
↳1803, Small 3, B-1, BB-251	*	199123	1,250	1,500	1,900	2,550	3,350	5,750	8,500	36,500
↳1803, Small 3, B-5, BB-252	*	199124	1,150	1,400	1,700	2,350	3,050	5,250	7,750	33,000
↳1803, Small 3, B-4, BB-254	*	199125	1,150	1,400	1,700	2,350	3,050	5,250	7,750	33,000
↳1803, Small 3, B-3, BB-256	*	199126	—	—	—	—	—	—	—	—
1803, Large 3	*	7181	1,150	1,400	1,700	2,350	2,750	4,500	7,500	31,000
	Auctions: $168,000, NGC MS-64 SBG 08/24; $705,000, NGC MS-65 HA 08/24									
↳1803, Large 3, B-6, BB-255	*	70434	1,150	1,400	1,700	2,350	2,750	4,500	7,500	31,000
↳1803, Large 3, B-8, BB-257	*	199153	—	—	—	—	—	—	—	—

* Included in number above.

1804 Dollar, Proof

1804, First Reverse, Proof

1804, Second Reverse, Proof

Note the position of the words STATES OF in relation to the clouds.

Proof Strikes

		GSID	AU-55	AU-58	PF-60	PF-63	PF-65	PF-66
1801, Proof Restrike (reverse struck from first die of 1804 dollar)	2 known	7175	—	—	—	—	$1,800,000	—
1802, Proof Restrike	4 known	7178	—	—	—	$540,000	1,020,000	—
	Auctions: $411,250, PCGS PF-64 HA 10/12							
1803, Proof Restrike	4 known	7182	—	—	$270,000	450,000	900,000	$1,320,000
	Auctions: $1,110,000, PCGS PF-66 HA 04/25							
1804, Class I, First Reverse (O Above Cloud)	8 known	7183	—	—	3,000,000	3,600,000	4,500,000	6,000,000
	Auctions: $7,680,000, PCGS PF-68 SBG 08/21							
1804, Class II, Second Reverse (O Above Space Between Clouds), Plain Edge (in Smithsonian Collection)	unique	374593	—	—	—	—	—	—
1804, Class III, Second Reverse (O Above Space Between Clouds), Lettered Edge	7 known	7184	$1,728,000	$2,100,000	3,000,000	4,320,000	6,000,000	—
	Auctions: $2,300,000, PCGS AU-58 HA 05/09							

GOBRECHT (1836–1839)

No Stars on Obverse, Stars on Reverse (1836):
Designer: *Christian Gobrecht.* **Weight:** *26.96 grams.*
Composition: *.8924 silver, .1076 copper (net weight .77352 oz. pure silver).*
Diameter: *39–40 mm.* **Edge:** *Plain.*

No Stars on Obverse, Stars on Reverse

Stars on Obverse, No Stars on Reverse (1838–1839): **Designer:** *Christian Gobrecht.*
Weight: *26.73 grams.* **Composition:** *.900 silver, .100 copper*
(net weight .77345 oz. pure silver). **Diameter:** *39–40 mm.* **Edge:** *Reeded.*

Stars on Obverse, No Stars on Reverse

History. Suspension of silver dollar coinage was lifted in 1831, but it was not until 1835 that steps were taken to resume their production. Late that year, Mint Director R.M. Patterson had engraver Christian Gobrecht prepare a pair of dies based on motifs by Thomas Sully and Titian Peale. The first obverse die, dated 1836, bore the seated figure of Liberty with the inscription C. GOBRECHT F. ("F." for the Latin word *Fecit*, or "made it") in the field above the date. On the reverse die was a large eagle flying left, surrounded by 26 stars and the legend UNITED STATES OF AMERICA • ONE DOLLAR •. It is unknown whether coins were struck from these dies at that time. A new obverse die with Gobrecht's name on the base of Liberty was prepared, and in December 1836, a thousand plain-edged pieces were struck for circulation. These coins weighed 416 grains, the standard enacted in 1792.

The feeder mechanism that was used, apparently designed for coins of half dollar size or smaller, damaged the reverse die's rim. Attempts were made to solve the problem by rotating the reverse die at various times during the striking run, but this only extended the damage to both sides of the rim. The original 1836 issue is thus known in multiple die alignments:

Die Alignment 1—head of Liberty opposite DO in DOLLAR; eagle flying upward.

Die Alignment 2—head of Liberty opposite ES in STATES; eagle flying upward.

Die Alignment 3—head of Liberty opposite N of ONE; eagle flying level.

Die Alignment 4—head of Liberty opposite F in OF; eagle flying level.

Original 1836 die orientation using either "coin" or "medal" turn.

Die alignment of original issues dated 1838 and 1839.

Restrikes were made from the late 1850s through the early 1870s. They were struck using the original obverse die and a different reverse die with cracks through NITED STATES O and OLLA, and in Die Alignment 3.

In January 1837, the standard weight for the dollar was lowered to 412-1/2 grains, and on January 8, 1837, Benjamin Franklin Peale wrote an internal memorandum to Mint Director Patterson noting, among other things, that the new dollar had received much criticism for looking too medallic, rather than like a coin. Peale felt this was due to the "smooth" edge and suggested striking with a segmented, lettered-edge collar like one he had seen in France. In March 1837, the dies of 1836 were used to strike 600 pieces (whether with plain or reeded edge is unknown). According to reports, the results were unsatisfactory and the coins were destroyed—although a single example, with a reeded edge, is known. It is unclear whether it was part of the March striking, from an earlier 1837 striking caused by the Peale memo, or struck at some later period.

Pattern pieces were struck in 1838 using modified dies with Gobrecht's name removed from the base, 13 stars added to the obverse, and the 26 stars removed from the reverse. These were struck in alignment 4 using a reeded-edge collar. In 1839, 300 pieces were struck for circulation, also in alignment 4. Both of these were restruck in alignment 3 and possibly alignment 4 in the late 1850s through early 1870s.

Striking and Sharpness. Striking is usually very good. Check the details on Liberty's head and the higher parts of the eagle. Note that the word LIBERTY is raised.

Availability. 1836 Gobrecht dollars are available in grades from so-called Very Fine upward (the coins were struck as Proofs, and worn examples are properly designated as PF-30, PF-40, and so on; however, sometimes they are found graded as Fine, VF, and EF for levels below PF-50). Most in the marketplace range from PF-50 to 62. Most have contact marks. Truly pristine PF-65 and better examples are very elusive. The demand for these coins is intense. For the 1839, circulated grades typically are PF-50 or higher, often with damage. Pristine Proofs are available, but virtually all are restrikes.

100 GREATEST UNITED STATES COINS

No. 65 1836, 1838, AND 1839 GOBRECHT SILVER DOLLARS

Grading Standards

PF-63

PF-60 to 70 (Proof). ***Obverse and Reverse:*** Many Proofs have been extensively cleaned and have many hairlines and dull fields. This is more applicable to 1836 than to 1839. Grades are PF-60 to 61 or 62. With medium hairlines and good reflectivity, an assigned grade of PF-64 is appropriate, and with relatively few hairlines, Gem PF-65. In various grades hairlines are most easily seen in the obverse field. PF-66 should have hairlines so delicate that magnification is needed to see them. Above that, a Proof should be free of such lines.

Illustrated coin: This is a restrike made at the Mint in or after spring 1859.

PF-58

PF-50, 53, 55, 58 (Proof). ***Obverse:*** Light wear is seen on the thighs and knees, bosom, and head. At PF-58, the Proof surface is extensive, but the open fields show abrasion. At PF-50 and 53, most if not all mirror surface is gone and there are scattered marks. ***Reverse:*** Wear is most evident on the eagle's breast and the top of the wings. Mirror surface ranges from perhaps 60 percent complete (at PF-58) to none (at PF-50).

Illustrated coin: This original 1836 Gobrecht dollar, of which 1,000 were coined in 1836, is nicely toned and has excellent eye appeal.

PF-45

PF-40 to 45 (Proof). ***Obverse:*** Further wear is seen on all areas, especially the thighs and knees, bosom, and head. The center of LIBERTY, which is in relief, is weak. Most at this level and lower are the 1836 issues. ***Reverse:*** Further wear is evident on the eagle, including the back edge of the closest wing, the top of the farthest wing, and the tail.

PF-20

PF-20, 25, 30, 35 (Proof). ***Obverse:*** Further wear is seen. Many details of the gown are worn away, but the lower-relief areas above and to the right of the shield remain well defined. Hair detail is mostly or completely gone. LIBERTY is weak at the center. ***Reverse:*** Even more wear is evident on the eagle, with only about 60 percent of the feathers visible.

Designer's Name on Rock

Designer's Name Below Rock

Proof Strikes

	Mintage	GSID	AU-50	PF-60	PF-63	PF-65
Gobrecht Dollar, Type of 1836, No Stars Obverse, Stars on Reverse	**n/a**	**69007**	**$15,000**	**$25,000**	**$37,000**	**$87,000**
Gobrecht Dollar, Type of 1839, Stars on Obverse, No Stars Reverse	**n/a**	**79501**	**30,000**	**36,000**	**48,000**	**102,000**
1836, Restrike, C. GOBRECHT F. Below Base; No Stars on Obverse. Plain Edge (J-58)	31 known	376670	—	50,500	69,500	120,000
1836, Original, C. GOBRECHT F. on Base; No Stars on Obverse. Plain Edge (J-60)	1,025	393844	—	—	—	—
↳1836, Original, C. GOBRECHT F. on Base; No Stars on Obverse, Alignment I. Plain Edge (J-60)	*	69008	15,000	25,000	37,000	87,000
↳1836, Original, C. GOBRECHT F. on Base; No Stars on Obverse, Alignment II. Plain Edge (J-60)	*	376550	—	—	—	—
↳1836, Original, C. GOBRECHT F. on Base; No Stars on Obverse, Alignment IV. Plain Edge (J-60)	*	7189	15,000	25,000	37,000	87,000
	Auctions: $264,000, PCGS PF-65 HA 08/21					
1836, Original, C. GOBRECHT F. on Base; No Stars on Obverse. Reeded Edge (J-61)	unique	376851	—	—	240,000	—
	Auctions: $195,500, PCGS PF-63 SBG 05/03					
1836, Restrike, C. GOBRECHT F. on Base; No Stars on Obverse. Plain Edge (J-60)	1,025	79500	15,000	25,000	37,000	87,000
↳1836, Restrike, C. GOBRECHT F. on Base; No Stars on Obverse, Alignment III. Plain Edge (J-60)	*	393845	—	—	—	—
1836, Restrike, C. GOBRECHT F. Below Base; No Stars on Obverse and Reverse. Plain Edge (J-63)	3	376689	—	—	180,000	—
1836, Restrike, C. GOBRECHT F. on Base; No Stars on Obverse and Reverse. Plain Edge (J-65)	4–5 known	376690	—	—	150,000	198,000
1838, Stars on Obverse. Reeded Edge (J-84)	31 est. known	135900	30,000	36,000	48,000	102,000
1838, Original, Stars on Obverse. Plain Edge (J-85)	8 known	376671	—	—	78,000	150,000
1838, Stars on Obverse and Reverse. Plain Edge (J-88)	3 known	135899	—	—	150,000	240,000
1839, Stars on Obverse. Reeded Edge (J-104)	70 est. known	68653	30,000	37,000	48,000	102,000
	Auctions: $168,000, PCGS PF-65 HA 08/21					
1839, Restrike, Stars on Obverse. Plain Edge (J-105)	10 known	376672	—	—	72,000	120,000
1839, Restrike, Stars on Obverse and Reverse. Plain Edge (J-108)	3	376691	—	—	120,000	—

Note: Restrikes were produced from the late 1850s to the 1870s, and are not official Mint issues. They were all oriented in either die alignment 3 (coin turn) or die alignment 4 (medal turn), with the eagle flying level. Almost all were struck from a cracked reverse die. For detailed analysis of these pieces, consult *United States Pattern Coins* (10th edition). For some issues, many originals were certified as restrikes in years past. for others, the grading services do not consistently distinguish between originals and restrikes.

LIBERTY SEATED (1840–1873)

No Motto (1840–1865): **Designer:** *Christian Gobrecht.* **Weight:** *26.73 grams.* **Composition:** *.900 silver, .100 copper (net weight .77344 oz. pure silver).* **Diameter:** *38.1 mm.* **Edge:** *Reeded.* **Mints:** *Philadelphia, New Orleans, and San Francisco.*

Mintmark location is on the reverse, below the eagle, for all varieties.

No Motto Above Eagle (1840–1865), Circulation Strike

No Motto Above Eagle, Proof Strike

With Motto IN GOD WE TRUST (1866–1873): **Designer:** *Christian Gobrecht.* **Weight:** *26.73 grams.* **Composition:** *.900 silver, .100 copper (net weight .77344 oz. pure silver).* **Diameter:** *38.1 mm.* **Edge:** *Reeded.* **Mints:** *Philadelphia, Carson City, and San Francisco.*

Motto Above Eagle, (1866–1873), Circulation Strike

Motto Above Eagle, Proof Strike

History. The Liberty Seated dollar was minted every year from 1840 to 1873, with an obverse design modified from that of the 1839 Gobrecht dollar. On the reverse, the flying eagle of the Gobrecht dollar was replaced with a perched eagle similar to that of contemporary quarter and half dollars. The dollars, minted in modest numbers, circulated in the United States through 1850. In that year the rising value of silver on the international markets brought the cost of minting each coin to more than $1. Production continued for the international, rather than domestic, market, through 1873, when the trade dollar took the Liberty Seated dollar's place.

Striking and Sharpness. On the obverse, check the head of Liberty and the centers of the stars. On the reverse, check the feathers of the eagle. The denticles usually are sharp. Dollars of 1857 usually are weakly struck, but have semi-prooflike surfaces. The word LIBERTY is in a high-relief area on the coin, with the result that it wore away quickly. Therefore this feature cannot be used as the only guide to grading an obverse. From EF downward, strike sharpness in the stars and the head does not matter to connoisseurs. Proof coins were made for all dates. All of 1851 and 1853 are restrikes, as are most of 1852. In 1858 only Proofs were struck, to the extent of an estimated 210 pieces, with no related circulation strikes. Most early dates were restruck at the Mint, augmenting the supply of originals. Nearly all Proofs are very well struck.

Availability. All issues from 1840 to 1850 are available in proportion to their mintages. Those of 1851 to the late 1860s are either scarce or rare in circulated grades, and in MS they range from rare to extremely rare, despite generous mintages in some instances. The later-date coins were shipped to China and later melted. Coins of the 1870s are more readily available, although some are scarce to rare. Today, Proofs from 1858 to 1873 are readily available, but high-quality examples with superb eye appeal are in the minority. Most Proofs prior to 1860 survive only in grades below PF-65 if strict grading is applied.

Grading Standards

MS-60 to 70 (Mint State). ***Obverse:*** At MS-60, some abrasion and contact marks are evident, most noticeably on the bosom and thighs and knees. Luster is present, but may be dull or lifeless. At MS-63, contact marks are very few, and abrasion is minimal. An MS-65 coin has no abrasion in the fields (but may have a hint on the knees), and contact marks are trivial. Check the knees of Liberty and the right field. Luster should be full and rich on later issues, not necessarily so for dates in the 1840s. Most Mint State coins of the 1861 to 1865 years, Philadelphia issues, have extensive die striae (from not completely finishing the die). ***Reverse:*** Comments apply as for the obverse, except that in lower Mint State grades, abrasion and marks are most noticeable on the eagle's head, the neck, the claws, and the top of the wings (harder to see there, however). At MS-65 or higher, there are no marks visible to the unaided eye. The field is mainly protected by design elements and does not show abrasion as much as does the obverse on a given coin.

MS-65

Illustrated coin: The fields show striations from incomplete polishing of the dies, but this does not affect the grade.

AU-50, 53, 55, 58 (About Uncirculated). ***Obverse:*** Light wear is seen on the thighs and knees, bosom, and head. At AU-58, the luster is extensive but incomplete, especially in the right field. At AU-50 and 53, luster is less. ***Reverse:*** Wear is visible on the eagle's neck, the claws, and the top of the wings. An AU-58 coin has nearly full luster. At AU-50 and 53, there still are traces of luster.

AU-58

Illustrated coin: This is an attractive example with much of the original luster.

EF-40

EF-40, 45 (Extremely Fine). ***Obverse:*** Further wear is seen on all areas, especially the thighs and knees, bosom, and head. Little or no luster is seen on most coins. From this grade downward, strike sharpness in the stars and the head does not matter to connoisseurs. ***Reverse:*** Further wear is evident on the eagle's neck, claws, and the wings, although on well-struck coins nearly all details are sharp.

VF-20

VF-20, 30 (Very Fine). ***Obverse:*** Further wear is seen. Many details of the gown are worn away, but the lower-relief areas above and to the right of the shield remain well defined. Hair detail is mostly or completely gone. The word LIBERTY is weak at BE (PCGS allows BER to be missing "on some coins"). ***Reverse:*** Wear is more extensive, with some feathers blended together, especially on the neck for a typical coin. Detail remains quite good overall.

F-12

F-12, 15 (Fine). ***Obverse:*** The seated figure is well worn, but with some detail above and to the right of the shield. BER in LIBERTY is visible only in part or missing entirely. ***Reverse:*** Wear is extensive, with about a third to half of the feathers flat or blended with others.

Illustrated coin: The reverse is stronger than the obverse on this coin.

VG-8

VG-8, 10 (Very Good). ***Obverse:*** The seated figure is more worn, but some detail can be seen above and to the right of the shield. The shield is discernible, but the upper-right section may be flat and blended into the seated figure. In LIBERTY two or three letters, or a combination totaling that, are readable. ***Reverse.*** Further wear has flattened half or slightly more of the feathers (depending on the strike). The rim is visible all around, as are the ends of the denticles. A Very Good Liberty Seated dollar usually has more detail overall than a lower-denomination coin of the same design.

G-4, 6 (Good). ***Obverse:*** The seated figure is worn nearly smooth. The stars and date are complete, but may be weak toward the periphery. ***Reverse:*** The eagle shows only a few details of the shield and feathers. The rim is worn down. The tops of the border letters are weak or worn away, although the inscription can still be read.

G-6

AG-3 (About Good). ***Obverse:*** The seated figure is visible in outline form. Much or all of the rim is worn away. The stars are weak and some may be missing. The date remains clear. ***Reverse:*** The border letters are partially worn away. The eagle is mostly in outline form, but with a few details discernible. The rim is weak or missing.

AG-3

PF-60 to 70 (Proof). ***Obverse and Reverse:*** Proofs that are extensively cleaned and have many hairlines, or that are dull and grainy, are lower level, such as PF-60 to 62. These are not widely desired, except for use as fillers for the dates (most circulation-strike dollars are rare after 1849 and before 1870). The rarities of 1851, 1852, and 1858 are in demand no matter what the grade. With medium hairlines and good reflectivity, an assigned grade of PF-64 is appropriate, and with relatively few hairlines, gem PF-65. In various grades hairlines are most easily seen in the obverse field. PF-66 should have hairlines so delicate that magnification is needed to see them. Above that, a Proof should be free of such lines.

PF-63

Illustrated coin: The frosty cameo motifs on this example contrast with the deeply mirrored fields.

1851, Circulation Strike, Original Strike, High Date

1851, Proof Strike, Restrike
Date is centered.

1852, Circulation Strike, Original Strike

1852, Proof Strike, Restrike

Circulation Strikes

	Mintage	GSID	G-4	VG-8	F-12	VF-20	EF-40	AU-50	MS-60	MS-63
Liberty Seated, No Motto (1840–1865)	**n/a**	**72401**	**$415**	**$470**	**$550**	**$625**	**$875**	**$1,150**	**$2,050**	**$4,750**
Liberty Seated, With Motto (1866–1873)	**n/a**	**72402**	**390**	**435**	**490**	**525**	**750**	**1,000**	**2,100**	**4,250**
1840	61,005	7190	450	525	600	700	950	1,600	5,500	19,000
1841	173,000	7191	455	500	575	700	950	1,500	3,500	8,750
1842	184,618	7192	415	470	550	625	950	1,200	3,000	5,500
↳1842, Three Cuds Obverse, FS-401	*	351906	460	525	600	675	1,050	1,300	3,300	6,000
1843	165,100	7193	415	470	550	625	875	1,150	2,500	6,250
1844	20,000	7194	470	525	600	800	1,500	2,750	7,000	12,500
1845	24,500	7195	490	575	775	950	1,400	2,800	6,250	23,000
1846	110,600	7196	415	470	550	625	875	1,150	2,050	5,250
	Auctions: $105,750, NGC MS-65 HA 11/13									
1846-O	59,000	7223	430	550	650	775	1,250	2,000	7,500	30,000
1847	140,750	7197	415	470	550	625	875	1,150	2,700	4,750
1848	15,000	7198	625	775	950	1,450	2,600	3,500	6,500	15,500
1849	62,600	7199	455	500	575	700	1,000	1,400	2,900	5,500
1850	7,500	7200	1,000	1,150	1,400	1,800	3,000	3,750	7,500	17,000
1850-O	40,000	7224	440	495	600	950	1,700	3,100	10,000	33,500
	Auctions: $141,000, PCGS MS-64 LGND 07/22									
1851, Original, High Date	1,300	7201	9,500	12,000	14,000	17,000	24,000	32,500	48,000	79,000
1852, Original	1,100	7202	12,000	15,000	19,000	26,500	32,500	35,000	44,000	90,000
1853	46,110	7203	575	725	950	1,200	2,100	2,600	4,250	8,500
	Auctions: $129,250, PCGS MS-66 SBG 10/14									
1854	33,140	7204	2,250	3,000	4,500	6,500	10,500	14,000	19,000	23,000
1855	26,000	7205	2,000	2,750	4,000	5,500	9,750	12,000	17,500	43,000
	Auctions: $149,500, NGC MS-64 HA 04/08									

* Included in number above.

1869, Repunched Date
FS-303

Circulation Strikes

	Mintage	GSID	G-4	VG-8	F-12	VF-20	EF-40	AU-50	MS-60	MS-63
1856	63,500	7206	$1,150	$1,600	$2,750	$3,750	$5,000	$6,250	$11,000	$19,000
1857	94,000	7207	900	1,250	1,750	2,950	4,250	5,000	8,750	12,500
1859	255,700	7208	525	650	725	850	1,200	1,900	4,000	6,000
1859-O	360,000	7225	415	470	550	625	875	1,150	2,050	4,750
1859-S	20,000	7226	700	950	1,400	2,000	3,250	5,500	10,500	19,000
1860	217,600	7209	455	500	575	775	1,150	1,550	3,000	5,250
	Auctions: $156,000, PCGS MS-66 HA 05/23									
1860-O	515,000	7227	415	470	550	625	875	1,150	2,050	4,750
1861	77,500	7210	1,750	2,800	3,250	3,600	4,750	6,000	10,000	14,500
1862	11,540	7211	650	850	1,250	2,000	3,750	5,500	7,500	9,000
1863	27,200	7212	1,100	1,500	2,100	2,800	3,750	4,300	5,750	8,250
	Auctions: $114,000, NGC MS-67 HA 12/21									
1864	30,700	7213	675	900	1,250	2,000	2,750	4,050	7,250	9,500
1865	46,500	7214	575	775	950	1,600	2,750	3,250	5,000	11,000
↳1865, Doubled Die Reverse, FS-801	*	351907	1,400	2,000	2,750	3,750	6,000	8,000	11,000	17,000
1866	48,900	7215	390	435	575	650	1,150	1,500	2,750	5,500
	Auctions: $150,000, PCGS MS-67 SBG 12/20									
1867	46,900	7216	550	650	850	1,000	1,500	2,000	4,250	7,500
1868	162,100	7217	420	525	600	850	1,600	2,400	4,250	8,250
1869	423,700	7218	390	470	525	725	1,000	1,400	2,900	5,000
↳1869, Repunched Date, FS-303	*	351910	430	525	575	775	1,150	1,500	3,150	5,500
1870	415,000	7219	390	435	490	575	825	1,100	2,500	4,750
	Auctions: $105,750, PCGS MS-66 HA 08/14									
1870-CC	11,758	7228	2,050	2,750	3,600	4,300	7,250	8,500	21,500	37,000
	Auctions: $148,638, PCGS MS-64 SBG 08/12									
1870-S (a)	9 known	7229	180,000	240,000	348,000	480,000	630,000	1,020,000	1,800,000	—
	Auctions: $805,000, NGC EF-40 HA 04/08									
1871	1,073,800	7220	390	435	490	525	800	1,150	2,300	5,250
1871-CC	1,376	7230	8,000	10,000	11,000	12,000	18,000	24,500	78,000	176,500
	Auctions: $204,000, NGC MS-64 HA 08/25									
↳1871-CC, Misplaced Date, FS-301	*	373727	8,000	10,000	11,000	12,000	18,000	24,500	78,000	176,500
1872	1,105,500	7221	390	435	490	525	750	1,000	2,100	4,250
↳1872, Misplaced Date, FS-301	*	373728	430	480	525	575	825	1,150	2,350	4,700
1872-CC	3,150	7231	2,500	3,250	4,000	5,000	9,000	14,000	20,500	102,000
	Auctions: $144,000, NGC MS-64 HA 08/25									
1872-S	9,000	7232	1,150	1,300	1,600	2,100	2,900	4,500	12,000	33,500
1873	293,000	7222	390	435	490	525	775	1,400	3,750	5,750
1873-CC	2,300	7233	12,000	17,000	20,000	23,000	34,000	46,000	108,000	270,000
	Auctions: $132,000, PCGS AU-58 HA 08/22									

* Included in number above. **a.** The Mint shows no record of 1870-S dollars being struck, but about a dozen are known to exist. The 1870-S silver dollars may have been struck as mementos of the laying of the cornerstone of the San Francisco Mint (May 25, 1870).

Proof Strikes

	Mintage	GSID	PF-60	PF-63	PF-65
Liberty Seated, No Motto (1840–1865), Proof	**n/a**	**73866**	**$3,000**	**$5,000**	**$9,000**
Same, Proof Cameo	**n/a**	**73867**	**—**	**5,750**	**10,000**
Same, Proof Deep Cameo	**n/a**	**73868**	**—**	**8,750**	**23,000**
Liberty Seated, With Motto (1866–1873), Proof	**n/a**	**73869**	**2,750**	**4,500**	**9,000**
Same, Proof Cameo	**n/a**	**73870**	**3,000**	**4,900**	**11,500**
Same, Proof Deep Cameo	**n/a**	**73871**	**—**	**6,500**	**17,500**
1840	40–60	7235	14,500	31,000	84,000
1841	10–15	7238	50,500	108,000	210,000
	Auctions: $156,000, PCGS PF-64 HA 02/25				
1842	10–15	7241	17,000	55,000	120,000
1843	10–15	7244	48,000	75,500	150,000
1844	10–15	7247	21,000	43,000	78,000
	Auctions: $132,250, NGC PF-66 ANR 08/04				
1845	10–15	7250	17,000	48,000	81,500
	Auctions: $207,000, NGC PF-67 HA 01/08				
1846	10–15	7253	12,000	29,000	102,000
	Auctions: $149,500, PCGS PF-65 HA 06/08				
1847	10–15	7256	14,500	31,000	69,500
1848	10–15	7259	13,000	38,500	81,500
	Auctions: $161,000, NGC PF-67 HA 08/08				
1849	10–15	7262	18,000	38,500	72,000
	Auctions: $230,000, NGC PF-67 HA 04/08				
1850	20–30	7265	11,000	21,500	50,500
1851, Restrike	35–50	7269	21,500	31,000	72,000
	Auctions: $373,750, PCGS PF-62 SBG 06/08				
1852, Original	20–30	7280	29,000	48,000	105,500
	Auctions: $129,250, PCGS PF-65 LGND 01/18				

	Mintage	GSID	PF-60	PF-63	PF-65
1852, Restrike	20–30	7277	$24,000	$31,000	$60,000
1853	15–20	7283	29,000	50,500	101,000
	Auctions: $105,750, PCGS PF-66 SBG 10/14				
1854, Original	unique	226248	—	—	—
1854, Restrike	40–60	7286	10,500	16,000	43,000
1855	40–60	7289	11,000	15,500	41,000
1856	40–60	7292	7,500	13,000	36,000
1857	50–70	7295	5,000	11,000	39,000
1858	300	7298	9,500	15,000	38,500
1859	800	7301	3,000	5,000	12,000
1860	1,330	7304	3,000	5,000	10,000
1861	1,000	7307	3,750	6,000	12,000
1862	550	7310	3,000	5,000	9,000
1863	460	7313	3,750	6,250	10,000
	Auctions: $184,000, NGC PF-69 ANR 08/06				
1864	470	7316	3,000	5,000	9,000
1865	500	7319	3,000	5,000	9,000
1866, No Motto	2 known	374594	—	—	—
	Auctions: $1,207,500, NGC PF-63 ANR 01/05				
1866, With Motto	725	7323	2,750	4,500	9,000
1867	625	7328	2,750	4,500	9,000
1868	600	7331	2,750	4,500	9,000
	Auctions: $102,000, PCGS PF-68 SBG 08/24				
↳1868, MPD, FS-302	*	373726	—	4,950	10,000
1869	600	7334	2,750	4,500	9,000
1870	1,000	7337	2,750	4,500	9,000
1871	960	7340	2,750	4,500	9,000
1872	950	7343	2,900	4,750	12,000
1873	600	7346	2,750	4,500	9,000

* Included in number above.

TRADE DOLLARS (1873–1885)

Designer: *William Barber.* **Weight:** *27.22 grams.*
Composition: *.900 silver, .100 copper (net weight .7874 oz. pure silver).*
Diameter: *38.1 mm.* **Edge:** *Reeded.* **Mints:** *Philadelphia, Carson City, and San Francisco.*

Circulation Strike

Mintmark location is on the reverse, below the fineness.

Proof Strike

History. Trade dollars were minted under the Coinage Act of 1873. Containing 420 grains of .900 fine silver, they were heavier than the Liberty Seated dollar (of 412.5 grains). They were made for use in the China export trade and proved to be a great success. Some circulated at par in the United States, until they were demonetized by the Act of July 22, 1876, after which they circulated at their silver value, which was slightly lower than their face value. The Bland-Allison Act of 1878 provided for the new "Morgan" silver dollar, and trade dollars were discontinued, although Proofs continued to be made through 1885. Modifications to the trade dollar design are distinguished as follows.

Reverse 1: With a berry under the eagle's left talon; the lowest arrowhead ends over the 0 in 420. (Used on all coins from all mints in 1873 and 1874, and occasionally in 1875 and 1876.)

Reverse 2: Without an extra berry under the talon; the lowest arrowhead ends over the 2 in 420. (Used occasionally at all mints from 1875 through 1876, and on all coins from all mints 1877 through 1885.)

Obverse 1: The ends of the scroll point to the left; the extended hand has only three fingers. (Used on coins at all mints, 1873 through 1876.)

Obverse 2: The ends of the scroll point downward; the extended hand has four fingers. (Used in combination with Reverse 2 on one variety of 1876-S, and on all coins at all mints from 1877 through 1885.)

Striking and Sharpness. Weakness is often seen. On the obverse, check Liberty's head and the star centers first. On the reverse, check the feathers on the eagle, particularly on the legs. Luster can range from dull to deeply frosty. In EF and lower grades, strike sharpness on the stars and the head does not matter to connoisseurs. Some Proofs are lightly struck on the head and the stars on the obverse and the leg feathers of the eagle on the reverse.

Availability. The 1878-CC is a rarity. Other dates and mintmarks are readily collected in grades from EF to MS. Lower grades are not often seen, for these coins did not circulate for a long time. Many used in China have counterstamps, called *chopmarks,* which are of interest to collectors. On an MS-63 or better coin a chopmark will decrease its value, but on EF and AU coins specialists eagerly seek them. MS coins are mostly in the lower ranges, often with unsatisfactory surfaces. True gems are very scarce. Proofs for collectors were made from 1873 to 1883 in quantity to supply the demand. In addition, a few were secretly made in 1884 and 1885. Most survivors are of high quality today, although gems of the 1873 to 1877 years are much harder to find than are those of 1878 to 1883.

Note: In recent years a flood of modern counterfeit trade dollars, many coming from China, has deluged the market.

Grading Standards

MS-60 to 70 (Mint State). ***Obverse:*** At MS-60, some abrasion and contact marks are evident, most noticeably on the left breast, left arm, and left knee. Luster is present, but may be dull or lifeless. Many of these coins are light in color or even brilliant, having been repatriated from China, and have been cleaned to remove sediment and discoloration. At MS-63, contact marks are very few, and abrasion is minimal. An MS-65 coin has no abrasion in the fields (but may have a hint on the higher parts of the seated figure), and contact marks are trivial. Luster should be full and rich. ***Reverse:*** Comments apply as for the obverse, except that in lower Mint State grades abrasion and contact marks are most noticeable on the eagle's head, the claws, and the top of the wings. At MS-65 or higher there are no marks visible to the unaided eye. The field is mainly protected by design elements and does not show abrasion as much as does the obverse on a given coin.

MS-61

Illustrated coin: Some friction in the fields is seen, but much of the original luster remains.

AU-50, 53, 55, 58 (About Uncirculated). ***Obverse:*** Light wear is seen on the knees, bosom, and head. At AU-58, the luster is extensive but incomplete. At AU-50 and 53, luster is less. ***Reverse:*** Wear is visible on the eagle's head, the claws, and the top of the wings. An AU-58 coin will have nearly full luster. At AU-50 and 53, there still are traces of luster.

AU-53

Illustrated coin: This example shows light, even wear. Most of the luster is gone, except in protected areas, but it has excellent eye appeal for the grade.

EF-40, 45 (Extremely Fine). ***Obverse:*** Further wear is seen on all areas, especially the head, the left breast, the left arm, the left leg, and the bale on which Liberty is seated. Little or no luster is seen on most coins. From this grade downward, strike sharpness on the stars and the head does not matter to connoisseurs. ***Reverse:*** Further wear is evident on the eagle's head, legs, claws, and wings, although on well-struck coins nearly all feather details on the wings are sharp.

EF-40

VF-20, 30 (Very Fine). ***Obverse:*** Further wear is seen on the seated figure, although more than half the details of her dress are visible. Details of the wheat sheaf are mostly intact. IN GOD WE TRUST and LIBERTY are clear. ***Reverse:*** Wear is more extensive; some feathers are blended together, with two-thirds or more still visible.

VF-30

F-12, 15 (Fine). ***Obverse:*** The seated figure is further worn, with fewer details of the dress visible. Most details in the wheat sheaf are clear. Both mottos are readable, but some letters may be weak. ***Reverse:*** Wear is extensive, with about half to nearly two-thirds of the feathers flat or blended with others. The eagle's left leg is mostly flat. Wear is seen on the raised E PLURIBUS UNUM, and one or two letters may be missing.

F-12

PF-60 to 70 (Proof). ***Obverse and Reverse:*** Proofs that are extensively cleaned and have many hairlines, or that are dull and grainy, are lower level, such as PF-60 to 62. These are not widely desired. With medium hairlines and good reflectivity, an assigned grade of PF-64 is appropriate, and with relatively few hairlines, gem PF-65. In various grades hairlines are most easily seen in the obverse field. PF-66 may have hairlines so delicate that magnification is needed to see them. Above that, a Proof should be free of such lines.

PF-62

Illustrated coin: This coin has medium-gray toning overall.

Chopmarked Trade Dollar

Examples of chopmarks.

Reverse 1
Arrowheads end over 0; berry under eagle's left talon.

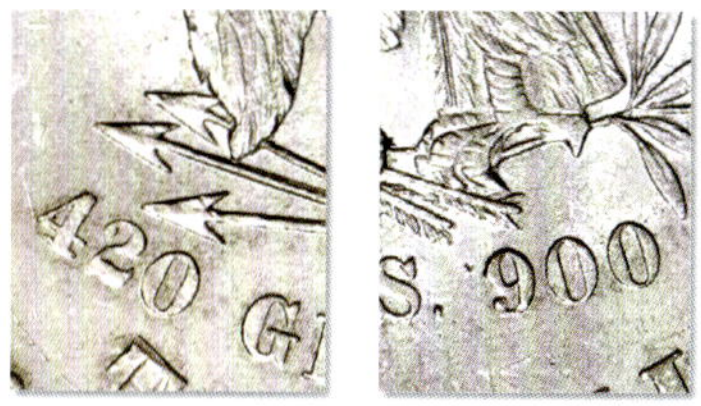

Reverse 2
Arrowheads end over 2; no berry under talon.

Obverse 1
Hand has three fingers; scroll points left.

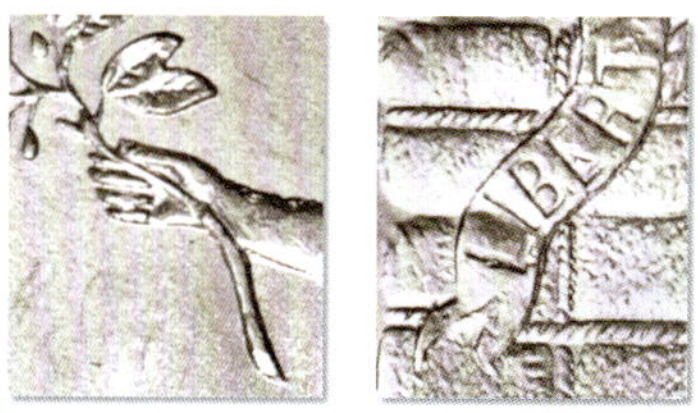

Obverse 2
Hand has four fingers; scroll points downward.

Circulation Strikes

	Mintage	GSID	G-4	VG-8	F-12	VF-20	EF-40	AU-50	MS-60	MS-63
Trade (1873–1885)	**n/a**	**72403**	**$170**	**$220**	**$260**	**$345**	**$455**	**$500**	**$1,150**	**$1,750**
1873	396,900	7349	180	235	275	365	550	650	1,300	3,200
1873-CC	124,500	7359	525	775	1,100	1,500	3,000	4,000	8,500	30,000
1873-S	703,000	7361	230	260	340	525	650	775	1,500	3,900
1874	987,100	7351	195	235	285	360	550	650	1,400	2,900
1874-CC	1,373,200	7363	325	405	500	725	1,200	1,500	2,750	6,500
1874-S	2,549,000	7365	170	220	260	345	455	500	1,150	2,100
1875	218,200	7353	340	420	525	775	1,200	1,500	2,500	4,400
	Auctions: $128,800, PCGS MS-68 HA 08/97									
↳1875, Obverse 1, Reverse 1	*	374596	340	420	525	775	1,200	1,500	2,500	4,400
↳1875, Obverse 1, Reverse 2	*	374597	340	420	525	775	1,200	1,650	2,750	5,250

* Included in number above.

1875-S, S Over CC
FS-501

1876-CC, Doubled Die Reverse
FS-801

Circulation Strikes

	Mintage	GSID	G-4	VG-8	F-12	VF-20	EF-40	AU-50	MS-60	MS-63
1875-CC	1,573,700	7367	$325	$390	$470	$750	$1,000	$1,250	$3,000	$5,000
↳1875-CC, Obverse 1, Reverse 1	*	213420	325	390	470	750	1,000	1,250	3,000	5,000
↳1875-CC, Obverse 1, Reverse 2	*	213421	325	390	470	750	1,000	1,250	3,000	5,000
1875-S	4,487,000	7369	170	220	260	345	455	500	1,150	1,750
↳1875-S, Obverse 1, Reverse 1	*	310742	170	220	260	345	455	500	1,150	1,750
↳1875-S, Obverse 1, Reverse 2	*	310744	185	245	285	380	525	600	1,300	2,100
1875-S, S Over CC	*	7371	440	525	675	950	1,400	1,800	5,250	13,000
↳1875-S, S Over CC, FS-501	*	351913	465	550	700	1,000	1,450	1,900	5,500	14,000
↳1875-S, S Over CC, FS-502	*	351915	440	525	675	950	1,400	1,800	5,250	13,000
1876	455,000	7355	185	245	285	380	490	575	1,150	2,000
↳1876, Obverse 1, Reverse 1	*	376166	205	265	315	415	525	625	1,250	2,200
↳1876, Obverse 1, Reverse 2	*	213422	185	245	285	380	490	575	1,150	2,000
↳1876, Obverse 2, Reverse 2	*	213423	—	625	950	1,500	2,750	5,000	8,000	13,000
1876-CC	509,000	7373	470	675	775	950	1,500	2,000	5,500	15,000
↳1876-CC, Obverse 1, Reverse 1	*	213424	470	675	775	950	1,500	2,000	5,500	15,000
↳1876-CC, Obverse 1, Reverse 2	*	213425	470	675	775	950	1,500	2,000	5,500	15,000
1876-CC, Doubled Die Reverse	*	7376	525	775	900	1,150	1,600	2,400	12,000	20,000
↳1876-CC, Doubled Die Reverse, FS-801	*	351917	550	850	1,100	1,700	2,500	3,750	12,500	21,000
1876-S	5,227,000	7377	170	220	260	345	455	500	1,200	1,900
↳1876-S, Obverse 1, Reverse 1	*	378719	170	220	260	345	455	500	1,200	1,900
↳1876-S, Obverse 1, Reverse 2	*	346948	170	220	260	345	455	500	1,200	1,900
↳1876-S, Obverse 2, Reverse 2	*	346949	170	220	260	345	455	500	1,200	1,900
↳1876-S, Obverse 2, Reverse 2, Doubled Die Obverse, FS-101	*	351918	170	220	260	345	455	500	1,200	1,900
1877	3,039,200	7357	170	220	285	345	455	600	1,250	1,800
1877-CC	534,000	7381	420	550	750	950	1,450	2,100	4,750	11,000

* Included in number above.

1877-S, Doubled Die Reverse
FS-801

1878-S, Doubled Die Reverse
FS-801

Circulation Strikes

	Mintage	GSID	G-4	VG-8	F-12	VF-20	EF-40	AU-50	MS-60	MS-63
1877-S	9,519,000	7383	$170	$220	$260	$345	$455	$500	$1,150	$1,750
↳**1877-S, Doubled Die Reverse, FS-801**	*	351920	205	265	310	415	550	600	1,300	2,100
1878-CC (a)	97,000	7385	850	1,150	1,600	2,500	5,000	7,000	15,000	30,000
	Auctions: $192,000, PCGS MS-65 HA 01/19									
1878-S	4,162,000	7387	170	220	260	345	475	550	1,200	1,900
	Auctions: $252,000, PCGS MS-68 HA 01/19									
↳**1878-S, Doubled Die Reverse, FS-801**	*	310746	185	245	285	380	525	600	1,300	2,050

* Included in number above. **a.** On July 19, 1878, a quantity of 44,148 trade dollars was melted by the Mint. Many of these may have been 1878-CC.

Proof Strikes

	Mintage	GSID	PF-60	PF-63	PF-65
Trade (1873–1885), Proof	**n/a**	**74085**	**$2,250**	**$3,000**	**$6,250**
Same, Proof Cameo	**n/a**	**74086**	**2,450**	**3,500**	**7,500**
Same, Proof Deep Cameo	**n/a**	**74087**	**—**	**6,000**	**13,000**
1873	865	7389	2,250	3,000	9,500
1874	700	7392	2,250	3,000	6,250
1875	700	7395	2,250	3,000	8,000
1876	1,150	7398	2,250	3,000	6,250
1877	510	7401	2,250	3,500	7,000

	Mintage	GSID	PF-60	PF-63	PF-65
1878	900	7404	$2,250	$3,000	$6,500
	Auctions: $120,750, PCGS PF-68 SU 01/06				
1879	1,541	7407	2,250	3,000	6,250
1880	1,987	7410	2,250	3,000	6,250
1881	960	7413	2,250	3,000	6,250
1882	1,097	7416	2,250	3,000	6,250
1883	979	7419	2,250	3,000	6,250
1884 (a)	10	7422	336,000	480,000	1,020,000
	Auctions: $1,140,000, PCGS PF-65 HA 01/25				
1885 (a)	5	7425	1,320,000	1,620,000	3,000,000
	Auctions: $3,960,000, NGC PF-66 HA 01/19				

* Included in number above. **a.** Trade dollars of 1884 and 1885 were unknown to the numismatic community until 1907 and 1908. None are listed in the Mint director's report, and numismatists believe that they are not a part of the regular Mint issue but were produced secretly for private sale to collectors.

MORGAN (1878–1921)

Designer: *George T. Morgan.* **Weight:** *26.73 grams.* **Composition:** *.900 silver, .100 copper (net weight .77344 oz. pure silver).* **Diameter:** *38.1 mm.* **Edge:** *Reeded.* **Mints:** *Philadelphia, New Orleans, Carson City, Denver, and San Francisco.*

Mintmark location is on the reverse, below the bow.

Circulation Strike

Proof Strike

History. The Morgan dollar, named for English-born designer George T. Morgan, was struck every year from 1878 to 1904, and again in 1921. The coin's production benefited Western silver interests by creating an artificial federal demand for the metal, whose market value had dropped sharply by 1878. Hundreds of millions of the coins, stored in cloth bags of 1,000 each, piled up in government vaults. In the 1900s some were melted, but immense quantities were bought by collectors and investors; today they are the most widely collected of all coins of their era.

The 1921 Silver Dollar Coin Anniversary Act, signed into law January 5, 2021, required the Treasury Department "to mint and issue coins in honor of the 100th anniversary of the completion of coinage of the Morgan dollar."

Striking and Sharpness. On coins of 1878 to 1900, check the hair above Liberty's ear and, on the reverse, the breast feathers of the eagle. These are weak on many issues, particularly those of the New Orleans Mint. From 1900 to 1904 a new reverse hub was used, and breast feathers, while discernible, are not as sharp. In 1921 new dies were made in lower relief, with certain areas indistinct. Many Morgan dollars have partially or fully prooflike surfaces. These are designated as Prooflike (PL), Deep Prooflike (DPL), or Deep Mirror Prooflike (DMPL). Certification practices can be erratic, and some DMPL-certified coins are not fully mirrored. All prooflike coins tend to emphasize contact marks, with the result that lower MS levels can be unattractive. *A Guide Book of Morgan Silver Dollars* (Bowers) and other references furnish information as to which dates and mintmarks are easily found with Full Details and which usually are weak, as well as the availability of the various levels of prooflike surface.

Proofs were struck from 1878 to 1904, with those of 1878 to 1901 generally having cameo contrast, and 1902 to 1904 having the portrait lightly polished in the die. Some are lightly struck; check the hair above Liberty's ear (in particular), and the eagle's breast feathers. In 1921 many so-called Zerbe Proofs (named thus after numismatic entrepreneur Farran Zerbe), with many microscopic die-finish lines, were made. A very few deeply mirrored 1921 coins were made, called Chapman Proofs (after coin dealer Henry Chapman, who started marketing them shortly after their production). Some Zerbe Proofs have been miscertified as Chapman Proofs.

Availability. All dates and mints of Morgan dollars are available in grades from well worn to MS. Some issues such as certain Carson City coins are rare if worn and common in MS. Other issues such as the

1901 Philadelphia coins are common if worn and are rarities at MS-65. The 1889-CC and 1893-S, and the Proof 1895, are considered to be the key issues. Varieties listed herein are some of those most significant to collectors. Numerous other variations exist, studied in the *Cherrypickers' Guide to Rare Die Varieties* and other specialized texts. Values shown herein are for the most common pieces. Values of varieties not listed in this guide depend on collector interest and demand.

Note: Values of common-date silver coins have been based on the current bullion price of silver, $45 per ounce, and may vary with the prevailing spot price.

Grading Standards

MS-60 to 70 (Mint State). ***Obverse:*** At MS-60, some abrasion and contact marks are evident, most noticeably on the cheek and on the hair above the ear. The left field also shows such marks. Luster is present, but may be dull or lifeless. At MS-63, contact marks are extensive but not distracting. Abrasion still is evident, but less than at lower levels. Indeed, the cheek of Liberty showcases abrasion. An MS-65 coin may have minor abrasion, but contact marks are so minute as to require magnification. Luster should be full and rich. Coins with prooflike surfaces such as PL, DPL, and DMPL display abrasion and contact marks much more noticeably than coins with frosty surfaces; in grades below MS-64 many are unattractive. With today's loose and sometimes contradictory interpretations, many at MS-64 appear to have extensive marks as well. ***Reverse:*** Comments apply as for the obverse, except that in lower Mint State grades abrasion and contact marks are most noticeable on the eagle's breast. At MS-65 or higher there are no marks visible to the unaided eye. The field is mainly protected by design elements, so the reverse often appears to grade a point or two higher than the obverse. A Morgan dollar can have an MS-63 obverse and an MS-65 reverse, as was indeed the nomenclature used prior to the single-number system. A careful cataloger may want to describe each side separately for a particularly valuable or rare Morgan dollar. An example with an MS-63 obverse and an MS-65 reverse should have an overall grade of MS-63, as the obverse is traditionally given prominence.

MS-61

Illustrated coin: This is a lustrous and attractive example.

AU-50, 53, 55, 58 (About Uncirculated). ***Obverse:*** Light wear is seen on the cheek and, to a lesser extent, on the hair below the coronet. Generally, the hair details mask friction and wear and it is not as easy to notice as on the cheek and in the fields. At AU-58, the luster is extensive, but incomplete, especially on the higher parts and in the left field. At AU-50 and 53, luster is less, but still is present. PL, DPL, and DMPL coins are not widely desired at these levels, as the marks are too distracting. ***Reverse:*** Wear is evident on the head, breast, wing tips, and, to a lesser extent, in the field. An AU-58 coin (as determined by the obverse) can have a reverse that appears to be full Mint State. (Incidentally, this is also true of Barber quarter dollars and half dollars.)

AU-58

Illustrated coin: This is a lustrous example of the rarest Carson City Morgan dollar. As is typical of AU-58 dollars of this design, the reverse appears to be full Mint State, as the field is protected by the design elements.

EF-40, 45 (Extremely Fine). ***Obverse:*** Further wear is seen on the cheek in particular. The hair near the forehead and temple has flatness in areas, most noticeable above the ear. Some luster can be seen in protected areas on many coins, but is not needed to define the EF-40 and 45 grades. ***Reverse:*** Further wear is seen on the breast of the eagle (most noticeably), the wing tips, and the leaves.

EF-40

VF-20, 30 (Very Fine). ***Obverse:*** The head shows more wear, now with most of the detail gone in the areas adjacent to the forehead and temple. The lower area has most hair fused into large strands. ***Reverse:*** Wear is more extensive on the breast and on the feathers in the upper area of the wings, especially the right wing, and on the legs. The high area of the leaves has no detail.

VF-20

F-12, 15 (Fine). ***Obverse:*** The head shows more wear, with most hair detail gone, and with a large flat area above the ear. Less detail is seen in the lower curls. ***Reverse:*** More wear is seen on the reverse, with the eagle's breast and legs flat and about a third of the feather detail gone, mostly near the tops of the wings.

F-15

VG-8, 10 (Very Good). ***Obverse:*** More hair details are gone, especially from the area from the top of the head down to the ear. The details of the lower part of the cap are gone. The rim is weak in areas, and some denticles are worn away. ***Reverse:*** Further wear has smoothed more than half of the feathers in the wing. The leaves are flat except for the lowest areas. The rim is weak in areas.

VG-8

100 GREATEST™ UNITED STATES COINS

No. 41 1893-S MORGAN SILVER DOLLAR

G-4, 6 (Good). ***Obverse:*** The head is in outline form, with most details gone. LIBERTY still is readable. The eye position and lips are discernible. Most of the rim is worn away. ***Reverse:*** The eagle shows some feathers near the bottom of the wings, but nearly all others are gone. The leaves are seen in outline form. The rim is mostly worn away. Some letters have details toward the border worn away.

G-4

Illustrated coin: Here is a well-worn example of this key issue.

PF-60 to 70 (Proof). ***Obverse and Reverse:*** Dull, grainy Proofs, or extensively cleaned ones with many hairlines, are lower level (PF-60 to 62). Only the 1895 is desirable at such low grades. Those with medium hairlines and good reflectivity may grade at about PF-64, and with relatively few hairlines, Gem PF-65. Hairlines are most easily seen in the obverse field. Horizontal slide marks on Liberty's cheek, caused by clear slides on some coin albums, are common. PF-66 may have hairlines so delicate that magnification is needed to see them. Above that, a Proof should be free of such lines, including slide marks.

PF-64

First Reverse
Eight tail feathers.

Second Reverse
Parallel top arrow feather, concave breast.

Third Reverse
Slanted top arrow feather, convex breast.

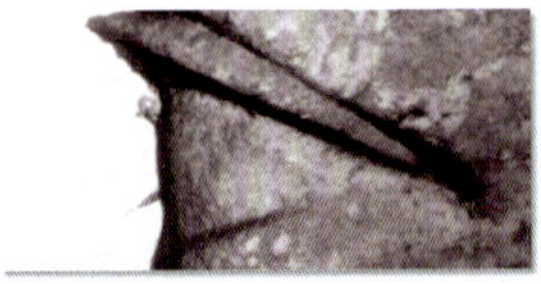

1878, 8 Feathers, Obverse Die Gouge
The "Wild Eye" variety. VAM-14.11

Circulation Strikes

	Mintage	GSID	VF-20	EF-40	AU-50	MS-60	MS-63	MS-64	MS-65	MS-66
Morgan, Pre-1921, non-Carson City Mint (1878–1904)	**n/a**	**72404**	**$50**	**$55**	**$60**	**$75**	**$90**	**$105**	**$180**	**$345**
Same, Prooflike	**n/a**	**72405**	**—**	**—**	**70**	**130**	**175**	**235**	**325**	**575**
Same, Deep Mirror Prooflike	**n/a**	**72406**	**—**	**—**	**100**	**180**	**325**	**500**	**850**	**2,100**
Morgan, Carson City Mint (1878–1893)	**n/a**	**85186**	**180**	**230**	**280**	**350**	**405**	**460**	**575**	**1,100**
Morgan, Type of 1921 (1921)	**n/a**	**71697**	**48**	**48**	**50**	**55**	**60**	**80**	**170**	**625**
Same, Prooflike	**n/a**	**76206**	**—**	**—**	**—**	**260**	**440**	**900**	**3,000**	**6,250**
Same, Deep Mirror Prooflike	**n/a**	**76205**	**—**	**—**	**—**	**2,250**	**8,000**	**15,500**	**36,000**	**—**
1878, 8 Tail Feathers	749,500	7444	95	100	145	260	550	650	2,100	4,400
↳1878, 8TF, Wild Eye, VAM-14.11	*	25043	2,500	3,500	5,000	7,500	10,000	14,000	18,500	—
↳1878, 8TF, Eye Dots, VAM-14.12	*	25044	2,750	6,250	9,500	—	—	—	—	—
↳1878, 8TF, Doubled Eyelid, VAM-14.13	*	25045	950	1,750	2,000	—	—	—	—	—
↳1878, 8TF, Eye Chip, VAM-14.14	*	25046	310	775	1,200	—	—	—	—	—
↳1878, 8TF, Lines in Hair, VAM-14.15	*	25047	455	650	950	—	—	—	—	—
↳1878, 8TF, Wild Lips, VAM-14.16	*	25048	—	525	1,250	3,750	7,500	—	—	—
↳1878, 8TF, Chip in Ear, VAM-14.17	*	25049	6,250	10,000	19,000	—	—	—	—	—
↳1878, 8TF, Broken 7, VAM-14.18	*	25050	7,000	10,000	12,500	—	—	—	—	—
↳1878, 8TF, Broken 8, VAM-14.19	*	25051	6,250	10,000	19,000	—	—	—	—	—
↳1878, 8TF, Boll Lines, VAM-14.20	*	25052	2,750	7,000	9,500	—	—	—	—	—
↳1878, 8TF, Doubled LIBERTY, VAM-15	*	25053	—	285	390	600	900	1,500	—	—
↳1878, 8TF, Crazy Lips, VAM-23	*	25061	—	110	155	285	600	875	—	—
1878, 8TF, Prooflike	*	7445	—	—	—	455	575	1,250	4,050	—
1878, 8TF, Deep Mirror Prooflike	*	7704	—	—	—	750	1,900	3,250	27,000	—

* Included in number above.

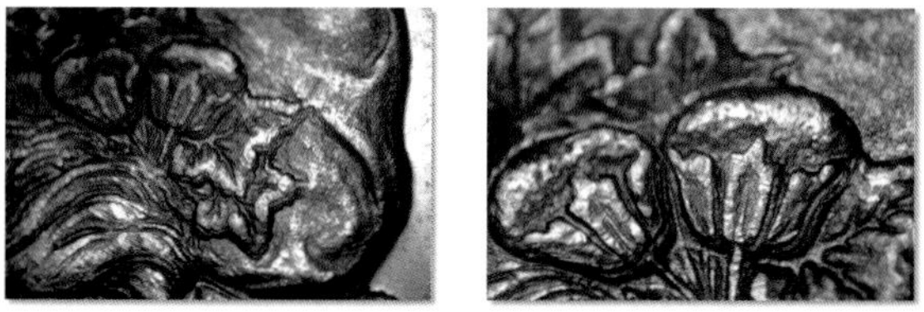

1878, 7 Over 8 Tail Feathers, Tripled Leaves
VAM-44

Circulation Strikes *(continued)*

	Mintage	GSID	VF-20	EF-40	AU-50	MS-60	MS-63	MS-64	MS-65	MS-66
1878, 7 Tail Feathers, Reverse of 1878	9,759,300	7440	$50	$55	$70	$115	$240	$325	$625	$2,700
↳1878, 7TF, Reverse of 1878, Doubled RIB, VAM-70	*	25079	55	60	75	125	265	360	675	—
↳1878, 7TF, Reverse of 1878, Fill in 8s, VAM-79	*	25072	55	60	75	125	265	360	675	—
↳1878, 7TF, Reverse of 1878, Doubled Liberty, VAM-85	*	193608	—	—	1,500	—	—	—	—	—
↳1878, 7TF, Reverse of 1878, Doubled P, VAM-116	*	193610	55	60	75	125	265	360	750	2,950
↳1878, 7TF, Reverse of 1878, Spiked Eye, VAM-123	*	193611	525	1,250	3,750	—	—	—	—	—
↳1878, 7TF, Reverse of 1878, Tripled Eye, VAM-166	*	25066	1,000	1,750	2,750	—	—	—	—	—
↳1878, 7TF, Reverse of 1878, Quad Stars, VAM-169	*	25075	55	65	85	135	290	—	—	—
↳1878, 7TF, Reverse of 1878, Doubled Date, VAM-170	*	25076	55	65	85	135	290	—	—	—
↳1878, 7TF, Reverse of 1878, Doubled R, VAM-187	*	25077	90	120	160	1,250	2,200	2,500	—	—
↳1878, 7TF, Reverse of 1878, Washed Out L, VAM-188	*	25068	130	195	260	3,750	—	—	—	—
↳1878, 7TF, Reverse of 1878, Re-engraved Wing, VAM-189	*	193613	130	285	725	2,500	—	—	—	—
↳1878, 7TF, Reverse of 1878, Tripled Blossoms, VAM-198	*	193614	80	110	170	575	—	—	—	—
1878, 7TF, Reverse of 1878, Prooflike	*	7442	—	—	95	195	350	500	2,100	7,000
1878, 7TF, Reverse of 1878, Deep Mirror Prooflike	*	7702	—	—	—	340	1,000	2,250	8,000	42,000
1878, 7 Over 8 Tail Feathers, Strong	*	7437	80	85	130	240	470	625	2,250	9,500
1878, 7 Over 8 TF, Strong, Prooflike	*	7438	—	—	—	325	575	1,100	4,750	10,500
1878, 7 Over 8 TF, Strong, Deep Mirror Prooflike	*	7700	—	—	—	—	1,750	4,600	15,000	26,500
1878, 7 Over 8 Tail Feathers, Weak	*	7436	55	60	75	130	195	285	625	2,700
↳1878, 7 Over 8 TF, Weak, 7/4, VAM-34A	*	376337	—	3,100	3,450	—	—	—	—	—
↳1878, 7 Over 8 TF, Weak, 7/0TF, Doubled Legs, VAM-43	*	25071	60	65	85	135	215	315	675	2,950
↳1878, 7 Over 8 TF, Weak, Tripled Blossoms, VAM-44	*	25017	1,500	2,000	2,400	6,250	12,000	—	—	—
↳1878, 7 Over 8 TF, Weak, 7/0TF, Doubled Talons, VAM-45	*	25078	60	65	85	135	215	315	675	2,950
1878, 7 Over 8 TF, Weak, Prooflike	*	7439	—	—	—	215	360	525	4,400	—
1878, 7 Over 8 TF, Weak, Deep Mirror Prooflike	*	7701	—	—	—	440	2,000	3,000	11,000	—

* Included in number above.

Circulation Strikes *(continued)*

	Mintage	GSID	VF-20	EF-40	AU-50	MS-60	MS-63	MS-64	MS-65	MS-66
1878, 7 Tail Feathers, Reverse of 1879	*	7441	$60	$70	$110	$190	$430	$675	$2,000	$5,500
↳1878, 7TF, Reverse of 1879, Short Leaf, VAM-203	*	25087	—	—	120	190	430	675	2,100	—
↳1878, 7TF, Reverse of 1879, Tripled R, VAM-220	*	25088	100	150	195	—	—	—	—	—
↳1878, 7TF, Reverse of 1879, Face Chips, VAM-222A	*	193617	—	95	195	950	2,400	—	—	—
↳1878, 7TF, Reverse of 1879, 168 Reeds, VAM-224	*	193618	60	70	110	190	430	675	2,000	5,500
↳1878, 7TF, Reverse of 1879, Slashed O, VAM-227-1	*	193619	—	—	—	—	—	—	—	—
↳1878, 7TF, Reverse of 1879, Slashed O, VAM-228B	*	193620	—	70	260	1,150	2,200	3,750	—	—
1878, 7TF, Reverse of 1879, Prooflike	*	7443	—	—	—	225	525	1,150	4,000	18,000
1878, 7TF, Reverse of 1879, Deep Mirror Prooflike	*	7703	—	—	—	440	2,000	3,000	11,000	—
1878-CC	2,212,000	7446	190	260	325	420	625	900	1,950	5,250
1878-CC, Prooflike	*	7447	—	—	365	575	900	1,550	2,900	8,000
1878-CC, Deep Mirror Prooflike	*	7705	—	—	—	850	2,050	3,900	8,750	30,000
1878-S	9,774,000	7448	55	55	70	105	155	210	390	850
↳1878-S, Long Nock, VAM-26	*	25101	230	390	675	—	—	—	—	—
↳1878-S, Long Nock, VAM-60	*	25107	1,250	6,250	8,750	—	—	—	—	—
↳1878-S, Long Nock, VAM-62	*	25108	775	1,400	—	—	—	—	—	—
↳1878-S, Doubled RIB, VAM-77	*	193624	390	1,250	—	—	—	—	—	—
↳1878-S, Doubled RIB, VAM-111	*	193626	3,500	4,700	—	—	—	—	—	—
1878-S, Prooflike	*	7449	—	—	70	135	230	390	625	3,450
1878-S, Deep Mirror Prooflike	*	7706	—	—	—	—	550	3,100	6,500	19,000
1879	14,806,000	7428	50	55	60	90	130	195	525	1,400
1879, Prooflike	*	7429	—	—	130	260	390	725	2,750	5,000
1879, Deep Mirror Prooflike	*	7672	—	—	—	360	625	2,100	8,250	24,000
1879-CC, Clear CC	756,000	7450	650	2,300	3,750	6,500	9,500	12,000	24,000	90,000
	Auctions: $192,000, PCGS MS-66 HA 01/23									
1879-CC, Clear CC, Prooflike	*	7453	—	—	4,500	7,500	11,000	17,000	37,000	—
1879-CC, Clear CC, Deep Mirror Prooflike	*	7708	—	—	4,950	8,250	13,000	22,000	84,000	—
1879-CC, Capped Die	*	7451	650	1,900	3,100	5,500	9,750	11,000	36,000	—
1879-CC, Capped Die, Prooflike	*	7452	—	—	4,000	7,750	12,000	18,000	60,000	—
1879-CC, Capped Die, Deep Mirror Prooflike	*	7707	—	—	—	—	13,000	36,000	84,000	—
1879-O	2,887,000	7454	60	65	85	145	525	750	2,500	11,000
1879-O, Prooflike	*	7455	—	—	130	260	625	1,300	11,000	—
1879-O, Deep Mirror Prooflike	*	7709	—	—	—	550	2,750	5,750	23,000	42,000
1879-S, Reverse of 1879	9,110,000	7456	50	55	60	75	110	120	185	345
1879-S, 1879-S, Reverse of 1879, Prooflike	*	7459	—	—	70	130	195	280	390	600
1879-S, 1879-S, Reverse of 1879, Deep Mirror Prooflike	*	7711	—	—	—	180	455	650	1,550	3,750
1879-S, Reverse of 1878	*	7457	100	130	175	500	1,300	3,250	7,000	48,000
↳1879-S, Reverse of 1878, VAM-4	*	25115	110	145	195	550	1,450	3,600	7,500	—
↳1879-S, Reverse of 1878, VAM-34B	*	193628	1,000	—	—	—	—	—	—	—
↳1879-S, Reverse of 1878, VAM-77	*	193632	850	—	—	—	—	—	—	—
↳1879-S, Reverse of 1878, VAM-77A	*	373130	1,150	—	—	—	—	—	—	—
1879-S, Reverse of 1878, Prooflike	*	7458	—	—	—	1,100	4,500	7,500	10,500	60,000
1879-S, Reverse of 1878, Deep Mirror Prooflike	*	7710	—	—	—	—	6,000	11,000	24,000	—

* Included in number above.

1880, 80 Over 79
VAM-6

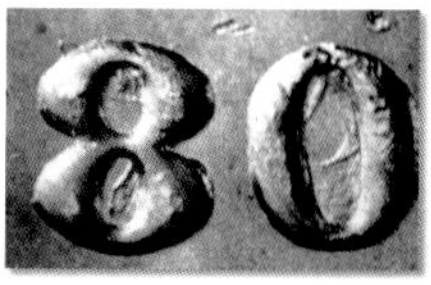

1880-CC, 80 Over 79
VAM-4

1880-CC, 8 Over High 7
VAM-5

1880-CC, 8 Over Low 7
VAM-6

1880-O, 80 Over 79
VAM-4

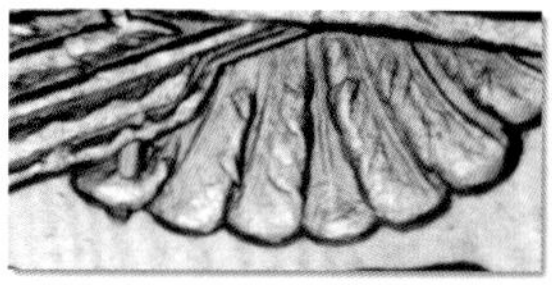

1880-O, Die Gouge
VAM-49: Hangnail

Circulation Strikes *(continued)*

	Mintage	GSID	VF-20	EF-40	AU-50	MS-60	MS-63	MS-64	MS-65	MS-66
1880	12,600,000	7430	$50	$55	$60	$80	$115	$130	$490	$1,600
↳1880, 80 Over 79	*	7432	70	100	160	360	950	1,500	7,000	10,000
↳1880, 80 Over 79, Ears, VAM-8	*	25135	—	1,150	3,100	11,000	—	—	—	—
1880, Prooflike	*	7433	—	—	70	155	340	525	1,200	6,250
↳1880, 80 Over 79, Prooflike	*	226387	—	—	—	—	2,500	—	—	—
1880, Deep Mirror Prooflike	*	7674	—	—	—	—	575	1,250	3,550	24,000
1880-CC	591,000	7465	275	310	390	725	850	1,000	1,250	2,700
↳1880-CC, 80 Over High 79, Reverse of 1879	*	79421	275	310	390	725	900	1,050	1,400	3,000
↳1880-CC, 80 Over Low 79, Reverse of 1879	*	79422	275	310	430	775	950	1,100	1,400	2,950
1880-CC, Prooflike	*	7473	—	—	—	—	1,050	1,200	1,600	4,400
↳1880-CC, 8 Over High 7, Prooflike	*	7469	—	—	—	—	1,150	1,300	1,800	4,800
↳1880-CC, 8 Over Low 7, Prooflike	*	7471	—	—	—	—	1,100	1,250	1,700	4,500
1880-CC, Deep Mirror Prooflike	*	7718	—	—	—	875	1,400	2,400	6,250	15,000
↳1880-CC, 8 Over High 7, Deep Mirror Prooflike	*	7716	—	—	—	925	1,500	2,600	7,000	30,000
↳1880-CC, 8 Over Low 7, Deep Mirror Prooflike	*	7717	—	—	—	1,100	1,600	4,400	8,250	—
1880-CC, 80 Over 79, Reverse of 1878)	*	7466	325	420	650	900	1,250	1,550	2,800	5,000
1880, 80 Over 79-CC, Reverse of 1878, Prooflike	*	7460	—	—	—	975	1,400	3,250	5,500	8,500
1880, 80 Over 79-CC, Reverse of 1878, Deep Mirror Prooflike	*	7712	—	—	—	—	2,600	7,000	12,000	—
1880-CC, Reverse of 1878, 8 Over 7, Prooflike	*	7467	—	—	—	—	—	—	—	—
1880-O	5,305,000	7474	50	55	70	120	675	1,400	12,000	66,000
↳1880-O, Doubled Ear, VAM-43	*	25147	70	130	260	500	775	—	—	—
↳1880-O, 8 Over 7, Spiked Ear, VAM-6D	*	193640	—	—	1,250	—	—	—	—	—
↳1880-O, 8 Over 7, Hangnail, VAM-49	*	25146	75	85	120	1,400	—	—	—	—
1880-O, 80 Over 79	*	7462	65	80	95	130	750	1,500	21,500	—
1880-O, Prooflike	*	7475	—	—	95	365	1,250	3,450	31,000	—
↳1880-O, 8 Over 7, Prooflike	*	347710	—	—	—	—	—	—	—	—
1880, 80 Over 79-O, Prooflike	*	7461	—	—	—	415	1,300	3,500	31,000	—
1880-O, Deep Mirror Prooflike	*	7719	—	—	—	575	3,250	7,000	72,000	—
↳1880-O, 8 Over 7, Deep Mirror Prooflike	*	226388	—	—	—	—	—	—	—	—

* Included in number above.

1882-O, O Over S
VAM-4

Circulation Strikes *(continued)*

	Mintage	GSID	VF-20	EF-40	AU-50	MS-60	MS-63	MS-64	MS-65	MS-66
1880-O, 80 Over 79, Deep Mirror Prooflike	*	7713	—	—	—	$575	$3,250	$7,000	$72,000	—
1880-S	8,900,000	7476	$50	$55	$60	75	90	105	180	$345
	Auctions: $162,000, PCGS MS-69 HA 01/21									
1880-S, 80 Over 79	*	7480	55	60	65	80	135	180	305	725
1880-S, Prooflike	*	7481	—	—	75	135	190	255	360	625
↳1880-S, 8 Over 7, Prooflike	*	297869	—	—	—	—	260	325	455	1,200
1880-S, 80 Over 79, Prooflike	*	7479	—	—	—	—	260	470	725	1,500
1880-S, 80 Over 9, 80 Over Date, Prooflike	*	7463	—	—	—	—	310	495	650	1,900
1880-S, Deep Mirror Prooflike	*	7722	—	—	—	—	325	500	850	2,100
↳1880-S, 8 Over 7, Deep Mirror Prooflike	*	297873	—	—	—	—	—	—	—	—
1880-S, 80 Over 79S, Deep Mirror Prooflike	*	7721	—	—	—	—	390	625	1,550	3,000
1880-S, 80 Over 9, 80 Over Date, Deep Mirror Prooflike	*	7714	—	—	—	—	430	850	1,200	3,400
1881	9,163,000	7434	50	55	60	80	105	120	470	1,500
1881, Prooflike	*	7435	—	—	90	155	230	455	2,450	—
1881, Deep Mirror Prooflike	*	7675	—	—	—	390	775	1,550	10,500	36,000
1881-CC	296,000	7482	440	470	490	725	875	875	1,150	1,300
1881-CC, Prooflike	*	7483	—	—	—	750	950	1,000	1,450	3,000
1881-CC, Deep Mirror Prooflike	*	7723	—	—	—	850	1,500	2,100	3,300	5,000
	Auctions: $228,000, PCGS MS-67 HA 01/24									
1881-O	5,708,000	7484	50	55	60	75	120	180	1,000	6,250
↳1881-O, Doubled Ear, VAM-27	*	25152	65	75	95	290	—	—	—	—
1881-O, Prooflike	*	7485	—	—	90	145	260	455	3,600	—
1881-O, Deep Mirror Prooflike	*	7724	—	—	—	230	490	1,150	5,500	—
1881-S	12,760,000	7486	50	55	60	75	90	105	180	345
1881-S, Prooflike	*	—	—	—	75	135	190	255	360	600
1881-S, Deep Mirror Prooflike	*	7725	—	—	—	195	360	575	1,050	3,100
1882	11,100,000	7488	50	55	60	80	130	130	390	1,200
1882, Prooflike	*	7489	—	—	80	135	210	455	1,250	2,900
1882, Deep Mirror Prooflike	*	7676	—	—	—	—	440	1,150	4,500	—
1882-CC	1,133,000	7508	180	230	280	350	390	420	625	1,250
1882-CC, Prooflike	*	7509	—	—	—	420	470	550	925	2,000
1882-CC, Deep Mirror Prooflike	*	7726	—	—	—	—	750	1,000	2,600	5,250
1882-O	6,090,000	7510	50	55	60	80	110	135	575	3,250
	Auctions: $108,688, PCGS MS-68 LGND 06/15									
1882-O, Prooflike	*	7512	—	—	75	130	195	290	1,400	—
1882-O, Deep Mirror Prooflike	*	7728	—	—	—	285	575	950	4,250	—
1882-O, O Over S, Strong	*	7513	80	95	120	260	575	1,400	45,500	—
↳1882-O, O Over S, O Over S Recessed EDS, VAM-4	*	25157	80	95	120	290	775	1,900	—	—

* Included in number above.

Circulation Strikes *(continued)*

	Mintage	GSID	VF-20	EF-40	AU-50	MS-60	MS-63	MS-64	MS-65	MS-66
1882-O, O Over S, Strong, Prooflike	*	241021	—	—	—	—	—	—	—	—
1882-O, O Over S, Strong, Deep Mirror Prooflike	*	7729	—	—	—	—	—	—	—	—
1882-O, O Over S, Weak	*	7511	$55	$60	$75	$175	$340	$775	$5,500	—
1882-S	9,250,000	7516	50	55	60	75	105	115	215	$375
1882-S, Prooflike	*	7517	—	—	75	135	195	255	390	900
1882-S, Deep Mirror Prooflike	*	7730	—	—	—	—	525	900	3,100	9,500
1883	12,290,000	7490	50	55	60	75	100	110	230	525
1883, Prooflike	*	7491	—	—	80	135	195	290	525	2,000
1883, Deep Mirror Prooflike	*	7677	—	—	—	—	420	600	1,300	5,500
1883-CC	1,204,000	7518	180	230	280	350	405	460	575	1,100
1883-CC, Prooflike	*	7519	—	—	—	375	490	575	775	1,450
1883-CC, Deep Mirror Prooflike	*	7731	—	—	—	390	575	850	1,700	3,100
1883-O	8,725,000	7520	50	55	60	80	100	115	195	395
1883-O, Prooflike	*	7521	—	—	70	130	190	245	430	950
1883-O, Deep Mirror Prooflike	*	7732	—	—	—	—	390	650	1,600	5,000
1883-S	6,250,000	7522	55	90	230	1,450	3,250	4,950	29,000	57,500
1883-S, Prooflike	*	7523	—	—	575	2,500	11,000	24,000	36,000	72,000
	Auctions: $161,000, PCGS MS-67 HA 01/09									
1883-S, Deep Mirror Prooflike	*	7733	—	—	—	21,500	60,000	108,000	—	—
	Auctions: $120,000, PCGS MS-64 HA 01/24									
1884	14,070,000	7492	50	55	60	75	100	115	210	575
↳1884, Partial E Reverse, VAM-2A	*	25164	—	—	—	80	130	160	430	1,000
↳1884, Doubled Ear, VAM-5	*	25165	—	—	—	—	—	—	—	—
1884, Prooflike	*	7493	—	—	70	130	195	255	750	1,900
1884, Deep Mirror Prooflike	*	7678	—	—	—	—	390	1,000	3,000	10,000
1884-CC	1,136,000	7524	180	230	280	350	405	460	575	1,100
1884-CC, Prooflike	*	7525	—	—	—	375	490	575	775	1,900
1884-CC, Deep Mirror Prooflike	*	7734	—	—	—	—	575	825	1,350	3,500
1884-O	9,730,000	7526	50	55	60	75	90	105	180	415
↳1884-O, O Over O, Repunched Mintmark, VAM-10	*	25169	50	55	60	75	90	105	180	415
1884-O, Prooflike	*	7527	—	—	70	130	190	255	360	900
1884-O, Deep Mirror Prooflike	*	7735	—	—	—	—	360	575	1,300	5,000
1884-S	3,200,000	7528	80	155	430	10,500	38,500	144,000	240,000	390,000
	Auctions: $600,000, PCGS MS-67 SBG 08/25; $120,000, NGC MS-65 SBG 08/25									
1884-S, Prooflike	*	7529	—	—	—	30,000	90,000	—	—	—
1884-S, Deep Mirror Prooflike	*	7736	—	—	—	36,000	—	—	—	—
1885	17,787,000	7494	50	55	60	80	100	110	195	375
1885, Prooflike	*	7495	—	—	70	130	190	260	360	700
1885, Deep Mirror Prooflike	*	7679	—	—	—	195	390	600	1,250	3,500
1885-CC	228,000	7530	650	675	700	775	975	1,100	1,400	2,300
	Auctions: $135,125, PCGS MS-68 LGND 06/15									
↳1885-CC, Doubled Dash, VAM-4	*	25176	700	750	775	850	1,050	1,200	1,500	4,500
1885-CC, Prooflike	*	7531	—	—	—	850	1,150	1,400	2,250	4,750
1885-CC, Deep Mirror Prooflike	*	7737	—	—	—	—	1,300	1,650	3,450	11,000
1885-O	9,185,000	7532	50	55	60	80	100	110	195	345
1885-O, Prooflike	*	7533	—	—	70	130	190	255	360	1,150
1885-O, Deep Mirror Prooflike	*	7738	—	—	—	—	345	650	1,300	3,250

* Included in number above.

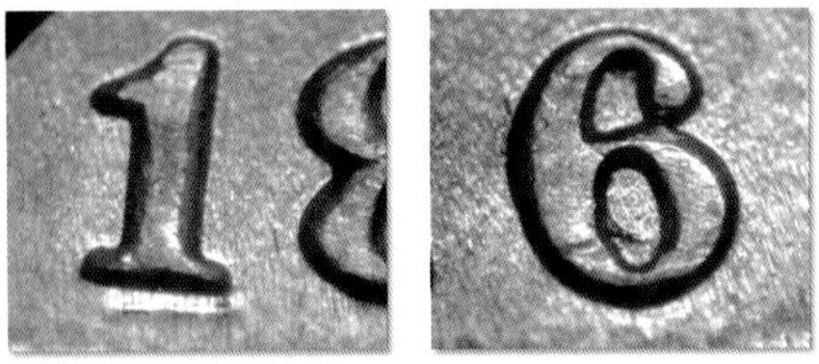
1886, Doubled Date
VAM-20

1887, 7 Over 6
VAM-2

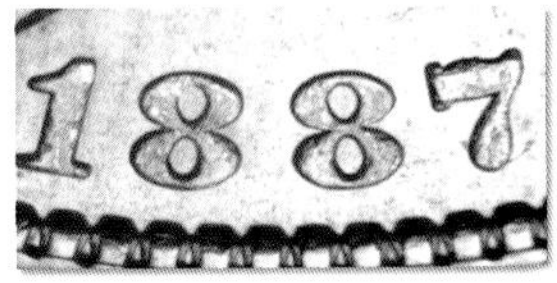
1887-O, 7 Over 6
VAM-3

Circulation Strikes *(continued)*

	Mintage	GSID	VF-20	EF-40	AU-50	MS-60	MS-63	MS-64	MS-65	MS-66
1885-S	1,497,000	7534	$70	$100	$195	$390	$675	$925	$1,950	$5,000
1885-S, Prooflike	*	7535	—	—	—	575	1,200	3,750	11,000	24,000
1885-S, Deep Mirror Prooflike	*	7739	—	—	—	—	3,750	10,000	90,000	—
1886	19,963,000	7496	50	55	60	80	100	105	180	395
↳1886, Doubled Date, VAM-20	*	25181	210	390	625	900	1,250	3,100	5,500	—
1886, Prooflike	*	7497	—	—	70	130	190	255	390	1,150
1886, Deep Mirror Prooflike	*	7680	—	—	—	—	325	575	950	3,400
1886-O	10,710,000	7536	55	105	160	1,400	3,900	12,000	144,000	—
	Auctions: $312,000, PCGS MS-65 SBG 08/25; $144,000, PCGS MS-65 SBG 08/25									
↳1886-O, Clashed Reverse BER, VAM-1A1	*	25184	70	130	180	1,500	4,250	—	—	—
↳1886-O, 2 + 2 Clash, VAM-11A	*	193676	—	—	—	—	—	—	—	—
1886-O, Prooflike	*	7537	—	—	725	3,250	18,000	36,000	—	—
1886-O, Deep Mirror Prooflike	*	7740	—	—	—	8,750	36,000	69,000	—	—
	Auctions: $780,000, PCGS MS-67 SBG 11/20									
1886-S	750,000	7538	95	130	230	490	875	1,300	2,050	5,500
1886-S, Prooflike	*	7539	—	—	260	525	950	1,750	5,000	13,000
1886-S, Deep Mirror Prooflike	*	7741	—	—	—	—	3,050	8,500	30,000	—
1887	20,290,000	7498	50	55	60	75	90	105	195	360
↳1887, Partial E Reverse, VAM-1B	*	25190	260	455	625	3,750	8,250	10,000	12,500	—
↳1887, Die Scratch Wing, VAM-3	*	374310	—	—	—	—	—	—	—	—
↳1887, Alligator Eye, Clashed Dies, VAM-12A	*	70603	—	60	65	80	110	125	215	395
↳1887, Donkey Tail, VAM-25A	*	25186	195	325	390	1,600	7,500	—	—	—
1887, Prooflike	*	7499	—	—	70	130	190	235	360	775
1887, Deep Mirror Prooflike	*	7681	—	—	100	180	390	625	1,250	3,500
1887, 7 Over 6	*	7540	130	195	310	650	950	1,250	2,200	7,750
↳1887, 7 Over 6, 7 Over Date, VAM-2	*	25187	130	195	310	650	950	1,250	2,200	7,750
1887, 7 Over 6, Prooflike	*	7541	—	—	—	750	1,250	1,600	3,100	10,000
1887, 7 Over 6, Deep Mirror Prooflike	*	7742	—	—	—	—	2,500	3,600	15,000	—
1887-O	11,550,000	7544	50	60	80	110	260	550	2,100	27,500
1887-O, Prooflike	*	7545	—	—	95	160	305	875	5,000	54,000
1887-O, Deep Mirror Prooflike	*	7744	—	—	—	405	900	3,750	10,500	60,000
1887-O, 7 Over 6	*	7542	130	325	390	850	2,100	4,400	39,000	57,500
↳1887-O, 7 Over 6, 7 Over Date, VAM-3	*	25193	130	325	390	850	2,100	4,400	39,000	57,500
1887-O, 7 Over 6, Prooflike	*	7543	—	—	—	—	—	—	—	—
1887-O, 7 Over 6, Deep Mirror Prooflike	*	7743	—	—	—	—	—	—	—	—
1887-S	1,771,000	7546	50	60	90	180	525	775	1,700	9,500
1887-S, Prooflike	*	7547	—	—	195	360	775	2,750	10,000	—
1887-S, Deep Mirror Prooflike	*	7745	—	—	—	—	3,500	8,000	31,000	—

* Included in number above.

1888-O, Doubled Die Obverse
VAM-4: Hot Lips

1888-O, Obverse Die Break
VAM-1B: Scarface

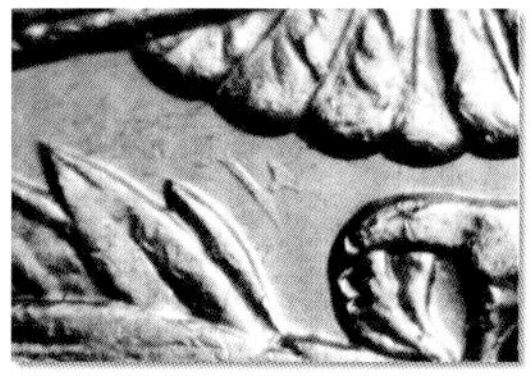

1889-O, Clashed Die
VAM-1A

Circulation Strikes *(continued)*

	Mintage	GSID	VF-20	EF-40	AU-50	MS-60	MS-63	MS-64	MS-65	MS-66
1888	19,183,000	7500	$50	$55	$60	$75	$100	$115	$195	$650
↳1888, Doubled Reverse, VAM-6	*	25199	—	—	—	110	170	285	650	—
1888, Prooflike	*	7501	—	—	70	130	190	255	575	—
1888, Deep Mirror Prooflike	*	7682	—	—	—	245	455	700	2,600	6,750
1888-O	12,150,000	7548	$55	$55	70	85	110	130	345	1,500
↳1888-O, Clashed E, VAM-1A	*	25204	60	65	75	95	140	165	450	—
↳1888-O, Oval O, VAM-2	*	25207	75	90	120	1,100	—	—	—	—
↳1888-O, Oval O, VAM-5	*	25208	260	525	1,150	—	—	—	—	—
↳1888-O, Shooting Star, VAM-7A	*	193648	290	490	950	—	—	—	—	—
↳1888-O, Doubled Arrows, VAM-9	*	25206	60	65	75	95	120	140	450	1,800
↳1888-O, Oval O, VAM-34	*	193649	160	220	365	1,150	—	—	—	—
1888-O, Prooflike	*	7551	—	—	—	135	235	285	825	3,000
1888-O, Deep Mirror Prooflike	*	7748	—	155	190	260	495	900	3,900	14,500
1888-O, Doubled Die Obverse	*	7603	155	310	750	11,000	—	—	—	—
↳1888-O, Hot Lips, VAM-4	*	193647	155	310	750	11,000	—	—	—	—
1888-O, Scarface	*	80063	550	950	1,500	3,000	7,500	9,000	—	—
↳1888-O, Scarface, VAM-1B3	*	377513	550	950	1,500	3,000	7,500	9,000	—	—
↳1888-O, Scarface, VAM 1B4	*	193646	950	1,900	3,000	5,500	8,500	12,000	—	—
1888-S	657,000	7552	145	160	245	455	950	1,250	2,300	6,000
1888-S, Prooflike	*	7553	—	—	—	525	1,100	2,050	3,750	14,500
1888-S, Deep Mirror Prooflike	*	7749	—	—	—	625	1,300	4,100	12,000	17,000
1889	21,726,000	7502	50	55	60	80	100	125	285	950
↳1889, Obverse Clashed Die, VAM-23A	7 known	25219	—	13,000	21,000	48,000	87,000	—	—	—
1889, Prooflike	*	7503	—	—	—	135	195	255	850	2,800
1889, Deep Mirror Prooflike	*	7683	—	—	—	—	525	1,250	2,500	11,500
1889-CC	350,000	7554	2,050	4,750	9,750	26,500	48,000	108,000	288,000	450,000
	Auctions: $168,000, PCGS MS-64 HA 08/25; $1,035,469, PCGS MS-68 SBG 08/25									
1889-CC, Prooflike	*	7555	—	—	11,000	30,000	54,000	120,000	378,000	—
	Auctions: $324,000, NGC MS-65 SBG 11/20									
1889-CC, Deep Mirror Prooflike	*	7750	—	—	—	33,000	90,000	180,000	—	—
	Auctions: $264,000, PCGS MS-64 SBG 11/24; $228,000, PCGS MS-64 HA 11/24									
1889-O	11,875,000	7556	50	70	130	415	650	875	3,000	14,500
↳1889-O, Clashed E, VAM-1A	*	25222	90	120	160	3,750	—	—	—	—
↳1889-O, Oval O, VAM-2	*	25223	—	80	130	450	1,150	—	—	—
1889-O, Prooflike	*	7557	—	—	—	550	1,150	2,250	7,500	21,000
1889-O, Deep Mirror Prooflike	*	7751	—	—	—	625	2,900	5,500	60,000	—

* Included in number above.

1890-CC, Die Gouge
VAM-4: Tailbar

1890-O, Die Gouges
VAM-10: Comet

1891-O, Pitted Reverse Die
VAM-1B

Circulation Strikes *(continued)*

	Mintage	GSID	VF-20	EF-40	AU-50	MS-60	MS-63	MS-64	MS-65	MS-66
1889-S	700,000	7558	$75	$95	$155	$340	$650	$825	$1,950	$3,450
1889-S, Prooflike	*	7559	—	—	—	420	850	1,500	4,800	18,000
1889-S, Deep Mirror Prooflike	*	7752	—	—	—	625	3,250	6,250	31,000	66,000
1890	16,802,000	7504	50	55	60	80	120	145	850	15,000
1890, Prooflike	*	7505	—	—	—	130	260	500	2,500	—
1890, Deep Mirror Prooflike	*	7684	—	—	—	370	900	2,250	12,000	—
1890-CC	2,309,041	7560	210	310	420	750	1,400	2,500	5,750	33,000
1890-CC, Prooflike	*	7563	—	—	465	950	1,750	2,600	8,750	—
1890-CC, Deep Mirror Prooflike	*	7754	—	—	—	1,100	2,250	4,100	17,000	93,500
1890-CC, Tail Bar, VAM-4	*	241022	420	700	850	2,000	3,750	7,000	32,500	—
1890-CC, Tail Bar, VAM-4, Prooflike	*	7561	—	—	—	—	6,000	9,000	—	—
1890-CC, Tail Bar, VAM-4, Deep Mirror Prooflike	*	7753	—	—	—	—	6,500	12,000	—	—
1890-O	10,701,000	7564	50	55	65	120	235	325	1,150	6,750
↳1890-O, Comet Die Gouge, VAM-10	*	25226	55	60	75	130	255	525	2,500	—
1890-O, Prooflike	*	7565	—	—	—	170	340	455	1,750	12,500
1890-O, Deep Mirror Prooflike	*	7755	—	—	—	—	575	1,450	8,000	—
1890-S	8,230,373	7566	50	60	65	115	220	370	875	2,250
1890-S, Prooflike	*	7567	—	—	—	180	360	525	2,500	7,500
1890-S, Deep Mirror Prooflike	*	7756	—	—	—	290	1,000	4,250	12,000	—
1891	8,693,556	7506	50	55	60	90	260	600	2,450	13,000
↳1891, Doubled Ear and Moustache, VAM-2A	*	25229	145	175	390	—	—	—	—	—
1891, Prooflike	*	7507	—	—	—	260	950	2,050	—	—
1891, Deep Mirror Prooflike	*	7685	—	—	—	625	2,250	5,250	26,500	38,500
1891-CC	1,618,000	7568	190	310	455	825	1,150	1,600	3,900	16,500
1891-CC, Prooflike	*	7569	—	—	—	900	1,250	2,000	7,000	—
	Auctions: $199,750, PCGS MS-68 LGND 06/15									
1891-CC, Deep Mirror Prooflike	*	7757	—	—	—	1,200	2,250	5,000	45,500	—
1891-O	7,954,529	7570	75	115	155	260	600	900	4,400	111,500
	Auctions: $108,688, PCGS MS-66 LGND 03/19									
↳1891-O, Pitted Reverse, VAM-1B	*	25232	95	195	325	—	—	—	—	—
1891-O, Prooflike	*	7571	—	—	—	390	2,050	4,600	—	—
1891-O, Deep Mirror Prooflike	*	7758	—	—	—	1,500	6,250	10,500	42,000	—
1891-S	5,296,000	7572	50	55	75	135	420	775	1,550	5,000
1891-S, Prooflike	*	7573	—	—	—	260	500	850	3,100	9,750
1891-S, Deep Mirror Prooflike	*	7759	—	—	—	—	1,050	3,750	15,500	33,500
1892	1,036,000	7574	55	110	175	450	1,100	1,200	3,050	50,500
1892, Prooflike	*	7575	—	—	—	775	1,200	2,850	8,000	—
1892, Deep Mirror Prooflike	*	7686	—	—	—	900	1,750	3,750	20,000	—

* Included in number above.

Circulation Strikes *(continued)*

	Mintage	GSID	VF-20	EF-40	AU-50	MS-60	MS-63	MS-64	MS-65	MS-66
1892-CC	1,352,000	7604	$455	$775	$1,000	$1,900	$3,000	$4,250	$7,500	$21,500
	Auctions: $135,125, PCGS MS-67 LGND 06/15									
1892-CC, Prooflike	*	7605	—	—	1,150	2,500	5,000	6,000	15,500	—
1892-CC, Deep Mirror Prooflike	*	7760	—	—	—	2,750	8,750	15,500	60,000	—
1892-O	2,744,000	7606	50	110	170	490	900	1,150	3,000	19,000
	Auctions: $111,625, PCGS MS-67 LGND 10/14									
1892-O, Prooflike	*	7607	—	—	1,400	4,000	11,000	18,000	36,000	—
1892-O, Deep Mirror Prooflike	*	7761	—	—	—	—	16,500	31,000	60,000	—
1892-S	1,200,000	7608	155	525	2,300	60,000	111,500	180,000	264,000	360,000
	Auctions: $456,000, PCGS MS-67 SBG 08/25; $180,000, PCGS MS-64 HA 08/25									
↳**1892-S, Doubled Date, VAM-2**	*	25236	220	575	2,300	66,000	—	—	—	—
↳**1892-S, Doubled Date, VAM-7**	*	193650	—	1,000	—	—	—	—	—	—
↳**1892-S, Tripled Hair, VAM-8**	*	193651	320	750	2,600	63,500	—	—	—	—
1892-S, Prooflike	*	7609	—	—	2,800	72,000	156,000	198,000	—	—
1892-S, Deep Mirror Prooflike	*	7762	—	—	—	—	—	—	—	—
1893	378,000	7576	470	675	850	1,900	2,750	3,600	6,500	60,000
1893, Prooflike	*	7577	—	—	1,100	4,400	14,500	24,000	—	—
1893, Deep Mirror Prooflike	*	7687	—	—	—	12,000	—	—	—	—
1893-CC	677,000	7610	1,050	2,500	4,100	6,000	9,750	20,000	111,500	216,000
	Auctions: $102,000, PCGS MS-65 HA 01/24									
1893-CC, Prooflike	*	7611	—	—	4,550	6,500	12,000	36,000	150,000	—
1893-CC, Deep Mirror Prooflike	*	7763	—	—	—	—	42,000	72,000	180,000	—
1893-O	300,000	7612	600	925	1,500	6,000	9,750	14,500	198,000	264,000
	Auctions: $108,000, NGC MS-65 HA 06/24; $228,000, PCGS MS-65 HA 06/24									
1893-O, Prooflike	*	7613	—	—	1,650	7,000	18,000	33,500	237,500	450,000
	Auctions: $458,250, PCGS MS-66 LGND 06/15									
1893-O, Deep Mirror Prooflike	*	7764	—	—	—	—	27,500	90,000	300,000	—
	Auctions: $360,000, PCGS MS-65 SBG 11/20									
1893-S (a)	100,000	7614	7,750	15,500	30,000	228,000	330,000	480,000	756,000	1,020,000
	Auctions: $444,000, PCGS MS-63 HA 01/24; $276,000, PCGS MS-63 HA 01/24									
1893-S, Prooflike (a)	*	7615	—	—	37,500	—	—	—	—	—
1894 (a)	110,000	7578	1,000	1,300	1,900	4,000	6,500	8,500	32,000	108,000
	Auctions: $152,750, PCGS MS-66 LGND 10/15									
1894, Prooflike (a)	*	7579	—	—	2,450	9,500	—	—	—	—
1894, Deep Mirror Prooflike (a)	*	7688					42,000	66,000	—	—
1894-O	1,723,000	7616	55	160	300	2,300	4,750	8,500	37,000	—
	Auctions: $192,000, PCGS MS-65 SBG 08/25									
1894-O, Prooflike	*	7617	—	—	2,500	8,000	42,000	—	—	—
1894-O, Deep Mirror Prooflike	*	7766	—	—	—	17,000	—	—	—	—
1894-S	1,260,000	7618	170	360	650	1,400	2,300	4,000	5,500	18,000
1894-S, Prooflike	*	7619	—	—	725	1,500	3,000	5,000	11,000	—
1894-S, Deep Mirror Prooflike	*	7767	—	—	—	2,750	15,500	36,000	54,000	84,000
1895-O	450,000	7620	470	900	1,650	16,000	48,000	96,000	156,000	390,000
	Auctions: $336,000, PCGS MS-66 SBG 08/25; $159,000, PCGS MS-65 HA 08/25									
1895-O, Prooflike	*	7621	—	—	2,000	19,500	66,000	112,000	—	—
1895-O, Deep Mirror Prooflike	*	7768	—	—	—	36,000	93,500	150,000	330,000	—
	Auctions: $253,000, PCGS MS-65 HA 11/05									

* Included in number above. **a.** Authentication is recommended. Beware of altered mintmark.

Circulation Strikes *(continued)*

	Mintage	GSID	VF-20	EF-40	AU-50	MS-60	MS-63	MS-64	MS-65	MS-66
1895-S	400,000	7622	$1,000	$1,800	$2,250	$6,000	$7,500	$12,000	$20,000	$96,000
	Auctions: $114,562, PCGS MS-66 LGND 10/15									
↳1895-S, S Over S, Repunched Mintmark, VAM-3	*	25239	1,000	1,800	2,250	6,000	7,500	12,000	20,000	—
↳1895-S, S Over S, S Over Horizontal S, VAM-4	*	25238	1,050	1,950	2,500	6,500	—	—	—	—
1895-S, Prooflike	*	7623	—	—	2,700	6,500	11,000	13,000	33,000	96,000
	Auctions: $108,000, PCGS MS-66 HA 09/19									
1895-S, Deep Mirror Prooflike	*	7769	—	—	—	7,750	13,000	18,000	42,000	96,000
	Auctions: $336,000, PCGS MS-67 SBG 11/20									
1896	9,976,000	7580	50	55	60	75	90	105	180	360
↳1896, Bar 6, VAM-20	*	25240	55	60	65	80	100	115	200	395
1896, Prooflike	*	7581	—	—	80	130	190	285	470	1,000
1896, Deep Mirror Prooflike	*	7689	—	—	100	200	460	675	1,300	4,900
1896-O	4,900,000	7624	60	90	155	1,800	6,250	26,500	210,000	510,000
	Auctions: $528,000, PCGS MS-66 SBG 11/20									
1896-O, Prooflike	*	7626	—	—	—	5,000	—	—	—	—
1896-O, Deep Mirror Prooflike	*	7770	—	—	—	15,500	31,000	45,500	—	—
1896-S	5,000,000	7627	170	525	1,250	3,250	4,400	5,500	12,000	78,000
	Auctions: $102,000, PCGS MS-66 SBG 08/25; $720,000, PCGS MS-69 SBG 08/25									
1896-S, Prooflike	*	7628	—	—	—	4,400	18,000	23,000	29,000	132,000
	Auctions: $111,625, PCGS MS-66 LGND 09/16									
1897	2,822,000	7582	50	55	60	75	145	170	280	875
1897, Prooflike	*	7583	—	—	75	135	200	280	440	1,250
1897, Deep Mirror Prooflike	*	7690	—	—	—	—	360	625	2,100	17,000
1897-O	4,004,000	7629	55	90	130	1,300	4,100	12,500	55,000	96,000
	Auctions: $300,000, PCGS MS-66 SBG 08/25									
1897-O, Prooflike	*	7630	—	—	750	3,250	12,000	30,000	—	—
1897-O, Deep Mirror Prooflike	*	7772	—	—	—	7,500	29,000	48,000	—	—
1897-S	5,825,000	7631	55	60	70	120	235	365	575	1,250
1897-S, Prooflike	*	7632	—	—	100	210	390	575	1,150	2,400
1897-S, Deep Mirror Prooflike	*	7773	—	—	—	390	900	2,000	3,500	11,000
1898	5,884,000	7584	50	55	60	80	110	130	210	575
1898, Prooflike	*	7585	—	—	70	130	200	300	525	1,450
1898, Deep Mirror Prooflike	*	7691	—	—	—	—	360	625	1,400	5,000
1898-O	4,440,000	7633	50	55	60	80	90	105	180	345
↳1898-O, Repunched Date, VAM-20	*	193673	3,100	—	—	—	—	—	—	—
1898-O, Prooflike	*	7634	—	—	70	130	190	255	360	850
1898-O, Deep Mirror Prooflike	*	7774	—	—	—	180	390	650	1,200	3,250
1898-S	4,102,000	7635	55	90	155	525	1,100	1,200	2,250	4,750
	Auctions: $117,500, PCGS MS-68 LGND 10/15									
1898-S, Prooflike	*	7636	—	—	—	575	1,200	1,650	4,500	10,000
1898-S, Deep Mirror Prooflike	*	7775	—	—	—	—	1,750	3,600	12,000	—
1899	330,000	7586	130	130	160	260	470	495	1,000	2,250
1899, Prooflike	*	7587	—	—	—	—	525	675	1,500	4,400
1899, Deep Mirror Prooflike	*	7692	—	—	—	—	775	1,400	2,500	6,250
1899-O	12,290,000	7637	50	55	60	75	90	110	180	345
1899-O, Prooflike	*	7638	—	—	70	130	195	280	430	900
1899-O, Deep Mirror Prooflike	*	7776	—	—	—	—	470	650	2,500	5,500

* Included in number above.

1899-O, Micro O
VAM-4, 5, 6, 31, and 32

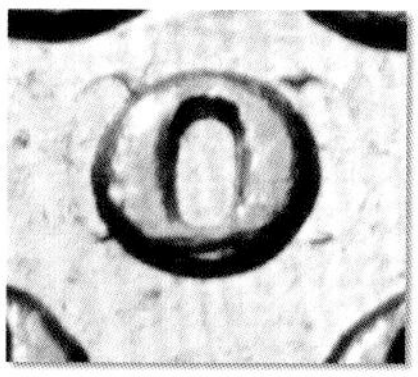

1900-O, O Over CC
Various VAMs

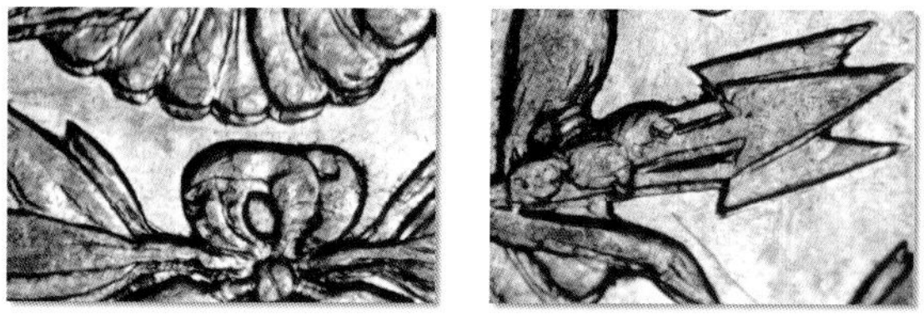

1901, Doubled Die Reverse
VAM-3: Shifted Eagle

Circulation Strikes *(continued)*

	Mintage	GSID	VF-20	EF-40	AU-50	MS-60	MS-63	MS-64	MS-65	MS-66
1899-O, Micro O	*	79426	$70	$130	$210	$3,750	$17,000	$24,000	$34,000	$60,000
↳1899-O, Micro O, VAM-4	*	25247	70	130	210	3,750	17,000	24,000	34,000	60,000
↳1899-O, Micro O, Wing Lines, VAM-5	*	25251	70	130	210	3,750	17,000	24,000	34,000	60,000
↳1899-O, Micro O, VAM-32	*	25250	130	195	290	—	20,500	—	—	—
1899-S	2,562,000	7639	80	145	360	725	1,250	1,400	2,100	6,250
↳1899-S, Doubled Date, VAM-7	*	195785	—	155	395	725	1,250	1,400	2,100	—
1899-S, Prooflike	*	7640	—	—	650	775	1,500	1,650	3,400	7,500
1899-S, Deep Mirror Prooflike	*	7777	—	—	—	1,100	2,500	4,600	21,000	36,000
1900	8,830,000	7588	50	55	60	80	95	115	205	600
↳1900, Two Olive Reverse, VAM-18	*	25257	—	—	—	—	—	—	—	—
1900, Prooflike	*	7589	—	—	130	260	455	775	3,500	8,000
1900, Deep Mirror Prooflike	*	7693	—	—	—	—	7,500	18,000	48,000	—
1900-O	12,590,000	7641	50	55	60	80	100	115	195	420
1900-O, Prooflike	*	7643	—	—	70	135	195	280	430	1,000
1900-O, Deep Mirror Prooflike	*	7778	—	—	—	—	1,000	1,900	7,500	—
1900-O, O Over CC	*	7644	180	260	390	725	1,350	1,700	2,500	5,500
1900-S	3,540,000	7646	55	100	180	455	950	1,250	1,400	2,500
1900-S, Prooflike	*	7647	—	—	200	500	1,150	1,600	3,000	6,000
1900-S, Deep Mirror Prooflike	*	7780	—	—	—	—	9,500	13,000	30,000	—
1901	6,962,000	7590	100	260	455	4,900	10,000	43,000	420,000	660,000
	Auctions: $720,000, PCGS MS-66 SBG 08/25									
↳1901, Doubled Ear, VAM-5	*	25268	145	285	500	6,250	—	—	—	—
1901, Prooflike	*	7593	—	—	—	—	42,000	—	—	—
1901, Deep Mirror Prooflike	*	7695	—	—	—	—	—	—	—	—
1901, Doubled Die Reverse	*	79424	490	850	1,500	33,500	—	—	—	—
↳1901, Doubled Die Reverse, Shifted Eagle, VAM-3	*	70532	1,000	1,750	2,500	33,500	—	—	—	—
1901-O	13,320,000	7648	50	55	60	75	95	105	180	550
1901-O, Prooflike	*	7649	—	—	80	170	280	390	850	2,400
1901-O, Deep Mirror Prooflike	*	7781	—	—	—	—	650	2,250	10,500	15,000
1901-S	2,284,000	7650	90	175	345	750	1,500	2,050	2,750	10,500
1901-S, Prooflike	*	7651	—	—	525	950	2,000	3,550	9,500	—
1901-S, Deep Mirror Prooflike	*	7782	—	—	—	—	17,000	24,000	24,000	40,500
1902	7,994,000	7594	55	60	80	145	310	325	420	850
1902, Prooflike	*	7595	—	—	—	900	1,600	2,400	3,450	6,500
1902, Deep Mirror Prooflike	*	7696	—	—	—	—	7,500	10,500	18,500	—
1902-O	8,636,000	7652	50	55	60	80	100	110	200	430
↳1902-O, Doubled Ear, VAM-25	*	193654	—	—	110	155	210	285	495	1,150
↳1902-O, Doubled Ear, VAM-54	*	193656	—	—	—	130	180	360	525	—
1902-O, Prooflike	*	7655	—	—	70	135	195	280	725	4,100
1902-O, Deep Mirror Prooflike	*	7784	—	—	—	—	1,100	2,500	7,500	19,000

* Included in number above.

1903-S, Small S Mintmark
VAM-2

Circulation Strikes *(continued)*

	Mintage	GSID	VF-20	EF-40	AU-50	MS-60	MS-63	MS-64	MS-65	MS-66
1902-S	1,530,000	7656	$175	$275	$325	$625	$1,200	$1,400	$2,400	$6,750
1902-S, Prooflike	*	7657	—	—	—	—	3,500	4,750	11,000	—
1902-S, Deep Mirror Prooflike	*	7785	—	—	—	—	—	—	—	—
1903	4,652,000	7596	55	55	70	95	150	175	300	600
1903, Prooflike	*	7597	—	—	130	260	650	1,000	1,900	3,000
1903, Deep Mirror Prooflike	*	7697	—	—	—	—	3,750	7,500	21,500	—
1903-O	4,450,000	7658	600	625	625	750	900	950	1,100	1,550
1903-O, Prooflike	*	7659	—	—	—	—	1,050	1,250	2,900	4,500
1903-O, Deep Mirror Prooflike	*	7786	—	—	—	—	1,450	2,100	6,000	15,500
1903-S	1,241,000	7660	235	775	2,500	7,250	10,000	12,000	15,500	31,000
1903-S, Micro S	*	79425	490	1,300	6,500	48,000	72,000	84,000	96,000	—
↳1903-S, Micro S, VAM-2	*	25252	490	1,300	6,500	48,000	72,000	84,000	96,000	—
1903-S, Prooflike	*	7663	—	—	—	8,500	18,000	24,000	36,000	—
1904	2,788,000	7598	50	60	90	160	550	750	2,000	5,500
1904, Prooflike	*	7599	—	—	—	1,000	3,750	6,000	22,500	—
1904, Deep Mirror Prooflike	*	7698	—	—	—	—	—	60,000	90,000	—
1904-O	3,720,000	7664	50	55	60	80	100	110	195	385
1904-O, Prooflike	*	7665	—	—	70	135	195	255	495	1,150
1904-O, Deep Mirror Prooflike	*	7789	—	—	—	—	390	575	1,250	3,900
1904-S	2,304,000	7666	170	500	1,600	4,100	6,250	7,000	8,750	22,000
1904-S, Prooflike	*	7667	—	—	—	—	10,000	13,000	24,000	42,000
1904-S, Deep Mirror Prooflike	*	7790	—	—	—	—	15,500	24,000	—	—
1921	44,690,000	7600	48	48	50	55	60	80	170	625
↳1921, Pitted Reverse, VAM-41B	*	374018	55	55	60	70	90	120	235	775
1921, Morgan, Prooflike	*	7601	—	—	—	260	440	900	3,000	6,250
1921, Morgan, Deep Mirror Prooflike	*	7699	—	—	—	2,250	8,000	15,500	36,000	—
1921-D	20,345,000	7668	48	48	50	75	180	430	495	900
↳1921-D, TRU_T Variety, VAM-1A2	*	25278	80	100	195	390	600	775	2,800	—
1921-D, Prooflike	*	7669	—	—	—	430	1,900	4,400	7,500	—
1921-D, Deep Mirror Prooflike	*	7791	—	—	—	2,250	8,000	26,500	43,000	—
1921-S	21,695,000	7670	48	48	50	80	180	310	900	3,050
↳1921-S, Thorn Head, VAM-1B	*	25280	—	—	325	—	—	—	—	—
↳1921-S, Thorn Head, VAM-1B5	*	193666	—	—	155	455	—	—	—	—
↳1921-S, Thorn Head, VAM-1B7	*	193668	950	1,250	3,450	—	—	—	—	—
1921-S, Prooflike	*	7671	—	—	—	—	12,000	21,500	33,500	—

* Included in number above.

GSA Releases. Starting in 1962, the Mint began releasing to the public older silver dollars discovered in Mint inventory. This practice was halted as of March 26, 1964, but nearly 3 million coins—mostly Morgan dollars from the Carson City Mint—remained. On December 31, 1970, President Richard M. Nixon signed legislation authorizing their sale through the General Services Administration (GSA). Those with CC mintmarks were set into black liners within sealed, transparent plastic holders impressed with the words "Carson City" and "Silver Dollar." About 2 million of those were also labeled "Uncirculated." Although the holders were protective, they were too large and inconvenient for transport or mail. Many buyers broke their coins out of them for ease of storage or to place them in albums. This practice accelerated in the mid-1980s, when the Professional Coin Grading Service (PCGS) and Numismatic Guaranty Corporation of America (NGC) introduced their own coin holders. Customers were happy to let their coins be "cracked out" of the GSA holders to get numerical grade designations that could increase their value, especially if a high number could be obtained.

Year after year, dealers and collectors continued to break coins out of the GSA holders. Those who did not were rewarded when, beginning early in the 21st century, Morgan dollars still in the GSA holders became highly collectible. A coin in an official GSA holder had a "pedigree" that was not available with a coin in a private company's slab. The grading services eventually made accommodations for GSA-holdered coins, and PCGS, NGC, CACG, and ANACS will grade them inside their holders. NGC, CACG, and ANACS will apply a tamper-resistant grading label to the holder itself, while PCGS will encase the coin and holder in a specially designed slab.

GSA Holders

	GSID	VF-20	EF-40	AU-50	MS-60	MS-63	MS-64	MS-65	MS-66
Morgan Dollar CC-Mint, Hard Package	**80062**	**—**	**—**	**—**	**$350**	**$405**	**$475**	**$600**	**$1,150**
1878-CC, Hard Package	72472	—	—	—	850	900	950	4,500	10,500
1878-S	76509	—	—	—	2,500	5,000	—	—	—
↳1879, Soft Package	381669	—	—	—	—	—	—	—	—
1879-CC, Clear CC, Hard Package	72473	—	—	—	9,000	11,000	14,500	31,000	—
1879-CC, Capped Die, Hard Package	72474	—	—	—	9,000	11,000	14,500	48,000	—
↳1879-O, Soft Package	381670	—	—	—	—	—	—	—	—
↳1879-S, Reverse of 1879	377784	—	—	—	160	340	495	675	1,250
1879-S, Reverse of 1878	76510	—	—	—	285	390	525	650	1,400
1880-CC, Hard Package	72475	—	—	—	925	950	1,100	1,400	4,500
1880-O, Soft Package	195837	—	—	—	—	—	—	—	—
1880-S	76511	—	—	—	260	285	330	360	525
1881	76512	—	—	—	290	310	330	550	1,800
1881-CC, Hard Package	71645	—	—	—	850	950	1,000	1,250	1,750
1881-O, Soft Package	76513	—	$110	$155	325	430	625	1,500	9,500
1881-O, Hard Package	374238	—	—	—	325	430	625	1,500	9,500
1881-S	76514	—	—	—	390	440	575	1,000	1,750

GSA Holders *(continued)*

	GSID	VF-20	EF-40	AU-50	MS-60	MS-63	MS-64	MS-65	MS-66
1882	76515	—	—	—	$2,500	$3,000	—	—	—
1882-CC, Hard Package	72477	—	—	—	370	435	$470	$650	$1,350
1882-O, Soft Package	193342	—	$100	$130	235	390	600	—	—
1882-O, Hard Package	193341	—	—	—	—	8,750	—	—	—
1882-S	76516	—	—	—	390	420	490	850	2,000
1883, Soft Package	213988	—	—	—	—	525	600	900	3,250
1883, Hard Package	373188	—	—	—	—	600	725	900	2,500
1883-CC, Hard Package	72478	—	—	—	350	405	475	600	1,150
1883-O	76517	—	—	160	235	325	365	455	3,500
1884, Soft Package	85187	—	—	—	—	2,000	—	—	—
1884-CC, Hard Package	72479	—	—	—	350	405	475	600	1,150
1884-O	151715	—	—	—	190	300	470	575	850
1884-S, Soft Package	195838	—	—	—	—	—	—	—	—
1885	76518	—	—	—	390	390	—	—	—
1885-CC, Hard Package	71646	—	—	—	950	1,000	1,100	1,500	2,550
1885-O	76519	—	—	—	230	260	575	675	—
1886	76520	—	—	—	325	325	455	—	—
1887	76521	—	—	—	230	260	330	525	1,250
1888	85188	—	—	—	—	—	—	—	—
1890-CC, Hard Package	72480	—	—	—	4,100	6,000	12,000	31,000	—
1890-S, Soft Package	85189	—	—	—	—	—	—	—	—
1891-CC, Hard Package	72481	—	—	—	2,700	4,250	12,000	31,000	—
1891-S, Soft Package	195840	—	—	—	—	—	—	—	—
1892-CC, Hard Package	195839	—	—	—	—	—	—	—	—
1895-S, Soft Package	195841	—	—	—	—	—	—	—	—
1898-O, Hard Package	195842	—	—	—	—	—	—	—	—
1898-S, Soft Package	195843	—	—	—	—	—	—	—	—
1899-O, Soft Package	76522	$70	75	80	160	260	390	—	—
1900-O, Hard Package	329335	—	—	—	—	—	—	—	—
↳1901-O, Soft Package	381671	—	—	—	—	—	—	—	—
1902-O, Soft Package	76523	—	—	—	2,500	2,500	—	—	—
1903-O	76524	—	—	—	1,250	1,250	—	—	—
1904-O, Soft Package	76525	—	—	—	2,500	2,500	—	—	—

Proof Strikes

	Mintage	GSID	PF-60	PF-63	PF-65
Morgan (1878–1921), Proof	**n/a**	**74167**	**$2,750**	**$4,050**	**$6,500**
Same, Proof Cameo	**n/a**	**74168**	**3,000**	**4,100**	**6,750**
Same, Proof Deep Cameo	**n/a**	**74169**	**4,250**	**7,000**	**12,000**
1878, 7 Tail Feathers, Reverse of 1878	250	7874	3,950	7,000	18,000
1878, 7 Tail Feathers, Reverse of 1879	*	7875	26,500	54,000	—
	Auctions: $155,250, NGC PF-64 DLRC 11/04				
1878, 8 Tail Feathers	500	7880	3,000	5,500	15,000
1879	1,100	7793	2,750	4,050	6,500
1880	1,355	7796	2,750	4,050	6,500
1881	984	7799	2,750	4,050	6,500
1882	1,100	7802	2,750	4,050	6,500
1883	1,039	7805	2,750	4,050	6,500
1884	875	7808	2,750	4,050	6,500
1885	930	7811	2,750	4,050	6,500
1886	886	7814	2,750	4,050	6,500
1887	710	7817	2,750	4,050	6,500
1888	833	7820	2,750	4,050	6,500
1889	811	7823	2,750	4,050	6,500
1890	590	7826	$2,750	$4,050	$6,500
1891	650	7829	2,750	4,050	6,500
1892	1,245	7832	2,750	4,050	6,500
1893	792	7835	2,750	4,050	6,500
1894	972	7838	2,800	4,200	6,500
1895 (a)	880	7841	60,000	69,000	89,000
	Auctions: $108,000, NGC PF-67 HA 08/25				
1896	762	7844	2,750	4,050	6,500
1897	731	7847	2,750	4,050	6,500
1898	735	7850	2,750	4,050	6,500
1899	846	7853	2,750	4,050	6,500
	Auctions: $126,500, NGC PF-69 HA 08/07				
1900	912	7856	2,750	4,050	6,500
1901	813	7859	2,750	4,050	7,000
1902	777	7862	2,750	4,050	6,500
1903	755	7865	2,750	4,050	6,500
1904	650	7868	2,750	4,050	6,500
1921, Chapman (b)		7872	29,000	48,000	120,000
	Auctions: $114,000, PCGS PF-65 HA 06/24; $240,000, PCGS PF-67 HA 06/24				
1921, Zerbe (c)		7871	5,000	12,000	21,500

* Included in number above. **a.** Beware of altered mintmark. Per Mint records, 12,000 Morgan dollars of 1895 were struck; only Proofs, many of them circulated, been seen, although there is no record of circulation strikes. **b.** Breen stated that 12 Chapman Proofs were minted (*Walter Breen's Encyclopedia of U.S. and Colonial Proof Coins, 1792–1977*); Bowers estimates fewer than 30 (*A Guide Book of Morgan Silver Dollars*, sixth edition). These are sometimes called *Chapman Proofs* because Philadelphia coin dealer Henry Chapman advertised them for sale within a few months of their production. **c.** From *A Guide Book of Morgan Silver Dollars* (sixth edition): "Pieces called Zerbe Proofs are simply circulation strikes with a semi-prooflike character, not as nice as on the earlier-noted [mirrorlike] prooflike pieces, struck from dies that were slightly polished, but that retained countless minute striae and preparation lines. In the view of the writer [Bowers], Zerbe Proofs have no basis in numismatic fact or history, although opinions differ on the subject. It seems highly unlikely that these were produced as Proofs for collectors. If indeed they were furnished to Farran Zerbe, a leading numismatic entrepreneur of the era, it is likely that they were simply regular production pieces. Zerbe had a fine collection and certainly knew what a brilliant Proof should look like, and he never would have accepted such pieces as mirror Proofs."

PEACE (1921–1935)

Designer: *Anthony de Francisci.* **Weight:** *26.73 grams.*
Composition: *.900 silver, .100 copper (net weight .77344 oz. pure silver).*
Diameter: *38.1 mm.* **Edge:** *Reeded.* **Mints:** *Philadelphia, Denver, and San Francisco.*

Circulation Strike

Mintmark location is on the reverse, to the left of the tail feathers.

Proof Strike

History. In 1921, following the melting of more than 270 million silver dollars as legislated by the Pittman Act of 1918, the U.S. Treasury struck millions more silver dollars of the Morgan type while a new Peace dollar was in development. Sculptor and medalist Anthony de Francisci created the Peace design, originally intended as a commemorative of the end of the hostilities of the Great War. The obverse features a flowing-haired Liberty wearing a spiked tiara, and the reverse an eagle perched before the rising sun. The designer's monogram is located in the field of the coin under the neck of Liberty. Coins of 1921 were struck in high relief; this caused weakness at the centers, so the design was changed to low relief in 1922. The dollars were struck until 1928, then again in 1934 and 1935. Legislation dated August 3, 1964, authorized the coinage of 45 million silver dollars, and 316,076 dollars of the Peace design dated 1964 were struck at the Denver Mint in 1965. Plans for completing this coinage were subsequently abandoned and all of these coins were melted. None were preserved or released for circulation; details are found in *A Guide Book of Peace Dollars* (Burdette).

Striking and Sharpness. Peace dollars of 1921 are always lightly struck at the center of the obverse, with hair detail not showing in an area. The size of this flat spot can vary. For this and other Peace dollars, check the hair detail at the center and, on the reverse, the feathers on the eagle. Many coins are struck from overly used dies, giving a grainy appearance to the fields, particularly the obverse. On many Peace dollars tiny white "milk spots" are seen, left over from when they were struck; these are not as desirable in the marketplace as unspotted coins.

Availability. All dates and mintmarks are readily available. Although some are well worn, they are generally collected in EF and finer grades. MS coins are available for each, with the 1934-S considered to be the key date. San Francisco issues of the 1920s, except for 1926-S, are often heavily bagmarked from coming into contact with other coins during shipment, storage, and other handling. The appearance of luster varies from issue to issue and can be deeply frosty, or—in the instance of Philadelphia Mint coins of 1928, 1934, and 1935—satiny or "creamy."

Proofs. Some Sandblast Proofs were made in 1921 and a limited issue in 1922 in high relief. These are rare today. Seemingly, a few Satin Proofs were also made in 1921. Sandblast Proofs of 1922 have a peculiar whitish surface in most instances, sometimes interrupted by small dark flecks or spots. There are a number of impostors among certified "Proofs."

Note: Values of common-date silver coins have been based on the current bullion price of silver, $45 per ounce, and may vary with the prevailing spot price.

Grading Standards

MS-64

MS-60 to 70 (Mint State). ***Obverse:*** At MS-60, some abrasion and contact marks are evident, most noticeably on the cheek and on the hair to the right of the face and forehead. Luster is present, but may be dull or lifeless. At MS-63, contact marks are extensive but not distracting. Abrasion still is evident, but less than at lower levels. MS-64 coins are slightly finer. Some Peace dollars have whitish "milk spots" in the field; while these are not caused by handling, but seem to have been from liquid at the mint or in storage, coins with these spots are rarely graded higher than MS-63 or 64. An MS-65 coin may have minor abrasion, but contact marks are so minute as to require magnification. Luster should be full and rich on earlier issues, and either frosty or satiny on later issues, depending on the date and mint. ***Reverse:*** At MS-60 some abrasion and contact marks are evident, most noticeably on the eagle's shoulder and nearby. Otherwise, comments apply as for the obverse.

Illustrated coin: Note the scattered marks that are practically definitive of the grade. The high relief of this particular year results in light striking at the center; this is normal and not to be mistaken for wear.

AU-53

AU-50, 53, 55, 58 (About Uncirculated). ***Obverse:*** Light wear is seen on the cheek and the highest-relief areas of the hair. The neck truncation edge also shows wear. At AU-58, the luster is extensive, but incomplete. At AU-50 and 53, luster is less but still present. ***Reverse:*** Wear is evident on the eagle's shoulder and back. Otherwise, comments apply as for the obverse.

Illustrated coin: This coin shows medium and somewhat mottled toning. Luster is still seen in protected areas.

EF-40

EF-40, 45 (Extremely Fine). ***Obverse:*** Further wear is seen on the highest-relief areas of the hair, with many strands now blended together. Some luster can usually be seen in protected areas on many coins, but is not needed to define the EF-40 and 45 grades. ***Reverse:*** Further wear is seen on the eagle, and the upper 60 percent of the feathers have most detail gone, except for the delineation of the edges of rows of feathers. PEACE shows light wear.

VF-20, 30 (Very Fine). ***Obverse:*** More wear shows on the hair, with more tiny strands now blended into heavy strands. ***Reverse:*** Further wear has resulted in very little feather detail except on the neck and tail. The rock shows wear. PEACE is slightly weak.

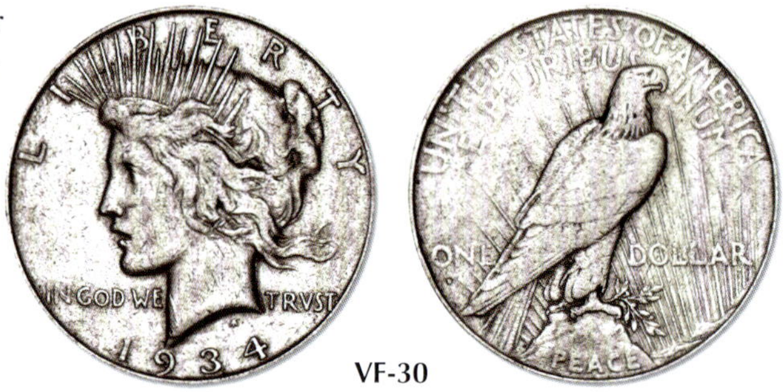

VF-30

F-12, 15 (Fine). ***Obverse:*** Most of the hair is worn flat, with thick strands blended together, interrupted by fewer divisions than on higher grades. The rim is full. ***Reverse:*** Fewer feather details show. Most of the eagle, except for the tail feathers and some traces of feathers at the neck, is in outline only. The rays between the left side of the eagle and PEACE are weak and some details are worn away.

F-12

PF-60 to 70 (Proof). ***Obverse and Reverse:*** Proofs of both types usually display very few handling marks or defects. To qualify as Satin PF-65 or Sandblast PF-65 or finer, contact marks must be microscopic.

Satin PF-64

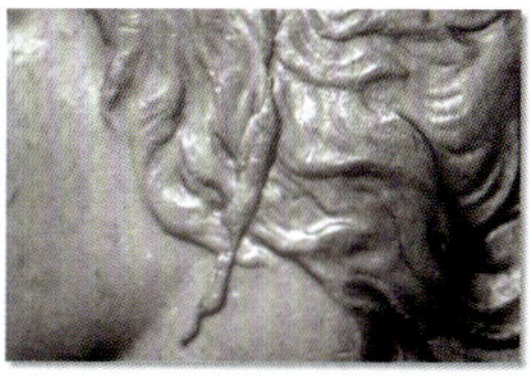

1922, Die Break at Ear
VAM-2A: Ear Ring

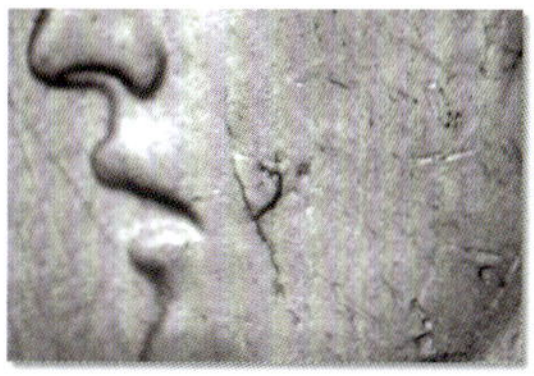

1922, Die Break on Cheek
VAM-5A: Scar Cheek

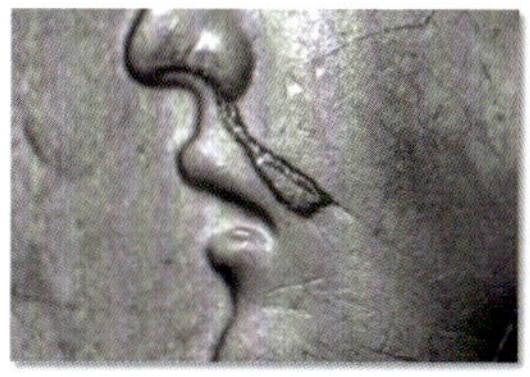

1922, Die Break at Nose
VAM-12A: Moustache

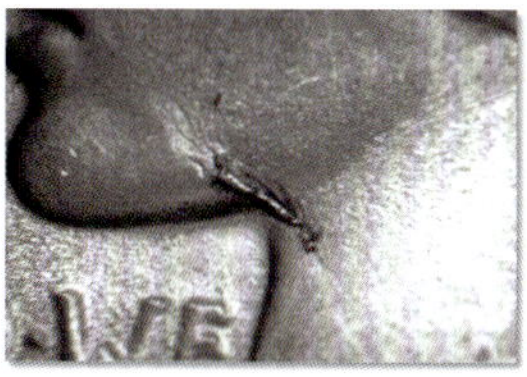

1923, Die Break at Jaw
VAM-1A: Whisker Jaw

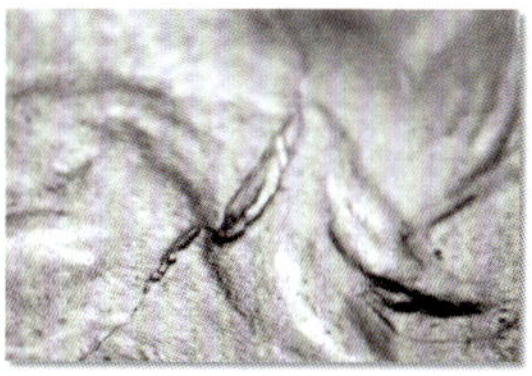

1923, Die Break in Hair
VAM-1B: Extra Hair

1923, Die Break on O in DOLLAR
VAM-1C: Tail on O

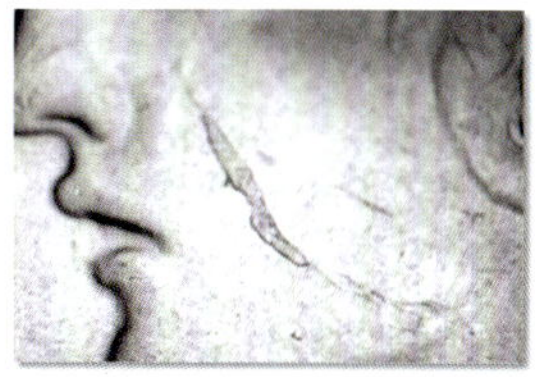

1923, Die Break on Cheek
VAM-1D: Whisker Cheek

Circulation Strikes

	Mintage	GSID	VF-20	EF-40	AU-50	MS-60	MS-63	MS-64	MS-65	MS-66
Peace (1921–1935)	**n/a**	**72407**	**$46**	**$46**	**$47**	**$49**	**$70**	**$85**	**$130**	**$550**
1921, High Relief	1,006,473	7887	160	215	260	600	1,100	1,500	2,900	9,000
	Auctions: $132,000, PCGS MS-67 SBG 08/18									
1922, Normal Relief	51,737,000	7889	46	46	47	49	70	85	130	550
↳1922, Earring, VAM-2A	*	25284	—	100	195	325	950	1,550	—	—
↳1922, Scar Cheek, VAM-5A	*	25290	—	80	100	170	360	775	1,150	—
↳1922, Tripled Die Reverse, Wing Break, VAM-5B	*	25295	—	—	—	—	—	—	—	—
↳1922, Moustache, VAM-12A	*	25294	—	—	100	195	390	775	—	—
1922-D	15,063,000	7899	46	46	47	55	130	240	600	1,350
1922-S	17,475,000	7900	46	46	47	70	115	290	1,250	21,500
↳1922-S, Reverse Rim Cud, VAM-2X	*	193581	—	—	—	—	—	—	—	—
1923	30,800,000	7891	46	46	47	49	70	85	130	550
↳1923, Whisker Jaw, VAM-1A1	*	25301	—	—	95	130	195	260	455	850
↳1923, Extra Hair, VAM-1B	*	25302	—	—	—	100	195	260	365	2,000
↳1923, Tail on O, VAM-1C	*	25303	—	—	145	260	525	1,500	2,000	—
↳1923, Whisker Cheek, VAM-1D	*	25304	—	70	80	115	155	495	1,400	—
1923-D	6,811,000	7901	46	49	70	130	290	420	1,100	3,900
	Auctions: $120,000, PCGS MS-67 HA 08/21									
↳1923-D, Reverse Rim Cud, VAM-1AZ	*	193590	—	—	—	—	—	—	—	—
↳1923-D, Doubled Eagle Head, VAM-2	*	351884	—	—	—	—	—	—	—	—
1923-S	19,020,000	7902	46	46	47	70	115	325	2,300	60,000

* Included in number above.

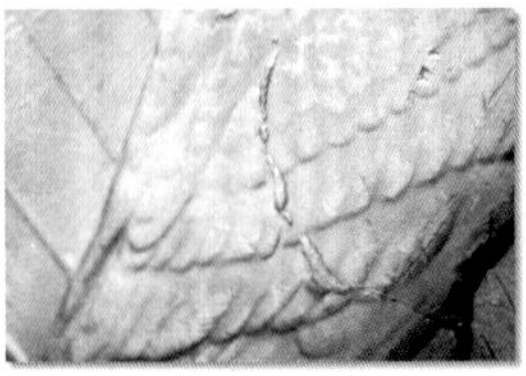

1924, Die Break on Wing
VAM-5A: Broken Wing

1926-S, Reverse Dot
VAM-4: Extra Berry

1934-D, Doubled Die Obverse, Small D
VAM-4

Circulation Strikes

	Mintage	GSID	VF-20	EF-40	AU-50	MS-60	MS-63	MS-64	MS-65	MS-66
1924	11,811,000	7892	$46	$46	$47	$49	$70	$85	$215	$550
↳**1924, Broken Wing, VAM-5A**	*	25315	—	—	80	130	210	390	725	1,150
1924-S	1,728,000	7903	55	65	100	325	725	1,300	7,000	48,000
1925	10,198,000	7893	46	46	47	49	70	85	135	550
1925-S	1,610,000	7904	50	60	75	160	420	825	19,000	90,000
	Auctions: $132,000, PCGS MS-65 HA 08/22									
1926	1,939,000	7894	46	49	60	95	160	360	575	1,750
	Auctions: $120,000, PCGS MS-67 HA 10/21									
1926-D	2,348,700	7905	46	49	70	180	440	550	1,150	2,400
1926-S	6,980,000	7906	46	46	70	120	230	405	975	2,500
↳**1926-S, Clashed E, VAM-1AF1**	*	373184	—	—	—	—	—	—	—	—
↳**1926-S, Dot Variety, VAM-4**	*	25323	—	—	95	180	290	485	1,150	3,000
1927	848,000	7895	50	65	80	155	310	600	1,500	24,000
1927-D	1,268,900	7907	50	80	120	340	900	1,300	3,250	31,000
	Auctions: $176,250, PCGS MS-66 LGND 03/19									
1927-S	866,000	7908	55	80	115	390	875	1,400	4,100	86,500
↳**1927-S, S Over S, VAM-4**	*	351885	—	—	—	—	—	—	—	—
1928	360,649	7896	310	330	360	575	1,000	1,100	3,600	21,000
	Auctions: $129,250, PCGS MS-66 LGND 04/23									
1928-S	1,632,000	7909	55	80	95	240	650	1,250	12,000	55,000
1934	954,057	7897	55	60	75	155	285	435	950	2,500
	Auctions: $108,000, PCGS MS-67 SBG 08/18									
1934-D (a)	1,569,500	7910	60	75	90	145	390	675	1,800	6,250
↳**1934-D, DDO, Medium D, VAM-3** (a)	*	25329	—	100	120	180	430	750	1,950	7,000
↳**1934-D, DDO, Micro D, VAM-4** (a)	*	25330	215	325	440	850	1,750	2,250	—	—
1934-S	1,011,000	7911	75	145	440	3,500	6,500	7,750	9,250	31,500
↳**1934-S, Doubled Tiara, VAM-3**	*	25331	95	180	525	3,850	7,250	8,500	9,250	—
1935	1,576,000	7898	55	70	80	155	245	370	775	2,600
1935-S (b)	1,964,000	7912	60	75	130	325	725	950	1,600	3,500

* Included in number above. **a.** Value is for variety with small mintmark on reverse. A second variety with larger, filled D mintmark is worth only about 20% more than the normal coin. **b.** Varieties exist with either three or four rays below ONE, and are of equal value.

Proof Strikes

		GSID	PF-60	PF-63	PF-65
1921, High Relief, Satin Finish	5–8 known	7888	$36,000	$72,000	$186,000
	Auctions: $264,000, NGC PF-66 SBG 02/25; $156,000, NGC PF-65 SBG 02/25				
1921, High Relief, Antique Finish	unique	377783	—	—	—
	Auctions: $129,250, PCGS MS-64 SBG 08/14				
1922, High Relief, Matte Finish	12 est. known	7890	60,000	120,000	210,000
	Auctions: $192,000, PCGS PF-63 HA 04/25; $460,200, PCGS PF-67 GLDB 04/25				
↳1922, High Relief, Matte Finish, FS-501	12 est. known	351883	60,000	120,000	210,000

Modern Dollars
1971 to Date

AN OVERVIEW OF MODERN DOLLARS

After the last Peace dollars rolled off the presses at the San Francisco and Philadelphia mints in 1935, there was a long lapse in silver dollar coinage until 1965. In that year the Denver Mint struck Peace dollars dated 1964—the start of production of 45 million coins authorized by legislation of August 3, 1964. This coinage ultimately was stopped after 316,076 of the new Peace dollars were made; they were held back from being released into circulation and melted. It would be another six years before the United States had a new dollar coin, and it would not be silver.

Scan for additional information.

Production of the next dollar started in 1971. The coin was the size of the twentieth century's earlier silver dollars, but made in copper-nickel for circulation (and, in much smaller quantities, in .400 fine silver for collectors). Its motifs honor the late President Dwight D. Eisenhower, and the Apollo 11 spaceflight that had landed the first men on the Moon in 1969. Silver dollars had long since disappeared from circulation, but there was demand for dollar coins in Las Vegas, Reno, and other centers of legalized gambling. Casinos otherwise had to depend on gaming chips and tokens.

The Eisenhower dollar was minted from 1971 to 1978, with those made in 1975 and 1976 being dual-dated 1776–1976 for the national bicentennial. In 1979 the "Ike" dollar was replaced by a smaller-format coin, the Susan B. Anthony dollar, honoring the famous women's-rights leader. Its reverse design shows an eagle landing on the Moon, similar to that of its predecessor (this design had in turn been based on the official insignia of the Apollo 11 mission). The Anthony dollar was struck in 1979, 1980, and 1981; then, in 1999 an additional final mintage of more than 40 million coins was produced to meet the needs of the vending-machine industry until distribution of the next year's new-design dollars could begin.

Presidential golden dollars cover the span from the 1st president of the United States, George Washington, to the 41st president, George H.W. Bush.

The year 2000 marked the debut of the first of several types of "golden" dollars, so called for the lustrous color of their manganese-brass surfaces. First came the Sacagawea dollar, minted from 2000 to 2008, with its conceptualized portrait of the young Shoshone Native American interpreter and guide who assisted the Lewis and Clark expedition of the early 1800s. A series of Native American dollars, each celebrating a different aspect of Native culture and historical importance, which began in 2009 and is ongoing today, is an offshoot of the Sacagawea dollar. And, since 2007, the golden-dollar format has been the canvas for a series of presidential portrait dollars honoring the nation's chief executives.

For the Collector and Investor: Modern Dollars as a Specialty

Eisenhower dollars, Susan B. Anthony dollars, and the golden dollars of various types are all easily found in today's marketplace. Dealers often have an abundance on hand of every date, mint, and most varieties. Banks sometimes have small quantities of Eisenhower or Anthony dollars. The current series are available directly from the U.S. Mint in collector formats and in rolls and bags of circulation strikes.

Eisenhower dollars are easily obtained in choice Mint State, although some of the coins made for circulation, especially of the earlier years, tend to be blemished with contact marks from jostling other coins during minting, transportation, and storage. Gems can be elusive. The Mint issued many options for collectors, including Proofs and .400 fine silver issues. Specialists look for die varieties including modified features, doubled dies, changes in depth of relief in the design, and other popular anomalies and variations that increase the challenge of building an extensive collection in what is otherwise a fairly short coinage series. Some Denver Mint dollars of 1974 and 1977 are also known to be struck in error, in silver clad composition rather than the intended copper-nickel.

Anthony dollars, too, are easy to assemble into a complete, high-grade collection of dates and mints. Specialists can focus on both varieties of 1979-P (Narrow Rim and Wide Rim), and varieties of S mintmark styles among the Proofs. Even these are common enough to easily acquire. Those seeking a harder challenge can search for the elusive 1980-S, Repunched Mintmark, Proof.

The Sacagawea dollar series includes several uncommon varieties that make an otherwise easy-to-collect type more challenging. The 2000-P coins include popular die varieties as detailed herein. Later dates were struck in smaller quantities and not issued for circulation, but still are readily available in high grades in the numismatic marketplace.

Native American dollars of 2009 to date are readily available in high grades.

The Presidential dollar series includes some error varieties with plain edges, instead of the normal lettered edge. These can be added to a date-and-mintmark collection for reasonable premiums. Otherwise the entire series is readily collectible from the secondary market and, for the current year of issue, in quantity directly from the U.S. Mint.

EISENHOWER (1971–1978)

Designer: *Frank Gasparro.* **Weight:** *Silver issue—24.59 grams; copper-nickel issue—22.68 grams.* **Composition:** *Silver issue—a core of .209 silver and .791 copper, clad in outer layers of .800 silver, .200 copper (net weight .3161 oz. pure silver); copper-nickel issue—a core of pure copper, clad in outer layers of copper-nickel (.750 copper, .250 nickel).* **Diameter:** *38.1 mm.* **Edge:** *Reeded.* **Mints:** *Philadelphia, Denver, and San Francisco.*

Circulation Strike

Proof Strike

Mintmark location is on the obverse, between the bust and the date.

Bicentennial variety: **Designers:** *Frank Gasparro and Dennis R. Williams.* **Weight:** *Silver issue—24.59 grams; copper-nickel issue—22.68 grams.* **Composition:** *Silver issue—a core of .209 silver, .791 copper, clad in outer layers of .800 silver, .200 copper (net weight .3161 oz. pure silver); copper-nickel issue—a core of pure copper, clad in outer layers of copper-nickel (.750 copper, .250 nickel).* **Diameter:** *38.1 mm.* **Edge:** *Reeded.* **Mints:** *Philadelphia, Denver, and San Francisco.*

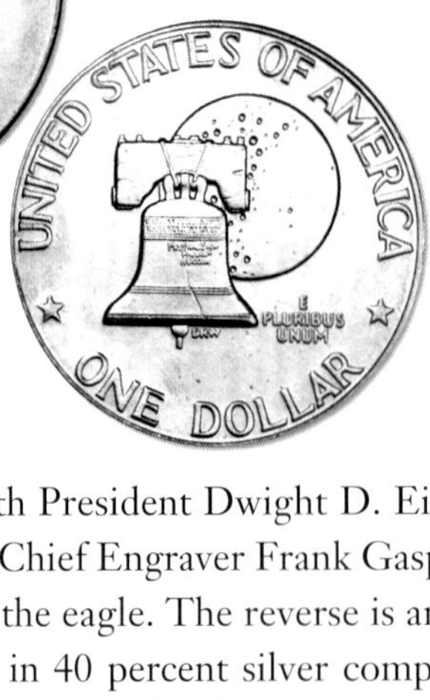

Bicentennial Variety, Circulation Strike

Bicentennial Variety, Proof Strike

History. Honoring both President Dwight D. Eisenhower and the first landing of man on the Moon, this coin is the work of Chief Engraver Frank Gasparro, whose initials are on the truncation of the president's neck and below the eagle. The reverse is an adaptation of the official Apollo 11 insignia. Collectors' coins were struck in 40 percent silver composition and sold by the Mint at a premium, and the circulation issue (for years a staple of the casino trade) was made in copper-nickel.

The dies for the Eisenhower dollar were modified several times by changing the relief, strengthening the design, and making Earth (above the eagle) more clearly defined.

Low-relief (Variety 1) dies, with a flattened Earth and three islands off the coast of Florida, were used for all copper-nickel issues of 1971, Uncirculated silver coins of 1971, and most copper-nickel coins of 1972.

High-relief (Variety 2) dies, with a round Earth and weak or indistinct islands, were used for all Proofs of 1971, all silver issues of 1972, and the reverse of some exceptional and scarce Philadelphia copper-nickel coins of 1972.

Improved high-relief reverse dies (Variety 3) were used for late-1972 Philadelphia copper-nickel coins and for all subsequent issues. Modified high-relief dies were also used on all issues beginning in 1973.

A few 1974-D and 1977-D dollars were made, in error, in silver clad composition.

A special reverse design was selected for the nation's Bicentennial. Nearly a thousand entries were submitted after the Treasury announced an open competition in October 1973. After the field was narrowed down to 12 semifinalists, the judges chose a rendition of the Liberty Bell superimposed on the Moon to appear on the dollar coins. The obverse remained unchanged except for the dual date 1776–1976, which appeared on all dollars made during 1975 and 1976. These dual-dated coins were included in the various offerings of Proof and Uncirculated coins made by the Mint. They were also struck for general circulation. The lettering was slightly modified early in 1975 to produce a more attractive design.

Striking and Sharpness. Striking generally is very good. For circulation strikes, on the obverse check the high parts of the portrait, and on the reverse, the details of the eagle. Nearly all Proofs are well struck and of high quality.

Availability. MS coins are common in the marketplace, although several early varieties are elusive at MS-65 or higher grades. Lower grades are not widely collected. Proofs were made of the various issues (both copper-nickel clad and silver clad from 1971 to 1976; copper-nickel only in 1977 and 1978). All are readily available in the marketplace today.

Note: Values of common-date silver coins have been based on the current bullion price of silver, $45 per ounce, and may vary with the prevailing spot price.

Grading Standards

MS-65

MS-60 to 70 (Mint State). ***Obverse:*** At MS-60, some abrasion and contact marks are evident, most noticeably on the cheek, jaw, and temple. Luster is present, but may be dull or lifeless. At MS-63, contact marks are extensive but not distracting. Abrasion still is evident, but less than at lower levels. MS-64 coins are slightly finer. An MS-65 coin may have minor abrasion, but contact marks are so minute as to require magnification. Luster should be full and rich. ***Reverse:*** At MS-60, some abrasion and contact marks are evident, most noticeably on the eagle's breast, head, and talons. Otherwise, the same comments apply as for the obverse.

AU-50, 53, 55, 58 (About Uncirculated). ***Obverse:*** Light wear is seen on the higher-relief areas of the portrait. At AU-58, the luster is extensive, but incomplete. At AU-50 and 53, luster is less but still present. ***Reverse:*** Further wear is evident on the eagle, particularly the head, breast, talons, and tops of the wings. Otherwise, the same comments apply as for the obverse.

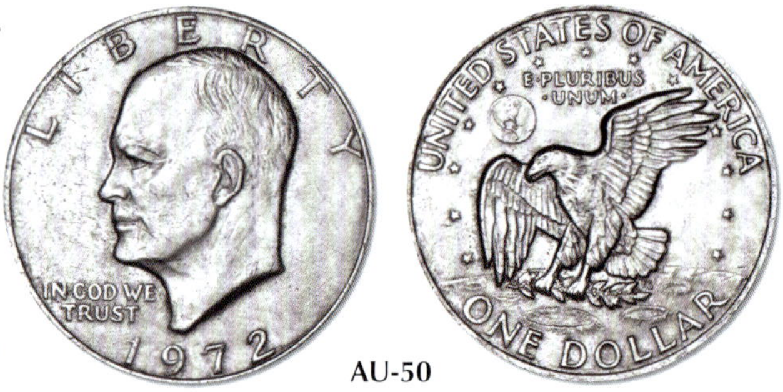

AU-50

PF-60 to 70 (Proof). ***Obverse and Reverse:*** Proofs that are extensively cleaned and have many hairlines, or that are dull and grainy, are lower level, such as PF-60 to 62. There are not many of these in the marketplace. With medium hairlines and good reflectivity, assigned grades of PF-63 or 64 are appropriate. With relatively few hairlines a rating of PF-65 can be given. PF-66 may have hairlines so delicate that magnification is needed to see them. Above that, a Proof should be free of any hairlines or other problems.

PF-68

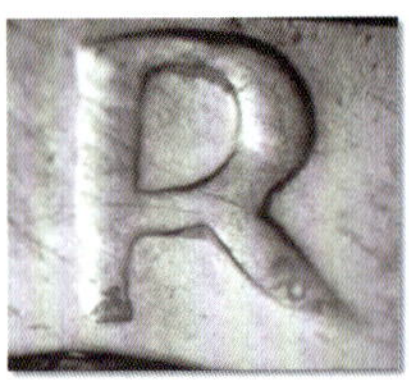

1971-S, Silver Clad, Polished Die
FS-401: Peg Leg R

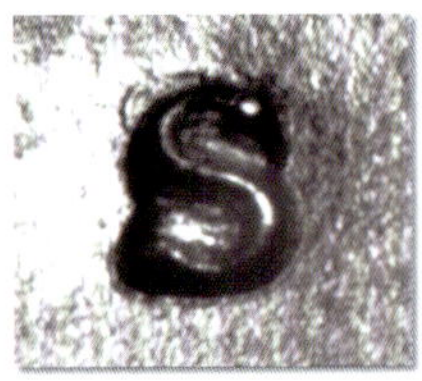

1971-S, Silver Clad, S Over S
FS-501

Circulation Strikes

	Mintage	GSID	MS-63	MS-65	MS-67
Eisenhower (1971–1978)	**n/a**	**376575**	**$4.10**	**$16**	**$32**
Eisenhower, Silver Clad (1971–1974)	**n/a**	**376878**	**19.50**	**20**	**27**
1971	47,799,000	7913	4.10	90	600
1971-D	68,587,424	7923	9.50	27	60
↳1971-D, Variety 1	68,587,424	374424	70.00	195	650
↳1971-D, Variety 2 (a)	*	374425	9.50	27	60
↳1971-D, Peg Leg, FS-401	*	351886	13.50	40	100
↳1971-D, Friendly Eagle, FS-901	*	226385	47.00	260	470
1971-S, Silver Clad	6,868,530	7924	21.00	24	31
↳1971-S, Silver Clad, Peg Leg, FS-401	*	298949	47.00	145	360
↳1971-S, S Over S, Silver Clad, FS-501	*	298950	38.00	110	245
1972, Variety 1	75,890,000	7915	12.00	95	2,500
1972, Variety 2	*	7916	120.00	1,600	8,250
↳1972, Variety 2, FS-901	*	298951	130.00	1,600	8,250
1972, Variety 3	*	7914	11.00	80	1,500

* Included in number above. **a.** Modified with accented crater lines.

Circulation Strikes *(continued)*

	Mintage	GSID	MS-63	MS-65	MS-67
1972-D	92,548,511	7925	$6.75	$20	$130
↳1972-D, Peg Leg, FS-401	*	351888	13.50	34	130
1972-S, Silver Clad	2,193,056	7926	21.00	27	34
1973 (b)	2,000,056	7917	5.50	55	495
1973-D (b)	2,000,000	7927	9.50	24	245
1973-S, Silver Clad	1,883,140	7928	20.00	20	30
1974	27,366,000	7918	4.10	55	155
1974-D	45,517,000	7929	4.10	24	75
↳1974-D, Peg Leg, FS-401	*	351889	11.00	38	130
↳1974-D, Goiter, FS-402	*	351890	16.00	50	155
1974-S, Silver Clad	1,900,156	7930	20.00	20	27
1776–1976, Variety 1	4,019,000	7919	5.50	110	1,100
1776–1976, Variety 2	113,318,000	7920	4.10	16	70
1776–1976-D, Variety 1	21,048,710	7931	4.10	40	115
↳1776–1976-D, Variety 1, Peg Leg, FS-401	*	351891	13.50	70	175
1776–1976-D, Variety 2	82,179,564	7932	4.10	20	75
1776–1976-S, Silver Clad, Variety 1	11,000,000	7933	20.00	24	35
1977	12,596,000	7921	4.10	27	32
1977-D	32,983,006	7934	4.10	30	70
1978	25,702,000	7922	4.10	24	80
↳1978, Clashed Die Obverse U, FS-402	*	351893	70.00	195	390
1978-D	33,012,890	7935	4.10	32	130
↳1978-D, Peg Leg, FS-401	*	351894	13.50	55	170

* Included in number above. **b.** 1,769,258 of each sold only in sets and not released for circulation. Unissued coins destroyed at mint.

1971-S, Silver Clad, Doubled Die Obverse, Proof

Proof Strikes

	Mintage	GSID	PF-68	PF-69	PF-70
Eisenhower, Clad (1971–1978), Proof	**n/a**	**376577**	**$13.50**	**$19**	**$325**
Eisenhower, Silver Clad (1971–1978), Proof	**n/a**	**376576**	**21.00**	**30**	**260**
1971-S, Silver Clad	4,265,234	373143	22.00	40	390
↳1971-S, Silver Clad, Doubled Die Obverse, FS-103	*	373144	455.00	1,750	—
↳1971-S, Silver Clad, Doubled Die Reverse, FS-801	*	351897	8,000.00	12,000	—
1971-S, Silver Clad, Variety 1 Reverse, FS-901	10 est. known	7939	36,000.00	—	—
1972-S, Silver Clad	1,811,631	7942	22.00	32	360
1973-S	2,760,339	7946	16.00	30	2,250
1973-S, Silver Clad	1,013,646	7948	32.00	43	625
↳1973-S, Silver Clad, Peg Leg, FS-401	*	351901	130.00	525	—
1974-S	2,612,568	7952	16.00	24	5,500
1974-S, Silver Clad	1,306,579	7954	23.00	80	575
1776–1976-S, Variety 1 (a)	2,845,450	7959	16.00	24	3,750
1976-S, Variety 2	4,149,730	7961	16.00	24	1,500
1776–1976-S, Silver Clad, Variety 1 (b)	4,000,000	7963	32.00	43	725
1776–1976, No S, Silver Clad, Variety 2	1 known	275425	—	—	—
1977-S	3,251,152	7966	16.00	24	435
1978-S	3,127,781	7969	16.00	24	340

* Included in number above. **a.** Only issued in Mint sets. **b.** Mintage is approximate.

SUSAN B. ANTHONY (1979–1999)

Designer: *Frank Gasparro.* **Weight:** *8.1 grams.*
Composition: *A core of pure copper, clad in outer layers of copper-nickel (.750 copper, .250 nickel).* **Diameter:** *26.5 mm.*
Edge: *Reeded.* **Mints:** *Philadelphia, Denver, and San Francisco.*

Circulation Strike

Mintmark location is on the obverse, above the left tip of the bust.

Proof Strike

History. The Susan B. Anthony dollar was designed by Frank Gasparro, chief engraver of the U.S. Mint, following a congressional mandate. It features a portrait of the famous suffragette, along with an eagle-and-Moon motif reduced from the coin's larger predecessor, the Eisenhower dollar. Legislators hoped that these so-called mini-dollars would be an efficient substitute for paper dollars, which wear much more quickly in circulation. A large mintage in 1979 was followed by smaller quantities in 1980 and 1981, and then a hiatus of almost 20 years. The coins were not popular in circulation, with some members of the public complaining that they were too easily confused with the similarly sized quarter dollar. A final coinage of Anthony dollars was struck in 1999—a stopgap measure to ensure the Treasury's supply of dollar coins before the Sacagawea dollar was launched in 2000.

Striking and Sharpness. Most are well struck, but check the highest areas of both sides.

Availability. Susan B. Anthony dollars are readily available in MS, although those of 1981 are less common than those of 1979 and 1980. Circulated coins are not widely sought by collectors. Proofs were made of all issues and are readily available today.

Grading Standards

MS-65

MS-60 to 70 (Mint State). ***Obverse:*** At MS-60, some abrasion and contact marks are evident, most noticeably on the cheek and upper center of the hair. Luster is present, but may be dull or lifeless. At MS-63, contact marks are extensive but not distracting. Abrasion still is evident, but less than at lower levels. MS-64 coins are slightly finer. An MS-65 coin may have minor abrasion, but contact marks are so minute as to require magnification. Luster should be full and rich. ***Reverse:*** At MS-60, some abrasion and contact marks are evident, most noticeably on the eagle's breast, head, and talons. Otherwise, the same comments apply as for the obverse.

AU-50

AU-50, 53, 55, 58 (About Uncirculated). ***Obverse:*** Light wear is seen on the higher-relief areas of the portrait. At AU-58, the luster is extensive but incomplete. At AU-50 and 53, luster is less but still present. ***Reverse:*** Further wear is evident on the eagle, particularly the head, breast, talons, and tops of the wings. Otherwise, the same comments apply as for the obverse.

PF-70
Deep Cameo

PF-60 to 70 (Proof). ***Obverse and Reverse:*** Proofs that are extensively cleaned and have many hairlines, or that are dull and grainy, are lower level, such as PF-60 to 62. This comment is more theoretical than practical, as nearly all Proofs have been well kept. With medium hairlines and good reflectivity, assigned grades of PF-63 or 64 are appropriate. With relatively few hairlines a rating of PF-65 can be given. PF-66 may have hairlines so delicate that magnification is needed to see them. Above that, all the way to PF-70, a Proof should be free of any hairlines or other problems under strong magnification.

1979-P, Narrow Rim
Also known as Far Date

1979-P, Wide Rim
Also known as Near Date

Circulation Strikes

	Mintage	GSID	PF-68	PF-69	PF-69	PF-70
Susan B. Anthony (1979–1999)	**n/a**	**375028**	**$2.60**	**$6.75**	**$15**	**$38**
1979-P, Narrow Rim (a)	360,222,000	7971	2.60	6.75	24	50
1979-P, Wide Rim (a)	*	7972	19.00	22.00	70	1,900
1979-D	288,015,744	7970	2.60	6.75	24	70
1979-S	109,576,000	7973	3.40	16.00	30	160
1980-P	27,610,000	7978	2.60	8.00	20	110
1980-D	41,628,708	7977	2.60	9.50	22	290
1980-S	20,422,000	7979	2.60	13.50	35	525
1981-P (b)	3,000,000	7982	2.60	20.00	32	1,400
1981-D (b)	3,250,000	7981	4.10	22.00	35	340
1981-S (b)	3,492,000	7983	2.60	22.00	245	6,500
1999-P	29,592,000	7987	5.50	6.75	15	70
1999-D	11,776,000	7986	5.50	8.00	19	38

* Included in number above. **a.** The obverse design was modified in 1979 to widen the border rim. Late issues of 1979-P and subsequent issues have the wide rim. Dies for the 1999 coins were further modified to strengthen details on the reverse. **b.** Issued only in Mint Sets.

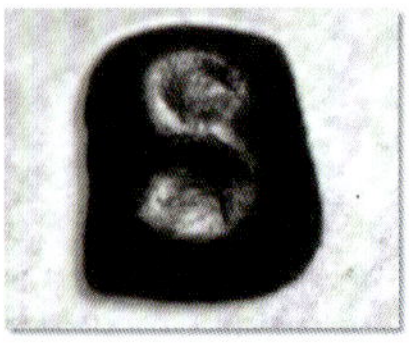
1979-S, Filled S (Variety 1), Proof

1979-S, Clear S (Variety 2), Proof

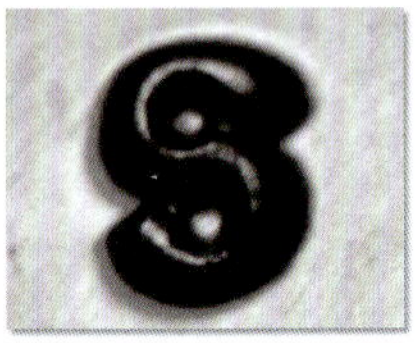
1981-S, Rounded S (Variety 1), Proof

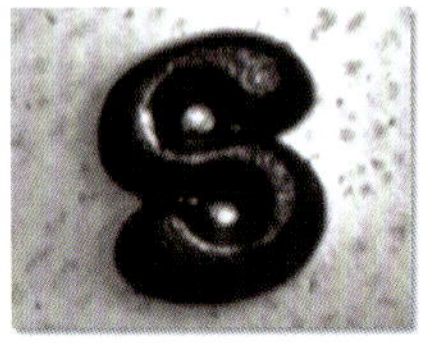
1981-S, Flat S (Variety 2), Proof

Proof Strikes

	Mintage	GSID	PF-68	PF-69	PF-70
Susan B. Anthony (1979–1999), Proof	**n/a**	**376578**	**$8**	**$11**	**$40**
1979-S, Variety 1	3,677,175	7975	10	16	55
1979-S, Variety 2	*	7976	32	35	160
1980-S	3,554,806	7980	8	11	40
↳1980-S, S Over S, FS-501	*	351903	55	80	—
1981-S, Variety 1	4,063,083	7984	8	11	55
1981-S, Variety 2	*	7985	90	95	360
↳1981-S, Variety 2, FS-501	*	394003	—	—	—
1999-P	750,000	7988	27	32	130

* Included in number above.

SACAGAWEA (2000–2008, 2025)

Designers: *Glenna Goodacre (obverse), Thomas D. Rogers Sr. (reverse).* **Weight:** *Golden issue—8.1 grams; gold issue—.5 ounce.* **Composition:** *Golden issue—a core of pure copper, clad in outer layers of manganese-brass (.770 copper, .120 zinc, .070 manganese, .040 nickel); Gold issue—.999 gold (net weight 0.5 oz. pure gold).* **Diameter:** *26.5 mm.* **Edge:** *Plain.* **Mints:** *Philadelphia, Denver, San Francisco, and West Point; 22-karat gold experimental specimens dated 2000-W were struck at West Point in 1999.*

Circulation Strike

Mintmark location is on the obverse, below the date.

Proof Strike

History. The Sacagawea dollar was launched in 2000, with a distinctive golden color and a plain edge to distinguish it from other denominations or coins of similar size. (One complaint leveled against the Susan B. Anthony dollar was that it too closely resembled the quarter dollar; both were silvery, with reeded edges, and with only about two millimeters' difference in diameter.) The new coinage alloy and the change in appearance were mandated by the United States Dollar Coin Act of 1997. The core of the coin is pure copper, and the golden outer layer is of manganese brass. The obverse shows a modern artist's conception of Sacagawea, the Shoshone Indian who assisted the Lewis and Clark expedition, and her infant son, Jean Baptiste. (No known contemporary portraits of them exist.) The reverse shows an eagle in flight.

In 1999, about a dozen Sacagawea dollars were struck in 22-karat gold at the West Point Mint, as experimental or presentation pieces. These featured a prototype reverse design with boldly detailed tail feathers on the eagle. The following year, a small number of early circulation strikes from the Philadelphia Mint also featured that same prototype design. These are popularly called "Cheerio" dollars, as the coins were packaged as a promotion in boxes of Cheerios cereal (their unusual nature was not recognized at the time). Today collectors seek them as rare and desirable varieties.

In addition to the regular Uncirculated or Mint State coins produced in large quantities, smaller numbers of Satin Finish dollars were made of the 2005 to 2008 years, Philadelphia and Denver mints. Sold at an additional premium, most of these exist today in grades of MS-67 and upward and are designated SP (Specimen) or SMS (Special Mint Set) by the commercial grading services.

Several distinct finishes can be identified on the Sacagawea dollars as a result of the Mint's attempts to adjust the dies, blanks, strikes, or finishing to produce coins with minimal spotting and better surface color. One group of 5,000 pieces, dated 2000 and with a special finish, was presented to sculptor Glenna Goodacre in payment for the obverse design. These have since entered the numismatic market and command a significant premium.

Another peculiarity in the Sacagawea series is a numismatic mule (a coin made from mismatched dies)—the combination of an undated State quarter obverse and a Sacagawea dollar reverse. Examples of this error are extremely rare.

Striking and Sharpness. Most are very well struck. Weakness sometimes is evident on the higher design points. Special issues are uniformly sharply struck.

Availability. These coins are common in high grades, and are usually collected in MS and Proof.

Grading Standards

MS-60 to 70 (Mint State). ***Obverse:*** At MS-60, some abrasion and contact marks are evident, most noticeably on the cheekbone and the drapery near the baby's head. Luster is present, but may be dull or lifeless. At MS-63, contact marks are extensive but not distracting. Abrasion still is evident, but less than at lower levels. MS-64 coins are slightly finer. An MS-65 coin may have minor abrasion, but contact marks are so minute as to require magnification. Luster should be full and rich. ***Reverse:*** At MS-60, some abrasion and contact marks are evident, most noticeably on the eagle's breast. Otherwise, the same comments apply as for the obverse.

MS-65

AU-50, 53, 55, 58 (About Uncirculated). ***Obverse:*** Light wear is seen on cheekbone, drapery, and elsewhere. At AU-58, the luster is extensive, but incomplete. At AU-50 and 53, luster is less but still present. ***Reverse:*** Further wear is evident on the eagle. Otherwise, the same comments apply as for the obverse.

AU-55

PF-60 to 70 (Proof). ***Obverse and Reverse:*** Proofs that are extensively cleaned and have many hairlines, or that are dull and grainy, are lower level, such as PF-60 to 62. This comment is more theoretical than practical, as nearly all Proofs have been well kept. With medium hairlines and good reflectivity, assigned grades of PF-63 or 64 are appropriate. With relatively few hairlines a rating of PF-65 can be given. PF-66 may have hairlines so delicate that magnification is needed to see them. Above that, all the way to PF-70, a Proof should be free of any hairlines or other problems under strong magnification.

PF-69

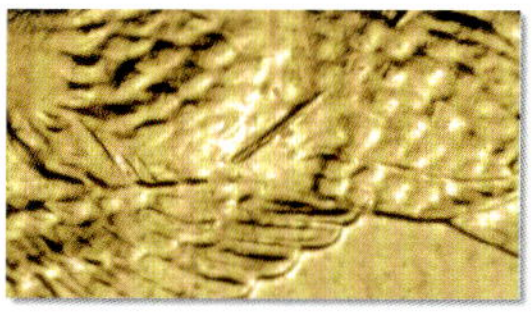

2000-P, Reverse Die Aberrations
FS-901: Wounded Eagle

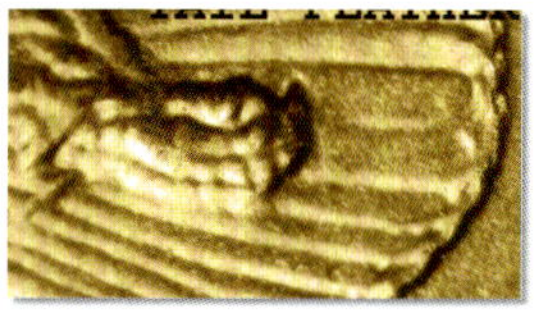

2000-P, Normal Feathers

2000-P, Boldly Detailed Tail Feathers

Circulation Strikes

	Mintage	GSID	MS-63	MS-65	MS-67
Sacagawea (2000–2008)	**n/a**	**82168**	**$3.00**	**$3.20**	**$5.50**
2000-P	767,140,000	7992	3.00	3.20	5.50
↳**2000-P, Speared Jaw, FS-401**	*	351904	4.40	4.50	9.50
↳**2000-P, Wounded Eagle, FS-901**	*	340427	210.00	390.00	900.00
2000-P, Cheerios (Boldly Detailed Tail Feathers) (a)	5,500	81740	1,000.00	2,050.00	6,500.00
↳**2000-P, Cheerios, FS-901** (a)	*	351905	1,000.00	2,050.00	6,500.00
2000-P, Goodacre Presentation Finish	5,000	7991	260.00	340.00	550.00
2000-D	518,916,000	7990	3.00	3.20	20.00
2001-P	62,468,000	7996	3.00	3.20	8.00
2001-D	70,939,500	7995	3.00	3.20	23.00
2002-P (b)	3,865,610	7999	3.00	3.20	8.00
2002-D (b)	3,732,000	7998	$3.00	$3.20	$22.00
2003-P (b)	3,080,000	8002	3.00	3.20	13.50
2003-D (b)	3,080,000	8001	3.00	3.20	27.00
2004-P (b)	2,660,000	8005	3.00	3.20	8.00
2004-D (b)	2,660,000	8004	3.00	3.20	13.50
2005-P (b)	2,520,000	69166	3.00	3.20	22.00
2005-P, Satin	1,160,000	24973	3.40	3.80	8.00
2005-D (b)	2,520,000	69167	3.00	3.20	80.00
2005-D, Satin	1,160,000	24974	3.40	3.80	8.00
2006-P (b)	4,900,000	68434	3.00	3.20	20.00
2006-P, Satin	847,631	69437	3.40	3.80	8.00
2006-D (b)	2,800,000	68431	3.00	5.50	80.00
2006-D, Satin	847,631	198231	3.40	3.80	8.00
2007-P (b)	3,640,000	69029	3.00	3.20	11.00
2007-P, Satin	895,628	69347	3.40	3.80	8.00
2007-D (b)	3,920,000	68984	3.00	3.20	27.00
2007-D, Satin	895,628	68985	3.40	3.80	8.00
2008-P (b)	1,820,000	69030	3.20	3.40	13.50
2008-P, Satin	745,464	69434	3.40	3.80	8.00
2008-D (b)	1,820,000	69031	3.20	3.40	20.00
2008-D, Satin	745,464	69433	3.40	3.80	8.00

Note: Satin Finish coins of 2005 through 2010 were produced for the annual Uncirculated Mint Sets, which were available only with the special finish during those years. * Included in number above. **a.** Released as a promotion with the breakfast cereal Cheerios, this variety was not noted as distinct until years later. About 100 are known today. **b.** Not issued for circulation. The U.S. Mint produced circulation-quality Sacagawea dollar coins at its Philadelphia and Denver facilities from 2002 to 2008. These were never issued for circulation through banks, but were made available to the general public by direct sales from the Mint.

Proof Strikes

	Mintage	GSID	PF-68	PF-69	PF-70
Sacagawea (2000–2008), Proof	**n/a**	**376579**	**$7.50**	**$8**	**$20**
2000-S	4,074,904	7994	7.50	8	40
2001-S	3,183,740	7997	12.00	13	25
2002-S	3,211,995	8000	7.50	8	20
2003-S	3,298,439	8003	7.50	8	24
2004-S	2,965,422	8006	7.50	8	20
2005-S	3,344,679	24972	$7.50	$8	$20
2006-S	3,054,436	65354	7.50	8	21
2007-S	2,577,166	69099	8.50	9	21
2008-S	2,169,561	69243	15.00	16	75
2025-W, 25th Anniversary Golden Dollar, $1, 1/2 oz., Gold		393716	—	2,950	3,150

PRESIDENTIAL (2007–2020)

Designers: *See below for obverse designers; Don Everhart (reverse).* **Weight:** *8.1 grams.* **Composition:** *A core of pure copper, clad in outer layers of manganese-brass (.770 copper, .120 zinc, .070 manganese, .040 nickel).* **Diameter:** *26.5 mm.* **Edge:** *Lettered.* **Mints:** *Philadelphia, Denver, and San Francisco.*

Obverse Designers:

2007, George Washington	Joseph Menna
2007, John Adams	Joel Iskowitz
2007, Thomas Jefferson	Joseph Menna
2007, James Madison	Joel Iskowitz
2008, James Monroe	Joseph Menna
2008, John Quincy Adams	Don Everhart
2008, Andrew Jackson	Joel Iskowitz
2008, Martin Van Buren	Joel Iskowitz
2009, William H. Harrison	Joseph Menna
2009, John Tyler	Phebe Hemphill
2009, James K. Polk	Susan Gamble
2009, Zachary Taylor	Don Everhart
2010, Millard Fillmore	Don Everhart
2010, Franklin Pierce	Susan Gamble
2010, James Buchanan	Phebe Hemphill
2010, Abraham Lincoln	Don Everhart
2011, Andrew Johnson	Don Everhart
2011, Ulysses S. Grant	Don Everhart
2011, Rutherford B. Hayes	Don Everhart
2011, James Garfield	Phebe Hemphill
2012, Chester Arthur	Don Everhart
2012, Grover Cleveland, First Term	Don Everhart
2012, Benjamin Harrison	Phebe Hemphill
2012, Grover Cleveland, Second Term	Don Everhart
2013, William McKinley	Phebe Hemphill
2013, Theodore Roosevelt	Joseph Menna
2013, William Howard Taft	Barbara Fox
2013, Woodrow Wilson	Don Everhart
2014, Warren Harding	Michael Gaudioso
2014, Calvin Coolidge	Phebe Hemphill
2014, Herbert Hoover	Phebe Hemphill
2014, Franklin. Roosevelt	Joseph Menna
2015, Harry S. Truman	Don Everhart
2015, Dwight Eisenhower	Joseph Menna
2015, John F. Kennedy	Don Everhart
2015, Lyndon Johnson	Michael Gaudioso
2016, Richard M. Nixon	Don Everhart
2016, Gerald R. Ford	Phebe Hemphill
2016, Ronald Reagan	Richard Masters
2020, George H.W. Bush	Elana Hagler

Obverse Style, 2007–2008, Circulation Strike
No motto on obverse.

Obverse Style, 2009–2020, Circulation Strike
Motto beneath portrait.

Common Reverse, Circulation Strike

Proof Strike

Date, Mintmark, and Mottos Incused on Edge

History. Presidential dollars debuted in 2007 and were issued at the rate of four designs per year through 2015, with the program's three final coins issued in 2016. The series started with George Washington and continued in order of office. Living presidents were ineligible, so the program ended with Ronald Reagan. Each coin has a common reverse showing the Statue of Liberty. The series began with the date, mintmark, and mottos IN GOD WE TRUST and E PLURIBUS UNUM incused on the edge of the coins; in 2009 IN GOD WE TRUST was moved from the edge to the obverse after some public criticism of the "Godless dollars." In 2020 the original program was expanded to include George H.W. Bush, who died in 2018.

In December 2011, Secretary of the Treasury Timothy Geithner directed that the U.S. Mint suspend minting and issuing circulating Presidential dollars. "Regular circulating demand for the coins will be met through the Federal Reserve Bank's existing inventory of circulating coins minted prior to 2012," the Mint announced. Collector formats, however, continued to be issued.

In addition to the regular Uncirculated or Mint State coins produced in large quantities, smaller numbers of Satin Finish dollars were made of the 2007 to 2010 years, Philadelphia and Denver Mints. Sold at an additional premium, most of these exist today in grades of MS-67 and upward and are designated SP (Specimen) or SMS (Special Mint Set) by the commercial grading services. Catching collectors, dealers, and others by surprise, the Coin and Chronicles sets of Presidential dollars were introduced in 2015. A small number of additional (to the regular Uncirculated) coins were made with Reverse Proof finish and sold at a sharp premium as part of Coin and Chronicles sets, which also included a brochure and a medal. Most collectors desired only the dollar. The Eisenhower and Truman sets, the first offered, sold out quickly, leaving many Mint clients disappointed. Letters of protest filled the columns of Coin World and Numismatic News when the only option to secure them seemed to be paying double or triple issue price on eBay and other venues. These were carefully produced, and nearly all grade MS-68 to 70. "First strike" and other notations on holders add little or nothing to the resale value of these or other modern coins.

Some Presidential dollars were inadvertently struck with the edge lettering missing. A 2009-D, John Tyler, variety has the wrong date, 2010, on the edge.

Striking and Sharpness. These usually are well struck, but check the higher-relief parts of each side. Special issues are uniformly sharp.

Availability. Presidential dollars are very common in MS. Most have from a few to many bagmarks, with true MS-65 and better coins in the minority.

Grading Standards

MS-60 to 70 (Mint State). ***Obverse:*** At MS-60, some abrasion and contact marks are evident, most noticeably on the highest-relief areas of the portrait, the exact location varying with the president depicted. Luster is present, but may be dull or lifeless. At MS-63, contact marks are extensive but not distracting. Abrasion still is evident, but less than at lower levels. MS-64 coins are slightly finer. An MS-65 coin may have minor abrasion, but contact marks are so minute as to require magnification. Luster should be full and rich. ***Reverse:*** At MS-60, some abrasion and contact marks are evident, most noticeably on the cheek and arm. Otherwise, the same comments apply as for the obverse.

MS-68

AU-50, 53, 55, 58 (About Uncirculated). ***Obverse:*** Light wear is seen on the portrait, most prominently on the higher-relief areas. At AU-58, the luster is extensive, but incomplete. At AU-50 and 53, luster is less, but still is present. ***Reverse:*** Further wear is evident on statue. Otherwise, the same comments apply as for the obverse.

AU-53

PF-60 to 70 (Proof). ***Obverse and Reverse:*** Proofs that are extensively cleaned and have many hairlines, or that are dull and grainy, are lower level, such as PF-60 to 62. This comment is more theoretical than practical, as nearly all Proofs have been well kept. With medium hairlines and good reflectivity, assigned grades of PF-63 or 64 are appropriate. With relatively few hairlines a rating of PF-65 can be given. PF-66 may have hairlines so delicate that magnification is needed to see them. Above that, all the way to PF-70, a Proof should be free of any hairlines or other problems under strong magnification.

PF-65

2007, Washington

2007, J. Adams

2007, Jefferson

2007, Madison

2008, Monroe

2008, J.Q. Adams

2008, Jackson

2008, Van Buren

2009, W.H. Harrison

2009, Tyler

2009, Polk

2009, Taylor

2010, Fillmore

2010, Pierce

2010, Buchanan

2010, Lincoln

2011, A. Johnson

2011, Grant

2011, Hayes

2011, Garfield

2012, Arthur

2012, Cleveland, First Term

2012, B. Harrison

2012, Cleveland, Second Term

2013, McKinley

2013, T. Roosevelt

2013, Taft

2013, Wilson

2014, Harding

2014, Coolidge

2014, Hoover

2014, F.D. Roosevelt

2015, Truman

2015, Eisenhower

2015, Kennedy

2015, L.B. Johnson

2016, Nixon

2016, Ford

2016, Reagan

2020, G.H.W. Bush

Circulation Strikes

	Mintage	GSID	MS-65	MS-67
Presidential (2007–2016, 2020)	**n/a**	**82242**	**$3.40**	**$19**
2007-P, Washington	176,680,000	68642	3.40	19
2007-P, Washington, Satin	895,628	82243	6.75	16
2007-D, Washington	163,680,000	68684	3.40	19
2007-D, Washington, Satin	895,628	82245	6.75	16
(2007), Washington, Missing Edge Lettering	176,680,000	68643	32.00	310
2007-P, J. Adams	112,420,000	69655	3.40	19
2007-P, J. Adams, Satin	895,628	82248	6.75	16
2007-D, J. Adams	112,140,000	69710	3.40	19
2007-D, J. Adams, Satin	895,628	82250	$6.75	$16
(2007), Adams, Missing Edge Lettering	112,140,000	68767	70.00	—
2007-P, Jefferson	100,800,000	69659	3.40	19
2007-P, Jefferson, Satin	895,628	82252	6.75	16
2007-D, Jefferson	102,810,000	69388	3.40	19
2007-D, Jefferson, Satin	895,628	82254	6.75	16
(2007), Jefferson, Missing Edge Lettering	*	373801	80.00	390
2007-P, Madison	84,560,000	69661	3.40	19
2007-P, Madison, Satin	895,628	82256	6.75	16

Note: Satin Finish coins of 2005 through 2010 were produced for the annual Uncirculated Mint Sets, which were available only with the special finish during those years. * Included in number above. **a.** Not issued for circulation.

Circulation Strikes *(continued)*

	Mintage	GSID	MS-65	MS-67
2007-D, Madison	87,780,000	68983	$3.40	$19
2007-D, Madison, Satin	895,628	82258	6.75	16
2008-P, Monroe	64,260,000	70555	3.40	19
2008-P, Monroe, Satin	745,464	82260	6.75	16
2008-D, Monroe	60,230,000	68947	3.40	19
2008-D, Monroe, Satin	745,464	82262	6.75	16
2008-P, J.Q. Adams	57,540,000	69284	3.40	19
2008-P, J.Q. Adams, Satin	745,464	82264	6.75	16
2008-D, J.Q. Adams	57,720,000	70556	3.40	19
2008-D, J.Q. Adams, Satin	745,464	82266	6.75	16
2008-P, Jackson	61,180,000	70554	3.40	19
2008-P, Jackson, Satin	745,464	82269	6.75	16
2008-D, Jackson	61,070,000	69289	3.40	19
2008-D, Jackson, Satin	745,464	82271	6.75	16
2008-P, Van Buren	51,520,000	70557	3.40	19
2008-P, Van Buren, Satin	745,464	82273	6.75	16
2008-D, Van Buren	50,960,000	70559	3.40	19
2008-D, Van Buren, Satin	745,464	82275	6.75	16
2009-P, W.H. Harrison	43,260,000	69653	3.40	19
2009-P, W.H. Harrison, Satin	784,614	82278	6.75	16
2009-D, W.H. Harrison	55,160,000	70535	3.40	19
2009-D, W.H. Harrison, Satin	784,614	82280	6.75	16
2009-P, Tyler	43,540,000	70654	3.40	19
2009-P, Tyler, Satin	784,614	82283	6.75	16
2009-D, Tyler	43,540,000	70655	3.40	19
2009-D, Tyler, Satin	784,614	82285	6.75	16
2009-P, Polk	46,620,000	70727	3.40	19
2009-P, Polk, Satin	784,614	82287	6.75	16
2009-D, Polk	41,720,000	70656	3.40	19
2009-D, Polk, Satin	784,614	82289	6.75	16
2009-P, Taylor	41,580,000	76272	3.40	19
2009-P, Taylor, Satin	784,614	82291	6.75	16
2009-D, Taylor	36,680,000	70657	3.40	19
2009-D, Taylor, Satin	784,614	82293	6.75	16
2010-P, Fillmore	37,520,000	70839	3.40	19
2010-P, Fillmore, Satin	583,897	82295	6.75	16
2010-D, Fillmore	36,960,000	70840	3.40	19
2010-D, Fillmore, Satin	583,897	82297	6.75	16
2010-P, Pierce	38,220,000	70841	3.40	19
2010-P, Pierce, Satin	583,897	82299	6.75	16
2010-D, Pierce	38,360,000	70842	3.40	19
2010-D, Pierce, Satin	583,897	82301	6.75	16
2010-P, Buchanan	36,820,000	76273	3.40	19
2010-P, Buchanan, Satin	583,897	82303	6.75	16
2010-D, Buchanan	36,540,000	70843	3.40	19
2010-D, Buchanan, Satin	583,897	82305	6.75	16
2010-P, Lincoln	49,000,000	76274	3.40	19
2010-P, Lincoln, Satin	583,897	82307	6.75	16
2010-D, Lincoln	48,020,000	70844	3.40	19
2010-D, Lincoln, Satin	583,897	82309	$6.75	$16
2011-P, A. Johnson	35,560,000	76275	3.40	19
2011-D, A. Johnson	37,100,000	76276	3.40	19
2011-P, Grant	38,080,000	76277	3.40	19
2011-D, Grant	37,940,000	76278	3.40	19
2011-P, Hayes	37,660,000	76279	3.40	19
2011-D, Hayes	36,820,000	76280	3.40	19
2011-P, Garfield	37,100,000	76281	3.40	19
2011-D, Garfield	37,100,000	76282	3.40	19
2012-P, Arthur (a)	6,020,000	73785	3.40	19
2012-D, Arthur (a)	4,060,000	73786	3.40	19
2012-P, Cleveland, 1st (a)	5,460,000	73787	3.40	19
2012-D, Cleveland, 1st (a)	4,060,000	73788	3.40	19
2012-P, B. Harrison (a)	5,640,001	73789	3.40	19
2012-D, B. Harrison (a)	4,200,000	73790	3.40	19
2012-P, Cleveland, 2nd (a)	10,680,000	73791	3.40	19
2012-D, Cleveland, 2nd (a)	3,920,000	73792	3.40	19
2013-P, McKinley (a)	4,760,000	73799	3.40	19
2013-D, McKinley (a)	3,365,100	73800	3.40	19
2013-P, T. Roosevelt (a)	5,310,700	73797	3.40	19
2013-D, T. Roosevelt (a)	3,920,000	73798	3.40	19
2013-P, Taft (a)	4,760,000	73795	3.40	19
2013-D, Taft (a)	3,360,000	73796	3.40	19
2013-P, Wilson (a)	4,620,000	73793	3.40	19
2013-D, Wilson (a)	3,360,000	73794	3.40	19
2014-P, Harding (a)	6,160,000	73801	3.40	19
2014-D, Harding (a)	3,780,000	73802	3.40	19
2014-P, Coolidge (a)	4,480,000	73803	3.40	19
2014-D, Coolidge (a)	3,780,000	73804	3.40	19
2014-P, Hoover (a)	4,480,000	73805	3.40	19
2014-D, Hoover (a)	3,780,000	73806	3.40	19
2014-P, F. Roosevelt (a)	4,760,000	73807	3.40	19
2014-D, F. Roosevelt (a)	3,920,000	73808	3.40	19
2015-P, Truman (a)	4,900,000	73809	3.40	19
2015-D, Truman (a)	3,500,000	73810	3.40	19
2015-P, Eisenhower (a)	4,900,000	73811	3.40	19
2015-D, Eisenhower (a)	3,645,998	73812	3.40	19
2015-P, Kennedy (a)	6,160,000	73813	3.40	19
2015-D, Kennedy (a)	5,180,000	73814	3.40	19
2015-P, L.B. Johnson (a)	7,840,000	73815	3.40	19
2015-D, L.B. Johnson (a)	4,200,000	73816	3.40	19
2016-P, Nixon (a)	5,460,000	73817	3.40	19
2016-D, Nixon (a)	4,340,000	73818	3.40	19
2016-P, Ford (a)	5,460,000	77330	3.40	19
2016-D, Ford (a)	5,040,000	77331	3.40	19
2016-P, Reagan (a)	7,140,000	77332	3.40	19
2016-D, Reagan (a)	5,880,000	77333	3.40	19
2020-P, G.H.W. Bush (a)	1,242,275	285878	3.40	19
2020-D, G.H.W. Bush (a)	1,502,425	285880	3.40	19

a. Not issued for circulation.

Proof Strikes

	Mintage	GSID	PF-68	PF-70
Presidential (2007–2016, 2020), Proof	**n/a**	**226245**	**$7.75**	**$27**
2007-S, Washington	3,965,989	68776	7.75	27
2007-S, J. Adams	3,965,989	68777	7.75	27
2007-S, Jefferson	3,965,989	68778	7.75	27
2007-S, Madison	3,965,989	69666	7.75	27
2008-S, Monroe	3,083,940	68948	9.50	40
2008-S, J.Q. Adams	3,083,940	69004	9.50	40
2008-S, Jackson	3,083,940	69005	9.50	40
2008-S, Van Buren	3,083,940	69006	9.50	40
2009-S, W.H. Harrison	2,809,452	73820	7.75	27
2009-S, Tyler	2,809,452	73821	7.75	27
2009-S, Polk	2,809,452	73822	7.75	27
2009-S, Taylor	2,809,452	73823	7.75	27
2010-S, Fillmore	2,224,613	73824	9.50	40
2010-S, Pierce	2,224,613	73825	9.50	40
2010-S, Buchanan	2,224,613	73827	9.50	40
2010-S, Lincoln	2,224,613	73826	12.00	40
2011-S, A. Johnson	1,972,863	73828	9.50	40
2011-S, Grant	1,972,863	73831	9.50	40
2011-S, Hayes	1,972,863	73830	9.50	40
2011-S, Garfield	1,972,863	73829	9.50	40
2012-S, Arthur	1,438,743	73832	23.00	55
2012-S, Cleveland, 1st	1,438,743	71475	23.00	55
2012-S, B. Harrison	1,438,743	73833	$23.00	$55
2012-S, Cleveland, 2nd	1,438,743	73834	23.00	55
2013-S, McKinley	1,488,798	73836	9.50	40
2013-S, T. Roosevelt	1,503,943	73835	9.50	40
2013-S, Taft	1,488,798	73837	9.50	40
2013-S, Wilson	1,488,798	73838	9.50	40
2014-S, Harding	1,373,569	73840	11.00	43
2014-S, Coolidge	1,373,569	73842	11.00	43
2014-S, Hoover	1,373,569	73839	11.00	43
2014-S, F. Roosevelt	1,392,619	73841	11.00	43
2015-P, Truman, RevPf (a)	16,812	76508	46.00	775
2015-S, Truman	1,272,462	73846	11.00	49
2015-P, Eisenhower, RevPf (a)	16,744	76506	46.00	2,000
2015-S, Eisenhower	1,272,462	73843	11.00	49
2015-P, Kennedy, RevPf (a)	49,051	346840	46.00	390
2015-S, Kennedy	1,272,462	73844	11.00	49
2015-P, L.B. Johnson, RevPf (a)	23,905	346841	46.00	1,900
2015-S, L.B. Johnson	1,272,462	73845	11.00	49
2016-S, Nixon	1,196,582	73847	9.50	40
2016-S, Ford	1,196,582	73848	9.50	40
2016-S, Reagan	1,196,582	73849	9.50	40
2016-S, Reagan, RevPf (a)	47,447	346842	46.00	95
2020-S, G.H.W. Bush, RevPf (a)	11,305	285882	80.00	325

a. Included in American $1 Coin and Chronicles sets dedicated to each president.

NATIVE AMERICAN (2009 TO DATE)

Designers: *Glenna Goodacre (obverse); see below for reverse designers.*
Weight: *8.1 grams.* **Composition:** *A core of pure copper, clad in outer layers of manganese-brass (.770 copper, .120 zinc, .070 manganese, .040 nickel).*
Diameter: *26.5 mm.* **Edge:** *Lettered.* **Mints:** *Philadelphia, Denver, San Francisco, and West Point.*

Reverse Designers:

2009, Three Sisters. . . . . Norman E. Nemeth
2010, Great Law. . . . . Thomas Cleveland
2011, Wampanoag Treaty. . . . . Richard Masters
2012, Trade Routes . . . . Thomas Cleveland
2013, Treaty With the Delawares. . . . . Susan Gamble
2014, Native Hospitality . . . . Chris Costello
2015, Mohawk Ironworkers. . . . . . Ronald D. Sanders
2016, Code Talkers . . . . Thomas D. Rogers Sr.
2017, Sequoyah. Chris Costello
2018, Jim Thorpe. . . . . .Michael Gaudioso
2019, American Indians in Space . . . . Emily Damstra
2020, Elizabeth Peratrovich and Alaska's Anti-Discrimination Law. . . . . . Phebe Hemphill
2021, American Indians in the U.S. Military . . . . Donna Weaver
2022, Ely S. Parker. . . . . .Paul C. Balan
2023, Maria Tallchief and American Indians in Ballet . . . . .Benjamin Sowards
2024, Indian Citizenship Act of 1924 Centennial. . . . . Phebe Hemphill
2025, Mary Kawena Pukui. . . . . .Christina Hess

Circulation Strike

Mintmark location is on the rim.

Proof Strike

History. Since 2009, the reverse of the golden dollar has featured an annually changing design that memorializes Native Americans and, in the words of the authorizing legislation, "the important contributions made by Indian tribes and individual Native Americans to the development [and history] of the United States." The coins are marked (incuse) on their edges with the year of minting, the mintmark, and the legend E PLURIBUS UNUM. The Native American $1 Coin Act also specified that at least 20 percent of the total mintage of dollar coins in any given year (including Presidential dollars) will be Native American dollars. Production of all dollar coins minted after 2011 has been limited to numismatic sales (Proofs and other collector formats, and circulation strikes in rolls and bags available directly from the U.S. Mint); none are issued for circulation, as they have proven unpopular in commerce.

The obverse of the Native American dollar coin is a modified version of the Sacagawea dollar, featuring that coin's central portraits (of Sacagawea and Jean Baptiste), and the legends LIBERTY and IN GOD WE TRUST. The date and mintmark, as noted above, are on the coin's edge. Each new reverse design is chosen by the secretary of the Treasury following consultation with the Senate Committee on Indian Affairs, the Congressional Native American Caucus of the House of Representatives, the Commission of Fine Arts, and the National Congress of American Indians. Design proposals are also reviewed by the Citizens Coinage Advisory Committee.

In addition to the regular Uncirculated or Mint State coins produced in large quantities, smaller numbers of Satin Finish dollars were made of the 2009-P, 2009-D, 2010-P, and 2010-D issues. Sold at an additional premium, most of these exist today in grades of MS-67 and upward and are designated SP (Specimen) or SMS (Special Mint Set) by the commercial grading services. 50,000 2014-D coins were made with Enhanced Uncirculated finish and were sold at an extra premium. Most of these grade MS-68 to 70. In

2015 at the West Point Mint 90,000 2015-W dollars were struck with Enhanced Uncirculated finish. These are unique up to this time as the only collectible West Point dollars in any of the three "golden dollar" series (Sacagawea, Native American, and Presidential). Nearly all are in grades MS-68 to 70.

Some error coins have been discovered without edge lettering.

Striking and Sharpness. Most examples are very well struck. Check the higher points of the design. Special issues are uniformly sharply struck.

Availability. Native American dollars are common in high grades, and are usually collected in MS and Proof. Distribution for public circulation has been slow despite Mint efforts such as the $1 Coin Direct Ship program (intended "to make $1 coins readily available to the public, at no additional cost [including shipping], so they can be easily introduced into circulation—particularly by using them for retail transactions, vending, and mass transit"). Proofs have been made each year and are readily available.

Grading Standards

MS-60 to 70 (Mint State). ***Obverse:*** At MS-60, some abrasion and contact marks are evident, most noticeably on the cheekbone and the drapery near the baby's head. Luster is present, but may be dull or lifeless. At MS-63, contact marks are extensive but not distracting. Abrasion still is evident, but less than at lower levels. MS-64 coins are slightly finer. An MS-65 coin may have minor abrasion, but contact marks are so minute as to require magnification. Luster should be full and rich. ***Reverse:*** At MS-60, some abrasion and contact marks are evident, most noticeably on the eagle's breast. Otherwise, the same comments apply as for the obverse.

MS-68

PF-60 to 70 (Proof). ***Obverse and Reverse:*** Proofs that are extensively cleaned and have many hairlines, or that are dull and grainy, are lower level, such as PF-60 to 62. This comment is more theoretical than practical, as nearly all Proofs have been well kept. With medium hairlines and good reflectivity, assigned grades of PF-63 or 64 are appropriate. With relatively few hairlines a rating of PF-65 can be given. PF-66 may have hairlines so delicate that magnification is needed to see them. Above that, all the way to PF-70, a Proof should be free of any hairlines or other problems under strong magnification.

PF-70
Deep Cameo

Three Sisters (2009)

Great Law of Peace (2010)

Wampanoag Treaty (2011)

Trade Routes in the 17th Century (2012)

Treaty With the Delawares (2013)

Native Hospitality (2014)

Mohawk Ironworkers (2015)

Code Talkers (2016)

Sequoyah (2017)

Jim Thorpe (2018)

American Indians in Space (2019)

Elizabeth Peratrovich and Alaska's Anti-Discrimination Law (2020)

American Indians in the U.S. Military (2021)

Ely S. Parker (2022)

Maria Tallchief and American Indians in Ballet (2023)

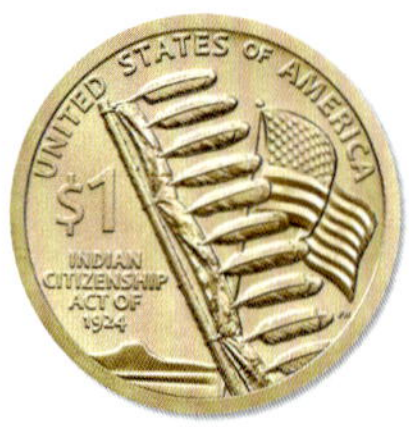

Indian Citizenship Act of 1924 Centennial (2024)

Mary Kawena Pukui (2025)

Circulation Strikes

	Mintage	GSID	MS-63	MS-65	MS-67
Native American (2009 to Date)	**n/a**	**82169**	**$3.00**	**$3.20**	**$5.50**
2009-P, Three Sisters	39,200,000	70508	3.40	3.80	12.00
2009-D, Three Sisters	35,700,000	70510	3.50	4.20	19.00
2010-P, Great Law	32,060,000	70845	3.50	4.20	27.00
2010-D, Great Law	48,720,000	70846	3.50	4.20	160.00
(2010), Great Law, Missing Edge Lettering	583,897	373800	—	—	—
2011-P, Wampanoag Treaty	29,400,000	71074	3.50	4.20	8.00
2011-D, Wampanoag Treaty	48,160,000	71075	3.50	4.20	8.00
2012-P, Trade Routes (a)	2,800,000	74214	3.10	3.40	12.00
2012-D, Trade Routes (a)	3,080,000	76263	3.10	3.40	9.50
2013-P, Treaty With the Delawares (a)	1,820,000	74215	3.10	3.40	6.75
2013-D, Treaty With the Delawares (a)	1,820,000	74216	3.10	3.40	6.75
2014-P, Native Hospitality (a)	3,080,000	74217	3.10	3.40	27.00
2014-D, Native Hospitality (a)	2,800,000	74218	3.10	3.40	9.50
2014-D, Native Hospitality, Enhanced Uncirculated (b)	50,000	198232	6.75	8.00	13.50
2015-P, Mohawk Ironworkers (a)	2,800,000	74219	3.10	3.40	9.50
2015-D, Mohawk Ironworkers (a)	2,240,000	74220	3.10	3.40	12.00
2015-W, Mohawk Ironworkers, Enhanced Uncirculated (b)	88,805	84809	3.50	4.20	8.00

a. Not issued for circulation. **b.** Special Native American dollars with Enhanced Uncirculated finish were struck for inclusion in American $1 Coin and Currency sets (listed under "Modern Commemorative Sets" in the "Commemoratives" chapter).

Circulation Strikes *(continued)*

	Mintage	GSID	MS-63	MS-65	MS-67
2016-P, Code Talkers (a)	2,800,000	74221	$3.00	$3.30	$27.00
2016-D, Code Talkers (a)	2,100,000	74222	3.00	3.30	20.00
2016-S, Code Talkers, Enhanced Uncirculated (b)	50,737	84810	3.50	4.20	8.00
2017-P, Sequoyah (a)	1,820,000	76264	3.00	3.30	16.00
2017-D, Sequoyah (a)	1,540,000	76265	3.00	3.30	16.00
2017-S, Sequoyah, Enhanced Uncirculated (c)	210,402	198234	3.50	4.20	6.75
2018-P, Jim Thorpe (a)	1,400,000	79388	3.00	3.20	5.50
2018-D, Jim Thorpe (a)	1,400,000	79390	3.00	3.20	5.50
2019-P, American Indians in Space (a)	1,400,000	79392	3.00	3.20	5.50
2019-P, American Indians in Space, Enhanced Uncirculated (b)	46,964	84811	3.50	4.20	6.75
2019-D, American Indians in Space (a)	1,540,000	79394	3.00	3.20	5.50
2020-P, Elizabeth Peratrovich and Alaska's Anti-Discrimination Law (a)	1,400,000	82164	3.00	3.20	5.50
2020-D, Elizabeth Peratrovich and Alaska's Anti-Discrimination Law (a)	1,260,000	82166	3.00	3.20	5.50
2021-P, American Indians in U.S. Military (a)	1,260,000	85157	3.00	3.20	5.50
2021-D, American Indians in U.S. Military (a)	1,260,000	85159	3.00	3.20	5.50
2022-P, Ely S. Parker (a)	980,000	193321	3.00	3.20	5.50
2022-D, Ely S. Parker (a)	980,000	193322	3.00	3.20	5.50
2023-P, Maria Tallchief and American Indians in Ballet (a)	1,120,000	199006	3.00	3.20	5.50
2023-D, Maria Tallchief and American Indians in Ballet (a)	1,120,000	199007	3.00	3.20	5.50
2024-P, Indian Citizenship Act of 1924 (a)		374002	3.00	3.20	5.50
2024-D, Indian Citizenship Act of 1924 (a)		374003	3.00	3.20	5.50
2025-P, Mary Kawena Pukui (a)		376197	3.00	3.20	5.50
2025-D, Mary Kawena Pukui (a)		376198	3.00	3.20	5.50

a. Not issued for circulation. **b.** Special Native American dollars with Enhanced Uncirculated finish were struck for inclusion in American $1 Coin and Currency sets (listed under "Modern Commemorative Sets" in the "Commemoratives" chapter). **c.** Included in the 2017-S set of Enhanced Uncirculated coins issued in honor of the 225th anniversary of the San Francisco Mint.

Proof Strikes

	Mintage	GSID	PF-68	PF-69	PF-70
Native American (2009 to Date), Proof	**n/a**	**376584**	**$12.00**	**$13.50**	**$20**
2009-S, Three Sisters	2,179,867	70653	12.00	13.50	26
2010-S, Great Law	1,689,216	71073	12.00	13.50	28
2011-S, Wampanoag Treaty	1,673,010	71076	12.00	13.50	40
2012-S, Trade Routes	1,189,445	74079	26.00	27.00	145
2013-S, Treaty With the Delawares	1,222,180	74080	12.00	13.50	34
2014-S, Native Hospitality	1,144,154	74081	12.00	13.50	34
2015-S, Mohawk Ironworkers	1,050,164	74082	16.00	17.50	24
2016-S, Code Talkers	931,866	74083	16.00	22.00	60
2017-S, Sequoyah	926,763	74084	16.00	19.00	27
2018-S, Jim Thorpe	849,321	79385	16.00	22.00	27
2018-S, Jim Thorpe, Reverse Proof	199,116	79387	32.00	34.00	35
2019-S, American Indians in Space	1,056,828	79386	15.00	16.00	20
2020-S, Elizabeth Peratrovich and Alaska's Anti-Discrimination Law	777,841	84808	16.00	23.00	26
2021-S, American Indians in U.S. Military	814,340	85161	16.00	20.00	20
2022-S, Ely S. Parker	646,177	193323	16.00	24.00	27
2023-S, Maria Tallchief and American Indians in Ballet		199008	15.00	16.00	26
2024-S, Indian Citizenship Act of 1924		374004	16.00	23.00	30
2025-S, Mary Kawena Pukui		376199	15.00	16.00	26

AMERICAN INNOVATION (2018–2032)

Designers: *Justin Kunz (obverse); see below for reverse designers.* **Weight:** *8.1 grams.* **Composition:** *A core of pure copper, clad in outer layers of manganese-brass (.770 copper, .120 zinc, .070 manganese, .040 nickel).* **Diameter:** *26.5 mm.* **Edge:** *Lettered.* **Mints:** *Philadelphia, Denver, and San Francisco.*

Reverse Designers:

2018, American Innovators . . . . . . Donna Weaver
2019, Delaware . . . . Donna Weaver
2019, Pennsylvania . . . . Richard Masters
2019, New Jersey . . . . Paul C. Balan
2019, Georgia . . . . Emily Damstra
2020, Connecticut . . . . Richard Masters
2020, Massachusetts . . . . Emily Damstra
2020, Maryland . . . . Joseph Menna
2020, South Carolina . . . . Justin Kunz
2021, New Hampshire . . . . Christina Hess
2021, Virginia . . . . Matt Swaim
2021, New York . . . . Ronald D. Sanders
2021, North Carolina . . . . Ronald D. Sanders
2022, Rhode Island . . . . Dennis Friel
2022, Vermont . . . . Justin Kunz
2022, Kentucky . . . . Christina Hess
2022, Tennessee . . . . Matt Swaim
2023, Ohio . . . . Beth Zaiken
2023, Louisiana . . . . Dennis Friel
2023, Indiana . . . . Ronald D. Sanders
2023, Mississippi . . . . Katelyn Arquette
2024, Illinois . . . . Justin Kunz
2024, Alabama . . . . Craig Campbell
2024, Maine . . . . Phebe Hemphill
2024, Missouri . . . . Eric David Custer
2025, Arkansas . . . . Elana Hagler
2025, Florida . . . . Ronald D. Sanders
2025, Michigan . . . . Ronald D. Sanders
2025, Texas . . . . Ronald D. Sanders

Circulation Strike

Mintmark location is on the rim, along with other inscriptions.

Proof Strike

On American Innovation dollars, the annual privy mark will be joined with the Semiquincentennial privy mark.

History. In 2018, the U.S. Mint issued the first coin in a new, 15-year series: the American Innovation $1 Coin Program. Authorized by Public Law 115-197, each of the golden dollars in the program features a reverse design that "symbolizes quintessentially American traits—the willingness to explore, to discover, and to create one's own destiny." Four new designs, in Uncirculated and Proof finishes, are issued each year from 2019 through 2032—one for each state, in the order in which the states ratified the Constitution or were admitted to the Union, and then for the District of Columbia and each of the five U.S. territories (Puerto Rico, Guam, American Samoa, the U.S. Virgin Islands, and the Northern Mariana Islands). Each year's designs share an obverse privy mark unique to that year (except 2018, which had no privy mark). The 2026 issues will share a gear privy mark overlaid with the Liberty Bell–250 privy in use on all 2026 coins in honor of the U.S. Semiquincentennial. Like all dollar coins minted after 2011, they are issued for numismatic sales only; none are distributed for circulation.

Design concepts that showcase "an innovation, innovator or group of innovators from each State or Territory" are submitted to the Mint by official state/territorial liaisons. The secretary of the Treasury selects the concepts deemed most appropriate for $1 coin designs, and the Mint—working in concert with its artists, the state liaisons, the U.S. Commission of Fine Arts (CFA), the Citizens Coinage Advisory Committee (CCAC), and technical and historical consultants (as needed)—produces the final design candidates. The Treasury secretary makes the final selection from the resulting designs.

Coins in the series bear the following required inscriptions: on the obverse, IN GOD WE TRUST and the denomination; on the reverse, the name of the state, the District of Columbia, or territory (as appropriate), along with UNITED STATES OF AMERICA; and incused into the edge, the date, the mintmark, and the inscription E PLURIBUS UNUM. The common obverse depicts a left-facing profile of the Statue of Liberty, as designed by Justin Kunz and sculpted by Phebe Hemphill.

While each issue from 2019 through 2032 represents an individual state, district, or territory, the 2018 inaugural issue (designed by Donna Weaver and sculpted by Renata Gordon) represents the program in general. A pattern of gears and cogs represents American industry; below, a facsimile of George Washington's signature with SIGNED FIRST PATENT beneath it together represent the presidential signature on the first-ever U.S. patent, issued July 31, 1790. On a cartouche at the right, an eagle crouches on an angled shield, its wings spread behind it, with tools representing innovation (hammer, plow, wheel, etc.) below it.

Striking and Sharpness. Most examples are very well struck; check the higher points of the design.

Availability. American Innovation dollars are common in high grades, and are collected in MS and Proof. Proofs are been as well and are readily available.

Grading Standards

MS-60 to 70 (Mint State). ***Obverse:*** At MS-60, some abrasion and contact marks are evident, most noticeably on Liberty's cheek and in the wide, empty field. Luster is present but may be dull or lifeless. At MS-63, contact marks are extensive but not distracting. Abrasion still is evident, but less than at lower levels. MS-64 coins are slightly finer. An MS-65 coin may have minor abrasion, but contact marks are so minute as to require magnification. Luster should be full and rich. ***Reverse:*** At MS-60, some abrasion and contact marks are evident, most noticeably on the gear wheels. Otherwise, the same comments apply as for the obverse.

MS-65

PF-60 to 70 (Proof). ***Obverse and Reverse:*** With medium hairlines and good reflectivity, assigned grades of PF-63 or 64 are appropriate. With relatively few hairlines a rating of PF-65 can be given. PF-66 may have hairlines so delicate that magnification is needed to see them. Above that, all the way to PF-70, a Proof should be free of any hairlines or other problems under strong magnification.

PF-70
Cameo

American Innovators (2018)
Note: No Privy Mark in 2018.

Delaware: Classifying the Stars (2019)

Pennsylvania: Polio Vaccine (2019)

New Jersey: Light Bulb (2019)

Georgia: Trustees' Garden (2019)

Privy Mark

2019

Connecticut: Gerber Variable Scale (2020)

Massachusetts: Telephone (2020)

Maryland: The Hubble Space Telescope (2020)

South Carolina: Septima Clark (2020)

Privy Mark

2020

New Hampshire: Ralph Baer (2021)

Virginia: Chesapeake Bay Bridge-Tunnel (2021)

New York: Erie Canal (2021)

North Carolina: Higher Learning (2021)

Privy Mark

2021

Rhode Island: Nautical Innovation (2022)

Vermont: Snowboarding (2022)

Kentucky: Bluegrass Music (2022)

Tennessee: Tennessee Valley Authority (2022)

Privy Mark

2022

Ohio: Underground Railroad (2023)

Louisiana: Higgins Boat (2023)

Indiana: Automobile Industry (2023)

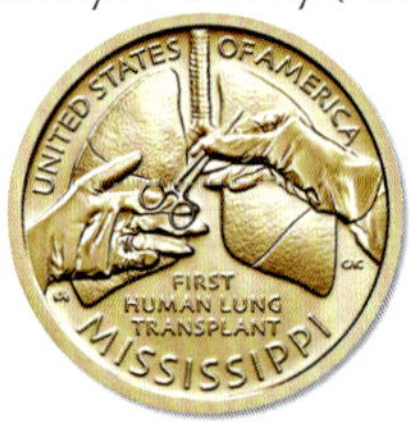

Mississippi: First Human Lung Transplant (2023)

Privy Mark

2023

Illinois:
Steel Plow (2024)

Alabama:
Saturn V Rocket (2024)

Maine:
Direct Current Defibrillator (2024)

Missouri:
George Washington Carver (2024)

Privy Mark

2024

Arkansas:
Raye Montague (2025)

Florida:
Space Shuttle (2025)

Michigan: Auto Assembly Line (2025)

Texas: Mission Control Center (2025)

Privy Mark

2025

Circulation Strikes

	Mintage	GSID	MS-65	MS-67
American Innovation (2018 to Date)	n/a	376580	$5.50	$27
2018-P, Innovators (a)	700,500	77884	6.75	34
2018-D, Innovators (a)	680,525	77886	5.50	27
2019-P, Delaware (a)	346,850	82126	5.50	27
2019-D, Delaware (a)	358,450	82128	6.75	34
2019-P, Pennsylvania (a)	317,550	82122	6.75	34
2019-D, Pennsylvania (a)	309,375	82124	6.75	34
2019-P, New Jersey (a)	334,500	82118	6.75	34
2019-D, New Jersey (a)	310,675	82120	6.75	34
2019-P, Georgia (a)	399,900	82114	5.50	27
2019-D, Georgia (a)	368,475	82116	5.50	27
2020-P, Connecticut (a)	436,000	82130	6.75	34
2020-D, Connecticut (a)	435,325	82132	5.50	27
2020-P, Massachusetts (a)	436,750	82134	9.50	47
2020-D, Massachusetts (a)	436,425	82136	8.00	40
2020-P, Maryland (a)	434,825	82138	12.00	60
2020-D, Maryland (a)	435,475	82140	11.00	55
2020-P, South Carolina (a)	432,850	82142	8.00	40
2020-D, South Carolina (a)	397,775	82144	5.50	27
2021-P, New Hampshire (a)	454,325	85162	5.50	27
2021-D, New Hampshire (a)	454,450	85164	5.50	27
2021-P, Virginia (a)	454,975	85166	5.50	27
2021-D, Virginia (a)	453,850	85168	5.50	27
2021-P, New York (a)	453,750	85170	5.50	27
2021-D, New York (a)	453,825	85172	5.50	27
2021-P, North Carolina (a)	454,150	85174	5.50	27
2021-D, North Carolina (a)	454,450	85176	5.50	27
2022-P, Rhode Island (a)	454,150	193293	5.50	27
2022-D, Rhode Island (a)	453,775	193295	5.50	27
2022-P, Vermont (a)	454,275	193309	$5.50	$27
2022-D, Vermont (a)	452,875	193311	5.50	27
2022-P, Kentucky (a)	451,900	193313	5.50	27
2022-D, Kentucky (a)	452,625	193315	5.50	27
2022-P, Tennessee (a)	452,325	193317	5.50	27
2022-D, Tennessee (a)	452,275	193319	5.50	27
2023-P, Ohio (a)		198977	5.50	27
2023-D, Ohio (a)		198979	5.50	27
2023-P, Louisiana (a)		198981	5.50	27
2023-D, Louisiana (a)		198983	5.50	27
2023-P, Indiana (a)		198985	5.50	27
2023-D, Indiana (a)		198987	5.50	27
2023-P, Mississippi (a)		198989	5.50	27
2023-D, Mississippi (a)		198991	5.50	27
2024-P, Illinois (a)		346892	5.50	27
2024-D, Illinois (a)		346894	5.50	27
2024-P, Alabama (a)		346896	5.50	27
2024-D, Alabama (a)		346898	5.50	27
2024-P, Maine (a)		346900	5.50	27
2024-D, Maine (a)		346902	5.50	27
2024-P, Missouri (a)		346904	5.50	27
2024-D, Missouri (a)		346906	5.50	27
2025-P, Arkansas (a)		377393	5.50	27
2025-D, Arkansas (a)		377395	5.50	27
2025-P, Florida (a)		377397	5.50	27
2025-D, Florida (a)		377399	5.50	27
2025-P, Michigan (a)		377401	5.50	27
2025-D, Michigan (a)		377403	5.50	27
2025-P, Texas (a)		377405	5.50	27
2025-D, Texas (a)		377407	5.50	27

a. Not issued for circulation.

Proof Strikes

	Mintage	GSID	PF-68	PF-70
American Innovation (2018 to Date), Proof	**n/a**	**376581**	**$8.00**	**$22**
2018-S, Innovators	206,886	82146	13.50	27
2018-S, Innovators, RevPf	74,720	82147	17.50	31
2019-S, Delaware	85,839	82154	8.00	22
2019-S, Delaware, RevPf	53,724	82155	11.00	24
2019-S, Pennsylvania	85,839	82152	8.00	22
2019-S, Pennsylvania, RevPf	36,337	82153	11.00	24
2019-S, New Jersey	85,839	82150	8.00	22
2019-S, New Jersey, RevPf	21,101	82151	11.00	24
2019-S, Georgia	85,839	82148	8.00	22
2019-S, Georgia, RevPf	46,915	82149	11.00	24
2020-S, Connecticut	107,052	82156	8.00	22
2020-S, Connecticut, RevPf	46,556	82157	11.00	24
2020-S, Massachusetts	107,052	82158	8.00	22
2020-S, Massachusetts, RevPf	48,529	82159	11.00	24
2020-S, Maryland	107,052	82160	8.00	22
2020-S, Maryland, RevPf	49,731	82161	11.00	24
2020-S, South Carolina	107,052	82162	8.00	22
2020-S, South Carolina, RevPf	41,083	82163	11.00	24
2021-S, New Hampshire	84,604	85178	8.00	22
2021-S, New Hampshire, RevPf	49,541	193298	11.00	24
2021-S, Virginia	84,604	85179	8.00	22
2021-S, Virginia, RevPf	49,541	193299	11.00	24
2021-S, New York	84,604	85180	8.00	22
2021-S, New York, RevPf	49,541	193300	11.00	24
2021-S, North Carolina	84,604	85181	8.00	22
2021-S, North Carolina, RevPf	49,541	193301	11.00	24
2022-S, Rhode Island	77,766	193297	8.00	22
2022-S, Rhode Island, RevPf	49,478	193302	11.00	24
2022-S, Vermont	77,766	193303	$8.00	$22
2022-S, Vermont, RevPf	49,478	193304	11.00	24
2022-S, Kentucky	77,766	193305	8.00	22
2022-S, Kentucky, RevPf	49,478	193306	11.00	24
2022-S, Tennessee	77,766	193307	8.00	22
2022-S, Tennessee, RevPf	49,478	193308	11.00	24
2023-S, Ohio	58,154	198993	8.00	22
2023-S, Ohio, RevPf	39,308	198994	11.00	24
2023-S, Louisiana	58,154	198995	8.00	22
2023-S, Louisiana, RevPf	39,308	198996	11.00	24
2023-S, Indiana	58,154	198997	8.00	22
2023-S, Indiana, RevPf	39,308	198998	11.00	24
2023-S, Mississippi	58,154	198999	8.00	22
2023-S, Mississippi, RevPf	39,308	199000	11.00	24
2024-S, Illinois		375536	8.00	22
2024-S, Illinois, RevPf		375537	11.00	24
2024-S, Alabama		375538	8.00	22
2024-S, Alabama, RevPf		375539	11.00	24
2024-S, Maine		375540	8.00	22
2024-S, Maine, RevPf		375541	11.00	24
2024-S, Missouri		375542	8.00	22
2024-S, Missouri, RevPf		375543	11.00	24
2025-S, Arkansas		377409	8.00	22
2025-S, Arkansas, RevPf		377410	11.00	24
2025-S, Florida		377411	8.00	22
2025-S, Florida, RevPf		377412	11.00	24
2025-S, Michigan		377413	8.00	22
2025-S, Michigan, RevPf		377414	11.00	24
2025-S, Texas		377415	8.00	22
2025-S, Texas, RevPf		377416	11.00	24

1921 SILVER DOLLAR ANNIVERSARY COINS (2021, 2023 TO DATE)

Designers: *George T. Morgan and Anthony de Francisci, as translated by modern Mint artists.* **Weight:** *2.67 grams.* **Composition:** *.999 silver (net weight 0.858 oz. pure silver).* **Diameter:** *38.1 mm.* **Edge:** *Reeded.* **Mints:** *Philadelphia, Denver, and San Francisco.*

Morgan Dollar

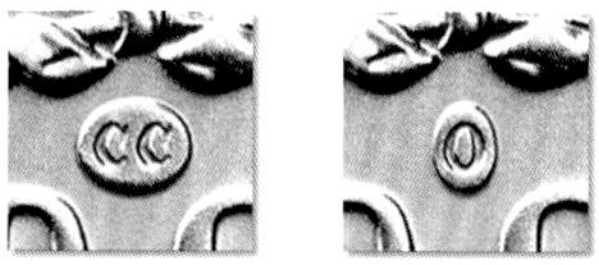

"CC" Privy Mark *"O" Privy Mark*

Peace Dollar

History. Congress passed the 1921 Silver Dollar Coin Anniversary Act "to mint and issue $1 coins in recognition of the 100th anniversary of completion of coinage of the Morgan dollar and the 100th anniversary of commencement of coinage of the Peace dollar." The resulting products, first minted in 2021, are not precise copies of the older coins, but, in the words of the legislation, "honor" the originals with "renditions" of the designs used on the original Morgan and Peace silver dollars.

The Mint's artists used modern technology and historical Mint assets to create the modern designs.

For the Morgan anniversary coins, some were minted in Philadelphia with "CC" and "O" privy marks to represent the historical mintages of Carson City and New Orleans.

In November 2021 the Mint announced plans to produce the coins as recurring annual products, in various finishes and using multiple Mint facilities.

Striking and Sharpness. Nearly every example is very well struck; check the higher points of the design.

Availability. American Innovation dollars are common in high grades, and are collected in MS.

Grading Standards

MS-60 to 70 (Mint State). ***Obverse:*** At MS-60, some abrasion and contact marks are evident, most noticeably on Liberty's cheek. Luster is present but may be dull or lifeless. At MS-63, contact marks are extensive but not distracting. Abrasion still is evident, but less than at lower levels. MS-64 coins are slightly finer. An MS-65 coin may have minor abrasion, but contact marks are so minute as to require magnification. Luster should be full and rich. ***Reverse:*** At MS-60, some abrasion and contact marks are evident. Otherwise, the same comments apply as for the obverse

MS-69

PF-60 to 70 (Proof). ***Obverse and Reverse:*** With medium hairlines and good reflectivity, assigned grades of PF-63 or 64 are appropriate. With relatively few hairlines a rating of PF-65 can be given. PF-66 may have hairlines so delicate that magnification is needed to see them. Above that, all the way to PF-70, a Proof should be free of any hairlines or other problems under strong magnification.

PF-70

Circulation Strikes

	Mintage	GSID	OGP*	MS-69	MS-70
1921 Silver Dollar Anniversary, Morgan (2021 to Date)	**n/a**	**85115**	**$50**	**$50**	**$70**
1921 Silver Dollar Anniversary, Peace (2021 to Date)	**n/a**	**85117**	**50**	**50**	**70**
2021-(P), Morgan, No Privy Mark	175,000	85110	145	145	245
2021-(P), Peace	200,000	85116	175	175	300
2021-(P), Morgan, CC Privy Mark	175,000	85111	190	190	300
2021-D, Morgan	175,000	85112	160	160	1,100
2021-(P), Morgan, O Privy Mark	175,000	85113	130	130	240
2021-S, Morgan	175,000	85114	130	130	235
2023-(P), Morgan	275,000	212722	50	50	70
2023-(P), Peace	275,000	212725	50	50	70
2024-(P), Morgan		375526	80	80	130
2024-(P), Peace	168,555	375527	80	80	130
2025-(P), Morgan		393384	110	110	130
2025-(P), Peace		393385	110	110	130

Note: Silver Dollar Anniversary coins are offered for sale directly to the public. None are issued for circulation. Production was paused in 2022 due to a shortage of silver blanks caused by the COVID-19 pandemic, with a return to production planned for 2023. * Value in original government packaging (OGP).

Proof Strikes

	Mintage	GSID	OGP*	PF-69	PF-70
1921 Silver Dollar Anniversary, Morgan (2021 to Date), Proof	**n/a**	**376582**	**$60**	**$60**	**$95**
1921 Silver Dollar Anniversary, Peace (2021 to Date), Proof	**n/a**	**376583**	**60**	**60**	**95**
2023-S, Morgan	400,000	212723	60	60	95
2023-S, Morgan, Reverse Proof	250,000	212724	70	70	100
2023-S, Peace	400,000	212726	60	60	95
2023-S, Peace, Reverse Proof	250,000	212727	70	70	100
2024-S, Morgan		375531	70	70	100
2024-S, Morgan, Reverse Proof	250,000	375532	75	75	110
2024-S, Peace	400,000	375533	70	70	100
2024-S, Peace, Reverse Proof		375534	75	75	110
2025-S, Morgan		393386	115	115	135
2025-S, Morgan, Reverse Proof	250,000	393387	135	135	160
2025-S, Peace	400,000	393388	115	115	135
2025-S, Peace, Reverse Proof		393389	135	135	160

* Value in original government packaging (OGP).

Sets

	GSID	OGP*	PF-69	PF-70
Two-Coin Set. 2023-S Morgan and Peace Reverse Proof silver dollars	376917	$130	$130	$195
2024-S Morgan and Peace Reverse Proof silver dollars	376918	135	135	200
2025-S Morgan and Peace Reverse Proof silver dollars	393390	275	275	325

* Value in original government packaging (OGP).

Gold Dollars
1849–1889

AN OVERVIEW OF GOLD DOLLARS

Coinage of the gold dollar was authorized by the Act of March 3, 1849, after the start of the California Gold Rush.

Scan for additional information.

Although a case could be made for designating the Small Head, Open Wreath, gold dollar as a separate type, it is not generally collected as such. Instead, pieces dated from 1849 through 1854 (whether Open Wreath or Close Wreath) are collectively designated as Variety 1. Examples today are readily available in all grades, although truly choice and gem Mint State pieces are in the minority.

In contrast, the Variety 2 design, produced at the Philadelphia Mint in part of 1854, and at the Philadelphia, Charlotte, Dahlonega, and New Orleans mints in 1855, and only at the San Francisco Mint in 1856, is a great challenge. Examples are scarcer in all grades than are those of types 1 and 3. Choice and gem coins are especially rare. Striking is a great problem, and while some sharp pieces exist, probably 80 percent or more have areas of weakness, typically at the 85 (center two digits) of the date, but also often on the headdress and elsewhere. Further, the borders are sometimes imperfect.

Variety 3 gold dollars, made from 1856 through 1889, are easier to acquire in nearly any grade desired, including choice and gem Mint State. Most are well struck and in Mint State have excellent eye appeal. Among Variety 3 gold dollars the dates from 1879 through 1889 inclusive are most often seen, as these were widely saved by coin dealers and collectors at the time and did not circulate to any appreciable extent. Gold dollar coins also were popular as Christmas gifts in the late 1800s. Some of these have very low mintage figures, making them very appealing to today's collectors.

North Carolina Representative James Iver McKay was among the proponents for the introduction of a gold dollar coin. He introduced a bill to authorize the denomination into the House of Representatives on February 20, 1849.

For the Collector and Investor: Gold Dollars as a Specialty

Forming a specialized collection of gold dollars is a fascinating pursuit, one that has drawn the attention of many numismatists over the years. A complete run of date-and-mintmark issues from 1849 through 1889 includes no impossible rarities, although the 1875, with just 20 Proofs and 400 circulation strikes made, is the key date and can challenge collectors. While the dollars of 1879 through 1889 often have remarkably low mintages, they were saved in quantity, and certain of these dates are easily obtainable (although not necessarily inexpensive).

The branch-mint gold dollars of the early years present a special challenge. Among the Charlotte Mint varieties the 1849 comes with an Open Wreath (of which just five are presently known, with a rumor of a sixth) and with a Close Wreath, the latter being scarce but available. Later Charlotte gold dollars, extending through 1859, range from scarce to rare. The 1857-C is notorious for its poor striking.

Gold dollars were struck at the Dahlonega Mint from 1849 through 1861. In the latter year the facility was under the control of the Confederate States of America, and thus the 1861-D gold dollars, rare in any event, are even more desirable as true Confederate coins. The New Orleans Mint also produced gold dollars, which in general are better struck than those of the Charlotte and Dahlonega mints. From 1854 intermittently to 1860, and then in 1870, gold dollars were struck in San Francisco. These Western issues are usually sharply defined and range from scarce to rare. In particular, choice and gem Mint State pieces are elusive.

LIBERTY HEAD (1849–1854)

Variety 1

Designer: *James B. Longacre.* **Weight:** *1.672 grams.*
Composition: *.900 gold, .100 copper (net weight .04837 oz. pure gold).*
Diameter: *13 mm.* **Edge:** *Reeded.* **Mints:** *Philadelphia, Charlotte, Dahlonega, New Orleans, and San Francisco.*

Open Wreath Reverse, Circulation Strike

Close Wreath Reverse, Circulation Strike

Proof Strike

Mintmark location is on the reverse, below the wreath.

History. U.S. Mint chief engraver James Barton Longacre designed the nation's gold dollars. This first type measured 13 mm in diameter, which proved to be inconvenient, and the two later types were enlarged to 15 mm.

Striking and Sharpness. As a rule, Variety 1 gold dollars struck in Philadelphia are sharper than those of the Charlotte and Dahlonega mints. On the obverse, check the highest areas of the hair below the coronet. On the reverse, check the wreath and the central two figures in the date. On both sides check the denticles, which can be mushy or indistinct (particularly on Charlotte and Dahlonega coins, which often have planchet roughness as well).

Availability. All dates and mintmarks are readily collectible, save for the 1849-C, Open Wreath, variety. MS coins often are found for the Philadelphia issues but can be elusive for the branch mints. Charlotte and Dahlonega coins often have striking problems. The few gold dollars of this type that are less than VF in grade usually are damaged or have problems. Although a few Proofs were coined in the early years, they are for all practical purposes unobtainable. Only about a dozen are known.

Grading Standards

MS-60 to 70 (Mint State). ***Obverse:*** At MS-60 to 62, there is abrasion on the hair below the coronet (an area that can be weakly struck as well) and on the cheeks. Marks may be seen. At MS-63, there may be slight abrasion. Luster is irregular. At MS-64, abrasion is less. Luster is rich on most coins, less so on Charlotte and Dahlonega varieties. At MS-65 and above, luster is deep and frosty. At MS-66 and higher, no marks at all are visible without magnification. ***Reverse:*** On MS-60 to 62 coins, there is abrasion on the 1, the highest parts of the leaves, and the ribbon. Otherwise, the same comments apply as for the obverse.

MS-62

Illustrated coin: Some friction is visible on the portrait and in the fields.

AU-50, 53, 55, 58 (About Uncirculated). ***Obverse:*** Light wear on the hair below the coronet and the cheek is very noticeable at AU-50, and progressively less at higher levels to AU-58. Luster is minimal at AU-50 and scattered and incomplete at AU-58. Some tiny nicks and contact marks are to be expected and should be mentioned if they are distracting. ***Reverse:*** Light wear on the 1, the wreath, and the ribbon characterize an AU-50 coin, progressively less at higher levels to AU-58. Otherwise, the same comments apply as for the obverse.

AU-58

Illustrated coin: Much of the luster remains, especially in protected areas.

EF-40, 45 (Extremely Fine). ***Obverse:*** Medium wear is seen on the hair below the coronet, extending to near the bun, and on the curls below. Detail is partially gone on the hair to the right of the coronet. Luster is gone on most coins. ***Reverse:*** Light wear is seen overall, and the highest parts of the leaves are flat. Luster is gone.

EF-45

VF-20, 30 (Very Fine). ***Obverse:*** Most hair detail is gone, except in the lower-relief areas and on the lower curls. Star centers are flat. ***Reverse:*** The wreath and other areas show more wear. Most detail is gone on the higher-relief leaves.

VF-25

PF-60 to 70 (Proof). ***Obverse and Reverse:*** PF-60 to 62 coins have extensive hairlines and may have nicks and contact marks. At PF-63, hairlines are prominent, but the mirror surface is very reflective. PF-64 coins have fewer hairlines. At PF-65, hairlines should be minimal and mostly seen only under magnification. One cannot be "choosy" with Proofs of this type, as only a few exist.

PF-64★ Cameo

1849, With L

1849, No L

Circulation Strikes

	Mintage	GSID	VF-20	EF-40	AU-50	AU-58	MS-60	MS-63	MS-65
Liberty Head, Variety 1 (1849–1854)	**n/a**	**72365**	**$305**	**$375**	**$390**	**$415**	**$430**	**$625**	**$1,900**
1849, Open Wreath, No L	688,567	8007	350	440	550	850	1,150	1,750	5,000
1849, Open Wreath, With L (a)	*	8008	335	415	470	525	625	1,000	4,500
1849, Closed Wreath	*	8009	335	415	430	500	650	1,150	5,000
1849-C, Closed Wreath	11,634	8053	2,250	3,250	4,400	8,750	11,000	21,500	—
1849-C, Open Wreath	5 known	8054	216,000	300,000	450,000	600,000	960,000	—	—
	Auctions: $1,560,000, PCGS MS-62 HA 01/25; $264,000, PCGS EF-45 SBG 01/25								
1849-D, Open Wreath	21,588	8055	2,750	3,600	4,300	5,750	6,250	20,000	96,000
1849-O, Open Wreath	215,000	8056	335	455	575	950	1,300	3,250	13,000
1850	481,953	8010	335	415	430	460	470	650	4,400
1850-C	6,966	8057	1,600	2,750	4,250	5,750	6,750	26,500	—
1850-D	8,382	8058	1,750	3,000	3,750	6,500	10,500	38,500	—
1850-O	14,000	8059	850	1,300	1,600	2,300	3,450	7,500	—
1851	3,317,671	8011	305	375	390	415	430	625	1,900
	Auctions: $108,000, PCGS MS-68 HA 02/21								
1851-C	41,267	8060	1,800	2,100	2,500	3,750	4,000	7,000	23,000
1851-D	9,882	8061	1,600	2,500	3,500	4,500	5,750	18,000	90,000
1851-O	290,000	8062	335	450	470	650	900	1,750	6,500
1852	2,045,351	8012	305	375	390	415	430	625	1,900
	Auctions: $312,000, PCGS MS-69 HA 08/22								
1852-C	9,434	8063	1,150	1,600	2,500	4,250	5,000	13,000	43,000
1852-D	6,360	8064	1,600	2,400	3,500	5,500	8,500	33,500	—
1852-O	140,000	8065	390	470	550	775	1,300	4,250	33,500
1853	4,076,051	8013	305	375	390	415	430	625	2,000
	Auctions: $264,000, PCGS MS-69 HA 01/24								
1853-C	11,515	8066	2,950	3,500	4,200	5,500	7,000	19,500	53,000
1853-D	6,583	8067	1,750	2,500	3,750	6,000	8,500	21,000	50,500
	Auctions: $108,000, PCGS MS-65 HA 08/22								
1853-O	290,000	8068	335	415	470	575	725	1,700	7,000
1854	855,502	8014	305	375	390	415	430	625	1,900
1854-D	2,935	8069	5,000	6,250	7,500	10,000	11,000	41,000	—
1854-S	14,632	8070	650	950	1,600	2,500	3,750	8,000	42,000

* Included in number above. **a.** Liberty's head appears slightly smaller than normal on some variations.

Proof Strikes

	Mintage	GSID	PF-60	PF-63	PF-65
1849, No L	2 known	8090	—	—	—
1850	2 known	8093	$210,000	$312,000	—
	Auctions: $129,250, PCGS PF-60 HA 01/13				
1854, Variety 1	1–2 known	8100	—	—	—

INDIAN PRINCESS HEAD, SMALL HEAD (1854–1856)

VARIETY 2

Designer: *James B. Longacre.* **Weight:** *1.672 grams.*
Composition: *.900 gold, .100 copper (net weight .04837 oz. pure gold).* **Diameter:** *15 mm.*
Edge: *Reeded.* **Mints:** *Philadelphia, Charlotte, Dahlonega, New Orleans, San Francisco.*

Circulation Strike

Mintmark location is on the reverse, below the wreath.

Proof Strike

History. The Variety 2 gold dollar, with the diameter increased from 13 mm to 15 mm, was first made in 1854. The headdress is decorated with *ostrich* plumes, which would not have been used in any genuine Native American headgear. The design proved difficult to strike, leading to its modification in 1856.

Striking and Sharpness. On the obverse, check the highest area of the hair below the coronet and the tips of the feathers. Check the letters. On the reverse, check the ribbon bow knot and in particular the two central digits of the dates. Examine the digits on both sides. Nearly all have problems. This type is often softly struck in the centers, with weak hair detail and the numerals 85 in the date sometimes faint—this should not be confused with wear. The 1855-C and 1855-D coins are often poorly struck and on rough planchets.

Availability. All Variety 2 gold dollars are collectible, but the Charlotte and Dahlonega coins are rare. With patience, Full Details coins are available of 1854, 1855, and 1856-S, but virtually impossible to find for the branch-mint issues of 1855. The few gold dollars of this type that are less than VF in grade usually are damaged or have problems. Proofs exist of the 1854 and 1855 issues, but were made in very small quantities.

GRADING STANDARDS

MS-61

MS-60 to 70 (Mint State). ***Obverse:*** At MS-60 to 62, there is abrasion on the hair below the band lettered LIBERTY (an area that can be weakly struck as well), on the tips of the feather plumes, and throughout the field. Contact marks may also be seen. At MS-63, there should be only slight abrasions. Luster is irregular. At MS-64, abrasions and marks are less. Luster is rich on most coins, less so on Charlotte and Dahlonega issues. At MS-65 and above, luster is deep and frosty, with no marks at all visible without magnification at MS-66 and higher. ***Reverse:*** At MS-60 to 62, there may be abrasions on the 1, on the highest parts of the leaves, on the ribbon knot, and in the field. Otherwise, the same comments apply as for the obverse.

Illustrated coin: Some loss of luster is evident in the fields, but strong luster remains among the letters and in other protected areas. Good eye appeal is elusive for this type.

AU-55

AU-50, 53, 55, 58 (About Uncirculated). ***Obverse:*** Light wear on the hair below the coronet, the cheek, and the tips of the feather plumes is very noticeable at AU-50, progressively less at higher levels to AU-58. Luster is minimal at AU-50 and scattered and incomplete at AU-58. Some tiny nicks and contact marks are to be expected and should be mentioned if they are distracting. ***Reverse:*** Light wear on the 1, the wreath, and the ribbon knot characterize an AU-50 coin, progressively less at higher levels to AU-58. Otherwise, the same comments apply as for the obverse.

Illustrated coin: This coin was lightly struck at the center. Clash marks appear on both sides, most prominent within the wreath on the reverse.

EF-40

EF-40, 45 (Extremely Fine). ***Obverse:*** Medium wear is seen on the hair below the coronet and on the feather plume tips. Detail is partially gone on the hair, although the usual light striking may make this moot. Luster is gone on most coins. ***Reverse:*** Light wear is seen overall, and the highest parts of the leaves are flat. Luster is gone on most coins.

Illustrated coin: This coin was lightly struck at the centers, but overall has extraordinary quality.

VF-25

VF-20, 30 (Very Fine). ***Obverse:*** Most hair detail is gone, except at the back of the lower curls. The feather plume ends are flat. ***Reverse:*** The wreath and other areas show more wear. Most detail is gone on the higher-relief leaves.

Illustrated coin: This coin is well worn, but has an exceptionally bold date, indicating that it must have been a very sharp strike.

PF-66

PF-60 to 70 (Proof). ***Obverse and Reverse:*** PF-60 to 62 coins have extensive hairlines and may have nicks and contact marks. At PF-63, hairlines are prominent, but the mirror surface is very reflective. PF-64 coins have fewer hairlines. At PF-65, hairlines should be minimal and mostly seen only under magnification. There should be no nicks or marks. PF-66 and higher coins have no marks or hairlines visible to the unaided eye.

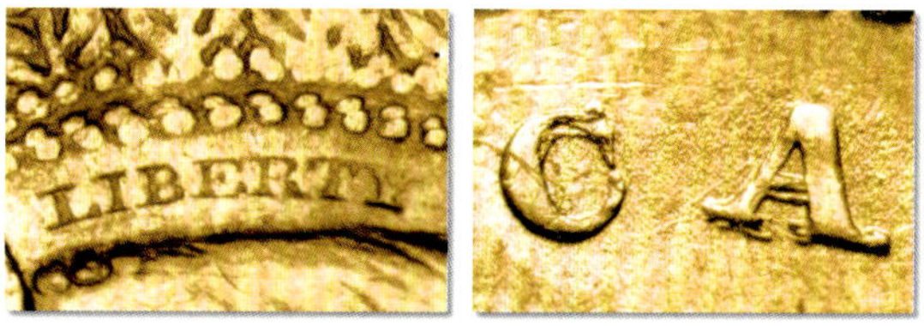

1854, Doubled Die Obverse
FS-1101

Circulation Strikes

	Mintage	GSID	VF-20	EF-40	AU-50	AU-58	MS-60	MS-63	MS-65
Indian Princess, Small Head, Variety 2 (1854–1856)	**n/a**	**72366**	**$525**	**$625**	**$650**	**$750**	**$1,400**	**$4,400**	**$20,500**
1854	783,943	8015	525	625	650	750	1,400	4,400	20,500
	Auctions: $161,000, NGC MS-68 SBG 01/09								
↳1854, Variety 2, Doubled Die Obverse, FS-101	*	322173	—	700	775	1,100	1,450	6,250	—
1855	758,269	8016	525	625	650	750	1,400	4,400	20,500
	Auctions: $180,000, PCGS MS-67 HA 08/22								
1855-C	9,803	8071	3,000	5,000	6,250	17,500	21,000	—	—
1855-D	1,811	8072	10,500	26,500	35,000	50,500	66,000	102,000	—
	Auctions: $164,500, PCGS MS-64 HA 08/15								
1855-O	55,000	8073	1,100	1,500	2,100	3,250	8,500	28,000	—
1856-S	24,600	8075	850	1,750	2,500	7,000	8,000	15,500	69,500
↳1856-S, S Over S, FS-501	*	351835	875	1,850	2,600	7,250	8,500	16,500	73,000

* Included in number above.

Proof Strikes

	Mintage	GSID	PF-60	PF-63	PF-65
Indian Princess, Small Head, Variety 2 (1849–1854), Proof	**n/a**	**74133**	**$96,000**	**$168,000**	**$288,000**
1854, Variety 2	4 known	8097	—	—	384,000
1855	8–9 known	8103	96,000	168,000	288,000
	Auctions: $287,500, PCGS PF-65 HA 01/05				

INDIAN PRINCESS HEAD, LARGE HEAD (1856–1889)

Variety 3

Designer: *James B. Longacre.* **Weight:** *1.672 grams.*
Composition: *.900 gold, .100 copper (net weight .04837 oz. pure gold).* **Diameter:** *15 mm.*
Edge: *Reeded.* **Mints:** *Philadelphia, Charlotte, Dahlonega, and San Francisco.*

Circulation Strike

Proof Strike

History. The design of the Indian Princess Head was modified in 1856. The new Variety 3 portrait is larger and in shallower relief. After this change, most (but not all) gold dollars were struck with strong detail. Gold dollars of this type did not circulate extensively after 1861, except in the West. As they did not see heavy use, today most pieces are EF or better. MS coins are readily available, particularly of the dates 1879 through 1889 (during those years the coins were popular among investors and speculators, and many were saved). These gold dollars were very popular with jewelers, who would purchase them at a price of $1.50 for use in a variety of ornaments.

Striking and Sharpness. These dollars usually are well struck, but many exceptions exist. Charlotte and Dahlonega coins are usually weak in areas and can have planchet problems. On all coins, check the hair details on the obverse. The word LIBERTY may be only partially present or missing completely, as the dies were made this way for some issues, particularly in the 1870s; this does not affect their desirability. On the reverse, check the ribbon knot and the two central date numerals. Check the denticles on both sides. Copper stains are sometimes seen on issues of the 1880s due to incomplete mixing of the alloy. Many coins of the 1860s onward have highly prooflike surfaces.

Availability. All Variety 3 gold dollars are collectible, but many issues are scarce. Most MS-65 or finer coins are dated from 1879 to 1889. The few gold dollars of this type that are less than VF usually are damaged or have problems. Proofs were made of all years. Most range from rare to very rare, some dates in the 1880s being exceptions. Some later dates have high Proof mintages, but likely many of these coins were sold to the jewelry trade (as the Mint was reluctant to release circulation strikes to this market sector). Such coins were incorporated into jewelry and no longer exist as collectible coins.

Grading Standards

MS-67

MS-60 to 70 (Mint State). ***Obverse:*** At MS-60 to 62, there is abrasion on the hair below the band lettered LIBERTY (an area that can be weakly struck as well), on the tips of the feather plumes, and throughout the field. Contact marks may also be seen. At MS-63, there should be only slight abrasions. Luster is irregular. At MS-64, abrasions and marks are less. Luster is rich on most coins, less so on Charlotte and Dahlonega issues. At MS-65 and above, luster is deep and frosty, with no marks at all visible without magnification at MS-66 and higher. ***Reverse:*** At MS-60 to 62, there may be abrasions on the 1, on the highest parts of the leaves, on the ribbon knot, and in the field. Otherwise, the same comments apply as for the obverse.

Illustrated coin: This exceptionally high-grade coin has superb eye appeal.

AU-50, 53, 55, 58 (About Uncirculated). ***Obverse:*** Light wear on the hair below the coronet, the cheek, and the tips of the feather plumes is very noticeable at AU-50, progressively less at higher levels to AU-58. Luster is minimal at AU-50 and scattered and incomplete at AU-58. Some tiny nicks and contact marks are to be expected and should be mentioned if they are distracting. ***Reverse:*** Light wear on the 1, the wreath, and the ribbon knot characterize an AU-50 coin, progressively less at higher levels to AU-58. Otherwise, the same comments apply as for the obverse.

AU-58

Illustrated coin: The obverse field is slightly bulged. This coin is lightly struck at the center, unusual for most Variety 3 gold dollars, but sometimes seen on Charlotte and Dahlonega varieties. Among 1857-C gold dollars this coin is exceptional. Most have poor striking and/or planchet problems.

EF-40, 45 (Extremely Fine). ***Obverse:*** Medium wear is seen on the hair below the coronet and on the feather plume tips. Detail is partially gone on the hair, although the usual light striking may make this moot. Luster is gone on most coins. ***Reverse:*** Light wear is seen overall, and the highest parts of the leaves are flat. Luster is gone on most coins.

EF-40

VF-20, 30 (Very Fine). ***Obverse:*** Most hair detail is gone, except at the back of the lower curls. The feather plume ends are flat. ***Reverse:*** The wreath and other areas show more wear. Most detail is gone on the higher-relief leaves.

Illustrated coin: This coin is lightly struck at the center obverse, as well as at the U and IC in the border lettering. It is lightly struck at the center of the reverse.

VF-20

PF-60 to 70 (Proof). ***Obverse and Reverse:*** PF-60 to 62 coins have extensive hairlines and may have nicks and contact marks. At PF-63, hairlines are prominent, but the mirror surface is very reflective. PF-64 coins have fewer hairlines. At PF-65, hairlines should be minimal and mostly seen only under magnification. There should be no nicks or marks. PF-66 and higher coins have no marks or hairlines visible to the unaided eye.

PF-67
Ultra Cameo

Illustrated coin: This splendid cameo Proof is one of the finest graded.

1862, Doubled Die Obverse
FS-101

Circulation Strikes

	Mintage	GSID	VF-20	EF-40	AU-50	AU-58	MS-60	MS-63	MS-65
Indian Princess, Large Head, Variety 3 (1856–1889)	**n/a**	**72367**	**$370**	**$385**	**$435**	**$450**	**$575**	**$850**	**$1,100**
1856, Slanted 5	1,762,936	8017	370	385	435	450	575	850	2,100
1856, Upright 5	*	8018	370	385	435	525	675	1,550	10,500
1856-D	1,460	8074	5,250	8,750	11,000	26,500	31,000	72,000	—
1857	774,789	8019	370	385	435	450	575	875	3,600
1857-C	13,280	8076	2,750	3,750	5,000	7,000	9,000	—	—
1857-D	3,533	8077	2,100	3,500	5,250	12,000	21,500	79,000	—
1857-S	10,000	8078	775	1,200	1,600	3,250	5,500	21,000	—
1858	117,995	8020	370	385	435	450	575	1,150	5,000
1858-D	3,477	8079	1,750	3,250	5,000	7,250	9,500	24,000	67,000
1858-S	10,000	8080	650	950	1,200	2,500	5,500	16,000	48,000
1859	168,244	8021	370	385	435	450	575	925	2,300
1859-C	5,235	8081	2,500	3,450	4,700	7,000	7,750	33,500	—
1859-D	4,952	8082	1,800	2,500	3,750	6,250	8,000	21,500	50,500
1859-S	15,000	8083	750	1,000	1,500	3,000	5,250	19,000	—
1860	36,514	8022	390	435	475	550	650	1,300	8,750
1860-D	1,566	8084	3,750	7,000	10,000	17,000	26,500	60,000	—
1860-S	13,000	8085	490	725	950	2,000	2,800	5,500	30,000
1861	527,150	8023	370	405	480	500	625	925	2,500
1861-D (a)	1,250	8086	38,500	55,000	69,500	103,000	120,000	180,000	300,000
	Auctions: $126,000, PCGS MS-61 HA 11/23; $102,000, PCGS AU-58 SBG 11/23								
1862	1,361,355	8024	370	385	435	450	575	900	2,000
↳1862, Doubled Die Obverse, FS-101	*	213850	—	525	600	950	1,000	2,500	3,750
1863	6,200	8025	1,400	2,250	3,750	7,000	8,250	12,000	21,000
	Auctions: $192,000, PCGS MS-68 SBG 11/24								
1864	5,900	8026	1,150	1,400	1,550	2,750	3,500	8,000	10,000
1865	3,700	8027	900	1,250	1,900	3,000	3,750	6,250	12,000
1866	7,100	8028	495	725	850	1,050	1,450	2,600	4,600
1867	5,200	8029	550	775	1,000	1,250	1,400	2,500	8,250
1868	10,500	8030	500	725	850	1,000	1,150	2,600	7,750

* Included in number above. **a.** All were struck under the auspices of the state of Georgia and the Confederate States of America after the Dahlonega Mint had been seized by Rebel troops.

Circulation Strikes *(continued)*

	Mintage	GSID	VF-20	EF-40	AU-50	AU-58	MS-60	MS-63	MS-65
1869	5,900	8031	$525	$750	$875	$1,200	$1,300	$2,250	$5,000
1870	6,300	8032	525	725	850	1,000	1,100	1,800	4,750
1870-S	3,000	8087	900	1,250	2,000	3,750	4,250	9,500	26,500
1871	3,900	8033	475	575	725	925	1,150	2,050	4,100
1872	3,500	8034	390	525	675	1,100	1,250	2,750	7,750
1873, Open 3	123,300	8035	370	385	435	450	575	850	1,250
1873, Closed 3	1,800	8036	525	800	950	1,100	1,600	3,750	14,000
1874	198,800	8037	370	385	435	450	575	850	1,100
1875	400	8038	4,050	6,000	7,500	12,000	13,000	20,000	45,000
	Auctions: $168,000, PCGS MS-66 HA 08/22								
1876	3,200	8039	475	700	825	1,050	1,150	1,750	5,250
1877	3,900	8040	500	600	725	950	1,000	1,900	5,000
1878	3,000	8041	470	575	725	875	950	1,550	5,000
1879	3,000	8042	390	490	550	750	1,000	1,450	2,750
1880	1,600	8043	395	430	490	575	650	1,500	2,050
1881	7,620	8044	405	435	525	600	650	950	1,900
1882	5,000	8045	405	435	525	600	775	1,200	1,900
1883	10,800	8046	405	435	525	600	650	950	1,500
1884	5,230	8047	405	435	525	625	675	1,050	1,700
	Auctions: $132,000, PCGS MS-69 HA 08/22								
1885	11,156	8048	405	435	525	600	650	950	2,000
1886	5,000	8049	405	435	525	600	650	950	1,700
1887	7,500	8050	405	435	525	600	650	925	1,300
1888	15,501	8051	405	435	525	600	650	950	1,300
1889	28,950	8052	405	435	525	600	650	900	1,100
↳1889, Doubled Die Reverse, FS-801	*	351836	—	480	575	675	725	975	1,200

* Included in number above.

Proof Strikes

	Mintage	GSID	PF-60	PF-63	PF-65
Indian Princess, Large Head, Variety 3 (1856–1889), Proof	**n/a**	**74136**	**$2,900**	**$4,100**	**$8,000**
Same, Proof Cameo	**n/a**	**74137**	**—**	**4,500**	**9,500**
Same, Proof Deep Cameo	**n/a**	**74138**	**—**	**6,250**	**11,000**
1856, Slanted 5	7–9 known	8106	11,500	20,000	60,000
1857	9–10 known	8109	8,750	14,000	48,000
1858	15–18 known	8112	8,750	14,000	31,000
1859	80	8115	3,250	5,250	19,000
1860	154	8118	3,000	7,250	17,500
1861	349	8121	5,000	8,000	19,000
1862	35	8124	3,500	5,500	23,500
1863	50	8127	3,550	5,750	20,500
1864	50	8130	3,750	7,500	20,500
1865	25	8133	5,000	10,500	24,000
1866	30	8136	3,550	5,750	18,000
1867	50	8139	6,750	10,000	19,000
1868	25	8142	3,750	6,750	16,000
1869	25	8145	3,750	6,750	15,000

	Mintage	GSID	PF-60	PF-63	PF-65
1870	35	8148	$3,550	$5,250	$15,000
1871	30	8151	3,550	5,250	17,000
1872	30	8154	3,550	7,000	17,500
1873, Closed 3	25	8157	6,500	15,000	32,500
1874	20	8160	4,600	12,000	21,000
1875	20	8163	10,500	14,000	31,000
1876	45	8166	3,550	5,250	15,000
1877	20	8169	8,000	10,500	18,000
1878	20	8172	3,550	5,250	15,000
1879	30	8175	6,250	7,500	17,000
1880	36	8178	6,250	10,000	18,000
1881	87	8181	3,550	5,000	11,500
1882	125	8184	2,900	4,100	8,000
1883	207	8187	2,900	4,100	8,000
1884	1,006	8190	2,900	4,100	8,000
1885	1,105	8193	2,900	4,100	8,000
1886	1,016	8196	2,900	4,100	8,000
1887	1,043	8199	2,900	4,100	8,000
1888	1,079	8202	2,900	4,100	8,000
1889	1,779	8205	2,900	4,100	8,000

Gold Quarter Eagles ($2.50)
1796–1929

AN OVERVIEW OF GOLD QUARTER EAGLES

The quarter eagle, denominated at one-fourth of an eagle, or $2.50, was authorized by the Act of April 2, 1792. Early types in the series range from rare to very rare. The first, the 1796 without stars on the obverse, Heraldic Eagle motif on the reverse, is a classic, one of the most desired of all pieces needed for a type set, and accordingly expensive. Most examples are in such grades as EF and AU.

Scan for additional information.

Quarter eagles with stars on the obverse and with the Heraldic Eagle reverse were produced from 1796 intermittently through 1807. Today they exist in modest numbers, particularly in grades such as EF and AU, but on an absolute basis are fairly rare.

The standalone 1808 Draped Bust type, by John Reich, of which only 2,710 were minted, is the rarest single type coin in the entire American copper, nickel, silver, and gold series, possibly excepting the 1839 Gobrecht dollar (in a different category, as Proof restrikes were made). Examples of the 1808 can be found in various grades from VF through AU, and only rarely higher.

The next style of quarter eagle, from 1821 through 1827, is scarce, but when seen is usually in grades such as EF, AU, or even the low levels of Mint State. The same can be said for the modified quarter eagle of 1829 through early 1834.

Finally, with the advent of the Classic Head in late 1834, continuing through 1839, quarter eagles become more readily available. Examples can be found in nearly any grade from VF into the lower levels of Mint State. Then come the Liberty Head quarter eagles, minted continuously from 1840 through 1907, in sufficient numbers and for such a long time that it is not difficult to obtain an example to illustrate the type, with choice and gem Mint State coins being plentiful for the dates of the early 20th century.

The last quarter eagles are of the Indian Head type, minted from 1908 through 1929. These pieces are plentiful today, but grading can be difficult, as they were struck in sunken relief and the highest part on the coin is the field (this area was immediately subject to contact marks and wear). Although many opportunities exist in the marketplace, a collector should approach a purchase with care, seeking an example that has frosty, lustrous fields.

For the Collector and Investor: Gold Quarter Eagles as a Specialty

Collecting quarter eagles by dates, mintmarks, and major varieties is a very appealing pursuit. Although many are scarce and rare—this description applies to any variety from 1796 through early 1834—none are truly impossible to obtain. Among the Classic Head issues of 1834–1839, branch-mint coins are especially scarce in higher grades.

Liberty Head quarter eagles, produced continuously from 1840 through 1907, include a number of key issues, such as the famous 1854-S (usually seen in well-circulated grades), the Proof-only 1863 (of which only 30 were struck), and a number of elusive mintmarks. Of particular interest is the 1848 coin with CAL. counterstamped on the reverse, signifying that the coin was made from gold bullion brought to the Philadelphia Mint in a special shipment from California.

DRAPED BUST TO RIGHT (1796–1807)

Designer: *Robert Scot.* **Weight:** *4.37 grams.* **Composition:** *.9167 gold, .0833 silver and copper.* **Diameter:** *Approximately 20 mm.* **Edge:** *Reeded.* **Mint:** *Philadelphia.*

No Stars on Obverse (1796)

Stars on Obverse (1796–1807)

History. The first quarter eagles were struck intermittently during the late 1790s and early 1800s, with consistently small mintages. The earliest issues of 1796 lack obverse stars. They likely circulated domestically, rather than being exported in international trade.

Striking and Sharpness. Most have light striking in one area or another. On the obverse, check the hair details and the stars. On the reverse, check the shield, stars, and clouds. Examine the denticles on both sides. Planchet adjustment marks (from a coin's overweight planchet being filed down to correct specifications) are seen on many coins and are not noted by the certification services. On high-grade coins the luster usually is very attractive. Certain reverse dies of this type were also used to make dimes of the era, which were almost exactly the same diameter.

Availability. Most Draped Bust to Right quarter eagles in the marketplace are EF or AU. MS coins are elusive; when seen, they usually are of later dates.

Grading Standards

MS-62

MS-60 to 70 (Mint State). ***Obverse:*** At MS-60, some abrasion and contact marks are evident, most noticeably on the hair to the left of Liberty's forehead and on the higher-relief areas of the cap. On the No Stars quarter eagles, there is some abrasion in the field—more so than the With Stars coins, on which the field is more protected. Luster is present, but may be dull or lifeless, and interrupted in patches. At MS-63, contact marks are few, and abrasion is very light. An MS-65 coin will have hardly any abrasion, and contact marks are so minute as to require magnification. Luster should be full and rich. Coins grading above MS-65 exist more in theory than in reality for this type—but they do exist, and are defined by having fewer marks as perfection is approached. ***Reverse:*** Comments apply as for the obverse, except that abrasion and contact marks are most noticeable on the upper part of the eagle and the clouds. The field area is complex; there is not much open space, with stars above the eagle, the arrows and olive branch, and other features. Accordingly, marks are not as noticeable as on the obverse.

Illustrated coin: Some friction appears on the higher areas of this example, but the fields retain nearly full luster, and the coin overall has nice eye appeal.

AU-50, 53, 55, 58 (About Uncirculated). ***Obverse:*** Light wear is seen on the cheek, the hair immediately to the left of the face, and the cap, more so at AU-50 than at AU–53 or 55. An AU-58 coin has minimal traces of wear. An AU-50 coin has luster in protected areas among the stars and letters, with little in the open fields or on the portrait. At AU-58 most luster is present in the fields, but is worn away on the highest parts of the motifs. The 1796 No Stars type has less luster in any given grade. ***Reverse:*** Comments as for Mint State, except that the eagle's neck, the tips and top of the wings, the clouds, and the tail now show noticeable wear, as do other features. Luster ranges from perhaps 40 percent remaining in protected areas at AU-50 to nearly full mint bloom at AU-58. Often the reverse of this type retains much more luster than does the obverse.

AU-58

EF-40, 45 (Extremely Fine). ***Obverse:*** Wear is evident all over the portrait, with some loss of detail in the hair to the left of Liberty's face. Excellent detail remains in low-relief areas of the hair, such as the front curl and the back of the head. The stars show wear, as do the date and letters. Luster, if present at all, is minimal and in protected areas. ***Reverse:*** Wear is greater than at the About Uncirculated level. The neck lacks feather detail on its highest points. Feathers have lost some detail near the edges of the wings, and some areas of the horizontal lines in the shield may be blended together. Some traces of luster may be seen, more so at EF-45 than at EF-40. Overall, the reverse appears to be in a slightly higher grade than the obverse.

EF-45

VF-20, 30 (Very Fine). ***Obverse:*** The higher-relief areas of hair are well worn at VF-20, less so at VF-30. The stars are flat at their centers. ***Reverse:*** Wear is greater, including on the shield and wing feathers. The star centers are flat. Other areas have lost detail as well. E PLURIBUS UNUM is easy to read.

VF-30

1798, Close Date

1798, Wide Date

1804, 13-Star Reverse

1804, 14-Star Reverse

Circulation Strikes

	Mintage	GSID	F-12	VF-20	EF-40	AU-50	AU-58	MS-60	MS-63
Draped Bust to Right, No Stars on Obverse (1796)	**n/a**	**72371**	**$69,500**	**$96,000**	**$144,000**	**$180,000**	**$270,000**	**$384,000**	**$1,200,000**
Draped Bust to Right, Stars on Obverse (1796–1807)	**n/a**	**72372**	**8,750**	**10,500**	**13,000**	**15,500**	**24,500**	**31,000**	**75,500**
1796, No Stars on Obverse	963	8208	69,500	96,000	144,000	180,000	270,000	384,000	1,200,000
	Auctions: $192,000, NGC AU-58 SBG 04/25; $1,725,000, PCGS MS-65 HA 04/25								
1796, Stars on Obverse	432	8209	60,000	72,000	96,000	126,000	186,000	192,000	600,000
	Auctions: $1,006,250, NGC MS-65 HA 01/08								
1797	427	8210	30,000	36,000	50,500	79,000	192,000	252,000	432,000
	Auctions: $276,000, NGC MS-64 SU 11/05								
1798, Close Date	1,094	8212	22,000	27,000	38,000	72,000	114,000	150,000	330,000
	Auctions: $268,500, PCGS MS-65 SOTH 06/00								
1798, Wide Date	*	8211	8,750	10,500	18,000	29,000	57,500	101,000	240,000
	Auctions: $115,000, PCGS MS-62 HA 01/11								
1802, 2 Over "1" (a)	3,035	8251	8,750	10,500	14,500	18,000	31,000	33,500	75,500
	Auctions: $185,150, NGC MS-65 SBG 11/10								
1804, 13-Star Reverse	3,327	8213	78,000	115,000	180,000	270,000	540,000	—	—
	Auctions: $322,000, NGC AU-55 HA 08/08								
1804, 14-Star Reverse	*	8214	10,500	13,000	17,000	20,500	31,000	42,000	137,000
1805	1,781	8215	8,750	10,500	13,000	17,500	24,500	31,000	153,500
1806, 6 Over 4, 8 Stars Left, 5 Stars Right	1,136	8252	9,500	11,000	14,500	20,500	36,000	57,500	138,000
	Auctions: $120,000, NGC MS-64 SBG 08/25								
1806, 6 Over 5, 7 Stars Left, 6 Stars Right	480	8253	9,500	11,000	16,000	32,500	66,000	96,000	360,000
	Auctions: $195,500, NGC MS-63 ANR 06/05								
1807	6,812	8216	8,750	10,500	13,000	15,500	24,500	31,000	75,500
	Auctions: $276,000, PCGS MS-65 GLDB 09/08								

* Included in number above. **a.** Some specialists believe this was a defective die punch and not a true overdate.

CAPPED BUST TO LEFT (1808)

Designer: *John Reich.* **Weight:** *4.37 grams.* **Composition:** *.9167 gold, .0833 silver and copper.* **Diameter:** *Approximately 20 mm.* **Edge:** *Reeded.*

History. John Reich's Draped Bust was an adaptation of the design introduced in 1807 on the half dollar. On the quarter eagle it was used for a single year only, with fewer than 3,000 coins struck, making it the rarest of the major gold coin types (indeed, the rarest of any U.S. coin type).

Striking and Sharpness. All examples are lightly struck on one area or another, particularly the stars and rims. The rims are low and sometimes missing or nearly so (on the obverse), causing quarter eagles of this type to wear more quickly than otherwise might be the case. Sharpness of strike is overlooked by most buyers.

Availability. Examples are rare in any grade. Typical grades are EF and AU. Lower grades are seldom seen, as the coins did not circulate to any great extent. Gold coins of this era were not seen in circulation after 1821, so they did not get a chance to acquire significant wear.

Grading Standards

MS-60 to 70 (Mint State). ***Obverse:*** At MS-60, some abrasion and contact marks are seen on the cheek, on the hair below the LIBERTY inscription, and on the highest-relief folds of the cap. Luster is present, but may be dull or lifeless, and interrupted in patches. At MS-63, contact marks are few, and abrasion is very light. Abrasion is even less at MS-64. (Discussion of such high grades in these early coins starts to enter the realm of theory.) Quarter eagles of this type are almost, but not quite, non-existent in a combination of high grade and nice eye appeal. ***Reverse:*** Comments apply as for the obverse, except that abrasion is most noticeable on the eagle's neck and highest area of the wings.

MS-63

Illustrated coin: Superbly struck, this coin is a "poster example" with few peers.

AU-50, 53, 55, 58 (About Uncirculated). ***Obverse:*** Light wear is seen on the cheek and higher-relief areas of the hair and cap. Friction and scattered marks are in the field, ranging from extensive at AU-50 to minimal at AU-58. The low rim affords little protection to the field of this coin, but the stars in relief help. Luster may be seen in protected areas, minimal at AU-50, but less so at AU-58. At

AU-50

AU-58 the field retains some luster as well. ***Reverse:*** Comments are as for a Mint State coin, except that the eagle's neck, the top of the wings, the leaves, and the arrowheads now show noticeable wear, as do other features. Luster ranges from perhaps 40 percent remaining in protected areas at AU-50 to nearly full mint bloom at AU-58. Often the reverse of this type retains much more luster than does the obverse, as on this type the motto, eagle, and lettering protect the surrounding flat areas.

Illustrated coin: Note some lightness of strike.

EF-40, 45 (Extremely Fine). ***Obverse:*** More wear is seen on the portrait, the hair, the cap, and the drapery near the clasp. Luster is likely to be absent on the obverse due to the low rim. ***Reverse:*** Wear is more extensive on the eagle, including the top of the wings, the head, the top of the shield, and the claws. Some traces of luster may be seen in protected areas, more so at EF-45 than at EF-40.

EF-40

VF-20, 30 (Very Fine). ***Obverse:*** Wear on the portrait has reduced the hair detail, especially to the right of the face and the top of the head, but much can still be seen. ***Reverse:*** Wear on the eagle is greater, and details of feathers near the shield and near the top of the wings are weak or missing. All other features show wear, but most are fairly sharp. Generally, Draped Bust gold coins at this grade level lack eye appeal.

VF-20

Illustrated coin: This is a nice, problem-free example of a lower but very desirable grade for this rare issue.

Circulation Strikes

	Mintage	GSID	F-12	VF-20	EF-40	AU-50	AU-58	MS-60	MS-63
Capped Bust to Left (1808)	**n/a**	**74467**	**$53,000**	**$65,000**	**$120,000**	**$144,000**	**$264,000**	**$318,000**	**$600,000**
1808	2,710	8217	53,000	65,000	120,000	144,000	264,000	318,000	600,000
	Auctions: $168,000, PCGS AU-53 SBG 11/24; $517,500, PCGS MS-63 SBG 11/24								

* Included in number above.

100 GREATEST™ UNITED STATES COINS

No. 89 1808 CAPPED BUST QUARTER EAGLE

CAPPED HEAD TO LEFT (1821–1834)

Designer: *John Reich.* **Weight:** *4.37 grams.* **Composition:** *.9167 gold, .0833 silver and copper.* **Diameter:** *1821–1827—18.5 mm; 1829–1834—approximately 18.2 mm.* **Edge:** *Reeded.* **Mint:** *Philadelphia.*

Large Diameter, Circulation Strike

Large Diameter, Proof Strike

Small Diameter, Circulation Strike

Small Diameter, Proof Strike

History. Capped Head to Left quarter eagles dated 1821 through 1827 have a larger diameter and larger letters, dates, and stars than those of 1829 to 1834. The same grading standards apply to both. Gold coins of this type did not circulate in commerce, because their face value was lower than their bullion value. Many legislators, who had the option to draw their pay in specie (silver and gold coinage), took advantage of this fact to sell their salaries at a premium for paper money. Most wear was due to use as pocket pieces, or from minor handling.

Striking and Sharpness. Most Capped Head to Left quarter eagles are well struck. On the obverse, check the hair details (which on the Large Diameter style can be light in areas) and the stars. On the reverse, check the eagle. On both sides inspect the denticles. Fields are often semi-prooflike on higher grades.

Availability. All Capped Head to Left quarter eagles are rare. Grades typically range from EF to MS, with choice examples in the latter category being scarce, and gems being very rare. Proof coins were made on a limited basis for presentation and for sale to numismatists. All Proof examples are exceedingly rare today, and are usually encountered only when great collections are dispersed.

Grading Standards

MS-65

MS-60 to 70 (Mint State). ***Obverse:*** At MS-60, some abrasion and contact marks are seen on the cheek, on the hair below the LIBERTY inscription, and on the highest-relief folds of the cap. Luster is present, but may be dull or lifeless, and interrupted in patches. At MS-63, contact marks are few, and abrasion is very light. Abrasion is even less at MS-64. (Discussion of such high grades in these early coins starts to enter the realm of theory.) Quarter eagles of this type are almost, but not quite, non-existent in a combination of high grade and nice eye appeal. ***Reverse:*** Comments apply as for the obverse, except that abrasion is most noticeable on the eagle's neck and highest area of the wings.

Illustrated coin: This is a well-struck lustrous gem.

AU-53

AU-50, 53, 55, 58 (About Uncirculated). ***Obverse:*** Light wear is seen on the cheek and higher-relief areas of the hair and cap. Friction and scattered marks are in the field, ranging from extensive at AU-50 to minimal at AU-58. The low rim affords little protection to the field of this coin, but the stars in relief help. Luster may be seen in protected areas, minimal at AU-50, but less so at AU-58. At AU-58 the field retains some luster as well. ***Reverse:*** Comments are as for a Mint State coin, except that the eagle's neck, the top of the wings, the leaves, and the arrowheads now show noticeable wear, as do other features. Luster ranges from perhaps 40 percent remaining in protected areas at AU-50 to nearly full mint bloom at AU-58. Often the reverse of this type retains much more luster than does the obverse, as on this type the motto, eagle, and lettering protect the surrounding flat areas.

EF-40

EF-40, 45 (Extremely Fine). ***Obverse:*** More wear is seen on the portrait, the hair, the cap, and the drapery near the clasp. Luster is likely to be absent on the obverse due to the low rim. ***Reverse:*** Wear is more extensive on the eagle, including the top of the wings, the head, the top of the shield, and the claws. Some traces of luster may be seen in protected areas, more so at EF-45 than at EF-40.

PF-67 Cameo

PF-60 to 70 (Proof). ***Obverse and Reverse:*** PF–60 to 62 coins have extensive hairlines and may have nicks and contact marks. At PF-63, hairlines are prominent, but the mirror surface is very reflective. PF-64 coins have fewer hairlines. At PF-65, hairlines should be minimal and mostly seen only under magnification. There should be no nicks or marks. PF-66 and higher coins should have no marks or hairlines visible to the unaided eye.

Circulation Strikes

	Mintage	GSID	F-12	VF-20	EF-40	AU-50	AU-58	MS-60	MS-63
Capped Head to Left, Large Diameter (1821–1827)	**n/a**	**72373**	**$8,000**	**$9,500**	**$12,500**	**$14,500**	**$24,000**	**$30,000**	**$70,000**
Capped Head to Left, Small Diameter (1829–1834)	**n/a**	**72374**	**6,500**	**7,750**	**11,000**	**14,500**	**21,500**	**24,000**	**39,500**
1821	6,448	8218	8,000	9,500	12,500	14,500	24,000	30,500	120,000
	Auctions: $149,500, PCGS MS-64 GLDB 09/08								
1824, 4 Over 1	2,600	8254	8,000	9,500	12,500	14,500	24,000	34,000	79,000
1825	4,434	8221	8,000	10,000	14,000	17,500	29,000	32,000	90,000
	Auctions: $240,000, NGC MS-65 SBG 08/25								
1826, 6 Over 6	760	8223	15,000	21,000	30,000	42,000	66,000	102,000	288,000
	Auctions: $132,000, PCGS MS-61 SBG 06/25								
1827	2,800	8224	8,250	9,750	16,000	19,000	33,500	36,000	72,000
	Auctions: $144,000, PCGS MS-64 SBG 11/24								
1829	3,403	8226	6,500	7,750	11,000	14,500	21,500	24,000	43,000
	Auctions: $316,250, PCGS MS-67 HA 08/06								
1830	4,540	8228	6,500	7,750	11,000	15,000	22,000	24,500	39,500
1831	4,520	8230	6,500	7,750	11,000	14,500	21,500	24,000	48,000
	Auctions: $240,000, PCGS MS-66 HA 09/20								
1832	4,400	8232	6,500	7,750	11,000	14,500	24,000	26,500	48,000
1833	4,160	8234	6,500	7,750	11,000	14,500	21,500	24,000	39,500
	Auctions: $124,998, NGC MS-67 SU 08/02								
1834, With Motto	4,000	8236	31,000	42,000	69,500	138,000	180,000	198,000	360,000

Proof Strikes

		GSID	PF-63
1821	4 known	8219	—
	Auctions: $241,500, PCGS PF-64 HA 01/07		
1824, 4 Over 1	2 known	8255	—
	Auctions: $1,740,000, PCGS PF-67 HA 05/23		
1825	unknown	8222	—
1826, 6 Over 5	unknown	8256	—
1827	unknown	8225	—
1829	unknown	8227	—
1830	unknown	8229	—
1831	2–3 known	8231	$240,000
	Auctions: $117,875, NGC PF-64 HA 04/12		
1832	2 known	8233	396,000
	Auctions: $336,000, PCGS PF-63 HA 08/23		
1833	unknown	8235	480,000
	Auctions: $408,000, PCGS PF-63 HA 09/22		
1834, Capped Head	1–2 known	8239	528,000
	Auctions: $384,000, PCGS PF-62 HA 01/23		

CLASSIC HEAD (1834–1839)

Designer: *William Kneass.* **Weight:** *4.18 grams.*
Composition: *.8992 gold, .1008 silver and copper (changed to .900 gold in 1837).*
Diameter: *18.2 mm.* **Edge:** *Reeded.* **Mints:** *Philadelphia, Charlotte, Dahlonega, and New Orleans.*

Circulation Strike

Mintmark location is on the obverse, above the date.

Proof Strike

History. Gold quarter eagles had not circulated at face value in the United States since 1821, as the price of bullion necessitated more than $2.50 worth of gold to produce a single coin. Accordingly, they traded at their bullion value. The Act of June 28, 1834, provided lower weights for gold coins, after which the issues (of new designs to differentiate them from the old) circulated effectively. The Classic Head design by William Kneass is an adaptation of the head created by John Reich for the cent of 1808. The reverse illustrates a perched eagle. The motto E PLURIBUS UNUM, seen on earlier gold coins, no longer is present. These coins circulated widely until mid-1861 (for this reason, many show extensive wear). After that, they were hoarded by the public because of financial uncertainty during the Civil War.

Striking and Sharpness. Weakness is often seen on the higher areas of the hair curls. Also check the star centers. On the reverse, check the rims. The denticles usually are well struck.

Availability. Most coins range from VF to AU or lower ranges of MS. Most MS coins are of the first three years. MS-63 to 65 examples are rare. Good eye appeal can be elusive. Proofs were made in small quantities, and today probably only a couple dozen or so survive, most bearing the 1834 date.

Grading Standards

MS-60 to 70 (Mint State). ***Obverse:*** At MS-60, some abrasion and contact marks are seen on the portrait, most noticeably on the cheek, as the hair details are complex on this type. Luster is present, but may be dull or lifeless, and interrupted in patches. Many low-level Mint State coins have grainy surfaces. At MS-63, contact marks are few, and abrasion is very light. Abrasion is even less at MS-64. An MS-65 coin has hardly any abrasion, and contact marks are minute. Luster should be full and rich and is often more intense on the obverse. Grades above MS-65 are defined by having fewer marks as perfection is approached. ***Reverse:*** Comments apply as for the obverse, except that abrasion is most noticeable on the eagle's neck and the highest area of the wings.

MS-65

Illustrated coin: This coin is especially well struck.

AU-55

AU-50, 53, 55, 58 (About Uncirculated). ***Obverse:*** Friction is seen on the higher parts, particularly the cheek and hair (under magnification) of Liberty. Friction and scattered marks are in the field, ranging from extensive at AU-50 to minimal at AU-58. Luster may be seen in protected areas, minimal at AU-50 but more visible at AU-58. On an AU-58 coin the field retains some luster as well. ***Reverse:*** Comments as for Mint State, except that the eagle's neck, the top of the wings, the leaves, and the arrowheads now show noticeable wear, as do other features. Luster ranges from perhaps 40 percent remaining in protected areas at AU-50 to nearly full mint bloom at AU-58. Often the reverse of this type retains much more luster than does the obverse.

Illustrated coin: The coin has light wear overall, but traces of luster can be seen here and there.

EF-40

EF-40, 45 (Extremely Fine). ***Obverse:*** Wear is seen on the portrait overall, with reduction or elimination of some separation of hair strands, especially in the area close to the face. The cheek shows light wear. Luster is minimal or nonexistent at EF-40, and may survive in among the letters of LIBERTY at EF-45. ***Reverse:*** Wear is greater than on an About Uncirculated coin. On most (but not all) coins the eagle's neck lacks some feather detail on its highest points. Feathers have lost some detail near the edges and tips of the wings. Some areas of the horizontal lines in the shield may be blended together. Some traces of luster may be seen, more so at EF-45 than at EF-40.

Illustrated coin: This coin is well struck.

VF-30

VF-20, 30 (Very Fine). ***Obverse:*** Wear on the portrait has reduced the hair detail, especially to the right of the face and the top of the head, but much can still be seen. ***Reverse:*** Wear is greater, including on the shield and wing feathers. Generally, Classic Head gold at this grade level lacks eye appeal.

Illustrated coin: This coin was lightly cleaned. It is lightly struck at the centers, although at this grade level that is not important.

PF-60 to 70 (Proof). ***Obverse and Reverse:*** PF–60 to 62 coins have extensive hairlines and may have nicks and contact marks. At PF-63, hairlines are prominent, but the mirror surface is very reflective. PF-64 coins have fewer hairlines. At PF-65, hairlines should be minimal and mostly seen only under magnification. There should be no nicks or marks. PF-66 and higher coins should have no marks or hairlines visible to the unaided eye.

PF-65 Cameo

1836, Script 8

1836, Block 8

Circulation Strikes

	Mintage	GSID	VF-20	EF-40	AU-50	AU-58	MS-60	MS-63	MS-65
Classic Head (1834–1839)	**n/a**	**72375**	**$900**	**$1,000**	**$1,250**	**$2,250**	**$3,250**	**$8,500**	**$45,500**
1834, No Motto	112,234	8237	900	1,000	1,250	2,250	3,250	8,500	45,500
1835	131,402	8240	900	1,100	1,400	2,750	3,500	12,000	54,000
1836, Block 8	547,986	8242	900	1,000	1,250	2,250	3,250	8,500	45,500
1836, Script 8	*	68429	900	1,000	1,250	2,250	3,250	8,500	45,500
1837	45,080	8245	1,050	1,250	2,000	4,000	5,000	10,500	66,000
1838	47,030	8247	900	1,100	1,750	2,800	3,450	10,500	45,500
	Auctions: $235,000, PCGS MS-67 SBG 09/15								
1838-C	7,880	8257	6,250	9,500	13,000	24,000	32,500	72,000	—
1839	27,021	8249	1,250	2,250	3,600	7,000	14,500	53,000	—
1839-C	18,140	8259	5,500	8,250	10,000	16,000	26,500	74,500	—
↳1839-C, 9 Over 8	18,140	8258	5,500	9,000	11,000	18,000	31,500	89,500	—
1839-D	13,674	8260	5,750	8,500	11,000	29,000	36,000	84,000	—
	Auctions: $168,000, PCGS MS-64 SBG 08/22								
1839-O	17,781	8261	2,100	4,100	5,500	12,000	14,500	45,500	138,000

Note: So-called 9 Over 8 varieties for Philadelphia, Charlotte, and Denver mints were made from defective punches. * Included in number above.

Proof Strikes

		GSID	PF-63	PF-65
1834, Classic Head	unknown	$8238	$132,000	$270,000
	Auctions: $138,000, NGC PF-64 HA 01/11			
1835	4 known	8241	—	—
1836	4–6 known	8244	—	—
	Auctions: $195,500, PCGS PF-64 HA 04/12			
1837	2 known	8246	—	—
1838	1–2 known	8248	$360,000	—
	Auctions: $396,000, PCGS PF-64 HA 08/23			
1839	3–4 known	8250	—	—
	Auctions: $188,000, PCGS PF-62 HA 08/12			

LIBERTY HEAD (1840–1907)

Designer: *Christian Gobrecht.* **Weight:** *4.18 grams.*
Composition: *.900 gold, .100 copper (net weight .12094 oz. pure gold).* **Diameter:** *18 mm.*
Edge: *Reeded.* **Mints:** *Philadelphia, Charlotte, Dahlonega, New Orleans, and San Francisco.*

Circulation Strike

Mintmark location is on the reverse, above the denomination.

Proof Strike

History. The Liberty Head quarter eagle debuted in 1840 and was a workhorse of American commerce for decades, being minted until 1907. Christian Gobrecht's design closely follows those used on half eagles and eagles of the same era.

In 1848, about 230 ounces of gold were sent to Secretary of War William L. Marcy by Colonel R.B. Mason, military governor of California. The gold was turned over to the Philadelphia Mint and made into quarter eagles. The distinguishing mark CAL. was punched above the eagle on the reverse of these coins, while they were in the die. Several pieces with prooflike surfaces are known.

A modified reverse design (with smaller letters and arrowheads) was used on Philadelphia quarter eagles from 1859 through 1907, and on San Francisco issues of 1877, 1878, and 1879. A few Philadelphia Mint pieces were made in 1859, 1860, and 1861 with the old Large Letters reverse design.

Striking and Sharpness. On the obverse, check the highest points of the hair, and the star centers. On the reverse, check the eagle's neck, and the area to the lower left of the shield and the lower part of the eagle. Examine the denticles on both sides. Branch-mint coins struck before the Civil War often are lightly struck in areas and have weak denticles. Often, a certified EF coin from the Dahlonega or Charlotte mint will not appear any sharper than a VF coin from Philadelphia. There are exceptions, and some C and D coins are sharp. The careful study of photographs is useful in acquainting you with the peculiarities of a given date or mint. Most quarter eagles from the 1880s to 1907 are sharp in all areas. Tiny copper staining spots (from improperly mixed alloy) can be a problem. Cameo contrast is the rule for Proofs prior to 1902, when the portrait was polished in the die (a few years later cameo-contrast coins were again made).

Availability. Early dates and mintmarks are generally scarce to rare in MS and very rare in MS-63 to 65 or finer, with only a few exceptions. Coins of Charlotte and Dahlonega (all of which are especially avidly collected) are usually EF or AU, or overgraded low MS. Rarities for the type include 1841, 1854-S, and 1875. Coins of the 1860s onward generally are seen with sharper striking and in higher average grades. Typically, San Francisco quarter eagles are in lower average grades than are those from the Philadelphia Mint, as Philadelphia coins did not circulate at par in the East and Midwest from late December 1861 until December 1878, and thus did not acquire as much wear. MS coins are readily available for the early-1900s years, and usually have outstanding eye appeal. Proofs exist relative to their original mintages; all prior to the 1890s are rare.

Note: Values of common-date gold coins have been based on the current bullion price of gold, $3,746 per ounce, and may vary with the prevailing spot price.

Grading Standards

MS-65

MS-60 to 70 (Mint State). ***Obverse:*** At MS-60, some abrasion and contact marks are evident, most noticeably on the hair to the right of Liberty's forehead, and on the jaw. Luster is present, but may be dull or lifeless, and interrupted in patches. At MS-63, contact marks are few, and abrasion is very light. An MS-65 coin has hardly any abrasion, and contact marks are so minute as to require magnification. Luster should be full and rich. Grades above MS-65 are usually found late in the series and are defined by having fewer marks as perfection is approached. ***Reverse:*** Comments apply as for the obverse, except that abrasion and contact marks are most noticeable on the eagle's neck and to the lower left of the shield.

Illustrated coin: Sharply struck, bright, and with abundant luster and great eye appeal, this is a "just right" coin for the connoisseur.

AU-55

AU-50, 53, 55, 58 (About Uncirculated). ***Obverse:*** Light wear is seen on the face, the hair to the right of the face, and the highest area of the hair bun, more so at AU-50 than at AU–53 or 55. An AU-58 coin has minimal traces of wear. An AU-50 coin has luster in protected areas among the stars and letters, with little in the open fields or on the portrait. At AU-58, most luster is present in the fields, but is worn away on the highest parts of the motifs. ***Reverse:*** Comments apply as for the preceding, except that the eagle shows wear in all of the higher areas, as well as the leaves and arrowheads. Luster ranges from perhaps 40 percent remaining in protected areas at AU-50 to nearly full mint bloom at AU-58. Often the reverse of this type retains more luster than the obverse.

Illustrated coin: The example has the bold rims often seen on Dahlonega Mint coins of this denomination.

EF-40

EF-40, 45 (Extremely Fine). ***Obverse:*** Wear is evident on all high areas of the portrait, including the hair to the right of the forehead, the tip of the coronet, and the hair bun. The stars show light wear at their centers. Luster, if present at all, is minimal and in protected areas such as between the star points. ***Reverse:*** Wear is greater than on an AU coin. The eagle's neck is nearly smooth, much detail is lost on the right wing, and there is flatness at the lower left of the shield, and on the leaves and arrowheads. Traces of luster may be seen, more so at EF-45 than at EF-40. Overall, the reverse appears to be in a slightly higher grade than the obverse.

Illustrated coin: This is an attractive coin with medium wear.

VF-20, 30 (Very Fine). ***Obverse:*** The higher-relief areas of hair are worn flat at VF-20, less so at VF-30. The hair to the right of the coronet is merged into heavy strands. The stars are flat at their centers. ***Reverse:*** Much of the eagle is flat, with less than 50 percent of the feather detail remaining. The vertical shield stripes, being deeply recessed, remain bold.

VF-20

PF-60 to 70 (Proof). ***Obverse and Reverse:*** PF–60 to 62 coins have extensive hairlines and may have nicks and contact marks. At PF-63, hairlines are prominent, but the mirror surface is very reflective. PF-64 coins have fewer hairlines; PF-65, minimal hairlines mostly seen only under magnification, and no nicks or marks. PF-66 and higher coins should have no marks or hairlines visible to the unaided eye.

Illustrated coin: This is an exceptional gem in rich yellow-orange gold.

PF-66

1843-C, Small Date, Crosslet 4

1843-C, Large Date, Plain 4

1843-O, Small Date, Crosslet 4

1843-O, Large Date, Plain 4

Circulation Strikes

	Mintage	GSID	VF-20	EF-40	AU-50	AU-58	MS-60	MS-63	MS-65
Liberty Head (1840–1907)	**n/a**	**72368**	**$700**	**$700**	**$700**	**$725**	**$725**	**$775**	**$950**
1840	18,859	8262	1,100	1,300	2,250	5,000	7,500	19,000	—
1840-C	12,822	8333	2,750	3,900	4,750	7,750	11,000	30,000	—
1840-D	3,532	8334	6,250	11,000	17,000	48,000	78,000	—	—
	Auctions: $144,000, NGC MS-62 SBG 08/22								
1840-O	33,580	8335	850	2,050	2,600	6,250	8,750	25,000	—
1841 (a)	10–12 known	374093	—	156,000	204,000	300,000	336,000	—	—
	Auctions: $288,000, PCGS MS-60 SBG 03/24; $138,000, PCGS EF-45 HA 03/24								
1841-C	10,281	8336	3,450	4,800	6,000	10,500	21,500	62,500	—
1841-D	4,164	8337	4,500	7,750	10,000	19,000	39,500	86,500	—
1842	2,823	8263	2,500	5,000	7,250	16,000	19,000	47,000	—
1842-C	6,729	8338	2,050	3,750	7,500	15,500	22,000	60,000	120,000
	Auctions: $182,500, PCGS MS-65 DLRC 05/21								
1842-D	4,643	8339	3,000	5,000	8,250	18,000	36,000	—	—
1842-O	19,800	8340	850	1,250	1,900	5,000	8,500	21,500	—
1843, Large Date	100,546	8264	750	800	875	1,750	2,250	12,000	—
1843-C, Large Date, Plain 4	23,076	8341	2,200	3,250	4,400	7,000	8,000	26,500	—
1843-C, Small Date, Crosslet 4	2,988	8342	3,750	6,000	8,000	16,500	24,000	—	—
1843-D, Small D, Crosslet 4	36,209	8343	2,100	2,900	3,600	5,750	7,500	36,000	—
1843-D, Large D	*	8344	2,000	3,000	4,700	7,000	11,000	—	—

* Included in number above. a. Values are for circulated proofs; existence of circulation strikes is unclear.

Note: Gold spot price at time of publication, $3,746 per ounce.

1848, CAL. Above Eagle

Circulation Strikes *(continued)*

	Mintage	GSID	VF-20	EF-40	AU-50	AU-58	MS-60	MS-63	MS-65
1843-O, Small Date, Crosslet 4	288,002	8345	$825	$875	$900	$1,350	$2,000	$8,250	$45,500
1843-O, Large Date, Plain 4	76,000	8346	800	1,100	1,800	5,250	7,000	24,000	—
1844	6,784	8265	900	1,250	2,500	7,500	9,500	26,500	—
1844-C	11,622	8347	1,900	3,000	4,550	8,250	13,000	43,000	—
1844-D	17,332	8348	2,900	3,750	4,700	8,500	10,000	31,000	—
1845	91,051	8266	750	800	900	1,150	1,750	5,000	21,500
1845-D	19,460	8349	2,900	3,750	4,750	9,500	11,000	48,000	—
1845-O	4,000	8350	3,750	8,000	10,000	26,500	33,500	102,000	—
	Auctions: $117,000, PCGS MS-63 SBG 03/21								
1846	21,598	8267	800	900	1,100	2,250	4,250	20,500	—
1846-C	4,808	8351	1,900	3,400	5,750	14,500	20,500	42,000	—
1846-D	19,303	8352	2,700	3,600	5,000	10,000	12,500	36,000	—
1846-D, D Over D	*	226374	2,950	4,000	5,500	11,000	14,000	39,500	—
1846-O	62,000	8354	825	900	1,250	3,000	6,500	17,000	45,500
1847	29,814	8268	750	775	1,000	1,550	3,300	12,000	18,500
1847-C	23,226	8355	2,500	3,250	4,100	6,250	6,750	18,000	—
1847-D	15,784	8356	3,100	4,250	6,500	9,000	10,500	26,500	108,000
1847-O	124,000	8357	825	925	1,400	3,100	6,250	18,000	—
1848	6,500	8269	1,000	1,550	2,750	5,500	6,250	16,000	—
1848, CAL. Above Eagle	1,389	8270	43,000	60,000	72,000	84,000	90,000	204,000	384,000
	Auctions: $288,000, PCGS MS-64 SBG 11/24								
1848-C	16,788	8358	3,050	3,750	4,250	8,750	12,000	41,000	—
1848-D	13,771	8359	3,000	3,500	4,200	7,500	9,250	36,000	—
1849	23,294	8271	775	1,000	1,200	2,400	3,400	10,000	—
1849-C	10,220	8360	4,800	6,250	8,000	12,000	14,500	41,000	102,000
	Auctions: $119,025, NGC MS-65 SBG 03/10								
1849-D	10,945	8361	2,800	3,750	5,000	9,000	15,000	—	—
1850	252,923	8272	750	775	775	900	950	4,100	24,000
1850-C	9,148	8362	1,750	3,250	4,400	7,500	12,500	42,000	—
1850-D	12,148	8363	2,000	3,000	4,400	7,500	12,000	39,500	—
1850-O	84,000	8364	825	925	1,150	2,750	4,400	19,000	—
1851	1,372,748	8273	750	775	800	900	925	1,100	6,500
↳1851, Repunched Date, FS-301	*	351838	850	850	900	975	1,000	1,200	7,250
1851-C	14,923	8365	1,750	2,600	3,750	6,250	9,500	36,000	—
1851-D	11,264	8366	1,900	3,000	4,500	9,500	19,000	33,500	84,000
1851-O	148,000	8367	775	900	1,000	2,000	4,000	12,500	—
1852	1,159,681	8274	750	775	775	850	900	1,200	4,900
1852-C	9,772	8368	1,500	2,500	3,750	7,250	9,000	36,000	—
1852-D	4,078	8369	1,800	3,450	6,750	9,500	18,000	48,000	—
1852-O	140,000	8370	825	900	1,000	2,000	4,500	11,500	—
1853	1,404,668	8275	750	775	775	850	900	1,100	4,700
1853-D	3,178	8371	2,200	3,600	6,250	9,500	15,000	57,000	—
	Auctions: $155,250, PCGS MS-61 GLDB 05/06								

* Included in number above.

Old Reverse (Pre-1859)

New Reverse

1862, 2 Over 1

Circulation Strikes *(continued)*

	Mintage	GSID	VF-20	EF-40	AU-50	AU-58	MS-60	MS-63	MS-65
1854	596,258	8276	$750	$775	$825	$950	$950	$1,250	$7,000
1854-C	7,295	8372	2,100	3,000	3,900	6,250	10,500	72,000	—
1854-D	1,760	8373	3,750	7,500	11,000	21,500	30,000	81,000	—
1854-O	153,000	8374	825	925	1,000	1,500	1,750	10,500	—
1854-S	12 known	8375	360,000	504,000	576,000	—	—	—	—
	Auctions: $408,000, NGC AU-50 SBG 08/24								
1855	235,480	8277	725	750	775	850	900	1,750	12,000
1855-C	3,677	8376	2,500	3,750	5,500	10,500	18,000	48,000	108,000
1855-D	1,123	8377	4,750	10,000	18,000	46,000	55,000	91,000	—
1856	384,240	8278	750	800	850	950	975	1,400	4,800
1856-C	7,913	8378	2,000	3,250	4,500	8,750	12,000	31,000	—
1856-D	874	8379	26,500	38,500	54,000	120,000	144,000	—	—
	Auctions: $120,000, PCGS AU-58 SBG 08/24								
1856-O	21,100	8380	825	1,150	1,800	4,000	9,000	—	—
1856-S	72,120	8381	825	925	1,000	2,750	4,500	12,500	36,000
1857	214,130	8279	750	775	850	950	950	1,500	6,500
1857-D	2,364	8382	1,800	2,900	5,000	11,000	12,000	30,500	—
1857-O	34,000	8383	800	975	1,250	2,250	4,750	18,000	—
1857-S	69,200	8384	725	800	1,150	2,700	4,200	14,000	—
1858	47,377	8280	750	775	850	1,000	1,250	3,750	—
1858-C	9,056	8385	1,900	2,750	3,750	4,800	7,750	23,000	—
1859, Old Reverse	39,364	8282	750	775	950	1,300	2,000	5,250	—
1859, New Reverse	*	8281	750	775	825	1,050	1,250	4,250	12,000
1859-D	2,244	8386	5,000	6,750	9,000	17,000	26,500	—	—
	Auctions: $132,000, PCGS MS-62 SBG 08/22								
1859-S	15,200	8387	775	1,150	1,900	3,750	5,500	18,000	—
1860, Old Reverse	22,563	8284	1,400	1,600	1,800	4,250	4,900	8,250	—
1860, New Reverse	*	8283	750	775	850	1,400	1,500	4,000	12,000
1860-C	7,469	8388	2,750	3,750	6,000	12,000	16,000	36,000	—
1860-S	35,600	8389	700	775	1,300	2,500	4,100	17,000	—
1861, Old Reverse	1,283,788	8286	900	1,200	1,600	2,750	3,250	8,500	25,000
1861, New Reverse	*	8285	750	800	825	950	950	1,550	5,500
1861-S	24,000	8390	1,750	3,000	5,000	14,000	20,000	—	—
1862	98,508	8287	750	800	1,600	3,000	4,100	10,500	—
1862, 2 Over 1	*	8391	950	1,900	3,750	6,500	11,000	30,000	—
1862-S	8,000	8392	2,800	5,000	6,000	10,000	17,000	45,500	—
1863-S	10,800	8393	1,900	3,500	5,500	9,250	15,500	30,000	—
1864	2,824	8288	33,500	50,500	84,000	120,000	138,000	—	—
	Auctions: $111,625, PCGS AU-58 LGND 12/20								
1865	1,520	8289	5,000	10,500	19,000	54,000	84,000	—	—
1865-S	23,376	8394	900	1,500	2,400	3,500	6,000	20,500	—

* Included in number above.

1873, Close 3

1873, Open 3

Circulation Strikes *(continued)*

	Mintage	GSID	VF-20	EF-40	AU-50	AU-58	MS-60	MS-63	MS-65
1866	3,080	8290	$1,250	$3,600	$5,500	$10,500	$14,500	$29,000	$51,000
1866-S	38,960	8395	750	875	1,250	3,900	8,750	26,500	—
1867	3,200	8291	950	1,500	2,100	5,500	7,250	18,000	42,000
1867-S	28,000	8396	775	900	1,300	2,250	4,250	15,000	—
1868	3,600	8292	750	850	950	1,850	2,750	12,000	—
1868-S	34,000	8397	725	775	1,000	2,250	3,300	8,000	—
1869	4,320	8293	750	800	900	1,700	3,250	11,000	—
1869-S	29,500	8398	750	775	850	1,550	3,000	12,000	31,000
1870	4,520	8294	725	775	950	1,950	4,400	12,000	30,000
1870-S	16,000	8399	725	775	950	3,250	4,400	15,000	—
1871	5,320	8295	750	800	950	1,300	2,000	5,250	29,000
1871-S	22,000	8400	700	775	800	1,250	2,200	4,600	20,000
1872	3,000	8296	825	1,200	2,100	4,000	5,250	19,000	—
1872-S	18,000	8401	750	800	975	2,000	5,000	11,000	—
1873, Open 3	122,800	8297	700	700	700	750	775	875	3,900
1873, Closed 3	55,200	8298	700	700	750	825	875	1,000	4,100
1873-S	27,000	8402	700	750	775	1,300	1,800	6,250	31,000
1874	3,920	8299	725	775	825	1,250	2,300	6,500	29,000
1875	400	8300	8,750	14,500	18,000	29,000	41,000	150,000	—
1875-S	11,600	8403	700	750	775	2,000	3,500	7,000	18,000
1876	4,176	8301	825	950	1,200	2,000	3,750	11,000	—
1876-S	5,000	8404	750	875	1,050	2,100	2,500	10,000	—
1877	1,632	8302	800	1,200	1,600	2,500	3,500	13,000	—
1877-S	35,400	8405	700	700	750	800	850	2,500	12,500
1878	286,240	8303	700	700	700	725	725	825	2,300
1878-S	178,000	8406	700	700	700	725	725	1,000	19,000
1879	88,960	8304	700	700	700	725	725	900	3,400
1879-S	43,500	8407	700	700	725	900	1,900	5,000	—
1880	2,960	8305	800	925	1,150	1,900	2,050	4,100	19,000
1881	640	8306	2,600	3,750	5,750	9,500	13,000	31,000	66,000
1882	4,000	8307	700	700	775	1,150	1,300	2,900	14,000
1883	1,920	8308	900	1,600	3,400	8,000	8,750	12,000	21,500
1884	1,950	8309	825	900	1,000	1,600	2,100	4,400	15,500
1885	800	8310	1,000	2,500	4,050	5,500	7,000	13,000	29,000
1886	4,000	8311	725	850	950	1,250	1,500	4,100	11,000
1887	6,160	8312	725	800	875	1,200	1,250	2,100	15,500
1888	16,001	8313	700	700	700	775	825	1,000	3,750
1889	17,600	8314	700	700	700	800	825	900	6,250
1890	8,720	8315	700	700	700	750	775	1,900	8,250
1891	10,960	8316	700	700	700	725	750	1,450	6,000
1892	2,440	8317	700	700	700	850	1,200	2,300	8,500
1893	30,000	8318	700	700	700	725	725	800	1,700
1894	4,000	8319	700	700	725	775	850	2,400	5,500
1895	6,000	8320	700	700	700	750	775	1,450	5,000
1896	19,070	8321	700	700	700	750	775	900	2,100
1897	29,768	8322	700	700	700	750	775	850	1,450
1898	24,000	8323	700	700	700	750	775	850	1,750

* Included in number above.

Circulation Strikes *(continued)*

	Mintage	GSID	VF-20	EF-40	AU-50	AU-58	MS-60	MS-63	MS-65
1899	27,200	8324	$700	$700	$700	$750	$775	$850	$1,600
1900	67,000	8325	700	700	700	725	725	775	950
1901	91,100	8326	700	700	700	725	725	775	950
1902	133,540	8327	700	700	700	725	725	775	950
1903	201,060	8328	700	700	700	725	725	775	950
1904	160,790	8329	700	700	700	725	725	775	950
1905	217,800	8330	700	700	700	725	725	775	1,000
1906	176,330	8331	700	700	700	725	725	775	950
1907	336,294	8332	700	700	700	725	725	800	1,000

* Included in number above.

Proof Strikes

	Mintage	GSID	PF-60	PF-63	PF-65
Liberty Head (1840–1907), Proof	**n/a**	**74139**	**$3,100**	**$5,250**	**$12,000**
Same, Proof Cameo	**n/a**	**74140**	**—**	**6,000**	**12,500**
Same, Proof Deep Cameo	**n/a**	**74141**	**—**	**6,750**	**17,000**
1840	unknown	8410	—	—	—
1841	16 known	8411	360,000	480,000	600,000
	Auctions: $228,000, NGC AU-50 HA 07/22				
1843	<10 known	8417	—	84,000	—
1844	5–6	8422	—	—	180,000
1845	5–6	8423	39,500	60,000	180,000
1846	7–9	8426	39,500	60,000	180,000
1848	5–7	8434	—	60,000	180,000
1850	2–3	8440	—	78,000	—
1854	unique	305408	—	—	—
	Auctions: $480,000, PCGS PF-64 HA 05/23				
1856	6–7	8447	33,500	48,000	168,000
1857	5–7	8450	30,000	43,000	144,000
	Auctions: $141,000, PCGS PF-65 HA 04/15				
1858	8–10	8453	24,000	36,000	90,000
1859, Old Reverse	80	8456	13,000	24,000	90,000
1859, New Reverse	11	226375	—	—	—
1860	112	8459	12,000	18,000	42,000
1861	90	8462	17,500	30,000	60,000
1862	35	8465	14,500	30,000	66,000
1863	30	8468	48,000	66,000	114,000
1864	50	8471	12,000	24,000	60,000
1865	25	8474	14,500	23,000	54,000
1866	30	8477	10,000	15,500	43,000
1867	50	8480	7,500	14,500	36,000
1868	25	8483	12,000	19,000	55,000
1869	25	8486	10,000	15,500	43,000
1870	35	8489	10,000	15,500	54,000
1871	30	8492	10,000	15,500	43,000
1872	30	8495	7,500	14,500	36,000
1873, Closed 3	25	8498	10,000	18,000	43,000
1874	20	8501	$12,000	$21,500	$48,000
1875	20	8504	33,500	48,000	114,000
	Auctions: $135,125, PCGS PF-65 SBG 08/16				
1876	45	8507	10,500	19,000	43,000
1877	20	8510	10,500	19,000	43,000
1878	20	8513	10,500	19,000	43,000
1879	30	8516	7,500	12,000	33,500
1880	36	8519	5,000	8,000	18,000
1881	51	8522	5,000	8,000	18,000
1882	67	8525	5,000	8,000	19,000
1883	82	8528	5,000	8,000	18,000
1884	73	8531	5,000	8,000	18,000
1885	87	8534	5,000	8,000	18,000
1886	88	8537	5,000	8,000	18,000
1887	122	8540	6,250	9,000	24,000
1888	97	8543	5,000	8,000	19,000
1889	48	8546	5,000	8,000	18,000
1890	93	8549	3,750	7,250	14,500
1891	80	8552	3,750	7,250	14,500
1892	105	8555	3,750	7,250	14,500
1893	106	8558	3,750	7,250	14,500
1894	122	8561	3,750	7,250	14,500
1895	119	8564	3,750	7,250	14,500
1896	132	8567	3,100	5,250	12,000
1897	136	8570	3,100	5,250	12,000
1898	165	8573	3,100	5,250	12,000
1899	150	8576	3,100	5,250	12,000
1900	205	8579	3,100	5,250	12,000
1901	223	8582	3,100	5,250	12,000
1902	193	8585	3,100	5,250	12,000
1903	197	8588	3,100	5,250	12,000
1904	170	8591	3,100	5,250	12,000
1905 (a)	144	8594	3,100	5,250	12,000
1906	160	8597	3,100	5,250	12,000
1907	154	8600	3,100	5,250	12,000

a. Pieces dated 1905-S are counterfeit.

INDIAN HEAD (1908–1929)

Designer: *Bela Lyon Pratt.* **Weight:** *4.18 grams.*
Composition: *.900 gold, .100 copper (net weight .12094 oz. pure gold).*
Diameter: *18 mm.* **Edge:** *Reeded.* **Mints:** *Philadelphia and Denver.*

Circulation Strike

Mintmark is on the reverse, to the left of arrows.

Sandblast Finish Proof Strike

Satin Finish Proof Strike

History. The Indian Head design—used on both the quarter eagle and the half eagle—is unusual in that the lettering and motifs are in sunken relief. (The design sometimes is erroneously described as incuse.) The designer, sculptor Bela Lyon Pratt, was chosen by President Theodore Roosevelt after Augustus Saint-Gaudens died before beginning his own design. Pratt modeled the head on Chief Hollow Horn Bear of the Lakota. The "standing eagle" reverse design was based on the reverse of Saint-Gaudens's Indian Head $10 gold coin of 1907; Pratt was a pupil of the famous sculptor.

Some Americans worried that the sunken designs of the Indian Head quarter eagle would accumulate dirt and germs—an unfounded fear. As the smallest gold denomination of the era, these coins were popular for use as souvenirs and gifts, but they did not circulate as money except in the West.

Striking and Sharpness. The striking quality of Indian Head quarter eagles varies. On many early issues the rims are flat, while on others, including most of the 1920s, they are slightly raised. Some have traces of a wire rim, usually on the reverse. Look for weakness on the high parts of the Indian's bonnet (particularly the garland of flowers) and in the feather details in the headdress. On the reverse, check the feathers on the highest area of the wing, the top of the shoulder. On some issues of the 1911-D, the D mintmark can be weak.

Availability. This design was not popular with collectors, and they saved relatively few of the coins. However, many coins were given as gifts and preserved in high quality. The survival of MS-63 and better coins is a matter of chance, especially for the issues dated from 1909 to 1915. The only scarce issue is 1911-D. Luster can range from deeply frosty to grainy. As the fields are the highest areas of the coin, luster diminished quickly as examples were circulated or jostled with others in bags. The Indian Head quarter eagle is one of the most challenging series for professional graders, and opinions can vary widely.

Proofs. Sandblast (also called Matte) Proofs were made in 1908 and 1911 to 1915, while Satin (also called Roman Finish) Proofs were made in 1909 and 1910. The Sandblast issues are usually somewhat dull, while the Satin Proofs are usually of a light-yellow gold. In their time the Proofs of both styles, made for all gold series, were not popular with numismatists. Today, they are in strong demand. As a class these are significantly more readily available than half eagles of the same date and style of finish. Most are in grades from PF-63 upward. At lower levels coins can show light contact marks. Some microscopic bright flecks may have been caused by the sandblasting process and, although they do not represent handling, usually result in a coin being assigned a slightly lower grade.

Note: Values of common-date gold coins have been based on the current bullion price of gold, $3,746 per ounce, and may vary with the prevailing spot price.

Grading Standards

MS-64

MS-60 to 70 (Mint State). ***Obverse:*** On MS–60 to 62 coins there is abrasion in the field, this representing the highest part of the coin. Abrasion is also evident on the headdress. Marks and, occasionally, a microscopic pin scratch may be seen. At MS-63, there may be some abrasion and some tiny marks. Luster is irregular. At MS-64, abrasion is less. Luster is rich. At MS-65 and above, luster is deep and frosty. No marks at all are visible without magnification at MS-66 and higher. ***Reverse:*** At MS–60 to 62, there is abrasion in the field, this representing the highest part of the coin. Abrasion is also evident on the eagle's wing. Otherwise, the same comments apply as for the obverse.

Illustrated coin: This lustrous example has excellent eye appeal.

AU-55

AU-50, 53, 55, 58 (About Uncirculated). ***Obverse:*** Friction on the cheek is very noticeable at AU-50, progressively less at higher levels to AU-58. The headdress shows light wear, most evident on the ribbon above the forehead and on the garland. Luster is minimal at AU-50 and scattered and incomplete at AU-58. Nicks and contact marks are to be expected. ***Reverse:*** Friction on the wing and neck is very noticeable at AU-50, increasingly less at higher levels to AU-58. Otherwise, the same comments apply as for the obverse.

Illustrated coin: Much of the original luster remains in the incuse areas but not in the fields, which are the highest points on this design.

EF-40

EF-40, 45 (Extremely Fine). ***Obverse:*** Light wear characterizes the portrait and headdress. Luster is gone. Marks and tiny scratches are to be expected, but not distracting. ***Reverse:*** Light wear is most evident on the eagle's head and wing, although other areas are lightly worn as well. Luster is gone. Marks and tiny scratches are to be expected, but not distracting.

VF-20

VF-20, 30 (Very Fine). ***Obverse:*** Many details of the ribbon above the forehead and the garland are worn away. Many feather vanes are blended together. The field is dull and has contact marks. ***Reverse:*** The neck and the upper part of the wing show extensive wear, other areas less so. The field is dull and has contact marks.

PF-60 to 70 (Proof). ***Obverse and Reverse:*** At PF–60 to 63, there is light abrasion and some contact marks; the lower the grade, the higher the quantity. On Sandblast Proofs these show up as visually unappealing bright spots. At PF-64 and higher levels, marks are fewer, with magnification needed to see any at PF-65. At PF-66, there should be none at all.

Illustrated coin: This is a Sandblast Proof of exceptionally high quality.

PF-66

Circulation Strikes

	Mintage	GSID	EF-40	AU-50	AU-58	MS-60	MS-63	MS-64	MS-65
Indian Head (1908–1929)	**n/a**	**72369**	**$700**	**$725**	**$725**	**$750**	**$775**	**$900**	**$1,600**
1908	564,821	8603	700	725	725	750	1,500	2,400	6,000
1909	441,760	8604	700	725	725	750	2,250	3,700	6,500
1910	492,000	8605	700	725	725	750	1,700	2,400	6,250
1911	704,000	8606	700	725	725	775	1,250	2,000	6,000
1911-D, Strong D (a)	55,680	8615	3,600	4,250	6,500	7,500	13,500	20,000	59,000
	Auctions: $312,000, PCGS MS-66 HA 01/25								
1911-D, Weak D (a)	*	8616	1,750	1,950	2,600	2,950	—	—	—
1912	616,000	8607	700	725	750	800	2,000	4,100	9,750
1913	722,000	8608	700	725	725	750	1,250	2,200	7,750
1914	240,000	8609	700	750	750	800	3,000	5,000	20,000
	Auctions: $168,000, PCGS MS-67 HA 01/25								
1914-D	448,000	8617	700	725	775	800	2,050	4,050	18,000
1915	606,000	8610	700	725	725	775	1,250	2,200	6,500
1925-D	578,000	8618	700	725	725	750	775	900	1,600
1926	446,000	8611	700	725	725	750	775	900	1,600
1927	388,000	8612	700	725	725	750	775	900	1,600
1928	416,000	8613	700	725	725	750	775	900	1,600
1929	532,000	8614	700	725	725	750	775	900	6,500

* Included in number above. **a.** Beware of counterfeit and altered pieces.

Proof Strikes

	Mintage	GSID	PF-63	PF-65	PF-66
Indian Head (1908–1929), Proof	**n/a**	**74142**	**$12,000**	**$29,000**	**$36,000**
1908	236	8619	12,000	29,000	36,000
1909	139	8620	12,000	54,000	66,000
1910	682	8621	12,000	31,500	41,500
1911	191	8622	12,000	35,000	36,000
1912	197	8623	$12,000	$32,000	$36,000
1913	165	8624	12,000	31,500	36,000
1914	117	8625	12,000	29,000	36,000
	Auctions: $138,000, PCGS PF-67 HA 04/19				
1915	100	8626	12,000	31,500	39,500
1914	117	8625	12,000	29,000	36,000

Note: Gold spot price at time of publication, $3,746 per ounce.

Three-Dollar Gold Pieces
1854–1889

AN OVERVIEW OF THREE-DOLLAR GOLD PIECES

The three-dollar gold coin denomination was conceived in 1853 and first produced for circulation in 1854. Although there were high hopes for it at the outset, and mintages were generous, the value was redundant given the $2.50 quarter eagle then in circulation. Mintages declined, and although pieces were struck each year through 1889, very few actually circulated after the 1850s.

Scan for additional information.

Although many different three-dollar dates are available at reasonable prices, most numismatists opt to acquire either a circulated or Mint State 1854 (significant as the first year of issue; also, in this year the word DOLLARS is in smaller letters than on later issues) or a Mint State coin from the low-mintage era of 1879–1889. Similar to the situation for gold dollars, although the mintages of these later pieces were low, they were popularly saved at the time, and many more have survived in high quality than might otherwise be the case.

For the Collector and Investor: Three-Dollar Gold Pieces as a Specialty

Collecting three-dollar pieces by date and mint would at first seem to be daunting, but it is less challenging than expected, outside of a handful of pieces. The 1870-S is unique (in the Harry W. Bass Jr. Collection on loan to the American Numismatic Association), the 1875 and 1876 were made only in Proof format to the extent of 20 and 45 pieces respectively, and the 1873 is quite rare. Beyond that, examples of coins in grades such as EF and AU (including some varieties with very low mintages) can be purchased for reasonable prices.

Some numismatists note that $3 gold pieces might have been used to purchase sheets of 100 3¢ stamps.

Choice examples can be elusive, this being particularly true of branch-mint issues of the 1854–1860 years. Generally, Mint State Philadelphia pieces are rare after 1855, but then come on the market with frequency for 1861 and later, with dates in the 1860s being scarcer than later issues. Coins of the years 1878 and 1879 were made in larger quantities, with the 1878 in particular being easy to find today, although examples usually are quite bag-marked. The low-mintage three-dollar pieces of 1879 through 1889 were popular at the time of issue, many were saved, and today Mint State pieces exist to a greater extent than would otherwise be the case.

INDIAN PRINCESS HEAD (1854–1889)

Designer: *James B. Longacre.* **Weight:** *5.015 grams.*
Composition: *.900 gold, .100 copper (net weight .14512 oz. pure gold).* **Diameter:** *20.5 mm.*
Edge: *Reeded.* **Mints:** *Philadelphia, Dahlonega, New Orleans, and San Francisco.*

Circulation Strike

Mintmark location is on the reverse, below the wreath.

Proof Strike

History. The three-dollar gold coin was designed by U.S. Mint chief engraver James B. Longacre, and first struck in 1854. The quarter eagle and half eagle had already been in use for a long time, and the reason for the creation of this odd new denomination is uncertain, although some numismatists note it could have been used to buy a sheet of current 3¢ postage stamps or a group of 100 silver trimes. After a large initial mintage in 1854, the coins were struck in smaller annual quantities. These coins were more popular on the West Coast, but, even in that region, use of this denomination dropped off sharply by the 1870s.

Striking and Sharpness. Points to observe on the obverse include the tips of the feathers in the headdress, and the hair details below the band inscribed LIBERTY. Focal points on the reverse are the wreath details (especially the vertical division in the ribbon knot), and the two central date numerals. Many of the later issues—particularly those of the early 1880s—are prooflike.

Availability. In circulated grades the issues of 1854 to 1860 survive in approximate proportion to their mintages. MS coins are plentiful for the first-year Philadelphia issue, 1854, but are scarce to rare for other years and for all branch-mint issues. For the 1860s and 1870s most are in grades such as EF, AU, and low MS, except for 1874 and in particular 1878, easily found in MS. Dates from 1879 to 1889 have a higher survival ratio and are mostly in MS, often at MS-65.

Proofs. Proofs were struck of all years. All prior to the 1880s are very rare today, with issues of the 1850s being exceedingly so. Coins of 1875 and 1876 were made only in Proof format, with no related circulation strikes. Most often seen in the marketplace are the higher-mintage Proofs of the 1880s. Some have patches of graininess or hints of non-Proof surface on the obverse, or an aura or "ghosting" near the portrait, an artifact of striking.

Grading Standards

MS-64

MS-60 to 70 (Mint State). ***Obverse:*** On MS-60 to 62 coins there is abrasion on the hair below the band lettered LIBERTY (an area that can be weakly struck as well) and on tips of the feather plumes. At MS-63, there may be slight abrasion. Luster can be irregular. At MS-64, abrasion is less. Luster is rich on most coins, less so on the 1854-D (which is often overgraded). At MS-65 and above, luster is deep and frosty, with no marks at all visible without magnification at MS-66 and higher. ***Reverse:*** On MS-60 to 62 coins there is abrasion on the 1, the highest parts of the leaves, and the ribbon knot. Otherwise, the same comments apply as for the obverse.

Illustrated coin: Satiny luster and partial mirror surfaces yield excellent eye appeal.

AU-55

AU-50, 53, 55, 58 (About Uncirculated). ***Obverse:*** Light wear on the hair below the coronet, the cheek, and the tips of the feather plumes is very noticeable at AU-50, increasingly less at higher levels to AU-58. Luster is minimal at AU-50 and scattered and incomplete at AU-58. Some tiny nicks and contact marks are to be expected and should be mentioned if they are distracting. ***Reverse:*** Light wear on the 1, the wreath, and the ribbon knot characterize an AU-50 coin, increasingly less at higher levels to AU-58. Otherwise, the same comments apply as for the obverse.

Illustrated coin: Most of the original luster is gone, but perhaps 15% remains in the protected areas.

EF-40

EF-40, 45 (Extremely Fine). ***Obverse:*** Medium wear is seen on the hair below the coronet and on the feather plume tips. Detail is partially gone on the hair. Luster is gone on most coins. ***Reverse:*** Light wear is seen overall, and the highest parts of the leaves are flat, but detail remains elsewhere. Luster is gone on most coins.

Illustrated coin: Note the mushy denticles (as seen on all but one specimen of this, the only Dahlonega variety in the series).

VF-20

VF-20, 30 (Very Fine). ***Obverse:*** Most hair detail is gone, except at the back of the lower curls. The feather plume ends are flat. ***Reverse:*** The wreath and other areas show more wear. Most detail is gone on the higher-relief leaves.

PF-61

PF-60 to 70 (Proof). ***Obverse and Reverse:*** PF-60 to 62 coins have extensive hairlines and may have nicks and contact marks. At PF-63, hairlines are prominent, but the mirror surface is very reflective. PF-64 coins have fewer hairlines. At PF-65, hairlines should be minimal and mostly seen only under magnification. There should be no nicks or marks. PF-66 and higher coins should have no marks or hairlines visible to the unaided eye.

Illustrated coin: Extensive friction is visible in the fields, but the mirror surface can be seen in protected areas. This is still a desirable example of a date of which only 45 were minted.

Circulation Strikes

	Mintage	GSID	VF-20	EF-40	AU-50	AU-58	MS-60	MS-63	MS-65
Indian Princess Head (1854–1889)	n/a	72370	$1,100	$1,400	$1,600	$2,100	$2,600	$4,000	$10,500
1854	138,618	8627	1,100	1,400	1,600	2,100	2,600	4,450	14,500
	Auctions: $112,125, PCGS MS-68 HA 06/04								
1854-D	1,120	8661	26,500	36,000	48,000	138,000	144,000	—	—
	Auctions: $138,000, PCGS AU-58 SBG 08/24; $528,000, PCGS MS-62 SBG 08/24								
1854-O	24,000	8662	2,500	3,500	4,750	27,000	54,000	168,000	—
	Auctions: $228,000, PCGS MS-63 HA 05/23								
1855	50,555	8628	1,100	1,400	1,600	2,300	2,600	6,500	28,000
1855-S	6,600	8663	2,550	4,250	7,750	30,000	54,000	144,000	—
	Auctions: $264,000, PCGS MS-64 HA 09/22								
1856	26,010	8629	1,100	1,400	1,750	3,050	3,250	7,500	42,000
1856-S (a)	34,500	8664	1,500	2,100	3,250	11,000	12,500	66,000	—
1857	20,891	8630	1,100	1,400	1,700	2,750	3,100	7,500	36,000
1857-S	14,000	8665	1,400	2,250	6,250	14,500	24,000	66,000	—
1858	2,133	8631	1,750	2,750	4,200	12,000	15,500	21,500	60,000
1859	15,558	8632	1,250	1,500	1,950	3,050	3,450	9,500	20,500
1860	7,036	8633	1,250	1,900	3,000	6,000	6,500	11,500	36,000
	Auctions: $114,562, PCGS MS-67 HA 01/14								
1860-S	7,000	8666	2,500	5,750	9,750	20,500	38,500	144,000	—
	Auctions: $360,000, PCGS MS-64 HA 09/22								
1861	5,959	8634	2,250	4,400	6,250	11,500	12,000	17,000	35,000
1862	5,750	8635	2,100	4,500	6,250	11,000	11,000	19,000	43,000
1863	5,000	8636	1,500	2,600	4,000	11,000	11,500	16,000	33,000
	Auctions: $211,500, PCGS MS-67 HA 01/14								
1864	2,630	8637	3,500	4,500	6,000	12,000	12,000	18,500	42,000
1865	1,140	8638	3,250	5,750	10,000	14,500	17,000	27,500	66,000
1866	4,000	8639	1,200	1,450	2,250	6,000	7,500	12,000	38,500
1867	2,600	8640	2,000	2,900	3,900	10,000	10,500	19,000	45,500
	Auctions: $141,000, PCGS MS-67 HA 01/14								
1868 (b)	4,850	8641	1,850	2,250	2,750	7,250	7,500	11,000	34,000
1869 (b)	2,500	8642	2,500	3,100	3,600	6,750	7,500	15,000	48,000
1870	3,500	8043	1,750	2,200	2,750	7,500	0,250	14,500	51,000
1870-S	unique	8667	—	—	6,600,000	—	—	—	—
	Auctions: $5,520,000, PCGS AU-50 HA 01/23								
1871	1,300	8644	1,750	2,300	3,100	8,750	9,000	13,000	38,500
1872	2,000	8645	2,000	2,750	3,500	7,000	7,500	14,500	60,000
1873, Closed 3 (c)	2,000	8646	7,500	12,000	17,000	29,000	33,000	57,500	—
1874	41,800	8647	1,100	1,400	1,600	2,100	2,600	4,000	10,500
1877	1,468	8648	6,250	8,750	12,500	26,500	31,000	72,000	132,000
	Auctions: $102,812, PCGS MS-64 LGND 05/22								
1878 (b)	82,304	8649	1,100	1,400	1,600	2,100	2,600	4,000	10,500
1879	3,000	8650	1,250	1,650	1,950	4,750	4,750	8,250	15,500
1880	1,000	8651	2,400	3,000	4,500	8,000	8,500	12,000	20,000
1881	500	8652	4,400	6,750	10,000	15,500	16,000	25,000	66,000

* Included in number above. **a.** Small S and Medium S varieties exist. **b.** Varieties showing traces of possible overdating include 1868, 8 Over 7; 1869, 9 Over 8; and 1878, 8 Over 7. **c.** The mintage of the 1873, Closed 3, coins is unknown. Research suggests that Proofs only may have been struck (none for circulation), and those perhaps as late as 1879. Mint records report 25 Proof coins, with no reference to the style of the 3 (Open or Closed); however, the actual mintage may be as high as 100 to 1,000 coins.

Circulation Strikes *(continued)*

	Mintage	GSID	VF-20	EF-40	AU-50	AU-58	MS-60	MS-63	MS-65
1882	1,500	8653	$2,450	$3,050	$3,750	$7,000	$7,500	$11,500	$26,500
	Auctions: $105,750, PCGS MS-67 HA 01/14								
↳1882, Repunched Date, FS-301	*	351837	2,450	3,050	3,750	7,000	8,000	12,000	29,000
1883	900	8654	2,750	3,400	4,500	8,000	8,500	12,000	26,500
1884	1,000	8655	3,100	3,600	4,500	8,500	9,500	17,000	29,000
1885	800	8656	2,600	3,500	4,700	8,500	8,500	13,500	29,000
1886	1,000	8657	2,500	3,100	4,000	7,000	7,500	12,500	55,000
1887	6,000	8658	1,850	2,300	2,700	5,000	5,500	8,250	12,000
1888	5,000	8659	1,750	2,000	2,450	4,550	5,000	7,750	13,500
1889	2,300	8660	2,000	2,500	3,000	4,550	4,750	7,500	15,500

* Included in number above.

Proof Strikes

	Mintage	GSID	PF-60	PF-63	PF-65
Indian Princess Head (1854–1889), Proof	**n/a**	**74143**	**$7,250**	**$13,000**	**$29,000**
Same, Proof Cameo	**n/a**	**74144**	**—**	**15,500**	**31,000**
Same, Proof Deep Cameo	**n/a**	**74145**	**—**	**26,500**	**41,000**
1854	15–20	8668	54,000	98,500	—
1855	4–8	8671	90,000	144,000	240,000
1855-S	unique	8778	—	—	—
	Auctions: $2,160,000, PCGS PF-64 HA 02/23				
1856	8–10	8674	—	120,000	192,000
1857	8–12	8677	18,000	36,000	144,000
	Auctions: $141,000, PCGS PF-65 HA 04/15				
1858	8–12	8680	13,000	24,000	93,500
1859	80	8683	8,000	16,000	62,500
1860	119	8686	8,000	19,000	62,500
1861	113	8689	12,000	21,500	108,000
1862	35	8692	8,000	18,000	60,000
1863	39	8695	8,000	14,500	66,000
1864	50	8698	8,000	14,500	66,000
1865, Original	25	8701	10,000	18,000	63,000
1865, Restrike	2 known	198922	—	—	—
1866	30	8703	12,000	21,500	65,000
1867	50	8706	8,750	17,500	62,500
1868	25	8709	8,750	17,500	62,500
1869	25	8712	$12,000	$24,000	$72,000
1870	35	8715	11,500	30,000	66,000
1871	30	8718	14,500	26,500	79,000
1872	30	8721	10,500	20,000	60,000
1873, Closed 3	unknown	8724	48,000	90,000	180,000
	Auctions: $156,000, PCGS PF-65 SBG 04/22				
1873, Open 3	25	8725	33,500	60,000	156,000
1874	20	8730	10,000	19,000	63,000
1875	20	8733	96,000	150,000	288,000
	Auctions: $218,500, NGC PF-66 HA 01/07				
1876	45	8736	48,000	65,000	102,000
1877	20	8739	11,000	24,000	57,500
1878	20	8742	11,000	26,500	66,000
1879	30	8745	8,000	14,500	41,000
1880	36	8748	8,750	19,000	41,000
1881	54	8751	8,750	17,000	38,500
1882	76	8754	8,000	14,500	29,000
1883	89	8757	7,250	13,000	29,000
1884	106	8760	7,250	13,000	29,000
1885	110	8763	7,250	13,000	29,000
1886	142	8766	8,750	14,500	31,500
1887	160	8769	7,250	13,000	29,000
1888	291	8772	7,250	13,000	29,000
1889	129	8775	7,250	13,000	29,000

Four-Dollar Gold Pieces
1879–1880

AN OVERVIEW OF FOUR-DOLLAR GOLD PIECES

Originally proposed by John A. Kasson, a former Iowa congressman, the four-dollar gold piece, or Stella, is not widely collected, simply because of its rarity. For type-set purposes some numismatists opt to acquire a single example of the only issue readily available, Charles Barber's 1879 Flowing Hair, although these are expensive. However, the Coiled Hair style is a different type, much rarer, and a collector with the means might acquire an example of that design as well.

Scan for additional information.

FOR THE COLLECTOR AND INVESTOR: FOUR-DOLLAR GOLD PIECES AS A SPECIALTY

Over the past century perhaps two dozen numismatists have put together complete sets of one of each gold striking of the 1879 and 1880 Flowing Hair and Coiled Hair Stella, this being made possible by collections being dispersed and sold to others, as it is unlikely that even as many as 20 complete sets could exist at one time.

John A. Kasson

100 GREATEST UNITED STATES COINS

No. 18 1879 AND 1880 $4 GOLD "STELLAS"

STELLA, FLOWING HAIR AND COILED HAIR (1879–1880)

Designers: *Charles E. Barber (Flowing Hair, and common reverse); George T. Morgan (Coiled Hair).* **Weight:** *7.0 grams.* **Composition:** *Approximately .857 gold, .042 silver, .100 copper.* **Diameter:** *22 mm.* **Edge:** *Reeded.* **Mint:** *Philadelphia.*

Flowing Hair

Coiled Hair

History. The four-dollar gold Stellas of 1879 and 1880 are Proof-only patterns, not regular issues. However, as they have been listed in popular references for decades, collectors have adopted them into the regular gold series. The obverse inscription notes the coins' metallic content in proportions of gold, silver, and copper in the metric system, intended to facilitate their use in foreign countries, where the value could be quickly determined. The Stella was proposed by John A. Kasson (formerly a U.S. representative from Iowa and chairman of the House Committee on Coinage, Weights, and Measures; in 1879 serving as envoy extraordinary and minister plenipotentiary to Austria-Hungary). It is believed that Charles E. Barber designed the Flowing Hair type (as well as the reverse common to both types), and George T. Morgan designed the Coiled Hair. Those dated 1879 were struck for congressional examination; popular testimony of the era suggests that the Flowing Hair Stella became a favorite gift for congressmen's lovers in the Washington demimonde. The only issue produced in quantity was the 1879, Flowing Hair. The others were made in secret and sold privately by Mint officers and employees. The Coiled Hair Stella was not generally known to the numismatic community until they were illustrated in *The Numismatist* in the early twentieth century. Stellas are cataloged by their Judd numbers, assigned in the standard reference, *United States Pattern Coins.*

Striking and Sharpness. On nearly all examples the high parts of the hair are flat, often with striations. The other areas of the coin are typically well struck. Tiny planchet irregularities are common.

Availability. The 1879 Flowing Hair is often available on the market—usually in PF-61 to 64, although higher-condition examples come on the market with regularity (as do lightly handled and impaired coins). The 1880 Flowing Hair is typically found in PF-63 or higher. Both years of Coiled Hair Stellas are great rarities; typical grades are PF-63 to 65, with a flat strike on the head and with some tiny planchet flaws.

Grading Standards

PF-60 to 70 (Proof). ***Obverse and Reverse:*** PF-60 to 62 coins have extensive hairlines and may have nicks and contact marks. At PF-63, hairlines are prominent, but the mirror surface is very reflective. PF-64 coins have fewer hairlines. At PF-65, hairlines should be minimal and mostly seen only under magnification. There should be no nicks or marks. PF-66 and higher coins should have no marks or hairlines visible to the unaided eye.

PF-62

Illustrated coin: A nick above the head and some light friction define the grade, but the coin has nice eye appeal overall.

PF-60 to 70 (Proof). ***Obverse and Reverse:*** PF-60 to 62 coins have extensive hairlines and may have nicks and contact marks. At PF-63, hairlines are prominent, but the mirror surface is very reflective. PF-64 coins have fewer hairlines. At PF-65, hairlines should be minimal and mostly seen only under magnification. There should be no nicks or marks. PF-66 and higher coins should have no marks or hairlines visible to the unaided eye.

PF-65

Proof Strikes

		GSID	PF-60	PF-63	PF-65	PF-66	PF-67
Stella, Flowing Hair (1879–1880), Proof	**n/a**	**74173**	**$127,000**	**$156,000**	**$222,000**	**$258,000**	**$384,000**
Same, Proof Cameo	**n/a**	**74174**	**—**	**168,000**	**240,000**	**276,000**	**403,000**
Same, Proof Deep Cameo	**n/a**	**74175**	**—**	**201,500**	**270,000**	**333,000**	**720,000**
Stella, Coiled Hair (1879–1880), Proof	**n/a**	**74252**	**432,000**	**810,000**	**1,200,000**	**1,560,000**	**1,920,000**
1879, Flowing Hair	425 est. known	8779	127,000	156,000	222,000	258,000	384,000
	Auctions: $228,000, PCGS PF-65 SBG 08/25; $600,000, PCGS PF-67 HA 08/25						
1879, Coiled Hair	13 known	8780	432,000	810,000	1,200,000	1,560,000	1,920,000
	Auctions: $1,440,000, PCGS PF-65 HA 08/25; $576,000, PCGS PF-62 HA 08/25						
1880, Flowing Hair	18 known	8785	156,000	210,000	510,000	600,000	1,080,000
	Auctions: $959,400, NGC PF-67 BON 09/13						
1880, Coiled Hair	9 known	8786	660,000	960,000	1,500,000	1,800,000	2,400,000
	Auctions: $2,280,000, NGC PF-67 HA 08/25						

Gold Half Eagles ($5)
1795–1929

AN OVERVIEW OF GOLD HALF EAGLES

The half eagle was the first gold coin actually struck for the United States. The five-dollar gold piece was authorized by the Act of April 2, 1792, and the first batch was minted in 1795.

Scan for additional information.

Forming a type set of half eagles is a daunting but achievable challenge—if a collector has the finances and some determination. Examples of the first type, with Draped Bust to Right (conical cap obverse), and with an eagle on a palm branch on the reverse, regularly come up on the market, usually of the date 1795. Typical grades range from EF to lower Mint State levels. Such pieces are scarce, and the demand for them is strong. The next type, the Heraldic Eagle motif, first struck in 1798, but also known from a 1795-dated die used later, was produced through 1807, and is easily enough obtained today. Again, typical grades range from EF to Mint State. MS-63 and better coins are available, but are in the distinct minority.

The short-lived Capped Bust to Left style, 1807–1812, can be found in similar grades, although such pieces did not circulate as extensively, and AU and Mint State levels are the rule, with VF pieces being unusual. Then follows the era of rarities. The Capped Head to Left, stars surrounding head, large diameter, 1813–1829 style is available largely courtesy of the first date of issue, 1813. This is the only date seen with some frequency. When available, examples tend to be choice. The later stretch of this series includes some formidable rarities, among which are the famous 1815 and the even rarer 1822, along with a whole string of other seldom-seen varieties in the 1820s. The same style, but of reduced diameter, 1829–1834, also is rare; examples of the 1830s turn up with some regularity, but these often lack eye appeal. For some reason, half eagles of the early 1830s are often heavily marked and abraded, which is not true at all for coins of the 1820s.

Classic Head half eagles, capless and without the motto E PLURIBUS UNUM, first minted in August 1834, are easily enough obtained. Those seen in today's marketplace are usually of the first several dates, and less frequently of 1837 or 1838. Grades range from VF upward, reflecting their extensive use in circulation. Mint State coins can be found on occasion and are scarce. Choice and gem pieces are rare.

With just a few exceptions, Liberty Head half eagles of the 1839–1866 type without the motto IN GOD WE TRUST are very plentiful in worn grades, including certain of the higher-mintage issues from the popular Charlotte and Dahlonega mints (permitting interesting varieties to be added to a type set). Mint State coins are scarce, and when seen are usually in lower levels such as MS-60 and 62. Gems of any date are rare. Then follow the Liberty Head pieces with the motto IN GOD WE TRUST on the reverse, 1866 through 1908; the earlier years are mostly encountered in worn grades, the later ones are easy enough to find in Mint State. Proofs were made of all Liberty Head half eagle dates, and today they are generally collectible from about 1860 onward.

With two exceptions (1909-O and 1929), the Indian Head half eagles of 1908 to 1929 are common enough in worn grades as well as low Mint State levels, but true gems, accurately graded and with lustrous, frosty surfaces, are quite rare. The field is the highest area of the coin and thus is quite susceptible to scuffs and marks. Probably the most readily available dates in higher grades are 1908 and 1909, with the 1909-D being plentiful due to a hoard that came on the market a generation ago.

For the Collector and Investor: Gold Half Eagles as a Specialty

While in the annals of American numismatics dozens of old-time numismatists collected half eagles by date (or, less often, by date *and* mint), today rarities are so widely scattered and are so expensive that few collectors can rise to the challenge.

Early half eagles can be collected by dates and basic varieties, and also by die varieties. The year 1795 in particular is rich in the latter, and years ago several scholars described such varieties, beginning with J. Colvin Randall in the 1870s, continuing to William H. Woodin in the early 1900s, then Edgar H. Adams, Thomas Ollive Mabbott, and Walter Breen. In more recent times Robert Miller, Harry W. Bass Jr., John Dannreuther, and others have added their research to the literature.

Among early half eagles there are two unique varieties: the 1797 with a 16-star obverse, and the 1797 with a 15-star obverse, both with the Heraldic Eagle reverse, likely struck in 1798. Of the later 1822, just three are known, two of which are in the National Numismatic Collection at the Smithsonian Institution. Of all early half eagles the 1815 was far and away the most famous during the nineteenth century. (In the 1880s a publication on the Mint Collection stated that the two highlights there were the 1815 half eagle and the unique 1849 double eagle.) At the time the rarer 1822 was not recognized for its elusive nature. Today an estimated 11 examples of the 1815 half eagles exist, mostly in higher circulated grades, including those in museums. There are only two known of the 1825, 5 Over 4, overdate, but it is not at all famous, probably because it is an overdate variety, not a single date on its own. Half eagles of 1826 through 1829 all are rare, with the 1829 being particularly well known. The latter date includes early pieces with regular diameter and later ones with the diameter reduced. Generally, all half eagles from 1815 through 1834 are scarce, some of them particularly so.

Classic Head half eagles of 1834 to 1838 include the scarce 1838-C and 1838-D, the first of the Charlotte and Dahlonega mints respectively; none are prohibitively rare. Generally, the higher-grade pieces are found toward the beginning of the Classic Head series, especially bearing the date 1834.

Liberty Head half eagles are readily available of most dates and mints from 1839 to 1908, save for the one great rarity, the 1854-S, of which just three are known (one is in the Smithsonian). There is a vast panorama of Charlotte and Dahlonega issues through 1861, most of which were made in fairly large quantities, as this was the highest denomination ever struck at each of these mints (larger-capacity presses were not on hand). Accordingly, they are highly collectible today. Some varieties are scarce, but none are completely out of reach. Typical grades range from VF to EF and AU, occasionally Mint State, though not often MS-63 or higher.

Among San Francisco half eagles most of the early issues are scarce, as such pieces circulated extensively and there was no thought to saving numismatic examples. However, there are not many specialists in the field, and for some varieties it can be said that collectors are harder to find than are the coins themselves, yielding the opportunity to purchase truly rare pieces for significantly less than would otherwise be the case. Carson City half eagles were minted beginning in 1870 and continuing intermittently through 1893. Most of the early issues range from scarce to rare, the 1870-CC being particularly well known in this regard. Proofs of the Liberty Head type are generally collectible from the 1860s onward, with most on the market being of the higher-mintage issues of the 1890s and 1900s.

Among Indian Head half eagles, 1908 to 1929, the 1909-O is the rarest of the early coins, and when seen is usually worn. A choice or gem Mint State 1909-O is an incredible rarity. However, enough worn 1909-O half eagles exist, including many brought from overseas hoards in recent decades, that a piece in VF or so grade presents no problem. Half eagles of 1929, of which just 662,000 were minted, were mostly melted, it seems. A couple hundred or so exist today, nearly all of which are Mint State, but nicked and with bagmarks, MS-60 to 62 or 63. Truly high-quality gems are exceedingly rare.

COLLECTING EARLY HALF EAGLES

by John Dannreuther

The object of collecting coins (or almost any collectible) is to complete a series or set. Some sets are short but cannot be completed because of one or more unavailable rarities. The New England (NE) shilling, sixpence, and threepence comprise such a set. Until recently, it was impossible to own all three of these rare first coins struck in America, as the only known threepence was ensconced in the Massachusetts Historical Society. The discovery of a second example in the Netherlands made this three-piece set completable (albeit quite expensive, as the threepence sold for just north of $2.5 million).

Other series have challenged collectors but have been completed. A few collectors finished the set of 29 early quarter eagle varieties (1796–1834), while three collectors (Bass, Taraszka, and Jacobson) came within one coin of completing the gold eagle Capped Bust date and variety set (1795–1804, including the 1804 Proof). The Tyrant Collector (Dan O'Dowd) obtained them all and stands alone as the owner of all 33 early eagle dates and varieties. Dr. Charles Link has completed the Proof Capped Bust quarters from 1818 to 1838, including the varieties.

Only a select group of collectors have attempted a collection of the early Draped and Capped Bust half eagles, as not only are there eight unique varieties, but the prices for this series are prohibitive for most collectors. Waldo Newcomer was the first to attempt a date and variety set and amazingly acquired 122 of the 145 issues (although fewer varieties were known during his lifetime). This total was bested by Harry W. Bass Jr., who obtained 133 pieces of this challenging set. The early half eagle series contains not only eight unique varieties but a legendary rarity (the 1822), of which a single example exists in collector hands. (The National Numismatic Collection at the Smithsonian Institution has the other two known for this date.) Also, two of the eight unique varieties reside in the NNC—one of them (the 1797, BD-6) has been ensconced there since the 19th century; the other (1797, BD-5) sold for $625 in the 1955 Farish Baldenhofer Collection and then was donated to the NNC as part of the 1968 Josiah K. Lilly Collection donation. That leaves only 143 collectible dates and varieties available.

The eight unique issues are:

- 1795, Large Eagle (BD-13)
- 1797, Small Eagle (BD-4)
- 1797, Large Eagle, 16-Star Obverse (BD-5; not collectible, as the only example is in the NNC)
- 1797, Large Eagle, 15-Star Obverse (BD-6; also not collectible, as the only example is in the NNC)
- 1819 (BD-3)
- 1825, 5 Over 4 Over 1 (BD-3)
- 1828, 8 Over 7 (BD-2)
- 1834, Capped Bust (BD-4)

Amazingly, all six collectible varieties from this list of unique coins will be sold at auction! As of this writing, the 2026 FUN auction is scheduled to make these coins available together for the first time. So a collector with the means could conceivably acquire all 143 collectible varieties of the 1795–1834 half eagles! The stopper, of course, is the 1822, which last sold for an eight-figure price a few years ago. There are numerous other hard-to-obtain issues, as there are six for which only two examples are known. These are slated to be sold in the same auction as the six collectible unique varieties.

Some of the unique half eagles that are scheduled to appear in a single auction for the first time ever in January 2026: 1795, Large Eagle (BD-13); 1797, Small Eagle (BD-4); and 1819 (BD-3).

The varieties with two known examples are:

- 1799 (BD-9)
- 1820, Square Base 2 (BD-4)
- 1821 (BD-2)
- 1826 (B-2)
- 1828 (BD-3)
- 1833, Small Date (BD-3)

The early half eagle series is the most challenging of all United States issues, as one can see by the number of unique and semi-unique examples. Yes, "semi-unique" is despised by some numismatists, but it is very descriptive, and calling them "R-8" examples does not do them justice. Some call unique examples "R-8+," but that does not convey their rarity! "Unique" is the ultimate description, as it implies that the owner has something that no one else can possess.

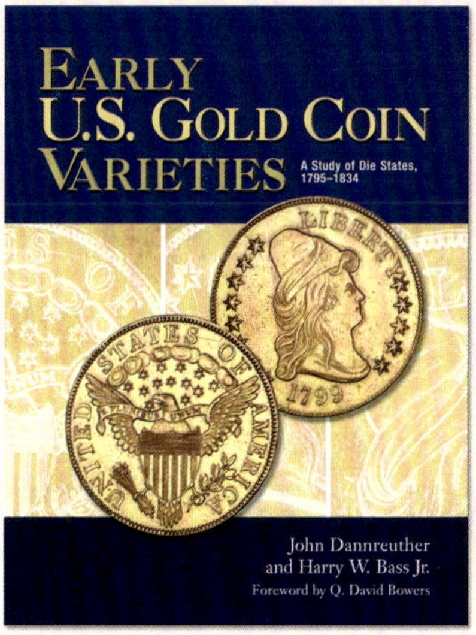

Early U.S. Gold Coin Varieties systematically catalogs die marriages and die states for early U.S. gold coins. Its BD numbers comprise the standard attribution system for these coins, allowing collectors, dealers and graders to precisely identify and compare specific die combinations.

Half eagles have many other varieties that are rarities, with several of those having only a handful known. This author was privileged to purchase (with Tom Phillips) an Extremely Fine example of the 1798, Small Eagle, issue (BD-1). This surfaced in an Alabama coin shop and was purchased with Tom describing the coin during a phone call. It was not a difficult decision, as Tom is a veteran dealer I have known since he was a teenager. Owning rarities is a thrill for any collector or dealer, as they appear so infrequently and their prices are prohibitive for most.

There are four varieties of the 1810 half eagle, with two available, one scarce, and the other rare. There are fewer than a handful of the Large Date, Small 5, variety (BD-3). There are numerous other scarce and rare issues for each type, and the reader should consult the Bass-Dannreuther book on early gold issues, *Early U.S. Gold Coin Varieties: A Study of Die States, 1795–1834* (Whitman, 2006). This work is based on the notes and work of Harry W. Bass Jr., the 20th-century connoisseur of early U.S. gold coins. Bass amassed more than 600 early gold issues, including multiple die states of some examples.

Harry W. Bass Jr., who assembled one of the greatest-ever collections of U.S. gold coins.

Few can afford to collect these treasures of our early Mint by variety, much less by die state as Bass did. However, there are many affordable alternative ways to collect. One can buy a single example. There are many nice, circulated examples in the mid–four-figure price range. Coins with nice original color, good luster, and eye appeal appear frequently at coin shows and in auctions. Problem-free coins are always available.

The type-coin collector, by definition, desires an example of each type. The four major (or five, to some) types are divided into "easily found" and "tough to find." The first and last types are the hardest to obtain and the most expensive. The Draped Bust, Small Eagle, design was issued for four years, with only the 1795 usually available—the other three dates are scarce to rare. A nice Very Fine or Extremely Fine example is a low-to-mid–five-figure coin, but examples are available at most coin shows and often appear at auction. The last type has an interesting moniker, as they are often called "Fat Head Fives." When the tight close collar was introduced in the late 1820s, rims were added to each denomination, with the dimes in late 1828 being the first to have this device. Half eagles followed in the middle of the next year, so the 1829–1834 issue has a rim to protect the devices. Thus, the flat Liberty of the obverse and the eagle of the reverse were "plumped" to create a more natural look. The contours of the head of Liberty are what led to the descriptive name. This type is more affordable than the Draped Bust, Small Eagle, type and is found with a little searching. The first and last years (1829 and 1834) are rare, so the other dates are the ones for type collectors.

The Draped Bust, Large Eagle (also called the Heraldic Eagle) is easily found even in About Uncirculated condition. It is a high–four-figure or low–five-figure price in this condition, but nice Very Fine and Extremely Fine examples are often seen. This type is very popular with collectors who just want a single early gold issue, as one can buy an example dated 1799 for not too much more than the later ones dated 1800 to 1807. The 1806, Knob 6, is the most often seen date and variety, so some collectors wait until a nice Uncirculated example appears to add to their collection. The next type (two types to some) is the Capped Bust half eagle struck from 1807 to 1829. The 1807 to 1812 variation has a slightly different head than the one from 1813 to 1829, but they are both the Capped Bust type. Both are the most readily available early half eagles; numerous dates are available for the one through 1812, while only the 1813 is common for the second group. Both are seen with frequency and in circulated grades are mid–four-figure items.

Of course, some collectors will want the varieties within each type, as there are variations in the Draped Bust, Large Eagle, series with eagles believed to have been produced by different engravers. The longer-neck variety is found only for those coins dated 1798 and earlier, while the short-neck version is seen on the rest of the series. There are reverse dies with 13 stars and others with 14 stars, so these are interesting varieties, too. The 15- and 16-star obverse issues are rarities and are seldom encountered, so they are beyond the reach of most collectors. There are numerous other variations, including the number of berries on the wreaths of the Draped Bust, Small Eagle, issues; but, again, the prices are prohibitive for these varieties.

No matter whether one possesses a single example, a type-coin set, a type set with varieties, a date set, or (as Bass and Newcomer assembled) the date-and-variety set, owning these early U.S. Mint issues is a source of pride for any collector. This denomination was the workhorse gold coin until the discovery of gold in California in 1848. It was the largest denomination after the eagle was discontinued in 1804 and remained so until the resumption of eagle production in 1838. Of course, after the California Gold Rush, the double eagle became the coin of preference for banks around the world. The half eagle was king before the crown passed to the double eagle.

AMERICAN GOLD COINS OF THE SOUTH

by Jeff Garrett

Contrary to popular belief, the first significant discovery of gold in America was not in California in 1848, but in the lower Piedmont area of North Carolina in 1799. Conrad Reed, the son of a local farmer, found a 17-pound, yellow-colored rock that later turned out to be gold (after it served a three-year stint as a doorstop!). By the early 1830s. the Bechtler family had established a private mint at Rutherford, North Carolina. Sufficient gold was found in the area to justify the opening of an official, U.S. branch mint at Charlotte, North Carolina, in 1838.

Around 1828, another gold rush began when gold was discovered in an obscure area of northern Georgia (once part of the Cherokee nation). By 1830, an average of 300 ounces of gold a day was being produced in the area. Private minters such as Templeton Reid and the Bechtler family produced their own coins from locally mined gold. In response, the U.S. Mint established a branch mint in 1838 at nearby Dahlonega, Georgia, to convert the raw gold into standardized coins.

Collecting coins by their various mintmarks did not come into vogue until the 1890s, after the publication by Augustus Heaton of a treatise on mintmarks. Many of the great collections formed before this time normally consisted of Proof gold coins produced by the U.S. Mint. The National Numismatic Collection at the Smithsonian lacked most mintmarked gold coins until the donation of the extensive Josiah Lilly collection in the 1960s.

Today, collectors find the short-lived gold issues from Charlotte and Dahlonega to be among the most desirable coins from that era, and the issues are eagerly collected.

Pre-1933 U.S. gold coins were produced at Philadelphia, Dahlonega , Charlotte, New Orleans, Denver, San Francisco, and Carson City, Nevada. Each of the mints (except Philadelphia) placed a mintmark (a small letter or letters) on every coin it produced, to identify the source—for example, the Charlotte Mint used a small C.. Each int seems to have had its own set of characteristics and quirks. Dahlonega and Charlotte coins are infamous for their poor strikes and general quality. Philadelphia appears to have produced the best coins of all the mints. Thus, a complete set of mintmarks includes coins of varying quality and even color (because of differences in the metallic composition of local ores).

Southern gold coins that were struck at the Dahlonega and Charlotte Mints were produced between 1838 and 1861, the year Confederate forces seized the Charlotte, Dahlonega, and New Orleans Mints. The first two facilities were shut down as a result, never to reopen, but the New Orleans Mint was recaptured by federal troops and produced coins until 1909.

Charlotte and Dahlonega gold coins are among the most popular series of United States coinage. The history surrounding their production makes them extremely desirable and collectible. The unique physical characteristics also add greatly to the charm of these fascinating coins.

Collecting Dahlonega Mint Gold Coins

The Dahlonega Mint opened in 1838 to process locally mined gold. Output at this facility was always low, yet it continued to operate until 1861, when Confederate forces seized the building at the outset of the Civil War. In 1878, the Dahlonega Mint was destroyed by fire. Today, Price Memorial Hall of North Georgia College sits on the original foundation of the Dahlonega Mint.

The only known picture of the Dahlonega Mint, taken before it was destroyed by fire in 1878.

The mintmark for Dahlonega is the letter D (the same as for the Denver Mint, but the two mints never operated simultaneously). The Dahlonega Mint produced only gold coins, of the following types and dates:

Gold Dollars, 1849–1861
Variety 1, Liberty Head, 1849–1854
Variety 2, Indian Princess, Small Head, 1855
Variety 3, Indian Princess, Large Head, 1856–1861

Quarter Eagles, 1838–1859
Classic Head, 1838
Liberty Head, 1839–1859

Three Dollar, 1854
Indian Princess Head, 1854

Half Eagles, 1838-1861
Classic Head, 1838
Liberty Head, No Motto, 1839–1842 (including 1842, Small Date and Large Date; and 1846, D Over D)

The websites for the Greysheet, Numismatic Guaranty Company (NGC), Professional Coin Grading Service (PCGS), and Certified Acceptance Corporation Grading (CACG) have population and price guide information for each coin. These are great resources for comparing relative rarity and availability in every grade.

A complete set of Dahlonega gold coins consists of the 62 coins listed above, including major *Red Book* varieties. Only the most advanced collectors usually attempt a collection of every coin issued.

Also, unlike with most series of U.S. coins, Mint State examples of Dahlonega gold coins are the true exception rather than the rule. Most collectors seek pleasing circulated examples in the best condition they can afford. Extremely Fine and About Uncirculated examples are the commonly collected grades for the series.

Many Dahlonega gold coins found on the market were cleaned years ago in their owners' attempts to get higher third-party grading ratings. Today's collectors place a considerable premium on original, "crusty"-looking circulated examples. As with any series you collect, spend some time trying to understand the issues of quality and eye appeal before making a substantial purchase. Examining auction lots is one of the best ways to accomplish this task.

The following are just a few of the different ways to collect these elusive coins.

Three-piece type set—Liberty Head gold dollar, quarter eagle, and half eagle. This is a relatively easy task, and can be done to fit your budget according to the grade collected.

Eight-piece type set—Varieties 1–3 gold dollars, Classic Head and Liberty Head quarter eagles, Indian Princess Head three-dollar gold coin, and Classic Head and Liberty Head half eagles. This set is relatively achievable, but much more expensive.

Denomination set—Many collectors choose one denomination and try to assemble a complete set. Although the Liberty Head quarter eagles do not contain major rarities like the 1861-D gold dollar and half eagle, many of the dates are among the most difficult to find in nice condition.

A few great coins—Over the years, quite a few of my customers have bought one or two coins from this interesting mint because of the history and charm of the era. The 1861-D gold dollar, which was struck by the Confederacy, is a prime example.

Complete set—As mentioned above, this is a daunting task and would cost about $750,000 in Extremely Fine to About Uncirculated condition. Over the years, I have assisted many collectors who have taken on this project. About four years ago, Atlanta dealer Robert Harwell and I assembled a complete collection of Dahlonega gold for John McMullan. The collection is now on permanent exhibit at the University of Georgia.

Regardless of the journey you choose, collecting Southern gold coins is both challenging and fun. These coins also provide the reassurance that they won't be found in bag quantities from overseas hoards. Attractive examples are becoming difficult to find, and as more collectors discover this area of the market, they will be even harder to locate.

Recommended Reading

Encyclopedia of United States Gold Coins, 1795–1933, by Jeff Garrett
Gold Coins of the Dahlonega Mint, 1838–1861, by Doug Winter

100 GREATEST™ UNITED STATES COINS

No. 17 1854-S LIBERTY HEAD HALF EAGLE

THE 1854-S HALF EAGLE

by John Dannreuther

The 1854-S half eagle is not only a great rarity—it is one of the greatest of the entire United States series.

With only 268 examples stuck, the 1854-S half eagle has one of the lowest regular-issue mintages of any United States coin. Today, only three examples survive, with one of those being a part of the Smithsonian's National Numismatic Collection (provenance from the Josiah Lilly collection). The 1854-S half eagle is much rarer than such famous rarities as the 1804 silver dollar, the 1933 double eagle, and the 1913 Liberty Head nickel. The Willis H. du Pont example of the 1854-S half eagle was stolen in 1967 and has never been recovered. A previously unknown example surfaced and was auctioned in 2018. Several numismatic experts suspected that it may have been the stolen du Pont example. Given the time that had elapsed, and the fact that photographic evidence could not prove otherwise, the coin was resold at auction in 2021 with a legal release from the du Pont family. The third and finest-known example (nearly mint condition), which was from the Brent Pogue collection, was sold in 2020 for $1,920,000—one of the best bargains of the Covid-19 pandemic.

The 1854-S half eagle is one of the great rarities of the Californian Gold Rush era. With only two examples known in private hands, the coin should also be considered one of the greatest coins of the United States series.

DRAPED BUST TO RIGHT, SMALL EAGLE REVERSE (1795–1798)

Designer: *Robert Scot.* **Weight:** *8.75 grams.*
Composition: *.9167 gold, .0833 silver and copper.*
Diameter: *Approximately 25 mm.* **Edge:** *Reeded.* **Mint:** *Philadelphia.*

History. Half eagles of this style, the first federal gold coins, were introduced in July 1795. The obverse features Liberty wearing a conical cap, a design generally called Draped Bust to Right. The reverse depicts a "small" eagle perched on a palm branch. The same motif was used on contemporary $10 gold coins. No Proofs or presentation strikes were made of this type.

Striking and Sharpness. On the obverse, check the star centers and the hair details. On the reverse, check the feathers of the eagle, particularly on the breast. Examine the denticles on both sides. Adjustment marks (from Mint workers filing down overweight planchets to acceptable standards) often are visible, but are not explicitly noted by the grading services.

Availability. Typical grades range from EF to AU and low MS. MS-63 and better coins are rare; when seen, they usually are of the 1795 date (of which many different die varieties exist). Certain varieties are rare, most famously the 1798 with Small Eagle reverse.

Grading Standards

MS-63

MS-60 to 70 (Mint State). ***Obverse:*** At MS-60, some abrasion and contact marks are evident, most noticeably on the hair to the left of Liberty's forehead and on the higher-relief areas of the cap. Luster is present, but may be dull or lifeless, and interrupted in patches. At MS-63, contact marks are few, and abrasion is very light. An MS-65 coin has hardly any abrasion, and contact marks are so minute as to require magnification. Luster should be full and rich. Grades above MS-65 for this type are more often theoretical than actual—but they do exist and are defined by having fewer marks as perfection is approached. ***Reverse:*** Comments apply as for the obverse, except that abrasion and contact marks are most noticeable on the breast and head of the eagle. The field area is mainly protected by the eagle, branch, and lettering.

Illustrated coin: This is the error die with the second S over an erroneous D in STATES (which originally read as STATED).

AU-58

AU-50, 53, 55, 58 (About Uncirculated). ***Obverse:*** Light wear is seen on the cheek, the hair immediately to the left of the face, and the cap, more at AU-50 than at AU-53 or 55. An AU-58 coin has minimal traces of wear. An AU-50 coin has luster in protected areas among the stars and letters, with little in the open fields or on the portrait. At AU-58, most luster is present in the fields but is worn away on the highest parts of the motifs. ***Reverse:*** Comments as preceding, except that the eagle shows light wear on the breast and head in particular, but also at the tip of the wing on the left and elsewhere. Luster ranges from perhaps 40 percent remaining in protected areas (at AU-50) to nearly full mint bloom (at AU-58).

EF-40

EF-40, 45 (Extremely Fine). ***Obverse:*** Wear is evident all over the portrait, with some loss of detail in the hair to the left of Liberty's face. Excellent detail remains in low-relief areas of the hair, such as the front curl and at the back of her head. The stars show wear, as do the date and letters. Luster, if present at all, is minimal and in protected areas. ***Reverse:*** Wear is greater than on an About Uncirculated coin. The breast, neck, and legs of the eagle lack nearly all feather detail. More wear is seen on the edges of the wing. Some traces of luster may be seen, more so at EF-45 than at EF-40.

VF-20, 30 (Very Fine). ***Obverse:*** The higher-relief areas of hair are well worn at VF-20, less so at VF-30. The stars are flat at their centers. ***Reverse:*** Wear is greater, the eagle is flat in most areas, and about 40 percent to 60 percent of the wing feathers can be seen.

Illustrated coin: While exhibiting typical wear for a VF-20 coin, this specimen also shows rim damage from having been mounted as jewelry at some point in time.

VF-20

1796, 6 Over 5

1797, 15-Star Obverse

1797, 16-Star Obverse

Circulation Strikes

	Mintage	GSID	F-12	VF-20	EF-40	AU-50	AU-58	MS-60	MS-63
Draped Bust to Right, Small Eagle Reverse (1795–1798)	**n/a**	**72376**	**$27,500**	**$31,000**	**$37,000**	**$50,500**	**$84,000**	**$90,000**	**$210,000**
1795, Small Eagle Reverse	8,707	8791	27,500	31,000	37,000	50,500	84,000	90,000	210,000
	Auctions: $156,000, NGC MS-63 SBG 08/24; $586,500, PCGS MS-65 SBG 08/24								
↳1795, S Over D	*	198172	27,500	31,000	37,000	50,500	84,000	90,000	210,000
1796, 6 Over 5	6,196	8870	30,500	34,500	41,000	55,500	93,000	108,000	300,000
	Auctions: $316,250, NGC MS-64 SBG 06/08								
1797, 16-Star Obverse	3,609	8793	30,000	42,000	78,000	132,000	288,000	360,000	—
	Auctions: $483,219, PCGS MS-61 SBG 08/13								
1797, 15-Star Obverse	*	8795	30,000	42,000	72,000	132,000	210,000	270,000	—
	Auctions: $210,000, PCGS AU-58 SBG 08/25								
1798, Small Eagle Reverse	6–7 est. known	8796	300,000	480,000	780,000	2,160,000	—	—	—
	Auctions: $264,500, PCGS EF-40 GLDB 06/00								

* Included in number above.

100 GREATEST™ UNITED STATES COINS

No. 35 1798 "SMALL EAGLE" DRAPED BUST HALF EAGLE

DRAPED BUST TO RIGHT, HERALDIC EAGLE REVERSE (1795–1807)

Designer: *Robert Scot.* **Weight:** *8.75 grams.*
Composition: *.9167 gold, .0833 silver and copper.*
Diameter: *Approximately 25 mm.* **Edge:** *Reeded.* **Mint:** *Philadelphia.*

History. For this type, the obverse design is the same as that of the preceding. The reverse features a heraldic eagle, as used on other silver and gold coins of the era. Some half eagles of the Heraldic Eagle Reverse design are dated 1795, but these were actually struck in 1798, from a leftover obverse coinage die. The *Encyclopedia of U.S. Gold Coins, 1795–1933* (second edition) notes that "No Proofs were made, but one 1795 half eagle with a Heraldic Eagle reverse has been certified as a Specimen."

Striking and Sharpness. On the obverse, check the star centers and the hair details. On the reverse, check the upper part of the shield, the lower part of the eagle's neck, the eagle's wing, the stars above the eagle, and the clouds. Inspect the denticles on both sides. Adjustment marks (from overweight planchets being filed down to correct standards by Mint workers) can be an aesthetic problem and are not explicitly identified by the grading services.

Availability. Although there are many rare die varieties, as a type this half eagle is plentiful. Typical grades are EF to lower MS. MS-63 and higher coins are seen with some frequency and usually are dated from 1802 to 1807. Sharply struck coins without adjustment marks are in the minority.

Grading Standards

MS-62

MS-60 to 70 (Mint State). ***Obverse:*** At MS-60, some abrasion and contact marks are evident, most noticeably on the hair to the left of Liberty's forehead and on the higher-relief areas of the cap. Luster is present, but may be dull or lifeless, and interrupted in patches. At MS-63, contact marks are few, and abrasion is very light. An MS-65 coin has hardly any abrasion, and contact marks are so minute as to require magnification. Luster should be full and rich. Grades above MS-65 are not often seen but are defined by having fewer marks as perfection is approached. ***Reverse:*** Comments apply as for the obverse, except that abrasion and contact marks are most noticeable on the upper part of the eagle and the clouds. The field area is complex, with not much open space, given the stars above the eagle, the arrows and olive branch, and other features. Accordingly, marks are not as noticeable as on the obverse.

Illustrated coin: This is an attractive coin with rich luster. Some friction is visible on the higher points and in the obverse field.

AU-50, 53, 55, 58 (About Uncirculated). ***Obverse:*** Light wear is seen on the cheek, the hair immediately to the left of the face, and the cap, more at AU-50 than at AU-53 or 55. An AU-58 coin has minimal traces of wear. An AU-50 coin has luster in protected areas among the stars and letters, with little in the open fields or on the portrait. At AU-58, most luster is present in the fields, but is worn away on the highest parts of the motifs. ***Reverse:*** Comments as preceding, except that the eagle's neck, the tips and top of the wings, the clouds, and the tail now show noticeable wear, as do other features. Luster ranges from perhaps 40 percent remaining in protected areas (at AU-50) to nearly full mint bloom (at AU-58). Often the reverse of this type retains much more luster than the obverse.

AU-58

Illustrated coin: An abrasion in the left obverse field keeps this otherwise lustrous and attractive coin below the Mint State level.

EF-40, 45 (Extremely Fine). ***Obverse:*** Wear is evident all over the portrait, with some loss of detail in the hair to the left of Liberty's face. Excellent detail remains in low-relief areas of the hair, such as the front curl and at the back of her head. The stars show wear, as do the date and letters. Luster, if present at all, is minimal and in protected areas. ***Reverse:*** Wear is greater than on an About Uncirculated coin. The neck lacks feather detail on its highest points. Feathers have lost some detail near the edges of the wings, and some areas of the horizontal lines in the shield may be blended together. Some traces of luster may be seen, more so at EF-45 than at EF-40. Overall, the reverse appears to be in a slightly higher grade than the obverse.

EF-45

VF-20, 30 (Very Fine). ***Obverse:*** The higher-relief areas of hair are well worn at VF-20, less so at VF-30. The stars are flat at their centers. ***Reverse:*** Wear is greater, including on the shield and wing feathers. The star centers are flat. Other areas have lost detail as well. E PLURIBUS UNUM may be light or worn away in areas.

VF-20

1797, 16-Star Obverse

1797, 15-Star Obverse

1797, 7 Over 5

1798, Small 8

1798, Large 8

1798, 13-Star Reverse

1798, 14-Star Reverse

1799, Small Stars Reverse

1799, Large Stars Reverse

1800, Pointed 1

1800, Blunt 1

1802, 2 Over 1
FS-301

1803, 3 Over 2

Circulation Strikes

	Mintage	GSID	F-12	VF-20	EF-40	AU-50	AU-58	MS-60	MS-63
Draped Bust to Right, Heraldic Eagle Reverse (1795–1807)	**n/a**	**72377**	**$4,500**	**$5,500**	**$7,750**	**$10,000**	**$12,500**	**$14,000**	**$27,000**
1795, Heraldic Eagle Reverse	unknown	8792	12,000	21,500	41,000	86,500	138,000	150,000	264,000
	Auctions: $180,000, PCGS MS-62 SBG 03/18								
1797, 16 Stars Obverse (in Smthsonian Collection)	unique	8794	—	—	—	—	—	—	—
1797, 15 Stars Obverse (in Smthsonian Collection)	unique	374607	—	—	—	—	—	—	—
1797, 7 Over 5	20 est. known	8871	31,000	38,500	55,000	90,000	180,000	216,000	—
	Auctions: $180,000, NGC MS-61 SBG 02/19								
1798, Normal 8	24,867	8799	7,500	10,000	19,000	29,000	51,500	66,000	150,000
1798, Large 8, 13-Star Reverse	*	8797	5,500	7,000	12,500	17,500	29,000	33,500	77,000
	Auctions: $155,250, NGC MS-64 HA 08/11								
1798, Large 8, 14-Star Reverse	<50 known	8798	7,000	8,750	14,000	27,500	45,500	120,000	—
1799, Small Stars Reverse	7,451	8800	6,500	7,750	11,000	14,500	24,500	33,000	86,500
1799, Large Stars Reverse	*	8801	—	7,750	11,000	14,500	25,000	36,500	93,500
1800	37,628	8802	5,000	6,250	9,000	11,500	14,500	15,500	42,000
	Auctions: $241,500, Uncert MS-67 SBG 03/05								
↳1800, Pointed 1	*	198190	5,000	6,250	9,000	11,500	14,500	15,500	42,000
↳1800, Blunt 1	*	198191	5,000	6,250	9,000	11,500	14,500	15,500	42,000
1802, 2 Over 1	53,176	8872	4,950	6,000	8,500	11,500	14,000	15,000	39,500
	Auctions: $138,000, PCGS MS-65 HA 01/09								
1803, 3 Over 2	33,506	8873	4,500	5,500	7,750	10,000	14,000	14,000	27,000
	Auctions: $168,000, PCGS MS-65 SBG 12/20								

* Included in number above.

1804, Small 8

1804, Small 8 Over Large 8

1806, Pointed-Top 6, 8 Stars Left, 5 Stars Right

Closeup of Pointed-Top 6

1806, Round-Top 6, 7 Stars Left, 6 Stars Right

Closeup of Round-Top 6

Circulation Strikes *(continued)*

	Mintage	GSID	F-12	VF-20	EF-40	AU-50	AU-58	MS-60	MS-63
1804, Small 8	30,475	8803	$4,500	$5,500	$7,750	$10,500	$17,000	$18,000	$38,500
1804, Small 8 Over Large 8	*	8804	5,000	5,750	8,500	13,000	23,000	26,500	57,500
1805	33,183	8805	4,500	5,500	7,750	11,500	14,000	15,000	27,000
	Auctions: $195,500, PCGS MS-65 HA 01/08								
1806, Pointed 6, 8 Stars Left, 5 Stars Right	9,676	8807	4,500	5,500	7,750	10,000	12,500	15,000	35,000
1806, Knob 6, 7 Stars Left, 6 Stars Right	54,417	8806	4,500	5,500	7,750	10,000	12,500	14,000	27,000
	Auctions: $126,500, PCGS MS-65 HA 01/10								
1807, Draped Bust to Right	32,488	8808	4,500	5,500	7,750	10,000	12,500	14,000	27,000
	Auctions: $195,500, PCGS MS-65 ANR 03/06								

* Included in number above.

100 GREATEST™ UNITED STATES COINS

No. 79 1797 "16 STARS OBVERSE" DRAPED BUST, HERALDIC REVERSE HALF EAGLE

CAPPED BUST TO LEFT (1807–1812)

Designer: *John Reich.* **Weight:** *8.75 grams.*
Composition: *.9167 gold, .0833 silver and copper.*
Diameter: *Approximately 25 mm.* **Edge:** *Reeded.* **Mint:** *Philadelphia.*

History. This half eagle motif, designed by John Reich and stylistically related to his Capped Bust half dollar of 1807, was used for several years in the early 1800s. Quantities minted were high, and the coins saw wide circulation. No Proof examples were made of this type.

Striking and Sharpness. The striking usually is quite good and is significantly better than on earlier half eagle types. Adjustment marks (from overweight planchets being filed down to acceptable weight) are seen only occasionally. On the obverse, check the star centers and the hair details. On the reverse, check the eagle, particularity at the shield and the lower left. Examine the denticles on both sides.

Availability. After 1821 gold coins of this standard no longer circulated, as their bullion value exceeded their face value. Accordingly, they never sustained extensive wear, and nearly all examples are in EF or higher grades (coins used as pocket pieces or incorporated into jewelry are exceptions). As a type this issue is readily available in grades up to MS-63, although MS-64 and 65 coins are seen on occasion. Most have excellent eye appeal.

Grading Standards

MS-60

MS-60 to 70 (Mint State). ***Obverse:*** At MS-60, some abrasion and contact marks are seen on the cheek, the hair below the LIBERTY inscription, and the highest-relief folds of the cap. Luster is present, but may be dull or lifeless, and interrupted in patches. At MS-63, contact marks are few, and abrasion is very light. At MS-64, abrasion is even less. An MS-65 coin has hardly any abrasion, and contact marks are minute. Luster should be full and rich and is often more intense on the obverse. Grades above MS-65 are defined by having fewer marks as perfection is approached. ***Reverse:*** Comments apply as for the obverse, except that abrasion is most noticeable on the eagle's neck and the highest area of the wings.

Illustrated coin: This attractive Capped Head to Left half eagle has nice luster.

AU-58

AU-50, 53, 55, 58 (About Uncirculated). ***Obverse:*** Light wear is seen on the cheek and the higher-relief areas of the hair and cap. Friction and scattered marks are in the field, ranging from extensive at AU-50 to minimal at AU-58. Luster may be seen in protected areas, minimal at AU-50 but more evident at AU-58. On an AU-58 coin the field retains some luster as well. ***Reverse:*** Comments as preceding, except that the eagle's neck, the top of the wings, the leaves, and the arrowheads now show noticeable wear, as do other features. Luster ranges from perhaps 40 percent remaining in protected areas (at AU-50) to nearly full mint bloom (at AU-58). Often the reverse of this type retains much more luster than the obverse, as the motto, eagle, and lettering protect the surrounding flat areas.

Illustrated coin: This lustrous example is well struck.

EF-40

EF-40, 45 (Extremely Fine). ***Obverse:*** More wear is seen on the portrait, the hair, the cap, and the drapery near the clasp. Luster is minimal or nonexistent at EF-40, and may be slight at EF-45. ***Reverse:*** Wear is more extensive on the eagle, including the top of the wings, the head, the top of the shield, and the claws. Some traces of luster may be seen, more so at EF-45 than at EF-40.

VF-20

VF-20, 30 (Very Fine). ***Obverse:*** Wear on the portrait has reduced the hair detail, especially to the right of the face and the top of the head, but much can still be seen. ***Reverse:*** Wear on the eagle is greater, and details of feathers near the shield and near the top of the wings are weak or missing. All other features show wear, but most are fairly sharp. Generally, Draped Bust gold coins at this grade level lack eye appeal.

1808, 8 Over 7

1808, Normal Date

1809, 9 Over 8

1810, Small Date

1810, Large Date

Small 5

Large 5

Tall 5

Circulation Strikes

	Mintage	GSID	F-12	VF-20	EF-40	AU-50	AU-58	MS-60	MS-63
Capped Bust to Left (1807–1812)	**n/a**	**72378**	**$4,250**	**$5,250**	**$7,750**	**$9,750**	**$12,000**	**$12,500**	**$20,000**
1807, Capped Bust to Left	51,605	8809	4,250	5,250	7,750	10,000	12,000	13,000	20,000
	Auctions: $115,000, PCGS MS-67 SU 02/02								
1808	55,578	8810	4,250	5,250	7,750	9,750	12,000	12,500	30,500
	Auctions: $138,000, PCGS MS-65 HA 08/11								
↳1808, Wide 5 D	*	197940	4,250	5,250	7,750	9,750	12,000	12,500	30,500
↳1808, 8 Over 7, Short 1	*	197941	—	—	—	—	23,000	24,000	43,000
↳1808, 8 Over 7, Tall 1	*	197942	4,250	5,250	7,750	10,000	16,000	18,500	42,000
	Auctions: $105,750, PCGS MS-65 SBG 02/16								
1809, 9 Over 8	33,875	8875	4,450	5,500	8,250	10,500	12,500	14,000	29,000
	Auctions: $126,500, PCGS MS-65 HA 01/11								
1810, Small Date, Tall 5	100,287	8812	4,250	5,250	7,750	9,750	12,000	13,000	33,500
	Auctions: $115,000, PCGS MS-65 HA 01/12								
1810, Small Date, Small 5	14 est. known	8811	17,000	26,500	43,000	60,000	102,000	132,000	—
	Auctions: $138,000, NGC MS-62 SBG 06/08								
1810, Large Date, Small 5	4 known	8813	66,000	96,000	156,000	264,000	360,000	420,000	—
1810, Large Date, Large 5	*	8814	4,250	5,250	7,750	9,750	12,000	12,500	21,500
	Auctions: $172,500, NGC MS-66 HA 01/08								
1811, Tall 5	99,581	8816	4,250	5,250	7,750	9,750	12,000	12,500	26,500
1811, Small 5	*	8815	4,250	5,250	7,750	9,750	13,000	14,500	24,000
1812	58,087	8817	4,250	5,250	7,750	9,750	12,000	12,500	26,500
	Auctions: $161,000, PCGS MS-65 HA 01/08								

* Included in number above.

CAPPED HEAD TO LEFT (1813–1834)

Designer: *John Reich (design modified by William Kneass in 1829).*
Weight: *8.75 grams.* **Composition:** *.9167 gold, .0833 silver and copper.*
Diameter: *25 mm (reduced to 23.8 mm in 1829).* **Edge:** *Reeded.* **Mint:** *Philadelphia.*

Circulation Strike

Proof Strike

History. Half eagles of the Capped Head to Left design are divided into issues of 1813 to 1829 (with a larger diameter), and issues of 1829 to 1834 (with a smaller diameter, and smaller letters, dates, and stars). Those dated 1813 to 1815 are in bold relief and sometimes collected as a separate variety.

Striking and Sharpness. On the obverse, check the star centers and the hair details (these details are usually less distinct on the 1829–1834 smaller-diameter coins). On the reverse, check the eagle. Most examples are well struck. Adjustment marks (from overweight planchets being filed down to acceptable specifications at the mint) are not often encountered. Proof coins were struck on a limited basis for inclusion in sets and for numismatists. Over the years some prooflike Mint State pieces have been classified as Proofs.

Availability. The 1813 and 1814, 4 Over 3, are seen with some frequency and constitute the main supply available for assembling type sets. Other dates range from very rare to extremely rare, with the 1822 topping the list (just three are known, two of which are in the Smithsonian Institution). As gold coins did not circulate after 1821, issues of 1813 to 1820 are usually seen in high-level AU or in MS, and those of the 1820s in MS. The half eagles of the early 1830s are exceptions; these usually show light wear and are much rarer in high-level MS. All Proofs are exceedingly rare.

Grading Standards

MS-63

MS-60 to 70 (Mint State). ***Obverse:*** At MS-60, some abrasion and contact marks are seen on the cheek, the hair below the LIBERTY inscription, and the highest-relief folds of the cap. Luster is present, but may be dull or lifeless, and interrupted in patches. At MS-63, contact marks are few, and abrasion is very light. At MS-64, abrasion is even less. An MS-65 coin has hardly any abrasion, and contact marks are minute. Luster should be full and rich and is often more intense on the obverse. Grades above MS-65 are defined by having fewer marks as perfection is approached. ***Reverse:*** Comments apply as for the obverse, except that abrasion is most noticeable on the eagle's neck and the highest area of the wings.

AU-50

AU-50, 53, 55, 58 (About Uncirculated). ***Obverse:*** Light wear is seen on the cheek and the higher-relief areas of the hair and cap. Friction and scattered marks are in the field, ranging from extensive at AU-50 to minimal at AU-58. Luster may be seen in protected areas, minimal at AU-50 but more evident at AU-58. On an AU-58 coin the field retains some luster as well. ***Reverse:*** Comments as preceding, except that the eagle's neck, the top of the wings, the leaves, and the arrowheads now show noticeable wear, as do other features. Luster ranges from perhaps 40 percent remaining in protected areas (at AU-50) to nearly full mint bloom (at AU-58). Often the reverse of this type retains much more luster than the obverse, as the motto, eagle, and lettering protect the surrounding flat areas.

EF-45

EF-40, 45 (Extremely Fine). ***Obverse:*** More wear is seen on the portrait, the hair, the cap, and the drapery near the clasp. Luster is minimal or nonexistent at EF-40, and may be slight at EF-45. ***Reverse:*** Wear is more extensive on the eagle, including the top of the wings, the head, the top of the shield, and the claws. Some traces of luster may be seen, more so at EF-45 than at EF-40.

PF-66+
Cameo

PF-60 to 70 (Proof). ***Obverse and Reverse:*** PF-60 to 62 coins have extensive hairlines and may have nicks and contact marks. At PF-63, hairlines are prominent, but the mirror surface is very reflective. PF-64 coins have fewer hairlines. At PF-65, hairlines should be minimal and mostly seen only under magnification. There should be no nicks or marks. PF-66 and higher coins should have no marks or hairlines visible to the unaided eye.

1820, Curved-Base 2

1820, Square-Base 2

1820, Small Letters

1820, Large Letters

1825, 5 Over Partial 4

1825, 5 Over 4

Circulation Strikes

	Mintage	GSID	F-12	VF-20	EF-40	AU-50	AU-58	MS-60	MS-63
Capped Head to Left, Large Size Planchet (1813–1829)	n/a	72379	$4,700	$6,000	$9,000	$10,500	$12,500	$13,000	$26,000
Capped Head to Left, Small Size Planchet (1829–1834)	n/a	72380	21,500	33,500	54,000	66,000	77,000	81,500	138,000
Variety 1: Large Size Planchet									
1813	95,428	8818	5,500	6,250	9,250	11,000	16,000	17,000	27,500
	Auctions: $316,250, PCGS MS-66 HA 01/07								
1814, 4 Over 3	15,454	8876	5,250	6,750	9,750	12,000	18,500	22,000	48,000
1815	10 est. known	8819	102,000	150,000	276,000	318,000	396,000	432,000	720,000
	Auctions: $822,500, PCGS MS-65 SBG 02/16								
1818	48,588	8820	5,750	7,750	14,500	17,500	22,000	26,500	60,000
1818, STATESOF	*	8822	6,250	8,500	16,000	19,000	24,500	29,000	60,000
	Auctions: $109,250, PCGS MS-64 HA 05/07								
1818, 5 D Over 5 0	*	8821	6,250	8,500	16,000	19,000	24,500	29,000	66,000
	Auctions: $135,125, PCGS MS-65 HA 01/14								
1819	5 est. known	8823	30,000	42,000	60,000	72,000	102,000	132,000	270,000
1819, 5 D Over 5 0	13 est. known	8824	30,000	42,000	62,500	74,500	114,000	144,000	252,000
	Auctions: $384,000, PCGS MS-64 SBG 08/23								
1820, Square-Base 2	263,806	8825	7,000	8,500	12,500	15,500	26,500	31,000	59,000
	Auctions: $108,000, PCGS MS-65 SBG 08/21								
1820, Curl-Base 2, Small Letters	*	8827	—	—	—	60,000	—	—	187,000
	Auctions: $300,000, PCGS MS-64 SBG 11/23								
1820, Curl-Base 2, Large Letters	*	8826	—	—	—	—	29,000	31,000	66,000
	Auctions: $253,000, PCGS MS-65 HA 04/08								
1821	17 est. known	8829	30,000	48,000	66,000	114,000	180,000	210,000	330,000
	Auctions: $540,500, PCGS MS-63 GLDB 01/14								
1822 (a)	3 known	8831	—	—	—	9,600,000	—	—	—
	Auctions: $8,400,000, PCGS AU-50 SBG 03/21								
1823	14,485	8832	5,250	6,750	13,000	15,500	25,000	27,500	50,500
	Auctions: $299,000, NGC MS-65 HA 01/11								
1824	17,340	8834	8,000	12,500	33,500	38,500	45,500	54,000	114,000
	Auctions: $199,750, NGC MS-65 HA 01/14								
1825, 5 Over 4 Over 1	29,060	8877	11,000	15,500	36,000	45,500	74,500	79,000	162,000
1825, 5 Over 4	2 known	8879	—	—	—	840,000	—	—	—
	Auctions: $940,000, PCGS MS-64 SBG 05/16								

* Included in number above. **a.** The reported mintage is 17,796.

1828, 8 Over 7

1829, Large Size Planchet

1829, Small Size Planchet

Small 5 D.

Large 5 D.

1832, Curved-Base 2, 12-Star Obverse

1832, Square-Base 2, 13-Star Obverse

1833, Large Date

1833, Small Date

1834, Plain 4

1834, Crosslet 4

Circulation Strikes

	Mintage	GSID	F-12	VF-20	EF-40	AU-50	AU-58	MS-60	MS-63
1826	18,069	8836	$6,250	$12,000	$26,000	$33,000	$60,000	$75,500	$156,000
	Auctions: $763,750, PCGS MS-66 HA 01/14								
1827	17 est. known	8838	6,250	11,000	24,000	31,000	45,000	54,000	144,000
	Auctions: $168,000, PCGS MS-64 SBG 04/25								
1828	9 est. known	8840	12,000	24,000	42,000	60,000	90,000	120,000	240,000
	Auctions: $499,375, PCGS MS-64 HA 04/13								
1828, 8 Over 7, Reverse of 1826	5 known	8880	14,000	31,000	69,500	78,000	102,000	150,000	390,000
	Auctions: $632,500, NGC MS-64 HA 01/12								
1829, Large Size	7 known	8842	—	—	—	—	—	420,000	—
	Auctions: $763,750, PCGS MS-66 SBG 05/16								
Variety 2: Small Size Planchet									
1829, Small Size	10 est. known	8843	—	—	—	150,000	240,000	312,000	576,000
	Auctions: $881,250, PCGS MS-65 SBG 05/16								
1830, Large 5 D.	126,351	197944	21,500	33,500	54,000	66,000	77,000	81,500	138,000
1830, Small 5 D.	*	197943	21,500	33,500	54,000	66,000	77,000	81,500	138,000
1831, Small 5 D.	140,594	197945	21,500	33,500	54,000	66,000	77,000	90,000	180,000
1831, Large 5 D.	*	197946	21,500	33,500	54,000	66,000	101,000	114,000	198,000
1832, Square-Base 2, 13 Stars	157,487	8850	21,500	33,500	54,000	66,000	77,000	81,500	138,000
	Auctions: $176,250, NGC MS-65 HA 01/14								
1832, Curved-Base 2, 12 Stars	5 known	8849	120,000	180,000	288,000	408,000	630,000	—	960,000
	Auctions: $822,500, PCGS MS-63 SBG 05/16								
1833, Large Date	193,630	8852	21,500	33,500	54,000	66,000	77,000	81,500	138,000
	Auctions: $129,250, PCGS MS-64 SBG 05/16								
1833, Small Date	*	8853	21,500	33,500	54,000	66,000	77,000	81,500	162,000
	Auctions: $192,000, PCGS MS-65 SBG 08/25								
1834, Capped Head, Plain 4	50,141	8855	21,500	33,500	54,000	66,000	77,000	81,500	138,000
	Auctions: $161,000, NGC MS-65 SU 11/06								
1834, Capped Head, Crosslet 4	*	8858	21,500	33,500	54,000	68,500	81,500	86,500	144,000
	Auctions: $205,625, PCGS MS-63 LGND 12/21								

* Included in number above.

Proof Strikes

		GSID	PF-63	PF-65
1820	unknown	8828	—	—
1821	unknown	8830	—	$4,800,000
1825, 5 Over 4 Over 1	3 known	8878	—	—
	Auctions: $1,080,000, PCGS PF-62 SBG 08/24			
1826	unknown	8837	—	—
1828	unknown	8841	—	—
1829, Large Size	2 known	226367	—	—
	Auctions: $1,380,000, PCGS PF-64 HA 01/12			
1829, Small Size	unknown	8844	—	—
1830	unknown	8846	$276,000	—
	Auctions: $300,028, NGC PF-63 HA 08/19			
1832	unknown	8851	—	—
1833, Large Date	unknown	8854	—	—
	Auctions: $1,351,250, PCGS PF-67 SBG 05/16			

CLASSIC HEAD (1834–1838)

Designer: *William Kneass.* **Weight:** *8.36 grams.*
Composition: *(1834–1836) .8992 gold, .1008 silver and copper; (1837–1838) .900 gold.*
Diameter: *22.5 mm.* **Edge:** *Reeded.* **Mints:** *Philadelphia, Charlotte, and Dahlonega.*

Circulation Strike

Mintmark location is on the obverse, above the date.

Proof Strike

History. U.S. Mint chief engraver William Kneass based the half eagle's Classic Head design on John Reich's cent of 1808. Minted under the Act of June 28, 1834, the coins' reduced size and weight encouraged circulation over melting or export, and they served American commerce until hoarding became extensive during the Civil War. Accordingly, many show considerable wear.

Striking and Sharpness. On the obverse, weakness is often seen on the higher areas of the hair curls. Also check the star centers. On the reverse, check the rims. The denticles are usually well struck.

Availability. Most coins range from VF to AU or lower grades of MS. Most MS coins are dated 1834. MS-63 and better examples are rare. Good eye appeal can be elusive. Proofs of the Classic Head type were made in small quantities, and today probably only a couple dozen or so survive, most bearing the 1834 date.

Grading Standards

MS-65

MS-60 to 70 (Mint State). ***Obverse:*** At MS-60, some abrasion and contact marks are seen on the portrait, most noticeably on the cheek, as the hair details are complex on this type. Luster is present, but may be dull or lifeless, and interrupted in patches. Many low-level Mint State coins have grainy surfaces. At MS-63, contact marks are few, and abrasion is very light. Abrasion is even less at MS-64. An MS-65 coin will have hardly any abrasion, and contact marks are minute. Luster should be full and rich and is often more intense on the obverse. Grades above MS-65 are defined by having fewer marks as perfection is approached. ***Reverse:*** Comments apply as for the obverse, except that abrasion is most noticeable in the field, on the eagle's neck, and on the highest area of the wings. Most Mint State coins in the marketplace are graded liberally, with slight abrasion on both sides of MS-65 coins.

Illustrated coin: This well-struck coin has some light abrasion, most evident in the reverse field.

AU-50

AU-50, 53, 55, 58 (About Uncirculated). ***Obverse:*** Friction is seen on the higher parts, particularly the cheek and the hair (under magnification) of Liberty. Friction and scattered marks are in the field, ranging from extensive at AU-50 to minimal at AU-58. Luster may be seen in protected areas, minimal at AU-50, more evident at AU-58. On an AU-58 coin the field retains some luster as well. ***Reverse:*** Comments as preceding, except that the eagle's neck, the top of the wings, the leaves, and the arrowheads now show noticeable wear, as do other features. Luster ranges from perhaps 40 percent remaining in protected areas (at AU-50) to nearly full mint bloom (at AU-58). Often the reverse of this type retains much more luster than the obverse.

EF-40

EF-40, 45 (Extremely Fine). ***Obverse:*** Wear is seen on the portrait overall, with reduction or elimination of some separation of hair strands, especially in the area close to the face. The cheek shows light wear. Luster is minimal or nonexistent at EF-40, and may survive in among the letters of LIBERTY at EF-45. ***Reverse:*** Wear is greater than on an About Uncirculated coin. On most (but not all) coins the neck lacks some feather detail on its highest points. Feathers have lost some detail near the edges and tips of the wings, and some areas of the horizontal lines in the shield may be blended together. Some traces of luster may be seen, more so at EF-45 than at EF-40.

VF-30

VF-20, 30 (Very Fine). ***Obverse:*** Wear on the portrait has reduced the hair detail, especially to the right of the face and the top of the head, but much can still be seen. ***Reverse:*** Wear is greater, including on the shield and the wing feathers. Generally, Classic Head gold at this grade level lacks eye appeal.

PF-60 to 70 (Proof). ***Obverse and Reverse:*** PF-60 to 62 coins have extensive hairlines and may have nicks and contact marks. At PF-63, hairlines are prominent, but the mirror surface is very reflective. PF-64 coins have fewer hairlines. At PF-65, hairlines should be minimal and mostly seen only under magnification. There should be no nicks or marks. PF-66 and higher coins should have no marks or hairlines visible to the unaided eye.

PF-65

1834, Plain 4

1834, Crosslet 4

Circulation Strikes

	Mintage	GSID	VF-20	EF-40	AU-50	AU-58	MS-60	MS-63	MS-65
Classic Head, No Motto Above Eagle (1834–1838)	**n/a**	**72381**	**$1,350**	**$1,450**	**$1,600**	**$2,500**	**$3,550**	**$10,500**	**$57,500**
1834, Classic Head, Plain 4	657,400	8856	1,350	1,450	1,600	2,750	4,000	12,000	63,500
	Auctions: $120,000, PCGS MS-65 SBG 12/20								
1834, Classic Head, Crosslet 4	*	8857	2,600	4,750	8,250	17,000	26,500	72,000	—
1835	371,534	8862	1,350	1,450	1,600	3,600	5,500	15,500	84,000
1836	553,147	8864	1,350	1,450	1,650	3,500	5,500	18,000	81,500
1837 (a)	207,121	8866	1,400	1,500	2,050	4,500	6,250	24,000	96,000
	Auctions: $264,000, PCGS MS-66 SBG 11/21								
1838	286,588	8868	1,400	1,600	2,750	4,250	5,250	12,000	108,000
	Auctions: $253,000, PCGS MS-66 HA 01/08								
1838-C	17,179	8881	8,000	15,000	20,000	36,000	72,000	264,000	—
	Auctions: $235,000, PCGS MS-63 SBG 05/16								
1838-D	20,583	8882	6,250	12,000	20,000	32,000	36,000	132,000	—
	Auctions: $228,000, PCGS MS-63 SBG 08/22								

* Included in number above. **a.** Varieties have either script 8 or block-style 8 in date.

Proof Strikes

	Mintage	GSID	PF-63
1834, Classic Head, Plain 4	unknown	8861	$312,000
	Auctions: $109,250, NGC PF-63 HA 01/11		
1835	unknown	8863	—
1836	unknown	8865	—
1837	unknown	8867	—
1838	unknown	8869	—

LIBERTY HEAD (1839–1908)

Designer: *Christian Gobrecht.* **Weight:** *8.359 grams.*
Composition: *.900 gold, .100 copper (net weight .24187 oz. pure gold).*
Diameter: *(1839–1840) 22.5 mm; (1840–1908) 21.6 mm.* **Edge:** *Reeded.*
Mints: *Philadelphia, Charlotte, Dahlonega, Denver, New Orleans, San Francisco, and Carson City.*

Large Diameter, Without Motto, (1839–1840), Circulation Strike

Mintmark location, 1839, is on the obverse, above the date.

Large Diameter, Without Motto, Proof Strike

Reduced Diameter, Without Motto, (1840–1865), Circulation Strike

Reduced Diameter, Without Motto, Proof Strike

Mintmark location, 1840–1908, is on the reverse, below the eagle.

With Motto, (1866–1908), Circulation Strike

With Motto, Proof Strike

History. Christian Gobrecht's Liberty Head half eagle design was introduced in 1839. The mintmark (for branch-mint coins) in that year was located on the obverse; for all later issues it was relocated to the reverse. The motto IN GOD WE TRUST was added to the reverse in 1866.

Striking and Sharpness. On the obverse, check the highest points of the hair and the star centers; the reverse, the eagle's neck, the area to the lower left of the shield, and the lower part of the eagle. Generally, the eagle on the $5 coins is better struck than on quarter eagles. Examine the denticles on both sides. Branch-mint coins struck before the Civil War are often lightly struck in areas. San Francisco half eagles are in lower average grades than are those from the Philadelphia Mint, as Philadelphia coins did not circulate at par in the East and Midwest from late December 1861 until December 1878, thus acquiring less wear. Most late nineteenth- and early twentieth-century coins are sharp in all areas; for these issues, tiny copper staining spots (from improperly mixed coinage alloy) can be a problem. Cameo contrast is the rule for Proofs prior to 1902. Beginning that year the portrait was polished in the die, although a few years later cameo-contrast coins were again made.

Availability. Early dates and mintmarks are typically scarce to rare in MS, very rare in MS-63 to 65. Charlotte and Dahlonega coins are usually EF or AU, or overgraded as low MS, as seen with quarter eagles. The 1854-S and several varieties in the 1860s and 1870s are rare. Coins from 1880 onward are seen in higher than average grades. Proof coins exist in relation to their original mintages; issues prior to the 1890s are rare.

Note: Values of common-date gold coins have been based on the current bullion price of gold, $3,746 per ounce, and may vary with the prevailing spot price.

Grading Standards

MS-60 to 70 (Mint State). ***Obverse:*** At MS-60, some abrasion and contact marks are evident, most noticeably on the hair to the right of Liberty's forehead and on the jaw. Luster is present, but may be dull or lifeless, and interrupted in patches. At MS-63, contact marks are few, and abrasion is very light. An MS-65 coin has only slight abrasion, and contact marks are so minute as to require magnification. Luster should be full and rich. Grades above MS-65 are defined by having fewer marks as perfection is approached. ***Reverse:*** Comments apply as for the obverse, except that abrasion and contact marks are most noticeable on the eagle's neck and to the lower left of the shield.

MS-63

Illustrated coin: Friction is seen in the obverse fields amid luster; on the reverse, luster is nearly complete.

AU-50, 53, 55, 58 (About Uncirculated). ***Obverse:*** Light wear is seen on the face, the hair to the right of the face, and the highest area of the hair bun, more so at AU-50 than at AU-53 or 55. An AU-58 coin has minimal traces of wear. An AU-50 coin has luster in protected areas among the stars and letters, with little in the open fields or on the portrait. At AU-58, most luster is present in the fields, but is worn away on the highest parts of the motifs. Striking must be taken into consideration, for a lightly struck coin can be About Uncirculated, but be weak in the central areas. ***Reverse:*** Comments as preceding, except that the eagle shows wear in all of the higher areas, as well as the leaves and arrowheads. From 1866 to 1908 the motto IN GOD WE TRUST helped protect the field, with the result that luster is more extensive on this side in comparison to the obverse. Luster ranges from perhaps 50 percent remaining in protected areas (at AU-50) to nearly full mint bloom (at AU-58).

AU-55

EF-40, 45 (Extremely Fine). ***Obverse:*** Wear is evident on all high areas of the portrait, including the hair to the right of the forehead, the tip of the coronet, the back of the head, and the hair bun. The stars show light wear at their centers (unless protected by a high rim). Luster, if present at all, is minimal and in protected areas such as between the star points. ***Reverse:*** Wear is greater than on an About Uncirculated coin, and flatness is seen on the feather ends, the leaves, and elsewhere. Some traces of luster may be seen, more so at EF-45 than at EF-40. Overall, the reverse appears to be in a slightly higher grade than the obverse on coins from 1866 to 1908 (With Motto).

EF-40

Illustrated coin: This coin is well struck on both sides.

VF-20, 30 (Very Fine). ***Obverse:*** The higher-relief areas of hair are worn flat at VF-20, less so at VF-30. The hair to the right of the coronet is merged into heavy strands. The stars are flat at their centers. ***Reverse:*** Feather detail is mostly worn away on the neck and legs, less so on the wings. The vertical shield stripes, being deeply recessed, remain bold.

VF-20

PF-60 to 70 (Proof). ***Obverse and Reverse:*** PF-60 to 62 coins have extensive hairlines and may have nicks and contact marks. At PF-63, hairlines are prominent, but the mirror surface is very reflective. PF-64 coins have fewer hairlines. At PF-65, hairlines should be minimal and mostly seen only under magnification. There should be no nicks or marks. PF-66 and higher coins should have no marks or hairlines visible to the unaided eye.

PF-55

Small Letters

Large Letters

Small Date

Large Date

Circulation Strikes

	Mintage	GSID	VF-20	EF-40	AU-50	AU-58	MS-60	MS-63	MS-64
Liberty Head, No Motto Above Eagle (1839–1866)	n/a	72382	$1,200	$1,300	$1,350	$1,600	$1,750	$5,750	$10,500
Liberty Head, Motto Above Eagle (1866–1908)	n/a	72383	1,150	1,150	1,150	1,150	1,200	1,200	1,250
Variety 1: No Motto Above Eagle									
1839	118,143	8883	1,250	1,600	2,100	7,250	8,750	33,500	66,000
1839-C	17,205	8955	4,750	8,750	17,000	26,500	33,500	57,500	144,000
	Auctions: $336,000, PCGS MS-64 SBG 08/22								
1839-D	18,939	8956	6,500	10,000	14,500	37,000	48,000	—	—
	Auctions: $252,000, PCGS MS-62 SBG 08/22								
1840	137,382	8884	1,200	1,400	1,650	2,750	4,000	11,000	29,000
	Auctions: $240,000, PCGS MS-65 HA 01/22								
1840-C	18,992	8957	3,000	5,000	8,000	14,500	21,500	54,000	72,000
	Auctions: $120,000, PCGS MS-64 HA 06/18								
1840-D, Tall D	22,896	8958	4,700	5,500	7,500	13,000	17,000	55,000	—
1840-D, Small D	*	8959	—	4,500	6,500	10,500	15,000	—	—
1840-O (a)	40,120	8960	1,250	1,500	2,600	5,500	11,000	41,500	—
1841	15,833	8885	1,750	2,250	3,000	5,250	5,500	14,500	29,000
1841-C	21,467	8961	4,000	5,500	8,250	13,000	17,000	43,000	66,000
1841-D, Small D	29,392	8962	2,500	4,400	6,000	9,750	14,500	35,000	60,000
1841-D, Medium D	*	8963	2,750	4,800	6,500	10,500	16,000	—	—
1842, Large Letters	27,578	8887	1,250	1,900	3,450	7,000	10,500	24,000	—
1842, Small Letters	*	8886	1,700	2,750	3,750	10,500	14,500	36,000	53,000
	Auctions: $108,000 PCGS MS-66 HA 08/25								
1842-C, Small Date	27,432	8965	9,500	18,500	28,000	54,000	84,000	132,000	—
	Auctions: $166,750, NGC MS-63 HA 01/12								
1842-C, Large Date	*	8966	2,000	2,750	4,250	7,000	11,000	29,000	41,000
1842-D, Small Date	59,608	8967	3,250	4,250	5,500	9,500	15,500	39,000	—
1842-D, Large Date	*	8968	5,000	9,500	13,000	36,000	48,000	—	—
1842-O	16,400	8969	2,500	3,800	10,500	13,000	23,500	43,000	—
1843	611,205	8888	1,200	1,300	1,350	1,600	1,750	12,000	18,000
1843-C	44,277	8970	3,250	4,750	7,750	15,000	17,000	41,000	66,000
1843-D, Medium D	98,452	8971	3,450	4,750	6,000	9,250	12,000	38,500	120,000
	Auctions: $282,000, NGC MS-65 HA 04/15								
1843-D, Small D	*	8972	4,400	5,500	7,250	14,500	16,000	43,000	—
1843-O, Large Letters	82,000	8973	1,350	1,750	3,500	7,000	11,000	27,500	48,000
1843-O, Small Letters	19,075	8974	1,250	2,250	4,400	9,500	20,000	39,000	60,000
1844	340,330	8889	1,200	1,300	1,350	1,800	1,900	11,000	15,500

* Included in number above. **a.** Scarce varieties of these 1840 coins have the fine edge-reeding and wide rims of the 1839 issues. These are known as "broad mill."

1846-D, High Second D Over D

1847, Extra 7 in Denticles
FS-301

1848-D, D Over D

1850-C, Normal C

1850-C, Weak C

1851-D, Normal D

1851-D, Weak D

Circulation Strikes *(continued)*

	Mintage	GSID	VF-20	EF-40	AU-50	AU-58	MS-60	MS-63	MS-64
1844-C	23,631	8975	$2,250	$3,400	$5,250	$8,750	$15,000	$32,500	—
1844-D	88,982	8976	3,100	4,500	5,750	8,750	11,000	33,500	$60,000
1844-O	364,600	8977	1,250	1,450	1,500	3,250	5,500	17,000	42,000
1845	417,099	8890	1,200	1,300	1,400	1,700	1,750	8,750	17,000
1845-D	90,629	8978	3,750	4,400	5,500	8,500	9,750	30,000	50,500
1845-O	41,000	8979	1,400	2,100	4,500	11,000	17,000	66,000	—
1846, Large Date	395,942	8891	1,200	1,300	1,350	1,600	2,300	13,000	21,500
1846, Small Date	*	8892	1,200	1,300	1,400	1,900	3,250	14,500	—
1846-C	12,995	8980	3,750	5,750	7,500	18,000	24,000	72,000	102,000
1846-D	80,294	8981	1,900	2,400	3,500	7,250	12,000	—	—
1846-D, D Over D	*	8982	2,250	3,500	4,700	8,750	12,000	43,000	60,000
1846-O	58,000	8983	1,350	2,250	4,000	11,000	14,500	66,000	—
1847	915,981	8893	1,200	1,300	1,350	1,600	1,750	5,750	12,000
↳1847, Extra 7 in Denticles, FS-301	*	8984	1,200	1,300	1,400	1,850	3,000	8,000	12,500
1847-C	84,151	8985	2,700	3,600	5,250	8,750	10,500	36,000	53,000
1847-D	64,405	8986	3,500	4,250	5,000	8,750	12,000	33,500	—
1847-O	12,000	8987	8,000	13,000	16,000	26,500	36,000	—	—
1848	260,775	8894	1,200	1,300	1,350	1,800	2,000	12,000	30,000
1848-C	64,472	8988	2,800	4,250	5,500	11,000	15,000	39,000	54,000
1848-D	47,465	8989	2,750	3,600	5,000	12,000	16,000	36,000	—
1848-D, D Over D	*	8990	5,500	10,500	14,000	26,500	29,500	—	—
↳1848-D, D Over D, FS-501	*	351841	5,500	10,500	14,000	26,500	29,500	—	—
1849	133,070	8895	1,250	1,350	1,600	2,500	3,250	15,000	24,000
1849-C	64,823	8991	1,750	2,200	3,250	6,500	9,750	24,000	43,000
1849-D	39,036	8992	4,400	5,500	6,250	11,000	18,000	60,000	102,000
1850	64,491	8896	1,200	1,400	1,600	2,500	3,500	19,000	33,500
1850-C	63,591	8993	2,600	3,500	5,000	8,500	12,000	26,500	54,000
↳1850-C, Weak C	*	8994	2,350	3,150	4,500	7,750	10,500	24,000	—
1850-D	43,984	8995	1,800	2,300	4,050	7,500	24,000	—	—
↳1850-D, Weak D	*	8996	1,450	1,850	3,250	6,000	17,000	—	—
1851	377,505	8897	1,200	1,300	1,350	1,600	2,000	9,500	26,500
1851-C	49,176	8997	3,000	4,000	6,000	10,000	14,500	43,000	66,000
1851-D	62,710	8998	3,200	3,900	5,250	8,750	12,000	29,000	50,500
↳1851-D, Weak D	*	8999	1,900	2,500	3,100	6,250	7,500	—	—

* Included in number above.

Note: Gold spot price at time of publication, $3,746 per ounce.

1854, Doubled Die Obverse
FS-101

1854-C, Normal C

1854-C, Weak C

1854-D, Normal D

1854-D, Weak D

Circulation Strikes *(continued)*

	Mintage	GSID	VF-20	EF-40	AU-50	AU-58	MS-60	MS-63	MS-64
1851-O	41,000	9000	$1,750	$2,750	$4,500	$8,000	$10,500	$26,500	$66,000
	Auctions: $144,000, PCGS MS-64 HA 07/22								
1852	573,901	8898	1,200	1,300	1,350	1,600	1,750	5,750	10,500
	Auctions: $123,375, PCGS MS-66 LGND 10/19								
1852-C	72,574	9001	3,450	4,500	5,500	7,000	9,000	29,000	43,000
1852-D	91,584	9002	3,100	4,250	6,750	9,500	10,500	36,000	—
1853	305,770	8899	1,200	1,300	1,350	1,700	1,750	7,000	17,000
1853-C	65,571	9003	3,300	4,400	5,500	8,000	9,500	24,000	66,000
1853-D	89,678	9004	3,300	4,250	5,500	7,250	10,000	27,000	72,000
1854	160,675	8900	1,200	1,300	1,350	1,700	1,950	9,000	18,000
1854-C	39,283	9007	1,900	2,750	3,950	5,000	12,500	42,500	51,000
↳1854-C, Weak C	39,283	9006	1,300	1,900	2,750	3,500	9,000	29,500	—
1854-D, Large D	56,413	9008	3,450	4,500	6,000	9,500	10,000	27,500	54,000
1854-D, Medium D	*	9009	3,800	4,950	6,500	12,000	14,000	—	—
↳1854-D, Weak D	*	9010	2,750	3,600	4,500	7,000	7,500	—	—
1854-O	46,000	9011	1,300	1,650	3,600	9,000	11,000	43,000	—
1854-S	3-4 known	9012	—	—	—	3,600,000	—	—	—
	Auctions: $2,400,000, PCGS EF-45 HA 08/21								
1855	117,098	8901	1,200	1,300	1,350	1,600	2,000	7,000	18,000
1855-C	39,788	9013	3,550	5,000	6,000	10,000	11,000	38,500	57,500
1855-D, Large D	22,432	9014	2,750	4,000	6,250	14,500	19,000	45,500	67,000
1855-D, Medium D	*	9015	3,300	4,800	7,000	16,000	21,000	—	—
1855-O	11,100	9016	1,700	3,750	5,500	11,000	22,000	—	—
1855-S	61,000	9017	1,350	2,100	3,450	7,250	12,000	—	—
1856	197,990	8902	1,200	1,300	1,350	1,700	1,750	7,750	16,000
1856-C	28,457	9018	2,000	2,500	3,500	6,250	12,000	50,500	60,000
1856-D	19,786	9019	2,250	3,000	4,100	7,250	10,000	26,500	50,500
1856-O	10,000	9020	1,600	2,500	4,500	12,000	15,500	150,000	—
1856-S	105,100	9021	1,300	1,500	2,050	6,250	9,000	41,000	60,000
1857	98,188	8903	1,200	1,300	1,350	1,650	2,250	7,000	17,500
1857-C	31,360	9022	2,750	3,750	5,500	8,000	12,000	50,500	66,000
1857-D	17,046	9023	2,500	3,500	4,750	8,750	15,500	48,000	—
1857-O	13,000	9024	1,750	3,000	5,000	8,750	14,500	49,000	—
1857-S	87,000	9025	1,450	1,750	2,400	7,500	9,500	22,000	34,000
1858	15,136	8904	1,750	2,200	2,700	5,500	7,500	17,000	24,000
1858-C	38,856	9026	2,250	3,500	4,300	8,250	10,500	36,000	66,000
1858-D	15,362	9027	3,550	4,250	6,000	11,000	15,500	67,000	105,500
1858-S	18,600	9028	2,000	5,000	6,750	19,000	33,500	—	—
1859	16,734	8905	1,200	1,550	2,050	4,400	7,000	24,000	60,000
1859-C	31,847	9029	2,800	4,100	5,500	11,000	12,000	41,000	—
1859-D, Medium D	10,366	9030	3,000	4,000	5,500	9,750	17,000	48,000	67,000
1859-D, Large D	*	9031	3,600	4,800	6,500	11,500	20,000	57,500	—
1859-S	13,220	9032	2,500	5,500	8,000	14,500	31,000	144,000	—
	Auctions: $144,000, PCGS MS-63 SBG 04/22								

* Included in number above.

1873, Closed 3

1873, Open 3

Circulation Strikes *(continued)*

	Mintage	GSID	VF-20	EF-40	AU-50	AU-58	MS-60	MS-63	MS-64
1860	19,763	8906	$1,200	$1,500	$2,000	$4,100	$7,500	$18,000	$36,000
1860-C	14,813	9033	2,900	4,100	6,250	10,000	14,000	29,000	60,000
1860-D, Medium D	14,635	9034	2,500	4,500	5,750	10,000	10,500	55,000	79,000
1860-D, Large D	*	9035	2,750	4,950	6,250	11,000	11,500	—	—
1860-S	21,200	9036	3,000	5,750	10,500	24,000	33,500	—	—
1861	688,084	8907	1,200	1,300	1,350	1,600	1,850	5,750	10,500
	Auctions: $152,750, PCGS MS-66 HA 04/15								
1861-C	6,879	9037	8,750	16,000	23,000	33,000	38,500	120,000	—
	Auctions: $164,500, PCGS MS-63 LGND 12/20								
1861-D	1,597	9038	31,000	48,000	57,500	90,000	108,000	330,000	480,000
	Auctions: $336,000, PCGS MS-63 SBG 08/24; $144,000, PCGS MS-62 SBG 08/24								
1861-S	18,000	9039	5,500	9,500	13,500	24,000	—	—	—
1862	4,430	8908	3,000	7,000	11,000	21,500	33,000	—	—
1862-S	9,500	9040	7,500	13,000	20,000	33,500	43,000	—	—
1863	2,442	8909	7,250	14,500	26,500	50,500	65,000	120,000	192,000
1863-S	17,000	9041	5,000	9,500	21,500	36,000	50,500	—	—
1864	4,170	8910	12,500	18,000	22,000	35,500	39,000	—	—
1864-S	3,888	9042	38,500	57,000	67,000	192,000	240,000	—	—
	Auctions: $192,000, PCGS AU-58 HA 01/25								
1865	1,270	8911	17,000	21,500	28,000	50,500	66,000	—	—
1865-S	27,612	9043	5,000	7,500	11,000	20,000	22,000	66,000	96,000
1866-S	9,000	9044	4,000	7,000	12,000	26,500	48,000	—	—
Variety 2: Motto Above Eagle									
1866	6,700	8912	1,500	2,500	4,550	11,000	14,500	43,000	—
1866-S	34,920	9045	1,400	3,000	8,000	13,000	22,000	—	—
1867	6,870	8913	2,600	3,750	5,000	12,000	19,000	66,000	—
1867-S	29,000	9046	1,500	2,500	7,500	19,000	—	—	—
1868	5,700	8914	1,450	2,050	4,000	11,000	12,000	38,500	—
1868-S	52,000	9047	1,450	2,050	3,600	7,500	27,500	102,000	168,000
1869	1,760	8915	1,250	3,250	5,500	10,500	14,500	29,500	39,500
1869-S	31,000	9048	1,250	1,600	2,500	7,250	20,500	—	—
1870	4,000	8916	1,350	1,900	3,100	9,500	15,500	—	—
1870-CC	7,675	9049	36,000	63,000	102,000	168,000	192,000	—	—
	Auctions: $168,000, PCGS AU-58 HA 08/22								
1870-S	17,000	9050	1,550	2,600	4,050	16,000	29,000	—	—
1871	3,200	8917	1,400	1,800	2,900	7,500	10,000	—	—
1871-CC	20,770	9051	5,750	14,500	18,000	49,000	55,000	96,000	—
1871-S	25,000	9052	1,250	1,600	2,400	7,000	14,500	36,000	—
1872	1,660	8918	1,250	2,250	4,700	7,500	12,000	21,000	26,500
1872-CC	16,980	9053	5,250	11,000	19,000	48,000	—	—	—
1872-S	36,400	9054	1,250	1,450	3,250	8,250	14,500	—	—
1873, Open 3	63,200	8919	1,150	1,150	1,150	1,250	1,300	2,750	7,250
1873, Closed 3	49,280	8920	1,150	1,150	1,150	1,250	1,300	5,000	7,500

* Included in number above.

1881, Repunched Date
FS-303

1881, Final 1 Over 0
FS-301

Circulation Strikes *(continued)*

	Mintage	GSID	VF-20	EF-40	AU-50	AU-58	MS-60	MS-63	MS-64
1873-CC	7,416	9055	$12,000	$20,000	$30,000	$54,000	$78,000	—	—
	Auctions: $168,000, PCGS MS-61 SBG 08/18								
1873-S	31,000	9056	1,500	2,000	2,900	9,500	12,000	—	—
1874	3,488	8921	1,400	2,250	3,000	6,250	11,000	$23,000	$36,000
1874-CC	21,198	9057	4,400	7,500	14,500	31,000	43,000	—	—
1874-S	16,000	9058	1,400	2,000	3,750	14,000	—	—	—
↳1874-S, Weak S	*	9059	1,200	1,350	2,050	—	—	—	—
1875	200	8922	—	192,000	360,000	660,000	—	—	—
	Auctions: $480,000, PCGS AU-53 SBG 04/22								
1875-CC	11,828	9060	5,000	11,500	17,000	30,000	43,000	108,000	—
1875-S	9,000	9061	2,000	3,250	5,250	12,000	19,000	33,500	45,500
1876	1,432	8923	5,000	6,250	9,500	19,000	21,000	31,000	41,000
1876-CC	6,887	9062	8,750	17,000	25,000	55,000	78,000	—	—
	Auctions: $780,000, PCGS MS-66 HA 08/22								
1876-S	4,000	9063	4,750	8,000	13,000	38,500	90,000	—	—
	Auctions: $336,000, PCGS MS-65 HA 01/25								
1877	1,132	8924	2,200	3,750	6,250	8,750	12,000	—	—
1877-CC	8,680	9064	4,500	10,500	14,500	31,000	50,500	—	—
1877-S	26,700	9065	1,250	1,350	1,600	7,000	8,250	20,000	31,000
1878	131,720	8925	1,150	1,150	1,200	1,250	1,300	2,400	4,250
1878-CC	9,054	9066	6,250	14,500	23,000	78,000	—	—	—
1878-S	144,700	9067	1,150	1,150	1,200	1,250	1,250	2,750	8,000
1879	301,920	8926	1,150	1,150	1,150	1,150	1,200	1,300	3,600
1879-CC	17,281	9068	3,750	5,500	7,750	19,000	27,000	—	—
1879-S	426,200	9069	1,150	1,150	1,150	1,200	1,250	1,600	6,250
1880	3,166,400	8927	1,150	1,150	1,150	1,150	1,200	1,250	1,400
1880-CC	51,017	9070	2,100	2,900	4,900	10,000	14,500	55,000	—
1880-S	1,348,900	9071	1,150	1,150	1,150	1,150	1,200	1,250	1,300
1881	5,708,760	8928	1,150	1,150	1,150	1,150	1,200	1,200	1,250
↳1881, Repunched Date, FS-302	*	329310	1,250	1,250	1,250	1,250	1,250	1,300	1,350
↳1881, Repunched Date, FS-303	*	329311	1,250	1,250	1,250	1,250	1,250	1,300	1,350
1881, Final 1 Over 0	*	9072	1,150	1,200	1,200	1,250	1,350	4,100	12,000
↳1881, Final 1 Over 0, FS-301	*	393279	1,150	1,200	1,200	1,250	1,350	4,100	12,000
1881-CC	13,886	9073	4,000	7,500	10,000	16,500	24,000	51,500	—
1881-S	969,000	9074	1,150	1,150	1,150	1,150	1,200	1,250	1,300
1882	2,514,520	8929	1,150	1,150	1,150	1,150	1,200	1,200	1,250
1882-CC	82,817	9075	1,800	3,000	4,750	9,750	11,000	41,000	—
1882-S	969,000	9076	1,150	1,150	1,150	1,150	1,200	1,250	1,250
1883	233,400	8930	1,150	1,150	1,150	1,150	1,200	1,300	2,050
1883-CC	12,598	9077	2,750	5,000	7,500	12,000	21,500	57,500	—
1883-S	83,200	9078	1,150	1,150	1,200	1,250	1,250	1,400	6,250
1884	191,030	8931	1,150	1,150	1,150	1,150	1,200	1,500	2,800

* Included in number above.

1901-S, Final 1 Over 0
FS-301

Circulation Strikes *(continued)*

	Mintage	GSID	VF-20	EF-40	AU-50	AU-58	MS-60	MS-63	MS-64
1884-CC	16,402	9079	$2,500	$4,000	$5,750	$13,000	$20,500	—	—
1884-S	177,000	9080	1,150	1,150	1,150	1,150	1,200	$1,250	$4,100
1885	601,440	8932	1,150	1,150	1,150	1,150	1,200	1,250	1,300
1885-S	1,211,500	9081	1,150	1,150	1,150	1,150	1,200	1,200	1,250
1886	388,360	8933	1,150	1,150	1,150	1,150	1,200	1,200	2,500
1886-S	3,268,000	9082	1,150	1,150	1,150	1,150	1,200	1,200	1,250
1887-S	1,912,000	9083	1,150	1,150	1,150	1,150	1,200	1,250	1,600
1888	18,201	8934	1,150	1,150	1,200	1,250	1,300	2,750	5,000
1888-S	293,900	9084	1,150	1,150	1,150	1,200	1,250	3,750	—
1889	7,520	8935	1,200	1,200	1,250	1,600	2,000	5,500	10,000
1890	4,240	8936	1,200	1,400	1,500	2,750	3,100	8,000	12,000
1890-CC	53,800	9085	1,350	1,600	1,950	2,750	3,250	9,000	15,500
1891	61,360	8937	1,150	1,150	1,150	1,150	1,200	1,500	2,600
1891-CC	208,000	9086	1,250	1,450	1,900	2,750	3,250	5,000	8,500
1892	753,480	8938	1,150	1,150	1,150	1,150	1,200	1,300	1,400
1892-CC	82,968	9087	1,500	1,850	2,200	3,250	3,750	13,000	26,500
1892-O	10,000	9088	2,400	3,250	4,400	8,250	8,750	31,000	—
1892-S	298,400	9089	1,150	1,150	1,150	1,150	1,200	1,500	4,600
1893	1,528,120	8939	1,150	1,150	1,150	1,150	1,200	1,250	1,300
1893-CC	60,000	9090	1,200	1,700	2,250	3,900	4,250	12,000	26,500
1893-O	110,000	9091	1,150	1,200	1,250	1,300	1,400	7,250	12,000
1893-S	224,000	9092	1,150	1,150	1,150	1,150	1,200	1,300	1,600
1894	957,880	8940	1,150	1,150	1,150	1,150	1,200	1,250	1,450
1894-O	16,600	9093	1,200	1,250	1,400	1,600	1,750	11,000	15,000
1894-S	55,900	9094	1,150	1,150	1,200	1,400	2,500	10,500	19,000
	Auctions: $176,250, NGC MS-69 HA 01/14								
1895	1,345,855	8941	1,150	1,150	1,150	1,150	1,200	1,200	1,250
1895-S	112,000	9095	1,150	1,150	1,200	1,250	1,350	5,250	6,500
1896	58,960	8942	1,150	1,150	1,150	1,150	1,200	1,350	1,350
1896-S	155,400	9096	1,150	1,150	1,150	1,250	1,250	3,750	8,750
1897	867,800	8943	1,150	1,150	1,150	1,150	1,200	1,200	1,300
1897-S	354,000	9097	1,150	1,150	1,150	1,150	1,250	3,550	5,500
1898	633,420	8944	1,150	1,150	1,150	1,150	1,200	1,250	1,300
1898-S	1,397,400	9098	1,150	1,150	1,150	1,150	1,200	1,250	2,250
1899	1,710,630	8945	1,150	1,150	1,150	1,150	1,200	1,200	1,250
↳1899, Repunched Date, FS-301	*	285491	1,250	1,250	1,250	1,250	1,250	1,300	1,350
1899-S	1,545,000	9099	1,150	1,150	1,150	1,150	1,200	1,250	1,900
	Auctions: $103,500, NGC MS-69 HA 01/10								
1900	1,405,500	8946	1,150	1,150	1,150	1,150	1,200	1,200	1,250
1900-S	329,000	9100	1,150	1,150	1,150	1,150	1,200	1,300	1,350
1901	615,900	8947	1,150	1,150	1,150	1,150	1,200	1,200	1,250
1901-S	3,648,000	9102	1,150	1,150	1,150	1,150	1,200	1,200	1,250
1901-S, Final 1 Over 0	*	9101	1,150	1,200	1,200	1,250	1,250	1,350	1,600

* Included in number above.

Circulation Strikes *(continued)*

	Mintage	GSID	VF-20	EF-40	AU-50	AU-58	MS-60	MS-63	MS-64
1902	172,400	8948	$1,150	$1,150	$1,150	$1,150	$1,200	$1,250	$1,350
1902-S	939,000	9103	1,150	1,150	1,150	1,150	1,200	1,200	1,250
	Auctions: $120,000, PCGS MS-68 HA 01/25								
1903	226,870	8949	1,150	1,150	1,150	1,150	1,200	1,250	1,300
1903-S	1,855,000	9104	1,150	1,150	1,150	1,150	1,200	1,300	1,350
1904	392,000	8950	1,150	1,150	1,150	1,150	1,200	1,200	1,250
1904-S	97,000	9105	1,150	1,150	1,150	1,250	1,300	3,000	5,000
1905	302,200	8951	1,150	1,150	1,150	1,150	1,200	1,200	1,250
1905-S	880,700	9106	1,150	1,150	1,150	1,150	1,200	1,350	3,100
↳1905-S, S Over S, FS-501	*	351844	1,250	1,250	1,250	1,250	1,300	1,450	3,450
1906	348,735	8952	1,150	1,150	1,150	1,150	1,200	1,200	1,250
1906-D	320,000	9107	1,150	1,150	1,150	1,150	1,200	1,200	1,250
1906-S	598,000	9108	1,150	1,150	1,150	1,150	1,200	1,350	2,000
1907	626,100	8953	1,150	1,150	1,150	1,150	1,200	1,200	1,250
1907-D	888,000	9109	1,150	1,150	1,150	1,150	1,200	1,200	1,250
1908	421,874	8954	1,150	1,150	1,150	1,150	1,200	1,200	1,250

* Included in number above.

Proof Strikes

	Mintage	GSID	PF-60	PF-63	PF-65
Liberty Head, No Motto Above Eagle (1839–1866), Proof	**n/a**	**74146**	**$21,000**	**$60,000**	**$144,000**
Same, Proof Cameo	**n/a**	**74147**	**—**	**72,000**	**158,500**
Same, Proof Deep Cameo	**n/a**	**74148**	**—**	**74,500**	**210,000**
Liberty Head, Motto Above Eagle (1866–1908), Proof	**n/a**	**74149**	**4,900**	**12,000**	**30,000**
Same, Proof Cameo	**n/a**	**74150**	**—**	**12,000**	**34,000**
Same, Proof Deep Cameo	**n/a**	**74151**	**—**	**14,500**	**41,000**
Variety 1: No Motto Above Eagle					
1839	unknown	9110	210,000	—	—
	Auctions: $199,750, PCGS PF-61 HA 08/12				
1840	unknown	9115	—	—	—
1841	unknown	9116	—	150,000	—
1842	unknown	9121	—	—	—
1843	unknown	9122	—	—	—
1844	unknown	9127	—	150,000	—
1845	unknown	9128	—	132,000	252,000
1846	unknown	9133	—	168,000	—
1847	unknown	9136	—	—	—
1848	unknown	9139	—	120,000	—
1849	unknown	9142	—	—	—
1850	unknown	9145	—	—	—
1854	unknown	9148	—	—	—
1855	unknown	9149	—	—	—
1856	unknown	9152	—	—	—
1857	unknown	9155	—	120,000	240,000
1858	unknown	9158	—	72,000	150,000
1859	80	9161	21,000	60,000	144,000
1860	62	9164	21,000	60,000	144,000
1861	66	9167	30,000	84,000	156,000
1862	35	9170	21,000	60,000	144,000

Proof Strikes *(continued)*

	Mintage	GSID	PF-60	PF-63	PF-65
1863	30	9173	$21,000	$60,000	$144,000
1864	50	9176	21,000	60,000	144,000
1865	25	9179	21,000	60,000	144,000
Variety 2: Motto Above Eagle					
1866	30	9182	36,000	81,500	168,000
	Auctions: $192,000, PCGS PF-65 SBG 03/24				
1867	50	9185	12,000	30,000	72,000
1868	25	9188	12,000	29,000	60,000
1869	25	9191	12,000	29,000	60,000
1870	35	9194	12,000	29,000	90,000
1871	30	9197	12,000	29,000	84,000
1872	30	9200	12,000	29,000	84,000
1873	25	9203	12,000	29,000	69,500
1874	20	9206	24,000	50,500	96,000
1875	20	9209	—	—	222,000
	Auctions: $161,000, Uncert PF-63 SBG 03/05				
1876	45	9212	14,500	33,500	78,000
1877	20	9215	12,000	29,000	84,000
1878	20	9218	12,000	29,000	72,000
1879	30	9221	13,000	31,000	67,000
1880	36	9224	8,750	15,500	60,000
1881	42	9227	8,750	14,000	43,000
1882	48	9230	8,750	14,000	45,500
1883	61	9233	12,000	20,000	41,000
1884	48	9236	8,750	14,000	43,000
1885	66	9239	11,000	18,000	41,000
1886	72	9242	8,750	14,000	43,000
1887	87	9245	26,500	45,500	111,000
1888	95	9248	10,000	15,500	38,500
1889	45	9251	8,750	14,000	38,500
1890	88	9254	9,250	17,000	43,000
1891	53	9257	8,750	12,500	38,500
1892	92	9260	8,750	12,500	38,500
1893	77	9263	8,750	12,500	43,000
1894	75	9266	8,750	12,500	36,000
1895	81	9269	7,500	12,000	33,000
1896	103	9272	4,900	12,000	30,000
1897	83	9275	4,900	12,000	33,000
1898	75	9278	4,900	12,000	30,000
1899	99	9281	4,900	12,000	30,000
1900	230	9284	4,900	12,000	30,000
1901	140	9287	4,900	12,000	30,000
1902	162	9290	4,900	12,000	30,000
1903	154	9293	4,900	12,000	30,000
1904	136	9296	5,250	12,000	30,000
1905	108	9299	4,900	12,000	33,000
1906	85	9302	4,900	12,000	30,000
1907	92	9305	4,900	12,000	30,000

Note: Gold spot price at time of publication, $3,746 per ounce.

INDIAN HEAD (1908–1929)

Designer: *Bela Lyon Pratt.* **Weight:** *8.359 grams.*
Composition: *.900 gold, .100 copper (net weight .24187 oz. pure gold).* **Diameter:** *21.6 mm.*
Edge: *Reeded.* **Mints:** *Philadelphia, Denver, New Orleans, and San Francisco.*

Circulation Strike

Sandblast Finish Proof Strike

Satin Finish Proof Strike

Mintmark location is on the reverse, to the left of the arrows.

History. The Indian Head half eagle made its first appearance in 1908; it was minted continuously through 1916, and again in 1929. Its design elements are in sunken relief (sometimes imprecisely called "incuse"), like those of the similar quarter eagle; the mintmark is raised. On most examples the rims are flat, while on others they are slightly raised. These coins saw limited circulation in the West, and were rarely encountered elsewhere.

Striking and Sharpness. Striking quality of Indian Head half eagles varies. Look for weakness on the high parts of the Indian's bonnet and in the feather details in the headdress. On the reverse, check the feathers on the highest area of the wing.

Proofs. Sandblast (also called Matte) Proofs were made in 1908 and from 1911 to 1915, while Satin (also called Roman Finish) Proofs were made in 1909 and 1910. At lower levels, these coins can show light contact marks. Some microscopic bright flecks may be caused by the sandblasting process and, although they do not represent handling, usually result in a coin being assigned a slightly lower grade.

Availability. Indian Head half eagles were not popular with numismatists of the time, who saved very few. Rare issues include the 1909-O, which usually is seen with evidence of circulation (often extensive) and the 1929, most of which are in MS. Luster can range from deeply frosty to grainy. Because the fields are the highest areas of the coin, luster diminished quickly as the coins were circulated or jostled with others in bags. When Proof examples are seen, they are usually in higher Proof grades, PF-64 and above. As a class these half eagles are rarer than quarter eagles of the same date and style of finish.

Note: Values of common-date gold coins have been based on the current bullion price of gold, $3,746 per ounce, and may vary with the prevailing spot price.

Grading Standards

MS-60 to 70 (Mint State). ***Obverse:*** At MS-60 to 62, there is abrasion in the field, this representing the highest part of the coin. Abrasion is also evident on the headdress. Marks and, occasionally, a microscopic pin scratch may be seen. At MS-63, there may be some abrasion and some tiny marks. Luster is irregular. At MS-64, abrasion is less. Luster is rich. At MS-65 and above, luster is deep and frosty, with no marks at all visible without magnification at MS-66 and higher. ***Reverse:*** At MS-60 to 62 there is abrasion in the field, this representing the highest part of the coin. Abrasion is also evident on the eagle's wing. Otherwise, the same comments apply as for the obverse.

MS-62

Illustrated coin: This example is lustrous and attractive. Most of the luster in the fields (the highest-relief area of this unusual design) is still intact.

AU-50, 53, 55, 58 (About Uncirculated). ***Obverse:*** Friction on the cheek is very noticeable at AU-50, increasingly less at higher levels to AU-58. The headdress shows light wear, most evident on the ribbon above the forehead and on the garland. Luster is minimal at AU-50 and scattered and incomplete at AU-58. Nicks and contact marks are to be expected. ***Reverse:*** Friction on the wing and neck is very noticeable at AU-50, increasingly less noticeable at higher levels to AU-58. Otherwise, the same comments apply as for the obverse.

AU-50

EF-40, 45 (Extremely Fine). ***Obverse:*** Light wear will characterize the portrait and headdress. Luster is gone. Marks and tiny scratches are to be expected, but not distracting. ***Reverse:*** Light wear is most evident on the eagle's head and wing, although other areas are lightly worn as well. Luster is gone. Marks and tiny scratches are to be expected, but not distracting.

EF-40

VF-20, 30 (Very Fine). ***Obverse:*** Many details of the garland and of the ribbon above the forehead are worn away. Many feather vanes are blended together. The field is dull and has contact marks. ***Reverse:*** The neck and the upper part of the wing show extensive wear, other areas less so. The field is dull and has contact marks.

VF-25

Illustrated coin: Some bumps are seen on the top obverse rim and should be mentioned in a description.

PF-60 to 70 (Proof). ***Obverse and Reverse:*** At PF-60 to 63, there is light abrasion and some contact marks (the lower the grade, the higher the quantity). On Sandblast Proofs these show up as visually unappealing bright spots. At PF-64 and higher levels, marks are fewer, with magnification needed to see any at PF-65. At PF-66, there should be none at all.

Illustrated coin: This is a particularly nice example.

PF-67

Circulation Strikes

	Mintage	GSID	EF-40	AU-50	AU-58	MS-60	MS-63	MS-64	MS-65
Indian Head (1908–1929)	**n/a**	**72384**	**$1,150**	**$1,150**	**$1,150**	**$1,200**	**$1,250**	**$1,750**	**$9,500**
1908	577,845	9308	1,150	1,150	1,150	1,200	1,700	2,750	9,500
1908-D	148,000	9317	1,150	1,150	1,150	1,200	2,000	3,600	27,500
1908-S	82,000	9318	1,250	1,500	3,900	5,750	12,500	14,500	21,500
	Auctions: $192,000, PCGS MS-68 HA 09/20								
1909	627,060	9309	1,150	1,150	1,150	1,200	1,900	3,250	9,500
1909-D	3,423,560	9319	1,150	1,150	1,150	1,200	1,250	1,750	9,500
1909-O (a)	34,200	9320	7,750	10,500	18,000	23,000	84,000	150,000	360,000
	Auctions: $216,000, PCGS MS-64 HA 09/24; $690,000, PCGS MS-66 HA 09/24								
1909-S	297,200	9321	1,200	1,250	1,400	4,100	13,000	19,000	60,000
	Auctions: $103,500, PCGS MS-66 HA 01/11								
1910	604,000	9310	1,150	1,150	1,150	1,200	1,950	3,900	10,000
1910-D	193,600	9322	1,150	1,150	1,150	1,200	3,500	9,500	33,000
	Auctions: $132,000, PCGS MS-66 HA 01/25								
1910-S	770,200	9323	1,150	1,200	1,350	1,350	9,750	24,500	75,000
	Auctions: $123,375, PCGS MS-65 GLDB 06/16								
1911	915,000	9311	1,150	1,150	1,150	1,200	1,800	3,100	9,500
1911-D	72,500	9324	1,450	2,400	4,750	6,000	29,000	60,000	312,000
	Auctions: $312,000, PCGS MS-65 HA 01/25								
1911-S	1,416,000	9325	1,150	1,250	1,250	1,300	5,500	11,500	57,500
↳1911-S, S Over S, FS-501	*	351846	1,250	1,350	1,350	1,450	6,250	12,500	63,500
↳1911-S, S Over S, FS-502	*	351847	1,350	1,450	1,500	1,600	6,750	13,500	69,000
1912	790,000	9312	1,150	1,150	1,150	1,200	1,950	3,250	10,500
1912-S	392,000	9326	1,200	1,250	1,400	1,750	11,000	41,000	186,000
	Auctions: $312,000, PCGS MS-65 HA 11/20								
1913	915,901	9313	1,150	1,200	1,200	1,200	1,750	3,300	10,000
1913-S	408,000	9327	1,150	1,200	1,250	2,000	12,000	21,000	114,000
	Auctions: $162,000, PCGS MS-66 HA 01/25								
1914	247,000	9314	1,150	1,150	1,150	1,200	2,100	3,400	10,500
	Auctions: $168,000, PCGS MS-66 HA 09/20								
1914-D	247,000	9328	1,150	1,150	1,200	1,200	3,550	4,300	15,500
1914-S	263,000	9329	1,200	1,250	1,550	2,000	12,000	50,500	132,000
	Auctions: $120,000, PCGS MS-65 HA 01/25								
1915 (b)	588,000	9315	1,150	1,150	1,150	1,200	1,950	3,000	10,000

* Included in number above. **a.** Beware spurious "O" mintmark. **b.** Pieces dated 1915-D are counterfeit.

Note: Gold spot price at time of publication, $3,746 per ounce.

	Mintage	GSID	EF-40	AU-50	AU-58	MS-60	MS-63	MS-64	MS-65
1915-S	164,000	9330	$1,200	$1,200	$1,900	$2,900	$12,000	$40,500	$132,000
	Auctions: $120,000, PCGS MS-64 HA 04/21								
1916-S	240,000	9331	1,250	1,250	1,400	1,550	6,000	7,500	33,000
	Auctions: $132,000, PCGS MS-66 HA 09/20								
1929	662,000	9316	18,000	22,000	29,000	31,000	43,000	54,000	102,000
	Auctions: $132,000, PCGS MS-65 HA 01/25								

* Included in number above. **a.** Beware spurious "O" mintmark. **b.** Pieces dated 1915-D are counterfeit.

Proof Strikes

	Mintage	GSID	PF-60	PF-63	PF-65
Indian Head (1908–1929)	**n/a**	**74152**	**$26,500**	**$66,000**	**$84,000**
1908	167	9332	26,500	66,000	84,000
	Auctions: $179,481, PCGS PF-67 SBG 08/13				
1909	78	9333	26,500	66,000	84,000
	Auctions: $175,662, NGC PF-67 SBG 08/12				
1910	250	9334	26,500	66,000	84,000
	Auctions: $146,250, NGC PF-68 BON 09/13				
1911	139	9335	26,500	66,000	84,000
	Auctions: $120,000, NGC PF-68 HA 09/20				
1912	144	9336	26,500	66,000	84,000
1913	99	9337	26,500	66,000	84,000
1914	125	9338	26,500	66,000	84,000
	Auctions: $246,750, PCGS PF-68 SBG 03/17				
1915	75	9339	26,500	78,000	102,000

Gold Eagles ($10) 1795–1933

AN OVERVIEW OF GOLD EAGLES

The ten-dollar gold coin, or *eagle*, was first produced in 1795. Coinage authority for the denomination, including its weight and fineness, had been specified by the Act of April 2, 1792.

Scan for additional information.

The Draped Bust to Right with Small Eagle reverse is the rarest of the early ten-dollar coin types. However, when seen they tend to be in higher grades such as EF, AU, or low levels of Mint State. The Heraldic Eagle reverse issues from 1797 through 1804 are much more readily available and in slightly higher average grade.

The Liberty Head eagles without the motto IN GOD WE TRUST, minted from 1838 through 1865, are elusive in any Mint State grade, although VF and EF pieces are plentiful, and there are enough AU coins to easily satisfy collector demands. Some collectors have considered the 1838 and 1839, 9 Over 8, with the head of Liberty tilted forward in relation to the date, to be a separate type. Eagles with IN GOD WE TRUST on the reverse, produced from 1866 to 1907, are plentiful in high grades, including choice and gem Mint State. Some of these were repatriated from overseas bank vaults beginning in the second half of the 20th century.

The Saint-Gaudens eagles of 1907, of the style with periods between and flanking the words E PLURIBUS UNUM, exist in the Wire Rim and Rounded Rim varieties. These can be collected as a distinct type, or not. Most readily available is the Wire Rim style, of which somewhat more than 400 are likely to exist today, nearly all in Mint State, often choice or gem. These coins were made as regular issues but soon became numismatic delicacies for Treasury officials to distribute as they saw fit. Some were to have gone to museums, but in reality most were secretly filtered out through favored coin dealers. Then comes the 1907–1908 style, without periods, easily available in EF, AU, and lower Mint State levels, although gems are elusive.

This pattern eagle of 1878, struck in copper and designated J-1580, was designed by George Morgan and strongly resembles the silver dollar design that bears his name.

The final eagle type, the 1908–1933 style with IN GOD WE TRUST on the reverse, is readily obtained in grades from EF through MS-63. Higher-grade pieces are elusive, and when seen are often dated 1932, a year in which 4,463,000 were struck—more than any other coin in the history of the denomination.

For the Collector and Investor: Gold Eagles as a Specialty

Collecting ten-dollar gold coins by die varieties is unusual, as the series includes so many scarce and rare coins. However, unlike other denominations, none is in the "impossible" category, and with some patience a full set of significant varieties, as listed in this book, can be obtained.

The early issues with a Small Eagle reverse, minted from 1795 through 1797, and those with the Heraldic Eagle reverse of 1797 through 1804, can be collected and studied by die varieties, with *United States Ten Dollar Gold Eagles 1795–1804*, by Anthony Teraskza, being one useful guide. *Early U.S. Gold Coin Varieties: A Study of Die States, 1795–1834*, by John W. Dannreuther and Harry W. Bass Jr., offers an abundance of information and enlarged photographs for study. In addition to the regular issues, a few 1804 restrike ten-dollar pieces exist from 1804-dated dies newly created in 1834.

Liberty Head eagles from 1838 through 1866 (without the motto IN GOD WE TRUST) comprise many scarce dates and mintmarks. Years ago the 1858, of which only 2,521 were minted, was highly acclaimed as a landmark issue, but since then the publicity has faded. In any event, although certain date-and-mintmark varieties are rare, the number of numismatists collecting them by date sequence is very small, and thus opportunities exist to acquire very elusive pieces at a much smaller proportionate premium than would be possible in, say, the gold dollar series. No full set of Mint State early eagles has ever been formed; probably none ever will be. EF and AU are typically the grades of choice, with Mint State pieces added when available.

Later Liberty Head eagles of the 1866–1907 style (with the motto IN GOD WE TRUST) include some low-mintage issues, but again these are not impossible to collect. The most famous is the 1875 Philadelphia coin, of which just 100 circulation strikes were made. Although smaller numbers exist for Proof-only mintages, in terms of those made for commerce the 1875 sets a record. The low-mintage 1879-O (1,500 made) and 1883-O (800) also have attracted much attention. Again, these pieces, while rare, are available to the specialist, as there is not a great deal of competition.

Among Indian Head eagles the 1907, With Periods, Wire Rim, is famous, popular, and rare. Examples come on the market with regularity but are expensive due to the demand they attract. The Rounded Rim style is much rarer and when seen is usually in choice Mint State.

The regular without-periods 1907 and 1908 eagles are easy enough to obtain in Mint State, although gems are elusive. The varieties from 1908 through 1916 include no great rarities, although some are scarcer than others. Not many such pieces were saved at the time they were issued, and, accordingly, gems are elusive. However, grades such as AU and low Mint State will present no problem. Among later eagles, the 1920-S, 1930-S, and 1933 are rarities. In particular the 1920-S is difficult to find in choice and gem Mint State. The 1933 eagle is usually found in Mint State, but is expensive due to the publicity given to it. Readily available at reasonable prices are the 1926 and 1932.

DRAPED BUST TO RIGHT, SMALL EAGLE REVERSE (1795–1797)

Designer: *Robert Scot.* **Weight:** *17.50 grams.*
Composition: *.9167 gold, .0833 silver and copper.*
Diameter: *Approximately 33 mm.* **Edge:** *Reeded.* **Mint:** *Philadelphia.*

History. Eagles of this style, the first in the denomination, debuted in the autumn of 1795. The obverse features Liberty dressed in a conical cap. The reverse shows a "small" eagle perched on a palm branch and holding a laurel in his beak. The same motif was used on contemporary gold half eagles.

Striking and Sharpness. On the obverse, check the star centers and the hair details. On the reverse, check the feathers of the eagle. In particular, the breast feathers often are weakly struck. Examine the denticles on both sides. Adjustment marks (from a Mint worker filing an overweight planchet down to the correct weight) often are visible, but are not noted by the grading services.

Availability. Typical grades range from EF to AU and low MS. MS-63 and higher coins are rare; when seen, they usually are of the 1795 or 1796 dates. Certain varieties are rare. While no Proofs of this type were made, certain eagles of 1796 have prooflike surfaces and are particularly attractive if in high grades.

Grading Standards

MS-63

MS-60 to 70 (Mint State). ***Obverse:*** At MS-60, some abrasion and contact marks are evident, most noticeably on the hair to the left of Liberty's forehead and on the higher-relief areas of the cap. Luster is present, but may be dull or lifeless, and interrupted in patches. At MS-63, contact marks are few, and abrasion is very light. An MS-65 coin has hardly any abrasion, and contact marks are so minute as to require magnification. Luster should be full and rich. On prooflike coins in any Mint State grade, abrasion and surface marks are much more noticeable. Coins above MS-65 exist more in theory than in reality for this type—but they do exist, and are defined by having fewer marks as perfection is approached. ***Reverse:*** Comments apply as for the obverse, except that abrasion and contact marks are most noticeable on the breast and head of the eagle. The field area is mainly protected by the eagle, branch, and lettering.

AU-58

AU-50, 53, 55, 58 (About Uncirculated). ***Obverse:*** Light wear is seen on the cheek, the hair immediately to the left of the face, and the cap, more so at AU-50 than at AU-53 or 55. An AU-58 coin has minimal traces of wear. An AU-50 coin has luster in protected areas among the stars and letters, with little in the open fields or on the portrait. At AU-58, most luster is present in the fields, but is worn away on the highest parts of the motifs. ***Reverse:*** Comments as preceding, except that the eagle shows light wear on the breast and head in particular, but also at the tip of the wing on the left and elsewhere. Luster ranges from perhaps 40 percent remaining in protected areas (at AU-50) to nearly full mint bloom (at AU-58).

Illustrated coin: This example shows light wear overall, with hints of original luster in protected areas.

EF-45

EF-40, 45 (Extremely Fine). ***Obverse:*** Wear is evident all over the portrait, with some loss of detail in the hair to the left of Liberty's face. Excellent detail remains in low-relief areas of the hair, such as the front curl and at the back of her head. The stars show wear, as do the date and letters. Luster, if present at all, is minimal and in protected areas. ***Reverse:*** Wear is greater than on an About Uncirculated coin. The breast, neck, and legs of the eagle lack nearly all feather detail. More wear is seen on the edges of the wing. Some traces of luster may be seen, more so at EF-45 than at EF-40.

VF-30

VF-20, 30 (Very Fine). ***Obverse:*** The higher-relief areas of hair are well worn at VF-20, less so at VF-30. The stars are flat at their centers. ***Reverse:*** Wear is greater, the eagle is flat in most areas, and about 40 percent to 60 percent of the wing feathers can be seen.

1795, 13 Leaves

1795, 9 Leaves

Circulation Strikes

	Mintage	GSID	F-12	VF-20	EF-40	AU-50	AU-58	MS-60	MS-63
Draped Bust to Right, Small Eagle Reverse (1795–1797)	**n/a**	**72385**	**$32,500**	**$39,500**	**$62,500**	**$84,000**	**$111,500**	**$138,000**	**$389,000**
1795, 13 Leaves	*	9340	32,500	39,500	62,500	84,000	111,500	138,000	389,000
	Auctions: $168,000, PCGS MS-61 SBG 08/25; $881,250, PCGS MS-65 HA 08/25								
1795, 9 Leaves	25 est. known	9341	93,500	114,000	144,000	180,000	300,000	462,000	1,680,000
	Auctions: $379,500, PCGS MS-61 SP 05/11								
1796	4,146	9342	32,500	39,500	62,500	84,000	111,500	138,000	427,500
	Auctions: $144,000, NGC MS-61 SBG 08/24; $322,000, NGC MS-63 SBG 08/24								
1797, Small Eagle Reverse	3,615	9343	43,000	57,500	78,000	96,000	165,500	264,000	522,000
	Auctions: $138,000 PCGS AU-58 SBG 11/24; $300,000, NGC MS-62 SBG 11/24								

* Included in number above.

100 GREATEST™ UNITED STATES COINS

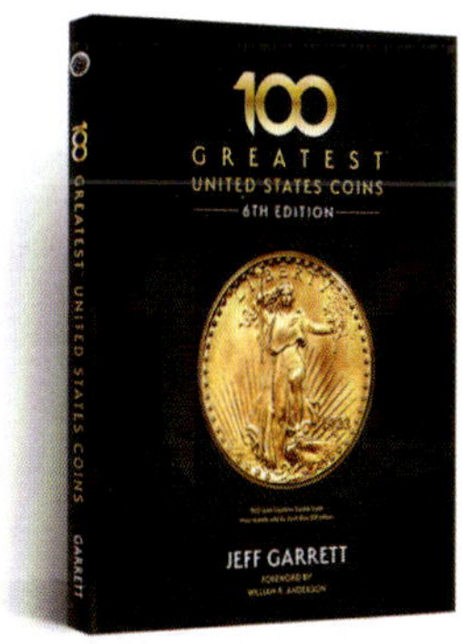

No. 52

1798, 8 OVER 7 CAPPED BUST EAGLES

DRAPED BUST TO RIGHT, HERALDIC EAGLE REVERSE (1797–1804)

Designer: *Robert Scot.* **Weight:** *17.50 grams.*
Composition: *.9167 gold, .0833 silver and copper.*
Diameter: *Approximately 33 mm.* **Edge:** *Reeded.* **Mint:** *Philadelphia.*

Circulation Strike

Proof Strike

History. Gold eagles of this type combine the previous obverse style with the Heraldic Eagle—a modification of the Great Seal of the United States—as used on other silver and gold coins of the era. Regarding the Proofs dated 1804: There were no Proofs coined in the era in which this type was issued, and all eagle and silver dollar production was suspended by President Thomas Jefferson in 1804. Years later, in 1834, the Mint made up new dies with the 1804 date (this time featuring a Plain 4 rather than a Crosslet 4) and struck a number of Proofs (the quantity unknown today, but perhaps a dozen or so) for inclusion in presentation Proof sets for foreign dignitaries.

Striking and Sharpness. On the obverse, check the star centers and the hair details. On the reverse, check the upper part of the shield, the lower part of the eagle's neck, the eagle's wing, the stars above the eagle, and the clouds. Inspect the denticles on both sides. Adjustment marks (from where an overweight planchet was filed down to correct specifications) can be problematic; these are not identified by the grading services.

Availability. Mintages of this type were erratic. Eagles of 1797 appear in the market with some regularity, while those of 1798 are rare. Usually seen are the issues of 1799 through 1803. Typical grades range from EF to lower MS. MS-62 and higher coins are seen with some frequency and usually are dated 1799 and later. The 1804 circulation strike is rare in true MS. Sharply struck coins without planchet adjustment marks are in the minority. Only a handful of the aforementioned 1804 Proofs survive today.

GRADING STANDARDS

MS-65

MS-60 to 70 (Mint State). ***Obverse:*** At MS-60, some abrasion and contact marks are evident, most noticeably on the hair to the left of Liberty's forehead and on the higher-relief areas of the cap. Luster is present, but may be dull or lifeless, and interrupted in patches. At MS-63, contact marks are few, and abrasion is very light. An MS-65 coin has even less abrasion (most observable in the right field), and contact marks are so minute as to require magnification. Luster should be full and rich. Coins graded above

MS-65 are more theoretical than actual for this type—but they do exist, and are defined by having fewer marks as perfection is approached. Large-size eagles are usually graded with slightly less strictness than the lower gold denominations of this type. ***Reverse:*** Comments apply as for the obverse, except that abrasion and contact marks are most noticeable on the upper part of the eagle and the clouds. The field area is complex, without much open space, given the stars above the eagle, the arrows and olive branch, and other features. Accordingly, marks are not as noticeable as on the obverse.

Illustrated coin: This coin has an exceptionally sharp strike overall, but with some lightness on the eagle's dexter (viewer's left) talon. Note some trivial abrasion in the right obverse field.

AU-50

AU-50, 53, 55, 58 (About Uncirculated). ***Obverse:*** Light wear is seen on the cheek, the hair immediately to the left of the face, and the cap, more so at AU-50 than at AU-53 or 55. An AU-58 coin has minimal traces of wear. An AU-50 coin has luster in protected areas among the stars and letters, with little in the open fields or on the portrait. At AU-58, most luster is present in the fields, but is worn away on the highest parts of the motifs. ***Reverse:*** Comments as preceding, except that the eagle's neck, the tips and top of the wings, the clouds, and the tail now show noticeable wear, as do other features. Luster ranges from perhaps 40 percent remaining in protected areas (at AU-50) to nearly full mint bloom (at AU-58). Often the reverse of this type retains much more luster than the obverse.

Illustrated coin: Note some lightness of strike at the center of the obverse. Significant luster remains.

EF-45

EF-40, 45 (Extremely Fine). ***Obverse:*** Wear is evident all over the portrait, with some loss of detail in the hair to the left of Liberty's face. Excellent detail remains in low-relief areas of the hair, such as the front curl and at the back of her head. The stars show wear as do the date and letters. Luster, if present at all, is minimal and in protected areas. ***Reverse:*** Wear is greater than on the preceding. The neck lacks some feather detail on its highest points. Feathers have lost some detail near the edges of the wings, and some areas of the horizontal lines in the shield may be blended together. Some traces of luster may be seen, more so at EF-45 than at EF-40. Overall, the reverse appears to be in a slightly higher grade than the obverse.

VF-30

VF-20, 30 (Very Fine). ***Obverse:*** The higher-relief areas of hair are well worn at VF-20, less so at VF-30. ***Reverse:*** Wear is greater, including on the shield and wing feathers. The star centers are flat. Other areas have lost detail as well. E PLURIBUS UNUM may be faint in areas, but is usually sharp.

PF-60 to 70 (Proof). ***Obverse and Reverse:*** PF-60 to 62 coins have extensive hairlines and may have nicks and contact marks. At PF-63, hairlines are prominent, but the mirror surface is very reflective. PF-64 coins have fewer hairlines. At PF-65, hairlines should be minimal and mostly seen only under magnification. There should be no nicks or marks.

PF-65+
Deep Cameo

1798, 8 Over 7,
9 Stars Left,
4 Stars Right

1798, 8 Over 7,
7 Stars Left, 6 Stars Right

1799, Small
Stars Obverse

1799, Large
Stars Obverse

1803, Small
Stars Reverse

1803, Large
Stars Reverse

Circulation Strikes

	Mintage	GSID	F-12	VF-20	EF-40	AU-50	AU-58	MS-60	MS-63
Draped Bust to Right, Heraldic Eagle Reverse (1797–1804)	**n/a**	**72386**	**$11,000**	**$12,000**	**$16,000**	**$19,000**	**$26,000**	**$30,000**	**$60,000**
1797, Heraldic Eagle Reverse	10,940	9344	12,000	16,000	25,000	31,000	51,500	60,000	228,000
	Auctions: $180,000, PCGS MS-62 SBG 11/22								
1798, 8 Over 7, 9 Stars Left, 4 Stars Right	900	9354	22,000	29,500	42,000	67,000	138,000	162,000	342,000
	Auctions: $176,250, PCGS MS-62 HA 04/14								
1798, 8 Over 7, 7 Stars Left, 6 Stars Right	842	9355	48,000	72,000	144,000	240,000	504,000	750,000	—
	Auctions: $352,500, PCGS AU-58 SBG 08/16								
1799, Large Stars Obverse	37,449	9345	11,000	12,000	16,000	19,000	26,000	30,000	68,500
	Auctions: $493,500, PCGS MS-66 SBG 04/16								
1799, Small Stars Obverse	*	9346	11,000	12,000	17,000	20,000	27,000	31,500	79,000
	Auctions: $156,000, PCGS MS-64 SBG 08/24								
1800	5,999	9347	11,000	12,000	16,000	19,000	27,000	33,000	84,000
	Auctions: $310,500, NGC MS-65 HA 01/08								
1801	44,344	9348	12,000	13,000	17,500	20,500	26,000	30,000	60,000
	Auctions: $264,000, PCGS MS-65 SBG 04/25								
1803, Small Stars Reverse	15,017	9349	13,000	15,000	18,500	23,000	33,000	35,000	71,000
	Auctions: $144,000, PCGS MS-64 SBG 02/25; $102,000, PCGS MS-63 SBG 02/25								
1803, Extra Star in Cloud	*	9350	14,500	16,500	20,500	27,500	39,500	60,000	132,000
	Auctions: $333,500, NGC MS-66 ANR 08/06								
1803, Large Stars Reverse	*	9351	12,000	13,000	18,500	24,000	33,000	42,000	72,000
	Auctions: $172,500, NGC MS-62 HA 06/08								
1804, Crosslet 4	3,757	9352	24,000	28,000	33,500	51,500	86,500	114,000	330,000
	Auctions: $174,000, PCGS MS-62 SBG 08/25; $168,000, NGC MS-62 SBG 08/25								

* Included in number above.

Proof Strikes

	Mintage	GSID	PF-63	PF-65
1804, Plain 4	4 known	9353	$3,360,000	$7,800,000

LIBERTY HEAD (1838–1907)

Designer: *Christian Gobrecht.* **Weight:** *16.718 grams.*
Composition: *.900 gold, .100 copper (net weight: .48375 oz. pure gold).* **Diameter:** *27 mm.*
Edge: *Reeded.* **Mints:** *Philadelphia, Carson City, Denver, New Orleans, and San Francisco.*

No Motto Above Eagle (1838–1866), Circulation Strike

No Motto Above Eagle, Proof Strike

Motto Above Eagle (1866–1907), Circulation Strike

Motto Above Eagle, Proof Strike

History. Production of the gold eagle, suspended after 1804, started up again in 1838 with the Liberty Head design. The coin's weight and diameter was reduced from the specifications of the earlier type. For the first time in the denomination's history, its value, TEN D., was shown. Midway through 1839 the style was modified slightly, including in the letters (made smaller) and in the tilt of Liberty's portrait. In 1866 the motto IN GOD WE TRUST was placed on a banner above the eagle's head.

Striking and Sharpness. On the obverse, check the highest points of the hair and the star centers. On the reverse, check the eagle's neck, and the area to the lower left of the shield and the lower part of the eagle. Examine the denticles on both sides. Branch-mint coins issued before the Civil War often are lightly struck in areas, and some Carson City coins of the early 1870s can have areas of lightness. Most late 19th-century and early 20th-century coins are sharp in all areas. Tiny copper staining spots (from improperly mixed alloy) can be a problem for those issues. Cameo contrast is the rule for Proofs prior to 1902. Beginning that year the portrait was polished in the die, imparting a mirror finish across the entire design, although a few years later cameo-contrast coins were again made.

Availability. Early dates and mintmarks are generally scarce to rare in MS and very rare in MS-63 and better grades, with only a few exceptions. These were workhorse coins in commerce; VF and EF grades are the rule for dates through the 1870s, and for some dates the finest known grade can be AU. In MS, Liberty Head eagles as a type are rarer than either quarter eagles or half eagles of the same design. Indeed, the majority of Mint State examples were only discovered in recent decades, resting in European banks, and some varieties are not known to exist at this level. Eagles of the 1880s onward generally are seen in higher average grades. Proof coins exist in relation to their original mintages, with all issues prior to the 1890s being very rare.

Note: Values of common-date gold coins have been based on the current bullion price of gold, $3,746 per ounce, and may vary with the prevailing spot price.

Grading Standards

MS-63

MS-60 to 70 (Mint State). ***Obverse:*** At MS-60, some abrasion and contact marks are evident, most noticeably on the hair to the right of Liberty's forehead and on the jaw. Luster is present, but may be dull or lifeless, and interrupted in patches. At MS-63, contact marks are few, and abrasion is very light. An MS-65 coin has hardly any abrasion, and contact marks are so minute as to require magnification. Luster should be full and rich. For most dates, coins graded above MS-65 exist more in theory than in actuality—but they do exist, and are defined by having fewer marks as perfection is approached. ***Reverse:*** Comments apply as for the obverse, except that abrasion and contact marks are most noticeable on the eagle's neck and to the lower left of the shield.

Illustrated coin: This coin is brilliant and lustrous with scattered marks in the field, as is typical for this grade.

AU-53

AU-50, 53, 55, 58 (About Uncirculated). ***Obverse:*** Light wear is seen on the face, the hair to the right of the face, and the highest area of the hair bun, more so at AU-50 than at AU-53 or 55. An AU-58 coin has minimal traces of wear. An AU-50 coin has luster in protected areas among the stars and letters, with little in the open fields or on the portrait. At AU-58 most luster is present in the fields, but is worn away on the highest parts of the motifs. ***Reverse:*** Comments as preceding, except that the eagle shows wear in all of the higher areas, as well as the leaves and arrowheads. Luster ranges from perhaps 40 percent remaining in protected areas (at AU-50) to nearly full mint bloom (at AU-58). Often the reverse of this type retains more luster than the obverse.

EF-40

EF-40, 45 (Extremely Fine). ***Obverse:*** Wear is evident on all high areas of the portrait, including the hair to the right of the forehead, the tip of the coronet, and the hair bun. The stars show light wear at their centers. Luster, if present at all, is minimal and in protected areas such as between the star points. ***Reverse:*** Wear is greater than on an About Uncirculated coin. On the $10 coins (in contrast to the $2.50 and $5 of the same design), most of the details on the eagle are sharp. There is flatness on the leaves and arrowheads. Some traces of luster may be seen, more so at EF-45 than at EF-40.

Illustrated coin: Note the many contact marks on both sides.

VF-20, 30 (Very Fine). ***Obverse:*** The higher-relief areas of hair are worn flat at VF-20, less so at VF-30. The hair to the right of the coronet is merged into heavy strands. The stars are flat at their centers. ***Reverse:*** The eagle is worn further, with most neck feathers gone and with the feathers in the wing having flat tips. The branch leaves have little or no detail. The vertical shield stripes, being deeply recessed, remain bold.

VF-25

PF-60 to 70 (Proof). ***Obverse and Reverse:*** PF-60 to 62 coins have extensive hairlines and may have nicks and contact marks. At PF-63, hairlines are prominent, but the mirror surface is very reflective. PF-64 coins have fewer hairlines. At PF-65, hairlines should be minimal and mostly seen only under magnification. There should be no nicks or marks. PF-66 and higher coins should have no marks or hairlines visible to the unaided eye.

PF-65

Illustrated coin: This is a museum-quality gem, with cameo-contrast motifs and mirror fields.

1839, Large Letters (Type of 1838)

1839, Small Letters (Type of 1840)

Circulation Strikes

	Mintage	GSID	VF-20	EF-40	AU-50	AU-58	MS-60	MS-63	MS-64
Liberty Head, No Motto Above Eagle, Type of 1838 (1838–1839)	**n/a**	**72387**	**$3,750**	**$6,250**	**$7,750**	**$19,000**	**$36,000**	**$108,000**	**$174,000**
Liberty Head, No Motto Above Eagle, Type of 1840 (1839–1866)	**n/a**	**72388**	**2,300**	**2,350**	**2,450**	**2,850**	**3,250**	**19,000**	**36,000**
Liberty Head, Motto Above Eagle (1866–1907)	**n/a**	**72389**	**2,250**	**2,250**	**2,250**	**2,300**	**2,300**	**2,350**	**2,450**
Variety 1: No Motto Above Eagle									
1838 (a)	7,200	9356	4,100	9,500	15,000	54,000	72,000	114,000	—
	Auctions: $115,000, NGC MS-63 HA 01/07								
1839, 9 Over 8, Large Letters, Type of 1838 (a)	25,801	9357	3,750	6,250	7,750	19,000	36,000	108,000	174,000
	Auctions: $402,500, PCGS MS-66 HA 01/05								
1839, Small Letters, Type of 1840	12,447	9358	6,250	10,000	11,000	45,500	72,000	144,000	228,000
	Auctions: $180,000, NGC MS-64 SBG 12/20								

a. The Liberty Head style of 1838 and 1839 (Large Letters) differs from that used for subsequent issues.

1842, Small Date

1842, Large Date

1846-O, 6 Over 5

1850, Large Date

1850, Small Date

1853, 3 Over 2

Circulation Strikes *(continued)*

	Mintage	GSID	VF-20	EF-40	AU-50	AU-58	MS-60	MS-63	MS-64
1840	47,338	9359	$2,450	$2,550	$2,850	$6,500	$18,000	—	—
1841	63,131	9360	2,300	2,450	2,700	7,000	12,000	$60,000	—
1841-O	2,500	9429	12,000	18,000	50,500	108,000	—	—	—
1842, Large Date	62,884	9361	2,300	2,400	2,550	7,000	12,000	30,000	$51,000
1842, Small Date	18,623	9362	2,450	2,600	2,900	8,000	12,000	66,000	—
1842-O	27,400	9430	2,550	3,100	6,250	18,000	60,000	300,000	—
	Auctions: $288,000, PCGS MS-63 HA 02/18								
1843	75,462	9363	2,300	2,500	2,800	17,000	30,000	—	—
1843-O	175,162	9431	2,450	2,700	3,200	8,750	18,500	108,000	180,000
1844	6,361	9364	5,000	7,000	10,500	24,000	29,000	93,500	—
1844-O	118,700	9432	2,450	2,650	3,200	7,000	17,000	90,000	—
1845	26,153	9365	2,700	2,950	3,500	9,500	16,000	—	—
1845-O	47,500	9433	2,600	2,900	4,500	12,000	24,000	69,500	—
1846	20,095	9366	2,400	3,000	6,000	18,500	36,000	—	—
1846-O	81,780	9436	2,550	3,000	4,500	19,000	33,000	90,000	144,000
↳1846-O, 6 Over 5	*	9435	2,800	4,000	6,250	43,000	60,000	—	—
↳1846-O, Over O/Repunched Date, FS-301/501	*	377754	—	—	—	—	—	—	—
1847	862,258	9367	2,300	2,350	2,450	2,850	4,500	29,000	50,500
1847-O	571,500	9437	2,400	2,500	2,700	5,250	9,750	48,000	102,000
1848	145,484	9368	2,300	2,350	2,450	2,950	7,000	30,000	48,000
1848-O	35,850	9438	2,550	4,000	5,000	12,500	18,000	57,500	81,500
	Auctions: $240,000, PCGS MS-66 SBG 03/20								
1849	653,618	9369	2,300	2,450	2,600	3,200	4,750	23,000	41,000
↳1849, Repunched Date, FS-301	*	351848	2,550	2,700	2,850	3,550	5,250	25,000	45,000
1849-O	23,900	9439	3,250	5,000	6,250	25,000	45,500	—	—
1850, Large Date	291,451	9370	2,300	2,350	2,450	2,850	7,500	33,500	66,000
1850, Small Date	*	9371	2,300	2,550	2,850	5,000	9,500	50,500	—
1850-O	57,500	9440	2,650	3,100	4,750	17,000	21,500	60,000	120,000
1851	176,328	9372	2,300	2,450	2,600	3,000	6,000	41,000	—
1851-O	263,000	9441	2,500	2,600	2,850	4,750	14,500	42,000	78,000
1852	263,106	9373	2,300	2,350	2,450	2,850	3,600	30,000	45,500
	Auctions: $288,000, PCGS MS-66 SBG 03/20								
1852-O	18,000	9442	3,250	6,250	8,500	24,000	102,000	—	—
	Auctions: $111,625, PCGS MS-60 SBG 11/16								
1853	201,253	9374	2,300	2,350	2,450	2,850	3,600	27,500	57,500
1853, 3 Over 2	*	9443	2,450	2,600	2,800	4,700	12,000	—	—
↳1853, 3 Over 2, FS-301	*	393367	2,450	2,600	2,800	4,700	12,000	—	—

* Included in number above.

1854-O, Large Date

1854-O, Small Date

1865-S, 865 Over Inverted 186

Circulation Strikes *(continued)*

	Mintage	GSID	VF-20	EF-40	AU-50	AU-58	MS-60	MS-63	MS-64
1853-O	51,000	9444	$2,450	$2,750	$3,100	$11,000	$24,000	—	—
	Auctions: $316,250, NGC MS-61 SBG 08/10								
1854	54,250	9375	2,550	2,600	2,700	3,000	8,000	$33,500	$57,500
1854-O, Small Date	52,500	9445	2,500	3,000	3,250	8,000	19,000	—	—
1854-O, Large Date	*	9446	2,500	3,000	3,250	9,250	20,000	42,000	—
1854-S	123,826	9447	2,450	2,550	2,750	6,500	23,000	—	—
1855	121,701	9376	2,300	2,350	2,450	2,850	3,900	23,000	43,000
1855-O	18,000	9448	3,500	5,000	9,250	31,000	36,000	—	—
1855-S	9,000	9449	4,000	5,250	7,750	31,000	—	—	—
1856	60,490	9377	2,300	2,350	2,450	2,850	3,250	21,000	39,500
1856-O	14,500	9450	2,700	3,750	6,000	19,000	42,000	—	—
1856-S	68,000	9451	2,500	2,650	2,850	6,250	13,000	57,500	—
1857	16,606	9378	2,550	2,850	3,250	7,500	11,000	—	—
1857-O	5,500	9452	3,750	7,500	10,500	31,000	—	—	—
1857-S	26,000	9453	2,500	3,500	4,750	11,000	13,000	38,500	66,000
1858	2,521	9379	5,500	7,500	10,500	26,500	36,000	168,000	331,000
	Auctions: $276,000, PCGS MS-64 HA 05/07								
1858-O	20,000	9454	2,500	2,800	3,250	8,750	17,000	53,000	—
1858-S	11,800	9455	3,900	5,500	8,750	19,000	24,000	—	—
1859	16,013	9380	2,300	2,600	3,250	5,750	18,000	72,000	—
1859-O	2,300	9456	10,000	19,000	29,000	66,000	—	—	—
1859-S	7,000	9457	6,250	10,000	15,500	33,500	53,000	—	—
1860	15,055	9381	2,300	2,350	2,650	5,500	10,000	33,500	90,000
1860-O	11,100	9458	2,700	4,000	5,250	14,500	24,000	—	—
1860-S	5,000	9459	8,750	12,500	15,500	38,500	48,000	—	—
1861	113,164	9382	2,300	2,350	2,550	4,000	6,250	25,000	47,000
1861-S	15,500	9400	5,750	8,750	12,000	21,500	48,000	—	—
1862	10,960	9383	4,000	5,500	7,500	12,000	19,000	60,000	86,500
1862-S	12,500	9461	6,250	9,250	13,000	50,500	84,000	—	—
	Auctions: $103,500, NGC MS-61 HA 05/11								
1863	1,218	9384	17,000	43,000	59,000	101,000	132,000	210,000	—
1863-S	10,000	9462	10,000	15,500	21,000	48,000	120,000	—	—
	Auctions: $132,000, PCGS MS-60 HA 02/18								
1864	3,530	9385	9,000	13,000	27,500	57,500	72,000	—	—
1864-S	2,500	9463	65,000	89,000	168,000	—	—	—	—
	Auctions: $219,005, NGC AU-55 HA 10/18								
1865	3,980	9386	5,000	8,750	20,500	33,500	48,000	—	—
1865-S	16,700	9464	8,750	17,000	21,000	45,500	114,000	—	—
	Auctions: $108,000, PCGS AU-58 SBG 04/22								
1865-S, 865 Over Inverted 186	*	9465	8,750	17,000	21,000	45,500	114,000	—	300,000
1866-S, No Motto	8,500	9466	8,000	10,000	12,500	38,500	60,000	—	—

* Included in number above.

Note: Gold spot price at time of publication, $3,746 per ounce.

Circulation Strikes (continued)

	Mintage	GSID	VF-20	EF-40	AU-50	AU-58	MS-60	MS-63	MS-64
Variety 2: Motto Above Eagle									
1866, Motto	3,750	9387	$2,550	$5,000	$7,000	$19,000	$41,000	—	—
1866-S, Motto	11,500	9467	4,100	7,000	10,000	21,500	29,000	—	—
1867	3,090	9388	4,000	5,250	7,500	26,500	33,500	—	—
1867-S	9,000	9468	6,000	9,000	14,500	54,000	—	—	—
1868	10,630	9389	2,450	2,500	2,750	7,250	12,500	—	—
1868-S	13,500	9469	2,450	3,250	5,250	20,500	—	—	—
1869	1,830	9390	3,000	7,000	10,000	29,000	48,000	$84,000	—
1869-S	6,430	9470	3,250	5,500	8,250	18,000	53,000	162,000	—
	Auctions: $162,000, PCGS MS-63 HA 01/25								
1870	3,990	9391	2,500	3,250	5,750	17,000	38,500	—	—
1870-CC	5,908	9471	96,000	120,000	210,000	1,020,000	—	—	—
	Auctions: $420,000, PCGS AU-55 SBG 08/24; $1,080,000, PCGS AU-58 SBG 08/24								
1870-S	8,000	9472	3,000	4,750	6,000	26,500	43,000	—	—
1871	1,790	9392	2,500	3,750	7,500	16,000	41,000	—	—
1871-CC	8,085	9473	7,500	19,000	27,500	50,500	67,000	—	—
	Auctions: $148,638, PCGS MS-62 SBG 08/12								
1871-S	16,500	9474	2,400	2,750	6,250	24,000	—	—	—
1872	1,620	9393	3,750	8,000	10,500	29,000	36,000	55,000	$89,000
1872-CC	4,600	9475	14,500	20,000	24,000	66,000	—	—	—
	Auctions: $240,000, NGC MS-62 HA 01/20								
1872-S	17,300	9476	2,500	2,750	4,000	11,000	33,000	—	—
1873	800	9394	12,000	16,000	26,500	78,000	101,000	—	—
	Auctions: $102,000, PCGS MS-61 HA 07/23								
1873-CC	4,543	9477	24,000	36,000	54,000	120,000	—	—	—
	Auctions: $102,000 PCGS AU-53 HA 01/25								
1873-S	12,000	9478	2,600	4,750	7,000	17,000	33,500	—	—
1874	53,140	9395	2,250	2,250	2,250	2,450	2,450	15,500	29,000
1874-CC	16,767	9479	4,500	8,000	12,500	48,000	74,500	216,000	336,000
	Auctions: $229,712, PCGS MS-63 SBG 08/12								
1874-S	10,000	9480	2,600	3,200	6,250	21,500	—	—	—
1875	10 known	9396	180,000	330,000	600,000	—	—	—	—
	Auctions: $1,020,000, PCGS AU-53 HA 10/22								
1875-CC	7,715	9481	9,000	18,000	29,000	90,000	113,000	204,000	—
1876	687	9397	6,250	12,000	24,000	48,000	90,000	—	—
1876-CC	4,696	9482	8,750	17,000	24,000	90,000	—	—	—
	Auctions: $192,000, PCGS AU-58 HA 01/22								
1876-S	5,000	9483	3,500	5,750	10,000	38,500	—	—	—
1877	797	9398	5,000	8,500	14,000	26,500	53,000	—	—
1877-CC	3,332	9484	11,500	17,000	43,000	144,000	—	—	—
	Auctions: $102,000, PCGS AU-58 HA 02/18								
1877-S	17,000	9485	2,400	2,600	3,500	12,500	30,000	—	—
1878	73,780	9399	2,250	2,250	2,250	2,350	2,450	5,250	11,000
1878-CC	3,244	9486	9,500	21,000	29,000	81,500	144,000	—	—
1878-S	26,100	9487	2,250	2,300	2,450	4,000	21,500	54,000	72,000
1879	384,740	9400	2,250	2,250	2,250	2,300	2,300	3,250	5,500
1879-CC	1,762	9488	24,000	33,500	48,000	79,000	—	—	—
1879-O	1,500	9489	12,500	20,000	29,500	66,000	86,500	—	—
1879-S	224,000	9490	2,250	2,250	2,250	2,300	2,400	7,500	16,000
1880	1,644,840	9401	2,250	2,250	2,250	2,300	2,300	2,450	4,500

1889-S, Repunched Mintmark
FS-501

Circulation Strikes *(continued)*

	Mintage	GSID	VF-20	EF-40	AU-50	AU-58	MS-60	MS-63	MS-64
1880-CC	11,190	9491	$3,250	$4,500	$6,250	$17,000	$43,000	—	—
1880-O	9,200	9492	2,450	2,900	4,100	8,000	18,000	$78,000	$150,000
	Auctions: $129,250, PCGS MS-64 SBG 03/17								
1880-S	506,250	9493	2,250	2,250	2,250	2,300	2,300	2,600	9,250
1881	3,877,220	9402	2,250	2,250	2,250	2,300	2,300	2,450	2,500
1881-CC	24,015	9494	3,200	3,900	5,500	9,500	11,000	66,000	120,000
	Auctions: $114,856, NGC MS-64 SBG 08/12								
1881-O	8,350	9495	2,500	3,250	4,400	6,500	13,000	—	—
1881-S	970,000	9496	2,250	2,250	2,250	2,300	2,300	2,500	5,750
1882	2,324,440	9403	2,250	2,250	2,250	2,300	2,300	2,350	2,550
1882-CC	6,764	9497	3,750	7,000	10,000	21,500	36,000	84,000	—
1882-O	10,820	9498	2,500	2,700	3,000	9,000	11,000	50,500	—
1882-S	132,000	9499	2,250	2,250	2,250	2,300	2,300	2,500	17,000
1883	208,700	9404	2,250	2,250	2,250	2,300	2,300	2,500	7,500
1883-CC	12,000	9500	3,550	6,000	8,750	21,500	38,500	—	—
1883-O	800	9501	30,000	54,000	102,000	198,000	240,000	—	—
	Auctions: $126,000, PCGS AU-58 HA 02/18								
1883-S	38,000	9502	2,250	2,250	2,250	2,300	2,400	7,250	12,000
↳1883-S, Misplaced Date, FS-301	*	393368	—	—	—	—	—	—	—
1884	76,860	9405	2,250	2,250	2,250	2,300	2,350	4,100	18,000
1884-CC	9,925	9503	2,750	3,950	7,250	15,500	21,500	84,000	—
	Auctions: $132,000, PCGS MS-62 SBG 08/21								
1884-S	124,250	9504	2,250	2,250	2,250	2,300	2,300	3,750	—
1885	253,462	9406	2,250	2,250	2,250	2,300	2,300	2,500	7,250
1885-S	228,000	9505	2,250	2,250	2,250	2,300	2,300	2,500	8,750
1886	236,100	9407	2,250	2,250	2,250	2,300	2,300	2,700	8,750
1886-S	826,000	9506	2,250	2,250	2,250	2,300	2,300	2,450	2,550
1887	53,600	9408	2,250	2,250	2,400	2,450	2,650	7,500	17,000
1887-S	817,000	9507	2,250	2,250	2,250	2,300	2,300	2,350	5,000
1888	132,921	9409	2,250	2,250	2,250	2,300	2,300	6,500	14,500
1888-O	21,335	9508	2,350	2,350	2,350	2,500	2,550	9,000	31,000
1888-S	648,700	9509	2,250	2,250	2,250	2,300	2,300	2,500	4,400
1889	4,440	9410	2,400	2,500	2,700	3,750	5,250	14,500	—
1889-S	425,400	9510	2,250	2,250	2,250	2,300	2,300	2,350	3,000
↳1889-S, S Over S, Doubled Die Reverse, FS-501	*	351850	2,400	2,400	2,400	2,400	2,400	2,500	3,150
1890	57,980	9411	2,250	2,250	2,250	2,300	2,300	3,500	9,500
1890-CC	17,500	9511	2,500	2,750	3,450	6,250	7,250	26,500	78,000
1891	91,820	9412	2,250	2,250	2,250	2,300	2,300	2,500	10,000
1891-CC	103,732	9512	2,400	2,650	2,950	3,450	3,550	8,250	30,000
↳1891-CC, CC Over CC, FS-501	*	226298	2,500	2,800	3,100	3,450	3,550	9,500	—
1892	797,480	9413	2,250	2,250	2,250	2,300	2,300	2,350	2,700

* Included in number above.

Circulation Strikes *(continued)*

	Mintage	GSID	VF-20	EF-40	AU-50	AU-58	MS-60	MS-63	MS-64
1892-CC	40,000	9513	$2,500	$2,900	$3,500	$5,000	$8,000	$39,500	$66,000
↳**1892-CC, Tripled Die Reverse, FS-801**	*	351851	2,650	3,050	3,700	5,500	8,500	41,500	69,500
1892-O	28,688	9514	2,400	2,400	2,400	2,500	2,500	11,000	—
1892-S	115,500	9515	2,250	2,250	2,250	2,300	2,300	3,000	10,000
1893	1,840,840	9414	2,250	2,250	2,250	2,300	2,300	2,350	2,550
1893-CC	14,000	9516	2,700	4,250	6,250	13,000	23,000	—	—
1893-O	17,000	9517	2,350	2,350	2,400	2,450	2,500	7,000	—
1893-S	141,350	9518	2,250	2,250	2,250	2,300	2,300	2,400	6,250
1894	2,470,735	9415	2,250	2,250	2,250	2,300	2,300	2,350	2,450
1894-O	107,500	9519	2,300	2,300	2,350	2,450	2,450	7,000	17,000
1894-S	25,000	9520	2,250	2,250	2,350	2,750	5,250	—	—
1895	567,770	9416	2,250	2,250	2,250	2,300	2,300	2,400	2,450
1895-O	98,000	9521	2,350	2,350	2,400	2,450	2,650	8,500	21,000
1895-S	49,000	9522	2,250	2,250	2,300	2,450	3,750	10,500	26,500
	Auctions: $160,000, PCGS MS-66 DLRC 05/21								
1896	76,270	9417	2,250	2,250	2,250	2,300	2,300	2,500	3,250
1896-S	123,750	9523	2,250	2,250	2,250	2,300	2,300	9,500	29,000
	Auctions: $156,000, PCGS MS-67 HA 02/25								
1897	1,000,090	9418	2,250	2,250	2,250	2,300	2,300	2,350	2,450
1897-O	42,500	9524	2,350	2,350	2,450	2,600	2,800	8,000	23,000
	Auctions: $264,000, PCGS MS-67 HA 02/18								
1897-S	234,750	9525	2,250	2,250	2,250	2,300	2,300	6,000	12,000
1898	812,130	9419	2,250	2,250	2,250	2,300	2,300	2,350	2,450
1898-S	473,600	9526	2,250	2,250	2,250	2,300	2,300	2,750	4,750
1899	1,262,219	9420	2,250	2,250	2,250	2,300	2,300	2,350	2,450
1899-O	37,047	9527	2,350	2,350	2,400	2,450	2,550	10,000	21,000
	Auctions: $336,000, PCGS MS-68 HA 09/20								
1899-S	841,000	9528	2,250	2,250	2,250	2,300	2,300	2,600	3,750
	Auctions: $288,000, PCGS MS-68 HA 11/20								
1900	293,840	9421	2,250	2,250	2,250	2,300	2,300	2,350	2,450
1900-S	81,000	9529	2,250	2,250	2,250	2,300	2,500	4,000	15,000
1901	1,718,740	9422	2,250	2,250	2,250	2,300	2,300	2,350	2,450
1901-O	72,041	9530	2,350	2,350	2,400	2,450	2,550	4,100	7,500
1901-S	2,812,750	9531	2,250	2,250	2,250	2,300	2,300	2,350	2,450
1902	82,400	9423	2,250	2,250	2,250	2,300	2,300	2,350	3,000
1902-S	469,500	9532	2,250	2,250	2,250	2,300	2,300	2,350	2,450
1903	125,830	9424	2,250	2,250	2,250	2,300	2,300	2,500	2,600
1903-O	112,771	9533	2,350	2,350	2,400	2,450	2,450	3,350	5,000
1903-S	538,000	9534	2,250	2,250	2,250	2,300	2,300	2,350	2,450
1904	161,930	9425	2,250	2,250	2,250	2,300	2,300	2,350	2,450
1904-O	108,950	9535	2,350	2,350	2,400	2,450	2,450	3,000	8,750
1905	200,992	9426	2,250	2,250	2,250	2,300	2,300	2,400	2,500
1905-S	369,250	9536	2,250	2,250	2,250	2,300	2,300	5,250	15,500
1906	165,420	9427	2,250	2,250	2,250	2,300	2,300	2,350	2,450
1906-D	981,000	9537	2,250	2,250	2,250	2,300	2,300	2,350	2,700
1906-O	86,895	9538	2,350	2,350	2,400	2,450	2,600	6,250	9,000
1906-S	457,000	9539	2,250	2,250	2,250	2,300	2,400	2,600	7,500
1907	1,203,899	9428	2,250	2,250	2,250	2,300	2,300	2,350	2,550
1907-D	1,030,000	9540	2,250	2,250	2,250	2,300	2,300	2,400	3,500
1907-S	210,500	9541	2,250	2,250	2,250	2,300	2,300	3,600	14,500

* Included in number above.

Proof Strikes

	Mintage	GSID	PF-60	PF-63	PF-65
Liberty Head, No Motto Above Eagle, Type of 1838 (1838–1839), Proof	n/a	74251	—	—	$2,400,000
Liberty Head, No Motto Above Eagle, Type of 1840 (1839–1866), Proof	n/a	74155	$55,000	$132,000	252,000
Same, Proof Cameo	n/a	74156	—	141,500	276,000
Same, Proof Deep Cameo	n/a	74157	—	144,000	288,000
Liberty Head, Motto Above Eagle (1866–1907), Proof	n/a	74176	9,750	16,000	46,000
Same, Proof Cameo	n/a	74177	12,000	19,000	53,000
Same, Proof Deep Cameo	n/a	74178	—	26,500	66,000
Variety 1: No Motto Above Eagle					
1838	unknown	9542	—	—	2,400,000
1839, 9 Over 8, Large Letters, Type of 1838	unknown	9545	—	—	—
	Auctions: $1,610,000, NGC PF-67 HA 01/07				
1840	unique	9548	—	—	—
1841	unique	9549	102,000	138,000	—
1843	unknown	9555	—	—	—
1844	unknown	9560	—	—	—
1845	unknown	9561	—	—	300,000
	Auctions: $120,750, PCGS PF-64 HA 08/99				
1846	unknown	9564	—	—	—
1847	unique	9569	—	—	—
1854	unique	393369	—	—	—
1857	unknown	9588	—	—	—
1858	unknown	9591	—	—	—
1859	80	9594	60,500	145,000	277,000
1860	50	9597	66,000	171,500	327,500
1861	69	9600	60,500	145,000	277,000
	Auctions: $126,500, PCGS PF-64 HA 01/11				
1862	35	9603	55,000	132,000	252,000
1863	30	9606	60,500	145,000	277,000
	Auctions: $144,000, PCGS PF-63 HA 10/22				
1864	50	9609	60,500	145,000	277,000
	Auctions: $149,500, PCGS PF-65 HA 01/05				
1865	25	9612	55,000	132,000	252,000

	Mintage	GSID	PF-60	PF-63	PF-65
Variety 2: Motto Above Eagle					
1866, Motto	30	9615	$29,000	$54,000	$120,000
	Auctions: $138,000, PCGS PF-65 HA 08/07				
1867	50	9618	29,000	54,000	120,000
1868	10–12 known	9621	29,000	54,000	120,000
1869	25	9624	33,500	60,000	132,000
1870	35	9627	24,000	50,500	108,000
1871	30	9630	24,000	50,500	108,000
1872	30	9633	24,000	50,500	108,000
1873	25	9636	24,000	50,500	108,000
1874	20	9639	29,000	54,000	120,000
1875	20	9642	26,500	66,000	180,000
	Auctions: $164,500, NGC AU-50 HA 01/14				
1876	45	9645	19,000	43,000	108,000
1877	20	9648	19,000	43,000	108,000
1878	20	9651	19,000	43,000	108,000
1879	30	9654	19,000	43,000	108,000
1880	36	9657	19,000	43,000	108,000
1881	40	9660	19,000	43,000	108,000
1882	40	9663	19,000	43,000	108,000
1883	40	9666	19,000	43,000	108,000
1884	45	9669	19,000	43,000	108,000
1885	65	9672	19,000	36,000	86,500
1886	60	9675	19,000	43,000	108,000
1887	80	9678	19,000	43,000	108,000
1888	75	9681	17,000	41,000	101,000
1889	45	9684	19,000	43,000	108,000
1890	63	9687	12,000	30,000	62,500
1891	48	9690	12,000	30,000	62,500
1892	72	9693	15,500	36,000	72,000
1893	55	9696	12,000	30,000	62,500
1894	43	9699	12,000	30,000	62,500
	Auctions: $105,750, PCGS PF-65 HA 01/14				
1895	56	9702	10,500	18,000	51,000
1896	78	9705	10,500	18,000	51,000
1897	69	9708	11,000	19,000	55,000
1898	67	9711	10,500	18,000	51,000
1899	86	9714	9,750	16,000	46,000
1900	120	9717	9,750	16,000	46,000
1901	85	9720	9,750	16,000	46,000
1902	113	9723	9,750	16,000	46,000
1903	96	9726	9,750	16,000	46,000
1904	108	9729	9,750	19,000	57,000
1905	86	9732	9,750	17,500	57,500
1906	77	9735	9,750	16,000	46,000
1907	74	9738	9,750	16,000	46,000

Note: Gold spot price at time of publication, $3,746 per ounce.

INDIAN HEAD (1907–1933)

Designer: *Augustus Saint-Gaudens.* **Weight:** *16.718 grams.*
Composition: *.900 gold, .100 copper (net weight: .48375 oz. pure gold).*
Diameter: *27 mm.* **Edge:** *1907–1911—46 raised stars; 1912–1933—48 raised stars.*
Mints: *Philadelphia, Denver, and San Francisco.*

No Motto (1907–1908), Circulation Strike

Mintmark location, 1908-D (No Motto), is on the reverse, at the tip of the branch.

Mintmark location, 1908 (With Motto)–1930, is on the reverse, to the left of the arrows.

With Motto (1908–1933), Circulation Strike

With Motto, Sandblast Finish Proof Strike

With Motto, Satin Finish Proof Strike

History. The Indian Head eagle, designed by sculptor Augustus Saint-Gaudens and championed by President Theodore Roosevelt, was struck from 1907 to 1916, and again in intermittent issues through the 1920s and early 1930s. Saint-Gaudens's original design proved impractical to strike and thus was modified slightly by Charles Barber before any large quantities were produced. Not long after (in July 1908), the motto IN GOD WE TRUST was added to the reverse, where it remained to the end of the series. These coins were widely used until 1918, in circulation in the American West and for export.

Striking and Sharpness. On the obverse, check the hair details and the vanes in the feathers. On the reverse, check the shoulder of the eagle. As well-struck coins are available for all varieties, avoid those that are weakly struck. Some examples may exhibit a pink-green color or rust-red "copper spots." Luster varies, but is often deeply frosty. On other coins, particularly from 1910 to 1916, it may be grainy.

Proofs. Sandblast (also called Matte) Proofs were made each year from 1907 through 1915. These have dull surfaces, much like fine-grained sandpaper. Satin (also called Roman Finish) Proofs were made in 1908, 1909, and 1910; they have satiny surfaces and are bright yellow.

Availability. Key rarities in this series are the rolled (or round) rim and wire rim 1907 coins, and the 1920-S, 1930-S, and 1933. Others are generally more readily available. MS-63 and higher coins are generally scarce to rare for the mintmarked issues. The Indian Head eagle is a very popular series. Most such coins in collectors' hands were exported in their time, then brought back to America after World War II. All of the Proofs are rare today.

Note: Values of common-date gold coins have been based on the current bullion price of gold, $3,746 per ounce, and may vary with the prevailing spot price.

Grading Standards

MS-62

MS-60 to 70 (Mint State). ***Obverse:*** At MS-60, some abrasion and contact marks are evident, most noticeably on the hair to the left of Liberty's forehead and in the left field. Luster is present, but may be dull or lifeless, and interrupted in patches. At MS-63, contact marks are few, and abrasion is very light. An MS-65 coin has hardly any abrasion, and contact marks are minute. Luster should be full and rich. Grades above MS-65 are defined by having fewer marks as perfection is approached. ***Reverse:*** Comments apply as for the obverse, except that abrasion and contact marks are most noticeable on the front of the left wing and in the left field.

Illustrated coin: This is a brilliant and lustrous example.

AU-58

AU-50, 53, 55, 58 (About Uncirculated). ***Obverse:*** Light wear is seen on the cheek, the hair to the right of the face, and the headdress, more so at AU-50 coin than at AU-53 or 55. An AU-58 coin has minimal traces of wear. An AU-50 coin has luster in protected areas among the stars and in the small field area to the right. At AU-58, most luster is present in the fields but is worn away on the highest parts of the Indian. ***Reverse:*** Comments as preceding, except that the eagle's left wing, left leg, neck, and leg show light wear. Luster ranges from perhaps 40 percent (at AU-50) to nearly full mint bloom (at AU-58).

Illustrated coin: With nearly full original luster, this coin has remarkable eye appeal.

EF-40

EF-40, 45 (Extremely Fine). ***Obverse:*** More wear is evident on the hair to the right of the face, and the feather vanes lack some details, although most are present. Luster, if present at all, is minimal. ***Reverse:*** Wear is greater than on the preceding. The front edge of the left wing is worn and blends into the top of the left leg. Some traces of luster may be seen, more so at EF-45 than at EF-40.

VF-20, 30 (Very Fine). ***Obverse:*** The Indian's forehead blends into the hair to the right. Feather-vane detail is gone except in the lower areas. ***Reverse:*** Wear is greater on the eagle, with only a few details remaining on the back of the left wing and the tail.

VF-25

PF-60 to 70 (Proof). ***Obverse and Reverse:*** At PF-60 to 63, there is light abrasion and some contact marks (the lower the grade, the higher the quantity). On Sandblast Proofs these show up as visually unappealing bright spots. At PF-64 and higher levels, marks are fewer, with magnification needed to see any at PF-65. At PF-66, there should be none at all.

PF-65

No Periods

Periods

Circulation Strikes

	Mintage	GSID	EF-40	AU-50	AU-58	MS-60	MS-63	MS-64	MS-65
Indian Head, No Motto on Reverse (1907–1908)	n/a	72391	$2,300	$2,300	$2,300	$2,400	$2,550	$4,500	$8,750
Indian Head, Motto on Reverse (1908–1933)	n/a	72392	2,300	2,300	2,300	2,350	2,400	2,500	3,450
Variety 1: No Motto on Reverse									
1907, Wire Rim, Periods	500	9744	21,500	33,500	43,000	45,500	60,000	72,000	97,000
	Auctions: $840,000, NGC MS-68 SBG 04/22								
1907, Rounded Rim, Periods (a)	50	9745	48,000	57,500	96,000	102,000	168,000	312,000	390,000
	Auctions: $660,000, PCGS MS-66 HA 08/24; $516,000, CAC MS-65 HA 08/24								
1907, No Motto	239,406	9746	2,300	2,300	2,300	2,400	2,550	4,500	8,750
	Auctions: $207,094, PCGS MS-68 SBG 08/13								
1908, No Motto	33,500	9747	2,300	2,300	2,400	2,500	6,000	9,500	18,000
	Auctions: $124,256, PCGS MS-67 SBG 08/13								
1908-D, No Motto	210,000	9759	2,300	2,300	2,400	2,550	7,500	13,000	45,500
	Auctions: $149,500, PCGS MS-66 HA 01/09								
Variety 2: Motto on Reverse									
1908, Motto	341,370	9748	2,300	2,300	2,350	2,400	2,850	3,750	8,500
	Auctions: $114,000, PCGS MS-68 SBG 08/25								
1908-D, Motto	836,500	9760	2,300	2,350	2,350	2,450	6,250	12,000	27,500
	Auctions: $230,000, PCGS MS-68 HA 04/06								

a. 31,500 were minted; all but 50 were melted at the mint.

Circulation Strikes *(continued)*

	Mintage	GSID	EF-40	AU-50	AU-58	MS-60	MS-63	MS-64	MS-65
1908-S	59,850	9761	$2,450	$2,500	$3,250	$5,250	$12,000	$15,500	$25,000
	Auctions: $240,000, NGC MS-69 SBG 11/23								
1909	184,789	9749	2,300	2,300	2,300	2,350	3,100	6,500	12,000
1909-D	121,540	9762	2,300	2,300	2,400	2,450	5,000	11,000	30,000
	Auctions: $138,000, PCGS MS-67 HA 11/05								
1909-S	292,350	9763	2,350	2,400	2,650	2,650	6,500	8,250	21,000
	Auctions: $146,875, PCGS MS-66 LGND 10/17								
1910	318,500	9750	2,300	2,300	2,300	2,350	2,500	2,600	7,750
1910-D	2,356,640	9764	2,300	2,300	2,300	2,350	2,650	2,800	6,500
1910-S	811,000	9765	2,300	2,300	2,400	2,500	7,500	13,000	60,000
	Auctions: $141,000, PCGS MS-66 LGND 10/17								
1911	505,500	9751	2,300	2,300	2,300	2,350	2,400	2,550	6,500
	Auctions: $110,450, NGC MS-68 SBG 08/13								
1911-D	30,100	9766	2,750	2,950	6,500	7,000	15,500	108,000	264,000
	Auctions: $195,500, PCGS MS-65 HA 01/07								
1911-S	51,000	9767	2,550	2,600	3,500	4,100	15,500	17,000	26,500
1912	405,000	9752	2,300	2,300	2,300	2,350	2,500	3,700	11,000
	Auctions: $138,000, PCGS MS-67 HA 04/06								
1912-S	300,000	9768	2,300	2,300	2,800	2,800	7,500	9,000	36,000
	Auctions: $115,000, PCGS MS-66 HA 11/05								
1913	442,000	9753	2,300	2,300	2,300	2,350	2,500	2,900	8,750
	Auctions: $126,500, PCGS MS-67 HA 04/06								
1913-S	66,000	9769	2,550	2,700	3,900	4,750	19,000	33,000	162,000
	Auctions: $299,000, PCGS MS-66 HA 01/09								
1914	151,000	9754	2,300	2,300	2,300	2,350	2,550	5,000	10,500
1914-D	343,500	9770	2,300	2,300	2,300	2,350	2,750	4,500	11,000
	Auctions: $135,125, PCGS MS-67 LGND 10/17								
1914-S	208,000	9771	2,350	2,350	2,500	2,550	6,500	11,000	35,000
	Auctions: $253,000, PCGS MS-66 ANR 06/06								
1915	351,000	9755	2,300	2,300	2,300	2,350	3,000	5,000	8,500
1915-S	59,000	9772	2,750	3,000	6,250	7,000	15,000	26,500	90,000
	Auctions: $126,500, PCGS MS-66 HA 01/09								
1916-S	138,500	9773	2,300	2,400	2,550	2,800	6,500	10,000	26,500
	Auctions: $131,159, PCGS MS-67 SBG 08/13								
1920-S	126,500	9774	43,000	49,000	72,000	96,000	162,000	240,000	432,000
	Auctions: $312,000, PCGS MS-64 HA 08/24; $1,725,000, PCGS MS-67 HA 08/24								
1926	1,014,000	9756	2,300	2,300	2,300	2,350	2,400	2,500	3,450
1930-S	96,000	9775	29,000	35,000	45,500	50,500	69,500	86,500	104,500
	Auctions: $132,000, PCGS MS-65 HA 08/25; $299,000, PCGS MS-67 HA 08/25								
1932	4,463,000	9757	2,300	2,300	2,300	2,350	2,400	2,500	3,450
1933 (b)	312,500	9758	—	162,000	174,000	210,000	288,000	432,000	600,000
	Auctions: $881,250, PCGS MS-66 GLDB 06/16								

b. Nearly all were melted at the mint.

Note: Gold spot price at time of publication, $3,746 per ounce.

Proof Strikes

	Mintage	GSID	PF-63	PF-65	PF-66
Indian Head, Motto on Reverse (1908–1933), Proof	**n/a**	**74153**	**$33,500**	**$84,000**	**$114,000**
Variety 2: Motto on Reverse					
1908	116	9776	36,000	91,000	126,000
	Auctions: $186,000, PCGS PF-67 SBG 08/25; $162,000, PCGS PF-67 HA 08/25				
1909	74	9777	36,000	91,000	126,000
	Auctions: $132,000, NGC PF-67 SBG 08/25				
1910	204	9778	36,000	91,000	126,000
	Auctions: $156,000, NGC PF-67 HA 05/24; $376,000, PCGS PF-67 LGND 05/24				
1911	95	9779	33,500	84,000	114,000
	Auctions: $126,000, NGC PF-67 SBG 08/25; $114,000, NGC PF-67 HA 08/25				
1912	83	9780	36,000	91,000	126,000
	Auctions: $126,000, PCGS PF-66 HA 01/24; $111,000, NGC PF-66 HA 01/24				
1913	71	9781	33,500	84,000	114,000
	Auctions: $138,000, NGC PF-67 HA 05/24; $120,000, NGC PF-67 SBG 05/24				
1914	50	9782	36,000	91,000	126,000
	Auctions: $138,000, PCGS PF-65 SBG 08/25; $132,000, NGC PF-67 HA 08/25				
1915	75	9783	38,500	108,000	132,000
	Auctions: $120,000, NGC PF-66 HA 05/24; $117,000, NGC PF-66 HA 05/24				

Gold Double Eagles ($20)
1850–1933

AN OVERVIEW OF GOLD DOUBLE EAGLES

Congress authorized the double eagle, or twenty-dollar coin—the largest denomination of all regular U.S. coinage issues—by the Act of March 3, 1849, in response to the huge amounts of gold coming from California.

Scan for additional information.

Double eagles are at once large and impressive to own. Many gold collectors form a type set of the six major double eagle designs (with the 1861 Paquet added as a sub-type if desired). Thanks to overseas hoards repatriated since the 1950s, finding choice and gem Mint State examples is no problem at all for the later types.

The first double eagle type, the Liberty Head of 1850 to 1866 without the motto IN GOD WE TRUST, is generally available in grades from VF up. Mint State pieces were elusive prior to the 1990s, but the market supply was augmented by more than 5,000 pieces—including some gems—found in the discovery of the long-lost treasure ship SS *Central America*. The SS *Brother Jonathan*, lost at sea in 1865, was recovered in the 1990s and yielded hundreds of Mint State 1865-S double eagles, along with some dated 1864 and a few earlier. The wreck of the SS *Republic*, lost in 1865 while on a voyage from New York City to New Orleans and salvaged in 2003, also yielded some very attractive Mint State double eagles of this first Liberty Head type.

The Liberty Head type from 1866 through 1876, with the motto IN GOD WE TRUST above the eagle and with the denomination expressed as TWENTY D., is the rarest in MS-63 and higher grades. Many EF and AU coins have been repatriated from overseas holdings, as have quite a few in such grades as MS-60 through 62. However, true gems are hardly ever seen.

Liberty Head double eagles of the 1877–1907 type with the IN GOD WE TRUST motto and with the denomination spelled out as TWENTY DOLLARS are exceedingly plentiful in just about any grade desired, with gems being readily available of certain issues of the early 20th century. While it is easy to obtain a gem of a common date, some collectors of type coins have opted to acquire a coin of special historical interest, such as a Carson City issue.

The famous Saint-Gaudens MCMVII High Relief double eagle of 1907 was saved in quantity by the general public as well as by numismatists, and today it is likely that at least 5,000 to 6,000 exist, representing about half of the mintage. Most of these are in varying degrees of Mint State, with quite a few graded as MS-64 and 65. Those in lower grades such as VF and EF often were used for jewelry or were polished, or have other problems. This particular design is a great favorite with collectors, and although the coins are not rarities, they are hardly inexpensive.

The so-called Arabic Numerals 1907–1908 Saint-Gaudens design is available in nearly any grade desired, with MS-60 through MS-63 or MS-64 pieces being plentiful and inexpensive. Double eagles of the final type, 1908–1933, are abundant in any grade desired, with choice and gem coins being plentiful.

For the Collector and Investor: Gold Double Eagles as a Specialty

Collecting double eagles by date and mint is more popular than one might think. Offhand, one might assume that these high denominations, laden with a number of rare dates, would attract few enthusiasts. However, over a long period of years more collectors have specialized in double eagles than have specialized in five-dollar or ten-dollar pieces.

Two particularly notable collections of double eagles by date and mint, from the earliest times to the latest, were formed by Louis E. Eliasberg of Baltimore, and Jeff Browning of Dallas. Both have been dispersed across the auction block. The first was cataloged by Bowers and Ruddy in 1982, and the second was offered by Stack's and Sotheby's in 2001. In addition, dozens of other collections over the years have had large numbers of double eagles, some specializing in the Liberty Head types of 1850–1907, others only with the Saint-Gaudens types from 1907 onward, and others addressing the entire range.

Among rarities in the double eagle series are the 1854-O and 1856-O, each known only to the extent of a few dozen pieces; the 1861 Philadelphia Mint coins with Paquet reverse (two known); the Proof-only issues of 1883, 1884, and 1887; several other low-mintage varieties of this era; the famous Carson City issue of 1870-CC; and various issues from 1920 onward, including 1920-S, 1921, mintmarked coins after 1923, and all dates after 1928. Punctuating these rarities is a number of readily available pieces, including the very common Philadelphia issues from 1922 through 1928 inclusive.

LIBERTY HEAD (1849–1907)

Designer: *James B. Longacre.* **Weight:** *33.436 grams.*
Composition: *.900 gold, .100 copper (net weight: .96750 oz. pure gold).* **Diameter** *34 mm.*
Edge: *Reeded.* **Mints:** *Philadelphia, Carson City, Denver, New Orleans, and San Francisco.*

Variety 1: No Motto Above Eagle (1849–1866), Circulation Strike

Variety 1: No Motto Above Eagle, Proof Strike

Variety 2: Motto Above Eagle, Value TWENTY D. (1866–1876), Circulation Strike

Variety 3: Motto Above Eagle, Value TWENTY D., Proof Strike

Variety 3: Motto Above Eagle, Value TWENTY DOLLARS (1866 1907), Circulation Strike

Variety 3: Motto Above Eagle, Value TWENTY DOLLARS, Proof Strike

Mintmark location is on the reverse, below the eagle.

History. The twenty-dollar denomination was introduced to circulation in 1850 (after a unique pattern, which currently resides in the Smithsonian's National Numismatic Collection, was minted in 1849). The large new coin was ideal for converting the flood of California gold rush bullion into federal legal tender. U.S. Mint chief engraver James B. Longacre designed the coin. A different reverse, designed by Anthony Paquet with taller letters than Longacre's design, was tested in 1861 but ultimately not used past that date. In 1866 the motto IN GOD WE TRUST was added to the reverse. In 1877 the denomination on the reverse, formerly given as TWENTY D., was changed to TWENTY DOLLARS. The double eagle denomination proved to be very popular, especially for export. By 1933, more than 75 percent of the American gold used to strike coins from the 1850s onward had been used to make double eagles. Oddly, some of the coins of 1850 to 1858 appear to have the word LIBERTY misspelled as LLBERTY.

Striking and Sharpness. On the obverse, check the star centers and the hair details. As made, the hair details are less distinct on many coins of 1859 (when a slight modification was made) through the 1890s, and knowledge of this is important. Later issues usually have exquisite detail. The reverse usually is well struck, but check the eagle and other features. The denticles are sharp on nearly all coins, but should be checked. Proofs were made in all years from 1858 to 1907, and a few were made before then. Proofs of 1902 onward, particularly 1903, have the portrait polished in the die, imparting a mirror finish across the design, and lack the cameo contrast of earlier dates.

Availability. Basic dates and mintmarks are available in proportion to their mintages. Key issues include the 1854-O, 1856-O, 1861 Paquet Reverse, 1861-S Paquet Reverse, 1866 No Motto, 1870-CC, 1879-O, and several Philadelphia Mint dates of the 1880s The vast majority of others are readily collectible. Among early coins, MS examples from about 1854 to 1857 are available, most notably the 1857-S and certain varieties of the 1860s. Most varieties of the 1880s onward, and particularly of the 1890s and 1900s, are easily available in MS, due to the repatriation of millions of coins that had been exported overseas. Proofs dated through the 1870s are all very rare today; those of the 1880s are less so; and those of the 1890s and 1900s are scarce. Many Proofs have been mishandled. Dates that are Proof-only (and those that are very rare in circulation-strike form) are in demand even if impaired. These include 1883, 1884, 1885, 1886, and 1887.

Note: Values of some gold coins have been based on a bullion price of gold of $3,746 per ounce, and may vary with the prevailing spot price.

Grading Standards

MS-60 to 70 (Mint State). ***Obverse:*** At MS-60, some abrasion and contact marks are evident, most noticeably on the hair to the right of Liberty's forehead and on the cheek. Luster is present, but may be dull or lifeless, and interrupted in patches. At MS-63, contact marks are few, and abrasion is light. An MS-65 coin has little abrasion, and contact marks are minute. Luster should be full and rich. Grades above MS-65 are defined by having fewer marks as perfection is approached. ***Reverse:*** Comments apply as for the obverse, except that abrasion and contact marks are most noticeable on eagle's neck, wingtips, and tail.

MS-64

AU-50, 53, 55, 58 (About Uncirculated). ***Obverse:*** Light wear is seen on the face, the hair to the right of the face, and the highest area of the hair behind the coronet, more so at AU-50 than at AU-53 or 55. An AU-58 coin has minimal traces of wear. An AU-50 coin has luster in protected areas among the stars and letters, with little in the open fields or on the portrait. At AU-58 most luster is present in the fields, but is worn away on the highest parts of the motifs. ***Reverse:*** Comments as preceding, except that the eagle and ornaments show wear in all of the higher areas. Luster ranges from perhaps 40 percent remaining in protected areas (at AU-50) to nearly full mint bloom (at AU-58). Often the reverse of this type retains more luster than the obverse.

AU-53

Illustrated coin: Much of the original luster still remains at this grade level, especially on the reverse.

EF-45

EF-40, 45 (Extremely Fine). ***Obverse:*** Wear is evident on all high areas of the portrait, including the hair to the right of the forehead, the tip of the coronet, and hair behind the coronet. The curl to the right of the neck is flat on its highest-relief area. Luster, if present at all, is minimal and in protected areas such as between the star points. ***Reverse:*** Wear is greater than on an About Uncirculated coin. The eagle's neck and wingtips show wear, as do the ornaments and rays. Some traces of luster may be seen, more so at EF-45 than at EF-40. Overall, the reverse appears to be in a slightly higher grade than the obverse.

VF-20

VF-20, 30 (Very Fine). ***Obverse:*** The higher-relief areas of hair are worn flat at VF-20, less so at VF-30. The hair to the right of the coronet is merged into heavy strands and is flat at the back, as is part of the bow. The curl to the right of the neck is flat. ***Reverse:*** The eagle shows further wear on the head, the tops of the wings, and the tail. The ornament has flat spots.

Illustrated coin: Note the small test cut or mark on the top rim.

PF-64

PF-60 to 70 (Proof). ***Obverse and Reverse:*** PF-60 to 62 coins have extensive hairlines and may have nicks and contact marks. At PF-63, hairlines are prominent, but the mirror surface is very reflective. PF-64 coins have fewer hairlines. At PF-65, hairlines should be relatively few. These large and heavy coins reveal hairlines more readily than do the lower denominations, mostly seen only under magnification. PF-66 and higher coins should have no marks or hairlines visible to the unaided eye.

Illustrated coin: A beautiful Proof, this is just a few hairlines away from a higher level.

1853, So-Called 3 Over 2
FS-301: Note rust under LIBERTY.

1854, Small Date

1854, Large Date

Circulation Strikes

	Mintage	GSID	VF-20	EF-40	AU-50	AU-58	MS-60	MS-63	MS-65
Liberty Head, No Motto Above Eagle (1849–1866)	**n/a**	**72393**	**$4,550**	**$4,600**	**$4,700**	**$4,800**	**$4,800**	**$8,500**	**$16,000**
Liberty Head, Motto Above Eagle, Value TWENTY D. (1866–1876)	**n/a**	**72394**	**4,500**	**4,550**	**4,550**	**4,650**	**4,650**	**6,500**	**180,000**
Liberty Head, Motto Above Eagle, Value TWENTY DOLLARS (1877–1907)	**n/a**	**73520**	**4,500**	**4,500**	**4,500**	**4,500**	**4,500**	**4,650**	**5,000**
Variety 1: No Motto Above Eagle									
1849 (Pattern; in Smithsonian Collection)	unique	9784	—	—	—	—	—	—	—
1850	1,170,261	9785	4,700	5,000	5,500	9,750	17,500	66,000	240,000
	Auctions: $199,750, PCGS MS-64 LGND 10/19								
1850-O	141,000	9843	5,500	8,000	12,000	43,000	60,000	—	—
	Auctions: $132,000, PCGS MS-61 HA 02/25								
1851	2,087,155	9786	4,550	4,650	4,700	5,000	6,000	30,000	192,000
	Auctions: $408,000, PCGS MS-65 HA 12/22								
1851-O	315,000	9844	4,700	5,000	5,500	16,500	25,000	114,000	—
1852	2,053,026	9787	4,550	4,600	4,850	5,000	5,500	31,000	216,000
	Auctions: $102,000, PCGS MS-64 HA 02/25; $288,000, PCGS MS-65 HA 02/25								
1852-O	190,000	9845	5,000	5,750	6,750	11,500	31,000	150,000	360,000
	Auctions: $102,000, NGC MS-63 SBG 02/25; $300,000, NGC MS-65 HA 02/25								
1853	1,261,326	9788	4,550	4,600	4,700	5,500	6,000	36,000	216,000
	Auctions: $152,750, NGC MS-65 HA 08/14								
1853, So-Called 3 Over 2 (a)	*	9846	4,550	4,700	4,950	8,750	11,000	—	—
↳1853, So-Called 3 Over 2, FS-301 (a)	*	351852	4,550	4,700	4,950	8,750	11,000	—	—
1853-O	71,000	9847	4,700	6,250	9,000	26,500	43,000	156,000	—
1854, Small Date	757,899	9789	4,550	4,600	4,700	4,900	5,500	38,500	114,000
1854, Large Date	*	9790	4,950	5,750	7,500	12,000	17,000	69,500	—
	Auctions: $102,000, NGC MS-64 HA 10/18								
1854-O	3,250	9848	150,000	240,000	360,000	540,000	—	—	—
	Auctions: $336,000, PCGS AU-53 HA 08/25; $312,000, PCGS EF-45 SBG 08/25								
1854-S	141,468	9849	5,750	10,500	12,500	23,000	29,000	60,000	150,000
	Auctions: $132,000, PCGS MS-65 SBG 03/20								
1855	364,666	9791	4,550	4,600	5,250	7,000	11,000	53,000	240,000
	Auctions: $126,500, PCGS MS-64 ANR 03/06								
1855-O	8,000	9853	15,000	29,000	48,000	84,000	120,000	—	—
	Auctions: $141,000, NGC MS-61 HA 01/14								
1855-S	879,675	9854	4,550	4,600	4,900	5,500	6,250	26,500	—
1856	329,878	9792	4,550	4,750	5,250	6,000	9,500	45,500	—
1856-O	2,250	9863	216,000	288,000	528,000	828,000	—	2,400,000	—
	Auctions: $690,000, PCGS AU-58 HA 02/25; $540,000, PCGS AU-53 HA 02/25								
1856-S	1,189,750	9864	4,550	4,600	4,700	5,000	5,750	17,000	41,000
1857	439,375	9793	4,550	4,600	4,700	5,000	5,250	43,000	—
1857-O	30,000	9883	6,500	9,000	15,000	29,000	84,000	240,000	—
	Auctions: $172,500, NGC MS-62 HA 01/11								

* Included in number above. **a.** Overlaid photographs indicate this is not a true overdate.

1861-S, Normal Reverse

1861-S, Paquet Reverse, Tall Letters

Circulation Strikes *(continued)*

	Mintage	GSID	VF-20	EF-40	AU-50	AU-58	MS-60	MS-63	MS-65
1857-S (b)	970,500	9884	$4,550	$4,600	$4,700	$4,800	$4,800	$8,500	$16,000
	Auctions: $168,000, NGC MS-67 HA 01/23								
1857-S, SS *Central America* Shipwreck Discovery (b)	*	9892	—	4,850	5,250	6,000	6,000	8,500	16,000
	Auctions: $198,000, NGC MS-67 HA 08/22								
1858	211,714	9794	4,700	5,000	5,250	6,500	10,500	48,000	—
1858-O	35,250	9893	8,500	12,000	15,000	41,000	60,000	216,000	—
	Auctions: $164,500, NGC MS-63 HA 01/15								
1858-S	846,710	9894	4,550	4,700	4,800	5,250	6,500	55,000	—
1859	43,597	9795	4,700	8,250	11,000	14,000	20,000	—	—
1859-O	9,100	9895	19,000	29,500	36,000	93,500	150,000	—	—
	Auctions: $150,000, PCGS MS-60 HA 04/21								
1859-S	636,445	9896	4,550	4,600	4,900	7,500	9,000	115,000	—
↳**1859-S, Doubled Die Obverse, FS-101**	*	347665	5,000	5,000	5,500	8,250	10,000	126,500	—
1860	577,611	9796	4,550	4,600	4,800	5,000	5,750	24,000	120,000
	Auctions: $141,000, PCGS MS-65 SBG 08/16								
1860-O	6,600	9897	19,000	31,000	43,000	101,000	144,000	—	—
	Auctions: $168,000, NGC MS-61 HA 07/18								
1860-S	544,950	9898	4,550	4,850	5,000	5,500	7,250	53,000	—
1861	2,976,453	9797	4,550	4,600	4,700	4,800	5,000	24,000	115,000
	Auctions: $414,188, PCGS MS-67 SBG 08/13								
1861, Paquet Reverse, Tall Letters	*	9798	—	—	—	—	1,800,000	—	—
	Auctions: $7,200,000, PCGS MS-67 HA 08/21								
1861-O	17,741	9899	24,000	33,000	48,000	108,000	270,000	—	—
	Auctions: $312,000, PCGS MS-60 HA 01/18								
1861-S	768,000	9900	4,550	5,000	5,250	6,250	11,000	60,000	—
1861-S, Paquet Reverse, Tall Letters	19,250	9901	42,000	81,500	108,000	288,000	—	—	—
	Auctions: $240,000, PCGS AU-58 SBG 11/24								
1862	92,133	9799	7,500	14,500	18,000	37,000	43,000	102,000	—
	Auctions: $174,000, NGC MS-63 HA 02/22								
1862-S	854,173	9902	4,550	4,950	5,250	6,500	11,000	72,000	—
1863	142,760	9800	5,750	8,250	12,000	23,000	31,000	108,000	—
1863-S	966,570	9903	4,550	5,000	5,250	6,000	7,000	30,000	—
1864	204,235	9801	4,750	7,000	10,000	21,500	29,000	78,000	240,000
	Auctions: $282,000, PCGS MS-65 HA 04/14								
1864-S	793,660	9904	4,550	4,600	4,800	6,750	8,000	48,000	156,000
	Auctions: $115,000, NGC MS-65 HA 01/12								
1865	351,175	9802	4,550	5,000	5,250	7,000	9,000	20,500	96,000
	Auctions: $105,750, PCGS MS-65 LGND 12/20								
1865-S	1,042,500	9905	4,550	4,850	5,250	5,500	6,250	15,000	39,500
1866-S	120,000	9906	12,000	19,000	29,000	86,500	168,000	—	—
	Auctions: $132,000, NGC MS-61 HA 02/25								

* Included in number above. **b.** Different size mintmark varieties exist; the Large S variety is rarest.

Note: Gold spot price at time of publication, $3,746 per ounce.

1866, With Motto, Doubled Die Reverse
FS-801

Open 3

Closed 3

Circulation Strikes *(continued)*

	Mintage	GSID	VF-20	EF-40	AU-50	AU-58	MS-60	MS-63	MS-65
Variety 2: Motto Above Eagle, Value TWENTY D.									
1866	698,745	9803	$4,550	$4,650	$4,800	$7,000	$8,750	$57,500	—
↳1866, Doubled Die Reverse, FS-801	*	351854	5,500	5,500	5,750	8,500	10,500	69,000	—
1866-S	842,250	9907	4,500	4,600	4,800	9,000	12,000	—	—
1867	251,015	9804	4,500	4,550	4,800	5,750	6,500	30,000	—
	Auctions: $258,500, NGC MS-66 HA 11/14								
1867-S	920,750	9908	4,500	4,550	4,700	5,250	9,500	78,000	—
	Auctions: $168,000, PCGS MS-64 SBG 04/22								
1868	98,575	9805	4,750	5,500	11,000	18,000	21,500	81,500	—
1868-S	837,500	9909	4,500	4,550	4,550	4,950	7,000	53,000	—
	Auctions: $120,000, PCGS MS-62 HA 01/19								
1869	175,130	9806	4,500	4,600	5,250	9,750	12,500	40,000	$180,000
	Auctions: $299,000, PCGS MS-65 HA 01/08								
1869-S	686,750	9910	4,500	4,550	4,600	4,750	7,000	36,000	—
1870	155,150	9807	4,500	4,900	5,500	9,500	10,500	51,500	—
1870-CC	3,789	9911	336,000	420,000	960,000	2,160,000	—	—	—
	Auctions: $1,440,000, PCGS AU-55 SBG 11/24; $840,000, PCGS AU-50 SBG 11/24								
1870-S	982,000	9912	4,500	4,550	4,550	4,800	5,500	60,000	—
1871	80,120	9808	4,600	5,250	5,500	9,500	12,000	48,000	—
1871-CC	17,387	9913	34,000	39,000	57,500	105,500	144,000	360,000	—
	Auctions: $108,000, PCGS AU-55 SBG 03/24; $414,000, NGC MS-64 HA 03/24								
1871-S	928,000	9914	4,500	4,550	4,550	4,650	6,000	21,000	216,000
	Auctions: $180,000, PCGS MS-64 HA 08/21								
1872	251,850	9809	4,500	4,550	4,550	5,250	5,500	29,000	—
1872-CC	26,900	9915	8,250	11,500	16,000	33,500	90,000	—	—
	Auctions: $102,000, PCGS MS-61 HA 02/25								
1872-S	780,000	9916	4,500	4,550	4,550	4,750	5,000	35,000	—
1873, Open 3	1,709,800	9811	4,500	4,550	4,550	4,650	4,650	6,500	180,000
	Auctions: $112,125, NGC MS-65 HA 01/11								
↳1873, Open 3, Doubled Die Obverse, FS-101	*	376707	5,000	5,000	5,000	5,000	5,000	7,250	—
1873, Closed 3	*	9810	4,500	4,550	4,550	5,750	7,500	48,000	—
1873-CC	22,410	9917	6,750	12,500	18,000	25,000	53,000	144,000	—
	Auctions: $138,000, PCGS MS-63 GLDB 09/07								
1873-S, Open 3	*	9919	4,500	4,550	4,550	4,900	5,500	—	—
1873-S, Closed 3	1,040,600	9918	4,500	4,550	4,550	4,650	4,900	20,500	—
1874	366,780	9812	4,500	4,550	4,550	5,250	5,500	21,500	—
1874-CC	115,085	9920	4,750	5,500	6,000	12,000	20,500	—	—
1874-S	1,214,000	9921	4,500	4,550	4,550	4,650	4,900	27,000	—
1875	295,720	9813	4,500	4,550	4,550	4,650	4,800	11,000	270,000
1875-CC	111,151	9922	4,750	5,250	5,500	8,250	10,000	36,000	—
1875-S	1,230,000	9923	4,500	4,550	4,550	4,650	4,650	9,750	180,000
	Auctions: $432,000, PCGS MS-67 SBG 03/20								
1876 (c)	583,860	9814	4,500	4,550	4,550	4,650	5,250	9,500	—

* Included in number above. **c.** A transitional Proof pattern also exists dated 1876 but of the type of 1877.

1888, Doubled Die Reverse
FS-801

Circulation Strikes *(continued)*

	Mintage	GSID	VF-20	EF-40	AU-50	AU-58	MS-60	MS-63	MS-65
1876-CC	138,441	9924	$4,900	$5,250	$5,500	$8,500	$12,000	$53,000	—
1876-S	1,597,000	9925	4,500	4,550	4,550	4,650	4,650	6,500	$180,000
	Auctions: $207,000, PCGS MS-65 HA 01/10								
Variety 3: Motto Above Eagle, Value TWENTY DOLLARS									
1877	397,650	9815	4,500	4,500	4,500	4,500	4,500	12,000	—
1877-CC	42,565	9926	4,850	6,250	9,250	19,500	27,000	—	—
	Auctions: $144,000, PCGS MS-62 HA 11/21								
1877-S	1,735,000	9927	4,500	4,500	4,500	4,500	4,550	12,000	69,000
1878	543,625	9816	4,500	4,500	4,500	4,500	4,550	11,000	—
1878-CC	13,180	9928	8,750	15,000	19,000	36,000	81,500	—	—
	Auctions: $120,000, PCGS MS-61 SBG 04/22								
1878-S	1,739,000	9929	4,500	4,500	4,500	4,500	4,500	13,000	—
1879	207,600	9817	4,500	4,500	4,500	4,650	4,850	24,000	96,000
↳1879, Doubled Die Reverse, FS-801	*	351857	4,500	4,500	4,500	4,650	4,850	24,000	96,000
1879-CC	10,708	9930	11,000	15,500	19,000	31,000	54,000	—	—
	Auctions: $102,000, PCGS MS-62 SBG 08/24								
1879-O	2,325	9931	48,000	62,000	86,500	138,000	153,500	300,000	—
	Auctions: $120,000, NGC MS-61 SBG 02/25								
1879-S	1,223,800	9932	4,500	4,500	4,500	4,500	4,600	31,000	—
1880	51,420	9818	4,500	4,500	4,750	5,500	11,000	36,000	—
1880-S	836,000	9933	4,500	4,500	4,500	4,500	4,900	17,000	108,000
	Auctions: $132,000, PCGS MS-65 HA 08/24								
1881	2,199	9819	29,000	39,500	62,500	101,000	115,000	—	—
	Auctions: $152,750, PCGS MS-61 HA 04/14								
1881-S	727,000	9934	4,500	4,500	4,500	4,500	4,600	19,000	—
1882	571	9820	48,000	89,000	114,000	132,000	156,000	—	—
	Auctions: $138,000, NGC AU-58 HA 03/24; $111,000, PCGS AU-58 SBG 03/24								
1882-CC	39,140	9935	4,950	5,500	7,250	11,000	12,000	114,000	
	Auctions: $156,000, PCGS MS-63 HA 06/21								
1882-S	1,125,000	9936	4,500	4,500	4,500	4,500	4,550	11,000	—
1883-CC	59,962	9937	4,850	5,250	6,250	9,000	11,000	57,500	—
1883-S	1,189,000	9938	4,500	4,500	4,500	4,500	4,600	7,250	—
1884-CC	81,139	9939	4,700	5,000	5,500	8,250	9,750	45,500	—
	Auctions: $120,000, PCGS MS-63 SBG 04/22								
1884-S	916,000	9940	4,500	4,500	4,500	4,500	4,750	5,500	48,000
1885	751	9821	21,500	33,500	53,000	69,500	77,000	156,000	—
	Auctions: $102,000, PCGS MS-61 HA 08/25								
1885-CC	9,450	9941	8,750	17,000	21,000	26,500	32,500	168,000	—
	Auctions: $264,000, PCGS MS-63 SBG 04/22								
1885-S	683,500	9942	4,500	4,500	4,500	4,500	4,500	5,500	53,000
1886	1,000	9822	42,000	78,000	96,000	150,000	168,000	222,000	—
	Auctions: $132,000, PCGS AU-55 SBG 04/22								
1887-S	283,000	9943	4,500	4,500	4,500	4,500	4,550	9,250	42,000
1888	226,161	9823	4,500	4,500	4,500	4,500	4,550	12,000	31,000
↳1888, Doubled Die Reverse, FS-801	*	226347	4,750	4,750	4,750	4,750	4,800	12,500	33,000

* Included in number above.

Circulation Strikes *(continued)*

	Mintage	GSID	VF-20	EF-40	AU-50	AU-58	MS-60	MS-63	MS-65
1888-S	859,600	9944	$4,500	$4,500	$4,500	$4,500	$4,500	$5,500	$33,500
1889	44,070	9824	4,500	4,500	4,500	4,550	4,650	18,500	—
1889-CC	30,945	9945	4,850	5,500	7,750	11,000	12,000	60,000	—
1889-S	774,700	9946	4,500	4,500	4,500	4,500	4,500	4,700	29,000
1890	75,940	9825	4,500	4,500	4,500	4,500	4,600	10,000	45,500
1890-CC	91,209	9947	4,950	5,250	5,750	6,250	9,500	45,500	—
1890-S	802,750	9948	4,500	4,500	4,500	4,500	4,500	6,500	30,000
1891	1,390	9826	27,000	36,000	48,000	66,000	72,000	162,000	—
	Auctions: $155,250, NGC MS-64 HA 01/05								
1891-CC	5,000	9949	17,000	25,000	30,000	34,000	36,000	180,000	—
	Auctions: $156,000, PCGS MS-62 HA 08/22								
1891-S	1,288,125	9950	4,500	4,500	4,500	4,500	4,500	4,750	33,000
↳1891-S, S Over S, FS-501	*	226348	4,500	4,500	4,500	4,500	4,550	4,750	33,000
1892	4,430	9827	6,750	9,250	11,500	13,000	18,500	43,000	74,500
1892-CC	27,265	9951	5,000	5,750	6,000	11,000	11,500	48,000	—
1892-S	930,150	9952	4,500	4,500	4,500	4,500	4,500	4,800	27,500
1893	344,280	9828	4,500	4,500	4,500	4,500	4,500	4,900	24,000
1893-CC	18,402	9953	5,250	6,750	8,250	12,000	12,500	42,000	—
1893-S	996,175	9954	4,500	4,500	4,500	4,500	4,500	4,900	36,000
1894	1,368,940	9829	4,500	4,500	4,500	4,500	4,500	4,900	25,000
1894-S	1,048,550	9955	4,500	4,500	4,500	4,500	4,500	4,750	31,000
1895	1,114,605	9830	4,500	4,500	4,500	4,500	4,500	4,900	21,500
1895-S	1,143,500	9956	4,500	4,500	4,500	4,500	4,500	4,750	14,500
1896	792,535	9831	4,500	4,500	4,500	4,500	4,500	4,700	18,500
1896-S	1,403,925	9957	4,500	4,500	4,500	4,500	4,500	4,800	30,000
1897	1,383,175	9832	4,500	4,500	4,500	4,500	4,500	4,950	21,500
1897-S	1,470,250	9958	4,500	4,500	4,500	4,500	4,500	4,700	16,000
1898	170,395	9833	4,500	4,500	4,500	4,500	4,950	5,500	—
1898-S	2,575,175	9959	4,500	4,500	4,500	4,500	4,500	4,750	8,000
1899	1,669,300	9834	4,500	4,500	4,500	4,500	4,500	4,650	8,000
1899-S	2,010,300	9960	4,500	4,500	4,500	4,500	4,500	4,850	24,000
1900	1,874,460	9835	4,500	4,500	4,500	4,500	4,500	4,650	5,500
1900-S	2,459,500	9961	4,500	4,500	4,500	4,500	4,500	4,750	26,500
1901	111,430	9836	4,500	4,500	4,500	4,500	4,500	4,650	5,500
1901-S	1,596,000	9962	4,500	4,500	4,500	4,500	4,500	4,950	21,500
1902	31,140	9837	4,500	4,500	4,500	4,700	4,700	14,500	78,000
1902-S	1,753,625	9963	4,500	4,500	4,500	4,500	4,500	5,000	31,000
1903	287,270	9838	4,500	4,500	4,500	4,500	4,500	4,750	5,500
1903-S	954,000	9964	4,500	4,500	4,500	4,500	4,500	5,000	14,000
1904	6,256,699	9839	4,500	4,500	4,500	4,500	4,500	4,650	5,000
	Auctions: $138,000, PCGS MS-67 SBG 06/22								
1904-S	5,134,175	9965	4,500	4,500	4,500	4,500	4,500	4,650	5,750
1905	58,919	9840	4,500	4,500	4,500	4,600	4,650	11,500	99,000
1905-S	1,813,000	9966	4,500	4,500	4,500	4,500	4,500	4,800	19,000
1906	69,596	9841	4,500	4,500	4,500	4,550	4,600	9,000	31,000
1906-D	620,250	9967	4,500	4,500	4,500	4,500	4,500	5,250	21,000
	Auctions: $172,500, PCGS MS-66 SBG 10/07								
1906-S	2,065,750	9968	4,500	4,500	4,500	4,500	4,500	5,000	19,000
	Auctions: $111,625, PCGS MS-66 SBG 06/14								
1907, Liberty Head	1,451,786	9842	4,500	4,500	4,500	4,500	4,500	4,700	15,500
1907-D	842,250	9969	4,500	4,500	4,500	4,500	4,500	4,900	9,500
1907-S	2,165,800	9970	4,500	4,500	4,500	4,500	4,500	4,750	20,500

* Included in number above.

Proof Strikes

	Mintage	GSID	PF-60	PF-63	PF-65
Liberty Head, No Motto Above Eagle (1849–1866), Proof	n/a	74158	$144,000	$264,000	$660,000
Liberty Head, Motto Above Eagle, Value TWENTY D. (1866–1876), Proof	n/a	74161	54,000	132,000	330,000
Same, Proof Cameo	n/a	74162	65,000	158,500	363,000
Same, Proof Deep Cameo	n/a	74163	—	174,000	399,500
Liberty Head, Motto Above Eagle, Value TWENTY DOLLARS (1877–1907), Proof	n/a	74164	24,000	51,500	168,000
Same, Proof Cameo	n/a	79402	26,500	60,000	192,000
Same, Proof Deep Cameo	n/a	74166	41,000	84,000	288,000
Variety 1: No Motto Above Eagle					
1850	unknown	9971	—	—	—
1854	unknown	9974	—	—	—
1856	unknown	9977	—	—	—
1856-O, Specimen	unique	376442	—	—	—
1857	unknown	9980	—	—	—
1858	unknown	9983	—	—	—
1859	80	9984	180,000	270,000	660,000
1860	59	9987	144,000	264,000	660,000
	Auctions: $230,000, NGC PF-64 HA 01/11				
1861	66	9990	240,000	360,000	840,000
1862	35	9993	158,500	290,500	726,000
1863	30	9996	144,000	264,000	660,000
	Auctions: $480,000, NGC PF-65 HA 01/25				
1864	50	9999	144,000	264,000	660,000
	Auctions: $161,000, PCGS PF-64 HA 01/05				
1865	25	10002	144,000	264,000	660,000
Variety 2: Motto Above Eagle, Value TWENTY D.					
1866	30	10005	60,000	146,500	528,000
1867	50	10008	54,000	132,000	330,000
1868	25	10011	54,000	132,000	330,000
1869	25	10014	54,000	132,000	330,000
1870	35	10017	54,000	132,000	330,000
	Auctions: $117,500, PCGS PF-63 HA 01/14				
1871	30	10020	54,000	132,000	330,000
1872	30	10023	54,000	132,000	330,000
	Auctions: $143,750, PCGS PF-66 SBG 06/02				
1873, Closed 3	25	10026	54,000	132,000	330,000
1874	20	10029	54,000	132,000	330,000
	Auctions: $103,500, NGC PF-64 HA 08/04				
1875	20	10032	90,000	174,000	390,000
	Auctions: $166,750, Uncert PF-64 SBG 03/05				
1876 (a)	45	10035	54,000	132,000	330,000
	Auctions: $117,500, PCGS PF-64 HA 08/12				
1875	20	10032	90,000	174,000	390,000

a. This transitional Proof pattern is dated 1876, but is of the type of 1877.

	Mintage	GSID	PF-60	PF-63	PF-65
Variety 3: Motto Above Eagle, Value TWENTY DOLLARS					
1877	20	10038	$31,000	$66,000	$192,000
1878	20	10041	31,000	66,000	192,000
1879	30	10044	31,000	66,000	192,000
1880	36	10047	50,500	90,000	240,000
1881	61	10050	43,000	77,000	168,000
1882	59	10053	45,500	102,000	330,000
	Auctions: $195,500, Uncert PF-65 SBG 01/08				
1883	92	10056	42,000	90,000	252,000
1884	71	10059	84,000	144,000	288,000
	Auctions: $207,000, PCGS PF-64 HA 10/08				
1885	77	10062	31,000	66,000	192,000
	Auctions: $103,500, NGC PF-66 HA 08/98				
1886	106	10065	31,000	66,000	192,000
1887	121	10068	96,000	134,500	180,000
	Auctions: $258,500, NGC PF-66 HA 01/14				
1888	105	10071	26,500	57,000	198,000
1889	41	10074	31,000	66,000	192,000
	Auctions: $352,500, PCGS PF-65 HA 01/14				
1890	55	10077	31,000	66,000	192,000
1891	52	10080	31,000	66,000	192,000
	Auctions: $161,000, PCGS PF-66 HA 10/06				
1892	93	10083	31,000	66,000	192,000
	Auctions: $132,000, PCGS PF-65 HA 01/18				
1893	59	10086	60,000	120,000	252,000
1894	50	10089	24,000	51,500	168,000
1895	51	10092	31,000	66,000	192,000
1896	128	10095	31,000	66,000	192,000
	Auctions: $126,500, PCGS PF-65 HA 01/10				
1897	86	10098	24,000	51,500	168,000
1898	75	10101	24,000	51,500	168,000
1899	84	10104	24,000	51,500	168,000
	Auctions: $109,250, Uncert F-12 SBG 03/05				
1900	124	10107	24,000	51,500	168,000
1901	96	10110	24,000	51,500	168,000
	Auctions: $115,000, Uncert PF-64 SBG 03/05				
1902	114	10113	27,000	55,000	180,000
	Auctions: $180,000, NGC PF-65 SBG 08/25				
1903	158	10116	24,000	51,500	168,000
1904	98	10119	24,000	51,500	168,000
1905	92	10122	24,000	51,500	180,000
	Auctions: $103,500, PCGS PF-65 ANR 03/06				
1906	94	10125	24,000	51,500	168,000
	Auctions: $264,000, NGC PF-66 HA 01/24; $174,000, PCGS PF-65 HA 01/24				
1906-D, Specimen	6	376443	—	—	—
	Auctions: $440,625, PCGS MS-66 HA 04/13				
1907	78	10128	24,000	51,500	168,000
	Auctions: $188,000, NGC PF-62 HA 01/13				
1907-D, Branch Mint Proof	3 known	213688	—	150,000	240,000
	Auctions: $432,000, PCGS PF-62 SBG 11/23				

SAINT-GAUDENS, HIGH RELIEF AND ULTRA HIGH RELIEF, MCMVII (1907)

Designer: *Augustus Saint-Gaudens.* **Weight:** *33.436 grams.*
Composition: *.900 gold, .100 copper (net weight: .96750 oz. pure gold).*
Diameter *34 mm.* **Edge:** *E PLURIBUS UNUM with words divided by stars (one specimen of the high-relief variety with plain edge is known).* **Mint:** *Philadelphia.*

Circulation Strike

Ultra High Relief Pattern, Proof Strike

History. Created by famous artist Augustus Saint-Gaudens under a commission arranged by President Theodore Roosevelt, this double eagle was first made (in pattern form) with ultra high relief, sculptural in its effect, on both sides and the date in Roman numerals. The story of its production is well known and has been described in several books, notably *Renaissance of American Coinage, 1905–1908* (Burdette) and *Striking Change: The Great Artistic Collaboration of Theodore Roosevelt and August Saint-Gaudens* (Moran). After the Ultra High Relief patterns of 1907, a modified High Relief version was developed to facilitate production. Each coin required three blows of the press to strike up properly. Most featured a flat rim (now known as the Flat Rim variety), but planchet metal would occasionally be squeezed up between the collar and the die, resulting in the Wire Rim variety; this can exist around part of or the entire circumference of the coin. The coins were made on a medal press in December 1907 and January 1908, to the extent of fewer than 13,000 pieces. In the meantime, production was under way for low-relief coins, easier to mint in quantities sufficient for commerce—these dated 1907 rather than MCMVII. Today the MCMVII double eagle is a favorite among collectors, and when surveys are taken of beautiful and popular designs (as in *100 Greatest U.S. Coins*, by Garrett and Guth), it always ranks near the top.

Striking and Sharpness. The striking usually is good. Check the left knee of Liberty, which sometimes shows lightness of strike and, most often, shows flatness or wear (sometimes concealed by post-mint etching or clever tooling). Check the Capitol at the lower left. On the reverse, check the high points at the top of the eagle. The surface on all is a delicate matte texture, grainy rather than deeply frosty. Under examination the fields show myriad tiny raised curlicues and other die-finish marks. There is no record of any MCMVII double eagles being made as *Proofs*, nor is there any early numismatic record of any being sold as Proofs. Walter Breen in the 1960s made up some guidelines for Proofs, which some graders have adopted. Some homemade "Proofs" have been made by pickling or sandblasting the surface of regular coins—*caveat emptor.*

Availability. Half or more of the original mintage still exist today, as many were saved, and these grade mostly from AU-50 to MS-62. Circulated examples often have been cleaned, polished, or used in jewelry. Higher-grade coins are seen with some frequency, up to MS-65. Overgrading is common.

Grading Standards

MS-60 to 70 (Mint State). ***Obverse:*** At MS-60, some abrasion and contact marks are seen on Liberty's chest. The left knee is flat on lower Mint State coins and all circulated coins. Scattered marks and abrasion are in the field. Satiny luster is present, but may be dull or lifeless, and interrupted in patches. Many coins at this level have been cleaned. At MS-63, contact marks are fewer, and abrasion is light, but the knee still has a flat spot. An MS-65 coin has little abrasion and few marks. Grades above MS-65 are defined by having fewer marks as perfection is approached. ***Reverse:*** Comments apply as for the obverse, except that abrasion and contact marks are most noticeable on the side of the eagle's body and the top of the left wing.

Illustrated coin: This is a splendid choice striking.

MS-63

AU-50, 53, 55, 58 (About Uncirculated). ***Obverse:*** Light wear is seen on the chest, the left leg, and the field, more so at AU-50 than at AU-53 or 55. An AU-58 coin has fewer traces of wear. An AU-50 coin has satiny luster in protected areas among the rays, with little in the open field above. At AU-58, most luster is present. ***Reverse:*** Comments as preceding, except that the side of the eagle below the front of the wing, the top of the wing, and the field show light wear. Satiny luster ranges from perhaps 40 percent (at AU-50) to nearly full mint bloom (at AU-58).

AU-55

EF-40, 45 (Extremely Fine). ***Obverse:*** Wear is seen on all the higher-relief areas of the standing figure and on the rock at the lower right. Luster is minimal, if present at all. Eye appeal is apt to be lacking. Nearly all Extremely Fine coins have been cleaned. ***Reverse:*** The eagle shows more wear overall, especially at the bottom and on the tops of the wings.

EF-45

VF-20, 30 (Very Fine). ***Obverse:*** Most details of the standing figure are flat, her face is incomplete, and the tips of the rays are weak. Eye appeal is usually poor. As these coins did not circulate to any extent, a Very Fine coin was likely carried as a pocket piece. ***Reverse:*** Wear is greater overall, but most evident on the eagle. Detail is good at the center of the left wing, but worn away in most other areas of the bird.

VF-30

Circulation Strikes

	Mintage	GSID	AU-50	AU-58	MS-60	MS-63	MS-64	MS-65	MS-66
Saint-Gaudens, No Motto on Reverse, High Relief, Roman Numerals (1907)	**n/a**	**72395**	**$12,500**	**$16,000**	**$18,000**	**$29,000**	**$40,000**	**$60,000**	**$108,000**
1907, Roman Numerals, Wire Edge	12,367	10131	12,500	16,000	18,000	29,000	40,000	60,000	108,000
	Auctions: $324,000, PCGS MS-67 HA 01/25; $312,000, PCGS MS-67 SBG 01/25								
1907, Roman Numerals, Flat Edge	*	10133	12,500	16,000	18,000	29,500	41,500	60,000	108,000
	Auctions: $384,000, PCGS MS-67 SBG 08/25; $108,000, NGC MS-66 SBG 08/25								

* Included in number above.

Proof Strikes

		GSID	PF-60	PF-63	PF-65
Saint-Gaudens, No Motto on Reverse, High Relief, Roman Numerals (1907), Proof	**n/a**	**68926**	**$57,500**	**$108,000**	**$180,000**
1907, High Relief, Small Edge Letters	3 known	10200	—	—	—
	Auctions: $1,680,000, PCGS PF-68 HA 01/23				
1907, High Relief, Large Edge Letters	unique	194815	—	—	—
1907, Ultra High Relief, Pattern, Plain Edge	unique	10156	—	—	—
1907, Ultra High Relief, Pattern, Lettered Edge	17 known	10157	—	—	2,700,000
	Auctions: $4,320,000, PCGS PF-69 HA 08/23				
1907, Ultra High Relief, Pattern, Inverted Edge Letters	2 known	194806	—	—	2,700,000
	Auctions: $264,000, NGC PF-67 HA 01/25; $660,000, NGC PF-69 HA 01/25				
1907, High Relief, Roman Numerals		10199	57,500	108,000	180,000
	Auctions: $870,000, PCGS MS-68 HA 01/23				

SAINT-GAUDENS, FLAT RELIEF, ARABIC NUMERALS (1907–1933)

Designer: *Augustus Saint-Gaudens.* **Weight:** *33.436 grams.*
Composition: *.900 gold, .100 copper (net weight: .96750 oz. pure gold).*
Diameter: *34 mm.* **Edge:** *E PLURIBUS UNUM with words divided by stars.*
Mints: *Philadelphia, Denver, and San Francisco.*

No Motto on Reverse (1907–1908), Circulation Strike

Mintmark location is on the obverse, above the date.

With Motto on Reverse (1908–1933), Circulation Strike

With Motto on Reverse, Proof Strike

History. In autumn 1907 U.S. Mint chief engraver Charles E. Barber modified Augustus Saint-Gaudens's design by lowering its relief and substituting Arabic (not Roman) numerals. Coins of this type were struck in large quantities from 1907 to 1916 and again from 1920 to 1933. In July 1908 the motto IN GOD WE TRUST was added to the reverse. Coins dated 1907 to 1911 have 46 stars on the obverse; coins of 1912 to 1933 have 48 stars. Sandblast (also called Matte) Proofs were made in 1908 and from 1911 to 1915; Satin (also called Roman Finish) Proofs were made in 1909 and 1910.

The vast majority of these coins were exported. Since World War II millions have been repatriated, supplying most of those in numismatic hands today.

Striking and Sharpness. The details are often light on the obverse. Check the bosom of Liberty, the covering of which tends to be weak on 1907 and, especially, 1908 No Motto coins. Check the Capitol building and its immediate area at the lower left. The reverse usually is well struck, but check the feathers on the eagle and the top of the wings. The Matte Proofs have dull surfaces, much like fine-grained sandpaper, while the Satin Proofs have satiny surfaces and are bright yellow.

Availability. Most dates and mintmarks range from very common to slightly scarce, punctuated with scarce to very rare issues such as 1908-S, 1920-S, 1921, mintmarked coins from 1924 to 1927, and all issues of 1929 to 1933. From their initial mintages, most of the double eagles of the 1920s were returned to the Mint and melted in the 1930s. Some, however, were unofficially saved by Treasury employees.

Estimates of the quantities saved range from a few dozen to several hundred thousand, depending on the date; this explains the high values for coins that, judged only by their initial mintages, should otherwise be more common. Probably a million or more MS coins exist of certain dates, most notably 1908 No Motto, 1924, 1925, 1926, and 1928 (especially common). Quality varies, as many have contact marks. Philadelphia Mint coins from 1922 onward usually are seen with excellent eye appeal. Common varieties are not usually collected in grades below MS. All of the Proofs are rare today.

Note: Values of some gold coins have been based on a bullion price of gold of $3,746 per ounce, and may vary with the prevailing spot price.

Grading Standards

MS-60 to 70 (Mint State). ***Obverse:*** At MS-60, some abrasion and contact marks are seen on Liberty's chest and left knee, and scattered marks and abrasion are in the field. Luster is present, but may be dull or lifeless, and interrupted in patches. At MS-63, contact marks are fewer, and abrasion is light. An MS-65 coin has little abrasion and few marks, although quality among certified coins can vary. On a conservatively graded coin the luster should be full and rich. Grades above MS-65 are defined by having fewer marks as perfection is approached. Generally, Mint State coins of 1922 onward are choicer and more attractive than the earlier issues. ***Reverse:*** Comments apply as for the obverse, except that abrasion and contact marks are most noticeable on the eagle's left wing.

MS-65

AU-50, 53, 55, 58 (About Uncirculated). ***Obverse:*** Light wear is seen on the chest, the left knee, the midriff, and across the field, more so at AU-50 than at AU-53 or 55. An AU-58 coin has minimal traces of wear. An AU-50 coin has luster in protected areas among the rays, with little in the open field above. At AU-58, most luster is present. ***Reverse:*** Comments as preceding, except that the side of the eagle below the front of the wing, the top of the wing, and the field show light wear. Luster ranges from perhaps 40 percent (at AU-50) to nearly full mint bloom (at AU-58).

AU-50

EF-40, 45 (Extremely Fine). ***Obverse:*** Wear is seen on all the higher-relief areas of the standing figure and on the rock at the lower right. Luster is minimal, if present at all. Eye appeal is apt to be lacking. ***Reverse:*** The eagle shows more wear overall, especially at the bottom and on the tops of the wings.

EF-40

VF-20, 30 (Very Fine). ***Obverse:*** Most details of the standing figure are flat, her face is incomplete, and the tips of the rays are weak. Eye appeal is usually poor. ***Reverse:*** Wear is greater overall, but most evident on the eagle. Detail is good at the center of the left wing, but worn away in most other areas of the bird.

VF-20

PF-60 to 70 (Proof). ***Obverse and Reverse:*** At PF-60 to 63, there is light abrasion and some contact marks (the lower the grade, the higher the quantity). On Sandblast Proofs these show up as visually unappealing bright spots. At PF-64 and higher levels, marks are fewer, with magnification needed to see any at PF-65. At PF-66, there should be none at all.

PF-66

1909, 9 Over 8

Circulation Strikes

	Mintage	GSID	AU-50	AU-58	MS-60	MS-63	MS-64	MS-65	MS-66
Saint-Gaudens, No Motto on Reverse, Normal Relief, Arabic Numerals (1907–1908)	**n/a**	**72396**	**$4,500**	**$4,500**	**$4,500**	**$4,650**	**$4,650**	**$4,650**	**$5,000**
Saint-Gaudens, With Motto on Reverse (1908–1933)	**n/a**	**72397**	**4,500**	**4,500**	**4,550**	**4,650**	**4,650**	**4,700**	**5,000**
1907, Arabic Numerals, No Motto	361,667	10132	4,500	4,500	4,700	4,950	5,000	5,500	10,000
	Auctions: $276,000, PCGS MS-67 HA 05/22								
1908, No Motto	4,271,551	10134	4,500	4,500	4,500	4,650	4,650	4,650	5,000
1908-D, No Motto	663,750	10159	4,500	4,500	4,500	4,900	5,000	9,000	43,000
	Auctions: $168,000, PCGS MS-66 HA 08/22								
1908, With Motto	156,258	10135	4,500	4,500	4,550	5,500	6,000	13,000	49,000
	Auctions: $168,000, PCGS MS-67 HA 01/23								
1908-D, With Motto	349,500	10160	4,500	4,500	4,550	5,000	5,500	8,000	26,000
	Auctions: $132,000, PCGS MS-67 HA 08/22								
1908-S	22,000	10161	6,000	8,500	10,500	36,000	48,000	84,000	132,000
	Auctions: $336,000, PCGS MS-67 HA 06/24; $312,000, PCGS MS-67 HA 06/24								
1909	161,282	10136	4,500	4,500	4,550	5,750	10,000	43,000	126,000
	Auctions: $312,000, PCGS MS-66 HA 05/22								
1909, 9 Over 8	*	10162	4,650	4,700	4,700	6,500	11,500	45,500	133,000
	Auctions: $108,000, PCGS MS-66 SBG 03/20								
↳1909, 9 Over 8, FS-301	*	374011	4,650	4,700	4,700	6,500	11,500	45,500	133,000
	Auctions: $111,000, PCGS MS-66 HA 08/25; $336,000, PCGS MS-66 HA 08/25								

Note: Most of the double eagles of the 1920s were returned to the Mint and melted in the 1930s. Some, however, were unofficially saved by Treasury employees. Estimates of the quantities saved range from a few dozen to several hundred thousand, depending on the date. This explains the high values for coins that, judged only by their initial mintages, should otherwise be more common.
* Included in number above.

1924, Doubled Die Obverse
FS-101

Circulation Strikes *(continued)*

	Mintage	GSID	AU-50	AU-58	MS-60	MS-63	MS-64	MS-65	MS-66
1910	482,000	10137	$4,500	$4,500	$4,550	$4,750	$4,900	$10,500	$53,000
1910-D	429,000	10165	4,500	4,500	4,550	4,650	4,900	5,000	12,000
1910-S	2,128,250	10166	4,500	4,500	4,550	4,750	4,950	10,000	39,500
1911	197,250	10138	4,500	4,500	4,550	4,950	5,000	16,000	43,000
	Auctions: $432,000, PCGS MS-67 HA 01/23								
1911-D	846,500	10167	4,500	4,500	4,550	4,750	4,850	4,950	5,750
1911-D, D Over D	*	70975	4,550	4,550	4,600	4,850	5,000	5,250	6,250
↳1911-D, D Over D, FS-501	*	393347	4,550	4,550	4,600	4,850	5,000	5,250	6,250
1911-S	775,750	10168	4,500	4,500	4,550	4,650	4,800	5,000	18,000
1912	149,750	10139	4,500	4,500	4,550	4,900	7,750	26,000	72,000
	Auctions: $114,000, PCGS MS-66 HA 08/25								
1913	168,780	10140	4,500	4,500	4,550	5,000	7,500	51,500	132,000
	Auctions: $192,000, PCGS MS-65 HA 08/22								
1913-D	393,500	10169	4,500	4,500	4,550	4,800	4,850	6,500	42,000
1913-S	34,000	10170	4,550	5,000	5,000	7,000	10,500	43,000	192,000
	Auctions: $149,500, PCGS MS-66 HA 11/05								
1914	95,250	10141	4,500	4,500	4,800	5,000	6,000	26,000	114,000
	Auctions: $132,000, PCGS MS-66 HA 08/22								
1914-D	453,000	10171	4,500	4,500	4,550	4,650	4,700	5,000	11,000
	Auctions: $204,000, PCGS MS-67 HA 01/23								
1914-S	1,498,000	10172	4,500	4,500	4,550	4,650	4,700	4,800	8,750
1915	152,000	10142	4,500	4,500	4,600	4,950	6,500	26,000	108,000
1915-S	567,500	10173	4,500	4,500	4,550	4,750	4,900	5,000	10,000
1916-S	796,000	10174	4,500	4,500	4,600	4,900	4,950	5,500	12,000
	Auctions: $108,000, PCGS MS-66 HA 01/23								
1920	228,250	10143	4,500	4,500	4,600	5,000	6,500	216,000	—
	Auctions: $188,000, PCGS MS-65 LGND 01/18								
1920-S	558,000	10175	41,000	60,000	72,000	132,000	216,000	648,000	912,000
	Auctions: $102,000, PCGS MS-62 SBG 04/25; $600,000, PCGS MS-65 HA 04/25								
1921	528,500	10144	70,000	93,500	101,000	312,000	396,000	720,000	1,800,000
	Auctions: $1,560,000, PCGS MS-66 HA 08/25; $144,000, NGC MS-62 HA 08/25								
1922	1,375,500	10145	4,500	4,500	4,550	4,650	4,650	5,250	40,000
↳1922, Tripled Die Obverse, FS-101	*	351861	4,500	4,500	4,500	4,600	4,650	5,250	40,000
1922-S	2,658,000	10176	4,700	4,900	5,250	6,000	8,250	44,500	162,000
	Auctions: $192,000, PCGS MS-66 SBG 08/19								
↳1922-S, Die Gouge Through 2, FS-401	*	351863	4,700	4,900	5,250	5,750	8,250	44,500	162,000
1923	566,000	10146	4,500	4,500	4,550	4,650	4,650	5,500	72,000
1923-D	1,702,250	10177	4,500	4,500	4,550	4,650	4,650	4,800	5,000
1924	4,323,500	10147	4,500	4,500	4,550	4,650	4,650	4,700	5,000
↳1924, Doubled Die Obverse, FS-101	*	351864	4,500	4,500	4,500	4,600	4,650	4,650	5,000
1924-D	3,049,500	10178	5,500	6,250	6,250	9,750	14,000	108,000	312,000
	Auctions: $264,000, PCGS MS-66 HA 08/25								

Note: Most of the double eagles of the 1920s were returned to the Mint and melted in the 1930s. Some, however, were unofficially saved by Treasury employees. Estimates of the quantities saved range from a few dozen to several hundred thousand, depending on the date. This explains the high values for coins that, judged only by their initial mintages, should otherwise be more common.
* Included in number above.

1933 Saint-Gaudens Double Eagle

Circulation Strikes *(continued)*

	Mintage	GSID	AU-50	AU-58	MS-60	MS-63	MS-64	MS-65	MS-66
1924-S	2,927,500	10179	$6,000	$7,250	$7,750	$13,000	$23,000	$120,000	$336,000
	Auctions: $102,000, PCGS MS-65 HA 08/24; $930,000, PCGS MS-67 HA 08/24								
1925	2,831,750	10148	$4,500	$4,500	$4,550	$4,650	$4,650	$4,900	$5,250
	Auctions: $132,000, PCGS MS-67 HA 05/22								
1925-D	2,938,500	10180	6,000	7,750	8,000	12,500	33,000	114,000	360,000
	Auctions: $105,000, NGC MS-65 HA 05/24; $336,000, PCGS MS-66 HA 05/24								
1925-S	3,776,500	10181	5,750	8,250	9,000	16,500	63,000	216,000	282,000
	Auctions: $240,000, NGC MS-66 HA 08/25								
1926	816,750	10149	4,500	4,500	4,550	4,650	4,650	4,750	5,500
1926-D	481,000	10182	14,500	15,500	16,500	31,000	48,000	216,000	420,000
	Auctions: $402,500, PCGS MS-66 HA 01/12								
1926-S	2,041,500	10183	5,250	5,750	6,000	9,000	11,000	23,000	90,000
	Auctions: $114,000, PCGS MS-67 HA 01/20								
1927	2,946,750	10150	4,500	4,500	4,550	4,650	4,650	4,700	5,000
	Auctions: $180,000, PCGS MS-67 HA 01/23								
1927-D	13 est. known	10184	900,000	1,140,000	1,200,000	1,800,000	2,280,000	3,360,000	5,280,000
	Auctions: $3,840,000, PCGS MS-65 HA 01/25								
1927-S	3,107,000	10185	22,000	31,000	33,000	65,000	129,500	240,000	336,000
	Auctions: $690,000, PCGS MS-67 HA 08/25; $108,000, PCGS MS-64 HA 08/25								
1928	8,816,000	10151	4,500	4,500	4,550	4,650	4,650	4,700	5,000
	Auctions: $204,000, PCGS MS-67 HA 08/22								
↳1928, Doubled Die Obverse, FS-101	*	351867	4,500	4,500	4,500	4,600	4,650	4,650	5,000
1929	1,779,750	10152	26,500	37,000	41,000	48,000	75,500	96,000	204,000
	Auctions: $114,000, PCGS MS-65 HA 03/24; $432,000, PCGS MS-66 HA 03/24								
1930-S	74,000	10186	60,000	84,000	91,000	156,000	210,000	288,000	396,000
	Auctions: $228,000, NGC MS-64 HA 01/25; $138,000, NGC MS-63 HA 01/25								
1931	2,938,250	10153	36,000	54,000	62,500	108,000	138,000	180,000	312,000
	Auctions: $264,000, PCGS MS-65 HA 01/25; $192,000, PCGS MS-65 SBG 01/25								
1931-D	106,500	10187	48,000	67,000	79,000	115,000	140,500	204,000	480,000
	Auctions: $504,000, PCGS MS-66 HA 08/25; $360,000, PCGS MS-66 HA 08/25								
1932	1,101,750	10154	53,000	74,500	79,000	134,500	156,000	201,500	312,000
	Auctions: $192,000, PCGS MS-65 SBG 11/24; $168,000, PCGS MS-65 HA 11/24								
1933 (a)	14 confirmed; only 1 legal to own	10155	—	—	—	—	—	21,600,000	—

Note: Most of the double eagles of the 1920s were returned to the Mint and melted in the 1930s. Some, however, were unofficially saved by Treasury employees. Estimates of the quantities saved range from a few dozen to several hundred thousand, depending on the date. This explains the high values for coins that, judged only by their initial mintages, should otherwise be more common. * Included in number above. a. All were to have been melted at the mint. Today at least 13 are known to have survived. Most are in government possession; only one, the King Farouk specimen, is legal to own and has ever been sold at auction.

Note: Gold spot price at time of publication, $3,746 per ounce.

Proof Strikes

	Mintage	GSID	PF-60	PF-63	PF-65
Saint-Gaudens, No Motto on Reverse, High Relief, Roman Numerals (1907), Proof	**n/a**	**68926**	**$57,500**	**$108,000**	**$180,000**
Saint-Gaudens, Motto on Reverse (1908–1933), Proof	**n/a**	**74154**	**50,500**	**114,000**	**162,000**
1907, Small Edge Letters	3 known	10200	—	—	—
	Auctions: $1,680,000, PCGS PF-68 HA 01/23				
1907, Large Edge Letters	unique	194815	—	—	—
1908, Roman Finish	possibly unique	10190	360,000	540,000	—
	Auctions: $329,000, NGC PF-65 HA 04/15				
1908, Matte Finish	101	10191	50,500	120,000	216,000
	Auctions: $222,000, NGC PF-67 HA 05/24; $216,000, PCGS PF-66 HA 05/24				
1909	67	10192	56,500	132,000	180,000
	Auctions: $336,000, NGC PF-68 SBG 08/25; $192,000, NGC PF-66 HA 08/25				
1910	167	10193	50,500	120,000	198,000
	Auctions: $252,000, NGC PF-66 HA 01/25; $252,000, NGC PF-67 HA 01/25				
1910, Experimental Finish	unique	194808	—	—	900,000
	Auctions: $840,000, PCGS MS-66 HA 01/22				
1911	100	10194	50,500	114,000	162,000
	Auctions: $222,000, NGC PF-67 HA 08/24; $150,000, NGC PF-66 HA 08/24				
1912	74	10195	50,500	126,000	162,000
	Auctions: $204,000, PCGS PF-65 SBG 08/25; $192,000, NGC PF-67 SBG 08/25				
1913	58	10196	50,500	120,000	186,000
	Auctions: $288,000, PCGS PF-66 SBG 08/25; $264,000, NGC PF-68 SBG 08/25				
1914	70	10197	56,500	120,000	168,000
	Auctions: $240,000, NGC PF-67 HA 01/25; $228,000, NGC PF-67 HA 01/25				
1915	50	10198	55,000	144,000	210,000
	Auctions: $210,000, NGC PF-66 HA 01/25; $132,000, NGC PF-65 HA 01/25				
1921, Special Strike	unique	194807	—	—	—
	Auctions: $2,010,000, NGC MS-64 HA 08/21				

U.S. Commemoratives
1892–1954 and 1982 to Date

AN OVERVIEW OF CLASSIC COMMEMORATIVES

Commemorative coins have been popular since the time of ancient Greece and Rome. In the beginning they recorded and honored important events and passed along the news of the day. Today commemorative coins, which are highly esteemed by collectors, have been issued by many modern nations—none of which has surpassed the United States when it comes to these impressive mementos.

Scan for additional information.

The unique position occupied by commemoratives in the United States coinage is largely due to the fact that, with few exceptions, all commemorative coins have real historical significance. The progress and advance of people in the New World are presented in an interesting and instructive manner on our commemorative coins. Such a record of history artistically presented on U.S. gold, silver, and other memorial issues appeals strongly to the collector who favors the romantic, storytelling side of numismatics. It is the historical features of our commemoratives, in fact, that create interest among many people who would otherwise have little interest in coins, and would not otherwise consider themselves collectors.

Proposed coin programs are considered by two congressional committees: the Senate Committee on Banking, Housing, and Urban Affairs; and the House Financial Services Committee. Once a program is approved by Congress, the independent Citizens Coinage Advisory Committee (ccac.gov) and the U.S. Commission of Fine Arts (cfa.gov) advise the secretary of the Treasury on its coin designs.

These special coins are usually issued either to commemorate events or to help pay for monuments, programs, or celebrations that commemorate historical persons, places, or things. Pre-1982 commemorative coins were offered in most instances by a commission in charge of the event to be commemorated and sold at a premium over face value.

Commemorative coins are popularly collected either by major types or in sets with mintmark varieties. The pieces covered in this section of the *Guide Book of United States Coins, Deluxe Edition*, are those of the "classic" era of U.S. commemoratives, 1892 to 1954. All commemoratives are of the standard weight and fineness of their regular-issue 20th-century gold and silver counterparts, and all are legal tender.

A note about price performance: It has mostly been in recent decades that the general public has learned about commemorative coins. They have long been popular with coin collectors who enjoy the artistry and history associated with them, as well as the profit to be made from owning these rare pieces. Very few of them ever reached circulation because they were all originally sold above face value, and because they are all so rare. Most of the early issues were of the half dollar denomination, often made in quantities of fewer than 20,000 pieces. This is minuscule when compared to the regular half dollar coins that are made by the millions each year, and are still rarely seen in circulation.

At the beginning of 1988, prices of classic commemoratives in MS-65 condition had risen so high that most collectors had to content themselves with pieces in lower grades. Investors continued to apply pressure to the high-quality pieces, driving prices even higher, while the collector community went after coins in grades from AU to MS-63. For several months the pressure from both influences caused prices to rise very rapidly (for all issues and grades) without even taking the price-adjustment breather that usually goes along with such activity.

By 1990, prices dropped to the point that several of the commemoratives began to look like bargains once again. Many of the MS-65 pieces held firm at price levels above the $3,000 mark, but others were still available at under $500 even for coins of similar mintage. Coins in MS-63 or 64 were priced at but a fraction of the MS-65 prices, which would seem to make them reasonably priced because the demand for these pieces is universal, and not keyed simply to grade, rarity, or speculator pressure.

Historically, the entire series of commemorative coins has frequently undergone a roller-coaster cycle of price adjustments. These cycles have usually been of short duration, lasting from months to years, with prices always recovering and eventually exceeding previous levels.

See page 893 for discussion of modern commemorative coins of 1982 to date.

Mintages: In many cases, not all commemorative coins that are minted are sold. The unsold coins are usually returned to the Mint and melted, although some have been placed in circulation at face value. The mintage figures in the charts are the net difference between the original total mintage (including assay coins) and the quantity of unsold coins. A limited number of Proof strikings or presentation pieces were made for some of the 1892 through 1954 issues; they are beyond the scope of this book, but all are very rare and valuable.

Composition: Unless otherwise stated, commemorative coins were struck with the same specifications as the regular issue of the same denomination at the their time of release, with modern silver coins changing from .900 silver / .100 copper to .999 silver starting in 2019.

Classic commemorative programs are listed ***alphabetically****. Their full names appear in the list below, but the charts use the names most familiar to collectors. If the program name is significantly different from the common name, the latter is noted in this list. Unless otherwise stated, coins issued over multiple years are identical to those from the first year of issue.*

Alabama Centennial (1921). ***Denomination(s):*** half dollar. ***Designer(s):*** Laura Gardin Fraser.

Albany, New York, Charter [250th Anniversary] (1936). ***Denomination(s):*** half dollar. ***Designer(s):*** Gertrude K. Lathrop.

Arkansas Centennial (1935–1939). ***Denomination(s):*** half dollar. ***Designer(s):*** Edward E. Burr. ***Notes:*** Although 1936 was the centennial year, the first of several issues was brought out in 1935 from all three mints.

Arkansas Centennial – Robinson (1936). ***Denomination(s):*** half dollar. ***Designer(s):*** Henry Kreis (obverse), Edward E. Burr (reverse). ***Notes:*** Senator Joseph T. Robinson, still living at the time his portrait was used, was the subject of a new reverse for the existing Arkansas Centennial series.

Battle of Antietam Anniversary [75th Anniversary] (1937). ***Denomination(s):*** half dollar. ***Designer(s):*** William M. Simpson.

Battle of Gettysburg Anniversary (1936). ***Denomination(s):*** half dollar. ***Designer(s):*** Frank Vittor.

Booker T. Washington Memorial (1946–1951). ***Denomination(s):*** half dollar. ***Designer(s):*** Isaac S. Hathaway.

Bridgeport, Connecticut, Centennial (1936). ***Denomination(s):*** half dollar. ***Designer(s):*** Henry Kreis.

California Diamond Jubilee (1925). ***Denomination(s):*** half dollar. ***Designer(s):*** Jo Mora.

California Pacific International Exposition (1935–1936). ***Denomination(s):*** half dollar. ***Designer(s):*** Robert Aitken.

Carver/Washington Commemorative (1951–1954). ***Denomination(s):*** half dollar; ***Designer(s):*** Isaac S. Hathaway.

Cincinnati Music Center (1936). ***Denomination(s):*** half dollar. ***Designer(s):*** Constance Ortmayer. ***Notes:*** Although the obverse features composer Stephen Foster, the series bears no relation to him, but was intended to commemorate the supposed 50th anniversary of Cincinnati as a center of music.

Cleveland Centennial / Great Lakes Exposition (1936). ***Denomination(s):*** half dollar. ***Designer(s):*** Brenda Putnam. ***Notes:*** Although half the coinage was struck in 1937, all were dated 1936.

Columbia, South Carolina, Sesquicentennial (1936). ***Denomination(s):*** half dollar. ***Designer(s):*** A. Wolfe Davidson.

Connecticut Tercentenary (1935). ***Denomination(s):*** half dollar. ***Designer(s):*** Henry Kreis.

Daniel Boone Bicentennial (1934–1938). ***Denomination(s):*** half dollar. ***Designer(s):*** Augustus Lukeman. ***Notes:*** For issues struck in 1935–1938, the date "1934" was added to the reverse field, above the word "Pioneer."

Delaware Tercentenary (1936). ***Denomination(s):*** half dollar. ***Designer(s):*** Carl L. Schmitz. ***Notes:*** This coin was authorized in 1936, struck in 1937, and dated 1938 on the reverse and 1936 on the obverse.

Elgin, Illinois, Centennial (1936). ***Denomination(s):*** half dollar. ***Designer(s):*** Trygve Rovelstad.

Fort Vancouver Centennial (1925). ***Denomination(s):*** half dollar. ***Designer(s):*** Laura Gardin Fraser.

Grant Memorial (1922). ***Denomination(s):*** half dollar, gold dollar. ***Designer(s):*** Laura Gardin Fraser *(both denominations)*. ***Notes:*** An incused (recessed) star that appeared on the first issues was later removed, creating a second variety. On a fake coin, the star usually has a flattened spot on the reverse. The star has no particular significance.

Hawaiian Sesquicentennial (1928). ***Denomination(s):*** half dollar. ***Designer(s):*** Juliette M. Fraser.

Hudson, New York, Sesquicentennial (1935). ***Denomination(s):*** half dollar. ***Designer(s):*** Chester Beach.

Huguenot-Walloon Tercentenary (1924). ***Denomination(s):*** half dollar. ***Designer(s):*** George T. Morgan (with model modifications by James Earle Fraser).

Illinois Centennial (1918). ***Denomination(s):*** half dollar. ***Designer(s):*** George T. Morgan (obverse), John R. Sinnock (reverse).

Iowa Centennial (1946). ***Denomination(s):*** half dollar. ***Designer(s):*** Adam Pietz. ***Notes:*** 500 examples were held back to be distributed in 1996, and another 500 in 2046.

Lafayette (1900). ***Denomination(s):*** silver dollar. ***Designer(s):*** Charles E. Barber.

Lewis and Clark Exposition (1904–1905). ***Denomination(s):*** gold dollar. ***Designer(s):*** Charles E. Barber. ***Notes:*** The coins are dual-dated 1904 and 1905.

Lexington-Concord Sesquicentennial (1925). ***Denomination(s):*** half dollar. ***Designer(s):*** Chester Beach.

Long Island Tercentenary (1936). ***Denomination(s):*** half dollar. ***Designer(s):*** Howard K. Weinman.

Louisiana Purchase Exposition (1903). ***Denomination(s):*** gold dollar (two designs). ***Designer(s):*** *Both designs:* Charles E. Barber (assisted by George T. Morgan).

Lynchburg, Virginia, Sesquicentennial (1936). ***Denomination(s):*** half dollar. ***Designer(s):*** Charles Keck.

Maine Centennial (1920). ***Denomination(s):*** half dollar. ***Designer(s):*** Anthony de Francisci.

Maryland Tercentenary (1934). ***Denomination(s):*** half dollar. ***Designer(s):*** Hans Schuler.

McKinley Memorial (1916–1917). ***Denomination(s):*** gold dollar. ***Designer(s):*** Charles E. Barber (obverse), George T. Morgan (reverse).

Missouri Centennial (1921). ***Denomination(s):*** half dollar. ***Designer(s):*** Robert Aitken. ***Notes:*** Coins were struck both with and without an incused "2H4" on the obverse, indicating that Missouri was the 24th star in the flag. Those with the marking were struck first, but were the last to be sold.

Monroe Doctrine Centennial (1923). ***Denomination(s):*** half dollar. ***Designer(s):*** Chester Beach. ***Notes:*** Many unsold coins were released into circulation at face value.

New Rochelle, New York, 250th Anniversary (1938). ***Denomination(s):*** half dollar. ***Designer(s):*** Gertrude K. Lathrop.

Norfolk, Virginia, Bicentennial (1936). ***Denomination(s):*** half dollar. ***Designer(s):*** William M. Simpson and Marjorie E. Simpson.

Old Spanish Trail [400th Anniversary of Cabeza de Vaca Expedition] (1935). ***Denomination(s):*** half dollar. ***Designer(s):*** L.W. Hoffecker.

Oregon Trail Memorial (1926–1939). ***Denomination(s):*** half dollar. ***Designer(s):*** James Earle Fraser and Laura Gardin Fraser. ***Notes:*** Originally struck in 1926, it was restruck in 1928 (released in 1933), and again in 1933, 1934, and 1936 through 1939.

Panama-Pacific International Exposition (1915). ***Denomination(s):*** half dollar, gold dollar, quarter eagle, $50 gold piece. ***Designer(s):*** *Half Dollar and Quarter Eagle:* Charles E. Barber (obverse), George T. Morgan (assisting Barber on half-dollar reverse); *Gold Dollar:* Charles Keck; *$50 Gold Piece:* Robert Aitken. ***Notes:*** The $50 gold piece was struck in both round and octagonal varieties.

Pilgrim Tercentenary (1920–1921). ***Denomination(s):*** half dollar. ***Designer(s):*** Cyrus E. Dallin. ***Notes:*** Coins struck in 1920 had no date on the obverse, while coins struck in 1921 added "1921" to the obverse.

Providence, Rhode Island, Tercentenary (1936). ***Denomination(s):*** half dollar. ***Designer(s):*** Arthur G. Carey and John H. Benson.

Roanoke Island, North Carolina, 350th Anniversary (1937). ***Denomination(s):*** half dollar. ***Designer(s):*** William M. Simpson.

San Francisco – Oakland Bay Bridge Opening (1936). ***Denomination(s):*** half dollar. ***Designer(s):*** Jacques Schnier.

Sesquicentennial of American Independence (1926). ***Denomination(s):*** half dollar, quarter eagle. ***Designer(s):*** *Both denominations:* John R. Sinnock.

Stone Mountain Memorial (1925). ***Denomination(s):*** half dollar. ***Designer(s):*** Gutzon Borglum. ***Notes:*** Some were counterstamped on the reverse with letters and numbers by the issuing commission, distributed to state sales agencies, and are valued much higher.

Texas Independence Centennial (1934–1938). ***Denomination(s):*** half dollar. ***Designer(s):*** John R. Sinnock.

Vermont Sesquicentennial (1927). ***Denomination(s):*** half dollar. ***Designer(s):*** Charles Keck.

Wisconsin Territorial Centennial (1936). ***Denomination(s):*** half dollar. ***Designer(s):*** David Parsons.

World's Columbian Exposition (1892–1893). ***Denomination(s):*** quarter dollar, half dollar. ***Designer(s):*** *Quarter Dollar:* Charles E. Barber; *Half Dollar:* Charles E. Barber (obverse), George T. Morgan (reverse). ***Notes:*** Many remained unsold and a substantial quantity was later released for circulation at face value or melted. Approximately 100 brilliant Proofs were struck for each date.

York County, Maine, Tercentenary (1936). ***Denomination(s):*** half dollar. ***Designer(s):*** Walter H. Rich.

Silver Commemoratives

Isabella Quarter Dollar (1893)

Lafayette Silver Dollar (1900)

Alabama Centennial, Plain (1921)

2X2 in Obverse Field

Albany, New York, Charter (1936)

Antietam, 75th Anniversary of Battle (1937)

Arkansas Centennial (1936)

Bay Bridge Opening (1936)

Boone Bicentennial (1934–1938)

Date in Obverse Field

Bridgeport, Connecticut, Centennial (1936)

California Diamond Jubilee (1925)

Cincinnati Music Center (1936)

Cleveland Centennial / Great Lakes Exposition (1936)

Columbia, South Carolina, Sesquicentennial (1936)

Columbian Expo (1892–1893)

Connecticut Tercentenary (1935)

Delaware Tercentenary (1936)

Elgin, Illinois, Centennial (1936)

Gettysburg, 75th Anniversary of Battle (1936)

Grant Memorial, Plain (1922)

Star in Obverse Field

Hawaiian Sesquicentennial (1928)

Hudson, New York, Sesquicentennial (1935)

Huguenot-Walloon Tercentenary (1924)

Iowa Centennial (1946)

Lexington-Concord Sesquicentennial (1925)

Lincoln–Illinois Centennial (1918)

Long Island Tercentenary (1936)

Lynchburg, Virginia, Sesquicentennial (1936)

Maine Centennial (1920)

Maryland Tercentenary (1934)

Missouri Centennial, Plain (1921)

2★4 in Obverse Field

Monroe Doctrine Centennial (1923)

New Rochelle, New York, 250th Anniversary (1938)

Norfolk, Virginia, Bicentennial (1936)

Oregon Trail Memorial (1926–1939)

Panama-Pacific International Expo (1915)

Pilgrim Tercentenary (1920–1921)

1921 in Obverse Field

Rhode Island—Providence, Tercentenary (1936)

Roanoke Island, North Carolina, 350th Anniversary (1937)

Robinson—Arkansas Centennial (1936)

San Diego–Pacific International Expo (1935–1936)

Sesquicentennial of American Independence (1926)

Spanish Trail (1935)

Stone Mountain Memorial (1925)

Texas Centennial (1934–1938)

Vancouver Centennial (1925)

Vermont Sesquicentennial (1927)

Booker T. Washington Memorial (1946–1951)

Washington-Carver Memorial (1951–1954)

Wisconsin Territorial Centennial (1936)

York County, Maine, Tercentenary (1936)

Classic Commemorative Silver Circulation Strikes

	Mintage	GSID	AU-50	MS-60	MS-63	MS-65	MS-66	MS-67
Arkansas Centennial, Single Type Coin	**n/a**	**193362**	**$105**	**$115**	**$130**	**$210**	**$365**	**$1,150**
Boone Bicentennial, Single Type Coin	**n/a**	**193363**	**140**	**150**	**160**	**195**	**240**	**650**
Oregon Trail Memorial, Single Type Coin	**n/a**	**193364**	**160**	**190**	**245**	**310**	**360**	**600**
Booker T. Washington Memorial, Single Type Coin	**n/a**	**193370**	**30**	**36**	**40**	**50**	**70**	**310**
Washington-Carver Memorial, Single Type Coin	**n/a**	**193371**	**30**	**35**	**43**	**75**	**100**	**900**
Isabella Quarter Dollar, 1893	24,214	10319	285	440	725	1,250	2,600	6,250
Lafayette Silver Dollar, 1900	36,026	10321	550	950	1,650	5,250	13,000	60,000
Alabama Centennial, Plain, 1921	16,014	10220	145	215	390	850	1,600	14,500
Alabama Centennial, 1921, "2X2" in Obverse Field	6,006	10221	240	345	470	1,100	2,000	12,000
Albany, New York, Charter, 1936	17,671	10222	215	225	240	310	455	725
Antietam, 75th Anniversary of Battle, 1937	18,028	10223	550	625	650	750	850	1,250
Arkansas Centennial, 1935	13,012	10224	105	115	130	210	365	1,750
Arkansas Centennial, 1935-D	5,505	10225	105	115	130	210	405	1,250
Arkansas Centennial, 1935-S	5,506	10226	105	115	130	230	390	1,150
Arkansas Centennial, 1936	9,660	10227	105	115	130	230	395	1,450
Arkansas Centennial, 1936-D	9,660	10228	105	115	130	230	390	1,150
Arkansas Centennial, 1936-S	9,662	10229	105	115	135	230	395	1,500
Arkansas Centennial, 1937	5,505	10230	125	130	140	275	430	2,500
Arkansas Centennial, 1937-D	5,505	10231	125	130	140	230	430	1,150
Arkansas Centennial, 1937-S	5,506	10232	125	130	155	310	650	5,000
Arkansas Centennial, 1938	3,156	10233	145	150	175	260	675	2,800
Arkansas Centennial, 1938-D	3,155	10234	145	150	215	325	455	3,250
Arkansas Centennial, 1938-S	3,156	10235	145	155	200	360	925	8,000
Arkansas Centennial, 1939	2,104	10236	245	260	290	500	1,250	11,000
Arkansas Centennial, 1939-D	2,104	10237	245	260	340	440	700	2,750
Arkansas Centennial, 1939-S	2,105	10238	255	280	340	650	825	2,800

Classic Commemorative Silver Circulation Strikes *(continued)*

	Mintage	GSID	AU-50	MS-60	MS-63	MS-65	MS-66	MS-67
Bay Bridge Opening, 1936-S	71,424	10244	$170	$180	$215	$300	$415	$1,000
Boone Bicentennial, 1934	10,007	10245	140	150	160	195	275	775
Boone Bicentennial, 1935	10,010	10246	140	150	160	200	245	750
Boone Bicentennial, 1935-D	5,005	10247	140	150	160	240	340	1,600
Boone Bicentennial, 1935-S	5,005	10248	140	150	160	215	260	1,000
Boone Bicentennial, 1935/34	10,008	10249	140	150	160	210	275	900
Boone Bicentennial, 1935/34-D	2,003	10250	275	310	390	625	875	1,400
Boone Bicentennial, 1935/34-S	2,004	10251	275	340	440	750	950	2,500
Boone Bicentennial, 1936	12,012	10252	140	150	160	200	255	650
Boone Bicentennial, 1936-D	5,005	10253	140	150	180	245	290	1,000
Boone Bicentennial, 1936-S	5,006	10254	140	150	210	245	325	950
Boone Bicentennial, 1937	9,810	10255	155	170	175	230	260	675
Boone Bicentennial, 1937-D	2,506	10256	255	260	280	405	450	975
Boone Bicentennial, 1937-S	2,506	10257	255	260	285	435	625	1,050
Boone Bicentennial, 1938	2,100	10258	340	350	385	470	575	1,300
Boone Bicentennial, 1938-D	2,100	10259	340	350	385	490	675	1,150
Boone Bicentennial, 1938-S	2,100	10260	340	350	395	500	850	1,400
Bridgeport, CT, Centennial, 1936	25,015	10266	145	155	195	275	370	1,000
California Diamond Jubilee, 1925-S	86,594	10291	200	225	245	575	1,000	1,900
Cincinnati Music Center, 1936	5,005	10293	320	340	390	470	650	1,250
Cincinnati Music Center, 1936-D	5,005	10294	320	340	370	470	625	1,450
Cincinnati Music Center, 1936-S	5,006	10295	320	340	385	525	900	6,500
Cleveland Centennial / Great Lakes Expo, 1936	50,030	10296	100	110	120	145	210	1,250
Columbia, SC, Sesquicentennial, 1936	9,007	10297	195	230	240	255	310	575
Columbia, SC, Sesquicentennial, 1936-D	8,009	10298	195	210	220	240	300	525
Columbia, SC, Sesquicentennial, 1936-S	8,007	10299	195	230	235	275	300	495
Columbian Expo, 1892	950,000	10302	30	40	110	280	625	3,250
↳Columbian Expo, 1892, Repunched Date, FS-301	*	351870	40	95	155	525	750	—
↳Columbian Expo, 1892, Repunched Date, FS-303	*	393348	55	95	155	950	—	—
Columbian Expo, 1893	1,550,405	10303	30	47	110	310	850	2,500
↳Columbian Expo, 1893, Repunched Date, FS-301	*	351872	37	80	150	410	1,050	—
Connecticut Tercentenary, 1935	25,018	10307	230	245	280	390	650	1,400
Delaware Tercentenary, 1936	20,993	10308	225	235	255	285	310	800
Elgin, IL, Centennial, 1936	20,015	10309	170	180	215	240	300	575
Gettysburg, 75th Anniversary of Battle, 1936	26,928	10310	525	550	625	825	900	1,450
Grant Memorial, 1922, Plain	67,405	10311	130	180	285	625	850	2,000
Grant Memorial, 1922, Star in Obverse Field	4,256	10313	1,100	1,500	2,750	4,750	6,000	27,500
Hawaiian Sesquicentennial, 1928 (a)	10,008	10314	1,750	2,500	3,100	4,250	5,750	79,000
Hudson, NY, Sesquicentennial, 1935	10,008	10316	750	750	800	925	1,200	4,600
Huguenot-Walloon Tercentenary, 1924	142,080	10317	110	120	160	190	430	1,200
Iowa Centennial, 1946	100,057	10318	95	100	110	135	155	235
Lexington-Concord Sesquicentennial, 1925	162,013	10322	80	95	120	235	420	3,250
Lincoln–Illinois Centennial, 1918	100,058	10323	155	195	285	525	900	3,100
Long Island Tercentenary, 1936	81,826	10324	90	100	115	170	275	1,000
Lynchburg, VA, Sesquicentennial, 1936	20,013	10325	175	195	235	280	345	900
Maine Centennial, 1920	50,028	10326	130	160	240	390	650	2,250
Maryland Tercentenary, 1934	25,015	10327	145	155	190	210	340	1,100
Missouri Centennial, 1921, Plain	11,400	10328	410	525	675	1,400	4,750	15,500
Missouri Centennial, 1921, 2★4 in Obverse Field	9,400	10329	700	875	1,200	1,600	5,750	48,000
Monroe Doctrine Centennial, 1923-S	274,077	10331	50	65	95	575	1,000	16,000
	Auctions: $102,000, PCGS MS-67 SBG 04/22							

* Included in number above. **a.** Fifty Sandblast Proof presentation pieces were also struck.

Classic Commemorative Silver Circulation Strikes *(continued)*

	Mintage	GSID	AU-50	MS-60	MS-63	MS-65	MS-66	MS-67
New Rochelle, NY, 250th Anniversary, 1938	15,266	10332	$255	$265	$310	$375	$455	$950
Norfolk, VA, Bicentennial, 1936	16,936	10333	290	305	320	340	360	495
Oregon Trail Memorial, 1926	47,955	10338	160	190	245	310	370	675
Oregon Trail Memorial, 1926-S	83,055	10339	160	210	270	330	390	675
Oregon Trail Memorial, 1928	6,028	10340	195	230	275	405	500	850
Oregon Trail Memorial, 1933-D	5,008	10341	405	430	495	600	775	1,200
↳Oregon Trail Memorial, 1933-D, Tripled Die Reverse, FS-801	*	351873	435	470	525	700	950	2,250
Oregon Trail Memorial, 1934-D	7,006	10342	200	230	285	350	455	850
Oregon Trail Memorial, 1936	10,006	10343	190	215	275	340	360	775
Oregon Trail Memorial, 1936-S	5,006	10344	190	215	275	340	390	725
Oregon Trail Memorial, 1937-D	12,008	10345	190	215	275	340	415	625
Oregon Trail Memorial, 1938	6,006	10346	200	230	275	330	365	750
Oregon Trail Memorial, 1938-D	6,005	10347	190	215	275	345	405	625
Oregon Trail Memorial, 1938-S	6,006	10348	200	230	285	365	415	750
Oregon Trail Memorial, 1939	3,004	10349	475	480	525	700	725	1,250
Oregon Trail Memorial, 1939-D	3,004	10350	475	480	525	575	725	1,000
Oregon Trail Memorial, 1939-S	3,005	10351	475	480	525	575	675	925
Panama-Pacific International Expo, 1915-S	27,134	10354	470	725	1,100	2,300	2,750	4,500
↳Panama-Pacific International Expo, 1915-S, Repunched Mintmark, FS-501	*	351874	525	800	1,200	2,550	3,000	4,950
Pilgrim Tercentenary, 1920	152,112	10355	90	95	120	285	435	2,100
Pilgrim Tercentenary, 1921	20,053	10356	180	195	230	340	625	1,600
Rhode Island–Providence, Tercentenary, 1936	20,013	10358	110	120	155	190	235	600
Rhode Island–Providence, Tercentenary, 1936-D	15,010	10359	110	120	145	175	245	575
Rhode Island–Providence, Tercentenary, 1936-S	15,011	10360	110	125	155	190	235	1,300
Roanoke Island, NC, 350th Anniversary, 1937	29,030	10361	175	180	190	230	280	575
Robinson–Arkansas Centennial, 1936	25,265	10362	115	120	130	150	260	1,100
San Diego–Pacific International Expo, 1935-S	70,132	10363	110	115	130	195	260	650
San Diego–Pacific International Expo, 1936-D	30,092	10364	110	120	150	240	275	900
↳San Diego–Pacific International Expo, 1936-D, FS-501	*	199157	130	150	180	285	405	1,200
Sesquicentennial of American Independence, 1926	141,120	10365	90	120	130	1,150	13,000	84,000
Spanish Trail, 1935	10,008	10366	1,000	1,100	1,150	1,450	1,950	2,400
Stone Mountain Memorial, 1925	1,314,709	10367	65	90	115	245	405	925
Texas Centennial, 1934	61,463	10368	150	170	195	260	340	900
Texas Centennial, 1935	9,996	10369	150	170	185	300	390	825
Texas Centennial, 1935-D	10,007	10370	150	170	185	275	350	775
Texas Centennial, 1935-S	10,008	10371	150	170	185	260	340	625
Texas Centennial, 1936	8,911	10372	150	170	200	305	350	850
Texas Centennial, 1936-D	9,039	10373	150	170	185	260	340	700
Texas Centennial, 1936-S	9,055	10374	150	170	185	285	365	825
Texas Centennial, 1937	6,571	10375	155	175	195	260	340	750
Texas Centennial, 1937-D	6,605	10376	155	175	195	275	350	700
Texas Centennial, 1937-S	6,637	10377	155	175	195	285	370	625
Texas Centennial, 1938	3,780	10378	235	245	285	390	525	1,400
Texas Centennial, 1938-D	3,775	10379	235	245	285	470	500	950
Texas Centennial, 1938-S	3,814	10380	235	245	300	405	470	925
Vancouver Centennial, 1925	14,994	10385	285	385	430	825	925	2,050
↳Vancouver Centennial, 1925, Doubled Die Obverse, FS-101	*	351878	315	420	470	900	1,000	2,250
Vermont Sesquicentennial, 1927	28,142	10387	255	270	285	420	650	2,400

* Included in number above.

Classic Commemorative Silver Circulation Strikes *(continued)*

	Mintage	GSID	AU-50	MS-60	MS-63	MS-65	MS-66	MS-67
Booker T. Washington Memorial, 1946	700,546	10267	$30	$36	$40	$50	$70	$310
Booker T. Washington Memorial, 1946-D	50,000	10268	30	36	40	60	95	500
Booker T. Washington Memorial, 1946-S	500,279	10269	30	36	40	50	70	340
Booker T. Washington Memorial, 1947	6,000	10270	30	36	48	70	100	1,500
Booker T. Washington Memorial, 1947-D	6,000	10271	30	36	48	70	190	1,400
Booker T. Washington Memorial, 1947-S	6,000	10272	30	36	48	80	130	850
Booker T. Washington Memorial, 1948	8,005	10273	30	36	48	80	110	1,200
Booker T. Washington Memorial, 1948-D	8,005	10274	37	44	48	85	100	1,000
Booker T. Washington Memorial, 1948-S	8,005	10275	37	44	48	65	80	650
Booker T. Washington Memorial, 1949	6,004	10276	44	50	75	120	150	650
Booker T. Washington Memorial, 1949-D	6,004	10277	50	60	65	75	95	495
Booker T. Washington Memorial, 1949-S	6,004	10278	50	65	75	100	130	440
Booker T. Washington Memorial, 1950	6,004	10279	37	44	50	60	90	950
Booker T. Washington Memorial, 1950-D	6,004	10280	34	39	60	90	180	1,100
Booker T. Washington Memorial, 1950-S	62,091	10281	34	39	43	60	75	345
Booker T. Washington Memorial, 1951	210,082	10282	30	38	40	50	75	1,250
Booker T. Washington Memorial, 1951-D	7,004	10283	37	50	65	90	195	575
Booker T. Washington Memorial, 1951-S	7,004	10284	34	44	55	70	90	455
Washington-Carver Memorial, 1951	20,018	10392	30	35	43	80	195	7,500
Washington-Carver Memorial, 1951-D	10,004	10393	34	40	50	80	175	3,750
Washington-Carver Memorial, 1951-S	10,004	10394	34	40	50	80	100	900
Washington-Carver Memorial, 1952	1,106,292	10395	30	36	45	75	100	900
Washington-Carver Memorial, 1952-D	8,006	10396	37	43	60	75	405	10,500
Washington-Carver Memorial, 1952-S	8,006	10397	37	43	50	80	110	1,100
Washington-Carver Memorial, 1953	8,003	10398	34	42	50	80	215	4,250
Washington-Carver Memorial, 1953-D	8,003	10399	30	49	60	85	525	13,000
Washington-Carver Memorial, 1953-S	88,020	10400	34	40	49	80	110	1,400
Washington-Carver Memorial, 1954	12,006	10401	33	39	47	75	245	4,800
Washington-Carver Memorial, 1954-D	12,006	10402	33	39	47	75	470	11,500
Washington-Carver Memorial, 1954-S	42,024	10403	33	39	47	85	155	1,450
Wisconsin Centennial, 1936	25,015	10404	150	170	190	230	285	625
York County, Maine, Tercentenary, 1936	25,015	10405	155	155	180	215	255	325
	Auctions: $102,000, PCGS MS-69 SBG 08/19							

Classic Commemorative Silver Proof and Special Strikes

	Mintage	GSID	PF-63	PF-65	PF-66
1893, Isabella	appx. 100	10320	$5,250	$14,000	$26,500
1937, Boone, Matte Finish	1	84302	90,000	—	—
1937-D, Boone, Matte Finish	1	84518	72,000	—	—
1937-S, Boone, Matte Finish	1	84519	66,000	—	—
1892, Columbian	100	10304	6,250	11,000	14,500
1893, Columbian	3–5	10301	27,500	—	—
1922, Grant, with Star, Matte Finish	16	10312	180,000	—	—
	Auctions: $184,000, PCGS PF-64 SBG 03/12				
1922, Grant, with Star	Unknown	198242	—	—	—
1928, Hawaiian	50	10315	38,500	72,000	132,000
	Auctions: $102,000, NGC PF-66 HA 01/24				
1921, Missouri, with 2x4	1–2 known	10330	—	—	—
1938, New Rochelle	est. 50	198243	3,750	6,250	7,500
1925, Fort Vancouver	2–3 known	10386	—	—	222,000
	Auctions: $188,000, PCGS PF-66 HA 04/15				

Gold Commemoratives

Classic Commemorative Gold Dollars

Jefferson–Louisiana Purchase (1903)

McKinley–Louisiana Purchase (1903)

Lewis and Clark Expo (1904–1905)

Panama-Pacific International Expo (1915)

McKinley Memorial (1916–1917)

Grant Memorial, Plain (1922)

Star in Obverse Field

Classic Commemorative Quarter Eagles

Panama-Pacific International Exposition (1915)

Sesquicentennial of American Independence (1926)

Classic Commemorative $50 Gold Coins

Panama-Pacific International Expo (1915)

Classic Commemorative Gold Circulation Strikes

	Mintage	GSID	MS-60	MS-63	MS-64	MS-65	MS-66	MS-67
Jefferson–Louisiana Purchase, 1903, Gold Dollar	17,500	10201	$625	$775	$850	$1,150	$1,300	$2,400
McKinley–Louisiana Purchase, 1903, Gold Dollar	17,500	10202	475	550	650	875	1,150	2,200
Lewis and Clark Expo, 1904, Gold Dollar	10,025	10205	875	1,100	1,250	2,750	4,950	9,000
Lewis and Clark Expo, 1905, Gold Dollar	10,041	10207	775	1,150	1,300	3,100	8,250	33,500
Panama-Pacific International Expo, 1915-S, Gold Dollar	15,000	10217	550	675	825	1,150	1,600	3,750
McKinley Memorial, 1916, Gold Dollar	15,000	10208	405	550	600	725	950	1,950
McKinley Memorial, 1917, Gold Dollar	5,000	10210	525	550	700	850	1,250	2,100

Classic Commemorative Gold Circulation Strikes *(continued)*

	Mintage	GSID	MS-60	MS-63	MS-64	MS-65	MS-66	MS-67
Grant Memorial, 1922, Plain, Gold Dollar	5,016	10211	$975	$1,250	$1,400	$1,600	$1,850	$2,600
Grant Memorial, 1922, Star in Obverse Field, Gold Dollar	5,016	10212	1,100	1,450	1,600	2,250	2,500	3,000
Panama-Pacific International Expo, 1915-S, Gold Quarter Eagle	6,749	10214	2,750	4,000	4,500	5,500	6,750	9,000
Sesquicentennial of American Independence, 1926, Gold Quarter Eagle	46,019	10213	675	775	850	1,400	4,100	36,000
Panama-Pacific International Expo, Round, 1915-S, Gold $50 Dollar	483	10215	69,500	86,500	108,000	180,000	258,000	330,000
	Auctions: $204,000 NGC MS-66 HA 01/24; $445,625, NGC MS-66 HA 01/24							
Panama-Pacific International Expo, Octagonal, 1915-S, Gold $50 Dollar	645	10216	72,000	93,500	108,000	173,000	228,000	312,000
	Auctions: $228,000, NGC MS-65 HA 08/25; $222,000, PCGS MS-66 HA 08/25							

Classic Commemorative Gold Proof and Special Strikes

	Mintage	GSID	PF-63	PF-65	PF-66
Jefferson–Louisiana Purchase, 1903, Gold Dollar	100	10203	$11,000	$13,000	$18,000
McKinley–Louisiana Purchase, 1903, Gold Dollar	100	10204	8,750	12,000	15,500
Lewis and Clark Expo, 1905, Gold Dollar	2–3 known	10206	24,000	—	—
McKinley Memorial, 1916, Gold Dollar	5–6 known	10209	36,000	—	—

AN OVERVIEW OF MODERN COMMEMORATIVES

No commemorative coins were made by the U.S. Mint from 1955 through 1981. As the years went by, the numismatic community missed having new commemoratives to collect, and many endorsements for events and subjects worthy of the honor were made through letters to congressmen and other officials, which were often reprinted in pages of *The Numismatist*, the *Numismatic Scrapbook Magazine*, *Numismatic News*, and *Coin World*.

Finally, in 1982, the Treasury Department issued the first commemorative coin since 1954—a silver half dollar celebrating the 250th anniversary of the birth of George Washington. This time around, distribution was placed in the hands of the Bureau of the Mint (today called the U.S. Mint) rather than with a commission or private individuals. The profits accrued to the Treasury Department and the U.S. government. The issue was well received in the numismatic community, with more than seven million of the half dollars sold nationwide.

Then came the 1983 and 1984 Los Angeles Olympiad coins, minted in the subject years for the Los Angeles Olympiad held in 1984. These comprised a diverse and somewhat experimental series, with dollars of two different designs and, for the first time, a commemorative ten-dollar gold coin. Sales were satisfactory, and the supply easily met the demand from collectors and investors.

The concept of a surcharge, or built-in fee, was introduced, with a certain amount per coin going to a congressionally designated beneficiary—in the instance of the Olympic coins, the Los Angeles Olympic Organizing Committee. These and related surcharges became controversial with collectors, some of whom resented making involuntary donations when they bought coins. Today the practice continues, though without as much controversy. Surcharges are the spark that has ignited most commemorative programs, as potential recipients of the earmarked profits launch intense lobbying campaigns in Congress.

In 1986 the 100th anniversary of the completion of the Statue of Liberty was commemorated by the issuance of a copper-nickel–clad half dollar (first of its kind in the commemorative series), a silver dollar, and a five-dollar gold coin, with varied motifs, each depicting on the obverse the Statue of Liberty or an element therefrom. Unprecedented millions of coins were sold.

Then followed a lull in commemorative purchases, although the Mint continued to issue coins celebrating more Olympic Games, various national anniversaries, and significant people, places, events, and other subjects. Some years saw four or five or more individual commemorative programs. Some were well received by the hobby community, but sales of most fell far short of projections. In certain cases these low sales would eventually prove beneficial for collectors who placed orders from the Mint. An example is the 1995 five-dollar commemorative honoring baseball star and Civil Rights hero Jackie Robinson. Only 5,174 Uncirculated pieces were sold, creating a modern rarity.

Most modern commemorative coins have seen only modest secondary-market appreciation, if any. Beyond their retail values, however, the coins will always have significant historical, cultural, and sentimental value. The 2001 American Buffalo silver dollar created a sensation with its bold design harkening back to the classic Buffalo nickel of 1913 to 1938; the issue sold out quickly and soon was commanding high premiums in the collector market. It remains popular and valuable today. In 2014, the National Baseball Hall of Fame commemoratives (a three-coin suite in copper-nickel, silver, and gold) captured mainstream-media headlines and national TV news coverage. Other modern commemoratives have honored American inventors and explorers, branches of the U.S. military, Boy Scouts and Girl Scouts, the Civil Rights Act of 1964, and other important themes, continuing a tradition of special coinage dating back to 1892 and giving today's collectors a broad spectrum of issues to study and cherish.

See pages 879 and 880 for discussion of classic commemorative coins of 1892 to 1954.

Modern commemorative programs are listed in **date** *order. Their full names appear in the following list, but the charts use the more common names familiar to most collectors.*

George Washington 250th Anniversary of Birth (1982). ***Denomination(s):*** half dollar. ***Designer(s):*** Elizabeth Jones.

Los Angeles Olympiad (1983–1984). ***Denomination(s):*** dollar (two designs), $10 gold coin. ***Designer(s):*** *Dollar Discus Thrower:* Elizabeth Jones; *Dollar Coliseum:* Robert Graham; *$10 Gold Coin:* James Peed.

Statue of Liberty Centennial (1986). ***Denomination(s):*** half dollar, dollar, $5 gold coin. ***Designer(s):*** *Half Dollar:* Edgar Z. Steever IV (obverse), Sherl Winter (reverse); *Dollar:* John Mercanti; *$5 Gold Coin:* Elizabeth Jones.

U.S. Constitution Bicentennial (1987). ***Denomination(s):*** dollar, $5 gold coin. ***Designer(s):*** *Dollar:* Patricia L. Verani; *$5 Gold Coin:* Marcel Jovine.

Seoul Olympiad (1988). ***Denomination(s):*** dollar, $5 gold coin. ***Designer(s):*** *Dollar:* Patricia Lewis Verani (obverse), Sherl Winter (reverse); *$5 Gold Coin:* Elizabeth Jones (obverse), Marcel Jovine (reverse).

Congress Bicentennial (1989). ***Denomination(s):*** half dollar, dollar, $5 gold coin. ***Designer(s):*** *Half Dollar:* Patricia Lewis Verani (obverse), William Woodward (reverse); *Dollar:* William Woodward; *$5 Gold Coin:* John Mercanti.

Eisenhower Centennial (1990). ***Denomination(s):*** dollar. ***Designer(s):*** John Mercanti (obverse), Marcel Jovine (reverse).

Mount Rushmore Golden Anniversary (1991). ***Denomination(s):*** half dollar, dollar, $5 gold coin. ***Designer(s):*** *Half Dollar:* Marcel Jovine (obverse), T. James Ferrell (reverse); *Dollar:* Marika Somogyi (obverse), Frank Gasparro (reverse); *$5 Gold Coin:* John Mercanti (obverse), William Lamb (reverse).

Korean War Memorial (1991). ***Denomination(s):*** dollar. ***Designer(s):*** John Mercanti (obverse), James Ferrell (reverse).

United Service Organizations (1991). ***Denomination(s):*** dollar. ***Designer(s):*** Robert Lamb (obverse), John Mercanti (reverse).

XXV Olympiad (1992). ***Denomination(s):*** half dollar, dollar, $5 gold coin. ***Designer(s):*** *Half Dollar:* William C. Cousins (obverse), Steven M. Bieda (reverse); *Dollar:* John R. Deecken (obverse), Marcel Jovine (reverse); *$5 Gold Coin:* James Sharpe (obverse), James Peed (reverse).

White House 200th Anniversary (1992). ***Denomination(s):*** dollar. ***Designer(s):*** Edgar Z. Steever IV (obverse), Chester Y. Martin (reverse).

Christopher Columbus Quincentenary (1992). ***Denomination(s):*** half dollar, dollar, $5 gold coin. ***Designer(s):*** *Half Dollar:* T. James Ferrell; *Dollar:* John Mercanti (obverse), Thomas D. Rogers Sr. (reverse); *$5 Gold Coin:* T. James Ferrell (obverse), Thomas D. Rogers Sr. (reverse).

Bill of Rights (1993). ***Denomination(s):*** half dollar, dollar, $5 gold coin. ***Designer(s):*** *Half Dollar:* T. James Ferrell (obverse), Dean McMullen (reverse); *Dollar:* William Krawczewicz (obverse), Dean McMullen (reverse); *$5 Gold Coin:* Scott R. Blazek (obverse), Joseph D. Peña (reverse). ***Notes:*** Some 9,656 of the Uncirculated version were privately marked on the edge with a serial number and the initials of the Madison Foundation and the American Numismatic Association.

50th Anniversary of World War II, 1991–1995 (1993). ***Denomination(s):*** half dollar, dollar, $5 gold coin. ***Designer(s):*** *Half Dollar:* George Klauba (obverse), Bill J. Leftwich (reverse); *Dollar:* Thomas D. Rogers Sr.; *$5 Gold Coin:* Charles J. Madsen (obverse), Edward Southworth Fisher (reverse).

Thomas Jefferson 250th Anniversary of Birth, 1993 (1994). ***Denomination(s):*** dollar. ***Designer(s):*** T. James Ferrell.

World Cup Tournament (1994). ***Denomination(s):*** half dollar, dollar, $5 gold coin. ***Designer(s):*** *Half Dollar:* Richard T. LaRoche (obverse), Dean McMullen (reverse); *Dollar:* Dean McMullen; *$5 Gold Coin:* William J. Krawczewicz (obverse), Dean McMullen (reverse).

Vietnam Veterans Memorial (1994). ***Denomination(s):*** dollar. ***Designer(s):*** John Mercanti (obverse), Thomas D. Rogers Sr. (reverse).

U.S. Prisoner of War Museum (1994). ***Denomination(s):*** dollar. ***Designer(s):*** Tom Nielsen (obverse), Edgar Z. Steever IV (reverse).

Women in Military Service Memorial (1994). ***Denomination(s):*** dollar. ***Designer(s):*** T. James Ferrell.

U.S. Capitol Bicentennial (1994). ***Denomination(s):*** dollar. ***Designer(s):*** William Cousins (obverse), John Mercanti (reverse).

Civil War Battlefield Preservation (1995). ***Denomination(s):*** half dollar, dollar, $5 gold coin. ***Designer(s):*** *Half Dollar:* Don Troiani (obverse), T. James Ferrell (reverse); *Dollar:* Don Troiani (obverse), John Mercanti (reverse); *$5 Gold Coin:* Don Troiani (obverse), Alfred F. Maletsky (reverse).

Atlanta Centennial Olympic Games (1995–1996). ***Denomination(s):*** half dollar (four designs), dollar (eight designs), $5 gold coin (4 designs). ***Designer(s):*** *Half Dollar Basketball:* Clint Hansen (obverse), T. James Ferrell (reverse); *Half Dollar Baseball:* Edgar Z. Steever IV (obverse), T. James Ferrell (reverse); *Half Dollar Swimming:* William Krawczewicz (obverse), Malcolm Farley (reverse); *Half Dollar Soccer:* Clint Hansen (obverse), Malcolm Farley (reverse); *Dollar Gymnastics and 1995 Paralympics:* James C. Sharpe (obverse), William Krawczewicz (reverse).; *Dollar Track and Field and Cycling:* John Mercanti (obverse), William Krawczewicz (reverse); *Dollar Tennis and 1996 Paralympics:* James C. Sharpe (obverse), Thomas D. Rogers Sr. (reverse); *Dollar Rowing:* Bart Forbes (obverse), Thomas D. Rogers Sr. (reverse); *Dollar High Jump:* Calvin Massey (obverse), Thomas D. Rogers Sr. (reverse); *$5 Gold Coin Torch Runner:* Frank Gasparro; *$5 Gold Coin Stadium:* Marcel Jovine (obverse), Frank Gasparro (reverse); *$5 Gold Coin Flag Bearer:* Patricia Lewis Verani (obverse), William Krawczewicz (reverse); *$5 Gold Coin Cauldron:* Frank Gasparro (obverse), William Krawczewicz (reverse).

Special Olympics World Games (1995). ***Denomination(s):*** dollar. ***Designer(s):*** T. James Ferrell from a portrait by Jamie Wyeth (obverse), Thomas D. Rogers Sr. (reverse).

National Community Service (1996). ***Denomination(s):*** dollar. ***Designer(s):*** Thomas D. Rogers Sr. from a medal by Augustus Saint-Gaudens (obverse), William C. Cousins (reverse).

Smithsonian Institution 150th Anniversary (1996). ***Denomination(s):*** dollar, $5 gold coin. ***Designer(s):*** *Dollar:* Thomas D. Rogers Sr. (obverse), John Mercanti (reverse); *$5 Gold Coin:* Alfred F. Maletsky (obverse), T. James Ferrell (reverse).

U.S. Botanic Garden (1997). ***Denomination(s):*** dollar. ***Designer(s):*** Edgar Z. Steever IV (obverse), William C. Cousins (reverse).

Jackie Robinson (1997). ***Denomination(s):*** dollar, $5 gold coin. ***Designer(s):*** *Dollar:* Alfred F. Maletsky (obverse), T. James Ferrell (reverse); *$5 Gold Coin:* William C. Cousins (obverse), James Peed (reverse).

Franklin D. Roosevelt (1997). ***Denomination(s):*** $5 gold coin. ***Designer(s):*** T. James Ferrell (obverse), James Peed (reverse).

National Law Enforcement Officers Memorial (1997). ***Denomination(s):*** dollar. ***Designer(s):*** Alfred F. Maletsky (obverse from a photograph by Larry Ruggieri).

Robert F. Kennedy (1998). ***Denomination(s):*** dollar. ***Designer(s):*** Thomas D. Rogers Sr.

Black Revolutionary War Patriots (1998). ***Denomination(s):*** dollar. ***Designer(s):*** John Mercanti (obverse), Ed Dwight (reverse).

Dolley Madison (1999). ***Denomination(s):*** dollar. ***Designer(s):*** Tiffany & Co.

George Washington Death Bicentennial (1999). ***Denomination(s):*** $5 gold coin. ***Designer(s):*** Laura Gardin Fraser.

Yellowstone National Park (1999). ***Denomination(s):*** dollar. ***Designer(s):*** Edgar Z. Steever IV (obverse), William C. Cousins (reverse).

Library of Congress Bicentennial (2000). ***Denomination(s):*** dollar, bi-metallic $10 coin; *Dollar:* Thomas D. Rogers Sr. (obverse), John Mercanti (reverse); *$10 Bi-metallic Coin:* John Mercanti (obverse), Thomas D. Rogers Sr. (reverse). ***Notes:*** The bi-metallic coin features an outer ring of gold and a core made of solid platinum.

Leif Ericson Millennium (2000). ***Denomination(s):*** dollar. ***Designer(s):*** John Mercanti (obverse), T. James Ferrell (reverse). ***Notes:*** Released as part of a joint issue with Iceland, whose mint issued a silver 1,000-kronur coin designed by Throstur Magnusson.

American Buffalo (2001). ***Denomination(s):*** dollar. ***Designer(s):*** James Earle Fraser.

U.S. Capitol Visitor Center (2001). ***Denomination(s):*** half dollar, dollar, $5 gold coin. ***Designer(s):*** *Half Dollar:* Dean McMullen (obverse), Alex Shagin and Marcel Jovine (reverse); *Dollar* Marika Somogyi (obverse), John Mercanti (reverse).; *$5 Gold Coin:* Elizabeth Jones.

Salt Lake City Olympic Games (2002). ***Denomination(s):*** dollar, $5 gold coin. ***Designer(s):*** *Dollar:* John Mercanti (obverse), Donna Weaver (reverse); *$5 Gold Coin:* Donna Weaver.

West Point Bicentennial (2002). ***Denomination(s):*** dollar. ***Designer(s):*** T. James Ferrell (obverse), John Mercanti (reverse).

First Flight Centennial (2003). ***Denomination(s):*** half dollar, dollar, $10 gold coin. ***Designer(s):*** *Half Dollar:* John Mercanti (obverse), Norman E. Nemeth (reverse); *Dollar:* T. James Ferrell (obverse), Norman E. Nemeth (reverse); *$10 Gold Coin:* Donna Weaver (obverse), Norman E. Nemeth (reverse).

Thomas Alva Edison (2004). ***Denomination(s):*** dollar. ***Designer(s):*** Donna Weaver (obverse), John Mercanti (reverse).

Lewis and Clark Bicentennial (2004). ***Denomination(s):*** dollar. ***Designer(s):*** Donna Weaver.

Chief Justice John Marshall (2005). ***Denomination(s):*** dollar. ***Designer(s):*** John Mercanti (obverse), Donna Weaver (reverse).

Marine Corps 230th Anniversary (2005). ***Denomination(s):*** dollar. ***Designer(s):*** Paul C. Balan (obverse), Don Everhart (reverse).

Benjamin Franklin Tercentenary (2006). ***Denomination(s):*** dollar (two designs). ***Designer(s):*** *Scientist:* Norman E. Nemeth (obverse), Charles L. Vickers (reverse); *Founding Father:* Don Everhart (obverse), Donna Weaver (reverse).

San Francisco Old Mint Centennial (2006). ***Denomination(s):*** dollar, $5 gold coin. ***Designer(s):*** *Dollar:* Sherl J. Winter (obverse), Joseph Menna after George T. Morgan (reverse); *$5 Gold Coin:* Charles L. Vickers (obverse), Don Everhart after Christian Gobrecht (reverse).

Jamestown 400th Anniversary (2007). ***Denomination(s):*** dollar, $5 gold coin. ***Designer(s):*** *Dollar:* Donna Weaver (obverse), Susan Gamble (reverse); *$5 Gold Coin:* John Mercanti (obverse), Susan Gamble (reverse).

Little Rock Central High School Desegregation (2007). ***Denomination(s):*** dollar. ***Designer(s):*** Richard Masters (obverse), Don Everhart (reverse).

Bald Eagle Recovery and National Emblem (2008). ***Denomination(s):*** half dollar, dollar, $5 gold coin. ***Designer(s):*** *Half Dollar:* Susan Gamble (obverse), Donna Weaver (reverse); *Dollar:* Joel Iskowitz (obverse), Jim Licaretz (reverse); *$5 Gold Coin:* Susan Gamble (obverse), Don Everhart (reverse).

Louis Braille Bicentennial (2009). ***Denomination(s):*** dollar. ***Designer(s):*** Joel Iskowitz (obverse), Phebe Hemphill (reverse).

Abraham Lincoln Bicentennial (2009). ***Denomination(s):*** dollar. ***Designer(s):*** Charles J. Madsen (obverse), Edward Southworth Fisher (reverse).

American Veterans Disabled for Life (2010). ***Denomination(s):*** dollar. ***Designer(s):*** Don Everhart.

Boy Scouts of America Centennial (2010). ***Denomination(s):*** dollar. ***Designer(s):*** Donna Weaver (obverse), Jim Licaretz from the universal logo of the Boy Scouts of America (reverse).

Medal of Honor (2011). ***Denomination(s):*** dollar, $5 gold coin. ***Designer(s):*** *Dollar:* Jim Licaretz (obverse), Richard Masters (reverse); *$5 Gold Coin:* Joseph Menna (obverse), Joel Iskowitz (reverse).

U.S. Army (2011). ***Denomination(s):*** half dollar, dollar, $5 gold coin. ***Designer(s):*** *Half Dollar:* Donna Weaver (obverse), Thomas Cleveland (reverse); *Dollar:* Richard Masters (obverse), Susan Gamble (reverse); *$5 Gold Coin:* Joel Iskowitz (obverse), Joseph Menna from the U.S. Army emblem (reverse).

Infantry Soldier (2012). ***Denomination(s):*** dollar. ***Designer(s):*** Joel Iskowitz (obverse), Ronald D. Sanders (reverse).

Star-Spangled Banner (2012). ***Denomination(s):*** dollar, $5 gold coin. ***Designer(s):*** *Dollar:* Joel Iskowitz (obverse), William C. Burgard II (reverse); *$5 Gold Coin:* Donna Weaver (obverse), Richard Masters (reverse).

Girl Scouts of the U.S.A. Centennial (2013). ***Denomination(s):*** dollar. ***Designer(s):*** Barbara Fox (obverse), Chris Costello (reverse).

5-Star Generals (2013). ***Denomination(s):*** half dollar, dollar, $5 gold coin. ***Designer(s):*** *Half Dollar:* Phebe Hemphill; *Dollar:* Richard Masters (obverse), Barbara Fox (reverse); *$5 Gold Coin:* Ronald D. Sanders (obverse), Barbara Fox (reverse).

John F. Kennedy Half Dollar Design 50th Anniversary (2014). ***Denomination(s):*** half dollar (nominal) gold. ***Designer(s):*** Gilroy Roberts (obverse), Frank Gasparro (reverse). ***Notes:*** This is a .9999 fine gold issue weighing .75 oz pure gold, dual-dated 1964–2014. Clad and silver dual-dated coins with various finishes are listed in the main half dollars section.

National Baseball Hall of Fame (2014). ***Denomination(s):*** half dollar, dollar, $5 gold coin. ***Designer(s):*** *All denominations:* Cassie McFarland (obverse), Don Everhart (reverse). ***Notes:*** The 2014 National Baseball Hall of Fame commemorative half dollar holds a unique place in U.S. Mint history as the country's first concave coin.

Civil Rights Act of 1964 (2014). ***Denomination(s):*** dollar. ***Designer(s):*** Justin Kunz (obverse), Donna Weaver (reverse).

U.S. Marshals Service 225th Anniversary (2015). ***Denomination(s):*** half dollar, dollar, $5 gold coin. ***Designer(s):*** *Half Dollar:* Joel Iskowitz (obverse), Susan Gamble (reverse); *Dollar:* Richard Masters (obverse), Frank Morris (reverse); *$5 Gold Coin:* Donna Weaver (obverse), Paul C. Balan (reverse).

March of Dimes 75th Anniversary (2015). ***Denomination(s):*** dollar. ***Designer(s):*** Paul C. Balan (obverse), Don Everhart (reverse).

Mark Twain (2016). ***Denomination(s):*** dollar, $5 gold coin. ***Designer(s):*** *Dollar:* Chris Costello (obverse), Patricia Lucas-Morris (reverse); *$5 Gold Coin:* Benjamin Sowers (obverse), Ronald D. Sanders (reverse).

National Park Service 100th Anniversary (2016). ***Denomination(s):*** half dollar, dollar, $5 gold coin. ***Designer(s):*** *Half Dollar:* Barbara Fox (obverse), Thomas Hipschen (reverse); *Dollar:* Joseph Menna (obverse), Chris Costello (reverse); *$5 Gold Coin:* Don Everhart.

Lions Club International Century of Service (2017). ***Denomination(s):*** dollar. ***Designer(s):*** Joel Iskowitz (obverse), Patricia Lucas-Morris (reverse).

Boys Town Centennial (2017). ***Denomination(s):*** half dollar, dollar, $5 gold coin. ***Designer(s):*** *Half Dollar:* Chris Costello; *Dollar:* Emily Damstra; *$5 Gold Coin:* Donna Weaver.

World War I Centennial (2018). ***Denomination(s):*** dollar. ***Designer(s):*** LeRoy Transfield.

Breast Cancer Awareness (2018). ***Denomination(s):*** half dollar, dollar, $5 gold coin. ***Designer(s):*** *All denominations:* Emily Damstra. ***Notes:*** The $5 gold coin was produced in "rose pink" gold, composed of .850 gold, .148 copper, and .002 zinc.

Apollo 11 50th Anniversary (2019). ***Denomination(s):*** half dollar, dollar, $5 gold coin. ***Designer(s):*** *All denominations and varieties:* Gary Cooper. ***Notes:*** The obverse of each denomination is concave; the reverse is convex. The Mint also issued a 5-ounce silver Proof, identical in design to the regular-issue dollar coin but enlarged to 3 inches in diameter.

American Legion 100th Anniversary (2019). ***Denomination(s):*** half dollar, dollar, $5 gold coin. ***Designer(s):*** *Half Dollar:* Richard Masters; *Dollar:* Paul C. Balan (obverse), Patricia Lucas-Morris (reverse); *$5 Gold Coin:* Chris Costello (obverse), Paul C. Balan (reverse).

Naismith Memorial Basketball Hall of Fame 60th Anniversary (2020). ***Denomination(s):*** half dollar, dollar, $5 gold coin. ***Designer(s):*** *All denominations:* Justin Kunz (obverse), Donna Weaver (reverse). ***Notes:*** The obverse of each denomination is concave; the reverse is convex. The Mint also issued the half dollar with Enhanced Uncirculated finish and as a Proof with elements colorized.

Women's Suffrage Centennial (2020). ***Denomination(s):*** dollar. ***Designer(s):*** Christina Hess.

Christa McAuliffe (2021). ***Denomination(s):*** dollar. ***Designer(s):*** Laurie J. Musser (obverse), Emily Damstra (reverse).

National Law Enforcement Memorial and Museum (2021). ***Denomination(s):*** half dollar, dollar, $5 gold coin. ***Designer(s):*** *Half Dollar:* Ronald D. Sanders (obverse), Heidi Wastweet (reverse); *Dollar and $5 Gold Coin:* Frank Morris (obverse), Ronald D. Sanders (reverse).

National Purple Heart Hall of Honor (2022). ***Denomination(s):*** half dollar, dollar, $5 gold coin. ***Designer(s):*** *Half Dollar:* Beth Zaiken; *Dollar:* Heidi Wastweet; *$5 Gold Coin:* Donna Weaver. ***Notes:*** The Mint also issued the Proof silver dollar with elements colorized.

Negro Leagues Baseball (2022). ***Denomination(s):*** half dollar, dollar, $5 gold coin. ***Designer(s):*** *Half Dollar:* Chris Costello (obverse), Justin Kunz (reverse); *Dollar:* Matt Swaim (obverse), Don Everhart (reverse); *$5 Gold Coin:* Laurie Musser (obverse), Donna Weaver (reverse). ***Notes:*** The Mint also issued the Proof silver dollar with a special privy mark.

Greatest Generation (2024). ***Denomination(s):*** half dollar, dollar, $5 gold coin. ***Designer(s):*** *Half Dollar:* Elana Hagler (obverse) Matt Swaim (reverse); *Dollar:* Beth Zaiken (obverse); Benjamin Sowards (reverse); *$5 Gold Coin:* Heidi Wastweet (obverse); Benjamin Sowards (reverse).

Harriet Tubman Bicentennial (2024). ***Denomination(s):*** half dollar, dollar, $5 gold coin. ***Designer(s):*** *Half Dollar:* Don Everhart (obverse), Thomas Hipschen (reverse); *Dollar:* Beth Zaiken; *$5 Gold Coin:* Chris Costello (obverse), Benjamin Sowards (reverse).

U.S. Marine Corps 250th Anniversary (2024). ***Denomination(s):*** half dollar, dollar, $5 gold coin. ***Designer(s):*** *Half Dollar:* Emily Damstra (obverse), Donna Weaver (reverse); *Dollar:* Ronald D. Sanders (obverse), Donna Weaver (reverse); *$5 Gold Coin:* Donna Weaver.

Modern Commemorative Half Dollars

George Washington Birth (1982)

Statue of Liberty (1986)

Congress Bicentennial (1989)

Mount Rushmore (1991)

XXV Olympiad (1992)

Christopher Columbus (1992)

World War II 50th Anniversary (1993)

Bill of Rights – James Madison (1993)

World Cup (1994)

Civil War Battlefields (1995)

Atlanta Olympics, Baseball (1995)

Atlanta Olympics, Basketball (1995)

Atlanta Olympics, Soccer (1996)

Atlanta Olympics, Swimming (1996)

U.S. Capitol Visitor Center (2001)

First Flight (2003)

Bald Eagle Recovery (2008)

U.S. Army (2011)

5-Star Generals (2013)

Baseball Hall of Fame (2014)

Kennedy 50th Anniversary (2015)

U.S. Marshals (2015)

National Park Service (2016)

Boys Town (2017)

Breast Cancer Awareness (2018)

Apollo 11 (2019)

American Legion (2019)

Basketball Hall of Fame (2020)

National Law Enforcement Memorial (2021)

Negro Leagues (2022)

Purple Heart (2022)

Greatest Generation (2024)

Harriet Tubman (2024)

U.S. Marine Corps 250th Anniversary (2025)

Modern Commemorative Half Dollar Circulation Strikes

	Mintage	GSID	OGP*	MS-69	MS-70
1982-D, George Washington Birth, Silver	2,210,458	10409	$23.00	$23.00	—
1986-D, Statue of Liberty	928,008	10411	2.60	5.50	$100
1989-D, Congress Bicentennial	163,753	10414	8.00	8.00	1,950
1991-D, Mount Rushmore	213,049	10418	15.00	15.00	47
1992-P, XXV Olympiad	161,607	10421	6.75	6.75	40
1992-D, Christopher Columbus	135,702	10420	12.00	12.00	47
1993-W, Bill of Rights–James Madison, Silver	193,346	10425	23.00	23.00	47
(1993-P), World War II 50th	197,072	10416	13.50	13.50	40
1994-D, World Cup	168,208	10426	9.50	9.50	40
1995-S, Civil War Battlefields	119,520	10431	20.00	20.00	40
1995-S, Atlanta Olympics, Basketball	171,001	10430	13.50	13.50	34
1995-S, Atlanta Olympics, Baseball	164,605	10429	19.00	19.00	34
1996-S, Atlanta Olympics, Swimming	49,533	10435	47.00	47.00	55
1996-S, Atlanta Olympics, Soccer	52,836	10436	27.00	27.00	50
2001-P, U.S. Capitol Visitor Center	99,157	10439	17.50	17.50	55
2003-P, First Flight	57,122	10441	19.00	19.00	47
2008-S, Bald Eagle Recovery	120,180	68924	13.50	13.50	40
2011-D, U.S. Army	39,442	70992	31.00	31.00	1,100
2013-D, 5-Star Generals	38,095	71649	20.00	20.00	130
2014-D, Baseball Hall of Fame	142,405	71631	27.00	27.00	60
2015-D, U.S. Marshals	30,231	73518	22.00	22.00	70
2016-D, National Park Service	21,328	76866	23.00	23.00	70
2017-S, Boys Town	15,561	76867	27.00	27.00	55
2018-D, Breast Cancer Awareness	11,301	76868	27.00	27.00	80
2019-D, Apollo 11	41,748	81963	27.00	27.00	47
2019-D, American Legion	11,429	81964	40.00	40.00	47
2020-D, Basketball Hall of Fame	13,369	84871	24.00	24.00	47
2020-S, Basketball Hall of Fame, Enhanced Uncirculated (a)	22,565	376894	40.00	35.00	47
2021-D, National Law Enforcement Memorial	10217	85118	20.00	20.00	47
2022-D, Negro Leagues	8,448	188855	34.00	34.00	47
2022-D, Purple Heart	12,456	195828	34.00	34.00	60

* Value in original government packaging (OGP). **a.** Included in the 2020-S Basketball Hall of Fame Kids Set.

Modern Commemorative Half Dollar Circulation Strikes *(continued)*

	Mintage	GSID	OGP*	MS-69	MS-70
2024-D, Harriet Tubman		346860	$34	$34	$60
2024-D, Greatest Generation		351805	34	34	55
2025-D, U.S. Marine Corps 250th		377388	70	70	90

* Value in original government packaging (OGP).

Modern Commemorative Half Dollar Proof Strikes

	Mintage	GSID	OGP*	PF-69	PF-70
1982-S, George Washington Birth, Silver	4,894,044	10410	$23.00	$23.00	$100
1986-S, Statue of Liberty	6,925,627	10412	2.60	8.00	32
1989-S, Congress Bicentennial	767,897	10415	5.50	5.50	110
1991-S, Mount Rushmore	618,488	10419	10.50	10.50	75
1992-S, XXV Olympiad (a)	519,645	10423	7.50	7.50	27
1992-S, Christopher Columbus	390,154	10422	12.00	12.00	70
1993-S, Bill of Rights–James Madison, Silver (a)	586,315	10424	23.00	23.00	100
(1993-P), World War II 50th	317,396	10417	17.00	17.00	75
1994-P, World Cup (a)	609,354	10428	9.50	9.50	195
1995-S, Civil War Battlefields	330,002	10434	27.00	27.00	90
1995-S, Atlanta Olympics, Basketball (a)	169,655	10433	22.00	22.00	130
1995-S, Atlanta Olympics, Baseball (a)	118,087	10432	19.00	19.00	170
1996-S, Atlanta Olympics, Swimming (a)	114,315	10438	24.00	24.00	145
1996-S, Atlanta Olympics, Soccer (a)	112,412	10437	27.00	27.00	195
2001-P, U.S. Capitol Visitor Center	77,962	10440	16.00	16.00	1,600
2003-P, First Flight	109,710	10442	15.00	15.00	55
2008-S, Bald Eagle Recovery	220,577	68951	20.00	20.00	47
2011-S, U.S. Army	68,332	70994	22.00	22.00	47
2013-S, 5-Star Generals	47,326	71486	13.50	80.00	80
2014-S, Baseball Hall of Fame	249,049	73513	24.00	24.00	80
2014-W, Kennedy 50th Anniversary Gold Half Dollar	73,772	71642	3,750.00	3,750.00	3,850
2015-S, U.S. Marshals	76,549	73519	17.50	17.50	90
2016-S, National Park Service	54,946	77474	33.00	33.00	60
2017-D, Boys Town	23,212	77475	20.00	20.00	55
2018-S, Breast Cancer Awareness	22,391	79398	32.00	32.00	55
2019-S, Apollo 11 (b)	181,735	77476	30.00	30.00	43
2019-S, American Legion	27,286	82375	43.00	43.00	47
2020-S, Basketball Hall of Fame, Colorized	26,572	81965	19.00	19.00	34
2020-S, Basketball Hall of Fame	32,581	84870	38.00	38.00	55
2021-S, National Law Enforcement Memorial	23,307	85119	38.00	38.00	60
2022-S, Negro Leagues	19,006	188856	43.00	43.00	70
2022-S, Purple Heart Hall of Honor	22,901	195829	47.00	47.00	75
2024-W, Harriet Tubman		346861	60.00	60.00	80
2024-W, Greatest Generation		351806	60.00	60.00	80
2025-S, U.S. Marine Corps 250th		377389	75.00	75.00	95

* Value in original government packaging (OGP). **a.** Proof half dollars from these series were also included in Prestige Sets; see "Proof Sets," listed in the "Proof and Mint Sets" chapter. **b.** Proof Apollo 11 sales figures include 10,000 coins for sets produced by the Royal Australian Mint and 5,000 coins for sets produced by the Royal Spanish Mint.

Modern Commemorative Dollars

L.A. Olympics, Discus Thrower (1983)

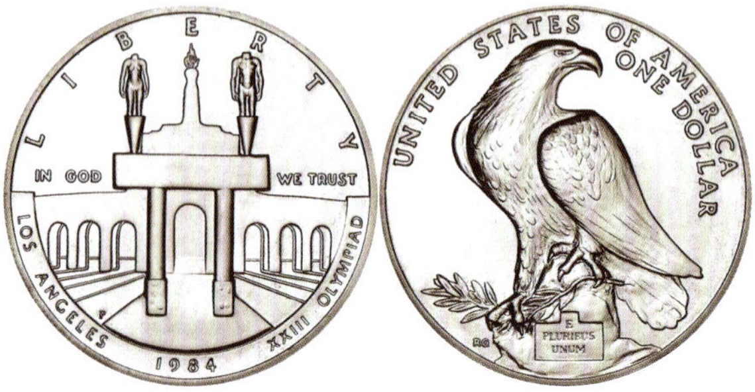

L.A. Olympics, Coliseum (1984)

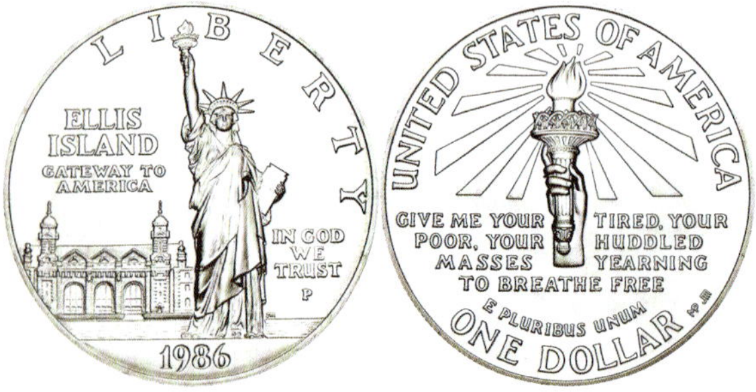

Statue of Liberty (1986)

Constitution Bicentennial (1987)

Seoul Olympiad (1988)

Congress Bicentennial (1989)

Eisenhower (1990)

Korean War Memorial (1991)

United Service Organizations (1991)

Mount Rushmore (1991)

Christopher Columbus (1992)

White House 200th Anniversary (1992)

XXV Olympiad (1992)

Bill of Rights – James Madison (1993)

World War II 50th Anniversary (1993)

Thomas Jefferson Birth (1994)

U.S. Capitol Bicentennial (1994)

World Cup Tournament (1994)

U.S. POW Museum (1994)

Vietnam Veterans Memorial (1994)

Women in Military (1994)

Atlanta Olympics, Cycling (1995)

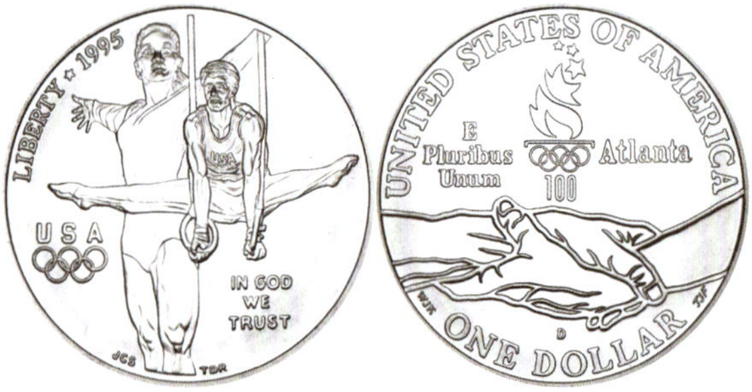

Atlanta Olympics, Gymnastics (1995)

Atlanta Olympics, Paralympics (1995)

Atlanta Olympics, Track and Field (1995)

Civil War Battlefields (1995)

Special Olympics (1995)

Atlanta Olympics, High Jump (1996)

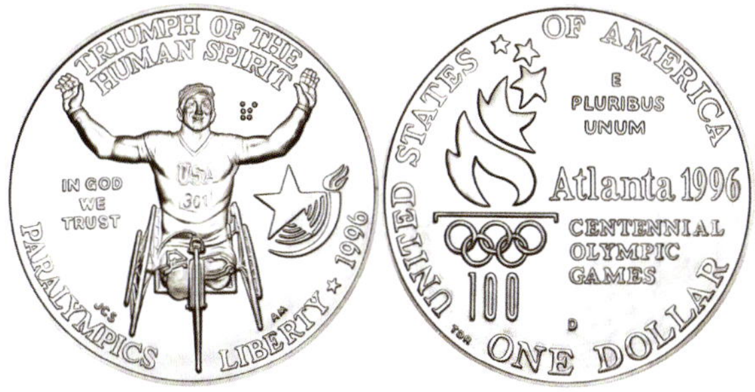

Atlanta Olympics, Paralympics (1996)

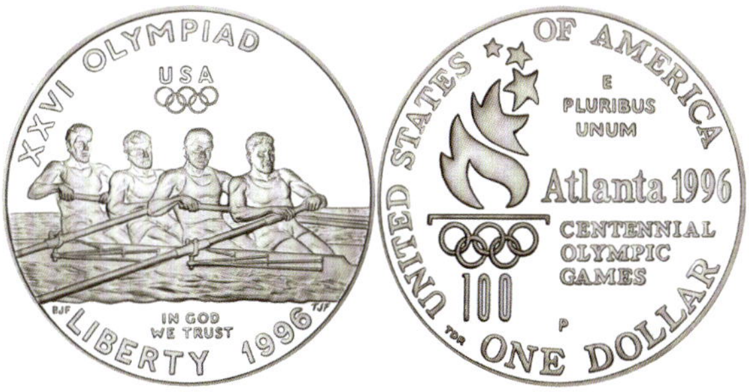

Atlanta Olympics, Rowing (1996)

Atlanta Olympics, Tennis (1996)

Smithsonian (1996)

National Community Service (1996)

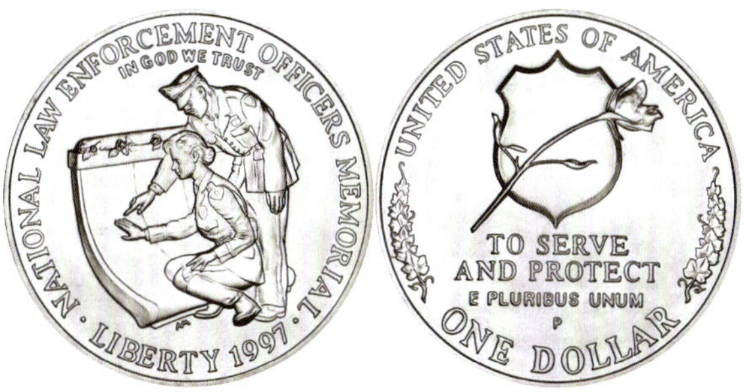

National Law Enforcement Officers Memorial (1997)

U.S. Botanic Garden (1997)

Jackie Robinson (1997)

Black Revolutionary War Patriots (1998)

Robert F. Kennedy (1998)

Dolley Madison (1999)

Yellowstone (1999)

Leif Ericson (2000)

Library of Congress (2000)

U.S. Capitol Visitor Center (2001)

American Buffalo (2001)

Salt Lake City Olympics (2002)

West Point Bicentennial (2002)

First Flight (2003)

Lewis and Clark (2004)

Thomas Alva Edison (2004)

Chief Justice Marshall (2005)

Marine Corps 230th Anniversary (2005)

Benjamin Franklin, Founding Father (2006)

Benjamin Franklin, Scientist (2006)

San Francisco Old Mint (2006)

Jamestown (2007)

Little Rock High School Desegregation (2007)

Bald Eagle Recovery (2008)

Abraham Lincoln (2009)

Louis Braille (2009)

Boy Scouts (2010)

American Veterans Disabled for Life (2010)

Medal of Honor (2011)

U.S. Army (2011)

Star-Spangled Banner (2012)

Infantry Soldier (2012)

5-Star Generals (2013)

Girl Scouts (2013)

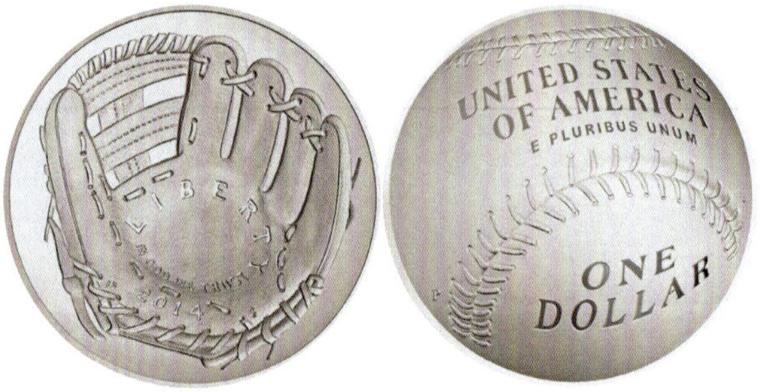

Baseball Hall of Fame (2014)

Civil Rights Act (2014)

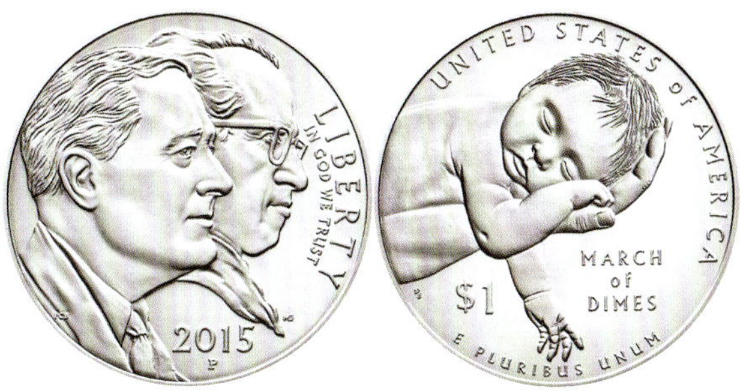

March of Dimes (2015)

U.S. Marshals (2015)

Mark Twain (2016)

National Park Service (2016)

Boys Town (2017)

Lions Club (2017)

Breast Cancer Awareness (2018)

World War I Centennial (2018)

American Legion (2019)

Apollo 11 (2019)

Christa McAuliffe (2021)

Naismith Memorial Basketball Hall of Fame 60th Anniversary (2020)

Women's Suffrage (2020)

National Law Enforcement Memorial (2021)

Negro Leagues Baseball (2022)

National Purple Heart Hall of Honor (2022)

Greatest Generation (2024)

Harriet Tubman (2024)

U.S. Marine Corps 250th Anniversary (2025)

Modern Commemorative Dollar Circulation Strikes

	Mintage	GSID	OGP*	MS-69	MS-70
Silver $1 (1983 to Date)	**n/a**	**84308**	**$55**	**$55**	**$70**
1983-P, L.A. Olympics, Discus Thrower	294,543	10444	55	55	340
1983-D, L.A. Olympics, Discus Thrower	174,014	10443	55	55	1,500
1983-S, L.A. Olympics, Discus Thrower	174,014	10445	55	55	1,400
1984-P, L.A. Olympics, Coliseum	217,954	10448	55	55	155
1984-D, L.A. Olympics, Coliseum	116,675	10447	55	55	925
1984-S, L.A. Olympics, Coliseum	116,675	10449	55	55	1,250
1986-P, Statue of Liberty	723,635	10451	55	55	90
1987-P, Constitution Bicentennial	451,629	10453	55	55	90
1988-D, Seoul Olympiad	191,368	10456	55	55	115
1989-D, Congress Bicentennial	135,203	10458	55	55	650
1990-W, Eisenhower	241,669	10461	60	60	100
(1993-D), World War II 50th	107,240	10462	55	55	80
1991-D, Korean War Memorial	213,049	10464	55	55	70
1991-D, United Service Organizations	124,958	10465	55	55	80
1991-P, Mount Rushmore	133,139	10468	60	60	110
1992-D, White House	123,803	10472	55	55	70
1992-D, Christopher Columbus	106,949	10473	60	60	90
1992-D, XXV Olympiad	187,552	10474	55	55	135
1993-D, Bill of Rights–James Madison	98,383	10478	60	55	70
1993-P, Thomas Jefferson Birth	266,927	10479	60	55	70
1994-D, World Cup	81,524	10482	55	55	490
1994-D, U.S. Capitol Bicentennial	68,332	10483	55	55	80
1994-W, U.S. POW Museum	54,893	10491	55	55	90
1994-W, Vietnam Veterans Memorial	57,290	10493	60	55	110
1994-W, Women in Military	69,860	10494	60	60	80
1995-D, Atlanta Olympics, Gymnastics	42,497	10499	55	55	95
1995-D, Atlanta Olympics, Paralympics	28,649	10496	70	55	95
1995-D, Atlanta Olympics, Track and Field	24,976	10497	60	55	115
1995-D, Atlanta Olympics, Cycling	19,662	10498	80	55	130
1995-P, Civil War Battlefields	45,866	10500	55	55	245
1995-W, Special Olympics	89,301	10507	55	55	75
1996-D, Atlanta Olympics, Tennis	15,983	10508	80	55	285
1996-D, Atlanta Olympics, Paralympics	14,497	10509	130	55	210
1996-D, Atlanta Olympics, Rowing	16,258	10510	90	55	220
1996-D, Atlanta Olympics, High Jump	15,697	10512	95	55	310
1996-D, Smithsonian	31,320	10511	55	55	120
1996-S, National Community Service	23,500	10518	80	55	200
1997-P, U.S. Botanic Garden	58,505	10520	55	55	110
1997-P, National Law Enforcement Officers Memorial	28,575	10521	95	55	175
1997-S, Jackie Robinson	30,180	10524	70	55	390
1998-S, Robert F. Kennedy	106,422	10526	60	60	75
1998-S, Black Revolutionary War Patriots	37,210	10527	70	55	135
1999-P, Dolley Madison	89,104	10530	60	60	75
1999-P, Yellowstone	82,563	10531	60	60	80
2000-P, Library of Congress	53,264	10535	55	55	90
2000-P, Leif Ericson	28,150	10534	75	55	220
2001-D, American Buffalo	227,131	10538	115	115	240
2001-P, U.S. Capitol Visitor Center	35,380	10539	55	55	115

* Value in original government packaging (OGP).

Modern Commemorative Dollar Circulation Strikes *(continued)*

	Mintage	GSID	OGP*	MS-69	MS-70
2002-W, West Point Bicentennial	103,201	10544	$60	$55	$75
2003-P, First Flight	53,533	10546	60	60	75
2004-P, Thomas Edison	92,510	10548	55	55	80
2004-P, Lewis and Clark	142,015	10549	55	55	75
2005-P, Chief Justice Marshall	67,096	15385	55	55	75
2005-P, U.S. Marine Corps 230th	49,671	15386	60	55	160
2006-P, Benjamin Franklin, Founding Father	58,000	65223	55	55	75
2006-P, Benjamin Franklin, Scientist	58,000	65221	55	55	70
2006-S, San Francisco Old Mint	67,100	68423	60	60	80
2007-P, Jamestown	81,034	68608	55	55	75
2007-P, Little Rock High School Desegregation	66,093	68925	55	55	75
2008-P, Bald Eagle Recovery	119,204	68944	60	55	75
2009-P, Abraham Lincoln	125,000	70399	60	60	80
2009-P, Louis Braille	82,639	70516	55	55	75
2010-W, American Veterans Disabled for Life	78,301	70816	55	55	75
2010-P, Boy Scouts	105,020	70833	60	60	70
2011-S, U.S. Army	43,512	70966	60	60	80
2011-S, Medal of Honor	44,752	71015	60	60	80
2012-W, Infantry Soldier	44,348	71439	60	60	75
2012-P, Star-Spangled Banner	41,686	71437	60	60	80
2013-W, Girl Scouts	37,462	71614	60	60	80
2013-W, 5-Star Generals	34,638	71489	60	55	80
2014-P, Baseball Hall of Fame	142,405	71624	60	60	90
2014-P, Civil Rights Act	24,720	71630	60	55	80
2015-P, U.S. Marshals	38,149	76855	55	55	75
2015-P, March of Dimes	24,742	76856	55	55	75
2016-P, Mark Twain	26,291	76857	60	60	75
2016-P, National Park Service	20,979	76858	60	60	80
2017-P, Lions Club	68,330	76859	55	55	75
2017-P, Boys Town	15,561	76860	60	60	75
2018-P, World War I Centennial	22,338	79397	65	55	85
2018-P, Breast Cancer Awareness	12,521	79396	65	65	85
2019-P, Apollo 11	50,711	70410	66	66	76
2019-P, American Legion	13,790	82376	55	55	75
2020-P, Basketball Hall of Fame	21,317	82365	70	55	90
2020-P, Women's Suffrage	21,317	82366	70	55	90
2020-P, Christa McAuliffe	16,025	84880	95	55	115
2021-P, National Law Enforcement Memorial	9,422	85120	95	55	115
2022-W, Negro Leagues	8,448	188857	95	55	115
2022-W, Purple Heart	14,316	195830	95	55	115
2024-P, Harriet Tubman	7,277	346862	95	55	115
2024-P, Greatest Generation		351807	95	55	115
2025-P, U.S. Marine Corps 250th		377391	115	115	135

* Value in original government packaging (OGP).

Modern Commemorative Dollar Proof Strikes

	Mintage	GSID	OGP*	PF-69	PF-70
1983-S, L.A. Olympics, Discus Thrower (a)	1,577,025	10446	$55	$55	$285
1984-S, L.A. Olympics, Coliseum (a)	1,801,210	10450	55	55	110
1986-S, Statue of Liberty (a)	6,414,638	10452	55	55	75
1987-S, Constitution Bicentennial (a)	2,747,116	10454	55	55	75
1988-S, Seoul Olympiad (a)	1,359,366	10457	55	55	75
1989-S, Congress Bicentennial (a)	762,198	10459	55	55	145
1990-P, Eisenhower (a)	1,144,461	10460	55	55	145
(1993-W), World War II 50th	342,041	10463	60	60	170
1991-S, United Service Organizations	321,275	10471	55	55	110
1991-S, Mount Rushmore (a)	738,419	10470	55	55	95
1991-P, Korean War Memorial	618,488	10469	55	55	155
1992-W, White House	375,851	10477	55	55	130
1992-P, Christopher Columbus	385,241	10475	55	55	160
1992-S, XXV Olympiad (a)	504,505	10476	55	55	170
1993-S, Bill of Rights–James Madison (a)	534,001	10480	55	55	160
1993-S, Thomas Jefferson Birth	332,891	10481	55	55	130
1994-S, World Cup (a,b)	577,090	10490	60	60	95
1994-S, U.S. Capitol Bicentennial	279,579	10489	60	60	130
1994-P, U.S. POW Museum	224,449	10485	60	60	470
1994-P, Vietnam Veterans Memorial	227,671	10484	60	60	415
1994-P, Women in Military	241,278	10487	60	60	285
1995-P, Atlanta Olympics, Gymnastics (a)	182,676	10502	60	60	180
1995-P, Atlanta Olympics, Paralympics (a)	138,337	10503	60	60	90
1995-P, Atlanta Olympics, Track and Field (a)	136,935	10505	60	60	260
1995-P, Atlanta Olympics, Cycling (a)	118,795	10501	60	60	360
1995-S, Civil War Battlefields (a)	437,114	10506	60	60	235
1995-P, Special Olympics	351,764	10504	60	60	115
1996-P, Atlanta Olympics, Tennis (a)	92,016	10517	70	70	850
1996-P, Atlanta Olympics, Paralympics (a)	84,280	10515	55	55	2,200
1996-P, Atlanta Olympics, Rowing (a)	151,890	10516	55	55	1,400
1996-P, Atlanta Olympics, High Jump (a)	124,502	10514	55	55	5,500
1996-P, Smithsonian	129,152	10513	60	60	575
1996-S, National Community Service	101,543	10519	60	60	95
1997-P, U.S. Botanic Garden (a)	189,671	10523	60	60	340
1997-P, National Law Enforcement Officers Memorial	110,428	10522	60	60	150
1997-S, Jackie Robinson	110,002	10525	60	60	275
1998-S, Robert F. Kennedy	99,020	10528	60	60	170
1998-S, Black Rev. War Patriots	75,070	10529	60	60	275
1999-P, Dolley Madison	224,403	10532	65	65	85
1999-P, Yellowstone	187,595	10533	60	60	235
2000-P, Library of Congress	198,503	10537	60	60	115
2000-P, Leif Ericson	144,748	10536	60	60	550
2001-P, American Buffalo	272,869	10540	115	115	260
2001-P, U.S. Capitol Visitor Center	143,793	10541	60	60	135
2002-P, Salt Lake City Olympics	166,864	10543	60	60	130
2002-W, West Point	288,293	10545	60	60	85
2003-P, First Flight	190,240	10547	60	60	195

* Value in original government packaging (OGP). **a.** Proof dollars from these series were also included in Prestige Sets; see "Proof Sets," listed in the "Proof and Mint Sets" chapter. **b.** The Mint also issued other minor sets under this program; they are not listed here.

Modern Commemorative Dollar Proof Strikes *(continued)*

	Mintage	GSID	OGP*	PF-69	PF-70
2004-P, Thomas Edison	211,055	10550	$60	$60	$75
2004-P, Lewis and Clark	351,989	10551	60	60	95
2005-P, U.S. Marine Corps 230th	548,810	15384	60	60	145
2006-P, Benjamin Franklin, Scientist	142,000	65224	60	60	80
2006-P, Benjamin Franklin, Founding Father	142,000	65222	65	65	85
2006-S, San Francisco Old Mint	160,870	68402	60	60	95
2007-P, Jamestown	260,363	68603	65	65	80
2007-P, Little Rock High School Desegregation	124,678	68742	60	60	75
2008-P, Bald Eagle Recovery	294,601	68950	60	60	130
2009-P, Abraham Lincoln Bicentennial	325,000	70400	60	60	80
2009-P, Louis Braille	135,235	70515	60	60	90
2010-W, American Veterans Disabled for Life	202,770	70817	55	55	75
2010-P, Boy Scouts	244,963	70832	60	60	80
2011-P, U.S. Army	119,829	70968	60	60	90
2011-P, Medal of Honor	112,833	71017	60	60	130
2012-W, Infantry Soldier	161,151	71440	60	60	90
2012-P, Star-Spangled Banner	169,065	71438	60	60	90
2013-W, Girl Scouts	86,355	71613	60	60	80
2013-P, 5-Star Generals	69,283	71487	65	65	85
2014-P, Civil Rights Act	61,992	76861	70	70	90
2014-P, Baseball Hall of Fame	249,049	71626	60	60	95
2015-P, U.S. Marshals	124,329	71679	55	55	110
2015-W, March of Dimes	32,030	71694	60	60	85
2016-P, Mark Twain	78,549	76862	60	60	85
2016-P, National Park Service	77,319	76863	60	60	90
2017-P, Lions Club	17,224	76864	65	65	85
2017-P, Boys Town	23,212	76865	60	60	110
2018-P, World War I Centennial	127,867	79399	65	65	95
2018-P, Breast Cancer Awareness	34,548	79400	75	75	95
2019-P, Apollo 11	224,010	79420	80	80	100
2019-P, Apollo 11, 5 oz. (c)	68,308	81966	260	260	390
2019-P, American Legion	63,100	82377	70	70	90
2020-P, Basketball Hall of Fame	60,756	81967	60	60	80
2020-P, Basketball Hall of Fame, colorized	25,719	82367	80	80	100
2020-P, Women's Suffrage	33,441	82368	80	80	100
2020-P, Christa McAuliffe	54,222	84879	100	100	120
2021-P, National Law Enforcement Memorial	29,701	85121	100	100	120
2022-P, Negro Leagues Baseball	22,687	188858	90	90	120
2022-P, Negro Leagues Baseball, with Privy Mark	19,674	188859	95	95	130
2022-W, Purple Heart	48,433	195831	100	100	130
2022-W, Purple Heart, colorized	24,949	195832	130	130	190
2024-W, Harriet Tubman		346863	100	100	130
2024-W, Greatest Generation		351808	100	100	130
2025-P, U.S. Marine Corps 250th		377392	120	115	135

* Value in original government packaging (OGP). **c.** Identical in design to the regular-issue dollar coin, but enlarged to 3 inches in diameter.

Modern Commemorative $5 Gold Coins

Statue of Liberty (1986)

Constitution Bicentennial (1987)

Seoul Olympiad (1988)

Congress Bicentennial (1989)

Mount Rushmore (1991)

Christopher Columbus (1992)

XXV Olympiad (1992)

Bill of Rights –
James Madison (1993)

World War II 50th Anniversary
(1993)

World Cup (1994)

Atlanta Olympics,
Stadium (1995)

Atlanta Olympics,
Torch Runner (1995)

Civil War Battlefields (1995)

Atlanta Olympics,
Cauldron (1996)

Atlanta Olympics,
Flag Bearer (1996)

Smithsonian (1996)

Franklin D. Roosevelt (1997)

Jackie Robinson (1997)

George Washington Death
(1999)

U.S. Capitol Visitor Center
(2001)

Salt Lake City Olympics
(2002)

San Francisco Old Mint (2006)

Jamestown (2007)

Bald Eagle Recovery (2008)

Medal of Honor (2011)

U.S. Army (2011)

Star-Spangled Banner (2012)

5-Star Generals (2013)

Baseball Hall of Fame (2014)

U.S. Marshals (2015)

Mark Twain (2016)

National Park Service (2016)

Boys Town (2017)

Breast Cancer Awareness (2018)

American Legion (2019)

Apollo 11 (2019)

Basketball Hall of Fame (2020)

National Law Enforcement Memorial (2021)

Negro Leagues (2022)

National Purple Heart (2022)

Greatest Generation (2024)

Harriet Tubman (2024)

U.S. Marine Corps 250th Anniversary (2025)

Modern Commemorative $5 Gold Circulation Strikes

	Mintage	GSID	OGP*	MS-69	MS-70
Gold $5 (1986 to Date)	**n/a**	**82371**	**$1,150**	**$1,150**	**$1,150**
1986-W, Statue of Liberty	95,248	10552	1,150	1,150	1,150
1987-W, Constitution Bicentennial	214,225	10554	1,150	1,150	1,150
1988-W, Seoul Olympiad	62,913	10556	1,150	1,150	1,200
1989-W, Congress Bicentennial	46,899	10558	1,150	1,150	1,150
1991-W, Mount Rushmore	31,959	10562	1,150	1,150	1,150
1992-W, Christopher Columbus	24,329	10567	1,150	1,150	1,150
1992-W, XXV Olympiad	27,732	10568	1,150	1,150	1,150
1993-W, Bill of Rights–James Madison	23,266	10571	1,150	1,150	1,150
(1993-W), World War II 50th	23,672	10560	1,150	1,150	1,150
1994-W, World Cup	22,447	10573	1,150	1,150	1,150
1995-W, Civil War Battlefields	12,735	10575	1,150	1,150	1,200
1995-W, Atlanta Olympics, Torch Runner	14,675	10576	1,150	1,150	1,200
1995-W, Atlanta Olympics, Stadium	10,579	10577	1,150	1,150	1,200
1996-W, Atlanta Olympics, Flag Bearer	9,174	10582	1,150	1,150	1,200
1996-W, Atlanta Olympics, Cauldron	9,210	10581	1,150	1,150	1,200
1996-W, Smithsonian	9,068	10583	1,150	1,150	1,200
1997-W, Jackie Robinson	5,174	10588	1,200	1,200	1,550
1997-W, Franklin D. Roosevelt	11,894	10587	1,150	1,150	1,150
1999-W, George Washington Death	22,511	10591	1,150	1,150	1,150
2001-W, Capitol Visitor Center	6,761	10593	1,150	1,150	1,150
2002-W, Salt Lake City Olympics	10,585	10595	1,150	1,150	1,150
2006-S, San Francisco Old Mint	17,500	68413	1,150	1,150	1,150
2007-W, Jamestown	18,623	68607	1,150	1,150	1,150
2008-W, Bald Eagle Recovery	15,009	68919	1,150	1,150	1,150
2011-P, U.S. Army	8,052	70956	1,150	1,150	1,150
2011-P, Medal of Honor	8,233	71002	1,150	1,150	1,150
2012-W, Star-Spangled Banner	7,027	76840	1,150	1,150	1,150
2013-P, 5-Star Generals	5,667	71622	1,150	1,150	1,150
2014-W, Baseball Hall of Fame	17,674	71623	1,150	1,150	1,150
2015-W, U.S. Marshals	6,743	77462	1,150	1,150	1,150
2016-W, Mark Twain	5,701	77463	1,150	1,150	1,150
2016-W, National Park Service	5,195	77464	1,150	1,150	1,150
2017-W, Boys Town	2,939	77465	1,150	1,150	1,250
2018-W, Breast Cancer Awareness (a)	4,477	77466	1,150	1,150	1,150
2019-W, Apollo 11	12,035	77467	1,150	1,150	1,150
2019-W, American Legion	2,929	82373	1,150	1,150	1,150
2020-W, Basketball Hall of Fame	3,263	84820	1,150	1,150	1,200
2021-W, National Law Enforcement Memorial	1,754	85122	1,150	1,150	1,250
2022-W, Purple Heart	1,689	195833	1,150	1,150	1,250
2022-W, Negro Leagues	1,507	188860	1,150	1,150	1,250
2024-W, Harriet Tubman	1,264	346864	1,150	1,150	1,250
2024-W, Greatest Generation	1,314	351809	1,150	1,150	1,250
2025-W, U.S. Marine Corps 250th		377386	1,200	1,200	1,250

* Value in original government packaging (OGP). **a.** Produced in "rose pink" gold, composed of .850 gold, .148 copper, and .002 zinc.

Modern Commemorative $5 Gold Proof Strikes

	Mintage	GSID	OGP*	PF-69	PF-70
1986-W, Statue of Liberty	404,013	10553	$1,200	$1,200	$1,200
1987-W, Constitution Bicentennial	651,659	10555	1,200	1,200	1,200
1988-W, Seoul Olympiad	281,465	10557	1,200	1,200	1,200
1989-W, Congress Bicentennial	164,690	10559	1,200	1,200	1,200
1991-W, Mount Rushmore	111,991	10563	1,200	1,200	1,200
1992-W, Christopher Columbus	79,730	10569	1,200	1,200	1,200
1992-W, XXV Olympiad	77,313	10570	1,200	1,200	1,200
1993-W, Bill of Rights–James Madison	78,651	10572	1,200	1,200	1,200
(1993-W), World War II 50th	67,026	10561	1,200	1,200	1,200
1994-W, World Cup	89,614	10574	1,200	1,200	1,200
1995-W, Civil War Battlefields	55,246	10578	1,200	1,200	1,200
1995-W, Atlanta Olympics, Torch Runner	57,442	10580	1,200	1,200	1,200
1995-W, Atlanta Olympics, Stadium	43,124	10579	1,200	1,200	1,200
1996-W, Atlanta Olympics, Flag Bearer	32,886	10585	1,200	1,200	1,200
1996-W, Atlanta Olympics, Cauldron	38,555	10584	1,200	1,200	1,200
1996-W, Smithsonian	21,772	10586	1,200	1,200	1,200
1997-W, Jackie Robinson	24,072	10589	1,200	1,200	1,250
1997-W, Franklin D. Roosevelt	29,474	10590	1,200	1,200	1,200
1999-W, George Washington Death	41,693	10592	1,200	1,200	1,200
2001-W, U.S. Capitol Visitor Center	27,652	10594	1,200	1,200	1,200
2002-W, Salt Lake City Olympics	32,877	10596	1,200	1,200	1,200
2006-S, San Francisco Old Mint	44,174	68409	1,200	1,200	1,200
2007-W, Jamestown	47,123	68604	1,200	1,200	1,200
2008-W, Bald Eagle Recovery	59,269	68920	1,200	1,200	1,200
2011-W, U.S. Army	17,148	70955	1,200	1,200	1,200
2011-W, Medal of Honor	17,999	71004	1,200	1,200	1,200
2012-W, Star-Spangled Banner	18,313	71589	1,200	1,200	1,200
2013-W, 5-Star Generals	15,844	71593	1,200	1,200	1,200
2014-W, Baseball Hall of Fame	32,428	71625	1,200	1,200	1,200
2015-W, U.S. Marshals	24,959	77468	1,200	1,200	1,200
2016-W, Mark Twain	13,271	77469	1,200	1,200	1,200
2016-W, National Park Service	19,503	77470	1,200	1,200	1,200
2017-W, Boys Town	7,377	77471	1,200	1,200	1,200
2018-W, Breast Cancer Awareness (a)	10,381	77472	1,200	1,200	1,200
2019-W, Apollo 11	34,036	77473	1,200	1,200	1,200
2019-W, American Legion	10,916	82374	1,200	1,200	1,200
2020-W, Basketball Hall of Fame	8,070	81968	1,200	1,200	1,200
2021-W, National Law Enforcement Memorial	1,473	85123	1,200	1,200	1,250
2022-W, Purple Heart	2,783	195834	1,200	1,200	1,250
2022-W, Negro Leagues Baseball	1,534	188861	1,200	1,200	1,250
2024-W, Harriet Tubman		346865	1,200	1,200	1,250
2024-W, Greatest Generation		351810	1,200	1,200	1,250
2025-W, U.S. Marine Corps 250th		377387	1,250	1,200	1,250

* Value in original government packaging (OGP). **a.** Produced in "rose pink" gold, composed of .850 gold, .148 copper, and .002 zinc.

Modern Commemorative $10 Gold and Bimetallic Coins

L.A. Olympics, Torch Bearer (1984)

Library of Congress (2000)

First Flight (2003)

Mayflower 400th Anniversary (2020)

Modern Commemorative $10 Gold and Bimetallic Circulation Strikes

	Mintage	GSID	OGP*	MS-69	MS-70
1984-W, L.A. Olympics, Torch Bearers	75,886	10600	$2,300	$2,300	$2,350
2000-W, Library of Congress, Bimetallic (Gold/Platinum) (a)	7,261	10602	1,450	1,450	1,550
2003-W, First Flight	10,009	10604	2,300	2,300	2,350

* Value in original government packaging (OGP). **a.** Composed of a ring of gold surrounding a platinum center.

Modern Commemorative $10 Gold and Bimetallic Proof Strikes

	Mintage	GSID	OGP*	PF-69	PF-70
1984-P, L.A. Olympics, Torch Bearers	33,309	10598	$2,300	$2,300	$2,450
1984-D, L.A. Olympics, Torch Bearers	34,533	10597	2,300	2,300	2,450
1984-S, L.A. Olympics, Torch Bearers	48,551	10599	2,300	2,300	2,350
1984-W, L.A. Olympics, Torch Bearers	381,085	10601	2,300	2,300	2,350
2000-W, Library of Congress, Bimetallic (Gold/Platinum) (a)	27,445	10603	1,450	1,450	1,550
2003-W, First Flight	21,676	10605	2,300	2,300	2,400
2020-W, Mayflower 400th Anniversary $10 Gold Coin, Reverse Proof	4,881	84819	1,300	1,300	1,400
2020-W, Mayflower 400th Anniversary $10 Gold Coin	4,743	84821	1,500	1,500	1,600

* Value in original government packaging (OGP). **a.** Composed of a ring of gold surrounding a platinum center.

Modern Commemorative $25 Gold Coins

WWII 75th Anniversary (2020)

Modern Commemorative $25 Gold Proof Strikes

	Mintage	GSID	OGP*	PF-69	PF-70
2020-W, World War II 75th Anniversary	7,367	152322	$2,450	$2,500	$2,950

* Value in original government packaging (OGP).

Modern Commemorative Sets

	GSID	OGP*
1983–1984, L.A. Olympics, Proof dollar set: $1 from each year	74349	$115.00
1983, L.A. Olympics 3-piece Unc set: P-D-S Discus Thrower $1	74333	165.00
1984, L.A. Olympics 3-piece Unc set: P-D-S Coliseum $1	70964	165.00
1983–1984, L.A. Olympics Gold and Silver 3-coin Unc set: 1983 and 1984 $1; 1984 $10	74334	2,500.00
1983–1984, L.A. Olympics Gold and Silver 3-coin Proof set: 1983 and 1984 $1; 1984 $10	74367	2,500.00
1983–1984, L.A. Olympics 6-coin set: Both years, P-S $1; 1984-W Proof and Unc $10 (a)	15379	4,950.00
1986, Statue of Liberty 2-coin set: Unc $1 and 50¢	74310	60.00
1986, Statue of Liberty 3-coin set: Unc $1, 50¢, and $5	74335	1,200.00
1986, Statue of Liberty 2-coin set: Proof $1 and 50¢	70921	60.00
1986, Statue of Liberty 3-coin set: Proof $1, 50¢, and $5	15380	1,250.00
1986, Statue of Liberty 6-coin set: Proof and Unc 50¢, $1, and $5 (a)	25338	2,450.00
1987, Constitution Bicentennial 2-coin set: Unc $1 and $5	74311	1,200.00
1987, Constitution Bicentennial 2-coin set: Proof $1 and $5	74350	1,250.00
1987, Constitution Bicentennial 4-coin set: Proof and Unc $1 and $5 (a)	25340	2,450.00
1988, Seoul Olympiad 2-coin set: Unc $1 and $5	74312	1,250.00
1988, Seoul Olympiad 2-coin set: Proof $1 and $5	74351	1,250.00
1988, Seoul Olympiad 4-coin set: Proof and Unc $1 and $5 (a)	25339	2,450.00
1989, Congress Bicentennial 2-coin set: Unc 50¢ and $1	74313	65.00
1989, Congress Bicentennial 2-coin set: Proof 50¢ and $1	74352	65.00
1989, Congress Bicentennial 3-coin set: Unc 50¢, $1, and $5	74336	1,250.00
1989, Congress Bicentennial 3-coin set: Proof 50¢, $1, and $5	74368	1,250.00
1989, Congress Bicentennial 6-coin set: Proof and Unc 50¢, $1, and $5 (a)	25336	2,450.00
1991, Mount Rushmore 2-coin set: Unc 50¢ and $1	74314	75.00
1991, Mount Rushmore 2-coin set: Proof 50¢ and $1	74353	70.00
1991, Mount Rushmore 3-coin set: Unc 50¢, $1, and $5	74337	1,250.00
1991, Mount Rushmore 3-coin set: Proof 50¢, $1, and $5	25337	1,250.00
1991, Mount Rushmore 6-coin set: Proof and Unc 50¢, $1, and $5 (a)	74385	2,450.00
1992, XXV Olympiad 2-coin set: Unc 50¢ and $1	74315	65.00
1992, XXV Olympiad 2-coin set: Proof 50¢ and $1	74354	65.00
1992, XXV Olympiad 3-coin set: Unc 50¢, $1, and $5	74338	1,250.00
1992, XXV Olympiad 3-coin set: Proof 50¢, $1, and $5	74369	1,250.00
1992, XXV Olympiad 6-coin set: Proof and Unc 50¢, $1, and $5 (a)	74386	2,450.00
1992, Christopher Columbus 2-coin set: Unc 50¢ and $1	74316	75.00
1992, Christopher Columbus 2-coin set: Proof 50¢ and $1	74355	70.00
1992, Christopher Columbus 3-coin set: Unc 50¢, $1, and $5	74339	1,250.00
1992, Christopher Columbus 3-coin set: Proof 50¢, $1, and $5	74370	1,250.00
1992, Christopher Columbus 6-coin set: Proof and Unc 50¢, $1, and $5 (a)	74387	2,450.00
1993, Bill of Rights–James Madison 2-coin set: Unc Silver 50¢ and $1	74317	80.00
1993, Bill of Rights–James Madison 2-coin set: Proof Silver 50¢ and $1	74356	80.00
1993, Bill of Rights–James Madison 3-coin set: Unc Silver 50¢, $1, and $5	74340	1,250.00
1993, Bill of Rights–James Madison 3-coin set: Proof 50¢, $1, and $5	25335	1,250.00
1993, Bill of Rights–James Madison 6-coin set: Proof and Unc Silver 50¢, $1, and $5 (a)	74388	2,450.00
1993, Bill of Rights–James Madison "Young Collector" set: Silver 50¢	81921	23.00
1993, Bill of Rights–James Madison Educational set: Unc Silver 50¢; Madison medal	81922	25.00
1993, Bill of Rights–James Madison Coin and Stamp set: Proof Silver 50¢; stamp	81923	24.00
1993, World War II 50th 2-coin set: Unc 50¢ and $1	74318	70.00
1993, World War II 50th 2-coin set: Proof 50¢ and $1	74357	80.00
1993, World War II 50th 3-coin set: Unc 50¢, $1, and $5	74341	1,250.00
1993, World War II 50th 3-coin set: Proof 50¢, $1, and $5	74371	1,250.00
1993, World War II 50th "Young Collector" set: Unc 50¢	81924	13.50
1993, World War II 50th 6-coin set: Proof and Unc 50¢, $1, and $5	74389	2,450.00
1993, World War II Victory Medal set: Unc 50¢; reproduction medal	81925	16.00

* Value in original government packaging (OGP). **a.** Packaged in a cherrywood box.

Modern Commemorative Sets *(continued)*

	GSID	OGP*
1993, Thomas Jefferson Birth "Coinage and Currency" set (issued in 1994), Unc $1 and Jefferson 5¢; $2 note	74320	$90.00
1994, World Cup 2-coin set: Unc 50¢ and $1	74319	70.00
1994, World Cup 2-coin set: Proof 50¢ and $1	74358	75.00
1994, World Cup 3-coin set: Unc 50¢, $1, and $5	74342	1,250.00
1994, World Cup 3-coin set: Proof 50¢, $1, and $5	15381	1,250.00
1994, World Cup 6-coin set: Proof and Unc 50¢, $1, and $5 (a)	74390	2,450.00
1994, World Cup "Young Collector" set: Unc 50¢	81926	9.50
1994, World Cup "Special Edition" set: Proof 50¢ and $1	81927	70.00
1994, U.S. Veterans 3-coin set: Unc POW, Vietnam, and Women in Military $1	74343	170.00
1994, U.S. Veterans 3-coin set: Proof POW, Vietnam, and Women in Military $1	74372	175.00
1995, Special Olympics 2-coin set: Proof $1 and 1995-S 50¢	81928	100.00
1995, Civil War Battlefields 2-coin set: Unc 50¢ and $1	74321	75.00
1995, Civil War Battlefields 2-coin set: Proof 50¢ and $1	74359	90.00
1995, Civil War Battlefields 3-coin set: Unc 50¢, $1, and $5	74344	1,250.00
1995, Civil War Battlefields 3-coin set: Proof 50¢, $1, and $5	74373	1,250.00
1995, Civil War Battlefields 6-coin set: Proof and Unc 50¢, $1, and $5 (a)	74391	2,500.00
1995, Civil War Battlefields "Young Collector" set: Unc 50¢	81929	20.00
1995, Civil War Battlefields 2-coin "Union" set: Unc 50¢ and $1	81930	75.00
1995, Civil War Battlefields 3-coin "Union" set: Unc 50¢, $1, and $5	81931	1,250.00
1995, Atlanta Olympics 2-coin set: Proof $1 (Gymnastics, Blind Runner)	74360	125.00
1995, Atlanta Olympics 2-coin set: Proof $1 (Track and Field, Cycling)	74361	125.00
1996, Atlanta Olympics 2-coin set: Proof $1 (Tennis, Wheelchair Athlete)	74362	125.00
1996, Atlanta Olympics 2-coin set: Proof $1 (High Jump, Rowing)	74363	120.00
1995, Atlanta Olympics 4-coin set: Unc 50¢ (Basketball), $1 (Blind Runner, Gymnastics), $5 (Torch Runner)	74345	1,250.00
1995, Atlanta Olympics 4-coin set: Proof 50¢ (Basketball), $1 (Blind Runner, Gymnastics), $5 (Torch Runner)	74377	1,300.00
1995, Atlanta Olympics 4-coin set: Unc 50¢ (Baseball), $1 (Cyclist, Track and Field), $5 (Olympic Stadium)	74346	1,300.00
1995, Atlanta Olympics 4-coin set: Proof 50¢ (Baseball), $1 (Cyclist, Track and Field), $5 (Olympic Stadium)	74378	1,300.00
1996, Atlanta Olympics 4-coin set: Unc 50¢ (Swimming), $1 (Tennis, Wheelchair Athlete), $5 (Flag Bearer)	74347	1,400.00
1996, Atlanta Olympics 4-coin set: Proof 50¢ (Swimming), $1 (Tennis, Wheelchair Athlete), $5 (Flag Bearer)	74380	1,300.00
1996, Atlanta Olympics 4-coin set: Unc 50¢ (Soccer), $1 (High Jump, Rowing), $5 (Cauldron)	74348	1,350.00
1996, Atlanta Olympics 4-coin set: Proof 50¢ (Soccer), $1 (High Jump, Rowing), $5 (Cauldron)	74381	1,300.00
1995–1996, Atlanta Olympics "Young Collector" 4-coin set: Unc 50¢ (Baseball, Basketball, Soccer, Swimming)	74379	90.00
1995–1996, Atlanta Olympics 8-coin Proof set: all Proof $1 coins in series	74392	470.00
1995–1996, Atlanta Olympics 16-coin set: all Unc coins in series (a)	74393	470.00
1995–1996, Atlanta Olympics 16-coin Proof set: all Proof coins in series (a)	74394	5,250.00
1995–1996, Atlanta Olympics 32-coin set: all Unc and Proof coins in series (a)	10406	10,500.00
1995, Atlanta Olympics "Young Collector" set: Unc 50¢ (Basketball)	81934	13.50
1995, Atlanta Olympics "Young Collector" set: Unc 50¢ (Baseball)	81935	19.00
1996, Atlanta Olympics "Young Collector" set: Unc 50¢ (Swimming)	81936	47.00
1996, Atlanta Olympics "Young Collector" set: Unc 50¢ (Soccer)	81937	27.00
1996, National Community Service set: Proof $1; stamp	81938	60.00
1996, Smithsonian 2-coin set: Proof $1 and $5	74364	1,250.00
1996, Smithsonian 4-coin set: Proof and Unc $1 and $5 (a)	74382	2,450.00
1996, Smithsonian "Young Collector" set: Proof $1	81939	60.00
1997, U.S. Botanic Garden "Coinage and Currency" set: Unc $1 and Jefferson 5¢; $1 note	74322	65.00
1997, Jackie Robinson 2-coin set: Proof $1 and $5	70889	1,250.00
1997, Jackie Robinson 4-coin set: Proof and Unc $1 and $5 (a)	74383	2,500.00
1997, Jackie Robinson 3-piece "Legacy" set: $5; baseball card and pin (a)	81940	1,300.00
1997, Franklin D. Roosevelt 2-coin set: Proof and Unc $5	74323	2,300.00

* Value in original government packaging (OGP). **a.** Packaged in a cherrywood box.

Modern Commemorative Sets *(continued)*

	GSID	OGP*
1997, National Law Enforcement Officers Memorial Insignia set: $1; pin and patch	81941	$110
1998, Robert F. Kennedy 2-coin set: Proof and Unc $1	74324	125
1998, Robert F. Kennedy 2-coin set: Unc $1 and 1998-S, Matte Finish Silver 50¢	74325	140
1998, Black Revolutionary War Patriots 2-coin set: Proof and Unc $1	74326	125
1998, Black Revolutionary War Patriots "Young Collector" set: Unc $1	81942	70
1998, Black Revolutionary War Patriots Black Revolutionary War Patriots set: $1; four stamps	81943	80
1999, Dolley Madison 2-coin set: Proof and Unc $1	74327	125
1999, Yellowstone 2-coin set: Proof and Unc $1	74329	120
1999, George Washington Death 2-coin set: Proof and Unc $5	74328	2,300
2000, Millennium Coin and Currency set: Unc 2000 Sacagawea $1 and Silver Eagle; Series 1999 $1 Federal Reserve Note	70996	85
2000, Leif Ericson 2-coin set: Proof $1; Icelandic 1,000 kronur	74365	90
2001, American Buffalo "Coinage and Currency" set: Unc $1; face reprint of 1899 Silver Certificate, two stamps	15382	145
2001, American Buffalo 2-coin set: Proof and Unc $1	74330	220
2001, U.S. Capitol Visitor Center 3-coin set: Proof 50¢, $1, and $5	74374	1,250
2002, Salt Lake City Olympics 2-coin set: Proof $1 and $5	74366	1,250
2002, Salt Lake City Olympics 4-coin set: Proof and Unc $1 and $5	74384	2,450
2003, First Flight Centennial 3-coin set: Proof 50¢, $1, and $10	81944	2,450
2003, Legacies of Freedom set: Unc 2003 $1 Silver Eagle; Unc 2002 £2 Silver Britannia	81945	130
2004, Thomas A. Edison set: Unc $1; working light bulb	81946	70
2004, Lewis and Clark Coin and Pouch set: Proof $1; beaded pouch	81947	100
2004, Lewis and Clark "Coinage and Currency" set: Unc $1, 2004-D Sacagawea $1, and two 2004 nickels; replica 1901 $10 note, Peace Medal replica, three stamps	69043	65
2004, Westward Journey Nickel Series Coin and Medal set: Proof Sacagawea $1 and two 2004 nickels; Peace Medal replica	68814	16
2005, Westward Journey Nickel Series Coin and Medal set: Proof Sacagawea $1 and two 2005 Proof nickels; Peace Medal replica	81948	16
2005, Marine Corps 230th Coin and Stamp set: Unc $1; stamp	81951	65
2005, American Legacy set: Proof Marine Corps and John Marshall commemorative Silver dollars, 11-piece Proof Set	71001	130
2006, American Legacy set: Proof Benjamin Franklin "Founding Father" commemorative Silver dollar, Proof San Francisco Old Mint Silver dollar, and Proof cent, nickel, dime, quarter, half dollar, and Sacagawea dollar	74463	135
2006, Benjamin Franklin "Coin and Chronicles" set: Unc "Scientist" $1; four stamps, Poor Richard's Almanack replica, intaglio print	70963	70
2007, American Legacy set: Proof Jamestown commemorative Silver dollar, Proof Little Rock Central High School Desegregation commemorative Silver dollar, and 14-piece Proof Set	72505	210
2007, Little Rock High School Desegregation Coin and Medal set: Unc $1; Bronze medal	70962	60
2008, Bald Eagle 3-piece set: Proof 50¢, $1, and $5	74375	1,250
2008, American Legacy set: Proof Bald Eagle commemorative Silver dollar and 14-piece Proof Set	72511	95
2008, Bald Eagle Bald Eagle Coin and Medal Set: Unc $1; Bronze medal	81954	65
2008, Bald Eagle "Young Collector" set: Unc 50¢	81955	60
2009, Louis Braille set: Unc $1 in tri-fold package	81957	65
2009, Abraham Lincoln "Coin and Chronicles" set: Proof $1 and four 2009-S cents	81958	85
2012, Star-Spangled Banner "Coin and Chronicles" set: Proof $1; replica document	84292	65
2012, Star-Spangled Banner 2-coin set: Proof $1 and $5	74331	1,250
2013, Theodore Roosevelt "Coin and Chronicles" set: Proof Presidential $1; Silver Presidential and Bronze National Wildlife Refuge medals; and Roosevelt print	81027	145
2013, 5-Star Generals 3-coin set: Proof 50¢, $1, and $5	74376	1,250
2013, 5-Star Generals Profile Collection, Unc 50¢ and $1; MacArthur Congressional Gold Medal replica	81959	85
2013, Girl Scouts "Young Collector" set: Unc $1	81960	60
2014, 50th Anniversary Kennedy Half Dollar Uncirculated Coin set: 2014-P and 2014-D clad half dollars	84293	43
2014, 50th Anniversary Kennedy Half Dollar Silver Coin Collection: P-Mint Pf, D-Mint Unc, S-Mint Enh Unc, and W-Mint Rev Pf Silver half dollars	77583	105

* Value in original government packaging (OGP).

Modern Commemorative Sets *(continued)*

	GSID	OGP*
2014, Franklin D. Roosevelt "Coin and Chronicles" set: Proof 10¢ and Presidential $1; Bronze and Silver Presidential medals; four stamps	81028	$75.00
2014, Baseball Hall of Fame "Young Collector" set: Unc 50¢	81961	27.00
2014, American $1 Coin and Currency set: 2014-D Native American Enh Unc $1; $1 Federal Reserve Note	81962	13.50
2015, Harry S. Truman "Coin and Chronicles" set: Rev Pf Presidential $1, Silver Presidential medal, stamp	77577	260.00
2015, Dwight D. Eisenhower "Coin and Chronicles" set: Rev Pf Presidential $1, Silver Presidential medal, stamp	77578	170.00
2015, John F. Kennedy "Coin and Chronicles" set: Rev Pf Presidential $1, Silver Presidential medal, stamp	77579	100.00
2015, Lyndon B. Johnson "Coin and Chronicles" set: Rev Pf Presidential $1, Silver Presidential medal, stamp	77580	70.00
2015, American $1 Coin and Currency set: 2015-W Native American Enh Unc $1 and $1 Federal Reserve Note	77581	13.50
2015, U.S. Marshals 3-coin set: Proof 50¢, $1, and $5	77563	1,250.00
2015, March of Dimes Special Silver Set: Proof $1, 2015-P Rev Pf Silver 10¢ and 2015-W Pf Silver 10¢	77564	90.00
2016, American $1 Coin and Currency set: 2016-S Native American Enh Unc dollar and $1 Federal Reserve Note	77582	13.50
2016, Ronald Reagan "Coin and Chronicles" set: Rev Pf Presidential $1, 2016-W Proof ASE, Bronze Ronald and Nancy Reagan medal, engraved Reagan Presidential portrait	81029	100.00
2016, National Park Service 3-coin set: Proof 50¢, $1, and $5	81906	1,250.00
2017, Boys Town 3-coin set: Proof 50¢, $1, and $5	81920	1,250.00
2018, Breast Cancer Awareness Coin and Stamp set: Proof 50¢; stamp	81914	90.00
2018, World War I Centennial Silver Dollar and Coast Guard Medal set: Proof $1; Proof Silver Coast Guard medal	81917	75.00
2018, World War I Centennial Silver Dollar and Navy Medal set: Proof $1; Proof Silver Navy medal	81919	75.00
2018, World War I Centennial Silver Dollar and Air Service Medal set: Proof $1; Proof Silver Air Service medal	81915	75.00
2018, World War I Centennial Silver Dollar and Marine Corps Medal set: Proof $1; Proof Silver Marine Corps medal	81918	75.00
2018, World War I Centennial Silver Dollar and Army Medal set: Proof $1; Proof Silver Army medal	81916	75.00
2019, Apollo 11 50th Anniversary 2-coin set: Unc and Proof 50¢	81392	55.00
2019, American Legion 3-coin set: Proof 50¢, $1, and $5	81910	80.00
2019, American Legion Silver Dollar and Medal set: Proof $1; American Veterans medal	81909	1,300.00
2019, American $1 Coin and Currency set: 2019-P Native American Enh Unc $1; $1 Federal Reserve Note	81911	13.50
2019, Youth Coin and Currency set: Five Proof 25¢; $2 Federal Reserve Note	376891	24.00
2020, Basketball Hall of Fame "Kids Set." 2020-S Enh Unc 50¢	82370	40.00
2020, Women's Suffrage Coin and Medal set: Proof $1; Silver medal	82369	95.00
2020-W, Mayflower 400th Anniversary Silver Coin and Medal set: Proof $10 Gold coin and Silver medal	85125	160.00
2020-W, Mayflower 400th Anniversary Proof Gold set: Proof and Reverse Proof $10 Gold coins	85126	3,050.00
2021, George H.W. Bush "Coin and Chronicles" set: Rev Pf Presidential $1; Silver Presidential medal, Barbara Bush Bronze medal, and postage stamp	376336	160.00
2021, National Law Enforcement Officers Memorial 3-coin set: Proof 50¢, $1, and $5	85124	1,350.00
2022, Negro Leagues 3-coin set: Proof 50¢, $1, and $5	193282	1,350.00
2022, Negro Leagues Coin and Medal set: Proof $1; Proof Jackie Robinson Silver medal	188863	190.00
2020, Purple Heart 3-coin set: Proof 50¢, $1, and $5	195835	1,350.00
2023-S, Morgan & Peace Dollar Set, 2 Coins	213987	130.00
2024, Greatest Generation 3-coin set: Proof 50¢, $1, and $5	346866	1,350.00
2024, Harriet Tubman 3-coin set: Proof 50¢, $1, and $5	351811	1,350.00
2025, U.S. Marine Corps 3-coin set: Proof 50¢, $1, and $5	377390	1,450.00

* Value in original government packaging (OGP).

Centennial Gold

In 2016 the Mint celebrated the centennial of three iconic American coins, all issued in 1916 to replace the unloved and much-maligned Barber design. The Mercury dime, Standing Liberty quarter, and Liberty Walking half dollar were produced in .9999 fine gold, but at slightly smaller dimensions than the original silver issues. (Regular production of the 2016 Roosevelt dimes, America the Beautiful quarters, and Kennedy half dollars continued without interruption.) Unlike most commemoratives, which are authorized by Congress, the gold Centennial coins were struck under the Treasury secretary's authority to issue gold coins "from time to time" without specific legislation. Although not commemoratives in the formal sense of the word, they are generally collected as such.

100th Anniversary of 1916 Coin Designs (2016)

Centennial Gold Circulation Strikes

	Mintage	GSID	OGP*	MS-69	MS-70
2016-W, Mercury Dime, 1/10 oz., Gold	124,885	74059	$525	$525	$550
2016-W, Standing Liberty Quarter, 1/4 oz., Gold	91,548	74060	1,250	1,250	1,250
2016-W, Liberty Walking Half Dollar, 1/2 oz., Gold	65,352	74061	2,400	2,400	2,550

* Value in original government packaging (OGP).

Best of the Mint Gold

In 2026, in conjunction with the U.S. Semiquincentennial issues authorized by the Circulating Collectible Coin Redesign Act of 2020, the Mint is producing a special Best of the Mint series. Five historic coin designs will be produced in .9999 fine gold, "reissued as faithful representations of the historic designs with the original dates of issue to acknowledge each coin's place in history." (Five 1-ounce silver companion medals, with modern designs inspired by each of the five gold coins, will also be released.) Like the circulating Semiquincentennial coins, each Best of the Mint issue will bear a privy mark in the form of the Liberty Bell inscribed with the number 250.

Unlike the Semiquincentennial circulating coinage and regular U.S. commemorative coins, the Best of the Mint issues are not associated with federal legislation. The coins in the series, like those in the 2016 Centennial Gold program, will be produced under the Treasury secretary's authority to issue gold coins "from time to time" without specific legislation.

The five coins to be honored in this program will be the 1916 Mercury dime, Standing Liberty quarter, and Liberty Walking half dollar; the 1804 silver dollar; and the 1907 Saint-Gaudens High Relief double eagle.

1804-W [2026], Draped Bust Dollar
U.S. Mint digital rendering; not an actual coin.

Privy Mark

Best of the Mint Circulation Strikes

	Mintage	GSID	OGP*	MS-69	MS-70
1916-W (2026), Mercury Dime, 1/10 oz., Gold		71686			
1916-W (2026), Standing Liberty Quarter, 1/4 oz., Gold		71693			
1916-W (2026), Liberty Walking Half Dollar, 1/2 oz., Gold		71698			
1804-W (2026), Draped Bust Dollar, 1 oz., Gold		394991			
1907-W (2026), Saint-Gaudens, Roman Numeral, High Relief $20, 1 oz., Gold		394992			

* Value in original government packaging (OGP).

Proof and Mint Sets
1936 to Date

AN OVERVIEW OF PROOF AND MINT SETS

Proof Coins and Sets

A Proof is a specimen coin struck for presentation, souvenir, exhibition, or numismatic purposes. Before 1968, Proofs were made only at the Philadelphia Mint, except in a few rare instances in which presentation pieces were struck at branch mints. Today Proofs are made at the San Francisco and West Point mints.

Scan for additional information.

The term *Proof* refers not to the condition of a coin, but to its method of manufacture. Regular-production coins (struck for circulation) in Mint State have coruscating, frosty luster; soft details; and minor imperfections. A Proof coin can usually be distinguished by its sharpness of detail, high wire edge, and extremely brilliant, mirrorlike surface. All Proofs are originally sold by the Mint at a premium.

Very few Proof coins were made prior to 1856. Because of their rarity and infrequent sales, they are not all listed in the regular edition of the *Guide Book of United States Coins*. However, here, in the *Deluxe Edition*, you will find them listed individually within their respective denominations.

Frosted Proofs were issued prior to 1936 and starting again in the late 1970s. These have a brilliant, mirrorlike field with contrasting dull or frosted design.

Matte Proofs have a granular, "sandblast" surface instead of the mirror finish. Matte Proof cents, nickels, and gold coins were issued from 1908 to 1916; a few 1921 and 1922 silver dollars and a 1998-S half dollar were also struck in this manner.

Brilliant Proofs have been issued from 1936 to date. These have a uniformly brilliant, mirrorlike surface and sharp, high-relief details.

Reverse Proofs were first struck for bullion coins in 2006, and regularly denominated, silver-struck coins have also been made with this finish since 2014. As their name implies, the devices, not the field, have a brilliant, mirrorlike finish, while the field has a matte finish.

"Prooflike" coins are occasionally seen. These are examples struck from dies that were lightly polished, often inadvertently during the removal of lines, contact marks, and other marks in the fields. In other instances, such as with certain New Orleans gold coins of the 1850s, the dies were polished in the machine shop of the mint. They are not true Proofs, but may have most of the characteristics of a Proof coin and generally command a premium. Collectors should beware of coins that have been buffed to look like Proofs; magnification will reveal polishing lines and loss of detail.

After a lapse of some 20 years, Proof coins were struck at the Philadelphia Mint from 1936 to 1942, inclusive. During these years the Mint offered Proof coins to collectors for individual sale, rather than in officially packaged sets, as such. In 1942, when the composition of the five-cent piece was changed from copper-nickel to copper-silver-manganese, there were two Proof types of this denomination available to collectors.

The striking of all Proof coins was temporarily suspended from 1943 through 1949, and again from 1965 through 1967; during the latter period, Special Mint Sets were struck. Proof sets were resumed in 1968. Sets from 1936 through 1972 included the cent, nickel, dime, quarter, and half dollar; from 1973 through 1981 the dollar was also included, and again from 2000 on. Regular Proof sets issued from 1982 to 1998 contain the cent through the half dollar. Specially packaged Prestige sets containing commemorative coins were sold from 1983 through 1997 at an additional premium. From 1999 to 2009, sets contain five different Statehood or Territorial quarters, and from 2010 to 2021, different National Parks quarters. In 1999 Proof dollars were sold separately. Four-piece Presidential dollar sets have been issued since 2007.

As part of a memorial John F. Kennedy half dollar set released in 2014, Reverse Proofs struck in silver at West Point were introduced. The Philadelphia mint first struck Reverse Proofs in 2015, also in silver, for inclusion in the March of Dimes commemorative set. Additionally, Coin and Chronicles sets of 2015 include Philadelphia-struck Reverse Proofs of the Presidential dollars of the year.

From time to time the Mint issues special Proof sets. One recent example is the four-piece 2009-S Lincoln Bicentennial set, which included each of the special cent designs issued that year, but coined in 95 percent copper (the Lincoln cent's original 1909 alloy).

Collectors are encouraged to consult David W. Lange's *Guide Book of Modern United States Proof Coin Sets* for detailed coverage and illustrations of Proof sets from 1936 to date.

From the advent of coinage programs featuring multiple annual designs within a denomination (an innovation that began with the State quarters), the U.S. Mint has offered Proof sets featuring each of the designs issued in the series for a particular year.

How Modern Proof Coins Are Made

Selected dies are inspected for perfection and are highly polished and cleaned. They are again wiped clean or polished after every 15 to 25 impressions and are replaced frequently to avoid imperfections from wear. Coinage blanks for Proof coins are polished and cleaned to ensure high quality in striking. They are then hand fed into the coinage press one at a time, each blank receiving two or more blows from the dies to bring up sharp, high-relief details. The coinage operation is done at slow speed with extra pressure. Finished Proofs are individually inspected and are handled with gloves or tongs. They also receive a final inspection by packers before being sonically sealed in special plastic cases.

Mint Sets

Official Uncirculated Mint sets are specially packaged by the government for sale to collectors. They contain Uncirculated examples of each year's coins for every denomination issued from each mint. Before 2005, the coins were the same as those normally intended for circulation and were not minted with any special consideration for quality. From 2005 to 2010, however, Mint sets were made with a satin finish rather than the traditional Uncirculated luster. As in the past, coins struck only as Proofs are not included.

Uncirculated Mint sets sold by the Treasury from 1947 through 1958 contained two examples of each regular-issue coin. These were packaged in cardboard holders that did not protect the coins from tarnish. Nicely preserved early sets generally command a 10 to 20 percent premium above average values. Since 1959, sets have been sealed in protective plastic envelopes.

Privately assembled Mint sets, and Souvenir sets produced for sale at the Philadelphia or Denver mints for special occasions, are valued according to the individual pieces they contain. Only the official, government-packaged full sets are included in the following list. No Mint Sets were produced in 1950, 1982, or 1983, though Souvenir sets were sold in the latter two years (see the final section of this overview).

From time to time the Mint issues special Mint sets. One recent example is the 1996-P-D Mint set, which also included a 1996-W dime (released only in those sets).

Special Mint Sets

In mid-1964 the Treasury department announced that the Mint would not offer Proof sets or Mint sets the following year. This was prompted by a nationwide shortage of circulating coins, which was wrongly blamed on coin collectors.

In 1966 the San Francisco Assay Office began striking coins dated 1965, for inclusion in so-called United States Special Mint Sets. These were issued in pliofilm packaging similar to that of recent Proof sets. The coins in early 1965 Special Mint Sets are semi-brilliant or satiny (distinctive, but not equal in quality to Proofs); the coins in later 1965 sets feature very brilliant fields (but again not reaching Proof brilliance).

The San Francisco Assay Office started striking 1966-dated coins in August of that year, and its Special Mint Sets were packaged in rigid, sonically sealed plastic holders. The coins were struck once on unpolished planchets, unlike Proof coins (which are struck at least twice on polished planchets). Also unlike Proofs, the SMS coins were allowed to come into contact with each other during their production, which accounts for minor contact marks and abrasions. To achieve a brilliant finish, Mint technicians overpolished the coinage dies. The result was a tradeoff: most of the coins have prooflike brilliance, but many are missing polished-off design details, such as Frank Gasparro's initials on the half dollar.

All 1967-dated coinage was struck in that calendar year. Nearly all SMS coins of 1967 have fully brilliant, prooflike finishes. This brilliance was achieved without overpolishing the dies, resulting in coins that approach the quality of true Proofs. Sales of the 1967 sets were lackluster, however. The popularity of coin collecting had dropped from its peak in 1964. Also, collectors and speculators did not anticipate much secondary-market profit from the sets, which had an issue price of $4.00, compared to $2.10 for a 1964 Proof set. As a result, fewer collectors bought multiples of the 1967 sets, and today they are generally worth more than those of 1965 and 1966. Similar SMS coins dated 1964 exist as single pieces and in sets. Like the 1965 through 1967 SMS coins, they have a semi-brilliant or satiny finish but are not equal in quality to Proofs. They are referred to as SP (Special Strike) coins and command much higher prices than their regular SMS counterparts. In August 2019, a 1964-dated Special Strike Kennedy half dollar (listed in the *100 Greatest U.S. Modern Coins*) sold at auction for $156,000, setting a new record for a non-error modern U.S. coin.

1936 Proof Set
Liberty Walking half dollar, Washington quarter dollar, Mercury or Winged Liberty dime, Buffalo nickel, and Lincoln cent with Wheat Ears reverse.

1938 Proof Set
Buffalo nickel replaced with the new Jefferson nickel.

1950 Proof Set
There was a seven-year hiatus (1943–1949) before Proof sets were issued again after World War II. By 1950 the Liberty Walking half dollar had been replaced by the Franklin half dollar (introduced 1948), and the Mercury dime by the Roosevelt dime (introduced 1946).

1955 Proof Set
Issued in traditional individual envelopes, or in the new pliofilm package (pictured), with a Philadelphia Mint embossed paper seal with a metallic finish.

Modern Proof Sets (1936 to Date)

	Mintage	GSID	OGP*
1936	3,837	10898	$6,500.00
1937	5,542	10899	2,950.00
1938	8,045	10900	1,250.00
1939	8,795	10901	1,200.00
1940	11,246	10902	975.00
1941	15,287	10903	950.00
1942, With one nickel	21,120	10904	900.00
1942, With both nickels	**	10967	1,000.00
1950	51,386	10908	800.00
1951	57,500	10910	650.00
1952	81,980	10912	305.00
1953	128,800	10914	255.00
1954	233,300	10916	145.00
1955, Box Pack	378,200	10917	145.00
1955, Flat Pack	**	10968	150.00
1956	669,384	10920	75.00
1957	1,247,952	10922	40.00
1958	875,652	10924	42.00
1959	1,149,291	10926	38.00
1960, With Large Date cent	1,691,602	10970	38.00
1960, With Small Date cent	**	10971	40.00
1961	3,028,244	10929	38.00
1962	3,218,019	10931	38.00
1963	3,075,645	10933	38.00
1964	3,950,762	10935	38.00
1968-S	3,041,506	10972	9.50
1968-S, With No S dime	**	10973	$14,500.00
1969-S	2,934,631	10974	10.00
1970-S, With Large Date cent	2,632,810	10977	15.00
1970-S, With No S dime	2,200 est.	10978	900.00
1970-S, With Small Date cent	**	10979	90.00
1971-S	3,220,733	10980	6.75
1971-S, With No S nickel	**	10981	1,250.00
1972-S	3,260,996	10982	5.50
1973-S	2,760,339	10983	12.00
1974-S	2,612,568	10984	12.00
1975-S, With 1976 quarter, half, and dollar	2,845,450	10985	16.00
1975-S, With No S dime	**	10986	660,000.00
1976-S	4,149,730	10988	12.00
1976-S, Silver clad, 3-piece set	3,998,621	10989	33.00
1977-S	3,251,152	10990	11.50
1978-S	3,127,781	10991	11.00
1979-S, Variety 1 (a)	3,677,175	10992	12.00
1979-S, Variety 2 (a)	**	10993	50.00
1980-S	3,554,806	10994	9.50
1981-S, Variety 1 (a)	4,063,083	10995	12.00
1981-S, Variety 2 (all six coins in set) (a)	**	10996	130.00
1982-S	3,857,479	10997	9.50
1983-S	3,138,765	10998	9.50
1983-S, With No S dime	**	10999	775.00

* Value in original government packaging (OGP). ** Included in number above. **a.** See "Susan B. Anthony (1979–1999)" in "Modern Dollars" for illustrations of Variety 1 and Variety 2.

Modern Proof Sets (1936 to Date) *(continued)*

	Mintage	GSID	OGP*
1983-S, Prestige set (Olympic dollar)	140,361	11000	$47.00
1984-S	2,748,430	11001	8.00
1984-S, Prestige set (Olympic dollar)	316,680	11002	65.00
1985-S	3,362,821	11003	8.00
1986-S	2,411,180	11004	8.00
1986-S, Prestige set (Statue of Liberty half, dollar)	599,317	11005	65.00
1987-S	3,792,233	11006	7.50
1987-S, Prestige set (Constitution dollar)	435,495	11007	65.00
1988-S	3,031,287	11008	6.75
1988-S, Prestige set (Olympic dollar)	231,661	11009	65.00
1989-S	3,009,107	11010	6.75
1989-S, Prestige set (Congressional half, dollar)	211,807	11011	65.00
1990-S	2,793,433	11012	9.50
1990-S, With No S cent	3,555	11013	5,500.00
1990-S, Prestige set (Eisenhower dollar)	506,126	11014	70.00
1990-S, Prestige set, with No S cent	**	11015	6,250.00
1991-S	2,610,833	11016	8.00
1991-S, Prestige set (Mt. Rushmore half, dollar)	256,954	11017	75.00
1992-S	2,675,618	11018	8.00
1992-S, Prestige set (Olympic half, dollar)	**	11020	75.00
1992-S, Silver	1,009,586	11021	38.00
1992-S, Silver Premier set	**	11019	38.00
1993-S	2,409,394	11022	8.00
1993-S, Prestige set (Bill of Rights half, dollar)	**	11024	90.00
1993-S, Silver	570,213	11025	38.00
1993-S, Silver Premier set	**	11023	38.00
1994-S	2,308,701	11026	8.00
1994-S, Prestige set (World Cup half, dollar)	**	11028	75.00
1994-S, Silver	636,009	11029	38.00
1994-S, Silver Premier set	**	11027	38.00
1995-S	2,010,384	11030	12.00
1995-S, Prestige set (Civil War half, dollar)	**	11033	100.00
1995-S, Silver	549,878	11032	38.00
1995-S, Silver Premier set	**	11031	38.00
1996-S	1,695,244	11034	12.00
1996-S, Prestige set (Olympic half, dollar)	**	11036	195.00
1996-S, Silver	623,655	11037	38.00
1996-S, Silver Premier set	**	11035	38.00
1997-S	1,975,000	11038	13.50
1997-S, Prestige set (Botanic dollar)	**	11040	75.00

	Mintage	GSID	OGP*
1997-S, Prestige set (Botanic dollar)	**	11040	$75.00
1997-S, Silver	605,473	11041	38.00
1997-S, Silver Premier set	**	11039	38.00
1998-S	2,086,507	11042	12.00
1998-S, Silver	638,134	11044	38.00
1998-S, Silver Premier set	240,658	11043	38.00
1999-S, 9-piece set	2,543,401	11045	13.50
1999-S, Silver 9-piece set	**	11046	85.00
1999-S, 5-piece quarter set	1,169,958	6053	5.00
2000-S, 10-piece set	3,082,572	11048	13.50
2000-S, Silver 10-piece set	965,421	11049	85.00
2000-S, 5-piece quarter set	937,600	6063	5.50
2001-S, 10-piece set	2,294,909	11051	13.50
2001-S, Silver 10-piece set	889,697	11052	85.00
2001-S, 5-piece quarter set	799,231	6075	5.50
2002-S, 10-piece set	2,319,766	11054	12.00
2002-S, Silver 10-piece set	892,229	11055	85.00
2002-S, 5-piece quarter set	764,479	6087	6.50
2003-S, 10-piece set	2,172,684	11057	13.50
2003-S, Silver 10-piece set	1,125,755	11058	85.00
2003-S, 5-piece quarter set	1,235,832	6102	3.40
2004-S, 11-piece set	1,789,488	11060	13.00
2004-S, Silver 11-piece set	1,175,934	11061	85.00
2004-S, 5-piece quarter set	951,196	6114	5.75
2004-S, Silver 5-piece quarter set	593,852	6115	60.00
2005-S, 11-piece set	2,275,000	11063	12.00
2005-S, Silver 11-piece set	1,069,679	11064	85.00
2005-S, 5-piece quarter set	987,960	6116	3.40
2005-S, Silver 5-piece quarter set	608,970	6117	60.00
2006-S, 10-piece set	2,000,428	71000	12.00
2006-S, Silver 10-piece set	1,054,008	68835	85.00
2006-S, 5-piece quarter set	882,000	65094	4.10
2006-S, Silver 5-piece quarter set	531,000	65095	60.00
2007-S, 14-piece set	1,702,116	72500	22.00
2007-S, Silver 14-piece set	875,050	72501	95.00
2007-S, 5-piece quarter set	672,662	68625	8.00
2007-S, Silver 5-piece quarter set	672,662	68626	60.00
2007-S, 4-piece Presidential set	1,285,972	72504	6.50
2008-S, 14-piece set	1,405,674	72506	38.00
2008-S, Silver 14-piece set	763,887	72507	95.00
2008-S, 5-piece quarter set	672,438	69163	16.00
2008-S, Silver 5-piece quarter set	429,021	72509	60.00
2008-S, 4-piece Presidential set	869,202	72510	12.00
2009-S, 18-piece set	1,482,502	72512	39.00
2009-S, Silver 18-piece set	697,365	72513	105.00
2009-S, 6-piece quarter set	630,976	72514	6.75
2009-S, Silver 6-piece quarter set	299,183	72515	70.00
2009-S, 4-piece Presidential set	629,585	72516	8.50
2009-S, 4-piece Lincoln Bicentennial set	201,107	72517	10.00

* Value in original government packaging (OGP). ** Included in number above.

Modern Proof Sets (1936 to Date) *(continued)*

	Mintage	GSID	OGP*
2009-S, Lincoln Chronology Proof set	1,103,815	72519	$40.00
2010-S, 14-piece set	585,401	72520	95.00
2010-S, Silver 14-piece set	276,296	72521	14.00
2010-S, 5-piece quarter set	274,034	72522	60.00
2010-S, Silver 5-piece quarter set	535,397	72523	16.00
2010-S, 4-piece Presidential set	1,098,835	72524	40.00
2011-S, 14-piece set	574,175	72525	95.00
2011-S, Silver 14-piece set	152,302	72526	15.00
2011-S, 5-piece quarter set	147,901	72527	60.00
2011-S, Silver 5-piece quarter set	299,853	72528	27.00
2011-S, 4-piece Presidential set	794,002	72529	95.00
2012-S, 14-piece set	395,443	72530	130.00
2012-S, Silver 14-piece set	44,952	72534	160.00
2012-S, Silver 8-piece Limited Edition Silver set	148,498	72531	17.00
2012-S, 5-piece quarter set	162,448	72532	60.00
2012-S, Silver 5-piece quarter set	249,265	72533	47.00
2012-S, 4-piece Presidential set	802,460	72535	40.00
2013-S, 14-piece set	419,720	72536	95.00
2013-S, Silver 14-piece set	47,791	73776	160.00
2013-S, Silver 8-piece Limited Edition Silver set	128,377	72537	15.00
2013-S, 5-piece quarter set	138,451	72538	60.00
2013-S, Silver 5-piece quarter set	266,677	72539	15.00
2013-S, 4-piece Presidential set	680,977	72540	40.00
2014-S, 14-piece set	387,310	72541	95.00
2014-S, Silver 14-piece set	41,609	77352	170.00
2014-S, Silver 8-piece Limited Edition Silver set	109,423	72542	16.00
2014-S, 5-piece quarter set	103,311	72543	60.00
2014-S, Silver 5-piece quarter set	218,976	72544	16.00
2014-S, 4-piece Presidential set	662,854	72545	47.00
2015-S, 14-piece set	387,310	72546	95.00
2015-S, Silver 14-piece set	99,466	72547	13.50
2015-S, 5-piece quarter set	103,311	72548	60.00
2015-S, Silver 5-piece quarter set	222,068	72549	15.00
2015-S, 4-piece Presidential set	575,183	72550	65.00
2016-S, 13-piece set	356,683	72551	90.00
2016-S, Silver 13-piece set	95,709	72553	130.00
2016-S, Silver 8-piece Limited Edition Silver set, with 2016-W American silver eagle	91,674	77906	15.00
2016-S, 5-piece quarter set	49,647	72552	60.00
2016-S, Silver 5-piece quarter set	231,549	77351	13.50
2016-S, 3-piece Presidential set	568,678	77562	47.00
2017-S, 10-piece set	517,053	77568	85.00
2017-S, Silver 10-piece set	48,901	81895	160.00
2017-S, Silver 8-piece Limited Edition Silver set	88,909	77955	15.00

	Mintage	GSID	OGP*
2017-S, 5-piece quarter set	89,632	77956	$60.00
2017-S, Silver 5-piece quarter set	517,053	79332	50.00
2018-S, 10-piece set	332,268	79333	85.00
2018-S, Silver 10-piece set	199,116	81897	100.00
2018-S, 50th Anniversary Silver 10-piece Reverse Proof set	49,480	81896	175.00
2018-S, Silver 8-piece Limited Edition Silver set	86,694	79334	17.00
2018-S, 5-piece quarter set	79,300	79335	60.00
2018-S, Silver 5-piece quarter set	600,423	79338	60.00
2019-S, 10-piece set, plus 2019-W Proof cent	412,508	79339	120.00
2019-S, Silver 10-piece set, plus 2019-W Reverse Proof cent	48,417	81898	180.00
2019-S, Silver 8-piece Limited Edition Silver set	78,777	79340	19.00
2019-S, 5-piece quarter set	78,585	79341	40.00
2019-S, Silver 5-piece quarter set	137,696	81907	30.00
2019-S, 4-piece American Innovation dollar set	465,080	81899	95.00
2020-S, 10-piece set, plus 2020-W Proof nickel	313,184	81900	190
2020-S, Silver 10-piece set, plus 2020-W Reverse Proof nickel	49,995	84862	260
2020-S, Silver 8-piece Limited Edition Silver set	64,242	81901	19
2020-S, 5-piece quarter set	64,012	81902	80
2020-S, Silver 5-piece quarter set	101,593	109864	30
2020-S, 4-piece American Innovation dollar set	511,147	193287	42
2021-S, 7-piece set	298,710	193288	130
2021-S, Silver 7-piece set	48,592	193289	260
2021-S, Silver 6-piece Limited Edition Silver set	82,539	193290	30
2021-S, 4-piece American Innovation dollar set	50,000	193291	35
2021-S, 4-piece American Innovation dollar Reverse Proof set	398,580	194799	60
2022-S, 10-piece set	236,373	194800	155
2022-S, Silver 10-piece set	50,000	198175	240
2022-S, Silver 8-piece Limited Edition Silver set	42,606	194801	24
2022-S, 5-piece quarter set	57,532	194802	85
2022-S, Silver 5-piece quarter set	72,948	194803	30
2022-S, 4-piece American Innovation dollar set		194804	35
2022-S, 4-piece American Innovation dollar Reverse Proof set		285289	49
2023-S, 10-piece set		285290	130
2023-S, Silver 10-piece set		315595	195

* Value in original government packaging (OGP).

Modern Proof Sets (1936 to Date) *(continued)*

	Mintage	GSID	OGP*
2023-S, Silver 8-piece Limited Edition Silver set		212684	$24
2023-S, 5-piece quarter set		212685	75
2023-S, Silver 5-piece quarter set		315593	30
2023-S, 4-piece American Innovation dollar set		315594	35
2023-S, 4-piece American Innovation dollar Reverse Proof set		373703	40
2024-S, 10-piece set		373704	180
2024-S, Silver 10-piece set		373705	290
2024-S, Silver 8-piece Limited Edition Silver set		373706	40
2024-S, 5-piece quarter set		373707	100
2024-S, Silver 5-piece quarter set		373708	34
2024-S, 4-piece American Innovation dollar set		373709	$35
2024-S, 4-piece American Innovation dollar Reverse Proof set		393360	47
2025-S, 10-piece set		393361	170
2025-S, Silver 10-piece set		393362	290
2025-S, Silver 8-piece Limited Edition Silver set		393363	31
2025-S, 5-piece quarter set		393364	110
2025-S, Silver 5-piece quarter set		393365	34
2025-S, 4-piece American Innovation dollar set		393366	35
2025-S, 4-piece American Innovation dollar Reverse Proof set		393366	35

* Value in original government packaging (OGP).

Uncirculated Mint Sets (1947 to Date)

	Mintage	GSID	OGP*
1947 P-D-S	5,000	10905	$1,500.00
1948 P-D-S	6,000	10906	1,100.00
1949 P-D-S	5,000	10907	1,250.00
1951 P-D-S	8,654	10909	1,000.00
1952 P-D-S	11,499	10911	925.00
1953 P-D-S	15,538	10913	775.00
1954 P-D-S	25,599	10915	420.00
1955 P-D-S	49,656	10918	360.00
1956 P-D	45,475	10919	360.00
1957 P-D	34,324	10921	360.00
1958 P-D	50,314	10923	230.00
1959 P-D	187,000	10925	100.00
1960 P-D	260,485	10927	100.00
1961 P-D	223,704	10928	100.00
1962 P-D	385,285	10930	100.00
1963 P-D	606,612	10932	100.00
1964 P-D	1,008,108	10934	95.00
1968 P-D-S	2,105,128	10939	11.50
1969 P-D-S	1,817,392	10940	11.50
1970 P-D-S, With Large Date cent	2,038,134	10975	34.00
1970 P-D-S, With Small Date cent	**	10976	80.00
1971 P-D-S (no Eisenhower dollar)	2,193,396	10941	5.50
1972 P-D-S (no Eisenhower dollar)	2,750,000	10942	4.70
1973 P-D-S	1,767,691	10943	16.00
1974 P-D-S	1,975,981	10944	15.00
1975 P-D, With 1976 quarter, half, dollar	1,921,488	10945	12.50
1976, Silver clad, 3-piece set	4,908,319	10946	12.00
1976 P-D	1,892,513	10987	32.00
1977 P-D	2,006,869	10947	12.00
1978 P-D	2,162,609	10948	12.00
1979 P-D (a)	2,526,000	10949	$8.00
1980 P-D-S	2,815,066	10950	8.00
1981 P-D-S	2,908,145	10951	9.50
1984 P-D	1,832,857	10952	4.10
1985 P-D	1,710,571	10953	4.10
1986 P-D	1,153,536	10954	8.00
1987 P-D	2,890,758	10955	5.50
1988 P-D	1,646,204	10956	5.50
1989 P-D	1,987,915	10957	4.10
1990 P-D	1,809,184	10958	4.10
1991 P-D	1,352,101	10959	4.10
1992 P-D	1,500,143	10960	5.50
1993 P-D	1,297,431	10961	5.50
1994 P-D	1,234,813	10962	4.10
1995 P-D	1,038,787	10963	5.50
1996 P-D, plus 1996-W dime	1,457,949	10964	16.00
1997 P-D	950,473	10965	6.75
1998 P-D	1,187,325	10966	5.50
1999 P-D (18 pcs) (b)	1,243,867	72482	8.00
2000 P-D (20 pcs)	1,490,160	72483	12.00
2001 P-D (20 pcs)	1,116,915	72484	12.00
2002 P-D (20 pcs)	1,139,388	72485	12.00
2003 P-D (20 pcs)	1,001,532	72486	12.00
2004 P-D (22 pcs)	842,507	72487	12.00
2005 P-D (22 pcs)	1,160,000	72488	12.00
2006 P-D (20 pcs)	847,361	72489	12.00
2007 P-D (28 pcs)	895,628	72490	27.00
2008 P-D (28 pcs)	745,464	72491	32.00
2009 P-D (36 pcs)	784,614	72492	27.00
2009 P-D, Presidential Dollar (8 pcs)		393822	19.00
2010 P-D (28 pcs)	583,897	72493	27.00

* Value in original government packaging (OGP). ** Included in number above. **a.** S-mint dollar not included. **b.** Dollar not included.

	Mintage	GSID	OGP*
2010 P-D, Presidential Dollar (8 pcs)		393823	$19
2011 P-D (28 pcs)	533,529	72494	27
2011 P-D, Presidential Dollar (8 pcs)		393824	19
2012 P-D (28 pcs)	392,224	72495	60
2012 P-D, Presidential Dollar (8 pcs)		77355	19
2013 P-D (28 pcs)	376,844	72496	34
2013 P-D, Presidential Dollar (8 pcs)		77356	19
2014 P-D (28 pcs)	327,969	72497	32
2014 P-D, Presidential Dollar (8 pcs)		77357	19
2015 P-D (28 pcs)	314,029	72498	31
2015 P-D, Presidential Dollar (8 pcs)		77358	19
2016 P-D (26 pcs)	296,582	72499	38

	Mintage	GSID	OGP*
2016 P-D, Presidential Dollar (8 pcs)		77359	$15
2017 P-D (20 pcs)	286,813	77954	36
2017-S, 225th Anniversary Enh Unc Set (10 pcs)	210,419	81908	27
2018 P-D (20 pcs)	257,531	79336	38
2019 P-D, plus 2019-W cent (21 pcs)	346,117	79337	47
2020 P-D (20 pcs) (c)	211,787	84881	27
2021 P-D (14 pcs)	210,931	84882	27
2022 P-D (20 pcs)	220,298	200003	43
2023 P-D (20 pcs)		285877	32
2024 P-D (20 pcs)		374691	30
2025 P-D (20 pcs)		393715	35

Note: From 2005 through 2010, Mint Set coins were produced with a Satin Finish. * Value in original government packaging (OGP). **c.** An Uncirculated nickel from the West Point Mint was intended to be a premium for the 2020 Mint Set, but was canceled due to COVID-19.

1965 Special Mint Set

Special Mint Sets (1965–1967)

	Mintage	GSID	OGP*
1965	2,360,000	10936	$13.50
1966	2,261,583	10937	12.00
1967	1,863,344	10938	$13

Note: See page 932 for details on the similar 1964 Special Strike coins. * Value in original government packaging (OGP).

U.S. Mint Bullion Coins

AN OVERVIEW OF U.S. MINT BULLION COINS

The United States' bullion-coin program was launched in 1986. Since then, American Eagle and other silver, gold, platinum, and palladium coins have provided investors with convenient vehicles to add physical bullion to their portfolios. They also have value as numismatic collectibles.

Scan for additional information.

In addition to regular investment-grade strikes, the U.S. Mint offers its bullion coins in various collectible formats. Proofs are created in a specialized minting process: a polished coin blank is manually fed into a press fitted with special dies; the blank is struck multiple times "so the softly frosted yet detailed images seem to float above a mirror-like field" (per Mint literature); a white-gloved inspector scrutinizes the coin; and it is then sealed in a protective plastic capsule and mounted in a satin-lined velvet presentation case along with a certificate of authenticity. Members of the public can purchase Proofs directly from the Mint, at fixed prices.

Burnished (called Uncirculated by the Mint) coins are also sold directly to the public. These coins have the same design as other bullion coins, but are distinguished from regular bullion strikes by a W mintmark (for West Point), and by their distinctive finish (the result of burnished coin blanks). Their blanks are individually fed by hand into specially adapted coining presses. After striking, each Burnished specimen is carefully inspected, encapsulated in plastic, and packaged in a satin-lined velvet presentation case, along with a certificate of authenticity. In recent years the Mint has also broadened its collectible bullion offerings with Reverse Proof and Enhanced Uncirculated formats. Various bullion coins have been offered in collector sets, as well.

Since the inception of the bullion-coin program in 1986, the Mint has marked several anniversaries with special issues and sets.

Mint-authorized purchasers (wholesalers, brokerage companies, precious-metal firms, coin dealers, and participating banks) buy regular bullion-strike coins in bulk. These authorized purchasers in turn sell them to secondary retailers, who then make them available to the general public. Authorized purchasers are required to meet financial and professional criteria, attested to by an internationally accepted accounting firm. They must be an experienced and established market-maker in bullion coins; provide a liquid two-way market for the coins; be audited annually; have an established and broad retail-customer base for distribution; and have a tangible net worth of $5 million (for American Silver Eagles) or $25 million (for gold and platinum American Eagles). Authorized purchasers of gold, platinum, and palladium must have sold 100,000 or more ounces of those metals (bullion, or bullion coins) in any 12-month period since 1990. For gold, the initial order must be for at least 1,000 ounces, with reorders in increments of 500 ounces; for platinum/palladium, 100 ounces for both the initial order and reorders; and for silver, a minimum order of 25,000 ounces. For American Eagles, an authorized purchaser's cost is based on the market value of the bullion, plus a premium to cover minting, distribution, and other overhead expenses. For ASEs, the premium is $2 per coin. For gold, the premiums are 3 percent (for the one-ounce coin), 5 percent (1/2 ounce), 7 percent (1/4 ounce), and 9 percent (1/10 ounce). For platinum the premium is 4 percent for the one-ounce coin; for palladium, 6.25 percent.

Note that the U.S. Mint does not release bullion mintage data on a regular basis; the numbers given herein reflect the most recently available official data.

The listed values of uncertified, average Mint State coins have been based on bullion prices of silver ($45 per ounce), gold ($3,746), platinum ($1,527.50), and palladium ($1,545).

For more detailed coverage of these coins, readers are directed to *American Silver Eagles: A Guide to the U.S. Bullion Coin Program* (Mercanti), *American Gold and Platinum Eagles: A Guide to the U.S. Bullion Coin Programs* (Moy), and *American Gold and Silver: U.S. Mint Collector and Investor Coins and Medals, Bicentennial to Date* (Tucker).

AMERICAN EAGLE PROGRAM

American Silver Eagles (1986 to Date)

Designers: *Adolph A. Weinman (obverse) and John Mercanti (reverse).*
Weight: *31.103 grams.* **Composition:** *.999 silver, .001 copper (net weight 1 oz. pure silver).*
Diameter: *40.6 mm.* **Edge:** *Reeded.* **Mints:** *Philadelphia, San Francisco, and West Point.*

Variety 1, Heraldic Eagle Reverse (1986–2021), Regular Finish

Variety 1, Burnished Finish

Variety 1, Enhanced Uncirculated Finish
This special format incorporates elements with a brilliant mirrored finish, a light frosted finish, and a heavy frosted finish.

Reverse Lettering Style of 1986–2007
Note the lack of spur or stem at bottom right of U.

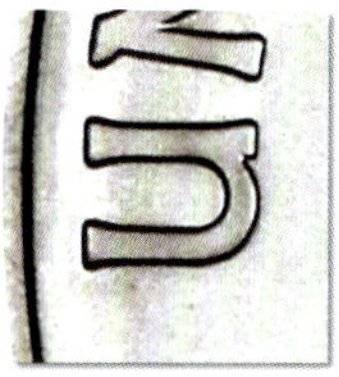

Reverse Lettering Style of 2008 to Date
Note the spur at bottom right of U.

Variety 1, Proof Finish

Variety 1, Reverse Proof Finish

2020-W Privy Mark, "V75," marking 75 years since Allied victory in World War II.

Variety 2, Flying Eagle Reverse (2021 to Date)

History. The American Silver Eagle (face value $1, actual silver weight one ounce) is a legal-tender bullion coin with weight, content, and purity guaranteed by the federal government. It is one of the few silver coins allowed in individual retirement accounts (IRAs).The obverse design features Adolph A. Weinman's Liberty Walking, as used on the circulating half dollar of 1916 to 1947. Weinman's initials appear on the hem of Liberty's gown. The reverse design of 1986–2021, by John Mercanti, is a heraldic eagle. In late 2021 a new Flying Eagle design, by Emily S. Damstra, was introduced.

Scan for additional information.

From 1986 to 1999 all American Silver Eagles were struck at the Philadelphia and San Francisco mints (with the exception of the 1995 West Point Proof). In 2000 they were struck at both Philadelphia (Proofs) and the U.S. Mint's West Point facility (bullion strikes). From 2001 to 2010, West Point was their sole producer (with one exception in 2006), making regular bullion strikes (without mintmarks) and Proof and "Burnished" specimens (with mintmarks). (The exception is the 2006 Reverse Proof, which was struck in Philadelphia.) In 2011, for the 25th anniversary of the American Eagle bullion program, the mints at West Point, San Francisco, and Philadelphia were all put into production to make several collectible formats of the coins. Since 2012, West Point has been their main production mint, with Philadelphia and San Francisco helping when demand is high.

In addition to the individually listed coins, American Silver Eagles were issued in two 2006 "20th Anniversary" sets and in several other special bullion coin sets.

Striking and Sharpness. Striking is generally sharp. The key elements to check on the obverse are Liberty's left hand, the higher parts and lines of her skirt, and her head. On the reverse, the eagle's breast is a main focal point.

Availability. The American Silver Eagle is one of the most popular silver-investment vehicles in the world. Between the bullion coins and various collectible formats, more than 400 million have been sold since 1986. The coins are readily available in the numismatic marketplace and from some banks, investment firms, and other non-numismatic channels.

MS-60 to 70 (Mint State). ***Obverse and Reverse:*** At MS-60, some abrasion and contact marks are evident on the higher design areas (Liberty's left arm, her hand, and the areas of the skirt covering her left leg). Luster may be dull or lifeless at MS-60 to 62, but there should be deep frost at MS-63 and better, particularly in the lower-relief areas. At MS-65 and above, the luster should be full and rich. These guidelines are more academic than practical, as American Silver Eagles are not intended for circulation, and nearly all are in high Mint State grades.

PF-60 to 70 (Proof). ***Obverse and Reverse:*** Proofs that are extensively cleaned and have many hairlines are lower level, such as PF-60 to 62. Those with fewer hairlines or flaws are deemed PF-63 to 65. (These exist more in theory than actuality, as nearly all Proof ASEs have been maintained in their original high condition by collectors and investors.) Given the quality of modern U.S. Mint products, even PF-66 and 67 are unusually low levels for ASE Proofs.

$1 1-Ounce Silver Eagle Bullion Strikes

	Mintage	GSID	OGP*	MS-69	MS-70
American Silver Eagle (ASE), $1 1 oz. (1986 to Date)	n/a	**72469**	**$65**	**$65**	**$80**
American Silver Eagle (ASE), $1 1 oz. (1986 to Date), Burnished	n/a	**84268**	**75**	**75**	**90**
1986	5,393,005	10644	100	95	1,000
1987	11,442,335	10645	70	80	650
1988	5,004,646	10646	75	75	1,100
1989	5,203,327	10647	65	70	675
1990	5,840,210	10648	75	80	3,000
1991	7,191,066	10649	70	70	1,200
1992	5,540,068	10650	70	70	1,150
1993	6,763,762	10651	65	80	2,600
1994	4,227,319	10674	90	70	5,000
1995	4,672,051	10675	75	75	1,250
1996	3,603,386	10676	100	100	2,700
1997	4,295,004	10677	85	85	1,150
1998	4,847,549	10678	70	70	950
1999	7,408,640	10679	75	75	5,500
2000-(W)	9,239,132	10680	70	70	2,300
2001-(W)	9,001,711	10681	70	70	1,000
2002-(W)	10,539,026	10652	70	70	120
2003-(W)	8,495,008	10653	70	70	110
2004-(W)	8,882,754	213165	—	70	120
2005-(W)	8,891,025	15388	65	70	90
2006-(W)	10,676,522	68740	65	65	130
2006-W, Burnished (a)	468,020	70901	95	95	160
2007-(W)	9,028,036	68989	65	70	95
2007-W, Burnished	621,333	68986	75	75	90
2008-(W)	20,583,000	213166	65	70	85
2008-W, Burnished, Rev of 2007	46,318	197930	525	455	1,100
2008-W, Burnished, Rev of 2008	533,757	68999	$75	$75	$90
2009-(W) (b)	30,459,000	69445	65	80	105
2010-(W)	34,764,500	71049	65	80	105
2011-S, Burnished	99,882	74464	155	145	235
2011-(S)	40,020,000	84266	65	65	80
2011-(W)	**	84267	65	80	85
2011-W, Burnished	409,776	71303	75	75	90
2012-(S)	33,121,500	71114	65	65	80
2012-(W)	**	84272	65	65	80
2012-W, Burnished	226,120	71116	75	75	90
2013-(S)	42,675,000	71551	65	65	80
2013-(W)	42,675,000	71554	$65	$65	$80
2013-W, Burnished	281,310	71493	75	75	130
2013-W, Enh Unc	222,091	71533	110	110	130
2014-(S)	44,006,000	84273	65	80	90
↳2014-(S), Gouged Shield, FS-801	44,006,000	376030	—	—	—
2014-(W)	**	84274	65	80	90
2014-W, Burnished	253,169	74223	75	75	90
2015-(P)	79,640	213361	480	470	4,500
2015-(W)	47,000,000	84275	65	80	90
2015-W, Burnished	223,879	74224	75	75	95
2016-(P)	37,701,500	213171	70	70	260
2016-(S) (c)	**	84276	65	80	90
2016-(W) (c)	**	84277	65	80	90
2016-W, Burnished (c)	216,501	74225	75	75	115
2017-(P)	18,065,500	198090	70	70	85
2017-(S)	**	84278	70	70	130
2017-(W)	**	84279	70	70	85
2017-W, Burnished	176,739	74226	75	75	90
2018-(W)	15,700,000	81693	80	80	90
2018-W, Burnished	131,935	84269	75	75	90
2019-(W)	14,863,500	81694	70	70	100

* Value in original government packaging (OGP). ** Included in number above. **a.** In celebration of the 20th anniversary of the Bullion Coinage Program, in 2006 the W mintmark was used on bullion coins produced in sets except for the Reverse Proof, which was struck at the Philadelphia Mint. **b.** No Proof American Silver Eagles were made in 2009. Beware of alterations made privately outside the Mint. **c.** To celebrate 30 years of the American Eagle, the edge is lettered 30TH ANNIVERSARY.

$1 1-Ounce Silver Eagle Bullion Strikes *(continued)*

	Mintage	GSID	OGP*	MS-69	MS-70
2019-W, Burnished (d)	140,779	84270	$75	$85	$100
2020-(P)	30,089,500	81905	65	65	80
2020-(S)	**	213172	65	65	80
2020-(W)	**	81904	65	65	80
2020-W, Burnished	154,864	84271	75	75	95
2021-(P), Variety 1 Rev	495,500	85128	65	65	80
2021-(S), Variety 1 Rev	**	85054	65	65	80
2021-(W), Variety 1 Rev	**	213362	65	65	80
2021-(S), Variety 2 Rev	**	213173	75	75	90
2021-(W), Variety 2 Rev	**	213363	65	65	80
2021-W, Variety 2 Rev, Burnished	185,791	193325	75	75	90
2022-(P)	16,000,000	193324	65	65	80
2022-(W)	16,000,000	213174	65	65	80

	Mintage	GSID	OGP*	MS-69	MS-70
2022-W, Burnished	219,640	194492	$75	$75	$90
2023-(P)	24,750,000	198246	65	65	80
2023-(W)	24,750,000	213175	65	65	80
2023-W, Burnished	199,533	213629	75	75	110
2024-(P)	22,860,000	346939	65	65	80
2024-(P), Star Privy Mark	500,000	376845	95	95	130
2024-(W)	22,860,000	347656	65	65	80
2024-W, Burnished	113,130	374796	75	75	90
2025-(P), Eagle Privy Mark	500,000	393377	160	160	195
2025-(W)		376287	65	65	80
2025-W, Burnished		376288	75	75	90

* Value in original government packaging (OGP). ** Included in number above. **d.** Included in the 2019 Pride of Two Nations set.

$1 1-Ounce Silver Eagle Proof Strikes

	Mintage	GSID	OGP*	PF-69	PF-70
American Silver Eagle (ASE), $1 1 oz. (1986 to Date), Proof	**n/a**	**72470**	**$85**	**$85**	**$105**
1986-S	1,446,778	10657	85	120	365
1987-S	904,732	10659	85	90	365
1988-S	557,370	10660	85	90	360
1989-S	617,694	10661	85	85	230
1990-S	695,510	10662	85	90	180
1991-S	511,925	10663	85	85	235
1992-S	498,654	10664	85	85	300
1993-P	405,913	10665	110	110	650
1994-P	372,168	10682	150	150	775
1995-P	438,511	10683	85	85	340
1995-W	30,125	10684	3,500	3,500	12,500
1996-P	500,000	10685	85	90	365
1997-P	435,368	10686	110	105	285
1998-P	450,000	10687	85	85	180
1999-P	549,769	10688	85	85	260
2000-P	600,000	10667	85	85	325
2001-W	746,398	10668	85	85	145
2002-W	647,342	10669	$85	$85	$155
2003-W	747,831	10670	85	85	145
2004-W	801,602	10672	85	85	155
2005-W	816,663	15391	85	85	130
2006-P, RevPf	248,875	68427	130	130	340
2006-W	1,092,477	65333	85	85	105
2007-W	821,759	68606	85	85	105
2008-W	700,979	68914	85	85	130
2010-W	849,861	71050	85	85	105
2011-W, 25th Anniv	947,355	71046	85	85	105
2011-P, RevPf, 25th Anniv	99,882	71375	235	235	365

	Mintage	GSID	OGP*	PF-69	PF-70
2012-W	869,386	71492	$85	$85	$105
2012-S	285,184	71644	85	85	115
2012-S, RevPf	224,981	71592	100	100	180
2013-W	934,812	71505	85	85	105
2013-W, RevPf	281,310	74465	100	100	145
2014-W	944,757	74074	85	85	105
2015-W	707,518	74075	85	85	105
2016-W, Lettered Edge, 30th Anniv	595,843	74076	85	85	130
2017-W	440,596	74077	85	85	105
2017-S	123,799	84294	100	100	145
2018-W	361,192	74078	85	85	105
2018-S	158,791	81462	85	85	105
2019-W	345,380	81463	85	85	105
2019-W, Pride of Two Nations, Enh RevPf	99,675	81903	130	130	210
2019-S	146,799	81737	85	85	120
2019-S, Enh RevPf	29,913	81738	1,150	1,150	2,250
2020-W	357,111	81464	85	85	105
2020-S	191,271	81739	85	85	105
2020-W, 75th Anniv of the End of WWII (with Privy Mark)	74,709	82111	420	410	675
2021-W, Variety 2 Rev	299,509	85060	85	85	105
2021-W, Variety 1 Rev	385,776	121151	85	85	105
2021-S, Variety 1 Rev	272,181	121152	85	85	135
2021-W, Variety 2 Rev, RevPf	124,822	152461	130	130	235
2021-S, Variety 1 Rev, RevPf	124,822	152462	$130	130	180
2022-S	199,398	200004	85	85	105
2022-W	496,686	194491	85	85	105

* Value in original government packaging (OGP).

$1 1-Ounce Silver Eagle Proof Strikes *(continued)*

	Mintage	GSID	OGP*	PF-69	PF-70
2023-W	213,357	198248	$85	$85	$105
2023-S	242,667	226242	85	85	105
2024-W	333,863	346867	85	85	105
2024-S	151,190	375535	85	85	105
2025-P, U.S. Marines (with Privy Mark)		393458	—	—	—
2025-S		376290	100	100	115
2025-S, U.S. Navy (with Privy Mark)		393459	—	—	—
2025-W		376289	$100	$100	$115
2025-W, 250th Anniv U.S. Army (with Privy Mark)	100,000	393460	290	290	420
2025-W, Laser Privy Mark		393461	230	230	455

* Value in original government packaging (OGP).

Silver Eagle Sets

	Mintage	GSID	OGP*
1995-W 10th Anniversary American Eagle Proof Set. $50, $25, $10, and $5 American Gold Eagles and $1 American Silver Eagle		70815	$12,000
1997 Impressions of Liberty Proof Set. 1997-W $100 American Platinum Eagle and $50 American Gold Eagle, and 1997-S $1 American Silver Eagle		376892	7,250
2006-W 20th Anniversary Three-Coin set: Uncirculated, Proof, and Reverse Proof American Silver Eagles		65334	270
2011 25th Anniversary Silver Eagle set: 2011 bullion, 2011-P Reverse Proof, 2011-S Uncirculated, and 2011-W Uncirculated and Proof American Silver Eagles		71571	600
2012-S 75th Anniversary of San Francisco Mint American Silver Eagle set: Proof and Reverse Proof		71491	175
2013-W 75th Anniversary of West Point Depository American Silver Eagle set: Reverse Proof and Enhanced Uncirculated		76851	175
2019-W Pride of Two Nations Limited Edition Two-Coin set: 2019-W Enhanced Reverse Proof American Silver Eagle and Royal Canadian Mint Silver Maple Leaf modified Proof	99,675	315631	195
2021, Reverse Proof American Silver Eagle set: 2021-W Variety 1 Reverse and 2021-S Variety 2 Reverse	125,000	152463	260

* Value in original government packaging (OGP).

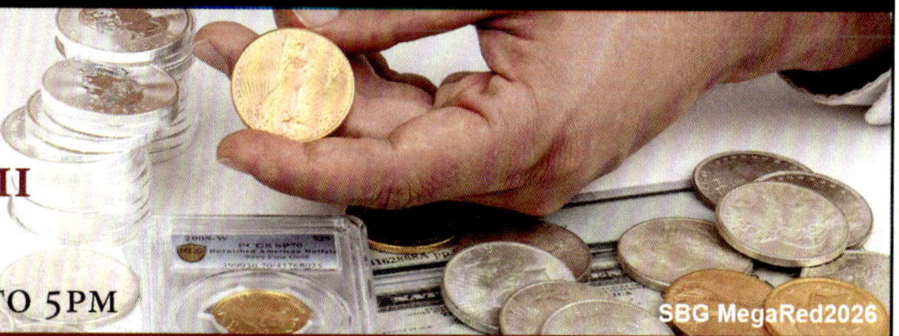

Note: Silver spot price at time of publication, $45 per ounce.

American Gold Eagles (1986 to Date)

Designers: *Augustus Saint-Gaudens (obverse) and Miley Busiek (reverse).* **Weight:** *$5 1/10 oz.—3.393 grams; $10 1/4 oz.—8.483 grams; $25 1/2 oz.—16.966 grams; $50 1 oz.—33.931 grams.* **Composition:** *.9167 gold, .03 silver, .0533 copper.* **Diameter:** *$5 1/10 oz.—16.5 mm; $10 1/4 oz.—22 mm; $25 1/2 oz.—27 mm; $50 1 oz.—32.7 mm.* **Edge:** *Reeded.* **Mints:** *Philadelphia and West Point.*

Regular Finish
Obverse design common to all denominations.

Mintmark location is on the obverse, below the date.

Burnished Finish

Proof Finish

Reverse Proof Finish

$5 1/10-Ounce

$10 1/4-Ounce

$20 1/2-Ounce

$50 1-Ounce

Variety 1: Family of Eagles Reverse, 1986–2021

Variety 2: Head of Eagle Reverse, 2021 to Date

History. American Eagle gold bullion coins are made in four denominations: $5 (1/10 ounce pure gold), $10 (1/4 ounce), $25 (1/2 ounce), and $50 (1 ounce). Each shares the same obverse and reverse designs: a modified rendition of Augustus Saint-Gaudens's famous Liberty (as depicted on the double eagle of 1907 to 1933), and a "family of eagles" motif by sculptor Miley Tucker-Frost (nee Busiek). From 1986 to 1991 the obverse bore a Roman numeral date, similar to the first Saint-Gaudens double eagles of 1907; this was changed to Arabic dating in 1992. The coins are legal tender—with weight, content, and purity guaranteed by the federal government—and are produced from gold mined in the United States. Investors can include them in their individual retirement accounts.

"American Eagles use the durable 22-karat standard established for gold circulating coinage over 350 years ago," notes the U.S. Mint. "They contain their stated amount of pure gold, plus small amounts of alloy. This creates harder coins that resist scratching and marring, which can diminish resale value."

Since the Bullion Coin Program started in 1986, these gold pieces have been struck in Philadelphia and West Point, in various formats similar to those of the American Silver Eagles—regular bullion strikes, Burnished, Proof, and Reverse Proof. Unlike their silver counterparts, none of the American Gold Eagles have been struck at San Francisco.

In addition to the individual coins listed below, American Eagle gold bullion coins have been issued in various sets (see page 1210).

Striking and Sharpness. Striking is generally sharp. The key elements to check on the obverse are Liberty's chest and left knee, and the open fields.

Availability. American Gold Eagles are the most popular gold-coin investment vehicle in the United States. The coins are readily available in the numismatic marketplace as well as from participating banks, investment firms, and other non-numismatic channels.

MS-60 to 70 (Mint State). ***Obverse and Reverse:*** At MS-60, some abrasion and contact marks are evident on the higher design areas (in particular, Liberty's chest and left knee) and the open fields. Luster may be dull or lifeless at MS-60 to 62, but there should be deep frost at MS-63 and better, particularly in the lower-relief areas. At MS-65 and above, the luster should be full and rich. Contact marks and abrasion are less and less evident at higher grades. These guidelines are more academic than practical, as these coins are not intended for circulation, and nearly all are in high Mint State grades.

PF-60 to 70 (Proof). ***Obverse and Reverse:*** Proofs that are extensively cleaned and have many hairlines are lower level, such as PF-60 to 62. Those with fewer hairlines or flaws are deemed PF-63 to 65. (These exist more in theory than actuality, as nearly all Proof American Eagle gold bullion coins have been maintained in their original high condition by collectors.) Given the quality of modern U.S. Mint products, even PF-66 and 67 are unusually low levels for these Proofs.

$5 1/10-Ounce Gold Eagle Bullion Strikes

	Mintage	GSID	OGP*	MS-69	MS-70
American Gold Eagle (AGE), $5 1/10 oz. (1986 to Date)	**n/a**	**74227**	**$525**	**$525**	**$575**
1986 (MCMLXXXVI)	912,609	15404	525	525	675
1987 (MCMLXXXVII)	580,266	15405	550	575	700
1988 (MCMLXXXVIII)	159,500	15406	525	575	5,250
1989 (MCMLXXXIX)	264,790	10689	550	575	850
1990 (MCMXC)	210,210	10690	550	575	1,500
1991 (MCMXCI)	165,200	10691	550	575	650
1992	209,300	10692	550	575	775
1993	210,709	15403	525	525	625
1994	206,380	10693	525	525	775
1995	223,025	10694	525	525	650
1996	401,964	10695	550	525	650
1997	528,266	10696	525	525	600
1998	1,344,520	10697	525	525	625
1999	2,750,338	10698	525	525	575
1999-W, Unc (a)	48,428	68755	900	850	2,700
2000	569,153	10699	$525	$525	$625
2001	269,147	10700	525	525	575
2002	230,027	10701	525	525	600
2003	245,029	10702	525	525	575
2004	250,016	10703	525	525	575
2005	300,043	15407	525	525	575
2006	285,006	65226	525	525	625
2006-W, Burnished	20,643	65225	525	525	600
2007	190,010	77480	525	525	575
2007-W, Burnished	22,501	69244	525	525	600
2008	305,000	71501	525	525	575
2008-W, Burnished	12,657	70891	525	525	750
2009	270,000	73772	525	525	600
2010	435,000	71502	525	525	600
2011, 25th Anniv	350,000	71690	525	525	600
2012	290,000	71281	525	525	600
2013	555,000	73770	525	525	600
2014	545,000	73771	525	525	600

* Value in original government packaging (OGP). **a.** Made from unfinished Proof dies.

$5 1/10-Ounce Gold Eagle Bullion Strikes *(continued)*

	Mintage	GSID	OGP*	MS-69	MS-70
2015	980,000	72466	$525	$525	$575
↳2015, Narrow Reeding	980,000	394987	525	525	550
↳2015, Wide Reeding	980,000	394988	550	550	600
2016, 30th Anniv	925,000	72467	525	525	575
2017	395,000	72468	525	525	575
2018	230,000	77313	525	525	575
2019	195,000	77314	$525	$525	$575
2020	350,000	84245	525	525	575
2021, Variety 1 Rev	490,000	85055	525	525	575
2021, Variety 2 Rev		188663	525	525	575
2022	575,000	193326	525	525	575
2023		199054	525	525	575
2024		346940	525	525	575
2025		377672	525	525	575

* Value in original government packaging (OGP).

$5 1/10-Ounce Gold Eagle Proof Strikes

	Mintage	GSID	OGP*	PF-69	PF-70
American Gold Eagle (AGE), $5 1/10 oz. (1986 to Date), Proof	**n/a**	**74286**	**$525**	**$525**	**$550**
1988-P (MCMLXXXVIII)	143,881	10704	525	525	575
1989-P (MCMLXXXIX)	84,647	10759	525	525	575
1990-P (MCMXC)	99,349	10705	525	525	600
1991-P (MCMXCI)	70,334	10706	525	525	600
1992-P	64,874	10707	525	525	575
1993-P	58,649	10708	525	525	575
1994-W	62,849	10709	525	525	575
1995-W	62,667	10710	525	525	575
1996-W	57,047	10711	525	525	575
1997-W	34,977	10712	525	525	575
1998-W	39,395	10713	525	525	575
1999-W	48,428	10714	525	525	575
2000-W	49,971	10715	525	525	575
2001-W	37,530	10716	525	525	575
2002-W	40,864	10717	525	525	575
2003-W	40,027	10718	525	525	575
2004-W	35,131	10719	525	525	575
2005-W	49,265	15409	525	525	575
2006-W	47,277	65227	$525	$525	$575
2007-W	58,553	68651	525	525	575
2008-W	28,116	70726	525	525	575
2010-W	54,285	71135	525	525	575
2011-W	42,697	71595	525	525	575
2012-W	20,637	71282	525	525	575
2013-W	21,738	71643	525	525	575
2014-W	22,725	74287	525	525	575
2015-W	26,769	74288	525	525	575
2016-W, 30th Anniv	38,889	74289	525	525	575
2017-W	20,974	74290	525	525	575
2018-W	22,155	77315	525	525	575
2019-W	19,612	77316	525	525	550
2020-W	24,033	84246	525	525	550
2021-W, Variety 1 Rev	20,062	188655	525	525	550
2021-W, Variety 2 Rev	26,342	188656	525	525	550
2022-W	23,712	194487	525	525	550
2023-W	22,821	213282	525	525	550
2024-W		346941	525	525	550
2025-W		377859	525	525	550
2024-W		346941	525	525	550

* Value in original government packaging (OGP).

$10 1/4-Ounce Gold Eagle Bullion Strikes

	Mintage	GSID	OGP*	MS-69	MS-70
American Gold Eagle (AGE), $10 1/4 oz. (1986 to Date)	**n/a**	**74228**	**$1,250**	**$1,250**	**$1,250**
1986 (MCMLXXXVI)	726,031	10737	1,250	1,250	1,450
1987 (MCMLXXXVII)	269,255	10738	1,250	1,250	1,900
1988 (MCMLXXXVIII)	49,000	10739	2,500	2,500	2,800
1989 (MCMLXXXIX)	81,789	10720	2,500	2,500	2,800
1990 (MCMXC)	41,000	10721	2,950	3,100	7,000
1991 (MCMXCI)	36,100	10722	2,850	2,850	3,100
1992	59,546	10723	2,300	2,300	2,550
1993	71,864	10725	2,300	2,300	2,400
1994	72,650	10726	1,750	2,300	2,500
1995	83,752	10727	$2,350	$2,350	$3,250
1996	60,318	10728	1,750	2,300	2,550
1997	108,805	10729	1,250	1,250	2,000
1998	309,829	10730	1,250	1,250	1,450
1999	564,232	10731	1,250	1,250	1,250
1999-W, Unfinished Proof Dies (a)	10,000	71683	1,850	1,850	7,500
↳1999-W, Unfinished Proof Dies, FS-401 (a)	10,000	393277	—	—	—
2000	128,964	10732	1,250	1,250	1,350
2001	71,280	10733	1,900	2,150	2,200

* Value in original government packaging (OGP). ** Included in number above. **a.** Made from unfinished Proof dies.

$10 1/4-Ounce Gold Eagle Bullion Strikes *(continued)*

	Mintage	GSID	OGP*	MS-69	MS-70
2002	62,027	10734	$1,250	$1,250	$1,450
2003	74,029	10735	1,250	1,250	1,250
2004	72,014	10736	1,250	1,250	1,250
2005	72,015	15410	1,250	1,250	1,250
2006	60,004	71451	1,250	1,250	1,250
2006-W, Burnished	15,188	65228	1,250	1,250	1,250
2007	34,004	71687	1,200	1,250	1,300
2007-W, Burnished	12,766	71027	1,250	1,250	1,250
2008	70,000	74242	1,250	1,250	1,250
2008-W, Burnished	8,883	71650	1,200	1,250	1,900
2009	110,000	74243	1,250	1,250	1,250
2010	86,000	71507	1,250	1,250	1,250
2011	80,000	74244	1,250	1,250	1,250
2012	90,000	74245	1,250	1,250	1,250
2013	114,500	74246	1,250	1,250	1,250
2014	90,000	74247	$1,250	$1,250	$1,250
2015	158,000	74248	1,250	1,250	1,250
2016, 30th Anniv	152,000	74249	1,250	1,250	1,250
2017	64,000	74250	1,250	1,250	1,250
2018	62,000	77317	1,250	1,250	1,250
2019	38,000	77318	1,250	1,250	1,300
2020	106,000	84247	1,250	1,250	1,250
2021, Variety 1 Rev	162,000	85056	1,250	1,250	1,250
2021, Variety 2 Rev		188661	1,250	1,250	1,250
2021-W, Variety 2 Rev (b)	**	226243	2,000	1,900	3,100
2022	140,000	193327	1,250	1,250	1,250
2023		199053	1,250	1,250	1,250
2024		346942	1,250	1,250	1,250
2025		377673	—	—	—

* Value in original government packaging (OGP). ** Included in number above. **b.** The Mint reported that 7,924 bullion-strike pieces were made in error with an unfinished Proof obverse die bearing a W mintmark. To date, just over 60 have been found.

$10 1/4-Ounce Gold Eagle Proof Strikes

	Mintage	GSID	OGP*	PF-69	PF-70
American Gold Eagle (AGE), $10 1/4 oz. (1986 to Date), Proof	n/a	**74291**	**$1,250**	**$1,250**	**$1,300**
1988-P (MCMLXXXVIII)	98,028	10757	1,250	1,250	1,400
1989-P (MCMLXXXIX)	54,170	10758	1,250	1,250	1,350
1990-P (MCMXC)	62,674	10742	1,250	1,250	1,300
1991-P (MCMXCI)	50,839	10743	1,250	1,250	1,300
1992-P	46,269	10744	1,250	1,250	1,300
1993-P	46,464	10745	1,250	1,250	1,300
1994-W	48,172	10746	1,250	1,250	1,300
1995-W	47,526	10747	1,250	1,250	1,300
1996-W	38,219	10748	1,250	1,250	1,300
1997-W	29,805	10749	1,250	1,250	1,300
1998-W	29,503	10750	1,250	1,250	1,300
1999-W	34,417	10751	1,250	1,250	1,300
2000-W	36,036	10752	1,250	1,250	1,300
2001-W	25,613	10753	1,250	1,250	1,300
2002-W	29,242	10754	1,250	1,250	1,300
2003-W	30,292	10755	1,250	1,250	1,300
2004-W	28,839	10756	1,250	1,250	1,300
2005-W	37,207	15411	1,250	1,250	1,300
2006-W	36,127	65230	$1,250	$1,250	$1,300
2007-W	46,189	68650	1,250	1,250	1,300
2008-W	18,877	70488	1,250	1,250	1,300
2010-W	44,507	71136	1,250	1,250	1,300
2011-W	28,782	71596	1,250	1,250	1,300
2012-W	13,926	71284	1,250	1,250	1,300
2013-W	12,782	74292	1,250	1,250	1,300
2014-W	14,790	74293	1,250	1,250	1,300
2015-W	15,775	74294	1,250	1,250	1,300
2016-W, 30th Anniv	24,405	74295	1,250	1,250	1,300
2017-W	14,516	74296	1,250	1,250	1,300
2018-W	12,769	77319	1,250	1,250	1,300
2019-W	11,861	77320	1,250	1,250	1,300
2020-W	15,806	84248	1,250	1,250	1,300
2021-W, Variety 1 Rev	13,531	188657	1,250	1,250	1,300
2021-W, Variety 2 Rev	10,865	188658	1,250	1,250	1,300
2022-W	14,370	194488	1,250	1,250	1,300
2023-W	13,884	213167	1,250	1,250	1,300
2024-W		346943	1,250	1,250	1,300
2025-W		377858	1,250	1,250	1,300
2024-W		346943	1,250	1,250	1,300

* Value in original government packaging (OGP).

Note: Gold spot price at time of publication, $3,746 per ounce.

$25 1/2-Ounce Gold Eagle Bullion Strikes

	Mintage	GSID	OGP*	MS-69	MS-70
American Gold Eagle (AGE), $25 1/2 oz. (1986 to Date)	**n/a**	**74229**	**$2,450**	**$2,450**	**$2,500**
1986 (MCMLXXXVI)	599,566	10778	2,600	2,600	2,650
1987 (MCMLXXXVII)	131,255	10779	3,250	3,250	5,000
1988 (MCMLXXXVIII)	45,000	10780	4,400	4,400	5,750
1989 (MCMLXXXIX)	44,829	10762	5,000	5,000	6,750
1990 (MCMXC)	31,000	10763	5,250	5,500	12,500
1991 (MCMXCI)	24,100	10764	6,500	6,750	6,750
1992	54,404	10765	3,100	3,100	3,300
1993	73,324	10766	3,150	3,200	3,600
1994	62,400	10767	3,150	3,200	3,600
1995	53,474	10768	4,350	4,400	4,950
1996	39,287	10769	4,000	4,000	5,500
1997	79,605	10770	3,100	3,150	3,250
1998	169,209	10771	2,450	2,450	2,500
1999	263,013	10772	2,450	2,450	3,750
2000	79,287	10773	3,050	3,100	3,600
2001	48,047	10774	3,050	3,100	3,400
2002	70,027	10775	2,500	2,450	2,900
2003	79,029	10776	2,450	2,450	2,500
2004	98,040	10777	2,450	2,450	2,500
2005	80,023	15413	2,450	2,450	2,500
2006	66,005	65232	2,450	2,450	2,500
2006-W, Burnished	15,164	65231	$2,500	$2,500	$2,650
2007	47,002	68766	2,450	2,450	2,550
2007-W, Burnished	11,455	70914	2,500	2,500	2,550
2008	61,000	71068	2,550	2,500	2,650
2008-W, Burnished	15,682	70898	2,500	2,500	2,550
2009	110,000	70899	2,450	2,450	2,500
2010	81,000	71278	2,450	2,450	2,500
2011	70,000	74230	2,550	2,500	2,650
2012	43,000	74231	2,500	2,500	2,650
2013	57,000	74232	2,500	2,500	2,650
2014	35,000	74233	2,500	2,500	2,650
2015	78,000	74234	2,450	2,450	2,500
2016, 30th Anniv	71,000	74235	2,450	2,450	2,500
2017	37,000	74236	2,450	2,450	2,500
2018	32,000	77321	2,450	2,450	2,500
2019	30,000	77322	2,450	2,450	2,500
2020	70,000	84242	2,450	2,450	2,500
2021, Variety 1 Rev	95,000	85057	2,450	2,450	2,500
2021, Variety 2 Rev		188662	2,450	2,450	2,500
2022	75,000	193328	2,450	2,450	2,500
2023		199052	2,450	2,450	2,500
2024		346944	2,450	2,450	2,500
2025		377674	—	—	—

* Value in original government packaging (OGP).

$25 1/2-Ounce Gold Eagle Proof Strikes

	Mintage	GSID	OGP*	PF-69	PF-70
American Gold Eagle (AGE),$10 1/2 oz. (1986 to Date), Proof	**n/a**	**74297**	**$2,450**	**$2,450**	**$2,550**
1987-P (MCMLXXXVII)	143,398	10798	2,450	2,450	2,550
1988-P (MCMLXXXVIII)	76,528	10781	2,450	2,450	2,550
1989-P (MCMLXXXIX)	44,798	10799	2,450	2,450	2,550
1990-P (MCMXC)	51,636	10782	2,450	2,450	3,750
1991-P (MCMXCI)	53,125	10783	2,450	2,450	2,550
1992-P	40,976	10784	2,450	2,450	2,550
1993-P	43,819	10785	2,450	2,450	3,400
1994-W	44,584	10786	2,450	2,450	2,550
1995-W	45,388	10788	2,450	2,450	2,550
1996-W	35,058	10789	2,450	2,450	2,550
1997-W	26,344	10790	2,450	2,450	2,550
1998-W	25,374	10791	2,450	2,450	2,550
1999-W	30,427	10792	2,450	2,450	2,550
2000-W	32,028	10793	2,450	2,450	2,550
2001-W	23,240	10794	2,450	2,450	2,550
2002-W	26,646	10795	2,450	2,450	2,550
2003-W	28,270	10796	2,450	2,450	2,550
2004-W	27,330	10797	2,450	2,450	2,550
2005-W	34,311	15415	$2,450	$2,450	$2,550
2006-W	34,322	65233	2,450	2,450	2,550
2007-W	44,025	68649	2,450	2,450	2,550
2008-W	22,602	69471	2,450	2,450	2,550
2010-W	44,527	70998	2,450	2,450	2,550
2011-W	26,781	71470	2,450	2,450	2,550
2012-W	12,919	71286	2,450	2,450	2,550
2013-W	12,716	74298	2,450	2,450	2,550
2014-W	14,693	74299	2,450	2,450	2,550
2015-W	15,820	74300	2,450	2,450	2,550
2016-W, 30th Anniv	23,578	74301	2,450	2,450	2,550
2017-W	12,715	74302	2,450	2,450	2,550
2018-W	9,961	77323	2,450	2,450	2,600
2019-W	10,703	84243	2,450	2,450	2,550
2020-W	14,020	84244	2,450	2,450	2,550
2021-W, Variety 1 Rev	12,180	188659	2,450	2,450	2,550
2021-W, Variety 2 Rev		188660	2,450	2,450	2,550
2022-W	11,876	194489	2,450	2,450	2,550
2023-W	11,408	213168	2,450	2,450	2,550
2024-W		346945	2,450	2,450	2,550
2025-W		377857	2,450	2,450	2,550

* Value in original government packaging (OGP).

$50 1-Ounce Gold Eagle Bullion Strikes

	Mintage	GSID	OGP*	MS-69	MS-70
American Gold Eagle (AGE), $10 1 oz. (1986 to Date)	n/a	74237	$4,800	$4,800	$4,850
American Gold Eagle (AGE), $10 1 oz. (1986 to Date), Burnished	n/a	84296	4,750	4,750	4,800
1986 (MCMLXXXVI)	1,362,650	10740	4,800	4,800	4,850
1987 (MCMLXXXVII)	1,045,500	10741	4,800	4,800	4,850
1988 (MCMLXXXVIII)	465,500	10800	4,800	4,800	6,000
1989 (MCMLXXXIX)	415,790	10801	4,800	4,800	5,250
1990 (MCMXC)	373,210	10802	4,800	4,800	5,000
1991 (MCMXCI)	243,100	10803	4,800	4,800	5,000
1992	275,000	10804	4,800	4,800	5,500
1993	480,192	10805	4,800	4,800	4,850
1994	221,663	10806	4,800	4,800	9,750
1995	200,636	10807	4,800	4,800	5,250
1996	189,148	10808	4,800	4,800	4,850
1997	664,508	10809	4,800	4,800	5,000
1998	1,468,530	10810	4,800	4,800	4,850
1999	1,505,026	10811	4,800	4,800	4,850
2000	433,319	10812	4,800	4,800	4,850
2001	143,605	10813	4,800	4,800	4,850
2002	222,029	10814	4,800	4,800	4,850
2003	416,032	10815	4,800	4,800	4,850
2004	417,019	10816	4,800	4,800	4,850
2005	356,555	15416	4,800	4,800	5,000
2006	237,510	65111	4,800	4,800	5,000
2006-W, Burnished	45,053	71028	4,750	4,750	4,850
2007	140,016	68768	4,850	4,800	5,000
2007-W, Burnished	18,066	69470	4,750	4,750	4,850
2008	710,000	71744	4,800	4,800	4,850
2008-W, Burnished	11,908	69468	4,750	4,750	4,800
2009	1,493,000	74254	4,800	4,800	4,850
2010	1,125,000	70910	$4,800	$4,800	$4,850
2011	857,000	74238	4,800	4,800	4,850
2011-W, Burnished	8,729	74255	4,750	4,750	4,800
2012	675,000	71745	4,800	4,800	4,850
2012-W, Burnished	6,118	74256	4,800	4,750	4,850
2013	758,500	74257	4,800	4,800	4,850
2013-W, Burnished	7,293	71674	4,750	4,750	4,850
2014	425,000	74258	4,800	4,800	4,850
2014-W, Burnished	7,902	74259	4,750	4,750	4,850
2015	626,500	74239	4,800	4,800	4,950
2015-W, Burnished	6,533	74260	4,750	4,750	4,800
2016, 30th Anniv	817,500	74240	4,800	4,800	4,850
2016-W, 30th Anniv, Burnished	6,887	74261	4,750	4,750	4,850
2017	228,500	74241	4,800	4,800	4,850
2017-W, Burnished	5,800	74262	4,800	4,750	4,800
2018	191,000	77325	4,800	4,800	4,850
2018-W, Burnished	8,518	77326	4,750	4,750	4,850
2019	108,000	77327	4,800	4,800	4,850
2019-W, Burnished	6,365	84297	4,750	4,750	4,800
2020	747,500	82362	4,800	4,800	4,850
2020-W, Burnished	6,284	84869	4,750	4,750	4,900
2021, Variety 1 Rev	1,115,500	85058	4,800	4,800	4,850
2021, Variety 2 Rev		85059	4,800	4,800	4,850
2021, Variety 2 Rev, Burnished		193688	4,750	4,750	4,800
2022	850,000	193329	4,800	4,800	4,850
2022-W, Burnished		213359	4,750	4,750	4,800
2023		199051	4,800	4,800	4,850
2023-W, Burnished		231560	4,750	4,750	4,800
2024		346946	4,800	4,800	4,850
2024-W, Burnished		375029	4,750	4,750	4,800
2025		377675	4,800	4,800	4,850
2025-W, Burnished		393392	—	—	—

* Value in original government packaging (OGP).

$50 1-Ounce Gold Eagle Proof Strikes

	Mintage	GSID	OGP*	PF-69	PF-70
American Gold Eagle (AGE), $10 1 oz. (1986 to Date), Proof	n/a	74303	$4,800	$4,700	$4,850
1986-W (MCMLXXXVI)	446,290	10821	4,850	4,800	5,250
1987-W (MCMLXXXVII)	147,498	10760	4,800	4,700	4,850
1988-W (MCMLXXXVIII)	87,133	10817	4,800	4,700	4,950
1989-W (MCMLXXXIX)	54,570	10761	4,800	4,700	4,850
1990-W (MCMXC)	62,401	10818	4,800	4,700	4,900
1991-W (MCMXCI)	50,411	10819	4,850	4,800	4,900
1992-W	44,826	10820	4,800	4,700	4,850
1993-W	34,369	10822	4,850	4,800	5,250
1994-W	46,674	10823	$4,800	$4,700	$4,850
1995-W	46,368	10824	4,850	4,800	4,850
1996-W	36,153	10825	4,850	4,800	5,250
1997-W	32,999	10826	4,800	4,700	4,850
1998-W	25,886	10827	4,850	4,800	5,250
1999-W	31,427	10828	4,850	4,800	4,900
2000-W	33,007	10829	4,800	4,700	4,850
2001-W	24,555	10830	4,800	4,700	4,850
2002-W	27,499	10831	4,800	4,700	4,850
2003-W	28,344	10832	4,800	4,700	4,850
2004-W	28,215	10833	4,800	4,700	4,850
2005-W	35,246	15418	4,850	4,800	5,250

* Value in original government packaging (OGP).

$50 1-Ounce Gold Eagle Proof Strikes *(continued)*

	Mintage	GSID	OGP*	PF-69	PF-70
2006-W	47,092	65113	$4,800	$4,700	$4,950
2006-W, 20th Anniv, RevPf	9,996	65313	4,950	4,850	5,250
2007-W	51,810	70918	4,800	4,700	4,850
2008-W	30,237	69461	4,800	4,700	4,850
2010-W	59,480	70999	4,800	4,700	4,850
2011-W	48,306	71597	4,800	4,700	4,850
2012-W	23,630	74304	4,800	4,700	4,850
2013-W	24,710	74305	4,800	4,700	4,850
2014-W	28,703	74306	4,800	4,700	4,850
2015-W	32,652	74307	4,800	4,700	4,850
2016-W, 30th Anniv	41,621	74308	4,800	4,700	4,850
2017-W	19,056	74309	4,800	4,700	4,850
2018-W	15,564	77328	$4,800	$4,700	$4,850
2019-W	14,695	77329	4,800	4,700	4,850
2020-W	5,784	82363	4,800	4,700	4,850
2020-W, 75th Anniv of End of WWII (with Privy Mark)	1,939	84815	14,500	14,500	23,000
2021-W, Variety 1 Rev	4,404	85184	4,800	4,700	4,850
2021-W, Variety 2 Rev	5,562	85185	4,800	4,700	4,850
2022-W	15,819	194490	4,800	4,700	4,850
2023-W	15,863	213170	4,800	4,700	4,850
2024-W		346947	4,800	4,700	4,850
2025-W		377856	4,800	4,700	4,850

* Value in original government packaging (OGP).

Gold Eagle Sets

	GSID	OGP*
American Gold Eagle (AGE) Set (1986 to Date), 4 Coins	**81695**	**$8,750**
1987 Proof Set. $50, $25	10607	7,000
1988 Proof Set. $50, $25, $10, $5	10609	8,750
1989 Proof Set. $50, $25, $10, $5	10612	8,750
1990 Proof Set. $50, $25, $10, $5	10614	8,750
1991 Proof Set. $50, $25, $10, $5	10616	8,750
1992 Proof Set. $50, $25, $10, $5	10618	8,750
1993 Proof Set. $50, $25, $10, $5	10620	8,750
1993 Philadelphia Mint Bicentennial Proof Set: 1993-W $25, $10, and $5 Gold Eagles, 1993-P $1 American Silver Eagle, and medal	79849	4,350
1994 Proof Set. $50, $25, $10, $5	10622	8,750
1995 Proof Set. $50, $25, $10, $5	10624	8,750
1996 Proof Set. $50, $25, $10, $5	10626	8,750
1997 Proof Set. $50, $25, $10, $5	10628	8,750
1998 Proof Set. $50, $25, $10, $5	10630	8,750
1999 Proof Set. $50, $25, $10, $5	10632	8,750
2000 Proof Set. $50, $25, $10, $5	10634	8,750
2001 Proof Set. $50, $25, $10, $5	10636	8,750
2002 Proof Set. $50, $25, $10, $5	10638	8,750
2003 Proof Set. $50, $25, $10, $5	10640	8,750
2004 Proof Set. $50, $25, $10, $5	10642	8,750
2005 Proof Set. $50, $25, $10, $5	65107	8,750
2006 Proof Set. $50, $25, $10, $5	65108	8,750
2006-W 20th Anniversary Gold and Silver Eagle Uncirculated set: $50 Gold Eagle and $1 American Silver Eagle	65332	4,850
2006-W 20th Anniversary American Gold Eagle Set. $50 Burnished, Proof, and Reverse Proof American Gold Eagles	65312	14,000
2006-W Burnished Set. $50, $25, $10, $5	65110	9,000
2007 Proof Set. $50, $25, $10, $5	68929	8,750
2007-W Burnished Set. $50, $25, $10, $5	77944	9,000
2008 Proof Set. $50, $25, $10, $5	70874	8,750
2008-W Burnished Set. $50, $25, $10, $5	77945	9,000
2010 Proof Set. $50, $25, $10, $5 (a)	70893	8,750
2011 Proof Set. $50, $25, $10, $5	77477	8,750
2012 Proof Set. $50, $25, $10, $5	77478	8,750
2013 Proof Set. $50, $25, $10, $5	71570	8,750
2014 Proof Set. $50, $25, $10, $5	77479	8,750
2015 Proof Set. $50, $25, $10, $5	77481	8,750
2016 Proof Set. $50, $25, $10, $5	77482	8,750
2017 Proof Set. $50, $25, $10, $5	77483	8,750
2018 Proof Set. $50, $25, $10, $5	213149	8,750
2019 Proof Set. $50, $25, $10, $5	213150	8,750
2020 Proof Set. $50, $25, $10, $5	315632	8,750
2021, Variety 1 Reverse Proof Set. $50, $25, $10, $5	213151	8,750
2021, Variety 2 Reverse Proof Set. $50, $25, $10, $5	213152	8,750
2022 Proof Set. $50, $25, $10, $5	213153	8,750
2023 Proof Set. $50, $25, $10, $5	213154	8,750
2024 Proof Set. $50, $25, $10, $5	347670	8,750
2025 Proof Set. $50, $25, $10, $5	393562	8,750

* Value in original government packaging (OGP). **a.** The U.S. Mint did not issue a 2009 gold set.

Note: Gold spot price at time of publication, $3,746 per ounce.

American Platinum Eagles (1997 to Date)

Designers: *John M. Mercanti (obverse), Thomas D. Rogers Sr. (original reverse) (see below for Proof designers).* **Weight:** *$10 1/10 oz.—3.112 grams; $25 1/4 oz.—7.780 grams; $50 1/2 oz.—15.560 grams; $100 1 oz.—31.120 grams.* **Composition:** *.9995 platinum.* **Diameter:** *$10 1/10 oz.—16.5 mm; $25 1/4 oz.—22 mm; $50 1/2 oz.—27 mm; $100 1 oz.—32.7 mm.* **Edge:** *Reeded.* **Mints:** *Philadelphia and West Point.*

$100 Proof Designers:

Reverses:

1997 . . . . Thomas D. Rogers Sr.
1998, Eagle Over New England . . Thomas D. Rogers Sr.
1999, Eagle Above Southeastern Wetlands . . . . John M. Mercanti
2000, Eagle Above America's Heartland . . . . John M. Mercanti
2001, Eagle Above America's Southwest . . . . Thomas D. Rogers Sr.
2002, Eagle Fishing in America's Northwest . . . . Al Maletsky
2003 . . . . Al Maletsky
2004 . . . . Donna Weaver
2005 . . . . Donna Weaver
2006, Legislative Branch . . . . Joel Iskowitz
2007, Executive Branch . . . . Tom Cleveland
2008, Judicial Branch . . . . Joel Iskowitz
2009, To Form a More Perfect Union. . . . Susan Gamble
2010, To Establish Justice . . . . Donna Weaver
2011, To Insure Domestic Tranquility . . . . Joel Iskowitz
2012, To Provide for the Common Defence Barbara Fox
2013, To Promote the General Welfare . . . Joel Iskowitz
2014, To Secure the Blessings of Liberty. . Susan Gamble
2015, Liberty Nurtures Freedom . . . . Joel Iskowitz
2016, Portrait of Liberty . . . . Paul C. Balan
2017 (same as 1997) . . . . Thomas D. Rogers Sr.

Obverses:

2018, Life . . . . Justin Kunz
2019, Liberty. . . . . Justin Kunz
2020, Pursuit of Hapiness . . . . Justin Kunz
2021, Freedom of Religion . . . . Donna Weaver
2022, Freedom of Speech . . . . Donna Weaver
2023, Freedom of the Press. . . . . Donna Weaver
2024, Right to Assemble . . . . Donna Weaver
2025, Right to Petition. . . . . Donna Weaver

Regular Finish

Burnished Finish

Proof Finish

Reverse Proof Finish

2007, Frosted FREEDOM

History. Platinum American Eagles (face values of $10 to $100) are legal-tender bullion coins with weight, content, and purity guaranteed by the federal government. They were added to the U.S. Mint's program of silver and gold bullion coinage in 1997.

In their debut year, Proofs had the same reverse design as regular bullion strikes. Since then, the regular strikes have continued with the 1997 reverse, while the Proofs have featured new reverse designs each year. From 1998 through 2002, these special Proof designs comprised a "Vistas of Liberty" subset, with eagles flying through various American scenes. Since 2003, they have featured patriotic allegories and symbolism. From 2006 to 2008 the reverse designs honored "The Foundations of Democracy"—the nation's legislative branch (2006), executive branch (2007), and judicial branch (2008). In 2009 the Mint introduced a new six-year program of reverse designs, exploring the core concepts of American democracy as embodied in the preamble to the Constitution. The designs—which were based on narratives by John Roberts, chief justice of the United States—began with *To Form a More Perfect Union* (2009), which features four faces representing the nation's diversity, with the hair and clothing interweaving symbolically. The tiny eagle privy mark is from an original coin punch from the Philadelphia Mint's archives. This design is followed by *To Establish Justice* (2010), *To Insure Domestic Tranquility* (2011), *To Provide for the Common Defence* (2012), *To Promote the General Welfare* (2013), and *To Secure the Blessings of Liberty to Ourselves and Our Posterity* (2014). In 2015, the Mint issued the first of a two-year series of new reverse designs emblematic of the core values of liberty and freedom called *Liberty Nurtures Freedom*. In 2017 the Proof reverse returned to the original 1997 design for the program's 20th anniversary. One-ounce Proofs of 2018 through 2020 feature new obverse designs in the theme of Life, Liberty, and the Pursuit of Happiness, and also share a new common reverse design. Beginning in 2021 the Mint will issue a new five-year series of one-ounce Proofs, for the five freedoms guaranteed under the First Amendment of the U.S. Constitution.

The Philadelphia Mint strikes regular bullion issues, which are sold to the public by a network of Mint-authorized precious-metal firms, coin dealers, banks, and brokerages. The West Point facility strikes Burnished pieces (called *Uncirculated* by the Mint, and featuring the reverse design of the Proof coins), which are sold directly to collectors. Proofs are also struck at West Point and, like the Burnished coins, are sold by the Mint to the public, without middlemen. Similar to their gold-bullion cousins, the platinum Proofs and Burnished coins bear a W mintmark and are specially packaged in plastic capsules and fancy presentation cases.

In addition to the individual coins listed below, platinum American Eagles were issued in the 1997 "Impressions of Liberty" bullion coin set; in 2007 "10th Anniversary" sets; and in annual platinum-coin sets.

Striking and Sharpness. Striking is generally sharp.

Availability. The platinum American Eagle is one of the most popular platinum-investment vehicles in the world. The coins are readily available in the numismatic marketplace and through some banks, investment firms, and other non-numismatic channels.

MS-60 to 70 (Mint State). ***Obverse and Reverse:*** At MS-60, some abrasion and contact marks are evident on the higher design areas. Luster may be dull or lifeless at MS-60 to 62, but there should be deep frost at MS-63 and better, particularly in the lower-relief areas. At MS-65 and above, the luster should be full and rich. These guidelines are more academic than practical, as platinum American Eagles are not intended for circulation, and nearly all are in high Mint State grades.

PF-60 to 70 (Proof). ***Obverse and Reverse:*** Proofs that are extensively cleaned and have many hairlines are lower level, such as PF-60 to 62. Those with fewer hairlines or flaws are deemed PF-63 to 65. (These exist more in theory than actuality, as nearly all Proof American Eagle platinum bullion coins have been maintained in their original high condition by collectors.) Given the quality of modern U.S. Mint products, even PF-66 and 67 are unusually low levels for these Proofs.

$10 1/10-Ounce Platinum Eagle Bullion Strikes

	Mintage	GSID	OGP*	MS-69	MS-70
American Platinum Eagle (APE), $10 1/10 oz. (1997–2008)	n/a	74263	$245	$245	$295
1997	70,250	10834	310	310	1,250
1998	39,525	10835	310	310	4,500
1999	55,955	10836	255	255	1,500
1999, DDR, FS-801	**	351881	—	2,050	3,100
2000	34,027	10837	245	245	775
2001	52,017	10838	245	245	525
2002	23,005	10839	250	250	320

	Mintage	GSID	OGP*	MS-69	MS-70
2003	22,007	10840	$245	$245	$490
2004	15,010	10841	245	245	360
2005	14,013	15419	245	245	295
2006	11,001	65118	245	245	295
2006-W, Burnished	3,544	74264	575	675	975
2007	13,003	71062	245	245	320
2007-W, Burnished	5,556	68779	420	500	725
2008	17,000	69036	245	245	295
2008-W, Burnished	3,706	70661	525	600	850
2008	17,000	69036	245	245	295

* Value in original government packaging (OGP). ** Included in number above.

$10 1/10-Ounce Platinum Eagle Proof Strikes

	Mintage	GSID	OGP*	PF-69	PF-70
American Platinum Eagle (APE), $10 1/10 oz. (1997–2008), Proof	n/a	74285	$235	$235	$300
1997-W	36,993	10842	265	265	365
1998-W	19,847	10843	235	235	300
1999-W	19,133	10844	235	235	300
2000-W	15,651	10845	235	235	300
2001-W	12,174	10846	235	235	300

	Mintage	GSID	OGP*	PF-69	PF-70
2002-W	12,365	10847	$235	$235	$300
2003-W	9,534	10848	235	235	300
2004-W	7,161	10849	235	235	365
2005-W	8,104	15420	275	275	330
2006-W	10,205	71590	235	235	300
2007-W	8,176	68930	235	235	300
2008-W	5,138	69037	265	265	365
2007-W	8,176	68930	235	235	300

* Value in original government packaging (OGP).

$25 1/4-Ounce Platinum Eagle Bullion Strikes

	Mintage	GSID	OGP*	MS-69	MS-70
American Platinum Eagle (APE), $25 1/4 oz. (1997–2008)	n/a	74265	$550	$550	$625
1997	27,100	10850	575	575	2,750
1998	38,887	10851	550	575	1,150
1999	39,734	10852	550	550	3,750
2000	20,054	10853	550	550	1,900
2001	21,815	10854	550	550	1,500
2002	27,405	10855	600	550	625

	Mintage	GSID	OGP*	MS-69	MS-70
2003	25,207	10856	$550	$550	$625
2004	18,010	10857	550	550	625
2005	12,013	15422	550	550	625
2006	12,001	65121	550	550	625
2006-W, Burnished	2,676	71019	1,000	1,000	1,450
2007	8,402	69373	550	550	650
2007-W, Burnished	3,690	71021	900	900	1,150
2008	22,800	69372	575	575	650
2008-W, Burnished	2,481	70658	1,350	1,350	1,900

* Value in original government packaging (OGP).

$25 1/4-Ounce Platinum Eagle Proof Strikes

	Mintage	GSID	OGP*	PF-69	PF-70
American Platinum Eagle (APE), $25 1/4 oz. (1997–2008), Proof	n/a	74284	$575	$575	$625
1997-W	18,628	10858	575	575	650
1998-W	14,873	10859	575	575	650
1999-W	13,507	10860	575	575	625
2000-W	11,995	10861	575	575	625
2001-W	8,847	10862	575	575	625
2002-W	9,282	10863	575	575	625

	Mintage	GSID	OGP*	PF-69	PF-70
2003-W	7,044	10864	$575	$575	$625
2004-W	5,193	10865	575	575	950
2005-W	6,592	15424	575	575	625
2006-W	7,813	65123	575	575	625
2007-W	6,017	69374	575	575	650
2007-W, Frosted FREEDOM	**	198091	—	—	48,000
2008-W	4,153	69375	575	575	850
2006-W	7,813	65123	575	575	625

* Value in original government packaging (OGP). ** Included in number above.

Note: Platinum spot price at time of publication, $1,527.50 per ounce.

$50 1/2-Ounce Platinum Eagle Bullion Strikes

	Mintage	GSID	OGP*	MS-69	MS-70
American Platinum Eagle (APE), $50 1/2 oz. (1997–2008)	**n/a**	**74266**	**$1,050**	**$1,050**	**$1,100**
1997	20,500	10866	1,050	1,050	2,400
1998	32,415	10867	1,050	1,050	9,500
1999	32,309	10868	1,050	1,050	10,000
2000	18,892	10869	1,050	1,050	6,250
2001	12,815	10870	1,050	1,050	5,250
2002	24,005	10871	1,050	1,050	1,200
2003	17,409	10872	$1,050	$1,050	$1,250
2004	13,236	10873	1,050	1,050	1,100
2005	9,013	15425	1,050	1,050	1,150
2006	9,602	74267	1,050	1,050	1,150
2006-W, Burnished	2,577	71020	1,250	1,400	1,950
2007	7,001	74268	1,050	1,050	1,100
2007-W, Burnished	3,635	71022	1,250	1,500	2,100
2008	14,000	74269	1,050	1,050	1,100
2008-W, Burnished	2,253	70659	2,100	2,100	2,900

* Value in original government packaging (OGP).

$50 1/2-Ounce Platinum Eagle Proof Strikes

	Mintage	GSID	OGP*	PF-69	PF-70
American Platinum Eagle (APE), $50 1/2 oz. (1997–2008), Proof	**n/a**	**74283**	**$1,150**	**$1,150**	**$1,200**
1997-W	15,431	10874	1,150	1,150	1,250
1998-W	13,836	10875	1,150	1,150	1,200
1999-W	11,103	10876	1,150	1,150	1,200
2000-W	11,049	10877	1,150	1,150	1,200
2001-W	8,254	10878	1,150	1,150	1,200
2002-W	8,772	10879	1,150	1,150	1,200
2003-W	7,131	10880	$1,150	$1,150	$1,200
2004-W	5,063	10881	1,150	1,150	1,200
2005-W	5,942	15427	1,150	1,150	1,200
2006-W	7,649	68614	1,150	1,150	1,250
2007-W	25,519	70952	1,150	1,150	1,200
2007-W, RevPf	19,583	121154	1,200	1,200	1,200
2007-W, Frosted FREEDOM	**	198092	—	—	93,500
2008-W	4,020	71029	1,150	1,150	1,250

* Value in original government packaging (OGP). ** Included in number above.

$100 1-Ounce American Platinum Eagles

Proof Reverse, 1998: Eagle Over New England. *Vistas of Liberty series.*

Proof Reverse, 1999: Eagle Above Southeastern Wetlands. *Vistas of Liberty series.*

Proof Reverse, 2000: Eagle Above America's Heartland. *Vistas of Liberty series.*

Proof Reverse, 2001: Eagle Above America's Southwest. *Vistas of Liberty series.*

Proof Reverse, 2002: Eagle Fishing in America's Northwest. *Vistas of Liberty series.*

Proof Reverse, 2003. *Designer: Alfred Maletsky.*

Proof Reverse, 2004.
Designer: Donna Weaver.

Proof Reverse, 2005.
Designer: Donna Weaver.

Proof Reverse, 2006: Legislative Branch.
Foundations of Democracy series.

Proof Reverse, 2007: Executive Branch.
Foundations of Democracy series.

Proof Reverse, 2008: Judicial Branch.
Foundations of Democracy series.

Proof Reverse, 2009: "To Form a More Perfect Union."
Preamble to the Constitution series.

Proof Reverse, 2010: "To Establish Justice."
Preamble to the Constitution series.

Proof Reverse, 2011: "To Insure Domestic Tranquility."
Preamble to the Constitution series.

Proof Reverse, 2012: "To Provide for the Common Defence."
Preamble to the Constitution series.

Proof Reverse, 2013: "To Promote the General Welfare."
Preamble to the Constitution series.

Proof Reverse, 2014: "To Secure the Blessings of Liberty to Ourselves and Our Posterity."
Preamble to the Constitution series.

Proof Reverse, 2015: Liberty Nurtures Freedom.

Proof Reverse, 2016: Portrait of Liberty.

Common Reverse, 2018 to date.

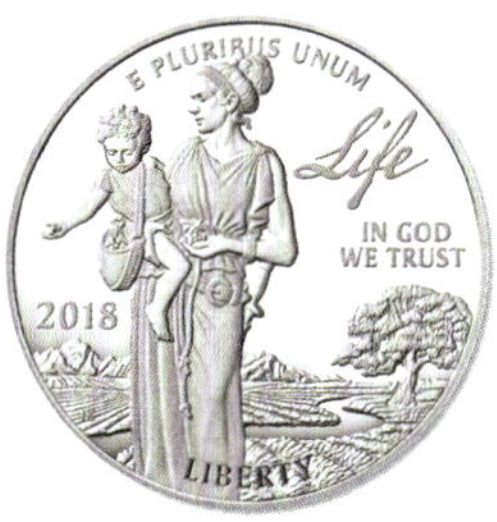

Proof Obverse, 2018: "Life."
Preamble to the Declaration of Independence series.

Proof Obverse, 2019: "Liberty."
Preamble to the Declaration of Independence series.

Proof Obverse, 2020:
"Happiness."
Preamble to the Declaration of Independence series.

Proof Obverse, 2021:
"Freedom of Religion."
First Amendment to the U.S. Constitution series.

Proof Obverse, 2022:
"Freedom of Speech."
First Amendment to the U.S. Constitution series.

Proof Obverse, 2023:
"Freedom of the Press."
First Amendment to the U.S. Constitution series.

Proof Obverse, 2024:
"Right to Assemble."
First Amendment to the U.S. Constitution series.

Proof Obverse, 2025:
"Right to Petition."
First Amendment to the U.S. Constitution series.

$100 1-Ounce Platinum Eagle Bullion Strikes

	Mintage	GSID	OGP*	MS-69	MS-70
American Platinum Eagle (APE), $100 1 oz. (1997 to Date)	**n/a**	**74270**	**$2,000**	**$2,000**	**$2,100**
1997	56,000	10882	2,000	2,000	27,000
1998	133,002	10883	2,000	2,000	60,000
1999	56,707	10884	2,750	2,750	36,000
2000	10,003	10885	2,000	2,000	36,000
2001	14,070	10886	3,250	3,250	36,000
2002	11,502	10887	2,150	2,150	9,000
2003	8,007	10888	2,200	2,200	6,250
2004	7,009	10889	2,000	2,000	2,750
2005	6,310	15428	2,000	2,000	3,000
2006	6,000	71066	2,000	2,000	2,500
2006-W, Burnished	3,068	71067	2,500	2,550	3,100
2007	7,202	74271	$2,000	$2,000	$3,100
2007-W, Burnished	4,177	71023	2,450	2,500	3,450
2008	21,800	71122	2,000	2,000	2,150
2008-W, Burnished	2,876	70660	2,600	2,700	3,750
2014	16,900	74272	2,000	2,000	2,150
2016	20,000	74273	2,000	2,000	2,250
2017	20,000	74274	2,000	2,000	2,100
2018	30,000	81972	2,000	2,000	2,100
2019	40,000	81973	2,000	2,000	2,100
2020	56,500	81974	2,000	2,000	2,100
2021	75,000	85182	2,000	2,000	2,100
2022	80,000	193334	2,000	2,000	2,100
2023		199056	2,000	2,000	2,100

* Value in original government packaging (OGP).

$100 1-Ounce Platinum Eagle Proof Strikes

	Mintage	GSID	OGP*	PF-69	PF-70
American Platinum Eagle (APE), $100 1 oz. (1997 to Date), Proof	**n/a**	**74275**	**$2,250**	**$2,250**	**$2,300**
1997-W	20,851	10890	2,250	2,250	2,550
1998-W	14,912	10891	2,250	2,250	2,300
1999-W	12,363	10892	2,250	2,250	2,350
2000-W	12,453	10893	2,250	2,250	2,300
2001-W	8,969	10894	2,250	2,250	2,300
2002-W	9,834	10895	2,250	2,250	2,300
2003-W	8,246	10896	2,250	2,250	2,450
2004-W	6,007	10897	2,250	2,250	2,800
2005-W	6,602	15430	2,300	2,300	2,700
2006-W	9,152	68754	2,300	2,300	2,700
2007-W	8,363	70886	2,250	2,250	2,300
2007-W, Frosted FREEDOM	*	198093	—	—	240,000
2008-W	4,769	70892	2,400	2,400	2,950
2009-W	7,945	70872	$2,250	$2,250	$2,300
2010-W	14,790	71026	2,250	2,250	2,300
2011-W	14,835	71025	2,250	2,250	2,300
2012-W	9,081	74276	2,250	2,250	2,300
2013-W	5,763	74277	2,250	2,250	2,300
2014-W	4,596	74278	2,500	2,500	3,250
2015-W	3,886	74279	2,300	2,300	2,950
2016-W	9,151	74280	2,250	2,250	2,300
2017-W	8,890	74281	2,250	2,250	2,300
2018-W	16,222	74282	2,300	2,300	2,350
2019-W	11,263	81975	2,250	2,250	2,300
2020-W	9,835	81976	2,300	2,300	2,350
2021-W	9,884	85183	2,300	2,300	2,350
2022-W	9,941	193383	2,300	2,300	2,700
2023-W	8,494	198247	2,250	2,250	2,300
2024-W	5,106	347668	2,250	2,250	2,300
2025-W	max. 9,000	377795	2,400	2,300	2,450

* Value in original government packaging (OGP).

Platinum Eagle Sets

	GSID	OGP*
1997-W Uncirculated Set. $100, $50, $25, $10	**376884**	**$3,000**
1997-W Proof Set.100, $50, $25, $10	11067	4,700
1998-W Proof Set.100, $50, $25, $10	11069	4,700
1999-W Proof Set.100, $50, $25, $10	11071	4,700
2000-W Proof Set.100, $50, $25, $10	11073	4,700
2001-W Proof Set.100, $50, $25, $10	11075	4,700
2002-W Proof Set.100, $50, $25, $10	11077	4,700
2003-W Proof Set.100, $50, $25, $10	11079	4,700
2004-W Proof Set.100, $50, $25, $10	11081	4,700
2005-W Proof Set.100, $50, $25, $10	65115	$4,700
2006-W Proof Set.100, $50, $25, $10	65117	4,700
2006-W Burnished Set. $100, $50, $25, $10	77484	5,000
2007-W Proof Set.100, $50, $25, $10	70870	4,700
2007-W Burnished Set. $100, $50, $25, $10	77485	4,800
2007-W, 10th Anniversary Two-Coin Set. $50 Proof and Reverse Proof	70953	2,300
2008-W Proof Set.100, $50, $25, $10	70871	4,650
2008-W Burnished Set. $100, $50, $25, $10	77486	5,750

* Value in original government packaging (OGP).

Note: Platinum spot price at time of publication, $1,527.50 per ounce.

American Palladium Eagles (2017 to Date)

Designer: *Adolph A. Weinman.* **Weight:** *31.120 grams (1 oz. pure palladium).* **Composition:** *.9995 palladium.* **Diameter:** *32.7 mm.* **Edge:** *Reeded.* **Mints:** *Philadelphia and West Point.*

A side view showing the coin's high relief.

History. In 2017 palladium was added to the U.S. Mint's American Eagle bullion programs, becoming the fourth precious metal in the lineup.

The American Palladium Bullion Act of 2010 (Public Law 111-303) required the secretary of the Treasury to mint and issue .9995 fine palladium bullion coins weighing one troy ounce and with a face value of $25, "in such quantities as the secretary determines appropriate to meet demand." Only coins in the one-ounce size are permitted; fractional sizes are not authorized. Title 31 U.S.C. Section 5112(v) authorizes the secretary to mint and issue Proof and Burnished ("Uncirculated") versions for collectors.

The American Palladium Eagle's designs were mandated by law. The obverse is a high-relief allegorical portrait derived from artist Adolph Weinman's Winged Liberty dime of 1916 to 1945. The reverse is a high-relief version of Weinman's 1907 American Institute of Architects gold medal reverse, showing an eagle grasping a branch. To develop the coin, the Mint was able to use the original reverse plaster of the AIA gold medal.

Although largely symbolic, the palladium coin's denomination of $25 provides proof of its authenticity as official U.S. coinage.

Bullion-strike coins are minted in Philadelphia on an annual basis, and distributed through the Mint's network of authorized purchasers. Proof and Reverse Proof numismatic versions struck at the West Point Mint are sold by the Mint directly to collectors.

Striking and Sharpness. Striking is generally sharp.

Availability. The American Palladium Eagle is a readily available bullion and collector coin. The coins are easily acquired in the numismatic marketplace and through some banks, investment firms, and other non-numismatic channels.

MS-60 to 70 (Mint State). *Obverse and Reverse:* Grading guidelines are more academic than practical for this program, since American Palladium Eagles are not intended for circulation, and nearly all are in high Mint State grades.

PF-60 to 70 (Proof). *Obverse and Reverse:* Impaired, cleaned, and otherwise low-level Proofs exist more in theory than in actuality for this series, as nearly all Proof American Palladium Eagle coins have been maintained in their original high condition by collectors. Given the quality of modern U.S. Mint products, even PF-66 or 67 would be unusually low for these Proofs.

$25 1-Ounce Palladium Eagle Bullion Strikes

	Mintage	GSID	OGP*	MS-69	MS-70
American Palladium Eagle, $25 1 oz. (2017 to Date)	**n/a**	**376573**	**$1,700**	**$1,700**	**$1,950**
2017-(P)	15,000	74210	1,700	1,700	2,600
2020-W, Burnished	9,746	193332	1,900	1,900	2,150
2021-(P)	8,700	193331	1,700	1,700	1,950
2023-W, Burnished	5,779	199004	1,700	1,700	1,950

* Value in original government packaging (OGP).

$25 Palladium Eagle Proof Strikes

	Mintage	GSID	OGP*	PF-69	PF-70
American Palladium Eagle, $25 1 oz. (2018 to Date), Proof	**n/a**	**376574**	**$2,400**	**$2,400**	**$2,550**
2018-W	14,988	74211	2,400	2,400	2,700
2019-W, Reverse Proof	18,839	81971	2,400	2,400	2,650
2021-W	5,170	121153	2,400	2,400	2,700
2022-W, Reverse Proof	7,439	197931	2,550	2,500	2,750
2024-W	6,000	376012	2,400	2,400	2,550
2025-W, Reverse Proof	6,000	393391	2,400	2,400	2,550

* Value in original government packaging (OGP).

Note: Palladium spot price at time of publication, $1,545 per ounce.

AMERICAN BUFFALO GOLD BULLION PROGRAM

Designer: *James Earle Fraser.* **Weight:** *\$5 1/10 oz.—3.393 grams; \$10 1/4 oz.—8.483 grams; \$25 1/2 oz.—16.966 grams; \$50 1 oz.—31.108 grams.* **Composition:** *.9999 gold.* **Diameter:** *\$5 1/10 oz.—16.5 mm; \$10 1/4 oz.—22 mm; \$25 1/2 oz.—27 mm; \$50 1 oz.—32.7 mm.* **Edge:** *Reeded.* **Mint:** *West Point.*

Regular Finish

Mintmark location is on the obverse, behind the neck.

Burnished Finish

Proof Finish

Reverse Proof Finish

\$5 1/10-oz. **\$10 1/4-oz.** **\$25 1/2-oz.** **\$50 1-oz.**

History. American Buffalo gold bullion coins, authorized by Congress in 2005 and produced since 2006, are the first 24-karat (.9999 fine) gold coins made by the U.S. Mint. They are coined, by mandate, of gold derived from newly mined sources in America. They feature an adaptation of James Earle Fraser's iconic Indian Head / Buffalo design, first used on circulating five-cent pieces of 1913 to 1938.

Only 1-ounce (\$50 face value) coins were struck in the American Buffalo program's first two years, 2006 and 2007. For 2008, the Mint expanded the coinage to include fractional pieces of 1/2 ounce (\$25), 1/4 ounce (\$10), and 1/10-ounce (\$5), in various finishes, individually and in sets.

The coins are legal tender, with weight, content, and purity guaranteed by the federal government. Investors can include them in some individual retirement accounts. Proofs and Burnished (*Uncirculated*, in the Mint's wording) pieces undergo special production processes, similar to the American Eagle gold-bullion coinage, and can be purchased directly from the Mint. As with other products in the Mint's bullion program, regular bullion-strike pieces are distributed through a network of authorized distributors.

All American Buffalo gold bullion coins (Proofs, Burnished, and regular bullion pieces) are struck at the U.S. Mint's West Point facility.

Striking and Sharpness. Striking is generally sharp.

Availability. American Buffalo .9999 fine gold bullion coins are a popular way to buy and sell 24-karat gold. The coins are readily available in the numismatic marketplace as well as from participating banks, investment firms, and other non-numismatic channels.

MS-60 to 70 (Mint State). ***Obverse and reverse:*** At MS-60, some abrasion and contact marks are evident on the higher design areas and the open areas of the design. Luster may be dull or lifeless at MS-60 to 62, but there should be deep frost at MS-63 and better, particularly in the lower-relief areas. At MS-65 and above, the luster should be full and rich. Contact marks and abrasion are less and less evident at higher grades. These guidelines are more academic than practical, as these coins are not intended for circulation, and nearly all are in high Mint State grades, as struck.

PF-60 to 70 (Proof). ***Obverse and reverse:*** Proofs that are extensively cleaned and have many hairlines are lower level, such as PF-60 to 62. Those with fewer hairlines or flaws are deemed PF-63 to 65. (These exist more in theory than actuality, as nearly all Proof American Buffalo gold coins have been maintained in their original high condition by collectors.) Given the quality of modern U.S. Mint products, even PF-66 and 67 are unusually low levels for these Proofs.

$5 1/10-Ounce American Buffalo Gold Bullion Strikes

	Mintage	GSID	OGP*	MS-69	MS-70
2008-W, Burnished	17,429	70612	$850	$850	$1,000

* Value in original government packaging (OGP).

$5 1/10-Ounce American Buffalo Gold Proof Strikes

	Mintage	GSID	OGP*	PF-69	PF-70
2008-W, Proof	18,884	70853	$800	$800	$950

$10 1/4-Ounce American Buffalo Gold Bullion Strikes

	Mintage	GSID	OGP*	MS-69	MS-70
2008-W, Burnished	9,949	70613	$1,300	$1,300	$1,900

* Value in original government packaging (OGP).

$10 1/4-Ounce American Buffalo Gold Proof Strikes

	Mintage	GSID	OGP*	PF-69	PF-70
2008-W, Proof	13,125	70888	$1,500	$1,500	$2,250

$25 1/2-Ounce American Buffalo Gold Bullion Strikes

	Mintage	GSID	OGP*	MS-69	MS-70
2008-W, Burnished	16,908	70614	$2,400	$2,450	$2,500

* Value in original government packaging (OGP).

$25 1/2-Ounce American Buffalo Gold Proof Strikes

	Mintage	GSID	OGP*	PF-69	PF-70
2008-W, Proof	12,169	70854	$2,500	$2,500	$3,100

$50 1-Ounce American Buffalo Gold Bullion Strikes

	Mintage	GSID	OGP*	MS-69	MS-70
American Buffalo, $50 1 oz. (2006 to Date)	n/a	**74456**	**$4,800**	**$4,850**	**$4,900**
2006	337,012	65236	4,800	4,850	4,900
2007	136,503	68692	4,800	4,850	4,900
2008	189,500	70979	4,800	4,850	4,900
2008-W, Burnished	9,074	70976	5,000	5,000	5,750
2009	200,000	70980	4,800	4,850	4,900
2010	209,000	70982	4,800	4,850	4,900
2011	174,500	70983	4,800	4,850	4,900
2012	132,000	74457	4,800	4,850	5,000
2013	198,500	71633	4,800	4,850	4,900
2014	180,500	74458	$4,800	$4,850	$4,900
2015	220,500	74459	4,800	4,850	4,900
2016	219,500	74460	4,800	4,850	4,900
2017	99,500	74461	4,800	4,850	4,900
2018	121,500	81696	4,800	4,850	5,000
2019	61,500	81697	4,800	4,850	5,000
2020	242,000	81698	4,800	4,850	5,000
2021	350,500	85193	4,800	4,850	4,900
2022		193330	4,800	4,850	4,900
2023		199001	4,800	4,850	4,900
2024		347667	4,800	4,850	4,900
2025		377683	4,800	4,850	4,900

* Value in original government packaging (OGP).

$50 1-Ounce American Buffalo Gold Proof Strikes

	Mintage	GSID	OGP*	PF-69	PF-70
American Buffalo, $50 1 oz. (2006 to Date), Proof	n/a	**81970**	**$4,800**	**$4,800**	**$4,900**
2006-W	246,267	65237	4,800	4,800	5,000
2007-W	58,998	68744	4,800	4,800	5,000
2008-W	18,863	68998	4,800	5,000	5,250
2009-W	49,306	70753	4,800	4,800	4,900
2010-W	49,263	70867	4,800	4,800	4,900
2011-W	28,693	71077	4,800	4,850	5,000
2012-W	19,765	71463	4,800	4,800	4,900
2013-W	18,594	74208	4,850	4,900	5,250
2013-W, RevPf	47,836	71495	4,900	4,900	5,000
2014-W	20,557	74209	$4,850	$4,900	$5,000
2015-W	16,591	71728	4,850	4,800	4,900
2016-W	21,878	76852	4,850	4,800	4,900
2017-W	15,810	76853	4,850	4,800	4,900
2018-W	15,283	76854	4,850	4,800	4,900
2019-W	14,836	81699	4,850	4,800	4,900
2020-W	11,887	81969	4,850	4,850	5,500
2021-W	16,958	85192	4,850	5,000	5,250
2022-W	15,943	193340	4,850	4,900	5,250
2023-W	13,731	199002	4,900	4,850	5,250
2024-W		347666	4,900	4,850	5,250
2025-W		377684	4,800	4,800	4,900

* Value in original government packaging (OGP).

American Buffalo Gold Sets

	Mintage	GSID	OGP*
2008-W Burnished Set. $50, $25, $10, $5	6,049	70873	$9,500
2008-W Proof Set. $50, $25, $10, $5		72816	9,500
2008-W Double Prosperity Uncirculated Set. $25 American Buffalo Gold and $25 American Gold Eagle	7,751	376893	4,950

* Value in original government packaging (OGP).

Note: Gold spot price at time of publication, $3,746 per ounce.

FIRST SPOUSE GOLD BULLION PROGRAM

Designers: *See below for list of designers.* **Weight:** *8.483 grams.* **Composition:** *.9999 gold.* **Diameter:** *26.5 mm.* **Edge:** *Reeded.* **Mint:** *West Point.*

Designers:

Coin	Designer
2007, Washington, Obverse	Joseph F. Menna
2007, Washington, Reverse	Susan Gamble
2007, A. Adams, Obverse	Joseph F. Menna
2007, A. Adams, Reverse	Thomas Cleveland
2007, Jefferson's Liberty, Obverse	Robert Scot
2007, Jefferson's Liberty, Reverse	Charles L. Vickers
2007, Madison	Don Everhard
2008, Monroe, Obverse	Joel Iskowitz
2008, Monroe, Reverse	Donna Weaver
2008, L. Adams, Obverse	Susan Gamble
2008, L. Adams, Reverse	Joseph F. Menna
2008, Jackson's Liberty, Obverse	John Reich
2008, Jackson's Liberty, Reverse	Justin Kunz
2008, Van Buren's Liberty, Obverse	Cristian Gobrecht
2008, Van Buren's Liberty, Reverse	Thomas Cleveland
2009, A. Harrison, Obverse	Donna Weaver
2009, A. Harrison, Reverse	Thomas Cleveland
2009, L. Tyler, Obverse	Phebe Hemphill
2009, L. Tyler, Reverse	Susan Gamble
2009, J. Tyler	Joel Iskowitz
2009, Polk	Phebe Hemphill
2009, Taylor, Obverse	Phebe Hemphill
2009, Taylor, Reverse	Mary Beth Zeitz
2010, Fillmore, Obverse	Phebe Hemphill
2010, Fillmore, Reverse	Susan Gamble
2010, Pierce	Donna Weaver
2010, Buchanan's Liberty, Obverse	Christian Gobrecht
2010, Buchanan's Liberty, Reverse	David Westwood
2010, Lincoln, Obverse	Phebe Hemphill
2010, Lincoln, Reverse	Joel Iskowitz
2011, E. Johnson, Obverse	Joel Iskowitz
2011, E. Johnson, Reverse	Gary Whitley
2011, Grant, Obverse	Donna Weaver
2011, Grant, Reverse	Richard Masters
2011, Hayes, Obverse	Susan Gamble
2011, Hayes, Reverse	Barbara Fox
2012, Garfield, Obverse	Barbara Fox
2012, Garfield, Reverse	Michael Gaudioso
2012, Paul, Obverse	Susan Gamble
2012, Paul, Reverse	Phebe Hemphill
2012, Cleveland (1st term), Obverse	Joel Iskowitz
2012, Cleveland (1st term), Reverse	Barbara Fox
2012, C. Harrison, Obverse	Frank Morris
2012, C. Harrison, Reverse	Donna Weaver
2012, Cleveland (2nd term), Obverse	Barbara Fox
2012, Cleveland (2nd term), Reverse	Joseph F. Menna
2013, McKinley, Obverse	Susan Gamble
2013, McKinley, Reverse	Donna Weaver
2013, Ed. Roosevelt, Obverse	Joel Iskowitz
2013, Ed. Roosevelt, Reverse	Chris Costello
2013, Taft, Obverse	William C. Burgard
2013, Taft, Reverse	Richard Masters
2013, El. Wilson, Obverse	Frank Morris
2013, El. Wilson, Reverse	Don Everhart
2013, Ed. Wilson, Obverse	David Westwood
2013, Ed. Wilson, Reverse	Joseph F. Menna
2014, Harding	Thomas Cleveland
2014, Coolidge, Obverse	Joel Iskowitz
2014, Coolidge, Reverse	Frank Morris
2014, Hoover, Obverse	Susan Gamble
2014, Hoover, Reverse	Richard Masters
2014, El. Roosevelt	Chris Costello
2015, Truman	Joel Iskowitz
2015, Eisenhower, Obverse	Richard Masters
2015, Eisenhower, Reverse	Barbara Fox
2015, Kennedy, Obverse	Susan Gamble
2015, Kennedy, Reverse	Benjamin Sowards
2015, L.B. Johnson, Obverse	Linda L. Fox
2015, L.B. Johnson, Reverse	Chris Costello
2016, Nixon	Richard Masters
2016, Ford, Obverse	Barbara Fox
2016, Ford, Reverse	Richard Masters
2016, Reagan, Obverse	Benjamin Sowards
2016, Reagan, Reverse	Joel Iskowitz
2020, B. Bush, Obverse	Benjamin Sowards
2020, B. Bush, Reverse	Barbara Fox

Burnished Finish

Mintmark location is on the obverse, below the date.

Proof Finish

History. The U.S. Mint's First Spouse bullion coins were struck in .9999 fine (24-karat) gold. Each weighs one-half ounce and bears a face value of $10. The coins honor the nation's first spouses and were struck on the same schedule as the Mint's Presidential dollars program. Each features a portrait on the obverse, and on the reverse a unique design symbolic of the spouse's life and work. In cases where a president held office widowed or unmarried, the coin bears "an obverse image emblematic of Liberty as depicted on a circulating coin of that era and a reverse image emblematic of themes of that president's life." All First Spouse gold bullion coins (Proofs and Burnished pieces) were struck at the U.S. Mint's West Point facility.

Note that the Mint does not release bullion mintage data on a regular basis; the numbers given herein reflect the most recently available official data.

Striking and Sharpness. Striking is generally sharp.

Availability. These coins are readily available in the numismatic marketplace. They could be purchased by the public, in both Burnished and Proof formats, directly from the U.S. Mint. Sales of later issues were low, leading to some issues being ranked among the 100 Greatest U.S. Modern Coins.

MS-60 to 70 (Mint State). ***Obverse and Reverse:*** At MS-60, some abrasion and contact marks are evident on the higher design areas and the open areas of the design. Luster may be dull or lifeless at MS-60 to 62, but there should be deep frost at MS-63 and better, particularly in the lower-relief areas. At MS-65 and above, the luster should be full and rich. Contact marks and abrasion are less and less evident at higher grades. These guidelines are more academic than practical, as these coins are not intended for circulation, and nearly all are in high Mint State grades, as struck.

PF-60 to 70 (Proof). ***Obverse and Reverse:*** Proofs that are extensively cleaned and have many hairlines are lower level, such as PF-60 to 62. Those with fewer hairlines or flaws are deemed PF-63 to 65. (These exist more in theory than actuality, as nearly all Proof First Spouse gold coins have been maintained in their original high condition by collectors.) Given the quality of modern U.S. Mint products, even PF-66 and 67 are unusually low levels for these Proofs.

2007, Martha Washington **2007, Abigail Adams** **2007, Jefferson's Liberty** **2007, Dolley Madison**

2008, Elizabeth Monroe

2008, Louisa Adams

2008, Jackson's Liberty

2008, Van Buren's Liberty

2009, Anna Harrison

2009, Letitia Tyler

2009, Julia Tyler

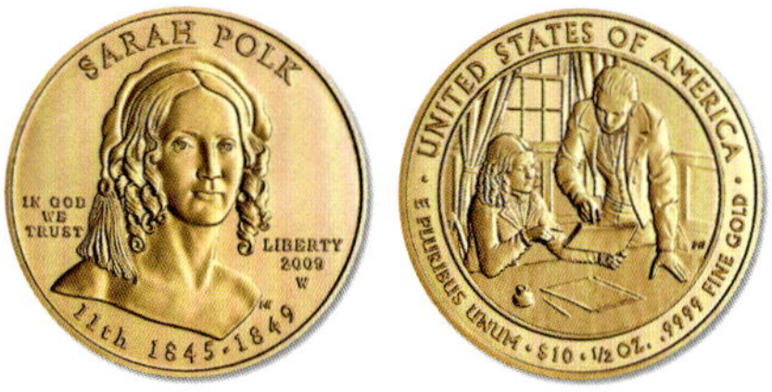

2009, Sarah Polk

2009, Margaret Taylor

2010, Abigail Fillmore

2010, Jane Pierce

2010, Buchanan's Liberty

2010, Mary Lincoln

2011, Eliza Johnson

2011, Julia Grant

2011, Lucy Hayes

2011, Lucretia Garfield

2012, Alice Paul

2012, Frances Cleveland (Variety 1)

2012, Caroline Harrison

2012, Frances Cleveland (Variety 2)

2013, Ida McKinley

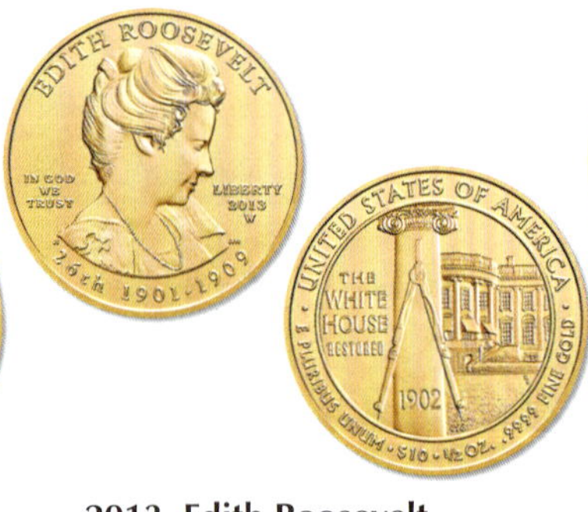

2013, Edith Roosevelt

2013, Helen Taft

2013, Ellen Wilson

2013, Edith Wilson

2014, Florence Harding

2014, Grace Coolidge

2014, Lou Hoover

2014, Eleanor Roosevelt

2015, Bess Truman

2015, Mamie Eisenhower

2015, Jacqueline Kennedy

2015, Claudia "Lady Bird" Johnson

2016, Patricia Nixon

2016, Betty Ford

2016, Nancy Reagan

2020, Barbara Bush

$10 1/2-Ounce First Spouse Gold Bullion Strikes

	Mintage	GSID	OGP*	MS-69	MS-70
First Spouse, $10 1/2 oz. (2007–2016, 2020)	**n/a**	**74415**	**$2,350**	**$2,350**	**$2,350**
2007-W, Washington	17,661	68871	2,350	2,350	2,350
2007-W, A. Adams	17,142	68873	2,350	2,350	2,350
2007-W, Jefferson's Liberty	19,823	68816	2,350	2,350	2,350
2007-W, Madison	12,340	68952	2,350	2,350	2,350
2008-W, Monroe	4,462	68957	2,350	2,350	2,450
2008-W, L. Adams	3,885	70428	2,350	2,350	2,450
2008-W, Jackson's Liberty	4,609	70429	$2,350	$2,350	$2,450
2008-W, Van Buren's Liberty	3,826	70430	2,350	2,350	2,350
2009-W, A. Harrison	3,645	70431	2,350	2,350	2,350
2009-W, Tyler	3,240	70863	2,350	2,350	2,350
2009-W, Tyler	3,143	70864	2,350	2,350	2,350
2009-W, Polk	3,489	70861	2,350	2,350	2,450
2009-W, Taylor	3,627	70862	2,350	2,350	2,350

* Value in original government packaging (OGP).

$10 1/2-Ounce First Spouse Gold Bullion Strikes *(continued)*

	Mintage	GSID	OGP*	MS-69	MS-70
2010-W, Fillmore	3,482	70865	$2,350	$2,350	$2,350
2010-W, Pierce	3,338	70866	2,350	2,350	2,350
2010-W, Buchanan's Liberty	5,162	71031	2,350	2,350	2,350
2010-W, Lincoln	3,695	71036	2,350	2,350	2,350
2011-W, E. Johnson	2,905	71040	2,350	2,350	2,450
2011-W, Grant	2,892	71042	2,350	2,350	2,350
2011-W, Hayes	2,196	71053	2,350	2,350	2,450
2011-W, Garfield	2,168	71058	2,350	2,350	2,450
2012-W, Paul	2,798	71594	2,350	2,350	2,350
2012-W, Cleveland, Variety 1	2,454	74416	2,350	2,350	2,350
2012-W, C. Harrison	2,436	74417	2,350	2,350	2,350
2012-W, Cleveland, Variety 2	2,425	74418	2,350	2,350	2,350
2013-W, McKinley	2,008	74419	2,350	2,350	2,350
2013-W, Edith Roosevelt	2,027	74420	2,350	2,350	2,350
2013-W, Taft	1,993	74421	$2,350	$2,350	$2,350
2013-W, El. Wilson	1,980	74422	2,350	2,350	2,450
2013-W, Ed. Wilson	1,974	74423	2,350	2,350	2,350
2014-W, Harding	1,944	74424	2,350	2,350	2,350
2014-W, Coolidge	1,949	74425	2,350	2,350	2,350
2014-W, Hoover	1,936	74426	2,350	2,350	2,350
2014-W, Eleanor Roosevelt	1,886	74427	2,350	2,350	2,350
2015-W, Truman	1,946	74428	2,350	2,350	2,350
2015-W, Eisenhower	2,102	74429	2,350	2,350	2,350
2015-W, Kennedy	6,771	74430	2,350	2,350	2,350
2015-W, Lady Bird Johnson	1,927	74431	2,350	2,350	2,350
2016-W, Nixon	1,839	74432	2,350	2,350	2,350
2016-W, Ford	1,824	74433	2,350	2,350	2,450
2016-W, Reagan	2,009	74434	2,350	2,350	2,350
2020-W, Bush	2,000	84298	2,350	2,350	2,350

* Value in original government packaging (OGP).

$10 1/2-Ounce First Spouse Gold Proof Strikes

	Mintage	GSID	OGP*	PF-69	PF-70
First Spouse, $10 1/2 oz. (2007–2016, 2020), Proof	**n/a**	**74435**	**$2,350**	**$2,350**	**$2,450**
2007-W, Washington	19,167	68872	2,350	2,350	2,450
2007-W, A. Adams	17,149	68874	2,350	2,350	2,450
2007-W, Jefferson's Liberty	19,815	68815	2,350	2,350	2,450
2007-W, Madison	17,943	68953	2,350	2,350	2,450
2008-W, Monroe	7,800	68954	2,350	2,350	2,450
2008-W, L. Adams	6,581	71032	2,350	2,350	2,550
2008-W, Jackson's Liberty	7,684	70890	2,350	2,350	2,450
2008-W, Van Buren's Liberty	6,807	70894	2,350	2,350	2,450
2009-W, A. Harrison	6,251	70849	2,350	2,350	2,550
2009-W, Polk	5,151	71033	2,350	2,350	2,450
2009-W, Taylor	4,936	71034	2,350	2,350	2,550
2009-W, Tyler	5,296	70912	2,350	2,350	2,550
2009-W, Tyler	4,844	71035	2,350	2,350	2,550
2010-W, Fillmore	6,130	71030	2,350	2,350	2,450
2010-W, Pierce	4,775	71038	2,350	2,350	2,450
2010-W, Buchanan's Liberty	7,110	71039	2,350	2,350	2,450
2010-W, Lincoln	6,861	71037	2,350	2,350	2,450
2011-W, E. Johnson	3,887	71041	2,350	2,350	2,550
2011-W, Grant	3,943	71043	2,350	2,350	2,550
2011-W, Hayes	3,868	71054	2,350	2,350	2,550
2011-W, Garfield	3,653	71056	$2,350	$2,350	$2,550
2012-W, Paul	3,505	74395	2,350	2,350	2,450
2012-W, Cleveland, Variety 1	3,151	74437	2,350	2,350	2,450
2012-W, C. Harrison	3,046	74397	2,350	2,350	2,450
2012-W, Cleveland, Variety 2	3,104	74439	2,350	2,350	2,450
2013-W, McKinley	2,724	74440	2,350	2,350	2,550
2013-W, Edith Roosevelt	2,840	74400	2,350	2,350	2,550
2013-W, Taft	2,598	74442	2,350	2,350	2,450
2013-W, El. Wilson	2,511	74402	2,350	2,350	2,450
2013-W, Ed. Wilson	2,464	74444	2,350	2,350	2,450
2014-W, Harding	2,372	74404	2,350	2,350	2,450
2014-W, Coolidge	2,315	74446	2,350	2,350	2,450
2014-W, Hoover	2,392	74406	2,350	2,350	2,450
2014-W, Eleanor Roosevelt	2,377	74448	2,350	2,350	2,450
2015-W, Truman	2,747	74408	2,350	2,350	2,450
2015-W, Eisenhower	2,704	74450	2,350	2,350	2,450
2015-W, Kennedy	11,222	74451	2,350	2,350	2,450
2015-W, Lady Bird Johnson	2,653	74452	2,350	2,350	2,550
2016-W, Nixon	2,645	74412	2,350	2,350	2,550
2016-W, Ford	2,471	74454	2,500	2,350	2,550
2016-W, Reagan	3,548	74414	2,500	2,500	2,750
2020-W, Bush	3,000	84299	2,500	2,500	2,750
2016-W, Reagan	3,548	74414	2,500	2,500	2,750

* Value in original government packaging (OGP).

Note: Gold spot price at time of publication, $3,746 per ounce.

AMERICA THE BEAUTIFUL SILVER BULLION PROGRAM

Designers: *See Specifications in quarter dollars section for designers.* **Weight:** *155.517 grams.* **Composition:** *.999 silver, .001 copper (net weight 5 oz. pure silver).* **Diameter:** *76.2 mm.* **Edge:** *Lettered.* **Mint:** *Philadelphia.*

Bullion Strike

Specimen Strike

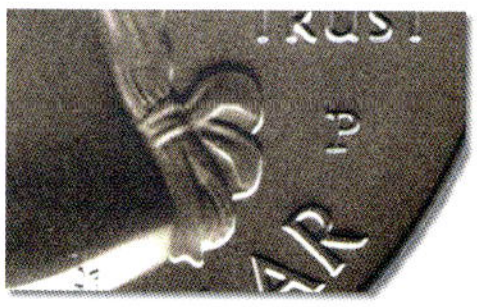

Mintmark location is on the obverse, to the right of the hair ribbon.

Details of the incused edge markings.

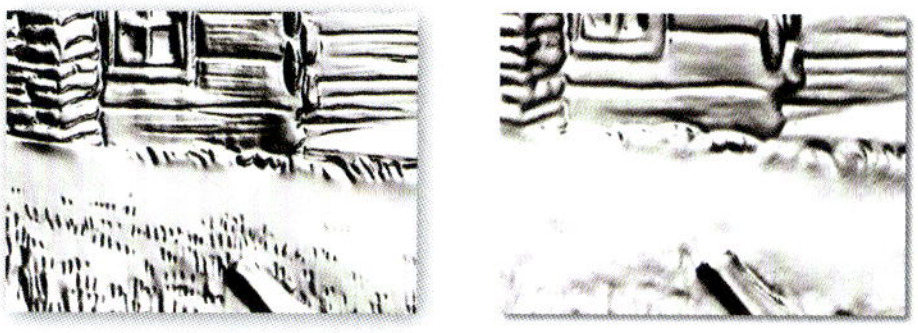

Details on 2014 Great Smoky Mountains National Park 5-ounce silver bullion coin (left) and quarter dollar (right). Note differences on window, cabin, and grass in foreground.

History. In conjunction with the National Park quarter dollars, the U.S. Mint issues silver-bullion coins based on each of the "America the Beautiful" program's circulation-strike coins. The coinage dies are cut on a CNC milling machine, bypassing a hubbing operation, which results in finer details than seen on the smaller quarter dollars. The bullion coins are made of .999 fine silver, have a diameter of three inches, weigh five ounces, and carry a face value of 25 cents. The fineness and weight are incused on each coin's edge. The Mint's German-made Gräbener press strikes 22 coins per minute, with two strikes per coin at 450 to 500 metric tons of pressure. In December 2010, the Mint announced it would produce Specimen versions (called *Uncirculated* by the Mint) for collectors. Detailed information on each issue is in *American Gold and Silver: U.S. Mint Collector and Investor Coins and Medals, Bicentennial to Date* (Tucker).

Striking and Sharpness. Striking is generally sharp.

Availability. The National Park silver bullion coins are distributed through commercial channels similar to those for the Mint's American Silver Eagle coins. Production of the 2010 coins was delayed (finally starting September 21) as the Mint worked out the technical details of striking such a large product. Production and distribution have been smoother since then.

MS-65 to 70 (Mint State). ***Obverse and Reverse:*** At MS-65, some abrasion and contact marks are evident on the higher design areas. Luster may be dull or lifeless at MS-65 to 66, but there should be deep frost at MS-67 and better, particularly in the lower-relief areas. At MS-68 and above, the luster should be full and rich. These guidelines are more academic than practical, as these coins are not intended for circulation, and nearly all are in high Mint State grades.

SP-68 to 70 (Specimen). ***Obverse and Reverse:*** These pieces should be nearly perfect and with full luster, in their original Mint packaging. Any with imperfections due to careless handling or environmental damage are valued lower.

The U.S. Mint produces the America the Beautiful™ 5-ounce silver coins in bullion and numismatic versions. The bullion version, which lacks the P mintmark, has a brilliant finish and is sold only through dealers. The numismatic version, with the mintmark, has a matte or burnished finish. These coins are designated "Specimens" (SP) by most collectors and grading services. They are sold directly to the public by the Mint.

25¢ 5-Ounce America the Beautiful Silver Bullion Strikes

	Mintage	GSID	OGP*	MS-69	MS-70
America the Beautiful, 25¢ 5 oz. (2010–2021)	**n/a**	**76715**	**$335**	**$380**	**$445**
America the Beautiful, 25¢ 5 oz. (2010–2021), Satin	**n/a**	**76716**	**330**	**360**	**395**
2010-(P), Hot Springs National Park	33,000	74123	335	380	445
2010-P, Hot Springs National Park, Satin	26,788	76797	340	375	405
2010-(P), Yellowstone National Park	33,000	71607	335	380	445
2010-P, Yellowstone National Park, Satin	26,711	76798	340	375	405
2010-(P), Yosemite National Park	33,000	71608	335	380	445
2010-P, Yosemite National Park, Satin	26,716	76799	340	375	405
2010-(P), Grand Canyon National Park	33,000	71609	335	380	445
2010-P, Grand Canyon National Park, Satin	25,967	76800	340	375	405
2010-(P), Mt. Hood National Forest	33,000	71606	335	380	445
2010-P, Mt. Hood National Forest, Satin	26,637	76801	340	375	405
2011-(P), Gettysburg National Military Park	126,700	70934	335	380	445
2011-P, Gettysburg National Military Park, Satin	24,625	76802	340	375	405
2011-(P), Glacier National Park	126,700	74124	335	380	445
2011-P, Glacier National Park, Satin	20,805	76803	340	375	405

* Value in original government packaging (OGP).

25¢ 5-Ounce America the Beautiful Silver Bullion Strikes *(continued)*

	Mintage	GSID	OGP*	MS-69	MS-70
2011-(P), Olympic National Park	95,600	71601	$335	$380	$445
2011-P, Olympic National Park, Satin	18,345	76804	340	375	405
2011-(P), Vicksburg National Military Park	41,200	71602	335	380	445
2011-P, Vicksburg National Military Park, Satin	18,528	76805	340	375	405
2011-(P), Chickasaw National Recreational Area	31,400	71603	335	380	445
2011-P, Chickasaw National Recreational Area, Satin	16,746	76806	340	375	405
2012-(P), El Yunque National Forest	24,000	71604	335	380	445
2012-P, El Yunque National Forest, Satin	17,314	76810	360	395	425
2012-(P), Chaco Culture National Historical Park	24,400	71605	335	380	445
2012-P, Chaco Culture National Historical Park, Satin	17,146	76811	340	375	405
2012-(P), Acadia National Park	25,400	74125	335	380	445
2012-P, Acadia National Park, Satin	14,978	76812	340	375	405
2012-(P), Hawai'i Volcanoes National Park	20,000	74126	390	430	575
2012-P, Hawai'i Volcanoes National Park, Satin	14,863	76813	470	500	525
2012-(P), Denali National Park and Preserve	20,000	74127	335	380	445
2012-P, Denali National Park and Preserve, Satin	15,225	76814	360	395	425
2013-(P), White Mountain National Forest	35,000	74129	335	380	445
2013-P, White Mountain National Forest, Satin	20,530	76815	330	360	395
2013-(P), Perry's Victory and International Peace Memorial	30,000	74128	335	380	445
2013-P, Perry's Victory and International Peace Memorial, Satin	17,707	76819	330	360	395
2013-(P), Great Basin National Park	30,000	74132	335	380	445
2013-P, Great Basin National Park, Satin	17,792	76816	330	360	395
2013-(P), Ft. McHenry National Monument and Historic Shrine	30,000	74131	335	380	445
2013-P, Ft. McHenry National Monument and Historic Shrine, Satin	19,802	76817	330	360	395
2013-(P), Mount Rushmore National Monument	35,000	74130	335	380	445
2013-P, Mount Rushmore National Monument, Satin	23,547	76818	330	360	395
2014-(P), Great Smoky Mountains National Park	33,000	74103	335	380	445
2014-P, Great Smoky Mountains National Park, Satin	24,710	76820	330	360	395
2014-(P), Shenandoah National Park	25,000	74104	335	380	445
2014-P, Shenandoah National Park, Satin	28,276	76821	330	360	395
2014-(P), Arches National Park	22,000	74105	335	380	445
2014-P, Arches National Park, Satin	28,183	76822	330	360	395
2014-(P), Great Sand Dunes National Park	22,000	85062	335	380	445
2014-P, Great Sand Dunes National Park, Satin	24,103	76823	330	360	395
2014-(P), Everglades National Park	34,000	74107	335	380	445
2014-P, Everglades National Park, Satin	19,772	76824	330	360	395
2015-(P), Kisatchie National Forest	42,000	74109	335	380	445
2015-P, Kisatchie National Forest, Satin	19,449	76826	330	360	395
2015-(P), Blue Ridge Parkway	45,000	74110	335	380	445
2015-P, Blue Ridge Parkway, Satin	17,461	76827	330	360	395
2015-(P), Bombay Hook National Wildlife Refuge	45,000	74111	335	380	445
2015-P, Bombay Hook National Wildlife Refuge, Satin	17,309	76828	330	360	395
2015-(P), Saratoga National Historic Park	45,000	74112	335	380	445
2015-P, Saratoga National Historic Park, Satin	17,563	76829	330	360	395
2015-(P), Homestead National Monument of America	35,000	74108	335	380	445
2015-P, Homestead National Monument of America, Satin	21,286	76825	330	360	395
2016-(P), Shawnee National Forest	105,000	85063	335	380	445
2016-P, Shawnee National Forest, Satin	18,781	76830	330	360	395

* Value in original government packaging (OGP).

25¢ 5-Ounce America the Beautiful Silver Bullion Strikes *(continued)*

	Mintage	GSID	OGP*	MS-69	MS-70
2016-(P), Harpers Ferry National Historical Park	75,000	74115	$335	$380	$445
2016-P, Harpers Ferry National Historical Park, Satin	18,896	76832	330	360	395
2016-(P), Theodore Roosevelt National Park	40,000	74116	335	380	445
2016-P, Theodore Roosevelt National Park, Satin	18,917	76834	330	360	395
2016-(P), Fort Moultrie	35,000	74117	335	380	445
2016-P, Fort Moultrie, Satin	17,882	76833	330	360	395
2017-(P), Effigy Mounds National Monument	35,000	85064	335	380	445
2017-P, Effigy Mounds National Monument, Satin	17,251	76835	330	360	395
2017-(P), George Rogers Clark National Historical Park	33,400	85065	335	380	445
2017-P, George Rogers Clark National Historical Park, Satin	14,731	76838	330	360	395
2017-(P), Frederick Douglass National Historic Site	20,000	84553	335	380	445
2017-P, Frederick Douglass National Historic Site, Satin	17,678	76836	330	360	395
2017-(P), Ozark National Scenic Riverways	20,000	85066	335	380	445
2017-P, Ozark National Scenic Riverways, Satin	17,694	76837	330	360	395
2017-(P), Ellis Island	40,000	84554	335	380	445
2017-P, Ellis Island, Satin	17,670	76839	330	360	395
2018-(P), Pictured Rocks National Lakeshore	30,000	85067	335	380	445
2018-P, Pictured Rocks National Lakeshore, Satin	17,773	84253	330	360	395
2018-(P), Apostle Islands National Lakeshore	30,000	85068	335	380	445
2018-P, Apostle Islands National Lakeshore, Satin	16,802	84254	330	360	395
2018-(P), Cumberland Island National Seashore	52,500	85069	335	380	445
2018-P, Cumberland Island National Seashore, Satin	16,376	84256	330	360	395
2018-(P), Voyageurs National Park	30,000	85070	335	380	445
2018-P, Voyageurs National Park, Satin	16,839	84255	330	360	395
2018-(P), Block Island National Wildlife Refuge	80,000	85071	335	380	445
2018-P, Block Island National Wildlife Refuge, Satin	15,912	84257	330	360	395
2019-(P), Lowell National Historical Park	80,000	85072	335	380	445
2019-P, Lowell National Historical Park, Satin	16,664	84258	330	360	395
2019-(P), American Memorial Park	80,000	85073	335	380	445
2019-P, American Memorial Park, Satin	16,287	84259	330	360	395
2019-(P), War in the Pacific National Historical Park	72,500	84555	335	380	445
2019-P, War in the Pacific National Historical Park, Satin	16,277	84260	330	360	395
2020-(P), San Antonio Missions National Historical Park	55,200	84556	335	380	445
2020-P, San Antonio Missions National Historical Park, Satin	16,211	84261	330	360	395
2019-(P), Frank Church River of No Return Wilderness	25,000	84557	335	380	445
2019-P, Frank Church River of No Return Wilderness, Satin	16,310	84262	330	360	395
2020-(P), National Park of American Samoa	45,000	84558	335	380	445
2020-P, National Park of American Samoa, Satin	15,781	84263	330	360	395
2020-(P), Marsh-Billings-Rockefeller National Historical Park	45,000	85074	335	380	445
2020-P, Marsh-Billings-Rockefeller National Historical Park, Satin	13,545	188666	330	360	395
2020-(P), Salt River Bay National Historical Park and Ecological Preserve	45,000	85075	335	380	445
2020-P, Salt River Bay National Historical Park and Ecological Preserve, Satin	13,544	84265	330	360	395
2020-(P), Weir Farm National Historic Site	45,000	85076	335	380	445
2020-P, Weir Farm National Historic Site, Satin	15,326	84264	330	360	395
2020-(P), Tallgrass Prairie National Preserve	45,000	85077	335	380	445
2020-P, Tallgrass Prairie National Preserve, Satin	13,613	213478	330	360	395
2021-(P), Tuskegee Airmen National Historic Site	52,900	213479	335	380	445
2021-P, Tuskegee Airmen National Historic Site, Satin	19,815	188667	330	360	395

* Value in original government packaging (OGP).

Note: Silver spot price at time of publication, $45 per ounce.

AMERICAN LIBERTY HIGH RELIEF GOLD COINS

Designers: *Various (see list of designers).* **Weight:** *$10 1/10 oz.—3.11 grams; $100 1 oz.—31.108 grams.* **Composition:** *.9999 gold.* **Diameter:** *$10 1/10 oz.—16.5 mm; $100 1 oz.—30.61 mm.* **Edge:** *Reeded.* **Mint:** *West Point.*

Designers:

2015, Obverse	Justin Kunz	2019, Reverse	Donna Weaver
2015, Reverse	Paul C. Balan	2021, Obverse	Beth Zaiken
2017, Obverse	Justin Kunz	2021, Reverse	Richard Masters
2017, Reverse	Chris Costello	2023, Obverse	Elana Hagler
2018, Obverse	Justin Kunz	2023, Reverse	John McGraw
2018, Reverse	Phebe Hemphill	2025, Obverse	Christopher Polentz
2019, Obverse	Richard Masters	2025, Reverse	Christopher Polentz

The first American Liberty High Relief .9999-fine gold coin, with a weight of one ounce and a face value of $100, was minted at West Point in 2015. The coin was not congressionally mandated, instead being created under authority granted to the Secretary of the Treasury by federal law—31 U.S.C. Section 5112 (i)(4)(C).

The design was strongly influenced by the Citizens Coinage Advisory Committee, who, according to a Mint spokesperson, "emphasized creating a 'modern' Liberty that reflects the nation's diversity." The U.S. Commission of Fine Arts also reviewed designs and made recommendations.

The designs for the American Liberty High Relief gold coins are created to take full advantage of the same high-relief techniques used to create the MMIX Ultra High Relief gold coin. The design of the 2015 American Liberty High Relief gold coin was adapted for a silver medal in 2016, but in 2017 the Mint continued the series with a 1792–2017 American Liberty High Relief gold coin. The series is slated to continue biennially, with a new design being issued every two years. In the years between new gold one-ounce designs, gold 1/10-ounce coins featuring the same designs are issued. The Mint also strikes high-relief silver medals based on each design.

2015-W

1792–2017-W

2018-W, $10

2019-W

2021-W

2023-W

2025-W

$100 1-Ounce American Liberty Gold Bullion Strikes

	Mintage	GSID	OGP*	MS-69	MS-70
2015-W $100 1 oz. Ultra High Relief, Uncirculated	49,325	74058	$4,800	$4,800	$4,950
2019-W $100 1 oz. Liberty, Enhanced Uncirculated	24,609	84430	4,850	4,900	5,000

* Value in original government packaging (OGP).

American Liberty Gold Proof Strikes *(multiple denominations/weights)*

	Mintage	GSID	OGP*	PF-69	PF-70
$100 1 oz. 1792–2017-W	30,823	78078	$4,800	$4,700	$4,950
$10 1/10 oz. 2018-W	29,590	78077	370	370	420
$100 1 oz. 2021-W, Mustang	12,470	193333	8,750	8,750	12,000
$100 1 oz. 2023-W, Bristlecone Pine	12,188	213482	5,500	5,500	8,000
$100 1 oz. 2025-W, Sunflower		393717	5,500	5,750	6,000

* Value in original government packaging (OGP).

MMIX ULTRA HIGH RELIEF GOLD COIN

Designer: *Augustus Saint-Gaudens.* **Weight:** *27 grams.* **Composition:** *.9999 gold.* **Diameter:** *31.1 mm.* **Edge:** *E★P★L★U★R★I★B★U★S★U★N★U★M★.* **Mint:** *West Point.*

A modern version of the famous United States 1907 Ultra High Relief double eagle gold pattern was produced in 2009 at the Philadelphia Mint. It was made as a tour de force to demonstrate how technical advances in minting techniques can now accommodate manufacturing such a coin. The original design was never made for commercial use because it was at that time impossible to make it in sufficient quantities.

The original striding-Liberty design used on these coins was the artistry of Augustus Saint-Gaudens. A version of it in much lower relief was used on double eagle coins minted from 1907 to 1933. In recreating the artist's attempt to mint a stunning coin in ultra high relief, the 2009 version was made in a slightly smaller diameter, and composed of 24-karat gold, thus making it easier to strike and maintain the fidelity of the design. Through 21st-century technology the original Saint-Gaudens plasters were digitally mapped by the Mint and used in the die-making process. The date was changed to 2009, and four additional stars were added to represent the current 50 states. Also included was the inscription "In God We Trust," which was not used on the 1907 version.

The MMIX Ultra High Relief gold coins are 4 mm thick and contain one ounce of .999 fine gold. All are Uncirculated. All were made at the U.S. Mint's West Point facility, and were packaged in a special mahogany box.

MMIX Ultra High Relief Gold Coin
Photographed at an angle to show the edge, lettered E PLURIBUS UNUM, and the depth of relief.

$20 1-Ounce MMIX (1909) Ultra High Relief Gold Bullion Strikes

	Mintage	GSID	OGP*	MS-69	MS-70
MMIX (2009) $20 1 oz. Ultra High Relief	114,427	69740	$4,800	$4,850	$5,250

* Value in original government packaging (OGP).

LIBERTY AND BRITANNIA GOLD COINS

Designers: *Joseph Menna and Gordon Summers (obverse); Joseph Menna (reverse).* **Weight:** *31.108 grams.* **Composition:** *.9999 gold.* **Diameter:** *30.61 mm.* **Edge:** *Reeded.* **Mint:** *West Point.*

In 2024, the Mint released the first issue in a new series produced in collaboration with the United Kingdom's Royal Mint. The one-ounce coins, struck at West Point with a face value of $100, are composed of .9999 fine gold and measure 32.7 mm in diameter. The obverse depicts the allegorical figures of Liberty and Britannia, representing America and Britain, respectively; this is the first time the two figures are shown together on a U.S. coin. Like the American Liberty High Relief gold coins and similar series, the Liberty and Britannia coins are produced under the authority of the Treasury secretary to issue gold coins "from time to time" without specific commemorative legislation.

2024-W

$100 1-Ounce Liberty and Britannia Gold Bullion Strikes

	Mintage	GSID	OGP*	PF-69	PF-70
2024-W $100 1 oz. Liberty and Britannia	5,549	351804	$5,000	$5,000	$5,250

* Value in original government packaging (OGP).

230TH ANNIVERSARY FLOWING HAIR HIGH RELIEF GOLD COINS

Designer: *Robert Scott.* **Weight:** *31.1 grams.* **Composition:** *.9999 gold.* **Diameter:** *30.61 mm.* **Edge:** *HUNDRED CENTS DOLLAR OR UNIT.* **Mint:** *West Point.*

In 2024, the Mint released a special gold coin in honor of the 230th anniversary of the first U.S. one-dollar coin: the Flowing Hair silver dollar, issued on October 15, 1794. The one-ounce bullion coins, measuring 30.61 mm in diameter, are produced in .9999 fine gold at the West Point Mint. The high-relief obverse and reverse designs are modern reproductions of those on the original dollar. The edge is lettered HUNDRED CENTS ONE DOLLAR OR UNIT, with one to three 6-pointed stars in the spaces between words. As with other coins in this section, the coins are produced under the Treasury secretary's authority to issue gold coins "from time to time" without specific commemorative legislation.

2024-W

2024-W With Privy Mark

Detail of privy mark.

$1 1-Ounce 230th Anniversary Flowing Hair High Relief Gold Bullion Strikes

	Mintage	GSID	OGP*	MS-69	MS-70
2024 230th Anniversary Flowing Hair Silver medal	49,932	376027	$290	$290	$490
2024 230th Anniversary Flowing Hair Silver medal with 230 Privy Mark	1,794	376692	5,500	5,500	7,000
2024-W $1 1 oz. 230th Anniversary Flowing Hair Gold dollar	9,975	376107	6,000	6,000	7,250
2024-W $1 1 oz. 230th Anniversary Flowing Hair Gold dollar with 230 Privy Mark	230	376919	—	46,000	60,000
	Auctions: $440,000, PCGS PF-70 SBG 12/24				

* Value in original government packaging (OGP).

COMIC ART GOLD COINS

Designer: *Joseph Menna (obverse); various (reverse; see list of designers).* **Weight:** *15.55 grams.* **Composition:** *.9999 gold.* **Diameter:** *27 mm.* **Edge:** *Reeded.* **Mint:** *West Point.*

Designers:

2025, Superman . . . . Joseph V. Noorigian
2025, Batman . . . . John P. McGraw
2025, Wonder Woman . . . . Phebe Hemphill

In 2025, through a licensing agreement with DC Comics, the U.S. Mint launched the Comic Art Coin and Medal Program. Spanning three years, the program presents nine iconic DC characters on special half-ounce gold Proof coins; each design is also rendered on a 1-ounce and a 2.5-ounce silver medal. The .9999 fine gold coins, denominated $50, are produced under the Treasury secretary's authority to issue gold coins "from time to time" without corresponding legislation.

The first year of the program, featuring Superman, Batman, and Wonder Woman, coincides with DC's 90th anniversary. In 2026, Supergirl, Robin, and the Green Lantern join the superhero lineup, followed in 2027 by The Flash, Batgirl, and Aquaman. Mint Director Ventris C. Gibson remarked that the coins "highlight the role that comic books have played in upholding American values." Two of the values associated with each superhero appear as legends on the silver-medal reverses: HOPE AND STRENGTH for Superman, JUSTICE AND COURAGE for Batman, and PEACE AND EQUALITY for Wonder Woman. The first year of the program, featuring Superman, Batman, and Wonder Woman, coincides with DC's 90th anniversary. In 2026, Supergirl, Robin, and the Green Lantern will join the superhero lineup, followed in 2027 by The Flash, Batgirl, and Aquaman. Mint Director Ventris C. Gibson remarked that the coins "highlight the role that comic books have played in upholding American values." Two of the values associated with each superhero appear as legends on the silver-medal reverses: HOPE AND STRENGTH for Superman, JUSTICE AND COURAGE for Batman, and PEACE AND EQUALITY for Wonder Woman.

2025-W, Superman

2025-W, Batman

2025-W, Wonder Woman

$50 1/2-Ounce Comic Art Gold Proof Strikes

	Mintage	GSID	OGP*	PF-69	PF-70
2025-W $50 1/2 oz. Superman		393394	$3,100	$3,100	$3,450
2025-W $50 1/2 oz. Batman		393393	3,100	3,100	3,450
2025-W $50 1/2 oz. Wonder Woman		393395	3,100	3,100	3,450

* Value in original government packaging (OGP)

Private and Territorial Gold

The expression *private gold*, used with reference to coins struck outside the United States Mint, is a general term. In the sense that no state or territory had authority to coin money, *private gold* simply refers to those necessity pieces of various shapes, denominations, and degrees of intrinsic worth that were coined by facilities other than official U.S. mints and circulated in isolated areas of the United States by assayers, bankers, and other private individuals and organizations. Some numismatists use the terms *territorial gold* and *state gold* to cover certain issues because they were coined and circulated in a territory or state. While the state of California properly sanctioned the ingots stamped by F.D. Kohler as state assayer, in no instance (except for the Mormon issues of Salt Lake City) were any of the gold pieces struck by authority of any of the territorial governments.

The stamped fifty-dollar and other gold coins, sometimes called *ingots*, but in coin form, were made by Augustus Humbert, the United States Assayer of Gold, but were not receivable at face value for government payments, despite the fact that Humbert was an official agent selected by the Treasury Department. However, such pieces circulated widely in commerce.

Usually, private coins were circulated due to a shortage of regular federal coinage. In the Western states particularly, official money became so scarce that gold itself—the very commodity the pioneers had come so far to acquire—was converted into a local medium of exchange.

Ephraim Brasher's New York doubloons of 1786 and 1787 are also private American gold issues; they are listed under "Post-Colonial Issues."

EXPLORING VARIETIES

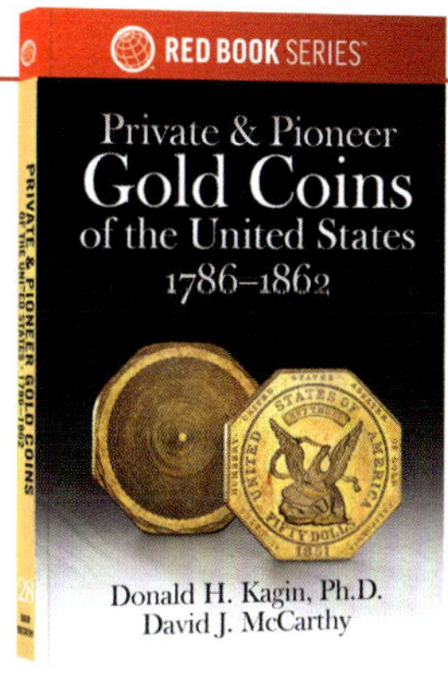

This is the definitive modern reference on all private and pioneer gold. It updates Kagin's earlier work with McCarthy, assigning catalog numbers and rarity ratings. Collectors and auction houses rely on Kagin numbers as the standard attributions for these coins.

Kagin, Donald H., and David J. McCarthy. *Private and Pioneer Gold Coins of the United States 1786–1862*. Whitman, 2025. (Formerly *America's Golden Age: Private & Pioneer Gold Coins of the United States 1786–1862*. Tiburon, CA: 2023.)

TEMPLETON REID

Georgia Gold, 1830

The first private gold coinage in the 19th century was struck by Templeton Reid, a jeweler and gunsmith, in Milledgeville, Georgia, in July 1830. To be closer to the mines he moved some 120 miles northwest to Gainesville, where most of his coins were made. Although their weights were accurate, Reid's assays were not and his coins were slightly short of their claimed value. He was severely attacked in the newspapers by a determined adversary, and soon lost the public's confidence. He closed his mint before the end of October in 1830; his output had amounted to only about 1,600 coins. Denominations struck were $2.50, $5, and $10. All are great rarities today.

Georgia Gold, $2.50 (1830)

Georgia Gold, $5 (1830)

Georgia Gold, $10 (1830)

		GSID	VF-20	EF-40	AU-50	AU-55	AU-58	MS-60
1830 $2.50, K-1		11874	—	—	$300,000	$330,000	$390,000	$450,000
	Auctions: $384,000, PCGS AU-58 HA 01/24							
1830 $5, K-2	7 known	11875	$510,000	$660,000	870,000	—	—	—
1830 $10, K-3	6 known	11876	1,200,000	1,440,000	—	—	—	—
(1830) $10, K-4	3 known	11878	1,500,000	—	—	—	—	—

California Gold, 1849

The enigmatic later issues of Templeton Reid, dated 1849 and marked CALIFORNIA GOLD, were probably made from California gold late in that year when bullion from California arrived in quantity in the East. Reid, who never went to California, was by then a cotton-gin maker in Columbus, Georgia (some 160 miles southwest of his former location of Gainesville), where he would die in 1851. The coins were in denominations of ten and twenty-five dollars. Struck copies of both exist in various metals.

California Gold, $10 (1849)

The only example known of the twenty-five–dollar piece was stolen from the cabinet of the U.S. Mint on August 16, 1858. It was never recovered.

		GSID	VF-20	EF-40	AU-50	AU-55	AU-58	MS-60
1849 $10 California Gold, K-1 (in Smithsonian Collection)	unique	11877	—	—	—	—	—	—
1849 $25 California Gold, K-2	unique	11879	—	—	—	—	—	—

THE BECHTLERS, RUTHERFORD COUNTY, NORTH CAROLINA, 1831–1852

A skilled German metallurgist, Christopher Bechtler, assisted by his son August and his nephew, also named Christopher, operated a private mint in Rutherford County, North Carolina. Rutherford County and other areas in the Piedmont region of North Carolina and Georgia (from the coastal plain to the mountains of north Georgia) were the principal sources of the nation's gold supply from the early 1800s until the California gold strikes in 1848.

The coins minted by the Bechtlers were of only three denominations, but they covered a wide variety of weights and sizes. Rotated dies are common throughout the series. In 1831, the Bechtlers produced the first gold dollar in the United States. (The Philadelphia Mint made patterns in 1836 and struck its first circulating gold dollar in 1849.) Bechtler coins were well accepted by the public and circulated widely in the Southeast without interference from the government.

The legend AUGUST 1. 1834 on several varieties of five-dollar pieces has a special significance. The secretary of the Treasury recommended to the director of the U.S. Mint that gold coins of the reduced weight introduced in 1834 bear the authorization date. This ultimately was not done on federal gold coinage, but the elder Christopher Bechtler evidently acted on the recommendation to avoid potential difficulty with Treasury authorities.

CHRISTOPHER BECHTLER (CAROLINA AND GEORGIA)

ONE GOLD DOLLAR N. CAROLINA, 30.G., Star

ONE GOLD DOLLAR N. CAROLINA, 28.G Centered, No Star

ONE DOLLAR CAROLINA, 28.G, N Reversed

2.50 NORTH CAROLINA GOLD, 20 C., Without 75.G.

2.50 NORTH CAROLINA GOLD, 20 C., 75.G., RUTHERFORD in a Circle.

2.50 CAROLINA GOLD, 67.G., 21 CARATS

2.50 GEORGIA GOLD, 64.G, 22 CARATS (Uneven "22")

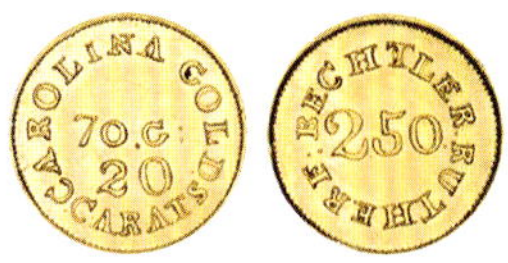

2.50 CAROLINA GOLD, 70.G, 20 CARATS

5 DOLLARS NORTH CAROLINA GOLD, 150.G., 20.CARATS

5 DOLLARS CAROLINA GOLD, RUTHERFORD, 140.G., 20 CARATS, AUGUST 1, 1834

5 DOLLARS CAROLINA GOLD, RUTHERF., 140.G., 20 CARATS, AUGUST 1, 1834

5 DOLLARS CAROLINA GOLD, 134.G., 21 CARATS, With Star

5 DOLLARS GEORGIA GOLD, RUTHERFORD, 128.G., 22 CARATS

		GSID	VF-20	EF-40	EF-45	AU-50	AU-55	AU-58	MS-60	MS-62	MS-63
ONE GOLD DOLLAR N. CAROLINA, 30.G., Reeded Edge, Star, 30 GR, K-1	150 est. known	11733	—	$5,500	$6,500	$8,250	$10,000	$12,000	$15,000	$26,500	$43,000
ONE GOLD DOLLAR N. CAROLINA, 30.G., Plain Edge, Star, K-1a	unique	375980	—	—	—	—	—	—	—	—	—
ONE GOLD DOLLAR N. CAROLINA, 28.G., High, No Star, Reeded Edge, K-2	20 est. known	11731	—	11,000	15,000	20,000	22,000	27,500	30,000	—	—
ONE GOLD DOLLAR N. CAROLINA, 28.G., High, No Star, Plain Edge, K-2a	2 est. known	375981	—	—	—	—	—	—	—	—	—
ONE GOLD DOLLAR N. CAROLINA, 28.G., Centered, No Star, Reeded Edge, K-3	35 est. known	11732	—	—	5,250	6,250	10,500	14,000	18,000	30,000	—
ONE GOLD DOLLAR N. CAROLINA, 28.G., Centered, No Star, Plain Edge, K-3a	2 known	375982	—	—	—	—	—	—	—	—	—
ONE DOLLAR N. CAROLINA, 28.G., N Reversed, K-4	100 est. known	11734	—	4,100	4,500	5,500	6,250	6,500	7,250	11,000	19,000
2.50 NORTH CAROLINA GOLD, 20 C., Without 75.G., Fine Beads, K-5	<10 known	11718	—	31,000	41,000	60,000	84,000	126,000	—	—	—
	Auctions: $105,000, PCGS AU-58 HA 01/22										
2.50 NORTH CAROLINA GOLD, 20 C., Without 75.G., Course Bead, K-6	10 known	11707	—	—	—	60,000	72,000	90,000	120,000	180,000	—
	Auctions: $180,000, PCGS MS-62 HA 01/22										
2.50 NORTH CAROLINA GOLD, 20 C., Without 75.G., CAROLINA above 250 instead of GOLD, K-7	2 known	11714	—	—	—	—	—	—	—	—	—
2.50 NORTH CAROLINA GOLD, 20 C., Without 75.G., 20 C. RUTHERFORD in a Circle. Border of Large Beads, K-8	15 est. known	11715	—	—	39,000	48,000	54,000	57,500	62,500	79,000	—
2.50 NORTH CAROLINA GOLD, 20 C. on Obverse, 75 G. and Star on Reverse. Border Finely Serrated, K-9	<10 known	11717	—	96,000	—	—	—	—	—	—	—
2.50 CAROLINA GOLD, 67.G., 21 CARATS, K-10	30 est. known	11712	$9,500	11,000	12,500	14,500	24,000	27,000	31,000	48,000	66,000
2.50 CAROLINA GOLD, 64.G., 22 CARATS (Uneven "22"), K-11	10 est. known	11711	9,000	11,000	12,000	14,000	19,000	23,000	26,500	36,000	—
2.50 CAROLINA GOLD, 64.G., 22 CARATS (Even "22"), K-12	<20 known	11716	8,500	10,500	12,000	15,000	17,000	20,000	30,000	54,000	72,000
2.50 CAROLINA GOLD, 70.G., 20 CARATS, K-13	30 est. known	11713	9,500	12,000	13,000	15,500	19,000	23,000	26,500	42,000	72,000
5 DOLLARS CAROLINA GOLD, RUTHERFORD, 20.CARATS, No 150.G., K-14	2 known	11729	—	—	—	—	—	—	—	—	—
5 DOLLARS CAROLINA GOLD, RUTHERFORD, 150.G., 20.CARATS, Beaded Border, K-15	20 est. known	11723	17,000	24,000	29,000	38,500	48,000	57,500	66,000	114,000	—
	Auctions: $139,443, PCGS MS-62 SBG 11/13										
5 DOLLARS CAROLINA GOLD, RUTHERFORD, 140.G., 20.CARATS, No Initial or Star, K-Transitional	unique	11710	—	—	—	—	—	—	—	—	—
5 DOLLARS CAROLINA GOLD, RUTHERFORD, 140.G., 20 CARATS, With Colon After C, Reeded Edge, K-16	5–6 known	11709	—	—	—	—	—	—	—	—	—
5 DOLLARS CAROLINA GOLD, RUTHERFORD, 140.G., 20 CARATS, With Colon After C, Plain Edge, K-16a	5–6 known	11708	—	—	—	—	—	—	—	—	—
5 DOLLARS CAROLINA GOLD, RUTHERFORD, 140.G., 20 CARATS, Plain Edge, K-17	100 est. known	11726	8,750	14,000	15,000	17,000	21,000	26,500	31,000	48,000	62,500

		GSID	VF-20	EF-40	EF-45	AU-50	AU-55	AU-58	MS-60	MS-62	MS-63
5 DOLLARS CAROLINA GOLD, RUTHERFORD, 140.G., 20 CARATS, Reeded Edge, K-17a	2 known	11727	—	—	—	—	—	—	—	—	—
5 DOLLARS CAROLINA GOLD, RUTHERF., 140.G., 20 CARATS, August 1, 1834, K-18	11 est. known	11728	$12,000	$17,000	$20,000	$24,000	—	—	—	—	—
5 DOLLARS CAROLINA GOLD, RUTHERF., 140.G., 20 CARATS, August 1, 1834, "20" Distant from CARATS, K-19	<40 known	11724	10,000	14,500	16,000	18,000	$26,500	$33,500	$43,000	$72,000	—
5 DOLLARS CAROLINA GOLD, RUTHERF., 134.G., 21 CARATS, With Star, Plain Edge, K-20	100 est. known	11721	8,250	10,500	12,000	14,000	18,000	20,500	24,000	42,000	$60,000
5 DOLLARS CAROLINA GOLD, RUTHERF., 134.G., 21 CARATS, With Star, Partially Reeded Edge, K-20a	unique	375984	—	—	—	—	—	—	—	—	—
5 DOLLARS GEORGIA GOLD, RUTHERFORD, 128.G., 22 CARATS, With Colon After G, K-21	14 est. known	11725	48,000	63,000	66,000	72,000	102,000	168,000	192,000	—	—
	Auctions: $228,000, PCGS AU-58 HA 01/24										
5 DOLLARS GEORGIA GOLD, RUTHERFORD, 128.G., 22 CARATS, K-22	20 est. known	11719	17,000	21,500	25,000	31,000	43,000	60,000	72,000	—	—
5 DOLLARS GEORGIA GOLD, RUTHERF, 128.G., 22 CARATS, K-23	40 est. known	11730	17,000	24,000	27,000	33,000	41,000	45,500	53,000	79,000	102,000

August Bechtler, Carolina

1 DOL:, CAROLINA GOLD, 27.G., 21.C

5 DOLLARS, CAROLINA GOLD, 134.G:, 21 CARATS

5 DOLLARS, CAROLINA GOLD, 128.G., 22 CARATS

5 DOLLARS, CAROLINA GOLD, 141.G., 20 CARATS

		GSID	VF-20	EF-40	EF-45	AU-50	AU-55	AU-58	MS-60	MS-62	MS-63	MS-65
1 DOL., CAROLINA GOLD, 27.G., 21 C., Plain Edge, K-24	300 est. known	11689	$2,000	$2,500	$2,800	$3,750	$4,700	$5,250	$6,250	$8,750	$11,000	—
1 DOL., CAROLINA GOLD, 27.G., 21 C., Reeded Edge, K-25	<5 known	11690	10,500	14,500	16,000	18,000	24,000	30,000	34,000	48,000	—	—
5 DOLLARS, CAROLINA, 134.G., 21 CARATS, K-27	40 est. known	11687	7,500	9,500	10,000	11,000	13,000	15,000	26,000	—	—	—
5 DOLLARS, CAROLINA, 134.G., 21 CARATS, Reverse of C. Bechtler, K-26	3 known	11720	10,000	12,000	13,000	15,000	18,000	—	—	—	—	—
5 DOLLARS, CAROLINA, 128.G., 22 CARATS, K-28	24 est. known	11686	—	18,000	20,500	24,000	36,000	50,500	60,000	—	—	—
5 DOLLARS, CAROLINA, 141.G., 20 CARATS, K-29	<15 known	11688	15,000	19,000	21,000	24,000	33,000	39,000	45,000	—	—	—
5 DOLLARS, CAROLINA, 141.G., 20 CARATS, Chapman Restrike, Proof, K-30		11691	—	—	—	—	—	—	36,000	45,500	53,000	—
5 DOLLARS CAROLINA, RUTHERF., 141.G., 20 CARATS, Chapman Restrike, Proof, K-31		11735	—	—	—	—	—	—	—	60,000	72,000	$102,000

Note: Restrikes in "Proof" of this type using original dies were made about 1920.

NORRIS, GREGG & NORRIS, SAN FRANCISCO, 1849

Collectors consider this piece the first of the California private gold coins. A newspaper account dated May 31, 1849, described a five-dollar gold coin, struck at Benicia City, though with the imprint of San Francisco. It mentioned the private stamp of Norris, Gregg & Norris, the California branch of a New York City plumbing and hardware firm.

		GSID	VF-20	EF-40	EF-45	AU-50	AU-55	AU-58	MS-60	MS-62	MS-63
1849 Half Eagle, Plain Edge, Period, K-2		11856	$10,000	$13,000	$15,000	$17,000	$24,000	$32,500	$36,000	$55,000	$77,000
1849 Half Eagle, Plain Edge, No Period, K-3		375854	12,000	16,000	18,000	20,000	29,000	39,000	43,000	—	—
1849 Half Eagle, Reeded Edge, K-4		11857	12,500	15,000	16,000	18,000	22,000	27,000	36,000	60,000	102,000
1849 Half Eagle, With STOCKTON Beneath Date, K-5 (in Smithsonian Collection)	unique	11858	—	—	—	—	—	—	—	—	—

MOFFAT & CO., SAN FRANCISCO, 1849–1853

The firm of Moffat & Co. (principals John Little Moffat, Joseph R. Curtis, Philo H. Perry, and Samuel H. Ward) was the most important of the California private coiners. The assay office they conducted became semi-official in character starting in 1851. The successors to this firm, Curtis, Perry, and Ward, later sold their coining facility to the Treasury Department, which in March 1854 reopened it as the branch mint of San Francisco.

In June or July 1849, Moffat & Co. began to issue small, rectangular ingots of gold in response to lack of coin in the locality, in values from $9.43 to $264. The $9.43, $14.25, and $16.00 varieties are the only types known today.

The dies for the five-dollar and ten-dollar Moffat & Co. pieces were cut by a Bavarian engraver, Albrecht Küner, who had moved to the United States in October 1848. On the coronet of Liberty appear the words MOFFAT & CO., instead of the word LIBERTY as in regular U.S. issues.

$16.00 Moffat Ingot

1849 FIVE DOL.

		GSID	VF-20	EF-40	EF-45	AU-50	AU-55	AU-58	MS-60	MS-62	MS-63	MS-65
(1849) $9.43 Moffat Ingot, K-1 (in Smithsonian Collection)	unique	375855	—	—	—	—	—	—	—	—	—	—
(1849) $14.25 Moffat Ingot, K-2 (in Smithsonian Collection)	unique	375856	—	—	—	—	—	—	—	—	—	—
(1849) $16.00 Moffat Ingot, K-3		11814	—	—	—	$360,000	$360,000	$432,000	—	—	—	—
	Auctions: $384,000, NGC AU-58 HA 01/22											
1849 FIVE DOL., K-4		11808	$4,750	$7,000	$7,500	9,000	12,000	14,500	$16,000	$30,000	—	—
	Auctions: $109,250, NGC MS-67 HA 06/04											
1849 TEN D., TEN D., K-5	50–60 known	11811	13,000	21,500	24,000	29,000	42,000	54,000	72,000	—	—	—
1849 TEN DOL., Period Below Arrowhead, K-6	4 known	11812	12,000	17,000	23,000	42,000	66,000	96,000	120,000	—	—	—
	Auctions: $102,000, PCGS AU-58 HA 01/24											
1849 TEN DOL., Period Above Arrowhead, K-6a	40–50 known	375853	12,000	17,000	23,000	33,500	—	—	—	—	—	—
1850 FIVE DOL., K-7		11809	4,700	7,000	7,750	8,750	11,000	12,000	14,500	24,000	$38,500	$150,000
	Auctions: $188,000, PCGS MS-65 HA 01/14											

a. This unique piece is housed in the Smithsonian's National Numismatic Collection. **a.** Multiple varieties exist.

UNITED STATES ASSAY OFFICE

Augustus Humbert / United States Assayer of Gold, 1851

Augustus Humbert, a New York watchcase maker, was appointed United States assayer by the Treasury Department in 1850 and arrived in California in early 1851. He placed his name and the government stamp on the ingots of gold issued by Moffat & Co., but without the Moffat imprint. The assay office, a provisional government mint, was a temporary expedient to accommodate the Californians until the establishment of a permanent federal branch mint.

The fifty-dollar gold piece was accepted by most banks and merchants as legal tender on a par with standard U.S. gold coins and was known variously as a *slug*, *quintuple eagle*, *five-eagle piece*, or *adobe* (the latter a type of construction brick). It was officially termed an *ingot*.

1851 50 D C 880 THOUS., No 50 on Reverse, Lettered Edge

1851 50 D C 887 THOUS., 50 on Reverse, Lettered Edge

1851 FIFTY DOLLS, 887 THOUS., "Target" Reverse, Reeded Edge

		GSID	VF-20	EF-40	EF-45	AU-50	AU-55	AU-58	MS-60	MS-62	MS-63	MS-65
1851 50 D C 880 THOUS., 50 on Reverse, Sunk in Edge: AUGUSTUS HUMBERT UNITED STATES ASSAYER OF GOLD, CALIFORNIA 1851, K-1	<15 known	11782	$51,000	$72,000	$90,000	$120,000	$180,000	$210,000	$330,000	$480,000	—	—
	Auctions: $287,500, NGC MS-62 HA 08/07											
1851 50 D C 880 THOUS., No 50 on Reverse, Sunk in Edge: AUGUSTUS HUMBERT UNITED STATES ASSAYER OF GOLD, CALIFORNIA 1851, K-2	100 est. known	11780	54,000	78,000	96,000	104,500	144,000	180,000	204,000	252,000	$312,000	—
	Auctions: $546,250, PCGS MS-63 HA 08/10											
1851 50 D C 887 THOUS., 50 on Reverse, K-4	60 est. known	11784	60,000	90,000	108,000	144,000	180,000	198,000	228,000	432,000	624,000	—
	Auctions: $456,000, PCGS MS-62 HA 02/25; $360,000, PCGS MS-62 SBG 02/25											

		GSID	VF-20	EF-40	EF-45	AU-50	AU-55	AU-58	MS-60	MS-62	MS-63	MS-65
1851 FIFTY DOLLS, 880 THOUS., "Target" Reverse, K-5	100–200 est. known	11785	$29,000	$36,000	$39,500	$43,000	$69,000	$90,000	$108,000	$180,000	—	—
	Auctions: $132,000, NGC MS-62 SBG 05/25											
1851 FIFTY DOLLS, 887 THOUS., "Target" Reverse, K-6	75 est. known	11786	28,000	41,000	45,500	53,000	67,000	90,000	114,000	165,500	$264,000	—
	Auctions: $204,000, PCGS MS-62 SBG 11/23; $440,625, PCGS MS-62 HA 11/23											
1851 FIFTY DOLLS, 887 THOUS., "Target" Reverse, Proof, K-6	2 known	11789	—	—	—	—	—	—	—	—	—	$6,000,000
1852 FIFTY DOLLS, 887 THOUS., "Target" Reverse, K-11	75 est. known	11787	26,500	38,500	47,000	57,500	83,000	108,000	162,000	264,000	—	—
	Auctions: $162,000, PCGS AU-55 HA 08/25											

Moffat & Co. / United States Assayer of Gold, 1852

In 1851, certain issues of the Miners' Bank, Baldwin, Pacific Company, and others were discredited, some unfairly, by newspaper accounts stating they were of reduced gold value. This provided an enhanced opportunity for Moffat and the U.S. Assay Office of Gold. Supplementing privately struck gold pieces and federal issues, coins of almost every nation were being pressed into service by the Californians, but the supply was too small to help to any extent. Moffat & Co. proceeded in January 1852 to issue a new ten-dollar gold piece bearing the stamp MOFFAT & CO.

1852 TEN D. MOFFAT & CO., Wide Date

1852 TEN DOLS.

Close Date

Wide Date

1852, Normal Date

1852, 2 Over 1

1852 TWENTY DOLS., 1852, 2 Over 1

		GSID	VF-20	EF-40	EF-45	AU-50	AU-55	AU-58	MS-60	MS-62	MS-63	MS-65
1852 TEN D., MOFFAT & CO., Close Date, K-8	20 est. known	11810	—	—	$72,000	$90,000	$117,500	—	—	—	—	—
1852 TEN D., MOFFAT & CO., Wide Date, K-9	<30 known	11813	—	$15,500	23,000	31,000	41,000	—	—	—	—	—
	Auctions: $276,000, Uncert MS-64 SBG 11/06											
1852 TEN D., Wide Date, Specimen, K-9	2 known	11816	—	—	—	—	—	—	—	—	$1,200,000	—
	Auctions: $948,750, PCGS MS-67 ANR 08/06											
1852 TEN DOLS., 1852, 2 Over 1, K-8	50–75 known	11778	$9,000	12,000	14,000	16,000	24,000	$36,000	$54,000	—	—	—
1852 TEN DOLS., K-10	150 est. known	11777	8,750	12,500	14,000	15,000	17,500	20,000	24,000	$38,500	—	—
	Auctions: $1,057,500, NGC MS-68 HA 04/13											
↳1852 TEN DOLS., CALIFORNIA Aligned Left, K-10b	<10 known	375998	—	—	—		—	—	—	—	—	—
1852 TWENTY DOLS., 1852, 2 Over 1, K-9	20 est. known	11779	18,000	23,000	26,500	31,000	48,000	79,000	108,000	162,000	186,000	—
	Auctions: $192,000, NGC MS-64 HA 08/24; $156,000, PCGS MS-63 HA 08/24											
1852 TWENTY DOLS., 1852, 2 Over 1, Proof, K-9	2 known	11788	—	—	—	—	—	—	—	—	660,000	$1,140,000
	Auctions: $434,500, NGC PF-64 SU 10/90											

United States Assay Office of Gold, 1852–1853

The firm of Moffat & Co. was dissolved in 1852 and a newly reorganized company known as the United States Assay Office of Gold took over the contract. Principals in the firm were Joseph Curtis, Philo Perry, and Samuel Ward.

1852 TEN DOLS., 884 THOUS.

1852 FIFTY DOLLS., 900 THOUS.

1853 TEN D., 900 THOUS.

1853 TWENTY D., 884 THOUS.

1853 TWENTY D., 900 THOUS.

		GSID	VF-20	EF-40	EF-45	AU-50	AU-55	AU-58	MS-60	MS-62	MS-63	MS-65
1852 TEN DOLS., 884 THOUS., First Reverse, K-12	12 est. known	375999	$8,000	$9,500	$10,500	$13,000	$18,000	$22,000	$24,000	$37,000	$53,000	—
1852 TEN DOLS., 884 THOUS., Second Reverse, K-12a	200 est. known	11692	7,250	8,750	9,750	12,000	16,500	20,000	21,500	33,500	48,000	—
1852 FIFTY DOLLS., 887 THOUS., K-13	110–150 known	11697	30,000	38,500	43,000	48,000	66,000	96,000	108,000	150,000	—	—
	Auctions: $111,000, NGC MS-62 HA 08/24											
1852 FIFTY DOLLS., 900 THOUS., K-14	100–150 known	11698	29,000	48,000	53,000	60,000	84,000	120,000	180,000	270,000	408,000	—
	Auctions: $690,000, PCGS MS-64 HA 08/25; $114,000, NGC MS-61 HA 08/25											
1853 TEN DOLS., 884 THOUS., K-15	12–15 known	11693	27,000	36,000	42,000	54,000	62,500	72,000	81,500	—	—	—
1853 TEN DOLS., 900 THOUS., K-16	45 est. known	11694	9,500	12,000	13,000	15,000	18,000	21,500	24,000	33,000	54,000	—
1853 TWENTY D., 884 THOUS., K-17	24 est. known	11695	17,000	21,500	24,000	29,000	38,500	50,500	60,000	108,000	156,000	—
	Auctions: $176,250, NGC MS-63 HA 04/14											
1853 TWENTY D., 900 THOUS., K-18	500–600 known	11696	7,250	8,500	9,500	11,000	12,000	13,000	14,500	20,000	26,000	$72,000
	Auctions: $129,250, PCGS MS-65 HA 01/14											
1853 TWENTY D., 900 THOUS., Proof, K-18		11700	—	—	—	—	—	—	—	—	180,000	—

Note: Modern prooflike forgeries exist.

Moffat & Co. Gold, 1853

The last Moffat & Co. issue, an 1853 twenty-dollar piece, is very similar to the U.S. double eagle of that period. It was struck after John L. Moffat retired from the Assay Office. The circumstances of its issue are unclear, but many were coined.

		GSID	VF-20	EF-40	XF45	AU-50	AU-55	AU-58	MS-60	MS-62	MS-63
1853 TWENTY D., K-19	50 est. known	11815	$15,000	$20,000	$22,000	$24,000	$36,000	$48,000	$60,000	$102,000	—
1853 TWENTY D., Proof, K-19 (both in Smithsonian Collection)	2 known	376013	—	—	—	—	—	—	—	—	—

CINCINNATI MINING & TRADING CO., 1849

The origin and location of this company are unknown.

		GSID	EF-45	AU-50	AU-55
1849 FIVE DOLLARS, K-1	unique	11736	—	—	—
1849 TEN DOLLARS, K-3	5 known	11737	$780,000	$840,000	$960,000

Note: Beware of spurious specimens cast in base metal with the word TRACING in place of TRADING.

MASSACHUSETTS AND CALIFORNIA COMPANY, 1849

This company was organized in Northampton, Massachusetts, in May 1849. Years later fantasy and copy dies were made and coins struck in various metals including gold. Pieces with the denomination spelled as 5D are not genuine.

		GSID	EF-40
1849 FIVE D., 16 Berries on Reverse, K-1	2 known	11801	$600,000
1849 FIVE D., 15 Berries on Reverse, K-2	unique	375861	—

MINERS' BANK, SAN FRANCISCO, 1849

The institution of Wright & Co., exchange brokers located in Portsmouth Square, San Francisco, was known as the Miners' Bank. The firm issued a ten-dollar gold piece in the autumn of 1849, and it saw wide use in commerce. However, the firm's coinage was ephemeral, and it was dissolved on January 14, 1850. Unlike the gold in most California issues, the gold in these coins was alloyed with copper.

		GSID	VF-20	EF-40	EF-45	AU-50	AU-55	AU-58	MS-60
(1849) TEN D., K-1	35 est. known	11806	$26,500	$45,500	$53,000	$66,000	$90,000	$96,000	$126,000
	Auctions: $264,000, PCGS MS-61 HA 01/22								

J.S. ORMSBY, SACRAMENTO, 1849

The initials J.S.O., which appear on certain issues of California privately coined gold pieces, represent the firm of J.S. Ormsby & Co., located in Sacramento. They struck five- and ten-dollar denominations, all undated.

		GSID	EF-40	AU-50
(1849) 5 DOLLS, Reeded Edge, K-1 (in Smithsonian Collection)	unique	375860	—	—
(1849) 5 DOLLS, Plain Edge, K-1a	unique	11861	—	—
(1849) 10 DOLLS, K-2	5 known	11862	$840,000	$1,140,000
	Auctions: $145,000, PCGS AU-50 GLDB 05/99			

PACIFIC COMPANY, SAN FRANCISCO, 1849

The origin of the Pacific Company is very uncertain. All data regarding the firm are based on conjecture.

Edgar H. Adams wrote that he believed that the coins bearing the stamp of the Pacific Company were produced by the coining firm of Broderick and Kohler. The coins were probably hand struck with the aid of a sledgehammer. Trial pieces exist in silver. All are rarities today.

		GSID	EF-40	AU-50	AU-58	MS-60
1849 1 DOLLAR, K-4	3 known	285887	—	—	—	$360,000
	Auctions: $305,500, NGC MS-61 HA 04/14					
1849 5 DOLLARS, K-1	4 known	11863	$690,000	$900,000	$1,080,000	—
	Auctions: $1,260,000, PCGS AU-58 SBG 02/25					
1849 10 DOLLARS, K-3	4 known	11866	—	—	—	1,320,000

F.D. KOHLER, CALIFORNIA STATE ASSAYER, 1850

The State Assay Office was authorized on April 12, 1850. That year, Governor Peter Burnett appointed to the position of state assayer Frederick D. Kohler, who thereupon sold his assaying business to Baldwin & Co. Kohler served at both the San Francisco and Sacramento offices. The State Assay Offices were discontinued at the time the U.S. Assay Office was established, on February 1, 1851.

Ingots issued ranged from $36.55 to $150. An Extremely Fine specimen sold in the Garrett Sale, 1980, for $200,000. Each is unique.

		GSID
$36.65 Sacramento, Ingot, K-7	unique	375864
$37.31 San Francisco, Ingot		375865
$40.07 San Francisco, Ingot		375866
$45.34 San Francisco, Ingot, K-4	unique	11775
$47.71 San Francisco, Ingot		11776
$50.00 San Francisco, Ingot		375867
$54.09 San Francisco, Ingot		375868

Note: A $40.07 ingot was stolen from the Mint Cabinet in 1858 and never recovered.

DUBOSQ & COMPANY, SAN FRANCISCO, 1850

Theodore Dubosq Sr., a Philadelphia jeweler, took melting and coining equipment to San Francisco in 1849 and minted five-dollar gold pieces.

		GSID	VF-20	EF-40	EF-45	AU-50	MS-60	MS-63
1850 FIVE D., K-1	2 known	11772	—	—	—	—	$36,000	$48,000
1850 TEN D., K-2	8 known	11773	$108,000	$210,000	$264,000	$360,000	660,000	—
	Auctions: $480,000, NGC MS-60 HA 01/22							

BALDWIN & CO., SAN FRANCISCO, 1850–1851

George C. Baldwin and Thomas S. Holman were in the jewelry business in San Francisco and were known as Baldwin & Co. They were the successors to F.D. Kohler & Co., taking over its machinery and other equipment in May 1850. The firm ceased minting coins in early 1851, at which time newspaper accounts stated that its coins fell short of their stated gold value. The 1850 Vaquero or Horseman ten-dollar design is one of the most famous of the California gold issues.

The Baldwin & Co. twenty-dollar piece was the first of that denomination issued in California. Baldwin coins are believed to have contained about 2 percent copper alloy.

1850 FIVE DOL.

1850 TEN DOLLARS, Horseman Type

1851 TEN D.

1851 TWENTY D.

		GSID	VF-20	EF-40	EF-45	AU-50	AU-55	AU-58	MS-60	MS-62	MS-63
1850 FIVE DOL., K-2	25–30 known	11701	—	$24,000	$27,000	$36,000	$50,500	$90,000	$150,000	—	—
	Auctions: $204,000, PCGS MS-61 HA 01/22										
1850 TEN DOLLARS, Horseman Type, K-3	20–25 known	11702	$120,000	150,000	168,000	198,000	264,000	330,000	420,000	$720,000	$1,080,000
	Auctions: $1,260,000, PCGS MS-63 SBG 11/24										
1851 TEN D., K-4		11703	42,000	62,500	72,000	84,000	114,000	174,000	240,000	360,000	—
	Auctions: $235,000, PCGS MS-61 HA 04/14										
1851 TWENTY D., K-5	5 known	11705	—	840,000	960,000	—	—	—	—	—	—
	Auctions: $646,250, PCGS EF-45 HA 04/14										

SCHULTZ & COMPANY, SAN FRANCISCO, 1851

The firm of Schultz & Co., a brass foundry, was operated by Judge G.W. Schultz and William T. Garratt. The surname is misspelled as SHULTZ on the coins.

		GSID	EF-40	AU-50	AU-55	AU-58	MS-60	MS-62
1851 FIVE D., K-1	12 est. known	11872	$312,000	$432,000	$552,000	$600,000	$720,000	$1,200,000
	Auctions: $1,020,000, PCGS MS-62 HA 01/24							

DUNBAR & COMPANY, SAN FRANCISCO, 1851

Edward E. Dunbar operated the California Bank in San Francisco. He later returned to New York City and organized the famous Continental Bank Note Co.

		GSID	VF-20	EF-40	AU-50
1851 FIVE D., K-1	4 known	11774	$480,000	$600,000	$750,000

WASS, MOLITOR & CO., SAN FRANCISCO, 1852–1855

The gold-smelting and assaying plant of Wass, Molitor & Co. was operated by two Hungarian patriots exiled after the Revolution of 1848, Count Samu Wass and A.P. Molitor. They maintained an excellent laboratory and complete apparatus for analysis and coinage of gold.

The company struck five-, ten-, twenty-, and fifty-dollar coins. In 1852 they produced a ten-dollar piece similar in design to the five-dollar denomination. The difference is in the reverse legend, which reads: S.M.V. [Standard Mint Value] CALIFORNIA GOLD TEN D.

No pieces were coined in 1853 or 1854, but they brought out the twenty- and fifty-dollar pieces in 1855. A considerable number of the fifty-dollar coins were made. There was a ten-dollar piece issued in 1855 also, with the Liberty Head design and small close date.

1852 FIVE DOLLARS, Small Head, Rounded Bust

1852 FIVE DOLLARS, Large Head, Pointed Bust

1852 TEN D., Large Head

1852 TEN D., Small Head

1852 TEN D., Small Close Date

1855 TEN D.

1855 TWENTY DOL., Large Head

1855 TWENTY DOL., Small Head

1855 50 DOLLARS

		GSID	VF-20	EF-40	EF-45	AU-50	AU-55	AU-58	MS-60	MS-62	MS-63
1852 FIVE DOLLARS, Small Head, Rounded Bust, K-1	10–12 known	11881	$17,000	$38,500	$43,000	$53,000	$62,500	$96,000	$156,000	—	—
	Auctions: $180,000, PCGS MS-60 HA 01/22										
1852 FIVE DOLLARS, Large Head, Rounded Bust, K-2	12 est. known	11880	19,000	31,000	38,500	51,000	66,000	81,500	101,000	—	—
1852 TEN D., Small Head, K-3	20–30 known	11885	8,750	18,000	21,000	27,000	33,000	—	—	—	—
1852 TEN D., Large Head, K-4	150 est. known	11884	7,500	11,000	13,000	15,500	17,000	18,000	27,000	$60,000	$86,500
1852 TEN D., Close Date, Short Neck, K-5	8 known	11883	45,500	67,000	78,000	96,000	—	—	—	—	—
1855 TEN D., K-6	30–35 known	11882	14,500	19,000	21,500	29,000	33,000	42,000	54,000	—	—
1855 TWENTY DOL., Small Head, K-7	25–30 known	11887	48,000	62,500	74,500	87,000	120,000	150,000	192,000	—	—
	Auctions: $180,000, NGC AU-55 HA 01/24										
1855 TWENTY DOL., Large Head, First Reverse, K-8a	unique	376018	—	—	—	—	—	—	—	—	—
1855 TWENTY DOL., Large Head, Second Reverse, K-8	3 known	11886	—	600,000	672,000	780,000	—	—	—	—	—
	Auctions: $558,125, NGC AU-53 HA 04/14										
1855 50 DOLLARS, K-9	75 est. known	11888	53,000	62,500	81,500	110,500	156,000	192,000	222,000	390,000	510,000
	Auctions: $411,250, NGC MS-63 HA 04/14										

KELLOGG & CO., SAN FRANCISCO, 1854–1855

John G. Kellogg went to San Francisco on October 12, 1849, from Auburn, New York. At first he was employed by Moffat & Co., and remained with that organization when control passed to Curtis, Perry, and Ward. When the U.S. Assay Office was discontinued, December 14, 1853, Kellogg became associated with George F. Richter, who had been an assayer in the U.S. Assay Office of Gold. These two set up business as Kellogg & Richter on December 19, 1853.

When the U.S. Assay Office ceased operations, a period ensued during which no private firm was striking gold. The new San Francisco branch mint did not produce coins for some months after Curtis & Perry took the contract for the government (Ward having died). The lack of coin was again keenly felt by businessmen, who petitioned Kellogg & Richter to "supply the vacuum" by issuing private coin. Their plea was soon answered: on February 9, 1854, Kellogg & Co. placed their first twenty-dollar piece in circulation.

The firm dissolved late in 1854 and reorganized as Kellogg & Humbert. The latter partner was Augustus Humbert, for some time identified as U.S. assayer of gold in California. Regardless of the fact that the San Francisco branch mint was then producing coins, Kellogg & Humbert issued twenty-dollar coins in 1855 in a quantity greater than before. On September 12, 1857, hundreds of the firm's rectangular gold ingots in transit to New York City were lost in the sinking of the SS *Central America*. They were the most plentiful of bars aboard the ill-fated ship from several different assayers.

The 1855 Kellogg & Co. twenty-dollar piece is similar to that of 1854. The letters on the reverse are larger and the arrows longer on one 1854 variety. There are die varieties of both.

In 1855, Ferdinand Grüner cut the dies for a round-format fifty-dollar gold coin for Kellogg & Co., but coinage seems to have been limited to presentation pieces in Proof format. Only 10 to 12 pieces are known to exist. A "commemorative restrike" was made in 2001 using transfer dies made from the original and gold recovered from the SS *Central America*. These pieces have the inscription S.S. CENTRAL AMERICA GOLD, C.H.S. on the reverse ribbon.

1854 TWENTY D.

1855 TWENTY D.

1855 FIFTY DOLLS.

		GSID	VF-20	EF-40	EF-45	AU-50	AU-55	AU-58	MS-60	MS-62	MS-63	MS-65
1854 TWENTY D., Short Arrows, K-1	180–220 known, all vars	11792	$7,500	$10,500	$12,000	$15,500	$19,500	$25,000	$36,000	$72,000	$162,000	$540,000
	Auctions: $552,000, PCGS MS-65 SBG 03/23											
1854 TWENTY D., Short Arrows, Specimen, K-1	unique	376014	—	—	—	—	—	—	—	—	—	—
1854 TWENTY D., Long Arrows, K-2	180–220 known, all vars	376015	—	—	—	—	—	—	—	—	—	—
1855 TWENTY D., Long Arrows, K-3		11793	8,000	12,000	15,000	20,000	24,000	29,000	33,500	57,500	—	—
1855 TWENTY D., Medium Arrows, K-3a		376016	—	—	—	—	—	—	—	—	—	—
1855 TWENTY D., Short Arrows, K-3b		376017	—	—	—	—	—	21,500	—	—	—	—
1855 FIFTY DOLLS., Proof, K-4	13 known	11799	—	—	—	390,000	438,000	450,000	510,000	660,000	870,000	—
	Auctions: $763,750, PCGS PF-64 HA 04/14											

OREGON EXCHANGE COMPANY, OREGON CITY, 1849

The Beaver Coins of Oregon

Upon the discovery of gold in California, a great exodus of Oregonians joined in the hunt for the precious metal. Soon, gold seekers returned with their gold dust, which became an accepted medium of exchange. As in other Western areas at that time, the uncertain qualities of the gold and weighing devices tended to irk tradespeople, and petitions were made to the legislature for a standard gold coin issue.

On February 16, 1849, the territorial legislature passed an act providing for a mint and specified five- and ten-dollar gold coins without alloy. Oregon City, the largest city in the territory with a population of about 1,000, was designated as the location for the mint. At the time this act was passed, Oregon had been brought into the United States as a territory by act of Congress. When the new governor arrived on March 2, he declared the coinage act unconstitutional.

The public-spirited people, however, continued to work for a convenient medium of exchange and soon took matters into their own hands by starting a private mint. Eight men of affairs, whose names were Kilborne, Magruder, Taylor, Abernethy, Willson, Rector, Campbell, and Smith, set up the Oregon Exchange Company.

The coins struck were of virgin gold as specified in the original act. Ten-dollar dies were made slightly later.

1849 5 D.

1849 TEN.D

	GSID	VF-20	EF-40	EF-45	AU-50	AU-55	AU-58	MS-60	MS-62
1849 5 D., K-1	11859	$50,500	$90,000	$102,000	$120,000	$174,000	$216,000	$288,000	$390,000
	Auctions: $336,000, PCGS MS-62 SBG 08/20								
1849 TEN D., K-2	11860	216,000	336,000	384,000	420,000	480,000	—	—	—
	Auctions: $340,750, PCGS AU-55 HA 04/14								

MORMON GOLD PIECES, SALT LAKE CITY, UTAH, 1849–1860

The first name given to the organized Mormon Territory was the "State of Deseret," the last word meaning "honeybee" in the Book of Mormon. The beehive, which is shown on the reverse of the five-dollar 1860 piece, was a favorite device of the followers of Joseph Smith and Brigham Young. The clasped hands appear on most Mormon coins and exemplify strength in unity. HOLINESS TO THE LORD was an inscription frequently used.

Brigham Young was the instigator of the coinage system and personally supervised the mint, which was housed in a little adobe building in Salt Lake City. The mint was inaugurated late in 1848 as a public convenience and to make a profit for the church. Each coin had substantially less gold than the face value stated.

1849 TWO.AND.HALF.DO.

1849 FIVE.DOLLARS

1849 TEN.DOLLARS

1849 TWENTY.DOLLARS

1850 FIVE DOLLARS

1860 5.D.

		GSID	VF-20	EF-40	EF-45	AU-50	AU-55	AU-58	MS-60	MS-62	MS-63
1849 TWO AND HALF DO., K-1		11818	$38,500	$54,000	$60,000	$72,000	$84,000	$96,000	$108,000	$180,000	$282,000
	Auctions: $235,000, PCGS MS-63 HA 04/14										
1849 FIVE DOLLARS, K-2		11822	27,000	38,500	41,000	45,500	60,000	72,000	79,000	—	—
1849 TEN DOLLARS, K-3		11831	600,000	810,000	900,000	1,020,000	1,200,000	1,320,000	—	—	—
	Auctions: $840,000, PCGS AU-53 SBG 12/20										
1849 TWENTY DOLLARS, K-4		11834	198,000	240,000	312,000	408,000	528,000	600,000	720,000	1,020,000	—
	Auctions: $720,000, PCGS MS-62 HA 01/21										
1850 FIVE DOLLARS, K-5		11823	24,000	36,000	43,000	54,000	90,000	102,000	114,000	—	—
	Auctions: $102,000, PCGS AU-58 HA 01/22										
1850 5.D., K-6	40–50 est. known	11824	30,000	55,000	62,500	77,000	103,000	120,000	138,000	228,000	—
	Auctions: $192,000, NGC MS-62 SBG 02/25; $144,000, PCGS AU-53 HA 02/25										

COLORADO GOLD PIECES

Clark, Gruber & Co., Denver, 1860–1861

Clark, Gruber & Co. was a well-known private minting firm in Denver, Colorado, in 1860 and 1861, formed by bankers from Leavenworth, Kansas Territory. In 1862 their operation was purchased by the Treasury Department and thenceforth operated as an assay office.

The $2.50 and $5 pieces of 1861 follow closely the designs of the 1860 issues. The main difference is found in the legends. The reverse side now has CLARK GRUBER & CO. DENVER. On the obverse, PIKES PEAK now appears on the coronet of Liberty.

1860 2 1/2 D

1860 FIVE D

1860 TEN D

1861 2 1/2 D

1861 FIVE D

1861 TEN D

1860 TWENTY D

1861 TWENTY D

	Mintage	GSID	VF-20	EF-40	EF-45	AU-50	AU-55	AU-58	MS-60	MS-62	MS-63	MS-65
1860 2 1/2 D., K-1	100 est. known	11738	$5,500	$8,000	$9,000	$10,000	$12,000	$12,500	$14,000	$21,500	$36,000	$90,000
1860 FIVE D., K-2	150–180 known	11742	4,550	5,750	6,750	9,500	12,000	12,500	15,500	24,000	31,000	162,000
	Auctions: $480,000, PCGS MS-66 HA 01/22											
1860 TEN D., K-3	100–150 known	11746	18,500	24,000	30,000	36,000	48,000	53,000	66,000	114,000	180,000	—
1860 TWENTY D., K-4	15–20 known	11751	330,000	432,000	468,000	570,000	660,000	720,000	840,000	—	—	—
	Auctions: $552,000, PCGS AU-55 SBG 11/23; $144,000, NGC AG0 SBG 11/23											
1860 TWENTY D., Proof, K-4	unique	376019	—	—	—	—	—	—	—	—	—	—
1861 2 1/2 D., K-5	100 est. known	11739	5,750	7,750	9,250	10,500	15,000	18,000	21,500	41,000	57,500	—
1861 FIVE D., K-6	50–75 known	11743	7,000	8,750	10,500	12,000	14,500	26,500	36,000	67,000	—	—
1861 TEN D., K-7	200 est. known	11747	8,250	11,000	12,500	14,000	18,000	26,500	36,000	66,000	108,000	—
1861 TWENTY D., K-8 (a)	25 est. known	11752	66,000	90,000	120,000	168,000	192,000	210,000	—	—	—	—
	Auctions: $144,000, PCGS AU-50 SBG 02/25; $102,025, PCGS EF-45 HA 02/25											

a. Beware of prooflike counterfeits.

John Parsons & Company, Tarryall Mines, Colorado, 1861

Very little is known regarding the mint of John Parsons and Co., although it is reasonably certain that it operated in the South Park section of Park County, Colorado, near the original town of Tarryall, in the summer of 1861.

		GSID	VF-20	EF-40
(1861) Undated 2 1/2 D.,K-1	6 known	11868	$540,000	$720,000
(1861) Undated FIVE D., K-2	5 known	11871	630,000	900,000

J.J. Conway & Co., Georgia Gulch, Colorado, 1861

Records show that the Conway mint operated for a short while in 1861. As in all gold-mining areas the value of gold dust caused disagreement among the merchants and the miners. The firm of J.J. Conway & Co. solved this difficulty by bringing out its gold pieces in August 1861.

(1861) Undated 2 1/2 D.

(1861) Undated FIVE D.

(1861) Undated TEN DOLLARS

		GSID	VF-20	EF-40	EF-45	AU-50
(1861) Undated 2 1/2 DOLL'S, K-1	9 known	11767	$480,000	$660,000	$720,000	$840,000
(1861) Undated FIVE DOLLARS, K-2	5 known	11769	600,000	840,000	—	—
(1861) Undated TEN DOLLARS, K-3	3 known	11770	—	1,020,000	—	—
	Auctions: $240,000, NGC AG-0 HA 01/19					

CALIFORNIA SMALL-DENOMINATION GOLD

Scan for additional information.

There was a scarcity of small coins during the California gold rush. Starting in 1852, quarter, half, and dollar coins were privately minted from native gold to alleviate the shortage. Period 1 California fractional gold coins were issued between 1852 and 1857 as Liberty Head denominations of 25 cents, 50 cents, and one dollar, in both octagonal and round formats. There is much credible evidence available to conclude these were used in daily commerce during the early stages of the gold rush. Beginning in 1859, various private entities continued to make them, but more as souvenirs, as charms, or for barter. These are called Period 2 California fractional gold coins and were issued up to 1882. Period 2 has both the Liberty Head and Indian Head designs and the coins are often prooflike. Most have a wreath on the reverse, but some have original designs.

Early coins contained up to 85 percent of face value in gold. The amount and quality of gold in the coins soon decreased, and some are merely gold plated.

The Coinage Act of April 22, 1864, made private coinage illegal, but the law was not fully enforced until 1883. In compliance with the law, non-denominated tokens were made, and from 1872 until 1883 both coins and tokens were produced. After 1883, most of the production was tokens. To circumvent the law, and to make them more acceptable, some pieces made after 1881 were backdated to the 1850s or 1860s.

About 35,000 pieces are believed to exist. More than 570 different varieties have been identified, many of them very rare. The quality of strike and edge treatment is inconsistent. Many bear their makers' initials: D, DERI, DERIB, DN, FD, G, GG, GL, H, L, N, or NR. Major denominated coins are listed below; values are for the most common variety of each type. Non-denominated tokens are not included in these listings. They are much less valuable. ***Beware of extremely common modern replicas*** (often having a bear in the design), which have little numismatic value.

The values in the following charts are only for coins made before 1883 with the denomination on the reverse expressed as CENTS, DOL., DOLL., or DOLLAR.

EXPLORING VARIETIES

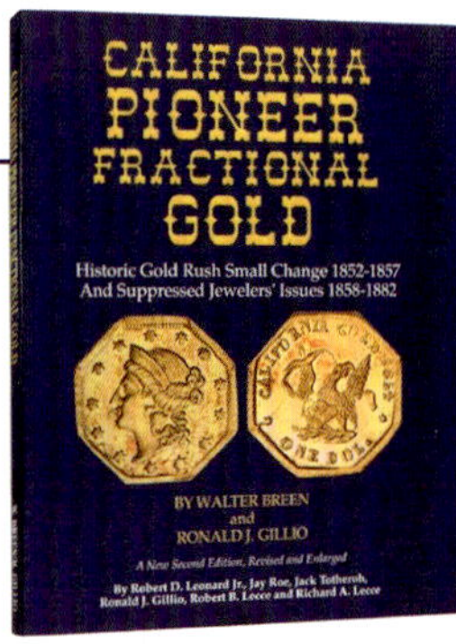

This catalog covers fractional gold pieces struck privately during and after the Gold Rush. The BG variety attributions provide a structured way to identify genuine coins and distinguish them from later jewelers' issues. Collectors use the system to navigate a complex and often misunderstood field.

Breen, Walter, and Ronald J. Gillio. *California Pioneer Fractional Gold: Historic Gold Rush Small Change 1852–1857 and Suppressed Jewelers' Issues 1858–1882.* Second edition. Wolfeboro, NH: Bowers & Merena, 2003.

California Gold Twenty-Five Cents

	GSID	AU-58	MS-60	MS-63	MS-65
1853, BG-101	11158	$675	$750	$1,750	$4,100
1853, BG-102	11159	240	275	455	900
1854, BG-103	11214	—	—	—	—
1854, BG-104	11215	240	275	455	1,000
1854, BG-105	11216	240	275	490	775
1855/4, BG-106	11653	300	340	575	1,000
1856, BG-107	11245	240	275	420	775
1854, BG-108	11217	240	275	420	775
1854, BG-109	11218	390	420	575	1,000
1855, BG-110	11234	285	310	575	1,250
1856, BG-111	11246	240	275	420	725
Cal. Gold, BG-201	11837	3,250	4,400	6,250	—
Cal. Gold, BG-202	11838	2,200	2,750	5,500	—
Cal. Gold, BG-203	11839	—	—	1,500	—
Cal. Gold, BG-204	11840	550	575	875	—
Cal. Gold, BG-204A	11850	—	—	—	—
Cal. Gold, BG-204B	11849	—	—	—	—
Cal. Gold, BG-204C	11851	—	—	24,000	—
Cal. Gold, BG-205	11841	—	—	4,400	—
Cal. Gold, BG-206	11842	365	455	775	2,500
Cal. Gold, BG-207	11843	490	525	650	—
1853, BG-208	11160	2,250	3,000	—	—
1853, BG-209	11161	2,050	2,750	7,000	—
Cal. Gold, BG-209A	11852	—	—	33,000	—
Cal. Gold, BG-209B	11853	—	—	—	—
1853, BG-210	11162	2,500	2,750	—	—
1853, BG-211	11163	—	—	—	—
1853, BG-212	11164	7,500	—	—	—
1853, BG-213	11165	—	—	24,000	—
1853, BG-214	11166	—	—	3,500	—
1853, BG-215	11167	1,750	2,000	3,250	—
1854, BG-216	11219	440	490	775	—
1853, BG-217	11168	—	—	—	—
1853, BG-217A	11171	—	—	—	—
1853, BG-218	11169	2,050	2,250	—	—
1853, BG-219	11170	2,250	—	—	—
1854, BG-220	11220	—	—	—	—
Cal. Gold, BG-221	11844	285	360	490	850

	GSID	AU-58	MS-60	MS-63	MS-65
Cal. Gold, BG-222	11845	$240	$260	$365	$725
Cal. Gold, BG-223	11846	240	275	370	650
Cal. Gold, BG-224	11847	260	275	420	650
1855, BG-225	11235	—	950	1,500	—
1855, BG-226	11236	390	420	775	2,500
1855, BG-226A	11238	390	420	575	1,000
1855, BG-227	11237	455	490	650	3,500
1856, BG-228	11247	1,500	3,100	8,250	—
1856, BG-229	11248	240	275	455	900
1856, BG-230	11249	240	275	405	775
1859, BG-701	11260	—	525	625	850
1859, BG-702	11261	230	260	360	550
1859, BG-703	11262	—	—	—	—
1856, BG-703A	11250	—	—	5,000	—
1859, BG-704	11263	—	—	—	—
1859, BG-705	11264	—	—	1,000	2,600
1864, BG-706	11281	420	455	725	1,300
1864, BG-707	11282	—	—	1,750	—
1866, BG-708	11298	360	390	455	675
1867, BG-709	11310	360	375	420	750
1868, BG-710	11320	390	455	650	950
1868, BG-711	11321	360	390	455	650
1869, BG-712	11341	360	390	455	675
1870, BG-713	11363	360	390	455	675
1871, BG-714	11401	310	325	370	575
1871, BG-715	11402	—	—	900	2,100
1871, BG-716	11403	—	775	900	1,400
1871, BG-716A	11404	—	—	—	—
1871, BG-717	11405	325	340	440	550
1871, BG-718	11406	—	—	775	1,000
1871, BG-718A (4 known)	11407	—	—	7,750	8,750
1871, BG-719	11408	—	—	—	—
1871, BG-720	11409	—	—	1,900	2,300
1872, BG-721	11467	—	—	—	—
1872, BG-721A	11468	—	—	—	—
1872, BG-722	11469	900	950	1,250	1,750
1872, BG-723	11470	1,550	1,750	2,400	—
1872, BG-724	11471	1,550	1,900	2,800	—

California Gold Twenty-Five Cents *(continued)*

	GSID	AU-58	MS-60	MS-63	MS-65
1872, BG-725	11472	—	$325	$525	$950
1872, BG-726	11473	—	325	525	950
1873, BG-727	11488	$240	260	420	725
1873, BG-728	11489	360	390	525	750
1860, BG-729	11274	—	—	—	—
1860, BG-730	11275	—	390	625	—
1860, BG-731	11276	390	430	600	—
1860, BG-732	11277	—	—	—	—
1863, BG-733	11278	—	—	—	—
1863, BG-734	11279	—	—	—	—
1864, BG-735	11283	370	420	600	775
1865, 5 Over 4, BG-736	11656	390	455	1,100	—
1866, BG-737	11299	390	430	650	—
1866, BG-738	11300	1,450	—	—	—
1866, BG-739	11301	—	—	—	—
1866, BG-740	11302	390	440	650	—
1867, BG-741	11311	390	—	—	—
1867, BG-742	11312	—	—	2,000	—
1867, BG-743	11313	3,250	—	—	—
1868, BG-744	11322	—	—	—	—
1868, BG-745	11323	455	525	1,900	—
1868, BG-746	11324	—	290	455	2,000
1868, BG-747	11325	280	290	550	—
1869, BG-748	11342	280	290	525	—
1869, BG-749	11343	290	360	1,100	—
1869, BG-750	11344	290	360	1,100	—
1869, BG-751	11345	280	290	455	—
1870, BG-752	11364	305	325	775	—
1870, BG-753	11365	455	575	—	—
1870, BG-754	11366	1,250	1,500	3,250	—
1870, BG-755	11367	280	290	455	—
1870, BG-756	11368	—	—	—	—
1870, BG-757	11369	—	—	775	—
1870, BG-758	11370	3,100	4,400	9,500	15,000
1870, BG-759	11371	280	290	390	850
1870, BG-760	11372	1,550	—	5,500	—
1870, BG-761	11373	280	290	390	850
1870, BG-762	11374	280	290	390	1,150
1870, BG-763	11375	280	290	495	1,150
1871, BG-764	11410	325	420	900	1,250
1871, BG-765	11411	280	290	365	850
1871, BG-766	11412	—	—	—	—
1871, BG-767	11413	280	290	390	850
1871, BG-768	11414	280	290	390	850
1871, BG-769	11415	280	290	525	—
1871, BG-770	11416	280	290	390	850
1871, BG-771	11417	325	360	725	1,000
1873, BG-772	11490	325	360	725	1,000
1874, BG-773	11508	—	—	—	—
1874, BG-774	11509	—	—	—	—
1874, BG-775	11510	325	360	725	1,000

	GSID	AU-58	MS-60	MS-63	MS-65
1874, 1874 Over 7874, BG-776	11670	$280	$290	$725	$1,600
1875, BG-777	11541	—	—	1,500	—
1876, BG-778	11574	—	—	1,100	—
1876, BG-779	11575	—	—	—	—
1876, BG-780	11576	280	290	390	850
1875, BG-781	11542	—	—	—	—
1875, BG-782	11543	—	—	—	—
1875, BG-783	11544	280	290	525	—
1875, BG-784	11545	280	290	525	1,000
1876, BG-785	11577	280	290	440	1,000
1876, BG-786	11578	325	360	725	1,000
1876, BG-787	11579	—	—	—	—
1881, BG-788	11625	—	—	950	1,750
1870, BG-789	11376	280	290	390	850
1872, 2 Over 1, BG-790	11657	280	290	390	850
1872, BG-791	11474	285	305	415	725
1873, 3 Over 2, BG-792	11664	—	1,150	1,500	2,050
1873, BG-793	11491	280	290	525	—
1873, BG-794	11492	280	290	525	950
1874, BG-795	11511	280	290	390	725
1875, BG-796	11546	280	290	525	—
1875, BG-797	11547	280	290	390	850
1875, BG-798	11548	280	290	525	—
1876, BG-799	11580	325	360	525	1,000
1876, BG-799A	11581	325	360	725	1,000
1876, BG-799B	11582	—	—	—	—
1876, BG-799C	11583	280	290	390	850
1876, BG-799D	11584	325	360	725	1,000
1876, BG-799E	11585	—	—	—	—
1876, BG-799F	11586	325	360	725	1,000
1878, 8 Over 6, BG-799G	11677	—	—	525	1,000
1880, 80 Over 70, BG-799H	11682	325	360	725	1,000
1880, 80 Over 70, BG-799I	11683	325	360	725	1,000
1880, BG-799J	11616	280	290	390	650
1880, BG-799K	11617	325	360	725	1,250
1880, BG-799L	11618	280	290	525	—
1881, BG-799M	11628	280	290	525	775
1881, BG-799N	11629	—	—	—	1,200
1881, BG-799O	11630	280	305	420	900
1874, BG-799P	11513	—	—	—	—
1874, BG-799Q	11514	280	290	525	1,400
1868, BG-799R	11326	—	—	—	2,000
1868, BG-799S	11327	—	—	—	—
1868, BG-799T	11328	280	290	525	850
1852, BG-799U	11127	280	325	525	950
1852, BG-799V	11128	—	—	—	2,500
1880, BG-799W	11619	—	—	—	1,100
1880, BG-799X	11620	390	415	575	775
1880, BG-799Y	11621	280	290	390	725
1881, BG-799Z	11631	—	—	—	—
1881, BG-799AA	11626	2,000	2,100	—	—

California Gold Twenty-Five Cents *(continued)*

	GSID	AU-58	MS-60	MS-63	MS-65
1881, BG-799BB	11627	—	—	$950	—
1882, BG-799CC	11644	—	—	1,600	$2,050
1852, BG-799DD	11126	—	—	—	—
1874, BG-799EE	11512	—	—	—	—
1874, BG-799P2	11521	—	—	—	—
1858, BG-800	11258	—	—	—	—
1859, BG-801	11265	$280	$290	370	625
1865, BG-802	11294	280	290	525	950
1865, BG-803	11295	280	290	525	950
1866, BG-804	11303	280	290	390	575
1867, BG-805	11314	280	290	420	575
1868, BG-806	11329	280	290	390	575
1870, BG-807	11377	575	650	925	1,900
1870, BG-808	11378	280	290	390	575
1870, BG-808A	11385	—	—	—	—
1871, BG-809	11418	280	290	390	650
1871, BG-810	11419	—	—	—	1,150
1871, BG-811	11420	—	—	—	—
1871, BG-812	11421	280	290	455	650
1871, BG-813	11422	280	290	390	575
1872, BG-814	11475	—	—	—	1,750
1872, BG-815	11476	—	—	3,100	—
1872, BG-816	11477	490	525	725	1,750
1873, BG-817	11493	310	340	430	625
1872, BG-818	11251	850	950	1,250	2,200
1860, 60 Over 50, BG-819	11654	390	470	725	—
1863, BG-820	11280	360	420	650	—
1864, BG-821	11284	290	360	725	—
1865, BG-822	11296	260	290	390	—
1866, BG-823	11304	—	—	2,500	—
1866, BG-824	11305	525	575	—	—
1867, BG-825	11315	260	290	390	—
1869, BG-826	11346	260	290	390	650
1869, BG-827	11347	260	290	455	—
1869, BG-828	11348	260	290	390	—
1869, BG-829	11349	290	325	775	—
1869, BG-830	11350	340	360	490	—
1869, BG-831	11351	—	—	—	—
1870, BG-832	11379	420	455	775	—
1870, BG-833	11380	420	455	775	—
(1871-71), BG-834	11848	290	325	650	—
1870, BG-835	11381	280	290	420	550
1870, BG-835A	11382	1,900	—	—	—
1870, BG-836	11383	—	—	—	—
1871, BG-837	11423	1,150	1,400	2,500	—
1871, BG-838	11424	280	290	430	775
1871, BG-839	11425	260	290	420	775
1871, BG-840	11426	260	290	420	650
1871, BG-841	11427	260	290	390	650
1873, BG-842	11494	725	900	1,250	—
1874, BG-843	11515	—	575	1,000	—

	GSID	AU-58	MS-60	MS-63	MS-65
1874, BG-844	11516	$325	$360	$650	—
1874, BG-845	11517	—	575	1,000	—
1875, BG-846	11549	470	725	1,250	—
1875, BG-847	11550	260	290	390	$950
1875, BG-848	11551	—	—	1,250	2,000
1876, BG-849	11588	340	360	490	—
1876, BG-850	11589	—	—	575	—
1876, BG-851	11590	—	—	—	1,400
1876, BG-852	11591	340	360	490	900
1876, BG-853	11592	340	360	490	900
1881, BG-853A	11635	—	—	—	—
1876, BG-854	11593	340	360	490	900
1876, BG-855	11594	1,250	—	—	5,000
1876, BG-856	11595	—	—	—	—
1871, BG-856A	11438	—	—	—	—
1871, BG-857	11428	260	290	360	1,000
1871, BG-859	11430	575	650	775	—
1871, BG-860	11431	—	—	525	—
1871, BG-861	11432	365	390	575	1,250
1871, BG-862	11433	—	650	1,250	2,500
1871, BG-864	11435	340	360	490	900
1871, BG-864A	11436	—	—	—	—
1871, BG-865	11437	340	360	490	950
1864, BG-866	11285	340	390	725	—
1870, BG-867	11384	260	290	390	1,250
1872, 2 Over 1, BG-868	11658	260	290	390	850
1872, 2 Over 1, BG-869	11659	260	290	390	575
1872, 2 Over 1, BG-870	11660	260	290	390	650
1873, BG-871	11495	—	775	1,050	—
1873, BG-872	11496	340	360	490	775
1873, BG-873	11497	—	—	—	—
1873, BG-874	11498	—	775	1,150	—
1874, BG-875	11518	310	340	525	775
1874, BG-876	11519	260	290	360	775
1875, BG-877	11552	340	360	490	—
1875, BG-878	11553	260	290	420	650
1876, BG-879	11596	260	290	390	725
1876, BG-880	11597	—	—	550	1,550
1876, BG-881	11598	340	360	525	950
1876, BG-882	11599	—	—	1,200	2,000
1878, 8 Over 6, BG-883	11678	260	290	455	850
1878, 8 Over 6, BG-884	11679	340	360	490	900
1880, 80 Over 76, BG-885	11685	325	365	470	775
1881, BG-886	11632	340	360	490	850
1881, BG-887	11633	260	290	390	650
1874, BG-888	11520	340	360	490	775
1868, BG-889	11330	260	290	390	650
1868, BG-890	11331	—	725	950	1,900
1852, BG-891	11129	260	290	390	650
1882, BG-892 (7–9 known)	11646	—	1,150	1,550	2,000
1881, BG-893	11634	—	—	—	—

California Gold Fifty Cents

	GSID	AU-58	MS-60	MS-63	MS-65
1853, BG-301	11172	$24,000	—	—	—
1853, BG-302	11173	1,750	$2,000	$2,750	$5,000
1853, BG-303	11174	10,500	—	—	—
1853, BG-304	11175	375	390	490	—
1854, BG-305	11221	360	390	525	1,000
1854, BG-306	11222	360	390	490	—
1856, BG-307	11252	455	525	1,000	4,900
1854, BG-308	11223	360	390	490	—
1855, BG-309	11239	490	525	1,150	—
1856, BG-310	11253	2,250	2,500	3,250	—
1856, BG-311	11254	600	650	925	—
1852, BG-401	11132	390	430	650	1,250
1853, BG-402	11176	—	—	—	—
1854, BG-403	11224	3,250	4,250	7,000	—
1854, BG-404	11225	—	—	—	—
1855, BG-405	11240	420	455	575	—
1855, BG-406	11241	—	900	—	—
1852, BG-407	11133	375	420	850	—
1853, BG-408	11177	1,200	1,400	2,050	6,000
1853, BG-409	11178	360	390	490	—
1853, BG-410	11179	—	—	—	—
1853, BG-411	11180	—	—	—	—
1853, BG-412	11181	—	—	—	—
1853, BG-413	11182	—	—	—	—
1853, BG-414	11183	525	625	—	—
1853, BG-415	11184	360	390	775	—
1853, BG-416	11185	2,250	2,500	6,250	—
1853, BG-416A	11196	—	—	—	—
1853, BG-417	11186	360	390	775	1,550
1853, BG-418	11187	—	—	5,500	—
1853, BG-419	11188	—	—	36,000	—
1853, BG-420	11189	—	7,500	9,750	—
1853, BG-421	11190	440	470	550	1,250
1853, BG-422	11191	—	—	9,750	—
1854, BG-422A	11232	—	—	—	—
1854, BG-423	11226	1,700	2,000	2,800	—
1854, BG-424	11227	—	4,400	—	—
1854, BG-425	11228	3,450	4,400	—	—
1852, BG-426	11134	—	—	—	—
1852, BG-427	11135	775	950	—	—
1853, BG-428	11192	340	375	525	2,250
1853, BG-429	11193	360	390	490	—
1853, BG-430	11194	325	360	470	725
1854, BG-431	11229	420	455	1,400	—
1855, BG-432	11242	360	390	900	—
1855, BG-433	11243	—	—	—	—
1856, BG-434	11255	360	390	575	—
1853, BG-435	11195	6,500	7,500	9,750	12,000
1854, BG-436	11230	3,500	4,000	18,000	—
1859, BG-901	11270	—	—	1,550	3,450
1859, BG-902	11271	240	275	455	1,500
1866, BG-903	11308	360	390	455	1,550
1866, BG-904	11309	—	—	—	—
1867, BG-905	11318	$360	$390	$525	$850
1868, BG-906	11336	240	275	455	575
1869, BG-907	11355	240	275	455	575
1870, BG-908	11391	360	390	525	1,000
1870, BG-909	11392	—	455	725	1,500
1871, BG-910	11454	390	455	650	1,250
1871, BG-911	11455	275	310	405	650
1871, BG-912	11456	240	285	415	750
1872, BG-913	11482	240	275	390	675
1872, BG-914	11483	290	325	420	775
1873, BG-915	11503	260	285	440	775
1856, BG-916	11256	1,150	1,500	—	—
1864, BG-917	11288	340	365	575	1,200
1864, BG-918	11289	240	285	725	1,600
1869, BG-919	11356	245	260	455	—
1870, BG-920	11393	245	260	455	—
1870, BG-921	11394	245	290	575	—
1870, BG-922	11395	240	275	370	—
1871, BG-923	11457	260	290	625	2,250
1871, BG-924	11458	240	275	370	850
1871, BG-925	11459	245	260	455	1,150
1871, BG-926	11460	490	550	950	2,500
1871, BG-927	11461	245	325	575	1,500
1873, BG-928	11504	775	850	—	—
1874, BG-929	11529	—	—	—	—
1874, BG-930	11530	245	260	455	1,150
1875, BG-930A	11566	—	—	—	—
1875/4, BG-931	11672	—	—	3,100	4,400
1876, BG-932	11610	245	290	550	850
1876, BG-932A	11615	—	—	—	—
1875, BG-933	11561	325	360	575	1,150
1875, BG-934	11562	360	390	575	1,150
1876, 1876 Over 6876, BG-935	11676	325	360	575	775
1870, BG-936	11396	325	360	575	1,150
1872, 2 Over 1, BG-937	11661	325	360	575	900
1872, BG-938	11484	—	—	725	1,550
1872, BG-939	11485	325	360	575	1,100
1872, BG-940	11486	245	290	550	850
1873, 3 Over 2, BG-941	11666	325	360	575	1,200
1873, BG-942	11505	325	360	575	1,200
1874, 4 Over 3, BG-943	11668	340	495	825	1,100
1874, BG-944	11531	—	—	390	—
1874, BG-944A	11534	—	—	5,500	—
1874, 4 Over 3, BG-945	11669	245	290	525	950
1875, BG-946	11563	245	290	525	1,150
1875, BG-947	11564	650	—	2,100	—
1875, BG-948	11565	245	290	525	1,400
1876, BG-949	11611	245	290	525	950
1876, BG-950	11612	—	—	950	2,500
1876, BG-951	11613	290	325	575	1,150
1878, 8 Over 6, BG-952	11681	245	290	525	1,400

California Gold Fifty Cents *(continued)*

	GSID	AU-58	MS-60	MS-63	MS-65
1880, BG-954	11623	$245	$290	$360	$725
1880, BG-955	11624	—	—	650	1,250
1881, BG-956	11638	245	290	525	850
1881, BG-957	11639	325	340	525	1,500
1881, BG-957A	11640	325	340	525	950
1874, BG-958	11532	325	340	525	950
1874, BG-958A	11535	—	—	—	—
1874, BG-959	11533	—	—	—	—
1868, BG-960	11337	—	—	850	1,400
1868, BG-960A	11339	—	—	850	1,400
1868, BG-961	11338	—	—	1,500	3,100
1852, BG-962	11136	—	—	—	3,100
1852, BG-962A	11138	—	—	—	—
1852, BG-963	11137	—	—	850	1,400
1881, BG-964	11641	—	—	850	1,400
1881, BG-965	11642	—	—	850	1,400
1881, BG-965A	11643	—	—	850	1,400
1882, BG-966	11647	—	—	1,800	4,400
1859, BG-1001	11266	—	—	4,500	—
1859, BG-1002	11267	245	290	525	850
1859, BG-1003	11268	—	—	1,250	—
1859, BG-1004	11269	390	455	950	—
1865, BG-1005	11297	325	360	525	1,250
1866, BG-1006	11306	325	360	525	750
1867, BG-1007	11316	245	290	360	775
1868, BG-1008	11332	325	360	525	850
1869, BG-1009	11352	325	360	490	725
1870, BG-1010	11386	245	260	325	775
1871, BG-1011	11440	280	290	375	675
1873, BG-1012	11499	325	360	525	1,150
1872, BG-1013	11479	360	390	575	—
1860, 60 Over 56, BG-1014	11655	360	390	575	1,150
1864, BG-1015	11286	1,300	1,550	—	—
1864, BG-1015A	11290	—	—	—	—
1864, BG-1016	11287	300	325	550	—
1864, BG-1016A	11291	1,550	—	4,400	—
1864, BG-1016B	11292	—	—	—	—
1866, BG-1017	11307	—	—	2,500	—
1867, BG-1018	11317	260	290	525	—
1868, BG-1019	11333	325	360	775	1,150
1869, BG-1020	11353	260	280	390	650
1869, BG-1021	11354	345	390	—	—
1870, BG-1022	11387	360	420	—	—
1870, BG-1023	11388	—	—	—	
1870, BG-1024	11389	260	280	420	1,250
1871, BG-1025	11441	370	390	675	—
1871, BG-1026	11442	260	280	390	650
1871, BG-1026A	11443	260	280	525	—
1871, BG-1027	11444	260	280	525	—
1871, BG-1028	11445	—	—	—	—
1871, BG-1029	11446	260	280	390	650

	GSID	AU-58	MS-60	MS-63	MS-65
1871, BG-1030	11447	$390	$455	$775	—
1873, BG-1031	11500	390	455	—	—
1873, BG-1032	11501	—	—	—	—
1874, BG-1033	11522	325	360	725	—
1874, BG-1034	11523	—	950	—	—
1875, BG-1035	11556	325	360	725	—
1875, BG-1036	11557	—	—	—	—
1875, BG-1037	11558	260	290	525	$900
1876, BG-1038	11600	260	280	390	850
1876, BG-1039	11601	850	—	—	—
1876, BG-1040	11602	325	360	725	—
1876, BG-1040A	11603	420	455	900	—
1871, BG-1041	11448	575	775	1,400	—
1871, BG-1042	11449	1,400	1,550	3,000	—
1871, BG-1043	11450	1,400	1,550	4,400	—
1871, BG-1044	11451	—	—	1,400	—
1871, BG-1045	11452	340	360	650	—
1871, BG-1046	11453	—	—	1,750	2,800
1870, BG-1047	11390	260	280	390	650
1872, BG-1048	11480	260	280	455	950
1872, BG-1049	11481	260	280	390	850
1873, 3 Over 2, BG-1050	11665	—	—	775	1,900
1873, BG-1051	11502	—	—	525	950
1874, 4 Over 3, BG-1052	11667	260	280	390	725
1874, BG-1053	11524	390	420	525	1,250
1874, BG-1054	11525	—	—	1,900	—
1874, BG-1055	11526	260	280	525	1,000
1875, BG-1056	11559	290	325	490	1,000
1875, BG-1057	11560	260	290	575	1,100
1875, 5 Over 3, BG-1058	11671	260	280	625	1,200
1876, 6 Over 5, BG-1059	11675	325	360	650	1,250
1876, BG-1060	11604	360	390	650	1,250
1876, BG-1061	11605	—	—	4,400	—
1876, BG-1062	11606	—	—	—	
1876, BG-1063	11607	420	455	775	1,900
1876, BG-1064	11608	—	—	725	—
1876, BG-1065	11609	—	—	575	1,250
1878, 8 Over 6, BG-1066	11680	—	—	575	—
1880, 80 Over 70, BG-1067	11684	360	390	525	1,150
1880, BG-1068	11622	—	—	1,100	1,300
1881, BG-1069	11636	260	280	390	850
1881, BG-1070	11637	260	290	525	1,100
1874, BG-1071	11527	1,500	1,600	2,100	3,750
1874, BG-1072	11528	—	—	1,000	1,900
1868, BG-1073	11334	—	1,750	3,000	—
1868, BG-1074	11335	—	525	625	1,250
1852, BG-1075	11130	—	—	1,900	3,000
1852, BG-1076	11131	360	390	625	—
1882, BG-1077	11645	1,200	1,250	1,500	—
Cal. Gold, BG-1078	11854	—	—	7,500	—
Cal. Gold, BG-1079	11855	—	11,000	—	—

California Gold Dollar

	GSID	AU-58	MS-60	MS-63	MS-65
Undated, BG-501	11836	$4,100	$9,000	$15,000	—
1853, BG-502	11139	—	—	—	—
1853, BG-503	11140	24,000	29,000	—	—
1854, BG-504	11197	3,550	3,900	9,500	—
1853, BG-505	11141	1,150	1,250	2,250	$3,750
1854, BG-506	11198	12,000	13,000	20,000	—
1854, BG-507	11199	1,950	2,300	5,000	—
1854, BG-508	11200	650	900	1,600	—
1854, BG-509	11201	2,750	3,750	7,500	—
1854, BG-510	11202	900	1,000	2,250	7,000
1855, 5 Over 4, BG-511	11652	875	1,000	2,000	—
1856, BG-512	11244	—	—	—	—
1854, BG-513	11203	—	—	—	—
1853, BG-514	11142	850	1,000	1,800	4,050
1853, BG-515	11143	—	—	—	—
1853, BG-516	11144	—	—	—	—
1853, BG-517	11145	—	—	—	—
1853, BG-518	11146	775	1,100	1,950	—
1853, BG-519	11147	725	775	1,750	—
1853, BG-520	11148	—	—	—	—
1853, BG-521	11149	—	—	—	—
1853, BG-522	11150	6,000	—	—	—
1853, BG-523	11151	1,000	1,050	—	—
1853, BG-524	11152	1,500	2,250	—	—
1853, BG-525	11153	1,950	3,000	6,250	—
1853, BG-526	11154	3,000	4,000	—	—
1853, BG-526a	152320	—	—	—	—
1854, BG-527	11204	—	—	—	—
1854, BG-528	11205	2,600	3,900	—	—
1854, BG-529	11206	18,000	—	—	—
1853, BG-530	11155	650	825	1,250	—
1853, BG-531	11156	725	800	1,400	—
1854, BG-532	11207	775	1,000	2,750	—
1855, BG-533	11233	850	900	1,900	3,450
1854, BG-534	11208	—	—	—	—
1854, BG-601	11209	—	—	—	—
1854, BG-602	11210	—	—	—	—
1854, BG-603	11211	—	—	—	—
1853, BG-604	11157	—	—	—	—
1854, BG-605	11212	14,500	—	—	—
1854, BG-606	11213	—	—	—	—
1857, BG-607	11257	—	—	—	—
1859, BG-1101	11259	—	—	—	—
1860, BG-1102	11272	650	725	1,250	2,200
1860, BG-1103	11273	—	—	—	—
1871, BG-1104	11397	650	775	1,200	3,750
1868, BG-1105	11319	$575	$625	$1,100	—
1869, BG-1106	11340	725	850	1,500	$3,450
1870, BG-1107	11357	950	1,000	1,900	4,400
1870, BG-1108	11358	—	—	3,100	—
1871, BG-1109	11398	675	775	1,250	3,100
1874, BG-1110	11506	—	—	3,250	—
1875, BG-1111	11536	—	—	—	—
1875, BG-1112	11537	650	900	1,200	—
1876, BG-1113	11567	—	—	—	—
1876, BG-1114	11568	—	—	4,700	—
1876, BG-1115	11569	—	—	3,000	—
1876, BG-1115A	11572	—	—	—	—
1876, BG-1116	11570	1,900	2,200	3,100	—
1876, BG-1117	11571	—	—	9,500	—
1876, BG-1117A	11573	—	—	—	—
1870, BG-1118	11359	850	950	1,600	—
1872, BG-1119	11462	1,900	2,000	2,400	—
1872, BG-1120	11463	1,100	1,250	2,500	3,450
1873, 3 Over 2, BG-1121	11662	1,250	1,550	2,800	—
1873, 3 Over 2, BG-1122	11663	1,200	1,500	3,750	5,500
1873, BG-1123	11487	675	850	1,900	4,400
1874, BG-1124	11507	875	950	1,300	3,100
1875, BG-1125	11538	850	950	1,500	2,600
1875, BG-1126	11539	1,200	1,400	2,050	3,750
1875, BG-1127	11540	850	950	1,500	—
1876, 6 Over 5, BG-1128	11673	850	950	1,700	2,750
1876, 6 Over 5, BG-1129	11674	775	900	1,750	3,500
1871, BG-1201	11399	1,900	2,050	3,750	—
1870, BG-1202	11360	1,250	1,400	—	—
1870, BG-1203	11361	1,750	2,000	5,000	—
1871, BG-1204	11400	1,750	2,200	5,000	—
1870, BG-1205	11362	1,600	1,900	3,750	—
1872, BG-1206	11464	3,100	3,750	—	—
1872, BG-1207	11465	1,200	1,400	2,500	6,250
1872, BG-1208	11466	1,900	2,800	3,750	—
1857, BG-1301	84520	—	—	550	—
1857, BG-1301A	84526	—	—	275	390
1855, BG-1302	84521	—	—	—	—
1868, BG-1303	84522	285	325	455	—
1854, BG-1304	84523	490	—	775	1,500
1854, BG-1304A	84527	—	—	—	260
1858, BG-1306	84524	—	—	—	—
1863, BG-1307	84525	—	—	—	—
1863, BG-1307A	84528	—	—	280	310
1858, BG-1323	84529	—	—	—	—
1858, BG-1324	84530	—	—	—	—

CALIFORNIA GOLD INGOT BARS

During the Gold Rush era, gold coins, ingots, and "dust" (actually flakes and nuggets) were sent by steamship from San Francisco to other ports, most importantly to New York City and London, where the gold was sold or, in some instances, sent to mints for conversion into coins. The typical procedure in the mid-1850s was to send the gold by steamship from San Francisco to Panama, where it was transported across 48 miles of territory by small water craft and pack animals from 1849 until the Panama Railroad opened in 1855, then loaded aboard another ship at the town of Aspinwall on the Atlantic side. On September 12, 1857, the SS *Central America*, en route from Aspinwall to New York City with more than 475 passengers, over 100 crew members, and an estimated $2.6 million in gold (in an era in which pure gold was valued at $20.67 per ounce) was lost at sea. Miraculously, more than 150 people, including all but one of the women and children, were rescued by passing ships. The *Central America* went to the bottom of the Atlantic Ocean off the Carolina coast.

In the 1980s a group of researchers secured financing to search for the long-lost ship. After much study and many explorations, they discovered the wreck of the *Central America* 7,200 feet below the surface. They used the robotic *Nemo*, a sophisticated device weighing several tons, to photograph the wreck and to carefully bring to the surface many artifacts. A king's ransom in gold ingots was found, along with more than 7,500 coins, the latter mostly consisting of Mint State 1857-S double eagles.

The 500-plus gold ingots furnished a unique opportunity to study specimens that, after conservation, were essentially in the same condition as they had been in 1857. These bore the imprints of five different California assayers, who operated seven offices. With few exceptions, each ingot bears individual stamps, indicating its maker, a serial number, the weight in ounces, the fineness (expressed in thousandths, e.g., .784 indicating 784/1000 pure gold), and the 1857 value in dollars. The smallest bar found was issued by Blake & Co., weighed 4.95 ounces, was .795 fine, and was stamped with a value of $81.34. The largest ingot, dubbed the "Eureka bar," bore the imprint of Kellogg & Humbert, and was stamped with a weight of 933.94 ounces, .903 fine, and a value of $17,433.57.

Blake & Co., Sacramento, California: From December 28, 1855, to May 1858, Blake & Co. was operated by Gorham Blake and W.R. Waters. • 34 ingots recovered. Serial numbers in the 5,100 and 5,200 series. Lowest weight and value: 4.95 ounces, $81.34. Highest weight and value: 157.40 ounces, $2,655.05. These bars have beveled or "dressed" edges and may have seen limited use in California commerce.

Harris, Marchand & Co., Sacramento and Marysville: This firm was founded in Sacramento in 1855 by Harvey Harris and Desiré Marchand, with Charles L. Farrington as the "& Co." The Marysville office was opened in January 1856. Serial numbers in the 6000 series are attributed to Sacramento, comprising 36 bars; a single bar in the 7000 series (7095) is attributed to Marysville. The Marchand bars each have a circular coin-style counterstamp on the face. Lowest weight and value (Sacramento): 9.87 ounces, $158.53. Highest weight and value (Sacramento): 295.20 ounces, $5,351.73. • Unique Marysville bar: 174.04 ounces, $3,389.06.

Henry Hentsch, San Francisco: Hentsch, a Swiss, was an entrepreneur involved in banking, real estate, assaying, and other ventures. In February 1856, he opened an assay office as an annex to his bank. It is likely that many of his ingots were exported to Europe, where he had extensive banking connections. • 33 ingots recovered. Lowest weight and value: 12.52 ounces, $251.82. Highest weight and value: 238.84 ounces, $4,458.35.

Justh & Hunter, San Francisco and Marysville: Emanuel Justh, a Hungarian, was a lithographer in San Francisco in the early 1850s. In 1854 and 1855 he worked as assistant assayer at the San Francisco Mint. Solomon Hillen Hunter came to California from Baltimore. The Justh & Hunter partnership was announced in May 1855. • Although study is continuing, the 60 ingots in the 4000 series are tentatively attributed to San Francisco, and the 26 ingots in the 9000 series are attributed to Marysville. • San Francisco—Lowest weight and value: 5.24 ounces, $92.18. Highest weight and value: 866.19 ounces, $15,971.93. • Marysville—Lowest weight and value: 19.34 ounces, $356.21. Highest weight and value: 464.65 ounces, $8,759.90.

Kellogg & Humbert, San Francisco: John Glover Kellogg and Augustus Humbert, two of the most famous names in the minting of California gold coins, formed the partnership of Kellogg & Humbert in spring 1855. The firm was one of the most active of all California assayers during the mid-1850s. • 346 ingots recovered, constituting the majority of those found. • Lowest weight and value: 5.71 ounces, $101.03. Highest weight and value: 933.94 ounces, $17,433.57.

A selection of gold ingots from the SS *Central America* treasure (with an 1857-S double eagle shown for scale, near lower left). (1) Harris, Marchand & Co., Marysville office, serial number 7095, 174.04 ounces, .942 fine, $3,389.06 (all values as stamped in 1857). (2) Henry Hentsch, San Francisco, serial number 3120, 61.93 ounces, .886 fine, $1,134.26. (3) Kellogg & Humbert, San Francisco, serial number 215, .944 fine, $1,045.96. (4) Blake & Co., Sacramento, 19.30 ounces, .946 fine, $297.42. (5) Another Blake & Co. ingot, serial number 5216, .915 fine, $266.12. (6) Justh & Hunter, Marysville office, serial number 9440, 41.79 ounces, $761.07. (7) Justh & Hunter, San Francisco office, serial number 4243, 51.98 ounces, .916 fine, $984.27. (8) Harris, Marchand & Co., Sacramento office, serial number 6514, 35.33 ounces, .807 fine, $589.38. (9) Harris, Marchand & Co., Sacramento office, serial number 6486, 12.64 ounces, .950 fine, $245.00.

Private Tokens

Privately issued tokens are by no means an American invention. They were common to most capitalist nations in the 1800s (and known even earlier), created and circulated by businessmen and others in periods of economic weakness or uncertainty, during financial panics, depressions, and times of war. Sometimes they were handed out as advertising trinkets or political propaganda pieces; more often they passed as makeshift currency when few real coins were available to make small change. Unlike real coins, which are government-issued as legal tender, tokens are minted by private citizens and companies. Commonly made of metal, usually round in shape, coins and tokens are very similar in appearance, but a token lacks a coin's official status as government-backed currency. Typically it would only have trade value, and then only in the vicinity in which it was issued (if, for example, a local merchant was prepared to redeem it in goods or services).

This section describes several of the more commonly encountered American tokens of the 1800s.

HARD TIMES TOKENS (1832–1844)

Hard Times tokens, as they are called, are pieces of Americana dating from the era of presidents Andrew Jackson and Martin Van Buren. They are mostly the size of a contemporary large copper cent. Privately minted from 1832 to 1844, they display diverse motifs reflecting political campaigns and satire of the era as well as carrying advertisements for merchants, products, and services. For many years these have been a popular specialty within numismatics, helped along with the publication of *Hard Times Tokens* by Lyman H. Low (1899; revised edition, 1906) and later works, continuing to the present day (see the *Guide Book of Hard Times Tokens*, 2015). In 1899 Low commented (adapted) that "the issues commonly called Hard Times tokens . . . had no semblance of authority behind them. They combine the character of political pieces with the catch-words of party cries; of satirical pieces with sarcastic allusions to the sentiments or speeches of the leaders of opposing parties; and in some degree also of necessity pieces, in a time when, to use one of the phrases of the day, 'money was a cash article,' hard to get for daily needs."

Although examples from the earlier 1830s are designated as Hard Times tokens, the true Hard Times period started in a serious way on May 10, 1837, when banks began suspending specie payments and would no longer exchange paper currency for coins. This date is memorialized on some of the token inscriptions. Difficult economic conditions continued through 1843; the first full year of recovery was 1844. From March 1837 to March 1841, President Martin Van Buren vowed to "follow in the steps of my illustrious predecessor," President Andrew Jackson, who had been in office from March 1829 until Van Buren's inauguration. Jackson was perhaps the most controversial president up to that time. His veto in 1832 of the impending (1836) recharter of the Bank of the United States set off a political firestorm, and the flames were fanned when his administration shifted deposits to favored institutions, derisively called "pet banks."

The Jackson era was one of unbridled prosperity. Due to sales of land in the West, the expansion of railroads, and a robust economy, so much money piled up in the Treasury that distributions were made in 1835 to all of the states. Seeking to end wild speculation, Jackson issued the "Specie Circular" on July 11, 1836, mandating that purchases of Western land, often made on credit, by paper money of uncertain worth, or by non-cash means, had to be paid in silver or gold coins. Almost immediately, the land boom settled and prices stabilized. A chill began to spread across the economy, which worsened in early 1837. Finally, many banks ran short of ready cash, causing the specie suspension.

After May 10, 1837, silver and gold coins completely disappeared from circulation. Copper cents remained, but were in short supply. Various diesinkers and others produced a flood of copper tokens. These were sold at discounts to merchants and banks, with $6 for 1,000 tokens being typical. Afterward, they were paid out in commerce and circulated for the value of one cent.

The actions of Jackson, the financial tribulations that many thought he precipitated, and the policies of Van Buren inspired motifs for a class of Hard Times tokens today known as "politicals." Several hundred other varieties were made with the advertisements of merchants, services, and products and are known as "store cards" or "merchants' tokens." Many of these were illustrated with elements such as a shoe, umbrella, comb, coal stove, storefront, hotel, or carriage.

One of the more famous issues depicts a slave kneeling in chains, with the motto "Am I Not a Woman & a Sister?" This token was issued in 1838, when abolition was a major rallying point for many Americans in the North. The curious small-size Feuchtwanger cents of 1837, made in Feuchtwanger's Composition (a type of German silver), were proposed to Congress as a cheap substitute for copper cents, but no congressional action was taken. Lewis Feuchtwanger produced large quantities on his own account and circulated them extensively (see page 1264).

As the political and commercial motifs of Hard Times tokens are so diverse, and reflect the American economy and political scene of their era, numismatists have found them fascinating to collect and study. Although there are major rarities in the series, most of the issues are very affordable. Expanded information concerning more than 500 varieties of Hard Times tokens can be found in Russell Rulau's *Standard Catalog of United States Tokens, 1700–1900* (fourth edition). Collectors and researchers are also encouraged to consult *A Guide Book of Hard Times Tokens* (Bowers). A representative selection is illustrated here.

L1, HT1

L57, HT76

L4, HT6

L56, HT75

	VF	EF	AU
L1, HT1. Andrew Jackson. Copper	$5,000	$8,500	—
L57, HT76. Van Buren Facing Left. Brass	2,200	3,250	$4,250
L4, HT6. Jackson President of the U.S. Brass	200	325	750
L56, HT75. Van Buren Facing Left. Copper	80	160	375

L66, HT24 · L54, HT81 · L55, HT63

L31, HT46 · L8, HT9 · L18, HT32

L51, HT70 · L47, HT66 · L60, HT18

L44, HT69 · L59, HT17 · L65, HT23

	VF	EF	AU
L66, HT24. Agriculture. Copper	$225	$350	$650
L54, HT81. A Woman & A Sister. Copper	180	300	500
L55, HT63. Loco Foco, 1838. Copper	55	160	275
L31, HT46. Not One Cent, Motto. Copper	45	60	135
L8, HT9. My Victory / Jackson. Copper	40	90	125
L18, HT32. Executive Experiment. Copper	30	65	110
L51, HT70. Roman Firmness. Copper	35	70	125
L47, HT66. Phoenix / May Tenth. Copper	25	65	110
L60, HT18. Ship/Lightning. Copper	25	65	110
L44, HT69. Ship/Jackson. Copper	25	70	125
L59, HT17. Ship / Wreath Border. Copper	25	65	110
L65, HT23. Ship / Liberty Head. Copper	100	200	350

FEUCHTWANGER TOKENS (1837–1864)

Lewis Feuchtwanger, a German-born chemist, moved to the United States in 1829 and settled in New York City. He produced a variety of German silver (an alloy of metals not including any actual silver) consisting of nickel, copper, and some zinc. Feuchtwanger suggested to Congress as early as 1837 that his metal be substituted for copper in U.S. coinage, and he made one-cent and three-cent trial pieces that circulated freely during the coin shortage of 1836 through 1844.

	GSID	VF-20	EF-40	AU-50	MS-60	MS-63
1837 One Cent, Eagle	15256	$155	$230	$310	$455	$675
1837 Three-Cent, New York Coat of Arms	15258	1,300	1,750	2,750	5,500	9,500
1837 Three-Cent, Eagle	15257	2,000	3,750	5,500	9,000	14,500
1864 Three-Cent, Eagle	15259	1,750	3,100	4,400	7,000	9,500

CIVIL WAR TOKENS (1860s)

Early Friday morning, April 12, 1861, the Confederate States Army fired shells from 10-inch siege mortars into the Union's Fort Sumter in Charleston Bay, South Carolina, touching off the American Civil War. The ensuing turmoil would bring many changes to America's financial and monetary systems, including a dramatic reworking of the banking structure, federalization of paper money, bold innovations in taxation, tariffs, and land grants, and radical government experiments in new kinds of currency. For the man on the street, one daily noticeable development of the war was the large-scale hoarding of coins, which began in late 1861 and early 1862—people squirreled away first their gold, then silver coins, and finally, as the war dragged on that summer, even small copper-nickel cents. This caused trouble for day-to-day commerce. There were no coins to buy a newspaper or a glass of soda, to get a haircut, or tip a doorman. The situation gave birth to the humble but ubiquitous Civil War token.

Tokens were a familiar sight on the American scene by the time the Civil War was ignited. In fact, Americans had been using tokens as monetary substitutes since the colonial era, during the early days of the new nation, and throughout the 1800s. Two main kinds of tokens entered into American commerce during the war: *patriotics*, so called for their political and nationalistic themes; and *store cards*, or merchant tokens. An estimated 50 million or more were issued—more than two for every man, woman, and child in the Union. Civil War tokens were mostly a Northern phenomenon; not surprising, considering that New York State alone produced four times as much manufacturing as the entire Confederacy at the start of the war. Southerners had to make do with weak government-backed paper money, which quickly depreciated in value; Yankee tradesmen had the industrial base and financial means to produce a hard-money substitute that at least *looked* like money, even if it was backed by nothing more substantial than a local grocery store's promise to accept it at the value of one cent.

Most Civil War tokens were made of copper, some were brass, and rare exceptions were struck in copper-nickel or white metal. In addition to patriotics and store cards, some issuers crafted *numismatic* tokens during the war. These were struck for collectors rather than for day-to-day commerce, and made in the typical alloys as well as (rarely) in silver and other metals. Some were overstruck on dimes or copper-nickel cents.

Many kinds of tokens and medals were issued during the war. This sometimes leads to the question, "What, exactly, counts as a *Civil War token?*" How about the small hard-rubber checks and tickets, in various shapes, of that era? Or encased postage stamps, another small-change substitute of the war years? Or sutler tokens, issued by registered vendors who supplied the Union Army and traveled with the troops? These and more are sometimes collected along with the main body of about 10,000 varieties of store cards and patriotics. There is a long tradition of collecting Civil War tokens, dating back to even before the end of the war, and the hobby community has developed various habits and traditions over the years. Ultimately what to include in a collection is up to the individual collector. The Civil War Token Society (www.cwtsociety.com), the preeminent club for today's collector, suggests that to be "officially" considered a Civil War token, a piece must be between 18 and 25 mm in diameter. (Most of the copper tokens issued to pass as currency during the war were 18 or 19 mm, the size of the federal government's relatively new Flying Eagle and Indian Head cents, introduced in the late 1850s.)

Civil War tokens can be collected by state and by city, by type of issuer (druggist, saloonkeeper, doctor, etc.), or by any number of designs and themes. If you live in New York City and would like to study store cards issued by local shops and businesses, you have hundreds to choose from. You might hail from a small town and still be able to find a Civil War token from where you grew up. In 1863 in Oswego, New York, M.L. Marshall—a general-store seller of the unlikely combination of toys, fancy goods, fishing tackle, and rare coins—issued a cent-sized copper token featuring a fish! Undertakers issued store cards with tiny coffins advertising their services. Booksellers, bootmakers, beer brewers, hat dealers, and hog butchers all pictured their products on small copper tokens. On the patriotic side, Civil War tokens show Abraham Lincoln, various wartime presidential candidates, national heroes, cannons at the ready, unfurled flags, defiant eagles, and soldiers on horseback. They shout out the slogans of the day, warning the South of the strength of THE ARMY & NAVY, urging Americans to STAND BY THE FLAG, and insisting that THE FEDERAL UNION MUST AND SHALL BE PRESERVED.

Many tokens were more or less faithful imitations of the federal copper-nickel Indian Head cent. A few of this type have the word NOT in small letters above the words ONE CENT. For a time the legal status of the Civil War tokens was uncertain. Mint Director James Pollock thought they were illegal; however, there was no law prohibiting the issue of tradesmen's tokens or of private coins not in imitation of U.S. coins. Finally a law was passed April 22, 1864, prohibiting the private issue of any one- or two-cent coins, tokens, or devices for use as money, and on June 8 another law was passed that abolished private coinage of every kind. By that summer the government's new bronze Indian Head cents, minted in the tens of millions, were plentiful in circulation.

Today Civil War tokens as a class are very accessible for collectors. Store-card tokens of Illinois, Massachusetts, Michigan, New York, Ohio, Pennsylvania, and Wisconsin are among those most frequently seen. A collector seeking special challenges will hunt for tokens from Iowa, Kansas, Maryland, and Minnesota—and, on the Confederate side, from Alabama, Louisiana (a counterstamped Indian Head cent), and Tennessee.

Three pieces of advice will serve the beginning collector. First, read the standard reference books, including *Patriotic Civil War Tokens* and *U.S. Civil War Store Cards*, both classics by George and Melvin Fuld, and the *Guide Book of Civil War Tokens*, by Q. David Bowers. These books lay the foundation and offer inspiration for building your own collection. Second, join the Civil War Token Society. This will put you in touch with other collectors who offer mentoring, friendship, and information. Third, visit a coin show and start looking for Civil War tokens in the inventories of the dealers there. Above all, enjoy the hobby and the many paths and byways it can lead you on through this important and turbulent era of American history.

Values shown are for the most common tokens in each composition.

	F	VF	EF	MS-63
Copper or Brass	$20	$30	$40	$150
Nickel or German Silver	55	75	130	290
White Metal	80	125	150	275
Copper-Nickel	75	125	175	325
Silver	200	300	500	1,200

Patriotic Civil War Tokens

Patriotic Civil War tokens feature leaders such as Abraham Lincoln; military images such as cannons or ships; and sociopolitical themes popular in the North, such as flags and slogans. Thousands of varieties are known.

	F	VF	AU	MS-63
Lincoln	$40	$85	$150	$300
Monitor	30	50	125	250
"Wealth of the South" (a)	200	400	600	1,000
Various common types	20	30	55	125

a. Dated 1860, but sometimes collected along with Civil War tokens.

Civil War Store Cards

Tradesmen's tokens of the Civil War era are often called store cards. These are typically collected by geographical location or by topic. The Fuld text (see bibliography) catalogs store cards by state, city, merchant, die combination, and metal. Values shown below are for the most common tokens for each state. Tokens from obscure towns or from merchants who issued only a few can be priced into the thousands of dollars and are widely sought.

	VG	VF	AU	MS-63
Alabama	$1,500	$3,000	$4,000	$6,500
Connecticut	15	30	55	150
Washington, D.C.	—	1,000	1,400	2,200
Idaho	400	700	1,300	—
Illinois	15	30	55	150
Indiana	15	35	65	150
Iowa	150	450	550	1,250
Kansas	900	2,500	3,500	5,500
Kentucky	50	125	200	350
Louisiana	2,000	3,500	4,500	—

	VG	VF	AU	MS-63
Maine	$50	$100	$200	$400
Maryland	150	350	550	1,000
Massachusetts	15	35	60	150
Michigan	15	30	55	150
Minnesota	150	450	550	750
Missouri	40	100	150	250
New Hampshire	80	130	175	300
New Jersey	15	30	55	150
New York	15	30	55	150
Ohio	15	30	55	150
Pennsylvania	15	30	55	150
Rhode Island	15	30	55	150
Tennessee	300	650	1,200	1,750
Virginia	250	500	1,000	—
West Virginia	55	120	225	500
Wisconsin	20	35	60	150
Sutlers' (a)	185	375	500	800

a. Sutler tokens were issued by registered contractors who operated camp stores that traveled with the military. These were made by coiners who also produced Civil War tokens, including John Stanton, Shubael Childs, and Francis X. Koehler. Each had a denomination, typically 5 cents to 50 cents. Some used on one side a die also used on Civil War tokens.

DC500A-1h

IN190D-3a

MI865A-1a

MN980A-1a

MO910A-2a

NY630AQ-4a

NY630Z-1a

OH165M-1a

NY630BJ-1a

WI510M-1a

PA750F-1a

WV890D-4a

	VG	VF	AU	MS-63
MI865A-1a, W. Darling, Saranac, MI, 1864	$7,500	$12,000	$15,000	—
MN980A-1a. C. Benson, Druggist, Winona, MN	300	700	900	$1,500
M0910A-4a. Drovers Hotel, St. Louis, MO, 1863	125	300	600	1,250
NY630AQ-4a. Gustavus Lindenmueller, New York, 1863	15	30	55	125
NY630Z-1a. Fr. Freise, Undertaker, New York, 1863	20	40	85	165
OH165M-1a. B.P. Belknp., "Teeth Extracted Without Pain"	125	250	400	700
NY630BJ-1a. Sanitary Commission, New York, 1864	400	850	1,100	1,750
WI510M-1a. Goes & Falk Malt House & Brewery, Milwaukee, WI, 1863	25	65	125	250
PA750F-1a. M.C. Campbell's Dancing Academy, Philadelphia, PA	20	35	50	150
WV890D-4a. R.C. Graves, News Dealer, Wheeling, WV, 1863	55	120	225	500

LESHER REFERENDUM DOLLARS (1900–1901)

Distributed in 1900 and 1901 by Joseph Lesher of Victor, Colorado, these private tokens manufactured in Denver were used in trade to some extent, and stocked by various merchants who redeemed them in goods. Lesher was an Ohio-born Civil War veteran and, after the war, an early pioneer of Colorado's mining fields. His coins, octagonal in shape, were numbered and a blank space left at bottom of 1901 issues, in which were stamped names of businessmen who bought them. All are quite rare; many varieties are extremely rare. Their composition is .950 fine silver (alloyed with copper). Lesher Referendum Dollars (tokens) are extensively cataloged and identified in the 2008 edition of *So-Called Dollars*, by Harold E. Hibler and Charles V. Kaplan.

	Mintage	GSID	EF-40	AU-50	AU-58	MS-60
1900, Bumstead, First Type, HK-787	100	15260	$3,750	$4,000	$5,000	$6,000
1900, Bumstead Type, First Reverse, HK-788	210	15261	—	3,000	3,600	3,750
1900, Bumstead Type, Second Reverse, HK-789	500	15263	3,000	3,450	4,600	5,000
1900, Bumstead Type, No Mountain Obverse, Second Reverse, HK-1016		79196	—	—	—	—
1900, Bank Type, HK-790	10	15264	—	—	—	—
1901, Imprint Type, HK-791		15275	—	3,750	4,750	5,500
1901, Imprint Type, Slusher stamp, HK-792	260	15279	3,300	3,750	6,250	—
1901, Imprint Type, Cohen stamp, HK-793	50	15269	8,750	11,000	—	—
1901, Imprint Type, Klein stamp, HK-794	100	15271	—	17,000	—	—
1901, Imprint Type, Mullen stamp, HK-795	100	15270	—	5,500	—	—
1901, Imprint Type, Boyd Park stamp, HK-796	150	15267	—	—	4,100	4,500
1901, Imprint Type, Alexander stamp, HK-797	50	15272	15,500	17,500	—	—
1901, Imprint Type, Goodspeeds stamp, HK-1017	15	79197	—	—	—	—
1901, Imprint Type, Nelson stamp, HK-1018	50	79198	—	—	—	—
1901, Imprint Type, White stamp, HK-1019	50	79199	—	—	—	—
1901, Imprint Type, Stein stamp, HK-1020		79200	—	—	—	—
1901, Imprint Type, Rosser stamp, HK-1021		79201	—	—	—	—
1901, Imprint Type, Clark stamp, HK-1021a	unique	79916	—	—	—	—

Confederate Issues

The Confederate States of America proclaimed itself in February 1861, a few weeks after Abraham Lincoln was elected president of the United States in November 1860. The newly formed nation based its monetary system on the Confederate dollar. Its paper currency was backed not by hard assets (such as gold) but by the promise to pay the bearer after the war was over—assuming Southern victory and independence. In addition to paper money, the Confederacy also explored creating its own coinage for day-to-day circulation. While this goal never came to fruition, interesting relics remain as testaments to the effort.

CONFEDERATE CENTS

Facts about the creation of the original Confederate cents are shrouded in mystery. However, a plausible storyline has developed based on research and recollections, through telling and retelling over the years. An order to make cents for the Confederacy is said to have been placed with Robert Lovett Jr., an engraver and diesinker of Philadelphia, through Bailey & Co., a jewelry firm of that city. Fearing arrest by the United States government for assisting the enemy, Lovett decided instead to hide the coins and the dies in his cellar. Captain John W. Haseltine, well known for finding numismatic rarities unknown to others, claimed that a bartender had received one of the coins over the counter and sold it to him. Haseltine recognized it as the work of Lovett, called on him, learned that he had struck 12 of the coins, and bought the remaining 11 and the dies. In 1874 Haseltine made restrikes in copper, silver, and gold.

Circa 1961, the dies were copied and additional pieces made by New York City coin dealer Robert Bashlow. These show prominent die cracks and rust marks that distinguish them from earlier examples.

	Mintage	GSID	MS-60	MS-62	MS-63	MS-65
1861 Cent, Original, Copper-Nickel, Uncirculated	13–16	15303	—	$186,000	$258,000	—
	Auctions: $216,000, PCGS MS-63 HA 05/24					
1861 Cent, Haseltine 1874 Restrike, Copper, Proof	55	15307	—	29,000	36,000	$57,500
1861 Cent, Haseltine 1874 Restrike, Gold, Proof	7	1210	—	—	78,000	—
1861 Cent, Haseltine 1874 Restrike, Silver, Proof	12	1211	—	72,000	114,000	—
	Auctions: $114,000, PCGS PF-63 SBG 11/24					
1861 Cent, 1961 Bashlow Restrike, Copper, Proof		69439	—	—	40	60
1861 Cent, 1961 Bashlow Restrike, Brass, Uncirculated		376885	$40	47	50	70
1861 Cent, 1961 Bashlow Restrike, Silver, Uncirculated		69440	—	—	70	100

CONFEDERATE HALF DOLLARS

According to records, only four original Confederate half dollars were struck (on a hand press). Regular silver planchets were used, as well as a regular federal obverse die. One of the coins was given to Secretary of the Treasury Christopher G. Memminger, who passed it on to President Jefferson Davis for his approval. Another was given to Professor John L. Riddell of the University of Louisiana. Edward Ames of New Orleans received a third specimen. The last was kept by chief coiner Benjamin F. Taylor. Lack of bullion prevented the Confederacy from coining more pieces.

The Confederate half dollar was unknown to collectors until 1879, when a specimen and its reverse die were found in Taylor's possession in New Orleans. E. Mason Jr., of Philadelphia, purchased both and later sold them to J.W. Scott and Company of New York. J.W. Scott acquired 500 genuine 1861-O half dollars, routed or otherwise smoothed away the reverses, and then restamped them with the Confederate die. Known as restrikes, these usually have slightly flattened obverses. Scott also struck some medals in white metal using the Confederate reverse die and an obverse die bearing this inscription: 4 ORIGINALS STRUCK BY ORDER OF C.S.A. IN NEW ORLEANS 1861 / ******* / REV. SAME AS U.S. (FROM ORIGINAL DIE•SCOTT)

Confederate Reverse

Scott Obverse

	Mintage	GSID	VF-20	EF-40	AU-50	AU-55	MS-60
1861 HALF DOL., Original	4 known	15304	—	$1,020,000	—	—	—
	Auctions: $960,000, NGC EF-40 HA 11/17						
1861 HALF DOL., Restrike	500	15305	$3,550	5,500	$7,750	$9,000	$11,000
1861 Scott Obverse, Confederate Reverse	500	15306	2,750	3,250	3,900	4,100	4,400

Hawaiian and Puerto Rican Issues

Although the following issues of Hawaii and Puerto Rico were not circulating U.S. coins, they have political, artistic, and sentimental connections to the United States. Generations of American numismatists have sought them for their collections.

HAWAIIAN ISSUES

Five official coins were issued for the Kingdom of Hawaii. These include the 1847 cent issued by King Kamehameha III and the 1883 silver dimes, quarters, halves, and dollars of King Kalakaua I. The silver pieces were all designed by U.S. Mint chief engraver Charles E. Barber and struck at the San Francisco Mint. The 1883 eighth-dollar piece is a pattern. The 1881 five-cent piece is an unofficial issue.

The Hawaiian dollar was officially valued equal to the U.S. dollar. After Hawaii became a U.S. territory in 1900, the legal-tender status of these coins was removed and most were withdrawn from circulation and melted.

1847, One Cent

1881, Five Cents
Unofficial issue.

1883, Ten Cents

1883, Quarter Dollar

1883, Half Dollar

1883, Dollar

Circulation Strikes

	Mintage	GSID	F-12	VF-20	EF-40	AU-50	MS-60	MS-63	MS-65
1847 Cent (a)	100,000	11082	$325	$455	$575	$725	$1,000	$2,100	$24,000
1881 Five Cents	26	11091	6,250	8,250	13,000	22,000	32,000	39,000	48,000
1883 Ten Cents	250,000	11094	75	115	190	290	850	2,000	4,400
1883 Quarter Dollar	234,478	11096	90	110	145	190	305	470	825
1883 Half Dollar	85,157	11097	150	210	310	390	950	1,900	7,250
1883 Dollar	45,182	11093	525	600	925	1,500	5,500	12,000	43,000

a. Values shown are for the most common of the six known varieties.

Proof Strikes

	Mintage	GSID	PF-60	PF-63	PF-65
1881 Five Cents Proof Aluminum Restrike, Thick Planchet (a)		377734	—	$11,000	—
1881 Five Cents Proof Aluminum Restrike, Thin Planchet (a)		377735	—	12,500	—
1881 Five Cents Proof Nickel Restrike, Thick Planchet (a)		377736	—	4,400	—
1883 Ten Cents	26	85092	$8,750	17,500	$26,500
1883 Quarter Dollar	26	11101	7,500	17,000	30,000
1883 Half Dollar	26	11102	12,000	26,500	54,000
1883 Dollar	26	11098	23,000	45,000	90,000

a. All were made circa 1900.

Plantation Tokens

During the 1800s, several private firms issued tokens for use as money in Hawaiian company stores. These are often referred to as Plantation tokens. The unusual denomination of 12-1/2 cents was equivalent to a day's wages in the sugar plantations, and was related to the fractional part of the Spanish eight-reales coin.

(1860) Undated, Waterhouse Token

(1871) Undated, Wailuku Plantation

1880, Wailuku Plantation

1882, Haiku Plantation

1891, Kahului Railroad

	Mintage	GSID	F-12	VF-20	EF-40	AU-50	MS-60	MS-63	AU-50	MS-60	MS-63
1891, 10 cents, Kahului Railroad		11105	—	—	—	—	—	—	—	—	—
1871, 12-1/2 cents, Wailuku, Narrow Starfish		11086	$900	$1,600	$2,500	$3,500	—	—	$3,500	—	—
1871, 12-1/2 cents, Wailuku, Broad Starfish		377801	1,400	1,900	5,500	7,250	—	—	7,250	—	—
1879, 12-1/2 cents, T.Hobron Railroad, 2/6 Stars		379389	—	1,000	1,250	1,450	$2,000	$2,900	1,450	$2,000	$2,900
↳1879, 12-1/2 cents, T.Hobron Railroad, 2/6 Stars, Thin Planchet		79441	—	1,000	1,250	1,450	2,000	2,900	1,450	2,000	2,900
↳1879, 12-1/2 cents, T.Hobron Railroad, 2/6 Stars, Thick Planchet		11087	—	1,000	1,250	1,450	2,000	2,900	1,450	2,000	2,900
1886, 12-1/2 cents, Grove Ranch		11103	—	—	4,400	6,250	—	—	6,250	—	—
1887, 12-1/2 cents, Grove Ranch		11104	—	—	—	11,000	—	—	11,000	—	—
1891, 15 cents, Kahului Railroad		11106	—	—	—	—	—	—	—	—	—
1891, 20 cents, Kahului Railroad		11107	—	—	—	—	—	—	—	—	—
1891, 25 cents, Kahului Railroad		11108	—	—	—	—	—	—	—	—	—
1891, 35 cents, Kahului Railroad		11109	—	—	—	—	—	—	—	—	—
1891, 75 cents, Kahului Railroad		11110	—	—	—	—	—	27,500	—	—	27,500
1871, 6-1/4 cents, Wailuku Plantation Token		11085	—	—	6,500	9,500	12,000	—	9,500	12,000	—
1880, Half Rial, Wailuku		11088	3,750	4,500	7,500	12,000	—	—	12,000	—	—
1880, One Rial, Wailuku		11089	—	—	2,750	4,750	—	—	4,750	—	—
1882, One Rial, Haiku		11092	—	850	1,050	1,150	2,800	4,200	1,150	2,800	4,200
(1860), Token, Waterhouse, Medcalf 2TE-1		79440	1,500	2,000	3,300	4,700	18,000	—	4,700	18,000	—
Kahului Railroad, 75 cents, 1891	3,500	3,500	6,500	6,500	6,500	6,500	12,000	16,000	—	—	—

PUERTO RICAN ISSUES

Puerto Rico, the farthest east of the Greater Antilles, lies about 1,000 miles southeast of Florida between the Atlantic Ocean and the Caribbean Sea. Settled by Spain in 1508, the island was ceded to the United States after the Spanish-American War in 1898. Puerto Ricans were granted U.S. citizenship in 1917. Today Puerto Rico is a self-governing territory of the United States with commonwealth status.

The Puerto Rican coins of 1895 and 1896 were minted at the Casa de Moneda de Madrid, in Spain. The peso was struck in .900 fine silver, and the others were .835 fine. The portrait is of King Alfonso XIII, and the arms are of the Bourbons, the royal house of Spain. These coins were in circulation at the time of the Spanish-American War of 1898, which ended with U.S. victory and with Spain's loss of sovereignty over Cuba (along with its cession of the Philippine Islands, Puerto Rico, and Guam to the United States for $20 million). Puerto Rico's Spanish coins continued to circulate after the war.

Collectors of United States coins often include Puerto Rican coins in their collections, even though they are not U.S. issues. After the Spanish-American War, exchange rates were set for these coins relative to the U.S. dollar, and the island transitioned to a dollar-based currency. Today in Puerto Rico the dollar is still popularly referred to as a "peso."

1896, 5 Centavos

1896, 10 Centavos

1895, 20 Centavos

1896, 40 Centavos

1895, One Peso

Circulation Strikes

	Mintage	GSID	F-12	VF-20	EF-40	AU-50	MS-60	MS-63	MS-65
1896 5 Centavos	600,000	337551	$17.50	$27	$80	$100	$155	$325	—
1896 10 Centavos	700,000	337553	22.00	34	90	195	260	340	—
1896 20 Centavos	3,350,000	337554	30.00	47	100	240	390	950	$4,050
1896 40 Centavos	725,002	337555	210.00	325	600	825	—	—	—
1895 1 Peso	8,500,021	337556	430.00	650	1,100	1,900	3,250	—	—

Philippine Issues

In April 1899, control of the Philippine Islands was officially transferred from Spain to the United States, as a condition of the treaty ending the Spanish-American War. The U.S. military suppressed a Filipino insurgency through 1902, and partway through that struggle, in July 1901, the islands' military government was replaced with a civilian administration led by American judge William Howard Taft. One of its first tasks was to sponsor a new territorial coinage that was compatible with the old Spanish issues, but also legally exchangeable for American money at the rate of two Philippine pesos to the U.S. dollar. The resulting coins—which bear the legend UNITED STATES OF AMERICA but are otherwise quite different in design from regular U.S. coins—today can be found in many American coin collections, having been brought to the States as souvenirs by service members after World War II or otherwise saved. The unusual designs, combined with the legend, have sometimes caused them to be confused with standard federal United States coins.

The coins, introduced in 1903, were designed by Filipino silversmith, sculptor, engraver, and art professor Melecio Figueroa, who had earlier worked for the Spanish *Casa de Moneda*, in Manila. They are sometimes called "Conant coins" or "Conants," after Charles Arthur Conant, an influential American journalist and banking expert who served on the commission that brought about the Philippine Coinage Act of March 2, 1903. "Both in the artistic quality of the designs and in perfection of workmanship, they compare favorably with anything of the kind ever done in America," wrote Secretary of War Elihu Root in his annual report to President Theodore Roosevelt. Figueroa died of tuberculosis on July 30, 1903, age 61, shortly after seeing his coins enter circulation.

Following Spanish custom, the dollar-sized peso was decimally equivalent to 100 centavos. Silver fractions were minted in denominations of fifty, twenty, and ten centavos, and minor coins (in copper-nickel and bronze) included the five-centavo piece, the centavo, and the half centavo.

In addition to the name of the United States, the coins bear the Spanish name for the islands: FILIPINAS. The silver coins feature a female personification of the Philippines, holding in one hand a hammer that she strikes against an anvil, and in the other an olive branch, with the volcanic Mount Mayon (northeast of the capital city of Manila) visible in the background. The minor coinage shows a young Filipino man, bare-chested and seated at an anvil with a hammer, again with Mount Mayon seen in the distance. The first reverse design, shared across all denominations, shows a U.S. federal shield surmounted by an eagle with outstretched wings, clutching an olive branch in its right talon and a bundle of arrows in its left. This reverse design was changed in 1937 to a new shield emblem derived from the seal of the 1936 Commonwealth.

Dies for the coins were made at the Philadelphia Mint by the U.S. Mint's chief engraver, Charles E. Barber. Mintmarks were added to the dies, as needed, at the branch mints. From 1903 to 1908 the coins were struck at the Philadelphia Mint (with no mintmark) and the San Francisco Mint (with an S mintmark). From

1909 through 1919, they were struck only at San Francisco. In the first part of 1920, one-centavo coins were struck in San Francisco; later in the year a new mint facility, the Mint of the Philippine Islands, was opened in Manila, and from that point into the early 1940s Philippine coins of one, five, ten, twenty, and fifty centavos were struck there. The coins produced at the Manila Mint in 1920, 1921, and 1922 bore no mintmark. No Philippine coins were struck in 1923 or 1924. The Manila Mint reopened in 1925; from then through 1941 its coinage featured an M mintmark. The Denver and San Francisco mints would be used for Philippine coinage in the final years of World War II, when the islands were under Japanese occupation.

Rising silver prices forced reductions in the fineness and weight for each Philippine silver denomination beginning in 1907, and subsequent issues are smaller in diameter. The new, smaller twenty-centavo piece was very close in size to the five-centavo piece (20.0 mm compared to 20.5 mm), resulting in a mismatching of dies for these two denominations in 1918. A small number of error coins were minted from this accidental combination, with some finding their way into circulation (often with the edge crudely reeded to induce them to pass as twenty-centavo coins). A solution was found by reducing the diameter of the five-centavo piece beginning in 1930.

It should be noted that, in addition to normal coins and paper currency, special token money in the form of coins and printed currency was made for use in the Culion Leper Colony. The token coinage saw six issues from 1913 to 1930, some produced at the Manila Mint. The leper colony was set up in May 1906 on the small island of Culion, one of the more than 7,000 islands comprising the Philippines, and the coinage was intended to circulate only there.

In 1935 the United States, responding to popular momentum for independence, approved the establishment of the Commonwealth of the Philippines, with the understanding that full self-governing independence would be recognized after a ten-year transition period. In 1936 a three-piece set of silver commemorative coins was issued to mark the transfer of executive power.

An adaptation of the new commonwealth's seal, introduced on the 1936 commemorative coins, was used for the reverse design of all circulating Philippine issues beginning in 1937. For their obverses, the Commonwealth coins retained the same Figueroa designs as those struck from 1903 to 1936. (A final transitional issue of more than 17 million 1936-dated one-centavo coins was minted using the federal-shield reverse design, rather than the new Commonwealth shield.)

After the bombing of Pearl Harbor, Japanese military forces advanced on the Philippines in late 1941 and early 1942, prompting the civil government to remove much of the Philippine treasury's bullion to the United States. Nearly 16 million pesos' worth of silver remained, mostly in the form of one-peso pieces of 1907 through 1912. These coins were hastily crated and dumped into Manila's Caballo Bay to prevent their capture by Japan. The Japanese occupied the Philippines, learned of the hidden treasure, and managed to recover some of the sunken coins (probably fewer than half a million). After the war, over the course of several years, more than 10 million of the submerged silver pesos were retrieved under the direction of the U.S. Treasury and, later, the Central Bank of the Philippines. Most of them show evidence of prolonged salt-water immersion, with dark corrosion that resists cleaning. This damage to so many coins has added to the scarcity of high-grade pre-war silver pesos.

Later during World War II, in 1944 and 1945, the U.S. Mint struck coins for the Philippines at its Philadelphia, Denver, and San Francisco facilities. These coins were brought over and entered circulation as U.S. and Philippine military forces fought to retake the islands from the Japanese.

After the war, the Commonwealth of the Philippines became an independent republic, on July 4, 1946, as had been scheduled by the Constitution of 1935. Today the Philippine coins of 1903 to 1945, including the set of commemoratives issued in 1936, remain significant mementoes of a colorful and important chapter in U.S. history and numismatics. They are a testament to the close ties and special relationship between the United States of America and the Republic of the Philippines.

PHILIPPINES UNDER U.S. SOVEREIGNTY (1903–1936)

The Philippine Islands were governed under the sovereignty of the United States from 1899 until early 1935. (In the latter year a largely self-governing commonwealth was established, followed by full independence in 1946.) Coinage under U.S. sovereignty began in 1903. There was a final issue of centavos dated 1936, minted in the style of 1903–1934, after which the design of all circulating coins changed to the new Commonwealth style.

BRONZE COINAGE

HALF CENTAVO (1903–1908)

Designer: *Melecio Figueroa.* **Weight:** *2.35 grams.* **Composition:** *.950 copper, .050 tin and zinc.* **Diameter:** *17.5 mm.* **Edge:** *Plain.* **Mint:** *Philadelphia.*

History. In 1903 and 1904 the United States minted nearly 18 million half centavos for the Philippines. By March of the latter year, it was obvious that the half centavo was too small a denomination, unneeded in commerce despite the government's attempts to force it into circulation. The recommendation of Governor-General Luke Edward Wright—that the coin be discontinued permanently—was approved, and on April 18, 1904, a new contract was authorized to manufacture one-centavo blanks out of unused half-centavo blanks. In April 1908, Governor-General James Francis Smith received permission to ship 37,827 pesos' worth of stored half centavos (7,565,400 coins) to the San Francisco Mint to be re-coined into one-centavo pieces. Cleared from the Philippine Treasury's vaults, the coins were shipped to California in June 1908, and most of them were melted and made into 1908 centavos.

Striking and Sharpness. Half centavos typically are well struck, except for the 1903 issue, of which some coins may show weak numerals in the date. Reverses sometimes show light flattening of the eagle's wing tips.

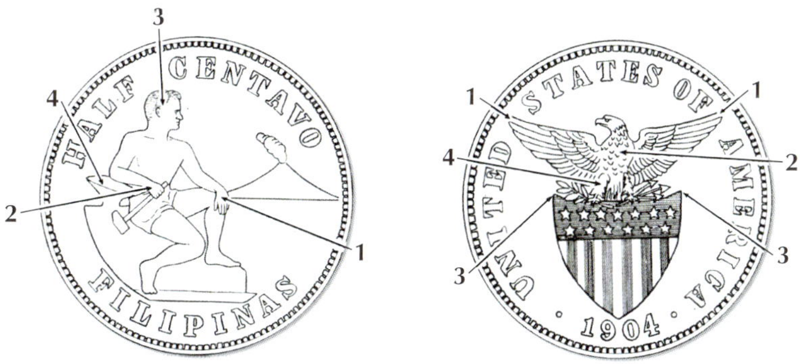

Half Centavo, 1903–1908

High Points of Wear. ***Obverse Checkpoints:*** 1. Figure's left hand. 2. Figure's right hand. 3. Face and frontal hair just above ear. 4. Edge of anvil. ***Reverse Checkpoints:*** 1. Eagle's wing tips. 2. Eagle's breast feathers. 3. Upper points of shield. 4. Eagle's right leg.

Proofs. The Philadelphia Mint struck small quantities of Proof half centavos for collectors throughout the denomination's existence, for inclusion in Proof sets (except for 1907, when no Proof sets were issued).

Circulation Strikes

	Mintage	GSID	AU-50	MS-60	MS-63	MS-65
1903	12,084,000	25725	$5.50	$13.50	$27	$60
1904	5,654,000	25731	$8	$20	$34	$115

Note: The half centavo was unpopular in circulation. More than 7,500,000 were withdrawn and melted to be recoined as one-centavo pieces in 1908. **a.** Proof only.

Proof Strikes

	Mintage	GSID	PF-60	PF-63	PF-65
1903	2,558	25728	$100	$160	$390
1904	1,355	25734	60	95	215
1905	471	25737	130	230	390
1906	500	25369	$110	$160	$525
1908	500	25740	110	230	525

One Centavo (1903–1936)

Designer: *Melecio Figueroa.* **Weight:** *4.7 grams.* **Composition:** *.950 copper, .050 tin and zinc.* **Diameter:** *24 mm.* **Edge:** *Plain.* **Mints:** *Philadelphia, San Francisco, and Manila.*

Mintmark location is on the reverse, to the left of the date.

History. Unlike the half centavo, the bronze centavo was a popular workhorse of Philippine commerce from the start of its production. Nearly 38 million coins were minted in the denomination's first three years. In 1920 the centavo was struck for circulation by two different mints (the only year this was the case). San Francisco produced the coins during the first part of 1920; later in the year, the coins were struck at the Manila Mint, after that facility opened. From that point forward all centavos struck under U.S. sovereignty were products of the Manila Mint. Those dated 1920, 1921, and 1922 bear no mintmark identifying their origin. Manila produced no coins (of any denomination) in 1923 and 1924.

Coin collectors, notably educator, writer, and American Numismatic Association member Dr. Gilbert S. Perez, urged Manila Mint officials to include an M mark on their coinage—similar to the way that, for example, San Francisco coins were identified by an S—and this change was made starting with the coinage of 1925.

Coinage of the centavo continued through the late 1920s and early 1930s. U.S. sovereignty was significantly altered in 1935 with the establishment of the Commonwealth of the Philippines, and this change was reflected in all Philippine currency. A final mintage of 1936-dated centavos (17,455,463 pieces) was struck using the federal-shield reverse of the denomination's 1903–1934 coinage. The coin then switched over to the Commonwealth shield design in 1937.

Several centavo die varieties exist to give the specialist a challenge. Among them is the 1918-S, Large S, whose mintmark appears to be the same size and shape of that used on fifty-centavo pieces of the era.

Striking and Sharpness. On the obverse, the figure's right hand (holding the hammer) is almost always found flatly struck. The reverse, especially of later-date centavos, often shows flattening of the eagle's breast and of the left part of the shield. Issues of the Manila Mint, especially of 1920, often are lightly struck. Those of San Francisco typically are better struck, with only occasional light strikes. On centavos of 1929 to 1936, the M mintmark often is nearly unidentifiable as a letter.

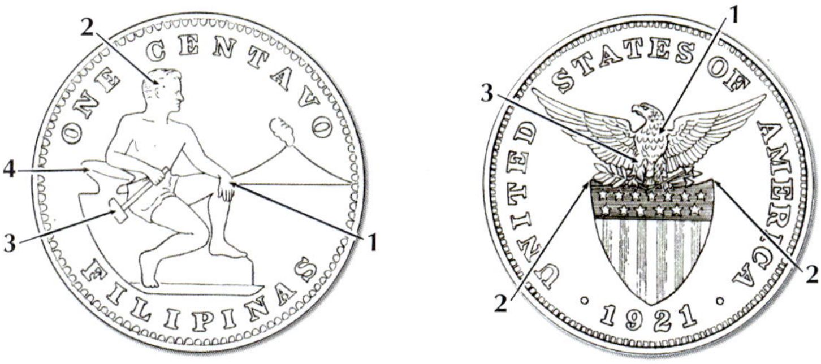

One Centavo, 1903–1936

High Points of Wear. ***Obverse Checkpoints:*** 1. Figure's left hand. 2. Frontal hair just above ear. 3. Head of hammer. 4. Left part of anvil. ***Reverse Checkpoints:*** 1. Eagle's breast feathers. 2. Upper points of shield. 3. Eagle's right leg.

Proofs. One-centavo Proofs were struck at the Philadelphia Mint for annual Proof sets in 1903, 1904, 1905, 1906, and 1908. Proof centavos of 1908 bear a date with numerals noticeably larger than those of circulation-strike 1908-S coins.

1908-S, S Over S

1918-S, Normal S

1918-S, Large S

Circulation Strikes

	Mintage	GSID	AU-50	MS-60	MS-63	MS-65
1903	10,790,000	25770	$6.75	$13.50	$27	$130
1904	17,040,400	25776	6.75	20.00	40	120
1905	10,000,000	25782	13.50	27.00	70	160
1908-S	2,187,000	25794	24.00	55.00	120	260
↳1908-S, S Over S, Allen-2.06a, FS-501	*	373165	230.00	650.00	1,250	2,050
↳1908-S, S Over S Over S, Allen-2.06b	*	373166	—	—	—	—
1909-S	1,737,612	25797	47.00	100.00	130	325
1910-S	2,700,000	25800	13.50	27.00	47	110
1911-S	4,803,000	25803	9.50	20.00	40	130
1912-S	3,001,000	25806	27.00	47.00	70	120
1913-S	5,000,000	25809	13.50	27.00	90	230
1914-S	5,000,500	25812	12.00	27.00	110	390
1915-S	2,500,000	25818	130.00	325.00	390	1,750
1916-S	4,330,000	25821	34.00	70.00	110	235
1917-S	7,070,000	25827	20.00	47.00	70	130
↳1917-S, 7 Over 6, Allen-2.15a, FS-301	*	25830	160.00	455.00	1,150	2,000

	Mintage	GSID	AU-50	MS-60	MS-63	MS-65
1917-S, 7 Over 8	*	25833	$455.00	$900	$1,700	$2,500
1918-S	1,160,000	25836	34.00	70	100	325
↳1918-S, Large S, Allen-2.16a, FS-501	*	25839	160.00	390	1,000	1,750
1919-S	454,000	25842	34.00	70	100	260
1920-(M)	3,552,256	25845	13.50	27	100	325
1920-S	2,500,000	25848	13.50	27	100	325
1921-(M)	7,282,673	25851	27.00	40	90	155
1922-(M)	3,519,100	25854	34.00	55	115	260
1925-M	9,325,000	25857	20.00	27	34	70
1926-M	9,000,000	25860	20.00	27	40	80
1927-M	92,700,000	25863	20.00	40	70	130
1928-M	91,500,000	25866	20.00	40	70	160
1929-M	5,657,161	25869	20.00	40	100	260
1930-M	5,577,000	25872	20.00	40	70	130
1931-M	5,659,355	25875	20.00	34	55	100
1932-M	4,000,000	25878	20.00	34	55	100
1933-M	8,392,692	25881	20.00	34	55	100
1934-M	3,179,000	25884	20.00	34	55	100
1936 M	17,455,463	25887	9.50	27	47	80

* Included in number above.

Proof Strikes

	Mintage	GSID	PF-60	PF-63	PF-65
1903	2,558	25773	$245	$375	$725
1904	1,355	25779	130	195	290
1905	471	25785	145	210	650

	Mintage	GSID	PF-60	PF-63	PF-65
1906	500	25788	$160	$230	$345
1908	500	25791	260	325	650

Copper-Nickel Coinage

Five Centavos (1903–1935)

Designer: *Melecio Figueroa.* **Weight:** *1903–1928, 5 grams; 1930–1935, 4.75 grams.* **Composition:** *.750 copper, .250 nickel.* **Diameter:** *1903–1908, 20.5 mm; 1930–1935, 19 mm.* **Edge:** *Plain.* **Mints:** *Philadelphia, San Francisco, and Manila.*

Five Centavos, Large Size (1903–1928, 20.5 mm)

Mintmark location is on the reverse, to the left of the date.

Five Centavos, Reduced Size (1930–1935, 19 mm)

History. Five-centavo coins were minted under U.S. sovereignty for the Philippines from 1903 to 1935, with several gaps in production over the years. Circulation strikes were made in Philadelphia in 1903 and 1904, then coinage resumed in 1916, this time at the San Francisco Mint. The newly inaugurated Manila Mint took over all five-centavo production starting in 1920, continuing through the end of direct U.S. administration, and under the Commonwealth government beginning in 1937.

The Manila Mint coins of 1920 and 1921 bore no mintmark indicating their producer, a situation noticed by coin collectors of the day. Gilbert S. Perez, superintendent of schools for Tayabas in the Philippines (and a member of the American Numismatic Association), wrote to Assistant Insular Treasurer Salvador Lagdameo in June 1922: "Several members of numismatic societies in Europe and America have made inquiries as to why the Manila mint has no distinctive mint mark. Some do not even know that there is a mint in the Philippine Islands and that the mint is operated by Filipinos." He recommended the letter M be used to identify Manila's coins. Lagdameo replied later that month, thanking Perez and informing him: "It is now being planned that the new dies to be ordered shall contain such mark, and it is hoped that the coins of 1923 and subsequent years will bear the distinctive mint mark suggested by you." Coinage would not resume at the Manila facility until 1925, but from that year forward the mintmark would grace the coins struck in the Philippines.

The diameter of the five-centavo coin was 20.5 mm diameter from 1903 to 1928. This was very close to the 20 mm diameter of the twenty-centavo coin of 1907 to 1929. By 1928 there had been two separate instances where a reverse die of one denomination was "muled" to an obverse of the other. In 1918 this occurred by accident when a small quantity of five-centavo pieces was struck in combination with the reverse die of the twenty centavos (identifiable by its wider shield and a smaller date, compared to the normal five-centavo reverse). This error was known to numismatists by 1922, by which time it was recognized as a scarce variety. The second instance of muling, in 1928, is discussed under twenty-centavo pieces. In 1930, to clearly differentiate the sizes of the coins, the diameter of the five-centavo piece was reduced from 20.5 to 19.0 mm.

Five-centavo coinage under U.S. sovereignty continued to 1935. From 1937 on, the Manila Mint's production of five-centavo coins would use the new Commonwealth shield design on the reverse.

Striking and Sharpness. The obverse of the 1918 and 1919 San Francisco Mint issues often is weakly struck, with considerable loss of detail. The Manila Mint started production in 1920, and many five-centavo coins from that year lack sharpness in the rims and have weak details overall.

Five Centavos, 1903–1928

High Points of Wear. ***Obverse Checkpoints:*** 1. Figure's right hand. 2. Frontal hair just above ear. 3. Figure's left hand. ***Reverse Checkpoints:*** 1. Eagle's breast feathers. 2. Eagle's wing tip (to viewer's right). 3. Upper points of shield.

Five Centavos, 1930–1935

High Points of Wear. ***Obverse Checkpoints:*** 1. Figure's right hand. 2. Frontal hair just above ear. 3. Edge of anvil. ***Reverse Checkpoints:*** 1. Eagle's breast feathers. 2. Eagle's wing tip (to viewer's right).

Proofs. Five-centavo Proofs were struck at the Philadelphia Mint for annual Proof sets in 1903, 1904, 1905, 1906, and 1908.

Circulation Strikes

	Mintage	GSID	AU-50	MS-60	MS-63	MS-65
1903	8,910,000	25967	$20	$47	$90	$360
1904	1,075,000	25969	20	47	90	155
1916-S	300,000	25974	130	575	1,300	3,000
1917-S	2,300,000	25975	34	80	130	1,000
1918-S	2,780,000	25976	60	160	415	—
↳1918-S, S/S, Allen-4.08a, FS-501	*	373171	160	875	1,500	—
↳1918-S, Mule, Allen-4.08b, FS-901 (a)	*	25977	1,250	3,100	7,500	—
1919-S	1,220,000	25978	75	130	455	2,500
1920-(M)	1,421,078	25979	70	195	525	2,500
1921-(M)	2,131,529	25980	$55	$120	$290	—
1925-M	1,000,000	25981	70	155	245	—
1926-M	1,200,000	25982	70	130	235	$950
1927-M	1,000,000	25983	34	80	130	435
1928-M	1,000,000	25984	27	70	115	285
1930-M	2,905,182	25985	27	49	130	775
1931-M	3,476,790	25986	20	60	90	1,250
1932-M	3,955,861	25987	20	40	60	—
1934-M	2,153,729	25988	34	90	260	1,000
↳1934-M, Repunched 1, Allen-5.04a, FS-301	*	85087	290	650	850	—
1935-M	2,754,000	25989	34	90	195	2,500

* Included in number above. **a.** Small Date Reverse of twenty centavos.

Proof Strikes

	Mintage	GSID	PF-60	PF-63	PF-65
1903	2,558	25968	$115	$175	$455
1904	1,355	25970	100	155	490
1905	471	25971	180	390	725
1906	500	25972	$155	$260	$650
1908	500	25973	155	260	625

Silver Coinage

Ten Centavos (1903–1935)

Designer: *Melecio Figueroa.* **Weight:** *1903–1906, 2.7 grams (.0779 oz. ASW); 1907–1935, 2 grams (.0482 oz. ASW).* **Composition:** *1903–1906, .900 silver, .100 copper; 1907–1935, .750 silver, .250 copper.* **Diameter:** *1903–1906, 17.5 mm; 1907–1935, 16.5 mm.* **Edge:** *Reeded.* **Mints:** *Philadelphia, San Francisco, and Manila.*

Ten Centavos, Large Size (1903–1906, 17.5 mm)

Mintmark location is on the reverse, to the left of the date.

Ten Centavos, Reduced Size (1907–1935, 16.5 mm)

History. The Philippine ten-centavo coin was minted from 1903 to 1935, in several facilities and with occasional interruptions in production.

In 1907 the silver ten-centavo coin's fineness was reduced from .900 to .750, and at the same time its diameter was decreased. This was in response to the rising price of silver, with the goal of discouraging exportation and melting of the silver coins. The net effect was nearly 40 percent less silver, by actual weight, in the new ten-centavo piece. The older coins continued to be removed from circulation, and by June 30, 1911, it was reported that only 35 percent of the ten-centavo pieces minted from 1903 to 1906 still remained in the Philippines.

The Manila Mint took over ten-centavo production from San Francisco in 1920. The ten-centavo coins of 1920 and 1921 bear no mintmark identifying them as products of Manila (this was the case for all Philippine coinage of those years, and of 1922). The efforts of Philippine numismatists, including American Numismatic Association member Gilbert S. Perez, encouraged mint officials to add the M mintmark when the facility reopened in 1925 after a two-year hiatus for all coinage.

Ten-centavo production after 1921 consisted of 1 million pieces struck in 1929 and just less than 1.3 million in 1935. The next ten-centavo mintage would be under the Commonwealth, not U.S. sovereignty.

Die varieties include a 1912-S with an S Over S mintmark, and date variations of the 1914-S.

Striking and Sharpness. The ten-centavo coins of 1903 to 1906 generally are well struck, although some show slight weakness of features. Those of 1907 to 1935 also are generally well struck; some obverses may have slight flattening of the hair just above the ear and on the upper part of the figure. On the reverse, check the eagle's breast feathers for flatness.

Ten Centavos, 1903–1906

High Points of Wear. ***Obverse Checkpoints:*** 1. Figure's left bosom. 2. Figure's right knee. 3. Figure's left knee. 4. Edge of anvil. ***Reverse Checkpoints:*** 1. Eagle's breast feathers. 2. Upper points of shield. 3. Eagle's wing tips. 4. Eagle's right leg.

Ten Centavos, 1907–1935

High Points of Wear. ***Obverse Checkpoints:*** 1. Figure's left thigh. 2. Figure's left bosom. 3. Figure's left hand. ***Reverse Checkpoints:*** 1. Eagle's breast feathers. 2. Upper points of shield. 3. Eagle's right leg.

Proofs. Ten-centavo Proofs were struck at the Philadelphia Mint for annual Proof sets in 1903, 1904, 1905, 1906, and 1908.

1912-S, S Over S

1914-S, Short Crossbar

1914-S, Long Crossbar

Circulation Strikes

	Mintage	GSID	AU-50	MS-60	MS-63	MS-65
1903	5,102,658	25743	$34	$80	$155	$340
1903-S	1,200,000	25744	235	1,150	2,250	6,250
1904	10,000	25745	47	95	145	260
1904-S	5,040,000	25364	34	75	130	195
1907	1,500,781	25747	34	60	100	280
1907-S	4,930,000	25748	34	70	110	390
↳1907-S, S/S, Allen-8.02a, FS-501	*	373172	40	100	180	—
1908-S	3363911	25750	34	70	130	260
1909-S	312199	25751	325	525	1,000	2,750
1911-S	1,000,505	25752	235	365	950	—
1912-S	1,010,000	25753	100.00	260.00	390	2,500
↳1912-S, S/S, Allen-8.08a, FS-501	*	373173	120.00	310.00	470	3,000
1913-S	1,360,693	25754	$100	$160	$260	$525
1914-S	1,180,000	25755	155	390	1,000	2,450
↳1914-S, Long Crossbar, Allen-8.10b, FS-301	*	373174	170	430	1,150	2,700
1915-S	450,000	25756	260	1,900	4,000	—
1917-S	5,991,148	25757	20	90	130	325
1918-S	8,420,000	25758	20	90	120	200
1919-S	1,630,000	25759	34	70	100	200
1920-(M)	520,000	25760	55	115	215	1,750
1921-(M)	3,863,038	25761	34	60	150	650
1929-M	1,000,000	25762	40	90	155	285
↳1929-M, RPD, Allen-8.17a	*	85085	70	130	230	725
1935-M	1,280,000	25763	20	47	80	195

* Included in number above.

Proof Strikes

	Mintage	GSID	PF-60	PF-63	PF-65
1903	2,558	25363	$130	$230	$550
1904	1,355	25373	110	160	345
1905	471	25372	325	525	900
1906	500	25746	$195	$260	$650
1908	500	25749	215	290	1,000

TWENTY CENTAVOS (1903–1929)

Designer: *Melecio Figueroa.* **Weight:** *1903–1906, 5.385 grams (.1558 oz. ASW); 1907–1929, 4 grams (.0964 oz. ASW).* **Composition:** *1903–1906, .900 silver, .100 copper; 1907–1929, .750 silver, .250 copper.* **Diameter:** *1903–1906, 23 mm; 1907–1929, 20 mm.* **Edge:** *Reeded.* **Mints:** *Philadelphia, San Francisco, and Manila.*

Twenty Centavos, Large Size (1903–1906, 23 mm)

Mintmark location is on the reverse, to the left of the date.

Twenty Centavos, Reduced Size (1907–1929, 20 mm)

History. In the early 1900s the rising value of silver was encouraging exportation and melting of the Philippines' silver twenty-centavo coins. As was the case with the ten-centavo piece, in 1907 the diameter of the twenty-centavo coin was reduced and its silver fineness decreased from .900 to .750. The net effect was about 40 percent less silver, by actual weight, in the new smaller coins. Attrition continued to draw the older coins out of circulation and into the melting pot, as their silver value exceeded their face value. A report of June 30, 1911, held that only about 25 percent of the twenty-centavo coins minted from 1903 to 1906 still remained in the Philippines.

Circulation strikes were made at the Philadelphia and San Francisco mints through 1919. In July 1920, a new "Mint of the Philippine Islands," located in Manila, started production. Its output during the period of U.S. sovereignty included twenty-centavo pieces in 1920, 1921, 1928, and 1929. (Production of the coins later continued under the Commonwealth, with a slightly modified design.) The first two years of coinage did not feature a mintmark identifying Manila as the producer of the coins. This was noticed by collectors of Philippine coins; they protested the oversight, and later coinage dies had an M mintmark added.

In 1928 a rush order for twenty-centavo coins was received at the Manila Mint—by that time the only producer of the denomination. Manila had not minted the coins since 1921, and the Philadelphia Mint had not shipped any new reverse dies (which would have featured their 1928 date). Under pressure to produce the coins, workers at the Manila Mint married a regular twenty-centavo obverse die with the 1928-dated reverse die of the five-centavo denomination, which was only .5 mm larger. As a result, the entire mintage of 100,000 1928 twenty centavos consists of these "mule" (mismatched-die) coins. The reverse of the 1928 coins, compared with others of 1907 to 1929, has a narrower shield and a larger date.

Striking and Sharpness. Most twenty centavos of 1903 to 1906 are well struck. The 1904-S usually shows weak striking on the figure's left bosom, the frontal hair just above her ear, and her left hand. Most of the coins of 1907 to 1929 show flattening of the figure's hair, sometimes extending into the area of her left bosom and her left hand.

Twenty Centavos, 1903–1906

High Points of Wear. ***Obverse Checkpoints:*** 1. Figure's left thigh and knee. 2. Figure's left bosom. 3. Figure's left hand. ***Reverse Checkpoints:*** 1. Eagle's breast feathers. 2. Upper points of shield. 3. Eagle's right leg.

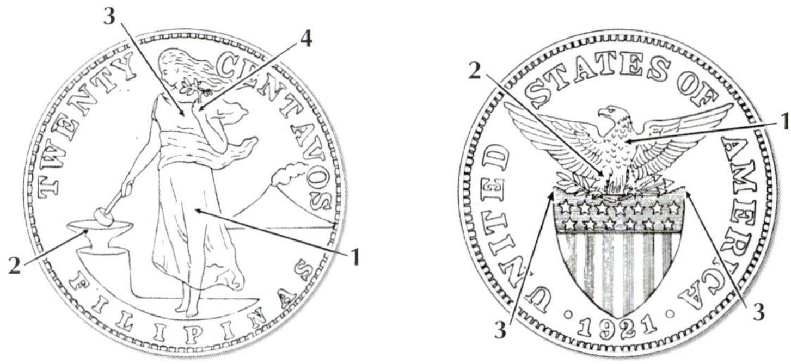

Twenty Centavos, 1907–1929

High Points of Wear. ***Obverse Checkpoints:*** 1. Figure's left thigh. 2. Edge of anvil. 3. Figure's left bosom. 4. Figure's left hand. ***Reverse Checkpoints:*** 1. Eagle's breast feathers. 2. Eagle's right leg. 3. Upper points of shield.

Proofs. Twenty-centavo Proofs were struck at the Philadelphia Mint for annual Proof sets in 1903, 1904, 1905, 1906, and 1908.

Circulation Strikes

	5,350,231	25911	70.00	120.00	260	1,100
1903	150,080	25912	$230	$1,000	$2,250	$8,750
1903-S	10,000	25913	55	130	210	430
1904	2,060,000	25915	60	115	195	435
1904-S	420,000	376195	1,100	2,250	3,500	6,000
↳1904-S, S/S, Allen-10.04b	*	25917	215	390	1,250	—
1905-S	1,250,651	25919	100	155	575	3,750
1907	3,165,000	25920	120	260	440	3,450
1907-S	1,535,000	25922	120	440	1,150	2,500
1908-S	450,000	25923	195	575	3,000	5,000
1909-S	500,259	25924	130	1,150	2,500	5,250
1910-S	505,000	25925	260	1,750	3,500	—
1911-S	750,000	25926	60	455	1,250	—
1912-S	795,000	25927	100	285	525	1,200
1913-S	795,000	25928	130	525	900	3,750
↳1913-S, S/S	*	25929	525	1,150	3,000	—
1914-S	795,000	25929	525	1,150	3,000	—

	Mintage	GSID	AU-50	MS-60	MS-63	MS-65
1915-S	655,000	25930	$195	$950	$2,250	—
1916-S (a)	1,435,000	25931	160	390	1,250	$4,300
↳1916-S, Tilted 6, Allen-11.12a, FS-301	*	85052	180	430	1,400	4,550
1917-S	3,150,655	25932	70	120	235	850
1918-S	5,560,000	25933	27	55	80	775
1919-S	850,000	25934	70	180	390	2,000
1920-(M)	1,045,415	25935	95	145	285	2,000
1921-(M)	1,842,631	25936	40	70	110	1,000
1928-M, Allen-11.18, FS-901	100,000	25937	625	1,250	2,000	5,500
1929-M	1,970,000	25938	27	55	80	390
↳1929-M, 2/2/2, Allen-11.19b, FS-301	*	373176	110	525	1,000	—

* Included in number above.

Proof Strikes

	Mintage	GSID	PF-60	PF-63	PF-65
1903	2,558	25365	$195	$325	$525
1904	1,355	25914	160	235	455
1905	471	25916	290	490	950
1906	500	25918	$325	$650	$950
1908	500	25921	235	390	1,000

FIFTY CENTAVOS (1903–1921)

Designer: *Melecio Figueroa.* **Weight:** *1903–1906, 13.48 grams (.3900 oz. ASW); 1907–1921, 10 grams (.2411 oz. ASW).* **Composition:** *1903–1906, .900 silver, .100 copper; 1907–1921, .750 silver, .250 copper.* **Diameter:** *1903–1906, 30 mm; 1907–1921, 27 mm.* **Edge:** *Reeded.* **Mints:** *Philadelphia, San Francisco, and Manila.*

Fifty Centavos, Large Size (1903–1906, 30 mm)

Mintmark location is on the reverse, to the left of the date.

Fifty Centavos, Reduced Size (1907–1921, 27 mm)

History. After four years of fifty-centavo coinage, in 1907 the denomination's silver fineness was lowered from .900 to .750, and its diameter was reduced by ten percent. This action was in response to rising silver prices. The new smaller coins contained 38 percent less silver, by actual weight, than their 1903–1906 forebears, making them unprofitable to melt for their precious-metal content. Gresham's Law being what it is ("Bad money will drive out good"), the older, heavier silver coins were quickly pulled from circulation; by June 30, 1911, it was officially reported that more than 90 percent of the 1903–1906 coinage had disappeared from the Philippines.

The reduced-size coins of the U.S. sovereignty type were minted from 1907 to 1921. The Manila Mint took over their production from the Philadelphia and San Francisco mints in 1920, using coinage dies shipped from Philadelphia. The fifty centavos was the largest denomination produced at the Manila Mint. Neither the 1920 nor the 1921 coinage featured a mintmark identifying Manila as its producer.

Production of the fifty-centavo denomination would again take place, in 1944 and 1945, in San Francisco, using the Commonwealth design introduced for circulating coins in 1937.

Striking and Sharpness. On fifty-centavo coins of 1903 to 1906, many obverses show slight flattening of the frontal hair just above the figure's ear. The reverses sometimes show slight flattening of the eagle's breast feathers. On the reverse, a high spot on the shield is the result of an unevenness in striking. The coins of 1907 to 1921 often show notable flatness of strike in the figure's hair just above her ear, and sometimes on her left hand. A flat strike on the abdomen and left leg should not be mistaken for circulation wear. The reverses are quite unevenly struck; observe the top part of the shield, which has a depressed middle and raised sides. The right side is slightly higher than the left and may show some flattening.

Fifty Centavos, 1903–1906

High Points of Wear. ***Obverse Checkpoints:*** 1. Edge of anvil. 2. Figure's left thigh and knee. 3. Figure's right knee. 4. Figure's right bosom. ***Reverse Checkpoints:*** 1. Part of shield just to left of lower-right star. 2. Eagle's breast feathers. 3. Eagle's right leg and claws.

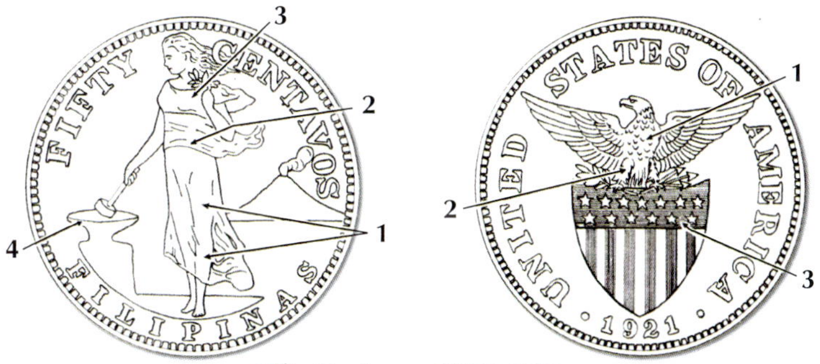

Fifty Centavos, 1907–1921

High Points of Wear. ***Obverse Checkpoints:*** 1. Figure's left thigh and lower leg. 2. Mid-drapery. 3. Figure's left bosom. 4. Edge of anvil. ***Reverse Checkpoints:*** 1. Eagle's breast feathers. 2. Eagle's right leg. 3. Part of shield just to left of lower-right star.

Proofs. Fifty-centavo Proofs were struck at the Philadelphia Mint for annual Proof sets in 1903, 1904, 1905, 1906, and 1908. Proofs of 1908 often are found with considerable flatness in the frontal hair above Liberty's hair and sometimes with flatness in her left hand.

Circulation Strikes

	Mintage	GSID	AU-50	MS-60	MS-63	MS-65
1903	3,099,061	25368	$40	$135	$200	—
1903-S		25947	60,000	—	—	—
1904	10,000	25948	115	195	390	$1,000
1904-S	216,000	25950	100	455	1,000	3,750
1905-S	852,000	25952	230	525	2,500	—
1907	1,200,625	25954	70	440	950	2,750
1907-S	2,112,000	25955	70	285	525	4,500
1908-S	1,601,000	25957	260	650	2,750	5,000
1909-S	528,000	25958	160	390	1,250	3,250

	Mintage	GSID	AU-50	MS-60	MS-63	MS-65
1917-S	674,369	25959	$70.00	$260	$525	$2,250
1918-S	2,202,000	25960	70.00	390	900	2,500
↳1918-S, S/S, Allen-14.07a, FS-501	*	373177	80.00	470	1,100	3,000
1919-S	1,200,000	25961	55.00	115	260	1,250
1920-(M)	420,000	25962	55.00	130	290	—
1921-(M)	2,316,763	25366	13.50	80	120	455

* Included in number above.

Proof Strikes

	Mintage	GSID	PF-60	PF-63	PF-65
1903	2,558	25946	$285	$490	$850
1904	1,355	25949	290	525	850
1905	471	25951	390	1,150	3,500

	Mintage	GSID	PF-60	PF-63	PF-65
1906	500	25953	$575	$1,000	$1,900
1908	500	25956	360	775	1,400

ONE PESO (1903–1912)

Designer: *Melecio Figueroa.* **Weight:** *1903–1906, 26.96 grams (.7800 oz. ASW); 1907–1912, 20 grams (.5144 oz. ASW).* **Composition:** *1903–1906, .900 silver, .100 copper; 1907–1912, .800 silver, .200 copper.* **Diameter:** *1903–1906, 38 mm; 1907–1912, 35 mm.* **Edge:** *Reeded.* **Mints:** *Philadelphia and San Francisco.*

Peso, Large Size
(1903–1906, 38 mm)

Peso, Reduced Size
(1907–1912, 35 mm)

Mintmark location is on the reverse, to the left of the date.

History. The Philippine silver peso was struck under U.S. sovereignty from 1903 to 1912. The key date among those struck for circulation is the issue of 1906-S. Although the San Francisco Mint produced more than 200,000 of the coins that year, nearly all of them were held back from circulation. They were instead stored and then later sold as bullion.

By 1906 natural market forces were driving the Philippine silver pesos out of commerce and into the melting pot: the rising price of silver made the coins worth more as precious metal than as legal tender. In 1907 the U.S. Mint responded by lowering the denomination's silver fineness from .900 to .800 and reducing its diameter from 38 mm to 35. The resulting smaller coins had about one-third less silver, by actual weight, than those of 1903 to 1906, guaranteeing that they would stay in circulation. The older coins, meanwhile, were still profitable to pull aside and melt for their silver value. An official report of June 30, 1911, disclosed that less than ten percent of the heavier silver coins still remained in the Philippines.

The new smaller pesos were minted every year from 1907 to 1912, with the San Francisco Mint producing them for commerce and the Philadelphia Mint striking a small quantity of Proofs in 1907 and 1908. Millions of the coins were stored as backing for Silver Certificates (and, later, Treasury Certificates) in circulation in the Philippines. Although the Manila Mint started operations in 1920, the silver peso was never part of its production for circulation.

In December 1941, Imperial Japan, immediately after attacking Pearl Harbor, began a fierce assault on the Philippines. Manila fell on January 2, 1942, and General Douglas MacArthur, commander of U.S. Army Forces in the Far East, fell back to the Bataan Peninsula. In late February President Franklin Roosevelt ordered him to leave the Philippines for Australia, prompting the general's famous promise to the Philippine people: "I shall return!" Not long after the fighting erupted it had become apparent that the Japanese would overtake the islands, and early in 1942 the U.S. military dumped crates holding 15,700,000 silver pesos, mostly of 1907–1912 coinage, into the sea near Corregidor, to avoid their seizure. Many millions of these coins were salvaged by the U.S. Treasury and the Central Bank of the Philippines after the war, with all but about five million pieces being reclaimed by 1958. Today a great majority of the salvaged "war pesos" show clear evidence of their prolonged submersion in saltwater. A typical effect is a dark corrosion strongly resistant to any manner of cleaning or conservation.

Striking and Sharpness. The silver pesos of 1903 to 1906 generally have well-struck obverses, but occasionally with some flattening of the figure's frontal hair above her ear, and sometimes her left bosom and hand. On the reverse, the feathers on the eagle's breast are indistinctly cut, and the wing tips can sometimes be found slightly flatly struck. Of the silver pesos of 1907 to 1912, some but not all exhibit flattened frontal hair, and sometimes a flattened left hand. On the reverse, the eagle's breast feathers are not clearly defined. On some examples the reverses are quite unevenly struck; check the top part of the shield, which has a depressed middle and raised sides, and the right side, which is slightly higher than the left and may show some flattening.

One Peso, 1903–1906

High Points of Wear. ***Obverse Checkpoints:*** 1. Figure's upper-left leg and knee. 2. Figure's right knee. 3. Figure's left bosom. 4. Frontal hair just above ear. ***Reverse Checkpoints:*** 1. Eagle's breast feathers. 2. Eagle's right leg. 3. Eagle's wing tips.

One Peso, 1907–1912

High Points of Wear. ***Obverse Checkpoints:*** 1. Figure's upper-left leg and knee. 2. Figure's lower-left leg. 3. Figure's left hand. 4. Frontal hair just above ear. ***Reverse Checkpoints:*** 1. Eagle's breast feathers. 2. Eagle's right leg.

Proofs. Proof pesos were struck at the Philadelphia Mint for annual Proof sets in 1903, 1904, 1905, 1906, and 1908. Unlike the smaller denominations, Proof pesos of 1907 also are known—but only to the extent of two examples.

1905-S, Curved Serif on "1"

1905-S, Straight Serif on "1"

Circulation Strikes

	Mintage	GSID	AU-50	MS-60	MS-63	MS-65
One Peso, Large Size (1903–1906)	**n/a**	**393671**	**$100**	**$575**	**$1,100**	**$6,000**
1903	2,788,901	25367	160	1,400	2,750	11,000
1903-S	11,361,000	25999	130	700	1,250	8,750
1904	11,355	26000	240	775	1,600	6,000
1904-S	6,600,000	26002	100	575	1,100	31,000
1905-S, Curved Serif, Allen-16.06	6,056,000	26004	405	3,750	17,000	—
1905-S, Straight Serif, Allen-16.06a, FS-301	*	26005	2,200	14,500	43,000	—
1906-S	201,000	26007	18,000	60,000	180,000	—
	Auctions: $156,000, PCGS MS-63 HA 08/24					
1907-S	10,278,000	26008	120	215	1,150	7,500

	Mintage	GSID	AU-50	MS-60	MS-63	MS-65
1908-S	20,954,944	25374	$150	$340	$850	$10,000
↳1908-S, S/S, Allen-17.03a	*	376194	1,250	3,500	6,250	—
1909-S	7,578,000	25375	130	260	950	7,000
↳1909-S, S/S, Allen-17.04a, FS-501	*	373179	775	1,900	3,250	—
↳1909-S, S/S/S, Allen-17.04b	*	373503	5,000	9,500	—	—
1910-S	3,153,559	26010	210	1,500	2,400	10,500
	Auctions: $102,000, PCGS MS-67 HA 01/22					
1911-S	463,000	26011	850	4,100	9,750	17,000
	Auctions: $120,000, PCGS MS-67 HA 08/24					
1912-S	680,000	26012	850	8,750	19,000	53,000

Note: Philippine silver pesos of 1907–1912 that were corroded from submersion in Caballo Bay during World War II are worth considerably less than their problem-free counterparts, but are avidly collected for their historical value. * Included in number above.

Proof Strikes

	Mintage	GSID	PF-60	PF-63	PF-65
1903	2,558	25998	$850	$1,300	$2,800
1904	1,355	26001	1,100	1,600	3,250
1905	471	26003	2,300	4,200	7,000

	Mintage	GSID	PF-60	PF-63	PF-65
1906	500	26006	$2,600	$5,500	$8,000
1908	500	26009	1,250	2,000	3,250

EXPLORING VARIETIES

This is the go-to reference for coins struck in the Philippines while under U.S. sovereignty (1903–1945). Allen numbers are widely used by collectors and dealers to identify varieties within the series. This cataloging system gives structure to a specialized but growing field of U.S.-related numismatics.

Allen, Lyman L. *U.S. Philippine Coins.* Oakland Park, FL: 1998.

COMMONWEALTH ISSUES FOR CIRCULATION (1937–1945)

The Philippine Islands were largely self-governed, as a commonwealth of the United States, from 1935 until full independence was recognized in 1946. Coinage under the Commonwealth began with three commemorative coins in 1936 (see next section). Circulating issues were minted from 1937 to 1941 (in Manila) and in 1944 and 1945 (in Philadelphia, Denver, and San Francisco).

The Commonwealth coinage retained the obverse motifs designed by Melecio Figueroa and used on the coinage of 1903 to 1936. Its new reverse design featured a shield derived from the official seal of the government of the Philippines, with three stars symbolizing Luzon, Mindanao, and the Visayas, the islands' three main geographical regions. In the oval set in the shield's center is a modification of the colonial coat of arms of the City of Manila: a fortress tower above with a heraldic crowned *morse* or sea-lion (half dolphin, half lion) below. An eagle with outstretched wings surmounts the entirety of the shield design, and beneath is a scroll with the legend COMMONWEALTH OF THE PHILIPPINES.

World War II forced the Commonwealth government to operate in exile during the Japanese occupation of 1942 to 1945. A pro-Japan puppet government was set up in Manila in 1943; it issued no coins of its own, and in fact during the Japanese occupation many coins were gathered from circulation to be melted and remade into Japanese coins. Barter and low-denomination emergency paper money took their place in day-to-day commerce. (Much of the money used in the Philippines during World War II consisted of hastily printed "guerrilla" currency.) The United States military knew of the local need for circulating coins, and the U.S. and Philippine governments included new coinage in the plans to liberate the islands. The U.S. Treasury Department used its Philadelphia, San Francisco, and Denver mints to produce brass, copper-nickel-zinc, and silver coins in 1944 and 1945, to be shipped to the Philippines during and after the liberation.

Note that mintage figures given for 1938, 1939, 1940, and 1941 are estimates, as many Manila Mint records were lost during the war.

BRONZE AND BRASS COINAGE

ONE CENTAVO (1937–1944)

Designer: *Melecio Figueroa (obverse).* **Weight:** *5.3 grams.*
Composition: *.950 copper, .050 tin and zinc (except for 1944-S: .950 copper, .050 zinc).*
Diameter: *24 mm.* **Edge:** *Plain.* **Mints:** *Manila and San Francisco.*

Bronze Alloy (1937–1941)

Mintmark location is on the reverse, to the left of the date.

Brass Alloy (1944)

History. The Manila Mint struck one-centavo coins for the Commonwealth of the Philippines every year from 1937 through 1941. This production was brought to an end by the Japanese invasion that started in December 1941, immediately after the bombing of Pearl Harbor. Part of the United States–Commonwealth plan to retake the islands included the San Francisco Mint's 1944 striking of 58 million one-centavo coins—a quantity greater than all of Manila's centavo output since 1937. Like the federal Lincoln cents of 1944 to 1946, these coins were made of *brass* rather than bronze—their alloy was derived in part from recycled cartridge cases, and their composition included copper and zinc, but no tin (a vital war material). The coins were transported to the islands to enter circulation as U.S. and Philippine military forces fought back the Japanese invaders. This would be the final mintage of centavos until the Republic of the Philippines, created on July 4, 1946, resumed the denomination's production in 1958.

The centavo was a popular coin that saw widespread circulation. As a result, many of the coins today are found with signs of wear or damage, exacerbated by corrosion and toning encouraged by the islands' tropical climate.

Striking and Sharpness. Well-struck examples are uncommon. Obverses of the Commonwealth centavos usually have very flat or depressed strikes in the left shoulder of the seated figure, and part of the face and chest. His right hand is better struck than in the coins struck under U.S. sovereignty. The left side of the anvil's edge is slightly rounded. On the reverse, many Uncirculated coins have flatness on the lower and central sections of the coat of arms, and some or most of the words COMMONWEALTH OF THE PHILIPPINES are unreadable.

On a perfectly struck coin, the eagle surmounting the Commonwealth shield would have a pattern of feathers visible on its breast; this level of detail is rarely evident, with the breast instead appearing smooth or flat.

Many 1937-M centavos have a barely readable mintmark. Issues of 1938 to 1941 used a narrow M mintmark, rather than a square version of the letter, resulting in better legibility.

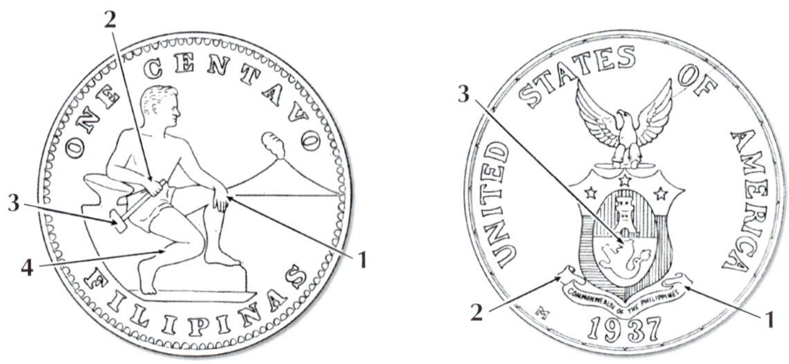

One Centavo, 1937–1944

High Points of Wear. ***Obverse Checkpoints:*** 1. Figure's left hand. 2. Figure's right hand. 3. Head of hammer. 4. Figure's right calf. ***Reverse Checkpoints:*** 1. Inner-right fold of ribbon. 2. Outer-left fold of ribbon. 3. Center of coat of arms.

Circulation Strikes

	Mintage	GSID	AU-50	MS-60	MS-63	MS-65
1937-M	15,790,492	25890	$9.50	$27	$40	$70
1938-M	10,000,000	25893	12.00	35	55	100
1939-M	6,500,000	25896	9.50	24	40	70
1940-M	4,000,000	25899	$9.50	$24	$40	$75
1941-M	5,000,000	25902	9.50	24	40	70
1944-S	58,000,000	25905	6.75	12	16	22

Copper-Nickel and Copper-Nickel-Zinc Coinage

Five Centavos (1937–1945)

Designer: *Melecio Figueroa (obverse).* **Weight:** *1937–1941, 4.8 grams; 1944–1945, 4.92 grams.* **Composition:** *1937–1941, .750 copper, .250 nickel; 1944–1945, .650 copper, .230 zinc, .120 nickel.* **Diameter:** *19 mm.* **Edge:** *Plain.* **Mints:** *Manila, Philadelphia, and San Francisco.*

Copper-Nickel (1937–1941)

Mintmark location is on the reverse, to the left of the date (Manila and San Francisco issues only; Philadelphia issues have no mintmark).

Copper-Nickel-Zinc (1944–1945)

Manila mintmark style of 1937 and 1941 (wide, with midpoint not extending to baseline).

Manila mintmark style of 1938 (narrow, with midpoint extending to baseline).

History. The Manila Mint switched its coinage of five-centavo pieces to the Commonwealth reverse design in 1937. Production of the coins increased in 1938, then skipped two years. The 1941 output would be Manila's last for the type; the Japanese invasion at year's end stopped all of its coinage.

Philippine commerce was starved for coins during the war. As part of the broader strategy for liberating the Philippines from Japanese occupation, the U.S. Treasury Department swung its mints into production of five-centavo coins in 1944 (Philadelphia and San Francisco) and 1945 (San Francisco alone). This effort dwarfed that of the Commonwealth's late-1930s coinage, producing in those two years more than ten times the combined output of 1937, 1938, and 1941. In order to help save copper and nickel for military use, the U.S. Mint reduced the proportions of those metals in the five-centavo coinage, making up for them with the addition of zinc. This substitution saved more than 4.2 million pounds of nickel and 3.2 million pounds of copper for the war effort. The Philadelphia and San Francisco coins were shipped to the islands during the combined American-Filipino military operations against Japan.

Striking and Sharpness. Most pre-war five-centavo coins are poorly struck. On the obverse, the seated figure's left hand is flat, and the left shoulder can be as well. The left side of the pedestal and the right side of Mount Mayon can be poorly detailed. The obverse rim typically lacks sharpness. On the reverse, the ribbon usually is flat, with its wording partially or completely illegible, and the coat of arms can lack detail especially at the top-left side. On a perfectly struck coin, the eagle surmounting the Commonwealth shield would have a pattern of feathers visible on its breast; this level of detail is rarely evident, with the breast instead appearing smooth or flat.

The mintmark style of 1937 and 1941—a wide M, with the middle point not descending to the letter's baseline—usually did not strike clearly, making it difficult to read. The mintmark style of 1938 was narrower, with the middle point descending to the base, and typically is more legible.

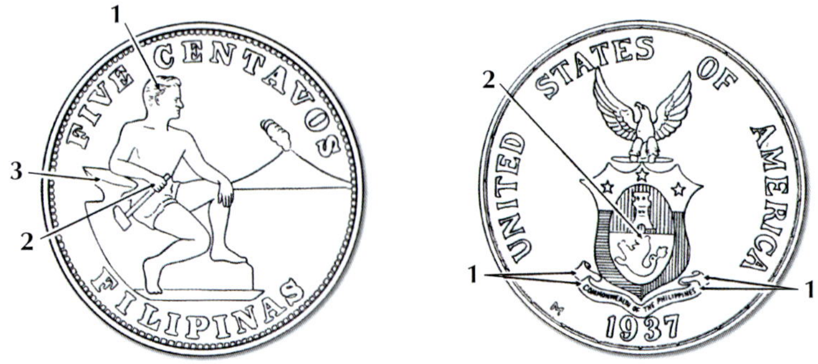

Five Centavos, 1937–1945

High Points of Wear. ***Obverse Checkpoints:*** 1. Frontal hair just above ear. 2. Figure's right hand. 3. Edge of anvil. ***Reverse Checkpoints:*** 1. Inner and outer folds of ribbon. 2. Center of coat of arms.

Circulation Strikes

	Mintage	GSID	AU-50	MS-60	MS-63	MS-65
1937-M	2,493,872	25990	$20	$40	$90	$155
1938-M	4,000,000	25991	20	40	70	260
1941-M	2,750,000	25992	20	70	145	1,250
1944-(P)	21,198,000	25993	$4.10	$13.50	$34	$160
1944-S	14,040,000	25994	4.10	13.50	34	70
1945-S	72,796.00	25995	5.50	13.50	34	115

Silver Coinage

Ten Centavos (1937–1945)

Designer: *Melecio Figueroa.* **Weight:** *2 grams (.0482 oz. ASW).* **Composition:** *.750 silver, .250 copper.* **Diameter:** *16.5 mm.* **Edge:** *Reeded.* **Mints:** *Manila and Denver.*

Mintmark location is on the reverse, to the left of the date.

History. As with its production of other denominations, the Manila Mint under Commonwealth governance struck ten-centavo coins in 1937 and 1938, followed by a hiatus of two years, and a final coinage in 1941. Normal mint functions were interrupted in 1941 when Imperial Japan invaded the Philippines as part of its war with the United States. The Japanese puppet government of 1943–1945 would not produce any of its own coins, and the Manila Mint, damaged by bombing during the Japanese assault, was later used as part of the invaders' defensive fortifications on the Pasig River.

Japan's wartime exportation of Philippine coins resulted in scarcity of coinage in day-to-day commerce. The U.S. Treasury geared up the Denver Mint for a massive production of Philippine ten-centavo coins in 1944 and 1945, to be shipped overseas and enter circulation as American and Philippine troops liberated the islands. The 1945 coinage was particularly heavy: more than 130 million ten-centavo coins, compared to the Denver Mint's production of just over 40 million Mercury dimes that year. This large mintage of silver coins continued to circulate in the Philippines into the 1960s.

Striking and Sharpness. Well-struck examples of the Commonwealth ten-centavo coin are unusual. Part of the figure's bust is nearly always flatly struck, especially along the left side. The hair and left arm may also be poorly struck. On the reverse, the coat of arms usually lacks detail, and COMMONWEALTH OF THE PHILIPPINES, on the ribbon, often is only partly legible. On a perfectly struck coin, the eagle surmounting the Commonwealth shield would have a pattern of feathers visible on its breast; this level of detail is rarely evident, with the breast instead appearing smooth or flat.

The Denver coinage of 1944 and 1945 often is weakly struck on the obverse, with loss of detail. The reverse typically is weakly struck on the ribbon, with indistinct lettering.

The mintmark style of 1937 and 1941—a wide M, with the middle point not descending to the letter's baseline—usually did not strike clearly, making it difficult to read. The mintmark style of 1938 was narrower, with the middle point descending to the base, and typically is more legible.

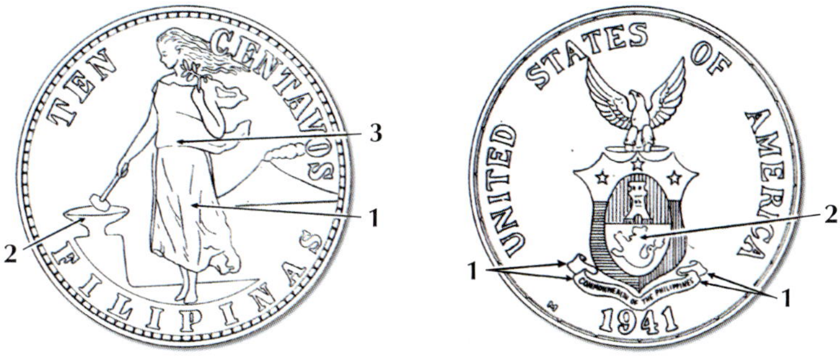

Ten Centavos, 1937–1945

High Points of Wear. ***Obverse Checkpoints:*** 1. Figure's left leg. 2. Edge of anvil. 3. Mid-drapery area. ***Reverse Checkpoints:*** 1. Inner and outer folds of ribbon. 2. Center of coat of arms.

Circulation Strikes

	Mintage	GSID	AU-50	MS-60	MS-63	MS-65
1937-M	3,500,000	25764	$6.75	$13.50	$38	$160
1938-M	3,750,000	25765	13.50	47.00	100	155
1941-M	2,500,000	25766	6.75	20.00	38	155
1944-D	31,592,000	25767	2.90	13.50	34	70
1945-D	137,208,000	25768	2.90	6.75	14	27
↳1945-D, D Over D, Allen-9.05a, FS-501	*	373175	27.00	70.00	130	230
↳1945-D, Doubled Die Reverse, Allen-9.05b	*	85086	325.00	900.00	1,500	2,750

* Included in number above.

Twenty Centavos (1937–1945)

Designer: *Melecio Figueroa (obverse).* **Weight:** *4 grams (.0964 oz. ASW).* **Composition:** *.750 silver, .250 copper.* **Diameter:** *20 mm.* **Edge:** *Reeded.* **Mints:** *Manila and Denver.*

Mintmark location is on the reverse, to the left of the date.

History. The twenty-centavo piece was the largest circulating coin struck by the Commonwealth of the Philippines at the Manila Mint. Production commenced in 1937 and 1938, followed by a hiatus of two years, and a final year of output in 1941 before Japan's December invasion put a halt to all coinage. During their occupation, the Japanese pulled many twenty-centavo pieces out of circulation and melted them as raw material for new imperial coins.

Anticipating driving the Japanese military out of the islands, the United States and Commonwealth governments planned an impressive production of coinage for the Philippines in 1944 and 1945. The Denver Mint was the source for twenty-centavo pieces, and its output was immense, in 1945 exceeding even the Philadelphia Mint's production of Washington quarters for domestic use. 111 million of the coins were shipped overseas to accompany the U.S. military as Americans and Filipinos fought to liberate the islands. The need was great, as legal-tender coins had largely disappeared from circulation. Most day-to-day commerce was transacted with small-denomination scrip notes and paper money issued by guerrilla military units, local governments, or anti-Japanese military and civilian currency boards.

Striking and Sharpness. Well-struck twenty-centavo Commonwealth coins are a challenge to locate. Nearly all obverses have flattened hair on the figure's head. On the reverse, the coat of arms usually lacks detail, and COMMONWEALTH OF THE PHILIPPINES, on the ribbon, often is only partly legible. The Denver coins typically lack sharp details on the obverse and have the same reverse weakness as earlier Manila issues.

On a perfectly struck coin, the eagle surmounting the Commonwealth shield would have a pattern of feathers visible on its breast; this level of detail is rarely evident, with the breast instead appearing smooth or flat.

The mintmark style of 1937 and 1941—a wide M, with the middle point not descending to the letter's baseline—usually did not strike clearly, making it difficult to read. The mintmark style of 1938 was narrower, with the middle point descending to the base, and typically is more legible.

Twenty Centavos, 1937–1945

High Points of Wear. ***Obverse Checkpoints:*** 1. Figure's left thigh and knee. 2. Figure's left hand. 3. Edge of anvil. ***Reverse Checkpoints:*** 1. Inner folds of ribbon. 2. Center of coat of arms.

1944-D, D Over S

Circulation Strikes

	Mintage	GSID	AU-50	MS-60	MS-63	MS-65
1937-M	2,665,000	25939	$13.50	$27.00	$50	$150
1938-M	3,000,000	25940	13.50	20.00	34	110
1941-M	1,500,000	25941	13.50	27.00	55	115
1944-D	28,596,000	25942	13.50	20.00	34	90
↳1944-D, D Over S, Allen-12.04a, FS-501	*	25943	115.00	170.00	215	525
1945-D	82,804,000	25944	9.50	13.50	16	34

* Included in number above.

Fifty Centavos (1944–1945)

Designer: *Melecio Figueroa.* **Weight:** *10 grams (.2411 oz. ASW).*
Composition: *.750 silver, .250 copper.* **Diameter:** *27 mm.*
Edge: *Reeded.* **Mint:** *San Francisco.*

Mintmark location is on the reverse, to the left of the date.

History. No fifty-centavo coins were struck at the Manila Mint for the Commonwealth of the Philippines. The denomination's first issue was a wartime production of the San Francisco Mint, in 1944, to the extent of some 19 million coins, or double that facility's production of Liberty Walking half dollars for the year. This was followed by a similar mintage in 1945. These coins were intended to enter circulation after being shipped overseas with the U.S. military during the liberation of the Philippines from Imperial Japan's 1942–1945 occupation. They were readily accepted in the coin-starved wartime economy and continued to circulate in the islands into the 1960s.

Striking and Sharpness. Many Commonwealth fifty-centavo coins are lightly struck, but they typically show flattening less severe than that of the 1907–1921 issues struck under U.S. sovereignty. On the reverse, the coat of arms usually is weakly struck, with COMMONWEALTH OF THE PHILIPPINES rarely completely legible. On a perfectly struck coin, the eagle surmounting the Commonwealth shield would have a pattern of feathers visible on its breast; this level of detail is rarely evident, with the breast instead appearing smooth or flat.

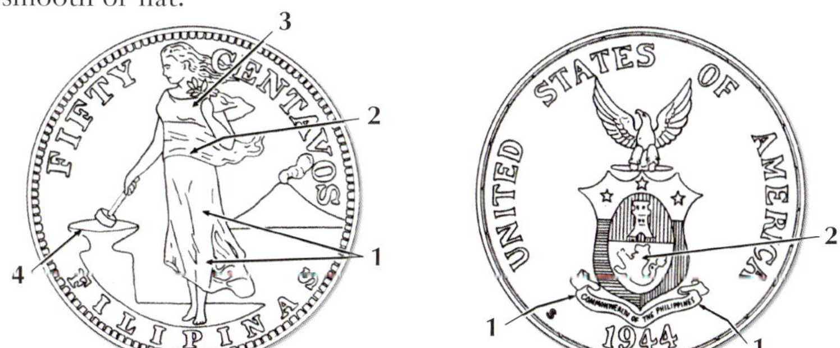

Fifty Centavos, 1944–1945

High Points of Wear. ***Obverse Checkpoints:*** 1. Figure's left thigh and lower leg. 2. Mid-drapery area. 3. Figure's left bosom. 4. Edge of anvil. ***Reverse Checkpoints:*** 1. Inner folds of ribbon. 2. Center of coat of arms.

1945-S, S Over S

Circulation Strikes

	Mintage	GSID	AU-50	MS-60	MS-63	MS-65
1944-S	19,187,000	25964	$13.50	$34	$40	$130
↳**1944-S, Obverse of 1907, FS-401, FS-401**	*	373178	70.00	210	370	—
1945-S	18,120,000	25965	13.50	27	34	90
↳**1945-S, S Over S, Allen-15.02a, FS-501**	*	68441	55.00	120	195	525

* Included in number above.

COMMONWEALTH COMMEMORATIVE ISSUES

The American territory of the Philippines was governed by the U.S. military from 1899 to mid-1901. Its executive branch was managed by the Bureau of Insular Affairs (part of the War Department) from mid-1901 to 1935. In the latter year the Philippines' status was changed to that of a commonwealth—a type of organized but unincorporated dependent territory, self-governed (except in defense and foreign policy) under a constitution of its own adoption, whose right of self-government would not be unilaterally withdrawn by Congress. This was a step in the direction of complete independence, scheduled to be recognized after an additional ten years of "nation building."

To celebrate this transfer of government, the Manila Mint in 1936 produced a set of three silver commemorative coins—one of the fifty-centavo denomination, and two of the one-peso. These were designed by Ambrosio Morales, professor of sculpture at the University of the Philippines School of Fine Arts.

The fifty-centavo coin and one of the set's pesos feature busts of Philippine president Manuel L. Quezon and the last U.S. governor-general, Frank Murphy, who served (largely ceremonially) as the first U.S. high commissioner to the Commonwealth of the Philippines. On the fifty-centavo piece the two men face each other with the rising sun between them; on the peso, they appear jugate (in conjoined profile portraits). The other peso has busts of Quezon and U.S. president Franklin D. Roosevelt. This was a rare instance of a living American president appearing on a coin, the only precedent being the 1926 Sesquicentennial commemorative half dollar, which showed President Calvin Coolidge.

On each of the three coins appears the date November 15, 1935, when the new commonwealth's government was inaugurated on the steps of the Legislative Building in Manila, witnessed by 300,000 people in attendance.

The set's issue price was $3.13, or about 2.5 times the coins' face value expressed in U.S. dollars. Commemorative coins were popular in the United States at the time, but still these sets sold poorly, and thousands remained within the Philippine Treasury at the onset of World War II. In early 1942 many if not all of the remainders were crated and thrown into Caballo Bay, to keep them (along with millions of older silver pesos) from being captured by the approaching forces of Imperial Japan. Today many of the coins are found with corrosion caused by their long exposure to saltwater before being salvaged.

FIFTY CENTAVOS (1936)

Designer: *Ambrosio Morales (obverse).* **Weight:** *10 grams (.2411 oz. ASW).*
Composition: *.750 silver, .250 copper.* **Diameter:** *27.5 mm.* **Edge:** *Reeded.* **Mint:** *Manila.*

Striking and Sharpness. This issue typically is found well struck.

Circulation Strikes

	Mintage	GSID	AU-50	MS-60	MS-63	MS-65
1936-M, Half Peso, Busts of Roosevelt and Quezon, Silver	20,000	25963	$70.00	$155	$260	$850
1947-S, Half Peso, MacArthur, Silver	200,000	25549	14.50	20	31	100

ONE PESO (1936)

Designer: *Ambrosio Morales (obverse).* **Weight:** *20 grams (.5144 oz. ASW).*
Composition: *.800 silver, .200 copper.* **Diameter:** *35 mm.* **Edge:** *Reeded.* **Mint:** *Manila.*

One Peso, Busts of Murphy and Quezon

One Peso, Busts of Roosevelt and Quezon

Striking and Sharpness. Sharply struck gems of the Murphy/Quezon peso can be a challenge to locate. Weak strike is evident on the reverse in particular, where the sea lion can be softly detailed. On some pieces, tiny bubbles resulting from improper fabrication of the planchet can be observed among the letters surrounding the rim.

The Roosevelt/Quezon peso typically is found well struck.

Circulation Strikes

	Mintage	GSID	AU-50	MS-60	MS-63	MS-65
1936-M, One Peso, Busts of Roosevelt and Quezon, Silver	10,000	26013	$70	$260	$390	$625
1936-M, One Peso, Busts of Murphy and Quezon, Silver	10,000	26014	80	195	340	750
1947-S, One Peso, MacArthur, Silver	100,000	25551	42	55	75	155

APPENDIX A

Misstrikes and Errors

With the production of millions of coins each year, it is natural that a few abnormal pieces escape inspection and are inadvertently released for circulation, usually in original bags or rolls of new coins. These are not considered regular issues because they were not made intentionally. They are all eagerly sought by collectors for the information they shed on minting techniques, and as a variation from normal date and mint series collecting.

MISSTRUCK COINS AND ERROR PIECES

Nearly every misstruck or error coin is unique in some way, and prices may vary from coin to coin. They may all be classified in general groups related to what kind of mint error they are, such as double-strikes, off-metals, and so on. Collectors value these pieces according to the scarcity and popularity of each kind of error. Non-collectors usually view them as curios and often believe that they must be worth much more than normal coins because they look so strange. In reality, the value assigned to various types of errors by collectors and dealers reflects both supply and demand, and is based on recurring transactions between willing buyers and sellers.

The following listings show current average values for the most frequently encountered kinds of error coins. In each case, the values shown are for coins that are unmarred by serious marks or scratches, and in Uncirculated condition for modern issues, and Extremely Fine condition for obsolete types. Exceptions are valued higher or lower. Error coins of rare-date issues generally do not command a premium beyond their normal values. In many cases each of these coins is unique in some respect and must be valued according to its individual appearance, quality, and eye appeal.

There are many other kinds of errors and misstruck coins beyond those listed in this book. Some are more valuable, and others less valuable. Those listed here are examples some of the most popular error types, and are some of what this interesting field of coin collecting contains. The pieces illustrated are general, average examples of the types described.

Early in 2002 the mints changed their production methods to a new system designed to eliminate deformed planchets, off-center strikes, and similar errors. They also changed the delivery system of bulk coinage, and no longer shipped loose coins in sewn bags to be counted and wrapped by banks or counting rooms, where error coins were often found and sold to collectors. Under the new system, coins are packaged in large quantities and go directly to automated counters that filter out deformed coins. The result has been that, for all but very minor errors, few error coins have entered the market since 2002. The values shown in these listings are for pre-2002 coins; those dated after that, with but a few exceptions, are valued considerably higher.

For additional details and information about these coins, the following books are recommended:

Margolis, Arnold, and Fred Weinberg. *The Error Coin Encyclopedia* (4th ed.). 2004.

Herbert, Alan. *Official Price Guide to Minting Varieties and Errors*. New York, 1991.

Fivaz, Bill, and J.T. Stanton. *The Cherrypickers' Guide to Rare Die Varieties*. Florence, AL. Updated regularly.

The coins discussed in this section must not be confused with others that have been mutilated or damaged after leaving the mint. Examples of such pieces include coins that have been scratched, hammered, engraved, impressed, acid etched, or plated by individuals to simulate something other than a normal coin. Those pieces have no numismatic value, and are considered altered coins not suitable for a collection.

TYPES OF ERROR COINS

***Clipped Planchet*—A coin with a portion of the planchet missing.** Clipped planchets result from accidents when the blanking dies, used to punch out blanks from the metal strip, either overlap a portion of the strip already punched or they overlap a portion of the strip's edge. The most common types of clips include curved, straight, ragged, incomplete, and elliptical clips. Values may be higher or lower depending on the nature and size of the clip. Coins with more than one clip usually command higher values.

***Multiple Strike*—A coin struck more than once.** The strike can be on top of the prior strike, or off-center. Values increase with the number of strikes. Double strikes occur when a struck coin goes back into the press and is struck again. The presence of a date, and having a large portion of both strikes visible can bring a higher value.

No Rim With Rim

***Blank or Planchet*—A blank disc of metal intended for coinage but not struck with dies.** In the process of preparation for coinage, the blanks are first punched from a strip of metal and then milled to upset the rim, which makes them a planchet. In most instances, blanks are slightly more valuable than the planchets. Values shown are for the planchets.

***Cud Die Break*—A coin showing raised metal originating from a broken die.** Cud die breaks are coins that have a raised area of metal that is connected to the coin's rim. Die breaks that are not touching the rim are simply called *die breaks* or *die cracks* and have little or no value. *Retained cuds* are very similar, but have the design still "on the cud," and have some "movement" that separates that portion of design from the rest of it. As a rule, the larger the cud, the more valuable it is.

***Off Center*—A coin that has been struck largely out of collar, with some of the design missing.** This error occurs when a planchet is fed between the dies so that it is not fully centered, resulting in an off-center strike. The ideal proportion off-center is generally considered to be 50 percent. Values are for coins with approximately 10 to 20 percent of the design missing from obsolete coins, or 20 to 60 percent missing from modern coins.

***Broadstrike*—A coin that was struck outside the collar die.** When coins are struck without being contained in the collar die, they spread out larger than normal pieces. A broadstrike may have a minor trace of reeding at two opposite poles of a coin, or a minor trace around no more than a quarter of the coin's edge. More than that amount makes it another error type called a *partial collar*.

***Lamination*—A flaw whereby a portion of metal is missing from the coin's surface.** This defect occurs when a foreign substance, such as gas oxides or dirt, becomes trapped in the strip as it is rolled out to the proper thickness, causing a area with metal missing. Lamination flaws may be missing or still attached to the coin's surface. Minor flaws may only decrease a coin's value, while a large lamination is worth more.

Brockage—**A mirror image of all or part of a coin's design impressed into its opposite side.** These errors are caused when a struck coin remains on or overlapping either die after striking, and when another planchet is fed between the dies, it strikes the prior coin into the new planchet, leaving a negative or mirror image. Full-mirror brockages are more valuable than partial-brockage coins; also, the sharper and larger the brockage, the higher the value. Other types of brockages can occur. Coins with negative impressions on both sides are usually mutilated pieces made outside the Mint when a coin is "sandwiched" between two others and all are pressed together.

Wrong or Off-Metal Planchet—**A coin struck on a planchet intended for another denomination or made of the wrong metal.** This can happen when Mint equipment is used for different coin denominations, as with the bins that transport planchets to coining presses. Examples of wrong-planchet errors are cents struck on dime planchets, nickels on cent planchets, and quarters on dime planchets. Values vary depending on the denominations involved and the rarity of the error. Those struck on existing coins of a different denomination are called *double denominations* and typically are of much greater value. Another type of error involves coins struck on planchets for the correct denomination but composed of the wrong metal—these are called *transitional off-metals* because they tend to occur when the Mint has switched from one metallic composition to another. One famous example (and also the most valuable error) is the 1943 cent struck in bronze (pictured), rather than in that year's new steel composition. (Fewer than three dozen are thought to exist.).

Mule—**A coin struck with an incorrect pairing of dies.** This error occurs when a coin is struck with the wrong design on the obverse die, the reverse die, or the collar die. Some such coins have two obverses, one on each side. Others have an incorrect design on one side, such as a dime obverse with a cent reverse. In such cases, the denomination is determined by the planchet; a dime obverse and cent reverse on a cent planchet would be considered a one-cent coin mule. Mules are generally the second most valuable error type, after the off-metal strikes.

Mint-Canceled Coins

In mid-2003, the U.S. Mint acquired machines to eliminate security concerns and the cost associated with providing Mint police escorts to private vendors for the melting of scrap, substandard struck coins, planchets, and blanks. Under high pressure, the rollers and blades of these machines cancel the coins and blanks by impressing them with a texture that resembles the surface of a waffle, and they are popularly known by that term. This process has effectively kept most misstruck coins produced after 2003 from becoming available to collectors. Waffled examples are known for all six 2003-dated coin denominations, from the Lincoln cent through the Sacagawea dollar. The Mint has not objected to these pieces' trading in the open market because they are not considered coins with legal tender status.

Misstruck and Error Pieces

	5% Clipped Planchet	Double Struck	Blank, No Raised Rim	Planchet, Raised Rim	Cud Die Break	Off Center	Broadstrike	Lamination	Brockage
Large Cent	$100	$1,250	—	$225	—	$600	$200	$50	$1,000
Indian Head 1¢	15	1,000	—	—	40	175	100	20	450
Lincoln 1¢ (95% Copper)	5	50	$4	3	35	12	15	3	45
Steel 1¢	25	1,000	175	150	50	175	100	15	400
Lincoln 1¢ (Zinc)	5	40	3	3	35	10	15	10	40
Liberty 5¢	30	1,500	—	—	—	350	200	20	1,500
Buffalo 5¢	8	2,500	—	—	100	400	350	30	1,500
Jefferson 5¢	4	50	12	15	50	15	15	10	50
Wartime 5¢	8	500	1,000	750	75	250	175	10	450
Barber 10¢	100	3,000	—	—	200	300	225	25	1,500
Mercury 10¢	15	1,750	—	—	175	200	150	15	1,250
Roosevelt 10¢ (Silver)	8	300	50	40	100	120	100	12	175
Roosevelt 10¢ (Clad)	4	65	5	4	40	15	18	10	50
Washington 25¢ (Silver)	40	1,000	175	150	150	400	200	25	500
Washington 25¢ (Clad)	5	250	125	7	75	80	50	25	75
Bicentennial 25¢	30	750	—	—	400	150	100	30	400
State 25¢	40	500	—	—	45	150	80	30	350
Franklin 50¢	35	3,500	—	—	—	5,000	2,500	40	1,500
Kennedy 50¢ (40% Silver)	30	1,000	165	150	—	450	400	40	650
Kennedy 50¢ (Clad)	15	800	125	100	100	300	100	25	400
Bicentennial 50¢	40	1,000	—	—	950	400	150	40	550
Silver $1	80	6,000	1,200	1,100	1,000	3,000	1,000	75	—
Eisenhower $1	40	1,500	150	120	500	600	200	50	950
Bicentennial $1	50	1,800	—	—	750	750	300	60	1,100
Anthony $1	40	750	175	100	300	300	100	30	450
Sacagawea $1	150	2,500	175	50	350	1,500	600	50	1,750

WRONG PLANCHETS

	Zinc 1¢	Copper 1¢	Steel 1¢	5¢	Silver 10¢	Copper-Nickel Clad 10¢	Silver 25¢	Copper-Nickel Clad 25¢	Copper-Nickel Clad 50¢
Indian Head 1¢	(a)	—	(a)	(a)	$18,000	(a)	(a)	(a)	(a)
Lincoln 1¢	—	—	—	(a)	1,300	$400	(a)	$12,500	$10,000
Buffalo 5¢	(a)	$5,000	(a)	—	10,000	(a)	(a)	(a)	(a)
Jefferson 5¢	$400	350	$3,000	—	550	400	(a)	(a)	(a)
Wartime 5¢	(a)	3,000	3,500	$5,000	2,300	(a)	(a)	(a)	(a)
Washington 25¢ (Silver)	(a)	1,000	10,000	750	1,300	—	—	—	(a)
Washington 25¢ (Clad)	—	900	(a)	275	6,000	400	$6,000	—	(a)
Bicentennial 25¢	(a)	3,000	(a)	2,500	—	3,500	—	—	(a)
State 25¢ (b)	7,000	(a)	(a)	1,250	(a)	7,000	(a)	—	(a)
Walking Liberty 50¢	(a)	—	35,000	—	35,000	(a)	20,000	(a)	(a)
Franklin 50¢	(a)	7,500	(a)	6,500	7,500	(a)	2,000	(a)	(a)
Kennedy 50¢ (c)	(a)	3,000	(a)	1,750	3,000	2,500	1,000	850	—
Bicentennial 50¢	(a)	7,000	(a)	3,000	—	—	—	1,500	—
Eisenhower $1	(a)	10,000	(a)	9,000	—	9,500	—	6,000	2,750
Anthony $1	—	4,000	(a)	6,000	(a)	—	—	850	(a)
Sacagawea $1	17,000	(a)	(a)	12,000	(a)	13,000	(a)	5,000	(a)

Note: Coins struck over other coins of different denominations are usually valued three to five times higher than these prices. Coins made from mismatched dies (State quarter obverse combined with Sacagawea dollar reverse) are extremely rare. **a.** Not possible. **b.** Values for State quarter errors vary with each type and state, and are generally much higher than for other quarters. **c.** The Kennedy fifty-cent piece struck on an Anthony one-dollar planchet is very rare.

APPENDIX B

Collectible Red and Blue Books

The book you are reading is the *Deluxe Edition* of a classic hobby reference, the *Guide Book of United States Coins*, popularly known as the *Red Book*. More than 25 million copies of the *Red Book* have been sold since 1946, making it one of the best-selling nonfiction titles in American publishing history. By 1959 more than 100,000 copies were being printed annually. The 1965 (18th) edition, published in 1964, reached a peak of 1,200,000 copies. That year the *Red Book* was ranked fifth on the list of best-selling nonfiction—ahead of Dale Carnegie's classic *How to Win Friends and Influence People* (at number 6) and John F. Kennedy's *Profiles in Courage* (at number 9).

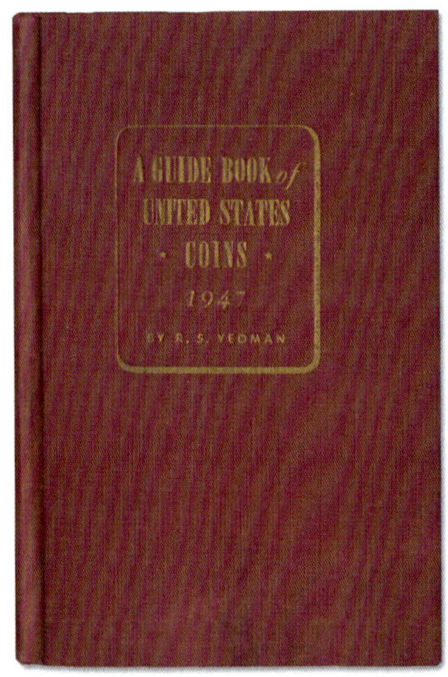

The first edition of *A Guide Book of United States Coins*, published in 1947.

The idea for the *Red Book* started in the 1940s with R.S. Yeoman. Employed by Whitman Publishing Company (part of Western Publishing), Yeoman at first created the *Blue Book* (official title, the *Handbook of United States Coins With Premium List*), which gave hobbyists an overview of American coinage and a detailed guide to the prices that dealers were paying for collectible coins. The first edition was published in 1942. Yeoman saw that collectors wanted even more information, and he began compiling data and records for an expanded *retail* version of the *Blue Book* (showing how much a collector could expect to pay a dealer for coins). After World War II ended, Yeoman and his team introduced the new volume, the *Guide Book of United States Coins*, soon nicknamed the *Red Book* because of its distinctive cover color.

Numismatist Kenneth E. Bressett joined the *Red Book* in 1956 as a freelance editor. He took a full-time editorial position with Whitman Publishing in 1959, and assumed full editorship of the *Red Book* in 1975. Today Bressett is the *Red Book*'s editor emeritus, with Jeff Garrett serving as senior editor and John Feigenbaum as publisher.

THE *RED BOOK* AS A COLLECTIBLE

The *Guide Book of United States Coins* holds the record as the longest-running annual retail coin-price guide. It has passed its 80th anniversary, and collectors seem to be almost as interested in assembling sets of old *Red Book*s as of old coins. The demand for old *Red Book*s has created a solid market. Some who collect these old editions maintain reference libraries of all kinds of coin publications. To them, having one of each edition is essential, because that is the way old books are collected. Others are speculators who believe that the value of old editions will go up as interest and demand increase. Many people who save old *Red Book*s do so to maintain a record of coin prices going back further than that in any other source.

Following price trends in old *Red Book*s is a good indicator of how well individual coins are doing in comparison to each other. The price information published in each year is an average of what collectors are paying for each coin. It is a valuable benchmark, showing how prices have gone up or down over the years. Information like this often gives investors an edge in predicting what the future may hold.

Old *Red Book*s are also a handy resource on collecting trends. They show graphically how grading has changed over the years, what new coins have been discovered and added to the listings, and which areas are growing in popularity. Studying these old books can be educational as well as nostalgic. It's great fun to see what your favorite coins sold for 15 or 25 years ago or more—and a bit frustrating to realize what might have been if we had only bought the right coins at the right time in years past.

Many collectors have asked about the quantities printed of each edition. That information has never been published, and now no company records exist specifying how many were made. The original author, R.S. Yeoman, told inquirers that the first press run in November 1946 was for 9,000 copies. In February 1947 an additional 9,000 copies were printed to satisfy the unexpected demand.

There were several edits between the first and second printings. The most well-known involves the wording at the bottom of page 135. In the first printing it reads, "which probably accounts for the scarcity of this date." In the second printing, those last few words were changed to "the scarcity of 1903 O."

The second edition had a press run of 22,000. The printing of each edition thereafter gradually increased, with the highest number ever being reached with the 18th edition, dated 1965 and published in 1964. At the top of a booming coin market, a whopping 1,200,000 copies were produced. Since that time the numbers have decreased, but the *Red Book* still maintains a record of being the world's largest-selling coin publication each year.

In some years a very limited number of *Red Book*s were made for use by price contributors. Those were interleaved with blank pages. No more than 50 copies were ever made for any one year. Perhaps fewer than 20 were made in the first few years. Three of these of the first edition, and one of the second edition, are currently known. Their value is now in four figures. Those made in the 1960s sell for about $300–$500 today.

There are other unusual *Red Book*s that command exceptional prices. One of the most popular is the 1987 special edition that was made for, and distributed only to, people who attended the 1986 American Numismatic Association banquet in Milwaukee. Only 500 of those were printed with a special commemorative cover.

Error books are also popular with collectors. The most common is one with double-stamped printing on the cover. The second most frequently seen are those with an upside-down cover. Probably the best known of the error books is the 1963 16th edition with a missing page. For some uncanny reason, page 239 is duplicated in some of those books, and page 237 is missing. The error was corrected on most of the printing.

The terminology used to describe book condition differs from that utilized in grading coins. A "Very Fine" book is one that is nearly new, with minimal signs of use. Early editions of the *Red Book* are rarely if ever found in anything approaching "New" condition. Exceptionally well-preserved older editions command a substantial premium and are in great demand. Nice used copies that are still clean and in good shape, but slightly worn from use, are also desirable. Only the early editions are worth a premium in badly worn condition.

For a more detailed history and edition-by-edition study of the *Red Book*, see Frank J. Colletti's *A Guide Book of The Official Red Book of United States Coins* (Whitman, 2009).

See also *A Penny Saved: R.S. Yeoman and His Remarkable Red Book*, by Kenneth Bressett (Whitman, 2021). That volume is a history of Whitman and the *Red Book*, and a biography of Yeoman as well as an autobiography of Bressett.

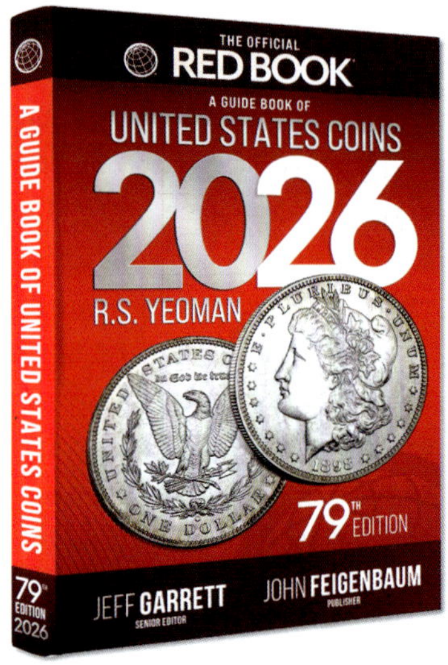

The *Red Book* received a much-needed update in 2025 (cover date 2026). The publisher embarked on a multi-year project to bring the content in line with modern collector usage, and the trim size was expanded accordingly.

Valuation Guide for Past Editions of the *Red Book*

Classic Hardcover Binding

See page 1058 for special editions in the classic hardcover binding.

Year/Edition	Issue Price	VG	F	VF	New
1947 (1st ed.), 1st Printing	$1.50	$225	$365	$600	$1,175 **(a)**
1947 (1st ed.), 2nd Printing	1.50	160	285	450	1,100 **(a)**
1948 (2nd ed.)	1.50	50	100	210	500 **(a)**
1949 (3rd ed.)	1.50	50	90	200	500 **(a)**
1951/52 (4th ed.)	1.50	50	80	175	350 **(a)**
1952/53 (5th ed.)	1.50	65	110	310	700 **(a)**
1953/54 (6th ed.)	1.75	25	40	55	85
1954/55 (7th ed.)	1.75	25	40	55	85
1955 (8th ed.)	1.75	25	35	50	75
1956 (9th ed.)	1.75	15	30	40	65
1957 (10th ed.)	1.75	10	15	35	40
1958 (11th ed.)	1.75		8	12	20
1959 (12th ed.)	1.75		8	10	20
1960 (13th ed.)	1.75		7	9	20
1961 (14th ed.)	1.75		4	6	20
1962 (15th ed.)	1.75		4	6	15
1963 (16th ed.)	1.75		2	6	15
1964 (17th ed.)	1.75		3	4	10
1965 (18th ed.)	1.75		3	4	10
1966 (19th ed.)	1.75		3	4	10
1967 (20th ed.)	1.75		2	3	8
1968 (21st ed.)	2		2	3	8
1969 (22nd ed.)	2		2	3	8
1970 (23rd ed.)	2.50		2	3	8
1971 (24th ed.)	2.50		2	3	7
1972 (25th ed.)	2.50		2	3	7
1973 (26th ed.)	2.50		2	3	7

Year/Edition	Issue Price	VG	F	VF	New
1974 (27th ed.)	$2.50		$2	$3	$7
1975 (28th ed.)	3.00			3	6
1976 (29th ed.)	3.95			3	6
1977 (30th ed.)	3.95			3	6
1978 (31st ed.)	3.95			3	6
1979 (32nd ed.)	3.95			3	6
1980 (33rd ed.)	3.95			3	6
1981 (34th ed.)	4.95			2	5
1982 (35th ed.)	4.95			2	5
1983 (36th ed.)	5.95			2	5
1984 (37th ed.)	5.95			2	5
1985 (38th ed.)	5.95			2	5
1986 (39th ed.)	5.95			2	5
1987 (40th ed.)	6.95			2	5
1988 (41st ed.)	6.95			2	5
1989 (42nd ed.)	6.95			2	5
1990 (43rd ed.)	7.95			2	5
1991 (44th ed.)	8.95			2	5
1992 (45th ed.)	8.95			2	5
1993 (46th ed.)	9.95				5
1994 (47th ed.)	9.95				3
1995 (48th ed.)	10.95				3
1996 (49th ed.)	10.95				3
1997 (50th ed.)	11.95				3
1998 (51st ed.)	11.95				2
1999 (52nd ed.)	11.95				2
2000 (53rd ed.)	12.95				2

Note: Values are for unsigned books. Those signed by R.S. Yeoman are worth substantially more. **a.** Values are for books in Near Mint condition, as truly New copies are effectively nonexistent.

Year/Edition	Issue Price	VG	F	VF	New
2001 (54th ed.)	$13.95				$2
2002 (55th ed.)	14.95				2
2003 (56th ed.)	15.95				2
2004 (57th ed.)	15.95				2
2005 (58th ed.)	15.95				2
2006 (59th ed.)	16.95				2
2007 (60th ed.)	16.95				2
2008 (61st ed.)	16.95				2
2009 (62nd ed.)	16.95				2
2010 (63rd ed.)	16.95				2
2011 (64th ed.)	16.95				2
2012 (65th ed.)	16.95				2
2013 (66th ed.)	16.95				2

Year/Edition	Issue Price	VG	F	VF	New
2014 (67th ed.)	$16.95				$2
2015 (68th ed.)	16.95				2
2016 (69th ed.)	16.95				2
2017 (70th ed.)	16.95				2
2018 (71st ed.) (b)	16.95				2
2019 (72nd ed.) (c)	17.95				2
2020 (73rd ed.)	17.95				2
2021 (74th ed.)	17.95				2
2022 (75th ed.) (d)	17.95				2
2023 (76th ed.)	19.95				2
2024 (77th ed.)	19.95				2
2025 (78th ed.)	19.95				2

b. The 2018 hardcover features a back-cover gold-foil portrait of David Rittenhouse, first director of the United States Mint, in celebration of 225 years of U.S. coinage at Philadelphia. **c.** The 2019 *Red Book* (in every format) includes a 10-page illustrated tribute to Editor Emeritus Kenneth Bressett. The back of the hardcover features a silver-foil portrait of Bressett. **d.** Features a silver-foil emblem for the 75th anniversary of the *Red Book.*

Softcovers (1993–2007)

The first softcover (trade paperback) *Red Book* was the 1993 (46th) edition. The softcover binding was offered (alongside other formats) in the 1993, 1994, 1995, and 1996 editions; again in the 1998 edition; and from 2003 through 2007. All are fairly common and easily collectible today. Values in New condition range from $2 up to $3–$4 for the earlier editions.

Spiralbound Softcovers (1997 to Date)

The first spiralbound softcover *Red Book* was the 1997 (50th) edition. The spiralbound softcover format was next available in the 1999 edition, and it has been an annually offered format every edition since then. Today the spiralbound softcovers all are easily collectible. The 1997 edition is worth $4 in New condition, and later editions are valued around $2.

Spiralbound Hardcovers (2008 to Date)

The first spiralbound hardcover *Red Book* was the 2008 (61st) edition. The format has been available (alongside other formats) every edition since. All spiralbound hardcovers are readily available to collectors, and are valued from $2 to $4.

Journal Edition (2009)

The large-sized Journal Edition, featuring a three-ring binder, color-coded tabbed dividers, and removable pages, was issued only for the 2009 (62nd) edition. Today it is valued at $5 in VF and $30 in New condition.

Large Print Editions (2010 to Date)

The oversized Large Print format of the *Red Book* has been offered annually since the 2010 (63rd) edition. All editions are readily available to collectors and are valued at $5 in New condition.

Essential Edition (2013–2017)

A magazine-sized softcover version of the *Red Book*, called the *Essential Edition*, was published annually from 2013 to 2017. Aimed at mainstream readers, it featured large print and focused on the most popular federal coins. Copies are rarely seen on the secondary market; valued around $10.

Leather Limited Editions (2005–2019)

	Print Run	Issue Price	Current Value
2005 (58th ed.)	3,000	$69.95	$60
2006 (59th ed.)	3,000	69.95	60
2007 (60th ed.)	3,000	69.95	60
2007 1947 Tribute Edition	500	49.95	85
2008 (61st ed.)	3,000	69.95	60
2008 (61st ed.), Numismatic Literary Guild (a)	135 **(b)**		550
2008 (61st ed.), American Numismatic Society (c)	250 **(b)**		350
2009 (62nd ed.)	3,000	69.95	60
2010 (63rd ed.)	1,500	$69.95	$60
2011 (64th ed.)	1,500	69.95	60
2012 (65th ed.)	1,000	69.95	60
2013 (66th ed.)	1,000	69.95	60
2014 (67th ed.)	1,000	69.95	60
2015 (68th ed.)	500	99.95	100
2016 (69th ed.)	500	99.95	100
2017 (70th ed.)	500	99.95	100
2018 (71st ed.)	500	99.95	100
2019 (72nd ed.)	500	99.95	100

a. One hundred thirty-five imprinted copies of the 2008 leather Limited Edition were created. Of these, 125 were distributed to members of the NLG at its 2007 literary awards ceremony; the remaining 10 were distributed from Whitman Publishing headquarters in Atlanta. **b.** Included in total print-run quantity. **c.** Two hundred fifty copies of the 2008 leather Limited Edition were issued with a special bookplate honoring the 150th anniversary of the ANS. They were distributed to attendees of the January 2008 celebratory banquet in New York.

Special Editions

Year/Edition	Print Run	Issue Price	VF	New
1987 (40th ed.), American Numismatic Association 95th Anniversary	*500*		$450	$675
1992 (45th ed.), American Numismatic Association 100th Anniversary	*600*		100	175
1997 (50th ed.), *Red Book* 50th Anniversary	1,200	$24.95	40	60
2002 (55th ed.), American Numismatic Association "Target 2001"	500	100.00	25	40
2002 (55th ed.), SS *Central America*		35.00	20	30
2005 (58th ed.), FUN (Florida United Numismatists) 50th Anniversary	*1,100*		35	60
2007 (60th ed.), American Numismatic Association 115th Anniversary	500		35	60
2007 (60th ed.), Michigan State Numismatic Society 50th Anniversary	*500*		35	60
2007 (1st ed.), 1947 Tribute Edition		17.95	5	20
2008 (61st ed.), ANA Milwaukee World's Fair of Money	*1,080*		25	55
2008 (61st ed.), Stack's Rare Coins			10	20
2010 (63rd ed.), Hardcover, Philadelphia Expo (a)		24.95	20	40
2011 (64th ed.), Boston Numismatic Society		85.00	40	75
2012 (65th ed.), American Numismatic Association	800	100.00	25	50
2013 (66th ed.), American Numismatic Society (b)	250		150	250
2015 (68th ed.), Central States Numismatic Society	500	15.00	25	60
2016 (69th ed.), American Numismatic Association 125th Anniversary		100.00	40	75
2018 (71st ed.), NGC 30th Anniversary			60	100
2020 (73rd ed.), Chicago Coin Club 100th Anniversary	250			90
2021 (74th ed.), Philippine Collectors Forum / 100th Anniversary Manila Mint (c)	250	25.00		125
2023 (76th ed.), American Numismatic Association "Celebrating 131 Years" (c)	1,500			10
2024 (77th ed.), American Numismatic Association 132nd Anniversary (d)	1,512			50
2025 (78th ed.), Central States Numismatic Society 85th Anniversary	500			50

a. Two thousand and nine copies of a special 2010 hardcover edition were made for distribution to dealers at the premiere Whitman Coin and Collectibles Philadelphia Expo (September 2009). Extra copies were sold at $50 apiece with proceeds benefiting the National Federation for the Blind. **b.** Two hundred fifty copies of the 2013 hardcover were issued with a special bookplate honoring ANS Trustees' Award recipient (and *Red Book* research contributor) Roger Siboni. **c.** Two hundred fifty copies were printed, but some were destroyed in shipping, resulting in total distribution of 212 books. **d.** The 2023 and 2024 ANA editions were distributed as membership premiums.

THE *BLUE BOOK* AS A COLLECTIBLE

The precursor to the *Red Book* was the *Handbook of United States Coins With Premium List*, popularly known as the *Blue Book*. Its mastermind was R.S. Yeoman, who had been hired by Western Publishing as a commercial artist in 1932. He distributed Western's Whitman line of "penny boards" to coin collectors, promoting them through department stores, along with children's books and games. He eventually arranged for Whitman to expand the line into other denominations, giving them the reputation of a numismatic endeavor rather than a "game" of filling holes with missing coins. He also developed these flat boards into a line of popular folders.

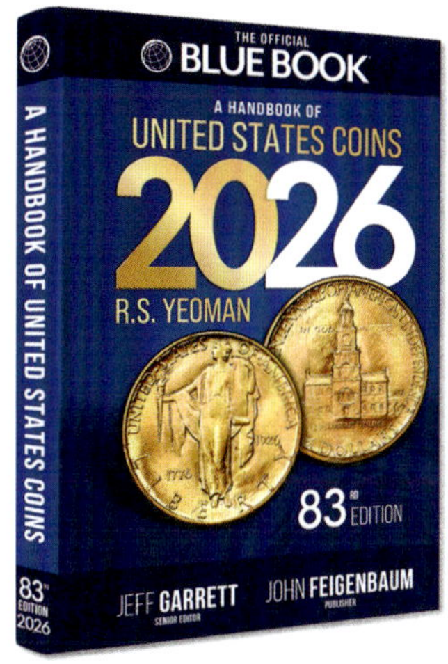

Although more collectors and dealers than ever before now get their pricing information online, the print edition of *A Handbook of United States Coins* remains a popular resource.

Yeoman began to compile coin-mintage data and market values to aid collectors. This research grew into the *Blue Book*: now collectors had a coin-by-coin guide to the average prices dealers would pay for U.S. coins. The first two editions were both published in 1942.

In the first edition of the *Red Book*, Whitman Publishing would describe the *Blue Book* as "a low-priced standard reference book of United States coins and kindred issues" for which there had been "a long-felt need among American collectors."

The *Blue Book* has been published annually (except in 1944 and 1950) since its debut. Past editions offer valuable information about the hobby of yesteryear as well as developments in numismatic research and the marketplace. Old *Blue Book*s are collectible; most editions after the 12th can be found for a few dollars in VF or better condition. Major variants were produced for the third, fourth, and ninth editions, including perhaps the only "overdate" books in American numismatic publishing. Either to conserve the previous years' covers or to correct an error in binding, the cloth on some third-edition covers was overstamped "Fourth Edition," and a number of eighth-edition covers were overstamped "Ninth Edition." The third edition was produced in several shades of blue ranging from light to dark. Some copies of the fourth edition were also produced in black cloth—the only time the *Blue Book* was bound in other than blue.

The history of the *Blue Book* is given by Kenneth Bressett in *A Penny Saved: R.S. Yeoman and His Remarkable Red Book* (Whitman, 2021). In that book, Bressett reveals recent archival research that shows there were two printings of the first edition of the *Blue Book*, with significant differences between them.

VALUATION GUIDE FOR SELECT PAST EDITIONS OF THE *BLUE BOOK*

Edition	Date (a)		VF	New
	Title Page	Copyright		
1st	1942	1942	$75	$210
2nd	1943	1942	35	50
3rd	1944	1943	25	45
4th	*none*	1945	25	40
5th	*none*	1946	20	40
6th	1948	1947	12	30
7th	1949	1948	11	20
8th	1950	1949	10	20
9th	1952	1951	5	10
10th	1953	1952	5	10

a. During its early years of production, the *Blue Book*'s date presentation was not standardized. Full information is given here to aid in precise identification of early editions.

APPENDIX C

Top 100 U.S. Coin Prices Realized at Auction

KEY

Price: The sale price of the coin, including the appropriate buyer's fee.

Attributions ("Coin" column): B = Baker (for pre-federal), Bolender (for silver dollars), Breen (for gold), or Browning (for quarter dollars); BB = Bowers/Borckardt; BD = Bass-Dannreuther; J = Judd; JR = John Reich Society; N = Newman; O = Overton; P = Pollock; S = Sheldon; T = Taraskza.

Rank	Price	Coin	Grade	Firm	Date
1	$18,872,250	$20, 1933	MS-65	Sotheby's	Jun-21
2	10,016,875	Silver $1, 1794	PCGS SP-66 CAC	Stack's Bowers	Jan-13
3	9,360,000	Prefederal, 1787, Brasher Doubloon, EB on Wing	NGC MS-65* CAC	Heritage	Jan-21
4	8,400,000	$5, 1822	PCGS AU-50	Stack's Bowers	Mar-21
5	7,680,000	Silver $1, 1804, Class I	PCGS PF-68	Stack's Bowers	Aug-21
6	7,590,020	$20, 1933	Gem BU	Sotheby's/Stack's	Jul-02
7	7,200,000	$20, 1861, Paquet Reverse	PCGS MS-67 CAC	Heritage	Aug-21
8	6,600,000	Silver $1, 1794	PCGS MS-66+ CAC	Heritage	Aug-21
9	5,520,000	$3, 1870-S	PCGS SP-50 893 Engraved	Heritage	Jan-23
10	5,280,000	$10, 1804, Plain 4, BD-2	PCGS 65+ DC CAC	Heritage	Jan-21
11	4,993,750	Silver $1, 1794	PCGS MS-66+	Stack's/Sotheby's	Sep-15
12	4,620,000	$5, 1821	PCGS PF65 Cam CAC	Heritage	Sep-22
13	4,582,500	Prefederal, 1787, Brasher Doubloon, EB on Wing	NGC MS-63 CAC	Heritage	Jan-14
14	4,560,000	5¢, 1913, Liberty Head	PCGS PF-66 CAC	Stack's Bowers	Aug-18
15	4,440,000	$20, 1927-D	PCGS MS-66	Heritage	Aug-22
16	4,320,000	$20, MCMVII, Ultra High Relief, Lettered Edge, Inverted	PCGS PF-69	Heritage	Aug-23
17	4,140,000	Silver $1, 1804, Class I	PCGS PF-68	B&M	Aug-99
18	4,080,000	$5, 1825/4/1, BD-1	PCGS PF-67 Cam CAC	Stack's Bowers	Aug-22
19	3,960,000	Trade $1, 1885	NGC PF-66	Heritage	Jan-19
20	3,877,500	Silver $1, 1804, Class I	PCGS PF-62	Heritage	Aug-13
21	3,840,000	$5, 1829, Small Date, BD-2	PCGS PF-66+ CAC	Heritage	Aug-23
22	3,737,500	5¢, 1913, Liberty Head	NGC PF-64	Heritage	Jan-10
23	3,737,500	Silver $1, 1804, Class I	NGC PF-62	Heritage	Apr-08
24	3,600,000	10¢, 1873-CC, No Arrows	PCGS MS-65	Heritage	Jan-23
25	3,600,000	$20, MCMVII, Ultra High Relief, Lettered Edge	NGC PF-68	Heritage	Feb-21
26	3,360,000	$10, 1795, 9 Leaves, BD-3	PCGS MS-63+	Heritage	Jan-22
27	3,360,000	Silver $1, 1804, Class I	PCGS PF-65	Stack's Bowers	Dec-20
28	3,290,000	Silver $1, 1804, Class I	PCGS PF-65	Stack's/Sotheby's	Mar-17
29	3,290,000	5¢, 1913, Liberty Head	NGC PF-64 CAC	Heritage	Jan-14
30	3,172,500	5¢, 1913, Liberty Head	PCGS PF-63	Heritage	Apr-13
31	3,120,000	1/2 10¢, 1870-S	PCGS MS-64 CAC	Heritage	Jun-23
32	2,990,000	$20, MCMVII, Ultra High Relief, Lettered Edge	PCGS PF-69	Heritage	Nov-05

Rank	Price	Coin	Grade	Firm	Date
33	$2,990,000	Prefederal, 1787, Brasher Doubloon, EB on Breast	NGC EF-45	Heritage	Jan-05
34	2,880,000	$5, 1829, Large Date JD-1	PCGS PF-66+	Heritage	May-23
35	2,820,000	Silver $1, 1794	PCGS MS-64	Stack's Bowers	Aug-17
36	2,760,000	$20, MCMVII, Ultra High Relief, Lettered Edge	PCGS PF-69	Stack's Bowers	Jun-12
37	2,711,250	$10, 1795, 9 Leaves, BD-3	PCGS MS-63+ CAC	GreatCollections	May-23
38	2,640,000	Silver $1, 1804, Class I	PCGS PF-62	Heritage	Jun-18
39	2,585,000	$10, 1795, 13 Leaves, BD-4	PCGS MS-66+	Stack's/Sotheby's	Sep-15
40	2,585,000	Pattern, 1792, Birch Cent LE, J-4	NGC MS-65* RB CAC	Heritage	Jan-15
41	2,574,000	$4, 1880, Coiled Hair	NGC PF-67 Cam	Bonhams	Sep-13
42	2,520,000	Prefederal, 1652, New England Threepence	PCGS EF-45	Stack's Bowers	Nov-24
43	2,520,000	Pattern, 1792, Silver Center Cent, J-1	PCGS SP-67 BN CAC	Heritage	Jan-21
44	2,415,000	Prefederal, 1787, Brasher Doubloon, EB on Wing	NGC AU-55	Heritage	Jan-05
45	$2,400,000	$5, 1854-S	NGC EF-45	Heritage	Aug-21
46	2,350,000	$2.50, 1808	PCGS MS-65	Stack's/Sotheby's	May-15
47	2,350,000	1¢, 1793, Chain AMERICA, S-4	PCGS MS-66 BN CAC	Heritage	Jan-15
48	2,300,000	Silver $1, 1804, Class III	PCGS PF-58	Heritage	Apr-09
49	2,280,000	$10, 1804, Plain 4, BD-2	PCGS PF-63	Heritage	Sep-22
50	2,232,500	Pattern, 1792, Quarter, Copper, J-12	NGC MS-63 BN CAC	Heritage	Jan-15
51	2,185,000	$10, 1907, Rounded Rim	NGC Satin PF-67	Heritage	Jan-11
52	2,160,000	$3, 1855-S	PCGSS PF-64 Cam	Heritage	Feb-23
53	2,160,000	$2.50, 1796, No Stars, BD-2	PCGS MS-62+ CAC	Heritage	Jan-22
54	2,160,000	$20, 1927-D	PCGS MS-65+ CAC	Heritage	Jan-20
55	2,160,000	$5, 1854-S	NGC EF-45	Heritage	Aug-18
56	2,115,000	$20, MCMVII, Ultra High Relief, Lettered Edge	PCGS PF-68	Heritage	Jan-15
57	2,100,000	$10, 1795, 9 Leaves, BD-3	PCGS MS-64	Heritage	Jan-23
58	2,100,000	Prefederal, 1786, Brasher Doubloon, Lima Style	NGC MS-61 CAC	Heritage	Jan-21
59	2,100,000	Trade $1, 1885	PCGS PF-63+ Cam CAC	Heritage	Jan-21
60	2,086,875	Silver $1, 1893-S	PCGS MS-67 CAC	GreatCollections	Aug-21
61	2,010,000	$20, 1921	NGC PF-64+ CAC	Heritage	Aug-21
62	1,997,500	10¢, 1894-S	PCGS PF-66 CAC	Heritage	Jan-16
63	1,997,500	Pattern, 1792, Silver Center Cent, J-1	PCGS MS-64 BN CAC	Heritage	Aug-14
64	1,997,500	$20, 1927-D	NGC MS-66	Heritage	Jan-14
65	1,980,000	$5, 1798, Small Eagle, BD-1	PCGS AU-53	Heritage	Aug-23
66	1,980,000	Pattern, 1874, Bickford $10, J-1373	PCGS PF-65+ Cam	Heritage	Jan-22
67	1,920,000	$5, 1854-S	PCGS AU-58+ CAC	Stack's Bowers	Mar-20
68	1,897,500	$20, 1927-D	PCGS MS-67	Heritage	Nov-05
69	1,880,000	Pattern, 1879, Quintuple Stella, J-1643	PCGS PF-64 DC	Legend	May-16
70	1,880,000	Silver $1, 1804, Class III	NGC PF-55	Stack's Bowers	Aug-14
71	1,860,000	$4, 1880, Coiled Hair	NGC PF-67 Cam	Heritage	Feb-21
72	1,840,000	10¢, 1873-CC, No Arrows	PCGS MS-65	Stack's Bowers	Aug-12
73	1,840,000	5¢, 1913, Liberty Head	NGC PF-66	Superior	Mar-08
74	1,840,000	$20, MCMVII, Ultra High Relief, Lettered Edge	PCGS PF-68	Heritage	Jan-07
75	1,840,000	Silver $1, 1804, Class I	PCGS PF-64	Stack's	Oct-00
76	1,821,250	$4, 1880, Coiled Hair	NGC PF-67 CAC	Heritage	Apr-15
77	1,815,000	Silver $1, 1804, Class I	PF-63	B&M/Stack's	Apr-97
78	1,800,000	50¢, 1794, O-101a, T-7	PCGS MS-64+ CAC	Heritage	Jan-23
79	1,800,000	50¢, 1796, 16 Stars, O-102, T-2	PCGS MS-66	Heritage	Jan-23
80	1,800,000	$20, 1861, JD-1	PCGS PF-66 DC	Heritage	Jan-22
81	1,740,000	$2.50, 1824/1, JD-1	PCGS PF-67	Heritage	May-23
82	1,740,000	25¢, 1796, B-2	PCGS MS-66	Heritage	Jan-22
83	1,740,000	Prefederal, 1792, Washington, Large Eagle, Gold	NGC EF-45*	Heritage	Aug-18
84	1,725,000	$2.50, 1796, No Stars	PCGS MS-65	Heritage	Jan-08

Rank	Price	Coin	Grade	Firm	Date
85	$1,725,000	$10, 1920-S	PCGS MS-67	Heritage	Mar-07
86	1,680,000	$20, 1907, Small Edge Letters	PCGS PF-68 CAC	Heritage	Jan-23
87	1,680,000	50¢, 1797, O-101a	PCGS MS-66 CAC	Stack's Bowers	Mar-21
88	1,645,000	$20, 1861, Paquet Reverse	PCGS MS-61	Heritage	Aug-14
89	1,620,000	$20, 1870-CC	PCGS AU-53	Heritage	Nov-21
90	1,610,000	$10, 1839/8, Type of 1838, Large Letters	NGC PF-67 UC	Heritage	Jan-07
91	1,610,000	$20, 1861, Paquet Reverse	PCGS MS-61	Heritage	Aug-06
92	1,560,000	50¢, 1797, O-101a, T-1	PCGS MS-65+ CAC	Heritage	Jan-23
93	1,552,500	10¢, 1894-S	PCGS PF-64	Stack's	Oct-07
94	1,527,500	25¢, 1796, B-2	PCGS MS-66	Stack's/Sotheby's	May-15
95	1,527,500	50¢, 1797, O-101a	PCGS MS-66	Stack's/Sotheby's	May-15
96	1,527,500	Prefederal, 1776, Continental $1, Silver, N-3D	NGC MS-62	Heritage	Jan-15
97	1,527,500	Prefederal, 1776, Continental $1, Silver, N-1C	NGC EF-40	Heritage	Jan-15
98	1,527,500	25¢, 1796, B-2	NGC MS-67+* CAC	Heritage	Nov-13
99	1,500,000	10¢, 1894-S	NGC PF-66	Heritage	Sep-20
100	1,500,000	1¢, 1793, Chain, S-1	PCGS MS-64+ BN CAC	Heritage	Jan-19

APPENDIX D

Numismatic Glossary

Over the years coin collectors have developed a special jargon to describe their coins. The following list includes terms that are used frequently by coin collectors or that have a special meaning other than their ordinary dictionary definitions. You will find them useful when you want to discuss or describe your coins.

alloy—A combination of two or more metals.

altered date—A false date on a coin; a date altered to make a coin appear to be one of a rarer or more valuable issue.

argent—Silver metal; also silver or white in color, represented in heraldry by a plain, blank area.

azure—A pattern of narrow horizontal lines representing the color blue.

bag mark—A surface mark, usually a small nick, acquired by a coin through contact with others in a mint bag.

billon—A low-grade alloy of silver (usually less than 50%) mixed with another metal, typically copper.

blank—The formed piece of metal on which a coin design will be stamped.

bronze—An alloy of copper, zinc, and tin.

bullion—Uncoined gold or silver in the form of bars, ingots, or plate.

cast coins—Coins that are made by pouring molten metal into a mold, instead of in the usual manner of striking blanks with dies.

cent—One one-hundredth of the standard monetary unit. Also known as a *centavo*, *centimo*, or *centesimo* in some Central American and South American countries; *centime* in France and various former colonies in Africa; and other variations.

certified coin—A coin that has been graded, authenticated, and encapsulated in plastic by an independent (neither buyer nor seller) grading service.

cherrypicker—A collector who finds scarce and unusual coins by carefully searching through unattributed items in old accumulations or dealers' stocks.

circulation strike—An Uncirculated coin intended for eventual use in commerce, as opposed to a Proof coin.

clad coinage—Issues of the United States dimes, quarters, halves, and some dollars made since 1965. Each coin has a center core of pure copper and a layer of copper-nickel or silver on both sides.

collar—The outer ring, or die chamber, that holds a blank in place in the coinage press while the coin is impressed by the obverse and reverse dies.

contact marks—Minor abrasions on an Uncirculated coin, made by contact with other coins in a bag or roll.

countermark—A stamp or mark impressed on a coin to verify its use by another government or to indicate revaluation.

crack-out—A coin that has been removed from a grading service holder.

crown—Any dollar-size coin (c. 38 mm in diameter) in general, often struck in silver; specifically, one from the United Kingdom and some Commonwealth countries.

cud—An area of raised metal at the rim of a coin where a portion of the die broke off, leaving a void in the design.

designer—The artist who creates a coin's design. An engraver is the person who cuts a design into a coinage die.

die—A piece of metal, usually hardened steel, with an incuse reverse image, engraved with a design and used for stamping coins.

die crack—A fine, raised line on a coin, caused by a broken die.

die defect—An imperfection on a coin, caused by a damaged die.

die variety—Any minor alteration in the basic design of a coin.

dipped, dipping—Refers to chemical cleaning of a coin to remove oxidation or foreign matter.

double eagle—The United States twenty-dollar gold coin.

doubled die—A die that has been given two misaligned impressions from a hub; also, a coin made from such a die.

doubloon—Popular name for a Spanish gold coin originally valued at $16.

eagle—A United States ten-dollar gold coin; also refers to U.S. silver, gold, and platinum bullion pieces made from 1986 to the present.

edge—Periphery of a coin, often with reeding, lettering, or other decoration.

electrotype—A reproduction of a coin or medal made by the electrodeposition process. Electrotypes are frequently used in museum displays.

electrum—A naturally occurring mixture of gold and silver. Some of the world's first coins were made of this alloy.

encapsulated coins—Coins that have been authenticated, graded, and sealed in plastic by a professional service.

engrailed edge—A coin edge marked with small curved notches.

engraver—The person who engraves or sculpts a model for use in translating to a coin die.

error—A mismade coin not intended for circulation.

exergue—That portion of a coin beneath the main design, often separated from it by a line, and typically bearing the date.

field—The background portion of a coin's surface not used for a design or inscription.

filler—A coin in worn condition but rare enough to be included in a collection.

fineness—The purity of gold, silver, or any other precious metal, expressed in terms of one thousand parts. A coin of 90% pure silver is expressed as .900 fine.

flan—A blank piece of metal in the size and shape of a coin; also called a *planchet*.

gem—A coin of exceptionally high quality, typically considered MS-65 or PF-65 or better.

gripped edge—An edge with irregularly spaced notches.

gules—On a shield or flag, the color red, represented by a pattern of narrow vertical lines.

half eagle—The United States five-dollar gold coin minted from 1795 to 1929.

hub—A positive-image punch to impress the coin's design into a die for coinage.

incuse—The design of a coin that has been impressed below the coin's surface. A design raised above the coin's surface is in relief.

inscription—The legend or lettering on a coin.

intrinsic value—Bullion or "melt" value of the actual precious metal in a numismatic item.

investment grade—Promotional term; generally, a coin in grade MS-65 or better.

junk silver—Common-date silver coins taken from circulation; worth only bullion value.

key coin—One of the scarcer or more valuable coins in a series.

laureate—Head crowned with a laurel wreath.

legal tender—Money that is officially issued and recognized for redemption by an authorized agency or government.

legend—A principal inscription on a coin.

lettered edge—The edge of a coin bearing an inscription, found on some foreign and some older United States coins, modern Presidential dollars, and the MMIX Ultra High Relief gold coin.

luster—The brilliant or "frosty" surface quality of an Uncirculated (Mint State) coin.

milled edge—The raised rim around the outer surface of a coin, not to be confused with the reeded or serrated narrow edge of a coin.

mint error—Any mismade or defective coin produced by a mint.

mint luster—Shiny "frost" or brilliance on the surface of an Uncirculated or Mint State coin.

mintmark—A small letter or other mark on a coin, indicating the mint at which it was struck.

Mint set—A set of Uncirculated coins packaged and sold by the Mint. Each set contains one of each of the coins made for circulation at each of the mints that year.

motto—An inspirational word or phrase used on a coin.

mule—A coin struck from two dies not originally intended to be used together.

obverse—The front or face side of a coin.

or—Gold metal; also gold in color, represented in heraldry by a pattern of evenly spaced dots.

overdate—Date made by superimposing one or more numerals on a previously dated die.

overgraded—A coin in poorer condition than stated.

overstrike—An impression made with new dies on a previously struck coin.

pale—On a shield or flag, a wide, vertical stripe or band.

patina—The green or brown surface film found on ancient copper and bronze coins, caused by oxidation over a long period of time.

pattern—Experimental or trial coin, generally of a new design, denomination, or metal.

pedigree—The record of previous owners of a rare coin.

planchet—The blank piece of metal on which a coin design is stamped.

Proof—Coins struck for collectors by the Mint using specially polished dies and planchets.

Proof set—A set of each of the Proof coins made during a given year, packaged by the Mint and sold to collectors.

quarter eagle—The United States $2.50 gold coin.

raw—A coin that has not been encapsulated by an independent grading service.

reeded edge—The edge of a coin with grooved lines that run vertically around its perimeter, as seen on modern United States silver and clad coins.

regula—The bar separating the numerator and the denominator in a fraction.

relief—Any part of a coin's design that is raised above the coin's field is said to be in relief. The opposite of relief is incuse, meaning sunk into the field.

restrike—A coin struck from genuine dies at a later date than the original issue.

reverse—The back side of a coin.

rim—The raised portion of a coin that protects the design from wear.

round—A round one-ounce silver medal or bullion piece.

series—A set of one coin of each year of a specific design and denomination issued from each mint. For example, Lincoln cents from 1909 to 1959.

slab—A hard plastic case containing a coin that has been graded and encapsulated by a professional service.

spot price—The daily quoted market value of precious metals in bullion form.

token—A privately issued piece, typically with an exchange value for goods or services, but not an official government coin.

trade dollar—Silver dollar issued especially for trade with a foreign country. In the United States, trade dollars were first issued in 1873 to stimulate commerce with the Orient. Many other countries have also issued trade dollars.

truncation—The sharply cut-off bottom edge of a bust or portrait.

type—A series of coins defined by a shared distinguishing design, composition, denomination, and other elements. For example, Barber dimes or Franklin half dollars.

type set—A collection consisting of one representative coin of each type, of a particular series or period.

Uncirculated—A circulation-strike coin that has never been used in commerce, and has retained its original surface and luster; also called Mint State.

unique—An item of which only one specimen is known to exist.

variety—A coin's design that sets it apart from the normal issue of that type.

wheaties—Lincoln cents with the wheat ears reverse, issued from 1909 to 1958.

year set—A set of coins for any given year, consisting of one of each denomination issued that year.

Bibliography

The reader may view a bibliography, if desired, via the QR code at right.

Image Credits

The reader may view the image credits, if desired, via the QR code at right.

Index

1792 proposed coinage, 166–168
1916 (2016) Centennial gold tribute coins, 71
  Standing Liberty tribute quarter, 927
  Walking Liberty tribute half dollar, 927
  Winged Liberty tribute dime, 927
1916 Centennial Gold series, 927
1921 Morgan and Peace Dollar Centennial coins, 72
1921 Silver Dollar Coin Anniversary Act, 698, 751
1922 Silver Dollar Coin Anniversary Act
  coins produced under, 751–753
230th Anniversary Flowing Hair High Relief gold bullion coin, 977

abbreviations
  in *Mega Red*, 95
Adams, Eva, 57
Alabama, 880
Albany Church Pennies, 151
Albany, New York, 880
albums and folders
  National, 46
  Whitman, 47, 52, 54
Alibaba, 85
AliExpress, 85
Allen, Lyman L., 1038
Allen numbers, 1038
altered coins, 83
altered surfaces, 83
Amazon, 85
American Arts Commemorative Series, 61
American Buffalo gold bullion program, 960–962
American Eagle bullion programs, 939–959
American Gold Eagles (1986 to date), 61, 944–950
  privy-marked, 950
American Half Cents: The "Little Half Sisters," 170, 171
American Independence
  Sesquicentennial of, 882, 891
  See also Bicentennial coinage
American Innovation dollars, 746–750
American Journal of Numismatics, 33
American Legion, 898, 901, 911, 919
American Liberty High Relief gold bullion coins, 71, 973–974
American Museum of Natural history, 66
  formation of, 36
  headquarters of, 59, 66
American Numismatic Association (ANA), 63, 74
  headquarters of, 60, 63
  official grading standards of, 76
  outreach to young collectors, 90
  World's Fair of Money, 90
American Palladium Eagles (2017 to date), 71, 958–959
American Plantations coinage, 117–118
American Platinum Eagles (1997 to date), 951–957
  privy-marked, 952
American Silver Eagles (1986 to date), 61, 939–943
America the Beautiful quarters (2010 to date), 67, 545–556
America the Beautiful silver bullion program, 969–972
ANACS, 62, 82
Andrews, Esao, 102, 102
Anthony dollars. *See* Susan B. Anthony dollars
Anti-Counterfeiting Educational Foundation (ACEF), 87
APMEX, 90
Apollo 11, 59, 898, 901, 912, 919
Arkansas, 880
Artazn, 105
artificial intelligence, 91
Artistic Infusion Program (AIP), 65
auction records
  in *Mega Red*, 95
  See also appendix C
auctions, streaming online, 89
Auctori Plebis tokens, 149, 149
authenticity
  aspects of, 82–84
  defined, 82–83
  See also counterfeits

bald eagle, 897, 909, 919
Baldwin & Co., 992
Bank of the United States, 16
Barber designs
  dimes, 37, 53, 444–449
  half dollars, 626–630
  quarter dollars, 509–514
Bar coppers, 149, 149
barter, 1, 107, 107
Bass, Harry W. Jr., 58, 800
Bath metal, 118, 118
Battle of Antietam, 880
Battle of Gettysburg, 881
Battle of Lexington and Concord, 881
B (Bolender) numbers, 658

B (Browning) numbers, 480
Bechtler, August, 983
Bechtler, Christopher, 17, 981
gold coinage of, 981–983
Bermuda, 110, 110
Bessent, Scott, 105
Best of the Mint Semiquincentennial gold coins, 100–104, 928
final designs for, 103–104
BG (Breen-Gillio) numbering system, 1000
Bicentennial coinage (1776–1976), 58
half dollars, 645, 649
modern dollars, 726, 728, 729
quarter dollars, 58, 522, 531
Bill of Rights, 894, 900, 905, 918
billon coinage (1709–1760), 129
bimetallic coins, 922–926
Birch cent, 167
bit, 9
Bland-Allison Act of February 28, 35
blank, unstruck, 1049
Blue Book, the. *See Handbook of United States Coins* (the *Blue Book*); *and appendix B*
Bolender, M.H., 658
Boone bicentennial, 47
Boone, Daniel, 881
Boudinot, Elias, 14
Boy Scouts of America, 897, 910
Boys Town, 898, 901, 911, 919
Braided Hair designs
half cents, 194–197
large cents, 245–258
Braille, Louis, 897, 910
branch mints, 17–54
breast-cancer awareness, 898, 901, 911, 919
Breen, Walter, 170
Bressett, Ken, 92
Bridgeport, Connecticut, 881
British copper coins, 144
British halfpence, 7
British New World issues, 110–116
British royal patent coinage, 117–122
British silver coinage, 110
broadstrike, 1050
brockage, 1051
Brothers, Eric, 96–99
Browning, Ard W., 480
Brown, Martin R., 75
Bryan, William Jennings, 38
buffalo, American, 896, 908. *See also* American Buffalo gold bullion coins
Bugert, Bill, 567
bullion coins, 61
background, 938–939
gold, 944–950, 960–969, 973–978
palladium, 958–959
platinum
silver, 939–943
See also specific U.S. Mint bullion programs
bullion prices, recent, 89
bungtown tokens, 125
Bushnell, Charlies I., 26
Bust coinage, 108–109
Bust reales, 108–109

CAC Grading (CACG), 72, 82, 90
California Diamond Jubilee, 881
California gold ingot bars, 1007–1008
California Gold Rush, 21
California Pacific International Exposition, 881
California Pioneer Fractional Gold, 1000
California private gold coins, 22, 980
California small-denomination gold coins, 999–1006
Calvert, Cecil, 5, 115
Campbell, Craig A., 101
Capped Bust designs
dimes, 424–432
half dimes, 396–402
half dollars, 585–613
half eagles, 811–813
quarter dollars, 489–497
quarter eagles, 770–771
Capped Head designs
half eagles, 814–818
quarter eagles, 772–774
Carolina Elephant tokens, 122–123
Carolina gold, 981–983
Carson City Mint, 33
Carver, George Washington, 881
Castorland medals, 154
CDN Publishing, 72
cents
Confederate, 1017
large (*see* large cents)
small (*see* small cents)
Certified Acceptance Corporation (CAC), 91. *See also* CAC Grading (CACG)
certified coins, 62
Chain cents, 11, 200–203
Chalmers issues, 127–128
Chalmers, John, 6, 7, 127–128
Charles I, 110
Charles II, 107
Charles III, 108
Charles IV, 108
Charlotte Mint, 18

charts. *See* pricing charts
Cheerios dollars, 64
Cincinnati Mining & Trading Co., 989
Cincinnati Music Center, 881
circulated coins, grade levels for, 77–79
Circulating Collectible Coin Redesign Act of 2020, 100
Citizens Coinage Advisory Committee (CCAC), 66, 68
Civil Rights Act of 1964, 898, 911
Civil War, 28
  battlefields, 895, 900, 906, 918
  tokens (*see* Civil War tokens)
Civil War–era coinage, 26–69. *See also* Confederate issues
clad composition, 57
Clark, Gruber & Co., 26–63, 998
Classic Head design
  half cents, 188–193
  half eagles, 819–821
  large cents, 227–230
  quarter eagles, 775–777
Cleveland / Great Lakes Exposition, 881
clipped planchet, 1049
cob coinage, 107–108
Cohen, Col. Mendes, 121
Cohen numbers, 171
Cohen, Roger S., 170, 171
coinage
  early American, 6–9
  federal (*see* federal coinage)
  history of U.S. (*see chapter on "The History of Coins in America, 1607 to Date"*)
coinage presses, 19
coin collectors
  young, 90
Coin Dealer Newsletter, 55, 76
coin holders. *See* slabs
coin market, in 2026, 89–91
coins
  history of in America (*see "The History of Coins in America, 1607 to Date" chapter*)
  as investments (*see* investment-grade coins)
coin shows, 90
Coin World, 54–91
Collector's Price Guide (CPG) Value, 94
colonial America, 1–2
colonial coins, 2–4
colonial issues, background, 106–107
Colonial Newsletter, 55
Colorado gold pieces, 998–999
colorized coins, 901, 903, 913
Columbia, South Carolina, 881
Columbus, Christopher, 894, 899, 905, 918
columnario, 109
Comic Art Coin and Medal Program, 73, 89
commemoratives, 60–61
commemoratives, classic
  background, 879–883
  gold, 891–892
  silver, 883–890
commemoratives, modern
  1916 Centennial Gold series, 927
  background, 893–899
  Best of the Mint Semiquincentennial gold coins, 928
  clad half dollars, 899–903
  five-dollar gold coins, 918–921
  sets, 923, 926
  silver dollars, 904–917
  ten-dollar gold and bimetallic coins, 922–926
community service, 895, 907
Complete Guide to Liberty Seated Half Dollars, The, 567
Comprehensive Catalogue and Encyclopedia of U.S. Morgan and Peace Silver Dollars, 658
Confederate States of America, 27–64
  issues of, 1017–1018
Confederatio and related tokens, 134–135
Connecticut
  coinage of, 7, 8, 139–141, 139–141
  state of, 881
Constitution, U.S., 894, 904, 918
continental currency, 4, 131–132
copper coinage, early, 10
Copper Company of Upper Canada tokens, 153
copper double, 128
coppers. *See* Bar coppers; Fugio coppers; Higley or Granby coppers; landscape coppers; Louisiana coppers; Nova Constellatio coppers; Vermont coppers
Coronet Head large cents, 231–244
counterfeiting
  circumstances leading to modern boom in, 84–85
  industrial-scale, 84–85
  U.S. laws and compliance, 88
counterfeits, 7
  of certified coin holders
  Chinese, 66, 70, 84–88
  fake websites, 87–88
  steps to avoid when buying online, 87–88
  types of, 83, 85
counterstamps
  as advertisements, 3
  on CAL. quarter eagles, 767, 778, 781
  on Civil War tokens
  on commemorative coins, 882

on French sou, 130
on gold ingot bars, 1007
on quarter dollars, 479, 493, 494
on trade dollars, 692
country pay, 1, 2, 107
COVID-19, 72
Cox, Albion, 98
Crime of '73, 34
Cripple Creek District, 38
crown (coin), 110
cud die break, 1050
Custer, Eric, 102

Dahlonega Mint, 18, 801–803
Dannreuther, John, 798–801, 804
Davis, David J., 414
Davis, Jefferson, 29
Dawson, Richard, 124
DC Comics, 73
D.C. and Territories quarters, 542–544
decimal coinage, proposed, 8
Deisher, Beth, 64, 70, 84–88
Delaware, 881
de minimis provision, 86–87
denarium, 116
deniers, 119, 128–130
Denver Mint, 31, 40
Depression-era coinage, 45–85
de Saussure, Henry William, 98
desegregation, 897, 909
details grade, 81
Dexter, "Lord" Timothy, 5
DHgate, 85
dimes
background, 413–414
Barber (1892–1916), 53, 444–449
Capped Bust (1809–1837), 424–432
Draped Bust (1796–1807), 415–423
gold, 927
Liberty Seated (1837–1891), 433–443
Mercury (Winged Liberty Head; 1916–1945), 43, 450–459
Roosevelt (1946 to date), 50, 460–472
dismes, 168
dollars. *See* commemoratives, modern, silver dollars; gold dollars; modern dollars; silver dollars; trade dollars
double de l'Amerique Françoise, 128
double eagles. *See* gold double eagles (1849–1933)
Draped Bust designs, 12
1804-W Best of the Mint Semiquincentennial gold coins, 928
dimes, 415–423
eagles, 839–844
half cents, 182–187
half dimes, 388–395
half dollars, 574–584
half eagles, 804–810
large cents, 215–226
quarter dollars, 481–488
quarter eagles, 767–769
silver dollars, 12, 664–680
Dubosq & Company, 991
Dudley, Benjamin, 8
Dunbar & Company, 993
Dunn, John W., 75

eagles ($20 coins, 1795–1933). *See* gold eagles (1795–1933)
Eagles (bullion coins, 1986 to date). *See* American Gold Eagles (1986 to date); American Silver Eagles (1986 to date); American Platinum Eagles (1997 to date); American Palladium Eagles (2017 to date)
early American and related tokens, 122–128
Early American Cents, 51
Early American Coppers Club (EACC), 171
Early Half Dollar Varieties 1794–1836, 567
Early Quarter Dollars of the United States, 1796–1838, 480
Early United States Dimes, 1796–1837, 414
Early U.S. Gold Coin Varieties, 798
eBay, 85
eBay Live, 89
écu, 106, 109, 128
Edison, Thomas Alva, 896, 909
eight reales, 13
Eisenhower dollars (1971–1978), 58, 726–729
Eisenhower, President Dwight, 894, 904
electrotypes, 83
Elephant tokens, 122–123
Elgin, Illinois, 881
Empire State Building, 45
encased postage, 30
Ericson, Leif, 896, 908
Erie Canal, 20
error coins, 1048–1049, 1052
types of, 1049–1051
See also appendix A
escudos, 108
Etsy, 85
European coins in early America, 5–6
eye appeal, 76

Facebook, 85
Fairmount Collection, 89

false coins, 83
Farouk, King, of Egypt, 74
farthing, 117, 118, 120–121, 125–126
F.D. Kohler, California State Assayer, 991
federal coinage
by decade, 10–73
Civil War, 20–62
Depression Era, 45–85
development of, 9–10
earliest, 10–11
early 19th-century, 14–51
pre–Civil War, 26–69
Federal Half Dimes 1792–1837, 383
Ferdinand VI, 108
Ferdinand VII, 108
Feuchtwanger tokens (1837–1864), 1012
fifty-dollar gold coins
classic commemorative, 891–892
private and territorial, 985–986, 988, 994–996
First Flight, 896, 900, 908, 922
First Spouse gold bullion coins (2007 to date), 963–969
flash grade, 80
Flowing Hair designs
half dimes, 384–387
half dollars, 568–573
large cents, 11, 200–207
silver dollars, 12, 98, 99, 659–663 (*see also* 230th Anniversary Flowing Hair High Relief gold bullion coin)
Flying Eagle cents, 261, 262–266
Flying Eagle and Indian Head Cents, 261
Foerster, Leroy, 92
foreign coins in the American colonies, 2–6, 9, 13, 106–110
Fort Knox Federal Bullion Depository, 48
Fort Sumter, 28
Fort Vancouver, 881
four-dollar gold pieces
background, 793
See also gold Stellas
fourpence, 116
Franklin, Benjamin, 897, 909
Franklin half dollars, 52, 638–644
Franklin Press tokens, 152, 152
Free Silverites, 35, 37
French New World issues, 128–130
French silver coinage, 109
Fugio cents, 8, 165–166
Fugio coppers, 8

Garrett, Jeff, 89–91, 801–803
generals, five-star, 897, 901, 910, 919
George II, 8
George III, 110
Georgia gold, 980, 981–983
Georgia Gulch, Colorado, 999
GEORGIVS/Britannia coinage, 145
Georgivs Triumpho pieces, 156
Girl Scouts of the U.S.A., 897, 910
Gloucester tokens, 124
Gobrecht, Christian, 18
Gobrecht dollars, 681–684
gold bullion coins. *See "Bullion Coins" chapter*
gold coins
in colonial America, 3
first federal, 12
struck in the South, 801–803
See also bullion coins, gold; commemoratives, classic, gold; commemoratives, modern, five-dollar gold coins; commemoratives, modern, ten-dollar gold and bimetallic coins; fifty-dollar gold coins; gold dollars; gold double eagles; gold eagles; gold half eagles; gold quarter eagles; gold Stellas; *"Bullion Coins" chapter; and "Private and Territorial Gold" chapter*
gold dollars
background, 754–755
classic commemorative, 891–892
Indian Princess Head (1854–1889), 759–765
Liberty Head (1849–1854), 755–758
gold double eagles (1849–1933)
1907-W Best of the Mint Semiquincentennial gold coin, 101,104, 928
background, 860–861
Liberty Head (1849–1907), 861–869
Saint-Gaudens (1907), 41, 870–878
from the SS *Central America*, 64
gold eagles (1795–1933)
background, 837–838
Draped Bust (1795–1804), 839–844
Indian Head (1907–1933), 41, 45, 854–858
Liberty Head (1838–1907), 845–853
modern commemorative, 922–926
golden dollars, 67
See also American Innovation dollars; Native American dollars; Presidential dollars; Sacagawea dollars
gold half eagles (1795–1929), 12, 16
1854-S, 804
background, 796–798
Capped Bust (1795–1807), 811–813
Capped Head (1813–1834), 814–818
Classic Head (1834–1838), 819–821
collecting early, 798–801
Draped Bust (1807–1812), 804–810

Indian Head (1908–1929), 833–836
Liberty Head (1839–1908), 822–832
modern commemorative, 918–921
gold quarter eagles (1796–1929)
background, 766–767
Capped Bust (1808), 770–771
Capped Head (1821–1834), 772–774
classic commemorative, 891–892
Classic Head (1834–1839), 775–777
Draped Bust (1808), 767–769
Indian Head (1908–1929), 785–787
Liberty Head (1840–1907), 778–784
gold standard, 45–82
gold Stellas, 794–795
Gordon, Renata, 102
Gould & Curry mine and mill, 34
grade, defined, 75
gradeflation, 82
grading
appropriate magnification level, 80–81
circulated coins, 77–79
coin handling, 80
lighting conditions, 80
Proof coins, 79–80
step-by-step guide to, 74–82
third-party, 81–82 (see also ANACS; CAC Grading [CACG]; Numismatic Guaranty Company [NGC]; Professional Coin Grading Service [PCGS])
Uncirculated coins, 76
visual examination, 80–81
grading scale
and detrimental surface conditions, 81
development of, 75–76
Grant, U.S., 881
Great Depression, coinage during, 45–85
Greatest Generation, the, 899, 902, 913, 919
Greysheet, 94
Greysheet ID (GSID) Number, 94
groat, 116
GSID. see *Greysheet* ID (GSID) Number
Guide Book of United States Coins, A (the *Red Book*), 50, 92, 1054–1058

hairlines, 79
half cents
background, 170–171, 258
Braided Hair (1840–1857), 194–197
Classic Head (1809–1836), 188–193
die-variety summary, 171
Draped Bust (1800–1808), 182–187
passing of, 258
Liberty Cap (1793–1797), 172–175
half dimes
background, 382–383
Capped Bust (1829–1837), 396–402
Draped Bust (1796–1805), 388–395
Flowing Hair (1794–1795), 384–387
Liberty Seated (1837–1873), 403–412
half dismes, 11, 168, 378–381
background, 378
half dollars
background, 564–567
Barber (1892–1915), 626–630
Bicentennial (1776–1976), 645, 649
Capped Bust (1807–1839), 585–613
commemorative, 883–890, 899–903
Confederate, 1018
Draped Bust (1796–1807), 574–584
Flowing Hair (1794–1795), 568–573
Franklin (1948–1963), 52, 638–644
gold, 70, 927
Kennedy (1964 to date), 56–93, 70, 645–654
Liberty Seated (1839–1891), 614–625
Liberty Walking (1916–1947), 43, 632–637
Paralympic designs (2027–2030), 100
half eagles. *See* gold half eagles (1795–1929)
halfpence, 6, 7
halfpennies, 5, 118–123, 125–126
Hamilton, Alexander, 9, 97
Handbook of United States Coins (the *Blue Book*), 1059
Hard Times tokens (1832–1844), 20, 1009–1011
Harris & Marchand, 25
Hawaii, 881
Hawaiian issues, 1019–1021
H.E. Harris & Co., 65
Hibernia coinage, 120–121
Hibernia–Voce Populi coins, 125–126
Higley, Dr. Samuel, 6, 124
Higley or Granby coppers, 7, 124–125
Hogge Money, 110–111
Holt, Richard, 5, 117
Howe, Lord Richard, 126
Hudson, Kathryn, 101
Hudson, New York, 881
Huguenots, 881
Hull, John, 112
Humbert, Augustus, 22, 985–986

Illinois, 881
Immune Columbia pieces, 133–134
Indian Head designs
eagles, 41, 45, 854–858
half eagles, 833–836
nickels, 43, 351–358
quarter eagles, 785–787

small cents, 41, 267–281
Indian Princess Head designs
gold dollars, 759–765
three-dollar gold pieces, 789–792
infantry, U.S., 897, 910
IN GOD WE TRUST, 31
ingots
gold, 25, 70, 1007–1008
silver, 37
International Association of Professional Numismatists (IAPN), 83
investment-grade coins, 62
Iowa, 881
Isabella quarter, 883

Jackson, Andrew, 16–53
Jackson, Darla, 102
James II, 117–118
Jamestown, 897, 909, 919
Jefferson nickels (1938 to date), 49, 359–377
Modified (2006 to date), 374–375
Westward Journey (2004–2005), 66, 372–373
Jefferson, Thomas, 8, 10, 97, 891, 895, 905
J.J. Conway & Co., 999
John Parsons & Company, 999
John Reich Collectors Society (JRCS), 414, 480
See also JR (John Reich) numbers
John Reich Journal, 414, 480
JR (John Reich) numbers, 414
J.S. Ormsby, 990
Julian, R.W., 98

Kellogg & Co., 995–996
Kennedy half dollars (1964 to date), 56–93, 70
2014 gold issue, 897, 901, 903
Kennedy, Robert F., 896, 907
Kentucky tokens, 151
"King of American Coins," 102
Klondike Gold Rush, 38–75
Korean War, 894, 904

Lafayette, Marquis de, 881
Lamasure, Edwin
lamination, 1050, 1056
landscape coppers, 7
large cents
advent of, 11
background, 198–199, 258
Braided Hair (1839–1857), 245–258
Classic Head (1808–1814), 227–230
Coronet Head (1816–1839), 231–244
Draped Bust (1796–1807), 215–226
passing of, 258
Flowing Hair (1793), 11, 200–207
Liberty Cap (1793–1796), 208–214
Lee, Robert E., 29
leeuwendaalder, 106, 109
Legal Tender Notes, 29–66
Lesher Referendum dollars (1900–1901), 1016
Lewis and Clark expedition, 881, 891, 896, 908
Libertas Americana medal, 169
Liberty and Britannia gold bullion coins, 976
Liberty Cap designs
half cents, 172–181
large cents, 208–214
Liberty Head designs
double eagles, 861–869
eagles, 845–853
gold dollars, 755–758
half eagles, 822–832
nickels, 35, 62, 345–350
quarter eagles, 778–784
Liberty Seated designs
dimes, 433–443
half dimes, 403–412
half dollars, 614–625
quarters, 498–508
silver dollars, 685–691
trade dollars, 692–697
twenty-cent pieces, 474–477
Liberty Walking half dollars, 43, 632–637
1916-W Best of the Mint Semiquincentennial gold coin, 101, 102, 103, 928
See also under 1916 (2016) Centennial gold tribute coins
Library of Congress, 896, 908, 922
Lincoln, Abraham, 897, 909
Lincoln cents (1909 to date)
Lincoln Birth Bicentennial Reverses (2009), 67, 313–315
Memorial Reverse (1959–2008), 54, 305–312
Shield Reverse (2010 to date), 68, 316–317
steel, 49–86
V.D.B., 42
Wheat Ears Reverse (1909–1958), 282–304
Lincoln token, 27
Lion dollar, 106, 106
Lions Club International, 898, 911
Little Rock Central High School, 897, 909
lliard, 129
LM (Logan-McCloskey) numbers, 383
Logan, Russell, 383, 414
London Elephant tokens, 122
Longacre, James B., 20–57, 96
Long Island, New York, 882
Lord Baltimore coinage, 5, 115–116

Louis d'or, 109
Louis I, 107
Louisiana coppers, 130
Louisiana Purchase Exposition, 40, 882, 891
Lovejoy, Allen F., 414
luster, 76
Lynchburg, Virginia, 882

Madison, Dolley, 896, 908
Madison, James, 894, 900, 905, 918
magnifiers, 80
Maine, 882
Mallis, A. George, 658
Manila Mint, 44, 1024, 1036, 1039,
  circulating coins struck by, 1026, 1028, 1030, 1032, 1034, 1039, 1041–1043
  commemorative issues, 1046
  Phililppine Collectors Forum / 100th Anniversary Manila Mint special-edition *Red Book* (2021), 1058
March of Dimes, 898, 911
mark, 8
Marshall, Chief Justice John, 896, 909
Maryland, 882
  colonial coinage of, 115–116
"Mason's Photographic Gallery of the Coin Collectors of the United States," 32
Massachusetts and California Company, 989
Massachusetts coinage, 111–115, 137–138
Matron Head design, 15
Mayflower, 400th anniversary of, 922
McAuliffe, Christa, 898, 912
McCloskey, John, 383, 414
McKinley, William, 38, 882, 891
McNally, Kristie, 91
Medal of Honor, 897, 910, 919
medals, silver, 100–104
Mega Red, 74, 92
Menna, Joseph F., 102
Mercury dimes, 43, 450–459, 450–459
  1916-W Best of the Mint Semiquincentennial gold coin, 101, 103, 928
  See also under 1916 (2016) Centennial gold tribute coins
micrograding, 80
Miners' Bank, 990
Mint Act of April 2, 1792, 10
mintages, 93–94
Mint Cabinet, 20
Mint-canceled coins, 1052
Missouri, state of, 882
misstrikes, 1048–1049, 1052. *See also appendix A*
MMIX Ultra High Relief gold bullion coins, 975
modern dollars
  1921 Silver Dollar Anniversary coins, 751–753
  American Innovation (2018–2032), 746–750
  Bicentennial (1776–1976), 726, 728, 729
  Eisenhower (1971–1978), 726–729
  Native American (2009 to date), 742–745
  Presidential (2007–2020), 736–741
  Sacagawea, 733–735
  Susan B. Anthony (1979–1999), 730–732
Moffat & Co., 989
  San Francisco, 984
  United States Assayer of Gold, 987
Monroe Doctrine, 882
Monthly Greysheet, 94
Morgan silver dollars (1878–1921), 35, 698–717
  1903-O Treasury find, 56
  1921 Silver Dollar Anniversary coins, 751–753
  See also 1921 Morgan and Peace Dollar Centennial coins; VAM (Van Allen–Mallis) numbers
Mormon gold pieces, 997
Morris, Robert, 8
Mott store cards, 150
Moulton, William, 7
Mount Rushmore, 894, 899, 905, 918
mousquetaires, 129
Moy, Edmund C., 69
mule, 1051
multiple-strike error, 1049
Myddelton tokens, 153

Naismith Memorial Basketball Hall of Fame, 898, 901, 912, 919
National Baseball Hall of Fame, 898, 901, 910, 919
National Law Enforcement Memorial and Museum, 899, 901, 913, 919
National Law Enforcement Officers Memorial, 895, 907
National Park Service, 898, 901, 911, 919
National Purple Heart Hall of Honor, 899, 902, 913, 919
Native American dollars (2009 to date), 67, 742–745
Negro Leagues Baseball, 899, 901, 913, 919
NE (New England) coinage, 111–112
Netherlands silver coinage, 109
Newby, Mark, 116
Newcomb, H.R., 199
Newcomb numbers, 199
New England Elephant tokens, 123
New England shilling, 1
New Hampshire coinage, 7, 136–137
New Jersey coinage, 116–117, 146–148
Newman Numismatic Portal, 72
New Orleans Mint, 18, 35

New Rochelle, New York, 882
New Spain (Texas) jola tokens, 155
New World, settlement of, 1
New York coinage, 141–143
New Yorke in America tokens, 123
Nice Gang, 942
nickels, 23
  background, 338–339
  Indian Head or Buffalo (1913–1938), 43, 351–358
  Jefferson (1938–2003), 49, 359–377
  Jefferson Modified (2006 to date), 374–375
  Liberty Head (1883–1913), 62, 345–350
  Semiquincentennial, 105
  Shield (1866–1883), 339–344
  Westward Journey (2004–2005), 66, 372–373
Noorigian, Joseph V., 104
Norfolk, Virginia, 882
Norris, Gregg & Norris, San Francisco, 22, 984
North American tokens, 148–149
Northwest Company tokens, 155–156
Nova Constellatio coppers, 132–133
Nova Constellatio patterns, 164
Numismatic Guaranty Company (NGC), 62, 82, 91
  counterfeited slabs of, 86
  verification numbers on slabs, 86
Numismatic News, 52
numismatist, first professional U.S., 16
Numismatist, The, 36

Oak Tree coinage, 113–114
Obama, President Barack, 100
off-center strike, 1050
Old Spanish Trail, 882
old tenor, 4
Olympics
  Atlanta (1995–1996), 895, 900, 906–907, 918
  Los Angeles (1984), 894, 904, 922
  Salt Lake City (2002), 896, 908, 918
  Seoul (1988), 894, 904, 918
  XXV (1992), 894, 899, 905, 918
online buying, hazards of, 87–88
Oregon Exchange Company, 996
Oregon Trail, 882
Overton, Al C., 567
Overton numbers, 567
Owl Creek bank note, 15

Pacific Company, 990
Panama-Pacific Exposition, 43, 882, 891
Panic of 1857, 25
Panic of 1893, 37
paper currency, colonial, 3–5
Paralympics, 100
Parsley, Donald L., 567
pattern coins, 26
  Birch cents, 166, 167
  Confederate, 28
  Continental Currency, 131
  early American, 11
  Flying Eagle cent, 260, 262, 266
  Fugio cent, 165
  Getz patterns, 161–162
  Gloucester tokens, 124
  Gobrecht dollar, 657, 682, 684
  gold double eagle, 861, 864, 869
  gold eagle, 837
  half dime, 412
  Indian Head cent, 267
  of New Hampshire, 7, 136–137
  nickels, 344
  Nova Constellatio, 8–9, 164
  Saint-Gaudens Ultra High Relief double eagle, 870, 872
  speculative, 132–135
  Virginia halfpennies, 121
  Washington pieces, 156, 161
  of William Wood, 118–121
  See also 1792 proposed coinage; dismes; half dismes; gold Stellas
Patterson, Robert, 14
Peace silver dollars (1921–1935), 45, 718–738
  1921 Silver Dollar Anniversary coins, 751–753
Peale, Charles Willson, 96
Pearl Harbor, 49
pence, 107
pennies, 118–120, 121–122
Penny Whimsy (1793–1814), 199
Penny-Wise, 55, 171
Peterson, Richard, 69
Philadelphia Mint, 10, 39
  First, 11, 97
Philadelphia Numismatic Society, 25
Philip II, 107
Philip III, 107
Philippines coinage, 50
  background, 1023–1024
  commemorative, 44, 1046–1047
  Commonwealth issues, 1039–1047
  under U.S. sovereignty (1903–1936), 39, 1025–1038
Philip V, 108
Photograde, 75
pieces of eight, 13, 106, 106
Pilgrims, 882
Pillar coinage, 106, 108
Pine Tree coinage, 7, 114–115

pistareens, 108, 109
Pitt tokens, 126
Pitt, William, 126
P.L. 114-196, 100
P.L. 116-330, 100
planchet
  clipped, 1049
  off-metal, 1051
  unstruck, 1049
  wrong, 1051, 1053
Plantation tokens, 1020–1021
Postage Currency, 30
post-colonial issues, background, 131
pounds, 107
Presidential dollars (2007–2016, 2020), 67, 68, 736–741
pricing charts, elements of, 93. *See also* valuations
prisoners of war, U.S., 895, 906
private and territorial gold, background, 979
privy marks
  "230" (230th anniversary of the Flowing Hair silver dollar), 977
  on 1921 Silver Dollar Anniversary coins, 751
  on American Eagle bullion coins, 940, 942, 943, 950, 952, 977
  on American Innovation dollars, 746, 748–749
  eagle privy in collaboration with Nice Gang, 942
  laser-engraved, 943
  on Negro Leagues Baseball commemorative, 913
  on quarter dollars, 549
  eagle privy on Preamble to the Constitution platinum bullion, 952
  Liberty Bell–250 (U.S. Semiquincentennial), 105, 746, 746, 928
  star privy in collaboration with Nice Gang, 942
  U.S. Army, Navy, and Marines privies, 943
  "V75" (75th anniversary of the end of World War II), 549, 940, 942, 950
Professional Coin Grading Service (PCGS), 62, 82, 91
  counterfeited slabs of, 86
  verification numbers on slabs, 86
Professional Numismatists Guild (PNG), 53, 83
  outreach to young collectors, 90
Proof and Mint Sets, 57
  background, 929–933
Proof coins, 931
  grading, 79–80
Providence, Rhode Island, 882
Puerto Rican issues, 1022
quarter dollars
  1792 proposed coinage, 168, 168
  American Women, 559–564
  America the Beautiful (2010 to date), 67, 545–556
  background, 478–480
  Barber (1892–1916), 509–514
  Bicentennial (1776–1976), 58, 531
  Capped Bust (1815–1838), 489–497
  Crossing the Delaware, 557–558
  D.C. and Territories (2009), 64, 542–544
  Draped Bust (1796–1807), 481–488
  gold, 927
  Isabella commemorative, 881
  Liberty Seated (1838–1891), 498–508
  obverse designs (2026 onward), 100
  Standing Liberty (1916–1930), 43, 515–521
  State (1999–2008), 62, 535–541
  Washington (1932 to date), 47, 522–564
  youth sports designs (2027–2030), 100
quarter eagles. *See* gold quarter eagles
quint, 8
raw coins
  defined, 74
reales, 106, 108, 108, 118
Red Book, the, 74
  podcast, 91
  See also A Guide Book of United States Coins (the *Red Book*); and appendix B
registry sets. *See* set registries
Reich, John, 14. *See also* John Reich Collectors Society; *John Reich Journal*
Reid, Templeton, 17, 980
replicas, 83
Revolutionary War, 96
  black patriots of, 896, 907
Rhode Island Ship medals, 126–127
Rittenhouse, David W., ii, 10, 96–99
Rittenhouse Society, 54
Roanoke Island, North Carolina, 882
Robinson, Jackie, 895, 907, 918
Robinson, Joseph T., 881
Roosevelt dimes (1946 to date), 50, 460–472
Roosevelt, Franklin D., 45, 896, 918
Roper, Dr. Lewis, 23
Rosa Americana coinage, 6, 118–120
Ruddy, James F., 75
Rush, Dr. Benjamin, 97
Rutherford Co., NC, 981–983
Ryder, David, 91
Sacagawea, 67
Sacagawea dollars (2000–2008), 63–64, 733–735
Saint-Gaudens, Augustus, 40–77, 104
Saint-Gaudens double eagles, 870–878
  See also Best of the Mint Semiquincentennial gold coins; MMIX Ultra High Relief gold bullion coin
San Francisco earthquake of 1906, 40

San Francisco Mint, 24, 34, 40, 41, 48, 897, 909, 919
San Francisco–Oakland Bay Bridge, 882
Schultz & Company, 992
Scot, Robert, 102
Semiquincentennial, 73
  Liberty Bell–250 privy mark, 746
  Mint plans for, 91
  See also Semiquincentennial coinage
Semiquincentennial Anniversary of the United States of America. *See* U.S. Semiquincentennial
Semiquincentennial coinage, 100–105
  Best of the Mint Semiquincentennial gold, 100–104, 928
  circulating, 105
  privy mark for. *See* privy mark, Semiquincentennial
Sesquicentennial of U.S. Independence, 62, 882, 891
set registries, 65
  competitions, 90
sets
  bullion, 941, 943, 950, 957, 962
  Best of the Mint (*see* Best of the Mint Semiquincentennial gold coins)
  Proof and Mint, 57, 929–933 *(see also "Proof and Mint Sets" chapter)*
  Semiquincentennial (*see* Best of the Mint Semiquincentennial gold coins)
Shein, 86
Sheldon, Dr. William H., 75
Sheldon grading scale, 76
Sheldon numbers, 199
Sheldon, William H., 51, 199
Shield nickels (1866–1883), 339–344
shillings, 7, 107, 110–115, 116, 121–122, 124, 127–128
Sides, Andrew, 102
silver center cent, 167
silver dollars
  1794, 98, 99
  1804 (original), 91, 657, 670–671
  1804-W Draped Bust, Class I Semiquincentennial gold coin, 101, 102, 104
  background, 655–658
  Bicentennial (1776–1976), 726
  commemorative, 883, 887, 904–917
  Draped Bust (1795–1804), 12, 664–680
  first struck for circulation, 11
  Flowing Hair (1794–1795), 12, 659–663 (*see also* 230th Anniversary Flowing Hair High Relief gold bullion coin)
  Gobrecht dollars (1836–1839), 681–684
  Liberty Seated (1840–1873), 685–691
  Morgan (1878–1921), 698–717 (*see also* 1921 Silver Dollar Anniversary coins)
  Peace (1921–1935), 45, 718–738 (*see also* 1921 Silver Dollar Anniversary coins)
  trade (*see* trade dollars [1873–1885])
sixpence, 5, 110–115, 116, 127–128
slabs, 62
  counterfeit, 86
  verification numbers on, 86
small cents
  background, 260–261
  discontinuation of in 2026, 73, 105
  Flying Eagle (1856–1858), 262–266
  Indian Head (1859–1909), 267–281
  Lincoln (1909 to date; *see* Lincoln cents)
  Semiquincentennial, 105
  steel, 49–86
Smithsonian Institution, 895, 907, 918
Snowden, James Ross, 26
Snow numbering system, 261
Snow, Richard, 261
so-called dollars, 1016
social media
  coin sales via, 89
  and counterfeit coins, 85
  and young collectors, 90
soldier, U.S. infantry, 897, 910
sols, 128–129
Somers, Admiral Sir George, 110
Sommer Islands (Bermuda) coinage, 6, 110–111
sou marque, 127
sous, 129–130
spade guinea, 110
Spanish-American coinage, 13, 107–109
Sparrow, Thomas, 127
Special Mint Sets (1965–1967), 931–932, 937
Special Olympics, 895, 906
Special Strike (SP) coins, 1964, 932, 937
Specie Circular, 19
speculative issues, 132–135
spot price. *See* bullion prices
SS *Central America*, 64, 66, 70
Stack, James A., 91
Standing Liberty quarters, 43, 515–521
  1916-W Best of the Mint Semiquincentennial gold coin, 101–102, 103, 928
  See also under 1916 (2016) Centennial gold tribute coins
Standish Barry threepence, 150
Star Rare Coin Encyclopedia, 46
"Star-Spangled Banner," 897, 910, 919
state coinage, early American, 135–148
State, D.C., and Territories quarters. *See* quarter dollars, D.C. and Territories; quarter dollars, State

Statue of Liberty, 894, 899, 904, 918
steel cents, 49–86
Stellas. *See* gold Stellas
Stone Mountain, 882
store cards, Civil War, 1016
St. Patrick or Mark Newby coinage, 5, 116–117
strike, off-center, 1050
strike quality, 76
struck copies, 83
surface quality, 76
surfaces, altered, 83
Susan B. Anthony dollars, 730–732
sutlers' tokens, 31
Sutter's Mill, 21

Talbot, Allum & Lee cents, 152
tariffs, 86
Tarryall Mines, Colorado, 999
Temu, 86
Texas, independence of, 883
Texas *jolas*, 155, 155
Theatre at New York tokens, 154–155
third-party grading. *See* grading, third-party
three-cent pieces (1851–1889)
  background, 325–326, 333
  nickel (1865–1889), 33, 333–337
  silver (1851–1873), 23, 325–332
three-dollar gold pieces, 788
threepence, 110–115, 127–128
tokens
  Civil War, 31, 1012–1016
  Hard Times, 20
  private, 148–156, 1009
  speculative, 132–135
  sutlers', 31
trade dollars, 692–697
transit of Venus (1769), 96
trimes, 23, 325–332
Trump, President Donald, 100, 105
  tariffs of, 86
Tubman, Harriet, 899, 902, 913, 919
Twain, Mark, 898, 911, 919
twenty-cent pieces, 34
  background, 473
twenty-five-dollar gold coins
  modern commemorative, 922
two bits, 107
two-cent pieces, 31
  background, 318–319
  Shield (1864–1873), 319–324
twopence, 110–111, 118–120

Ultra High Relief coins
  Saint-Gaudens double eagles, 870–872
Uncirculated coins
  attributes of, 76
  grade levels for, 76–77
Uniform Commercial Code (UCC), 84
United Service Organizations, 894, 905
United States Assayer of Gold
  Humbert, Augustus, 985–986
  Moffat & Co., 987
United States Assay Office, 984–989
United States Assay Office of Gold, 988
United States Copper Cents 1816–1857, 199
United States Early Silver Dollars from 1794 to 1803, The, 658
U.S./Philippine Coins, 1038
U.S. Army, 897, 900, 910, 919
U.S. Botanic Garden, 895, 907
U.S. Capitol, 895, 900, 905
U.S. Capitol Visitor Center, 896, 908, 918
U.S. Congress, 894, 899, 904, 918
U.S. Constitution, 894, 904, 918
U.S. Marine Corps, 896, 899, 902, 902, 909, 913, 919
U.S. Marshals Service, 898, 901, 911, 919
U.S. Mint
  and digital technology, 84
  creation of, 9–10
  first facility, 97
U.S. Mint Sets
  Proof, 929–930, 932–936
  Silver Proof (*see* U.S. Mint Sets, Proof)
  Uncirculated, 931, 936–937
U.S. Semiquincentennial, 100
  See also Semiquincentennial coinage
U.S. Silver Bullion Depository, 61
U.S. Treasury Building, 56

valuations, 94
VAM (Van Allen–Mallis) numbers, 658
Van Allen, Leroy C., 658
V.D.B. cents, 42
Vermont coppers, 7–8
Vermont, Republic of, coinage, 135–136
Vermont, state of, 883
veterans, disabled American, 897, 910
Vietnam Veterans Memorial, 895, 906
Virginia Company, 110
Virginia halfpennies, 121–122
Voight, Henry, 97

Walloons, 881
Walter Breen's Encyclopedia of United States Half Cents, 170
wampum, 106, 111–112
exchange rate of, 2
Washington, Booker T., 881
Washington (George) portrait pieces, 156–163, 156–163
Washington, President George, 97
birth, 894, 899
death, 896, 918
on quarter dollar obverses, 100
Washington quarters
America the Beautiful (2010 to date), 67
background, 522–523
Bicentennial (1976), 58
Crossing the Delaware (2021), 557–558
D.C. and Territories (2009), 542–544
Eagle Reverse (1932–1998), 47, 522–534
John Flanagan obverse, 522
Laura Gardin Fraser obverse, 559
State (1999–2008), 535–541
updated portrait on, 559, 559
Wass, Moliter & Co., 993–994
WB (Wiley-Bugert) numbers, 567
websites
fake, 87–88
secure vs. legitimate, 88
Weinman, Adolph A., 102
West Point Mint, 61
West Point (U.S. Military Academy), 896, 908
Westward Journey nickels, 66
Whatnot, 89
Wheat cents, 282–304
White House, 894, 905
Whitman Coin and Collectibles Expo, 65
Whitman Publishing, 47, 65
purchase of by CDN Publishing, 72
whizzing, 83
Wiley, Randy, 567
Willow Tree coinage, 112–113
Wilson dollar, 44
Winged Liberty Head or "Mercury" dimes. *See* Mercury dimes (1916–1945)
Wisconsin territorial government, 883
Wish (website), 85
Women in Military Service Memorial, 895, 906
women's suffrage, 898, 913
Wood, William, 5–6
coinage of, 118–121
world coinage in colonial America, 109–110
World Cup Tournament (1994), 895, 900, 918
World's Columbian Exposition, 37, 883
commemorative half dollar, 37
World's Fair of Money, 90
World War I, 43–80
Centennial commemorative coins (2018), 898, 911
World War II
50th Anniversary of (1993, dated 1991–1995), 895, 900, 905, 918
75th anniversary of, 899, 922
outbreak of, 49
World War II–era coinage, 49–90
Wray, Dr. Nicholas, 97
Wright, Orville and Wilbur, 42, 896, 900, 908, 922

Yellowstone National Park, 896, 908
Yeoman, R.S., 92

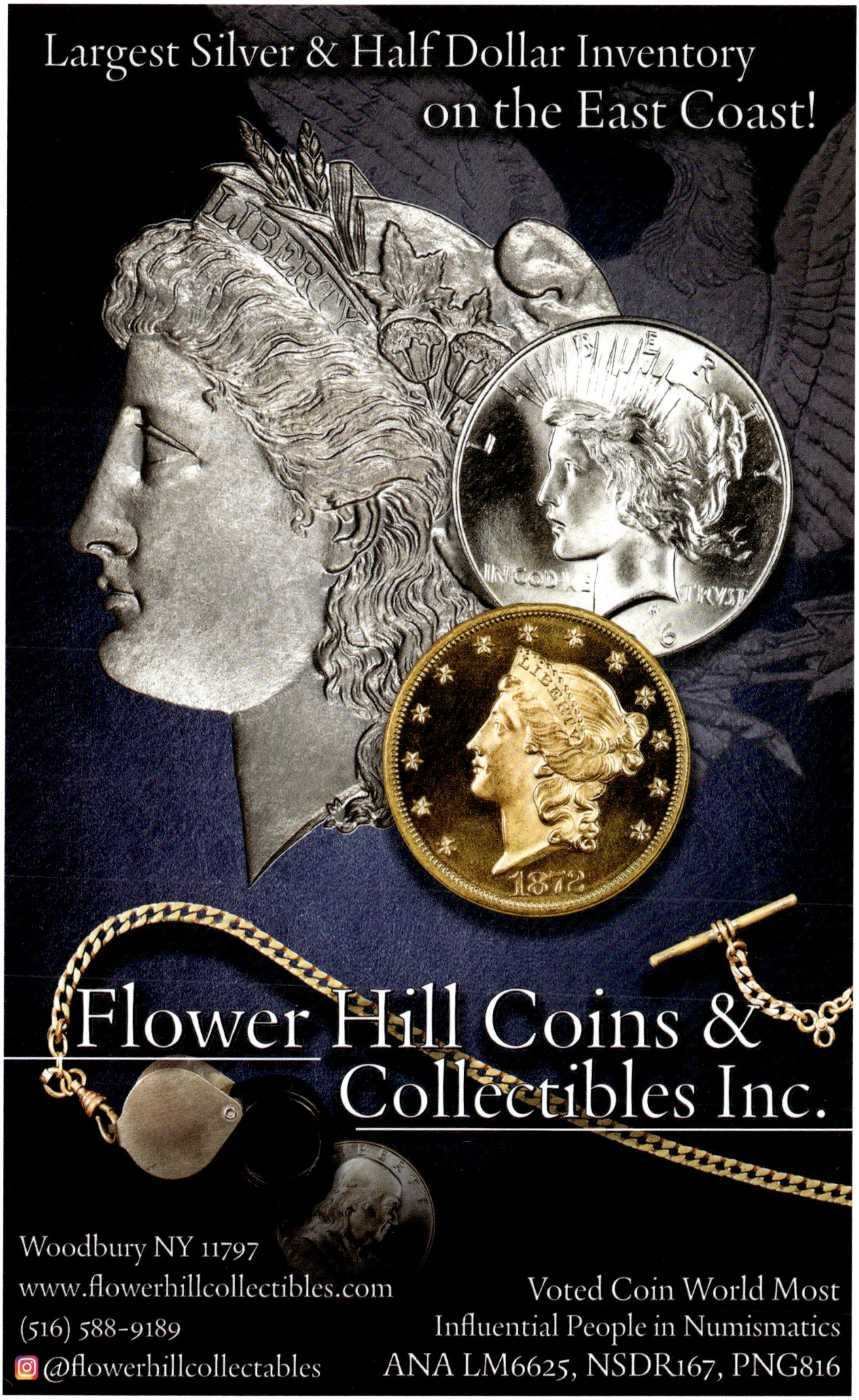
Largest Silver & Half Dollar Inventory
on the East Coast!
Flower Hill Coins &
Collectibles Inc.
Woodbury NY 11797
www.flowerhillcollectibles.com
(516) 588-9189
@flowerhillcollectables
Voted Coin World Most
Influential People in Numismatics
ANA LM6625, NSDR167, PNG816